Welcome to
OPERATIONS MANAGEMENT

Operations Management – it's important, it's exciting, it's challenging, and everywhere you look!

Important, because it's concerned with creating all of the products and services upon which we depend. Exciting, because it's at the centre of so many of the changes affecting the world of business. Challenging, because the solutions that we find need to work globally and responsibly within society and the environment. And everywhere, because every service and product that you use – the cereal you eat at breakfast, the chair you sit on, and the radio station you listen to while you eat – is the result of an operation or process.

Our aim in writing *Operations Management* is to give you a **comprehensive understanding** of the issues and techniques of operations management, and to **help you get a great final result** in your course. Here's how you might make the most of the text:

● Get ahead with the latest developments – from the up-to-the-minute *Operations in practice* features in every chapter to the focus on corporate social responsibility in the final chapter – these **put you at the cutting edge**.

● Use the *Worked examples* and *Problems and applications* to improve your use of key quantitative and qualitative techniques, and work your way to **better grades in your assignments and exams**.

● Follow up on the recommended readings at the end of each chapter. They're specially selected to enhance your learning and **give you an edge** in your course work.

And in particular, look out for the references to **MyOMLab** in the text, and log on to **www.myomlab.com*** where you can

● check and reinforce your understanding of key concepts using self-assessment questions, video clips and more;

● practise your problem-solving with feedback, guided solutions and an almost limitless supply of questions!

We want *Operations Management* to give you what you need: a comprehensive view of the subject, an ambition to put that into practice, and – of course – success in your studies. So, read on and good luck!

Nigel Slack
Alistair Brandon-Jones
Robert Johnston

OPERATIONS MANAGEMENT

Seventh edition

Nigel Slack

Alistair Brandon-Jones

Robert Johnston

PEARSON

Harlow, England • London • New York • Boston • San Francisco • Toronto • Sydney • Auckland • Singapore • Hong Kong
Tokyo • Seoul • Taipei • New Delhi • Cape Town • São Paulo • Mexico City • Madrid • Amsterdam • Munich • Paris • Milan

Pearson Education Limited
Edinburgh Gate
Harlow CM20 2JE
United Kingdom
Tel: +44 (0)1279 623623
Fax: +44 (0)1279 431059
Web: www.pearson.com/uk

First published under the Pitman Publishing imprint 1995
Second edition (Pitman Publishing) 1998
Third edition 2001
Fourth edition 2004
Fifth edition 2007
Sixth edition 2010
Seventh edition 2013

ISBN: 978-0-273-77620-8 (print)
978-0-273-77628-4 (PDF)
978-0-273-77621-5 (eText)

British Library Cataloguing-in-Publication Data
A catalogue record for the print edition is available from the British Library

Library of Congress Cataloging-in-Publication Data
A catalog record for the print edition is available from the Library of Congress

10 9 8 7 6 5 4 3
17 16 15

Print edition typeset in 9.25/12 by Charter ITC Std by 75
Print edition printed and bound in Italy by L.E.G.O. S.p.A

NOTE THAT ANY PAGE CROSS REFERENCES REFER TO THE PRINT EDITION

Brief contents

Contents

Guide to 'operations in practice', examples, short cases and case studies

Chapter	Location	Company/example	Region	Sector/activity	Company size
Chapter 1 **Operations** **management**	p. 5	IKEA	Global	Retail	Large
	p. 11	Torchbox	UK	Web design	Small
	p. 12	MSF	Global	Charity	Large
	p. 15	First Direct	UK	Banking	Large
	p. 18	Pret A Manger	Europe/USA	Retail	Medium
	p. 24	Formule 1	Europe	Hospitality	Large
	p. 25	Anantara Bangkok Riverside Resort & Spa	Thailand	Hospitality	Medium
	p. 28	To be a great operations manager you need to . . .	General	General	N/A
	p. 31	Concept Design Services	UK	Design/manufacturing/distribution	Medium
Chapter 2 **Operations** **performance**	p. 37	A tale of two terminals	UK	Airport	Medium
	p. 44	Patagonia, a B Corp	Global	Garment manufacturing	Large
	p. 49	Organically good quality	UK	Agricultural	Small
	p. 50	When speed means life or death	General	Health care	Medium
	p. 51	How UPS maintains its dependability	Global	Distribution	Large
	p. 53	566 quadrillion individual muesli mixes	German	Web retail	Small
	p. 56	Everyday low prices at Aldi	Europe	Retail	Large
	p. 57	Can cost cutting go too far?	China	Manufacturing	Large
	p. 64	The Penang Mutiara	Malaysia	Hospitality	Medium
Chapter 3 **Operations** **strategy**	p. 69	Flextronix and Ryanair	Europe	MSC/airline	Large
	p. 76	Apple's retail operations strategy	Global	Retail	Large
	p. 83	Amazon, so what exactly is your core competence?	Global	Web retail	Large
	p. 85	Apple's supply operations strategy	Global	Manufacturing	Large
	p. 89	Sometimes any plan is better than no plan	European	Military	Large
	p. 91	Long Ridge Gliding Club	UK	Sport	Small
Chapter 4 **Process design**	p. 97	Fast-food drive-throughs	USA	Quick service restaurant	Large
	p. 101	Ecover's ethical operation design	Belgium/France	Manufacturing	Large
	p. 109	Space4 housing processes	UK	Construction	Medium
	p. 119	Heathrow delays caused by capacity utilization	UK	Airport	Large
	p. 121	The Action Response Applications Processing Unit	UK	Charity	Small

Chapter	Location	Company/example	Region	Sector/activity	Company size
Chapter 5 Innovation and design in services and products	p. 126	Innovative design from Dyson	Global	Design/manufacturing	Large
	p. 129	The sad tale of Kodak and its digital camera	Global	Manufacturing	Large
	p. 133	Square watermelons!	Global	Agriculture/retail	Large
	p. 136	Daniel Hersheson Blow Dry Bar	UK	Hairdresser	Small
	p. 138	Customizing for kids	UK	Media	Small
	p. 144	The troubled history of the Airbus A380	Global	Aerospace	Large
	p. 148	Chatsworth	UK	Tourism	Medium
Chapter 6 Supply network design	p. 153	Dell	Global	Computer manufacturing	Large
	p. 159	HTC	Taiwan	Design/telecoms	Large
	p. 162	Tata Nano	India	Car manufacturing	Large
	p. 164	Counting clusters	Global	Various	Various
	p. 170	Economies of scale in heart surgery and shipping	Various	Health care/shipping	Medium/Large
	p. 176	Disneyland Resort Paris	France	Entertainment	Large
Chapter 7 Layout and flow	p. 192	Tesco	UK	Retail	Large
	p. 195	'Factory flow' helps surgery productivity	UK	Health care	Medium
	p. 199	Apple's shop-within-a-shop in Harrods	UK	Retail	Large
	p. 201	Cadbury's	UK	Entertainment/ manufacturing	Large
	p. 204	The transparent factory	Germany	Manufacturing	Large
	p. 218	North West Constructive Bank	UK	Financial services	Medium
Chapter 8 Process technology	p. 224	I, Robot	All	Various	Various
	p. 228	Customers are not always human	Netherlands	Agriculture	Medium
	p. 229	QB House	Asia	Hairdressing	Medium
	p. 244	Who's in the cockpit?	All	Airlines	Large
	p. 247	Rochem Ltd	UK	Food processing	Medium
Chapter 9 People, jobs and organization	p. 252	W.L. Gore	Global	Manufacturing	Large
	p. 255	Google	Global	Internet	Large
	p. 266	McDonald's	UK	Restaurants	Large
	p. 268	Lloyds TSB	UK	Banking	Large
	p. 274	Service Adhesives	Europe	Manufacturing	Large
Chapter 10 The nature of planning and control	p. 289	BMW dealership	UK	Service and repair	Medium
	p. 293	Air France	Global	Airline	Large
	p. 297	Taxi App replaces dispatching office	Germany	Software development	Medium
	p. 302	Can airline passengers be sequenced?	Global	Airlines	Large
	p. 304	The hospital triage system	All	Health care	Large
	p. 309	Chicken salad sandwich – part one	All	Food processing	Large
	p. 317	subText Studios	Singapore	CGI	Small

Chapter	Location	Company/example	Region	Sector/activity	Company size
Chapter 18 Operations improvement	p. 579	TNT	Global	Logistics	Large
	p. 583	The Checklist Manifesto	Global	Health care	Various
	p. 589	Heineken International	Netherlands	Brewery	Large
	p. 595	Six Sigma at Xchanging	UK	Financial services	Medium
	p. 605	GCR Insurance	Global	Insurance	Large
Chapter 19 Risk management	p. 611	Cadbury	UK	Food	Large
	p. 614	Risk and human error	All	Airlines	Large
	p. 630	Otis Maintenance Management System	Global	Facilities services	Large
	p. 636	Slagelse Industrial Services (SIS)	Denmark	Manufacturing	Large
Chapter 20 Organizing for improvement	p. 641	Sonae Corporation	Portugal	Retail	Large
	p. 649	Taxing quality	Denmark	Government service	Large
	p. 660	Learning from Formula 1	Global	Distribution	Large
	p. 662	Work-Out at GE	Global	Various	Large
	p. 666	Re-inventing Singapore's Libraries	Singapore	Government services	Large
Chapter 21 Corporate social responsibility	p. 673	Marmite	UK	Food processing	Large
	p. 676	Holcim	Global	Quarrying	Large
	p. 679	Hewlett-Packard	USA	Information systems	Large
	p. 684	The Gap	Global	Retail	Large
	p. 690	CSR as it is presented: HSBC, Orange, John Lewis Partnership and Starbucks	Various	Various	Large

Making the most of this book and MyOMLab

Check your understanding

Each chapter opens with a set of **Key questions** to identify major topics. **Summary answers** conclude the chapter. You can check your understanding of each chapter by taking the **Sample tests of self-assessment questions** on MyOMLab at **www.myomlab.com**.

Practice makes perfect

Worked examples show how quantitative and qualitative techniques can be used in operations management. **Problems and applications** at the end of the chapter allow you to apply these techniques, and you can get more practice as well as guided solutions from the **Study plan** on MyOMLab at **www.myomlab.com**.

Analyse operations in action

The **Operations in practice** and **Case study** features in each chapter illustrate and encourage you to analyse operations management in action. You can see and hear more about how theory is applied in practice in the video clips in the **Multimedia library** in MyOMLab at www.myomlab.com.

Take a different view

Critical commentaries, together with **Selected further reading** and **Useful websites** at the end of each chapter, show a diversity of viewpoint and encourage you to think critically about operations management. You can link to the **Useful websites** in the **Multimedia library** of MyOMLab at www.myomlab.com.

Preface

Introduction

Operations management is *important*. It is concerned with creating the services and products upon which we all depend. And all organizations produce some mixture of services and products, whether that organization is large or small, manufacturing or service, for profit or not for profit, public or private. Thankfully, most companies have now come to understand the importance of operations. This is because they have realized that effective operations management gives the potential to improve both efficiency and customer service simultaneously. But more than this, operations management is *everywhere*, it is not confined to the operations function. All managers, whether they are called Operations or Marketing or Human Resources or Finance, or whatever, manage processes and serve customers (internal or external). This makes at least part of their activities 'operations'.

Operations management is also *exciting*. It is at the centre of so many of the changes affecting the business world – changes in customer preference, changes in supply networks brought about by internet-based technologies, changes in what we want to do at work, how we want to work, where we want to work, and so on. There has rarely been a time when operations management was more topical or more at the heart of business and cultural shifts.

Operations management is also *challenging*. Promoting the creativity which will allow organizations to respond to so many changes is becoming the prime task of operations managers. It is they who must find the solutions to technological and environmental challenges, the pressures to be socially responsible, the increasing globalization of markets and the difficult-to-define areas of knowledge management.

The aim of this book

This book provides a clear, authoritative, well-structured and interesting treatment of operations management as it applies to a variety of businesses and organizations. The text provides both a logical path through the activities of operations management and an understanding of their strategic context.

More specifically, this text is:

- *Strategic* in its perspective. It is unambiguous in treating the operations function as being central to competitiveness.
- *Conceptual* in the way it explains the reasons why operations managers need to take decisions.
- *Comprehensive* in its coverage of the significant ideas and issues which are relevant to most types of operation.
- *Practical* in that the issues and challenges of making operations management decisions *in practice* are discussed. The 'Operations in practice' feature, which starts every chapter, the short cases that appear through the chapters and the case studies at the end of each chapter all explore the approaches taken by operations managers in practice.
- *International* in the examples which are used. There are over 120 descriptions of operations practice from all over the world.
- *Balanced* in its treatment. This means we reflect the balance of economic activity between service and manufacturing operations. Around seventy-five per cent of examples are from service organizations and twenty-five per cent from manufacturing.

Who should use this book?

Anyone who is interested in how services and products are created.

- *Undergraduates* on business studies, technical or joint degrees should find it sufficiently structured to provide an understandable route through the subject (no prior knowledge of the area is assumed).
- *MBA students* should find that its practical discussions of operations management activities enhance their own experience.
- *Postgraduate students* on other specialist masters degrees should find that it provides them with a well-grounded and, at times, critical approach to the subject.

Distinctive features

Clear structure

The structure of the book uses a model of operations management which distinguishes between direct, design, deliver and develop.

Illustrations-based

Operations management is a practical subject and cannot be taught satisfactorily in a purely theoretical manner. Because of this, we have used examples and 'boxed' short cases which explain issues faced by real operations.

Worked examples

Operations management is a subject that blends qualitative and quantitative perspectives; 'worked examples' are used to demonstrate how both types of technique can be used.

Critical commentaries

Not everyone agrees about what is the best approach to the various topics and issues with operations management. This is why we have included 'critical commentaries' that pose alternative views to the one being expressed in the main flow of the text.

Summary answers to key questions

Each chapter is summarized in the form of a list of bullet points. These extract the essential points which answer the key questions posed at the beginning of each chapter.

Case studies

Every chapter includes a case study suitable for class discussion. The cases are usually short enough to serve as illustrations, but have sufficient content also to serve as the basis of case sessions.

Problems and applications

Every chapter includes a set of problem-type exercises. These can be used to check out your understanding of the concepts illustrated in the worked examples. There are also activities that support the learning objectives of the chapter that can be done individually or in groups.

Selected further reading

Every chapter ends with a short list of further reading which takes the topics covered in the chapter further, or treats some important related issues. The nature of each further reading is also explained.

Useful websites

A short list of web addresses is included in each chapter for those who wish to take their studies further.

To the Instructor . . .

Teaching and learning resources for the 7th edition

New for the seventh edition

Our users have been, as usual, very generous in answering our questions as to how we can improve the book. Our research for the 7th edition resulted in maintaining the successful structure of previous editions and incorporating the following key changes:

- The topic of Corporate Social Responsibility (CSR) has been emphasized further, both in the final chapter and throughout the book.
- We have further strengthened the emphasis on the idea that 'operations management' is relevant to every functional area of the organization.
- The 'Operations in Practice' that are used to introduce the topic at the beginning of each chapter and the 'Short case' sections have been substantially refreshed.
- New ideas in operations management have been included in order to keep the text up to date with the latest trends while retaining its emphasis on the foundations of the subject.
- Several of the cases at the end of the chapter are new (but the old ones are still available on the website), and provide an up-to-date selection of operations issues.
- The book has been visually redesigned to aid learning.

Instructor's resources

A completely new instructor's manual is available to lecturers adopting this textbook, together with PowerPoint presentations for each chapter and a Testbank of assessment questions. Visit **www.pearsoned.co.uk/slack** to access these.

Most importantly, a new set of online resources to enable students to check their understanding, practise key techniques and improve their problem-solving skills now accompanies the book. Please see below for details of MyOMLab.

 The key to greater understanding and better grades in Operations Management!

MyOMLab for instructors

MyOMLab is designed to save you time in preparing and delivering assignments and assessments for your course, and to enable your students to study independently and at their own pace. Using MyOMLab, you can take advantage of:

- A wide range of engaging resources, including PowerPoint slides and video.
- Hundreds of self-assessment questions, including algorithmically-generated quantitative values which generate a different problem every time.
- A Homework feature, allowing you to assign work for your students to prepare for your next class or seminar.
- A Gradebook which tracks students' performance on sample tests as well as assessments of your own design.

If you'd like to learn more or find out how MyOMLab could help you, please contact your local Pearson representative at **www.pearsoned.co.uk/replocator** or visit **www.myomlab.com**.

Making the most of this book

All academic textbooks in business management are, to some extent, simplifications of the messy reality which is actual organizational life. Any book has to separate topics, in order to study them, which in reality are closely related. For example, technology choice impacts on job design which in turn impacts on quality control; yet we have treated these topics individually. The first hint therefore in using this book effectively is to look out for all the links between the individual topics. Similarly with the sequence of topics, although the chapters follow a logical structure, they need not be studied in this order. Every chapter is, more or less, self-contained. Therefore, study the chapters in whatever sequence is appropriate to your course or your individual interests. But because each part has an introductory chapter, those students who wish to start with a brief 'overview' of the subject may wish first to study Chapters 1, 4, 10 and 18 and the chapter summaries of selected chapters. The same applies to revision – study the introductory chapters and summary answers to key questions.

The book makes full use of the many practical examples and illustrations which can be found in all operations. Many of these were provided by our contacts in companies, but many also come from journals, magazines and newspapers. So if you want to understand the importance of operations management in everyday business life, look for examples and illustrations of operations

management decisions and activities in newspapers and magazines. There are also examples which you can observe every day. Whenever you use a shop, eat a meal in a restaurant, borrow a book from the library or ride on public transport, consider the operations management issues of all the operations for which you are a customer.

The case exercises and study activities are there to provide an opportunity for you to think further about the ideas discussed in the chapters. Study activities can be used to test out your understanding of the specific points and issues discussed in the chapter and discuss them as a group, if you choose. If you cannot answer these you should revisit the relevant parts of the chapter. The case exercises at the end of each chapter will require some more thought. Use the questions at the end of each case exercise to guide you through the logic of analysing the issue treated in the case. When you have done this individually, try to discuss your analysis with other course members. Most important of all, every time you analyse one of the case exercises (or any other case or example in operations management), start off your analysis with the two fundamental questions:

- How is this organization trying to compete (or satisfy its strategic objectives if a not-for-profit organization)?
- What can the operation do to help the organization compete more effectively?

 The key to greater understanding and better grades in Operations Management!

MyOMLab for students

MyOMLab has been developed to help students make the most of their studies in operations management. Visit MyOMLab at **www.myomlab.com** to find valuable teaching and learning material including:

- Self-assessment questions and a personalized Study Plan to diagnose areas of strength and weakness, direct students' learning, and improve results.
- Unlimited practice on quantitative techniques and solving problems.
- Flashcards to aid exam revision.
- Video clips and short cases to illustrate operations management in action.
- Questions that are mapped to learning objectives (rather than just to chapters).

Ten steps to getting a better grade in operations management

We could say that the best rule for getting a better grade is to be good. We mean really, really good! But, there are plenty of us who, while fairly good, don't get as good a grade as we really deserve. So, if you are studying operations management, and you want a really good grade, try following these simple steps:

Step 1 Practise, practise, practise. Use the Key questions and the Problems and applications to check your understanding. Use the Study plan feature in MyOMLab and practise to master the topics which you find difficult.

Step 2 Remember a few **key models**, and apply them wherever you can. Use the diagrams and models to describe some of the examples that are contained within the chapter. You can also use the revision pod casts on MyOMLab.

Step 3 Remember to use both **quantitative and qualitative analysis.** You'll get more credit for appropriately mixing your methods: use a quantitative model to answer a quantitative question and vice versa, but qualify this with a few well-chosen sentences. Both the chapters of the book, and the exercises on MyOMLab, incorporate qualitative and quantitative material.

Step 4 There's always a *strategic* **objective** behind any operational issue. Ask yourself, 'Would a similar operation with a different strategy do things differently?' Look at the Short cases, Case studies, and Operations in practice pieces in the book.

Step 5 Research widely around the topic. Use websites that you trust – we've listed some good websites at the end of each chapter and on MyOMLab. You'll get more credit for using references that come from genuine academic sources.

Step 6 Use **your own experience.** Every day, you're experiencing an opportunity to apply the principles of operations management. Why is the queue at the airport check-in desk so long? What goes on behind the 'hole in the wall' of your bank's ATM machines? Use the videos on MyOMLab to look further at operations in practice.

Step 7 Always answer the question. Think 'What is really being asked here? What topic or topics does this question cover?' Find the relevant chapter or chapters, and search the Key questions at the beginning of each chapter and the Summary at the end of each chapter to get you started.

Step 8 Take account of the three tiers of accumulating marks for your answers.

(a) First, demonstrate your knowledge and understanding. Make full use of the text and MyOMLab to find out where you need to improve.
(b) Second, show that you know how to illustrate and apply the topic. The Short cases, Case studies and 'Operations in practice' sections, combined with those on MyOMLab, give you hundreds of different examples.
(c) Third, show that you can discuss and analyse the issues critically. Use the Critical commentaries within the text to understand some of the alternative viewpoints.

Generally, if you can do (a) you will pass; if you can do (a) and (b) you will pass well, and if you can do all three, you will pass with flying colours!

Step 9 Remember not only **what** the issue is about, but also **understand why!** Read the text and apply your knowledge on MyOMLab until you really understand why the concepts and techniques of operations management are important, and what they contribute to an organization's success. Your new-found knowledge will stick in your memory, allow you to develop ideas, and enable you to get better grades.

Step 10 Start now! Don't wait until two weeks before an assignment is due. Log on (**www.myomlab.com**), read on, and GOOD LUCK!

Nigel Slack
Alistair Brandon-Jones
Robert Johnston

About the authors

Nigel Slack is the Professor of Operations Management and Strategy at Warwick University. Previously he has been Professor of Service Engineering at Cambridge University, Professor of Manufacturing Strategy at Brunel University, a University Lecturer in Management Studies at Oxford University and Fellow in Operations Management at Templeton College, Oxford.

He worked initially as an industrial apprentice in the hand-tool industry and then as a production engineer and production manager in light engineering. He holds a Bachelor's degree in Engineering and Master's and Doctor's degrees in Management, and is a chartered engineer. He is the author of many books and papers in the operations management area, including *The Manufacturing Advantage*, published by Mercury Business Books, 1991, and *Making Management Decisions* (with Steve Cooke), 1991, published by Prentice Hall, *Service Superiority* (with Robert Johnston), published in 1993 by EUROMA and *Cases in Operations Management* (with Robert Johnston, Alan Harrison, Stuart Chambers and Christine Harland) third edition published by Financial Times Prentice Hall in 2003, *The Blackwell Encyclopedic Dictionary of Operations Management* (with Michael Lewis) published by Blackwell in 2005, *Operations Strategy* together with Michael Lewis, the third edition published by Financial Times Prentice Hall in 2011 and *Perspectives in Operations Management (Volumes I to IV)* also with Michael Lewis, published by Routledge in 2003, *Operations and Process Management*, with Alistair Brandon-Jones, Robert Johnston and Alan Betts, now in its 3rd edition, 2012. He has authored numerous academic papers and chapters in books. He also acts as a consultant to many international companies around the world in many sectors, especially financial services, transport, leisure and manufacturing. His research is in the operations and manufacturing flexibility and operations strategy areas.

Alistair Brandon-Jones is a Reader in Operations and Supply Management at Manchester Business School, University of Manchester, Visiting Research Fellow at the University of Bath, and Visiting Lecturer at Warwick Medical School. Prior to his move, he was a Senior Lecturer (Associate Professor) and Lecturer (Assistant Professor) at the University of Bath, a Teaching Fellow at Warwick Business School, and worked in a number of operations and logistics roles. He has a PhD and Bachelor's degree from the University of Warwick and is widely published in leading operations and supply management journals. In addition to *Operations Management*, Alistair has three other co-authored books, *Operations and Process Management, Essentials of Operations Management* and *Quantitative Analysis in Operations Management*, published by Pearson. He has been nominated for the Times Higher Education Most Innovative Teacher of the Year Award, is a University of Bath Mary Tasker Teaching Prize winner, and has received a number of other awards for teaching innovation at both Bath and Warwick. Alistair has consulting and executive development experience with a range of organizations around the world including Eni S.p.A Oil & Gas, Italy, Crompton Greaves, India, The Royal Bank of Scotland, Schroders Investment Management, QinetiQ Defense & Security, NHS Purchasing & Supply Agency, The Welsh Assembly, Bahrain Olympic Association, and the Improvement & Development Agency.

Robert Johnston was Professor of Operations Management at Warwick Business School and its Deputy Dean. He was the founding editor of the *International Journal of Service Industry Management* and he also served on the editorial board of the *Journal of Operations Management* and the *International Journal of Tourism and Hospitality Research*. He was the author of the market leading text, *Service Operations Management* (with Graham Clark), now in its 4th edition (2012), published by Financial Times Prentice Hall. Before moving to academia Dr Johnston held several line management and senior management posts in a number of service organizations in both the public and private sectors. As a specialist in service operations, his research interests included service design, service recovery, performance measurement and service quality. He was the author or co-author of many books, as well as chapters in other texts, numerous papers and case studies.

We very much regret that our friend and colleague Bob Johnston passed away shortly after the manuscript for this edition was completed. He will be greatly missed by all his many friends, colleagues and students.

Acknowledgements

During the preparation of the seventh edition of this book, the authors conducted a number of 'faculty workshops' and the many useful comments from these sessions have influenced this and the other books for the 'Warwick group'. Our thanks go to everyone who attended these sessions and other colleagues. We thank Pär Åhlström of Stockholm School of Economics and Alan Betts of ht2.org for case writing help and support, Dr Ran Bhamra, Lecturer in Engineering Management, Loughborough University and Shirley Johnston for case writing help and support. Also, Dr Maggie Zeng of Gloucestershire University, Dr Abhijeet Ghadge, Heriot Watt University, Professor Sven Åke Hörte of Lulea University of Technology, Eamonn Ambrose of University College, Dublin, Colin Armistead of Bournemouth University, Ruth Boaden of Manchester Business School, Emma Brandon-Jones of Manchester Business School, Peter Burcher of Aston University, John K. Christiansen of Copenhagen Business School, Philippa Collins of Heriot-Watt University, Henrique Correa of Rollins College, Florida, Paul Coughlan, Trinity College Dublin, Simon Croom, University of San Diego, Stephen Disney, Cardiff University, Doug Davies of University of Technology, Sydney, Tony Dromgoole of the Irish Management Institute, Dr J.A.C. de Haan of Tilburg University, Carsten Dittrich, University of Southern Denmark, David Evans of Middlesex University, Paul Forrester of Keele University, Keith Goffin, Cranfield University, Ian Graham of Edinburgh University, Alan Harle of Sunderland University, Norma Harrison of Macquarie University, Catherine Hart of Loughborough Business School, Chris Hillam of Sunderland University, Ian Holden of Bristol Business School, Matthias Holweg, Cambridge University, Mickey Howard, Exeter University, Tom Kegan of Bell College of Technology, Hamilton, Denis Kehoe, Liverpool University, Mike Lewis, Bath University, John Maguire of the University of Sunderland, Charles Marais of the University of Pretoria, Roger Maull, Exeter University, Bart McCarthy, Nottingham University, Harvey Maylor of Cranfield University, John Meredith Smith of EAP, Oxford, Michael Milgate of Macquarie University, Keith Moreton of Staffordshire University, Chris Morgan, Cranfield University, Adrian Morris of Sunderland University, Steve New, Oxford University, John Pal of Manchester University, Peter Race of Henley College, Reading University, Ian Sadler of Victoria University, Richard Small, Supply Network Solutions, Andi Smart, Exeter University, Amrik Sohal of Monash University, Alex Skedd of Northumbria Business School, Martin Spring of Lancaster University, Dr Ebrahim Soltani of the University of Kent, R. Stratton of Nottingham Trent University, Dr Nelson Tang of the University of Leicester, David Twigg of Sussex University, Helen Valentine of the University of the West of England, Professor Roland van Dierdonck of the University of Ghent, Dirk Pieter van Donk of the University of Groningen and Peter Worthington.

Our academic colleagues in the Operations Management Group at Warwick Business School, Bath University and Manchester Business School also helped, both by contributing ideas and by creating a lively and stimulating work environment. We are also grateful to many friends, colleagues and company contacts. In particular, thanks for help with this edition goes to Philip Godfrey and Cormac Campbell and their expert colleagues at OEE, David Garman and Carol Burnett of The Oakwood Partnership, Clive Buesnel of Xchanging, Hans Mayer of Nestlé, Peter Norris of the Royal Bank of Scotland, Joanne Cheung of Synter BMW, Tom Dyson of Torchbox, Michael Purtill of Four Seasons Hotel Group, John Matthew of HSPG.

We were lucky to receive continuing professional and friendly assistance from a great publishing team. Especial thanks to Rufus Curnow, Kate Brewin, Philippa Fiszzon, Colin Reed, Rhian McKay, Alison Prior, Kay Holman and Annette Abel.

Finally, all seven editions were organized, and largely word processed, by Angela Slack. It was, yet again, an heroic effort. To Angela – our thanks.

Nigel Slack
Alistair Brandon-Jones
Robert Johnston

Publisher's acknowledgements

We are grateful to the following for permission to reproduce copyright material:

Figures

Figure 2.11b from Spidergram to check on police forces, *The Times* (Miles, A. and Baldwin, T.), 10 July 2002; Figure 3.9 from *Operations Strategy*, 3rd ed., Pearson Education Limited (Slack, N. and Lewis, M.A. 2011) p. 33, Figure 1.12, © Nigel Slack and Michael Lewis 2002, 2008, 2011; Figure 7.6 from For Toyota, patriotism and profits may not mix, *Wall Street Journal* (Dawson, C.), 29 November 2011, republished with permission of Dow Jones & Company, Inc., permission conveyed through Copyright Clearance Center; Figure 9.7 adapted from A new strategy for job enrichment, *California Management Review*, Vol. 17 (3) (Hackman, J.R., Oldham, G., Janson, R. and Purdy, K. 1975), republished with permission of University of California Press, permission conveyed through Copyright Clearance Center; Figure 10.10 from Northamptonshire Police incident grading; Figure 13.7 adapted from What is the right supply chain for your product?, *Harvard Business Review*, March-April, pp. 105–16 (Fisher, M.C. 1997); Figure 15.13 from C.A. Voss and A. Harrison, Strategies for implementing JIT, in *Just-in-Time Manufacture* (Voss, C.A. (ed.) 1987), IFS/Springer-Verlag, Copyright © 1987 Springer; Figure 16.2 adapted from *Project Management for Engineering, Business and Technology*, 4th ed., Routledge (Nicholas, J.M. and Steyn, H. 2012) p. 6, Figure 1.3, © 2012 Routledge, used with permission of Taylor & Francis Books (UK); Figure 16.13 adapted from *Collaboration, Integrated Information, and the Project Life Cycle in Building Design and Construction and Operation*, Construction Users Roundtables (CURT); Figure 17.4 adapted from A conceptual model of service quality and implications for future research, *Journal of Marketing*, Vol. 49, Fall, pp. 41–50 (Parasuraman, A., Zeithaml, V.A. and Berry, L.B. 1985), American Marketing Association; Figure 21.2 Marmite image, reproduced with kind permission of Unilever PLC and group companies.

Tables

Table 8.1 after E-commerce and its impact on operations management, *International Journal of Production Economics*, Vol. 75, pp. 185–97 (Gunasekaran, A., Marri, H.B., McGaughey, R.E. and Nebhwani, M.D. 2002), Elsevier; Table S9.2 adapted from *Principles of Motion Economy: Revisited, Reviewed and Restored*, Proceedings of the Southern Management Association Annual Meeting (Atlanta, GA 1983) (Barnes, F.C. 1983) p. 298; Table 15.1 adapted from *What is the theory of constraints, and how does it compare to lean thinking?* (Rattner, S. 2009) The Lean Enterprise Institute, Copyright © 1999 Sergio Rattner, all rights reserved; Table 21.1 from How Corporate Social Responsibility is Defined: an Analysis of 37 Definitions, *Corporate Social Responsibility and Environment Management*, Vol. 12, No. 2 (Dahlsrud, A. 2006) p. 4, Table 1, John Wiley and Sons.

Text

Case Study on pages 148–9 from *Operations and Process Management*, 2nd ed., Pearson Education (Slack, N., Chambers, S., Johnston, R. and Betts, A. 2009) p. 204, © Pearson Education Limited 2006, 2009; Case Study on pages 218–20 adapted from *Operations and Process Management*, Pearson Education Limited (Slack, N., Chambers, S., Johnston, R. and Betts, A. 2005) © Pearson Education Limited 2006; Case Study on pages 274–6 by Dr Ran Bhamra, Lecturer in Engineering Management, Loughborough University; Case Study on page 317 adapted from *Operations and Process Management*, 3rd ed., Pearson Education (Slack, N., Brandon-Jones, A., Johnston, R. and Betts, A. 2012) © Pearson Education Limited 2006, 2009, 2012; General Displayed Text on page 440 from My way - IT at Butcher's Pet Care, *Engineering and Technology Magazine*, Vol. 4 (13) (Allan, K. 2009), 21 July; Case Study on pages 490–2 by Robert Johnson and Zoe Radnor, with the help of Giovanni Bucci; General Displayed Text on pages 641–2 adapted from a case study by Professors Rui Sousa and Sofia Salgado Pinto, Católica Porto Business School, Portugal, with permission from the authors; Case Study on pages 666–7 by Professors Robert Johnson, Warwick Business School, Chai Kah Hin and Jochen Wirtz, National University of Singapore, and Christopher Lovelock, Yale University; Case Study on page 690 includes extract from *Responsible Sourcing Supplier Workbook*, John Lewis plc © Copyright John Lewis plc.

Photographs

(Key: b-bottom; c-centre; l-left; r-right; t-top)

Alamy Images: Apex News & Pictures Agency 83, 579, Art Kowalsky 477, Candy Box Images 136, Clivestock 101, Corbis Bridge 91, Hannu Liivaar 465, Helen Sessions 417, Hugh Threlfall 31, Ingram Publishing 605, Itar-Tass Photo Agency 144, Jack Sullivan 51, Justin Kase 405, 418, Lucia Lanpur 673, M4OS Photos 323, Numb 444, Paul Marriot 201, Roger Bamber 119, Stephen Woods 252, Thomas Jackson 86, Vario images GmbH & Co.KG 204; **Alistair Brandon-Jones:** 44, 89, 148,

170r, 228, 339, 356, 440, 503, 540; **Andy Maluche/ Photographers Direct:** 229; **Corbis:** 50b, Ultraf 690; **Courtesy of Dyson:** 126; **Digital Vision:** 378; **Getty Images:** 24l, 57, 162, Jasper James 2, 94, 286, 576, 670; **Imagemore Co., Ltd:** 400, 546; **Imagestate Media:** John Foxx 553, John Foxx Collection 535, John Foxx Images 354, Michael Duerinckx 334; **Pearson Education Ltd:** Sozaijiten 614; **PhotoDisc:** Don Farrell 328b, Kim Steele 557, Mitch Hrdlicka 538, Nick Rowe 369, Ryan McVay 266b, Tracy Montana 449; **Photolibrary.com:** Tetra Images 491; **Press Association Images:** 247; **Rex Features:** Voisin Phanic 268; **Shutterstock.com:** Aaron Amat 527, Adisa 641, Ahmad Faizal Yahya 255, Ajay Bhaskar 170l, Alhovik 293, alphaspirit 480, Anna Subbotina 24r, Annette Shaff 551, antipathique 138, anyunov 637, aodaodaodaod 676, Archman 109, 231, Argus 235, Blaz Kure 47tr, 48tr, 50tr, 53tr, 55tr, Buruhtan 47cr, 48cr, 50cr, 53cr, 55cr, cappi thompson 412, Chen WS 452, Cuiphoto 328tl, 336bl, 337bl, Daniel M. Nagy 38, Derek Audette 318, Deymos 176, Diego Cervo 5, 9 (c), Dmitry Kalinovsky 103b, Dragon Images 160, Ecliptic Blue 49, Eimantas Buzas 106, Evgeny Varlamov 9 (a), Filipchuk Oleg Vasiliovich 153, Food Pics 18, Food Pictures 104t, Francisco Amaral Leitão 244, Gyn9037 192, Hadrian 47tl, 48tl, 50tl, 53tl, 55tl, Hana 545, Hannamariah 342, Highviews 547, ID1974 448, ifong 105b, Ingrid W 195, InnervisionArt 435, Ioana Davies 649, Jacqueline Abromeit 37, Jimmi 224, jl661227 218, Jordan Tan 289, justasc 432, Kencko Photography 297, Kzenon 56, 595, Light & Magic Photography 328cl, 335tl, 337tl, Losevsky Photo and Video 97, Luciano Mortula 9 (e), Lucky Photo 328cr, 336br, 337br, Mama-Mia 232, March Cattle 630, Markus 29, Massimiliano Pieraccini 335b, Matusciac Alexandru 387, Max Photographer 611, Michael Rolands 47cl, 48cl, 50cl, 53cl, 55cl, Minerva Studio 129, Mironov 164, Monkey Business Images 443, Montebasso 269, Natursports 660, nostal6ie 104b, Nui7711 76, PENGYOU91 104cl, PeterPhoto123 69r, Pics Five 53b, Prill 662, PT Images 9 (b), RA2 Studio 679, Richard Semik 496, Rob Wilson 69l, Robyn Mackenzie 583, Ronen 64, Santiago Cornejo 15, Scott Cornell 513, Silver John 103t, Silver-John 666, Sinisa Botas 275, Stuart Monk 199, StudioSmart 302, Suzanne Tucker 12, SV Luma 304, Toria 11, Tupungato 430, Valentyn Volkov 133, 589, Viorel Sima 684, Yeko Photo Studio 309, Yuri Acurs 105t, yuyangc 328tr, 335tr, 337tr, 341, zhangyang13576997233 121, Zurijeta 9 (d), 266t.

Cover images: *Front:* **Getty Images**.

In some instances we have been unable to trace the owners of copyright material, and we would appreciate any information that would enable us to do so.

OPERATIONS MANAGEMENT

1   **Operations management**

2   **Operations performance**

3   **Operations strategy**

Part One
INTRODUCTION

This part of the book introduces the idea of the operations function in different types of organization. It identifies the common set of objectives to which operations managers aspire in order to serve their customers, and it explains how operations can have an important strategic role.

Operations management

Key questions

> What is operations management?

> Why is operations management important in all types of organization?

> What is the input-transformation–output process?

> What is the process hierarchy?

> How do operations processes have different characteristics?

> What do operations managers do?

INTRODUCTION

Operations management is about how organizations create and deliver services and products. Everything you wear, eat, sit on, use, read or knock about on the sports field comes to you courtesy of the operations managers who organized its creation and delivery. Every book you borrow from the library, every treatment you receive at the hospital, every service you expect in the shops and every lecture you attend at university – all have been created by operations. While the people who supervised their creation and delivery may not always be called operations managers, that is what they really are. And that is what this book is concerned with – the tasks, issues and decisions of those operations managers who have made the services and products on which we all depend. This is an introductory chapter, so we will examine what we mean by 'operations management', how operations processes can be found everywhere, how they are all similar yet different, and what it is that operations managers do (*see* Fig. 1.1).

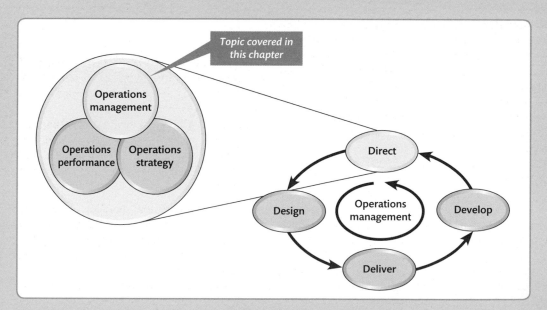

Figure 1.1 This chapter examines operations management

MyOMLab

Check and improve your understanding of this chapter using self-assessment questions and a personalized study plan, a video case study, and an eText – all at www.myomlab.com.

(All chapters start with an 'Operations in practice' example that illustrates some of the issues that will be covered in the chapter.)

Love it or hate it, IKEA is the most successful furniture retailer ever. With 276 stores in 36 countries, they have managed to develop their own special way of selling furniture. Their stores' layout means customers often spend two hours in the store – far longer than in rival furniture retailers. IKEA's philosophy goes back to the original business, started in the 1950s in Sweden by Ingvar Kamprad. He built a showroom on the outskirts of Stockholm where land was cheap and simply displayed suppliers' furniture as it would be in a domestic setting. Increasing sales soon allowed IKEA to start ordering its own self-designed products from local manufacturers. But it was innovation in its operations that dramatically reduced its selling costs. These included the idea of selling furniture as self-assembly flat packs, which reduced production and transport costs, and its 'showroom-warehouse' concept, which required customers to pick the furniture up themselves from the warehouse (which reduced retailing costs). Both of these operating principles are still the basis of IKEA's retail operations process today.

Stores are designed to facilitate the smooth flow of customers, from parking, moving through the store itself, to ordering and picking up goods. At the entrance to each store large notice boards provide advice to shoppers. For young children, there is a supervised children's play area, a small cinema, and a parent and baby room so parents can leave their children in the supervised play area for a time. Parents are recalled via the loudspeaker system if the child has any problems. IKEA 'allow customers to make up their minds in their own time' but 'information points' have staff who can help. All furniture carries a ticket with a code number which indicates its location in the warehouse. (For larger items customers go to the information desks for assistance.) There is also an area where smaller items are displayed, and can be picked directly. Customers then pass through the warehouse where they pick up the items viewed in the showroom. Finally, customers pay at the checkouts, where a ramped conveyor belt moves purchases up to the checkout staff. The exit area has service points, and a loading area that allows customers to bring their cars from the car park and load their purchases.

Behind the public face of IKEA's huge stores is a complex worldwide network of suppliers, 1,300 direct suppliers, about 10,000 sub-suppliers, and wholesale and transport operations, including 26 distribution centres. This supply network is vitally important to IKEA. From purchasing raw materials, right through to finished products arriving in its customers' homes, IKEA relies on close partnerships with its suppliers to achieve both ongoing supply efficiency and new product development. However, IKEA closely controls all supply and development activities from IKEA's hometown of Älmhult in Sweden.

Source: Shutterstock.com/Diego Cervo

But success brings its own problems and some customers became increasingly frustrated with overcrowding and long waiting times. In response IKEA launched a programme 'designing out' the bottlenecks. The changes included:

● clearly marked in-store short cuts allowing those customers who just want to visit one area to avoid having to go through all the preceding areas;
● express checkout tills for customers with a bag only rather than a trolley;
● extra 'help staff' at key points to help customers;
● redesign of the car parks, making them easier to navigate;
● dropping the ban on taking trolleys out to the car parks for loading (originally implemented to stop vehicles being damaged);
● a new warehouse system to stop popular product lines running out during the day;
● more children's play areas.

IKEA spokeswoman Nicki Craddock said: '*We know people love our products but hate our shopping experience. We are being told that by customers every day, so we can't afford not to make changes. We realized a lot of people took offence at being herded like sheep on the long route around stores. Now if you know what you are looking for and just want to get in, grab it and get out, you can.*'

Operations management is a vital part of IKEA's success

IKEA shows how important operations management is for its own success and the success of any type of organization. Of course, IKEA understands its market and its customers. But, just as important, it knows that the way it manages the network of operations that design, produce and deliver its products and services must be right for its market. No organization can survive in the long term if it cannot supply its customers effectively. And this is essentially what operations management is about – designing, producing and delivering products and services that satisfy market requirements. For any business, it is a vitally important activity. Consider just some of the activities that IKEA's operations managers are involved in:

- Arranging the store's layout to give a smooth and effective flow of customers (called process design).
- Designing stylish products that can be flat-packed efficiently (called product design).
- Making sure that all staff can contribute to the company's success (called job design).
- Locating stores of an appropriate size in the most effective place (called supply network design).
- Arranging for the delivery of products to stores (called supply chain management).
- Coping with fluctuations in demand (called capacity management).
- Maintaining cleanliness and safety of storage areas (called failure prevention).
- Avoiding running out of products for sale (called inventory management).
- Monitoring and enhancing quality of service to customers (called quality management).
- Continually examining and improving operations practice (called operations improvement).

And these activities are only a small part of IKEA's total operations management effort. But they do give an indication, first of how operations management should contribute to the business's success, and second, what would happen if IKEA's operations managers failed to be effective in carrying out any of its activities. Yet, although the relative importance of these activities will vary between different organizations, operations managers in all organizations will be making the same *type* of decision (even if *what* they actually decide is different).

WHAT IS OPERATIONS MANAGEMENT?

Operations management is the activity of managing the resources that create and deliver services and products. The operations function is the part of the organization that is responsible for this activity. Every organization has an operations function because every organization creates some type of services and/or products. However, not all types of organization will necessarily call the operations function by this name. (Note in addition that we also use the shorter terms 'the operation' or 'operations' interchangeably with the 'operations function'.) Operations managers are the people who have particular responsibility for managing some, or all, of the resources which comprise the operations function. Again in some organizations, the operations manager could be called by some other name. For example, he or she might be called the 'fleet manager' in a distribution company, the 'administrative manager' in a hospital, or the 'store manager' in a supermarket.

> **✻ Operations principle**
>
> All organizations have 'operations' that produce some mix of services and products.

Operations in the organization

The operations function is central to the organization because it creates and delivers services and products, which is its reason for existing. The operations function is one of the three core functions of any organization. These are:

- **the marketing (including sales) function** – which is responsible for communicating the organization's services and products to its markets in order to generate customer requests;

- **the product/service development function** – which is responsible for coming up with new and modified services and products in order to generate future customer requests;
- **the operations function** – which is responsible for the creation and delivery of services and products based on customer requests.

In addition, there are the support functions which enable the core functions to operate effectively. These include, for example, the accounting and finance function, the technical function, the human resources function, and the information systems function. Remember that different organizations will call their various functions by different names and will have a different set of support functions. Almost all organizations, however, will have the three core functions, because all organizations have a fundamental need to sell their products and services, meet customer requests for services and products, and come up with new services and products to satisfy customers in the future. Table 1.1 shows the activities of the three core functions for a sample of organizations.

In practice, there is not always a clear division between the three core functions or between core and support functions. This leads to some confusion over where the boundaries of the operations function should be drawn. In this book we use a relatively broad definition of operations. We treat much of the product/service development, technical and information systems activities and some of the human resource, marketing, and accounting and finance activities as coming within the sphere of operations management. We view the operations function as comprising all the activities necessary for the day-to-day fulfilment of customer requests. This includes sourcing services and products from suppliers and delivering services and products to customers.

It is a fundamental of modern management that functional boundaries should not hinder efficient internal processes. Figure 1.2 illustrates some of the relationships between operations and other functions in terms of the flow of information between them. Although it is not comprehensive, it gives an idea of the nature of each relationship. However, note that the support functions have a different relationship with operations than the other core functions. Operations management's responsibility to support functions is primarily to make sure that they understand operations' needs and help them to satisfy these needs. The relationship with the other two core functions is more equal – less of *'this is what we want'* and more *'this is what we can do currently – how do we reconcile this with broader business needs?'*

> **✱ Operations principle**
> Operations managers need to co-operate with other functions to ensure effective organizational performance.

Table 1.1 The activities of core functions in some organizations

Core functional activities	Internet service provider (ISP)	Fast food chain	International aid charity	Furniture manufacturer
Operations	Maintain hardware, software and content Implement new links and services	Make burgers, etc. Serve customers Maintain equipment	Give service to the beneficiaries of the charity	Make components Assemble furniture
Marketing and sales	Promote services to users and get registrations Sell advertising space	Advertise on TV Devise promotional materials	Develop funding contracts Mail out appeals for donations	Advertise in magazines Determine pricing policy Sell to stores
Product/service development	Devise new services and commission new information content	Design hamburgers, pizzas, etc. Design decor for restaurants	Develop new appeals campaigns Design new assistance programmes	Design new furniture Co-ordinate with fashionable colours

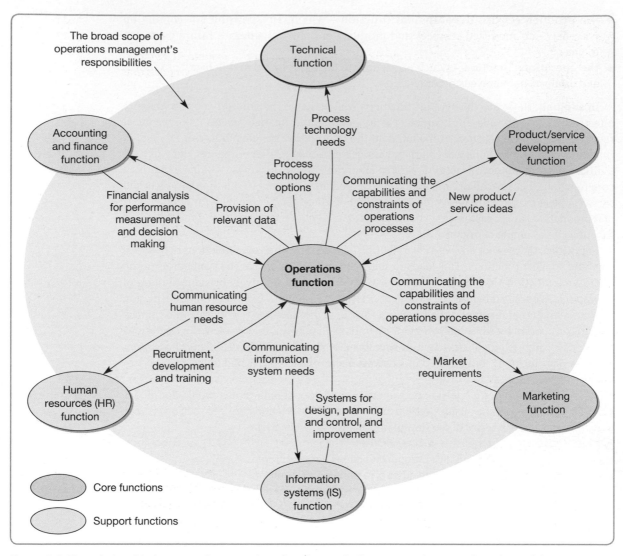

The broad scope of operations management's responsibilities

Technical function

Process technology needs

Process technology options

Accounting and finance function

Financial analysis for performance measurement and decision making

Provision of relevant data

Product/service development function

Communicating the capabilities and constraints of operations processes

New product/ service ideas

Operations function

Communicating human resource needs

Communicating information system needs

Communicating the capabilities and constraints of operations processes

Recruitment, development and training

Market requirements

Human resources (HR) function

Systems for design, planning and control, and improvement

Marketing function

Information systems (IS) function

Core functions

Support functions

Figure 1.2 The relationship between the operations function and other core and support functions of the organization

OPERATIONS MANAGEMENT IS IMPORTANT IN ALL TYPES OF ORGANIZATION

In some types of organization it is relatively easy to visualize the operations function and what it does, even if we have never seen it. For example, most people have seen images of an automobile assembly. But what about an advertising agency? We know vaguely what they do – they create the advertisements that we see in magazines and on television – but what is their operations function? The clue lies in the word 'create'. Any business that creates something must use resources to do so, and so must have an operations activity. Also the automobile plant and the advertising agency do have one important element in common: both have a higher objective – to make a profit from creating and delivering their products or services. Yet not-for-profit organizations also use their resources to create and deliver services, not to make a profit, but to serve society in some way. Look at the following examples of what operations management does in five very different organizations and some common themes emerge.

> ✳ **Operations principle**
>
> The economic sector of an operation is less important in determining how it should be managed than its intrinsic characteristics.

Automobile assembly factory – *operations management uses machines to efficiently assemble products that satisfy current customer demands*

Source: Shutterstock/Evgeny Varlamov

Physician (general practitioner) – *operations management uses knowledge to effectively diagnose conditions in order to treat real and perceived patient concerns*

Source: Shutterstock/PT Images

Management consultant – *operations management uses people to effectively create the services that will address current and potential client needs*

Source: Shutterstock/Diego Cervo

Disaster relief charity – *operations management uses our and our partners' resources to speedily provide the supplies and services that relieve community suffering*

Source: Shutterstock/Zurijeta

Advertising agency – *operations management uses our staff's knowledge and experience to creatively present ideas that delight clients and address their real needs*

Source: Shutterstock/Luciano Mortula

Start with the statement from the 'easy to visualize' automobile plant. Its summary of what operations management does is . . . '*Operations management uses machines to efficiently assemble products that satisfy current customer demands.*' The statements from the other organizations were similar, but used slightly different language. Operations management used not just machines but also . . . '*knowledge, people, our and our partners' resources*', and '*our staff's experience and knowledge*', to '*efficiently (or effectively, or creatively) assemble (or produce, change, sell, move, cure, shape, etc.) products (or services or ideas) that satisfy (or match or exceed or delight) customer (or client or citizens' or society) demands (or needs or concerns or even dreams)*'. So whatever terminology is used there is a common theme and a common purpose to how we can visualize the operations activity in any type of organization; small or large, service or manu-facturing, public or private, profit or not-for-profit. Operations management uses '*resources to appropriately create outputs* that *fulfil defined market requirements*' (*see* Fig. 1.3). However, although the essential nature and purpose of operations management is the same in any type of organization, there are some special issues to consider, particularly in smaller organizations and those whose purpose is to maximize something other than profit.

Operations management in the smaller organization

Operations management is just as important in small organizations as it is in large ones. Irrespective of their size, all companies need to create and deliver their services and products efficiently and effectively. However, in practice, managing operations in a small or medium size organization has its own set of problems. Large companies may have the resources to dedicate individuals to specialized tasks but smaller companies often cannot, so people may have to do different jobs as the need arises. Such an informal structure can allow the company to respond quickly as opportunities or problems present themselves. But decision making can also become confused as individuals' roles overlap. Small companies may have exactly the same operations management issues as large ones but they can be more difficult to separate from the mass of other issues in the organization. However, small operations can also have significant advantages; the short case on Torchbox illustrates this.

Operations management in not-for-profit organizations

Terms such as *competitive advantage*, *markets* and *business*, which are used in this book, are usually associated with companies in the for-profit sector. Yet operations management is also relevant to organizations whose purpose is not primarily to earn profits. Managing the operations in an animal welfare charity, hospital, research organization or govern-ment department is essentially the same as in commercial organizations. Operations have to take the same decisions – how to create and deliver services and products, invest in technology, contract out some of their activities, devise performance measures, improve their operations performance, and so on. However, the strategic objectives of not-for-profit organizations may be more complex and involve a mixture of political, economic, social or environmental objectives. Because of this there may be a greater chance of operations decisions being made under conditions of conflicting objectives. So, for example, it is the

Operations management uses . . .

resources	to	appropriately	create	outputs	that	fulfil	defined	market	requirements
			produce						
experience			change				potential	citizens'	
people		effectively	sell	ideas		match	perceived	client	dreams
machines		efficiently	assemble	products		satisfy	current	customer	demands
knowledge		creatively	move	services		exceed	emerging	society	needs
partners		etc.	cure	etc.		delight	real	etc.	concerns
etc.			shape			etc.	etc.		etc.
			etc.						

Figure 1.3 Operations management uses resources to appropriately create outputs that fulfil defined market requirements

We may take it for granted, yet browsing websites, as part of your studies, your job, or your leisure, is an activity that we all do; probably every day, probably many times each day. So it's important. All organizations need to have a web presence if they want to sell products and services, interact with their customers, or promote their cause. And, not surprisingly, there is a whole industry devoted to designing websites so that they have the right type of impact. In fact, taken over the years, web development has been one of the fastest-growing industries in the world. But it's also a tough industry. Not every web design company thrives, or even survives beyond a couple of years. To succeed, web designers need technology skills, design capabilities, business awareness and operational professionalism.

Source: Shutterstock.com/Toria

One company that has succeeded is Torchbox, an independently owned web design and development company based in Oxfordshire. Founded back in 2000, it now employs 30 people, providing *'high-quality, cost-effective, and ethical solutions for clients who come primarily, but not exclusively, from the charity, non-governmental organizations and public sectors'*.

Co-founder and Technical Director Tom Dyson has been responsible for the technical direction of all major developments. *'There are a number of advantages about being a relatively small operation'*, he says. *'We can be hugely flexible and agile, in what is still a dynamic market. But at the same time we have the resources and skills to provide a creative and professional service. Any senior manager in a firm of our size cannot afford to be too specialized. All of us here have our own specific responsibilities; however, every one of us shares the overall responsibility for the firm's general development. We can also be clear and focused on what type of work we want to do. Our ethos is important to us. We set out to work with clients who share our commitment to environmental sustainability and responsible, ethical business practice; we take our work, and that of our clients, seriously. If you're an arms dealer, you can safely assume that we're not going to be interested.'*

Nevertheless, straightforward operational effectiveness is also essential to Torchbox's business. *'We know how to make sure that our projects run not only on time and to budget'*, says Olly Willans, also a co-founder and the firm's Creative Director, *'but we also like to think that we provide an enjoyable and stimulating experience – both for our customers' development teams and for our staff too. High standards of product and service are important to us: our clients want accessibility, usability, performance and security embedded in their web designs, and of course, they want things delivered on-time and on-budget. We are in a creative industry that depends on fast-moving technologies, but that doesn't mean that we can't also be efficient. We back everything we do with a robust feature-driven development process using a kanban project management methodology which helps us manage our obligations to our clients.'*

The 'kanban' approach used by the Torchbox web development teams originated from car manufacturers like Toyota (it is fully explained in Chapter 15). *'Using sound operations management techniques helps us constantly to deliver value to our clients'*, says Tom Dyson. *'We like to think that our measured and controlled approach to handling and controlling work helps ensure that every hour we work produces an hour's worth of value for our clients and for us.'*

operations staff in a children's welfare department who have to face the conflict between the cost of providing extra social workers and the risk of a child not receiving adequate protection. Nevertheless the vast majority of the topics covered in this book have relevance to all types of organization, including non-profit, even if the context is different and some terms may have to be adapted.

Médecins Sans Frontières MSF (also called Doctors Without Borders) is an independent humanitarian organization providing medical aid where it is most needed, regardless of race, religion, politics or gender, and raising awareness of the plight of the people it helps in countries around the world. Its core work takes place in crisis situations – armed conflicts, epidemics, famines and natural disasters such as floods and earthquakes. Their teams deliver both medical aid (including consultations with a doctor, hospital care, nutritional care, vaccinations, surgery, obstetrics and psychological care) and material aid (including food, shelter, blankets, etc.). Each year, MSF sends around 3,000 doctors, nurses, logisticians, water-and-sanitation experts, administrators and other professionals to work alongside around 25,000 locally hired staff. It is one of the most admired and effective relief organizations in the world. But no amount of fine intentions can translate into effective action without superior operations management. As MSF says, it must be able to react to any crisis with *fast response, efficient logistics systems, and efficient project management*.

Source: Shutterstock.com/Suzanne Tucker

MSF makes every effort to respond quickly and efficiently to crises around the world. Their response procedures are continuously being developed to ensure that they reach those most in need as quickly as possible.

The process has five phases: proposal, assessment, initiation, running the project, and closing. The information that prompts a possible mission can come from governments, the international community, humanitarian organizations such as the United Nations, financial bodies such as the Humanitarian Aid Department of the European Commission (ECHO), or MSF teams already present in the region. Once the information has been checked and validated, MSF sends a team of medical and logistics experts to the crisis area to carry out a quick evaluation. The team assesses the situation, the number of people affected, and the current and future needs, and sends a proposal back to the MSF office. When the proposal is approved, MSF staff start the process of selecting personnel, organizing materials and resources and securing project funds.

Initiating a project involves sending technical equipment and resources to the area. In large crises, planes fly in all the necessary materials so that the work can begin immediately. Thanks to their pre-planned processes, specialized kits and the emergency stores, MSF can distribute material and equipment within 48 hours, ready for the response team to start work as soon as they arrive. Most MSF projects generally run for somewhere between 18 months and three and a half years. Whether an emergency response or a long-term health-care project, the closing process is roughly similar. Once the critical medical needs have been met (which could be after weeks,

months or years depending on the situation), MSF begins to close the project with a gradual withdrawal of staff and equipment. At this stage, the project closes or is passed on to an appropriate organization. MSF will also close a project if risks in the area become too great to ensure staff safety.

Whether they are dealing with urgent emergencies, when material might need to be on a plane within 24 hours, or a long-running programme where a steady supply of equipment and drugs is vital, everything MSF does on the ground depends on an efficient logistics system. It is based on the principle that MSF staff should always have exactly the right materials for the job at hand. So MSF has developed and produced pre-packaged disaster kits ready for transport within hours, including a complete surgical theatre the size of a small conference table and an obstetrics kit the size of a two-drawer filing cabinet. There is an ongoing process of revising the kits every time a new drug or medical tool becomes available.

To make sure they are reacting as quickly as possible, MSF have four logistical centres based in Europe and East Africa plus stores of emergency materials in Central America and East Asia. These purchase, test and store equipment so that aircraft can be loaded and flown into crisis areas within 24 hours. The pre-packaged disaster kits are custom-cleared within the logistics centres ready for flight. But not all supplies are needed quickly. If it is not a dire emergency, MSF reduces its costs by shipping the majority of material and drugs by sea. Because of this, it is vital to monitor stock levels and anticipate future needs so that orders can be placed up to three months in advance of expected requirements.

The new operations agenda

The business environment has a significant impact on what is expected from operations management. In recent years there have been new pressures for which the operations function has needed to develop responses. Table 1.2 lists some of these business pressures and the operations responses to them. These operations responses form a major part of a *new agenda* for operations. Parts of this agenda are trends which have always existed but have accelerated, such as globalization and increased cost pressures. Part of the agenda involves seeking ways to exploit new technologies, most notably the internet. Of course, the list in Table 1.2 is not comprehensive, nor is it universal. But very few operations functions will be unaffected by at least some of these concerns.

THE INPUT–TRANSFORMATION–OUTPUT PROCESS

All operations create and deliver services and products by changing *inputs* into *outputs* using an 'input–transformation–output' process. Figure 1.4 shows this general transformation process model. Put simply, operations are processes that take in a set of input resources which are used to transform something, or are transformed themselves, into outputs of services and products. And although all operations conform to this general input–transformation–output model, they differ in the nature of their specific inputs and outputs. For example, if you stand far enough away from a hospital or a car plant, they might look very similar, but move closer and clear differences do start to emerge. One is a service operation delivering 'services' that change the physiological or psychological condition of patients, the other is a manufacturing operation creating and delivering 'products'. What is inside each operation will also be different. The hospital contains diagnostic, care and therapeutic processes whereas the motor vehicle plant contains metal forming machinery and assembly processes. Perhaps the most important difference between the two operations, however, is the nature of their inputs. The hospital transforms the customers themselves. The patients form part of the input to, and the output from, the operation. The vehicle plant transforms steel, plastic, cloth, tyres and other materials into vehicles.

> **✱ Operations principle**
> All processes have inputs of transforming and transformed resources that they use to create products and services.

Table 1.2 Changes in the business environment are shaping a new operations agenda

The business environment is changing . . .	*Prompting operations responses . . .*
For example . . .	For example . . .
• Increased cost-based competition	• Globalization of operations networking
• Higher quality expectations	• Information-based technologies
• Demands for better service	• Co-creation of service
• More choice and variety	• Internet-based integration of operations activities
• Rapidly developing technologies	• Supply chain management
• Frequent new product/service introduction	• Customer relationship management
• Increased ethical sensitivity	• Flexible working patterns
• Environmental impacts are more transparent	• Mass customization
• More legal regulation	• Fast time-to-market methods
• Greater security awareness	• Lean process design
	• Environmentally sensitive design
	• Supplier 'partnership' and development
	• Failure analysis
	• Business recovery planning

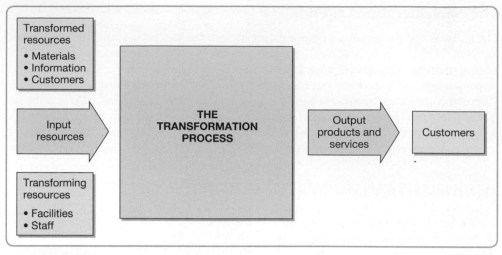

Figure 1.4 All operations are input–transformation–output processes

Inputs to the process

One set of inputs to any operation's processes are transformed resources. These are the resources that are treated, transformed or converted in the process. They are usually a mixture of the following:

- **Materials** – operations which process materials could do so to transform their *physical properties* (shape or composition, for example). Most manufacturing operations are like this. Other operations process materials to change their *location* (parcel delivery companies, for example). Some, like retail operations, do so to change the *possession* of the materials. Finally, some operations *store* materials, such as warehouses.
- **Information** – operations which process information could do so to transform their *informational properties* (that is the purpose or form of the information); accountants do this. Some change the *possession* of the information, for example market research companies sell information. Some *store* the information, for example archives and libraries. Finally, some operations, such as telecommunication companies, change the *location* of the information.
- **Customers** – operations which process customers might change their *physical properties* in a similar way to materials processors: for example, hairdressers or cosmetic surgeons.

> **✱ Operations principle**
>
> Transformed resource inputs to a process are materials, information or customers.

Some *store* (or more politely *accommodate*) customers: hotels, for example. Airlines, mass rapid transport systems and bus companies transform the *location* of their customers, while hospitals transform their *physiological state*. Some are concerned with transforming their *psychological state*, for example most entertainment services such as music, theatre, television, radio and theme parks. But customers are not always simple 'passive' items to be processed. They can also play a more active part in many operations and processes. For example, they create the atmosphere in a restaurant; they provide the stimulating environment in learning groups in education; they provide information at check-in desks, and so on. When customers play this role it is usually referred to as co-production (or co-creation for new services) because the customer plays a vital part in the provision of the product/service offering.

Some operations have inputs of materials *and* information *and* customers, but usually one of these is dominant. For example, a bank devotes part of its energies to producing printed statements by processing inputs of material but no one would claim that a bank is a printer. The bank also is concerned with processing inputs of customers at its branches and contact centres. However, most of the bank's activities are concerned with processing inputs

It isn't the biggest bank in Europe, but many judge it to be the best as far as its customer service is concerned. Now part of the giant HSBC Group, First Direct has no high street branches, but relies on internet-based and telephone transactions with its customers. Yet the bank has consistently been voted the best at customer service, not just when measured against other banks, but in comparison with all types of service companies. More than one in four of First Direct customers joins because of personal recommendation.

Source: Shutterstock.com/Santiago Cornejo

So how has it managed this? First, it focuses uncompromisingly on its customers and how best to serve them. Staff in all parts of its operations – whether they are in direct contact with customers (such as the bank's call centres) or in its 'back office' operations (such as their Information Technology provision) – are trained to understand the importance of customer care. As one of the bank's trainers puts it, *'They have continued with their philosophy of putting people first, not resting on their laurels and valuing training and development as an investment not a cost. When staff are treated in an excellent way, they deliver excellent customer service – the old saying you reap what you sow is so true! I've come across a few companies that have used some of the techniques and models in training that First Direct use, but they don't always have the thorough knowledge to embed them strongly.'*

First Direct is renowned for the quality of its customer service. So it's no surprise that the bank is inviting customers to collaborate on new ideas. One of the most innovative ideas is the 'First Direct Labs website'. The idea sounds simple, but is effective. The bank posts new ideas on the site and visitors comment on them. Natalie Cowen, Head of Brand and Communications at the bank, is enthusiastic about the idea of the 'co-creation' of new services. *'The First Direct Lab is a straightforward concept that I'm surprised more innovative companies aren't using. We have a method of directly engaging with our customers and the general public to influence and drive the direction we take with products, services and, well, everything*

really. One of the main reasons people feel let down by a brand, from financial institutions to supermarkets, is that they believe their opinions and frustrations haven't been considered. Customer service is at the heart of everything we do at First Direct, so it seemed obvious to turn to co-creation to make sure we're on the right path. It seems obvious, but surely it's better to discover what your customers really want before spending time, money and resources on a project – co-creation allows us to do just that.'

However, customers' ideas and preferences do not always agree with the bank's. One of its first initiatives was to ask for feedback on plans to redesign its debit card. Customer feedback indicated that the proposed design looked too similar to its credit card, and the two were hard to tell apart when paying at the checkout. *'When we asked customers for feedback it turned out they liked the existing design for the debit card and would prefer any changes to be made to the credit card instead'*, says Natalie Cowen.

Nor are all customer suggestions positive. For example, a proposal to develop a mobile app for finding a mortgage proved unpopular. Customers said that this was something they would do on a PC at home, not on the move. Yet even negative responses are valued by the bank because it is *'a demonstration of the bank's commitment to transparency and its willingness to throw open the design process to customers'*.

of information about its customers' financial affairs. As customers, we may be unhappy with badly printed statements and we may be unhappy if we are not treated appropriately in the bank. But if the bank makes errors in our financial transactions, we suffer in a far more fundamental way. Table 1.3 gives examples of operations with their dominant transformed resources.

Table 1.3 Dominant transformed resource inputs of various operations

Predominantly processing inputs of materials	Predominantly processing inputs of information	Predominantly processing inputs of customers
All manufacturing operations	Accountants	Hairdressers
Mining companies	Bank headquarters	Hotels
Retail operations	Market research company	Hospitals
Warehouses	Financial analysts	Mass rapid transports
Postal services	News service	Theatres
Container shipping line	University research unit	Theme parks
Trucking companies	Telecoms company	Dentists

The other set of inputs to any operations process are transforming resources. These are the resources which act upon the transformed resources. There are two types which form the 'building blocks' of all operations:

- **facilities** – the buildings, equipment, plant and process technology of the operation;
- **staff** – the people who operate, maintain, plan and manage the operation. (Note we use the term 'staff' to describe all the people in the operation, at any level.)

The exact nature of both facilities and staff will differ between operations. To a five-star hotel, its facilities consist mainly of 'low-tech' buildings, furniture and fittings. To a nuclear-powered aircraft carrier, its facilities are 'high-tech' nuclear generators, and sophisticated electronic equipment. Staff will also differ between operations. Most staff employed in a factory assembling domestic refrigerators may not need a very high level of technical skill. In contrast, most staff employed by an accounting company are, hopefully, highly skilled in their own particular 'technical' skill (accounting). Yet although skills vary, all staff can make a contribution. An assembly worker who consistently misassembles refrigerators will dissatisfy customers and increase costs just as surely as an accountant who cannot add up. The balance between facilities and staff also varies. A computer chip manufacturing company, such as Intel, will have significant investment in physical facilities. A single chip fabrication plant can cost in excess of $4 billion, so operations managers will spend a lot of their time managing their facilities. Conversely, a management consultancy firm depends largely on the quality of its staff. Here operations management is largely concerned with the development and deployment of consultant skills and knowledge.

> ✳ **Operations principle**
>
> All processes have transforming resources of facilities (equipment, technology, etc.) and people.

Outputs from the process

Products and services are different. Products are usually tangible things, whereas services are activities or processes. A car or a newspaper or a restaurant meal is a product, whereas a service is the activity of the customer using or consuming that product. Some services do not involve products. Consultancy advice or a haircut is a process (though some products may be supplied in support of the service, such as a report or a hair gel). Also, while most products can be stored, at least for a short time, service only happens when it is consumed or used. So accommodation in an hotel room, for example, will perish if it is not sold that night; a restaurant table will remain empty unless someone uses it that evening.

Most operations produce both products and services

Some operations create and deliver just services and others just products, but most operations combine both elements. Figure 1.5 shows a number of operations (including some described as examples in this chapter) positioned in a spectrum from 'pure' products to 'pure' services. Crude oil producers are concerned almost exclusively with the product which comes from their

Figure 1.5 The output from most operations is a mixture of products and services. Some general examples are shown here together with some of the operations featured as examples in this chapter

oil wells. So are aluminium smelters, but they might also deliver some services such as technical advice. Services in these circumstances are called facilitating services. To an even greater extent, machine tool manufacturers deliver facilitating services such as technical advice and applications engineering. The services delivered by a restaurant are an essential part of what the customer is paying for. It is both a manufacturing operation which creates and delivers meals and a provider of service in the advice, ambience and service of the food. An information systems provider may create software 'products', but primarily it is providing a service to its customers, with facilitating products. Certainly, a management consultancy, although it produces reports and documents, would see itself primarily as a service provider. Finally, pure services solely create and deliver services – a psychotherapy clinic, for example. Of the short cases and examples in this chapter, IKEA and Pret A Manger both create and deliver products and services, but IKEA's customers are probably more interested in the 'products' they collect from the store than any idea of 'service'. Torchbox produces intangible 'products' and web design advice 'services' in close collaboration with its clients, as does MSF. Formule 1 and the resort hotel are close to being pure services, although they both have some tangible elements such as food.

Increasingly the distinction between services and products is difficult to define and not particularly useful. Software is both a product (sold on a disc) and a service when sold over the internet or used by the customer. A restaurant meal is both a product and also a service as it is delivered and consumed. Indeed we would argue that *all* operations are service providers which may create and deliver products as part of the offering to their customers. This is why operations management is important to all organizations. Whether they see themselves as manufacturers or service providers is very much a secondary issue.

> *** Operations principle**
>
> Most operations produce a mixture of tangible products and intangible services.

> *** Operations principle**
>
> Whether an operation produces tangible products or intangible services is becoming increasingly irrelevant. In a sense all operations produce service for their customers.

Customers

Customers may be an input to many operations (see earlier) but they are also the reason for their existence. If there were no customers (whether business customers, users or consumers), there would be no operation. So it is critical that operations managers are aware of

Customer service at Pret A Manger[5]

Pret A Manger are proud of their customer service. *'We'd like to think we react to our customers' feelings (the good, the bad, the ugly) with haste and absolute sincerity'*, they say. *'Pret customers have the right to be heard. Do call or email. Our UK Managing Director is available if you would like to discuss Pret with him. Alternatively, our CEO hasn't got much to do; hassle him!'*

It's a bold approach to customer service, but Pret has always been innovative. Described by the press as having 'revolutionized the concept of sandwich making and eating', Pret A Manger opened their first shop in London and now they have over 260 shops in the UK, New York, Hong Kong and Tokyo. They say that their secret is to focus continually on the quality of their food and of their service. They avoid the chemicals and preservatives common in most 'fast' food. *'Many food retailers focus on extending the shelf life of their food, but that's of no interest to us. We sell food that can't be beaten for freshness. At the end of the day, we give whatever we haven't sold to charity to help feed those who would otherwise go hungry.'*

Pret A Manger shops have their own kitchen where fresh ingredients are delivered every morning, with food prepared throughout the day. The team members serving on the tills at lunchtime will have been making sandwiches in the kitchen that morning. *'We are determined never to forget that our hardworking people make all the difference. They are our heart and soul. When they care, our business is sound. If they cease to care, our business goes down the drain. In a retail sector where high staff turnover is normal, we're pleased to say our people are much more likely to stay around! We work hard at building great teams. We take our reward schemes and career opportunities very seriously. We don't work nights (generally), we wear jeans, we party!'*

Customer feedback is regarded as being particularly important at Pret. Examining customers' comments for improvement ideas is a key part of weekly management

Source: Shutterstock.com/Food Pics

meetings, and of the daily team briefs in each shop. Moreover, staff at Pret are rewarded in cash for being nice to customers. They collect bonuses for delivering outstanding customer service. Every week, each Pret's outlet is visited by a secret shopper who scores the shop on such performance measures as speed of service, product availability and cleanliness. In addition the mystery shopper rates the 'engagement level' of the staff; questions include, 'did servers connect with eye contact, a smile and some polite remarks?' Assessors score out of 50. If the store gets 43 points or more every team member receives an extra payment for every hour worked; and if an individual is mentioned by the mystery shopper for providing outstanding service, they get an extra payment. *'The emphasis on jollity and friendliness has been a winner'*, said James Murphy of the Future Foundation, a management consultant. *'In the highly competitive sandwich market, that's been a big contributor to their success.'* But not everyone agrees with using mystery shoppers. *'It is the equivalent of asking one customer in a shop what they thought at that exact moment, and then planning an entire store-improvement strategy around the one piece of feedback'*, says Jeremy Michael of the Service Management Group, another consultancy.

customer needs, both current and potential. This information will determine what the operation has to do and how it has to do it (the operation's strategic performance objectives), which in turn defines the service/product offering to be designed, created and delivered.

THE PROCESS HIERARCHY

So far we have discussed operations management, and the input–transformation–output model, at the level of 'the operation'. For example, we have described 'the web designer', 'the bank', 'the sandwich shop', 'the disaster relief operation', and so on. But look inside any of these operations and one will see that all operations consist of a collection of processes (though these processes may be called 'units' or 'departments') interconnecting with each other to form a network. Each process acts as a smaller version of the whole operation of which they form a part, and transformed resources flow in between them. In fact within any operation, the mechanisms that actually transform inputs into outputs are these processes. A process is an arrangement of resources that create some mixture of service and products. They are the 'building blocks' of all operations, and they form an 'internal network' within an operation. Each process is, at the same time, an internal supplier and an internal customer for other processes. This 'internal customer' concept provides a model to analyse the internal activities of an operation. It is also a useful reminder that, by treating internal customers with the same degree of care as external customers, the effectiveness of the whole operation can be improved. Table 1.4 illustrates how a wide range of operations can be described in this way.

Within each of these processes is another network of individual units of resource such as individual people and individual items of process technology (machines, computers, storage facilities, etc.). Again transformed resources flow between each unit of transforming resource. So any business, or operation, is made up of a network of processes and any process is made up of a network of resources. But also any business or operation can itself be viewed as part of a greater network of businesses or operations. It will have operations that supply it with the services and products it needs and, unless it deals directly with the end consumer, it will supply customers who themselves may go on to supply their own customers. Moreover, any operation could have several suppliers, several customers and may be in competition with other operations creating similar services or products to itself. This network of operations is called the supply network. In this way the input–transformation output model can be used at a number of different 'levels of analysis'. Here we have used the idea to analyse businesses at three levels, the process, the operation and the supply network. But one could define many different 'levels of analysis', moving upwards from small to larger processes, right up to the huge supply network that describes a whole industry.

> *** Operations principle**
>
> A process perspective can be used at three levels: the level of the operation itself, the level of the supply network, and the level of individual processes.

Table 1.4 Some operations described in terms of their processes

Operation	Some of the operation's inputs	Some of the operation's processes	Some of the operation's outputs
Airline	Aircraft Pilots and air crew Ground crew Passengers and freight	Check passengers in Board passengers Fly passengers and freight around the world Care for passengers	Transported passengers and freight
Department store	Products for sale Sales staff Information systems Customers	Source and store products Display products Give sales advice Sell products	Customers and products 'assembled' together.
Police	Police officers Computer systems Information systems Public (law-abiding and criminals)	Crime prevention Crime detection Information gathering Detaining suspects	Lawful society, public with a feeling of security
Frozen food manufacturer	Fresh food Operators Processing technology Cold storage facilities	Source raw materials Prepare food Freeze food Pack and freeze food	Frozen food

This idea is called the hierarchy of operations and is illustrated for a business that makes television programmes and videos in Figure 1.6. It will have inputs of production, technical and administrative staff, cameras, lighting, sound and recording equipment, and so on. It transforms these into finished programmes, music videos, etc. At a more macro level, the business itself is part of a whole supply network, acquiring services from creative agencies, casting agencies, and studios, liaising with promotion agencies, and serving its broadcasting company customers. At a more micro level, within this overall operation there are many individual processes; workshops manufacturing the sets; marketing processes that liaise with potential customers; maintenance and repair processes that care for, modify and design technical equipment; production units that shoot the programmes and videos; and so on. Each of these individual processes can be represented as a network of yet smaller processes, or even individual units of resource. So, for example, the set manufacturing process could comprise of four smaller processes: one that designs the sets, one that constructs them, one that acquires the props, and one that finishes (assembles and paints) the set.

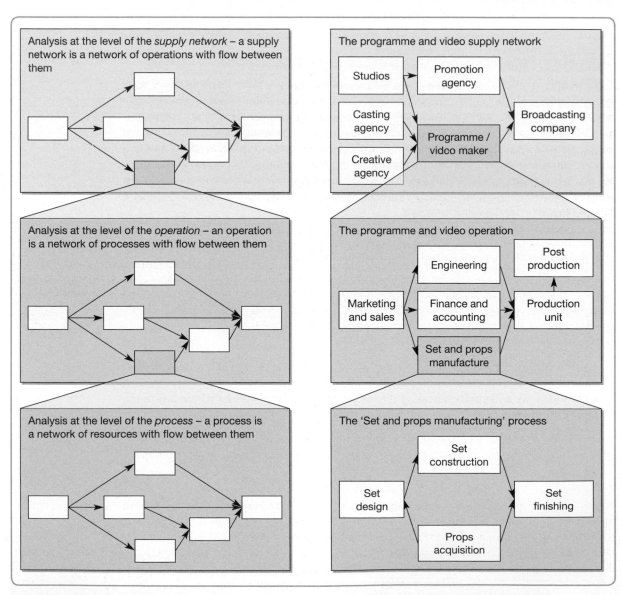

Figure 1.6 Operations and process management requires analysis at three levels: the supply network, the operation, and the process

The idea of the internal network of processes is seen by some as being over-simplistic. In reality the relationship between groups and individuals is significantly more complex than that between commercial entities. One cannot treat internal customers and suppliers exactly as we do external customers and suppliers. External customers and suppliers usually operate in a free market. If an organization believes that in the long run it can get a better deal by purchasing services and products from another supplier, it will do so. But internal customers and suppliers are not in a 'free market'. They cannot usually look outside either to purchase input resources or to sell their output services and products (although some organizations are moving this way). Rather than take the 'economic' perspective of external commercial relationships, models from organizational behaviour, it is argued, are more appropriate.

Operations management is relevant to all parts of the business

The example in Figure 1.6 demonstrates that it is not just the operations function that manages processes; all functions manage processes. For example, the marketing function will have processes that create demand forecasts, processes that create advertising campaigns and processes that create marketing plans. These processes in the other functions also need managing using similar principles to those within the operations function. Each function will have its 'technical' knowledge. In marketing, this is the expertise in designing and shaping marketing plans; in finance, it is the technical knowledge of financial reporting. Yet each will also have a 'process management' role of producing plans, policies, reports and services.

The implications of this are very important. Because all managers have some responsibility for managing processes, they are, to some extent, operations managers. They all should want to give good service to their (often internal) customers, and they all will want to do this efficiently. So, operations management is relevant for all functions, and all managers should have something to learn from the principles, concepts, approaches and techniques of operations management. It also means that we must distinguish between two meanings of 'operations':

> *** Operations principle**
> All parts of the business manage processes so all parts of the business have an operations role and need to understand operations management principles.

- **'operations' as a function**, meaning the part of the organization which creates and delivers services and products for the organization's external customers;
- **'operations' as an activity**, meaning the management of the processes within any of the organization's functions.

Table 1.5 illustrates just some of the processes that are contained within some of the more common non-operations functions, the outputs from these processes and their 'customers'.

Business processes

Whenever a business attempts to satisfy its customers' needs it will use many processes, both in its operations and its other functions. Each of these processes will contribute some part to fulfilling customer needs. For example, the television programme and video production company, described previously, creates and delivers two types of 'product'. Both of these involve a slightly different mix of processes within the company. The company decides to reorganize its operations so that each product is created from start to finish by a dedicated process that contains all the elements

> *** Operations principle**
> Processes are defined by how the organization chooses to draw process boundaries.

Table 1.5 Some examples of processes in non-operations functions

Organizational function	Some of its processes	Outputs from its process	Customer(s) for its outputs
Marketing and sales	Planning process	Marketing plans	Senior management
	Forecasting process	Sales forecasts	Sales staff, planners, operations
	Order-taking process	Confirmed orders	Operations, finance
Finance and accounting	Budgeting process	Budgets	Everyone
	Capital approval processes	Capital request evaluations	Senior management, requesters
	Invoicing processes	Invoices	External customers
Human resources management	Payroll processes	Salary statements	Employees
	Recruitment processes	New hires	All other processes
	Training processes	Trained employees	All other processes
Information technology	Systems review process	System evaluation	All other processes
	Help desk process	Advice	All other processes
	System implementation project processes	Implemented working systems and aftercare	All other processes

necessary for its production, as in Figure 1.7. So customer needs for each product are entirely fulfilled from within what is called an 'end-to-end' business process. These often cut across conventional organizational boundaries. Reorganizing (or 're-engineering') process boundaries and organizational responsibilities around these business processes is the philosophy behind business process re-engineering (BPR) which is discussed further later (see Chapter 18).

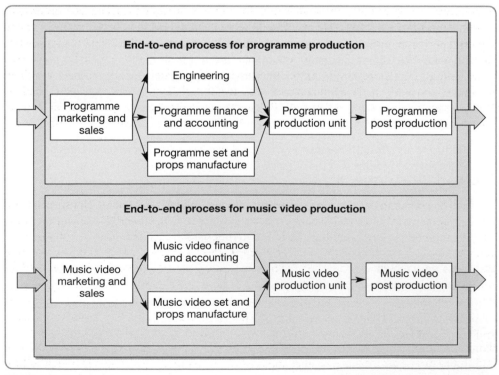

Figure 1.7 The television and video company divided into two 'end-to-end' business processes, one dedicated to creating programmes and the other dedicated to creating music videos

OPERATIONS PROCESSES HAVE DIFFERENT CHARACTERISTICS

Although all operations processes are similar in that they all transform inputs, they do differ in a number of ways, four of which, known as the four Vs, are particularly important:

- The **volume** of their output;
- The **variety** of their output;
- The **variation** in the demand for their output;
- The degree of **visibility** which customers have of the creation of their output.

The volume dimension

Let us take a familiar example. The epitome of high-volume hamburger production is McDonald's, which serves millions of burgers around the world every day. Volume has important implications for the way McDonald's operations are organized. The first thing you notice is the repeatability of the tasks people are doing and the systemization of the work where standard procedures are set down specifying how each part of the job should be carried out. Also, because tasks are systematized and repeated, it is worthwhile developing specialized fryers and ovens. All this gives *low unit costs*. Now consider a small local cafeteria serving a few 'short order' dishes. The range of items on the menu may be similar to the larger operation, but the volume will be far lower, so the repetition will also be far lower and the number of staff will be lower (possibly only one person) and therefore individual staff are likely to perform a wider range of tasks. This may be more rewarding for the staff, but less open to systemization. Also, it is less feasible to invest in specialized equipment. So the cost per burger served is likely to be higher (even if the price is comparable).

The variety dimension

A taxi company offers a relatively high-variety service. It is prepared to pick you up from almost anywhere and drop you off almost anywhere. To offer this variety it must be relatively *flexible*. Drivers must have a good knowledge of the area, and communication between the base and the taxis must be effective. However, the cost per kilometre travelled will be higher for a taxi than for a less customized form of transport such as a bus service. Although both provide the same basic service (transportation), the taxi service has a higher variety of routes and times to offer its customers, while the bus service has a few well-defined routes, with a set schedule. If all goes to schedule, little, if any, flexibility is required from the bus operation. All is standardized and regular which results in relatively low costs compared with using a taxi for the same journey.

The variation dimension

Consider the demand pattern for a successful summer holiday resort hotel. Not surprisingly, more customers want to stay in summer vacation times than in the middle of winter. At the height of 'the season' the hotel could be full to its capacity. Off-season demand, however, could be a small fraction of its capacity. Such a marked variation in demand means that the operation must change its capacity in some way, for example by hiring extra staff for the summer. The hotel must try to predict the likely level of demand. If it gets this wrong, it could result in too much or too little capacity. Also, recruitment costs, overtime costs and under-utilization of its rooms all have the effect of increasing the hotel's costs operation compared with a hotel of a similar standard with level demand. A hotel which has relatively level demand can plan its activities well in advance. Staff can be scheduled, food can be bought and rooms can be cleaned in a *routine* and *predictable* manner. This results in a high utilization of resources and unit costs which are likely to be lower than those hotels with a high-variation demand pattern.

The visibility dimension

Visibility is a slightly more difficult dimension of operations to envisage. It means how much of the operation's activities its customers experience, or how much the operation is exposed to its customers. Generally, customer-processing operations are more exposed to their customers than material- or information-processing operations. But even customer-processing operations have some choice as to how visible they wish their operations to be. For example, a retailer could operate as a high visibility 'bricks and mortar', or a lower visibility web-based operation. In the 'bricks and mortar', high visibility operation, customers will directly experience most of its 'value-adding' activities. Customers will have a relatively *short waiting tolerance*, and may walk out if not served in a reasonable time. Customers' perceptions, rather than objective criteria, will also be important. If they perceive that a member of the operation's staff is discourteous to them, they are likely to be dissatisfied (even if the staff member meant no discourtesy), so high-visibility operations require staff with good customer contact skills. Customers could also request services or products which clearly would not be sold in such a shop, but because the customers are actually in the operation they can ask what they like! This is called high received variety. This makes it difficult for high-visibility operations to achieve high productivity of resources, so they tend to be relatively high-cost operations. Conversely, a web-based retailer, while not a pure low-contact operation, has far lower visibility. Behind its website, it can be more 'factory-like'. The *time lag* between the order being placed and the items ordered by the customer being retrieved and dispatched does not have to be minutes as in the shop, but can be hours or even days. This allows the tasks of finding the items, packing and dispatching them to be *standardized* by staff who need few customer contact skills. Also, there can be relatively *high staff utilization*. The web-based organization can also centralize its operation on one (physical) site, whereas the 'bricks and mortar' shop needs many shops close to centres of demand. Therefore, the low-visibility web-based operation will have lower costs than the shop.

> **✳ Operations principle**
>
> The way in which processes need to be managed is influenced by volume, variety, variation and visibility.

SHORT CASE | **Two very different hotels**

Formule 1

Hotels are high-contact operations – they are staff-intensive and have to cope with a range of customers, each with a variety of needs and expectations. So, how can a highly successful chain of affordable hotels avoid the crippling costs of high customer contact? Formule 1, a subsidiary of the French Accor group, manage to offer outstanding value by adopting two principles not always associated with hotel operations – standardization and an innovative use of technology. Formule 1 hotels are usually located close to the roads, junctions and cities which make them visible and accessible to prospective customers. The hotels themselves are made from state-of-the-art volumetric prefabrications. The prefabricated units are arranged in various configurations to suit the characteristics of each individual site. All rooms are nine square metres in area, and are designed to be attractive, functional, comfortable and soundproof. Most important, they are designed to be easy to clean and maintain. All have the same fittings, including a double bed, an additional bunk-type bed, a wash basin, a storage area, a working table with seat, a wardrobe and a television set. The reception of a Formule 1 hotel is staffed only from 6.30 am to 10.00 am and from 5.00 pm to 10.00 pm. Outside these times an automatic machine sells rooms to credit card users, provides access to the hotel, dispenses a security code for the room and even prints a receipt. Technology is also evident in the washrooms. Showers and toilets are automatically cleaned after each use by using nozzles and heating elements to spray the room with a disinfectant solution and dry it before it is used again. To keep things even simpler, Formule 1 hotels do not include a restaurant as they are usually located near existing ones. However, a continental breakfast is available, usually between 6.30 am and 10.00 am, and of course on a 'self-service' basis!

Anantara Bangkok Riverside Resort & Spa

In Sanskrit the word means 'without end', and Anantara really does evoke, as its publicity states, the freedom, movement and harmony that are the spirit of the 'Anantara experience'. The Anantara Bangkok Riverside Resort and Spa, which is a member of the exclusive 'Small Luxury Hotels of the World', is to be found luxuriating in 11 acres of tropical gardens beside the Chao Phraya River just 3 kilometres from the centre of Bangkok. Its concept is about providing guests with laid-back luxury, sensitive service, with an experience of local culture. The resort's owners say that it draws its strength from the rich cultural traditions, historic heritage and natural beauty of its destination; every customer experience being a 'unique voyage of discovery and inspiration that is distinctly Anantara'. It employs over 550 staff and has 407 spacious rooms and suites decorated in a Thai style making use of colourful Thai silks, hardwood floors and fine furniture. All rooms have internet access, TVs and DVD players with iPod docks and private balconies that have spectacular views over the city, garden or river. The hotel's ten restaurants and bars serve local, international and fusion cuisines. The outdoor tropical pool and Jacuzzi provide areas for enjoyment and relaxation. Should any guests want to venture outside the luxury, the hotel also offers river cruises in converted rice barges, supervised activities for children, and Thai cooking classes. A frequent complimentary boat service takes guests to the Sky Train and the heart of the city. An alternative to city centre shopping is provided in the mall adjacent to the hotel.

Mixed high- and low-visibility processes

Some operations have both high- and low-visibility processes within the same operation. In an airport, for example, some activities are totally 'visible' to its customers, such as information desks answering people's queries. These staff operate in what is termed a front-office environment. Other parts of the airport have little, if any, customer 'visibility', such as the baggage handlers. These rarely seen staff perform the vital but low-contact tasks, in what is called the back-office part of the operation.

The implications of the four Vs of operations processes

All four dimensions have implications for the cost of creating and delivering services and products. Put simply, high volume, low variety, low variation and low customer contact all help to keep processing costs down. Conversely, low volume, high variety, high variation and high customer contact generally carry some kind of cost penalty for the operation. This is why the volume dimension is drawn with its 'low' end at the left, unlike the other dimensions, to keep all the 'low cost' implications on the right. To some extent the position of an operation in the four dimensions is determined by the demand of the market it is serving. However, most operations have some discretion in moving themselves on the dimensions. Figure 1.8 summarizes the implications of such positioning.

> *** Operations principle**
>
> Operations and processes can (other things being equal) reduce their costs by increasing volume, reducing variety, reducing variation, and reducing visibility.

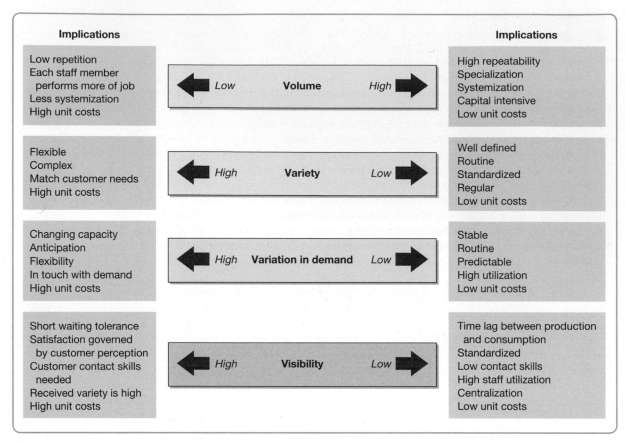

Implications		Implications
Low repetition Each staff member performs more of job Less systemization High unit costs	← Low **Volume** High →	High repeatability Specialization Systemization Capital intensive Low unit costs
Flexible Complex Match customer needs High unit costs	← High **Variety** Low →	Well defined Routine Standardized Regular Low unit costs
Changing capacity Anticipation Flexibility In touch with demand High unit costs	← High **Variation in demand** Low →	Stable Routine Predictable High utilization Low unit costs
Short waiting tolerance Satisfaction governed by customer perception Customer contact skills needed Received variety is high High unit costs	← High **Visibility** Low →	Time lag between production and consumption Standardized Low contact skills High staff utilization Centralization Low unit costs

Figure 1.8 A typology of operations

WHAT DO OPERATIONS MANAGERS DO?

The exact details of what operations managers do will, to some extent, depend on the way an organization defines the boundaries of the function. Yet there are some general classes of activities that apply to all types of operation irrespective of whether they are service, manufacturing, private or public sector, and no matter how the operations function is defined. We classify operations management activities under four headings: direct, design, deliver and develop.

- **Directing** the overall nature and strategy of the operation. A general understanding of operations and processes and their strategic purpose and performance, together with an appreciation of how strategic purpose is translated into reality, is a prerequisite to the detailed design of operations and process. This is treated in Chapters 1 to 3.
- **Designing** the operation's services, products and processes. Design is the activity of determining the physical form, shape and composition of operations and processes together with the services and products that they create. This is treated in Chapters 4 to 9.
- Planning and control process **delivery**. After being designed, the delivery of services and products from suppliers and through the total operation to customers must be planned and controlled. This is treated in Chapters 10 to 17.
- **Developing** process performance. Increasingly it is recognized that operations managers, or indeed any process managers, cannot simply routinely deliver services and products in the same way that they always have done. They have a responsibility to develop the capabilities of their processes to improve process performance. This is treated in Chapters 18 to 21.

Figure 1.9 illustrates the different positions on the dimensions of the Formule 1 hotel chain and the Anantara Bangkok Riverside Resort & Spa (*see* the short case on 'Two very different hotels', p. 24). Both provide the same basic service as any other hotel. However, one is a luxurious and intimate hotel whose customers tend to stay for relatively long periods. Its variety of services is almost infinite in the sense that customers can make individual requests in terms of food and entertainment. Variation is high with many customers avoiding the rainy season. Customer contact, and therefore visibility, is also very high (in order to ascertain customers' requirements and provide for them). All of which is very different from the Formule 1 branded hotels, whose customers usually stay one night, where the variety of services is strictly limited, and business and holiday customers use the hotel at different times, which limits variation. Most notably, though, customer contact is kept to a minimum. The Anantara resort hotel has very high levels of service but provides them at a high cost (and therefore a high price). Conversely, Formule 1 has arranged its operation in such a way as to provide a highly standardized service at minimal cost.

Figure 1.9 The four Vs profiles of two very different hotel operations

The model of operations management

We can now combine two ideas to develop the model of operations and process management that will be used throughout this book. The first is the idea that *operations* and the *processes* that make up both the operations and other business functions are transformation systems that take in inputs and use process resources to transform them into outputs. The second idea is that the resources both in an organization's operations as a whole and in its individual processes need to be managed in terms of how they are *directed*, how they are *designed*, how *delivery* is planned and controlled and how they are *developed* and improved. Figure 1.10 shows how these two ideas go together. This book will use this model to examine the more important decisions that should be of interest to all managers of operations and processes.

> **❋ Operations principle**
>
> Operations management activities can be grouped into four broad categories, directing the overall strategy of the operation, designing the operation's products, services and processes, planning and controlling delivery, and developing performance.

Figure 1.10 A general model of operations management

The image above contains the following text boxes:

Chapter 4 Process design
Chapter 5 Innovation and design in services and products
Chapter 6 Supply network design
Chapter 7 layout and flow
Chapter 8 Process technology
Chapter 9 People, jobs and organization

Chapter 1 Operations management
Chapter 2 Operations performance
Chapter 3 Operations strategy

Transformed resources
• Materials
• Information
• Customers

Input resources

Transforming resources
• Facilities
• Staff

Direct
Steering operations and processes

Design
Shaping processes, products and services

Operations management

Develop
Improving the operation's capabilities

Deliver
Planning and controlling ongoing operations

Output products and services

Value-added for customers

Chapter 10 The nature of planning and control
Chapter 11 Capacity management
Chapter 12 Inventory planning and control
Chapter 13 Supply chain management
Chapter 14 Enterprise resource planning (ERP)
Chapter 15 Lean synchronization
Chapter 16 Project management
Chapter 17 Quality management

Chapter 18 Operations improvement
Chapter 19 Risk management
Chapter 20 Organizing for improvement
Chapter 21 Corporate social responsibility (CSR)

To be a great operations manager you need to . . .[6]

So, you are considering a career in operations management, and you want to know, 'is it for you?' What skills and personal qualities will you need to make a success of the job as well as enjoying yourself as you progress in the profession? Well, the first thing to recognize is that there are many different roles encompassed within the general category of 'operations management'. Someone who makes a great risk control system designer in an investment bank may not thrive as a site manager in a copper mine. A video game project manager has a different set of day-to-day tasks when compared with a purchasing manager for a hospital. So the first skill you need is to understand the range of operations-related responsibilities that exist in various industries; and there is no better way to do this than by reading this book! However, there are also some generic skills that an effective operations manager must possess. Here are some of them. How many of them do you share?

- *Enjoys getting things done* – operations management is about doing things. It takes energy and/or commitment to finishing tasks. It means hitting deadlines and not letting down customers, whether they are internal or external.

- *Understands customer needs* – operations management is about adding value for customers. This means fully understanding what 'value' means for customers. It means putting yourself in the customer's place: knowing what it is like to be the customer, and knowing how to ensure that your services or products make the customer's life better.

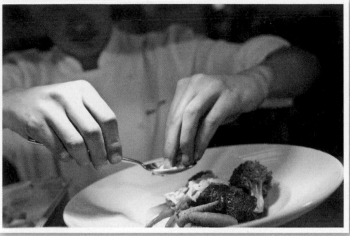

Source: Shutterstock.com/Markus

- *Communicates and motivates* – operations management is about directing resources to produce services or products in an efficient and effective manner. This means articulating what is required and persuading people to do it. Interpersonal skills are vital. Operations managers must be 'people people'.

- *Learns all the time* – every time an operations manager initiates an action (of any kind) there is an opportunity to learn from the result. Operations management is about learning, because without learning there can be no improvement, and improvement is an imperative for all operations.

- *Committed to innovation* – operations management is always seeking to do things better. This means creating new ways of doing things, being creative, imaginative, and (sometimes) unconventional.

- *Knows their contribution* – operations management may be the central function in any organization, but it is not the only one. It is important that operations managers know how they can contribute to the effective working of other functions.

- *Capable of analysis* – operations management is about making decisions. Each decision needs to be evaluated (sometimes with very little time). This involves looking at both the quantitative and the qualitative aspects of the decision. Operations managers do not necessarily have to be mathematical geniuses, but they should not be afraid of numbers!

- *Keeps cool under pressure* – operations managers often work in pressured situations. They need to be able to remain calm no matter what problems occur.

Critical commentary

The central idea in this introductory chapter is that all organizations have operations processes which create and deliver services and products and all these processes are essentially similar. However, some believe that by trying to characterize processes in this way (perhaps by calling them 'processes') one loses or distorts their nature, depersonalizes or takes the 'humanity' out of the way in which we think of the organization. This point is often raised in not-for-profit organizations, especially by 'professional' staff. For example, the head of one European 'Medical Association' (a doctors' trade union) criticized hospital authorities for expecting a *sausage factory service based on productivity targets*. No matter how similar they appear on paper, it is argued, a hospital can never be viewed in the same way as a factory. Even in commercial businesses, professionals, such as creative staff, often express discomfort at their expertise being described as a 'process'.

MyOMLab *Check and improve your understanding of this chapter using self-assessment questions and a personalized study plan, a video case study, and an eText – all at* **www.myomlab.com**.

> ❯ **What is operations management?**

- Operations management is the activity of managing the resources which are devoted to the creation and delivery of services and products. It is one of the core functions of any business, although it may not be called operations management in some industries.
- Operations management is concerned with managing processes. And all processes have internal customers and suppliers. But all management functions also have processes. Therefore, operations management has relevance for all managers.

> ❯ **Why is operations management important in all types of organization?**

- Operations management uses the organization's resources to create outputs that fulfil defined market requirements. This is *the* fundamental activity of any type of enterprise.
- Operations management is increasingly important because today's business environment requires new thinking from operations managers.

> ❯ **What is the input–transformation–output process?**

- All operations can be modelled as input–transformation–output processes. They all have inputs of transforming resources, which are usually divided into 'facilities' and 'staff', and transformed resources, which are some mixture of materials, information and customers.
- Most operations create and deliver a combination of services and products, rather than being a 'pure' service or 'product' operation.

> ❯ **What is the process hierarchy?**

- All operations are part of a larger supply network which, through the individual contributions of each operation, satisfies end customer requirements.
- All operations are made up of processes that form a network of internal customer–supplier relationships within the operation.
- End-to-end business processes that satisfy customer needs often cut across functionally based processes.

> ❯ **How do operations processes have different characteristics?**

- Operations differ in terms of their volume of their outputs, the variety of outputs, the variation in demand for their outputs, and the degree of 'visibility' they have.
- High volume, low variety, low variation and low customer 'visibility' are usually associated with low cost.

❯ What do operations managers do?

- Responsibilities can be classed in four categories – direct, design, deliver, and develop.
- Direct includes understanding relevant performance objectives and setting an operations strategy.
- Design includes the design of the operation and its processes and the design of its services and products.
- Delivery includes the planning and controlling of the activities of the operation.
- Develop includes the improvement of the operation over time.

CASE STUDY	**Design house partnerships at Concept Design Services**[7]

'I can't believe how much we have changed in a relatively short time. From being an inward-looking manufacturer, we became a customer-focused "design and make" operation. Now we are an integrated service provider. Most of our new business comes from the partnerships we have formed with design houses. In effect, we design products jointly with specialist design houses that have a well-known brand, and offer them a complete service of manufacturing and distribution. In many ways we are now a "business-to-business" company rather than a "business-to-consumer" company.' (Jim Thompson, CEO, Concept Design Services (CDS))

CDS had become one of Europe's most profitable homeware businesses. Originally founded in the 1960s, the company had moved from making industrial mouldings, mainly in the Aerospace sector, and some cheap 'homeware' items such as buckets and dustpans, sold under the 'Focus' brand name, to making very high quality (expensive) stylish home wares with a high 'design value'.

The move into 'Concept' products

The move into higher margin homeware had been masterminded by Linda Fleet, CDS's Marketing Director, who had previously worked for a large retail chain of paint and wallpaper retailers. 'Experience in the decorative products industry had taught me the importance of fashion and product development, even in mundane products such as paint. Premium-priced colours and new textures would become popular for one or two years, supported by appropriate promotion and features in lifestyle magazines. The manufacturers and retailers who created and supported these products were dramatically more profitable than those who simply provided standard ranges. Instinctively, I felt that this must also apply to homeware. We decided to develop a whole coordinated range of such items, and to open up a new distribution network for them to serve up-market stores, kitchen equipment and specialty retailers. Within a year of

Source: Alamy Images/Hugh Threlfall

launching our first new range of kitchen homeware under the 'Concept' brand name, we had over 3,000 retail outlets signed up, provided with point-of-sale display facilities. Press coverage generated an enormous interest which was reinforced by the product placement on several TV cookery and 'life style' programmes. We soon developed an entirely new market and within two years 'concept' products were providing over 75 per cent of our revenue and 90 per cent of our profits. The price realization of Concept products is many times higher than for the Focus range. To keep ahead we launched new ranges at regular intervals.'

The move to the design house partnerships

'Over the last four years, we have been designing, manufacturing and distributing products for some of the more prestigious design houses. This sort of business is likely to grow, especially in Europe where the design houses appreciate our ability to offer a full service. We can design products in conjunction with their own design staff and offer them a level of manufacturing expertise they can't get elsewhere. More significantly, we can offer a distribution service which is tailored to their needs. From the customer's point of view the distribution arrangements appear to belong to the design house itself. In fact they are based exclusively on our own call centre, warehouse and distribution resources.'

The most successful collaboration was with Villessi, the Italian designers. Generally it was CDS's design expertise which was attractive to 'design house' partners. Not only did CDS employ professionally respected designers, they had also acquired a reputation for being able to translate difficult technical designs into manufacturable and saleable products. Design house partnerships usually involved relatively long lead times but produced unique products with very high margins, nearly always carrying the design house's brand. 'This type of relationship plays to our strengths. Our design expertise gains us entry to the partnership but we are soon valued equally for our marketing, distribution and manufacturing competence.' (Linda Fleet, Marketing Director)

Manufacturing operations

All manufacturing was carried out in a facility located 20 km from head office. Its moulding area housed large injection-moulding machines, most with robotic material handling capabilities. Products and components passed to the packing hall, where they were assembled and inspected. The newer, more complex, products often had to move from moulding to assembly and then back again for further moulding. All products followed the same broad process route but with more products needing several progressive moulding and assembly stages, there was an increase in 'process flow re-cycling' which was adding complexity. One idea was to devote a separate cell to the newer and more complex products until they had 'bedded in'. This cell could also be used for testing new moulds. However, it would need investment in extra capacity that would not always be fully utilized. After manufacture, products were packed and stored in the adjacent distribution centre.

'When we moved into making the higher-margin 'Concept' products, we disposed of most of our older, small injection-moulding machines. Having all larger machines allowed us to use large multi-cavity moulds. This increased productivity by allowing us to produce several products, or components, each machine cycle. It also allowed us to use high-quality and complex moulds which, although cumbersome and more difficult to change over, gave a very high quality product. For example, with the same labour we could make three items per minute on the old machines, and 18 items per minute on the modern ones using multi moulds. That's a 600 per cent increase in productivity. We also achieved high dimensional accuracy, excellent surface finish, and extreme consistency of colour. We could do this because of our expertise derived from years making aerospace products. Also, by standardizing on single large machines, any mould could fit any machine. This was an ideal situation from a planning perspective, as we were often asked to make small runs of Concept products at short notice.' (Grant Williams, CDS Operations Manager)

Increasing volume and a desire to reduce cost had resulted in CDS subcontracting much of its Focus products to other (usually smaller) moulding companies. 'We would never do it with any complex or design house partner products, but it should allow us to reduce the cost of making basic products while releasing capacity for higher margin ones. However, there have been quite a few 'teething problems'. Co-ordinating the production schedules is currently a problem, as is agreeing quality standards. To some extent it's our own fault. We didn't realize that subcontracting was a skill in its own right. And although we have got over some of the problems, we still do not have a satisfactory relationship with all of our subcontractors.' (Grant Williams, CDS Operations Manager)

Planning and distribution services

The distribution services department of the company was regarded as being at the heart of the company's customer service drive. Its purpose was to integrate the efforts of design, manufacturing and sales by planning the flow of products from production, through the distribution centre, to the customer. Sandra White, the Planning Manager, reported to Linda Fleet and was responsible for the scheduling of all manufacturing and distribution, and for maintaining inventory levels for all the warehoused items. 'We try to stick to a preferred production sequence for each machine and mould so as to minimize set-up times by starting on a light colour, and progressing through a sequence to the darkest. We can change colours in 15 minutes, but because our moulds are large and technically complex, mould changes can take up to three hours. Good scheduling is important to maintain high plant utilization. With a higher variety of complex products, batch sizes have reduced and it has brought down average utilization. Often we can't stick to schedules. Short-term changes are inevitable in a fashion market. Certainly better forecasts would help . . . but even our own promotions are sometimes organized at such short notice that we often get caught with stockouts. New products in particular are difficult to forecast, especially when they are 'fashion' items and/or seasonal. Also, I have to schedule production time for new product mould trials; we normally allow 24 hours for the testing of each new mould received, and this has to be done on production machines. Even if we have urgent orders, the needs of the designers always have priority.' (Sandra White)

Customer orders for Concept and design house partnership products were taken by the company's sales call centre located next to the warehouse. The individual orders would then be dispatched using the company's own fleet of medium and small distribution vehicles for UK orders, but using carriers for the Continental European market. A standard delivery timetable was used and an 'express delivery' service was offered for those customers prepared to pay a small delivery premium. However, a recent study had shown that almost 40 per cent of express deliveries were initiated by the company rather than customers. Typically this would be to fulfil deliveries of orders containing products out of stock at the time of ordering. The express delivery service was not required for Focus products because almost all deliveries were to five large customers. The size of each order was usually very large, with deliveries to customers' own distribution depots. However, although the organization of Focus delivery was relatively straightforward, the consequences of failure were large. Missing a delivery meant upsetting a large customer.

Challenges for CDS

Although the company was financially successful and very well regarded in the homeware industry, there were a number of issues and challenges that it knew it would have to address. The first was the role of the design department and its influence over new product development.

New product development had become particularly important to CDS, especially since they had formed alliances with design houses. This had led to substantial growth in both the size and the influence of the design department, which reported to Linda Fleet. 'Building up and retaining design expertise will be the key to our future. Most of our growth is going to come from the business which will be brought in through the creativity and flair of our designers. Those who can combine creativity with an understanding of our partners' business and design needs can now bring in substantial contracts. The existing business is important of course, but growth will come directly from these people's capabilities.' (Linda Fleet)

But not everyone was so sanguine about the rise of the design department. 'It is undeniable that relationships between the designers and other parts of the company have been under strain recently. I suppose it is, to some extent, inevitable. After all, they really do need the freedom to design as they wish. I can understand it when they get frustrated at some of the constraints which we have to work under in the manufacturing or distribution parts of the business. They also should be able to expect a professional level of service from us. Yet the truth is that they make most of the problems themselves. They sometimes don't seem to understand the consequences or implications of their design decisions or the promises they make to the design houses. More seriously they don't really understand that we could actually help them do their job better if they co-operated a bit more. In fact, I now see some of our design house partners' designers more than I do our own designers. The Villessi designers are always in my factory and we have developed some really good relationships.' (Grant Williams)

The second major issue concerned sales forecasting, and again there were two different views. Grant Williams was convinced that forecasts should be improved. 'Every Friday morning we devise a schedule of production and distribution for the following week. Yet, usually before Tuesday morning, it has had to be significantly changed because of unexpected orders coming in from our customers' weekend sales. This causes tremendous disruption to both manufacturing and distribution operations. If sales could be forecast more accurately we would achieve far high utilization, better customer service, and I believe, significant cost savings.'

However, Linda Fleet saw things differently. 'Look, I do understand Grant's frustration, but after all, this is a fashion business. By definition it is impossible to forecast accurately. In terms of month-by-month sales volumes we are in fact pretty accurate, but trying to make a forecast for every week and every product is almost impossible to do accurately. Sorry, that's just the nature of the business we're in. In fact, although Grant complains about our lack of forecast accuracy, he always does a great job in responding to unexpected customer demand.'

Jim Thompson, the Managing Director, summed up his view of the current situation. 'Particularly significant has been our alliances with the Italian and German design houses. In effect we are positioning ourselves as a complete service partner to the designers. We have a world-class design capability together with manufacturing, order processing, order-taking and distribution services. These abilities allow us to develop genuinely equal partnerships which integrate us into the whole industry's activities.'

Linda Fleet also saw an increasing role for collaborative arrangements. 'It may be that we are seeing a fundamental change in how we do business within our industry. We have always seen ourselves as primarily a company that satisfies consumer desires through the medium of providing good service to retailers. The new partnership arrangements put us more into the "business-to-business" sector. I don't have any problem with this in principle, but I'm a little anxious as to how much it gets us into areas of business beyond our core expertise.'

The final issue which was being debated within the company was longer term, and particularly important. 'The two big changes we have made in this company have both happened because we exploited a strength we already had within the company. Moving into Concept products was only possible because we brought our high-tech precision expertise that we had developed in the aerospace sector into the homeware sector where none of our new competitors could match our manufacturing excellence. Then, when we moved into design house partnerships we did so because we had a set of designers who could command respect from the world-class design houses with whom we formed partnerships. So what is the next move for us? Do we expand globally? We are strong in Europe but nowhere else in the world. Do we extend our design scope into other markets, such as furniture? If so, that would take us into areas where we have no manufacturing expertise. We are great at plastic injection moulding, but if we tried any other manufacturing processes, we would be no better than, and probably worse than, other firms with more experience. So what's the future for us?' (Jim Thompson, CEO CDS)

QUESTIONS

1 Why is operations management important in CDS?

2 Draw a four Vs profile for the company's products and services.

3 What would you recommend to the company if they asked you to advise them in improving their operations?

MyOMLab

These problems and applications will help to improve your analysis of operations. You can find more practice problems as well as worked examples and guided solutions on MyOMLab at www.myomlab.com.

1 Read the short case on Pret A Manger (p. 18) and (**a**) identify the processes in a typical Pret A Manger shop together with their inputs and outputs. (**b**) Pret A Manger also supply business lunches (of sandwiches and other take-away food). What are the implications for how it manages its processes within the shop? (**c**) What would be advantages and disadvantages if Pret A Manger introduced 'central kitchens' that made the sandwiches for a number of shops in an area?

2 Compare and contrast Torchbox and Pret A Manger in terms of the way that they need to manage their operations.

3 Visit a furniture store (other than IKEA) and a sandwich or snack shop (other than Pret A Manger). Observe how each shop operates, for example, where customers go, how staff interact with them, how big it is, how the shop has chosen to use its space, what variety of products it offers, and so on. Think about how these shops are similar to IKEA and Pret A Manger, and how they differ.

4 Visit and observe three restaurants. Compare them in terms of the four Vs. Think about the impact of volume, variety, variation and visibility on the day-to-day management of each of the operations and consider how each operation attempts to cope with its volume, variety, variation and visibility.

5 (**Advanced**) Find a copy of a financial newspaper (*Financial Times, Wall Street Journal, The Economist*, etc.) and identify one company which is described in the paper that day. Using the list of issues identified in Table 1.2, what do you think would be the *new operations agenda* for this company?

SELECTED FURTHER READING

Brandon-Jones, A. and Slack, N. (2008) *Quantitative Analysis in Operations Management*, **FT Prentice Hall, Harlow.** A useful short book covering some of the more advanced quantitative aspects of operations management.

Chase, R.B., Jacobs, F.R. and Aquilano, N.J. (2004) *Operations Management for Competitive Advantage* (10th edn), **McGraw-Hill/Irwin, Boston, MA.** There are many good general textbooks on operations management. This is a good one, though written very much for an American audience.

Chopra, S., Deshmukh, S., Van Mieghem, J., Zemel E. and Anupindi R. (2005) *Managing Business Process Flows: Principles of Operations Management*, **Prentice Hall, Upper Saddle River, NJ.** Takes a 'process' view of operations. Mathematical but rewarding.

Hall, J.M. and Johnson, M.E. (2009) When should a process be art, not science?, *Harvard Business Review*, **March.** One of the few articles that looks at the boundaries of conventional process theory.

Hammer, M. and Stanton, S. (1999) How process enterprises really work, *Harvard Business Review*, **Nov.** Hammer is one of the gurus of process design. This paper is typical of his approach.

Johnston, R., Clark, E. and Shulver, M. (2012) *Service Operations Management*, 4th edn, Pearson, Harlow. What can we say! A great treatment of service operations from the same stable as this textbook.

Slack, N. and Lewis, M.A. (eds) (2005) *The Blackwell Encyclopedic Dictionary of Operations Management*, 2nd edn, Blackwell Business, Oxford. For those who like technical descriptions and definitions.

USEFUL WEBSITES

www.myomlab.com Test which sections you have mastered and which you need to review, with questions, a personalized study plan, video clips, revision tips, and cases.

www.opsman.org Useful materials.

http://operationsroom.wordpress.com/ Stanford University's take on topical operations stories.

www.iomnet.org.uk The Institute of Operations Management site. One of the main professional bodies for the subject.

www.poms.org A US academic society for production and operations management. Academic, but some useful material, including a link to an encyclopedia of operations management terms.

http://sites.google.com/site/tomiportal/home One of the longest-established portals for the subject. Useful for academics and students alike.

www.ft.com Good for researching topics and companies.

www.economist.com/ *The Economist's* site, well written and interesting stuff on business generally.

Now that you have finished reading this chapter, why not visit MyOMLab at www.myomlab.com where you'll find more learning resources to help you make the most of your studies and get a better grade.

2 Operations performance

Key questions

> Why is operations performance vital in any organization?

> Why is quality important?

> Why is speed important?

> Why is dependability important?

> Why is flexibility important?

> Why is cost important?

> How do operations performance objectives trade off against each other?

INTRODUCTION

Operations are judged by the way they perform. However, there are many ways of judging performance and there are many different individuals and groups doing the judging. So in this chapter we start by describing a very broad approach to measuring operations performance that uses the 'triple bottom line' to judge an operation's social, environmental and economic impact. We also introduce the related ideas of the operation's 'stakeholders', and how they judge performance, and corporate social responsibility (CSR, a topic that is treated in far more detail in Chapter 21). The chapter then looks at the more directly operations-related aspects of performance – quality, speed, dependability, flexibility, and cost. Finally we examine how performance objectives trade off against each other. On our general model of operations management the topics covered in this chapter are represented by the area marked on Figure 2.1.

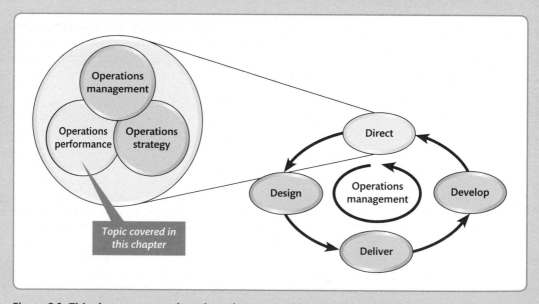

Figure 2.1 This chapter covers the role and strategic objectives of operations management

On 15 April 2008 British Airways (BA) ann-ounced that two of its most senior executives, its director of operations and its director of customer services, would leave the company. They were paying the price for the disastrous opening of British Airways' new Terminal 5 at London's Heathrow Airport. The opening of the £4.3bn terminal, said BA's boss Willie Walsh with magnificent understatement, *'was not the company's finest hour'*. The chaos at the terminal on its opening days made news around the world and was seen by many as one of the most public failures of basic operations management in the mod-ern history of aviation. *'It's a terrible, terrible PR nightmare to have hanging over you'*, said David Learmount, an aviation expert. *'Somebody who may have been a faithful customer and still not have their luggage after three weeks, is not good for their [BA's] image. The one thing that's worse than having a stack of 15,000 bags is adding 5,000 a day to that heap.'* According to a BA spokeswoman it needed an extra 400 volunteer staff and courier companies to wade through the backlog of late baggage. So the new terminal that had opened on 27 March could not even cope with BA's full short-haul service until 8 April (two hundred flights in and out of T5 were cancelled in its first three days). This delayed moving its long-haul operations to the new building from Terminal 4 as sched-uled on 30 April, which, in turn, disrupted the operations of other airlines, many of whom were scheduled to move into Terminal 4 once BA had moved its long-haul flights from there. Sharing the blame with BA was the British Airports Authority (BAA) which was already suffering criticism, from passenger groups, airlines, and businesses for allegedly poor performance. BAA's non-executive chairman, Sir Nigel Rudd, said he was *'bitterly disappointed'* about the opening of the terminal. *'It was clearly a huge embarrassment to the com-pany, me personally, and the board. Nothing can take away that failure. We had all believed genuinely that it would be a great opening, which clearly it wasn't.'*

Yet it all should have been so different. T5 took more than six years and around 60,000 workers to build. And it's an impressive building. It is Europe's largest free-standing structure. It was also keenly anticipated by travellers and BA alike. Willie Walsh had said that the terminal *'will com-pletely change his passengers' experience'*. He was right, but not in the way he imagined! So what went wrong? As is often the case with major operations failures, it was not one thing, but several interrelated problems (all of which

Source: Shutterstock.com/Jacqueline

could have been avoided). Press reports initially blamed glitches with the state-of-the-art baggage handling system that consisted of 18 km of conveyor belts and was (theo-retically) capable of transporting 12,000 bags per hour. And indeed the baggage handling system did experience problems which had not been exposed in testing. But BAA, the airport operator, doubted that the main problem was the baggage system itself. The system had worked until it became clogged with bags that were overwhelming BA's handlers loading them onto the aircraft. Partly this may have been because staff were not sufficiently familiar with the new system and its operating processes, but handling staff had also suffered delays getting to their new (and unfamiliar) work areas, negotiating (new) security checks and finding (again, new) car parking spaces. Also, once staff were airside they had problems logging-in. The cumulative effect of these problems meant that the airline was unable to get ground handling staff to the correct locations for loading and unloading bags from the aircraft, so baggage could not be loaded onto aircraft fast enough, so baggage backed up clogging the baggage handling system, which in turn meant closing baggage check-in and baggage drops, leading eventually to baggage check-in being halted.

However, not every airline underestimates the opera-tional complexity of airport processes. During the same year that Terminal 5 at Heathrow was suffering queues, lost bags and bad publicity, Dubai International Airport's Terminal 3 opened quietly with little publicity and fewer problems. Like T5, it is also huge and designed to impress. Its new shimmering facilities are solely dedicated to Emirates Airline. Largely built underground (20 metres beneath the taxiway area), the multi-level environ-ment reduces passenger walking by using 157 elevators,

Source: Shutterstock.com/Daniel M. Nagy

lot of arrogance and hubris around the opening of T5, with all the . . . publicity that BA generated,' Mr Griffiths says. *'The first rule of customer service is under-promise and over-deliver because that way you get their loyalty. BA was telling people that they were getting a glimpse of the future with T5, which created expectation and increased the chances of disappointment. Having watched the development of T5, it was clear that we had to make sure that everyone was on-message. We just had to bang heads together so that people realized what was at stake. We knew the world would be watching and waiting after T5 to see whether T3 was the next big terminal fiasco. We worked very hard to make sure that didn't happen.'*

Paul Griffiths was also convinced that Terminal 3 should undergo a phased programme with flights added progressively, rather than a *'big bang'* approach where the terminal opened for business on one day. *'We exhaustively tested the terminal systems throughout the summer . . . We continue to make sure we're putting large loads on it, week by week, improving reliability. We put a few flights in bit by bit, in waves rather than a big bang.'* Prior to the opening he also said that Dubai Airport would never reveal a single opening date for its new Terminal 3 until all pre-opening test programmes had been completed. *'T3 opened so quietly'*, said one journalist, *'that passengers would have known that the terminal was new only if they had touched the still-drying paint.'*

97 escalators and 82 moving walkways. Its underground baggage handling system is the deepest and the largest of its kind in the world with 90 km of baggage belts handling around 15,000 items per hour, with 800 RFID (see Chapter 8) read/write stations for 100 per cent accurate tracking. Also like T5 it handles about 30 million passengers a year.

But one difference between the two terminals was that Dubai's T3 could observe and learn lessons from the botched opening of Heathrow's Terminal 5. Paul Griffiths, the former head of London's Gatwick Airport, who is now Dubai Airport's chief executive, insisted that his own new terminal should not be publicly shamed in the same way. *'There was a*

OPERATIONS PERFORMANCE IS VITAL FOR ANY ORGANIZATION

It is no exaggeration to view operations management as being able to either 'make or break' any business. Not just because the operations function is large and, in most businesses, represents the bulk of its assets and the majority of its people, but because the operations function gives the ability to compete by providing the ability to respond to customers and by developing the capabilities that will keep it ahead of its competitors in the future. For example, operations management principles and the performance of its operations function proved hugely important in the Heathrow T5 and Dubai T3 launches. It was a basic failure to understand the importance of operations processes that (temporarily) damaged British Airways' reputation. It was Dubai's attention to detail and thorough operational preparation that avoided similar problems.

Of course, operations managers will always face new challenges, not only when they have major new projects to manage like Terminal 5, but also more generally as their economic, social, political and technological environment changes. Many of these decisions and challenges seem largely economic in nature. What will be the impact on our costs of adding a new product or service feature? Can we generate an acceptable return if we invest in new technology? Other decisions have more of a 'social' aspect. How do we make sure that all our suppliers treat their staff fairly? Yet others have an environmental impact. Are we doing enough to reduce our carbon footprint? What's more, the 'economic' decisions also have an environmental aspect to them. Will a new product

✳ **Operations principle**

Operations management is fundamental to the sustainable success of any organization.

feature make end-of-life recycling more difficult? Will the new technology increase pollution? Similarly the 'social' decisions must be made in the context of their economic consequences. Sure, we want suppliers to treat staff well, but we also need to make a profit. And this is the great dilemma. How do operations managers try to be, simultaneously, economically viable whilst being socially and environmentally responsible?

The triple bottom line

One common term that tries to capture the idea of a broader approach to assessing an organization's performance is the 'triple bottom line'[2] (TBL, or 3BL), also known as 'people, planet and profit'. Essentially, it is a straightforward idea – simply that organizations should measure themselves not just on the traditional economic profit that they generate for their owners, but also on the impact their operations have on society (broadly, in the sense of communities, and individually, for example in terms of their employees) and the environment. The influential initiative that has come out of this triple bottom line approach is that of 'sustainability'. A sustainable business is one that creates an acceptable profit for its owners, but minimizes the damage to the environment and enhances the existence of the people with whom it has contact. In other words, it balances economic, environmental and societal interests. This gives the organization its 'licence to operate' in society. The assumption underlying the triple bottom line (which is not universally accepted) is that a sustainable business is more likely to remain successful in the long term than one which focuses on economic goals alone. Only a company that produces a balanced TBL is really accounting for the total cost of running its operations. Figure 2.2 illustrates some of the issues involved in achieving the triple bottom line.

The social bottom line

The idea behind the social bottom line performance is not just that there is a connection between businesses and the society in which they operate – that is self-evident. Rather it is that businesses should accept that they bear some responsibility for the impact they have on society and balance the external 'societal' consequences of their actions with the more direct internal consequences, such as profit. At the level of the individual, social bottom line performance means devising jobs and work patterns which allow individuals to contribute their talents without undue stress. At a group level, it means recognizing and dealing honestly with employee representatives. In addition, businesses are also a part of the larger community and, it is argued, should be recognizing their responsibility to local communities by helping to promote their economic and social well-being.

> ✳ **Operations principle**
>
> Operations should judge themselves on the triple bottom line principle of people, planet and profit.

The environmental bottom line

Environmental sustainability (according to the World Bank) means 'ensuring that the overall productivity of accumulated human and physical capital resulting from development actions more than compensates for the direct or indirect loss or degradation of the environment'. Put more directly, it is generally taken to mean the extent to which business activity negatively impacts on the natural environment. It is clearly an important issue, not only because of the obvious impact on the immediate environment of hazardous waste, air and even noise pollution, but also because of the less obvious, but potentially far more damaging issues around global warming. Operations managers cannot avoid responsibility for environmental performance. It is often operational failures which are at the root of pollution disasters and operations decisions (such as product design) which impact on longer-term environmental issues.

The economic bottom line

The organization's top management represent the interests of the owners (or trustees, or electorate, etc.) and therefore are the direct custodians of the organization's economic

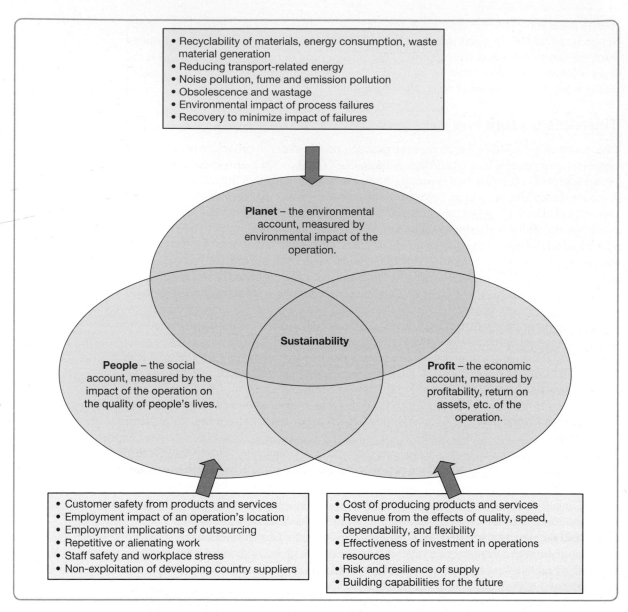

Figure 2.2 Some ways in which operations management can impact triple bottom line performance

performance. Broadly this means that operations managers must use the operation's resources effectively, and there are many ways of measuring this 'economic bottom line'. Finance specialists have devised various measures (such as return on assets, etc.), which are beyond the scope of this book, to do this. But from an operations perspective, five aspects of performance have a significant impact on economic performance (*see* Fig. 2.3).

* Operations principle

All operations should be expected to contribute to their business by controlling costs, increasing revenue, reducing risks, making investment more effective and growing long-term capabilities.

- It can reduce the costs of producing its services and products.
- It can achieve customer satisfaction (and therefore secure revenue) through good quality and service.
- It can reduce the risk of operational failure, because well-designed and well-run operations should be less likely to fail, and if they do they should be able to recover faster and with less disruption (this is called *resilience*).

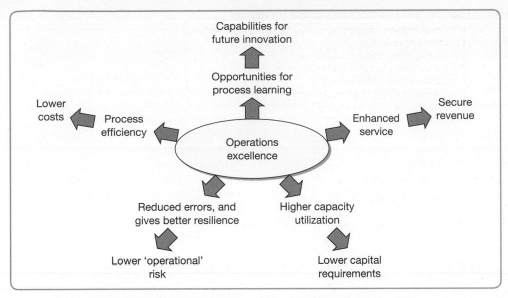

Figure 2.3 Operations can contribute to the economic bottom line through low costs, high levels of service (securing revenue), lower operational risk, lower capital requirements, and providing the capabilities that determine future innovation

- It can reduce the amount of investment (sometimes called *capital employed*) that is necessary to produce the required type and quantity of products and services by increasing the effective capacity of the operation and by being innovative in how it uses its physical resources.
- It can provide the basis for *future* innovation by learning from its experience of operating its processes, so building a solid base of operations skills, knowledge and capability within the business.

How operations can affect profits

As a simple illustration of how operations management can have a very significant effect on a business, look at how it can influence the profitability of a company. Consider two information technology (IT) support companies. Both design, supply, install, and maintain IT systems for business clients. Table 2.1 shows the effect that good operations management could have on a business's performance.

Company A believes that the way it produces and delivers its services can be used for long-term competitive advantage. Company B, by contrast, does not seem to be thinking about how its operations can be managed creatively in order to add value for its customers and sustain its own profitability. Company A is paying its service engineers higher salaries, but expects them to contribute their ideas and enthusiasm to the business without excessive supervision. Perhaps this is why Company A is 'wasting' less of its expenditure on overheads. Its purchasing operations are also spending less on buying in the computer hardware that it installs for its customers, perhaps by forming partnerships with its hardware suppliers. Finally, Company A is spending its own money wisely by investing in 'appropriate rather than excessive' technology of its own.

So, operations management can have a very significant impact on a business's financial performance. Even when compared with the contribution of other parts of the business, the contribution of operations can be dramatic. Consider the following example. Kandy Kitchens currently produce 5,000 units a year. The company is considering three options for boosting its earnings. Option 1 involves organizing a sales campaign that would involve spending an

Table 2.1 Some operations management characteristics of two companies

Company A has operations managers who . . .	*Company B has operations managers who . . .*
Employ skilled, enthusiastic people, and encourage them to contribute ideas for cutting out waste and working more effectively.	Employ only people who have worked in similar companies before and supervise them closely to make sure that they 'earn their salaries'.
Carefully monitor their customers' perception of the quality of service they are receiving and learn from any examples of poor service and always apologize and rectify any failure to give excellent service.	Have rigid 'completions of service' sheets that customers sign to say that they have received the service, but they never follow up to check on customers' views of the service that they have received.
Have invested in simple but appropriate systems of their own that allow the business to plan and control its activities effectively.	Have bought an expensive integrative system with extensive functionality, because 'you might as well invest in state-of-the art technology'.
Hold regular meetings where staff share their experiences and think about how they can build their knowledge of customer needs, new technologies, and how their services will have to change in the future to add value for their customers and help the business to remain competitive.	At the regular senior managers' meeting always have an agenda item entitled 'Future business'.

Last year's financial details for Company A:			**Last year's financial details for Company B:**		
Sales revenue	=	€10,000,000	Sales revenue	=	€9,300,000
Wage costs	=	€2,000,000	Wages costs	=	€1,700,000
Supervisor costs	=	€300,000	Supervisor costs	=	€800,000
General overheads	=	€1,000,000	General overheads	=	€1,300,000
Bought-in hardware	=	€5,000,000	Bought-in hardware	=	€6,500,000
Margin	=	€1,700,000	Margin	=	€700,000
Capital expenditure	=	€600,000	Capital expenditure	=	€1,500,000

extra €100,000 in purchasing extra market information. It is estimated that sales would rise by 30 per cent. Option 2 involves reducing operating expenses by 20 per cent through forming improvement teams that will eliminate waste in the firm's operations. Option 3 involves investing €70,000 in more flexible machinery that will allow the company to respond faster to customer orders and therefore charge 10 per cent extra for this 'speedy service'. Table 2.2 illustrates the effect of these three options.

Increasing sales volume by 30 per cent certainly improves the company's sales revenue, but operating expenses also increase. Nevertheless, earnings before investment and tax (EBIT) rise to €1,000,000. But reducing operating expenses by 20 per cent is even more effective, increasing EBIT to €1,200,000. Furthermore, it requires no investment to achieve this. The third

Table 2.2 The effects of three options for improving earning at Kandy Kitchens

	Original (sales volume = 50,000 units) (€,000)	Option 1 – Sales campaign Increase sales volumes by 30% to 65,000 units (€,000)	Option 2 – Operations efficiency Reduce operating expenses by 20% (€,000)	Option 3 – 'Speedy service' Increase price by 10% (€,000)
Sales revenue	5,000	6,500	5,000	5,500
Operating expenses	4,500	5,550	3,800	4,500
EBIT*	500	1,000	1,200	1,000
Investment required		100		70

*EBIT = Earnings before interest and tax = Net sales − Operating expenses. It is sometimes called 'operating profit'.

option involves improving customer service by responding more rapidly to customer orders. The extra price this will command improves EBIT to €1,000,000 but requires an investment of €70,000. Note how options 2 and 3 involve operations management in changing the way the company operates. Note also how, potentially, reducing operating costs and improving customer service can equal and even exceed the benefits that come from improving sales volume.

The 'stakeholder' perspective on operations performance

The triple bottom line is an increasingly adopted approach to reaching a broad and comprehensive assessment of operations performance, but there are other similar concepts. One is to judge the impact an operation has on its stakeholders. Stakeholders are the people and groups who have a legitimate interest in the operation's activities. Some stakeholders are internal, for example the operation's employees; others are external, for example customers, society or community groups, and a company's shareholders. Some external stakeholders have a direct commercial relationship with the organization, for example suppliers and customers; others do not, for example industry regulators. In not-for-profit operations, these stakeholder groups can overlap. So, voluntary workers in a charity may be employees, shareholders and customers all at once. However, in any kind of organization, it is a responsibility of the operations function to understand the (sometimes conflicting) objectives of its stakeholders and set its objectives accordingly.

> ✳ **Operations principle**
>
> All operations decisions should reflect the interests of stakeholder groups.

Figure 2.4 illustrates just some of the stakeholder groups who would have an interest in how an organization's operations function performs. But although each of these groups, to different extents, will be interested in operations performance, they are likely to have very different views of which aspect of performance is important. Table 2.3 identifies typical stakeholder requirements. But stakeholder relationships are not just one way. It is also useful to consider what an individual organization or business wants of the stakeholder groups themselves. Some of these requirements are also illustrated in Table 2.3.

Corporate social responsibility (CSR)

Yet another idea related to the triple bottom line approach is that of corporate social responsibility (generally known as CSR). According to the UK government's definition: '*CSR is essentially about how business takes account of its economic, social and environmental impacts in the way it operates – maximizing the benefits and minimizing the downsides . . . Specifically, we see CSR as the voluntary actions that business can take, over and above compliance with minimum legal requirements, to address both its own competitive interests and the interests of wider society.*' A more direct link with the stakeholder concept is to be found in the definition used by Marks & Spencer, the UK-based retailer. '*Corporate social responsibility . . . is listening and responding*

Figure 2.4 Stakeholder groups with a legitimate interest in the operation's activities

In most countries it's a principle that is enshrined in law. Companies must look after the interests of their owners; in other words their shareholders. But that is beginning to change. Since 2005 Britain, for example, has allowed people to form 'community interest companies' that have a broader set of objectives. Some argue that conventional 'for-profit firms' come under pressure to discard social goals in favour of increasing profits. Charities and 'non-profit firms' are constrained in their ability to raise capital when they need to grow. Similarly, in 2012, Yvon Chouinard, founder and owner of Patagonia Inc, the outdoor clothing firm that designs, develops and markets clothing and gear for a wide range of outdoor sports, became the first business person to take advantage of a new law in California that gave

Source: Alistair Brandon-Jones

businesses greater freedom to follow strategies which they believe benefit society as a whole rather than simply concentrating on maximizing profits. According to Mr Chouinard, Patagonia is one of the new 'benefit corporations' (usually called 'B Corps'). To meet the criteria as a B Corp, a firm should have a clear and unequivocal social and/or environmental mission, and a legal responsibility to respect the interests of workers, the community and the environment, as well as its shareholders. It must also issue independently verified information on its social and environmental impact in addition to its financial results.

Patagonia's mission statement goes like this: 'Build the best product, cause no unnecessary harm, and use business to inspire and implement solutions to the environmental crisis.' They use environmentally sensitive materials (organic cotton, recycled and recyclable polyester, and hemp among them) and both sponsor and participate in a host of environmental initiatives that range from promoting wildlife corridors to combating genetic engineering. Their employees enjoy good benefits, including generous health care, subsidized day care, flexible work schedules and paid time off for environmental internships. Many employees share their values,

care about quality and are active in environmental and community causes.

But, like most clothing companies, Patagonia outsources its production. So how does it ensure that the company's values are also upheld in their supply chain? It is important, they say, to work with suppliers, *'that share our values of integrity and environmentalism. In the past, we found we didn't have to make a lot of extra effort to achieve this. Our demand for high quality and our close relationships with the small number of factories we did business with pretty much assured it. It really is true that you can't make good products in a bad factory, and we did business with some of the world's best. They were, for the most part, efficient and well run. The people who worked in them tended to have a lot of experience. Despite high employee turnover elsewhere in the garment industry, these factories were able to retain employees because they paid them fairly and treated them humanely.'* Transparency is also important. In an effort to understand the social and environmental impacts of their supply chain, Patagonia launched its *Footprint Chronicles*, in which they trace the environmental and social impact of products from design through fibre creation to construction to shipment to their warehouse.

to the needs of a company's stakeholders. This includes the requirements of sustainable development. We believe that building good relationships with employees, suppliers and wider society is the best guarantee of long-term success. This is the backbone of our approach to CSR.'

The issue of how CSR objectives can be included in operations management's activities is of increasing importance, both from an ethical and a commercial point of view. It is treated again at various points throughout this text (and the final chapter, Chapter 21, is devoted entirely to the topic).

Table 2.3 Typical stakeholders' performance objectives

Stakeholder	What stakeholders want from the operation	What the operation wants from stakeholders
Shareholders	Return on investment Stability of earnings Liquidity of investment	Investment capital Long-term commitment
Directors/top management	Low/acceptable operating costs Secure revenue Well-targeted investment Low risk of failure Future innovation	Coherent, consistent, clear, and achievable strategies Appropriate investment
Staff	Fair wages Good working conditions Safe work environment Personal and career development	Attendance Diligence/best efforts Honesty Engagement
Staff representative bodies (e.g. trade unions)	Conformance with national agreements Consultation	Understanding Fairness Assistance in problem solving
Suppliers (of materials, services, equipment, etc.)	Early notice of requirements Long-term orders Fair price On-time payment	Integrity of delivery, quality and volume Innovation Responsiveness Progressive price reductions
Regulators (e.g. financial regulators)	Conformance to regulations Feedback on effectiveness of regulations	Consistency of regulation Consistency of application of regulations Responsiveness to industry concerns
Government (local, national, regional)	Conformance to legal requirements Contribution to (local/national/regional) economy	Low/simple taxation Representation of local concerns Appropriate infrastructure
Lobby groups (e.g. environmental lobby groups)	Alignment of the organization's activities with whatever the group are promoting	No unfair targeting Practical help in achieving aims (if the organization wants to achieve them)
Society	Minimize negative effects from the operation (noise, traffic, etc.) and maximize positive effects (jobs, local sponsorship, etc.)	Support for organization's plans

Critical commentary

The dilemma with using this wide range of triple bottom line, stakeholders, or CSR to judge operations performance is that organizations, particularly commercial companies, have to cope with the conflicting pressures of maximizing profitability on one hand, with the expectation that they will manage in the interests of (all or part of) society in general with accountability and transparency. Even if a business wanted to reflect aspects of performance beyond its own immediate interests, how is it to do it? According to Michael Jensen of Harvard Business School, '*At the economy-wide or social level, the issue is this: If we could dictate the criterion or objective function to be maximized by firms (and thus the performance criterion by which corporate executives choose among alternative policy options), what would it be? Or, to put the issue even more*

The five operations performance objectives

Triple bottom line, stakeholder and CSR objectives form the backdrop to operations decision making, but running operations at an operational day-to-day level requires a more tightly defined set of objectives. These are the five basic 'performance objectives' and they apply to all types of operation. Imagine that you are an operations manager in any kind of business – a hospital administrator, for example, or a production manager at a car plant. What kind of things are you likely to want to do in order to satisfy customers and contribute to competitiveness?

- You would want to do things right; that is, you would not want to make mistakes, and would want to satisfy your customers by providing error-free goods and services which are 'fit for their purpose'. This is giving a quality advantage.
- You would want to do things fast, minimizing the time between a customer asking for goods or services and the customer receiving them in full, thus increasing the availability of your goods and services and giving a speed advantage.
- You would want to do things on time, so as to keep the delivery promises you have made. If the operation can do this, it is giving a dependability advantage.
- You would want to be able to change what you do; that is, being able to vary or adapt the operation's activities to cope with unexpected circumstances or to give customers individual treatment. Being able to change far enough and fast enough to meet customer requirements gives a flexibility advantage.
- You would want to do things cheaply; that is, produce goods and services at a cost which enables them to be priced appropriately for the market while still allowing for a return to the organization; or, in a not-for-profit organization, give good value to the taxpayers or whoever is funding the operation. When the organization is managing to do this, it is giving a cost advantage.

> ✳ **Operations principle**
>
> Operations performance objectives can be grouped together as quality, speed, dependability, flexibility and cost.

The next part of this chapter examines these five performance objectives in more detail by looking at what they mean for four different operations: a general hospital, an automobile factory, a city bus company and a supermarket chain.

WHY IS QUALITY IMPORTANT?

Quality is consistent conformance to customers' expectations, in other words, 'doing things right', but the things which the operation needs to do right will vary according to the kind of operation. All operations regard quality as a particularly important objective. In some ways quality is the most visible part of what an operation does. Furthermore, it is something that a customer finds relatively easy to judge about the operation. Is the product or service as it is supposed to be? Is it right or is it wrong? There is something fundamental about quality. Because of this, it is clearly a major influence on customer satisfaction or dissatisfaction. A customer perception of high-quality products and services means customer satisfaction and therefore the likelihood that the customer will return. Figure 2.5 illustrates how quality could be judged in four operations.

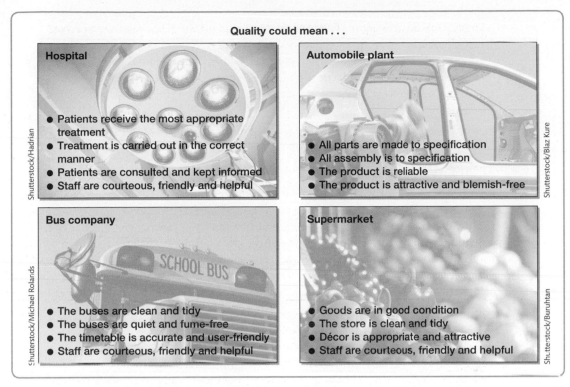

Quality could mean . . .

Hospital
- Patients receive the most appropriate treatment
- Treatment is carried out in the correct manner
- Patients are consulted and kept informed
- Staff are courteous, friendly and helpful

Shutterstock/Hadrian

Automobile plant
- All parts are made to specification
- All assembly is to specification
- The product is reliable
- The product is attractive and blemish-free

Shutterstock/Blaz Kure

Bus company
- The buses are clean and tidy
- The buses are quiet and fume-free
- The timetable is accurate and user-friendly
- Staff are courteous, friendly and helpful

Shutterstock/Michael Rolands

Supermarket
- Goods are in good condition
- The store is clean and tidy
- Décor is appropriate and attractive
- Staff are courteous, friendly and helpful

Shutterstock/Buruhtan

Figure 2.5 Quality means different things in different operations

Quality inside the operation

When quality means consistently producing services and products to specification it not only leads to external customer satisfaction, but makes life easier inside the operation as well.

Quality reduces costs The fewer mistakes made by each process in the operation, the less time will be needed to correct the mistakes and the less confusion and irritation will be spread. For example, if a supermarket's regional warehouse sends the wrong goods to the supermarket, it will mean staff time – and therefore cost – being used to sort out the problem.

Quality increases dependability Increased costs are not the only consequence of poor quality. At the supermarket it could also mean that goods run out on the supermarket shelves with a resulting loss of revenue to the operation and irritation to the external customers. Sorting the problem out could also distract the supermarket management from giving attention to the other parts of the supermarket operation. This in turn could result in further mistakes being made. So, quality (like the other performance objectives, as we shall see) has both an external impact which influences customer satisfaction, and an internal impact which leads to stable and efficient processes.

> **❋ Operations principle**
>
> Quality can give the potential for better services and products and save costs.

WHY IS SPEED IMPORTANT?

Speed means the elapsed time between customers requesting products or services and them receiving them. Figure 2.6 illustrates what speed means for the four operations. The main benefit to the operation's (external) customers of speedy delivery of goods and services is that the faster they can have the product or service, the more likely they are to buy it, or the more they will pay for it, or the greater the benefit they receive (see the short case below, 'When speed means life or death').

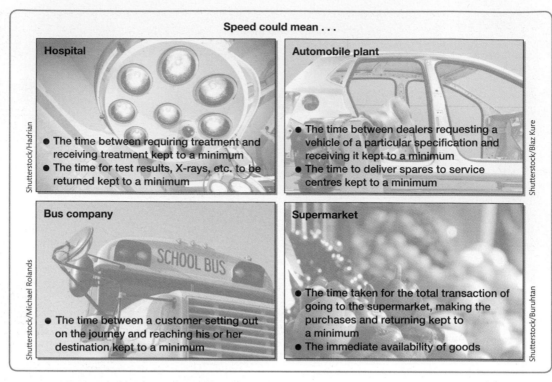

Figure 2.6 Speed means different things in different operations

Speed inside the operation

Inside the operation, speed is also important. Fast response to external customers is greatly helped by speedy decision making and speedy movement of materials and information inside the operation. And there are other benefits.

Speed reduces inventories Take, for example, the automobile plant. Steel for the vehicle's door panels is delivered to the press shop, pressed into shape, transported to the painting area, coated for colour and protection, and moved to the assembly line where it is fitted to the automobile. This is a simple three-stage process, but in practice material does not flow smoothly from one stage to the next. First, the steel is delivered as part of a far larger batch containing enough steel to make possibly several hundred products. Eventually it is taken to the press area, pressed into shape, and again waits to be transported to the paint area. It then waits to be painted, only to wait once more until it is transported to the assembly line. Yet again it waits by the trackside until it is eventually fitted to the automobile. The material's journey time is far longer than the time needed to make and fit the product. It actually spends most of its time waiting as stocks (inventories) of parts and products. The longer items take to move through a process, the more time they will be waiting and the higher inventory will be. This is an important idea which will be explored in Chapter 15 on lean operations.

Speed reduces risks Forecasting tomorrow's events is far less of a risk than forecasting next year's. The further ahead companies forecast, the more likely they are to get it wrong. The faster the throughput time of a process, the later forecasting can be left. Consider the automobile plant again. If the total throughput time for the door panel is six weeks, door panels are being processed through their first operation six weeks before they reach their final destination. The quantity of door panels being processed will be determined by the forecasts for demand six weeks ahead. If instead of six weeks, they take only one week to move through the plant, the door panels being processed through their first stage are intended to meet demand only one week ahead. Under these

> **✱ Operations principle**
>
> Speed can give the potential for faster delivery of services and products and save costs.

'Organic farming means taking care and getting all the details right. It is about quality from start to finish. Not only the quality of the meat that we produce but also quality of life and quality of care for the countryside.' Nick Fuge is the farm manager at Lower Hurst Farm located within the Peak District National Park of the UK. He has day-to-day responsibility for the well-being of all the livestock and the operation of the farm on strict organic principles. The 85-hectare farm has been producing high-quality beef for almost 20 years but changed to fully organic production in 1998. Organic farming is a tough regime. No artificial fertilizers, genetically modified feedstuff or growth-promoting agents are used. All beef sold from the farm is home bred and can be traced back to the animal from which it came. 'The quality of the herd is most important,' says Nick, 'as is animal care. Our customers trust us to ensure that the cattle are organically and humanely reared, and slaughtered in a manner that minimizes any distress. If you want to understand the difference between conventional and organic farming, look at the way we use veterinary help. Most conventional farmers use veterinarians like an emergency service to put things right when there is a problem with an animal. The amount we pay for veterinary assistance is lower because we try to avoid problems with the animals from the start. We use veterinaries as consultants to help us in preventing problems in the first place.'

Catherine Pyne runs the butchery and the mail-order meat business. 'After butchering, the cuts of meat are individually vacuum-packed, weighed and then blast frozen. We worked extensively with the Department of Food and

Source: Shutterstock.com/Ecliptic Blue

Nutrition at Oxford Brooks University to devise the best way to encapsulate the nutritional, textural and flavoursome characteristics of the meat in its prime state. So, when you defrost and cook any of our products you will have the same tasty and succulent eating qualities associated with the best fresh meat.' After freezing, the products are packed in boxes, designed and labelled for storage in a home freezer. Customers order by phone or through the internet for next-day delivery in a special 'mini deep freeze' reusable container which maintains the meat in its frozen state. 'It isn't just the quality of our product which has made us a success', says Catherine. 'We give a personal and inclusive level of service to our customers that makes them feel close to us and maintains trust in how we produce and prepare the meat. The team of people we have here is also an important aspect of our business. We are proud of our product and feel that it is vitally important to be personally identified with it.'

circumstances it is far more likely that the number and type of door panels being processed are the number and type which eventually will be needed.

WHY IS DEPENDABILITY IMPORTANT?

Dependability means doing things in time for customers to receive their goods or services exactly when they are needed, or at least when they were promised. Figure 2.7 illustrates what dependability means in the four operations. Customers might only judge the dependability of an operation after the product or service has been delivered. Initially this may not affect the likelihood that customers will select the service – they have already 'consumed' it. Over time, however, dependability can override all other criteria. No matter how cheap or fast a bus service is, if the service is always late (or unpredictably early) or the buses are always full, then potential passengers will be better off calling a taxi.

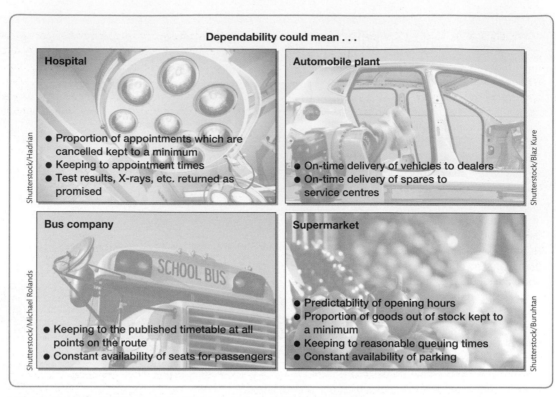

Dependability could mean . . .

Hospital
- Proportion of appointments which are cancelled kept to a minimum
- Keeping to appointment times
- Test results, X-rays, etc. returned as promised

Automobile plant
- On-time delivery of vehicles to dealers
- On-time delivery of spares to service centres

Bus company
- Keeping to the published timetable at all points on the route
- Constant availability of seats for passengers

Supermarket
- Predictability of opening hours
- Proportion of goods out of stock kept to a minimum
- Keeping to reasonable queuing times
- Constant availability of parking

Figure 2.7 Dependability means different things in different operations

SHORT CASE   When speed means life or death[6]

Of all the operations which have to respond quickly to customer demand, few have more need of speed than the emergency services. In responding to road accidents especially, every second is critical. The treatment you receive during the first hour after your accident (what is called the 'golden hour') can determine whether you survive and fully recover or not. Making full use of the golden hour means speeding up three elements of the total time to treatment – the time it takes for the emergency services to find out about the accident, the time it takes them to travel to the scene of the accident, and the time it takes to get the casualty to appropriate treatment.

Alerting the emergency services immediately is the idea behind Mercedes-Benz's TeleAid system. As soon as the vehicle's airbag is triggered, an on-board computer reports through the mobile phone network to a control centre (drivers can also trigger the system manually if not too badly hurt); satellite tracking allows the vehicle to be precisely located and the owner identified (if special medication is needed). Getting to the accident quickly is the next hurdle. Often the fastest method is by helicopter. When most rescues are only a couple of minutes' flying time back to the hospital, speed can really save lives. However, it is not always possible to land a helicopter safely at night (because of possible overhead wires and other hazards) so conventional ambulances will always be needed, both to get paramedics quickly to accident victims and to speed them to hospital. One increasingly common method of ensuring that ambulances arrive quickly at the accident site is to position them, not at hospitals, but close to where accidents are likely to occur. Computer analysis of previous accident data helps to select the ambulance's waiting position, and global positioning systems help controllers to mobilize the nearest unit. At all times a key requirement for fast service is effective communication between all who are involved in each stage of the emergency. Modern communications technology can play an important role in this.

SHORT CASE   How UPS maintains its dependability[7]

What do you do when it's coming up to the biggest gift-giving time of the year, you are responsible for the gifts' delivery and your aircraft, which are vital for dependable delivery, are grounded by a freak snowstorm a continent away, or mechanical problems, or an air traffic controllers' dispute in France?

That is the potential problem facing all global parcel delivery companies; and it's made worse when customers blame you for any non-delivery. Generally freight operators have to absorb the cost when a delivery doesn't arrive on time, so weather and other disruptions directly affect their customer service, reputation and, ultimately, profitability. UPS, the largest express carrier and package delivery company in the world, reckons that each late shipment will cost them between $5 and $30 in revenue. And with almost 16 million packages and documents delivered worldwide every day it only takes a fraction of a percentage point of lateness for the total cost of any lack of dependability to be huge.

So what do UPS do to minimize disruption to their delivery network when it's coming up to a peak demand time like Christmas and there is a possibility of bad weather? The obvious thing is to very carefully keep a constant watch on the weather forecast, and indeed they do have meteorologists and other staff who do this. But they also build in a buffer of extra operational capacity. At UPS headquarters a 'hot status board' on the wall identifies cities and regions where the company has spare pilots and planes whose task is to 'rescue volume': that is, the spare resources are used to come to the aid of packages stuck somewhere. UPS says that this 'hot spares programme' rescues more than 1 million packages annually and saves the company more than $20 million in revenue.

Dependability inside the operation

Inside the operation internal customers will judge each other's performance partly by how reliable the other processes are in delivering material or information on time. Operations where internal dependability is high are more effective than those which are not, for a number of reasons.

Dependability saves time Take, for example, the maintenance and repair centre for the city bus company. If the centre runs out of some crucial spare parts, the manager of the centre will need to spend time trying to arrange a special delivery of the required parts and the resources allocated to service the buses will not be used as productively as they would have been without this disruption. More seriously, the fleet will be short of buses until they can be repaired and the fleet operations manager will have to spend time rescheduling services. So, entirely due to the one failure of dependability of supply, a significant part of the operation's time has been wasted coping with the disruption.

Dependability saves money Ineffective use of time will translate into extra cost. The spare parts might cost more to be delivered at short notice and maintenance staff will expect to be paid even when there is not a bus to work on. Nor will the fixed costs of the operation, such as heating and rent, be reduced because the two buses are not being serviced. The rescheduling of buses will probably mean that some routes have inappropriately sized buses and some services could have to be cancelled. This will result in empty bus seats (if too large a bus has to be used) or a loss of revenue (if potential passengers are not transported).

Dependability gives stability The disruption caused to operations by a lack of dependability goes beyond time and cost. It affects the 'quality' of the operation's time. If everything in an operation is always perfectly dependable, a level of trust will have built up between the different parts of the operation. There will be no 'surprises' and everything will be predictable. Under such circumstances, each part of the operation can concentrate on improving its own area of responsibility without having its attention continually diverted by a lack of dependable service from the other parts.

> *** Operations principle**
>
> Dependability can give the potential for more reliable delivery of services and products and save costs.

WHY IS FLEXIBILITY IMPORTANT?

Flexibility means being able to change the operation in some way. This may mean changing what the operation does, how it is doing it, or when it is doing it. Specifically, customers will need the operation to change so that it can provide four types of requirement:

- **product/service flexibility** – the operation's ability to introduce new or modified products and services;
- **mix flexibility** – the operation's ability to produce a wide range or mix of products and services;
- **volume flexibility** – the operation's ability to change its level of output or activity to produce different quantities or volumes of products and services over time;
- **delivery flexibility** – the operation's ability to change the timing of the delivery of its services or products.

Figure 2.8 gives examples of what these different types of flexibility mean to the four different operations.

Mass customization

One of the beneficial external effects of flexibility is the increased ability of operations to do different things for different customers. So, high flexibility gives the ability to produce a high variety of products or services. Normally high variety means high cost (see Chapter 1). Furthermore, high-variety operations do not usually produce in high volume. Some companies have developed their flexibility in such a way that products and services are customized for each individual customer. Yet they manage to produce them in a high-volume, mass-production manner which keeps costs down. This approach is called mass customization. Sometimes this is achieved through flexibility in design. For example, Dell is one of the largest volume producers of personal computers in the world, yet allows each customer to 'design' (albeit in a limited sense) their own configuration. Sometimes flexible technology is used to achieve the same effect. Another example is Paris Miki, an upmarket eyewear retailer which has the largest number of eyewear stores in the world, which uses its own 'Mikissimes Design System' to capture a digital image of the customer and analyse facial characteristics. Together with a list of customers' personal preferences, the system then recommends a particular design and displays it on the image of the customer's face. In consultation with the optician the customer can adjust shapes and sizes until the final

Flexibility could mean . . .

Hospital

- Product/service flexibility – the introduction of new types of treatment
- Mix flexibility – a wide range of available treatments
- Volume flexibility – the ability to adjust the number of patients treated
- Delivery flexibility – the ability to reschedule appointments

Shutterstock/Hadrian

Automobile plant

- Product/service flexibility – the introduction of new models
- Mix flexibility – a wide range of options available
- Volume flexibility – the ability to adjust the number of vehicles manufactured
- Delivery flexibility – the ability to reschedule manufacturing priorities

Shutterstock/Blaz Kure

Bus company

- Product/service flexibility – the introduction of new routes or excursions
- Mix flexibility – a large number of locations served
- Volume flexibility – the ability to adjust the frequency of services
- Delivery flexibility – the ability to reschedule trips

Shutterstock/Michael Rolands

Supermarket

- Product/service flexibility – the introduction of new goods or promotions
- Mix flexibility – a wide range of goods stocked
- Volume flexibility – the ability to adjust the number of customers served
- Delivery flexibility – the ability to obtain out-of-stock items (very occasionally)

Shutterstock/B.ruhtan

Figure 2.8 Flexibility means different things in different operations

566 quadrillion individual muesli mixes – now that's flexible[8]

The idea might sound somewhat unusual, but it has proved a great success. Three university students, Hubertus Bessau, Philipp Kraiss and Max Wittrock, in the small city of Passau, Germany, came up with the concept of mymuesli – the first web-based platform where you can mix your own organic muesli online, with a choice of 75 different ingredients. This makes it possible to create 566 quadrillion individual muesli mixes – and you can even name your own muesli. So, irrespective of whether you are a chocolate addict, a raisin hater or an athlete, this incredible variety will make it easy, say mymuesli, for anyone to invent their all-time favourite muesli. 'We wanted to provide customers with nothing else but the perfect muesli', they say. 'Of course the idea of custom-mixing muesli online might sound wacky . . . but think about it – it's the breakfast you were always looking for.' All muesli is mixed in the Passau production site according to strict quality standards and hygiene law requirements. Ingredients are strictly organic, without additional sugar, additives, preservatives or artificial colours. On first visiting the website customers first have to pick a muesli base (full nutritional information is provided). After this customers can add other basics and ingredients such as

Source: Shutterstock.com/Pics Five

fruit, nuts and seeds, and extras. And the company will deliver it direct by courier to your door! The name for the muesli (chosen by the customer) is printed on the can to make it even more personal. Names chosen by customers for their individual muesli mixes include: 'reindeer food', 'donkey's breakfast', 'sweet dream', 'paradise meal' and, rather charmingly, 'darling's breakfast'.

The company purchase their ingredients from selected suppliers and dealers throughout the world. One of mymuesli's great assets is the multitude of eccentric and exotic ingredients (from over 20 countries) included in the product range, like carrots, Tibetan goji-berries, cedar nuts or jelly babies. Philipp Kraiss, one of the company founders, is constantly on the lookout for 'new crazy and tasty' muesli ingredients. During its first year mymuesli was awarded several business prizes (one of which was awarded by the *Financial Times* Germany), and has now grown to have annual sales worth over 1 million euros, with over 40 people working for the company. It has now expanded its operations to the United Kingdom. *'We seriously hope that mymuesli will find just as many friends here in the UK as in Germany and Austria'*, says Max Wittrock, another of the three founding members. *'And we are looking forward to a great deal of feedback, so we can continue to improve our products. Last year thousands of emails and user replies in Germany really have helped us immensely with the project. Because after all,'* Wittrock says, *'it is supposed to be a user-generated breakfast.'*

design is chosen. Within the store the frames are assembled from a range of pre-manufactured components and the lenses ground and fitted to the frames. The whole process takes around an hour. Another example is mymuesli (see the short case above).

Agility

Judging operations in terms of their agility has become popular. Agility is really a combination of all the five performance objectives, but particularly flexibility and speed. In addition, agility implies that an operation and the supply chain of which it is a part (supply chains are described in Chapter 6) can respond the uncertainty in the market. Agility means responding to market requirements by producing new and existing products and services fast and flexibly.

Flexibility inside the operation

Developing a flexible operation can also have advantages to the internal customers within the operation.

Flexibility speeds up response Fast service often depends on the operation being flexible. For example, if the hospital has to cope with a sudden influx of patients from a road accident, it clearly needs to deal with injuries quickly. Under such circumstances a flexible hospital which can speedily transfer extra skilled staff and equipment to the Accident and Emergency department will provide the fast service which the patients need.

Flexibility saves time In many parts of the hospital, staff have to treat a wide variety of complaints. Fractures, cuts or drug overdoses do not come in batches. Each patient is an individual with individual needs. The hospital staff cannot take time to 'get into the routine' of treating a particular complaint; they must have the flexibility to adapt quickly. They must also have sufficiently flexible facilities and equipment so that time is not wasted waiting for equipment to be brought to the patient. The time of the hospital's resources is being saved because they are flexible in 'changing over' from one task to the next.

> **✳ Operations principle**
>
> Flexibility can give the potential to create new services and products, in a wider variety and with differing volumes and with differing delivery dates, as well as save costs.

Flexibility maintains dependability Internal flexibility can also help to keep the operation on schedule when unexpected events disrupt the operation's plans. For example, if the sudden influx of patients to the hospital requires emergency surgical procedures, routine operations will be disrupted. This is likely to cause distress and considerable inconvenience. A flexible hospital might be able to minimize the disruption by possibly having reserved operating theatres for such an emergency, and being able to bring in medical staff quickly that are 'on call'.

WHY IS COST IMPORTANT?

To the companies which compete directly on price, cost will clearly be their major operations objective. The lower the cost of producing their goods and services, the lower can be the price to their customers. Even those companies which do not compete on price will be interested in keeping costs low. Every euro or dollar removed from an operation's cost base is a further euro or dollar added to its profits. Not surprisingly, low cost is a universally attractive objective. The short case 'Everyday low prices at Aldi' describes how one retailer keeps its costs down.

The ways in which operations management can influence cost will depend largely on where the operation costs are incurred. The operation will spend its money on staff (the money spent on employing people), facilities, technology and equipment (the money spent on buying, caring for, operating and replacing the operation's 'hardware') and materials (the money spent on the 'bought-in' materials consumed or transformed in the operation). Figure 2.9 shows typical cost breakdowns for the hospital, car plant, supermarket and bus company.

> ✳ **Operations principle**
>
> Cost is always an important objective for operations management, even if the organization does not compete directly on price.

Keeping operations costs down

All operations have an interest in keeping their costs as low as is compatible with the levels of quality, speed, dependability, and flexibility that their customers require. The measure that is most frequently used to indicate how successful an operation is at doing this is

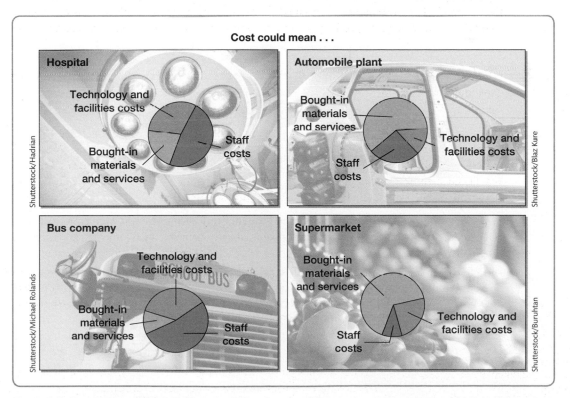

Figure 2.9 Cost means different things in different operations

Everyday low prices at Aldi[9]

Aldi is an international *'limited assortment'* supermarket specializing in 'private label', mainly food, products. It has carefully focused its service concept and delivery system to attract customers in a highly competitive market. The company believe that their unique approach to operations management make it, '... *virtually impossible for competitors to match our combination of price and quality'.*

Aldi operations challenge the norms of retailing. They are deliberately simple, using basic facilities to keep down overheads. Most stores stock only a limited range of goods (typically around 700, compared with 25,000 to 30,000 stocked by conventional supermarket chains). The private label approach means that the products have been produced according to Aldi quality specifications and are only sold in Aldi stores. Without the high costs of brand marketing and advertising and with Aldi's formidable purchasing power, prices can be 30 per cent below their branded equivalents. Other cost-saving practices include open carton displays which eliminate the need for special shelving, no grocery bags to encourage recycling as well as saving costs, and using a 'cart rental' system which requires customers to return the cart to the store to get their coin deposit back.

Source: Shutterstock.com/Kzenon

productivity. Productivity is the ratio of what is produced by an operation to what is required to produce it.

$$\text{Productivity} = \frac{\textbf{Output from the operation}}{\textbf{Input to the operation}}$$

Often partial measures of input or output are used so that comparisons can be made. So, for example, in the automobile industry productivity is sometimes measured in terms of the number of cars produced per year per employee. This is called a single-factor measure of productivity.

$$\text{Single-factor productivity} = \frac{\textbf{Output from the operation}}{\textbf{One input to the operation}}$$

This allows different operations to be compared excluding the effects of input costs. One operation may have high total costs per car but high productivity in terms of number of cars per employee per year. The difference between the two measures is explained in terms of the distinction between the cost of the inputs to the operation and the way the operation is managed to convert inputs into outputs. Input costs may be high, but the operation itself is good at converting them to goods and services. Single-factor productivity can include the effects of input costs if the single input factor is expressed in cost terms, such as 'labour costs'. Total factor productivity is the measure that includes all input factors.

$$\text{Multi-factor productivity} = \frac{\textbf{Output from the operation}}{\textbf{All inputs to the operation}}$$

A health-check clinic has five employees and 'processes' 200 patients per week. Each employee works 35 hours per week. The clinic's total wage bill is £3,900 and its total overhead expenses are £2,000 per week. What is the clinic's single-factor labour productivity and its multi-factor productivity?

$$\text{Labour productivity} = \frac{200}{5} = 40 \text{ patients/employees/week}$$

$$\text{Labour productivity} = \frac{200}{(5 \times 35)} = 1.143 \text{ patients/labour hour}$$

$$\text{Multi-factor productivity} = \frac{200}{(3900 + 2000)} = 0.0339 \text{ patients/£}$$

SHORT CASE   Can cost cutting go too far?[10]

There is a good reason why most electronic components are made in China: it's cheap. Companies such as Taiwan's Foxconn, who produce many of the world's computer, consumer electronics, and communications products for customers such as Apple, Dell, Nokia and Sony, have perfected the art and science of squeezing cost out of their operations processes. But, although Foxconn is known for having an obsession with cutting its costs and has moved much of its manufacturing into China and other low-cost areas, with plants in South-East Asia, Eastern Europe, and South America, it has been criticized for pushing its workers too far. In 2010 there was a cluster of suicides at its factories, with 18 workers throwing themselves from the tops of the company's buildings; 14 people died. The firm operates a huge industrial park, which it calls Foxconn City, in Shenzhen, just across the border from Hong Kong, with 15 multi-storey manufacturing buildings, each devoted to one customer. This is where the suicides took place. It prompted Foxconn to install safety nets in some of its factories and hire counsellors to help its workers.

Source: Getty Images

However, Boy Lüthje of the Institute of Social Research in Frankfurt says that conditions at the firm are actually not that bad when compared with many others. Food and lodging are free, as are extensive recreational facilities. But workers routinely put in overtime in excess of the 36 hours a month permitted under Chinese law and plenty of people seek jobs with the company. Moreover, the suicide rate at the company is lower than that among the general population in China. Yet the deaths raised questions about working conditions in electronics manufacturing in general and in particular at Foxconn. Nor was this the last time concern was raised over working conditions. In 2012 around 150 workers at Wuhan threatened to commit suicide by leaping from their factory roof in protest at their working conditions. They were eventually coaxed down by managers after two days on top of the three-floor plant. 'We were put to work without any training, and paid piecemeal', said one of the protesting workers. 'The assembly line ran very fast and after just one morning we all had blisters and the skin on our hands was black. The factory was also really choked with dust and no one could bear it.' Some reports indicate that Foxconn is more advanced in designing its processes than many of its competitors, but it is run in a regimented fashion that is not always popular with workers.

Improving productivity

One obvious way of improving an operation's productivity is to reduce the cost of its inputs while maintaining the level of its outputs. This means reducing the costs of some or all of its transformed and transforming resource inputs. For example, a bank may choose to relocate its call centres to places where its facility-related costs (for example rent) are cheaper. A software developer may relocate its entire operation to India or China where skilled labour is available at rates significantly less than in European countries. A computer manufacturer may change the design of its products to allow the use of cheaper materials. Productivity can also be improved by making better use of the inputs to the operation. For example, garment manufacturers attempt to cut out the various pieces of material that make up the garment by positioning each part on the strip of cloth so that material wastage is minimized. All operations are increasingly concerned with cutting out waste, whether it is waste of materials, waste of staff time, or waste through the under-utilization of facilities.

Cost reduction through internal effectiveness

Our previous discussion distinguished between the benefits of each performance objective to externally and internally. Each of the various performance objectives has several internal effects, but *all of* them affect cost. So one important way to improve cost performance is to improve the performance of the other operations objectives (*see* Fig. 2.10).

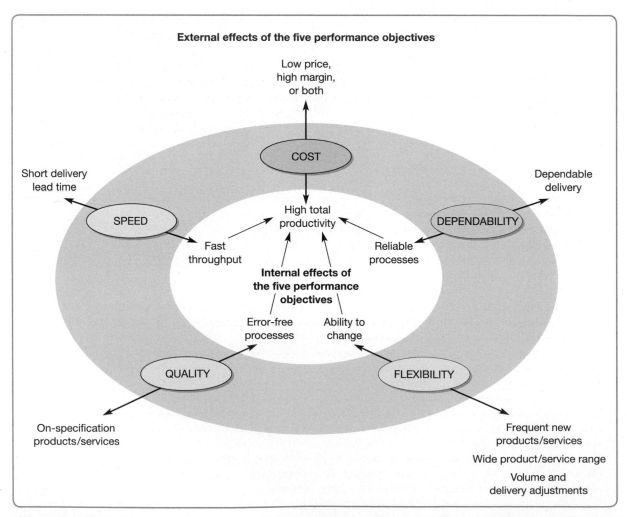

Figure 2.10 Performance objectives have both external and internal effects. Internally, cost is influenced by the other performance objectives

- High-quality operations do not waste time or effort having to re-do things, nor are their internal customers inconvenienced by flawed service.
- Fast operations reduce the level of in-process inventory between processes as well as reducing administrative overheads.
- Dependable operations do not spring any unwelcome surprises on their internal customers. They can be relied on to deliver exactly as planned. This eliminates wasteful disruption and allows the other processes to operate efficiently.
- Flexible operations adapt to changing circumstances quickly and without disrupting the rest of the operation. Flexible processes can also change over between tasks quickly and without wasting time and capacity.

Worked example

Slap.com is an internet retailer of speciality cosmetics. It orders products from a number of suppliers, stores them, packs them to customers' orders, and then dispatches them using a distribution company. Although broadly successful, the business is very keen to reduce its operating costs. A number of suggestions have been made to do this. These are as follows:

- Make each packer responsible for his or her own quality. This could potentially reduce the percentage of mis-packed items from 0.25 per cent to near zero. Repacking an item that has been mis-packed costs €2 per item.
- Negotiate with suppliers to ensure that they respond to delivery requests faster. It is estimated that this would cut the value of inventories held by slap.com by €1,000,000.
- Institute a simple control system that would give early warning if the total number of orders that should be dispatched by the end of the day actually is dispatched in time. Currently 1 per cent of orders is not packed by the end of the day and therefore has to be sent by express courier the following day. This costs an extra €2 per item.

Because demand varies through the year, sometimes staff have to work overtime. Currently the overtime wage bill for the year is €150,000. The company's employees have indicated that they would be willing to adopt a flexible working scheme where extra hours could be worked when necessary in exchange for having the hours off at a less busy time and receiving some kind of extra payment. This extra payment is likely to total €50,000 per year.

If the company dispatch 5 million items every year and if the cost of holding inventory is 10 per cent of its value, how much cost will each of these suggestions save the company?

Analysis

Eliminating mis-packing would result in an improvement in quality. Currently 0.25 per cent of 5 million items are mis-packed. This amounts to 12,500 items per year. At €2 repacking charge per item, this is a cost of €25,000 that would be saved.

Getting faster delivery from suppliers helps reduce the amount of inventory in stock by €1,000,000. If the company is paying 10 per cent of the value of stock for keeping it in storage the saving will be €1,000,000 × 0.1 = €100,000.

Ensuring that all orders are dispatched by the end of the day increases the dependability of the company's operations. Currently, 1 per cent are late – in other words, 50,000 items per year. This is costing €2 × 50,000 = €100,000 per year, which would be saved by increasing dependability.

Changing to a flexible working hours system increases the flexibility of the operation and would cost €50,000 per year, but it saves €150,000 per year. Therefore, increasing flexibility could save €100,000 per year.

So, in total, by improving the operation's quality, speed, dependability, and flexibility, a total of €325,000 can be saved.

The polar representation of performance objectives

A useful way of representing the relative importance of performance objectives for a product or service is shown in Figure 2.11(a). This is called the polar representation because the scales which represent the importance of each performance objective have the same origin. A line describes the relative importance of each performance objective. The closer the line is to the common origin, the less important is the performance objective to the operation. Two services are shown, a taxi and a bus service. Each essentially provides the same basic service, but with different objectives. The differences between the two services are clearly shown by the diagram. Of course, the polar diagram can be adapted to accommodate any number of different performance objectives. For example, Figure 2.11(b) shows a proposal for using a polar diagram to assess the relative performance of different police forces in the UK.[11]

TRADE-OFFS BETWEEN PERFORMANCE OBJECTIVES

Earlier we examined how improving the performance of one objective inside the operation could also improve other performance objectives. Most notably better quality, speed, dependability and flexibility can improve cost performance. But externally this is not always the case. In fact there may be a 'trade-off' between performance objectives. In other words improving the performance of one performance objective might only be achieved by sacrificing performance in another. So, for example, an operation might wish to improve its cost efficiencies by reducing the variety of products or services that it offers to its customers. 'There is no such thing as a free lunch' could be taken as a summary of this approach. Probably the best-known summary of the trade-off idea comes from Professor Wickham Skinner, who said:

> 'most managers will readily admit that there are compromises or trade-offs to be made in designing an airplane or truck. In the case of an airplane, trade-offs would involve matters such as cruising speed, take-off and landing distances, initial cost, maintenance, fuel consumption, passenger comfort and cargo or passenger capacity. For instance, no one today can design a 500-passenger plane that can land on an aircraft carrier and also break the sound barrier. Much the same thing is true in . . . [operations]'.[12]

But there are two views of trade-offs. The first emphasizes 'repositioning' performance objectives by trading-off improvements in some objectives for a reduction in performance in others. The other emphasizes increasing the 'effectiveness' of the operation by overcoming trade-offs so that improvements in one or more aspects of performance can be achieved

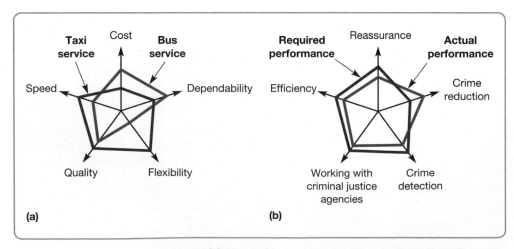

Figure 2.11 Polar representations of (a) the relative importance of performance objectives for a taxi service and a bus service, and (b) a police force targets and performance

without any reduction in the performance of others. Most businesses at some time or other will adopt both approaches. This is best illustrated through the concept of the 'efficient frontier' of operations performance.

Trade-offs and the efficient frontier

Figure 2.12(a) shows the relative performance of several companies in the same industry in terms of their cost efficiency and the variety of products or services that they offer to their customers. Presumably all the operations would ideally like to be able to offer very high variety while still having very high levels of cost efficiency. However, the increased complexity that a high variety of product or service offerings brings will generally reduce the operation's ability to operate efficiently. Conversely, one way of improving cost efficiency is to severely limit the variety on offer to customers. The spread of results in Figure 2.12(a) is typical of an exercise such as this. Operations A, B, C, D all have chosen a different balance between variety and cost efficiency. But none is dominated by any other operation in the sense that another operation necessarily has 'superior' performance. Operation X, however, has an inferior performance because operation A is able to offer higher variety at the same level of cost efficiency, and operation C offers the same variety but with better cost efficiency. The convex line on which operations A, B, C and D lie is known as the 'efficient frontier'. They may choose to position themselves differently (presumably because of different market strategies) but they cannot be criticized for being ineffective. Of course any of these operations that lie on the efficient frontier may come to believe that the balance they have chosen between variety and cost efficiency is inappropriate. In these circumstances they may choose to reposition themselves at some other point along the efficient frontier. By contrast, operation X has also chosen to balance variety and cost efficiency in a particular way but is not doing so effectively. Operation B has the same ratio between the two performance objectives but is achieving them more effectively.

However, a strategy that emphasizes increasing effectiveness is not confined to those operations that are dominated, such as operation X. Those with a position on the efficient frontier will generally also want

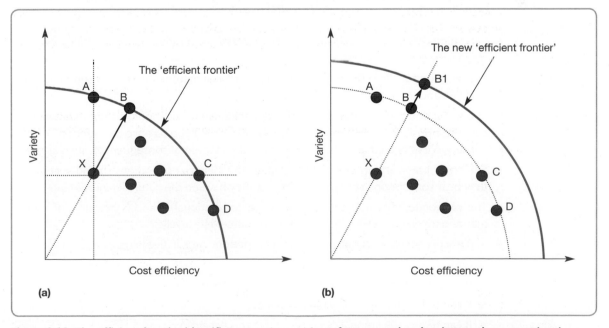

Figure 2.12 The efficient frontier identifies operations with performances that dominate other operations' performance

to improve their operations effectiveness by overcoming the trade-off that is implicit in the efficient frontier curve. For example, suppose operation B in Figure 2.12(b) wants to improve both its variety and its cost efficiency simultaneously and move to position B1. It may be able to do this, but only if it adopts operations improvements that extend the efficient frontier. For example, one of the decisions that any supermarket manager has to make is how many checkout positions to open at any time. If too many checkouts are opened then there will be times when the checkout staff do not have any customers to serve and will be idle. The customers, however, will have excellent service in terms of little or no waiting time. Conversely, if too few checkouts are opened, the staff will be working all the time but customers will have to wait in long queues. There seems to be a direct trade-off between staff utilization (and therefore cost) and customer waiting time (speed of service). Yet even the supermarket manager might, for example, allocate a number of 'core' staff to operate the checkouts but also arrange for those other staff who are performing other jobs in the supermarket to be trained and 'on-call' should demand suddenly increase. If the manager on duty sees a build-up of customers at the checkouts, these other staff could quickly be used to staff checkouts. By devising a flexible system of staff allocation, the manager can both improve customer service and keep staff utilization high.

> ✳ **Operations principle**
>
> An operation's improvement path can be described in terms of repositioning and/or overcoming its performance trade-offs.

This distinction between positioning on the efficient frontier and increasing operations effectiveness by extending the frontier is an important one. Any business must make clear the extent to which it is expecting the operation to reposition itself in terms of its performance objectives and the extent to which it is expecting the operation to improve its effectiveness in several ways simultaneously.

SUMMARY ANSWERS TO KEY QUESTIONS

MyOMLab *Check and improve your understanding of this chapter using self-assessment questions and a personalized study plan, a video case study, and an eText – all at* **www.myomlab.com**.

〉 Why is operations performance vital in any organization?

- Operations management can either 'make or break' any business. In most businesses it represents the bulk of its assets.

- The triple bottom line (TBL, or 3BL), includes the social bottom line, the environmental bottom line and the economic bottom line.

- The social bottom line incorporates the idea that businesses should accept that they bear some responsibility for the impact they have on society and balance the external 'societal' consequences of their actions with the more direct internal consequences, such as profit.

- The environmental bottom line incorporates the idea that operations should accept that they bear some responsibility for the impact they have on the natural environment.

- The economic bottom line incorporates the conventional financial measures of performance derived from using the operation's resources effectively.

- In particular, operations can affect economic performance in five ways:
  - It can reduce the costs.
  - It can achieve customer satisfaction through service.
  - It can reduce the risk of operational failure.
  - It can reduce the amount of investment that is necessary.
  - It can provide the basis for *future* innovation.

› Why is quality important?

- By 'doing things right', operations seek to influence the quality of the company's goods and services.
- Externally, quality is an important aspect of customer satisfaction or dissatisfaction.
- Internally, quality operations both reduce costs and increase dependability.

› Why is speed important?

- By 'doing things fast', operations seek to influence the speed with which goods and services are delivered.
- Externally, speed is an important aspect of customer service.
- Internally, speed both reduces inventories by decreasing internal throughput time and reduces risks by delaying the commitment of resources.

› Why is dependability important?

- By 'doing things on time', operations seek to influence the dependability of the delivery of goods and services.
- Externally, dependability is an important aspect of customer service.
- Internally, dependability within operations increases operational reliability, thus saving the time and money that would otherwise be taken up in solving reliability problems and also giving stability to the operation.

› Why is flexibility important?

- By 'changing what they do', operations seek to influence the flexibility with which the company produces goods and services.
- Externally, flexibility can:
  - produce new products and services (product/service flexibility);
  - produce a wide range or mix of products and services (mix flexibility);
  - produce different quantities or volumes of products and services (volume flexibility);
  - produce products and services at different times (delivery flexibility).
- Internally, flexibility can help speed up response times, save time wasted in changeovers, and maintain dependability.

› Why is cost important?

- By 'doing things cheaply', operations seek to influence the cost of the company's goods and services.
- Externally, low costs allow organizations to reduce their price in order to gain higher volumes or, alternatively, increase their profitability on existing volume levels.
- Internally, cost performance is helped by good performance in the other performance objectives.

- Trade-offs are the extent to which improvements in one performance objective can be achieved by sacrificing performance in others. The 'efficient frontier' concept is a useful approach to articulating trade-offs and distinguishes between repositioning performance on the efficient frontier and improving performance by overcoming trade-offs.

CASE STUDY — Operations objectives at the Penang Mutiara[13]

There are many luxurious hotels in the South-East Asia region but few can compare with the Penang Mutiara, a 440-room top-of-the-market hotel which nestles in the lush greenery of Malaysia's Indian Ocean Coast. Owned by Pernas–OUE of Malaysia and managed by Singapore Mandarin International Hotels, the hotel's General Manager is under no illusions about the importance of running an effective operation. *'Managing a hotel of this size is an immensely complicated task,'* he says. *'Our customers have every right to be demanding. They expect first-class service and that's what we have to give them. If we have any problems with managing this operation, the customer sees them immediately and that's the biggest incentive for us to take operations performance seriously. Our quality of service just has to be impeccable. This means dealing with the basics. For example, our staff must be courteous at all times and yet also friendly towards our guests. And of course they must have the knowledge to be able to answer guests' questions. The building and equipment – in fact all the hardware of the operation – must support the luxury atmosphere which we have created in the hotel. Stylish design and top-class materials not only create the right impression but, if we choose them carefully, are also durable so the hotel still looks good over the years. Most of all, though, quality is about anticipating our guests' needs, thinking ahead so you can identify what will delight or irritate a guest.'*

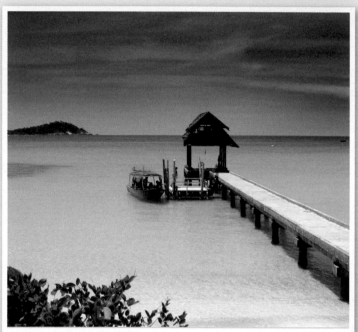

Source: Shutterstock.com/Ronen

The hotel tries to anticipate guests' needs in a number of ways. For example, if guests have been to the hotel before, staff avoid having to repeat the information they gave on the previous visit. Reception staff simply check to see if guests have stayed before, retrieve the information and take them straight to their room without irritating delays. Quality of service also means helping guests sort out their own problems. If the airline loses a guest's luggage en route to the hotel, for example, he or she will arrive at the hotel understandably irritated. *'The fact that it is not us who have irritated them is not really the issue. It is our job to make them feel better.'*

Speed, in terms of fast response to customers' requests is something else that is important. *'A guest just should not be kept waiting. If a guest has a request, he or she has that request now so it needs to be sorted out now. This is not always easy but we do our best. For example, if every guest in the hotel tonight decided to call room service and request a meal instead of going to the restaurants, our room service department would obviously be grossly overloaded and customers would have to wait an unacceptably long time before the meals were brought up to their rooms. We cope with this by keeping a close watch on how demand for room service is building up. If we think it's going to get above the level where response time to customers would become unacceptably long, we will call in staff from other restaurants in the hotel. Of course, to do this we have to make sure that our staff are multiskilled. In fact we have a policy of making sure that restaurant staff can always do more than one job. It's this kind of flexibility which allows us to maintain fast response to the customer.'*

Dependability is also a fundamental principle of a well-managed hotel. *'We must always keep our promises. For example, rooms must be ready on time and accounts must be ready for presentation when a guest departs; the guests expect a dependable service and anything less than full dependability is a legitimate cause for dissatisfaction.'* It is on the grand occasions, however, when dependability is particularly important in the hotel. When staging a banquet, for example, everything has to be on time. Drinks, food, entertainment have to be available exactly as planned. Any deviation from the plan will very soon be noticed by customers. *'It is largely a matter of planning the details and anticipating what could go wrong. Once we've done the planning we can anticipate possible problems and plan how to cope with them, or better still, prevent them from occurring in the first place.'*

Flexibility means a number of things to the hotel. First of all it means that they should be able to meet a guest's requests. *'We never like to say NO! For example, if a guest asks for some Camembert cheese and we don't have it in stock, we will make sure that someone goes to the supermarket and tries to get it. If, in spite of our best efforts, we can't get any we will negotiate an alternative solution with the guest. This has an important side-effect – it greatly helps us to maintain the motivation of our staff. We are constantly being asked to do the seemingly impossible – yet we do it, and our staff think it's great. We all like to be part of an organization which is capable of achieving the very difficult, if not the impossible.'* Flexibility in the hotel also means the ability to cope with the seasonal fluctuations in demand. They achieve this partly by using temporary part-time staff. In the back-office parts of the hotel this isn't a major problem. In the laundry, for example, it is relatively easy to put on an extra shift in busy periods by increasing staffing levels. However, this is more of a problem in the parts of the hotel that have direct contact with the customer. *'New temporary staff can't be expected to have the same customer contact skills as our more regular staff. Our solution to this is to keep the temporary staff as far in the background as we possibly can and make sure that our skilled, well-trained staff are the ones who usually interact with the customer. So, for example, a waiter who would normally take orders, service the food, and take away the dirty plates would in peak times restrict his or her activities to taking orders and serving the food. The less skilled part of the job, taking away the plates, could be left to temporary staff.'*

As far as cost is concerned, around 60 per cent of the hotel's total operating expenses go on food and beverages, so one obvious way of keeping costs down is by making sure that food is not wasted. Energy costs, at 6 per cent of total operating costs, are also a potential source of saving. However, although cost savings are welcome, the hotel is very careful never to compromise the quality of its service in order to cut costs. *'It is impeccable customer service which gives us our competitive advantage, not price. Good service means that our guests return again and again. At times, around half our guests are people who have been before. The more guests we have, the higher is our utilization of rooms and restaurants, and this is what really keeps cost per guest down and profitability reasonable. So in the end we've come full circle: it's the quality of our service which keeps our volumes high and our costs low.'*

QUESTIONS

1 Describe how you think the hotel's management will:
   (a) make sure that the way it manages the hotel is appropriate to the way it competes for business;
   (b) implement any change in strategy;
   (c) develop its operation so that it drives the long-term strategy of the hotel.
2 The case study describes how quality, speed, dependability, flexibility and cost impact on the hotel's external customers. Explain how each of these performance objectives might have internal benefits.

PROBLEMS AND APPLICATIONS

These problems and applications will help to improve your analysis of operations. You can find more practice problems as well as worked examples and guided solutions on MyOMLab at www.myomlab.com.

MyOMLab

1 The 'forensic science' service of a European country has traditionally been organized to provide separate forensic science laboratories for each police force around the country. In order to save costs, the government has decided to centralize this service in one large central facility close to the country's capital. What do you think are the external advantages and disadvantages of this to the stakeholders of the operation? What do you think are the internal implications to the new centralized operation that will provide this service?

2 The health clinic described in the worked example earlier in the chapter has expanded by hiring one extra employee and now has six employees. It has also leased some new health

monitoring equipment which allows patients to be processed faster. This means that its total output is now 280 patients per week. Its wage costs have increased to £4,680 per week and its overhead costs to £3,000 per week. What are its single-factor labour productivity and its multi-factor productivity now?

3 A publishing company plans to replace its four proofreaders who look for errors in manuscripts with a new scanning machine and one proofreader in case the machine breaks down. Currently the proofreaders check 15 manuscripts every week between them. Each is paid €80,000 per year. Hiring the new scanning machine will cost €5,000 each calendar month, but it could check 50 manuscripts per week. How will this new system affect the proofreading department's productivity?

4 Bongo's Pizzas have a service guarantee that promises you will not pay for your pizza if it is delivered more than 30 minutes from the order being placed. An investigation shows that 10 per cent of all pizzas are delivered between 15 and 20 minutes from order, 40 per cent between 20 and 25 minutes from order, 40 per cent between 25 and 30 minutes from order, 5 per cent between 30 and 35 minutes from order, 3 per cent between 35 and 40 minutes from order, and 2 per cent over 40 minutes from order. If the average profit on each pizza delivered on time is €1 and the average cost of each pizza delivered is €5, is the fact that Bongo's does not charge for 10 per cent of its pizzas a significant problem for the business? How much extra profit per pizza would be made if 5 minutes was cut from all deliveries?

5 *Step 1.* Look again at the figures in the chapter which illustrate the meaning of each performance objective for the four operations. Consider the bus company and the supermarket, and in particular consider their external customers.
Step 2. Draw the relative required performance for both operations on a polar diagram.
Step 3. Consider the internal effects of each performance objective. For both operations, identify how quality, speed, dependability and flexibility can help to reduce the cost of producing their services.

6 Visit the websites of two or three large oil companies such as Exxon, BP, Shell, Elf, etc. Examine how they describe their policies towards their customers, suppliers, shareholders, employees and society at large. Identify areas of the company's operations where there may be conflicts between the needs of these different stakeholder groups. Discuss or reflect on how (if at all) such companies try and reconcile these conflicts.

SELECTED FURTHER READING

Bourne, M., Kennerley, M. and Franco, M. (2005) Managing through measures: a study of the impact on performance, *Journal of Manufacturing Technology Management*, vol. 16, issue 4, 373–395. What it says on the tin.

Kaplan, R.S. and Norton, D.P. (2005) The balanced scorecard: measures that drive performance, *Harvard Business Review*, Jul/Aug. The latest pronouncements on the Balanced Scorecard approach (which we cover in Chapter 18).

Neely, A. (2012) *Business Performance Measurement: Unifying Theory and Integrating Practice*, Cambridge University Press, Cambridge. A collection of papers on the details of measuring performance objectives.

Pine, B.J. (1993) *Mass Customization*, Harvard Business School Press, Boston, MA. The first substantial work on the idea of mass customization. Still a classic.

Savitz, A.W. and Weber, K. (2006) *The Triple Bottom Line: How Today's Best-Run Companies Are Achieving Economic, Social and Environmental Success—and How You Can Too*, Jossey-Bass, San Francisco. Good on the triple bottom line.

Waddock, S. (2003) Stakeholder performance implications of corporate responsibility, *International Journal of Business Performance Management*, vol. 5, numbers 2–3, 114–124. An introduction to stakeholder analysis.

USEFUL WEBSITES

www.myomlab.com Test which sections you have mastered and which you need to review, with questions, a personalized study plan, video clips, revision tips, and cases.

www.opsman.org Useful materials.

http://operationsroom.wordpress.com/ Stanford University's take on topical operations stories.

www.iomnet.org.uk The Institute of Operations Management site. One of the main professional bodies for the subject.

www.poms.org A US academic society for production and operations management. Academic, but some useful material, including a link to an encyclopedia of operations management terms.

http//sites.google.com/site/tomiportal/home One of the longest-established portals for the subject. Useful for academics and students alike.

www.ft.com Good for researching topics and companies.

www.economist.com *The Economist's* site, well written and interesting stuff of business generally.

www.worldbank.org Global issues. Useful for international operations strategy research.

www.weforum.org Global issues, including some operations strategy ones.

Now that you have finished reading this chapter, why not visit MyOMLab at www.myomlab.com where you'll find more learning resources to help you make the most of your studies and get a better grade.

3 Operations strategy

Key questions

> What is strategy and what is operations strategy?

> What is the difference between a 'top-down' and a 'bottom-up' view of operations strategy?

> What is the difference between a 'market requirements' and an 'operations resources' view of operations strategy?

> How can an operations strategy be put together?

INTRODUCTION

No organization can plan in detail every aspect of its current or future actions, but all organizations need some strategic direction and so can benefit from some idea of where they are heading and how they could get there. Once the operations function has understood its role in the business and after it has articulated its performance objectives, it needs to formulate a set of general principles which will guide its decision making. This is the operations strategy of the company. Yet the concept of 'strategy' itself is not straightforward; neither is operations strategy. Here we consider four perspectives, each of which goes partway to illustrating the forces that shape operations strategy. Figure 3.1 shows the position of the ideas described in this chapter in the general model of operations management.

Figure 3.1 This chapter examines operations strategy

Two operations strategies: Flextronics and Ryanair[1]

The two most important attributes of any operations strategy are first that it aligns operations activities with the strategy of the whole organization, and second that it gives clear guidance. Here are two examples of very different businesses and very different strategies which nonetheless meet both criteria.

Ryanair is today Europe's largest low-cost airline (LCAs) and whatever else can be said about its strategy, it does not suffer from any lack of clarity. It has grown by offering low-cost basic services and has devised an operations strategy which is in line with its market position. The efficiency of the airline's operations supports its low-cost market position. Turnaround time at airports is kept to a minimum. This is achieved partly because there are no meals to be loaded onto the aircraft and partly through improved employee productivity. All the aircraft in the fleet are identical, giving savings through standardization of parts, maintenance and servicing. It also means large orders to a single aircraft supplier and therefore the opportunity to negotiate prices down. Also, because the company often uses secondary airports, landing and service fees are much lower. Finally, the cost of selling its services is reduced where possible.

Ryanair has developed its own low-cost internet booking service. In addition, the day-to-day experiences of the company's operations managers can also modify and refine these strategic decisions. For example, Ryanair changed its baggage handling contractors at Stansted Airport in the UK after problems with misdirecting customers' luggage. The company's policy on customer service is also clear. 'We patterned Ryanair after Southwest Airlines, the most consistently profitable airline in the US,' says Michael O'Leary, Ryanair's Chief Executive. 'Southwest founder Herb Kelleher created a formula for success that works by flying only one type of airplane – the 737, using smaller airports, providing no-frills service on-board, selling tickets directly to customers and offering passengers the lowest fares in the market. We have adapted his model for our marketplace and are now setting the low-fare standard for Europe. Our customer service,' says O'Leary, 'is about the most well defined in the world. We guarantee to give you the lowest air fare. You get a safe flight. You get a normally on-time flight. That's the package. We don't, and won't, give you anything more. Are we going to say sorry for our lack of customer service? Absolutely not. If a plane is cancelled, will we put you up in a hotel overnight? Absolutely not. If a plane is delayed, will we give you a voucher for a restaurant? Absolutely not.'

Flextronics is a global company based in Singapore that lies behind such well-known brand names as Nokia and Dell, who are increasingly using Electronic Manufacturing Services (EMS) companies, such as Flextronics, which specialize in providing the outsourced design, engineering, manufacturing and logistics operations for the big brand names. It is amongst the biggest of those EMS suppliers that offer the broadest worldwide capabilities, from design to end-to-end vertically integrated global supply chain services. Flextronics' operations strategy must balance their customers' need for low costs (electronic goods are often sold in a fiercely competitive market) with their need for responsive and flexible service (electronics markets can also be volatile). The company achieves this in a number of ways. First, it has an extensive network of design, manufacturing, and logistics facilities in the world's major electronics markets, giving them significant scale and the flexibility to move activities to the most appropriate location to serve customers. Second, Flextronics offers vertical integration capabilities that simplify global product development and supply processes, moving a product from its initial design through volume production, test, distribution, and into post-sales service, responsively and

Source: Shutterstock.com/Rob Wilson

Source: Shutterstock.com/PeterPhoto123

efficiently. Finally, Flextronics has developed integrated industrial parks to exploit fully the advantages of their global, large-scale, high-volume capabilities. Positioned in low-cost regions, yet close to all major world markets, Flextronics industrial parks can significantly reduce the cost of production. Locations include Gdansk in Poland; Sárvàr in Hungary; Guadalajara in Mexico; Sorocaba in Brazil; Chennai in India; and Shanghai in China. Flextronics' own suppliers are encouraged to locate within these parks, from which products can be produced on-site and shipped directly from the industrial park to customers, greatly reducing freight costs of incoming components and outgoing products. Products not produced on-site can be obtained from Flextronics' network of regional manufacturing facilities located near the industrial parks. Using this strategy, Flextronics says it can provide cost-effective delivery of finished products within 1–2 days of orders.

WHAT IS STRATEGY AND WHAT IS OPERATIONS STRATEGY?

Surprisingly, 'strategy' is not particularly easy to define. Linguistically the word derives from the Greek word 'strategos' meaning 'leading an army'. And although there is no direct historical link between Greek military practice and modern ideas of strategy, the military metaphor is powerful. Both military and business strategy can be described in similar ways, and include some of the following:

- Setting broad objectives that direct an enterprise towards its overall goal.
- Planning the path (in general rather than specific terms) that will achieve these goals.
- Stressing long-term rather than short-term objectives.
- Dealing with the total picture rather than stressing individual activities.
- Being detached from, and above, the confusion and distractions of day-to-day activities.

Here, by strategic decisions, we mean those decisions which are widespread in their effect on the organization to which the strategy refers, define the position of the organization relative to its environment, and move the organization closer to its long-term goals. But 'strategy' is more than a single decision; it is the *total pattern of the decisions* and actions that influence the long-term direction of the business. Thinking about strategy in this way helps us to discuss an organization's strategy even when it has not been explicitly stated. Observing the total pattern of decisions gives an indication of the *actual* strategic behaviour.

Operations strategy

Operations strategy concerns the pattern of strategic decisions and actions which set the role, objectives and activities of the operation. The term 'operations strategy' sounds at first like a contradiction. How can 'operations', a subject that is generally concerned with the day-to-day creation and delivery of goods and services, be strategic? 'Strategy' is usually regarded as the opposite of those day-to-day routine activities. But 'operations' is not the same as 'operational'. 'Operations' are the resources that create products and services. 'Operational' is the opposite of strategic, meaning day-to-day and detailed. So, one can examine both the operational *and* the strategic

> **∗ Operations principle**
>
> Operations is not the same as operational, it does have a strategic role.

aspects of operations. It is also conventional to distinguish between the 'content' and the 'process' of operations strategy. The *content* of operations strategy is the specific decisions and actions which set the operations role, objectives and activities. The *process* of operations strategy is the method that is used to make the specific 'content' decisions.

From implementing to supporting to driving strategy

Most businesses expect their operations strategy to improve operations performance over time. In doing this they should be progressing from a state where they contribute very little to the competitive success of the business through to the point where they are directly responsible for its competitive success. This means that they should be able to, in turn, master the skills to first 'implement', then 'support', and then 'drive' operations strategy.

Implementing business strategy The most basic role of operations is to implement strategy. You cannot, after all, touch a strategy; you cannot even see it; all you can see is how the operation behaves in practice. For example, if an insurance company has a strategy of moving to an entirely online service, its operations function will have to supervise the design of all the processes which allow customers to access online information, issue quotations, request further information, check credit details, send out documentation and so on. Without effective implementation even the most original and brilliant strategy will be rendered totally ineffective.

Supporting business strategy Support strategy goes beyond simply implementing strategy. It means developing the capabilities which allow the organization to improve and refine its strategic goals. For example, a mobile phone manufacturer wants to be the first in the market with new product innovations so its operations need to be capable of coping with constant innovation. It must develop processes flexible enough to make novel components, organize its staff to understand the new technologies, develop relationships with its suppliers which help them respond quickly when supplying new parts, and so on.

Driving business strategy The third, and most difficult, role of operations is to drive strategy by giving it a unique and long-term advantage. For example, a specialist food service company supplies restaurants with frozen fish and fish products. Over the years it has built up close relationships with its customers (chefs) as well as its suppliers around the world (fishing companies and fish farms). In addition it has its own small factory which develops and produces a continual stream of exciting new products. In fact the whole company's success is based largely on these unique operations capabilities. The operation drives the company's strategy.

> **✱ Operations principle**
> Operations should try to, progressively, implement, support and drive strategy.

Hayes and Wheelwright's four stages of operations contribution

The ability of any operation to play these roles within the organization can be judged by considering the organizational aims or aspirations of the operations function. Professors Hayes and Wheelwright of Harvard University[2] developed a four-stage model which can be used to evaluate the role and contribution of the operations function. The model traces the progression of the operations function from what is the largely negative role of stage 1 operations to it becoming the central element of competitive strategy in excellent stage 4 operations. Figure 3.2 illustrates the four stages.

Stage 1: Internal neutrality This is the very poorest level of contribution by the operations function. It is holding the company back from competing effectively. It is inward-looking and, at best, reactive with very little positive to contribute towards competitive success. Paradoxically, its goal is 'to be ignored' (or, 'internally neutral'). At least then it isn't holding the company back in any way. It attempts to improve by 'avoiding making mistakes'.

Stage 2: External neutrality The first step of breaking out of stage 1 is for the operations function to begin comparing itself with similar companies or organizations in the outside market (being 'externally neutral'). This may not immediately take it to the 'first division' of companies in the market, but at least it is measuring itself against its competitors' performance and trying to implement 'best practice'.

Stage 3: Internally supportive Stage 3 operations are amongst the best in their market. Yet, stage 3 operations still aspire to be clearly and unambiguously *the* very best in the market. They achieve this by gaining a clear view of the company's competitive or strategic goals and supporting it by developing appropriate operations resources. The operation is trying to be 'internally supportive' by providing a credible operations strategy.

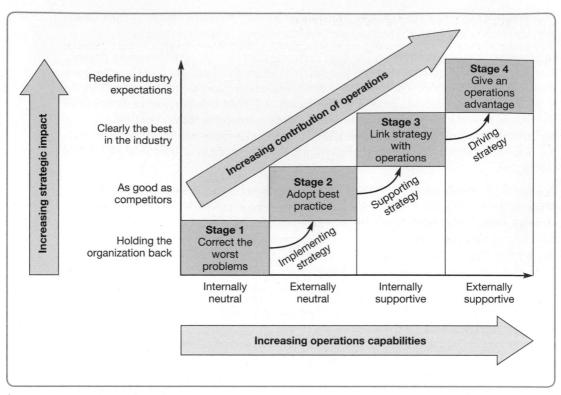

Figure 3.2 The Four-stage model of operations contribution

Stage 4: Externally supportive Yet Hayes and Wheelwright suggest a further stage – stage 4, where the company views the operations function as providing the foundation for its competitive success. Operations look to the long term. It forecasts likely changes in markets and supply, and it develops the operations-based capabilities which will be required to compete in future market conditions. Stage 4 operations are innovative, creative and proactive and are driving the company's strategy by being 'one step ahead' of competitors – what Hayes and Wheelwright call being 'externally supportive'.

Critical commentary

The idea that operations can have a leading role in determining a company's strategic direction is not universally supported. Both Hayes and Wheelwright's stage 4 of their four-stage model and the concept of operations 'driving' strategy do not only imply that it is possible for operations to take such a leading role, but are explicit in seeing it as a 'good thing'. A more traditional stance taken by some authorities is that the needs of the market will always be pre-eminent in shaping a company's strategy. Therefore, operations should devote all their time to understanding the requirements of the market (as defined by the marketing function within the organization) and devote themselves to their main job of ensuring that operations processes can actually deliver what the market requires. Companies can only be successful, they argue, by positioning themselves in the market (through a combination of price, promotion, product design and managing how products and services are delivered to customers) with operations very much in a 'supporting' role. In effect, they say, Hayes and Wheelwright's four-stage model should stop at stage 3. The issue of an 'operations resource' perspective on operations strategy is discussed later in the chapter.

Perspectives on operations strategy

Different authors have slightly different views and definitions of operations strategy. Between them, four 'perspectives' emerge: [3]

- Operations strategy is a top-down reflection of what the whole group or business wants to do.
- Operations strategy is a bottom-up activity where operations improvements cumulatively build strategy.
- Operations strategy involves translating market requirements into operations decisions.
- Operations strategy involves exploiting the capabilities of operations resources in chosen markets.

None of these four perspectives alone gives the full picture of what operations strategy is. But together they provide some idea of the pressures which go to form the content of operations strategy. We will treat each in turn (*see* Fig. 3.3).

Figure 3.3 The four perspectives on operations strategy

THE 'TOP-DOWN' AND 'BOTTOM-UP' PERSPECTIVES

Top-down strategies

A large corporation will need a strategy to position itself in its global, economic, political and social environment. This will consist of decisions about what types of business the group wants to be in, what parts of the world it wants to operate in, how to allocate its cash between its various businesses, and so on. Decisions such as these form the corporate strategy of the corporation. Each business unit within the corporate group will also need to put together its own business strategy which sets out its individual mission and objectives. This business strategy guides the business in relation to its customers, markets and competitors, and also the strategy of the corporate group of which it is a part. Similarly, within the business, functional strategies need to consider what part each function should play in contributing to the strategic objectives of the business.

So, one perspective on operations strategy is that it should take its place in this hierarchy of strategies. Its main influence, therefore, will be whatever the business sees as its strategic direction. For example, a printing services group has a company which prints packaging for consumer products. The group's management figures that, in the long term, only companies with significant market share will achieve substantial profitability. Its corporate objectives therefore stress market dominance. The consumer packaging company decides to achieve volume growth, even above short-term profitability or return on investment. The implication for operations strategy is that it needs to expand rapidly, investing in extra capacity (factories, equipment and labour) even if it means some excess capacity in some areas. It also needs to establish new factories in all parts of its market to offer relatively fast delivery. The important point here is that different business objectives would probably result in a very different operations strategy. The role of operations is therefore largely one of implementing or 'operationalizing' business strategy. Figure 3.4 illustrates this strategic hierarchy, with some of the decisions at each level and the main influences on the strategic decisions.

'Bottom-up' strategies

The 'top-down' perspective provides an orthodox view of how functional strategies *should* be put together. But in fact the relationship between the levels in the strategy hierarchy is more complex than this. When any group is reviewing its corporate strategy, it will also take

Corporate strategy decisions
- What businesses to be in?
- Allocation of cash to businesses?
- How to manage the relationships between different businesses?

Business strategy decisions
- Defining the mission of the business, e.g.
  - growth targets
  - return on investment
  - profitability targets
  - cash generation
- Setting competitive objectives

Functional strategy decisions
- The role of the function
- Translating business objectives into functional objectives
- Allocation of resources so as to achieve functional objectives
- Performance improvement priorities

Printing services group corporate strategy
- Specialize in packaging businesses
- Become a major player in all its markets

Consumer packaging business strategy
- Rapid volume growth
- Fast service
- Economies of scale

Operations strategy
- Capacity expansion
- Tolerate some overcapacity in the short term
- New locations established

Figure 3.4 The top-down perspective of operations strategy and its application to the printing services group into account the circumstances, experiences and capabilities of the various businesses that form the group. Similarly, businesses, when reviewing their strategies, will consult the individual functions within the business about their constraints and capabilities. They may also incorporate the ideas which come from each function's day-to-day experience. Therefore an alternative view to the top-down perspective is that many strategic ideas emerge over time from operational experience. Sometimes companies move in a particular strategic direction because the ongoing experience of providing products and services to customers at an operational level convinces them that it is the right thing to do. There may be no high-level decisions examining alternative strategic options and choosing the one which provides the best way forward. Instead, a general consensus emerges from the operational level of the organization.

Suppose the printing services company described previously succeeds in its expansion plans. However, in doing so it finds that having surplus capacity and a distributed network of factories allows it to offer an exceptionally fast service to customers. It also finds that some customers are willing to pay considerably higher prices for such a responsive service. Its experiences lead the company to set up a separate division dedicated to providing fast, high-margin printing services to those customers willing to pay. The strategic objectives of this new division are not concerned with high-volume growth but high profitability.

This idea of strategy being shaped by operational level experience over time is sometimes called the concept of emergent strategies [4] (*see* Fig. 3.5). This view of operations strategy is perhaps more descriptive of how things really happen, but at first glance it seems less useful in providing a guide for specific decision making. Yet while emergent strategies are less easy to categorize, the principle governing a bottom-up perspective is clear: shape the operation's objectives and action, at least partly, by the knowledge it gains from its day-to-day activities. The key virtues required for shaping strategy from the bottom up are an ability to learn from experience and a philosophy of continual and incremental improvement.

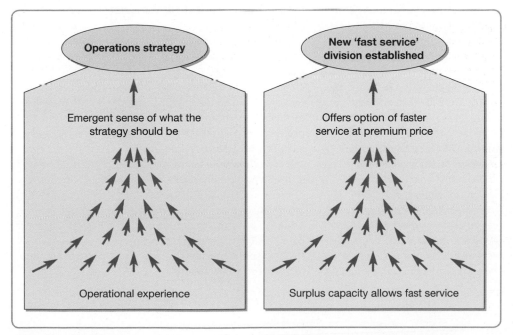

Figure 3.5 The bottom-up perspective of operations strategy and its application to the printing services group

This is the first of two short cases in this chapter that features operations strategy at Apple. Why? Because Apple is comprised of different parts, and different parts of a business often need different operations strategies. This case looks at Apple's retail operations strategy, the one later in the chapter looks at their supply strategy.

Apple has not always had a retail operations strategy, because Apple has not always sold its products through its own shops. It was back in 1990 when Steve Jobs, then Apple's boss, decided to build Apple Stores because conventional computer retailers were reluctant to stock its Mac computers. They said that the Apple brand was too weak (which, at the time, it was). The original Apple stores were heavily influenced by Gap (the clothing retailer) and so many Gap employees moved to work for Apple that they joked about working for 'Gapple'. However, even with the experienced Gap retailers, Apple wanted to develop its own ideas. Consequently they built a 'prototype store' near their Californian headquarters and tested its retail concepts for a year before opening the first Apple Stores. This early learning period was important. It allowed Apple to come to the conclusion that the two key issues for their retail operations strategy were store location and the experience that customers would have within the stores.

Source: Shutterstock.com/Nui 7711

First, store location: Apple has stores in some of the highest profile locations on earth. This is expensive, but the large number of customers it attracts together with the Apple range of products allows the company to produce very high sales. In fact its sales productivity (sales per square metre) is above many luxury goods retailers, for example Tiffany.

Second, the customer experience: according to Ron Johnson, who built up Apple's shop network, says, '*People come to the Apple Store for the experience, and they're willing to pay a premium for that. There are lots of components to that experience, but maybe the most important is that the staff isn't focused on selling stuff, it's focused on building relationships and trying to make people's lives better. The staff is exceptionally well trained, and they're not on commission, so it makes no difference to them if they sell you an expensive new computer or help you make your old one run better so you're happy with it. Their job is to figure out what you need and help you get it, even if it's a product Apple doesn't carry. Compare that with other retailers where the emphasis is on encouraging customers to buy more, even if they don't want or need it. That doesn't enrich their lives, and it doesn't deepen the retailer's relationship with them. It just makes their wallets lighter.*'

Yet creating the customer experience is not a matter of chance – it is carefully designed into Apple's strategy. Employees are helped to cultivate their air of cool confidence through extensive training, and it's easier to be approachable and calm when there is little pressure to push sales. Training emphasizes the importance of problem solving rather than selling and treating customers with courtesy. For example, staff have been told never to correct a customer's mispronunciation of a product in case it is seen as patronizing. Of course, Apple's products are attractive and Apple customers are famously passionate about the brand – but if Apple products were the only reason for the Stores' success, it's difficult to explain why customers flock to the stores to buy Apple products at full price when discount retailers sell them cheaper.

THE MARKET REQUIREMENTS AND OPERATIONS RESOURCES PERSPECTIVES

Market-requirements-based strategies

No operation that continually fails to serve its markets adequately is likely to survive in the long term. Without an understanding of what markets require, it is impossible to ensure that operations is achieving the right priority between its performance objectives (quality, speed, dependability, flexibility and cost).

The market influence on performance objectives

Operations seek to satisfy customers through developing their five performance objectives. For example, if customers particularly value low-priced products or services, the operation will place emphasis on its cost performance. Alternatively, a customer emphasis on fast delivery will make speed important to the operation, and so on. These factors which define the customers' requirements are called competitive factors.[6] Figure 3.6 shows the relationship between some of the more common competitive factors and the operation's performance objectives. This list is not exhaustive; whatever competitive factors are important to customers should influence the priority of each performance objective.

> ✳ **Operations principle**
> Operations strategy should reflect the requirements of the business's markets.

Order-winning and qualifying objectives

A particularly useful way of determining the relative importance of competitive factors is to distinguish between 'order-winning' and 'qualifying' factors.[7] Order-winning factors are those things which directly and significantly contribute to winning business. They are regarded by customers as key reasons for purchasing the product or service. Raising performance in an order-winning factor will either result in more business or improve the chances of gaining more business. Qualifying factors may not be the major competitive determinants

Figure 3.6 Different competitive factors imply different performance objectives

of success, but are important in another way. They are those aspects of competitiveness where the operation's performance has to be above a particular level just to be considered by the customer. Performance below this 'qualifying' level of performance will possibly disqualify the company from being considered by many customers. But any further improvement above the qualifying level is unlikely to gain the company much competitive benefit. To order-winning and qualifying factors can be added less important factors which are neither order-winning nor qualifying. They do not influence customers in any significant way. They are worth mentioning here only because they may be of importance in other parts of the operation's activities.

Figure 3.7 shows the difference between order-winning, qualifying and less important factors in terms of their utility or worth to the competitiveness of the organization. The curves illustrate the relative amount of competitiveness (or attractiveness to customers) as the operation's performance at the factor varies. Order-winning factors show a steady and significant increase in their contribution to competitiveness as the operation gets better at providing them. Qualifying factors are 'givens'; they are expected by customers and can severely disadvantage the competitive position of the operation if it cannot raise its performance above the qualifying level. Less important objectives have little impact on customers no matter how well the operation performs in them.

Different customer needs imply different objectives

If, as is likely, an operation produces goods or services for more than one customer group, it will need to determine the order-winning, qualifying and less important competitive factors for each group. For example, Table 3.1 shows two 'product' groups in the banking industry. Here the distinction is drawn between the customers who are looking for banking services for their private and domestic needs (current accounts, overdraft facilities, savings accounts, mortgage loans, etc.) and those corporate customers who need banking services for their (often large) organizations. These latter services would include such things as letters of credit, cash transfer services and commercial loans.

The product/service life cycle influence on performance objectives

One way of generalizing the behaviour of both customers and competitors is to link it to the life cycle of the products or services that the operation is producing. The exact form of product/service life cycles will vary, but generally they are shown as the sales volume passing

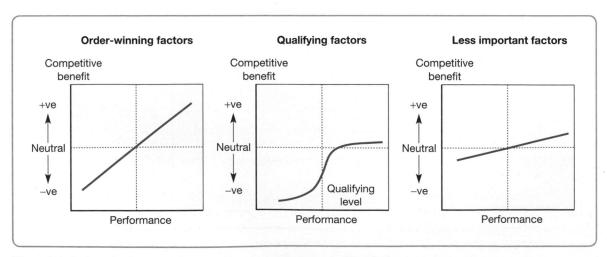

Figure 3.7 Order-winning, qualifying and less important competitive factors

Table 3.1 Different banking services require different performance objectives

	Retail banking	Corporate banking
Products	Personal financial services such as loans and credit cards	Special services for corporate customers
Customers	Individuals	Businesses
Product range	Medium but standardized, little need for special terms	Very wide range, many need to be customized
Design changes	Occasional	Continual
Delivery	Fast decisions	Dependable service
Quality	Means error-free transactions	Means close relationships
Volume per service type	Most service are high volume	Most services are low volume
Profit margins	Most are low to medium, some high	Medium to high

Competitive factors		
Order winners	Price	Customization
	Accessibility	Quality of service
	Speed	Reliability
Qualifiers	Quality	Speed
	Range	Price
Less important		Accessibility

Internal performance	Cost	Flexibility
objectives	Speed	Quality
	Quality	Dependability

through four stages – introduction, growth, maturity and decline. The implication of this for operations management is that products and services will require different operations strategies in each stage of their life cycle (*see* Fig. 3.8).

Introduction stage When a product or service is first introduced, it is likely to be offering something new in terms of its design or performance, with few competitors offering the same product or service. The needs of customers are unlikely to be well understood, so operations management needs to develop the flexibility to cope with any changes and be able to give the quality to maintain product/service performance.

Sales volume	Introduction into market	Growth in market acceptance	Maturity of market, sales level off	Decline as market becomes saturated
Customers	Innovators	Early adopters	Bulk of market	Laggards
Competitors	Few/none	Increasing numbers	Stable number	Declining number
Likely order winners	Product/service specification	Availability	Low price Dependable supply	Low price
Likely qualifiers	Quality Range	Price Range	Range Quality	Dependable supply
Dominant operations performance objectives	Flexibility Quality	Speed Dependability Quality	Cost Dependability	Cost

Figure 3.8 The effects of the product/service life cycle on operations performance objectives

Worked example

'It is about four years now since we specialized in the small to medium firms' market. Before that we also used to provide legal services for anyone who walked in the door. So now we have built up our legal skills in many areas of corporate and business law. However, within the firm, I think we could focus our activities even more. There seem to be two types of assignment that we are given. About 40 per cent of our work is relatively routine. Typically these assignments are to do with things like property purchase and debt collection. Both these activities involve a relatively standard set of steps which can be automated or carried out by staff without full legal qualifications. Of course, a fully qualified lawyer is needed to make some decisions; however, most work is fairly routine. Customers expect us to be relatively inexpensive and fast in delivering the service. Nor do they expect us to make simple errors in our documentation; in fact if we did this too often we would lose business. Fortunately our customers know that they are buying a standard service and don't expect it to be customized in any way. The problem here is that specialist agencies have been emerging over the last few years and they are starting to undercut us on price. Yet I still feel that we can operate profitably in this market and anyway, we still need these capabilities to serve our other clients. The other 60 per cent of our work is for clients who require far more specialist services, such as assignments involving company merger deals or major company restructuring. These assignments are complex, large, take longer, and require significant legal skill and judgement. It is vital that clients respect and trust the advice we give them across a wide range of legal specialisms. Of course they assume that we will not be slow or unreliable in preparing advice, but mainly it's trust in our legal judgement which is important to the client. This is popular work with our lawyers. It is both interesting and very profitable. But should I create two separate parts to our business: one to deal with routine services and the other to deal with specialist services? And, what aspects of operations performance should each part be aiming to excel at?' (Managing Partner, Branton Legal Services)

Analysis

Table 3.2 has used the information supplied above to identify the order winners, qualifiers and less important competitive factors for the two categories of service. As the Managing Partner suspects, the two types of service are very different. Routine services must be relatively inexpensive and fast, whereas the clients for specialist services must trust the quality of advice and range of legal skills available in the firm. The customers for routine services do not expect errors and those for specialist services assume a basic level of dependability and speed. These are the qualifiers for the two categories of service. Note that qualifiers are not 'unimportant'; on the contrary, failure to be 'up to standard' at them can lose the firm business. However, it is the order winner which attracts new business. Most significantly, the performance objectives which each operations partner should stress are very different. Therefore there does seem to be a case for separating the sets of resources (e.g. lawyers and other staff) and processes (information systems and procedures) that produce each type of service.

Table 3.2 Competitive factors and performance objectives for the legal firm

Service category	Routine services	Specialist services
Examples	Property purchase	Company merger deals
	Debt collection	Company restructuring
Order winner	Price	Quality of service
	Speed	Range of skills
Qualifiers	Quality (conformance)	Dependability
		Speed
Less important	Customization	Price
Operations partners should stress	Cost	Quality of relationship
	Speed	Legal skills
	Quality	Flexibility

Growth stage As volume grows, competitors may enter the growing market. Keeping up with demand could prove to be the main operations preoccupation. Rapid and dependable response to demand will help to keep demand buoyant, while quality levels must ensure that the company keeps its share of the market as competition starts to increase.

Maturity stage Demand starts to level off. Some early competitors may have left the market and the industry will probably be dominated by a few larger companies. So operations will be expected to get the costs down in order to maintain profits or to allow price cutting, or both. Because of this, cost and productivity issues, together with dependable supply, are likely to be the operation's main concerns.

Decline stage After time, sales will decline with more competitors dropping out of the market. There might be a residual market, but unless a shortage of capacity develops the market will continue to be dominated by price competition. Operations objectives continue to be dominated by cost.

> **✳ Operations principle**
> Operations strategy objectives will change depending on the stage of the business's services and products.

The operations resources perspective

The fourth and final perspective we shall take on operations strategy is based on a particularly influential theory of business strategy – the resource-based view (RBV) of the firm.[8] Put simply, the RBV holds that firms with an 'above average' strategic performance are likely to have gained their sustainable competitive advantage because of the core competences (or capabilities) of their resources. This means that the way an organization inherits, or acquires, or develops its operations resources will, over the long term, have a significant impact on its strategic success. Furthermore, the impact of its 'operations resource' capabilities will be at least as great as, if not greater than, that which it gets from its market position. So understanding and developing the capabilities of operations resources, although often neglected, is a particularly important perspective on operations strategy.

Resource constraints and capabilities

No organization can merely choose which part of the market it wants to be in without considering its ability to produce services and products in a way that will satisfy that market. In other words, the constraints imposed by its operations must be taken into account. For example, a small translation company offers general translation services to a wide range of customers who wish documents such as sales brochures to be translated into another language. A small company, it operates an informal network of part-time translators who enable the company to offer translation into or from most of the major languages in the world. Some of the company's largest customers want to purchase their sales brochures on a 'one-stop shop' basis and have asked the translation company whether it is willing to offer a full service, organizing the design and production, as well as the translation, of export brochures. This is a very profitable market opportunity; however, the company does not have the resources, financial or physical, to take it up. From a market perspective, it is good business; but from an operations resource perspective, it is not feasible.

However, the operations resource perspective is not always so negative. This perspective may identify *constraints* to satisfying some markets but it can also identify *capabilities* which can be exploited in other markets. For example, the same translation company has recently employed two new translators who have translation software skills so now the company can offer a new 'fast response' service which has been designed specifically to exploit the capabilities within the operations resources. Here the company has chosen to be driven by its resource capabilities rather than the obvious market opportunities.

Intangible resources

An operations resource perspective must start with an understanding of the resource capabilities and constraints within the operation. It must answer the simple questions, what do we have, and what can we do? An obvious starting point here is to examine the transforming and transformed resource inputs to the operation. These, after all, are the 'building blocks' of the operation. However, merely listing the type of *resources* an operation has does not give a complete picture of what it can do. Trying to understand an operation by listing its resources alone is like trying to understand an automobile by listing its component parts. To describe it more fully, we need to describe how the component parts form the internal mechanisms of the motor car. Within the operation, the equivalent of these mechanisms is its *processes*. Yet, even for an automobile, a technical explanation of its mechanisms still does not convey everything about its style or 'personality'. Something more is needed to describe these. In the same way, an operation is not just the sum of its processes. In addition, the operation has some intangible resources. An operation's intangible resources include such things as its relationship with suppliers, the reputation it has with its customers, its knowledge of its process technologies and the way its staff can work together in new product and service development. These intangible resources may not always be obvious within the operation, but they are important and have real value. It is these intangible resources, as well as its tangible resources, that an operation needs to deploy in order to

Amazon, so what exactly is your core competence?[9]

The founder and boss of Amazon, Jeff Bezos, was at a conference speaking about the company's plans. Although Amazon was generally seen as an internet book retailer and then a more general internet retailer, Jeff Bezos was actually pushing three of Amazon's 'utility computing' services. These were: a company that provides cheap access to online computer storage, a company that allows program developers to rent computing capacity on Amazon systems, and a service that connects firms with other firms who perform specialist tasks that are difficult to automate. The problem with online retailing, said Bezos, is its seasonality. At peak times, such as Christmas, Amazon has far more computing capacity than it needs for the rest of the year. At low points it may be using as little as 10 per cent of its total capacity. Hiring out that spare capacity is an obvious way to bring in extra revenue. In addition, Amazon had developed a search engine, a video download business, a service (Fulfilment By Amazon) that allowed other companies to use Amazon's logistics capability, including the handling of returned items, and a service that provided access to Amazon's 'back-end' technology.

Amazon's apparent redefinition of its strategy was immediately criticized by some observers. 'Why not,' they said, 'stick to what you know, focus on your core competence of internet retailing?' Bezos's response was clear. 'We *are* sticking to our core competence; this is what we've been doing for the last 11 years. The only thing that's changed is that we are exposing it for (the benefit of) others.' At least for Jeff Bezos, Amazon is not so much an internet retailer as a provider of internet-based technology and logistics services.

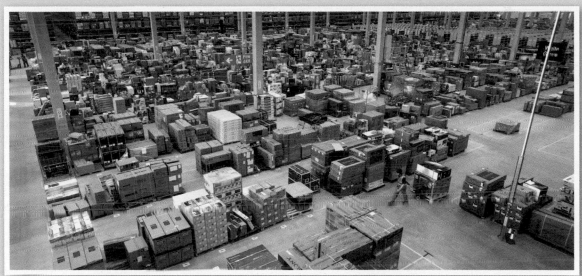

Source: Alamy Images/Apex News & Pictures

satisfy its markets. The central issue for operations management, therefore, is to ensure that its pattern of strategic decisions really does develop appropriate capabilities within its resources and processes.

Strategic resources and sustainable competitive advantage

The 'resource-based' explanation of why some companies manage to gain sustainable competitive advantage is that they have accumulated better or more appropriate resources. Put simply, 'above average' competitive performance is more likely to be the result of the core capabilities (or competences) inherent in a firm's resources than its competitive positioning in its industry. And resources can have a particularly influential impact on strategic success if they exhibit some or all of the following properties. [10]

They are scarce Unequal access to resources, so that not all competing firms have scarce resources such as an ideal location, experienced engineers, proprietary software, etc., can strengthen competitive advantage. So, for example, if a firm did not have the good foresight (or luck) to acquire a strategic resource (such as a supply contract with a specialist supplier) when it was inexpensive, it will have to try and acquire it after it has become expensive (because other firms are also now wanting it).

They are not very mobile Some resources are difficult to move out of a firm. For example, if a new process is developed in a company's Stockholm site and is based on the knowledge and experience of the Stockholm staff, the process will be difficult (although not totally impossible) to sell to another company based elsewhere in Europe (or even in Sweden if the staff do not want to move). As a result, the advantages that derive from the process's resources are more likely to be retained over time.

They are difficult to imitate or substitute for These two factors help define how easily a resource-based advantage can be sustained over time. It is not enough only to have resources

> **✳ Operations principle**
>
> The long-term objective of operations strategy is to build operations-based capabilities.

which are unique and immobile. If a competitor can copy these resources or, less predictably, replace them with alternative resources, then their value will quickly deteriorate. However, the less tangible are the resources and more connected with the tacit knowledge embedded within the organization, the more difficult they are for competitors to understand and to copy.

Structural and infrastructural decisions

A distinction is often drawn between the strategic decisions which determine an operation's structure and those which determine its infrastructure. An operation's structural decisions are those which we have classed as primarily influencing design activities, while infrastructural decisions are those which influence the workforce organization and the planning and control, and improvement activities. This distinction in operations strategy has been compared to that between 'hardware' and 'software' in computer systems. The hardware of a computer sets limits to what it can do. In a similar way, investing in advanced technology and building more or better facilities can raise the potential of any type of operation. Within the limits which are imposed by the hardware of a computer, the software governs how effective the computer actually is in practice. The most powerful computer can only work to its full potential if its software is capable of exploiting its potential. The same principle applies with operations. The best and most costly facilities and technology will only be effective if the operation also has an appropriate infrastructure which governs the way it will work on a day-to-day basis. Table 3.3 illustrates both structural and infrastructural decision areas, arranged

Table 3.3 Structural and infrastructural strategic decision areas

Structural strategic decisions	Typical questions which the strategy should help to answer
New product/service design	• How should the operation decide which products or services to develop and how to manage the development process?
Supply network design	• Should the operation expand by acquiring its suppliers or its customers? If so, what customers and suppliers should it acquire? • How should it develop the capabilities of its customers and suppliers? • What capacity should each operation in the network have? • What number of geographically separate sites should the operation have and where should they be located? • What activities and capacity should be allocated to each plant?
Process technology	• What types of process technology should the operation be using? • Should it be at the leading edge of technology or wait until the technology is established?

Infrastructural strategic decisions	Typical questions which the strategy should help to answer
Job design and organization	• What role should the people who staff the operation play in its management? • How should responsibility for the activities of the operations function be allocated between different groups in the operation? • What skills should be developed in the staff of the operation?
Planning and control	• How should the operation forecast and monitor the demand for its products and services? • How should the operation adjust its activity levels in response to demand fluctuations? • What systems should the operation use to plan and control its activities? • How should the operation decide the resources to be allocated to its various activities?
Inventory	• How should the operation decide how much inventory to have and where it is to be located? • How should the operation control the size and composition of its inventories?
Supplier development	• How should the operation choose its suppliers? • How should it develop its relationship with its suppliers? • How should it monitor its suppliers' performance?
Improvement	• How should the operation's performance be measured? • How should the operation decide whether its performance is satisfactory? • How should the operation ensure that its performance is reflected in its improvement priorities? • Who should be involved in the improvement process? • How fast should the operation expect improvement in performance to be? • How should the improvement process be managed?
Failure prevention risk and recovery	• How should the operation maintain its resources so as to prevent failure? • How should the operation plan to cope with a failure if one occurs?

SHORT CASE · Apple's supply operations strategy[11]

Earlier in this chapter we looked at Apple's retail operations strategy. Here we move on to how Apple supplies those, and other, of its retail outlets.

Behind the impressive corporate facade of Apple's Silicon Valley headquarters there are no factories churning out the millions of products that Apple sells every year. Apple, like most of its competitors, outsources its production to supplier operations around the world; mainly in the manufacturing powerhouses of South East Asia. So does this mean that Apple's operations strategy is also outsourced along with its manufacturing? Not at all. What it does mean is that operations strategy for Apple is concerned with 'supply'. In other words, making sure that current products are always supplied fast enough to meet demand and new products always meet their launch dates. Over the years Apple has put together a remarkable supply network that is recognized as one of the most efficient in the world, and what is more important, gives them significant competitive advantage. The company's (outsourced) manufacturing, purchasing and supply logistics gives it the ability to accomplish substantial new product launches without having to build up huge and expensive pre-launch stocks. In the words of Tim Cook, who developed Apple's operations strategy, *'nobody wants to buy sour milk'*.

The way that Apple beats its competitors is to use its cash to secure exclusive deals on new component technologies (touch-screens, chips, LED displays, etc.).

When a new component first comes out, it is usually very expensive to produce, and constructing a factory that can produce it in high volume is even more expensive. Combine this with the relatively small profit margin of many components and it becomes difficult for suppliers to make enough profit to guarantee that they can make an acceptable return on their investment. But, thanks to its successful stream of products, Apple can afford to pay for some or all of a supplier's construction cost of the new factory. In exchange the supplier gives exclusive rights to Apple for the new component over an agreed period. This has two advantages for Apple. First, it gives Apple access to new component technology months (or even years) before its rivals, allowing it to launch radical new products that are literally impossible for competitors to duplicate. Second, even when the exclusive agreement expires, Apple will often have negotiated a discounted price. So it can source the component at a lower cost from the supplier that is now the most experienced and skilled provider of those parts.

In summary, according to Marty Lariviere, at Stanford University, '[Apple's operations strategy is to] *bet big on technology that lets them have distinctive products. With* their limited product line and high volume, they can make commitments that other tech firms may shy away from. It also means that (if they are right) other firms are going to be hard pressed to catch up if Apple has locked up a large amount of supplier capacity.'

Source: Alamy Images/Thomas Jackson

to correspond approximately to the chapter headings used in this book. The table also shows some typical questions which each strategic decision area should be addressing.

HOW CAN AN OPERATIONS STRATEGY BE PUT TOGETHER?

The process of strategy formulation is concerned with 'how' operations strategies are put together. But, putting an operations strategy together and making it happen in practice is a complex and difficult thing to achieve. Even the most sophisticated organizations would probably admit that they do not always get it right. And although any simple step-by-step model of how to 'do' operations strategy will inevitably be a simplification of a messy reality, we shall use a four-stage model to illustrate some of the elements of 'process'. This stage model is shown in Figure 3.9. It divides the process of operations strategy into formulation, implementation, monitoring and control.[12]

> *** Operations principle**
>
> The process of operation strategy involves formulation, implementation, monitoring and control.

Operations strategy formulation

Formulation of operations strategy is the process of clarifying the various objectives and decisions that make up the strategy, and the links between them. Unlike day-to-day operations management, formulating an operations strategy is likely to be only an occasional activity. Some firms will have a regular (e.g. annual) planning cycle and operations strategy consideration may form part of this but the extent of any changes made in each annual cycle is likely to be limited. In other words, the 'complete' process of formulating an entirely new operations strategy will be a relatively infrequent event. There are many 'formulation processes' which are, or can be, used to formulate operations strategies. Most consultancy companies have developed their own frameworks, as have several academics.

Figure 3.9 The four stages of the process of operations strategy

Source: *Operations Strategy*, 3rd ed., Pearson Education Limited (Slack, N. and Lewis, M.A. 2011) p.33, Figure 1.12, © Nigel Slack and Michael Lewis 2002, 2008, 2011

What should the formulation process be trying to achieve?

Before putting an operations strategy together, it is necessary to ask the question, 'What should it be trying to achieve?' Clearly, it should provide a set of actions that, with hindsight, have provided the 'best' outcome for the organization. But that really does not help us. What do we mean by 'the best', and what good is a judgement that can only be applied in hindsight? Yet, even if we cannot assess the 'goodness' of a strategy for certain in advance, we can check it out for some attributes that could stop it being a success, as follows.

Is operations strategy comprehensive? In other words, does it include all important issues? Business history is littered with companies that simply failed to notice the potential impact of, for instance, new process technology, or emerging changes in their supply network.

Is operations strategy coherent? As a strategy evolves over time, tensions can emerge that threaten to pull the overall strategy in different directions. This can result in a loss of coherence. Coherence is when the choices made in each decision area all direct the operation in the same strategic direction, with all strategic decisions complementing and reinforcing each other in the promotion of performance objectives. For example, if new internet-based remote diagnostic technology for heating systems is introduced which allows service engineers to customize their service advice to individual clients' needs, it would be 'incoherent' not to devise a new operating process which did not enable service staff to exploit the technology's potential, for example by emailing customers with service options before the service engineer visits.

Does operations strategy have correspondence? The strategies pursued in each part of the strategy should correspond to the true priority of each performance objective. So, for example, if cost reduction is the main objective for an operation then its process technology investment decisions might err towards the purchase of 'off-the-shelf' (as opposed to customized) equipment, which would reduce the capital cost of the technology and may also imply lower maintenance and running costs. However, it is unlikely to be as flexible. Implicitly the strategy is accepting that cost is more important than flexibility. So, we would expect all other decisions to correspond with the same prioritization of objectives; for example, capacity strategies that exploit natural economies of scale; supply network strategies that reduce purchasing costs; performance measurement systems that stress efficiency and productivity; continuous improvement strategies that emphasize continual cost reduction; and so on.

Does operations strategy identify critical issues? The more critical the decision, the more attention it deserves. Although no strategic decision is unimportant, in practical terms some decisions are more critical than others. The judgement over exactly which decisions are particularly critical is very much a pragmatic one which must be based on the particular circumstances of an individual firm's operations strategy. But they must be identified.

> *** Operations principle**
>
> Operations strategies should be comprehensive, coherent, correspond to stated objectives and identify the critical issues.

Operations strategy implementation

Operations strategy implementation is the way that strategies are operationalized or executed. It means attempting to make sure that intended strategies are actually achieved. It is important because no matter how sophisticated the intellectual and analytical underpinnings of a strategy, it remains only a document until it has been implemented. But, the way one implements any strategy will very much depend on the specific nature of the changes implied by that strategy, and the organizational and environmental conditions that apply during its implementation. However, three issues are often mentioned by strategy practitioners as being important in achieving successful implementation.

Clarity of strategic decisions There is a strong relationship between the formulation stage and the implementation stage of operations strategy. The crucial attribute of the formulation stage is clarity. If a strategy is ambiguous it is difficult to translate strategic intent into specific actions. With clarity, however, it should be easier to define the intent behind the strategy, the few important issues that need to be developed to deliver the intent, the way that projects will be led and resourced, who will be responsible for each task, and so on.

Motivational leadership Leadership that motivates, encourages and provides support is a huge advantage in dealing with the complexity of implementation. Leadership is needed to bring sense and meaning to strategic aspirations, maintain a sense of purpose over the implementation period, and, when necessary, modify the implementation plan in the light of experience.

Project management Implementation means breaking a complex plan into a set of relatively distinct activities. Fortunately there is a well-understood collection of ideas of how to do this. It is called 'project management' and a whole chapter is devoted to this subject (Chapter 16).

Operations strategy monitoring

Especially in times when things are changing rapidly, as during strategic change, organizations often want to track ongoing performance to make sure that the changes are proceeding as planned. Monitoring should be capable of providing early indications (or a 'warning bell' as some call it) by diagnosing data and triggering appropriate changes in how the operations strategy is being implemented. Having created a plan for the implementation, each part of it has to be monitored to ensure that planned activities are indeed happening. Any deviation from what should be happening (that is, its plans) can then be rectified through some kind of intervention in the operation.

Operations strategy control

Strategic control involves the evaluation of the results from monitoring the implementation. Activities, plans and performance are assessed with the intention of correcting future action if that is required. In some ways this strategic view of control is similar to how it works operationally (which is discussed in Chapter 10), but there are differences. At a strategic level, control can be difficult because strategic objectives are not always clear and unambiguous. Ask any experienced managers; they will acknowledge that it is not always possible to articulate every aspect of a strategic decision in detail. Many strategies are just too complex for that. So, rather than adhering dogmatically to a predetermined plan, it may be better to adapt as circumstances change. And, the more uncertain the environment, the more an operation needs to emphasize this form of strategic flexibility and develop its ability to learn from events.

The argument has been put forward that strategy does not lend itself to a simple 'stage model' analysis that guides managers in a step-by-step manner through to the eventual 'answer' that is a final strategy. Therefore, the models put forward by consultants and academics are of very limited value. In reality, strategies (even those that are made deliberately, as opposed to those that simply 'emerge') are the result of very complex organizational forces. Even descriptive models such as the four-stage model described above in Figure 3.9 can do little more than sensitize managers to some of the key issues that they should be taking into account when devising strategies. In fact, they argue, it is the articulation of the 'content' of operations strategy that is more useful than adhering to some over-simplistic description of a strategy process.

SHORT CASE Sometimes any plan is better than no plan[13]

There is a famous story that illustrates the importance of having some kind of plan, even if hindsight proves it to be the wrong plan. During manoeuvres in the Alps, a detachment of Hungarian soldiers got lost. The weather was severe and the snow was deep. In these freezing conditions, after two days of wandering, the soldiers gave up hope and became reconciled to a frozen death on the mountains. Then, to their delight, one of the soldiers discovered a map in his pocket. Much cheered by this discovery, the soldiers were able to escape from the mountains. When they were safe back at their headquarters, they discovered that the map was not of the Alps at all, but of the Pyrenees. And what is the moral of the story? It is that a plan (or a map) may not be perfect but it gives a sense of purpose and a sense of direction! If the soldiers had waited for the right map they would have frozen to death. Yet their renewed confidence motivated them to get up and create opportunities.

Source: Alistair Brandon-Jones

SUMMARY ANSWERS TO KEY QUESTIONS

Check and improve your understanding of this chapter using self-assessment questions and a personalized study plan, a video case study, and an eText – all at www.myomlab.com.

MyOMLab

❯ What is strategy and what is operations strategy?

● Strategy is the total pattern of decisions and actions that position the organization in its environment and that are intended to achieve its long-term goals.

- Operations strategy concerns the pattern of strategic decisions and actions which set the role, objectives and activities of the operation.
- Operations strategy has content and process. The content concerns the specific decisions which are taken to achieve specific objectives. The process is the procedure which is used within a business to formulate its strategy.

> ### ❯ What is the difference between a 'top-down' and a 'bottom-up' view of operations strategy?

- The 'top-down' perspective views strategic decisions at a number of levels. Corporate strategy sets the objectives for the different businesses which make up a group of businesses. Business strategy sets the objectives for each individual business and how it positions itself in its marketplace. Functional strategies set the objectives for each function's contribution to its business strategy.
- The 'bottom-up' view of operations strategy sees overall strategy as emerging from day-to-day operational experience.

> ### ❯ What is the difference between a 'market requirements' and an 'operations resources' view of operations strategy?

- A 'market requirements' perspective of operations strategy sees the main role of operations as satisfying markets. Operations performance objectives and operations decisions should be primarily influenced by a combination of customers' needs and competitors' actions. Both of these may be summarized in terms of the product/service life cycle.
- The 'operations resource' perspective of operations strategy is based on the resource-based view (RBV) of the firm and sees the operation's core competences (or capabilities) as being the main influence on operations strategy. Operations capabilities are developed partly through the strategic decisions taken by the operation. Strategic decision areas in operations are usually divided into structural and infrastructural decisions. Structural decisions are those which define an operation's shape and form. Infrastructural decisions are those which influence the systems and procedures that determine how the operation will work in practice.

> ### ❯ How can an operations strategy be put together?

- Putting an operations strategy together is called 'the process' of operations strategy. There are four stages in the process of operations strategy.
- Formulation – which is the process of clarifying the various objectives and decisions that make up the strategy, and the links between them. This should produce strategies that are comprehensive, coherent, provide correspondence and prioritize the most critical activities or decisions.
- Implementation – the way that strategy is operationalized or executed. Three issues are often mentioned by strategy practitioners as being important in achieving successful implementation: the clarity of the strategy, the nature of the leadership provided by top management, and effective project management.
- Monitoring – involves tracking ongoing performance and diagnosing data to make sure that the changes are proceeding as planned and providing early indications of any deviation from the plan.

● Control – involves the evaluation of the results from monitoring the implementation so that activities, plans and performance can be assessed with the intention of correcting future action if that is required.

Long Ridge Gliding Club[14]

Long Ridge Gliding Club is a not-for-profit organization run by its members. The large grass airfield is located on the crest of a ridge about 400 metres above sea level. It is an ideal place to practise ridge soaring and cross-country flying. The gliders are launched using a winch machine which can propel them from a standing start to around 110 kilometres per hour (70 mph), 300 metres above the airfield, in just five seconds. The club is housed in a set of old farm buildings with simple but comfortable facilities for members. A bar and basic catering services are provided by the club steward and inexpensive bunkrooms are available for club members wishing to stay overnight.

The club has a current membership of nearly 150 pilots who range in ability from novice to expert. While some members have their own gliders, the club has a fleet of three single-seater and three twin-seater gliders available to its members. The club also offers trial flights to members of the public. (In order to provide insurance cover they actually sell a three-month membership with a 'free' flight at the start.) These 'casual flyers' can book flights in advance or just turn up and fly on a first-come, first-served basis. The club sells trial flight gift vouchers which are popular as birthday and Christmas presents. The club's brochure and website encourage people to:

Source: Alamy Images/Corbis Bridge

'Experience the friendly atmosphere and excellent facilities and enjoy the thrill of soaring above Long Ridge's dramatic scenery. For just £70 you could soon be in the air. Phone now or just turn up and our knowledgeable staff will be happy to advise you. We have a team of professional instructors dedicated to make this a really memorable experience.'

The average flight for a trial lesson is around 10 minutes. If the conditions are right the customer may be lucky and get a longer flight, although at busy times the instructors may feel under pressure to return to the ground to give another lesson. Sometimes when the weather is poor, or there is low cloud and wind in the wrong direction, almost not fit for flying at all, the instructors still do their best to get people airborne but they are restricted to a 'circuit': a takeoff, immediate circle and land. This only takes two minutes. Circuits are also used to help novice pilots practise landings and takeoffs. At the other end of the scale many of the club's experienced pilots can travel long distances and fly back to the airfield. The club's record for the longest flight is 755 kilometres taking off from the club's airfield and landing back on the same airfield eight hours later, never having touched the ground. (They take sandwiches and drinks and a bottle they can use to relieve themselves!)

The club has three part-time employees: a club steward, an office administrator and a mechanic. In the summer months the club also employs a winch driver (for launching the gliders) and two qualified flying instructors. Throughout the whole year essential tasks such as maintaining the gliders, getting them out of the hangar and towing them to the launch point, staffing the winches, keeping the flying log, bringing back gliders, and providing look-out cover are undertaken on a voluntary basis by club members. It takes a minimum of five experienced people (club members) to be able to launch one glider. The club's membership includes ten qualified instructors who, together with the two paid summer instructors, provide instruction in two-seater gliders for the club's members and the casual flyers.

When club members come to fly they are expected to arrive by 9.30 am and be prepared to stay all day to help each other and any casual flyers get airborne while they wait their turn to fly. On a typical summer's day there might be ten club members requiring instruction plus four casual flyers and also six members with their own gliders who have to queue up with the others for a launch hoping for a single long-distance flight. In the winter months there would typically be six members, one casual flyer and six experienced pilots. Club members would hope to have three flights on a good day, with durations of between 2 and 40 (average 10) minutes per flight, depending on conditions. However, if the weather conditions change they may not get a flight. Last year there were 180 days when flying took place, 140 in the 'summer' season and 40 in the 'winter'. Club members are charged an £8.00 winch fee each time they take to the air. In addition, if they are using one of the club's gliders, they are charged 50p per minute that they are in the air.

Bookings for trial flights and general administration are dealt with by the club's administrator who is based in a cabin close to the car park and works most weekday mornings from 9.00 am to 1.00 pm. An answerphone takes messages at other times. The launch point is out of sight and 1.5 km from the cabin but a safe walking route is signposted. Club members can let themselves onto the airfield and drive to the launch point. At the launch point the casual flyers might have to stand and wait for some time until a club member has time to find out what they want. Even when a flight has been pre-booked, casual flyers may then be kept waiting on the exposed and often windy airfield for up to two hours before their flight, depending on how many club members are present. Occasionally they will turn up for a pre-booked trial flight and will be turned away because either the weather is unsuitable or there are not enough club members to get a glider into the air. The casual flyers are encouraged to help out with the routine tasks but often seem reluctant to do so. After their flight they are left to find their own way back to their cars.

Income from the casual flyers is seen to be small compared to membership income and launch fees but the club's management committee views casual flying as a 'loss leader' to generate club memberships, which are £350 per annum. The club used to generate a regular surplus of around £10,000 per year which is used to upgrade the gliders and other facilities. However, insurance costs have risen dramatically due to their crashing and severely damaging four gliders during the last two years. Two of the accidents resulted in the deaths of one member and one casual flyer and serious injuries to three other members.

The club's committee is under some pressure from members to end trial flights because they reduce the number of flights members can have in a day. Some members have complained that they sometimes spend most of their day working to get casual flyers into the air and miss out on flying themselves. Although they provide a useful source of income for the hard-pressed club (around 700 were sold in the previous year), only a handful have been converted into club memberships.

QUESTIONS

1 **Evaluate the service to club members and casual flyers by completing a table similar to Table 3.1.**

2 **Chart the five performance objectives to show the differing expectations of club members and casual flyers and compare these with the actual service delivered.**

3 **What advice would you give to the club chairman?**

PROBLEMS AND APPLICATIONS

MyOMLab *These problems and applications will help to improve your analysis of operations. You can find more practice problems as well as worked examples and guided solutions on MyOMLab at www.myomlab.com.*

1 Explain how the four perspectives of operations strategy would apply to Ryanair and Flextronics.

2 Compare the operations strategies of Ryanair and a full-service airline such as British Airways or KLM.

3 What do you think are the qualifying and order-winning factors for (a) a top-of-the-range Ferrari, and (b) a Renault Clio?

4 What do you think are the qualifying or order-winning factors for IKEA described in Chapter 1?

5   Search the internet site of Intel, the best known microchip manufacturer, and identify what appear to be its main structural and infrastructural decisions in its operations strategy.

6   **(Advanced)** McDonald's has come to epitomize the 'fast food' industry. When the company started in the 1950s it was the first to establish itself in the market. Now there are hundreds of 'fast food' brands in the market competing in different ways. Some of the differences between these fast food chains are obvious. For example, some specialize in chicken products, others in pizza and so on. However, some differences are less obvious. Originally, McDonald's competed on low price, fast service and a totally standardized service offering. They also offered a very narrow range of items on their menu. Visit a McDonald's restaurant and deduce what you believe to be its most important performance objectives. Then try to identify two other chains which appear to compete in a slightly different way. Then try to identify how these differences in the relative importance of competitive objectives must influence the structural and infrastructural decisions of each chain's operations strategy.

SELECTED FURTHER READING

Boyer, K.K., Swink, M. and Rosenzweig, E.D. (2006) **Operations strategy research in the POMS Journal**, *Production and Operations Management*, vol. 14, issue 4, 442–449. A survey of recent research in the area.

Hayes, R.H., Pisano, G.P., Upton, D.M. and Wheelwright, S.C. (2005) *Operations, Strategy, and Technology: Pursuing the competitive edge*, John Wiley & Sons, Inc., Hoboken, NJ. The gospel according to the Harvard school of operations strategy. Articulate, interesting and informative.

Slack, N. and Lewis, M. (2011) *Operations Strategy*, third edn, FT Prentice Hall, Harlow. What can we say – just brilliant!

Spring, M. and Araujo, L. (2009) **Service, services and products: rethinking operations strategy**, *International Journal of Operations & Production Management*, vol. 29, issue 5, 444–467. Academic, but interesting.

USEFUL WEBSITES

www.myomlab.com Test which sections you have mastered and which you need to review, with questions, a personalized study plan, video clips, revision tips, and cases.

www.opsman.org Useful materials.

http://operationsroom.wordpress.com/ Stanford University's take on topical operations stories.

www.iomnet.org.un The Institute of Operations Management site. One of the main professional bodies for the subject.

www.poms.org A U.S. academic society for production and operations management. Academic, but some useful material, including a link to an encyclopedia of operations management terms.

www.ft.com Good for researching topics and companies.

www.economist.com *The Economist's* site, well written and interesting stuff of business generally.

www.worldbank.org Global issues. Useful for international operations strategy research.

www.weforum.org Global issues, including some operations strategy ones.

 Now that you have finished reading this chapter, why not visit MyOMLab at www.myomlab.com where you'll find more learning resources to help you make the most of your studies and get a better grade.

Source: Getty Images/Jasper James

Part Two
DESIGN

All operations managers are designers, because design is the process of satisfying people's requirements through shaping or configuring products, services and processes. This part of the book looks at how managers can manage the design of the products and services they produce and the processes that produce them. At the most strategic level 'design' means shaping the networks of operations that supply products and services. At a more operational level it means the arrangements of the processes, technology and people that constitute operations processes.

4

Process design

Key questions

❯ What is process design?

❯ What objectives should process design have?

❯ How do volume and variety affect process design?

❯ How are processes designed in detail?

❯ What are the effects of process variability?

INTRODUCTION

As a job description, 'designer' sounds like someone who is exclusively concerned with how a product looks. But the design activity is much broader than that and, while there is no universally recognized definition of 'design', we take it to mean 'the process by which some functional requirement of people is satisfied through the shaping or configuration of the resources and/or activities that comprise a product, or a service, or the transformation process that produces them'. All operations managers are designers. When they purchase or rearrange the position of a piece of equipment, or when they change the way of working within a process, it is a design decision because it affects the physical shape and nature of their processes. Here we examine the design of processes. Figure 4.1 shows where this topic fits within the overall model of operations management.

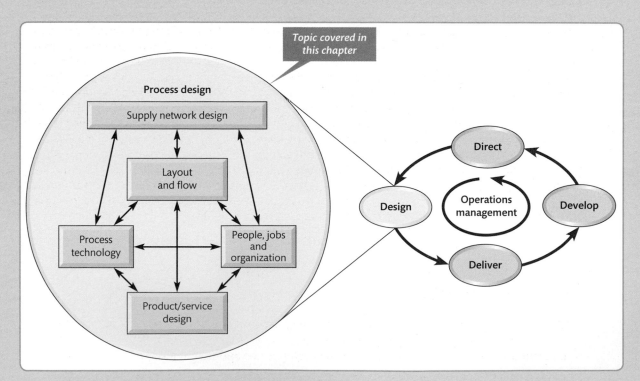

Figure 4.1 The design activities in operations management

Fast-food drive-throughs[1]

The quick service restaurant (QSR) industry reckon that the very first drive-through dates back to 1928 when Royce Hailey first promoted the drive-through service at his Pig Stand restaurant in Los Angeles. Customers would simply drive by the back door of the restaurant where the chef would come out and deliver the restaurant's famous 'Barbequed Pig' sandwiches. Today, drive-through processes are slicker and faster. They are also more common – in 1975, McDonald's did not have any drive-throughs, and now more than 90 per cent of its US restaurants incorporate a drive-through process. In fact 80 per cent of recent fast-food growth has come through the growing number of drive-throughs. Says one industry specialist, *'There are a growing number of customers for whom fast food is not fast enough. They want to cut waiting time to the very minimum without even getting out of their car. Meeting their needs depends on how smooth we can get the process.'*

Source: Shutterstock.com/Losevsky Photo and Video

The competition to design the fastest and most reliable drive-through process is fierce. Starbucks' drive-throughs have strategically placed cameras at the order boards so that servers can recognize regular customers and start making their order even before it's placed. Burger King has experimented with sophisticated sound systems, simpler menu boards and see-through food bags to ensure greater accuracy (no point in being fast if you don't deliver what the customer ordered).

These details matter. McDonald's reckon that their sales increase one per cent for every six seconds saved at a drive-through, while a single Burger King restaurant calculated that its takings increased by 15,000 dollars a year each time it reduced queuing time by one second. Menu items must be easy to read and understand. Designing 'combo meals' (burger, fries and a cola), for example, saves time at the ordering stage. Perhaps the most remarkable experiment in making drive-through process times slicker is being carried out by McDonald's in the USA. On California's central coast 150 miles from Los Angeles, a call centre takes orders remotely from 40 McDonald's outlets around the country. The orders are then sent back to the restaurants through the internet and the food is assembled only a few metres from where the order was placed. It may only save a few seconds on each order, but that can add up to extra sales at busy times of the day. But not everyone is thrilled by the boom in drive-throughs. People living in the vicinity may complain of the extra traffic they attract and the unhealthy image of fast food, combined with a process that does not even make customers get out of their car, is, for some, a step too far.

WHAT IS PROCESS DESIGN?

To 'design' is to conceive the looks, arrangement, and workings of something *before it is created*. In that sense it is a conceptual exercise. Yet it is one which must deliver a solution that will work in practice. Design is also an activity that can be approached at different levels of detail. One may envisage the general shape and intention of something before getting down to defining its details. This is certainly true for process design. At the start of the process design activity it is important to understand the design objectives, especially at first, when the overall shape and nature of the process is being decided. The most common way of doing this is by positioning it according to its volume and variety characteristics. Eventually the details of the process must be analysed to ensure that it fulfils its objectives effectively. Yet, it is often only through getting to grips with the detail of a design that the feasibility of its overall shape can be assessed. But don't think of this as a simple sequential process. There may be aspects concerned with the objectives, or the broad positioning of the process, that will need to be modified following its more detailed analysis.

Process design and service/product design are interrelated

Often we will treat the design of services and products, on the one hand, and the design of the processes which make them, on the other, as though they were separate activities. Yet they are clearly interrelated. It would be foolish to commit to the detailed design of any product or service without some consideration of how it is to be produced. Small changes in the design of products and services can have profound implications for the way the operation eventually has to produce them. Similarly, the design of a process can constrain the freedom of product and service designers to operate as they would wish (*see* Fig. 4.2). This holds good whether the operation is producing products or services. However, the overlap between the two design activities is generally greater in operations which produce services. Because many services involve the customer in being part of the transformation process, the service, as far as the customer sees it, cannot be separated from the process to which the customer is subjected. Overlapping product and process design has implications for the organization of the design activity (as will be discussed in Chapter 5). Certainly, when product designers also have to make or use the things which they design, it can concentrate their minds on what is important. For example, in the early days of flight, the engineers who designed the aircraft were also the test pilots who took them out on their first flight. For this reason, if no other, safety was a significant objective in the design activity.

> ✳ **Operations principle**
>
> The design of processes cannot be done independently of the services and/or products that they are creating.

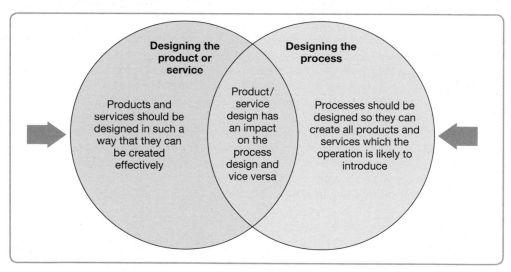

Figure 4.2 The design of products/services and processes are interrelated and should be treated together

WHAT OBJECTIVES SHOULD PROCESS DESIGN HAVE?

The whole point of process design is to make sure that the performance of the process is appropriate for whatever it is trying to achieve. For example, if an operation competed primarily on its ability to respond quickly to customer requests, its processes would need to be designed to give fast throughput times. This would minimize the time between customers requesting a product or service and them receiving it. Similarly, if an operation competed on low price, cost-related objectives would be likely to dominate its process design. Some kind of logic should link what the operation as a whole is attempting to achieve, and the performance objectives of its individual processes. This is illustrated in Table 4.1.

Operations performance objectives translate directly to process design objectives, as shown in Table 4.1. But, because processes are managed at a very operational level, process design also needs to consider a more 'micro' and detailed set of objectives. These are largely concerned with flow through the process. When whatever are being 'processed' enter a process they will progress through a series of activities where they are 'transformed' in some way. Between these activities they may dwell for some time in inventories, waiting to be transformed by the next activity. This means that the time that a unit spends in the process (its throughput time) will be longer than the sum of all the transforming activities that it passes through. Also the resources that perform the process's activities may not be used all the time because not all items will necessarily require the same activities and the capacity of each resource may not match the demand placed upon it. So neither the items moving through the process, nor the resources performing the activities may be fully utilized. Because of this the way that items leave the process is unlikely to be exactly the same as the way they arrive at the process. It is common for more 'micro' performance flow objectives to be used that describe process flow performance. For example:

- Throughput rate (or flow rate) is the rate at which items emerge from the process, i.e. the number of items passing through the process per unit of time.
- Cycle time, or takt time, is the reciprocal of throughput rate – it is the time between items emerging from the process. The term 'takt' time is the same, but is normally applied to

Table 4.1 The impact of strategic performance objectives on process design objectives and performance

Operations performance objective	Typical process design objectives	Some benefits of good process design
Quality	- Provide appropriate resources, capable of achieving the specification of products or services - Error-free processing	- Products and services produced 'on-specification' - Less recycling and wasted effort within the process
Speed	- Minimum throughput time - Output rate appropriate for demand	- Short customer waiting time - Low in-process inventory
Dependability	- Provide dependable process resources - Reliable process output timing and volume	- On-time deliveries of products and services - Less disruption, confusion and rescheduling within the process
Flexibility	- Provide resources with an appropriate range of capabilities - Change easily between processing states (what, how, or how much is being processed?)	- Ability to process a wide range of products and services - Low cost/fast product and service change - Low cost/fast volume and timing changes - Ability to cope with unexpected events (e.g. supply or a processing failure)

Cost	- Appropriate capacity to meet demand
	- Eliminate process waste in terms of:
	  - excess capacity
	  - excess process capability
	  - in-process delays
	  - in-process errors
	  - inappropriate process inputs
		- Low processing costs
		- Low resource costs (capital costs)
		- Low delay/inventory costs (working capital costs)

'paced' processes like moving belt assembly lines. It is the 'beat', or tempo, of working required to meet demand.[2]

- Throughput time is the average elapsed time taken for inputs to move through the process and become outputs.
- The number of items in the process (also called the 'work in progress', or in-process inventory), as an average over a period of time.
- The utilization of process resources is the proportion of available time that the resources within the process are performing useful work.

Standardization of processes

One of the most important process design objectives, especially in large organizations, concerns the extent to which process designs should be standardized. By standardization in this context we mean 'doing things in the same way', or more formally, 'adopting a common sequence of activities, methods and use of equipment'. It is a significant issue in large organizations because very often different ways of carrying out similar or identical tasks emerge over time in the various parts of the organization. But, why not allow many different ways of doing the same thing? That would give a degree of autonomy and freedom for individuals and teams to exercise their discretion. The problem is that allowing numerous ways of doing things causes confusion, misunderstandings, and eventually, inefficiency. In healthcare processes, it can even cause preventable deaths. For example, in 2012, the Royal College

of Physicians in the UK revealed that there were more than 100 types of charts that were used for monitoring patients' vital signs in use in UK hospitals.[3] This leads to confusion, they said. Potentially, thousands of hospital deaths could be prevented if doctors and nurses used a standardized bed chart. Because hospitals can use different charts, doctors and nurses have to learn how to read new ones when they move. They recommended that there should be just one chart and one process for all staff that check on patients' conditions. Professor Derek Bell said: '*Developing and adopting a standardized early warning system will be one of the most significant developments in healthcare in the next decade.*'

Standardization is also an important objective in the design of some services and products, for similar reasons (see Chapter 5). The practical dilemma for most organizations is how to draw the line between processes that are required to be standardized, and those that are allowed to be different.

Environmentally sensitive process design

With the issues of environmental protection becoming more important, process designers have to take account of 'green' issues (see Chapter 21). In many developed countries, legislation has already provided some basic standards. Interest has focused on some fundamental issues:

- *The sources of inputs* to a product or service. (Will they damage rainforests? Will they use up scarce minerals? Will they exploit the poor or use child labour?)
- *Quantities and sources of energy* consumed in the process. (Do plastic beverage bottles use more energy than glass ones? Should waste heat be recovered and used in fish farming?)
- *The amounts and type of waste material* that are created in the manufacturing processes. (Can this waste be recycled efficiently, or must it be burnt or buried in landfill sites?)
- *The life of the product itself*. (If a product has a long useful life will it consume fewer resources than a short-life product?)
- *The end-of-life of the product*. (Will the redundant product be difficult to dispose of in an environmentally friendly way?)

Designers are faced with complex trade-offs between these factors, although it is not always easy to obtain all the information that is needed to make the 'best' choices. To help make more rational decisions in the design activity, some industries are experimenting with *life-cycle analysis.* This technique analyses all the production inputs, the life-cycle use of the product and its final disposal, in terms of total energy used and all emitted wastes. The inputs and wastes are evaluated at *every* stage of a service or product's creation, beginning with the extraction or farming of the basic raw materials. The short case below, 'Ecover's ethical operation design', demonstrates that it is possible to include ecological considerations in all aspects of product and process design.

PROCESS TYPES – THE VOLUME–VARIETY EFFECT ON PROCESS DESIGN

Earlier (in Chapter 1) we saw how processes range from those producing at high volume (for example, credit card transaction processing) to low volume (for example, funding a large complex take-over deal). Also processes can range from producing a very low variety

---

SHORT CASE | **Ecover's ethical operation design[4]**

Ecover cleaning products, such as washing liquid, are famously ecological. In fact it is the company's whole rationale. *'We clean with care'*, say Ecover. *'Whether you're washing your sheets, your floors, your hands or your dishes, our products don't contain those man-made chemicals that can irritate your skin.'* But it isn't just their products that are based on an ecologically sustainable foundation. Ecover's ecological factories in France and Belgium also embody the company's commitment to sustainability. Whether it's their factory roof, their use of energy or the way they treat the water used in the production processes, Ecover point out that they do their best to limit environmental impact. For

Source: Alamy Images/Clivestock

example, the Ecover factory operates entirely on green electricity – the type produced by wind generators, tidal generators and other natural sources. What is more, they make the most of the energy they do use by choosing energy-efficient lighting, and then only using it when needed. And, although the machinery they use in the factories is standard for the industry, they keep their energy and water consumption down by choosing low-speed appliances that can multi-task and don't require water to clean them. For example, the motors on their mixing machines can mix 25 tonnes of Ecover liquid while 'consuming no more electricity than a few flat irons'. And they have a 'squeezy gadget that's so efficient at getting every last drop of product out of the pipes, they don't need to be rinsed through'. Ecover say that they *'hate waste, so we're big on recycling. We keep the amount of packaging used in our products to a minimum, and make sure whatever cardboard or plastic we do use can be recycled, reused*

or re-filled. It's an ongoing process of improvement; in fact, we've recently developed a new kind of green plastic we like to call "Plant-astic" that's 100% renewable, reusable and recyclable – and made from sugarcane.'

Even the building is ecological. It is cleverly designed to follow the movement of the sun from east to west, so that production takes place with the maximum amount of natural daylight (good for saving power and good for working conditions). The factory's frame is built from pine rather than more precious timbers and the walls are constructed using bricks that are made from clay, wood pulp and mineral waste. They require less energy to bake, yet they're light, porous and insulate well. The factories' roofs are covered in thick, spongy Sedum (a flowering plant, often used for natural roofing) that gives insulation all year round. In fact it's so effective that they don't need heating or air conditioning – the temperature never drops below 4°C and never rises above 26°C.

of products or services (for example, in an electricity utility) to a very high variety (for example, in an architects' practice). Usually the two dimensions of volume and variety go together – but in a reversed way. So low-volume processes often produce a high variety of products and services, and high-volume operations processes often produce a narrow variety of products and services. Thus there is a continuum from low volume/high variety through to high volume/low variety, on which we can position processes. And within a single operation there could be processes with very different positions on this volume–variety spectrum. So, for example, compare the approach taken in a medical service during mass medical treatments, such as large-scale immunization programmes, with that taken in transplant surgery where the treatment is designed specifically to meet the needs of one person. In other words, no one type of process design is best for all types of requirement in all circumstances – different products or services with different volume–variety positions require different processes.

Process types

The position of a process on the volume–variety continuum shapes its overall design and the general approach to managing its activities. These 'general approaches' to designing and managing processes are called process types. Different terms are used to identify process types depending on whether they are predominantly manufacturing or service processes, and there is some variation in the terms used. For example, it is not uncommon to find the 'manufacturing' terms used in service industries. Figure 4.3 illustrates how these 'process types' are used to describe different positions on the volume–variety spectrum.

Project processes

Project processes deal with discrete, usually highly customized products; often with a relatively long timescale between the completion of each item, where each job has a well-defined start and finish. Project processes have low volume and high variety. Activities involved in the process can be ill-defined and uncertain. Transforming resources may have to be organized especially for each item (because each item is different). The process may be complex, partly because the activities in such processes often involve significant discretion to act according to

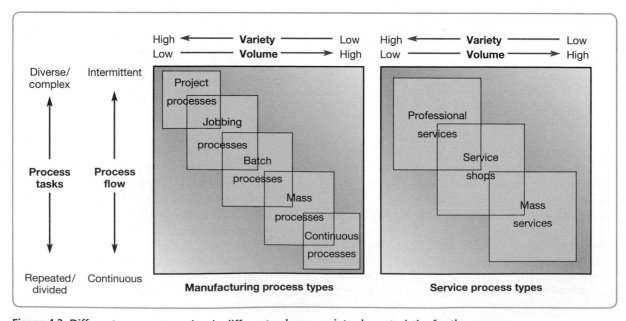

Figure 4.3 Different process types imply different volume–variety characteristics for the process

professional judgement. Examples of project processes include software design, movie production, most construction companies, and large fabrication operations such as those manufacturing turbo generators.

The major construction site shown in the picture is a project process. Each 'item' (building) is different and poses different challenges to those running the process (civil engineers)

Jobbing processes

Jobbing processes also deal with high variety and low volumes. However, while in project processes each item has resources devoted more or less exclusively to it, in jobbing processes each product has to share the operation's resources with many others. Resources will process a series of items but, although each one will require similar attention, they may differ in their exact needs. Many jobs will probably be 'one-offs' that are never repeated. Again, jobbing processes could be relatively complex; however, they usually produce physically smaller products and, although sometimes requiring considerable skill, such processes often involve fewer unpredictable circumstances. Examples of jobbing processes include made-to-measure tailors, many precision engineers such as specialist toolmakers, furniture restorers, and the printer who produces tickets for the local social event.

This craftsman is using general purpose wood-cutting technology to make a product for an individual customer. The next product made will be different (although maybe similar) for a different customer

Batch processes

Batch processes may look like jobbing processes, but do not have the same degree of variety. As the name implies, each time batch processes produce more than one item at a time. So each part of the process has periods when it is repeating itself, at least while the 'batch' is being processed. If the size of the batch is just two or three items, it is little different to jobbing. Conversely, if the batches are large, and especially if the products are familiar to the operation, batch processes can be fairly repetitive. Because of this, the batch type of process can be found over a wide range of volume and variety levels. Examples of batch processes include machine tool manufacturing, the production of some special gourmet frozen foods, and the manufacture of most of the component parts which go into mass-produced assemblies such as automobiles.

In this kitchen, food is being prepared in batches. All batches go through the same sequence (preparation, cooking and storage) but each batch is of a different dish

Mass processes

Mass processes are those which produce items in high volume and relatively narrow variety (narrow in terms of its fundamentals – an automobile assembly process might produce thousands of variants, yet essentially the variants do not affect the basic process of production). The activities of mass processes are usually repetitive and largely predictable. Examples of mass processes include frozen food production, automatic packing lines, automobile plants, television factories, and DVD production.

The automobile plant is everyone's idea of a mass process. Each product is almost (but not quite) the same, and made in large quantities

Continuous processes

Continuous processes have even higher volume and usually lower variety than mass processes. They also usually operate for longer periods of time. Sometimes they are literally continuous in that their products are inseparable, being produced in an endless flow. They often have relatively inflexible, capital-intensive technologies with highly predictable flow and, although products may be stored during the process, their predominant characteristic is of smooth flow from one part of the process to another. Examples of continuous processes include water processing, petrochemical refineries, electricity utilities, steel making and some paper making.

This continuous water treatment plant almost never stops (it only stops for maintenance) and performs only one task (filtering impurities). Often we only notice the process if it goes wrong

Professional services

Professional services are high-contact processes where customers spend a considerable time in the service process. They can provide high levels of customization (the process being highly adaptable in order to meet individual customer needs). Professional services tend to be people-based rather than equipment-based, and usually staff are given considerable discretion in servicing customers. Professional services include management consultants, lawyers' practices, architects, doctors' surgeries, auditors, health and safety inspectors and some computer field service operations.

Here consultants are preparing to start a consultancy assignment. They are discussing how they might approach the various stages of the assignment, from understanding the real nature of the problem through to the implementation of their recommended solutions. This is a process map, although a very high-level one. It guides the nature and sequence of the consultants' activities

Service shops

Service shops have levels of volume and variety (and customer contact, customization and staff discretion) between the extremes of professional and mass services (see next paragraph). Service is provided via mixes of front- and back-office activities. Service shops include banks, high street shops, holiday tour operators, car rental companies, schools, most restaurants, hotels and travel agents.

The health club shown in the picture has front-office staff who can give advice on exercise programmes and other treatments. To maintain a dependable service the staff need to follow defined processes every day

Mass services

Mass services have many customer transactions, involving limited contact time and little customization. Staff are likely to have a relatively defined division of labour and have to follow set procedures. Mass services include supermarkets, a national rail network, an airport, telecommunications service, library, television station, the police service and the enquiry desk at

Operations principle

Process types indicate the position of processes on the volume–variety spectrum.

a utility. For example, one of the most common types of mass service are the call centres used by almost all companies that deal directly with consumers. Coping with a very high volume of enquiries requires some kind of structuring of the process of communicating with customers. This is often achieved by using a carefully designed enquiry process (sometimes known as a script).

Source: Shutterstock/Eimantas Buzas

This is an account management centre at a retail bank. It deals with thousands of customer requests every day. Although each customer request is different, thay are all of the same type – involving customer accounts

The product–process matrix

The most common method of illustrating the relationship between a process's volume–variety position and its design characteristics is shown in Figure 4.4. Often called the 'product–process' matrix,[5] it can in fact be used for any type of process whether producing products or services. The underlying idea of the product–process matrix is that many of the more important elements of process design are strongly related to the volume–variety position of the process. So, for any process, the tasks that it undertakes, the flow of items through the process, the layout of its resources, the technology it uses, and the design of jobs, are all strongly influenced by its volume–variety position. This means that most processes should lie close to the

Critical commentary

Although the idea of process types can be useful, it is in many ways simplistic. In reality there is no clear boundary between process types. For example, many processed foods are manufactured using mass production processes but in batches. So, a 'batch' of one type of cake (say) can be followed by a 'batch' of a marginally different cake (perhaps with different packaging), followed by yet another, etc. Essentially this is still a mass process, but not quite as pure a version of mass processing as a manufacturing process that only makes one type of cake. Similarly, the categories of service processes are likewise blurred. For example, a specialist camera retailer would normally be categorized as a service shop, yet it also will give, sometimes very specialized, technical advice to customers. It is not a professional service like a consultancy, of course, but it does have elements of a professional service process within its design. This is why the volume and variety characteristics of a process are sometimes seen as being a more realistic way of describing processes. The product-process matrix described next adopts this approach.

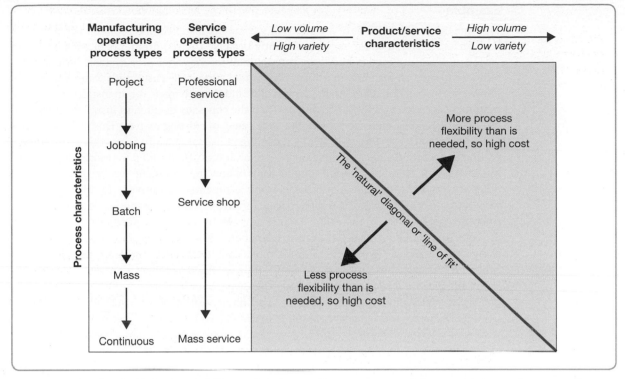

Figure 4.4 Deviating from the 'natural' diagonal on the product–process matrix has consequences for cost and flexibility

Source: Based on Hayes and Wheelwright

diagonal of the matrix that represents the 'fit' between the process and its volume–variety position. This is called the 'natural' diagonal, or the 'line of fit'.

Moving off the natural diagonal

A process lying on the natural diagonal of the matrix shown in Figure 4.4 will normally have lower operating costs than one with the same volume variety position that lies off the diagonal. This is because the diagonal represents the most appropriate process design for any volume–variety position. Processes that are on the right of the 'natural' diagonal would normally be associated with lower volumes and higher variety. This means that they are likely to be more flexible than seems to be warranted by their actual volume–variety position. That is, they are not taking advantage of their ability to standardize their activities. Because of this, their costs are likely to be higher than they would be with a process that was closer to the diagonal. Conversely, processes that are on the left of the diagonal have adopted a position that would normally be used for higher volume and lower variety processes. Processes will therefore be 'over-standardized' and probably too inflexible for their volume–variety position. This lack of flexibility can also lead to high costs because the process will not be able to change from one activity to another as readily as a more flexible process.[6] So a first step in examining the design of an existing process is to check if it is on the natural diagonal of the product–process matrix. The volume–variety position of the process may have changed without any corresponding change in its design. Alternatively, design changes may have been introduced without considering their suitability for the process's volume–variety position.

> **❋ Operations principle**
>
> Moving off the 'natural diagonal' of the product-process matrix will incur excess cost.

Example

The 'meter installation' unit of a water utility company installed and repaired water meters. Each installation job could vary significantly because the requirements of each customer varied and because meters had to be fitted into different water pipe systems. When a customer requested an installation a supervisor would survey the customer's water system and inform the installation team. An appointment would then be made for an installer to visit the customer's location and install the meter. Then the company decided to install a new 'standard' remote-reading meter to replace the wide range of existing meters. This new meter was designed to make installation easier by including universal quick-fit joints that reduced pipe cutting and jointing during installation. As a pilot, it was also decided to prioritize those customers with the oldest meters and conduct trials of how the new meter worked in practice. All other aspects of the installation process were left as they were. However, after the new meters were introduced, the costs of installation were far higher than forecast and the installers were frustrated at the waste of their time and the now relatively standardized installation job. So the company decided to change its process. It cut out the survey stage of the process because, using the new meter, 98 per cent of installations could be fitted in one visit, minimizing disruption to the customer. Just as significantly, fully qualified installers were often not needed, so installation could be performed by less expensive labour.

This example is illustrated in Figure 4.5. The initial position of the installation process is at point A. The installation unit were required to install a wide variety of meters into a very wide variety of water systems. This needed a survey stage to assess the nature of the job and the use of skilled labour to cope with the complex tasks. The installation of the new type of meter changed the volume–variety position for the process by reducing the variety the jobs tackled by the process and increasing the volume it had to cope with. However, the process was not changed and therefore the design of the process was appropriate for its old volume–variety position, but not the new one. In effect it had moved to point B in Figure 4.5. It was off the diagonal, with unnecessary flexibility and high operating costs. Redesigning the process to take advantage of the reduced variety and complexity of the job (position C on Figure 4.5) allowed installation to be performed far more efficiently.

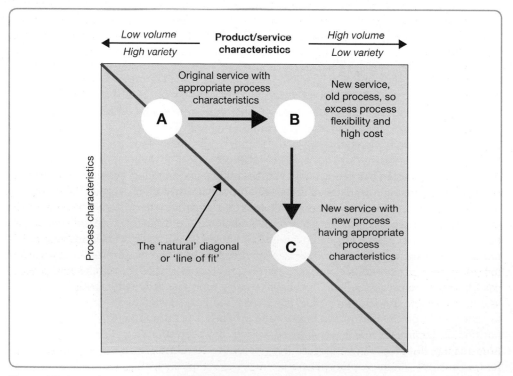

Figure 4.5 A product–process matrix with process positions from the water meter example

Space4 housing processes[7]

You don't usually build a house this way. It's more like the way you would expect an automobile to be made. Nevertheless, Space4's huge building in Birmingham (UK) contains what some believe could be the future of house building. Space4 is a division of Persimmon, who are the UK's largest house builder. It has a production line whose 90 operators, many of whom have automobile assembly experience, are capable of producing the timber-framed panels that form the shell of the new homes at a rate of a house every hour. The automated, state-of-the-art electronic systems within the production process control all facets of the operation, ensuring that scheduling and operations are timely and accurate. There is a direct link between the Computer Aided Design (CAD) systems that design the houses and the manufacturing processes that make them, reducing the time between design and manufacture. The machinery itself incorporates automatic predictive and preventative maintenance routines that minimize the chances of unexpected breakdowns. But not everything about the process relies on automation. Because of their previous automobile assembly experience, staff are used to the just-in-time high-efficiency culture of modern mass production. After production, the completed panels are stacked in three-metre-high piles and are then forklifted into trucks where they are dispatched to building sites across the UK. Once the panels arrive at the building site,

Source: Shutterstock.com/ArchMan

the construction workforce can assemble the exterior of a 1,200 sq ft (average size) new home in a single day. Because the external structure of a house can be built in a few hours, and enclosed in a weatherproof covering, staff working on the internal fittings of the house, such as plumbers and electricians, can have a secure and dry environment in which to work, irrespective of external conditions. Furthermore, the automated production process uses a type of high-precision technology which means there are fewer mistakes in the construction process on site. This means that the approval process from the local regulatory authority takes less time. This process, says Space4, speeds up the total building time from 12–14 weeks to 8–10 weeks.

DETAILED PROCESS DESIGN

After the overall design of a process has been determined, its individual activities must be configured. At its simplest, this detailed design of a process involves identifying all the individual activities that are needed to meet the objectives of the process, and deciding on the sequence in which these activities are to be performed and who is going to do them. There will, of course, be some constraints to this. Some activities must be carried out before others and some activities can only be done by certain people or equipment. Nevertheless, for a process of any reasonable size, the number of alternative process designs is usually large. Because of this, process design is often done using some simple visual approach, such as process mapping.

Process mapping

Process mapping simply involves describing processes in terms of how the activities within the process relate to each other. There are many techniques which can be used for *process mapping* (or process blueprinting, or process analysis, as it is sometimes called). However, all the techniques identify the different *types of* activity that take place during the process and show the flow of materials or people or information through the process.

Process mapping symbols

Process mapping symbols are used to classify different types of activity. And although there is no universal set of symbols used all over the world for any type of process, there are some that are commonly used. Most of these derive either from the early days of 'scientific' management around a century ago (see Chapter 9) or, more recently, from information system flowcharting. Figure 4.6 shows the symbols we shall use here.

These symbols can be arranged in order, and in series or in parallel, to describe any process. For example, Figure 4.7 shows one of the processes used in a theatre lighting operation. The company hires out lighting and stage effects equipment to theatrical companies and event organizers. Customers' calls are routed to the store technician. After discussing their requirements, the technician checks the equipment availability file to see if the equipment can be supplied from the company's own stock on the required dates. If the equipment cannot

be supplied, in-house customers may be asked whether they want the company to try and obtain it from other possible suppliers. This offer depends on how busy and how helpful individual technicians are. Sometimes customers decline the offer and a 'Guide to Customers' leaflet is sent to the customer. If the customer does want a search, the technician will call potential suppliers in an attempt to find available equipment. If this is not successful the customer is informed, but if suitable equipment is located it is reserved for delivery to the company's site. If equipment can be supplied from the company's own stores, it is reserved on the equipment availability file and the day before it is required a 'kit wagon' is taken to the store where all the required equipment is assembled, taken back to the workshop and checked. If any equipment is faulty it is repaired at this point. After that it is packed in special cases and delivered to the customer.

Different levels of process mapping

For a large process, drawing process maps at this level of detail can be complex. This is why processes are often mapped at a more aggregated level, called high-level process mapping, before more detailed maps are drawn. Figure 4.8 illustrates this for the total '*supply and install lighting*' process in the stage lighting operation. At the highest level the process can be drawn simply as an input–transformation–output process with materials and customers as its input

Figure 4.6 Some common process mapping symbols

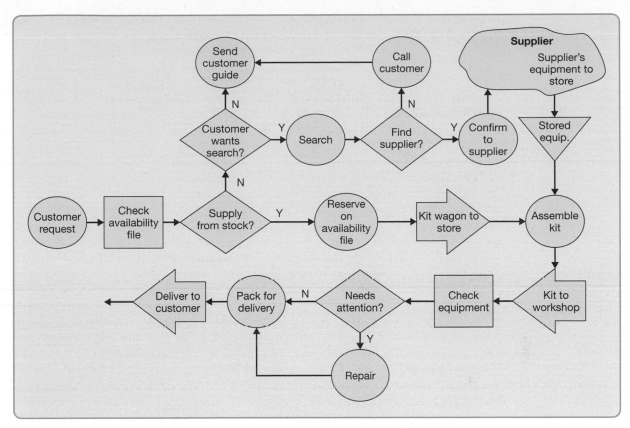

Figure 4.7 Process map for 'enquire to delivery' process at stage lighting operation

resources and lighting services as outputs. No details of how inputs are transformed into outputs are included. At a slightly lower or more detailed level, what is sometimes called an outline process map (or chart) identifies the sequence of activities but only in a general way. So the process of '*enquire to delivery*' that is shown in detail in Figure 4.7 is here reduced to a single activity. At the more detailed level, all the activities are shown in a 'detailed process map' (the activities within the process 'install and test' are shown).

Although not shown in Figure 4.8, an even more micro set of process activities could be mapped within each of the detailed process activities. Such a micro-detailed process map could specify every single motion involved in each activity. Some quick service restaurants, for example, do exactly that. In the lighting hire company example, most activities would not be mapped in any more detail than that shown in Figure 4.8. Some activities, such as 'return to base', are probably too straightforward to be worth mapping any further. Other activities, such as 'rectify faulty equipment', may rely on the technician's skills and discretion to the extent that the activity has too much variation and is too complex to map in detail. Some activities, however, may need mapping in more detail to ensure quality or to protect the company's interests. For example, the activity of safety-checking the customer's site to ensure that it is compliant with safety regulations will need specifying in some detail to ensure that the company can prove it exercised its legal responsibilities.

Process visibility

It is sometimes useful to map such processes in a way that makes the degree of visibility of each part of the process obvious. This allows those parts of the process with high visibility to be designed so that they enhance the customer's perception of the process. Figure 4.9 shows yet another part of the lighting equipment company's operation: the 'collect and check' process. The process is mapped to show the visibility of each activity to the customer. Here four levels of visibility are used. There is no hard and fast rule about this; many processes simply

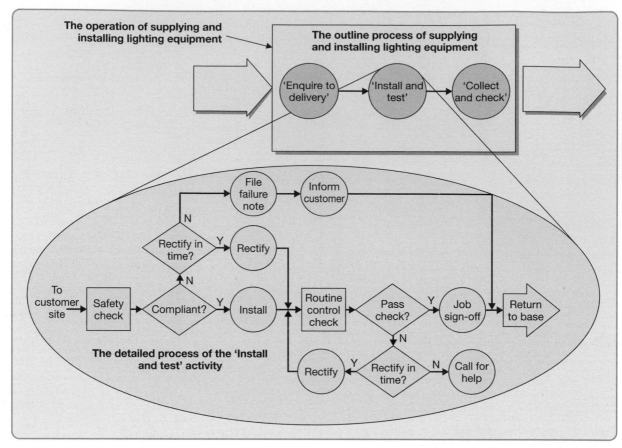

Figure 4.8 The 'supply and install' operations process mapped at three levels

distinguish between those activities that the customer *could* see and those that they couldn't. The boundary between these two categories is often called the 'line of visibility'. In Figure 4.9 three categories of visibility are shown. At the very highest level of visibility, above the 'line of interaction', are those activities that involve direct interaction between the lighting company's staff and the customer. Other activities take place at the customer's site or in the presence of the customer but involve less or no direct interaction. Yet further activities (the two transport activities in this case) have some degree of visibility because they take place away from the company's base and are visible to potential customers, but are not visible to the immediate customer.

Throughput time, cycle time and work in progress

So far we have looked at the more conceptual (process types) and descriptive (process mapping) aspects of process design. We now move on the equally important analytical perspective. And the first stage is to understand the nature of, and relationship between, throughput time, cycle time and work-in-progress. As a reminder: throughput time is the elapsed time between an item entering the process and leaving it, cycle time is the average time between items being processed, and work-in-progress is the number of items within the process at any point in time. In addition the work content for each item will also be important for some

> ✳ **Operations principle**
>
> Process analysis derives from an understanding of the required process cycle time.

analysis. It is the total amount of work required to produce a unit of output. For example, suppose that in an assemble-to-order sandwich shop, the time to assemble and sell a sandwich (the work content) is two minutes and that two people are staffing the process. Each member of staff will serve a customer every two minutes: therefore every two minutes, two customers are being served, and so on average

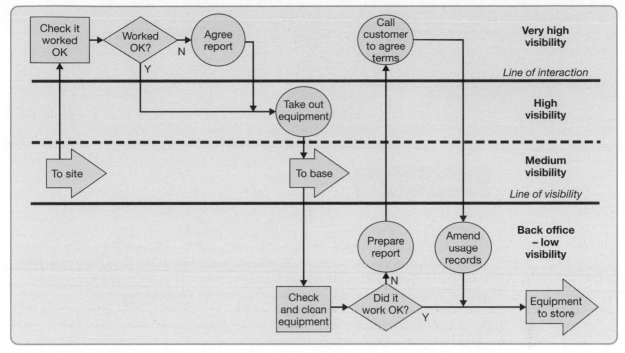

Figure 4.9 The 'collect and check' process mapped to show different levels of process visibility

a customer is emerging from the process every minute (the cycle time of the process). When customers join the queue in the process they become work-in-progress (sometimes written as WIP). If the queue is ten people long (including that customer) when the customer joins it, he or she will have to wait ten minutes to emerge from the process. Or put more succinctly...

$$\textbf{Throughput time} = \textbf{Work-in-progress} \times \textbf{Cycle time}$$

In this case: 10 minutes' wait = 10 people in the system × 1 minute per person

Little's law

This mathematical relationship (throughput time = work-in-progress × cycle time) is called Little's law. It is simple but very useful, and it works for any stable process. Little's law states that the average number of things in the system is the product of the average rate at which things leave the system and average time each one spends in the system. Or, put another way, the average number of objects in a queue is the product of the entry rate and the average holding time.

For example, suppose it is decided that in a new sandwich assembly and sales process, the average number of customers in the process should be limited to around ten and the maximum time a customer is in the process should be on average four minutes. If the time to assemble and sell a sandwich (from customer request to the customer leaving the process) in the new process has been reduced to 1.2 minutes, how many staff should be serving?

Putting this into Little's law:

$$\text{Throughput time} = 4 \text{ minutes}$$

and

$$\text{Work-in-progress, WIP} = 10$$

So since:

$$\text{Throughput time} = \text{WIP} \times \text{cycle time}$$

$$\text{Cycle time} = \frac{\text{Throughput time}}{\text{WIP}}$$

$$\text{Cycle time for the process} = \frac{4}{10} = 0.4 \text{ minute}$$

That is, a customer should emerge from the process every 0.4 minutes, on average.
Given that an individual can be served in 1.2 minutes:

✱ Operations principle

Little's law states that Throughput time = Work-in-progress $\times$ Cycle time.

$$\text{Number of servers required} = \frac{1.2}{0.4} = 3$$

In other words, three servers would serve three customers in 1.2 minutes. Or one customer in 0.4 minute.

Worked example

Mike was totally confident in his judgement. *'You'll never get them back in time'*, he said. *'They aren't just wasting time, the process won't allow them to all have their coffee and get back for 11 o'clock.'* Looking outside the lecture theatre, Mike and his colleague Dick were watching the 20 business people who were attending the seminar queuing to be served coffee and biscuits. The time was 10.45 and Dick knew that unless they were all back in the lecture theatre at 11 o'clock there was no hope of finishing his presentation before lunch.

'I'm not sure why you're so pessimistic', said Dick. *'They seem to be interested in what I have to say and I think they will want to get back to hear how operations management will change their lives.'* Mike shook his head. *'I'm not questioning their motivation,'* he said, *'I'm questioning the ability of the process out there to get through them all in time. I have been timing how long it takes to serve the coffee and biscuits. Each coffee is being made fresh and the time between the server asking each customer what they want and them walking away with their coffee and biscuits is taking 48 seconds. Remember that, according to Little's law, throughput equals work in process multiplied by cycle time. If the work in process is the 20 managers in the queue and cycle time is 48 seconds, the total throughput time is going to be 20 multiplied by 0.8 minutes which equals 16 minutes. Add to that sufficient time for the last person to drink their coffee and you must expect a total throughput time of a bit over 20 minutes. You just haven't allowed long enough for the process.'* Dick was impressed. *'Err . . . what did you say that law was called again?'* *'Little's law'*, said Mike.

Worked example

Every year it was the same. All the workstations in the building had to be renovated (tested, new software installed, etc.) and there was only one week in which to do it. The one week fell in the middle of the August vacation period when the renovation process would cause minimum disruption to normal working. Last year the company's 500 workstations had all been renovated within one working week (40 hours). Each renovation last year took on average 2 hours and 25 technicians had completed the process within the week. This year there would be 530 workstations to renovate but the company's IT support unit had devised a faster testing and renovation routine that would only take on average 1 and a half hours instead of 2 hours. How many technicians will be needed this year to complete the renovation processes within the week?

Last year:

$$\text{Work-in-progress (WIP)} = 500 \text{ work stations}$$

$$\text{Time available } (T_t) = 40 \text{ hours}$$

$$\text{Average time to renovate} = 2 \text{ hours}$$

$$\text{Therefore throughput rate } (T_r) = 1/2 \text{ hours per technician}$$

$$= 0.5N$$

where $\quad N = $ Number of technicians

Little's law:

$$WIP = T_t \times T_r$$

$$500 = 40 \times 0.5N$$

$$N = \frac{500}{40 \times 0.5}$$

$$= 25 \text{ technicians}$$

This year:

$$\text{Work-in-progress (WIP)} = 530 \text{ workstations}$$

$$\text{Time available} = 40 \text{ hours}$$

$$\text{Average time to renovate} = 1.5 \text{ hours}$$

$$\text{Throughput rate } T_r = 1/1.5 \text{ per technician}$$

$$= 0.67N$$

where $\quad N = $ Number of technicians

Little's law:

$$WIP = T_t \times T_r$$

$$530 = 40 \times 0.67N$$

$$N = \frac{530}{40 \times 0.67}$$

$$= 19.88 \text{ (say 20) technicians}$$

Throughput efficiency

This idea that the throughput time of a process is different from the work content of whatever it is processing has important implications. What it means is that for significant amounts of time no useful work is being done to the materials, information, or customers that are progressing through the process. In the case of the simple example of the sandwich process described earlier, customer throughput time is restricted to 4 minutes, but the work content of the task (serving the customer) is only 1.2 minutes. So, the item being processed (the customer) is only being 'worked on' for $1.2/4 = 30$ per cent of its time. This is called the throughput efficiency of the process.

$$\textbf{Percentage throughput efficiency} = \frac{\textbf{Work content}}{\textbf{Throughput time}} \times \textbf{100}$$

In this case the throughput efficiency is very high, relative to most processes, perhaps because the 'items' being processed are customers who react badly to waiting. In most material and information transforming processes, throughput efficiency is far lower, usually in single percentage figures.

A vehicle licensing centre receives application documents, keys in details, checks the information provided on the application, classifies the application according to the type of licence required, confirms payment and then issues and mails the licence. It is currently processing an average of 5,000 licences every 8-hour day. A recent spot check found 15,000 applications that were 'in progress' or waiting to be processed. The sum of all activities that are required to process an application is 25 minutes. What is the throughput efficiency of the process?

$$\text{Work in progress} = 15{,}000 \text{ applications}$$

$$\text{Cycle time} = \text{time producing}$$

$$\frac{\text{Time producing}}{\text{Number produced}} = \frac{8\text{hours}}{5{,}000} = \frac{480 \text{ minutes}}{5{,}000} = 0.096 \text{ minutes}$$

From Little's law,

$$\text{Throughput time} = \text{WIP} \times \text{Cycle time}$$

$$\text{Throughput time} = 15{,}000 \times 0.096$$

$$= 1{,}440 \text{ minutes} = 24 \text{ hours} = 3 \text{ days of working}$$

$$\text{Throughput efficiency} = \frac{\text{Work content}}{\text{Throughput time}} = \frac{25}{1{,}440} = 1.74 \text{ per cent}$$

Although the process is achieving a throughput time of 3 days (which seems reasonable for this kind of process) the applications are only being worked on for 1.7 per cent of the time they are in the process.

Value-added throughput efficiency

The approach to calculating throughput efficiency that is described above assumes that all the 'work content' is actually needed. Changing a process can significantly reduce the time that is needed to complete the task. Therefore, work content is actually dependent upon the methods and technology used to perform the task. It may be also that individual elements of a task may not be considered 'value-added'. So, value-added throughput efficiency restricts the concept of work content to only those tasks that are literally adding value to whatever is being processed. This often eliminates activities such as movement, delays and some inspections.

For example, if in the vehicle licensing worked example, of the 25 minutes of work content only 20 minutes were actually adding value, then:

$$\text{Value-added throughput efficiency} = \frac{20}{1{,}440} = 1.39 \text{ per cent}$$

Workflow[8]

When the transformed resource in a process is information (or documents containing information), and when information technology is used to move, store and manage the information, process design is sometimes called 'workflow' or 'workflow management'. It is defined as 'the automation of procedures where documents, information or tasks are passed between participants according to a defined set of rules to achieve, or contribute to, an overall business goal'. Although workflow may be managed manually, it is almost always managed using an IT system. The term is also often associated with Business Process Re-engineering (see Chapter 1 and Chapter 18). More specifically, workflow is concerned with the following:

- Analysis, modelling, definition and subsequent operational implementation of business processes.
- The technology that supports the processes.
- The procedural (decision) rules that move information/documents through processes.
- Defining the process in terms of the sequence of work activities, the human skills needed to perform each activity, and the appropriate IT resources.

The effects of process variability

So far in our treatment of process design we have assumed that there is no significant variability either in the demand to which the process is expected to respond, or in the time taken for the process to perform its various activities. Clearly, this is not the case in reality. So, it is important to look at the variability that can affect processes and take account of it.

There are many reasons why variability occurs in processes. These can include: the late (or early) arrival of material, information or customers; a temporary malfunction or breakdown of process technology within a stage of the process; the recycling of 'mis-processed' materials, information or customers to an earlier stage in the process; variation in the requirements of items being processed, etc. All these sources of variation interact with each other, but result in two fundamental types of variability:

- Variability in the demand for processing at an individual stage within the process, usually expressed in terms of variation in the inter-arrival times of items to be processed.
- Variation in the time taken to perform the activities (i.e. process a unit) at each stage.

To understand the effect of arrival variability on process performance it is first useful to examine what happens to process performance in a very simple process as arrival time changes under conditions of no variability. For example, the simple process shown in Figure 4.10 is comprised of one stage that performs exactly 10 minutes of work. Items arrive at the process at a constant and predictable rate. If the arrival rate is 1 unit every 30 minutes, then the process will be utilized for only 33.33 per cent of the time, and the items will never have to wait to be processed. This is shown as point A on Figure 4.10. If the arrival rate increases to 1 arrival every 20 minutes, the utilization increases to 50 per cent,

> *** Operations principle**
> Variability in a process acts to reduce its efficiency.

and again the items will not have to wait to be processed. This is point B on Figure 4.10. If the arrival rate increases to 1 arrival every 10 minutes, the process is now fully utilized, but, because a unit arrives just as the previous one has finished being processed, no unit has to wait. This is point C on Figure 4.10. However, if the arrival rate ever exceeded 1 unit every 10 minutes, the waiting line in front of the process activity would build up indefinitely, as is shown as point D in Figure 4.10. So, in a perfectly constant and predictable world, the relationship between process waiting time and utilization is a rectangular function as shown by the red line in Figure 4.10.

However, when arrival and process times are variable, then sometimes the process will have items waiting to be processed, while at other times the process will be idle, waiting for items to arrive. Therefore the process will both have a 'non-zero' average queue and be under-utilized in the same period. So, a more realistic point is that shown as point X in Figure 4.10. If the average arrival time were to be changed with the same variability, the blue line in Figure 4.10 would show the relationship between average waiting time and process

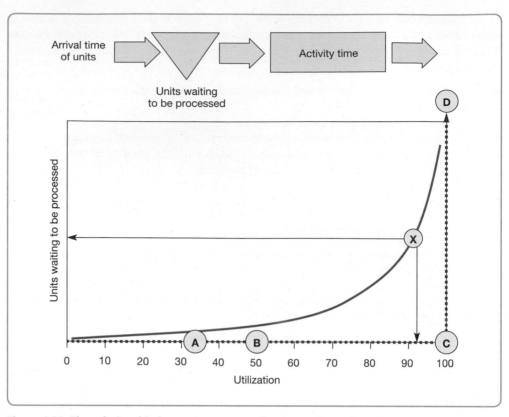

Figure 4.10 The relationship between process utilization and number of items waiting to be processed for constant, and variable, arrival and process times

utilization. As the process moves closer to 100 per cent utilization, the higher the average waiting time will become. Or, to put it another way, the only way to guarantee very low waiting times for the items is to suffer low process utilization.

The greater the variability in the process, the more the waiting time utilization deviates from the simple rectangular function of the 'no variability' conditions that was shown in Figure 4.10. A set of curves for a typical process is shown in Figure 4.11(a). This phenomenon has important implications for the design of processes. In effect it presents three options to process designers wishing to improve the waiting time or utilization performance of their processes, as shown in Figure 4.11(b). Either,

- accept long average waiting times and achieve high utilization (point X);
- accept low utilization and achieve short average waiting times (point Y); or
- reduce the variability in arrival times, activity times, or both, and achieve higher utilization and short waiting times (point Z).

To analyse processes with both inter-arrival and activity time variability, queuing or 'waiting line' analysis can be used. This is treated in the supplement to Chapter 11. But, do not dismiss the relationship shown in Figures 4.10 and 4.11 as some minor technical phenomenon. It is far more than this. It identifies an important choice in process design that could have strategic implications. Which is more important to a business, fast throughput time, or high utilization of its resources? The only way to have both of these simultaneously is to reduce variability in its processes, which may itself require strategic decisions such as limiting the degree of customization of products or services,

> *** Operations principle**
>
> Process variability results in simultaneous waiting and resource under-utilization.

Figure 4.11 The relationship between process utilization and number of items waiting to be processed for variable arrival and activity times

or imposing stricter limits on how products or services can be delivered to customers, and so on. It also demonstrates an important point concerned with the day-to-day management of process – the only way to absolutely guarantee a 100 per cent utilization of resources is to accept an infinite amount of work-in-progress and/or waiting time.

SHORT CASE   **Heathrow delays caused by capacity utilization[9]**

It may be the busiest international airport in the world, but it is unlikely to win any prizes for being the most loved. Long delays, overcrowding and a shortage of capacity have meant that Heathrow is often a cause of frustration to harassed passengers. Yet to the airlines it is an attractive hub. Its size and location give it powerful 'network effects'. This means that it can match incoming passengers with outgoing flights to hundreds of different cities. Actually it is its attractiveness to the airlines that is one of its main problems. Heathrow's runways are in such demand that they are almost always operating at, or close to, their maximum capacity. In fact its runways operate at 99 per cent of capacity. This compares with about 70 per cent at most other large airports. This means that any slightest variability (bad weather or an unscheduled landing, such as a plane having to turn back with engine trouble) causes delays, which in turn cause more delays. (See Figure 4.11 for the theoretical explanation of this effect.) The result is that a third of all flights at Heathrow are delayed by at least 15 minutes. This is poor when compared with other large European airports such as Amsterdam and Frankfurt, which have 21 per cent and 24 per cent of flights delayed respectively.

Source: Alamy Images/Roger Bamber

SUMMARY ANSWERS TO KEY QUESTIONS

MyOMLab *Check and improve your understanding of this chapter using self-assessment questions and a personalized study plan, a video case study, and an eText – all at* **www.myomlab.com.**

❭ What is process design?

- Design is the activity which shapes the physical form and purpose of both products and services and the processes that produce them.

- This design activity is more likely to be successful if the complementary activities of product or service design and process design are coordinated.

❭ What objectives should process design have?

- The overall purpose of process design is to meet the needs of customers through achieving appropriate levels of quality, speed, dependability, flexibility and cost.

- The design activity must also take account of environmental issues. These include examination of the source and suitability of materials, the sources and quantities of energy consumed, the amount and type of waste material, the life of the product itself, and the end-of-life state of the product.

❭ How do volume and variety affect process design?

- The overall nature of any process is strongly influenced by the volume and variety of what it has to process.

- The concept of process types summarizes how volume and variety affect overall process design.

- In manufacturing, these process types are (in order of increasing volume and decreasing variety) project, jobbing, batch, mass and continuous processes. In service operations, although there is less consensus on the terminology, the terms often used (again in order of increasing volume and decreasing variety) are professional services, service shops and mass services.

❭ How are processes designed in detail?

- Processes are designed initially by breaking them down into their individual activities. Often common symbols are used to represent types of activity. The sequence of activities in a process is then indicated by the sequence of symbols representing activities. This is called 'process mapping'. Alternative process designs can be compared using process maps and improved processes considered in terms of their operations performance objectives.

- Process performance in terms of throughput time, work-in-progress, and cycle time are related by a formula known as Little's law: throughput time equals work-in-progress multiplied by cycle time.

- Variability has a significant effect on the performance of processes, particularly the relationship between waiting time and utilization.

CASE STUDY | The Action Response Applications Processing Unit (ARAPU)

Introduction

Action Response is a London-based charity dedicated to providing fast responses to critical situations throughout the world. It was founded by Susan N'tini, its Chief Executive, to provide relatively short-term aid for small projects until they could obtain funding from larger donors. The charity receives requests for cash aid, usually from an intermediary charity, and looks to process the request quickly, providing funds where and when they are needed. *'Give a man a fish and you feed him today, teach him to fish and you feed him for life. It's an old saying and it makes sense but – and this is where Action Response comes in – he might starve while he's training to catch fish.'* (Susan N'tini)

Nevertheless, Susan does have some worries. She faces two issues in particular. First she is receiving complaints that funds are not getting through quickly enough. Second the costs of running the operation are starting to spiral. She explains. *'We are becoming a victim of our own success. We have striven to provide greater accessibility to our funds; people can access application forms via the internet, by post and by phone. But we are in danger of losing what we stand for. It is taking longer to get the money to where it is needed and our costs are going up. We are in danger of failing on one of our key objectives: to minimize the proportion of our turnover that is spent on administration. At the same time we always need to be aware of the risk of bad publicity through making the wrong decisions. If we don't check applications thoroughly, funds may go to the "wrong" place and if the newspapers gets hold of the story we would run a real risk of losing the goodwill, and therefore the funds, from our many supporters.'*

Susan held regular meetings with key stakeholders. One charity that handled a large number of applications for people in Nigeria told her of frequent complaints about the delays over the processing of the applications. A second charity representative complained that when he telephoned to find out the status of an application the ARAPU staff did not seem to know where it was or how long it might be before it was complete. Furthermore he felt that this lack of information was eroding his relationship with his own clients, some of whom were losing faith in him as a result. *'Trust is so important in the relationship'*, he explained.

Some of Susan's colleagues, while broadly agreeing with her anxieties over the organization's responsiveness and efficiency, took a slightly different perspective. *'One of the*

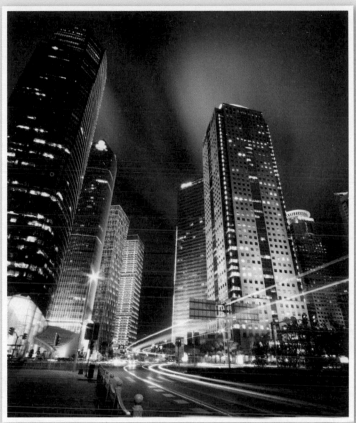

really good things about Action Response is that we are more flexible than most charities. If there a need and if they need support until one of the larger charities can step in, then we will always consider a request for aid. I would not like to see any move towards high process efficiency harming our ability to be open-minded and consider requests that might seem a little unusual at first.' (Jacqueline Horton, Applications Assessor)

Others saw the charity as performing an important counselling role. *'Remember that we have gained a lot of experience in this kind of short-term aid. We are often the first people that are in a position to advise on how to apply for larger and longer-term funding. If we developed this aspect of our work we would again be fulfilling a need that is not adequately supplied at the moment.'* (Stephen Nyquist, Applications Assessor)

The ARAPU process

Potential aid recipients, or the intermediary charities representing them, apply for funds using a standard form. These forms can be downloaded from the internet or requested via a special helpline. Sometimes the application will come directly from an individual community leader but more usually it will come via an intermediary charity that will help the applicant to complete the form. The application is sent to ARAPU, usually by fax or post (some were submitted online, but few communities have this facility).

ARAPU employs seven applications assessors with support staff who are responsible for data entry, coding, filing and 'completing' (staff who prepare payment, or explain why no aid can be given). In addition, a board of unpaid trustees meets every Thursday, to approve the assessors' decisions. The unit's IT system maintained records of all transactions, providing an update on the number of applications received, approved, declined, and payments allocated. These reports identified that the Unit received about 300 new applications per week and responded to about the same number (the Unit operates a 35-hour week). But whilst the Unit's financial targets were being met, the trend indicated that cost per application was increasing. The target for the turnaround of an application, from receipt of application to response, was 20 days, and although this was not measured formally, it was generally assumed that turnaround time was longer than this. Accuracy had never been an issue as all files were thoroughly assessed to ensure that all the relevant data was collected before the applications were processed. Productivity seemed high and there was always plenty of work waiting for processing at each section, with the exception that the 'completers' were sometimes waiting for work to come from the committee on a Thursday. Susan had conducted an inspection of all sections' in-trays that had revealed a rather shocking total of about 2,000 files waiting within the process, not counting those waiting for further information.

Processing applications

The processing of applications is a lengthy procedure requiring careful examination by applications assessors who are trained to make well-founded assessments in line with the charity's guidelines and values. Incoming applications are opened by one of the four 'receipt' clerks who check that all the necessary forms have been included in the application. The receipt clerks take about 10 minutes per application. These are then sent in batches to the coding staff, twice a day. The five coding clerks allocate a unique identifier to each application and key the information on the application into the system. The coding stage takes about 20 minutes for each application. Files are then sent to the senior applications assessors' secretary's desk. As assessors become available, the secretary provides the next job in the line to the assessor.

About one hundred of the cases seen by the assessors each week are put aside after only 10 minutes 'scanning'

because the information is ambiguous so further information is needed. The assessor returns these files to the secretaries, who write to the applicant (usually via the intermediate charity) requesting additional information, and return the file to the 'receipt' clerks who 'store' the file until the further information eventually arrives (usually between 1 and 8 weeks). When it does arrive, the file enters the process and progresses through the same stages again. Of the applications that require no further information, around half (150) are accepted and half (150) declined. On average, those applications that were not 'recycled' took around 60 minutes to assess.

All the applications, whether approved or declined, are stored prior to ratification. Every Thursday the Committee of Trustees meets to formally approve the applications assessors' decisions. The committee's role is to sample the decisions to ensure that the guidelines of the charity are upheld. In addition they will review any particularly unusual cases highlighted by the applications assessors. Once approved by the committee the files are then taken to the completion officers. There are three 'decline' officers whose main responsibility is to compile a suitable response to the applicant pointing out why the application failed and offering, if possible, helpful advice. An experienced 'decline' officer takes about 30 minutes to finalize the file and write a suitable letter. Successful files are passed to the four 'payment' officers where again the file is completed, letters (mainly standard letters) are created and payment instructions are given to the bank. This usually takes around 50 minutes, including dealing with any queries from the bank about payment details. Finally the paperwork itself is sent, with the rest of the file, to two 'dispatch' clerks who complete the documents and mail them to the applicant. The dispatch activity takes, on average, 10 minutes for each application.

The feeling amongst the staff was generally good. When Susan consulted the team they said their work was clear and routine, but their life was made difficult by charities that rang in expecting them to be able to tell them the status of an application they had submitted. It could take them hours, sometimes days, to find any individual file. Indeed two of the 'receipt' clerks now were working almost full time on this activity. They also said that charities frequently complained that decision making seemed slow.

QUESTIONS

1 What objectives should the ARAPU process be trying to achieve?
2 What is the main problem with the current ARAPU process?
3 How could the ARAPU process be improved?

These problems and applications will help to improve your analysis of operations. You can find more practice problems as well as worked examples and guided solutions on MyOMLab at www.myomlab.com.

MyOMLab

1 Read again the description of fast food drive-through processes at the beginning of this chapter.

(a) Draw a process map that reflects the types of process described.

(b) What advantage do you think is given to McDonald's through its decision to establish a call centre for remote order-taking for some of its outlets?

2 A laboratory process receives medical samples from hospitals in its area and then subjects them to a number of tests that take place in different parts of the laboratory. The average response time for the laboratory to complete all its tests and mail the results back to the hospital (measured from the time that the sample for analysis arrives) is 3 days. A recent process map has shown that, of the 60 minutes that are needed to complete all the tests, the tests themselves took 30 minutes, moving the samples between each test area took 10 minutes, and double-checking the results took a further 20 minutes. What is the throughput efficiency of this process? What is the value-added throughput efficiency of the process? (State any assumptions that you are making.) If the process is rearranged so that all the tests are performed in the same area, thus eliminating the time to move between test areas, and the tests themselves are improved to half the amount of time needed for double-checking, what effect would this have on the value-added throughput efficiency?

3 The regional government office that deals with passport applications is designing a process that will check applications and issue the documents. The number of applications to be processed is 1,600 per week and the time available to process the applications is 40 hours per week. What is the required cycle time for the process?

4 For the passport office, described above, the total work content of all the activities that make up the total task of checking, processing and issuing a passport is, on average, 30 minutes. How many people will be needed to meet demand?

5 The same passport office has a 'clear desk' policy that means that all desks must be clear of work by the end of the day. How many applications should be loaded onto the process in the morning in order to ensure that every one is completed and desks are clear by the end of the day? (Assume a 7.5 hour (450 minutes) working day.)

6 Visit a drive-through quick service restaurant and observe the operation for half an hour. You will probably need a stopwatch to collect the relevant timing information. Consider the following questions:

(a) Where are the bottlenecks in the service (in other words, what seems to take the longest time)?

(b) How would you measure the efficiency of the process?

(c) What appear to be the key design principles that govern the effectiveness of this process?

(d) Using Little's law, how long would the queue have to be before you think it would be not worth joining the queue?

SELECTED FURTHER READING

Chopra, S., Anupindi, R., Deshmukh, S.D., Van Mieghem, J.A. and Zemel, E. (2012) *Managing Business Process Flows*, 2nd edn, Prentice Hall, Upper Saddle River, NJ. An excellent, although mathematical, approach to process design in general.

Hammer, M. (1990) Reengineering Work: Don't automate, obliterate, *Harvard Business Review*, July–August. This is the paper that launched the whole idea of business processes and process management in general to a wider managerial audience. Slightly dated but worth reading.

Hopp, W.J. and Spearman, M.L. (2001) *Factory Physics*, 2nd edn, McGraw-Hill, New York. Very technical so don't bother with it if you aren't prepared to get into the maths. However, some fascinating analysis, especially concerning Little's law.

Smith, H. and Fingar, P. (2003) *Business Process Management: The Third Wave*, Meghan-Kiffer Press, Tampa, FL. A popular book on process management from a BPR perspective.

USEFUL WEBSITES

www.bpmi.org Site of the Business Process Management Initiative. Some good resources including papers and articles.

www.bptrends.com News site for trends in business process management generally. Some interesting articles.

www.iienet.org The American Institute of Industrial Engineers site. They are an important professional body for process design and related topics.

www.waria.com A Workflow and Reengineering association website. Some useful topics.

www.myomlab.com Test which sections you have mastered and which you need to review, with questions, a personalized study plan, video clips, revision tips, and cases.

www.opsman.org Useful materials.

http://operationsroom.wordpress.com/ Stanford University's take on topical operations stories.

http://sites.google.com/site/tomiportal/home One of the longest-established portals for the subject. Useful for academics and students alike.

www.ft.com Good for researching topics and companies.

www.economist.com *The Economist's* site, well written and interesting stuff of business generally.

Now that you have finished reading this chapter, why not visit MyOMLab at www.myomlab.com where you'll find more learning resources to help you make the most of your studies and get a better grade.

5 | Innovation and design in services and products

INTRODUCTION

New service and product design is concerned with putting new ideas into practice by embedding them in services and products. And innovation is the act of introducing new ideas. So the activity of service and product design and the objective of 'innovation' are closely linked. Innovation is about novel ideas. Design is about making ideas practical. Both are important because services and products are often the first thing that customers see of a company. And although operations managers may only have partial responsibility for service and product design, they always have some responsibility, if only to provide the information and advice upon which successful service or product development depends. But increasingly operations managers are expected to take a more active part in service and product design. Unless a service, however well conceived, can be implemented, and unless a product, however well designed, can be produced to a high standard, it can never bring its full benefits. Figure 5.1 shows where the issues covered here fit into the overall operations model.

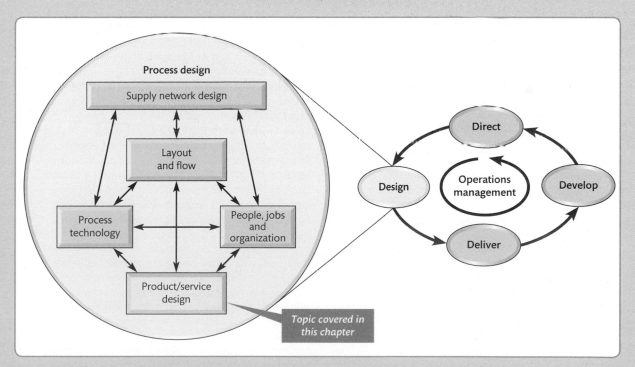

Figure 5.1 The design activities in operations management covered in this chapter

Innovative design from Dyson[1]

In 1907 a janitor called Murray Spangler put together a pillowcase, a fan, an old biscuit tin, and a broom handle. It was a great innovation – the world's first vacuum cleaner – but not one that he ever capitalized on. One year later he had sold his patented idea to William Hoover whose company went on to dominate the vacuum cleaner market for decades, especially in its United States homeland. Yet between 2002 and 2005 Hoover's market share dropped from 36 per cent to 13.5 per cent. Why? Because a futuristic-looking and comparatively expensive rival product, the Dyson vacuum cleaner, had jumped from nothing to over 20 per cent of the market. In fact, the Dyson product dates back to 1978 when James (now Sir James) Dyson noticed how the air filter in the spray-finishing room of a company where he had been working was constantly clogging with power particles (just like a vacuum cleaner bag clogs with dust). So he designed and built an industrial cyclone tower, which removed the powder particles by exerting centrifugal forces. The question intriguing him was, *'Could the same principle work in a domestic vacuum cleaner?'*

Five years and five *thousand* prototypes later he had a working design, since praised for its 'uniqueness and functionality'. However, existing vacuum cleaner manufacturers were not as impressed – two rejected the design outright. So Dyson started making his new design himself. Within a few years Dyson cleaners were, in the UK, outselling the rivals who had once rejected them. The aesthetics and functionality of the design help to keep sales growing in spite of a higher retail price. To Dyson, good design *'is about looking at everyday things with new eyes and working out how they can be made better. It's about challenging existing technology.'*

The Dyson engineers then took the technology one stage further and developed core separator technology to capture even more microscopic dirt. Dirt now goes through three stages of separation. Firstly, dirt is drawn into a powerful outer cyclone. Centrifugal forces fling larger debris such as pet hair and dust particles into the clear bin at 500Gs (the maximum G-force the human body can take is 8Gs). Second, a further cyclonic stage, the core separator, removes dust particles as small as 0.5 microns from the airflow; particles so small you could fit 200 of them on this full stop. Finally, a cluster of smaller, even faster cyclones generate centrifugal forces of up to 150,000G – extracting particles as small as mould and bacteria.

Other innovations followed. In 2006 came the Dyson Airblade™, an electric hand dryer. Rather than using a broad, relatively unfocused hot air jet, the Dyson engineers decided to use a 'blade' of cool air that emerges from the dryer at around four hundred miles per hour (643 km/hr). The advantage of this

Source: Dyson Ltd.

innovation is that it dries hands quicker (around 10 seconds) and uses less electricity than conventional hand dryers. Then came the Dyson Air Multiplier™. These are fans and fan heaters that work very differently to conventional fans and electric heaters. They don't have fast-spinning blades that chop the air and cause uncomfortable buffeting. Instead, they use Air Multiplier™ technology to draw in air and amplify it up to 18 times, producing an uninterrupted stream of smooth air. Sir James, who remains chief engineer and sole shareholder in Dyson, is enthusiastic about the Air Multiplier™. *'This* [electric heaters] *business is at least as large as the vacuum cleaner sector and I hope we will do as well in this as we have done in floor cleaners'*, he said. *'One of the benefits of the new device is that it will heat all the air in the room to reduce the effect of hot and cold spots. Sensors measure the temperature of the surrounding air so that once the desired temperature is reached, the system cuts out, making the product much more efficient and useful than comparable heaters.'* He said the new heater was part of the company's effort to turn itself into a *'broad-line technology company'* rather than being seen as only an appliance maker. *'I would not limit the company to particular areas of technology or markets. We are developing a range of technologies to improve both industrial and consumer products so that the people using them get a better experience than with the comparable items that currently exist.'*

HOW DOES INNOVATION IMPACT ON DESIGN?

So, what is 'innovation'? There are many definitions: it is 'a new method, idea, product, etc.' (Oxford English Dictionary); 'change that creates a new dimension of performance' (Peter Drucker, a well-known management writer); 'the act of introducing something new' (the American Heritage Dictionary); 'a new idea, method or device' (Webster Online Dictionary). What runs through all these definitions is the idea of novelty and change. Innovation is simply about doing something new. 'Design' (as we described it in Chapter 4) is to *conceive the looks, arrangement, and workings of something...* [a design] *must deliver a solution that will work in practice.* Innovation creates the novel idea; design makes it work in practice. The two concepts are intimately related, which is why we treat them in the same chapter. First we will look at some of the basic ideas that help to understand innovation.

The innovation S-curve

When new ideas are introduced in services, products or processes, they rarely have an impact that increases uniformly over time. Usually performance follows an S-shaped progress. So, in the early stages of a new idea's introduction, although often large amounts of resources, time and effort are needed to introduce the idea, relatively small performance improvements are experienced. However, with time, as experience and knowledge about the new idea grow, performance increases. But as the idea becomes established, extending its performance further becomes increasingly difficult (see Fig. 5.2 (a)). But when one idea reaches its mature, 'levelling off' period, it is vulnerable to a further new idea being introduced which, in turn, moves through its own S shaped progress. This is how innovation works: the limits of one idea being reached which prompts a newer, better idea, with each new S-curve requiring some degree of re-design (*see* Fig. 5.2 (b)).

> **✳ Operations principle**
> The innovation activity is an important part of service and product design.

Incremental or radical innovation

An obvious difference between how the pattern of new ideas emerges in different operations or industries is the rate and scale of innovation. Some industries, such as telecommunications, enjoy frequent and often significant innovations. Others, such as house building, do have innovations, but they are usually less dramatic. So some innovation is radical, resulting in discontinuous, 'breakthrough' change, while other innovations are more incremental, leading to smaller, continuous changes. Radical innovation often includes large technological advancements which may require completely new knowledge and/or resources, making existing services and products obsolete and therefore non-competitive. Incremental innovation, by contrast, is more likely to involve relatively modest technological changes, building upon existing knowledge and/or resources so existing services and products are not fundamentally changed. This is why established companies may favour incremental innovation because they have the experience to have built up a significant pool of knowledge (on which incremental innovation is based). In addition, established companies are more likely to have a mindset that emphasizes continuity, perhaps not even recognizing potential innovative opportunities (see the short case on Kodak). New entrants to markets, however, have no established position to lose, nor do they have a vast pool of experience. They may be more likely to try for more radical innovation.

The Henderson–Clark model

Although distinguishing between incremental and radical innovation is useful, it does not fully make clear why some companies succeed or fail at innovation. Two researchers, Henderson and Clark,[2] looked at the question of why some established companies sometimes fail to exploit seemingly obvious incremental innovations. They answered this question by

Figure 5.2 The S-shaped curve of innovation

dividing the technological knowledge required to develop new services and products into 'knowledge of the components of knowledge' and 'knowledge of how the components of knowledge link together'. They called this latter knowledge 'architectural knowledge'. Figure 5.3 shows what has become known as the Henderson–Clark model. It refines the simpler idea of the split between incremental and radical innovation. In this model incremental innovation is built upon existing component and architectural knowledge, whereas radical innovation changes both component and architectural knowledge. Modular innovation is built on existing architectural knowledge, but requires new knowledge for one or more components. By contrast, architectural innovation will have a great impact upon the linkage of components (or the architecture), but the knowledge of single components is unchanged.

So, for example, in health-care services, simple (but useful and possibly novel at the time) innovations in a primary care (general practitioner) doctors' clinic, such as online appointment websites, would be classed as incremental innovation because neither any elements nor

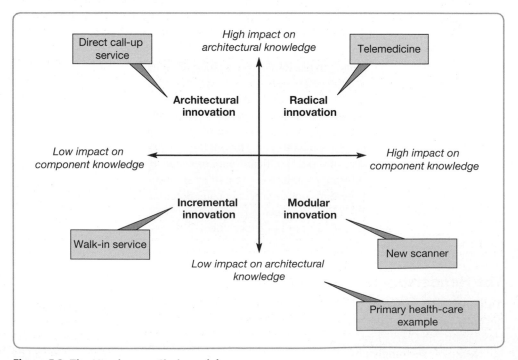

Figure 5.3 The Henderson–Clark model

The once mighty Eastman Kodak Company dominated the photographic and film markets for decades. But no longer: thirty years ago it employed over 140,000 people and made substantial profits; by 2010 it had shrunk to around 19,000, with regular quarterly losses. This dramatic fall from grace is usually put down to the company's failure to see the approach of digital photography or fully appreciate how it would totally undermine Kodak's traditional products. Yet, ironically, Kodak was more than ahead of its competitors than most people outside the company realized. It actually invented the digital camera. Sadly though, it lacked the foresight to make the most of it. For years the company had, as one insider put it, '*too much technology in its labs rather than in the market*'.

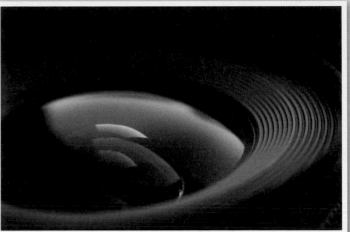

Source: Shutterstock.com/Minerva Studio

It was back in 1975 when a newly hired scientist at Kodak, Steve Sasson, was given the task of researching how to build a camera using a comparatively new type of electronic sensor – the charged-couple device (CCD). He found little previous research so he used the lens from a Kodak motion-picture camera, an analogue-to-digital convertor, some CCD chips and some digital circuitry that he made himself. By December 1975 he had an operational prototype. Yet the advance was largely, although not completely, ignored inside the company. '*Some people talked about reasons it would never happen, while others looked at it and realized it was important*', he says. He also decided not to use the word 'digital' to describe his trial product. '*I proposed it as filmless photography, an electronic stills camera. Calling it "digital"*

would not have been an advantage. Back then "digital" was not a good term. It meant new, esoteric technology.' Some resistance came from genuine, if mistaken, technical reservations. But others feared the magnitude of the changes that digital photography could bring. Objections '*were coming from the gut: a realization that [digital] would change everything – and threaten the company's entire film-based business model*'. Some see Kodak's reluctance to abandon its traditional product range as understandable. It was making vast profits and as late as 1999 it was making over three billion dollars from film sales. Todd Gustavson, curator of technology at the George Eastman House museum, says that, '*Kodak was almost recession-proof until the rise of digital. A film-coating machine was like a device that printed money.*' So Kodak's first digital camera, the Quicktake, was licensed to and sold by Apple in 1994.

In 2012 Kodak filed for bankruptcy protection.

---

the relationship between them is changed. If the practice invests in a new diagnostic heart scanner, that element of their diagnosis task has been changed and will probably need new knowledge, but the overall architecture of the service has not been changed. This innovation would be classed as 'modular'. An example of architectural innovation would be the practice providing 'walk-in' facilities in the local city centre. It would provide more or less the same service as the regular surgery (no new components), but the relationship between the service and patients has changed. Finally, if the practice adopted some of the 'telemedicine' technology (see Chapter 8) that monitors patient signs and can react to significant changes in patient condition, then this would be radical innovation. The components are novel (monitors) as is the overall architecture of the service (distance diagnosis).

> **＊ Operations principle**
>
> Innovation can be classified on two dimensions: innovation of components of a design and innovation of the linkages between them.

WHY IS GOOD DESIGN SO IMPORTANT?

Good design takes innovative ideas and makes them practical. Good design also communicates the purpose of the service or product to its market, and brings financial rewards to the business. Service and product design, therefore, can be seen as starting and ending with the customer. So the design activity has one overriding objective: to provide products, services and processes which will satisfy the operation's customers. *Product* designers try to achieve aesthetically pleasing designs which meet or exceed customers' expectations. They also try to design a product which performs well and is reliable during its lifetime. Further, they should design the product so that it can be manufactured easily and quickly. Similarly, service designers try to put together a service which meets, or even exceeds, customer expectations. Yet at the same time the service must be within the capabilities of the operation and be delivered at reasonable cost.

Critical commentary

Remember that not all new services and products are created in response to a clear and articulated customer need. While this is usually the case, especially for services and products that are similar to (but presumably better than) their predecessors, more radical innovations are often brought about by the innovation itself creating demand. Customers don't usually know that they need something radical. For example, in the late 1970s people were not asking for microprocessors; they did not even know what they were. They were improvised by an engineer in the USA for a Japanese customer who made calculators. Only later did they become the enabling technology for the PC and after that the innumerable devices that now dominate our lives.

What is designed in a service or product?

All services and products can be considered as having three aspects:

- A concept which articulates the nature, use and value of the service or product. Developing the concept is a crucial stage in the design of services and products because customers are buying more than just physical and evident components; they are buying into a particular concept. Patients consuming a new drug are not concerned about the ingredients nor the way they were made, they are concerned about the benefits it will provide. This is why designers often talk about a 'new concept'.
- A package of 'component' services and products that provide those benefits defined in the concept. A service or product is not a single homogenous entity; it is a package of elements. The purchase of an automobile includes the vehicle itself with its associated services such as 'warranties', 'after-sales services', etc. A restaurant meal is more than the food: it is also about serving the food, the attentions of the waiting staff, etc. Some parts of the package are 'core' in that they are fundamental to achieving the concept and could not be removed without destroying the nature of the service or product. Other parts are supporting; they serve to enhance the core.

> **✳ Operations principle**
>
> The design of a service or product must include its concept, package and process.

- The process defines the way in which the component services and products will be created and delivered. For an automobile, an assembly line has to be designed and built which will assemble the various components. In the restaurant, the processes of food purchase, preparation and cooking need to be designed, as do the way customers are moved from reception to the table, and the way that table service is performed.

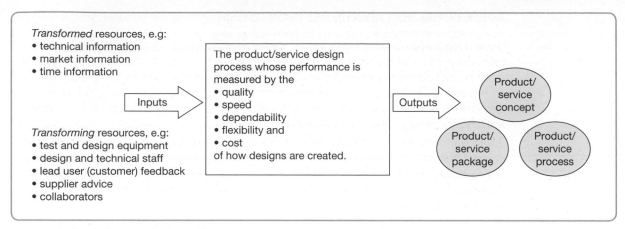

Figure 5.4 The design activity is itself a process

The design activity is itself a process

Producing designs for services and products is itself a process which conforms to the input–transformation–output model (described in Chapter 1). It therefore has to be designed and managed like any other process. Figure 5.4 illustrates the design activity as an input–transformation–output diagram. The transformed resource inputs will consist mainly of information in the form of market forecasts, market preferences, technical data, and so on. Transforming resource inputs includes operations managers and specialist technical staff, and design equipment and software. One can describe the objectives of the design activity in the same way as we do any transformation process. All operations satisfy customers by producing their services and goods according to customers' desires for quality, speed, dependability, flexibility and cost. In the same way, the design activity attempts to produce designs to the same objectives.

> **✳ Operations principle**
>
> The design activity is a process that can be managed using the same principles as other processes.

THE STAGES OF DESIGN – FROM CONCEPT TO SPECIFICATION

Fully specified designs rarely spring, fully formed, from a designer's imagination. The design activity must pass through several key stages. These form the sequence shown in Figure 5.5, although in practice designers will often recycle or backtrack through the stages. Nor is this sequence of stages descriptive of the stages used by all companies, yet most will use some stage model similar to this one. It moves from the concept generation stage to a screening stage, a preliminary design stage that produces a design to be evaluated and prototyped, before reaching the final design.

> **✳ Operations principle**
>
> *Design processes involve a number of stages that move an innovation from a concept to a fully specified state.*

Concept generation

This is where innovative ideas become the inspiration for new service or product concepts. And innovation can come from many different sources.

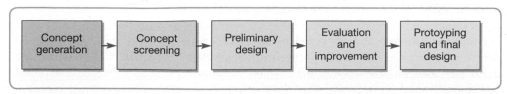

Figure 5.5 The stages of product/service design

Ideas from customers Marketing, the function generally responsible for identifying new service or product opportunities, may use market research tools for gathering data from customers in a structured way to test out ideas or check services or products against predetermined criteria.

Listening to customers Ideas may come from customers on a day-to-day basis: from complaints, or from everyday transactions. Although some organizations may not see gathering this information as important (and may not even have mechanisms in place to facilitate it), it is an important potential source of ideas.

Ideas from competitor activity Most organizations follow the activities of their competitors. A new idea from a competitor may be worth imitating, or better still, improving. Taking apart a competitor's service or product to explore potential new ideas is called 'reverse engineering'. Some aspects of services may be difficult to reverse engineer (especially 'back-office' services) as they are less transparent to competitors.

Ideas from staff The contact staff in a service organization or the salesperson in a product-orientated organization could meet customers every day. These staff may have good ideas about what customers like and do not like. They may have gathered suggestions from customers or have ideas of their own. One well-known example – which may be an urban myth – is that an employee at Swan Vestas, the matchmaker, suggested having one instead of two sandpaper strips on the matchbox. It saved a fortune!

Ideas from research and development Many organizations have a formal research and development (R&D) function. As its name implies, its role is twofold. Research develops new knowledge and ideas in order to solve a particular problem or to grasp an opportunity. Development utilizes and operationalizes the ideas that come from research. And although 'development' may not sound as exciting as 'research', it often requires as much creativity and even more persistence. One product has commemorated the persistence of its development engineers in its company name. Back in 1953 the Rocket Chemical Company set out to create a rust-prevention solvent and degreaser to be used in the aerospace industry. It took them 40 attempts to get the water displacing formula worked out. So that is what they called the product. WD-40 literally stands for Water Displacement, fortieth attempt.

Open sourcing – using a 'development community'[4]

Not all 'products' or services are created by professional, employed designers for commercial purposes. Many of the software applications that we all use, for example, are developed by an open community, including the people who use the products. If you use Google, the internet search facility, or use Wikipedia, the online encyclopaedia, or shop at Amazon, you are using open-source software. The basic concept of open-source software is extremely simple. Large communities of people around the world, who have the ability to write software code, come together and produce a software product. The finished product is not only available to be used by anyone or any organization for free but is regularly updated to ensure it keeps pace with the necessary improvements. The production of open-source software is very well organized and, like its commercial equivalent, is continuously supported and maintained. However, unlike its commercial equivalent, it is absolutely free to use.

Over the last few years the growth of open-source has been phenomenal, with many organizations transitioning over to using this stable, robust and secure software. With the maturity open-source software now has to offer, organizations have seen the true benefits of using free software to drive down costs and to establish themselves on a secure and stable platform. Open-source has been the biggest change in software development for decades and is setting new open standards in the way software is used. The open nature of this type of development also encourages compatibility between products. BMW, for example, was reported to be developing an open-source platform for vehicle electronics. Using an open-source approach, rather than using proprietary software, BMW can allow providers of 'infotainment' services to develop compatible, plug-and-play applications.

Crowdsourcing[5]

Closely related to the open-sourcing idea is that of 'crowdsoucing'. Crowdsourcing is the act of taking a job traditionally performed by a designated agent (usually an employee) and outsourcing it to an undefined, generally large group of people in the form of an open call. Although in essence it is not a totally new idea, it has become a valuable source of ideas largely through the use of the internet and social networking. For example, Procter & Gamble, the consumer products company, asked amateur scientists to explore ideas for a detergent dye whose colour changed when enough has been added to dishwater. Other uses of the idea involve government agencies asking citizens to prioritize spending (or cutting spending) projects.

Concept screening

Not all concepts which are generated will necessarily be capable of further development into services and products. Designers need to be selective as to which concepts they progress to the next design stage. The purpose of the concept-screening stage is to evaluate concepts by assessing the worth or value of design options. This involves assessing each concept or option against a number of design criteria. While the criteria used in any particular design exercise will depend on the nature and circumstances of the exercise, it is useful to think in terms of three broad categories of design criteria:

- The feasibility of the design option – can we do it?
  - Do we have the skills (quality of resources)?
  - Do we have the organizational capacity (quantity of resources)?
  - Do we have the financial resources to cope with this option?

SHORT CASE Square watermelons![6]

Source: Shutterstock.com/Valentyn Volkov

It sounds like a joke, but it is a genuine product innovation motivated by a market need. It's green, it's square and it comes originally from Japan. It's a square watermelon! Why square? Because Japanese grocery stores are not large and space cannot be wasted. Also a round watermelon does not fit into a refrigerator very conveniently. There is also the problem of trying to cut the fruit when it keeps rolling around. So an innovative farmer from Japan's south-western island of Shikoku solved the problem by devising the idea of making a cube-shaped watermelon which could easily be packed and stored. But there is no genetic modification or clever science involved in growing watermelons. It simply involves placing the young fruit into wooden boxes with clear sides. During its growth, the fruit naturally swells to fill the surrounding shape. Now the idea has spread from Japan. *'Melons are among the most delicious and refreshing fruit around but some people find them a problem to store in their fridge or to cut because they roll around'*, said Damien Sutherland, the exotic fruit buyer for Tesco, the UK supermarket. *'We've seen samples of these watermelons and they literally stop you in their tracks because they are so eye-catching. These square melons will make it easier than ever to eat because they can be served in long strips rather than in the crescent shape.'* But not everyone liked the idea. Comments on news websites included: *'Where will engineering everyday things for our own unreasonable convenience stop? I prefer melons to be the shape of melons!'* and *'They are probably working on straight bananas next!'*. Other were more enthusiastic. *'I would like to buy square sausages so then they would be easier to turn over in the frying pan. Round sausages are hard to keep cooked all over.'*

- The acceptability of the design option – do we want to do it?
  - Does the option satisfy the performance criteria which the design is trying to achieve? (These will differ for different designs.)
  - Will our customers want it?
  - Does the option give a satisfactory financial return?
- The vulnerability of each design option – do we want to take the risk?
  - Do we understand the full consequences of adopting the option?
  - Being pessimistic, what could go wrong if we adopt the option? What would be the consequences of everything going wrong? (This is called the 'downside risk' of an option.)

The design 'funnel'

Applying these evaluation criteria progressively reduces the number of options which will be available further along in the design activity. For example, deciding to make the outside casing of a camera case from aluminium rather than plastic limits later decisions, such as the overall size and shape of the case. This means that the uncertainty surrounding the design reduces as the number of alternative designs being considered decreases. Figure 5.6 shows what is sometimes called the design funnel, depicting the progressive reduction of design options from many to one. But reducing design uncertainty also impacts on the cost of changing one's mind on some detail of the design. In most stages of design the cost of changing a decision is bound to incur some sort of rethinking and recalculation of costs. Early on in the design activity, before too many fundamental decisions have been made, the costs of change are relatively low. However, as the design progresses the interrelated and cumulative decisions already made become increasingly expensive to change.

Critical commentary

Not everyone agrees with the concept of the design funnel. For some it is just too neat and ordered an idea to reflect accurately the creativity, arguments and chaos that sometimes characterize the design activity. First, they argue, managers do not start out with an infinite number of options. No one could process that amount of information – and anyway, designers often have some set solutions in their mind, looking for an opportunity to be used. Second, the number of options being considered often *increases* as time goes by. This may actually be a good thing, especially if the activity was unimaginatively specified in the first place. Third, the real process of design often involves cycling back, often many times, as potential design solutions raise fresh questions or become dead ends. In summary, the idea of the design funnel does not describe what actually happens in the design activity. Nor does it necessarily even describe what *should* happen.

Balancing evaluation with creativity

The systematic process of evaluation is important but it must be balanced by the need for design creativity. Creativity is a vital ingredient in effective design. The final quality of any design of service or product will be influenced by the creativity of its designers. Increasingly, creativity is seen as an essential ingredient not just in the design of services and products, but also in the design of operations processes. Partly because of the fast-changing nature of many industries, a lack of creativity (and consequently of innovation) is seen as a major risk. Of course, creativity can be expensive. By its nature it involves exploring sometimes unlikely possibilities. Many of these will die as they are proved to be inappropriate. Yet, to some extent, the process of creativity depends on these many seemingly wasted investigations. As Art Fry, the inventor of 3M's Post-it note products, said: '*You have to kiss a lot of frogs to find the prince. But remember, one prince can pay for a lot of frogs.*'

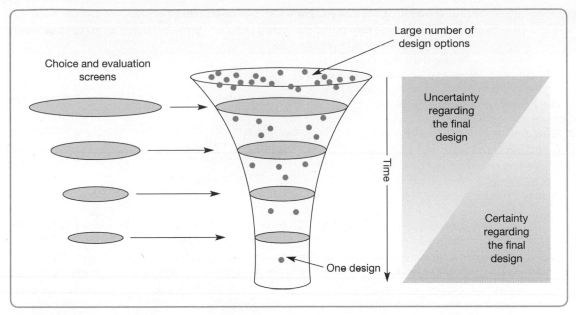

Figure 5.6 The design funnel – progressively reducing the number of possibilities until the final design is reached

Preliminary design

Having generated an acceptable, feasible and viable service or product concept, the next stage is to create a preliminary design. The objective of this stage is to have a first attempt at both specifying the component services and products in the *package*, and defining the *processes* to create the package.

Specify the components of the package

The first task in this stage of design is to define exactly what will go into the service or product: that is, specifying the components of the package. This will require the collection of information about such things as the *constituent component parts* which make up the service or product package and the component (or product) structure – the order in which the component parts of the package have to be put together. For example, the components for a remote mouse for a computer may include upper and lower casings, and a control unit and packaging, which are themselves made up of other components. The component structure shows how these components fit together to make the mouse (*see* Fig. 5.7).

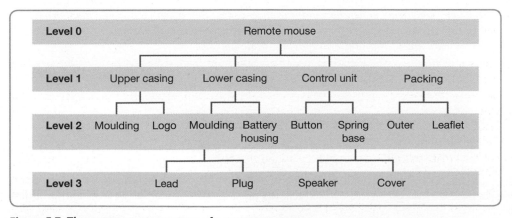

Figure 5.7 The component structure of a remote mouse

Even at the chic and stylish end of the hairdressing business, close as it is to the world of changing fashion trends, true innovation and genuinely novel new services are a relative rarity. Yet real service innovation can reap significant rewards, as Daniel and Luke Hersheson, the father and son team behind the Daniel Hersheson salons, fully understand. The Hersheson brand has successfully bridged the gap between salon, photo session and the fashion catwalk. The team first put themselves on the fashion map with a salon in London's Mayfair followed by a salon and spa in Harvey Nichols' flagship London store.

Their latest innovation is the 'Blow Dry Bar at Topshop'. This is a unique concept that is aimed at customers who want fashionable and catwalk quality styling at an affordable price without the full 'cut and blow dry' treatment. The Hersheson Blow Dry Bar was launched to ecstatic press coverage in Topshop's flagship Oxford Circus store. The four-seater pink pod within the Topshop store is a scissor-free zone dedicated to styling on the go. Originally seen as a walk-in, no-appointment-necessary format, demand has proved to be so high that an appointment system has been implemented to avoid disappointing customers. Once in the pod, customers can choose from a tailor-made picture menu of nine fashion styles with names like 'The Super Straight', 'The Classic Big and Bouncy', and 'Wavy Gravy'. Typically, the wash and blow dry takes around 30 minutes. *'It's just perfect for a client who wants to look that bit special for a big night out but who doesn't want a full cut'*, says Ryan Wilkes, one of the stylists at the Blow Dry Bar. *'Some clients will "graduate" to become regular customers at the main Daniel Hersheson salons. I have clients who started out using the Blow Dry Bar but now also get their hair cut with me in the salon.'*

Partnering with Topshop is an important element in the design of the service, says Daniel Hersheson. *'We are delighted to be opening the UK's first blow dry bar at Topshop. Our philosophy of constantly relating hair back to fashion means we will be perfectly at home in the most creative store on the British high street.'* Topshop also

Source: Alamy Images/Candy Box Images

recognizes the fit. *'The Daniel Hersheson Blow Dry Bar is a really exciting service addition to our Oxford Circus flagship and offers the perfect finishing touch to a great shopping experience at Topshop'*, says Jane Shepherdson, Brand Director of Topshop.

But the new service has not just been a success in the market; it also has advantages for the operation itself. *'It's a great opportunity for young stylist not only to develop their styling skills, but also to develop the confidence that it takes to interact with clients'*, says George Northwood, Manager of Daniel Hersheson's Mayfair salon. *'You can see a real difference after a trainee stylist has worked in the Blow Dry Bar. They learn how to talk to clients, to understand their needs, and to advise them. It's the confidence that they gain that is so important in helping them to become fully qualified and successful stylists in their own right.'*

✳ Operations principle

A key design objective should be the simplification of the design through standardization, commonality, modularization and mass customization.

Reducing design complexity

Simplicity is usually seen as a virtue amongst designers of services and products. The most elegant design solutions are often the simplest. However, when an operation produces a variety of services or products (as most do), the range of services and products considered as a whole can become complex, which, in turn, increases costs. Designers adopt a number of approaches to reducing the inherent complexity in the design of their service or product range. Here we describe some common approaches to complexity reduction – standardization, commonality and modularization.

Standardization

Operations sometimes attempt to overcome the cost penalties of high variety by standardizing their products, services or processes. This allows them to restrict variety to that which has real value for the end customer. Often it is the operation's outputs which are standardized. Examples of this are fast-food restaurants, discount supermarkets or telephone-based insurance companies. Perhaps the most common example of standardization are the clothes which most us of buy. Although everyone's body shape is different, garment manufacturers produce clothes in only a limited number of sizes. The range of sizes is chosen to give a reasonable fit for most body shapes. To suit all their potential customers and/or to ensure a perfect fit, garment manufacturers would have to provide an unfeasibly large range of sizes. Alternatively, they would need to provide a customized service. Both solutions would have a significant impact on cost. This control of variety is an important issue with most companies. A danger facing established operations is that they allow variety to grow excessively. They are then faced with the task of *variety reduction*, often by assessing the real profit or contribution of each service or product. Many organizations have significantly improved their profitability by careful variety reduction. In order to overcome loss of business, customers may be offered alternative services or products which provide similar value.

Commonality

Using common elements within a service or product can also simplify design complexity. Using the same components across a range of automobiles is a common practice. Likewise, standardizing the format of information inputs to a process can be achieved by using appropriately designed forms or screen formats. The more different services and products can be based on common components, the less complex it is to produce them. For example, the European aircraft maker, Airbus, has designed its aircraft with a high degree of commonality. This meant that ten aircraft models, ranging from the 100-seat A318 through to the world's largest aircraft, the over 500-seat A380, feature virtually identical flight decks, common systems and similar handling characteristics. In some cases, such as the entire A320 family, the aircraft even share the same 'pilot-type rating', which enables pilots with a single licence to fly any of them. The advantages of commonality for the airline operators include a much shorter training time for pilots and engineers when they move from one aircraft to another. This offers pilots the possibility of flying a wide range of routes from short-haul to ultra-long-haul and leads to greater efficiencies because common maintenance procedures can be designed with maintenance teams capable of servicing any aircraft in the same family. Also, when up to 90 per cent of all parts are common within a range of aircraft, there is a reduced need to carry a wide range of spare parts.

Modularization

The use of modular design principles involves designing standardized 'sub-components' of a service or product which can be put together in different ways. It is possible to create wide choice through the fully interchangeable assembly of various combinations of a smaller number of standard sub-assemblies; computers are designed in this way, for example. These standardized modules, or sub-assemblies, can be produced in higher volume, thereby reducing their cost. Similarly, the package holiday industry can assemble holidays to meet a specific customer requirement, from pre-designed and purchased air travel, accommodation, insurance, and so on. In education also there is an increasing use of modular courses which allow 'customers' choice but permit each module to have economical volumes of students. The short case 'Customizing for kids' describes an example of modularization in TV programme production.

Design evaluation and improvement

The purpose of this stage in the design activity is to take the preliminary design and see if it can be improved before the service or product is tested in the market. There are a number of techniques that can be used at this stage. Here we treat just two – quality function deployment (QFD) and value engineering (VE).

Quality function deployment

The key purpose of quality function deployment (QFD) is to try to ensure that the eventual design of a service or product actually meets the needs of its customers. Customers may not have been considered explicitly since the concept generation stage, and therefore it is appropriate to check that what is being proposed for the design of the service or product will meet their needs. It is also known as the 'house of quality' (because of its shape) and the 'voice of the customer' (because of its purpose). The technique tries to capture *what* the customer needs and *how* it might be achieved. Figure 5.8 shows an example of quality function deployment being used in the design of a new information system product. The QFD matrix is a formal articulation of how the company sees the relationship between the requirements of the customer (the *whats*) and the design characteristics of the new product (the *hows*). The matrix contains various sections, as explained opposite:

- The *whats*, or 'customer requirements', are the list of competitive factors which customers find significant. Their relative importance is scored, in this case on a 10-point scale, with *accurate* scoring the highest.
- The competitive scores indicate the relative performance of the product, in this case on a 1 to 5 scale. Also indicated are the performances of two competitor products.
- The *hows*, or 'design characteristics' of the product, are the various 'dimensions' of the design which will operationalize customer requirements within the service or product.
- The central matrix (sometimes called the relationship matrix) represents a view of the interrelationship between the *whats* and the *hows*. This is often based on value judgements made by the design team. The symbols indicate the strength of the relationship – for example, the relationship between the ability to link remotely to the system and the intranet compatibility of the product is strong. All the relationships are studied, but in many cases, where the cell of the matrix is blank, there is none.
- The bottom box of the matrix is a technical assessment of the product. This contains the absolute importance of each design characteristic. (For example, the design characteristic 'interfaces' has a relative importance of $(9 \times 5) + (1 \times 9) = 54$.) This is also translated into a ranked relative importance. In addition, the degree of technical difficulty to achieve high levels of performance in each design characteristic is indicated on a 1 to 5 scale.

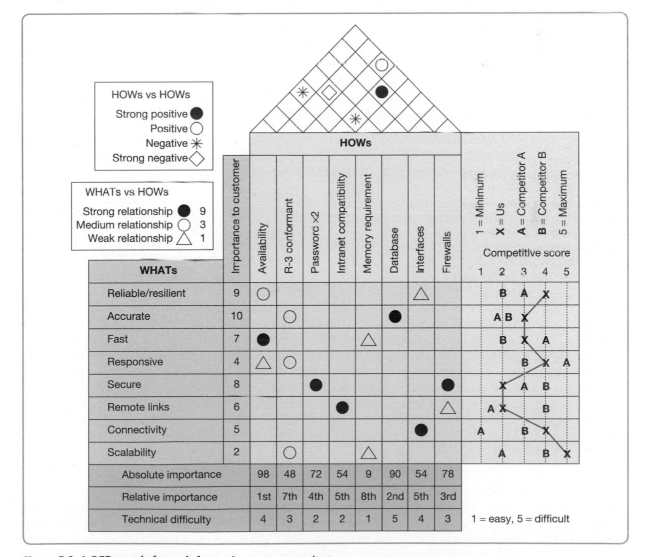

Figure 5.8 A QFD matrix for an information system product

- The triangular 'roof' of the 'house' captures any information the team has about the correlations (positive or negative) between the various design characteristics.

Although the details of QFD may vary between its different variants, the principle is generally common: namely to identify the customer requirements for a service or product (together with their relative importance) and to relate them to the design characteristics which translate those requirements into practice. In fact, this principle can be continued by making the *hows* from one stage become the *whats* of the next.

Value engineering

The purpose of value engineering is to try to reduce costs, and prevent any unnecessary costs, before producing the service or product. Simply put, it tries to eliminate any costs that do not contribute to the value and performance of the service or product. (Value analysis is the name given to the same process when it is concerned with cost reduction after the service or product has been introduced.) Value-engineering programmes are usually conducted by project teams consisting of designers, purchasing specialists, operations managers and financial analysts. The chosen elements of the package are subject to rigorous scrutiny, by analysing their function and cost, then trying to find any similar components that could do the same job at lower cost. The team may attempt to reduce the number of components, or use cheaper materials, or simplify processes. It requires innovative and critical thinking, but is also carried out using a formal procedure that examines the purpose of the service or product, its basic functions and its secondary functions. Taking the example of the remote mouse used previously:

- The purpose of the remote mouse is to communicate with the computer.
- The basic function is to control presentation slide shows.
- The secondary function is to be plug-and-play compatible with any system.

Team members would then propose ways to improve the secondary functions by combining, revising or eliminating them. All ideas would then be checked for feasibility, acceptability, vulnerability and their contribution to the value and purpose of the service or product.

Prototyping and final design

At around this stage in the design activity it is necessary to turn the improved design into a prototype so that it can be tested. It may be too risky to go into full production of the telephone, or the holiday, before testing it out, so it is usually more appropriate to create a prototype. Product prototypes include everything from clay models to computer simulations. Service prototypes may also include computer simulations but also the actual implementation of the service on a pilot basis. Many retailing organizations pilot new services and products in a small number of stores in order to test customers' reaction to them. Increasingly, it is possible to store the data that defines a service or product in a digital format on computer systems, which allows this virtual prototype to be tested in much the same way as a physical prototype. Virtual-reality-based simulations allow businesses to test new services and products as well as visualize and plan the processes that will produce them. Individual component parts can be positioned together virtually and tested for fit or interference. Even virtual workers can be introduced into the prototyping system to check for ease of assembly or operation.

Computer-aided design (CAD)

CAD systems provide the computer-aided ability to create and modify product drawings. These systems allow conventionally used shapes, such as points, lines, arcs, circles and text, to be added to a computer-based representation of the product. Once incorporated into the design, these entities can be copied, moved about, rotated through angles, magnified or deleted. The designs thus created can be saved in the memory of the system and retrieved for later use. This enables a library of standardized drawings of parts and components to be built up. The simplest CAD systems model only in two dimensions in a similar way to a conventional engineering 'blueprint'. More sophisticated systems model products in three dimensions. The most obvious advantage of CAD systems is that their ability to store and retrieve design data quickly, as well as their ability to manipulate design details, can considerably increase the productivity of the design activity. In addition to this, however, because changes can be made rapidly to designs, CAD systems can considerably enhance the flexibility of the design activity, enabling modifications to be made much more rapidly. Further, the use of standardized libraries of shapes and entities can reduce the possibility of errors in the design.

Skunkworks[9]

Encouraging creativity in design, while at the same time recognizing the constraints of everyday business life, has always been one of the great challenges of industrial design. One well-known approach to releasing the design and development creativity of a group has been called a 'Skunkworks'. It is usually taken to mean a small team who are taken out of their normal work environment and granted the freedom from their normal management activities and constraints. It was an idea that originated in the Lockheed aircraft company in the 1940s, where designers were set up outside the normal organizational structure and given the task of designing a high-speed fighter plane. The experiment was so successful that the company continued with it to develop other innovative products. Since that time many other companies have used a similar approach, although 'Skunkworks' is a registered trademark of Lockheed Martin Corporation.

WHAT ARE THE BENEFITS OF INTERACTIVE DESIGN?

Earlier we made the point that in practice it is a mistake to separate the design of services and products from the design of the processes which will produce them. Operations managers should have some involvement from the initial evaluation of the concept right through to the production of the service or product and its introduction to the market. Merging the design of products/services and the processes which create them is sometimes called interactive design. Its benefits come from the reduction in the elapsed time for the whole design activity, from concept through to market introduction. This is often called the time to market (TTM). The argument in favour of reducing time to market is that doing so gives increased competitive advantage. For example, if it takes a company five years to develop a product from concept to market, with a given set of resources, it can introduce a new product only once every five years. If its rival can develop products in three years, it can introduce its new product, together with its (presumably) improved performance, once every three years. This means that the rival company does not have to make such radical improvements in performance each time it introduces a new product, because it is introducing its new products more frequently. In other words, shorter TTM means that companies get more opportunities to improve the performance of their services or products.

If the development process takes longer than expected (or even worse, longer than competitors') two effects are likely to show. The first is that the costs of development will increase. Having to use development resources, such as designers, technicians, subcontractors, and so on, for a longer development period usually increases the costs of development. Perhaps more seriously, the late introduction of the service or product will delay the revenue from its sale (and possibly reduce the total revenue substantially if competitors have already got to the market with their own services or products). The net effect of this could be not only a considerable reduction in sales but also reduced profitability – an outcome which could considerably extend the time before the company breaks even on its investment in the new service or product. This is illustrated in Figure 5.9.

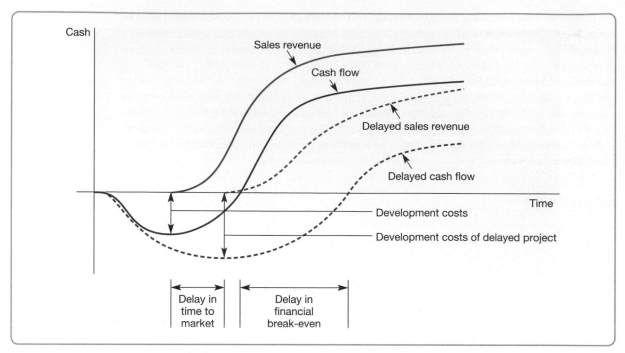

Figure 5.9 Delay in the time to market of new services and products not only reduces and delays revenues, it also increases the costs of development. The combination of both these effects usually delays the financial break-even point far more than the delay in the time to market

A number of factors have been suggested which can significantly reduce time to market for a service or product, including the following:

- simultaneous development of the various stages in the overall process;
- an early resolution of design conflict and uncertainty;
- an organizational structure which reflects the development project.

Simultaneous development

Earlier in the chapter we described the design process as essentially a set of individual, pre-determined stages. Sometimes one stage is completed before the next one commences. This step-by-step, or sequential, approach has traditionally been the typical form of product/service development. It has some advantages. It is easy to manage and control design projects organized in this way, since each stage is clearly defined. In addition, each stage is completed before the next stage is begun, so each stage can focus its skills and expertise on a limited set of tasks. The main problem of the sequential approach is that it is both time-consuming and costly. When each stage is separate, with a clearly defined set of tasks, any difficulties encountered during the design at one stage might necessitate the design being halted while responsibility moves back to the previous stage. This sequential approach is shown in Figure 5.10(a).

Yet often there is really little need to wait until the absolute finalization of one stage before starting the next. For example, perhaps while generating the concept, the evaluation activity of screening and selection could be started. It is likely that some concepts could be judged as 'non-starters' relatively early on in the process of idea generation. Similarly, during the screening stage, it is likely that some aspects of the design will become obvious before the phase is finally complete. Therefore, the preliminary work on these parts of the design could be commenced

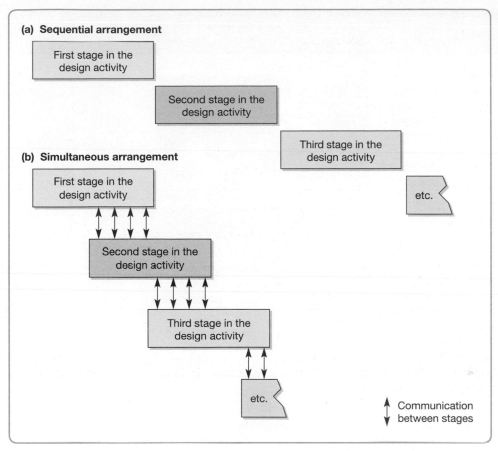

(a) Sequential arrangement

First stage in the design activity

Second stage in the design activity

Third stage in the design activity

etc.

(b) Simultaneous arrangement

First stage in the design activity

Second stage in the design activity

Third stage in the design activity

etc.

Communication between stages

Figure 5.10 (a) Sequential arrangement of the stages in the design activity; (b) simultaneous arrangement of the stages in the design activity

at that point. This principle can be taken right through all the stages, one stage commencing before the previous one has finished, so there is simultaneous or concurrent work on the stages (*see* Fig. 5.10(b)). (Note that simultaneous development is often called simultaneous, or concurrent, engineering in manufacturing operations.)

✳ Operations principle

Effective simultaneous development reduces time-to-market.

Early conflict resolution

Characterizing the design activity as a whole series of decisions is a useful way of thinking about design. However, a decision, once made, need not totally and utterly commit the organization. For example, if a design team is designing a new vacuum cleaner, the decision to adopt a particular style and type of electric motor might have seemed sensible at the time the decision was made but might have to be changed later, in the light of new information. It could be that a new electric motor becomes available which is clearly superior to the one initially selected. Under those circumstances the designers might very well want to change their decision.

There are other, more avoidable, reasons for designers changing their minds during the design activity, however. Perhaps one of the initial design decisions was made without sufficient discussion among those in the organization who have a valid contribution to make.

It is perhaps inevitable that a major new and complex product like a passenger aircraft will experience a few problems during its development. But the history of the Airbus A380 was a long and incident-packed journey from drawing board to reality that illustrates the dangers when the design activity goes wrong. This is the story in brief:

1991: Airbus consults with international Airlines about their requirements for a super-large passenger aircraft.

June 1993: Airbus and its partners set up the A3XX team to start the 'super-jumbo' project.

1996: Airbus forms its 'Large Aircraft' Division. Because of the size of the aircraft, it is decided to develop specially designed engines rather than adapt existing models.

2000: The commercial launch of the A3XX (later to be named the A380).

2002: Work starts on manufacturing the aircraft's key components.

2004: Rolls-Royce delivers the first Airbus engines to the assembly plant in Toulouse (February) and the first Airbus wings are completed in the North Wales factory. London's Heathrow airport starts to redevelop its facilities so that it can accommodate the new aircraft (April). Assembly begins in the Toulouse plant (May). EADS reveals the project is €1.45 billion over budget, and will now cost more than €12 billion (December).

2005: Airbus unveils the A380 to the world's press and European leaders (January). The aircraft makes its maiden flight, taking off in Toulouse and circling the Bay of Biscay for four hours before returning to Toulouse. A year of flight-testing and certification work begins (April). Airbus announces that the plane's delivery schedule will slip by six months (June).

2006: The plane passes important safety tests involving 850 passengers and 20 crew, safely leaving the aircraft in less than 80 seconds with half the exits blocked (March). The A380 suffers another production delay. Airbus now predicts a delay of a further six to seven months. This caused turmoil in the boardrooms of both Airbus and its parent company EADS. The Company's Directors were accused of suppressing the news for months before revealing it to shareholders. It leads to the resignations of Airbus' chief executive, EADS co-chief executive, and the A380 programme manager (July). Airbus infuriates customers by announcing yet a further delay for the A380, this time of a whole year. The first

Source: Alamy Images/Itar-Tass Photo Agency

plane is now forecast enter commercial service around twenty months later than had been originally planned. The delays will cost Airbus another estimated €4.8billion over the next four years. The company announces a drastic cost-cutting plan to try to recoup some of the losses (October).

2007: The super-jumbo eventually takes off in full service as a commercial airliner for Singapore Airlines. It wins rave reviews from both airlines and passengers – even if it is two years late (October).

So what caused the delays? First, the A380 was the most complex passenger jet ever to be built. Second, the company was notorious for its internal rivalries and constant political infighting, particularly by the French and German governments and frequent changes of management. According to one insider, *'the underlying reason for the mess we were in was the hopeless lack of integration [between the French and German sides] within the company'*. Eventually it was this lack of integration between design and manufacturing processes that was the main reason for the delays to the aircraft's launch. During the early design stages the firm's French and German factories had used incompatible software to design the 500 km of wiring that each plane needs. Eventually, to resolve the cabling problems, the company had to transfer 2,000 German staff from Hamburg to Toulouse. Processes that should have been streamlined had to be replaced by temporary and less efficient ones, described by one French union official as a *'do-it-yourself system'*. Feelings ran high on the shop floor, with tension and arguments between French and German staff. *'The German staff will first have to succeed at doing the work they should have done in Germany'*, said the same official. Electricians had to resolve the complex wiring problems one by one, with the engineers having to adjust the computer blueprints as they modified them so they could be used on future aircraft. *'Normal installation time is two to three weeks'*, said Sabine Klauke, a team leader. *'This way it is taking us four months.'* Mario Heinen, who ran the cabin and fuselage cross-border division, admitted the pressure to keep up with intense production schedules and the overcrowded conditions made things difficult: *'We have been working on these initial aircraft in a handmade way.'* But, he claimed, there was no choice: *'We have delivered five high-quality aircraft this way. If we had left* the work in Hamburg, to wait for a new wiring design, we would not have delivered one by now.' *But the toll taken by these delays was high. The improvised wiring processes were far more expensive than the planned 'streamlined' processes and the delay in launching the aircraft meant two years without the revenue that the company had expected.*

But Airbus was not alone. Its great rival, Boeing, was also having problems. Supply chain problems and mistakes by its own design engineers delayed its '787 Dreamliner' aircraft. When it carried its first passengers in 2011 the Dreamliner was three years late.

It may even be that when the decision was made there was insufficient agreement to formalize it, and the design team decided to carry on without formally making the decision. Yet subsequent decisions might be made as though the decision had been formalized. For example, suppose the company could not agree on the correct size of electric motor to put into its vacuum cleaner. It might well carry on with the rest of the design work while further discussions and investigations take place on what kind of electric motor to incorporate in the design. Yet much of the rest of the product's design is likely to depend on the choice of the electric motor. The plastic housings, the bearings, the sizes of various apertures, and so on, could all be affected by this decision. Failure to resolve these conflicts and/or decisions early on in the process can prolong the degree of uncertainty in the total design activity. In addition, if a decision is made (even implicitly) and then changed later on in the process, the costs of that change can be very large. However, if the design team manages to resolve conflict early in the design activity, this will reduce the degree of uncertainty within the project and reduce the extra cost and, most significantly, the time associated with either managing this uncertainty or changing decisions already made. Figure 5.11 illustrates two patterns of design changes through the life of the total design, which imply different time-to-market performances.

> *** Operations principle**
> The design process requires strategic attention early, when there is most potential to affect design decisions.

Project-based organization structures

The total process of developing concepts through to market will almost certainly involve personnel from several different areas of the organization. To continue the vacuum cleaner example, it is likely that the vacuum cleaner company would involve staff from its research and development department, engineering, production management, marketing and finance. All these different functions will have some part to play in making the decisions which will shape the final design. Yet any design project will also have an existence of its own. It will have a project name, an individual manager or group of staff championing the project, a budget and, hopefully, a clear strategic purpose in the organization. The organizational question is which of these two ideas – the various organizational functions which contribute to the design or the design project itself – should dominate the way in which the design activity is managed?

Before answering this, it is useful to look at the range of organizational structures which are available – from pure functional to pure project forms. In a pure functional organization, all staff associated with the design project are based unambiguously in their functional groups. There is no project-based group at all. They may be working full-time on the project but all communication and liaison are carried out through their functional manager. The project exists because of agreement between these functional managers. At the other extreme, all

Figure 5.11 Sorting out problems early saves greater disruption later in the design activity

Figure 5.12 Organization structures for the design activity

the individual members of staff from each function who are involved in the project could be moved out of their functions and perhaps even physically relocated to a task force dedicated solely to the project. The task force could be led by a project manager who might hold the entire budget allocated to the design project. Not all members of the task force necessarily have to stay in the team throughout the development period, but a substantial core might see the project through from start to finish. Some members of a design team may even be from other companies. In between these two extremes there are various types of matrix organization with varying emphasis on these two aspects of the organization (*see* Fig. 5.12). Although the 'task force' type of organization, especially for small projects, can sometimes be a little cumbersome, it seems to be generally agreed that, for substantial projects at least, it is more effective at reducing overall time to market.

SUMMARY ANSWERS TO KEY QUESTIONS

Check and improve your understanding of this chapter using self-assessment questions and a personalized study plan, a video case study, and an eText – all at www.myomlab.com.

MyOMLab

❯ How does innovation impact on design?

- Innovation is the act of introducing something new. Design is to 'conceive the looks, arrangement, and workings of something'. The two concepts are intimately related.
- The innovation S-curve describes the impact of an innovation over time, slow at first, increasing in impact, then slowing down before levelling off.
- Incremental and radical innovations differ in how they use knowledge. Radical innovation often requires completely new knowledge and/or resources, making existing services and products obsolete. Incremental innovation builds upon existing knowledge and/or resources.
- The Henderson–Clark model goes further by distinguishing between 'knowledge of the components of innovation' and 'knowledge of how the components of innovation link together' (called architectural knowledge).

❯ Why is good service and product design important?

- Good design makes good business sense because it translates customer needs into the shape and form of the service or product and so enhances profitability.
- Design includes formalizing three particularly important issues: the concept, package and process implied by the design.
- Design is a process that itself must be designed according to the process design principles described earlier (see previous chapter).

❯ What are the stages in service and product design?

- *Concept generation* transforms an idea for a service or product into a concept which captures the nature of the service or product and provides an overall specification for its design.

- *Screening* the concept involves examining its feasibility, acceptability and vulnerability in broad terms to ensure that it is a sensible addition to the company's service or product portfolio.
- *Preliminary design* involves the identification of all the component parts of the service or product and the way they fit together. Typical tools used during this phase include component structures and flow charts.
- *Design evaluation and improvement* involve re-examining the design to see if it can be done in a better way, more cheaply or more easily. Typical techniques used here include quality function deployment and value engineering.
- *Prototyping and final design* involve providing the final details which allow the service or product to be produced. The outcome of this stage is a fully developed specification for the package of services and products, as well as a specification for the processes that will make and deliver them to customers.

❭ What are the benefits of interactive design?

- Looking at the stages of design together can improve the quality of both service and product design and process design. It helps a design 'break even' on its investment earlier than would otherwise have been the case.
- Employ *simultaneous development* where design decisions are taken as early as they can be, without necessarily waiting for a whole design phase to be completed.
- Ensure early *conflict resolution* which allows contentious decisions to be resolved early in the design process, thereby not allowing them to cause far more delay and confusion if they emerge later in the process.
- Use a *project-based organizational structure* which can ensure that a focused and coherent team of designers is dedicated to a single design or group of design projects.

CASE STUDY   Chatsworth – the adventure playground decision

Chatsworth, the home of the 12th Duke and Duchess of Devonshire, is one of the finest and most palatial houses in the UK, set in over 1,000 acres of parkland in the Peak District National Park, England. The original house was built over 400 years ago and rebuilt starting in the 17th century. The house is vast, with 175 rooms, lit by over 2,000 light bulbs, and with a roof that covers 1.3 acres. Chatsworth's many rooms are full of treasures including famous works of art by painters such as Rembrandt, and tapestries, sculptures, valuable furniture, musical instruments and even 63 antique clocks which need winding every day. The gardens cover over 105 acres with over five miles of footpaths that guide visitors past fountains small and large (the largest is 28 metres high), cascades, streams and ponds, all of which are fed by gravity from four large man-made lakes on the moors above the

Source: Alistair Brandon-Jones

grounds. The gardens are a mix of formal and informal areas. There are sculptures, statues, rock gardens, a maze and garden views that constantly change with the seasons; all managed and maintained by a small team of 20 gardeners. Both the house and gardens are open from March to December and are just two of the experiences available to visitors. Others include an orangery gift shop, restaurant, and farm shop, which are open all year round, and the surrounding park land which is open to visitors for walking, picnics and swimming in the river. The whole estate is owned and managed by an independent charity.

Close to the house and gardens, with a separate admission charge, is the farmyard and adventure playground. The farmyard is a popular attraction for families and provides for close encounters with a variety of livestock, including pigs, sheep, cows, chickens and fish. The staff provide daily milking demonstrations and animal handling sessions. The woodland adventure playground is accessed through the farmyard and is one of the largest in the country with a range of frames, bridges, high level walkways, swings, chutes and slides.

Simon Seligman was the Promotions and Education Manager at Chatsworth. As head of marketing he was closely involved in the design and development of new services and facilities. He explained the way they do this at Chatsworth. *'It is a pretty abstract and organic process. Looking back over the last 25 years we either take occasional great leaps forward or make frequent little shuffles. The little shuffles tend to be organic changes usually in response to visitor feedback. The great leaps forward have been the few major changes that we decided we wanted to bring about.'*

One of those great leaps forward was the need to consider removing or replacing the children's adventure playground attached to the farmyard. Simon explained. *'The existing adventure playground was coming to the end of its life and it was time to make a decision about what to do with it. It was costing us about £18,000 each winter to maintain it and these costs were increasing year on year. We believed we could get a better one for around £100,000. The trustees asked me, the deputy estate manager with line responsibility for the farmyard and the farmyard manager to form a group and put forward a report to the trustees setting out all the options. We asked ourselves several detailed questions and some fundamental ones too, such as why are we replacing it, and should we replace it at all. We came up with four options, remove it, do nothing, replace with similar, replace with substantially better.'*

It was felt that removing the playground altogether was a realistic option. The Duke and Duchess had a view that Chatsworth should be true to its roots and traditions. Whereas one could make an argument for a farmyard being part of a country estate, an adventure playground was considered to fit less well. The downside would be that the lack of an adventure playground, which is a big attraction for families with young children, could have an impact on visitor numbers. However, there would be a savings in terms of site maintenance.

The 'do nothing' option would entail patching up the playground each year and absorbing the increasing maintenance costs. This could be a low impact option, in the short term at least. However, it was felt that this option would simply delay the replace/remove decision by five years at most.

The current playground was no longer meeting international safety standards so this could be a good opportunity to replace the playground with something similar. It was estimated that a like-for-like replacement would cost around £100,000. Replacing the playground with a substantially better one would entail a much greater cost but could have an impact on visitor numbers. Simon and his team keep a close eye on their competitors and visit them whenever they can. They reported that several other attractions had first-rate adventure playgrounds. Installing a substantially better playground could provide an opportunity for Chatsworth to leapfrog over them and provide something really special.

'We tried to cost out all four alternatives and estimate what we thought the impact on visitor numbers might be. We presented an interim report to the Duke and the other trustees. We felt that maintaining the status quo was inappropriate and a like-for-like replacement was expensive especially given that it would attract little publicity and few additional visitors. We strongly recommended two options: either remove the playground or go for a great leap forward. The trustees asked us to bear in mind the "remove" option and take a closer look at the "substantially better" option.'

Three companies were asked to visit the site, propose a new adventure playground and develop a site plan and initial design to a budget of £150,000. All three companies provided some outline proposals for such a figure but they all added that for £200,000 they could provide something really quite special. Furthermore, the team realized that they would have to spend some additional money putting in a new ramp and a lift into the farmyard at an estimated £50,000. It was starting to look like a very expensive project. Simon takes up the story. *'One of the companies came along with a complete idea for the site based on water, which is a recurring theme in the garden at Chatsworth. They had noticed the stream running through the playground and thought it could make a wonderful feature. They told us they were reluctant to put up a single solution but wanted to work with us, really engage with us, to explore what would really work for us and how it could be achieved. They also wanted to take us to visit their German partner who made all the major pieces of equipment. So, over the next few months, together, we worked up a complete proposal for a state-of-the-art adventure playground, including the structural changes in the farmyard. The budget was £250,000. To be honest, it was impossible to know what effect this would have on visitor numbers so in the end we put in a very conservative estimate that suggested that we would make the investment back in seven years. Over the next few years we reckon the playground led to an increase in visitor numbers of 85,000 per year and so we recouped our investment in just three years.'*

QUESTIONS

1 What do you think comprise the concept, package, and process for the adventure playground?

2 Describe the four options highlighted in the case in terms of their feasibility, acceptability, and vulnerability.

3 What does the concept of interactive design mean for a service such as the adventure playground described here?

MyOMLab

These problems and applications will help to improve your analysis of operations. You can find more practice problems as well as worked examples and guided solutions on MyOMLab at **www.myomlab.com**.

1   How would you evaluate the design of this book?

2   A company is developing a new app that will allow customers to track the progress of their orders. The app developers charge €10,000 for every development week and it is estimated that the design will take 10 weeks from the start of the design project to the launch of the app. Once launched, it is estimated that the new app will attract extra business that will generate profits of €5,000 per week. However, if the app is delayed by more than 5 weeks, the extra profit generated would reduce to €2,000 per week. How will a delay of 5 weeks affect the time when the design will break even in terms of cash flow?

3   How can the concept of modularization be applied to package holidays sold through an online travel agent?

4   One product where a very wide range of product types is valued by customers is that of domestic paint. Most people like to express their creativity in the choice of paints and other home-decorating products that they use in their homes. Clearly, offering a wide range of paint must have serious cost implications for the companies which manufacture, distribute and sell the product. Visit a store which sells paint and get an idea of the range of products available on the market. How do you think paint manufacturers and retailers manage to design their services and products so as to maintain high variety but keep costs under control?

SELECTED FURTHER READING

Bangle, C. (2001) The ultimate creativity machine: how BMW turns art into profit, *Harvard Business Review,* **Jan, 47–55.** A good description of how good aesthetic design translates into business success.

Bruce, M. and Bessant, J. (2002) *Design In Business: Strategic Innovation through Design***, FT Prentice Hall and The Design Council, Harlow.** Probably one of the best overviews of design in a business context available today.

Christensen, C. (2000) *The Innovator's Dilemma***, Harvard Business School Press, 1997; Harper Business, New York.** A major influence on innovation theory.

Dyson, J. (1997) *Against the Odds: An autobiography***, Orion Business Books, London.** One of Europe's most famous designers tells of his philosophy.

Nambisan, S. and Sawhney, M. (2007) A buyer's guide to the innovation bazaar, *Harvard Business Review***, June.** Provocative innovation ideas.

The Industrial Designers Society of America (2003) *Design Secrets: Products: 50 Real-Life Projects Uncovered (Design Secrets)***, Rockport Publishers Inc., Gloucester, MA.** Very much a practitioner book with some great examples.

USEFUL WEBSITES

www.cfsd.org.uk The centre for sustainable design's site. Some useful resources, but obviously largely confined to sustainability issues.

www.conceptcar.co.uk A site devoted to automotive design. Fun if you like new car designs!

www.betterproductdesign.net A site that acts as a resource for good design practice. Set up by Cambridge University and the Royal College of Art. Some good material that supports all aspects of design.

www.designcouncil.org.uk Site of the UK's Design Council. One of the best sites in the world for design-related issues.

www.myomlab.com – Test which sections you have mastered and which you need to review, with questions, a personalized study plan, video clips, revision tips, and cases.

www.opsman.org Useful materials.

http://operationsroom.wordpress.com Stanford University's take on topical operations stories.

Now that you have finished reading this chapter, why not visit MyOMLab at www.myomlab.com where you'll find more learning resources to help you make the most of your studies and get a better grade.

6 Supply network design

Key questions

Key questions

> ❯ Why should an organization take a total supply network perspective?

> ❯ What is involved in configuring a supply network?

> ❯ Where should an operation be located?

> ❯ How much capacity should an operation plan to have?

INTRODUCTION

No operation exists in isolation. Every operation is part of a larger and interconnected network of other operations. This *supply network* will include suppliers and customers. It will also include suppliers' suppliers and customers' customers, and so on. At a strategic level, operations managers are involved in 'designing' the shape and form of their network. Network design starts with setting the network's strategic objectives. This helps the operation to decide how it wants to influence the overall shape of its network, the location of each operation, and how it should manage its overall capacity within the network. Here we treat all these strategic design decisions in the context of supply networks (*see* Fig. 6.1).

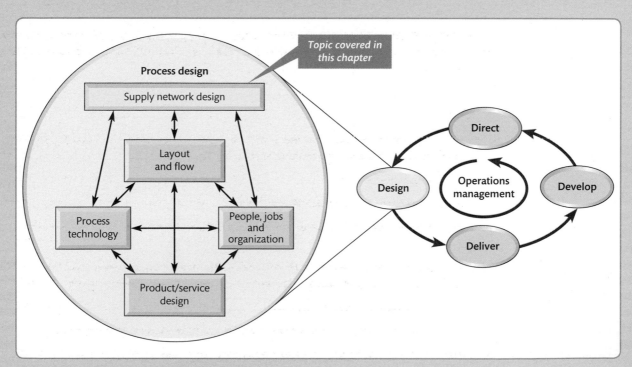

Figure 6.1 This chapter covers supply network design

Dell: the customer is still king of the supply network[1]

Michael Dell, the founder of Dell, has always stressed that his customers are the driving force behind how he shapes the company's supply networks. As a student in Texas he realized that he could add value by modifying PCs bought from local dealers so that they represented better value for local businesses. He quit university and founded the computer company which was to revolutionize the industry. But his fledgling company was just too small to make their own components. Better, he figured, to learn how to outsource to a network of specialist component manufacturers. Dell says that his commitment to outsourcing was always done for the most positive of reasons. *'We*

Source: Shutterstock.com/Filipchuk Oleg

focus on how we can coordinate our activities to create the most value for customers.' To save costs further, Dell still decided to sell its computers directly to its customers, allowing them to cut out the retailer's (often considerable) margin, which in turn allowed Dell to offer lower prices. Also, dealing directly with customers provided them with the opportunity to get to know their customers' needs far more intimately. They could forecast based on the thousands of customer contact calls every hour and could talk with customers about what they really wanted. Most importantly it allowed Dell to learn how to run its supply networks so that products get to end customers fast and efficiently, reducing Dell's level of inventory and giving it a significant cost advantage. However, two decades after its foundation, Dell seems to have forgotten supply network management's golden rule – understand the customer.

Selling computers to individuals (as opposed to the corporate market) was changing. Maybe influenced by Apple, customers increasingly wanted up-to-date computers with a high design value, and most significantly, they wanted to see, touch, and feel the products before buying them. This was clearly a problem for a

company like Dell who had spent 20 years investing in its telephone- and later, internet-based sales channels. What the market wanted had changed but Dell's supply network had not. However, Dell did recover. It focused on consumers. *'Let's say you wanted to buy a Dell computer in a store – you'd have searched a long time and not found one. Now we have over 10,000 stores that sell our products.'*

In a recent move, Dell has re-emphasized its commitment to matching its supply networks with what customers want. It has established the 'Social Media Listening Command Center' which monitors more than 25,000 posts and Twitter messages every day that in some way relate to Dell. Using an analytics tool, this allows the monitoring team to gather and sort conversations, evaluate trends and problems and, if necessary, react rapidly to customers. Dell says it has a 'resolution rate' of 99 per cent customer satisfaction and succeeds in converting more than a third of its online critics to fans. *'Today a single customer complaint from someone with influence can have more impact on your company's reputation than your best marketing'*, said Jason Duty, head of Dell's global social outreach service.

THE SUPPLY NETWORK PERSPECTIVE

A supply network perspective means setting an operation in the context of all the other operations with which it interacts, some of which are its suppliers and its customers. Materials, parts, other information, ideas and sometimes people all flow through the network of customer–supplier relationships formed by all these operations. On its supply side, an operation has its suppliers of parts, or information, or services. These suppliers themselves have their own suppliers who in turn could also have suppliers, and so on. On the demand side, the operation has customers. These customers might not be the final consumers of the operation's products or services; they might have their own set of customers. On the supply side, is a group of operations that directly supply the operation; these are often called first-tier suppliers. They are supplied by second-tier suppliers. However, some second-tier suppliers may also supply an operation directly, thus missing out a link in the network. Similarly, on the demand side of the network, 'first-tier' customers are the main customer group for the operation. These in turn supply 'second-tier' customers, although again the operation may at times supply second-tier customers directly. The suppliers and customers who have direct contact with an operation are called its immediate supply network, whereas all the operations which form the network of suppliers' suppliers and customers' customers, etc., are called the total supply network.

Figure 6.2 illustrates the total supply network for two operations. First is a plastic homeware (kitchen bowls, etc.) manufacturer. On the demand side it supplies products to wholesalers who supply retail outlets. However, it also supplies some retailers directly, bypassing a stage in the network – not an uncommon situation. As products flow from suppliers to customers, orders and information flow the other way from customers to suppliers. It is a two-way process with goods flowing one way and information flowing the other. But do not think that only manufacturers can be part of supply networks. The second illustration in Figure 6.2 shows a supply network centred on a shopping mall. It also has suppliers and customers who themselves have their own suppliers and customers.

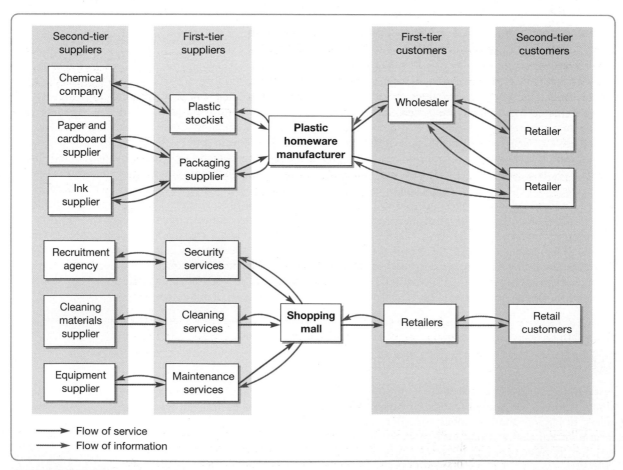

Figure 6.2 Operations network for a plastic homeware company and a shopping mall

Why consider the whole supply network?

So why is it important to stand back and look at the whole (or a large part of) a supply network rather than an individual operation? There are three reasons:

It helps an understanding of competitiveness Immediate customers and immediate suppliers, quite understandably, are the main concern for companies. Yet sometimes they need to look beyond these immediate contacts to understand *why* customers and suppliers act as they do. Any operation has only two options if it wants to understand its ultimate customers' needs at the end of the network. It can rely on all the intermediate customers and customers' customers, etc., which form the links in the network between the company and its end customers. Alternatively, it can look beyond its immediate customers and suppliers. Relying on one's immediate network is seen as putting too much faith in someone else's judgement of things which are central to an organization's own competitive health.

It helps identify significant links in the network Not everyone in a supply network has the same degree of influence over the performance of the network as a whole. Some operations contribute more to the performance objectives that are valued by end customers. So an analysis of networks needs to understand the downstream and the upstream operations which contribute most to end customer service. For example, the important end customers for domestic plumbing parts and appliances are the installers and service companies who deal directly with consumers. They are supplied by 'stock holders' who must have all parts in stock and deliver them fast. Suppliers of parts to the stock holders can best contribute to their end customers' competitiveness partly by offering a short delivery lead time but mainly through dependable delivery. The key players in this example are the stock holders. The best way of winning end customer business in this case is to give the stock holder prompt delivery, which helps keep costs down while providing high availability of parts.

It helps focus on long-term issues There are times when circumstances render parts of a supply network weaker than its adjacent links. High street music stores, for example, have been largely displaced by music streaming and downloading services. A long-term supply network view would involve constantly examining technology and market changes to see how each operation in the supply networks might be affected.

> **✳ Operations principle**
>
> A supply network perspective helps to make sense of competitive, relationship, and longer-term operations issues.

Design decisions in supply networks

The supply network view is useful because it prompts three particularly important design decisions. These are the most strategic of all the design decisions treated in this part of the book. It is necessary to understand them at this point, however, because, as well as having a particularly significant impact on the strategy of the organization, they set the context in which all other process design decisions are made. The three decisions are:

1 How should the network be configured?
2 Where should each part of the network be located? The location decision.
3 What physical capacity should each part of the network have? The long-term capacity management decision.

In this chapter we deal with these three related strategic decisions. Note, however, that all three of these decisions rely on forecasts of future demand which the supplement to this chapter explores in more detail. Also, in Chapter 13 we will cover the more operational day-to-day issues of managing operations networks.

CONFIGURING THE SUPPLY NETWORK

'Configuring' a supply network means determining its overall pattern. This includes two main sets of decisions. First, what should be the pattern, shape or arrangement of the various operations that make up the supply network? Second, how much of the network should a specific operation own? This may be called the outsourcing, vertical integration, or the do-or-buy decision.

Changing the shape of the supply network

Even when an operation does not directly own, or even control, other operations in its network, it may still wish to change the shape of the network. This involves attempting to manage network behaviour by reconfiguring the network so as to change the scope of the activities performed in each operation and the nature of the relationships between them. Reconfiguring a supply network sometimes involves parts of the operation being merged – not necessarily in the sense of a change of ownership of any parts of an operation, but rather in the way responsibility is allocated for carrying out activities. The most common example of network reconfiguration has come through the many companies that have recently reduced the number of direct suppliers. The complexity of dealing with many hundreds of suppliers may both be expensive for an operation and (sometimes more important) prevent the operation from developing a close relationship with a supplier. It is not easy to be close to hundreds of different suppliers.

Disintermediation

Another trend in some supply networks is that of companies within a network bypassing customers or suppliers to make contact directly with customers' customers or suppliers' suppliers. 'Cutting out the middle men' in this way is called disintermediation. An obvious example of this is the way the internet has allowed some suppliers to 'disintermediate' traditional retailers in supplying goods and services to consumers. So, for example, many services in the travel industry that used to be sold through retail outlets (travel agents) are now also available direct from the suppliers. The option of purchasing the individual components of a vacation through the websites of the airline, hotel, car-hire operation, etc., is now easier for consumers. Of course, they may still wish to purchase an 'assembled' product from retail travel agents which can have the advantage of convenience. Nevertheless the process of disintermediation has developed new linkages in the supply network.

Co-opetition

One approach to thinking about supply networks sees any business as being surrounded by four types of players: suppliers, customers, competitors and complementors. Complementors enable one's products or services to be valued more by customers because they can also have the complementor's products or services, as opposed to having yours alone. Competitors are the opposite: they make customers value your product or service less when they can have their product or service, rather than yours alone. Competitors can also be complementors and vice versa. For example, adjacent restaurants may see themselves as competitors for customers' business. A customer standing outside and wanting a meal will choose between the two of them. Yet in another way they are complementors. Would that customer have come to this part of town unless there was more than one restaurant to choose from? Restaurants, theatres, art galleries, and tourist attractions generally, all cluster together in a form of co-operation to increase the total size of their joint market. It is important to distinguish between the way companies co-operate in increasing the total size of a market and the way in which they then compete for a share of that market. Customers and suppliers, it is argued, should have 'symmetric' roles. Harnessing the value of suppliers is just as important as listening to the needs of customers. Destroying value in a supplier in order to create it in a customer does not increase the value of the network as a whole. So, pressurizing suppliers will not necessarily add value. In the long term it creates value for the total network to find ways of increasing value for suppliers and well as customers. All the players in the network, whether they are customers, suppliers, competitors or complementors, can be both friends and enemies at different times. The term used to capture this idea is 'co-opetition'.

Outsourcing

No single business does everything that is required to produce its products and services. Bakers do not grow wheat or even mill it into flour. Banks do not usually do their own credit checking – they retain the services of specialist credit checking agencies that have the specialized information systems and expertise to do it better. This process is called outsourcing (also known as the do-or-buy, or the vertical integration decision) and it has become an important issue for most businesses. This is because, although most companies have always outsourced some of their activities, a larger proportion of direct activities are now being bought from suppliers. Also many indirect processes are now being outsourced. This is often referred to as business process outsourcing (BPO). Financial service companies in particular are outsourcing some of their more routine back-office processes. In a similar way, many processes within the human resource function, from simple payroll services through to more complex training and development processes, are being outsourced to specialist companies. The processes may still be physically located where they were before, but the staff and technology are managed by the outsourcing service provider. The reason for doing this is often primarily to reduce cost. However, there can sometimes also be significant gains in the quality and flexibility of service offered. *'People talk a lot about looking beyond cost cutting when it comes to outsourcing companies' human resource functions'*, says Jim Madden, CEO of Exult, the California-based specialist outsourcing company. *'I don't believe any company will sign up for this [outsourcing] without cost reduction being part of it, but for the clients whose human resource functions we manage, such as BP, and Bank of America, it is not just about saving money.'*

The outsourcing debate is just part of a far larger issue which will shape the fundamental nature of any business. Namely, what should the scope of the business be? In other words, what should it do itself and what should it buy in? This is often referred to as the 'do-or-buy decision' when individual components or activities are being considered, or 'vertical integration' when it is the ownership of whole operations that are being decided. Vertical integration is the extent to which an organization owns the network of which it is a part. It usually involves an organization assessing the wisdom of acquiring suppliers or customers. And different companies, even in the same industry, can make very different decisions over how much and where in the network they want to be. Figure 6.3 illustrates the (simplified) supply network for the wind turbine power generation industry. Original equipment

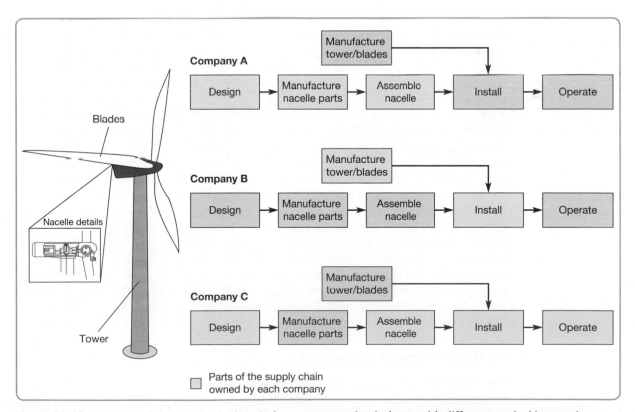

Figure 6.3 Three companies operating in the wind power generation industry with different vertical integration positions

manufacturers (OEMs) assemble the wind turbine nacelle (the nacelle houses the generator and gearbox). Towers and blades are often built to the OEM's specifications, either in-house or by outside suppliers. Installing wind turbines involves assembling the nacelle, tower and blades on site, erecting the tower and connecting to the electricity network. The extent of vertical integration varies by company and component. The three companies illustrated in Figure 6.3 have all chosen different vertical integration strategies. Company A is primarily a nacelle designer and manufacturer that also makes the parts. Company B is primarily an installer that also makes the tower and blades (but buys in the nacelle itself). Company C is primarily an operator that generates electricity and also designs and assembles the nacelles as well as installing the whole tower (but it outsources the manufacture of the nacelle parts, tower and blades).

Making the outsourcing or vertical integration decision

Whether it is referred to as do-or-buy, vertical integration or no vertical integration, in-house or outsourced supply, the choice facing operations is rarely simple. Organizations in different circumstances with different objectives are likely to take different decisions. Yet the question itself is relatively simple, even if the decision itself is not: 'Does in-house or outsourced supply in a particular set of circumstances give the appropriate performance objectives that it requires to compete more effectively in its markets?' For example, if the main performance objectives for an operation are dependable delivery and meeting short-term changes in customers' delivery requirements, the key question should be: 'How does in-house or outsourcing give better dependability and delivery flexibility performance?' This means judging two sets of opposing factors – those which give the potential to improve performance, and those which work against this potential being realized. Table 6.1 summarizes some arguments for in-house supply and outsourcing in terms of each performance objective.

> * **Operations principle**
>
> Assessing the advisability of outsourcing should include how it impacts on relevant performance objectives.

Outsourcing as a strategic decision

Although the effect of outsourcing on the operation's performance objective is important, there are other factors that companies take into account when deciding if outsourcing an activity is a sensible option. For example, if an activity has long-term strategic importance to a company, it is unlikely to outsource it. For instance, a retailer might choose to keep the design and development of its website in-house even though specialists could perform the activity at less cost because it plans to move into web-based retailing at some point in the future. Nor would a company usually outsource an activity where it had specialized skills or knowledge. For example, a company making laser printers may have built up specialized knowledge in the production of sophisticated laser drives. This capability may allow it to introduce product or process innovations in the future. It would be foolish to 'give away' such capability. After these two more strategic factors have been considered, the company's operations performance can be taken into account. Obviously if its operation's performance is already superior to any potential supplier, it would unlikely to outsource the activity. But also even if its performance was currently below that of potential suppliers, it may not outsource the activity if it feels that it could significantly improve its performance. Figure 6.4 illustrates this decision logic.

> * **Operations principle**
>
> Assessing the advisability of outsourcing should include consideration of the strategic importance of the activity and the operation's relative performance.

Outsourcing and offshoring

Two supply network strategies that are often confused are those of outsourcing and offshoring. Outsourcing means deciding to buy in products or services rather than perform the activities in-house. Offshoring means obtaining products and services from operations that are based outside one's own country. Of course, one may both outsource and offshore as illustrated in

Table 6.1 How in-house and outsourced supply may affect an operation's performance objectives

Performance objective	'Do it yourself' in-house supply	'Buy it in' outsourced supply
Quality	The origins of any quality problems usually easier to trace in-house and improvement can be more immediate but can be some risk of complacency.	Supplier may have specialized knowledge and more experience, also may be motivated through market pressures, but communication more difficult.
Speed	Can mean synchronized schedules which speed throughput of materials and information, but if the operation has external customers, internal customers may be low priority.	Speed of response can be built into the supply contract where commercial pressures will encourage good performance, but there may be significant transport/delivery delays.
Dependability	Easier communications can help dependability, but, if the operation also has external customers, internal customers may receive low priority.	Late delivery penalties in the supply contract can encourage good delivery performance, but organizational barriers may inhibit in communication.
Flexibility	Closeness to the real needs of a business can alert the in-house operation to required changes, but the ability to respond may be limited by the scale and scope of internal operations.	Outsource suppliers may be larger with wider capabilities than in-house suppliers and more ability to respond to changes, but may have to balance conflicting needs of different customers.
Cost	In-house operations do not have to make the margin required by outside suppliers so the business can capture the profits which would otherwise be given to the supplier, but relatively low volumes may mean that it is difficult to gain economies of scale or the benefits of process innovation.	Probably the main reason why outsourcing is so popular. Outsourced companies can achieve economies of scale and they are motivated to reduce their own costs because it directly impacts on their profits, but costs of communication and coordination with supplier need to be taken into account.

Figure 6.4 The decision logic of outsourcing

SHORT CASE   HTC moves downstream[2]

A few years ago, even mobile communication enthusiasts might not have heard of Taiwan's HTC. Yet the firm has long been one of the most important suppliers to better-known brands. HTC was an 'original design manufacturer', or ODM, developing and building high-end 'smart' phones for better-known Western mobile operators, including Verizon and Orange. And it's a good business. HTC had built an enviable reputation as an innovative and reliable supplier of sophisticated hand-held computers and mobile phones. However, Peter Chou, the Chief

Executive Officer of HTC, believed that the industry was changing. Regarded by many as a pioneer and visionary in the mobile industry, Chou could see the market becoming more difficult. Although still a profitable business, the margins from supplying other brands were shrinking. Chinese suppliers, with their lower labour costs, were providing stiff competition and customers had started to look for rival suppliers (which would increase their bargaining power). *'We needed to establish a new competency before we got into trouble'*, explained Mr Chou. The way ahead, the company decided, was to move forward in the supply network and start developing their own brand. This new supply network strategy meant HTC had to develop new capabilities. More talent was recruited to strengthen its in-house design and software skills so that HTC products would have a unique look and feel. But the strategy was not without its risks. It meant investing in the marketing and sales operations that had, up till then, been the province of their customers. HTC also lost of much of its existing business, because some customers were reluctant to do business with a budding rival. Just as significant, the culture and objectives of the company had to move from

Source: Shutterstock.com/Dragon Images

'efficiently implementing what had been decided by one's customers' to that of *'constantly developing radical and innovative new ideas'*.

Figure 6.5. Offshoring is very closely related to outsourcing and the motives for each may be similar. Offshoring to a lower cost region of the world is usually done to reduce an operation's overall costs, as is outsourcing to a supplier who has greater expertise or scale or both.[3]

Critical commentary

In many instances there has been fierce opposition to companies outsourcing some of their processes. Trade unions often point out that the only reason that outsourcing companies can do the job at lower cost is that they either reduce salaries, reduce working conditions, or both. Furthermore, they say, flexibility is only achieved by reducing job security. Employees who were once part of a large and secure corporation could find themselves as far less secure employees of a less benevolent employer with a philosophy of permanent cost-cutting. Even some proponents of outsourcing are quick to point out the problems. There can be significant obstacles, including understandable resistance from staff who find themselves 'outsourced'. Some companies have also been guilty of 'outsourcing a problem'. In other words, having failed to manage a process well themselves, they ship it out rather than face up to why the process was problematic in the first place. There is also evidence that, although long-term costs can be brought down when a process is outsourced, there may be an initial period when costs rise as both sides learn how to manage the new arrangement.

WHERE SHOULD AN OPERATION BE LOCATED?

There is an old saying in retail operations management, *'There are three important things in retailing – location, location and location'*, and any retailing operation knows exactly what that means. Get the location wrong and it can have a significant impact on profits, or service. In fact the same is true for all types of operation. For example, mislocating a fire service station

Figure 6.5 Offshoring and outsourcing are related but different

can delay fire crews getting to the fires; siting a data centre where potential staff with appropriate skills will not live will affect its performance. Location decisions will usually have an effect on an operation's costs as well as its ability to serve its customers (and therefore its revenues). Also, location decisions, once taken, are difficult to undo. The costs of moving an operation can be hugely expensive and the risks of inconveniencing customers very high. No operation wants to move very often.

Reasons for location decisions

Not all operations can logically justify their location. Some are where they are for historical reasons. Yet even the operations that are 'there because they're there' are implicitly making a decision not to move. Presumably their assumption is that the cost and disruption involved in changing location would outweigh any potential benefits of a new location. When operations do move, it is usually for one or both of two reasons – changes in demand or changes in supply.

Changes in demand A change in location may be prompted by customer demand shifting. For example, as garment manufacture moved to Asia, suppliers of zips, threads, etc., started to follow them. Changes in the volume of demand can also prompt relocation. To meet higher demand, an operation could expand its existing site, or choose a larger site in another location, or keep its existing location and find a second location for an additional operation; the last two options will involve a location decision. High-visibility operations may not have the choice of expanding on the same site to meet rising demand. A dry cleaning service may attract only marginally more business by expanding an existing site because it offers a local, and therefore convenient, service. Finding a new location for an additional operation is probably its only option for expansion.

Changes in supply The other stimulus for relocation is changes in the cost, or availability, of the supply of inputs to the operation. For example, a mining or oil company will need to relocate as the minerals it is extracting become depleted. The reason why so many software companies are located in India is the availability of talented, well-educated, but relatively cheap staff.

The objectives of the location decision

The aim of the location decision is to achieve an appropriate balance between three related objectives:

- The spatially variable costs of the operation (spatially variable means that something changes with geographical location).

Finding a suitable site for any operation can be a political as well as an economic problem. It certainly was when Tata, the Indian company, unveiled their plans for the Nano. Named the '1 lakh' car (in India 1 lakh means 100,000), it was to be the cheapest car in the world, with the basic model priced at 100,000 rupees, or $2,500, excluding taxes. The price was about half of existing low cost cars. And the site chosen by Tata was equally bold. It was to be made at Singur, in the Indian state of West Bengal. Although the Communist Party had ruled the state for four decades, the West Bengal government was keen to encourage the Nano plant. It would bring much needed jobs and send a message that the state welcomed inward investment. In fact, the state had won the plant against stiff competition from rival states.

Source: Getty Images

Controversially, the state government had expropriated land for the factory using an old law dating from 1894, which requires private owners sell land for a 'public purpose'. The government justified this action by pointing out that over 13,000 people had some kind of claim to parts of the land required for new plant and Tata could not be expected to negotiate, one by one, with all of them. Also financial compensation was being offered at significantly above market rates. Unfortunately about 2,250 people refused to accept the offered compensation. The political opposition organized mass protests in support of the farmers who did not want to move. They blocked roads, threatened staff and even assaulted an employee of a Tata supplier. In response, Ratan Tata, chairman of the Tata group, threatened to move the site of the Nano plant from the state if the company really was not wanted, even though the company had already invested 15 billion rupees in the project. Eventually, exasperated with being caught in the 'political crossfire', Tata said it would abandon its factory in the state. Instead, the company selected a location in Gujarat, one of India's most industrialized states, which quickly approved even more land than the West Bengal site.

However, the delay and uncertainty over the location decision took their toll and things got worse. Moving the production plant from one state to another was traumatic, and as Mr Tata, then the boss of the company, admitted, 'after that we never really got our act together'. All the company's plans had to be pushed back to cope with moving the location of the plant. It was rushed into operation and eventually opened in the summer of 2010, but not enough cars came off the production line to meet a huge surge of early orders for the new car. Production was increased, but then orders fell away. Some commentators say that, distracted by the location problem, Tata devoted too little attention to marketing and distributing the new car. If that wasn't enough, a few early production model cars caught fire, raising fears about the Nano's safety.

- The service the operation is able to provide to its customers.
- The revenue potential of the operation.

In for-profit organizations the last two objectives are related. The assumption is that the better the service the operation can provide to its customers, the better will be its potential to attract custom and therefore generate revenue. In not-for-profit organizations, revenue potential might not be a relevant objective and so cost and customer service are often taken as the twin objectives of location. In making decisions about where to locate an operation, operations managers are concerned with minimizing spatially variable costs and maximizing revenue/customer service. Location affects both of these but not

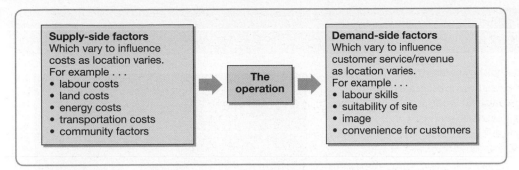

Figure 6.6 Supply-side and demand-side factors in location decisions

always equally. For example, customers may not care very much where some products are made, so location is unlikely to affect revenues significantly. However, the costs could be very greatly affected by location. Services, on the other hand, often have both costs and revenues affected by location. The location decision for any operation is determined by the relative strength of supply-side and demand-side factors (*see* Fig. 6.6).

Supply-side influences

Labour costs The costs of employing people with particular skills can vary between different areas in any country, but are likely to be more significant when international comparisons are made. Labour costs can be expressed in two ways. The 'hourly cost' is what firms have to pay workers on average per hour. However, the 'unit cost' is an indication of the labour cost per unit of production. This includes the effects both of productivity differences between countries and of differing currency exchange rates. Exchange rate variation can cause unit costs to change dramatically over time. Yet in spite of this, labour costs exert a major influence on the location decision, especially in some industries such as clothing, where labour costs as a proportion of total costs are relatively high.

Land costs The cost of acquiring the site itself is sometimes a relevant factor in choosing a location. Land and rental costs vary between countries, cities and districts. A retail operation, when choosing 'high street' sites, will pay a particular level of rent only if it believes it can generate a certain level of revenue from the site.

Energy costs Operations which use large amounts of energy, such as aluminium smelters, can be influenced in their location decisions by the availability of relatively inexpensive energy. This may be direct, as in the availability of hydroelectric generation in an area, or indirect, such as low-cost coal which can be used to generate inexpensive electricity.

Transportation costs Transportation costs include both the cost of transporting inputs from their source to the site of the operation, and the cost of transporting outputs to customers. Whereas almost all operations are concerned to some extent with the former, not all operations transport goods to customers; rather, customers come to them (for example, hotels). Even for operations that do transport their goods to customers (most manufacturers, for example), we consider transportation as a supply-side factor because as location changes, transportation costs also change. Proximity to sources of *supply* dominates the location decision where the cost of transporting input materials is high or difficult. Food processing and other agricultural-based activities, for example, are often carried out close to growing areas. Conversely, transportation to *customers* dominates location decisions where this is expensive or difficult. Civil engineering projects, for example, are constructed mainly where they will be needed.

Community factors Community factors are those influences on an operation's costs which derive from the social, political and economic environment of its site. These include such things as local tax rates, government financial assistance and planning assistance, political

Similar companies with similar needs often cluster together in the same geographical area. Why? For a number of reasons. Michael Porter of Harvard Business School, the famous strategy professor and an authority on industrial clusters, says that firms' geographical proximity helps to promote economies of scale, learning and productivity, as well as boosting innovation and encouraging the growth of new supplier firms. This is a winning combination, according to Professor Porter, and accounts for the existence of such clusters around the world. Here are just a few examples:

Financial services. These are clustered in a relatively few centres globally, even after the recent turbulence in financial services. London, New York, Hong Kong, Singapore, Tokyo, Chicago and Zurich dominate the industry. According to Deutsche Bank: *'Big is beautiful – and will remain so.'* It is far easier to build on existing market strength than start afresh. Banks have to trade with each other and, even in an increasingly globalized world, being close helps. Combine this with good regulation and free markets and it becomes a significant competitive advantage.

High-tech Industries. These industries provide one of the most famous location clusters in the area south of San Francisco known as Silicon Valley, probably the most important intellectual and commercial hub of technological innovation. Yet other locations are developing. For example, Bangalore in India is fast becoming a cluster for the computer industry; because of the ready availability of well-educated, low-cost English-speaking software technicians, it has now attracted more, and more sophisticated, business. Something similar is happening in Shanghai in China. *'Over the next ten years, China will become a ferociously formidable competitor for companies that run the entire length of the technology food chain'*, says Michael J. Moritz, owner of a Californian venture-capital firm.

Even in higher cost countries, new clusters are growing. One is around 'silicon roundabout', in East London, where old Victorian warehouses are home to a growing

Source: Shutterstock.com/Mironov

number of web and technology start-ups, working on everything from online game design to streaming music services and general web services (Google has offices there). The history of start-ups in the area stretches back a couple of decades because of relatively low office rents, a creative atmosphere generated by an influx of artists and designers, London's world-class universities, art galleries and the kind of cafes, bars, shops and clubs that help attract creative staff. So, again the cluster developed for clear reasons, then grew because size and focus attract other companies.

Racing cars. These are mostly made in Britain, in particular in the area around Oxfordshire and Northamptonshire. Most Formula 1 teams are based in Britain, as are many IndyCar teams. Even those who are not are likely to use British services. Motorsport is a flourishing cluster with around 4,500 firms working at building, maintaining, modifying and restoring cars, making engines and components, and providing technical and management services. Almost everything a racing team needs can be found without leaving the area.

stability and corruption, language, local amenities (schools, theatres, shops, etc.), availability of support and supply infrastructure, labour relations, environmental regulations and waste disposal, planning procedures, etc.

Demand-side influences

Labour skills The abilities of a local labour force can have an effect on customer reaction to the products or services which the operation produces. For example, 'science parks' are usually located close to universities because they hope to attract companies who are interested in using the skills available at the university.

The suitability of the site itself Different sites may have different intrinsic characteristics which can affect an operation's ability to serve customers and generate revenue. For examvple, locate a luxury resort hotel next to a beach, surrounded by waving palm trees and overlooking a picturesque bay and the hotel is very attractive to its customers. Move it a few kilometres away into the centre of an industrial estate and it rapidly loses its attraction.

Image of the location Some locations are firmly associated in customers' minds with a particular image. Suits from Savile Row (the centre of the up-market bespoke tailoring district in London) may be no better than high-quality suits made elsewhere but, by locating its operation there, a tailor has probably enhanced its reputation and therefore its revenue. The product and fashion design houses of Milan and the financial services in the City of London also enjoy a reputation shaped partly by that of their location.

Convenience for customers This is often the most important demand-side factor. Locating a general hospital, for instance, in the middle of the countryside may have many advantages for its staff, and even perhaps for its costs, but it clearly would be very inconvenient to its customers (patients). So, hospitals are usually located close to centres of demand. Similarly with other public services and restaurants, stores, banks, petrol filling stations, etc., location determines the effort to which customers have to go in order to use the operation.

Location techniques

Although operations managers must exercise considerable judgement in the choice of alternative locations, there are some systematic and quantitative techniques which can help the decision process. We describe two here – the weighted-score method and the centre-of-gravity method.

Weighted-score method

The procedure involves, first of all, identifying the criteria which will be used to evaluate the various locations. Second, it involves establishing the relative importance of each criterion and giving weighting factors to them. Third, it means rating each location according to each criterion. The scale of the score is arbitrary. In our example we shall use 0 to 100, where 0 represents the worst possible score and 100 the best.

Worked example

An Irish company which prints and makes specialist packaging materials for the pharmaceutical industry has decided to build a new factory somewhere in the Benelux countries so as to provide a speedy service for its customers in continental Europe. In order to choose a site it has decided to evaluate all options against a number of criteria, as follows:

- the cost of the site;
- the rate of local property taxation;
- the availability of suitable skills in the local labour force;
- the site's access to the motorway network;
- the site's access to the airport;
- the potential of the site for future expansion.

After consultation with its property agents the company identifies three sites which seem to be broadly acceptable. These are known as sites A, B and C. The company also investigates each site and draws up the weighted-score table shown in Table 6.2. It is important to remember that the scores shown in Table 6.2 are those which the manager has given as an indication of how each site meets the company's needs specifically. Nothing is necessarily being implied regarding any intrinsic worth of the locations. Likewise, the weightings are an indication of how important the company finds each criterion in the circumstances it finds itself. The 'value' of a site for each criterion is then calculated by multiplying its score by the weightings for each criterion. For location A, its score for the 'cost-of-site' criterion is 80 and the weighting of this criterion is 4, so its value is $80 \times 4 = 320$. All these values are then summed for each site to obtain its total weighted score.

Table 6.2 Weighted-score method for the three sites

Criteria	Importance weighting	Scores		
		Sites		
		A	B	C
Cost of the site	4	80	65	60
Local taxes	2	20	50	80
Skills availability	1	80	60	40
Access to motorways	1	50	60	40
Access to airport	1	20	60	70
Potential for expansion	1	75	40	55
Total weighted scores		585	580	605*

*Preferred option.

Table 6.2 indicates that location C has the highest total weighted score and therefore would be the preferred choice. Yet location C has the lowest score on the most important criterion – cost of the site. The high total scores that it achieves in other criteria, however, outweigh this deficiency. If, on examination of this table, a company cannot accept what appears to be an inconsistency, then either the weights which have been given to each criterion, or the scores that have been allocated, do not truly reflect the company's preference.

The centre-of-gravity method

The centre-of-gravity method is used to find a location which minimizes transportation costs. It is based on the idea that all possible locations have a 'value' which is the sum of all transportation costs to and from that location. The best location, the one which minimizes costs, is represented by what in a physical analogy would be the weighted centre of gravity of all points to and from which goods are transported. So, for example, two suppliers, each sending 20 tonnes of parts per month to a factory, are located at points A and B. The factory must then assemble these parts and send them to one customer located at point C. Since point C receives twice as many tonnes as points A and B (transportation cost is assumed to be directly related to the tonnes of goods shipped), it has twice the weighting of points A or B. The lowest transportation cost location for the factory is at the centre of gravity of a (weightless) board where the two suppliers' and one customer's locations are represented to scale and have weights equivalent to the weightings of the number of tonnes they send or receive.

A company which operates four out-of-town garden centres has decided to keep all its stocks of products in a single warehouse. Each garden centre, instead of keeping large stocks of products, will fax its orders to the warehouse staff who will then deliver replenishment stocks to each garden centre as necessary. The location of each garden centre is shown on the map in Figure 6.7.

Figure 6.7 Centre-of-gravity location for the garden centre warehouse

A reference grid is superimposed over the map. The centre-of-gravity coordinates of the lowest cost location for the warehouse, $\bar{x}$ and $\bar{y}$, are given by the formulae:

$$\bar{x} = \frac{\sum x_i V_i}{\sum V_i}$$

and

$$\bar{y} = \frac{\sum y_i V_i}{\sum V_i}$$

where

x_i = the x coordinate of source or destination i
y_i = the y coordinate of source or destination i
V_i = the amount to be shipped to or from source or destination i.

Each of the garden centres is of a different size and has different sales volumes. In terms of the number of truckloads of products sold each week, Table 6.3 shows the sales of the four centres.

Table 6.3 The weekly demand levels (in truckloads) at each of the four garden centres

	Sales per week (truck loads)
Garden centre A	5
Garden centre B	10
Garden centre C	12
Garden centre D	8
Total	35

In this case

$$\bar{x} = \frac{(1 \times 5) + (5 \times 10) + (5 \times 12) + (9 \times 8)}{35}$$

$$= 5.34$$

and

$$\bar{y} = \frac{(2 \times 5) + (3 \times 10) + (1 \times 12) + (4 \times 8)}{35}$$

$$= 2.4$$

So the minimum cost location for the warehouse is at point (5.34, 2.4) as shown in Figure 6.7. That is, at least, theoretically. In practice, the optimum location might also be influenced by other factors such as the transportation network. The technique does go some way, however, towards providing an indication of the area in which the company should be looking for sites for its warehouse.

LONG-TERM CAPACITY MANAGEMENT

The next set of supply network decisions concern the size or capacity of each part of the network. Here we shall treat capacity in a general long-term sense. The specific issues involved in measuring and adjusting capacity in the medium and short terms are examined later (see Chapter 11).

The optimum capacity level

Most organizations need to decide on the size (in terms of capacity) of each of their facilities. An air-conditioning unit company, for example, might operate plants each of which has a capacity (at normal product mix) of 800 units per week. At activity levels below this, the average cost of producing each unit will increase because the fixed costs of the factory are being covered by fewer units produced. The total production costs of the factory have some elements which are fixed – they will be incurred irrespective of how much, or little, the factory produces. Other costs are variable – they are the costs incurred by the factory for each unit it produces. Between them, the fixed and variable costs comprise the total cost at any output level. Dividing this cost by the output level itself will give the theoretical average cost of producing units at that output rate. This is the green line shown as the theoretical unit cost curve for the 800-unit plant in Figure 6.8. However, the actual average cost curve may be different from this line for a number of reasons:

> **✳ Operations principle**
>
> All types of operation exhibit economy of scale effects where operating costs reduce as the scale of capacity increases.

- All fixed costs are not incurred at one time as the factory starts to operate. Rather they occur at many points (called fixed cost breaks) as volume increases. This makes the theoretically smooth average cost curve more discontinuous.
- Output levels may be increased above the theoretical capacity, by using prolonged overtime, for example.
- There may be less obvious cost penalties of operating at levels close to or above its nominal capacity. For example, long periods of overtime may reduce productivity levels and cost more in extra payments to staff; operating equipment for long periods with reduced maintenance may increase the chances of breakdown, and so on. This usually means that average costs start to increase after a point which may be lower than theoretical capacity.

Figure 6.8 Unit cost curves for individual plants of varying capacities and the unit cost curve for this type of plant as its capacity varies

The blue dotted line in Figure 6.8 shows this effect. The two other blue lines show similar curves for a 600-unit plant and a 1,000-unit plant. Figure 6.8 also shows that a similar relationship occurs between the average cost curves for plants of increasing size. As the nominal capacity of the plants increases, the lowest cost points at first reduce. There are two main reasons for this:

- The fixed costs of an operation do not increase proportionately as its capacity increases. An 800-unit plant has less than twice the fixed costs of a 400-unit plant.
- Capital costs do not increase proportionately to capacity. An 800-unit plant costs less to build than twice the cost of a 400-unit plant.

These two factors, taken together, are often referred to as economies of scale. However, above a certain size, the lowest cost point may increase. In Figure 6.8 this happens with plants above 800 units capacity because of what are called diseconomies of scale, two of which are particularly important. First, transportation costs can be high for large operations. For example, if a manufacturer supplies its global market from one major plant in Denmark, materials may have to be brought in to, and shipped from, several countries. Second, complexity costs increase as size increases. The communications and coordination effort necessary to manage an operation tends to increase faster than capacity. Although not seen as a direct cost, it can nevertheless be very significant.

> **✻ Operations principle**
>
> Diseconomies of scale increase operating costs above a certain level of capacity, resulting in a minimum cost level of capacity.

Scale of capacity and the demand–capacity balance

Large units of capacity also have some disadvantages when the capacity of the operation is being changed to match changing demand. For example, suppose that the air-conditioning unit manufacturer forecasts demand increase over the next three years, as shown in Figure 6.9, to level off at around 2,400 units a week. If the company seeks to satisfy all demand by building three plants, each of 800 units capacity, the company will have substantial amounts of over-capacity for much of the period when demand is increasing. Over-capacity means low capacity utilization, which in turn means higher unit costs. If the company builds smaller plants, say 400-unit plants, there will still be over-capacity but to a lesser extent, which means higher capacity utilization and possibly lower costs.

> **✻ Operations principle**
>
> Changing capacity using large units of capacity reduces the chance of achieving demand–capacity balance.

Figure 6.9 The scale of capacity increments affects the utilization of capacity

---

SHORT CASE — Economies of scale in heart surgery and shipping[6]

Don't think that the idea of economies of scale only applies to manufacturing operations. It's a universal concept. Here are just two examples.

Narayana Hrudayalaya hospital

In the 1,000-bed Narayana Hrudayalaya hospital, in Bangalore, India, Dr Devi Shetty (who has been called the 'Henry Ford' of heart surgery) has created what, according to *Forbes* magazine, is the world's largest heart factory. It is a radical new approach, he says, and proves that economies of scale can transform the cost of cardiology. Dr Shetty calls his approach the 'Wal-Martization'

of surgery – referring to the high-volume approach of the world's largest supermarket chain, Wal-Mart. The hospital has 42 surgeons who perform 6,000 heart operations each year, including 3,000 on children. This makes the hospital the busiest facility of its type in the world. And it's needed: it is estimated that India requires 2.5 million heart operations every year yet only 90,000 are performed.

'*It's a numbers game,*' said Dr Shetty, who has performed 15,000 heart operations. '*Surgeons are technicians. The more practice they get, the more specialized they become and the better the results.*' The result is that costs are slashed and the hospital can be profitable even though many patients are poor. The hospital's charges for open-heart surgery are, on average, a tenth of the cost of the cheapest procedures in the United States. But even then, treatment is too expensive for many, so wealthier patients are charged more to subsidize the poorest.

The *Eleonora Maersk*

The *Eleonora Maersk* is one of seven ships in her class that are owned by Maersk Lines, the world's biggest container-shipping company. At almost 400m long (the length of four football pitches), it is among the biggest ships ever built. The *Eleonora Maersk* is also powerful: it has the largest internal-combustion engine ever built, as powerful as 1,000 family cars, which enables it to move all its cargo from China to Europe in just over three weeks. Yet the ship is so automated that it requires only 13 people to crew it. On board, the ship can carry 15,000 20-foot containers, each one of which can hold 70,000 T-shirts. It is these economies of scale that allow a T-shirt made in China to be sent to the Netherlands for just 2.5 cents. And the economies of scale involved in building and running these ships means that things will get bigger still. Hoping to drive costs down further, the ship's owners have ordered 20 even larger ships with a capacity of 18,000 20-foot containers, costing $200 million each.

Balancing capacity

As we discussed earlier (see Chapter 1), all operations are made up of separate processes, each of which will itself have its own capacity. So, for example, the 800-unit air-conditioning plant may not only assemble the products but may also manufacture the parts from which they are made, pack, store and load them in a warehouse and distribute them to customers. If demand is 800 units per week, not only must the assembly process have a capacity sufficient for this output, but the parts manufacturing processes, warehouse and distribution fleet of trucks must also have sufficient capacity. For the network to operate efficiently, all its stages must have the same capacity. If not, the capacity of the network as a whole will be limited to the capacity of its slowest link.

The timing of capacity change

Changing the capacity of an operation is not just a matter of deciding on the best size of a capacity increment. The operation also needs to decide when to bring 'on-stream' new capacity. For example, Figure 6.10 shows the forecast demand for the new air-conditioning unit. The company has decided to build 400-unit-per-week plants in order to meet the growth in demand for its new product. In deciding *when* the new plants are to be introduced, the company must choose a position somewhere between two extreme strategies:

> ✱ **Operations principle**
> Capacity-leading strategies increase opportunities to meet demand.

Figure 6.10 (a) Capacity-leading and capacity-lagging strategies. (b) Smoothing with inventories means using the excess capacity in one period to produce inventory that supplies the under-capacity period

- capacity leads demand – timing the introduction of capacity in such a way that there is always sufficient capacity to meet forecast demand;
- capacity lags demand – timing the introduction of capacity so that demand is always equal to or greater than capacity.

Figure 6.10(a) shows these two extreme strategies, although in practice the company is likely to choose a position somewhere between the two. Each strategy has its own advantages and disadvantages. These are shown in Table 6.4. The actual approach taken by any company will depend on how it views these advantages and disadvantages. For example, if the company's access to funds for capital expenditure is limited, it is likely to find the delayed capital expenditure requirement of the capacity-lagging strategy relatively attractive.

> **✳ Operations principle**
>
> Capacity-lagging strategies increase capacity utilization.

'Smoothing' with inventory

The strategy on the continuum between pure leading and pure lagging strategies can be implemented so that no inventories are accumulated. All demand in one period is satisfied (or not) by the activity of the operation in the same period. Indeed, for customer-processing operations there is no alternative to this. A hotel cannot satisfy demand in one year by using rooms which were vacant the previous year. However, for some operations output which is not required in one period can be stored for use in the next (inventory management is explored in Chapter 12). Using inventories can combine the advantages of both capacity leading and capacity lagging. Figure 6.10(b) shows how this can be done. Capacity is introduced such that demand can always be met by a combination of production and inventories, and capacity is, with the occasional exception, fully utilized. This may seem like an ideal state, but there is a price to pay – that is the cost of carrying the inventories. Not only will these have to be funded but the risks of obsolescence and deterioration of stock are introduced. Table 6.5 summarizes the advantages and disadvantages of the 'smoothing-with-inventory' strategy.

> **✳ Operations principle**
>
> Using inventories to overcome demand–capacity imbalance tends to increase working capital requirements.

Table 6.4 The arguments for and against pure leading and pure lagging strategies of capacity timing

Advantages	Disadvantages
Capacity-leading strategies	
• Always sufficient capacity to meet demand, therefore revenue is maximized and customers satisfied • Most of the time there is a 'capacity cushion' which can absorb extra demand if forecasts are pessimistic • Any critical start-up problems with new plants are less likely to affect supply to customers	• Utilization of the plants is always relatively low, therefore costs will be high • Risks of even greater (or even permanent) over-capacity if demand does not reach forecast levels • Capital spending on plant early
Capacity-lagging strategies	
• Always sufficient demand to keep the plants working at full capacity, therefore unit costs are minimized • Over-capacity problems are minimized if forecasts are optimistic • Capital spending on the plants is delayed	• Insufficient capacity to meet demand fully, therefore reduced revenue and dissatisfied customers • No ability to exploit short-term increases in demand • Under-supply position even worse if there are start-up problems with the new plants

Table 6.5 The advantages and disadvantages of a smoothing-with-inventory strategy

Advantages	Disadvantages
• All demand is satisfied, therefore customers are satisfied and revenue is maximized • Utilization of capacity is high and therefore costs are low • Very short-term surges in demand can be met from inventories	• The cost of inventories in terms of working capital requirements can be high. This is especially serious at a time when the company requires funds for its capital expansion • Risks of product deterioration and obsolescence

Worked example

A business process outsourcing (BPO) company is considering building some processing centres in India. The company has a standard call centre design that it has found to be the most efficient around the world. Demand forecasts indicate that there is already demand from potential clients to fully utilize one process centre that would generate $10 million of business per quarter (three-month period). The forecasts also indicate that by quarter 6 there will be sufficient demand to fully utilize one further processing centre. The costs of running a single centre are estimated to be $5 million per quarter and the lead time between ordering a centre and it being fully operational is two quarters. The capital costs of building a centre is $10 million, $5 million of which is payable before the end of the first quarter after ordering, and $5 million payable before the end of the second quarter after ordering. How much funding will the company have to secure on a quarter-by-quarter basis if it decides to build one processing centre as soon as possible and a second processing centre to be operational by the beginning of quarter 6?

Analysis

The funding required for a capacity expansion such as this can be derived by calculating the amount of cash coming in to the operation each time period, then subtracting the operating and capital costs for the project eacwh time period. The cumulative cash flow indicates the funding required for the project. In Table 6.6 these calculations are performed for eight quarters. For the first two quarters there is a net cash outflow because capital costs are incurred but no revenue is being earned. After that, revenue is being earned but in quarters 4 and 5 this is partly offset by further capital costs for the second processing centre. However, from quarter 6 onwards the additional revenue from the second processing centre brings the cash flow positive again. The maximum funding required occurs in quarter 2 and is $10 million.

Table 6.6 The cumulative cash flow indicating the funding required for the project

	Quarters							
	1	2	3	4	5	6	7	8
Sales revenue ($ millions)	0	0	10	10	10	20	20	20
Operating costs ($ millions)	0	0	−5	−5	−5	−10	−10	−10
Capital costs ($ millions)	−5	−5	−0	−5	−5	0	0	0
Required cumulative funding ($ millions)	−5	−10	−5	−5	−5	+5	+15	+25

BREAK-EVEN ANALYSIS OF CAPACITY EXPANSION

An alternative view of capacity expansion can be gained by examining the cost implications of adding increments of capacity on a break-even basis. Figure 6.11 shows how increasing capacity can move an operation from profitability to loss. Each additional unit of capacity results in a *fixed-cost break* that is a further lump of expenditure which will have to be incurred before any further activity can be undertaken in the operation. The operation is unlikely to be profitable at very low levels of output. Eventually, assuming that prices are greater than marginal costs, revenue will exceed total costs. However, the level of profitability at the point where the output level is equal to the capacity of the operation may not be sufficient to absorb all the extra fixed costs of a further increment in capacity. This could make the operation unprofitable in some stages of its expansion.

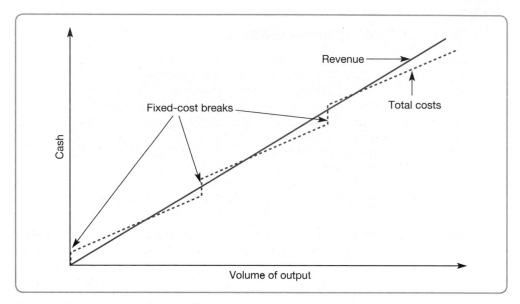

Figure 6.11 Repeated incurring of fixed costs can raise total costs above revenue

Worked example

A specialist graphics company is investing in a new machine which enables it to make high-quality prints for its clients. Demand for these prints is forecast to be around 100,000 units in year 1 and 220,000 units in year 2. The maximum capacity of each machine the company will buy to process these prints is 100,000 units per year. They have a fixed cost of €200,000 per year and a variable cost of processing of €1 per unit. The company believe they will be able to charge €4 per unit for producing the prints.

Question
What profit are they likely to make in the first and second years?

$$\text{Year 1 demand} = 100{,}000 \text{ units; therefore company will need one machine}$$
$$\text{Cost of manufacturing} = \text{fixed cost for one machine} + \text{variable cost} \times 100{,}000$$
$$= €200{,}000 + (€1 \times 100{,}000)$$
$$= €300{,}000$$
$$\text{Revenue} = \text{demand} \times \text{price}$$
$$= 100{,}000 \times €4$$
$$= €400{,}000$$

$$\text{Therefore profit} = €400{,}000 - €300{,}000$$
$$= €100{,}000$$

$$\text{Year 2 demand} = 220{,}000; \text{therefore company will need three machines}$$
$$\text{Cost of manufacturing} = \text{fixed cost for three machines} + \text{variable cost} \times 220{,}000$$
$$= (3 \times €200{,}000) + €1 \times 220{,}000)$$
$$= €820{,}000$$
$$\text{Revenue} = \text{demand} \times \text{price}$$
$$= 220{,}000 \times €4$$
$$= €880{,}000$$
$$\text{Therefore profit} = €880{,}000 - €820{,}000$$
$$= €60{,}000$$

Note: the profit in the second year will be lower because of the extra fixed costs associated with the investment in the two extra machines.

SUMMARY ANSWERS TO KEY QUESTIONS

Check and improve your understanding of this chapter using self-assessment questions and a personalized study plan, a video case study, and an eText – all at **www.myomlab.com**.

MyOMLab

❯ Why should an organization take a total supply network perspective?

- The main advantage is that it helps any operation to understand how it can compete effectively within the network. This is because a supply network approach requires operations managers to think about their suppliers and their customers *as operations*. It can also help to identify particularly significant links within the network and hence identify long-term strategic changes which will affect the operation.

❯ What is involved in configuring a supply network?

- There are two main issues involved in configuring the supply network. The first concerns the overall shape of the supply network. The second concerns the nature and extent of *outsourcing* or *vertical integration*.
- Changing the shape of the supply network may involve reducing the number of suppliers to the operation so as to develop closer relationships, and bypassing or disintermediating operations in the network.
- Outsourcing or vertical integration concerns the nature of the ownership of the operations within a supply network. The direction of vertical integration refers to whether an organization wants to own operations on its supply side or demand side (backwards or forwards integration). The extent of vertical integration relates to whether an organization wants to own a wide span of the stage in the supply network. The balance of vertical integration refers to whether operations can trade with only their vertically integrated partners or with any other organizations.

❯ Where should an operation be located?

- The stimuli which act on an organization during the location decision can be divided into supply-side and demand-side influences. Supply-side influences are the factors such as labour, land and utility costs which change as location changes. Demand-side influences include such things as the image of the location, its convenience for customers and the suitability of the site itself.

❯ How much capacity should an operation plan to have?

- The amount of capacity an organization will have depends on its view of current and future demand. It is when its view of future demand is different from current demand that this issue becomes important.

- When an organization has to cope with changing demand, a number of capacity decisions need to be taken. These include choosing the optimum capacity for each site, balancing the various capacity levels of the operation in the network, and timing the changes in the capacity of each part of the network.

- Important influences on these decisions include the concepts of economy and diseconomy of scale, supply flexibility if demand is different from that forecast, and the profitability and cash-flow implications of capacity timing changes.

CASE STUDY Disneyland Resort Paris (abridged)[7]

In August 2006, the company behind Disneyland Resort Paris reported a 13 per cent rise in revenues, saying that it was making encouraging progress with new rides aimed at getting more visitors. '*I am pleased with year-to-date revenues and especially with third quarter's, as well as with the success of the opening of Buzz Lightyear Laser Blast, the first step of our multi-year investment program. These results reflect the group's strategy of increasing growth through innovative marketing and sales efforts as well as a multi-year investment program. This performance is encouraging as we enter into the important summer months*', said Chairman and Chief Executive Karl L. Holz. Yet it hadn't always been like that. The 14-year history of Disneyland Paris had more ups and downs than any of its rollercoasters. From 12 April 1992 when Euro Disney opened, through to this more optimistic report, the resort had been subject simultaneously to both wildly optimistic forecasts and widespread criticism and ridicule. An essay on one critical internet site (called 'An Ugly American in Paris') summarized the whole venture in this way: '*When Disney decided to *expand its hugely successful theme park operations to Europe, it brought American management styles, American cultural tastes, American labor practices, and American marketing pizzazz to Europe. Then, when the French stayed away in droves, it accused them of cultural snobbery.'*

The 'magic' of Disney

Since its founding in 1923, the Walt Disney company had striven to remain faithful in its commitment to *'producing unparalleled entertainment experiences based on its rich legacy of quality creative content and exceptional storytelling'*. In the Parks and Resorts division, according to the company's description, customers could experience the 'Magic of Disney's beloved characters'. It was founded in 1952, when Walt Disney formed what is now known as 'Walt Disney Imagineering' to build Disneyland in Anaheim, California. By 2006, Walt Disney Parks and Resorts operated or licensed 11 theme parks at five Disney destinations around the world. They were: Disneyland Resort, California; Walt Disney World Resort, Florida; Tokyo Disneyland; Disneyland Resort Paris; and their latest park, Hong Kong Disneyland. In addition, the division operated 35 resort hotels, two luxury cruise ships and a wide variety of other entertainment offerings. But perhaps none of its ventures proved to be as challenging as its Paris Resort.

Service delivery at Disney resorts and parks

The core values of the Disney company and, arguably, the reason for its success, originated in the views and personality of Walt Disney, the company's founder. He had what some call an obsessive focus on creating images, products and experiences for customers that epitomized fun, imagination and service. Through the 'magic' of legendary fairytale and story characters, customers could escape the cares of the real world. Different areas of each Disney Park are themed, often around various 'lands' such as Frontierland and Fantasyland. Each land contains attractions and rides, most of which are designed to be acceptable to a wide range of ages. Very few rides are 'scary' when compared to many other entertainment parks. The architectural styles, décor, food, souvenirs and cast costumes were all designed to reflect the theme of the 'land', as were the films and shows. And although there were some regional differences, all the theme parks followed the same basic setup. The terminology used by the company reinforced its philosophy of consistent entertainment. Employees, even those working 'back stage', were called cast members. They did not wear uniforms but 'costumes', and, rather than being given a job, they were 'cast in a role'. All park visitors were called 'guests'.

Disney employees were generally relatively young, often of school or college age. Most were paid hourly for tasks that could be repetitive even though they usually involved constant contact with customers. Yet employees were still expected to maintain a high level of courtesy and work performance. All cast members were expected to conform to strict dress and grooming standards. Applicants to become cast members were screened for qualities such as how well

they responded to questions, how well they listened to their peers, how well they smiled and used body language, and whether they had an 'appropriate attitude'. Disney parks had gained a reputation for their obsession with delivering a high level of service and experience through attention to operations detail. All parks employed queue management techniques such as providing information and entertainment for visitors, who were also seen as having a role within the park; they were not merely spectators or passengers on the rides, they were considered to be participants in a play. Their needs and desires were analysed and met through frequent interactions with staff (cast members). In this way they could be drawn into the illusion that they were actually part of the fantasy.

Disney's stated goal was to exceed their customers' expectations every day. Service delivery was mapped and continuously refined in the light of customer feedback and the staff induction programme emphasized the company's quality assurance procedures and service standards based on the four principles of safety, courtesy, show, and efficiency. Parks were kept fanatically clean. The same Disney character never appears twice within sight – how could there be two Mickeys? Staff were taught that customer perceptions are the key to customer delight, but also are extremely fragile. Negative perceptions can be established after only one negative experience. Disney University trained Disney's employees in their strict service standards as well as providing the skills to operate new rides as they were developed. Staff recognition programmes attempted to identify outstanding service delivery performance as well as 'energy, enthusiasm, commitment, and pride'. All parks contained phones connected to a central question hot-line for employees to find the answer to any question posed by customers.

Tokyo Disneyland

Tokyo Disneyland, opened in 1982, was owned and operated by the Oriental Land Company. Disney had designed the park and advised on how it should be run, and it was considered a great success. Japanese customers revealed a significant appetite for American themes, American brands, and already had a good knowledge of Disney characters. Feedback was extremely positive, with visitors commenting on the cleanliness of the park, the courtesy and the efficiency of staff members. Visitors also appreciated the Disney souvenirs because giving gifts is deeply embedded in the Japanese culture. The success of the Tokyo Park was explained by one American living in Japan: *'Young Japanese are very clean-cut. They respond well to Disney's clean-cut image, and I am sure they had no trouble filling positions. Also, young Japanese are generally comfortable wearing uniforms, obeying their bosses, and being part of a team. These are part of the Disney formula. Also, Tokyo is very crowded and Japanese here are used to crowds and waiting in line. They are very patient. And above all, Japanese are always very polite to strangers.'*

Disneyland Paris

By 2006 Disneyland Paris consisted of three parks: the Disney village; Disneyland Paris itself; and the Walt Disney

Studios Park. The village was comprised of stores and restaurants; Disneyland Paris was the main theme park; and Disney Studio Park has a more general movie-making theme. At the time of the European park's opening more than two million Europeans visited the US Disney parks. The company's brand was strong and it had over half a century of translating the Disney brand into reality. The name 'Disney' had become synonymous with wholesome family entertainment that combined childhood innocence with high-tech 'imagineering'.

Initially, as well as France, Germany, Britain, Italy and Spain were all considered as possible locations, though Germany, Britain and Italy were soon discarded from the list of potential sites. The decision soon came to a straight contest between the Alicante area of Spain, which had a similar climate to Florida for a large part of the year, and the Marne-la-Vallée area just outside Paris. Certainly, winning the contest to host the new park was important for all the potential host countries. The new park promised to generate more than 30,000 jobs. The major advantage of locating in Spain was the weather. However, the eventual decision to locate near Paris was thought to have been driven by a number of factors that weighed more heavily with Disney executives. These included the following:

- There was a suitable site available just outside Paris.
- The proposed location put the park within a 2-hour drive for 17 million people, a 4-hour drive for 68 million people, a 6-hour drive for 110 million people and a 2-hour flight for a further 310 million or so.
- The site also had potentially good transport links. The Channel Tunnel that was to connect England with France was due to open in 1994. In addition, the French autoroutes network and the high-speed TGV network could both be extended to connect the site with the rest of Europe.
- Paris was already a highly attractive vacation destination.
- Europeans generally take significantly more holidays each year than Americans (five weeks of vacation as opposed to two or three weeks).
- Research indicated that 85 per cent of French people would welcome a Disney park.
- Both national and local government in France were prepared to give significant financial incentives (as were the Spanish authorities) including an offer to invest in local infrastructure, reduce the rate of value added tax on goods sold in the park, provide subsidized loans, and value the land artificially low to help reduce taxes. Moreover, the French government were prepared to expropriate land from local farmers to smooth the planning and construction process.

Early concerns that the park would not have the same sunny, happy feel in a cooler climate than Florida were allayed by the spectacular success of Disneyland Tokyo in a location with a similar climate to Paris, and construction started in August 1988. But from the announcement that the park would be built in France, it was subject to a wave of criticism. One critic called the project a 'cultural Chernobyl' because of how it might affect French cultural values. Another described it as 'a horror made of cardboard, plastic, and appalling colours; a construction of hardened chewing-gum and idiot folk lore taken straight out of comic books written for obese Americans'. However, as some commentators noted, the cultural arguments and anti-Americanism of the French intellectual elite did not seem to reflect the behaviour of most French people, who 'eat at McDonald's, wear Gap clothing, and flock to American movies'.

Designing Disneyland Resort Paris

Phase 1 of the Euro Disney Park was designed to have 29 rides and attractions, a championship golf course, together with many restaurants, shops, live shows, and parades as well as six hotels. Although the park was designed to fit in with Disney's traditional appearance and values, a number of changes were made to accommodate what was thought to be the preferences of European visitors. For example, market research indicated that Europeans would respond to a 'wild west' image of America. Therefore, both rides and hotel designs were made to emphasize this theme. Disney was also keen to diffuse criticism, especially from French left-wing intellectuals and politicians, that the design of the park would be too 'Americanized' and would become a vehicle for American 'cultural imperialism'. To counter charges of American imperialism, Disney gave the park a flavour that stressed the European heritage of many of the Disney characters, and increased the sense of beauty and fantasy. They were, after all, competing against Paris's exuberant architecture and sights. For example, Discoveryland featured storylines from Jules Verne, the French author. Snow White and her dwarfs were located in a Bavarian village. Cinderella was located in a French inn. Even Peter Pan was made to appear more 'English Edwardian' than in the original US designs.

Because of concerns about the popularity of American 'fast-food', Euro Disney introduced more variety into its restaurants and snack bars, featuring foods from around the world. In a bold publicity move, Disney invited a number of top Paris chefs to visit and taste the food. Some anxiety was also expressed concerning the different 'eating behaviour' between Americans and Europeans. Whereas Americans preferred to 'graze', eating snacks and fast meals throughout the day, Europeans generally preferred to sit down and eat at traditional meal times. This would have a very significant impact on peak demand levels at dining facilities. A further concern was that in Europe (especially French) visitors would be intolerant of long queues. To overcome this, extra diversions such as films and entertainments were planned for visitors as they waited in line for a ride.

Before the opening of the park, Euro Disney had to recruit and train between 12,000 and 14,000 permanent, and around 5,000 temporary, employees. All these new employees were required to undergo extensive training in order to prepare them to achieve Disney's high standard of customer service as well as understand operational routines and safety procedures. Originally, the company's objective was to hire 45 per cent of its employees from France, 30 per cent from other European countries, and 15 per cent from outside Europe. However, this proved difficult and when the park opened around 70 per cent of employees were French. Most cast members were paid around 15 per cent above the French minimum wage.

An information centre was opened in December 1990 to show the public what Disney was constructing. The 'casting centre' was opened on 1 September 1991 to recruit the 'cast members' needed to staff the park's attractions. But the hiring process did not go smoothly. In particular, Disney's grooming requirements, which insisted on a 'neat' dress code, a ban on facial hair, set standards for hair and fingernails, and an insistence on 'appropriate undergarments', proved controversial. Both the French press and trade unions strongly objected to the grooming requirements, claiming they were excessive and much stricter than was generally held to be reasonable in France. Nevertheless, the company refused to modify its grooming standards. Accommodating staff also proved to be a problem, when the large influx of employees swamped the available housing in the area. Disney had to build its own apartments as well as rent rooms in local homes just to accommodate its employees. Notwithstanding all the difficulties, Disney did succeed in recruiting and training all its cast members before the opening.

The park opens

The park opened to employees for testing during late March 1992, during which time the main sponsors and their families were invited to visit the new park, but the opening was not helped by strikes on the commuter trains leading to the park, staff unrest, threatened security problems (a terrorist bomb had exploded the night before the opening) and protests in surrounding villages who demonstrated against the noise and disruption from the park. The opening day crowds, expected to be 500,000, failed to materialize, however, and at close of the first day only 50,000 people had passed through the gates. Disney had expected the French to make up a larger proportion of visiting guests than they did in the early days. This may have been partly due to protests from French locals who feared their culture would be damaged by Euro Disney. Also all Disney parks had traditionally been alcohol-free. To begin with Euro Disney was no different. However, this was extremely unpopular, particularly with French visitors who like to have a glass of wine or beer with their food. But whatever the cause, the low initial attendance was very disappointing for the Disney Company.

It was reported that, in the first nine weeks of operation, approximately 1,000 employees left Euro Disney, about one half of whom 'left voluntarily'. The reasons cited for leaving varied. Some blamed the hectic pace of work and the long hours that Disney expected. Others mentioned the 'chaotic' conditions in the first few weeks. Even Disney conceded that conditions had been tough immediately after the park opened. Some leavers blamed Disney's apparent difficulty in understanding 'how Europeans work'. *'We can't just be told what to do, we ask questions and don't all think the same.'* Some visitors who had experience of the American parks commented that the standards of service were noticeably below what would be acceptable in America. There were reports that some cast members were failing to meet Disney's normal service standard. *'. . . even on opening weekend some clearly couldn't care less . . . My overwhelming impression . . . was that they were out of their depth. There is much more to being a cast member than endlessly saying "Bonjour". Apart from having a detailed knowledge of the site, Euro Disney staff have the anxiety of not knowing in what language they are going to be addressed . . . Many were struggling.'*

It was also noticeable that different nationalities exhibited different types of behaviour when visiting the park. Some nationalities always used the waste bins while others were more likely to drop litter on the floor. Most noticeable were differences in queuing behaviour. Northern Europeans tend to be disciplined and content to wait for rides in an orderly manner. By contrast some Southern European visitors *'seem to have made an Olympic event out of getting to the ticket taker first'*. Nevertheless, not all reactions were negative. European newspapers also quoted plenty of positive reaction from visitors, especially children. Euro Disney was so different from the existing European theme parks, with immediately recognizable characters and a wide variety of attractions. Families who could not afford to travel to the United States could now interact with Disney characters and 'sample the experience at far less cost'.

The next 15 years

By August 1992 estimates of annual attendance figures were being drastically cut from 11 million to just over 9 million. Euro Disney's misfortunes were further compounded in late 1992 when a European recession caused property prices to drop sharply, and interest payments on the large start-up loans taken out by Euro Disney forced the company to admit serious financial difficulties. Also the cheap dollar resulted in more people taking their holidays in Florida at Walt Disney World. At the first anniversary of the park's opening, in April 1993, Sleeping Beauty's Castle was decorated as a giant birthday cake to celebrate the occasion; however, further problems were approaching. Criticized for having too few rides, the rollercoaster 'Indiana Jones and the Temple of Peril' was opened in July. This was the first Disney rollercoaster that included a 360-degree loop, but just a few weeks after opening emergency brakes locked on during a ride, causing some guest injuries. The ride was temporarily shut down for investigations. Also in 1993 the proposed Euro Disney phase 2 was shelved due to financial problems, which meant Disney MGM Studios Europe and 13,000 hotel rooms would not be built to the original 1995 deadline originally agreed upon by the Walt Disney company. However, Discovery Mountain, one of the planned phase 2 attractions, did get approval.

By the start of 1994 rumours were circulating that the park was on the verge of bankruptcy. Emergency crisis talks were held between the banks and backers with things coming to a head during March when Disney offered the banks an ultimatum. It would provide sufficient capital for the park to continue to operate until the end of the month, but unless the banks agreed to restructure the park's $1bn debt, the Walt Disney company would close the park, and walk away from the whole European venture, leaving the banks with a bankrupt theme park and a massive expanse of virtually worthless real estate. Michael Eisner, Disney's CEO, announced that Disney were planning to pull the plug on the venture at the end of March 1994 unless the banks were prepared to restructure the loans. The banks agreed to Disney's demands.

In May 1994 the connection between London and Marne-La-Vallée was completed, along with a TGV link, providing a connection between several major European cities. By August the park was starting to find its feet at last, and all of the park's hotels were fully booked during the peak holiday season. Also, in October, the park's name was officially changed from Euro Disney to 'Disneyland Paris', in order to 'show that the resort now was named much more like its counterparts in California and Tokyo'. The end-of-year figures for 1994 showed encouraging signs despite a 10 per cent fall in attendance caused by the bad publicity over the earlier financial problems. For the next few years new rides continued to be introduced – 1995 saw the opening of the new rollercoaster, 'Space Mountain De la Terre à la Lune' – and Euro Disney did announce its first annual operating profit in November 1995. New attractions were added steadily, but in 1999 the planned Christmas and New Year celebrations were disrupted when a freak storm caused havoc, destroying the Mickey Mouse glass statue that had just been installed for the Lighting Ceremony and many other attractions.

Disney's 'Fastpass' system was introduced in 2000: a new service that allowed guests to use their entry passes to gain a ticket at certain attractions and return at the time stated and gain direct entry to the attraction without queuing. Two new attractions were also opened, 'Indiana Jones et la Temple du Peril' and 'Tarzan le Recontre' starring a cast of acrobats along with Tarzan, Jane and all their jungle friends with music from the movie in different European languages. In 2001 the 'ImagiNations Parade' was replaced by the 'Wonderful World of Disney Parade' which received some criticism for being 'less than spectacular', with only eight parade floats. Also Disney's 'California Adventure' was opened in California. The resort's 10th anniversary saw the opening of the new Walt Disney Studios Park attraction, based on a similar attraction in Florida that had already proved to be a success.

Andre Lacroix from Burger King was appointed as CEO of Disneyland Resort Paris in 2003, to 'take on the challenge of a failing Disney park in Europe and turn it around'. Increasing investment, he refurbished whole sections of the park and introduced the Jungle Book Carnival in February to increase attendance during the slow months. By 2004 attendance had increased but the company announced that it was still losing money. And even the positive news of 2006, although generally well received, still left questions unanswered. As one commentator put it, 'Would Disney, the stockholders, the banks, or even the French government, make the same decision to go ahead if they could wind the clock back to 1987? Is this a story of a fundamentally flawed concept, or was it just mishandled?'

QUESTIONS

1 What markets are the Disney resorts and parks aiming for?

2 Was Disney's choice of the Paris site a mistake?

3 What aspects of their parks' design did Disney change when it constructed Euro Disney?

4 What did Disney *not* change when it constructed Euro Disney?

5 What were Disney's main mistakes from the conception of the Paris resort through to 2006?

PROBLEMS AND APPLICATIONS

MyOMLab   *These problems and applications will help to improve your analysis of operations. You can find more practice problems as well as worked examples and guided solutions on MyOMLab at www.myomlab.com.*

1 A company is deciding between two locations (location A and location B). It has six location criteria, the most important being the suitability of the buildings that are available in each location. About half as important as the suitability of the buildings are the access to the site and the supply of skills available locally. Half as important as these two factors are the potential for expansion on the sites and the attractiveness of the area. The attractiveness of the buildings themselves is also a factor, although a relatively unimportant one, rating one half as important as the attractiveness of the area. Table 6.8 indicates the scores for each of these factors, as judged by the company's senior management. What would you advise the company to do?

Table 6.8 The scores for each factor in the location decision as judged by the company's senior management

	Location A	Location B
Access	4	6
Expansion	6	5
Attractiveness (area)	10	6
Skills supply	5	7
Suitability of buildings	8	7
Attractiveness of buildings	4	6

2 A company which assembles garden furniture obtains its components from three suppliers. Supplier A provides all the boxes and packaging material; supplier B provides all metal components; and supplier C provides all plastic components. Supplier A sends one truckload of the materials per week to the factory and is located at the position (1,1) on a grid reference which covers the local area. Supplier B sends four truckloads of components per week to the factory and is located at point (2,3) on the grid. Supplier C sends three truckloads of components per week to the factory and is located at point (4,3) on the grid. After assembly, all the products are sent to a warehouse which is located at point (5,1) on the grid. Assuming there is little or no waste generated in the process, where should the company locate its factory so as to minimize transportation costs? Assume that transportation costs are directly proportional to the number of truckloads of parts, or finished goods, transported per week.

3 A rapid response maintenance company serves its customers who are located in four industrial estates. Estate A has 15 customers and is located at grid reference (5,7). Estate B has 20 customers and is located at grid reference (6,3). Estate C has 15 customers and is located at grid reference (10,2) but these customers are twice as likely to require service as the company's other customers. Estate D has 10 customers and is located at grid reference (12,3). At what grid reference should the company be looking to find a suitable location for its service centre?

4 A private health-care clinic has been offered a leasing deal where it could lease a CAT scanner at a fixed charge of €2,000 per month and a charge per patient of €6 per patient scanned. The clinic currently charges €10 per patient for taking a scan.
   (a) At what level of demand (in number of patients per week) will the clinic break even on the cost of leasing the CAT scan?
   (b) Would a revised lease that stipulated a fixed cost of €3,000 per week and a variable cost of €0.2 per patient be a better deal?

5 Visit sites on the internet that offer (legal) downloadable music using MP3 or other compression formats. Consider the music business supply chain, a) for the recordings of a well-known popular music artist, and b) for a less well-known (or even largely unknown) artist struggling to gain recognition. How might the transmission of music over the internet affect each of these artists' sales? What implications does electronic music transmission have for record shops?

6 Visit the websites of companies that are in the paper manufacturing/pulp production/packaging industries. Assess the extent to which the companies you have investigated are vertically integrated in the paper supply chain that stretches from foresting through to the production of packaging materials.

SELECTED FURTHER READING

Carmel, E. and Tjia, P. (2005) *Offshoring Information Technology: Sourcing and Outsourcing to a Global Workforce*, Cambridge University Press, Cambridge. An academic book on outsourcing.

Corbett, M.F. (2010) *The Outsourcing Revolution: Why it Makes Sense and How to Do it Right*, Kaplan, New York. A non-academic book on outsourcing.

Dell, M. (with Fredman, C.) (1999) *Direct from Dell: Strategies that Revolutionized an Industry*, HarperBusiness, New York. Michael Dell explains how his supply network strategy (and other decisions) had such an impact on the industry. Interesting and readable, but not a critical analysis!

Schniederjans, M.J. (1998) *International Facility Location and Acquisition Analysis*, Quorum Books, New York. Very much one for the technically-minded.

Vashistha, A. and Vashistha, A. (2006) *The Offshore Nation: Strategies for Success in Global Outsourcing and Offshoring*, McGraw-Hill Professional, New York. Another topical book on outsourcing.

USEFUL WEBSITES

www.thesla.org The site of the Society for Location Analysis (SLA), a not-for-profit networking group for professionals working in location analysis.

www.plittinternational.com/assets/docs/selectingTheCorrectChineseSupplier.pdf An interesting perspective on how Chinese partners can be selected.

www.transparency.org A leading site for international business (including location) that fights corruption.

www.intel.com More details on Intel's 'Copy Exactly' strategy and other capacity strategy issues.

www.outsourcing.com Site of the Institute of Outsourcing. Some good case studies and some interesting reports, news item, etc.

www.myomlab.com Test which sections you have mastered and which you need to review, with questions, a personalized study plan, video clips, revision tips, and cases.

www.opsman.org Useful materials.

http://operationsroom.wordpress.com/ Stanford University's take on topical operations stories.

www.poms.org A US academic society for production and operations management. Academic, but some useful material, including a link to an encyclopedia of operations management terms.

http://sites.google.com/site/tomiportal/home One of the longest-established portals for the subject. Useful for academics and students alike.

www.ft.com Good for researching topics and companies.

www.economist.com/ *The Economist's* site, well written and interesting stuff on business generally.

Supplement to Chapter 6
Forecasting

INTRODUCTION

Some forecasts are accurate. We know exactly what time the sun will rise at any given place on earth tomorrow or one day next month or even next year. Forecasting in a business context, however, is much more difficult and therefore prone to error. We do not know precisely how many orders we will receive or how many customers will walk through the door tomorrow, next month, or next year. Such forecasts are nonetheless necessary to help managers make decisions about resourcing the organization for the future.

FORECASTING – KNOWING THE OPTIONS

Simply knowing that demand for your goods or services is rising or falling is not enough in itself. Knowing the rate of change is likely to be vital to business planning. A firm of lawyers may have to decide the point at which, in their growing business, they will have to take on another partner. Hiring a new partner could take months so they need to be able to forecast when they expect to reach that point and then when they need to start their recruitment drive. The same applies to a plant manager who will need to purchase new equipment to deal with rising demand. She may not want to commit to buying an expensive piece of machinery until absolutely necessary but she will need to allow enough time to order the machine and have it built, delivered, installed and tested. The same is so for governments whether planning new airports or runway capacity or deciding where and how many primary schools to build.

The first question is to know how far you need to look ahead and this will depend on the options and decisions available to you. Take the example of a local government where the number of primary-age children (5–11 year olds) is increasing in some areas and declining in other areas within its boundaries. It is legally obliged to provide school places for all such children. Government officials will have a number of options open to them and they may each have different lead times associated with them. One key step in forecasting is to know the possible options and the lead times required to bring them about (see Table S6.1).

1 Individual schools can hire (or lay off) short-term (supply) teachers from a pool, not only to cover for absent teachers, but also to provide short-term capacity while teachers are

Table S6.1 Options available and lead time required for dealing with changes in numbers of schoolchildren

Options available	Lead time required
Hire short-term teachers	Hours
Hire staff	
Build temporary classrooms	
Amend school catchment areas	
Build new classrooms	
Build new schools	Years

hired to deal with increases in demand. Acquiring (or dismissing) such temporary cover may only require a few hours' notice. (This is often referred to as short-term capacity management.)

2 Hiring new (or laying off existing) staff is another option but both of these may take months to complete. (Medium-term capacity management.)

3 A shortage of accommodation may be fixed in the short to medium term by hiring or buying temporary classrooms. It may only take a couple of weeks to hire such a building and equip it ready for use.

4 It may be possible to amend catchment areas between schools to try to balance an increasing population in one area against a declining population in another. Such changes may require lengthy consultation processes.

5 In the longer term new classrooms or even new schools may have to be built. The planning, consultation, approval, commissioning, tendering, building and equipping process may take one to five years depending on the scale of the new build. (Long-term capacity planning – see Chapter 6.)

Knowing the range of options managers can then decide the timescale for their forecasts; indeed several forecasts might be needed for the short term, medium term and long term.

IN ESSENCE FORECASTING IS SIMPLE

In essence forecasting is easy. To know how many children may turn up in a local school tomorrow you can use the number that turned up today. In the long term, in order to forecast how many primary-age children will turn up at a school in five years' time, one need simply look at the birth statistics for the current year for the school's catchment area – see Figure S6.1.

However, such simple extrapolation techniques are prone to error and indeed such approaches have resulted in some local governments committing themselves to building schools which five or six years later, when complete, had few children and other schools bursting at the seams with temporary classrooms and temporary teachers, often resulting in falling morale and declining educational standards. The reason why such simple approaches are prone to problems is that there are many contextual variables (see Figure S6.2) which will have a potentially significant impact on, for example, the school population five years hence. For example:

1 One minor factor in developed countries, though a major factor in developing countries, might be the death rate in children between birth and five years of age. This may be dependent upon location, with a slightly higher mortality rate in the poorer areas compared to the more affluent areas.

2 Another more significant factor is immigration and emigration as people move into or out of the local area. This will be affected by housing stock and housing developments, the ebb and flow of jobs in the area, and the changing economic prosperity in the area.

3 One key factor which has an impact on the birth rate in an area is the amount and type of the housing stock. City-centre tenement buildings tend to have a higher proportion of children per dwelling, for example, than suburban semi-detached houses. So not only will existing housing stock have an impact on the child population but so also will the type of housing developments under construction, planned and proposed.

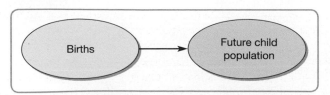

Figure S6.1 Simple prediction of future child population

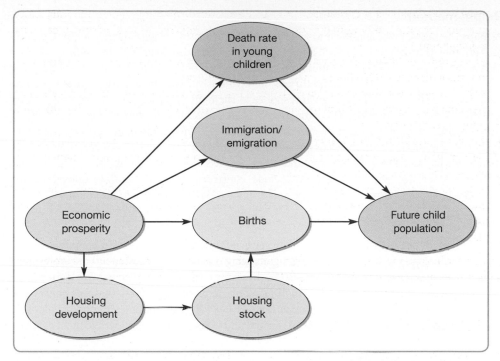

Figure S6.2 Some of the key causal variables in predicting child populations

APPROACHES TO FORECASTING

There are two main approaches to forecasting. Managers sometimes use qualitative methods based on opinions, past experience and even best guesses. There is also a range of qualitative forecasting techniques available to help managers evaluate trends, causal relationships and make predictions about the future. Also quantitative forecasting techniques can be used to model data. Although no approach or technique will result in an accurate forecast, a combination of qualitative and quantitative approaches can be used to great effect by bringing together expert judgements and predictive models.

Qualitative methods

Imagine you were asked to forecast the outcome of a forthcoming football match. Simply looking at the teams' performance over the last few weeks and extrapolating it is unlikely to yield the right result. Like many business decisions, the outcome will depend on many other factors. In this case the strength of the opposition, their recent form, injuries to players on both sides, the match location and even the weather will have an influence on the outcome. A qualitative approach involves collecting and appraising judgements, options, even best guesses from 'experts' to make a prediction, as well as past performances. There are several ways this can be done: a panel approach, the Delphi method and scenario planning.

Panel approach

Just as panels of football pundits gather to speculate about likely outcomes, so too do politicians, business leaders, stock market analysts, banks and airlines. The panel acts like a focus group, allowing everyone to talk openly and freely. Although there is the great advantage of several brains being better than one, it can be difficult to reach a consensus, or sometimes the views of the loudest or highest status may emerge (the bandwagon effect). Although more reliable than one person's views, the panel approach still has the weakness that everybody, even the experts, can get it wrong.

Delphi method[1]

Perhaps the best-known approach to generating forecasts using experts is the Delphi method. This is a more formal method which attempts to reduce the influences from procedures of face-to-face meetings. It employs a questionnaire that is emailed or posted to the experts. The replies are analysed and summarized and returned, anonymously, to all the experts. The experts are then asked to reconsider their original response in the light of the replies and arguments put forward by the other experts. This process is repeated several more times to conclude either with a consensus or at least a narrower range of decisions. One refinement of this approach is to allocate weights to the individuals and their suggestions based on, for example, their experience, their past success in forecasting and other people's views of their abilities. The obvious problems associated with this method include constructing an appropriate questionnaire, selecting an appropriate panel of experts and trying to deal with their inherent biases.

Scenario planning

One method for dealing with situations of even greater uncertainty is scenario planning. This is usually applied to long-range forecasting, again using a panel. The panel members are usually asked to devise a range of future scenarios. Each scenario can then be discussed and the inherent risks considered. Unlike the Delphi method, scenario planning is not necessarily concerned with arriving at a consensus but looking at the possible range of options and putting plans in place to try to avoid the ones that are least desired and taking action to follow the most desired.

Quantitative methods

There are two main approaches to qualitative forecasting: time series analysis and causal modelling techniques.

Time series examine the pattern of past behaviour of a single phenomenon over time, taking into account reasons for variation in the trend in order to use the analysis to forecast the phenomenon's future behaviour.

Causal modelling is an approach which describes and evaluates the complex cause effect relationships between the key variables (such as in Figure S6.2).

Time series analysis

Simple time series plot a variable over time then, by removing underlying variations with assignable causes, use extrapolation techniques to predict future behaviour. The key weakness with this approach is that it simply looks at past behaviour to predict the future, ignoring causal variables which are taken into account in other methods such as causal modelling or qualitative techniques. For example, suppose a company is attempting to predict the future sales of a product. The past three years' sales, quarter by quarter, are shown in Figure S6.3(a). This series of past sales may be analysed to indicate future sales. For instance, underlying the series might be a linear upward trend in sales. If this is taken out of the data, as in Figure S6.3(b), we are left with a cyclical seasonal variation. The mean deviation of each quarter from the trend line can now be taken out, to give the average seasonality deviation. What remains is the random variation about the trends and seasonality lines, Figure S6.3(c). Future sales may now be predicted as lying within a band about a projection of the trend, plus the seasonality. The width of the band will be a function of the degree of random variation.

Forecasting unassignable variations The random variations which remain after taking out trend and seasonal effects are without any known or assignable cause. This does not mean that they do not have a cause, however, just that we do not know what it is. Nevertheless, some attempt can be made to forecast it, if only on the basis that future events will, in some way, be based on past events. We will examine two of the more common approaches to forecasting which are based on projecting forward from past behaviour. These are:

- moving-average forecasting;
- exponentially smoothed forecasting.

Figure S6.3 Time series analysis with (a) trend, (b) seasonality and (c) random variation

Moving-average forecasting The moving-average approach to forecasting takes the previous n periods' actual demand figures, calculates the average demand over the n periods, and uses this average as a forecast for the next period's demand. Any data older than the n periods plays no part in the next period's forecast. The value of n can be set at any level, but is usually in the range 4 to 7.

Example – Eurospeed parcels
Table S6.2 shows the weekly demand for Eurospeed, a European-wide parcel delivery company. It measures demand, on a weekly basis, in terms of the number of parcels which it is given to deliver (irrespective of the size of each parcel). Each week, the next week's demand is forecast by taking the moving average of the previous four weeks' actual demand. Thus if the forecast demand for week t is F_t and the actual demand for week t is A_t, then:

$$F_t = \frac{A_{t-1} + A_{t-2} + A_{t-3} + A_{t-4}}{4}$$

For example, the forecast for week 35:

$$F_{35} = (72.5 + 66.7 + 68.3 + 67.0)/4$$

$$= 68.6$$

Exponential smoothing There are two significant drawbacks to the moving-average approach to forecasting. First, in its basic form, it gives equal weight to all the previous n periods which are used in the calculations (although this can be overcome by assigning different weights to each of the n periods). Second, and more important, it does not use data from beyond the n periods over which the moving average is calculated. Both these problems are overcome by *exponential smoothing*, which is also somewhat easier to calculate. The exponential-smoothing approach forecasts demand in the next period by taking into account

Table S6.2 Moving-average forecast calculated over a four-week period

Week	Actual demand (thousands)	Forecast
20	63.3	
21	62.5	
22	67.8	
23	66.0	
24	67.2	64.9
25	69.9	65.9
26	65.6	67.7
27	71.1	66.3
28	68.8	67.3
29	68.4	68.9
30	70.3	68.5
31	72.5	69.7
32	66.7	70.0
33	68.3	69.5
34	67.0	69.5
35		68.6

the actual demand in the current period and the forecast which was previously made for the current period. It does so according to the formula:

$$F_t = \alpha A_{t-1} + (1 - \alpha)F_{t-1}$$

where $\alpha = $ the smoothing constant.

The smoothing constant α is, in effect, the weight which is given to the last (and therefore assumed to be most important) piece of information available to the forecaster. However, the other expression in the formula includes the forecast for the current period which included the previous period's actual demand, and so on. In this way all previous data has a (diminishing) effect on the next forecast.

Table S6.3 shows the data for Eurospeed's parcels forecasts using this exponential-smoothing method, where $\alpha = 0.2$. For example, the forecast for week 35 is:

$$F_{35} = 0.2 \times 67.0 + 0.8 \times 68.3 = 68.04$$

The value of α governs the balance between the *responsiveness* of the forecasts to changes in demand, and the *stability* of the forecasts. The closer α is to 0 the more forecasts will be dampened by previous forecasts (not very sensitive but stable). Figure S6.4 shows the Eurospeed volume data plotted for a four-week moving average, exponential smoothing with $\alpha = 0.2$ and exponential smoothing with $\alpha = 0.3$.

Causal models

Causal models often employ complex techniques to understand the strength of relationships between the network of variables and the impact they have on each other. Simple regression models try to determine the 'best fit' expression between two variables. For example, suppose an ice-cream company is trying to forecast its future sales. After examining previous demand, it figures that the main influence on demand at the factory is the average temperature of the previous week. To understand this relationship, the company plots demand against the previous week's temperatures. This is shown in Figure S6.5. Using this graph, the company can make a reasonable prediction of demand, once the average temperature is known, provided that the other conditions prevailing in the market are reasonably stable. If they are not, then these other factors which have an influence on demand will need to be included in the regression model, which becomes increasingly complex.

Table S6.3 Exponentially smoothed forecast calculated with smoothing constant $\alpha = 0.2$

Week (t)	Actual demand (thousands) (A)	Forecast $(F_t = \alpha A_{t-1} + (1 - \alpha)F_{t-1})$ ($\alpha = 0.2$)
20	63.3	60.00
21	62.5	60.66
22	67.8	60.03
23	66.0	61.58
24	67.2	62.83
25	69.9	63.70
26	65.6	64.94
27	71.1	65.07
28	68.8	66.28
29	68.4	66.78
30	70.3	67.12
31	72.5	67.75
32	66.7	68.70
33	68.3	68.30
34	67.0	68.30
35		68.04

These more complex networks comprise many variables and relationships, each with their own set of assumptions and limitations. While developing such models and assessing the importance of each of the factors and understanding the network of interrelationships is beyond the scope of this text, many techniques are available to help managers undertake this more complex modelling and also feed back data into the model to further refine and develop it, in particular structural equation modelling.

The performance of forecasting models

Forecasting models are widely used in management decision making, and indeed most decisions require a forecast of some kind, yet the performance of this type of model is far from impressive.

Figure S6.4 A comparison of a moving-average forecast and exponential smoothing with the smoothing constant $\alpha = 0.2$ and 0.3

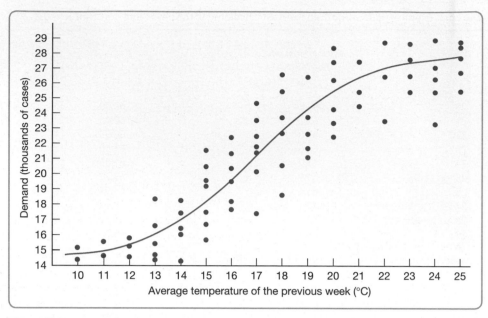

Figure S6.5 Regression line showing the relationship between the previous week's average temperature and demand

Hogarth and Makridakis,[2] in a comprehensive review of the applied management and finance literature, show that the record of forecasters using both judgement and sophisticated mathematical methods is not good. What they do suggest, however, is that certain forecasting techniques perform better under certain circumstances. In short-term forecasting there is:

> . . . considerable inertia in most economic and natural phenomena. Thus the present states of any variables are predictive of the short-term future (i.e. three months or less). Rather simple mechanistic methods, such as those used in time series forecasts, can often make accurate short-term forecasts and even out-perform more theoretically elegant and elaborate approaches used in econometric forecasting.[3]

Long-term forecasting methods, although difficult to judge because of the time lapse between the forecast and the event, do seem to be more amenable to an objective causal approach. In a comparative study of long-term market forecasting methods, Armstrong and Grohman[4] conclude that econometric methods offer more accurate long-range forecasts than do expert opinion or time series analysis, and that the superiority of objective causal methods improves as the time horizon increases.

SELECTED FURTHER READING

Hoyle, R.H. (ed) (1995) *Structural Equation Modeling*, Sage, Thousand Oaks, CA. For the specialist.

Maruyama, G.M. (1997) *Basics of Structural Equation Modeling*, Sage, Thousand Oaks, CA. For the specialist.

Now that you have finished reading this chapter, why not visit MyOMLab at www.myomlab.com where you'll find more learning resources to help you make the most of your studies and get a better grade.

Layout and flow

> **What is layout?**

> **What are the basic layout types used in operations?**

> **What type of layout should an operation choose?**

> **How should each basic layout type be designed in detail?**

INTRODUCTION

The layout of an operation is concerned with the physical positioning of its transforming resources. It is often the first thing most of us would notice when we enter an operation because it governs its appearance. It means deciding where to put all the facilities, machines, equipment and staff in the operation. It is important because the layout of facilities determines the way in which transformed resources – the materials, information and customers – flow through an operation. Relatively small changes in layout – moving displays in a supermarket, or the changing rooms in a sports centre, or the position of a machine in a factory – can affect the flow through the operation which, in turn, affects the costs and general effectiveness of the operation. Figure 7.1 shows the position of layout and flow in design activities.

Figure 7.1 The design activities in operations management covered in this chapter

Successful supermarkets, like Tesco, know that the design of their stores has a huge impact on profitability. They must maximize their revenue per square metre and minimize the costs of operating the store, while keeping customers happy. At a basic level, supermarkets have to get the amount of space allocated to the different areas right. Tesco's 'One in front' campaign, for example, tries to avoid long waiting times by opening additional tills if more than one customer is waiting at a checkout. Tesco also uses technology to understand exactly how customers flow through their stores. The 'Smartlane' system from Irisys, a specialist in intelligent infrared technologies, counts the number and type of customers entering the store (in family or other groups known as 'shopping units'), tracks their movement using infrared sensors, and predicts the likely demand at the checkouts well in advance. And it's important to Tesco. Its CEO commented on having the ability to *'sense the number of customers entering a store and predicting the checkouts that need to be open in an hour. We can monitor and manage the service customers get much more precisely – by customer, by store and by the minute. Thanks to this, a quarter of a million more customers every week don't have to queue.'*

Source: Shutterstock.com/Gyn9037

The circulation of customers through the store must be right and the right layout can make customers buy more. Some supermarkets put their entrance on the left-hand side of a building with a layout designed to take customers in a clockwise direction around the store. Aisles are made wide to ensure a relatively slow flow of trolleys so that customers pay more attention to the products on display (and buy more). However, wide aisles can come at the expense of reduced shelf space that would allow a wider range of products to be stocked. Also, the actual location of all the products is a critical decision, directly affecting the convenience to customers, their level of spontaneous purchase, and the cost of filling the shelves. Although the majority of supermarket sales are packaged, tinned or frozen goods, the displays of fruit and vegetables are usually located adjacent to the main entrance, as a signal of freshness and wholesomeness, providing an attractive and welcoming point of entry. Basic products that figure on most people's shopping lists, such as flour, sugar and bread, may be located at the back of the store and apart from each other so that customers have to pass higher-margin items as they search. High-margin items are usually put at eye level on shelves (where they are more likely to be seen) and low-margin products lower down or higher up. Some customers also go a few paces up an aisle before they start looking for what they need. Some supermarkets call the shelves occupying the first metre of an aisle 'dead space', not a place to put impulse-bought goods. But the prime site in a supermarket is the 'gondola-end', the shelves at the end of the aisle. Moving products to this location can increase sales 200 or 300 per cent. Not surprising that suppliers are willing to pay for their products to be located here.

The supermarkets themselves are keen to point out that, although they obviously lay out their stores with customers' buying behaviour in mind, it is counterproductive to be too manipulative. Nor are some commonly held beliefs about supermarket layout always true. They deny that they periodically change the location of foodstuffs in order to jolt customers out of their habitual shopping patterns so that they are more attentive to other products and end up buying more. Occasionally layouts are changed, they say, but mainly to accommodate changing tastes and new ranges.

WHAT IS LAYOUT?

The 'layout' of an operation or process means how its transforming resources are positioned relative to each other and how its various tasks are allocated to these transforming resources. Together these two decisions will dictate the pattern of flow for transformed resources as they progress through the operation or process (*see* Fig. 7.2). It is an important decision because, if the layout proves wrong, it can lead to over-long or confused flow patterns, customer queues, long process times, inflexible operations, unpredictable flow and high cost. Also, re-laying out an existing operation can cause disruption, leading to customer dissatisfaction or lost operating time. So, because the layout decision can be difficult and expensive, operations managers are reluctant to do it too often. Therefore layout must start with a full appreciation of the objectives that the layout should be trying to achieve. However, this is only the starting point of what is a multi-stage process, which leads to the final physical layout of the operation.

What makes a good layout?

To a large extent the objectives of any layout will depend on the strategic objectives of the operation, but there are some general objectives which are relevant to all operations. All layouts should be inherently safe; constituting no danger to either staff or customers. Generally, layout should (usually) minimize the length of flow through the operation and preferably make the flow clear. Staff should be located away from noisy or unpleasant parts of the operation and all equipment should be accessible. Layouts should achieve an appropriate use of space and allow for flexibility in the longer term.

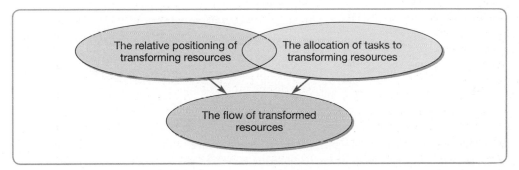

Figure 7.2 Layout involves the relative positioning of transforming resources within operations and processes and the allocation of tasks to the resources, which together dictate the flow of transformed resources through the operation or process

THE BASIC LAYOUT TYPES

Most practical layouts are derived from only four basic layout types. These are:

- fixed-position layout
- functional layout
- cell layout
- product (line) layout.

These layout types are loosely related to the process types described earlier (see Chapter 4). As Table 7.1 indicates, a process type does not necessarily imply only one particular basic layout.

Table 7.1 The relationship between process types and basic layout types

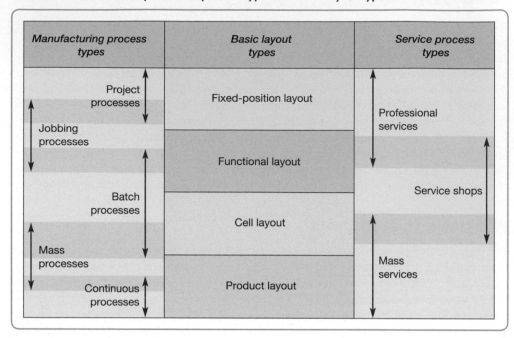

Manufacturing process types	Basic layout types	Service process types
Project processes / Jobbing processes	Fixed-position layout	Professional services
Batch processes	Functional layout	Service shops
	Cell layout	
Mass processes / Continuous processes	Product layout	Mass services

Fixed-position layout

Fixed-position layout is in some ways a contradiction in terms, since the transformed resources do not move between the transforming resources. Instead of materials, information or customers flowing through an operation, the recipient of the processing is stationary and the equipment, machinery, plant and people who do the processing move as necessary. This could be because the product or the recipient of the service is too large to be moved conveniently, or it might be too delicate to move, or perhaps it could object to being moved; for example:

- *Motorway construction* – the product is too large to move.
- *Open-heart surgery* – patients are too delicate to move.
- *High-class service restaurant* – customers would object to being moved to where food is prepared.
- *Shipbuilding* – the product is too large to move.
- *Mainframe computer maintenance* – the product is too big and probably also too delicate to move, and the customer might object to bringing it in for repair.

Functional layout

In functional layout, similar resources or processes are located together. This may be because it is convenient to group them together, or so that the utilization of transforming resources is improved. It means that when products, information or customers flow through the operation, they will take a route from activity to activity according to their needs. Different products or customers will have different needs and therefore take different routes. Usually this makes the flow pattern in the operation very complex. Examples of functional layouts include:

- *Hospital* – some processes (e.g. X-ray machines and laboratories) are required by several types of patient; some processes (e.g. general wards) can achieve high staff and bed utilization.
- *Machining the parts which go into aircraft engines* – some processes (e.g. heat treatment) need specialist support (heat and fume extraction); some processes (e.g. machining

'Factory flow' helps surgery productivity[2]

Even surgery can be seen as a process, and like any process, it can be improved. Normally patients remain stationary with surgeons and other theatre staff performing their tasks around the patient. But this idea has been challenged by John Petri, an Italian consultant orthopaedic surgeon at a hospital in Norfolk in the UK. Frustrated by spending time drinking tea while patients were prepared for surgery, he redesigned the process so now he moves continually between two theatres. While he is operating on a patient in one theatre, his anaesthetist colleagues are preparing a patient for surgery in another theatre. After finishing with the first patient, the surgeon 'scrubs up', moves to the second operating theatre and begins the surgery on the second patient. While he is doing this the first patient is moved out of the first operating theatre and the third patient is prepared. This method of overlapping operations in different theatres allows him to work for five hours at a time rather than the previous standard three-and-a-half-hour session. *'If you were running a factory',* says the surgeon, *'you wouldn't allow your most important and most expensive machine to stand idle. The same is true in a hospital.'* Currently used on hip and knee replacements, this layout would not be suitable for all surgical procedures. But since its introduction the surgeon's waiting list has fallen to zero and his productivity has doubled.

Source: Shutterstock.com/Ingrid W

'For a small increase in running costs we are able to treat many more patients', said a spokesperson for the hospital management. *'What is important is that clinicians . . . produce innovative ideas and we demonstrate that they are effective.'*

1 7.20am Anaesthetist prepares patient for surgery in theatre one

2 8.00am Surgeon begins first hip operation in theatre one

3 8.20am Halfway through first operation another anaesthetist prepares second patient in theatre two

4 9.00am Surgeon finishes first operation, scrubs up and starts operating in theatre two

5 9.20am Halfway through second operation third patient prepared in theatre one

Anaesthetist

Surgeon

THEATRE 1

THEATRE 2

Figure 7.3 Assembly line surgery

centres) require the same technical support from specialist setter–operators; some processes (e.g. grinding machines) get high machine utilization as all parts which need grinding pass through a single grinding section.

- *Supermarket* – some products, such tinned goods, are convenient to restock if grouped together. Some areas, such as those holding frozen vegetables, need the common technology of freezer cabinets. Others, such as the areas holding fresh vegetables, might be together because that way they can be made to look attractive to customers (see the opening short case (p. 192)).

Like most functional layouts, a library has different types of users with different traffic patterns. The college library in Figure 7.4 has put its users into three categories, as follows (in fact, very similar categories are used for retail customers).[3]

Browsers These seek interesting or useful materials by surfing the internet, browsing shelves and examining items, and moving around slowly while assessing the value of items.

Destination traffic These have a specific purpose or errand and are not deterred from it by their surroundings or other library materials.

Beeline traffic These concentrate on goals unconnected with personal use of the library. For example, messengers, delivery staff or maintenance workers.

Based on studies tracking these different types of customer, the library derived the following guide rules for the layout of its library:

- Position displays and services that need to be brought to users' attention at the front of the facility.
- To the right of the entrance should be new acquisitions; items that might be selected on impulse and have no satisfactory substitutes; and items that require repeated exposure before users select them.
- On the left at the front should be items that probably will not be used unless there is maximum convenience for the user, such as the dictionary and the atlas and encyclopedias.
- The circulation desk should be on the left of the entrance, the last thing the user passes before leaving.
- The rear of the library should house items for which user motivation is strong, such as classroom-assigned materials and meeting rooms, or which the user is willing to spend time and effort obtaining, such as microfiche printouts.

Figure 7.4 An example of a functional layout in a library

Cell layout

A cell layout is one where the transformed resources entering the operation are pre-selected (or pre-select themselves) to move to one part of the operation (or cell) in which all the transforming resources, to meet their immediate processing needs, are located. The cell itself may be arranged in either a functional or product layout (*see* next section). After being processed in the cell, the transformed resources may go on to another cell. In effect, cell layout is an attempt to bring some order to the complexity of flow which characterizes functional layout. Examples of cell layouts include:

- *Some computer component manufacture* – the processing and assembly of some types of computer parts may need a special area dedicated to the manufacturing of parts for one particular customer who has special requirements, such as particularly high quality levels.
- *'Lunch' products area in a supermarket* – some customers use the supermarket just to purchase sandwiches, savoury snacks, cool drinks, yoghurt, etc., for their lunch. These products are often located close together so that customers who are just buying lunch do not have to search around the store.
- *Maternity unit in a hospital* – customers needing maternity attention are a well-defined group who can be treated together and who are unlikely to need the other facilities of the hospital at the same time that they need the maternity unit.

Although the idea of cell layout is often associated with manufacturing, the same principle can be, and is, used in services. In Figure 7.5 the ground floor of a department store is shown, comprising displays of various types of goods in different parts of the store. In this sense the predominant layout of the store is a functional layout. Each display area can be considered a separate process devoted to selling a particular class of goods shoes, clothes, books, and so on. The exception is the sports shop. This area is a shop-within-a-shop area devoted to many goods which have a common sporting theme. For example, it will stock sports clothes, sports shoes, sports bags, sports magazines, sports books and videos, sports equipment and gifts and sports energy drinks. Within the 'cell' there are all the 'processes' which are also located elsewhere in the store. They have been located in the 'cell' not because they are similar goods (shoes, books and drinks would not usually be located together) but because they are needed to satisfy the needs of a particular type of customer. The store management calculates that enough customers come to the store to buy 'sports goods' in particular (rather than shoes, clothes, books, etc.) to devote an area specifically for them. The store is also aware that someone coming to the store with the intention of purchasing some sports shoes might also be persuaded to buy other sports goods if they are placed in the same area.

Product (line) layout

Product layout involves locating the transforming resources entirely for the convenience of the transformed resources. Each product, piece of information or customer follows a pre-arranged route in which the sequence of activities that are required matches the sequence in which the processes have been located. The transformed resources 'flow' along a 'line' of processes. This is why this type of layout is sometimes called flow or line layout. Flow is clear, predictable and therefore relatively easy to control. Usually, it is the standardized requirements of the product or service which lead to operations choosing product layouts. Examples of product layout include:

- *Automobile assembly* – almost all variants of the same model require the same sequence of processes.
- *Mass-immunization programme* – all customers require the same sequence of clerical, medical and counselling activities.
- *Self-service cafeteria* – generally the sequence of customer requirements (starter, main course, dessert, and drink) is common to all customers, but layout also helps control customer flow.

Figure 7.5 The ground floor plan of a department store showing the sports goods shop-within-a-shop retail 'cell'

But don't think that product (line) layouts are not changing. Even Toyota, the best known of all automobile companies that routinely use this type of layout, are rethinking the assembly line. The appreciation of the Japanese yen has made it difficult for vehicles made in Japan to compete; and while Toyota, like other Japanese firms, have built factories in other parts of the world, cost savings had to be made to enable them to continue to manufacture in Japan. Figure 7.6 shows just two of the ideas that Toyota are employing at their Miyagi factory in Japan to make assembly lines even more efficient.[4] The top illustration shows how Toyota have positioned vehicles sideways rather than the conventional lengthways positioning. A simple idea, but it has the advantage of shortening the line by 35 per cent (which saves on the cost of constructing the line and requires fewer steps by workers) and shortening the distance that workers have to walk between cars (which increases productivity). The bottom illustration shows how, instead of the vehicle chassis hanging from overhead conveyor belts, they are positioned on raised platforms. This costs only half as much to construct and allows ceiling heights to be lowered, which is more space efficient and reduces heating and cooling costs by 40 per cent.

Mixed layouts

Many operations either design themselves hybrid layouts which combine elements of some or all of the basic layout types, or use the 'pure' basic layout types in different parts of the operation. For example, a hospital would normally be arranged on functional-layout principles – each department representing a particular type of function (the X-ray department, the surgical theatres, the blood-processing laboratory, and so on). Yet within each department, quite different

Apple has opened a string of over 300 Apple Stores all over the world in leading locations like London's Regent Street and Covent Garden, Grand Central Station and Fifth Avenue in New York, the Louvre in Paris, and the spectacular Beijing store with its 40-foot curved glass exterior. These stores are large, beautifully architected, and in keeping with Apple's brand. Then in 2012 it was reported that Apple would be opening a store-within-a-store in one of the world's most famous department stores. Harrods is a huge 'upmarket' department store in the heart of London. It covers over five acres of land and the store itself features over one million square feet of selling space. Across the million square feet are over 330 departments that cover clothing, technology accessories, and food. Commentators declared that the Apple brand would fit in well within the Harrods' surroundings, and the Harrods Apple Store, itself, would blend in nicely with the store's noted architecture. The Apple Store will feature most of what makes an Apple Store an Apple Store, like wooden tables and signage. Like most retail 'cells', all the products sold in the Apple Store in Harrods could be sold in other departments. But they are collected together for another purpose. In this case the internal Apple Store supports the Apple brand, yet does not inconvenience customers. In fact, for Apple fans, it is more convenient.

Figure 7.6 Contrasting arrangements in product (line) layout for automobile assembly plants

layouts are used. The X-ray department is probably arranged in a functional layout, the surgical theatres in a fixed-position layout, and the blood-processing laboratory in a product layout.

Another example is shown in Figure 7.7. Here a restaurant complex is shown with three different types of restaurant and the kitchen which serves them all. The kitchen is arranged in a functional layout, with the various processes (food storage, food preparation, cooking processes, etc.) grouped together. The traditional service restaurant is arranged in a fixed-position layout. The customers stay at their tables while the food is brought to (and sometimes cooked at) the tables. The buffet restaurant is arranged in a cell-type layout with each buffet area having all the processes (dishes) necessary to serve customers with their starter, main course or dessert. Finally, in the cafeteria restaurant, all customers take the same route when being served with their meal. They may not take the opportunity to be served with every dish but they move through the same sequence of processes.

Figure 7.7 A restaurant complex with all four basic layout types

WHAT TYPE OF LAYOUT SHOULD AN OPERATION CHOOSE?

The importance of flow to an operation will depend on its volume and variety characteristics. When volume is very low and variety is relatively high, 'flow' is not a major issue. For example, in telecommunications satellite manufacture, a fixed-position layout is likely to be appropriate because each product is different and because products 'flow' through the operation very infrequently, so it is just not worth arranging facilities to minimize the flow of parts through the operation. With higher volume and lower variety, flow becomes an issue. If the variety is still high, however, an entirely flow-dominated arrangement is difficult because there will be different flow patterns. For example, the library in Figure 7.4 will arrange its different categories of books and its other services partly to minimize the average distance its customers have to 'flow' through the operation. But, because its customers' needs vary, it will arrange its layout to satisfy the majority of its customers (but perhaps inconvenience a minority). When the variety of products or services reduces to the point where a distinct 'category' with similar requirements becomes evident but variety is still not small, cell layout could become appropriate, as in the sports goods cell in Figure 7.5. When variety is relatively small and volume is high, flow can become regularized and a product-based layout is likely to be appropriate, as in an assembly plant (*see* Fig. 7.8).

Although the volume–variety characteristics of the operation will narrow the choice down to one or two layout options, there are other associated advantages and disadvantages, some

> **✳ Operations Principle**
>
> Resources in low volume/high variety processes should be arranged to cope with irregular flow.

> **✳ Operations principle**
>
> Resources in high volume/low variety processes should be arranged to cope with smooth, regular flow.

Chocolate and customers both have a 'product' layout at Cadbury's[6]

Flow of chocolate in the factory

In the famous Cadbury's chocolate factory at Bourneville, on the outskirts of Birmingham, UK, production processes are based on a *product (line) layout*. This has allowed Cadbury's engineers to develop the technology to meet the technical and capacity requirements of each stage of the process. Consider, for example, the production of Cadbury's Dairy Milk bars. First, the standard liquid chocolate is prepared from cocoa beans, fresh milk and sugar using specialized equipment, connected together with pipes and conveyors. These processes operate continuously, day and night, to ensure consistency of both the chocolate itself and the rate of out-

Source: Alamy Images/Paul Marriot

put. Next, the liquid is pumped through to the moulding department, where it is dispensed into a moving line of plastic moulds which form the chocolate bars and vibrate them to remove any trapped air bubbles. The moulds then move through a large refrigerator so the chocolate can harden. The moulded bars then pass directly to automated wrapping and packing machines, from where they go to the warehouse.

Flow of customers in the visitor attraction

Cadbury also has a large visitor centre called 'Cadbury World' alongside the factory. It is a permanent exhibition devoted entirely to chocolate and the part Cadbury has played in its fascinating history. The design is also based on a 'product' (line) layout with a single route for all customers that promotes a smooth flow of customers, avoiding bottlenecks and delays where possible. Entry to the Exhibition Area is by timed ticket, to ensure a constant flow of input customers, who are free to walk around at

their preferred speed, but are constrained to keep to the single track through the sequence of displays. On leaving this section, they are directed upstairs to the Chocolate Packaging Plant, where a guide escorts standard-sized batches of customers to the appropriate positions where they can see the packing processes and a video presentation. The groups are then led down to and around the Demonstration Area, where skilled employees demonstrate small-scale production of handmade chocolates. Finally, visitors are free to roam unaccompanied through a long, winding path of the remaining exhibits.

Cadbury has chosen to use the line layout design for both the production of chocolates and the processing of its visitors. In both cases, volumes are large and the variety offered is limited. Sufficient demand exists for each standard 'product', and the operations objective is to achieve consistent high quality at low cost. Both operations have little volume flexibility, and both would be expensive to change.

---

of which are shown in Table 7.2. However, the type of operation will also influence the relative importance of these advantages and disadvantages. For example, a high-volume television manufacturer may find the low-cost characteristics of a product layout attractive, but an amusement theme park may adopt the same layout type primarily because of the way it 'controls' customer flow.

Cost analysis

Of all the characteristics of the various layout types, perhaps the most generally significant are the unit cost implications of layout choice. This is best understood by distinguishing between the fixed- and variable-cost elements of adopting each layout type. For any particular product

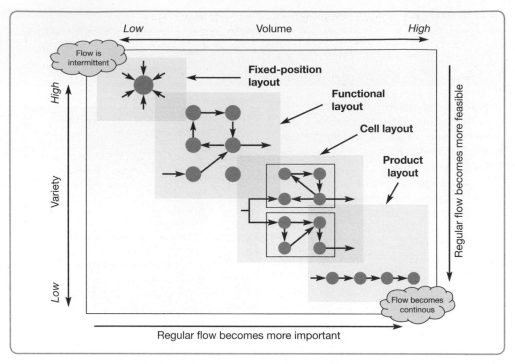

Figure 7.8 Different process layouts are appropriate for different volume-variety combinations

or service, the fixed costs of physically constructing a fixed-position layout are relatively small compared with any other way of producing the same product or service. However, the variable costs of producing each individual product or service are relatively high compared to the alternative layout types. Fixed costs then tend to increase as one moves from fixed-position, through process and cell, to product layout. Variable costs per product or service tend to decrease, however. The total costs for each layout type will depend on the volume of products or services produced and are shown in Figure 7.9(a). This seems to show that for any volume there is a lowest-cost basic layout. However, in practice, the cost analysis of layout selection is rarely as clear as this. The exact cost of operating the layout is difficult to forecast and will probably depend on many often difficult to predict factors. Rather than use lines to represent the cost of layout as volume increases, broad bands, within which the real cost is likely to lie, are prob-

> **✴ Operations principle**
>
> Different layout types have different fixed and variable costs which determine the appropriateness of layout for varying volume–variety characteristics.

ably more appropriate (*see* Fig. 7.9b). The discrimination between the different layout types is now far less clear. There are ranges of volume for which any of two or three layout types might provide the lowest operating cost. The less certainty there is over the costs, the broader the cost 'bands' will be, and the less clear the choice will be. The probable costs of adopting a particular layout need to be set in the broader context of advantages and disadvantages in Table 7.2.

Servicescapes

In operations that transform customers (high-visibility operations, see Chapter 1) the general look and feel of the operation will be as important as, if not more important than, cost and distance criteria. The term that is often used to describe the look and feel of the environment within an operation is its 'servicescape'. There are many academic studies that have shown that the servicescape of an operation plays an important role, both positive and negative, in shaping customers' views.[7] The general idea is that ambient conditions, space factors and signs and symbols in a service operation will create an 'environment experience' both for employees and customers; and this environmental experience should support the service

Table 7.2 The advantages and disadvantages of the basic layout types

	Advantages	*Disadvantages*
Fixed-position	● Very high mix and product flexibility ● Product or customer not moved or disturbed ● High variety of tasks for staff	● Very high unit costs ● Scheduling of space and activities can be difficult ● Can mean much movement of plant and staff
Process	● High mix and product flexibility ● Relatively robust in the case of disruptions ● Relatively easy supervision of equipment or plant	● Low facilities utilization ● Can have very high work-in-progress or customer queuing ● Complex flow can be difficult to control
Cell	● Can give a good compromise between cost and flexibility for relatively high-variety operations ● Fast throughput ● Group work can result in good motivation	● Can be costly to rearrange existing layout ● Can need more plant and equipment ● Can give lower plant utilization
Product	● Low unit costs for high volume ● Gives opportunities for specialization of equipment ● Materials or customer movement is convenient	● Can have low mix flexibility ● Not very robust if there is disruption ● Work can be very repetitive

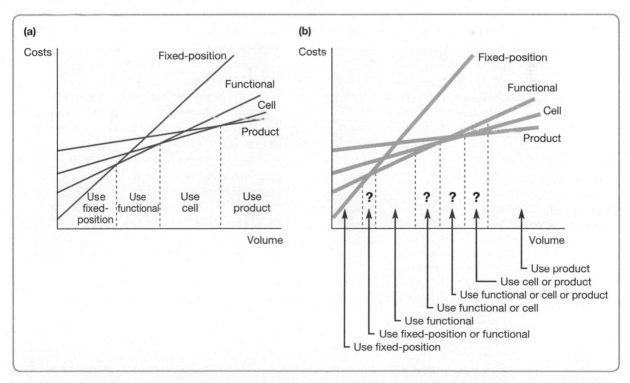

Figure 7.9 (a) The basic layout types have different fixed- and variable-cost characteristics which seem to determine which one to use. (b) In practice the uncertainty about the exact fixed and variable costs of each layout means the decision can rarely be made on cost alone

concept (see Chapter 5). The individual factors that influence this experience will then lead to certain responses (again, in both employees and customers). These responses can be put into three main categories:

- cognitive (what people think);
- emotional (what they feel); and
- physiological (what their bodies experience).

However, remember that a servicescape will contain not only objective, measureable and controllable stimuli but also subjective, immeasurable and often uncontrollable stimuli, which will influence customer behaviour. The obvious example is other customers frequenting an operation. As well as controllable stimuli – such as the colour, lighting, design, space and music – other issues such as the number, demographics and appearance of one's fellow customers will also shape the impression of the operation.

HOW SHOULD EACH BASIC LAYOUT TYPE BE DESIGNED IN DETAIL?

Once the basic layout type has been decided, the next step is to decide the detailed design of the layout. Detailed design is the act of operationalizing the broad principles which were implicit in the choice of the basic layout type.

SHORT CASE   The transparent factory[8]

Source: Alamy Images/Vario Images GmbH & Co.KG

Do not assume that the idea of servicescapes applies only to high-contact service operations. VW's 'transparent factory' in the heart of Dresden in Germany certainly is visually impressive and does not look like a traditional automobile assembly plant. Inside the factory that makes the very upmarket Phaeton sedan, the floors are expensive Canadian maple, the factory walls are made of clear glass (a loudspeaker outside imitates territorial bird sounds to keep birds from flying into the glass) and the workers all wear white coats and gloves. In fact the operation has the atmosphere of a research lab rather than a factory. Partly this is because the dirtier, noisier processes such as pressing, welding and the painting of steel bodies take place in another facility. Partly though, it is because the facility is as much a customer relations and marketing device as it is a production plant. Thousands of visitors visit the plant for tours each year. Its layout is visitor-friendly and is designed to receive 250 tourists per day by advance reservation, who are charged 5 euros each. Customers or prospective customers are not charged. The ground floor houses a restaurant, and on the lower level there is a simulator that provides visitors a virtual test drive of the Phaeton. Yet the 'Transparent Factory' is also a serious manufacturing operation, producing an average of 44 Phaetons a day, most of which are destined for China, Germany and South Korea.

Detailed design in fixed-position layout

In fixed-position arrangements the location of resources will be determined, not on the basis of the flow of transformed resources, but on the convenience of transforming resources themselves. The objective of the detailed design of fixed-position layouts is to achieve a layout for the operation which allows all the transforming resources to maximize their contribution to the transformation process by allowing them to provide an effective 'service' to the transformed resources. The detailed layout of some fixed-position layouts, such as building sites, can become very complicated, especially if the planned schedule of activities is changed frequently. Imagine the chaos on a construction site if heavy trucks continually (and noisily) drove past the site office, delivery trucks for one contractor had to cross other contractors' areas to get to where they were storing their own materials, and the staff who spent most time at the building itself were located furthest away from it. Although there are techniques which help to locate resources on fixed-position layouts, they are not widely used.

Detailed design in functional layout

The detailed design of functional layouts is complex, as is flow in this type of layout. Chief among the factors which lead to this complexity is the very large number of different options. For example, in the very simplest case of just two work centres, there are only two ways of arranging these *relative to each other*. But there are six ways of arranging three centres and 120 ways of arranging five centres. This relationship is a factorial one. For N centres there are factorial N ($N!$) different ways of arranging the centres, where:

$$N! = N \times (N-1) \times (N-2) \times \ldots \times (1)$$

So for a relatively simple functional layout with, say, 20 work centres, there are $20! = 2.433 \times 10^{18}$ ways of arranging the operation. This combinatorial complexity of functional layouts makes optimal solutions difficult to achieve in practice. Most functional layouts are designed by a combination of intuition, common sense, and systematic trial and error.

> ✴ **Operations principle**
>
> Functional layouts are combinatorially complex; there are many alternative layouts.

The information for functional layouts

Before starting the process of detailed design in functional layouts there are some essential pieces of information which the designer needs:

- the area required by each work centre;
- the constraints on the shape of the area allocated to each work centre;
- the degree and direction of flow between each work centre (for example, number of journeys, number of loads or cost of flow per distance travelled);
- the desirability of work centres being close together or close to some fixed point in the layout.

The degree and direction of flow are usually shown on a flow record chart like that shown in Figure 7.10(a) which records in this case the number of loads transported between departments. This information could be gathered from routing information, or where flow is more random, as in a library for example, the information could be collected by observing the routes taken by customers over a typical period of time. If the direction of the flow between work centres makes little difference to the layout, the information can be collapsed as shown in Figure 7.10(b), an alternative form of which is shown in Figure 7.10(c). There may be significant differences in the costs of moving materials or customers between different work centres. For example, in Figure 7.10(d) the unit cost of transporting a load between the five work centres is shown. Combining the unit cost and flow data gives the cost per distance travelled data shown in Figure 7.10(e). This has been collapsed as before into Figure 7.10(f).

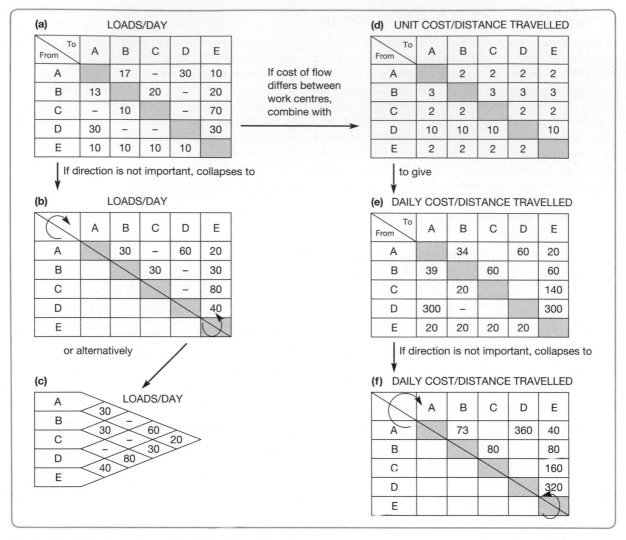

Figure 7.10 Collecting information in functional layout

Minimizing distance travelled

In most examples of functional layout, the prime objective is to minimize the costs to the operation which are associated with flow through the operation. This usually means minimizing the total distance travelled in the operation. For example, Figure 7.11(a) shows a simple six-centre functional layout with the total number of journeys between centres each day. The effectiveness of the layout, at this simple level, can be calculated from:

$$\text{Effectiveness of layout} = \sum F_{ij}D_{ij} \text{ for all } i \neq j$$

where F_{ij} = the flow in loads or journeys per period of time from work centre i to
work centre j
D_{ij} = the distance between work centre i and work centre j.

The lower the effectiveness score, the better the layout. In this example the total of the number of journeys multiplied by the distance for each pair of departments where there is some flow is 4,450 metres. This measure will indicate whether changes to the layout improve its effectiveness (at least in the narrow terms defined here). For example, if centres C and E are exchanged as in Figure 7.11(b), the effectiveness measure becomes 3,750, showing that the new layout now has reduced the total distance travelled in the operation. These calculations assume that all journeys are the same in that their cost to the operation is the same. In some operations this

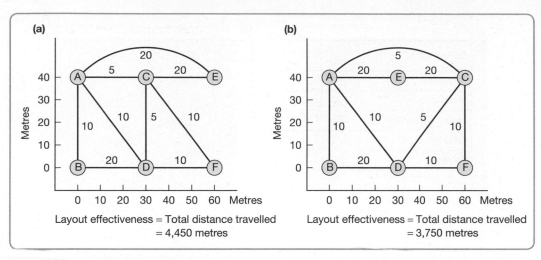

(a) Layout effectiveness = Total distance travelled = 4,450 metres

(b) Layout effectiveness = Total distance travelled = 3,750 metres

Figure 7.11 (a) and (b) The objective of most functional layouts is to minimize the cost associated with movement in the operation, sometimes simplified to minimizing the total distance travelled

is not so, however. For example, in the hospital some journeys involving healthy staff and relatively fit patients would have little importance compared with other journeys where very sick patients need to be moved from the operating theatres to intensive-care wards. In these cases a cost (or difficulty) element is included in the measure of layout effectiveness:

$$\text{Effectiveness of layout} = \sum F_{ij} D_{ij} C_{ij} \text{ for all } i \neq j$$

where C_{ij} = the cost per distance travelled of making a journey between departments i and j.

The steps in determining the location of work centres in a functional layout is illustrated in the worked example: Rotterdam Educational Group.

Worked example

Rotterdam Educational Group (REG) is a company which commissions, designs and manufactures education packs for distance-learning courses and training. It has leased a new building with an area of 1,800 square metres, into which it needs to fit 11 'departments'. Prior to moving into the new building it has conducted an exercise to find the average number of trips taken by its staff between the 11 departments. Although some trips are a little more significant than others (because of the loads carried by staff), it has been decided that all trips will be treated as being of equal value.

Step 1 – Collect information

The areas required by each department together with the average daily number of trips between departments are shown in the flow chart in Figure 7.12. In this example the direction of flow is not relevant and very low flow rates (fewer than five trips per day) have not been included.

Step 2 – Draw schematic layout

Figure 7.13 shows the first schematic arrangement of departments. The thickest lines represent high flow rates between 70 and 120 trips per day; the medium lines are used for flow rates between 20 and 69 trips per day; and the thinnest lines for flow rates between 5 and 19 trips per day. The objective here is to arrange the work centres so that those with the thick lines are closest together. The higher the flow rate, the shorter the line should be.

DEPARTMENT	AREA (m²)	CODE
Reception	85	A
Meeting room	160	B
Layout and design	100	C
Editorial	225	D
Printing	200	E
Cutting	75	F
Receiving and shipping	200	G
Binding	120	H
Video production	160	I
Packing	200	J
Audio production	100	K

Dimensions of the building = 30 metres × 60 metres

Figure 7.12 Flow information for Rotterdam Educational Group

Step 3 – Adjust the schematic layout

If departments were arranged exactly as shown in Figure 7.13(a), the building which housed them would be of an irregular, and therefore high-cost, shape. The layout needs adjusting to take into account the shape of the building. Figure 7.13(b) shows the departments arranged in a more ordered fashion which corresponds to the dimensions of the building.

Step 4 – Draw the layout

Figure 7.14 shows the departments arranged with the actual dimensions of the building and occupying areas which approximate to their required areas. Although the distances between the centroids of departments have changed from Figure 7.14 to accommodate their physical shape, their relative positions are the same. It is at this stage that a quantitative expression of the cost of movement associated with this relative layout can be calculated.

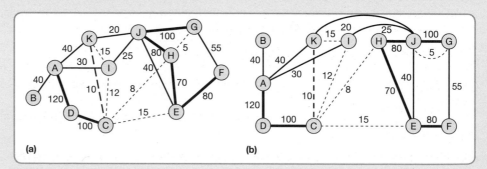

(a)

(b)

Figure 7.13 (a) Schematic layout placing centres with high traffic levels close to each other. (b) Schematic layout adjusted to fit building geometry

Step 5 – Check by exchanging

The layout in Figure 7.14 seems to be reasonably effective but it is usually worthwhile to check for improvement by exchanging pairs of departments to see if any reduction in total flow can be obtained. For example, departments H and J might be exchanged, and the total distance travelled calculated again to see if any reduction has been achieved.

Figure 7.14 Final layout of building

Computer-aided functional layout design

The combinatorial complexity of functional layout has led to the development of several heuristic procedures to aid the design process. Heuristic procedures use what have been described as 'shortcuts in the reasoning process' and 'rules of thumb' in the search for a reasonable solution. They do not search for an optimal solution (though they might find one by chance) but rather attempt to derive a good suboptimal solution. One such computer-based heuristic procedure is called CRAFT (Computerized Relative Allocation of Facilities Technique). The reasoning behind this procedure is that, whereas it is infeasible to evaluate factorial N ($N!$) different layouts when N is large, it is feasible to start with an initial layout and then evaluate all the different ways of exchanging two work centres.

There are:

$$\frac{N!}{2!(N-2)}$$

possible ways of exchanging two out of N work centres. So for a 20-work-centre layout, there are 190 ways of exchanging two work centres.

Three inputs are required for the CRAFT heuristic: a matrix of the flow between departments; a matrix of the cost associated with transportation between each of the departments; and a spatial array showing an initial layout. From these:

- the location of the centroids of each department is calculated;
- the flow matrix is weighted by the cost matrix, and this weighted flow matrix is multiplied by the distances between departments to obtain the total transportation costs of the initial layout;
- the model then calculates the cost consequence of exchanging every possible pair of departments.

The exchange giving the most improvement is then fixed, and the whole cycle is repeated with the updated cost flow matrix until no further improvement is made by exchanging two departments.

Detailed design in cell layout

Figure 7.15 shows how a functional layout has been divided into four cells, each of which has the resources to process a 'family' of parts. In doing this the operations management has implicitly taken two interrelated decisions regarding:

- the extent and nature of the cells it has chosen to adopt;
- which resources to allocate to which cells.

Figure 7.15 Cell layout groups together the processes which are necessary for a family of products/services

Production flow analysis

The detailed design of cellular layouts is difficult, partly because the idea of a cell is itself a compromise between process and product layout. To simplify the task, it is useful to concentrate on either the process or product aspects of cell layout. If cell designers choose to concentrate on processes, they could use cluster analysis to find which processes group naturally together. This involves examining each type of process and asking which other types of processes a product or part using that process is also likely to need. One approach to allocating tasks and machines to cells is production flow analysis (PFA), which examines both product requirements and process grouping simultaneously. In Figure 7.16(a) a manufacturing operation has grouped the components it makes into eight families – for example, the components in family 1 require machines 2 and 5. In this state the matrix does not seem to exhibit any natural groupings. If the order of the rows and columns is changed, however, to move the crosses as close as possible to the diagonal of the matrix which goes from top left to bottom right, then a clearer pattern emerges. This is illustrated in Figure 7.16(b) and shows that the machines could conveniently be grouped together in three cells, indicated on the diagram as cells A, B and C. Although this procedure is a particularly useful way to allocate machines to cells, the analysis is rarely totally clean. This is the case here where component family 8 needs processing by machines 3 and 8 which have been allocated to cell B. There are some partial solutions for this. More machines could be purchased

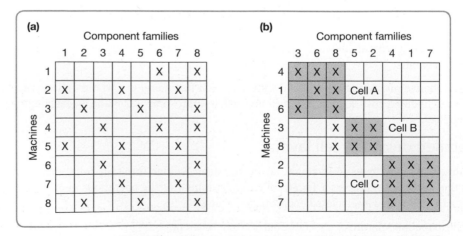

Figure 7.16 (a) and (b) Using production flow analysis to allocate machines to cells

and put into cell A. This would clearly solve the problem but requires investing capital in a new machine which might be under-utilized. Or, components in family 8 could be sent to cell B after they have been processed in cell A (or even in the middle of their processing route if necessary). This solution avoids the need to purchase another machine but it conflicts partly with the basic idea of cell layout – to achieve a simplification of a previously complex flow. Or, if there are several components like this, it might be necessary to devise a special cell for them (usually called a remainder cell) which will almost be like a mini-functional layout. This remainder cell does remove the 'inconvenient' components from the rest of the operation, however, leaving it with a more ordered and predictable flow.

Detailed design in product layout

The nature of the product layout design decision is a little different to the other layout types. Rather than 'where to place what', product layout is concerned more with 'what to place where'. Locations are frequently decided upon and then work tasks are allocated to each location. For example, it may have been decided that four stations are needed to make computer cases. The decision then is which of the tasks that go into making the cases should be allocated to each station. The main product layout decisions are as follows:

- What cycle time is needed?
- How many stages are needed?
- How should the task-time variation be dealt with?
- How should the layout be balanced?

The cycle time of product layouts

The cycle time (as was mentioned in Chapter 4) is the time between completed products, pieces of information or customers emerging from the process. Cycle time is a vital factor in the design of product layouts and has a significant influence on most of the other detailed design decisions. It is calculated by considering the likely demand for the products or services over a period and the amount of production time available in that period.

Worked examtple

Suppose the regional back-office operation of a large bank is designing an operation which will process its mortgage applications. The number of applications to be processed is 160 per week and the time available to process the applications is 40 hours per week.

$$\text{Cycle time for the layout} = \frac{\text{time available}}{\text{number to be processed}}$$

$$= \frac{40}{160} = \frac{1}{4}\text{ hours}$$

$$= 15 \text{ minutes}$$

So the bank's layout must be capable of processing a completed application once every 15 minutes.

The number of stages

The next decision concerns the number of stages in the layout and depends on the cycle time required and the total quantity of work involved in producing the product or service. This latter piece of information is called the total work content. The larger the total work content and the smaller the required cycle time, the more stages will be necessary.

Task-time variation

Imagine a line of four stages, each contributing a quarter of the total work content of processing the mortgage, and passing the documentation on to the next stage every 15 minutes. In practice, of course, the flow would not be so regular. Each station's allocation of work might on average take 15 minutes, but almost certainly the time will vary each time a mortgage application is processed. This is a general characteristic of all repetitive processing (and indeed of all work performed by humans) and can be caused by such factors as differences between each product or service being processed along the line (in the mortgage-processing example, the time some tasks require will vary depending on the personal circumstances of the person applying for the loan), or slight variations in coordination and effort on the part of staff performing the task. This variation can introduce irregularity into the flow along the line, which in turn can lead to both periodic queues at the stages and lost processing time. It may even prove necessary to introduce more resources into the operation to compensate for the loss of efficiency resulting from work-time variation.

Balancing work-time allocation

One of the most important design decisions in product layout is that of line balancing. In the mortgage-processing example we have assumed that the 15 minutes of work content are allocated equally to the four stations. This is nearly always impossible to achieve in practice and some imbalance in the work allocation results. Inevitably this will increase the effective cycle time of the line. If it becomes greater than the required cycle time, it may be necessary to devote extra resources, in the shape of a further stage, to compensate for the imbalance. The effectiveness of the line-balancing activity is measured by balancing loss. This is the time wasted through the unequal allocation of work as a percentage of the total time invested in processing the product or service.

> ✳ **Operations principle**
>
> Allocating work equally to each stage in a process (balancing) smooths flow and avoids bottlenecks.

Balancing techniques

There are a number of techniques available to help in the line-balancing task. Again, in practice, the most useful (and most used) 'techniques' are the relatively simple such as the precedence diagram. This is a representation of the ordering of the elements which comprise the total work content of the product or service. Each element is represented by a circle. The circles are connected by arrows which signify the ordering of the elements. Two rules apply when constructing the diagram:

- the circles which represent the elements are drawn as far to the left as possible;
- none of the arrows which show the precedence of the elements should be vertical.

The precedence diagram, either using circles and arrows or transposed into tabular form, is the most common starting point for most balancing techniques. We do not treat the more complex of these techniques here but it is useful to describe the general approach to balancing product layouts.

Worked example

In Figure 7.17 the work allocations in a four-stage line are illustrated. The total amount of time invested in producing each product or service is four times the cycle time because, for every unit produced, all four stages have been working for the cycle time. When the work is equally allocated between the stages, the total time invested in each product or service produced is $4 \times 2.5 = 10$ minutes. However, when work is unequally allocated, as illustrated, the time invested is $3.0 \times 4 = 12$ minutes, i.e. 2.0 minutes of time, 16.67 per cent of the total, is wasted.

Figure 7.17 Balancing loss is that proportion of the time invested in processing the product or service which is not used productively

This general approach is to allocate elements from the precedence diagram to the first stage, starting from the left, in order of the columns until the work allocated to the stage is as close to, but less than, the cycle time. When that stage is as full of work as is possible without exceeding the cycle time, move on to the next stage, and so on until all the work elements are allocated. The key issue is how to select an element to be allocated to a stage when more than one element could be chosen. Two heuristic rules have been found to be particularly useful in deciding this:

- Simply choose the largest that will 'fit' into the time remaining at the stage.
- Choose the element with the most 'followers': that is the highest number of elements which can only be allocated when that element has been allocated.

Worked example

Karlstad Kakes (KK) is a manufacturer of speciality cakes, which has recently obtained a contract to supply a major supermarket chain with a speciality cake in the shape of a space rocket. It has been decided that the volumes required by the supermarket warrant a special production line to perform the finishing, decorating and packing of the cake. This line would have to carry out the elements shown in Figure 7.18, which also shows the precedence diagram for the total job. The initial order from the supermarket is for 5,000 cakes a week and the number of hours worked by the factory is 40 per week. From this:

$$\text{The required cycle time} = \frac{40 \text{ hrs} \times 60 \text{ mins}}{5,000}$$

$$= 0.48 \text{ mins}$$

Element a – De-tin and trim	0.12 mins
Element b – Reshape with off-cuts	0.30 mins
Element c – Clad in almond fondant	0.36 mins
Element d – Clad in white fondant	0.25 mins
Element e – Decorate, red icing	0.17 mins
Element f – Decorate, green icing	0.05 mins
Element g – Decorate, blue icing	0.10 mins
Element h – Affix transfers	0.08 mins
Element i – Transfer to base and pack	0.25 mins

Total work content = 1.68 mins

Figure 7.18 Element listing and precedence diagram for Karlstad Kakes

$$\text{The required number of stages} = \frac{1.68 \text{ mins (the total work content)}}{0.48 \text{ mins (the required cycle time)}}$$

$$= 3.5 \text{ stages}$$

This means four stages.

Working from the left on the precedence diagram, elements a and b can be allocated to stage 1. Allocating element c to stage 1 would exceed the cycle time. In fact, only element c can be allocated to stage 2 because including element d would again exceed the cycle time. Element d can be allocated to stage 3. Either element e or element f can also be allocated to stage 3, but not both or the cycle time would be exceeded. Following the 'largest element' heuristic rule, element e is chosen. The remaining elements then are allocated to stage 4. Figure 7.19 shows the final allocation and the balancing loss of the line.

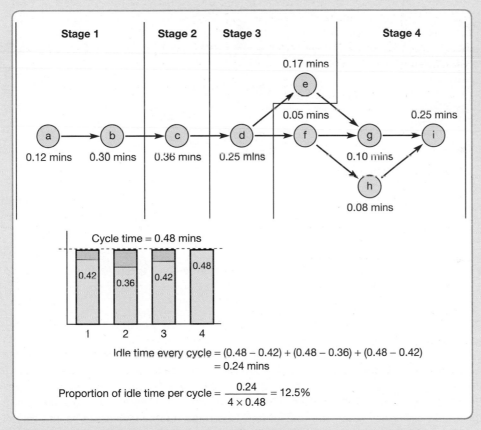

Figure 7.19 Allocation of elements to stages and balancing loss for Karlstad Kakes

Arranging the stages

All the stages necessary to fulfil the requirements of the layout may not be arranged in a sequential 'single line'. Return to the mortgage-processing example, which requires four stages working on the task to maintain a cycle time of one processed application every 15 minutes. The conventional arrangement of the four stages would be to lay them out in one line, each stage having 15 minutes' worth of work. However, nominally, the same output rate could also be achieved by arranging the four stages as two shorter lines, each of two stages with 30 minutes' worth of work each. Alternatively, following this logic to its ultimate conclusion, the stages could be arranged as four parallel stages, each responsible for the whole work content. Figure 7.20 shows these options.

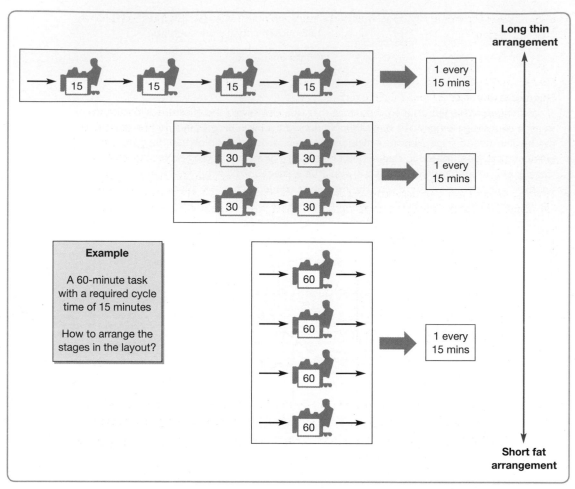

Figure 7.20 The arrangement of stages in product layout can be described on a spectrum from 'long thin' to 'short fat'

This may be a simplified example, but it represents a genuine issue. Should the layout be arranged as a single long thin line, as several short fat parallel lines, or somewhere in between? (Note that 'long' means the number of stages and 'fat' means the amount of work allocated to each stage.) In any particular situation there are usually technical constraints which limit either how 'long and thin' or how 'short and fat' the layout can be, but there is usually a range of possible options within which a choice needs to be made. The advantages of each extreme of the long thin to short fat spectrum are very different and help to explain why different arrangements are adopted.

The advantages of the long thin arrangement These include:

- *Controlled flow of materials or customers* – which is easy to manage.
- *Simple materials handling* – especially if a product being manufactured is heavy, large or difficult to move.
- *Lower capital requirements*. If a specialist piece of equipment is needed for one element in the job, only one piece of equipment would need to be purchased; on short fat arrangements every stage would need one.
- *More efficient operation*. If each stage is performing only a small part of the total job, the person at the stage will have a higher proportion of direct productive work as opposed to the non-productive parts of the job, such as picking up tools and materials.

This latter point is particularly important and is fully explained later (*see* Chapter 9) when we discuss job design.

The advantages of the short fat arrangement These include:

- *Higher mix flexibility*. If the layout needs to process several types of product or service, each stage or line could specialize in different types.
- *Higher volume flexibility*. As volume varies, stages can simply be closed down or started up as required; long thin arrangements would need rebalancing each time the cycle time changed.
- *Higher robustness*. If one stage breaks down or ceases operation in some way, the other parallel stages are unaffected; a long thin arrangement would cease operating completely.
- *Less monotonous work*. In the mortgage example, the staff in the short fat arrangement are repeating their tasks only every hour; in the long thin arrangement it is every 15 minutes.

SUMMARY ANSWERS TO KEY QUESTIONS

Check and improve your understanding of this chapter using self-assessment questions and a personalized study plan, a video case study, and an eText – all at **www.myomlab.com**.

MyOMLab

❯ What is layout?

- The 'layout' of an operation or process is how its transforming resources are positioned relative to each other and how its various tasks are allocated to these transforming resources.
- These two decisions will dictate the pattern of flow for transformed resources as they progress through the operation or process.

❯ What are the basic layout types used in operations?

- There are four basic layout types. They are fixed-position layout, functional layout, cell layout and product (line) layout.

❯ What type of layout should an operation choose?

- Partly this is influenced by the nature of the process type, which in turn depends on the volume–variety characteristics of the operation. Partly also the decision will depend on the objectives of the operation. Cost and flexibility are particularly affected by the layout decision.
- The fixed and variable costs implied by each layout differ such that, in theory, one particular layout will have the minimum costs for a particular volume level. However, in practice, uncertainty over the real costs involved in layout make it difficult to be precise on which is the minimum-cost layout.
- In addition to the conventional operations objectives which will be influenced by the feel and general impression of the layout design, this is often called the 'servicescape' of the operation.

❯ How should each basic layout type be designed in detail?

- In fixed-position layout the materials or people being transformed do not move but the transforming resources move around them. Techniques are rarely used in this type of layout, but some, such as resource location analysis, bring a systematic approach to minimizing the costs and inconvenience of flow at a fixed-position location.

- In functional layout all similar transforming resources are grouped together in the operation. The detailed design task is usually (although not always) to minimize the distance travelled by the transformed resources through the operation. Either manual or computer-based methods can be used to devise the detailed design.

- In cell layout the resources needed for a particular class of product or service are grouped together in some way. The detailed design task is to group the products or customer types such that convenient cells can be designed around their needs. Techniques such as production flow analysis can be used to allocate products or services to cells.

- In product (line) layout, the transforming resources are located in sequence specifically for the convenience of products or product types. The detailed design of product layouts includes a number of decisions, such as the cycle time to which the design must conform, the number of stages in the operation, the way tasks are allocated to the stages in the line, and the arrangement of the stages in the line. The cycle time of each part of the design, together with the number of stages, is a function of where the design lies on the 'long thin' to 'short fat' spectrum of arrangements. This position affects costs, flexibility, robustness and staff attitude to work. The allocation of tasks to stages is called line balancing, which can be performed either manually or through computer-based algorithms.

CASE STUDY   North West Constructive Bank (abridged)[9]

It had been a long day for Andy Curtis when he emerged from the meeting. 'It was terrible in there. The marketing people gave me a really tough time when I told them our current average turnaround times. They were quite happy to remind me that I had told them our "discount rate" product was killing us operationally and that we had to pull it if we were to survive the reorganization. I've been made to look stupid. Four weeks after reorganization and after the product has been pulled, our turnaround times are even worse. I think they are right, we really are a shambles.' Mary Godfrey, his deputy, was protective of her staff. 'It's no use blaming us, we are all working flat out but we can't seem to make any inroads to the piles of work.'

Andy Curtis was the Mortgage Operations Manager for North West Constructive Bank (NWCB), a large retail banking group. His main responsibility was running the new applications process in the bank's new mortgage centre. For twelve months Andy had led a project team that had been planning the consolidation of the bank's original three mortgage-processing centres into one new site. Prior to the consolidation, the bank's mortgage business had been divided into three regions: 'Northern', 'Southern', and 'Western' applications. 'The driver for the consolidation was to achieve economies of

Source: Shutterstock.com/Jj661227

scale. There is no reason why a processing centre need be located close to its market and we could make significant savings by giving up our city centre leases on the three old sites, consolidating all our operations. We also felt that there would be room to develop more flexibility between the three regions when demand varied.' Andy and his team had always known that the merger of the three centres could be difficult, which is why they had planned it for early February, before the spring peak in applications. It was also why they had decided to (at least initially) keep the three regional sets of processing cells located close to each other. Figure 7.21 shows the current layout of the new mortgage floor.

Seven months ago, it became clear that the bank's portfolio of mortgage products would be changing. *'We had a confusing and incoherent legacy of products that even our branches didn't fully understand'* (Parminder Singh, Mortgage Product Manager). The introduction of the new product portfolio was scheduled to start in June. And Andy's team was delighted by the idea of a simplified product portfolio. *'We can see two operational advantages. First, by consolidating all three centres into one we can get greater economies of scale. Second, the new product portfolio could considerably reduce the variety, and hopefully complexity, of our processing.'*

Demand

Demand fluctuated according to the time of year and specific offers. The 'discounted rate' product had been seen as very attractive by the market. Although intended as a short-term offer, Marketing had wanted the product to continue for another few months, but Andy persuaded them to discontinue it to reduce the demand on the new applications process during the reorganization. Unfortunately, when the news of the imminent demise of the discounted rate product broke there was a final surge in demand.

The new applications process

The processing of a mortgage application involves four sets of activities:

- 'Input' where applications are keyed into the computer and initial checks carried out.

- 'Underwriting' where the decision to lend is made.
- 'Offer' where the team liaises with surveyors to obtain surveys.
- 'Completion' where sanction letters are sent to solicitors.

When the processes were moved to the new centre, the only significant change from the old way of working was the grouping together of all the 'keying in' activities associated with the input stage. *'Input is a fairly simple activity and there is relatively little difference between different types of product and it has worked very well. Also bringing the teams together has allowed us to examine marginal differences between the ways we used to do it and adopt the best method. The input section have reduced from 19 to 13. It has also allowed staff to specialize to some extent, which can be useful at times.'*

Problems with the new process

In spite of his irritation at the recent meeting, Andy was broadly optimistic. *'We have three problems, which have hit us at the same time. First, the move itself was bound to cause some disruption and has created an uncertain and unstable environment in which to cope with our other problems. Second, the last-minute rush on our discounted rate product meant an extra load above what we expected and hit us just at the wrong time. Third, although we have only been operating with the new layout for four weeks, it's clearly not working as it should.'* Andy's team debated this last point and identified a list of key problems:

- Staff were having to move about more than at the old centres. There, the information was within easy reach of all staff. Now, the files had been consolidated to avoid duplication, so the filing room was further away for most staff.

Figure 7.21 Floor plan for new mortgage processing centre

- Therefore because of the effort in retrieving a file, staff were keeping it on their desk, out of the filing system, for longer than necessary, 'in case it was required again', making it unavailable to any other member of staff.
- All the scanning machines were located together in one location to maintain a high utilization of the machines, but again, this meant that staff had further to walk. Even the southern area team, for whom the scanning machines were convenient, resented the other teams constantly walking through their area.
- There was no clarity of flow. The high level of in-process inventory of partially processed applications (both physical files and virtual files on the IT system) had resulted in a 'black hole syndrome', with applications disappearing into people's in-trays.

'We must get the flow through our process right. Processing a mortgage is a relatively standard task. The only activity where a specialized knowledge matters is at the offer stage, where knowledge of the region is required. We have already put all the input activities together and that has worked well. I don't see why we can't have work flowing from the input section, to underwriting, then to offer, and then to completion, just like a smooth running assembly line.' (Andy Curtis)

Redesigning the process

Three separate options for the design of the process were being actively considered by the management team.

Option 1. Keep the process as it is currently at the new centre, with a common data entry stage serving all regions, and with the three regions each having their own underwriting, offer and completion stages working in series. This arrangement had the advantage of not disrupting the existing way of working and of maintaining the organizational coherence of the three teams, which were each already developing their own cultures.

Option 2. Reorganize the whole process by abandoning the current regional structure and organizing four sequential teams around each of the four stages of data entry, underwriting, offer and completion. The advantage of this arrangement was seen as being more appropriate for the higher volume that the new combined centre was processing. It would also allow some skills, such as underwriting skills and legal skills, to be developed because of the larger number of staff with these skills working together. However, there were some disadvantages. First, it would affect the morale of the existing regionally based teams, especially the southern team who had worked together for many years. Second, for some activities in the offer stage it was still an advantage to have some local knowledge of the regional property markets. Even if this option were adopted, the offer team would probably still have to retain some local 'cells' within the process.

Option 3. In some ways this was the most radical design option being considered. It involved reorganizing into four teams around the four stages within the process, but operating the underwriting stage and offer stage in parallel. This was seen as risky, especially with such high levels of recycled applications, but offered the advantage of short throughput times.

QUESTIONS

1 What appears to be the volume–variety position of the new centre? Is it different from the old centres?

2 Should the process be redesigned, and if so, which option should be adopted?

3 How would you recommend that Andy sets about making any changes?

PROBLEMS AND APPLICATIONS

These problems and applications will help to improve your analysis of operations. You can find more practice problems as well as worked examples and guided solutions on MyOMLab at www.myomlab.com.

1 A loan application process involves 8 separate tasks. Task A takes 10 minutes and does not require any other of the tasks to be performed before it can be started. Similarly, Task B can be started without any other task being completed and takes 8 minutes. Task C takes 16 minutes and cannot be performed until Task A has been done. Task D cannot be done until both A and B have been performed and takes 8 minutes. Task E requires Task C and D to be finished and takes 8 minutes. After Task E has been performed, Tasks F and G, taking respectively 5 and 17 minutes, can be performed. Finally (but only after Tasks F and G have been performed), Task H can be performed and takes 11 minutes. Devise a precedence diagram for this process, and, assuming a required cycle time of 18 minutes, determine how many people will be required to perform the task, and, if they are arranged in a 'product' layout, how the tasks will be allocated to each person. Calculate the balancing loss for this layout.

2 A simple product has 8 elements (a to h) whose times and immediate predecessors are shown in Table 7.4. Devise a product layout that will produce products at a rate of at least 6 products an hour. How many people will be required for this layout, and what will be its balancing loss?

Table 7.4 The immediate predecessors table for a simple product

Task	Time (mins)	Immediate predecessor task
a	5	–
b	4	a
c	3	b
d	4	b
e	2	c
f	6	c
g	3	d, e, f
h	4	g

3 The flow of materials through eight departments is shown in Table 7.5. Assuming that the direction of the flow of materials is not important, construct a relationship chart, a schematic layout and a suggested layout, given that each department is the same size and the eight departments should be arranged four along each side of a corridor.

Table 7.5 Flow of materials

	D1	D2	D3	D4	D5	D6	D7	D8
D1	\	30						
D2	10	\	15	20				
D3		5	\	12	2		15	
D4		6		\	10	20		
D5				8	\	8	10	12
D6	3				2	\	30	
D7	3					13	\	2
D8				10	6		15	\

4 Sketch the layout of your local shop, coffee bar or sports hall reception area. Observe the area and draw onto your sketch the movements of people through the area over a sufficient period of time to get over 20 observations. Assess the flow in terms of volume, variety and type of layout.

5 Revisit the opening short case in this chapter (p. 192) which examines some of the principles behind supermarket layout. Then visit a supermarket and observe people's behaviour. You may wish to try and observe which areas they move slowly past and which areas they seem to move past without paying attention to the products. (You may have to exercise some discretion when doing this; people generally don't like to be stalked round the supermarket too obviously!) Try and verify, as far as you can, some of the principles that were outlined in the opening short case. If you were to redesign the supermarket, what would you recommend?

SELECTED FURTHER READING

This is a relatively technical chapter and, as you would expect, most books and articles on the subject are technical. Here are a few of the more accessible.

Karlsson, C. (1996) **Radically new production systems**, *International Journal of Operations and Production Management*, **vol. 16, no. 11.** An interesting paper because it traces the development of Volvo's factory layouts over the years.

Meyers, F.E. (2000) *Manufacturing Facilities Design and Material Handling*, **Prentice Hall, Upper Saddle River, NJ.** Exactly what it says; thorough.

Rosenbaum, M.S. and Massiah, C. (2011) **An expanded servicescape perspective**, *Journal of Service Management*, **vol. 22, issue 4.** Academic but a good review of the research literature.

White, J.A., White, J.A. Jnr and McGinnis, L.F. (1998) *Facility Layout and Location: An Analytical Approach*, **Prentice Hall Professional, Upper Saddle River, NJ.** One for the practitioners but including many quantitative techniques.

Wu, B. (1994) *Handbook of Manufacturing and Supply Systems Design*, **Taylor and Francis, London.** A general treatment that includes layout and related subjects.

USEFUL WEBSITES

www.bpmi.org Site of the Business Process Management Initiative. Some good resources including papers and articles.

www.bptrends.com News site for trends in business process management generally. Some interesting articles.

www.iienet.org The American Institute of Industrial Engineers site. They are an important professional body for process design and related topics.

www.waria.com Workflow and Reengineering International Association website. Some useful topics.

www.strategosinc.com Some useful briefings, mainly in a manufacturing context.

www.myomlab.com Test which sections you have mastered and which you need to review, with questions, a personalized study plan, video clips, revision tips, and cases.

www.opsman.org Useful materials.

www.iomnet.org.uk The Institute of Operations Management site. One of the main professional bodies for the subject.

www.poms.org A US academic society for production and operations management. Academic, but some useful material, including a link to an encyclopedia of operations management terms.

http://sites.google.com/site/tomiportal.home One of the longest-established portals for the subject. Useful for academics and students alike.

 Now that you have finished reading this chapter, why not visit MyOMLab at **www.myomlab.com** *where you'll find more learning resources to help you make the most of your studies and get a better grade.*

8

Process technology

INTRODUCTION

There is a lot of new process technology around. Few, if any, operations have been unaffected by the advances in process technology that have radically changed everyday life over the last two or three decades. And all indications are that the pace of technological development is not slowing down. This has important implications for operations managers because all operations use some kind of process technology, whether it is a simple internet link or the most complex and sophisticated of automated factories. But whatever the technology, all operations managers need to understand what emerging technologies can do, in broad terms how they do it, what advantages the technology can give, and what constraints it might impose on the operation. Figure 8.1 shows where the issues covered here relate to the overall model of operations management activities.

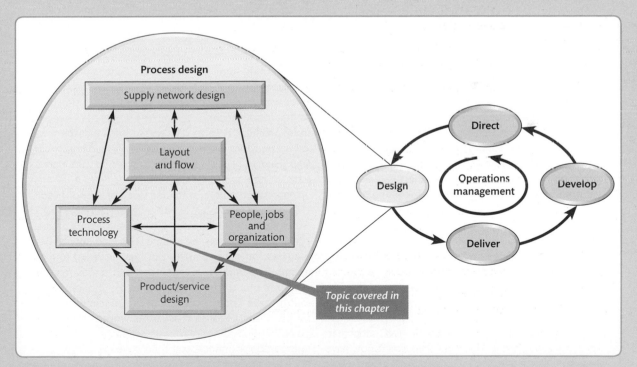

Figure 8.1 The design activities in operations management covered in this chapter

I, Robot[1]

Back in 1920, a Czech playwright, Karel Capek, first coined the name 'robot' (it comes from the Slavonic word for 'work'). Since then, robots have moved from the stuff of science fiction to become a common, if not ubiquitous, element of mass production operations. There are more than a million industrial robots doing routine jobs on production lines. Robots do not take meal breaks, fall ill, complain, or leave for better pay. They perform repetitive tasks more cheaply than humans, give greater accuracy and repeatability, and can also be used where conditions are hazardous or uncomfortable for humans. Anyone who has seen the way that robots weld together automobile bodies, assemble complex products or load and unload work pieces onto a machine cannot fail to recognize the impact that robotics has had on manufacturing operations since they were first introduced in the 1960s.

Source: Shutterstock.com/Jimmi

However, like most new process technologies, the effect of robotics on operations management practice can be both positive and negative, depending on one's perspective. (Film critics, who voted on Hollywood's 50 greatest good guys and 50 greatest baddies, included a robot – the Terminator – on both lists.) Certainly they can save humans from exposure to danger. Robots were used during the clear-up operation amongst the rubble of the Twin Towers in New York. 'Enough people have died here', said a spokesperson for the emergency services. 'We don't want to risk anyone.' Bomb disposal squads use specialized robots which can take at least some of the risk from what remains a hazardous job. Nuclear power stations are decommissioned by using robots to move, dismantle and manipulate hazardous radioactive material. They are also becoming both cheaper and more versatile in their production role. For example, Canon has announced plans to move toward fully automating its digital camera production. Decades ago, Canon, like other manufacturers, began using cell production (see Chapter 7) with teams or a single worker assembling a major part of the product, rather than repeating a simple task. And over the years robots have been routinely used as part of production cells. Canon calls it a 'man-machine cell', and says that 'human involvement will be phased out in making some products'.

Only by substituting robots for people will production be kept in Japan, according to Canon, reversing the trend of Japanese manufacturers moving production to China, India and the rest of Asia, where labour costs are cheaper. 'When machines become more sophisticated, human beings can be transferred to do new kinds of work', Jun Misumi, a Canon spokesperson, said. But it is the nature of the interface between people and robots that is concerning some experts. Akihito Sano, a professor at Nagoya Institute of Technology, has stressed the need for some way in which workers can communicate effectively so that robotic technology can be fine-tuned to become more practical. He also says, reassuringly, that there will always be room for human intelligence and craftsmanship. 'Human beings are needed to come up with innovations on how to use robots. Going [totally] to a no-man operation at that level is still the world of science fiction.' Yet people have always been nervous that new process technologies will take away their jobs. (Capek's original play that gave robots their name described how, at first, they brought many benefits but eventually led to mass unemployment and unhappiness.) But there are some examples of a smooth introduction of robotics. Audi is said to have been successful in introducing industrial robots partly because it asked its workers to suggest potential applications of robotics where they could both improve performance and then gave the same workers jobs supervising, maintaining and programming the robots. It may even be that robots can help defend manufacturing jobs in the rich world. For example, it has been pointed out that one reason why Germany has lost fewer such jobs than Britain is that it has five times as many robots for every 10,000 workers.

OPERATIONS MANAGEMENT AND PROCESS TECHNOLOGY

How operations managers deal with process technology is now one of the most important decisions that shape the capabilities of operations. This was not always the case, at least not for all operations. There used to be a simple division between those operations that used a lot of process technology, usually manufacturing operations, and those that used little or no process technology, usually service operations. But this is no longer true, and arguably has not been true for decades. High-volume services have for years understood the value of process technology. Online transactions for retail and other services are vital for their success. Yet even professional services such as legal and medical services can benefit from new and value-adding technologies (see the piece on telemedicine later in this chapter).

So what do operations managers need to know about process technology? It must be important to them because they are continually involved in the choice, installation and management of process technology. But operations managers are not (or need not be) technologists as such. They do not need to be experts in engineering, computing, biology, electronics or whatever constitutes the core science of the technology. Yet they should be able to do three things. First, they need to understand the technology to the extent that they are able to articulate what it should be able to do. Second, they should be able to evaluate alternative technologies and share in the decisions of which technology to choose. Third, they must implement the technology so that it can reach its full potential in contributing to the performance of the operation as a whole. These are the three issues which this chapter deals with. This is illustrated in Figure 8.2 and forms the structure of the chapter.

Figure 8.2 The three stages of process technology management

WHAT DO OPERATIONS MANAGERS NEED TO KNOW ABOUT PROCESS TECHNOLOGY?

First, let us define what is meant by process technology. It is 'the machines, equipment, and devices that *create* and/or *deliver* products and services'. Process technologies range from milking machines to marking software, from body scanners to bread ovens, from mobile phones to milling machines. Disney World uses flight-simulation technologies to create the thrill of space travel on its rides; just one stage in a long history of Disney Corporation and its 'imagineers' using technology to engineer the experience for their customers. In fact, process technology is pervasive in all types of operations. Without it many of the products and services we all purchase would be less reliable, take longer to arrive and arrive unexpectedly, only be available in a limited variety, and be more expensive. Process technology has a very significant effect on quality, speed, dependability, flexibility and cost. That is why it is so important to operations managers, and that is why we devote a whole chapter to it. Even when technology seems peripheral to the actual creation of goods and services, it can play a key role in *facilitating* the direct transformation of inputs to an operation. For example, the computer systems which run planning and control activities, accounting systems and stock control systems can be used to help managers and operators control and improve the processes. This type of technology is called indirect process technology. It is becoming increasingly important. Many businesses spend more on the computer systems which control their processes than they do on the direct process technology which acts on its material, information or customers.

Process technology and transformed resources

One common method of distinguishing between different types of process technology is by what the technology actually processes – materials, information or customers. We used this distinction earlier (see Chapter 1) when we discussed inputs to operations and processes.

Material-processing technologies

These include any technology that shapes, transports, stores, or in any way changes physical objects. It obviously includes the machines and equipment found in manufacturing operations (such as the robots described in the 'operations in practice' section at the start of this chapter), but also includes trucks, conveyors, packing machines, warehousing systems, and even retail display units. In manufacturing operations, technological advances have meant that the ways in which metals, plastics, fabric and other materials are processed have improved over time. Generally, it is the initial forming and shaping of materials at the start, and the handling and movement through the supply network, that have been most affected by technology advances. Assembling parts to make products, although far more automated that once it was, presents more challenges.

Information-processing technology

Information-processing technology, or just information technology (IT), is the most common single type of technology within operations, and includes any device which collects, manipulates, stores or distributes information. Arguably, it is the use of internet-based technology (generally known as e-business) that has had the most obvious impact on operations – especially those that are concerned with buying and selling activity (e-commerce). Its advantage is that it increases both reach (the number of customers who can be reached and the number of items they can be presented with) and richness (the amount of detail which can be provided concerning both the items on sale and customers' behaviour in buying them). Traditionally, selling involved a trade-off between reach and richness. The internet effectively overcame this trade-off. Also, the internet has equally powerful implications on many other operations management tasks. Table 8.1 illustrates just a few of these.

Customer-processing technology

Although customer-processing operations were once seen as 'low technology', now this technology is very much in evidence in many services. In any airline flight, for example, e-ticket reservation technology, check-in technology, the aircraft and its in-flight entertainment, all play vital parts in service delivery. Increasingly the human element of service is being reduced, with customer-processing technology being used to give an acceptable level of service while significantly reducing costs.

There are three types of customer-processing technologies:

● The first category includes active interaction technology such as automobiles, telephones, internet bookings and purchases, fitness equipment and cash machines (ATMs). In all of these, customers themselves are using the technology to create the service.
● The second category, by contrast, is passive interactive technologies; they 'process' and control customers by constraining their actions in some way. Examples include aircraft, mass transport systems, moving walkways and lifts, cinemas and theme parks.

Table 8.1 Some applications of e-business to operations management

Organizational tasks	E-business applications and/or contributions
Design	Customer feedback on requirements, testing and information exchange in new service/product designs, data mining to understand retail consumer behaviour better
Purchasing	Ordering, fund transfer, supplier selection, supplier portals
Supplier development	Partnership, supplier development
Human resource management	E-recruiting, benefit selection and management, online and multi-media training and education
Planning and control	Production planning and control, scheduling, inventory management, quality monitoring and control, Enterprise Resource Planning (ERP)
Customer service	Online help desks, reduced cycle time, customer services, selection of distribution channels, transportation, scheduling, third-party logistics

Source: Based on E-commerce and its impact on operations management, *International Journal of Production Economics*, Vol. 75, pp. 185–97 (Gunasekaran, A., Marri, H.B., McGaughey, R.E. and Nebhwani, M.D. 2002)

- The third category includes those technologies that are 'aware' of customers but not the other way round; for example, security monitoring technologies in shopping malls or at national frontier customs areas. The objective of these 'hidden technologies' is to track customers' movements or transactions in an unobtrusive way.

Integrating technologies

Of course, some technologies process more than one type of resource. Many newer technologies process combinations of materials, people and customers. These technologies are called integrating technologies. Electronic point of sale (EPOS) technology in shops, for example, processes shoppers, products and information.

Understanding process technologies – the four key questions

Understanding process technology does not (necessarily) mean knowing the details of the science and engineering embedded in the technology. But it does mean knowing enough about the principles behind the technology to be comfortable in evaluating some technical information, capable of dealing with experts in the technology and confident enough to ask relevant questions. In particular the following four key questions can help operations managers to grasp the essentials of the technology.

> ✱ **Operations principle**
>
> Operations managers should understand enough about process technology to evaluate alternatives.

- What does the technology do that is different from other similar technologies?
- How does it do it? That is, what particular characteristics of the technology are used to perform its function?
- What benefits does using the technology give to the operation?
- What constraints or risks does using the technology place on the operation?

For example, return to the 'operations in practice' section that discussed some developments in robotics. Now think through the four key questions in relation to robotics.

What does the technology do? Primarily used for handling materials, for example loading and unloading work pieces onto a machine, for processing where a tool is gripped by the

Customers are not always human[2]

The first milking machines were introduced to grateful farmers over 100 years ago. Until recently, however, they could not operate without a human hand to attach the devices to the cows. This problem has been overcome by a consortium in the Netherlands which includes the Dutch government and several private firms. They hope that the 'robot milkmaid' will do away with the farmers' early morning ritual of milking. Each machine can milk between 60 and 100 cows a day and 'processes' the cows through a number of stages. Computer-controlled gates activated by transmitters around the cows' necks allow the cows to enter. The machine then checks their health, connects them to the milking machine and feeds them while they are being milked. If illness is detected in any cow, or if the machine for some reason fails to connect the milking cups to the cow after five attempts, automatic gates divert it into special pens where the farmer can inspect it later. Finally, the machine ushers the cows out of the system. It also self-cleans periodically and can detect and reject any impure milk. Rather than herding all the cows in a 'batch' to the milking machine twice a day, the system relies on the cows being able to find their own way to the machine. Cows, it would appear, are creatures of habit. Once they have been shown the

Source: Alistair Brandon-Jones

way to the machine a few times, they go there of their own volition because they know that it will relieve the discomfort in their udders, which grow heavier as they fill up. The cows may make the journey to the machine three or more times per day (see Fig. 8.3). Farmers also appear to be as much creatures of habit as their cows, however. Mr Riekes Uneken of Assen, the Dutch farmer who bought the very first robot milking machine, admitted, *'I have a bleeper if things go wrong. But I still like to get up early in the morning. I just like to see what goes on.'*

1 Cows enter, two at a time
2 Robot locates udders with scanners and positions milking cups
3 Cows are fed and milked simultaneously
4 Robot nudges cows to exit

Figure 8.3 Cows are also customers

robot, and for assembly where the robot places parts together. Some robots have some limited sensory feedback through vision control and touch control.

How does it do it? Through a programmable and computer-controlled (sometimes multi-jointed) arm with an effector end piece, which will depend on the task being performed.

What benefits does it give? Can be used where conditions are hazardous or uncomfortable for humans, or where tasks are highly repetitive. Performs repetitive tasks at a lower cost than using humans and gives greater accuracy and repeatability. Some robots are starting to mimic human abilities.

What constraints or risks does it impose? Although the sophistication of robotic movement is increasing, their abilities are still more limited than popular images of robot-driven factories suggest. They are not always good at performing tasks which require delicate sensory feedback or sophisticated judgement. The human–robot interface needs managing carefully, especially where robotics could replace human jobs.

Worked example

QB House speeds up the cut[3]

It was back in 1996 when Kuniyoshi Konishi, frustrated by having to wait to get his hair cut and then pay over 3,000 yen for the privilege, decided that there must be a better way to offer this kind of service. *'Why not',* he said, *'create a no-frills barber's shop where the customer could get a haircut in ten minutes at a cost of 1,000 yen (€7)?'* He realized that a combination of technology and process design could eliminate all non-essential elements from the basic task of cutting hair. How is this done? Well, first QB House's barbers never handle cash. Each shop has a ticket vending machine that accepts 1,000 yen bills (and gives no change!) and issues a ticket that the customer gives the barber in exchange for the haircut. Second, QB House

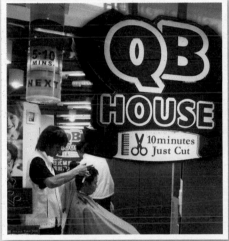

Source: Andy Maluche

does not take reservations. The shops don't even have telephones. Therefore, no receptionist is needed, nor anyone to schedule appointments. Third, QB House developed a lighting system to indicate how long customers will have to wait. Electronic sensors under each seat in the waiting area and in each barber's chair track how many customers are waiting in the shop and different coloured lights are displayed outside the shop. Green lights indicate that there is no waiting, yellow lights indicate a wait of about 5 minutes, and red lights indicate that the wait may be around 15 minutes. This system can also keep track of how long it takes for each customer to be served. Fourth, QB has done away with the traditional Japanese practice of shampooing their customers after the haircut to remove any loose hairs. Instead, the barbers use QB House's own 'air wash' system where a vacuum cleaner hose is pulled down from the ceiling and used to vacuum the customer's hair clean. The QB House system has proved so popular that its shops (now over 200) can be found not only in Japan but in many other South East Asian countries such as Singapore, Malaysia and Thailand. Each year almost 4 million customers experience QB House's 10-minute haircuts.

Analysis

What does the technology do?
Signals availability of servers, thus managing customers' expectations. It avoids hairdressers having to handle cash. Speeds service by substituting 'air wash' for traditional shampoo.

Emerging technologies – assessing their implications

The four questions are universal, in the sense that they can help to understand the implications for operations management of any new or emerging technology. By 'implications', we mean the natural consequence for the operation of adopting the technology. In other words, what would (or could) be the effects on the operation if the technology was included in the operation's transforming resources.

In the rest of this section we look at three technologies that, at the time of writing, were new(ish). One processes materials (3D printing), one processes information (the Internet of Things) and one processes customers (telemedicine). The intention is not to provide a comprehensive survey of technologies – that could be expanded into a whole book – nor is it to delve into technical details. Rather it is to demonstrate how operations managers have to look beyond the technology in order to start to understand their implications.

> ✳ **Operations principle**
>
> Emerging technologies can have a potentially significant impact on how operations are managed.

3D printing (additive manufacturing)

For decades – and in some industries, for centuries – producing physical products has been dominated by the principles of mass production. Standardized designs, repetitive processes and rigid, but productive process technology help to produce most of the items we use every day at (relatively) low cost. The downside of mass production was that variety and customization are difficult to achieve at the same time as economies of scale. However, a process technology called 3D printing (also known as 'additive manufacturing') could have the potential to fundamentally change the economics of manufacturing, and in doing so challenge the dominance of mass production. But 3D printing is not a new technology as such. Since the 1990s designers have been using the technology to make prototype products or parts quickly and cheaply prior to committing to the expense of equipping a factory to produce the real thing. Yet the technology has advanced to the point where it is used, not just to make prototypes, but to produce finished products for real customers.

A 3D printer produces a three-dimensional object by laying down layer upon layer of material until the final form is obtained. This is why it is also known as 'additive manufacturing', because, starting from nothing, successive layers are built up. This contrasts with 'subtractive manufacturing', which starts with more material than an item requires and reduces it through cutting, drilling, squeezing and otherwise removing material until the finished form is reached. The process starts with a computer-based design which is 'digitally deconstructed' by software that takes a series of virtual digital slices through the design. Details of each slice are then sent to the 3D printer to 'print' the respective layers on top of one other to create the 3D object. Different materials can be used to build up the object, from plastic to metals (and even food), and in various sizes limited only by the capacity of the printer.

There are many different techniques used by 3D printers. Some use a process very much like an inkjet printer, spraying each layer as a very thin but precise layer of liquid plastic which

Source: Shutterstock.com/ArchMan

is then hardened by exposure to ultraviolet light. Another melts plastic through an extrusion head which deposits a thin filament thread of material layer by layer. Other printers spread powder as a thin layer onto a 'build tray'. The powder is then solidified with a spray of liquid binder. Yet others fuse the powder using an electron beam operating in a vacuum.

Implications

The obvious implication of 3D printing is the effect it has on the economics of production, especially the economics of making small quantities of novel and/or complicated items economically. The technology's more enthusiastic proponents claim that, at last, the trade-off between speed and efficiency on one hand, and flexibility and variety on the other, has been overcome. Most conventional process technology is at its most efficient when standardized products are made in large batches. But with 3D printing the cost of changing from one product to another is effectively zero. Also, because the technology is 'additive' it reduces waste significantly; sometimes as much as 90 per cent of material is wasted in machining some aerospace parts, for example. It also enables a single 'experimental' item to be made quickly and cheaply, followed by another one after the design has been refined. As Ian Harris, from the Additive Manufacturing Consortium, says, '*It adds up to a new industry which reduces immensely the gap between design and production. Manufacturers will be able to say to their customers, "Tell us what you want" and then they will be able to make specific products for them.*' Some commentators even believe that 3D printing will challenge the advantage of low-cost, low-wage countries. As labour costs become less important, it is argued, manufacturers will return to make items close to their market.

However, like any new technology, it is not without its problems. At the time of writing, 3D printers need to become appreciably more efficient and reliable in order to significantly reduce manufacturing costs (yet most new technologies do get better over time). Similarly, the cost of 3D printing machines is relatively high, but again should reduce over time. Also the accuracy and surface finish of products made using this technology are not always as good as those produced by more conventional technologies. Perhaps more importantly, the technology may have implications for intellectual-property ownership rules. As we have all witnessed in the music industry, when something can be transferred as a digital file it is much easier to copy and distribute, both legally and illegally. It is possible the manufacturing files for new products, toys, or designer shoes will be pirated just like music files are swapped.

The Internet of Things[4]

Back in 1973 the Universal Product Code, or bar code, was developed, enabling a part or product type to be identified when read by a bar-code scanner. Now bar codes are used to speed up checkout operations in most large supermarkets. However, they also have a role to

Source: Shutterstock.com/Mama-Mia

play in many of the stages in the supply chain that delivers products into retail outlets: during manufacture and in warehouses, bar codes are used to keep track of products passing through processes. But bar codes do have disadvantages: it is sometimes difficult to align the item so that the bar code can be read conveniently; items can only be scanned one by one; and, most significantly, the bar code only identifies the *type* of item, not a specific item itself. That is, the code identifies that an item is, say, a can of one type of drink rather than one specific can.

Yet these drawbacks can be overcome through the use of automatic identification technologies such as Radio Frequency Identification (RFID). Here an Electronic Product Code (ePC) that is a unique number, 96 bits long, is embedded in a memory chip or smart tag. These tags are put on individual items so that each item has its own unique identifying code. At various points during its manufacture, distribution, storage and sale, each smart tag can be scanned by a wireless radio frequency 'reader'. This can transmit the item's embedded identity code to a network such as the internet.

Over the last several years the full potential of RFID technology has gone to a more revolutionary level, and one which has some important implications for operations management. Embedding physical objects with sensors and actuators (from vehicles to pharmaceuticals), and connecting them using wireless networks and the protocol that connects the internet, allows information networks and physical networks to merge to form what has become known as 'the Internet of Things' (IoT) (*see* Fig. 8.4). SAP, the developer of Enterprise Resource systems, describes the Internet of Things as follows: '*A world where physical objects are seamlessly integrated into the information network, and where the physical objects can become active participants in business processes. Services are available to interact with these "smart objects" over the internet, query and change their state and any information associated with them, taking into account security and privacy issues.*'[5]

Implications

According to some authorities, the IoT promises to create new ways of doing business, the potential to improve processes, and more possibilities to reduce costs and risks. Putting sensors on 'things' gives information networks the ability to generate huge volumes of current data that can both sense the environment and communicate between the 'things'. Operations managers can track and analyse the data to understand what is happening, even in complex

232 PART TWO DESIGN

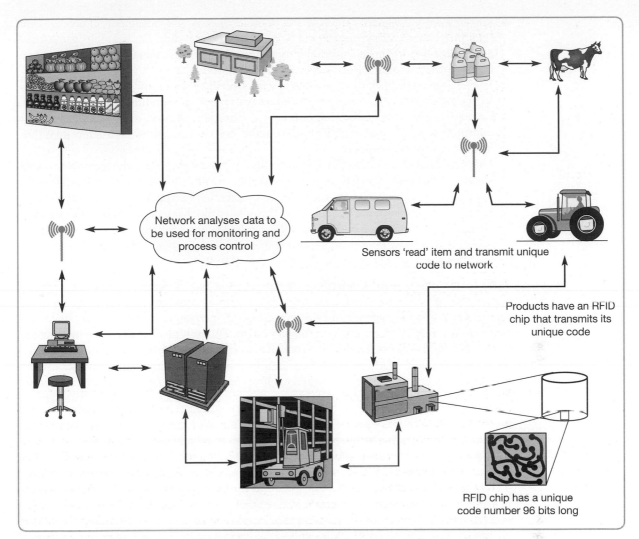

Figure 8.4 The Internet of Things (IOT) is a combination of RFID chips, sensors and internet protocols that allows information on the location and state of physical objects to be networked

systems, and respond quickly if necessary. This helps operations save significant amounts of money in lost, stolen or wasted products by helping manufacturers, distribution companies and retailers to pinpoint exactly the position and state of every item in the supply chain. So, for example, if a product had to be recalled because of a health-risk scare, the exact location of every potentially dangerous product could be immediately identified. Shoppers could easily scan products to learn more about its characteristics and features while they are in the store, waiting at checkout counters could be eliminated because items will be scanned automatically by readers, and the bill could even be automatically debited from your personal account as you leave the store. There are also potential benefits in tracking products after they leave the store. Data on how customers use products can be collected automatically and accurate recycling of waste materials could be made considerably easier. McKinsey, the consultants, see six distinct types of emerging applications with implications for operations managers. These implications fall in two broad categories: first, information and analysis; second, automation and control.

Information and analysis Because IoT networks link data from products, equipment, processes and the operating environment, they will produce enhanced information and more sophisticated analysis, which can augment operations management decisions. In particular, three aspects of information and analysis could be affected:

- *Knowing where things are* – tracking will be easier because the movements of products and their interactions with processes will be monitored in real time. For example, some insurance companies will install location sensors in customers' cars, allowing the insurer to base its fees on how a car is driven as well as where it travels.
- *Knowing what is happening* – the data from large numbers of sensors, located in such infrastructural resources as roads and buildings, can report on conditions so that managers have an instantaneous awareness of events. For example, security systems can use sensor information from a combination of video, audio, and vibration sensors to detect unauthorized entry to restricted areas.
- *Knowing what to do* – the IOT's storage and computing power, when combined with advanced decision support systems, could significantly enhance decision making. For example, in health care, sensors and data links can monitor a patient's behaviour and their symptoms at low cost and in real time. This allows physicians to diagnose disease more accurately. Similarly, in retailing, shoppers can be monitored as they move through stores. Sensors record how long customers loiter at individual displays and what they ultimately buy. The resulting data can help to optimize retail layouts.

Automation and control Controlling any operation or process involves monitoring what is actually happening within the operation or process, comparing what is *actually* happening with what *should* be happening, then making any necessary interventions to correct any deviations from what should be happening (see Chapter 10 for a fuller explanation). So monitoring and data collection are at the heart of the control activity, and monitoring and data collection is what the IoT is particularly good at. When information is fed back through a network to some kind of automation that can intervene and modify processes behaviour, control can be exercised (theoretically at least) without human intervention. Again, three aspects could be affected:

- *Process optimization* – processes that can be controlled can be more easily optimized. For example, in some semi-continuous processes in pulp and paper manufacturing, the requirement for the temperature of lime kilns to be continually adjusted limits their productivity. Yet by embedding temperature sensors in the process, the kiln's flame can be automatically adjusted to reduce temperature variance (and therefore increase quality) to near zero without frequent operator intervention.
- *Optimized resource usage* – knowing exactly how much resource is being used can help in reducing costs. For example, some energy companies are providing customers with 'smart' meters that give visual displays showing energy usage and the real-time costs of providing it. This allows domestic commercial customers to do things such as moving the use of energy-intensive processes away from peak energy demand (and therefore high-priced) periods to off-peak periods.
- *Fast reactions* – the most demanding use of the IoT involves rapid, real-time sensing of unpredictable circumstances and immediate responses governed by automated systems. The idea is for the IoT to imitate human decision makers' reactions, but at a faster and more accurate level. For example, it could be possible for a group of robots to clean up toxic waste spills when detected.

However, the IoT does pose problems. There are technical challenges in integrating RFID chips into physical objects in such a way that makes sure that information is accurately transmitted. And although, as volume has increased, the cost of such chips and sensors has fallen, cost is still a factor in adopting the technology. But perhaps the most contested issues are those relating to customer privacy in extending data capture from products beyond the checkout. People see the potential and the dangers of the IoT in very different ways. Take the following two statements:

> 'We are on the brink of a revolution of "smart products" that will interconnect everyday objects, consumers and manufacturers in a dynamic cycle of world commerce … The vision … is to create a universal environment in which computers understand the world without help from human beings.'

'*Supermarket cards and other retail surveillance devices are merely the opening volley of the marketers' war against consumers. If consumers fail to oppose these practices now our long-term prospects may look like something from a dystopian science fiction novel . . . though many [applications] appear [to be] focused on inventory and supply chain efficiency, others are developing financial and consumer applications that, if adopted, will have chilling effects on consumers' ability to escape the oppressive surveillance of manufacturers, retailers, and marketers. Of course, government and law enforcement will be quick to use the technology to keep tabs on citizens as well.*'

It is this last issue which particularly scares some civil liberties activists. Keeping track of items within a supply chain is a relatively uncontentious issue. Keeping track of items when those items are identified with a particular individual going about their everyday lives is far more problematic. So, beyond the checkout, for every arguably beneficial application there is also potential for misuse. For example, smart tags could drastically reduce theft because items could automatically report when they are stolen, their tags serving as a homing device to pinpoint their exact location. But similar technology could be used to trace any citizen, honest or not.

Telemedicine[6]

The technological breakthroughs in medical care reported in the press often focus on those dramatic 'miracle cures' which have undoubtedly improved the quality of medical care. Yet a whole collection of changes in medical process technology has also had a huge impact on the way health-care operations manage themselves. In particular, telemedicine has challenged one of the most fundamental assumptions of medical treatment – that medical staff need to be physically present to examine and diagnose a patient. No longer: web-connected devices are now able to monitor an individual's health-related data and communicate the information to health-care professionals located anywhere in the world, allowing medical staff to be alerted to changing conditions as they occur and providing a status report of a person's health so that the appropriate care can be administered. Telemedicine generally refers to the use of communications and information technologies for the delivery of clinical care. Formally, telemedicine is the ability to provide interactive health care utilizing modern technology and telecommunications. It allows patients to virtually 'visit' with physicians: sometimes live (perhaps by using video links); sometimes automatically in the case of an emergency; sometimes by storing patient data and sending it to physicians for diagnosis and follow-up treatment at a later time. Telemedicine may be as simple as two health professionals discussing a case over

Source: Shutterstock.com/Argus

the telephone, or as complex as using diagnostic algorithms and video-conferencing equipment to conduct a real-time consultation between medical specialists in different countries.

The first interactive telemedicine system was developed and marketed in the USA by MedPhone Corporation in 1989. It operated over standard telephone landlines and was used for remotely diagnosing and treating patients requiring cardiac resuscitation. A year later the company introduced a mobile cellular version. Broadly, there are three types of telemedicine: store-and-forward, remote monitoring and interactive services.

Store-and-forward telemedicine. Involves acquiring medical data such as medical images, blood test results, dermatological data, biosignals, etc., and then transmitting this data to a (remote) medical specialist at a convenient time for assessment offline. Because this does not require the presence of both parties at the same time, there is no actual physical examination and sometimes no opportunity to collect a medical history. The store-and-forward process requires the clinician to rely on a medical record report and maybe audio/video information as a substitute for a physical examination.

Remote monitoring. Allows medical professionals to monitor a patient remotely using various technological devices. This method is primarily used for managing chronic (long lasting) diseases or specific conditions, such as heart disease. Because monitoring can be almost continuous, remote monitoring services can provide better, or at least comparable, health outcomes to traditional physician–patient interactions. In addition, they could be more convenient for both patient and doctor.

Interactive telemedicine. Involves real-time interactions between patient and provider. These could include online communication, telephone conversations, and facilitated home visits by a non-specialist. This type of telemedicine is similar to traditional face-to-face visits by a physician, and normal activities such as history review, physical examination, psychiatric evaluations, etc., can be performed, at least partially.

Implications

Telemedicine can be particularly beneficial for communities in remote or isolated areas. Where previously no, or only a partial (or delayed), service was available, it allows medical services to be delivered. This is particularly important in developing countries. Known as 'Primary Remote Diagnostic Visits', a doctor uses devices to remotely examine and treat a patient. Telemedicine can also be useful in facilitating communication between a general practitioner and a specialist. All doctors need to seek advice. The easier, faster and cheaper it is to get this advice, the more likely they are to do it. The approach can also make use of decision support diagnostic systems, which give accurate and consistent diagnoses. The quality of medical care in terms of accuracy of diagnosis and appropriateness of treatment is therefore enhanced by 'virtually' bringing specialist expertise to patients. New knowledge, improved medical practice, novel pharmaceuticals, the latest guidelines, and so on, can all be communicated more effectively. Monitoring patients at home using standard equipment like blood pressure monitors and transmitting the information to a carer also provides the basis for a faster emergency service. This is certainly true for situations where a physician is needed, but no physician is present, such as on a passenger aircraft. For example, telemedicine kits are regularly used by pilots, cabin crew and other attending staff – i.e. non-medical experts who may have to deal with possible medical emergencies. They can use the kits to collect and transmit the data that would normally be collected in a hospital emergency room. This enables doctors, at a remote advice service, to help manage the medical emergency, make sure the right decisions are made and determine what treatment can be carried out and whether a diversion or medical evacuation is necessary. Airlines such as Emirates, Etihad and Virgin Atlantic use this type of technology, as do commercial shipping companies, yacht owners and the military.

Just as important in a world where some health-care costs are likely to increase substantially, telemedicine has the potential to bring substantial cost savings. Requiring patients to visit physicians at their surgeries or hospitals is costly for the patient. Requiring doctors to visit patients at home can be even more expensive. Connecting through telemedicine reduces these costs dramatically. Patients, having convenient access to medical advice, may make fewer visits to the hospital. It is also family-friendly in the sense that the patient's family life and work is less disrupted. More significantly, nurses can see up to 15 patients in 4 hours, whereas visiting them in their home, they can see only 5 or 6 patients a day. Even when the costs of the technology are taken into account, telemedicine can represent a significant cost saving. Similarly, telemedicine can make the outsourcing of medical services easier. Primary care physicians routinely outsource some services. For example, they take blood samples, but send them to a specialist laboratory for analysis. With the more extensive use of telemedicine the data required for diagnostic decisions (for example, X-ray images) can be processed by a large-scale (therefore less expensive) specialist facility, possibly in a less expensive part of the world.

However, there are issues with the adoption of telemedicine technology. One study[7] found that there were three major barriers to the adoption of telemedicine in emergency and critical care units. The first of these is the regulatory environment in some regions. Medicine must be (of course) a regulated activity, but the difficulty and cost of obtaining permission and/or licences, especially when multiple states and multiple facilities are involved, can be prohibitive. Second, there can be a lack of acceptance of telemedicine by whoever pays for the medical care, whether this is government or commercial insurance companies. This creates a major financial barrier because it puts the payment responsibility upon the hospital or health-care system. Third, there may be cultural barriers, with some physicians unable or unwilling to adapt clinical procedures for telemedicine applications.

HOW ARE PROCESS TECHNOLOGIES EVALUATED?

The most common technology-related decision in which operations managers will be involved is the choice between alternative technologies. It is an important decision because process technology can have a significant effect on the operation's long-term strategic capability; no one wants to change expensive technologies too frequently. This means that the characteristics of alternative technologies need to be evaluated so that they can be compared. Here we use three sets of criteria for evaluation:

> **✳ Operations principle**
>
> Process technologies can be evaluated in terms of their fit with process tasks, their effect on performance and their financial impact.

- Does the technology fit the processing task for which it is intended?
- How does the technology improve the operation's performance?
- Does the technology give an acceptable financial return?

Does the process technology fit the processing task?

Different process technologies will be appropriate for different types of operations, not just because they process different transformed resources, but also because they do so at different levels of volume and variety. High-variety, low-volume processes generally require process technology that is *general purpose,* because it can perform the wide range of processing activities that high variety demands. High-volume, low-variety processes can use technology that is more *dedicated* to its narrower range of processing requirements. Within the spectrum from general-purpose to dedicated-process technologies three dimensions in particular tend to vary with volume and variety. Figure 8.5 illustrates these three dimensions of process technology:

- its degree of 'automation';
- the capacity of the technology to process work, that is, its 'scale' or 'scalability';
- the extent to which it is integrated with other technologies; that is, its degree of 'coupling' or 'connectivity'.

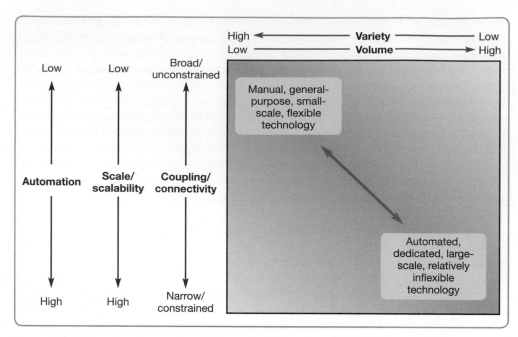

Figure 8.5 Different process technologies are important for different volume–variety combinations

The degree of automation of the technology

To some extent, all technology needs human intervention. It may be minimal, for example the periodic maintenance interventions in a petrochemical refinery. Conversely, the person who operates the technology may be the entire 'brains' of the process, for example the surgeon using keyhole surgery techniques. The ratio of technological to human effort it employs is sometimes called the capital intensity of the process technology. Generally processes that have high variety and low volume will employ process technology with lower degrees of automation than those with higher volume and lower variety. For example, investment banks trade in highly complex and sophisticated financial 'derivatives', often customized to the needs of individual clients, and each may be worth millions of dollars. The back office of the bank has to process these deals to make sure that payments are made on time, documents are exchanged, and so on. Much of this processing will be done using relatively general-purpose technology such as spreadsheets. Skilled back-office staff are making the decisions rather than the technology. Contrast this with higher-volume, low-variety products, such as straightforward equity (stock) trades. Most of these products are simple and straightforward and are processed in very high volume of several thousand per day by 'automated' technology.

The scale/scalability of the technology

There is usually some discretion as to the scale of individual units of technology. For example, the duplicating department of a large office complex may decide to invest in a single, very large, fast copier, or alternatively in several smaller, slower copiers distributed around the operation's various processes. An airline may purchase one or two wide-bodied aircraft or a larger number of smaller aircraft. The advantage of large-scale technologies is that they can usually process items cheaper than small-scale technologies, but usually need high volume and can cope only with low variety. By contrast, the virtues of smaller-scale technology are often the nimbleness and flexibility that is suited to high-variety, lower-volume processing. For example, four small machines can between them produce four different products simultaneously (albeit slowly), whereas a single large machine with four times the output can produce only one product at a time (albeit faster). Small-scale technologies are also more robust. Suppose the choice is between three small machines and one larger one. In the first case, if one machine breaks down, a third of the capacity is lost, but in the second, capacity is reduced to zero. The advantages of large-scale technologies are similar to those of large-capacity increments (as discussed in Chapter 6).

The equivalent to scale for some types of information-processing technology is *scalability*. By scalability we mean the ability to shift to a different level of useful capacity quickly and cost-effectively. Scalability is similar to absolute scale insomuch as it is influenced by the same volume–variety characteristics. IT scalability relies on consistent IT platform architecture and the high process standardization that is usually associated with high-volume and low-variety operations.

The coupling/connectivity of the technology

Coupling means the linking together of separate activities within a single piece of process technology to form an interconnected processing system. Tight coupling usually gives fast process throughput. For example, in an automated manufacturing system products flow quickly without delays between stages, and inventory will be lower – it can't accumulate when there are no 'gaps' between activities. Tight coupling also means that flow is simple and predictable, making it easier to keep track of parts when they pass through fewer stages, or information when it is automatically distributed to all parts of an information network. However, closely coupled technology can be both expensive (each connection may require capital costs) and vulnerable (a failure in one part of an interconnected system can affect the whole system). The fully integrated manufacturing system constrains parts to flow in a predetermined manner, making it difficult to accommodate products with very different processing requirements. So, coupling is generally more suited to relatively low variety and high volume. Higher-variety processing generally requires a more open and unconstrained level of coupling because different products and services will require a wider range of processing activities.

> **✳ Operations principle**
> Process technology in high-volume, low-variety processes is relatively automated, large-scale and closely coupled when compared to that in low-volume, high-variety processes.

How does the technology improve the operation's performance?

Earlier (in Chapters 2 and 3) we identified the five operations *performance objectives*. So a sensible approach to evaluating the impact of any process technology on an operation is to assess how it affects the quality, speed, dependability, flexibility and cost performance of the operation. For example, consider a warehouse that stores spare parts which it packs and distributes to its customers. It is considering investing in a new 'retrieval and packing' system which converts sales orders into 'retrieval lists' and uses materials-handling equipment to automatically pick up the goods from its shelves and bring them to the packing area. The market requirements evaluation for this warehouse might be as follows:

- *Quality*. The impact on quality could be the fact that the computerized system is not prone to human error, which may previously have resulted in the wrong part being picked off the shelves.
- *Speed*. The new system may be able to retrieve items from the shelves faster than human operators can do safely.
- *Dependability*. This will depend on how reliable the new system is. If it is less likely to break down than the operators in the old system were likely to be absent (through illness, etc.), then the new system may improve dependability of service.
- *Flexibility*. New service flexibility is not likely to be as good as the previous manual system. For example, there will be a physical limit to the size of products able to be retrieved by the automatic system, whereas people are capable of adapting to doing new things in new ways. Mix flexibility will also be poorer than was previously the case, for the same reason. Volume (and perhaps delivery) flexibility, however, could be better. The new system can work for longer hours when demand is higher than expected or deadlines are changed.

- *Cost*. The new system is certain to require fewer direct operatives to staff the warehouse, but will need extra engineering and maintenance support. Overall, however, lower labour costs are likely.

Does the technology give an acceptable financial return?

Assessing the financial value of investing in process technology is in itself a specialized subject. And while it is not the purpose of this book to delve into the details of financial analysis, it is important to highlight one important issue that is central to financial evaluation: while the benefits of investing in new technology can be spread over many years into the future, the costs associated with investing in the technology usually occur up front. So we have to consider the time value of money. Simply, this means that receiving €1,000 now is better than receiving €1,000 in a year's time. Receiving €1,000 now enables us to invest the money so that it will be worth more than the €1,000 we receive in a year's time. Alternatively, reversing the logic, we can ask ourselves how much would have to be invested now to receive €1,000 in one year's time. This amount (lower than €1,000) is called the net present value of receiving €1,000 in one year's time.

For example, suppose current interest rates are 10 per cent per annum; then the amount we would have to invest to receive €1,000 in one year's time is:

$$€1,000 \times \frac{1}{(1.10)} = €909.10$$

So the present value of €1,000 in one year's time, *discounted for the fact that we do not have it immediately*, is €909.10. In two years' time, the amount we would have to invest to receive €1,000 is:

$$€1,000 \times \frac{1}{(1.10)} \times \frac{1}{(1.10)} = €1,000 \times \frac{1}{(1.10)^2} = €826.50$$

The rate of interest assumed (10 per cent in our case) is known as the discount rate. More generally, the present value of €x in n years' time, at a discount rate of r per cent, is:

$$€\frac{x}{(1 + r/100)^n}$$

Worked example

The warehouse which we have been using as an example has been subjected to a costing and cost savings exercise. The capital cost of purchasing and installing the new technology can be spread over three years, and from the first year of its effective operation, overall operations cost savings will be made. Combining the cash that the company will have to spend and the savings that it will make, the cash flow year by year is shown in Table 8.2.

Table 8.2 Cash flows for the warehouse process technology

Year	0	1	2	3	4	5	6	7
Cash flow (€000s)	–300	30	50	400	400	400	400	0
Present value (discounted at 10%)	–300	27.27	41.3	300.53	273.21	248.37	225.79	0

However, these cash flows have to be discounted in order to assess their 'present value'. Here the company is using a discount rate of 10 per cent. This is also shown in Table 8.2. The effective life of this technology is assumed to be six years:

$$\text{total cash flow (sum of all the cash flows)} = \text{€1.38 million}$$

However,

$$\text{net present value (NPV)} = \text{€816,500}$$

This is considered to be acceptable by the company.

Calculating discount rates, although perfectly possible, can be cumbersome. As an alternative, tables are usually used such as the one in Table 8.3.

So now the net present value, $P = DF \times FV$

where:

DF = the discount factor from Table 8.3

FV = future value

To use the table, find the vertical column and locate the appropriate discount rate (as a percentage). Then find the horizontal row corresponding to the number of years it will take to receive the payment. Where the column and the row intersect is the present value of €1. You can multiply this value by the expected future value, in order to find its present value.

Table 8.3 Present value of €1 to be paid in future

Years	3.0%	4.0%	5.0%	6.0%	7.0%	8.0%	9.0%	10.0%
1	€0.970	€0.962	€0.952	€0.943	€0.935	€0.926	€0.918	€0.909
2	€0.942	€0.925	€0.907	€0.890	€0.873	€0.857	€0.842	€0.827
3	€0.915	€0.889	€0.864	€0.840	€0.816	€0.794	€0.772	€0.751
4	€0.888	€0.855	€0.823	€0.792	€0.763	€0.735	€0.708	€0.683
5	€0.862	€0.822	€0.784	€0.747	€0.713	€0.681	€0.650	€0.621
6	€0.837	€0.790	€0.746	€0.705	€0.666	€0.630	€0.596	€0.565
7	€0.813	€0.760	€0.711	€0.665	€0.623	€0.584	€0.547	€0.513
8	€0.789	€0.731	€0.677	€0.627	€0.582	€0.540	€0.502	€0.467
9	€0.766	€0.703	€0.645	€0.592	€0.544	€0.500	€0.460	€0.424
10	€0.744	€0.676	€0.614	€0.558	€0.508	€0.463	€0.422	€0.386
11	€0.722	€0.650	€0.585	€0.527	€0.475	€0.429	€0.388	€0.351
12	€0.701	€0.626	€0.557	€0.497	€0.444	€0.397	€0.356	€0.319
13	€0.681	€0.601	€0.530	€0.469	€0.415	€0.368	€0.326	€0.290
14	€0.661	€0.578	€0.505	€0.442	€0.388	€0.341	€0.299	€0.263
15	€0.642	€0.555	€0.481	€0.417	€0.362	€0.315	€0.275	€0.239
16	€0.623	€0.534	€0.458	€0.394	€0.339	€0.292	€0.252	€0.218
17	€0.605	€0.513	€0.436	€0.371	€0.317	€0.270	€0.231	€0.198
18	€0.587	€0.494	€0.416	€0.350	€0.296	€0.250	€0.212	€0.180
19	€0.570	€0.475	€0.396	€0.331	€0.277	€0.232	€0.195	€0.164
20	€0.554	€0.456	€0.377	€0.312	€0.258	€0.215	€0.179	€0.149

A health-care clinic is considering purchasing a new analysis system. The net cash flows from the new analysis system are as follows:

Year 1: −€10,000 (outflow of cash)

Year 2: €3,000

Year 3: €3,500

Year 4: €3,500

Year 5: €3,000

Assuming that the real discount rate for the clinic is 9 per cent, using the net present value table (Table 8.4), demonstrate whether the new system would at least cover its costs. Table 8.4 shows the calculations. It shows that, because the net present value of the cash flow is positive, purchasing the new system would cover its costs, and will be (just) profitable for the clinic.

Table 8.4 Present value calculations for the clinic

Year	Cash flow		Table factor		Present value
1	(€10,000)	×	1.000	=	(€10,000.00)
2	€3,000	×	0.917	=	€2,752.29
3	€3,500	×	0.842	=	€2,945.88
4	€3,500	×	0.772	=	€2,702.64
5	€3,000	×	0.708	=	€2,125.28
			Net present value =		€526.09

HOW ARE PROCESS TECHNOLOGIES IMPLEMENTED?

Implementating process technology means organizing all the activities involved in making the technology work as intended. No matter how potentially beneficial and sophisticated the technology, it remains only a prospective benefit until it has been implemented successfully. So implementation is an important part of process technology management. Yet it is not always straightforward to make general points about the implementation process because it is very context dependent. That is, the way one implements any technology will very much depend on its specific nature, the changes implied by the technology and the organizational conditions that apply during its implementation. In the remainder of this chapter we look at three particularly important issues that affect technology implementation: the idea of resource and process 'distance'; the need to consider customer acceptability; and the idea that if anything can go wrong, it will.

Resource and process 'distance'

The degree of difficulty in the implementation of process technology will depend on the degree of novelty of the new technology resources and the changes required in the operation's processes. The less that the new technology resources are understood (influenced perhaps by the degree of innovation), the greater their 'distance' from the current technology resource base of the operation. Similarly, the extent to which an implementation requires an operation

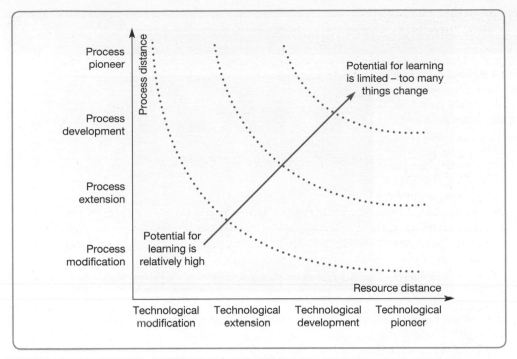

Figure 8.6 Learning potential depends on both technological resource and process 'distance'

to modify its existing processes, the greater the process 'distance'. The greater the resource and process distance, the more difficult any implementation is likely to be. This is because such distance makes it difficult to adopt a systematic approach to analysing change and learning from mistakes. Those implementations which involve relatively little process or resource 'distance' provide an ideal opportunity for organizational learning. As in any classic scientific experiment, the more variables that are held constant, the more confidence you have in determining cause and effect. Conversely, in an implementation where the resource and process 'distance' means that nearly everything is 'up for grabs', it becomes difficult to know what has worked and what has not. More importantly, it becomes difficult to know why something has or has not worked.[8] This idea is illustrated in Figure 8.6.

> *** Operations principle**
> The difficulty of process technology implementation depends on its degree of novelty and the changes required in the operation's processes.

Customer acceptability

When an operation's customers interact with its process technology it is essential to consider the customer interaction when evaluating it. If customers are to have direct contact with technology, they must have some idea of how to operate it. Where customers have an active interaction with technology, the limitations of their understanding of the technology can be the main constraint on its use. For example, even some domestic technology such as DVD recorders cannot be used to their full potential by most owners. Other customer-driven technologies can face the same problem, with the important addition that if customers cannot use technologies such as internet banking, there are serious commercial consequences for a bank's customer service. Staff in manufacturing operations may require several years of training before they are given control of the technology they operate. Service operations may not have the same opportunity for customer training. Walley and Amin[9] suggest that the ability of the operation to train its customers in the use of its technology depends on three factors: complexity, repetition, and the variety of tasks performed by the customer. If services are complex, higher levels of 'training' may be needed; for example, the technologies in theme parks and fast-food outlets rely on customers copying the behaviour of others. Frequency of use is

Who's in the cockpit?[10]

Modern aircraft fly on automatic-pilot for most of their time, certainly more than most passengers realize. *'Most people are blissfully unaware that when an aircraft lands in mist or fog, it is a computer that is landing it'*, says Paul Jackson of 'Jane's All The World's Aircraft'. *'It is the only sensible thing to do'*, agrees Ken Higgins of Boeing. *'When auto-pilots can do something better than a human pilot, we obviously use auto-pilots.'* Generally this means using auto-pilots to do two jobs. First, they can take control of the plane during the long and (for the pilot) monotonous part of the flight between take-off and landing. Automatic pilots are not prone to the tedium or weariness which can affect humans and which can cause pilot error. The second job is to make landings, especially when visibility is poor because of fog or light conditions. The auto-pilot communicates with automatic equipment on the ground which allows the aircraft to be landed, if necessary, under conditions of zero visibility. In fact, automatic landings when visibility is poor are safer than when the pilot is in control. Even in the unlikely event of one of the aircraft's two engines failing, an auto-pilot can land the plane safely. This means that on some flights, the auto-pilot is switched on within seconds of the aircraft wheels leaving the ground and then remains in charge throughout the flight and the landing. One of the few reasons not to use the auto-pilot is if the pilot is training or needs to log up the required number of landings to keep licensed.

As yet, commercial flights do not take off automatically, mainly because it would require airports and airlines to invest in extra guidance equipment which would be expensive to develop and install. Also take-off is technically more complex than landing. More things could go wrong and some situations (for example, an engine failure during take-off) require split-second decision making from the pilot. Industry analysts agree that it would be technically feasible to develop automatic take-off technology that met required safety standards but it could be prohibitively expensive.

Yet some in the airline industry believe that technology could be developed to the point where commercial flights can do without a pilot on the aircraft entirely. This is not as farfetched as it seems. In April 2001 the Northrop Grumman Global Hawk, an 'unmanned aerial vehicle' (UAV), completed the first entirely unmanned flight of the Pacific when it took off from California and landed nearly twenty-four hours later in South Australia. The Global Hawk made the journey without any human intervention whatsoever. *'We made a historic flight with two clicks of the mouse'*, said Bob Mitchell of Northrop Grumman. The first mouse click told the aircraft to take off; the second, made after landing, told it to switch off its engine. UAVs are used for military reconnaissance purposes but enthusiasts point out that most aircraft breakthroughs, such as the jet engine and radar, were developed for military use before they found civilian applications. However, even the enthusiasts admit that there are some significant problems to overcome before pilotless aircraft could become commonplace. The entire commercial flight infrastructure, from air-traffic control through to airport control, would need to be restructured, a wholly automatic pilotless aircraft would have to be shown to be safe, and perhaps most important, passengers would have to be persuaded to fly in them. If all these objections could be overcome, the rewards are substantial. Airlines' largest single cost is the wages of its staff (far more than fuel costs or maintenance cost, etc.) and of all staff, pilots are by far the most costly. Automated flights would cut costs significantly – but no one is taking bets on it happening soon!

Source: Shutterstock.com/Francisco Amaral

important because the payback for the 'investment' in training will be greater if the customer uses the technology frequently. Also, customers may, over time, forget how to use the technology, but regular repetition will reinforce the training. Finally, training will be easier if the customer is presented with a low variety of tasks. For example, vending machines tend to concentrate on one category of product, so that the sequence of tasks required to operate the technology remains consistent.

In other cases the technology may not be trusted by customers because it is technology and not a person. Sometimes we prefer to put ourselves in the care of a person, even if their performance is inferior to a technology. For example, the use of robot technologies in surgery has distinct advantages over conventional surgery, but in spite of the fact that the surgeon is in control, it is viewed with suspicion by some patients and physicians. When robot surgeons operate without any direct human control, rather than simply mirroring the movement of human surgeons, resistance is likely to be even greater. Similarly the idea of pilotless aircraft is difficult to 'sell' to customers; see the short case 'Who's in the cockpit?'.

Anticipating implementation problems

The implementation of any process technology will need to account for the 'adjustment' issues that almost always occur when making any organizational change. By adjustment issues we mean the losses that could be incurred before the improvement is functioning as intended. But estimating the nature and extent of any implementation issues is notoriously difficult. This is particularly true because more often than not, Murphy's Law seems to prevail. This law is usually stated as, 'if anything can go wrong, it will'. This effect has been identified empirically in a range of operations, especially when new types of process technology are involved. Specifically discussing technology-related change (although the ideas apply to almost any implementation), Bruce Chew of Massachusetts Institute of Technology[11] argues that adjustment 'costs' stem from unforeseen mismatches between the new technology's capabilities and needs and the existing operation. New technology rarely behaves as planned and as changes are made their impact ripples throughout the organization. Figure 8.7 is an example of what Chew calls a Murphy Curve. It shows a typical pattern of performance reduction (in this case, quality) as a new process technology is introduced. It is recognized that implementation may take some time; therefore allowances are made for the length and cost of a 'ramp-up' period. However, as the operation prepares for the implementation, the distraction causes performance actually to deteriorate. Even after the start of the implementation this downward trend continues and it is only weeks, indeed maybe months, later that the old performance level is reached. The area of the dip indicates the magnitude of the adjustment costs, and therefore the level of vulnerability faced by the operation.

Figure 8.7 The reduction in performance during and after the implementation of a new process reflects 'adjustments costs'

MyOMLab *Check and improve your understanding of this chapter using self-assessment questions and a personalized study plan, a video case study, and an eText – all at* **www.myomlab.com.**

❯ What do operations managers need to know about process technology?

- Process technologies are the machines, equipment or devices that help operations to create or deliver products and services. Indirect process technology helps to facilitate the direct creation of products and services.

- Operations managers do not need to know the technical details of all technologies, but they do need to know the answers to four key questions: What does it do? How does it do it? What advantages does it give? What constraints does it impose?

- Process technologies can also be classified according to the transformed resources that they process, namely material-processing technologies, information-processing technologies and customer-processing technologies. In addition some technologies process more than one type of resource; they are called integrating technologies.

- An important element in understanding process technologies is understanding their implications for the operations where they will be used.

❯ How are process technologies evaluated?

- All technologies should be appropriate for the activities that they have to undertake. In practice this means making sure that the degree of automation of the technology, the scale or scalability of the technology and the degree of coupling or connectivity of the technology fit the volume and variety characteristics of the operation.

- All technologies should be evaluated by assessing the impact that the process technology will have on the operation's performance objectives (quality, speed, dependability, flexibility and cost).

- All technologies should be evaluated financially. This usually involves the use of some of the more common evaluation approaches, such as net present value (NPV).

❯ How are process technologies implemented?

- Implementating process technology means organizing all the activities involved in making the technology work as intended.

- The resource and process 'distance' implied by the technology implementation will indicate the degree of difficulty.

- Customer acceptability may be a barrier to implementation in customer processing technologies.

- It is necessary to allow for the adjustment costs of implementation.

Rochem Ltd

Dr Rhodes was losing his temper. *'It should be a simple enough decision. There are only two alternatives. You are only being asked to choose a machine!'*

The Management Committee looked abashed. Rochem Ltd was one of the largest independent companies supplying the food-processing industry. Its initial success had come with a food preservative used mainly for meat-based products and marketed under the name of 'Lerentyl'. Other products were subsequently developed in the food colouring and food container coating fields, so that now Lerentyl accounted for only 25 per cent of total company sales, which were now slightly over £10 million.

Source: Press Association Images (PA Photos)

The decision

The problem over which there was such controversy related to the replacement of one of the process units used to manufacture Lerentyl. Only two such units were used; both were 'Chemling' machines. It was the older of the two Chemling units which was giving trouble. High breakdown figures, with erratic quality levels, meant that output-level requirements were only just being reached. The problem was: should the company replace the ageing Chemling with a new Chemling, or should it buy the only other plant on the market capable of the required process, the 'AFU' unit? The Chief Chemist's staff had drawn up a comparison of the two units, shown in Table 8.5.

The body considering the problem was the newly formed Management Committee. The committee consisted of the four senior managers in the firm: the Chief Chemist and the Marketing Manager, who had been with the firm since its beginning, together with the Production Manager and the Accountant, both of whom had joined the company only six months before.

What follows is a condensed version of the information presented by each manager to the committee, together with their attitudes to the decision.

The Marketing Manager

The current market for this type of preservative had reached a size of some £5 million, of which Rochem Ltd supplied approximately 48 per cent. There had, of late, been significant changes in the market – in particular, many of the users

Table 8.5 A comparison of the two alternative machines

	CHEMLING	AFU
Capital cost	£590,000	£880,000
Processing costs	Fixed: £15,000/month	Fixed: £40,000/month
	Variable: £750/kg	Variable: £600/kg
Design capacity	105 kg/month	140 kg/month
	98 ± 0.7% purity	99.5 ± 0.2% purity
Quality	Manual testing	Automatic testing
Maintenance	Adequate but needs servicing	Not known – probably good
After-sales services	Very good	Not known – unlikely to be good
Delivery	Three months	Immediate

of preservatives were now able to buy products similar to Lerentyl. The result had been the evolution of a much more price-sensitive market than had previously been the case. Further market projections were somewhat uncertain. It was clear that the total market would not shrink (in volume terms) and best estimates suggested a market of perhaps £6 million within the next three or four years (at current prices). However, there were some people in the industry who believed that the present market only represented the tip of the iceberg.

Although the food preservative market had advanced by a series of technical innovations, 'real' changes in the basic product were now few and far between. Lerentyl was sold in either solid powder or liquid form, depending on the particular needs of the customer. Prices tended to be related to the weight of chemical used, however. Thus, for example, the current average market price was approximately £10.50 per kg. There were, of course, wide variations depending on order size, etc.

'At the moment I am mainly interested in getting the right quantity and quality of Lerentyl each month and although Production has never let me down yet, I'm worried that unless we get a reliable new unit quickly, it soon will. The AFU machine could be on line in a few weeks, giving better quality too. Furthermore, if demand does increase (but I'm not saying it will), the AFU will give us the extra capacity. I will admit that we are not trying to increase our share of the preservative market as yet. We see our priority as establishing our other products first. When that's achieved, we will go back to concentrating on the preservative side of things.'

The Chief Chemist

The Chief Chemist was an old friend of John Rhodes and together they had been largely responsible for every product innovation. At the moment, the major part of his budget was devoted to modifying basic Lerentyl so that it could be used for more acidic food products such as fruit. This was not proving easy and as yet nothing had come of the research, although the Chief Chemist remained optimistic.

'If we succeed in modifying Lerentyl the market opportunities will be doubled overnight and we will need the extra capacity. I know we would be taking a risk by going for the AFU machine, but our company has grown by gambling on our research findings, and we must continue to show faith. Also the AFU technology is the way all similar technologies will be in the future. We have to start learning how to exploit it sooner or later.'

The Production Manager

The Lerentyl Department was virtually self-contained as a production unit. In fact, it was physically separate, located in a building a few yards detached from the rest of the plant. Production requirements for Lerentyl were currently at a steady rate of 190 kg per month. The six technicians who staffed the machines were the only technicians in Rochem who did all their own minor repairs and full quality control. The reason for this was largely historical since, when the firm started, the product was experimental and qualified technicians were needed to operate the plant. Four of the six had been with the firm almost from its beginning.

'It's all right for Dave and Eric [Marketing Manager and Chief Chemist] to talk about a big expansion of Lerentyl sales; they don't have to cope with all the problems if it doesn't happen. The fixed costs of the AFU unit are nearly three times those of the Chemling. Just think what that will do to my budget at low volumes of output. As I understand it, there is absolutely no evidence to show a large upswing in Lerentyl. No, the whole idea [of the AFU plant] is just too risky. Not only is there the risk, I don't think it is generally understood what the consequences of the AFU would mean. We would need twice the variety of spares for a start. But what really worries me is the staff's reaction. As fully qualified technicians they regard themselves as the elite of the firm; so they should, they are paid practically the same as I am! If we get the AFU plant, all their most interesting work, like the testing and the maintenance, will disappear or be greatly reduced. They will finish up as highly paid process workers.'

The Accountant

The company had financed nearly all its recent capital investment from its own retained profits, but would be taking out short-term loans the following year for the first time for several years.

'At the moment, I don't think it wise to invest extra capital we can't afford in an attempt to give us extra capacity we don't need. This year will be an expensive one for the company. We are already committed to considerably increased expenditure on promotion of our other products and capital investment in other parts of the firm, and Dr Rhodes is not in favour of excessive funding from outside the firm. I accept that there might eventually be an upsurge in Lerentyl demand but, if it does come, it probably won't be this year and it will be far bigger than the AFU can cope with anyway, so we might as well have three Chemling plants at that time.'

QUESTIONS

1 How do the two alternative process technologies (Chemling and AFU) differ in terms of their scale and automation? What are the implications of this for Rochem?

2 Remind yourself of the distinction between feasibility, acceptability and vulnerability discussed earlier (see Chapter 5). Evaluate both technologies using these criteria.

3 What would you recommend the company should do?

PROBLEMS AND APPLICATIONS

These problems and applications will help to improve your analysis of operations. You can find more practice problems as well as worked examples and guided solutions on MyOMLab at **www.myomlab.com**.

MyOMLab

1 In the early part of this chapter, three technologies are described – 3D printing, the Internet of Things, and telemedicine. Try to describe the technologies by answering the 'four key questions' that are also described.

2 A new machine requires an investment of €500,000 and will generate profits of €100,000 for 10 years. Will the investment have a positive net present value assuming that a realistic interest rate is 6 per cent?

3 A local government housing office is considering investing in a new computer system for managing the maintenance of its properties. The system is forecast to generate savings of around £100,000 per year and will cost £400,000. It is expected to have a life of 7 years. The local authority expects its departments to use a discount rate of 0.3 to calculate the financial return on its investments. Is this investment financially worthwhile?

4 In the example above, the local government's finance officers have realized that their discount rate has been historically too low. They now believe that the discount rate should be doubled. Is the investment in the new computer system still worthwhile?

5 A new optical reader for scanning documents is being considered by a retail bank. The new system has a fixed cost of €30,000 per year and a variable cost of €2.5 per batch. The cost of the new scanner is €100,000. The bank charges €10 per batch for scanning documents and it believes that the demand for its scanning services will be 2,000 batches in year 1, 5,000 batches in year 2, 10,000 batches in year 3, and then 12,000 batches per year from year 4 onwards. If the realistic discount rate for the bank is 6 per cent, calculate the net present value of the investment over a 5-year period.

SELECTED FURTHER READING

Arthur, W.B. (2010) *The Nature of Technology: What It Is and How It Evolves*, **Penguin, New York.** Popular science in a way, but very interesting on how technologies evolve.

Brain, M. (2001) *How Stuff Works*, **John Wiley & Sons, Inc., Hoboken, NJ.** Exactly what it says. A lot of the 'stuff' is product technology, but the book also explains many process technologies in a clear and concise manner without sacrificing relevant detail.

Carr, N.G. (2000) Hypermediation: 'Commerce and Clickstream', *Harvard Business Review*, **January–February.** Written at the height of the internet boom, it gives a flavour of how internet technologies were seen.

Chew, W.B., Leonard-Barton, D. and Bohn, R.E. (1991) Beating Murphy's Law, *Sloan Management Review*, **vol. 5, Spring.** One of the few articles that treats the issue of why everything seems to go wrong when any new technology is introduced. Insightful.

Cobham, D. and Curtis, G. (2004) *Business Information Systems: Analysis, Design and Practice*, **FT Prentice Hall, Harlow.** A good solid text on the subject.

Evans, P. and Wurster, T. (1999) *Blown to Bits: How the New Economics of Information Transforms Strategy*, **Harvard Business School Press, Boston, MA.** Interesting exposition of how internet-based technologies can change the rules of the game in business.

USEFUL WEBSITES

www.bpmi.org Site of the Business Process Management Initiative. Some good resources including papers and articles.

www.iienet.org The American Institute of Industrial Engineers site. They are an important professional body for technology, process design and related topics.

www.waria.com Workflow and Reengineering International Association website. Some useful topics.

www.myomlab Test which sections you have mastered and which you need to review, with questions, a personalized study plan, video clips, revision tips, cases.

www.opsman.org Useful materials.

http://operationsroom.wordpress.com Stanford University's take on topical operations stories.

www.iomnet.org.uk The Institute of Operations Management site. One of the main professional bodies for the subject.

www.poms.org A US academic society for production and operations management. Academic, but some useful material, including a link to an encyclopedia of operations management terms.

http://sites.google.com/site/tomiportal/home One of the longest-established portals for the subject. Useful for academics and students alike.

www.ft.com Good for researching topics and companies.

www.economist.com *The Economist*'s site, well written and interesting stuff on business generally.

MyOMLab   *Now that you have finished reading this chapter, why not visit MyOMLab at www.myomlab.com where you'll find more learning resources to help you make the most of your studies and get a better grade.*

9

People, jobs and organization

Key questions

❯ Why are people issues so important in operations management?

❯ How do operations managers contribute to human resource strategy?

❯ What forms can organization designs take?

❯ How do we go about designing jobs?

❯ How are work times allocated?

INTRODUCTION

Operations management is often presented as a subject the main focus of which is on technology, systems, procedures and facilities – in other words the non-human parts of the organization. This is not true of course. On the contrary, the manner in which an organization's human resources are managed has a profound impact on the effectiveness of its operations function. In this chapter we look especially at the elements of human resource management which are traditionally seen as being directly within the sphere of operations management. These are: how operations managers contribute to human resource strategy, organization design, selection and development, designing the working environment, job design, and the allocation of 'work times' to operations activities. The more detailed (and traditional) aspects of these last two elements are discussed further in the supplement on work study. Figure 9.1 shows how the issues covered here fit into the overall model of operations activities

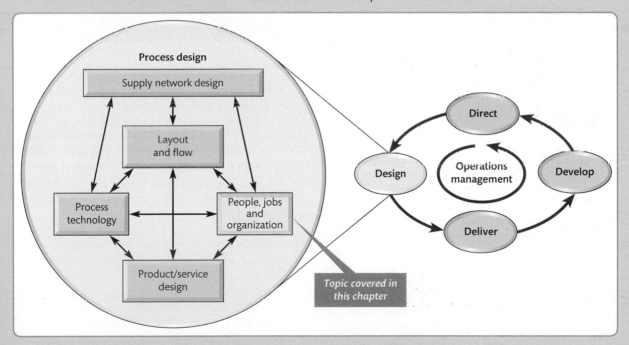

Figure 9.1 The design activities in operations management covered in this chapter

Most famous for its high performance fabrics such as GORE-TEX™, Gore also has an enviable reputation as being one of the best companies to work for wherever it operates. In a recent 'Best Companies to work for' list, its associates (the company does not use the term 'employees') gave it the very top marks for 'feeling you can make a difference'. More than half of its staff have been with the firm for at least a decade, a consequence of its philosophy ('to make money and have fun'), and its unique organizational culture and job design practices. Few in the company have any formal job titles, or job descriptions. There are no managers, only leaders and associates, people are paid 'according to their contribution' and staff help to determine each other's pay – ideas which seem revolutionary yet are based on the company's founding principles from over 50 years ago. Started by Bill and Vieve Gore in the basement of their home in Delaware, it has now become a global business with facilities in more than 45 locations around the world. Its skilled staff develop, manufacture and sell a range of innovative products, virtually all of which are based on just one material (expanded polytetrafluoroethylene) which was discovered by Bob Gore (the founders' son) in 1969. It now has approximately 8,000 associates in its four main divisions (textiles, electronic, medical and industrial products) and annual revenues of over $2 billion.

Gore's approach to how it works with its staff is at the heart of the company's success. On almost every level Gore is different to other global companies. Associates are hired for general work areas rather than specific jobs, and with the guidance of their 'sponsors' (not bosses) and as they develop experience, they commit to projects that match their skills. Teams organize around opportunities as they arise, with associates committing to the projects that they have chosen to work on, rather than having tasks delegated to them. Project teams are small, focused, multi-disciplined, and foster strong relationships between team members. Personal initiative is encouraged, as is 'hands-on' innovation, which involves those closest to a project in its decision making. There are, says Gore, no traditional organizational charts, no chains of command, no predetermined channels of communication. Instead, team members communicate directly with each other and are accountable to the other members of their team. Groups are led by whoever is the most appropriate person at each stage of a project. Leaders are not appointed by senior management; they 'emerge' naturally by demonstrating special knowledge, skill, or experience that advances a business objective. Everyone's performance is assessed using

Source: Alamy Images/Stephen Woods

a peer-level rating system. Even the Group's CEO (one of the few people with a title), Terri Kelly, 'emerged' in this way. When the previous CEO retired, no shortlist of preferred candidates was interviewed; instead, along with board discussions, a wide range of associates were invited to nominate people they would be willing to follow. 'We weren't given a list of names – we were free to choose anyone in the company', she says. 'To my surprise, it was me.'

The explicit aim of the company's culture is to 'combine freedom with co-operation and autonomy with synergy'. Everyone can earn the credibility to define and drive projects. Sponsors help associates chart a course in the organization that will offer personal fulfilment while maximizing their contribution to the enterprise. Associates adhere to four basic guiding principles, originally expressed by Bill Gore:

● Fairness to each other and everyone with whom we come in contact.
● Freedom to encourage, help, and allow other associates to grow in knowledge, skill, and scope of responsibility.

- The ability to make one's own commitments and keep them.
- Consultation with other associates before undertaking actions that could impact the reputation of the company.

This degree of personal commitment and control by associates would not sit happily with a large 'corporate'-style organization. It is no surprise, then, that Gore have unusual notions of economies of scale. Bill Gore believed in the need 'to divide so that you can multiply'. So when units grow to around 200 people, they are usually split up, with these small facilities organized in clusters or campuses. Ideally a dozen or so sites are close enough to permit good communication and knowledge exchange, but still be intimate yet separate enough to promote a feeling of ownership. Bill Gore also believed that people come to work to be innovative and had a desire to invent great products. This, he said, 'would be the glue holding the company together', rather than the official procedures other companies rely on. And at Gore's Livingstone plant in Scotland the story of 'the breathable bagpipes' is used to illustrate this type of creative innovation generated from the company's culture of trust that allows people to follow their passion. The story goes that an associate who worked in Gore's filter bags department at Livingstone was also a keen exponent of his national instrument – the bagpipes. By day he'd be working on filter systems, in the evening he'd play his bagpipes. It occurred to him that the physical properties of the product he was putting together during the day could make a synthetic bag for the pipes he played in the evening. Traditionally, bagpipes have a bag made from sheepskin or cow leather which fills up with moisture and becomes a smelly health hazard. He recognized that if you added GORE-TEX™, it would be breathable and it would be dry. He put a prototype together, tried it, and it worked. So he decided to spend time developing it, created a team to develop it further, and now almost all Scottish bagpipes have a GORE-TEX™ bag in them.

PEOPLE IN OPERATIONS

To say that an organization's human resources are its greatest asset is something of a cliché. Yet it is worth reminding ourselves of the importance of human resources, especially in the operations function, where most 'human resources' are to be found. It follows that it is operations managers who are most involved in the leadership, development and organization of human resources. In this chapter we examine some of the issues that most directly affect, or are affected by, operations management; these are illustrated in Figure 9.2. But the influence of operations management on the organization's staff is not limited to the topics covered in this chapter. Almost everything discussed in this book has a 'people' dimension. Yet, in some chapters, the human perspective is particularly important. In addition to this chapter, Chapters 18 and 20, for example, are concerned largely with how the contribution of the operation's staff can be harnessed. In essence the issues covered in this chapter define how people go about their working lives. It positions their expectations of what is required of them, and it influences their perceptions of how they contribute to the organization. It defines their activities in relation to their work colleagues and it channels the flows of communication between different parts of the operation. But, of most importance, it helps to develop the culture of the organization – its shared values, beliefs and assumptions.

> **✷ Operations principle**
> Human resources aspects are especially important in the operations function, where most 'human resources' are to be found.

HUMAN RESOURCE STRATEGY

Human resource strategy is the overall long-term approach to ensuring that an organization's human resources provide a strategic advantage. It involves two interrelated activities. First, identifying the number and type of people that are needed to manage, run and develop the organization so that it meets its strategic business objectives. Second, putting in place the programmes and initiatives that attract, develop and retain appropriate staff. It is an essential activity. Here is what Accenture, one of the top consultancies in the world, has to say about it.[2] 'Attention to people is more critical than ever . . . a company's workforce has become increasingly important to

Figure 9.2 People in operations

business success – so much so that most senior executives now view people and workforce issues as a critical competitive differentiator and one of their top agenda items . . . A superior workforce – supported by highly effective, flexible and business-oriented HR and learning organizations – will be essential to achieving these objectives and taking greater strides toward high performance.'

Developing the specific details of an HR strategy is outside the scope of this book. Yet one set of issues is directly relevant, namely, how can operations managers make sure that they are well served by, and contribute to, the strategy?

An influential contribution to the strategic role of HR comes from Dave Ulrich,[3] at the University of Michigan. His assumption is that traditional HR departments are often inadequate at fulfilling a meaningful strategic role. He proposes four elements to the HR activity: being a 'strategic partner' to the business, administering HR procedures and processes, being an 'employee champion', and being a 'change agent'. Figure 9.3 illustrates these roles, and Table 9.1 explains each role and suggests how operations managers can be associated with each role.

It is important to recognize the interdependence of all the activities in Table 9.1. Managers may focus only on whatever of these activities currently demands attention. But, just as in the operations function generally, people issues are inter-reliant. There is little point in attempting, for example, to develop a more egalitarian team-based structure and then fail to change the organization's training or reward procedures. This is why a strategic perspective aimed at identifying the relationship between all four roles is necessary, and why the first step in **developing an HR strategy** is to understand the organization's overall strategy. In particular, key questions are: What are the implications of the strategy for human resources? And how can the people in the organization contribute to successfully achieving the strategy?

Figure 9.3 Human resource strategy

Table 9.1 Ulrich's HR roles and their relevance to operations managers

Human resources (HR) role	What it involves	Relevance to operations management (OM)
Strategic partner	Aligning HR and business strategy: 'organizational diagnosis', manpower planning, environmental monitoring, etc.	OM integrates operations strategy with HR strategy. OM both specifies its long-term skills requirements and relies on HR to supply/develop them informed by labour market forecasts, succession planning, etc.
Administrative expert	Running the organization's HR processes and 'shared services': payroll, appraisal, selection and recruitment, communication, etc.	OM is largely an 'internal customer' for HR's processes. OM must be clear in its requirements with agreed service levels mutually negotiated. Note OM should also be able to advise HR on how to design and manage its processes efficiently and effectively.
Employee champion	Listening and responding to employees: 'providing resources to employees', conciliation, career advice, grievance procedures, etc.	OM and HR must develop a good working relationship and clear procedures to deal with any 'emergency' issues that arise. Also OM must be sensitive to feedback from HR on how it manages day-to-day operations.
Change agent	Managing transformation and change: 'ensuring capacity for change', management development, performance appraisal, organization development, etc.	OM and HR are jointly responsible for operations improvement activities. HR has a vital role in all the cultural, developmental and evaluation activities associated with improvement.

SHORT CASE — Is it 'Googley'?[4]

Do a company's resources, particularly its people, come to reflect the vision and culture of the company? Some companies are keen to make sure that they do. For example, drivers on Highway 101 that passes through Silicon Valley, if they were paying attention, would have noticed a billboard that read '[first10-digit prime found in consecutive digits of e].com'. Those drivers with both the intellectual curiosity and the mathematical knowledge would have realized that the number in question is 7427466391, and is a sequence that starts at the 101st digit of the constant e (the base of the natural logarithm). Those that looked up the website then found a mathematically more difficult riddle to solve. Solving that led to another webpage where they were invited to submit their CVs to Google. It was one of Google's ideas for attracting the type of clever but inventive staff that they need, and also a way of further establishing Google as the type of company that has the quirky vision to make it attractive to such people. The tone of the billboard was, as its employees like to say, 'Googley – something that evokes a "humble, cosmopolitan,

Source: Shutterstock.com/Ahmad Faizal Yahya

different, toned down, classiness."' At a recent conference, instead of the rock music and flashing lights used by most firms to introduce their speakers, Google played Bach's Brandenburg Concerto No 3 and had a 'thought puzzle' placed on every seat. Whatever else it is, Google is an organization that thinks hard about what it is, what it wants to be, and how its people can sustain its position.

Table 9.2 Causes of stress at work and what can be done about it

Causes of stress	What can be done about it
Staff can become overloaded if they cannot cope with the amount of work or type of work they are asked to do	Change the way the job is designed and investigate training needs and whether it is possible for employees to work more flexible hours
Staff can feel disaffected and perform poorly if they have no control or say over how and when they do their work	Actively involve staff in decision making, the contribution made by teams, and how reviewing performance can help identify strengths and weaknesses
Staff feel unsupported: levels of sick absence often rise if employees feel they cannot talk to managers about issues that are troubling them	Give staff the opportunity to talk about the issues causing stress; be sympathetic and keep them informed
A failure to build relationships based on good behaviour and trust can lead to problems related to discipline, grievances and bullying	Check the organization's policies for handling grievances, unsatisfactory performance, poor attendance and misconduct, and for tackling bullying and harassment
Staff will feel anxious about their work and the organization if they don't know their role and what is expected of them	Review the induction process, work out an accurate job description and maintain a close link between individual targets and organizational goals
Change can lead to huge uncertainty and insecurity	Plan ahead so change is not unexpected; consult with employees so they have a real input, and work together to solve problems

Work-related stress

The idea that there is a link between human resource strategy and the incidence of stress at work is not new. Even some of the early 'scientific management' pioneers accepted that working arrangements should not result in conditions that promoted stress. Now it is generally accepted that stress can seriously undermine the quality of people's working lives and, in turn, their effectiveness in the workplace. Here stress is defined as 'the adverse reaction people have to excessive pressures or other types of demand placed on them'.[5] In addition to the obvious ethical reasons for avoiding work-related stress, there are also business-related benefits, such as the following:[6]

● Staff feel happier at work, their quality of working life is improved and they perform better.
● Introducing improvements is easier when 'stress' is managed effectively.
● Employment relations – problems can be resolved more easily.
● Attendance levels increase and sickness absence reduces.

Table 9.2 illustrates some of the causes of stress at work and what operations managers can do about it.

ORGANIZATION DESIGN

There are many different ways of defining 'organization structure'; here it is seen as the way in which tasks and responsibilities are divided into distinct groupings, and how the responsibility and co-ordination relationships between the groupings are defined. This includes the informal relationships which build up between groups as well as their more formal relationships.

Perspectives on organizations[7]

How we illustrate organizations says much about our underlying assumptions of what an 'organization' is and how it is supposed to work. For example, the illustration of an organization as a conventional 'organogram' implies that organizations are neat and controllable with unambiguous lines of accountability. But this is rarely the case. In fact taking such a mechanistic view may be neither appropriate, nor desirable. Seeing an organization as though it was unambiguously machine-like is just one of several metaphors commonly used to understand organizations. One well-known analysis by Gareth Morgan proposes a number of 'images' or 'metaphors' which can be used to understand organizations as follows.

Organizations are machines The resources within organizations can be seen as 'components' in a mechanism whose purpose is clearly understood. Relations within the organization are clearly defined and orderly, processes and procedures that should occur usually do occur, and the flow of information through the organization is predictable. Such mechanical metaphors appear to impose clarity on what is actually messy organizational behaviour. But, where it is important to impose clarity (as in much operations analysis) such a metaphor can be useful, and is the basis of the 'process approach' used in this and similar books.

Organizations are organisms Organizations are living entities. Their behaviour is dictated by the behaviour of the individual humans within them. Individuals, and their organizations, adapt to circumstances just as different species adapt to the environment. This is a particularly useful way of looking at organizations if parts of the environment (such as the needs of the market) change radically. The survival of the organization depends on its ability to exhibit enough flexibility to respond to its environment.

Organizations are brains Like brains, organizations process information and make decisions. They balance conflicting criteria, weigh up risks and decide when an outcome is acceptable. They are also capable of learning and changing their model of the world in the light of experience. This emphasis on decision making, accumulating experience and learning from that experience is important in understanding organizations. They consist of conflicting groups where power and control are key issues.

Organizations are cultures An organization's culture is usually taken to mean its shared values, ideology, pattern of thinking and day-to-day ritual. Different organizations will have different cultures stemming from their circumstances and their history. A major strength of seeing organizations as cultures is that it draws attention to their shared 'enactment of reality'. Looking for the symbols and shared realities within an organization allows us to see beyond what the organization says about itself.

Organizations are political systems Organizations, like communities, are governed. The system of government is rarely democratic, but nor is it usually a dictatorship. Within the mechanisms of government in an organization are usually ways of understanding alternative philosophies, ways of seeking consensus (or at least reconciliation) and sometimes ways of legitimizing opposition. Individuals and groups seek to pursue their aims through the detailed politics of the organization. They form alliances, accommodate power relationships and manage conflict. Such a view is useful in helping organizations to legitimize politics as an inevitable aspect of organizational life.

Forms of organization structure

Most organization designs attempt to divide an organization into discrete parts which are given some degree of authority to make decisions within their part of the organization. All but the very smallest of organizations need to delegate decision making in this way; it allows specialization so decisions can be taken by the most appropriate people. The main issue is what dimension of specialization should be used when grouping parts of the organization together. There are three basic approaches to this:

- Group resources together according to their *functional purpose* – so, for example, sales, marketing, operations, research and development, finance, etc.

- Group resources together by the *characteristics of the resources themselves* – this may be done, for example, by clustering similar technologies together (extrusion technology, rolling, casting, etc.). Alternatively, it may be done by clustering similar skills together (audit, mergers and acquisitions, tax, etc.). It may also be done according to the resources required for particular products or services (chilled food, frozen food, canned food, etc.).
- Group resources together by the *markets* which the resources are intended to serve – again this may be done in various ways. Markets may be defined by location, with distinct geographical boundaries (North America, South America, Europe and Middle East, South East Asia, etc.). Alternatively, markets may be defined by the type of customer (small firms, large national firms, large multinational firms, etc.).

Within an organization, resources can be grouped in several different ways, and the lines of responsibility linking the resource clusters can also be configured in different ways. There are an almost infinite number of possible organizational structures. However, some pure types of organization have emerged that are useful in illustrating different approaches to organizational design, even if, in their pure form, they are rarely found.

The U-form organization The unitary form, or U-form, organization clusters its resources primarily by their functional purpose. Figure 9.4(a) shows a typical U-form organization with a pyramid management structure, each level reporting to the managerial level above. Such structures can emphasize process efficiency above customer service and the ability to adapt to changing markets. The classic disease of such bureaucratic structures is that efficiency becomes an end in itself. Functions may even become primarily concerned with their own survival and power. But, the U-form keeps together expertise and can promote the creation and sharing of technical knowledge. The problem then with the U-form organization is not so much the development of capabilities, but the flexibility of their deployment.

The M-form organization This form of organizational structure emerged because the functionally based structure of the U-form was cumbersome when companies became large, often with complex markets. It groups together either the resources needed for each product or service group, or alternatively, those needed to serve a particular geographical market, in separate divisions. The separate functions such as operations may be distributed throughout the different divisions (*see* Fig. 9.4(b)), which can reduce economies of scale and the operating efficiency of the structure. However, it does allow each individual division to focus on the specific needs of their markets.

Matrix forms Matrix structures are a hybrid, usually combining the M-form with the U-form. In effect, the organization has simultaneously two different structures (*see* Fig. 9.4(c)). In a matrix structure each resource cluster has at least two lines of authority, for example both to the division and to the functional groups. So an operations manager may be directly responsible to his or her division head, while at the same time having a (sometimes weaker) reporting responsibility to the head of the operations function for the whole company. While a matrix organization ensures the representation of all interests within the company, it can be complex and sometimes confusing.

The N-form organization The 'N' in N-form stands for 'network'. In N-form organizations, resources are clustered into groups as in other organizational forms, but with more delegation of responsibility for the strategic management of those resources. N-forms have relatively little hierarchical reporting and control. Each cluster of resources is linked to the others to form a network, with the relative strength of the relationships between clusters changing over time, depending on circumstances (*see* Fig. 9.4(d)). Senior management set broad goals and attempt to develop a unifying culture but do not 'command and control' to the same extent as in other organization forms. They may, however, act to encourage any developments they see as beneficial to the organization as a whole.

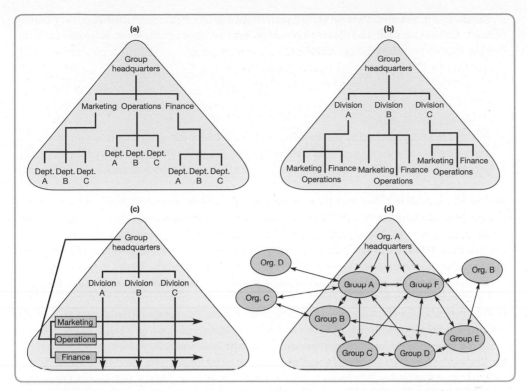

Figure 9.4 (a) U-form organizations give prominence to functional groupings of resources. (b) The M-form separates the organization's resources into separate divisions. (c) Matrix-form structures the organization's resources so that they have two (or more) levels of responsibility. (d) N-form organizations form loose networks internally between groups of resources and externally with other organizations

JOB DESIGN

In the remainder of this chapter we deal with three interrelated topics; the design of individuals' and groups' jobs, the allocation of work times to people's activities, and the design of the working environment. We look at them together because they are influenced by and use a more or less common set of concepts and frameworks. These are illustrated in Figure 9.5.

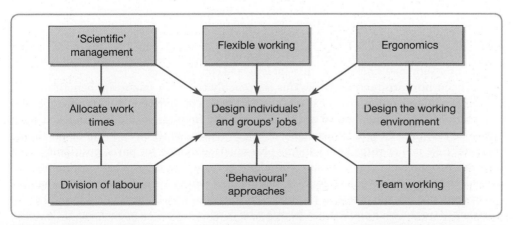

Figure 9.5 The main influences on job design, work time allocation and the design of the working environment

Job design is about how we structure each individual's job, the team to which they belong (if any), their workplace and their interface with the technology they use. It involves a number of separate yet related elements:

- *What tasks are to be allocated to each person in the operation?* Producing goods and services involves a whole range of different tasks which need to be divided between the people who staff the operation. Different approaches to the division of labour will lead to different task allocations.
- *What is the best method of performing each job?* Every job should have an approved (or best) method of completion. And although there are different ideas of what is 'best', it is generally the most efficient method that fits the task, and does not unduly interfere with other tasks.
- *How long will it take and how many people will be needed?* Work measurement helps us calculate the time required to do a job, and therefore how many people will be needed.
- *How do we maintain commitment?* Understanding how we can encourage people and maintain job commitment is, arguably, the most important of the issues in job design. This is why behavioural approaches, including empowerment, teamwork and flexible working, are at the core of job design.
- *What technology is available and how will it be used?* Many operational tasks require the use of technology. Not only does the technology need to be appropriately designed, but so also does the interface between the people and the hardware.
- *What are the environmental conditions of the workplace?* The conditions under which jobs are performed will have a significant impact on people's effectiveness. Although often considered a part of job design, we treat it separately in this chapter.

Task allocation – the division of labour

Any operation must decide on the balance between using specialists and generalists. This idea is related to the division of labour – dividing the total task down into smaller parts, each of which is accomplished by a single person or team. It was first formalized as a concept by the economist Adam Smith in his *Wealth of Nations* in 1746. Perhaps the epitome of the division of labour is the assembly line, where products move along a single path and are built up by operators continually repeating a single task. This is the predominant model of job design in most mass-produced products and in some mass-produced services (fast food, for example). There are some *real advantages* in division-of-labour principles:

- **It promotes faster learning**. It is obviously easier to learn how to do a relatively short and simple task than a long and complex one. This means that new members of staff can be quickly trained and assigned to their tasks when those tasks are short and simple.
- **Automation becomes easier**. Dividing a total task into small parts raises the possibility of automating some of those small tasks. Substituting technology for labour is considerably easier for short and simple tasks than for long and complex ones.
- **Reduced non-productive work**. This is probably the most important benefit of division of labour. In large, complex tasks the proportion of time spent picking up tools and materials, putting them down again and generally finding, positioning and searching can be very high indeed. For example, one person assembling a whole motor-car engine would take two or three hours and involve much searching for parts, positioning, and so on. Around half the person's time would be spent on these reaching, positioning and finding tasks (called non-productive elements of work). Now consider how a motor-car engine is actually made in practice. The total job is probably divided into 20 or 30 separate stages, each staffed by a person who carries out only a proportion of the total. Specialist equipment and materials-handling devices can be devised to help them carry out their job more efficiently. Furthermore, there is relatively little finding, positioning

and reaching involved in this simplified task. Non-productive work can be considerably reduced, perhaps to under 10 per cent, which would be very significant to the costs of the operation.

There are also serious drawbacks to highly divided jobs:

- **Monotony.** The shorter the task, the more often operators will need to repeat it. Repeating the same task, for example every 30 seconds, eight hours a day and five days a week, can hardly be called a fulfilling job. As well as any ethical objections, there are other, more obviously practical objections to jobs which induce such boredom. These include the increased likelihood of absenteeism and staff turnover, the increased likelihood of error and even the deliberate sabotage of the job.
- **Physical injury.** The continued repetition of a very narrow range of movements can, in extreme cases, lead to physical injury. The over-use of some parts of the body (especially the arms, hands and wrists) can result in pain and a reduction in physical capability. This is sometimes called repetitive strain injury (RSI).
- **Low flexibility.** Dividing a task up into many small parts often gives the job design a rigidity which is difficult to alter under changing circumstances. For example, if an assembly line has been designed to make one particular product but then has to change to manufacture a quite different product, the whole line will need redesigning. This will probably involve changing every operator's set of tasks, which can be a long and difficult procedure.
- **Poor robustness.** Highly divided jobs imply materials (or information) passing between several stages. If one of these stages is not working correctly, for example because some equipment is faulty, the whole operation is affected. On the other hand, if each person is performing the whole of the job, any problems will only affect that one person's output.

> ✳ **Operations principle**
> There are both positive and negative effects of the division of labour, but it is still a significant factor in job design.

Designing job methods – scientific management[*]

The term 'scientific management' became established in 1911 with the publication of the book of the same name by Fredrick Taylor (this whole approach to job design is sometimes referred to, pejoratively, as Taylorism). In this work he identified what he saw as the basic tenets of scientific management:[8]

- All aspects of work should be investigated on a scientific basis to establish the laws, rules and formulae governing the best methods of working.
- Such an investigative approach to the study of work is necessary to establish what constitutes a 'fair day's work'.
- Workers should be selected, trained and developed methodically to perform their tasks.
- Managers should act as the planners of the work (analysing jobs and standardizing the best method of doing the job), while workers should be responsible for carrying out the jobs to the standards laid down.
- Co-operation should be achieved between management and workers based on the 'maximum prosperity' of both.

The important thing to remember about scientific management is that it is not particularly 'scientific' as such, although it certainly does take an 'investigative' approach to improving operations. Perhaps a better term for it would be 'systematic management'. It gave birth to two separate, but related, fields of study: method study, which determines the methods and activities to be included in jobs; and work measurement, which is concerned with measuring the time that should be taken for performing jobs. Together, these two fields are often referred to as work study and are explained in detail in the supplement to this chapter.

Even in 1915, criticisms of the scientific management approach were being voiced. In a submission to the United States Commission on Industrial Relations, scientific management is described as:

- being in 'spirit and essence a cunningly devised speeding up and sweating system';
- intensifying the 'modern tendency towards specialization of the work and the task';
- condemning 'the worker to a monotonous routine';
- putting 'into the hands of employers an immense mass of information and methods that may be used unscrupulously to the detriment of workers';
- tending to 'transfer to the management all the traditional knowledge, the judgement and skills of workers';
- greatly intensifying 'unnecessary managerial dictation and discipline';
- tending to 'emphasize quantity of product at the expense of quality'.

Two themes evident in this early criticism do warrant closer attention. The first is that scientific management inevitably results in standardization of highly divided jobs and thus reinforces the negative effects of excessive division of labour previously mentioned. Second, scientific management formalizes the separation of the judgemental, planning and skilled tasks, which are done by 'management', from the routine, standardized and low-skill tasks, which are left for 'operators'. Such a separation, at the very least, deprives the majority of staff of an opportunity to contribute in a meaningful way to their jobs (and, incidentally, deprives the organization of their contribution). Both of these themes in the criticisms of scientific management lead to the same point: that the jobs designed under strict scientific management principles lead to low motivation among staff, frustration at the lack of control over their work, and alienation from the job.

Designing the human interface – ergonomic workplace design

Ergonomics is concerned primarily with the physiological aspects of job design. Physiology is about the way the body functions. It involves two aspects: first, how a person interfaces with his or her immediate working area; second, how people react to environmental conditions. We will examine the second aspect of ergonomics later in this chapter. Ergonomics is sometimes referred to as human factors engineering or just 'human factors'. Both aspects are linked by two common ideas:

- There must be a fit between people and the jobs they do. To achieve this fit there are only two alternatives. Either the job can be made to fit the people who are doing it, or, alternatively, the people can be made (or perhaps less radically, recruited) to fit the job. Ergonomics addresses the former alternative.
- It is important to take a 'scientific' approach to job design, for example collecting data to indicate how people react under different job design conditions and trying to find the best set of conditions for comfort and performance.

Anthropometric aspects

Many ergonomic improvements are primarily concerned with what are called the anthropometric aspects of jobs – that is, the aspects related to people's size, shape and other physical abilities. The design of an assembly task, for example, should be governed partly by the size and strength of the operators who do the job. The data which ergonomists use when doing this

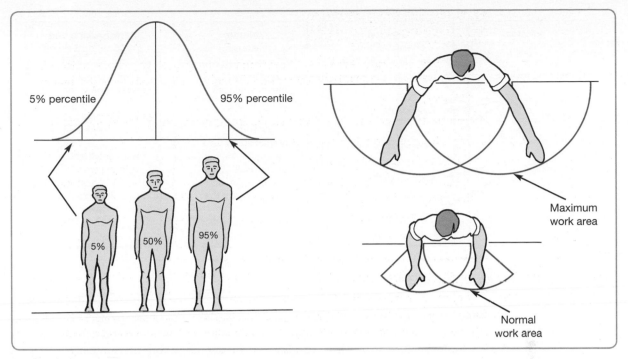

Figure 9.6 The use of anthropometric data in job design

is called anthropometric data. Because we all vary in our size and capabilities, ergonomists are particularly interested in our range of capabilities, which is why anthropometric data is usually expressed in percentile terms. Figure 9.6 illustrates this idea. This shows the idea of size (in this case height) variation. Only 5 per cent of the population are smaller than the person on the extreme left (5th percentile), whereas 95 per cent of the population are smaller than the person on the extreme right (95th percentile). When this principle is applied to other dimensions of the body, for example arm length, it can be used to design work areas. Figure 9.6 also shows the normal and maximum work areas derived from anthropometric data. It would be inadvisable, for example, to place frequently used components or tools outside the maximum work area derived from the 5th percentile dimensions of human reach.

> **✳ Operations principle**
>
> Ergonomic considerations in job design can prevent excessive physical strain and increase efficiency.

Designing for job commitment – behavioural approaches to job design

Jobs which are designed purely on division of labour, scientific management or even purely ergonomic principles can alienate the people performing them. Job design should also take into account the desire of individuals to fulfil their needs for self-esteem and personal development. This is where motivation theory and its contribution to the behavioural approach to job design is important. This achieves two important objectives of job design. First, it provides jobs which have an intrinsically higher quality of working life – an ethically desirable end in itself. Second, because of the higher levels of motivation it engenders, it is instrumental in achieving better performance for the operation, in terms of both the quality and the quantity of output. This approach to job design involves two conceptual steps: first, exploring how the various characteristics of the job affect people's motivation; second, exploring how individuals' motivation towards the job affects their performance at that job.

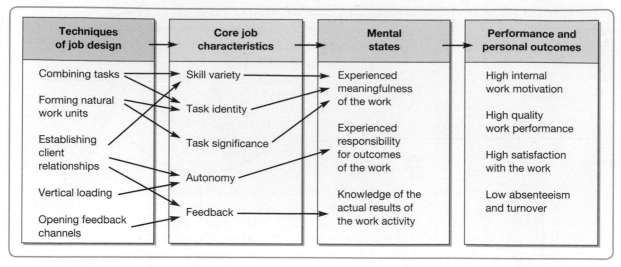

Figure 9.7 A typical 'behavioural' job design model

Typical of the models which underlie this approach to job design is that by Hackman, Oldham et al shown in Figure 9.7. Here a number of 'techniques' of job design are recommended in order to affect particular core 'characteristics' of the job. These core characteristics of the job are held to influence various positive 'mental states' towards the job. In turn, these are assumed to give certain performance outcomes. In Figure 9.7 some of the 'techniques' (which Hackman, Oldham et al originally called 'implementing concepts') need a little further explanation:[9]

- Combining tasks means increasing the number of activities allocated to individuals.
- Forming natural work units means putting together activities which make a coherent whole.
- Establishing client relationships means that staff make contact with their internal customers directly.
- Vertical loading means including 'indirect' activities (such as maintenance).
- Opening feedback channels means that internal customers feed back perceptions directly.

Hackman, Oldham et al also indicate how these techniques of job design shape the core characteristics of the resulting job, and further, how the core characteristics influence people's 'mental states'. Mental states are the attitude of individuals towards their jobs, specifically, how meaningful they find the job, how much responsibility and control they feel they have over the way the job is done, and how much they understand about the results of their efforts. All of these mental states influence people's performance at their job in terms of their motivation, quality of work, satisfaction with their work, turnover and absenteeism.

Job rotation

If increasing the number of related tasks in the job is constrained in some way, for example by the technology of the process, one approach may be to encourage job rotation. This means moving individuals periodically between different sets of tasks to provide some variety in their activities. When successful, job rotation can increase skill flexibility and make a small contribution to reducing monotony. However, it is not viewed as universally beneficial either by management (because it can disrupt the smooth flow of work) or by the people performing the jobs (because it can interfere with their rhythm of work).

Job enlargement

The most obvious method of achieving at least some of the objectives of behavioural job design is by allocating a larger number of tasks to individuals. If these extra tasks are broadly of the same type as those in the original job, the change is called job enlargement. This may not involve more demanding or fulfilling tasks, but it may provide a more complete and therefore slightly more meaningful job. If nothing else, people performing an enlarged job will not repeat themselves as often, which could make the job marginally less monotonous. So, for example, suppose that the manufacture of a product has traditionally been split up on an assembly-line basis into 10 equal and sequential jobs. If that job is then redesigned so as to form two parallel assembly lines of five people, the output from the system as a whole would be maintained but each operator would have twice the number of tasks to perform. This is job enlargement. Operators repeat themselves less frequently and presumably the variety of tasks is greater, although no further responsibility or autonomy is necessarily given to each operator.

Job enrichment

Job enrichment not only means increasing the number of tasks, but also allocating extra tasks which involve more decision making, greater autonomy and greater control over the job. For example, the extra tasks could include maintenance, planning and control, or monitoring quality levels. The effect is both to reduce repetition in the job and to increase autonomy and personal development. So, in the assembly-line example, each operator, as well as being allocated a job which is twice as long as that previously performed, could also be allocated responsibility for carrying out routine maintenance and such tasks as record-keeping and managing the supply of materials. Figure 9.8 illustrates the difference between what are called horizontal and vertical changes. Broadly, horizontal changes are those which extend the variety of *similar* tasks assigned to a particular job. Vertical job changes are those which add responsibilities, decision making or autonomy to the job. Job enlargement implies movement only in the horizontal scale, whereas job enrichment certainly implies movement on the vertical scale and perhaps on both scales.

Empowerment

Empowerment is an extension of the *autonomy* job characteristic prominent in the behavioural approach to job design. However, it is usually taken to mean more than autonomy. Whereas autonomy means giving staff the *ability* to change how they do their jobs, empowerment means giving staff the *authority* to make changes to the job itself, as well as how it is performed. This can be designed into jobs to different degrees. At a minimum, staff could be asked to contribute their suggestions for how the operation might be improved. Going further, staff could be empowered to redesign their jobs. Further still, staff could be included in the strategic direction and performance of the whole organization. The *benefits* of empowerment are generally seen as providing fast responses to customer needs (including dissatisfied customers), employees who feel better about their jobs and who will interact with customers with more enthusiasm, promoting 'word-of-mouth' advertising and customer retention. However, there are *costs* associated with empowerment, including higher selection and training costs, perceived inequity of service and the possibility of poor decisions being made by employees.

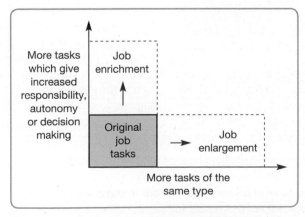

Figure 9.8 Job enlargement and job enrichment

In what was thought to be the first contract of its type in the UK, McDonald's, the quick-service restaurant chain, announced in 2005 that it was to allow family members to cover each other's jobs. Under the deal, members of the same family working in the same outlet would be able to work each other's shifts without giving any prior notice or getting a manager's permission. The company said that it hoped the contracts would, *'encourage people to become fully trained and fully rotatable'*. But that the main aim was to, *'cut absenteeism and improve staff retention'*. *'It's great'*, said one McDonald's employee. *'Depending on how we feel in a morning, we decide which one of us wants to go in and work.'* Although the scheme is currently limited to family members only, McDonald's said that they might consider extending it to cover friends who work at the same restaurant.

Source: Shutterstock.com/Zurijeta

Teamworking

A development in job design which is closely linked to the empowerment concept is that of team-based work organization (sometimes called self-managed work teams). This is where staff, often with overlapping skills, collectively perform a defined task and have a high degree of discretion over how they actually perform the task. The team would typically control such things as task allocation between members, scheduling work, quality measurement and improvement, and sometimes the hiring of staff. To some extent most work has always been a group-based activity. The concept of teamwork, however, is more prescriptive and assumes a shared set of objectives and responsibilities. Groups are described as teams when the virtues of working together are being emphasized, such as the ability to make use of the various skills within the team. Teams may also be used to compensate for other organizational changes, such as the move towards flatter organizational structures. When organizations have fewer managerial levels, each manager will have a wider span of activities to control. Teams which are capable of autonomous decision making[10] have a clear advantage in these circumstances. The benefits of teamwork can be summarized as:

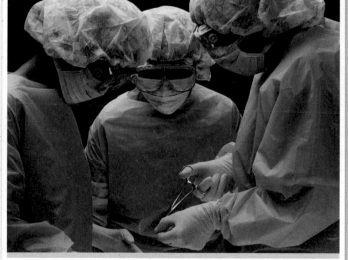

Source: AL RF (PhotoDisc/Ryan McVay)

- improving productivity through enhanced motivation and flexibility;
- improving quality and encouraging innovation;
- increasing satisfaction by allowing individuals to contribute more effectively;
- making it easier to implement technological changes in the workplace because teams are willing to share the challenges this brings.

Teamwork is not only difficult to implement successfully, but it can also place undue stress on the individuals who form the teams. Some teams are formed because more radical solutions, such as total reorganization, are being avoided. Teams cannot compensate for badly designed organizational processes; nor can they substitute for management's responsibility to define how decisions should be made. Often teams are asked to make decisions but are given insufficient responsibility to carry them out. In other cases, teams may provide results but at a price. The Swedish car maker Volvo introduced self-governing teams in the 70s and 80s which improved motivation and morale but eventually proved prohibitively expensive. Perhaps most seriously, teamwork is criticized for substituting one sort of pressure for another. Although teams may be autonomous, this does not mean they are stress-free. Top-down managerial control is often replaced by excessive peer pressure, which is in some ways more insidious.

Flexible working

The nature of most jobs has changed significantly over the last 25 years. New technologies, more dynamic marketplaces, more demanding customers and a changed understanding of how individuals can contribute to competitive success have all had their impact. Also changing is our understanding of how home life, work and social life need to be balanced. Alternative forms of organization and alternative attitudes to work are being sought which allow, and encourage, a degree of flexibility in working practice which matches the need for flexibility in the marketplace. From an operations management perspective, three aspects of flexible working are significant: skills flexibility, time flexibility, and location flexibility.

Skills flexibility A flexible workforce that can move across several different jobs could be deployed (or deploy themselves) in whatever activity is in demand at the time. In the short term, staff at a supermarket may be moved from warehouse activities to shelf replenishment in the store to the checkout, depending on what is needed at the time. In the longer-term sense, multi-skilling means being able to migrate individuals from one skill set to another as longer-term demand trends become obvious. So, for example, an engineer who at one time maintained complex equipment by visiting the sites where such equipment was installed may now perform most of his or her activities by using remote computer diagnostics and 'helpline' assistance. The implication of job flexibility is that a greater emphasis must be placed on training, learning and knowledge management. Defining what knowledge and experience are required to perform particular tasks and translating these into training activities are clearly prerequisites for effective multi-skilling.

Time flexibility Not every individual wants to work full-time. Many people, often because of family responsibilities, only want to work for part of their time, sometimes only during specific parts of the day or week (because of childcare responsibilities, etc.). Likewise, employers may not require the same number of staff at all times. They may, for example, need extra staff only at periods of heavy demand. Bringing both the supply of staff and the demand for their work together is the objective of 'flexible time' or flexi-time working systems. These may define a *core* working time for each individual member of staff and allow other times to be accumulated flexibly. Other schemes include annual hours schemes, one solution to the capacity management issue described later (see Chapter 11).

Location flexibility The sectoral balance of employment has changed. The service sector in most developed economies now accounts for between 70 and 80 per cent of all employment. Even within the manufacturing sector, the proportion of people with indirect jobs (those not directly engaged in making products) has also increased significantly. One result of all this is that the number of jobs which are not 'location-specific' has increased. Location-specific means that a job must take place in one fixed location. So a shop worker must work in a shop and an assembly line worker must work on the assembly line. But many jobs could be performed at any location where there are communication links to the rest of the organization. The realization of this has given rise to what is known as teleworking, which is also known as using 'alternative workplaces' (AW), 'flexible working', 'home working', mobile working, and creating the 'virtual office'.

Critical commentary

There is always a big difference between what is technically possible and what is organizationally feasible. Mobile working does have its problems. In particular, those types that deny individuals the chance to meet with colleagues often face difficulties. Problems can include the following:

- *Lack of socialization* – offices are social places where people can adopt the culture of an organization as well as learn from each other. It is naïve to think that all knowledge can be codified and learnt formally at a distance.

- *Effectiveness of communication* – a large part of the essential communication we have with our colleagues is unplanned and face-to-face. It happens on 'chance meet' occasions, yet it is important in spreading contextual information as well as establishing specific pieces of information necessary to the job.

- *Problem-solving* – it is still often more efficient and effective informally to ask a colleague for help in resolving problems than formally to frame a request using communications technology.

- *It is lonely* – isolation amongst mobile or home workers is a real problem. For many of us, the workplace provides the main focus for social interaction. A computer screen is no substitute.

SHORT CASE — Flexible working at Lloyds TSB[11]

Not too long ago in many organizations, employees were expected to work fixed hours. There was a fixed start time; miss it and you were late, and subject to some form of penalty. There was a fixed finish time; why would anyone want to work later than this 'for free'? And although there are some places where the vestiges of this attitude remain, many enterprises now understand the benefits of taking a more flexible attitude. Amongst the first large organizations to take flexible working seriously in Europe was Lloyds TSB Group, one of the UK's biggest banking groups, employing over 66,000 people worldwide and serving more than 16 million customers. The Group was prompted to take up flexible working because it was sensitive to the social and economic changes that were affecting, not only its customers, but its staff as well. People's lives were becoming more complex. There seemed to be clear benefits of adapting work patterns so they reflected its staff's needs and constraints and yet still offered the best quality and quantity of service to its customers. Recruiting and keeping talented

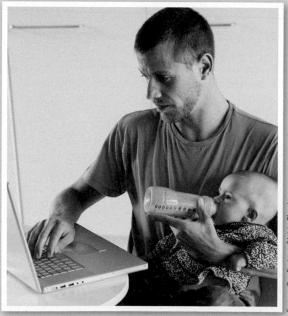

Source: Rex Features/Voisin Phanic

and committed people who wanted to build a career in the Group meant understanding and implementing the right balance between staff's individual needs, the business's requirement to control the costs of delivering service, and the customers' expectation of excellent service. So, to further its interest in flexible working, the Group researched its employee's views. The results showed that one of their main issues was trying to balance a demanding job with outside commitments, such as family and leisure. In response the Group introduced its flexible working policy. Called 'Work Options', it allowed staff to reconfigure their working activities by requesting a different working pattern from the conventional working day. This can be done in several ways. Sometimes it may simply involve starting and finishing earlier or later each day, while maintaining the same weekly hours. This could allow for other commitments such as childcare activities, or simply cater for working preferences. Also it could benefit the business. Customer demand does not necessarily follow a traditional working day. Varying staff's work patterns could mean staffing is more closely aligned with actual customer demand. The business may also be able to extend staff without paying overtime premiums.

Job sharing is also used, where two members of staff share one job role. It suits both staff members, who may not want full-time employment, and the business can have two people's combined experience, skills and creativity. Job-sharing staff can also be more productive than full-time colleagues. As one Customer Service Manager at Lloyds TSB says, '*We have job shared for nine years now. We cover a full working week between us with handover*

meetings every Tuesday morning. We talk about any issues that have arisen. We are very different characters and react in completely different ways to problems. However, we find our skills complement each other well. The bank benefits because it wouldn't get this from just one person.'

Another form of flexible working is 'compressed working', which allows staff to work a standard one or two weeks within a shorter timescale, for example by working some longer days a week, then taking extra time off to compensate. For example: '*I have worked a compressed week for five years. This means I can pursue the two hobbies I love, scuba diving and genealogy. I feel motivated, enthused and energized about my role in Lloyds TSB. I take my non-working day when it suits both me and the branch. My manager knows I will get the job done. It has transformed my work and my non-work life!*' Working from home may also be an option. A Process Designer in Group Operations says, '*I have two children and my husband is self-employed. I work from home five days a week. I have been able to continue my career with the bank and deliver 100 per cent commitment.*'

To some extent, the introduction of flexible working has been motivated by demographic and social changes. There are also increasing regulatory and legal requirements promoting working flexibility in some parts of the world. However, Lloyds TSB believes its ability to deal effectively with the need for flexibility makes good business sense. It helps to bolster its reputation as an employer of choice, and allows it to deliver differentiated levels of service; customers can deal with a skilled, friendly and enthusiastic member of staff, and the best staff are more likely to stay.

Designing the working environment – ergonomics

One aspect of ergonomics is concerned with how a person interfaces with the physical aspects of his or her immediate working area, such as its dimensions, as we examined earlier. Here we look at how people interface with their working environment. By this we mean the temperature, lighting, noise environment, and so on. The immediate environment in which jobs take place will influence the way they are performed. Working conditions which are too hot or too cold, insufficiently illuminated or glaringly bright, excessively noisy or irritatingly silent will all influence the way jobs are carried out. Many of these issues are often covered by occupational health and safety legislation which controls environmental conditions in workplaces throughout the world. A thorough understanding of this aspect of ergonomics is necessary to work within the guidelines of such legislation.

Source: Shutterstock.com/Montebasso

Working temperature

Predicting the reactions of individuals to working temperature is not straightforward. Individuals vary in the way their performance and comfort vary with temperature. Furthermore, most of us judging 'temperature' will also be influenced by other factors such as humidity and air movement. Nevertheless, some general points regarding working temperatures provide guidance to job designers:

- Comfortable temperature range will depend on the type of work being carried out; lighter work requiring higher temperatures than heavier work.
- The effectiveness of people at performing vigilance tasks reduces at temperatures above about 29°C; the equivalent temperature for people performing light manual tasks is a little lower.
- The chances of accidents occurring increase at temperatures which are above or below the comfortable range for the work involved.

Illumination levels

The intensity of lighting required to perform any job satisfactorily will depend on the nature of the job. Some jobs which involve extremely delicate and precise movement, surgery for example, require very high levels of illumination. Other, less delicate, jobs do not require such high levels. Table 9.3 shows the recommended illumination levels (measured in lux) for a range of activities.

Noise levels

The damaging effects of excessive noise levels are perhaps easier to understand than some other environmental factors. Noise-induced hearing loss is a well-documented consequence of working environments where noise is not kept below safe limits. The noise levels of various activities are shown in Table 9.4. When reading this list, bear in mind that the recommended (and often legal) maximum noise level to which people can be subjected over the working day is 90 decibels (dB) in the UK (although in some parts of the world the legal level is lower than this). Also bear in mind that the decibels unit of noise is based on a logarithmic scale, which means that noise intensity doubles about every 3 dB. In addition to the damaging effects of high levels of noise, intermittent and high-frequency noise can also affect work performance at far lower levels, especially on tasks requiring attention and judgement.

Ergonomics in the office

As the number of people working in offices (or office-like workplaces) has increased, ergonomic principles have been applied increasingly to this type of work. At the same time,

Table 9.3 Examples of recommended lighting levels for various activities[12]

Activity	Illuminance (lx)
Normal activities in the home, general lighting	50
Furnace rooms in glass factory	150
General office work	500
Motor vehicle assembly	500
Proofreading	750
Colour matching in paint factory	1,000
Electronic assembly	1,000
Close inspection of knitwear	1,500
Engineering testing inspection using small instruments	3,000
Watchmaking and fine jewellery manufacture	3,000
Surgery, local lighting	10,000–50,000

Table 9.4 Noise levels for various activities

Noise	Decibels (dB)
Quiet speech	40
Light traffic at 25 metres	50
Large busy office	60
Busy street, heavy traffic	70
Pneumatic drill at 20 metres	80
Textile factory	90
Circular saw – close work	100
Riveting machine – close work	110
Jet aircraft taking off at 100 metres	120

legislation has been moving to cover office technology such as computer screens and keyboards. For example, European Union directives on working with display screen equipment require organizations to assess all workstations to reduce the risks inherent in their use, plan work times for breaks and changes in activity and provide information and training for users. Figure 9.9 illustrates some of the ergonomic factors which should be taken into account when designing office jobs.

ALLOCATE WORK TIMES

Without some estimate of how long it takes to complete an activity, it would not be possible to know how much work to allocate to teams or individuals, to know when a task will be completed, to know how much it costs, to know if work is progressing according to schedule, and many other vital pieces of information that are needed to manage any operation. Without some estimate of work times, operations managers are 'flying blind'. At the same time it does not need much thought before it becomes clear that measuring work times must be difficult to do with any degree of accuracy, or confidence. The time you take to do any task will depend on how skilled you are at the task, how much experience you have, how energetic or motivated you are, whether you have the appropriate tools, what the environmental conditions are, how tired you are, and so on. So, at best, any 'measurement' of how long a task will, or should, take will be an estimate. It will be our 'best guess' of how much time to allow for the task. That is why we call this process of estimating work times, 'work time allocation'. We are allocating a time for completing a task because we need to do so for many important operations management decisions. For example, work times are needed for:

- planning how much work a process can perform (its capacity);
- deciding how many staff are needed to complete tasks;
- scheduling individual tasks to specific people;
- balancing work allocation in processes (see Chapter 7);
- costing the labour content of a product or service;
- estimating the efficiency or productivity of staff and/or processes;
- calculating bonus payments (less important than it was at one time).

Notwithstanding the weak theoretical basis of work measurement, understanding the relationship between work and time is clearly an important part of job design. The advantage of structured and systematic work measurement is that it gives a common currency for the evaluation and comparison of all types of work. So, if work time allocation is important, how should it be done? In fact, there is a long-standing body of knowledge and experience in this area. This is generally referred to as 'work measurement'; although, as we have said, 'measurement' could be regarded as indicating a somewhat spurious degree of accuracy. Formally, work measurement is defined as, 'the process of establishing the time for a

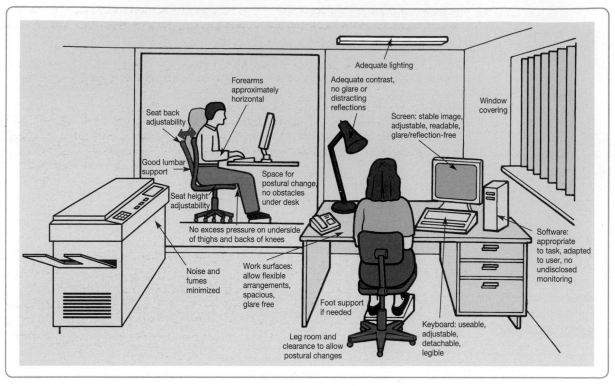

Figure 9.9 Ergonomics in the office environment

qualified worker, at a defined level of performance, to carry out a specified job'. Although not a precise definition, generally it is agreed that a *specified job* is one for which specifications have been established to define most aspects of the job. A *qualified worker* is 'one who is accepted as having the necessary physical attributes, intelligence, skill, education and knowledge to perform the task to satisfactory standards of safety, quality and quantity'. Standard performance is 'the rate of output which qualified workers will achieve without over-exertion as an average over the working day, provided they are motivated to apply themselves to their work'.

The techniques of work measurement

At one time, work measurement was firmly associated with an image of the 'efficiency expert', 'time and motion' man, or 'rate fixer', who wandered around factories with a stopwatch, looking to save a few cents or pennies. And although that idea of work measurement has (almost) died out, the use of a stopwatch to establish a basic time for a job is still relevant, and used in a technique called 'time study'. Time study and the general topic of work measurement is treated in the supplement to this chapter – work study.

As well as time study, there are other work measurement techniques in use. They include the following.

- **Synthesis from elemental data** is a work measurement technique for building up the time for a job at a defined level of performance by totalling element times obtained previously from studies in other jobs containing the elements concerned or from synthetic data.
- **Predetermined motion-time systems (PMTS)** is a work measurement technique whereby times established for basic human motions (classified according to the nature of the motion and the conditions under which it is made) are used to build up the time for a job at a defined level of performance.

- **Analytical estimating** is a work measurement technique which is a development of estimating whereby the time required to carry out the elements of a job at a defined level of performance is estimated from knowledge and experience of the elements concerned.
- **Activity sampling** is a technique in which a large number of instantaneous observations are made over a period of time of a group of machines, processes or workers. Each observation records what is happening at that instant and the percentage of observations recorded for a particular activity or delay is a measure of the percentage of time during which that activity or delay occurs.

Critical commentary

The criticisms aimed at work measurement are many and various. Amongst the most common are the following:

- All the ideas on which the concept of a standard time is based are impossible to define precisely. How can one possibly give clarity to the definition of qualified workers, or specified jobs, or especially a defined level of performance?

- Even if one attempts to follow these definitions, all that results is an excessively rigid job definition. Most modern jobs require some element of flexibility, which is difficult to achieve alongside rigidly defined jobs.

- Using stopwatches to time human beings is both degrading and usually counter-productive. At best it is intrusive, at worst it makes people into 'objects for study'.

- The rating procedure implicit in time study is subjective and usually arbitrary. It has no basis other than the opinion of the person carrying out the study.

- Time study, especially, is very easy to manipulate. It is possible for employers to 'work back' from a time which is 'required' to achieve a particular cost. Also, experienced staff can 'put on an act' to fool the person recording the times.

SUMMARY ANSWERS TO KEY QUESTIONS

Check and improve your understanding of this chapter using self-assessment questions and a personalized study plan, a video case study, and an eText – all at www.myomlab.com.

MyOMLab

❯ Why are people issues so important in operations management?

- Human resources are any organization's, and therefore any operation's, greatest asset. Often, most 'human resources' are to be found in the operations function.

❯ How do operations managers contribute to human resource strategy?

- Human resource strategy is the overall long-term approach to ensuring that an organization's human resources provide a strategic advantage. It involves identifying the number and type of people that are needed to manage, run and develop the organization so that it meets its strategic business objectives, and putting in place the programmes and initiatives that attract, develop and retain appropriate staff.

❯ What forms can organization designs take?

- One can take various perspectives on organizations. How we illustrate organizations says much about our underlying assumptions of what an 'organization' is. For example, organizations can be described as machines, organisms, brains, cultures, or political systems.

- There are an almost infinite number of possible organizational structures. Most are blends of two or more 'pure types', such as:
  - the U-form
  - the M-form
  - matrix forms
  - the N-form.

❯ How do we go about designing jobs?

- There are many influences on how jobs are designed. These include:
  - division of labour
  - scientific management
  - method study
  - work measurement
  - ergonomics
  - behavioural approaches, including job rotation, job enlargement and job enrichment
  - empowerment
  - teamworking
  - flexible working.

❯ How are work times allocated?

- The best-known method is time study, but there are other work measurement techniques including:
  - synthesis from elemental data
  - predetermined motion-time systems (PMTS)
  - analytical estimating
  - activity sampling.

CASE STUDY   Service Adhesives try again

By Dr Ran Bhamra, Lecturer in Engineering Management, Loughborough University.

'I'm not sure why we've never succeeded in really getting an improvement initiative to take hold in this company. It isn't that we haven't been trying. TQM, Lean, even a limited attempt to adopt Six Sigma; we've tried them all. I guess that we just haven't yet found the right approach that fits us. That is why we're quite excited about what we saw at Happy Products.' (James Broadstone, Operations Director, Service Adhesives Limited)

Service Adhesives Ltd was a mid-sized company founded over 20 years ago to produce specialist adhesives, mainly used in the fast-moving consumer goods (FMCG) business, where any adhesive had to be guaranteed 'non-irritating' (for example, in personal care products) and definitely 'non-toxic' (for example, in food-based products). Largely because of its patented adhesive formulation, and its outstanding record in developing new adhesive products, it has always been profitable. Yet, although its sales revenue had continued to rise, the last few years had seen a slowdown in the company's profit margins. According to Service Adhesives' senior management there were two reasons for this: first, production costs were rising more rapidly than sales revenues; second, product quality, while acceptable, was no longer significantly better than competitors. These issues had been recognized by senior management for a number of years and several improvement initiatives, focusing on product quality and process improvement, had attempted to reverse their declining position relative to competitors. However, none of the initiatives had fully taken hold and delivered as promised.

Source: Shutterstock.com/Sinisa Botas

In recent years, Service Adhesives Ltd had tried to embrace a number of initiatives and modern operations philosophies such as TQM (Total Quality Management) and Lean, but all had proved disappointing, with little resulting change within the business. It was never clear why these steps towards modern ways of working had not been successful. Some senior management viewed the staff as being of 'below average' skills and motivation, and very reluctant to change. There was a relatively high staff turnover rate and the company had recently started employing short-term contract labour as an answer to controlling its fluctuating orders. The majority of the short-term labour force were from eastern European Union member states such as Poland and the Czech Republic and accounted for almost 20 per cent of the total shop-floor personnel. There had been some issues with temporary staff not adhering to quality procedures or referring to written material, all of which was written in English. Despite this, the company's management saw the use of migrant labour as largely positive; they were hard-working and provided an opportunity to save costs. However, there had been some tension between temporary and permanent employees over what was seen as a perceived threat to their jobs.

James Broadstone, the Operations Director of Service Adhesives, was particularly concerned about the failure of their improvement initiatives and organized a number of visits to other companies with similar profiles and also to a couple of Service Adhesives' customers. It was a visit to one of their larger customers, called (bizarrely) 'Happy Products', that had particularly enthused the senior management team. '*It was like entering another world. Their processes are different from ours, but not that different. But their plant was cleaner, the flow of materials seemed smoother, their staff seemed purposeful, and above all, it seemed an efficient and happy place to work. Everybody really did work as a team. I think we have a lot to learn from them. I'm sure that team-based approach could be implemented just as successfully in our plant.*' (James Broadstone)

Happy Products were a global company and the market leaders in their field. And although their various plants in different parts of the world had slightly different approaches to how they organized their production operations, the group as a whole had a reputation for excellent human resource management. The plant visited by Service Adhesives was in the third year of a five-year programme to introduce and embed a team-based work structure and culture. It had won the coveted international 'Best Plant' in Division Award twice within three years. The clear driver of this success had been identified by the award judging panel as its implementation of a team-based work structure. The Happy Products plant operated a three-shift system over a 24/7 operation cycle making diapers (nappies) and health-care products and was organized into three distinct product areas, each containing at least two production lines utilizing highly complex technology. Each production line was staffed by five operators (with additional support staff serving the whole plant). One operator was a team leader responsible for 'first-line management'. A second operator was a specially trained health and safety representative. A third was a trained quality representative who also liaised with the Quality Department. A fourth operator was a trained maintenance engineer, while a fifth was a non-specialist, 'floating' operator. The team had support from the production process engineering, quality and logistics departments.

Most problems encountered in the day-to-day operation of the line could be dealt with immediately, on the line. This ensured that production output, product quality and line efficiency were controlled exceptionally well. Individual team roles enabled team members to contribute and take great satisfaction in the knowledge that they played a key part in the success of the organization. The team specialist roles also gave the opportunity for networking with counterparts in other plants across the world. This international communication was encouraged and added to the sense of belonging and organizational goal orientation. Teams were also involved in determining annual performance targets for their specific areas. Annually, corporate strategy identified business direction, and developed performance requirements for each business division which, in turn, filtered down to individual plants. Plants devised strategic targets for their sections and the teams themselves created a list of projects and activities to meet (and hopefully exceed) targets. In this way the individual operator on the shop floor had direct influence over their future and the future of their business.

So impressed were Service Adhesives with what they perceived to be a world-class operation that they decided that they should also consider following a similar path towards a team-based work organization. They were obviously missing the organizational 'cohesiveness' that their customer seemed to be demonstrating. Until that time, however, the management at Service Adhesives Ltd had prided themselves on their traditional, hierarchical organization structure. The organization had five layers of operational management, from the plant director at the top, to the shop floor operatives at the bottom. The chain of command was strictly enforced by operating procedures entwined with their long-established and comprehensive quality assurance system. Now, it seemed, a very different approach was needed. 'We are very interested in learning from the visit. We have to change the way we work and make some radical improvements to our organization's operational effectiveness. I have come to believe that we have fallen behind in our thinking. A new kind of organizational culture is needed for these challenging times and we must respond by learning from the best practice that we can find. We also must be seen by our customers as forward thinking. We have to prove that we are in the same league as the "big boys". (James Broadstone)

At the next top team meeting, Service Adhesives formally committed itself to adopting a 'team-based organizational structure' with the aim of 'establishing a culture of improvement and operational excellence'.

QUESTIONS

1 Service Adhesive Ltd currently employs up to 20 per cent of their workforce on short-term contracts. What effect will this have on the proposed team-based working structure?

2 In considering a transition from a traditional, organizational work structure to a team-based work structure, what sort of barriers are Service Adhesives Ltd likely to encounter? Think about formal structures (e.g. roles and procedures) and informal structures (e.g. social groups and communication).

3 The senior management of Service Adhesives thought that the reason for ineffective improvement initiatives in the past was due mainly to the apparent lack of cohesion amongst the organization's human resource. Could a team-based work organization be the answer to their organizational difficulties? Why do you think that previous initiatives at Service Adhesives had failed?

4 Employee empowerment is a key element of team-based working; what difficulties could Service Adhesives face in implementing empowerment?

PROBLEMS AND APPLICATIONS

MyOMLab *These problems and applications will help to improve your analysis of operations. You can find more practice problems as well as worked examples and guided solutions on MyOMLab at www.myomlab.com.*

1 A hotel has two wings, an east wing and a west wing. Each wing has 4 'room service maids' working 7-hour shifts to service the rooms each day. The east wing has 40 standard rooms, 12 deluxe rooms, and 5 suites. The west wing has 50 standard rooms and 10 deluxe rooms. The standard times for servicing rooms are as follows: standard rooms 20 standard minutes, deluxe rooms 25 standard minutes, and suites 40 standard minutes. In addition, an allowance of 5 standard minutes per room is given for any miscellaneous jobs such as collecting extra items for the room or dealing with customer requests. What is the productivity of the maids in each wing of the hotel? What other factors might also influence the productivity of the maids?

2 In the example above, one of the maids in the west wing wants to job share with his partner, each working 3 hours per day. His colleagues have agreed to support him and will guarantee to service all the rooms in the west wing to the same standard each day. If they succeed in doing this, how has it affected their productivity?

3 *Step 1* – Make a sandwich. Any type of sandwich, preferably one that you enjoy, and document the tasks you have to perform in order to complete the job. Make sure you include all the activities, including the movement of materials (bread, etc.) to and from the work surface.

Step 2 – So impressed were your friends with the general appearance of your sandwich that they have persuaded you to make one each for them every day. You have 10 friends so every morning you must make 10 identical sandwiches (to stop squabbling). How would you change the method by which you make the sandwiches to accommodate this higher volume?

Step 3 – The fame of your sandwiches has spread. You now decide to start a business making several different types of sandwich in high volume. Design the jobs of the 2 or 3 people who will help you in this venture. Assume that volumes run into at least 100 of 3 types of sandwich every day.

 A little-known department of your local government authority has the responsibility for keeping the area's public lavatories clean. It employs 10 people who each have a number of public lavatories that they visit, clean and also report any necessary repairs every day. Draw up a list of ideas for how you would keep this fine body of people motivated and committed to performing this unpleasant task.

 Visit a supermarket and observe the people who staff the checkouts:
(a) What kind of skills do people who do this job need to have?
(b) How many customers per hour are they capable of 'processing'?
(c) What opportunities exist for job enrichment in this activity?
(d) How would you ensure motivation and commitment amongst the staff who do this job?

SELECTED FURTHER READING

Apgar, M. (1998) **The alternative workplace: changing where and how people work,** *Harvard Business Review*, **May–June.** Interesting perspective on homeworking and teleworking amongst other things.

Argyris, C. (1998) **Empowerment: the emperor's new clothes,** *Harvard Business Review*, **May–June.** A critical but fascinating view of empowerment.

Bond, F. W. and Bunce, D. (2001) **Job control mediates change in a work reorganization intervention for stress reduction,** *Journal of Occupational Health Psychology*, **vol. 6, 290–302.**

Bridger, R. (2003) *Introduction to Ergonomics*, **Taylor and Francis, London.** Exactly what it says in the title: an introduction (but a good one) to ergonomics. A revised edition of a core textbook that gives a comprehensive introduction to ergonomics.

Hackman, R.J. and Oldham, G. (1980) *Work Redesign*, **Addison-Wesley, Reading, MA.** Somewhat dated but, in its time, ground-breaking and certainly hugely influential.

Herzberg, F. (1987) **One more time: how do you motivate employees? (with retrospective commentary),** *Harvard Business Review*, **vol. 65, no. 5.** An interesting look back by one of the most influential figures in the behavioural approach to job design school.

Lantz, A. and Brav, A. (2007) **Job design for learning in work groups,** *Journal of Workplace Learning*, **vol. 19, issue 5, 269–285.**

USEFUL WEBSITES

www.bpmi.org Site of the Business Process Management Initiative. Some good resources including papers and articles.

www.bptrends.com News site for trends in business process management generally. Some interesting articles.

www.bls.gov/oes US Department of Labour employment statistics.

www.fedee.com/labour-relations Federation of European Employers guide to employment and job trends in Europe.

www.waria.com A Workflow and Reengineering association website. Some useful topics.

www.myomlab.com Test which sections you have mastered and which you need to review, with questions, a personalized study plan, video clips, revision tips, and cases.

Supplement to Chapter 9
Work study

INTRODUCTION

A tale is told of Frank Gilbreth (the founder of method study) addressing a scientific conference with a paper entitled 'The best way to get dressed in a morning'. In his presentation, he rather bemused the scientific audience by analysing the 'best' way of buttoning up one's waistcoat in the morning. Among his conclusions was that waistcoats should always be buttoned from the bottom upwards. (To make it easier to straighten his tie in the same motion; buttoning from the top downwards requires the hands to be raised again.) Think of this example if you want to understand scientific management and method study in particular. First of all, he is quite right. Method study and the other techniques of scientific management may often be without any intellectual or scientific validation, but by and large they work in their own terms. Second, Gilbreth reached his conclusion by a systematic and critical analysis of what motions were necessary to do the job. Again, these are characteristics of scientific management – detailed analysis and painstakingly systematic examination. Third (and possibly most important), the results are relatively trivial. A great deal of effort was put into reaching a conclusion that was unlikely to have any earth-shattering consequences. Indeed, one of the criticisms of scientific management, as developed in the early part of the twentieth century, is that it concentrated on relatively limited, and sometimes trivial, objectives.

The responsibility for its application, however, has moved away from specialist 'time and motion' staff to the employees who can use such principles to improve what they do and how they do it. Further, some of the methods and techniques of scientific management, as opposed to its philosophy (especially those which come under the general heading of 'method study'), can in practice prove useful in critically re-examining job designs. It is the practicality of these techniques which possibly explains why they are still influential in job design almost a century after their inception.

METHOD STUDY IN JOB DESIGN

Method study is a systematic approach to finding the best method. There are six steps:

1 Select the work to be studied.
2 Record all the relevant facts of the present method.
3 Examine those facts critically and in sequence.
4 Develop the most practical, economic and effective method.
5 Install the new method.
6 Maintain the method by periodically checking it in use.

Step 1 – Selecting the work to be studied

Most operations have many hundreds and possibly thousands of discrete jobs and activities which could be subjected to study. The first stage in method study is to select those jobs to be studied which will give the most return on the investment of the time spent studying them. This means it is unlikely that it will be worth studying activities which, for example, may soon be discontinued or are only performed occasionally. On the other hand, the types of job which should be studied as a matter of priority are those which, for example, seem to offer the greatest scope for improvement, or which are causing bottlenecks, delays or problems in the operation.

Step 2 – Recording the present method

There are many different recording techniques used in method study. Most of them:

- record the sequence of activities in the job;
- record the time interrelationship of the activities in the job; or
- record the path of movement of some part of the job.

Perhaps the most commonly used recording technique in method study is process mapping which was discussed earlier (see Chapter 4). Note that we are here recording the present method of doing the job. It may seem strange to devote so much time and effort to recording what is currently happening when, after all, the objective of method study is to devise a better method. The rationale for this is, first of all, that recording the present method can give a far greater insight into the job itself, and this can lead to new ways of doing it. Second, recording the present method is a good starting point from which to evaluate it critically and therefore improve it. In this last point the assumption is that it is easier to improve the method by starting from the current method and then criticizing it in detail than by starting with a 'blank sheet of paper'.

Step 3 – Examining the facts

This is probably the most important stage in method study and the idea here is to examine the current method thoroughly and critically. This is often done by using the so-called 'questioning technique'. This technique attempts to detect weaknesses in the rationale for existing methods so that alternative methods can be developed (*see* Table S9.1). The approach may

Table S9.1 The method study questioning technique

Broad question	Detailed question
The purpose of each activity (questions the fundamental need for the element)	• What is done? • Why is it done? • What else could be done? • What should be done?
The place in which each element is done (may suggest a combination of certain activities or operations)	• Where is it done? • Why is it done there? • Where else could it be done? • Where should it be done?
The sequence in which the elements are done (may suggest a change in the sequence of the activity)	• When is it done? • Why is it done then? • When should it be done?
The person who does the activity (may suggest a combination and/or change in responsibility or sequence)	• Who does it? • Why does that person do it? • Who else could do it? • Who should do it?
The means by which each activity is done (may suggest new methods)	• How is it done? • Why is it done in that way? • How else could it be done? • How should it be done?

appear somewhat detailed and tedious, yet it is fundamental to the method study philosophy – everything must be critically examined. Understanding the natural tendency to be less than rigorous at this stage, some organizations use pro forma questionnaires, asking each of these questions and leaving space for formal replies and/or justifications, which the job designer is required to complete.

Step 4 – Developing a new method

The previous critical examination of current methods has by this stage probably indicated some changes and improvements. This step involves taking these ideas further in an attempt to:

- eliminate parts of the activity altogether;
- combine elements together;
- change the sequence of events so as to improve the efficiency of the job; or
- simplify the activity to reduce the work content.

A useful aid during this process is a checklist such as the revised principles of motion economy. Table S9.2 illustrates these.

Steps 5 and 6 – Install the new method and regularly maintain it

The method study approach to the installation of new work practices concentrates largely on 'project managing' the installation process. It also emphasizes the need to monitor regularly the effectiveness of job designs after they have been installed.

Table S9.2 The principles of motion economy

Broad principle	How to do it
Use the human body the way it works best	• Work should be arranged so that a natural rhythm can become automatic • Motion of the body should be simultaneous and symmetrical if possible • The full capabilities of the human body should be employed • Arms and hands as weights are subject to the physical laws and energy should be conserved • Tasks should be simplified
Arrange the workplace to assist performance	• There should be a defined place for all equipment and materials • Equipment, materials and controls should be located close to the point of use • Equipment, materials and controls should be located to permit the best sequence and path of motions • The workplace should be fitted both to the tasks and to human capabilities
Use technology to reduce human effort	• Work should be presented precisely where needed • Guides should assist in positioning the work without close operator attention • Controls and foot-operated devices can relieve the hands of work • Mechanical devices can multiply human abilities • Mechanical systems should be fitted to human use

Source: Adapted from Barnes, Frank C. (1983) 'Principles of Motion Economy: Revisited, Reviewed, and Restored', *Proceedings of the Southern Management Association Annual Meeting* (Atlanta, GA 1983), p. 298.

WORK MEASUREMENT IN JOB DESIGN

Basic times

Terminology is important in work measurement. When a *qualified worker* is working on a *specified job* at *standard performance*, the time he or she takes to perform the job is called the basic time for the job. Basic times are useful because they are the 'building blocks' of time estimation. With the basic times for a range of different tasks, an operations manager can construct a time estimate for any longer activity which is made up of the tasks. The best-known technique for establishing basic times is probably time study.

Time study

Time study is 'a work measurement technique for recording the times and rate of working for the elements of a specified job, carried out under specified conditions, and for analysing the data so as to obtain the time necessary for the carrying out of the job at a defined level of performance'. The technique takes three steps to derive the basic times for the elements of the job:

- observing and measuring the time taken to perform each element of the job;
- adjusting, or 'normalizing', each observed time;
- averaging the adjusted times to derive the basic time for the element.

Step 1 – Observing, measuring and rating

A job is observed through several cycles. Each time an element is performed, it is timed using a stopwatch. Simultaneously with the observation of time, a rating of the perceived performance of the person doing the job is recorded. Rating is 'the process of assessing the worker's rate of working relative to the observer's concept of the rate corresponding to standard performance. The observer may take into account, separately or in combination, one or more factors necessary to carrying out the job, such as speed of movement, effort, dexterity, consistency, etc.'. There are several ways of recording the observer's rating. The most common is on a scale which uses a rating of 100 to represent standard performance. If an observer rates a particular observation of the time to perform an element at 100, the time observed is the actual time which anyone working at standard performance would take.

Step 2 – Adjusting the observed times

The adjustment to normalize the observed time is:

$$\frac{\text{observed rating}}{\text{standard rating}}$$

where standard rating is 100 on the common rating scale we are using here. For example, if the observed time is 0.71 minutes and the observed rating is 90, then:

$$\text{Basic time} = \frac{0.71 \times 90}{100} = 0.64 \text{ mins}$$

Step 3 – Average the basic times

In spite of the adjustments made to the observed times through the rating mechanism, each separately calculated basic time will not be the same. This is not necessarily a function of inaccurate rating, or even the vagueness of the rating procedure itself; it is a natural phenomenon of the time taken to perform tasks. Any human activity cannot be repeated in *exactly* the same time on every occasion.

Standard times

The standard time for a job is an extension of the basic time and has a different use. Whereas the basic time for a job is a piece of information which can be used as the first step in estimating the time to perform a job under a wide range of conditions, standard time refers to the time *allowed* for the job under specific circumstances. This is because standard time includes allowances which reflect the rest and relaxation allowed because of the conditions under which the job is performed. So the standard time for each element consists principally of two parts, the basic time (the time taken by a qualified worker, doing a specified job at standard performance) and an allowance (this is added to the basic time to allow for rest, relaxation and personal needs).

Allowances

Allowances are additions to the basic time intended to provide the worker with the opportunity to recover from the physiological and psychological effects of carrying out specified work under specified conditions and to allow for personal needs. The amount of the allowance will depend on the nature of the job. The way in which relaxation allowance is calculated, and the exact allowances given for each of the factors which determine the extent of the allowance, varies between different organizations. Table S9.3 illustrates the allowance table used by one company which manufactures domestic appliances. Every job has an allowance of 10 per cent; the table shows the further percentage allowances to be applied to each element of the job. In addition, other allowances may be applied for such things as unexpected contingencies, synchronization with other jobs, unusual working conditions, and so on.

Table S9.3 An allowances table used by a domestic appliance manufacturer

Allowance factors	Example	Allowance (%)
Energy needed		
Negligible	none	0
Very light	0–3 kg	3
Light	3–10 kg	5
Medium	10–20 kg	10
Heavy	20–30 kg	15
Very heavy	Above 30 kg	15–30
Posture required		
Normal	Sitting	0
Erect	Standing	2
Continuously erect	Standing for long periods	3
Lying	On side, face or back	4
Difficult	Crouching, etc.	4–10
Visual fatigue		
Nearly continuous attention		2
Continuous attention with varying focus		3
Continuous attention with fixed focus		5
Temperature		
Very low	Below 0°C	over 10
Low	0–12°C	0–10
Normal	12–23°C	0
High	23–30°C	0–10
Very high	Above 30°C	over 10
Atmospheric conditions		
Good	Well ventilated	0
Fair	Stuffy/smelly	2
Poor	Dusty/needs filter	2–7
Bad	Needs respirator	7–12

Element		Observation										Average basic time	Allowances	Element standard time
		1	2	3	4	5	6	7	8	9	10			
Make box	Observed time	0.71	0.71	0.71	0.69	0.75	0.68	0.70	0.72	0.70	0.68			
	Rating	90	90	90	90	80	90	90	90	90	90			
	Basic time	0.64	0.64	0.63	0.62	0.60	0.61	0.63	0.65	0.63	0.61	0.626	10%	0.689
Pack x 20	Observed time	1.30	1.32	1.25	1.33	1.33	1.28	1.32	1.32	1.30	1.30			
	Rating	90	90	100	90	90	90	90	90	90	90			
	Basic time	1.17	1.19	1.25	1.20	1.20	1.15	1.19	1.19	1.17	1.17	1.168	12%	1.308
Seal and secure	Observed time	0.53	0.55	0.55	0.56	0.53	0.53	0.60	0.55	0.49	0.51			
	Rating	90	90	90	90	90	90	85	90	100	100			
	Basic time	0.48	0.50	0.50	0.50	0.48	0.48	0.51	0.50	0.49	0.51	0.495	10%	0.545
Assemble outer,	Observed time	1.12	1.21	1.20	1.25	1.41	1.27	1.11	1.15	1.20	1.23			
fix and label	Rating	100	90	90	90	90	90	100	100	90	90			
	Basic time	1.12	1.09	1.08	1.13	1.27	1.14	1.11	1.15	1.08	1.21	1.138	12%	1.275

Raw standard time		3.817
Allowances for total job	5%	0.191
Standard time for job		4.01 SM

Figure S9.1 Time study of a packing task – standard time for the whole task calculated

Figure S9.1 shows how average basic times for each element in the job are combined with allowances (low in this example) for each element to build up the standard time for the whole job.

Worked example

Two work teams in the Monrovian Embassy have been allocated the task of processing visa applications. Team A processes applications from Europe, Africa and the Middle East. Team B processes applications from North and South America, Asia and Australasia. Team A has chosen to organize itself in such a way that each of its three team members processes an application from start to finish. The four members of Team B have chosen to split themselves into two sub-teams. Two open the letters and carry out the checks for a criminal record (no one who has been convicted of any crime other than a motoring offence can enter Monrovia), while the other two team members check for financial security (only people with more than Monrovian $1000 may enter the country). The head of consular affairs is keen to find out if one of these methods of organizing the teams is more efficient than the other. The problem is that the mix of applications differs region by region. Team A typically processes around two business applications to every one tourist application. Team B processes around one business application to every two tourist applications.

A study revealed the following data:

Average standard time to process a business visa = 63 standard minutes

Average time to process a tourist visa = 55 standard minutes

Average weekly output from Team A is:
  85.2   Business visas
  39.5   Tourist visas

Average weekly output from Team B is:
  53.5   Business visas
  100.7 Tourist visas

All team members work a 40-hour week.

The efficiency of each team can be calculated by comparing the actual output in standard minutes and the time worked in minutes.

So Team A processes:

$$(85.2 \times 63) + (39.5 \times 55) = 7{,}540.1 \text{ standard minutes of work}$$

$$\text{in } 3 \times 40 \times 60 \text{ minutes} = 7{,}200 \text{ minutes}$$

$$\text{So its efficiency} = \frac{7{,}540.1}{7{,}200} \times 100 = 104.72\%$$

Team B processes:

$$(53.5 \times 63) + (100.7 \times 55) = 8{,}909 \text{ standard minutes of work}$$

$$\text{in } 4 \times 40 \times 60 \text{ minutes} = 9{,}600 \text{ minutes}$$

$$\text{So its efficiency} = \frac{8{,}909}{9{,}600} \times 100 = 92.8\%$$

The initial evidence therefore seems to suggest that the way Team A has organized itself is more efficient.

Now that you have finished reading this chapter, why not visit MyOMLab at www.myomlab.com where you'll find more learning resources to help you make the most of your studies and get a better grade.

The nature of planning and control

Key questions

> **What is planning and control?**

> **What is the difference between planning and control?**

> **How do supply and demand affect planning and control**

> **What are the activities of planning and control?**

INTRODUCTION

The design of an operation determines the resources with which it creates its services and products, but the operation then has to deliver those services and products on an ongoing basis. And central to an operation's ability to deliver is the way it plans its activities and controls them so that customers' demands are satisfied. This chapter introduces and provides an overview of some of the principles and methods of planning and control. Later chapters in this part of the book develop some specific issues that are vital to an operation delivering its services and products. These issues start with managing capacity and move through managing inventory, providing an overview of supply chain management and looking at how enterprise resources planning (ERP) manages the information that ensures effective delivery. We then examine how 'lean' philosophy has influenced operations practice before examining the special case of project management and finally the role that quality management plays in delivering appropriate services and products. But whatever aspect of delivery is being examined, they can all be viewed as representing the reconciliation of supply with demand (*see* Fig. 10.1).

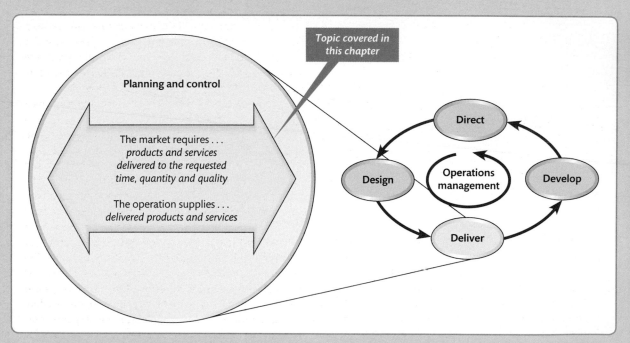

Figure 10.1 This chapter introduces planning and control

Joanne manages the schedule[1]

Source: Shutterstock.com/Jordan Tan

Joanne Cheung is the Senior Service Adviser at a premier BMW dealership. She and her team act as the interface between customers who want their cars serviced and repaired, and the 16 technicians who carry out the work in their state-of-the-art workshop. *'There are three types of work that we have to organize'*, says Joanne. *'The first is performing repairs on customers' vehicles. They usually want this doing as soon as possible. The second type of job is routine servicing. It is usually not urgent so customers are generally willing to negotiate a time for this. The remainder of our work involves working on the pre-owned cars which our buyer has bought-in to sell on to customers. Before any of these cars can be sold they have to undergo extensive checks. To some extent we treat these categories of work slightly differently. We have to give good service to our internal car buyers, but there is some flexibility in planning these jobs. At the other extreme, emergency repair work for customers has to be fitted into our schedule as quickly as possible. If someone is desperate to have their car repaired at very short notice, we sometimes ask them to drop their car in as early as they can and pick it up as late as possible. This gives us the maximum amount of time to fit it into the schedule.*

'There are a number of service options open to customers. We can book short jobs in for a fixed time and do it while they wait. Most commonly, we ask the customer to leave the car with us and collect it later. To help customers we have 10 loan cars which are booked out on a first-come first-served basis. Alternatively, the vehicle can be collected from the customer's home and delivered back there when it is ready. Our 4 drivers who do this are able to cope with up to 12 jobs a day.

'Most days we deal with 50 to 80 jobs, taking from half-an-hour up to a whole day. To enter a job into our process all Service Advisers have access to the computer-based scheduling system. On-screen it shows the total capacity we have day-by-day, all the jobs that are booked in, the amount of free capacity still available, the number of loan cars available, and so on. We use this to see when we have the capacity to book a customer in, and then enter all the customer's details. BMW have issued "standard times" for all the major jobs. However, you have to modify these standard times a bit to take account of circumstances. That is where the Service Adviser's experience comes in.

'We keep all the most commonly used parts in stock, but if a repair needs a part which is not in stock, we can usually get it from the BMW parts distributors within a day. Every evening our planning system prints out the jobs to be done the next day and the parts which are likely to be needed for each job. This allows the parts staff to pick out the parts for each job so that the technicians can collect them first thing the next morning without any delay.

'Every day we have to cope with the unexpected. A technician may find that extra work is needed, customers may want extra work doing, and technicians are sometimes ill, which reduces our capacity. Occasionally parts may not be available so we have to arrange with the customer for the vehicle to be rebooked for a later time. Every day up to 4 or 5 customers just don't turn up. Usually they have just forgotten to bring their car in so we have to rebook them in at a later time. We can cope with most of these uncertainties because our technicians are flexible in terms of the skills they have and also are willing to work overtime when needed. Also, it is important to manage customers' expectations. If there is a chance that the vehicle may not be ready for them, it shouldn't come as a surprise when they try and collect it.'

WHAT IS PLANNING AND CONTROL?

Planning and control is concerned with the activities that attempt to reconcile the demands of the market and the ability of the operation's resources to deliver. It provides the systems, procedures and decisions which bring different aspects of supply and demand together. Consider, for example, the way in which routine surgery is organized in a hospital. When a patient arrives and is admitted to the hospital, much of the planning for the surgery will already have happened. The operating theatre will have been reserved, and the doctors and nurses who staff the operating theatre will have been provided with all the information regarding the patient's condition. Appropriate pre-operative and post-operative care will have been organized. All this will involve staff and facilities in different parts of the hospital, all of whom must have been given the same information and their activities co-ordinated. Soon after the patient arrives, he or she will be checked to make sure that the condition is as expected (in much the same way as material is inspected on arrival in a factory). Blood, if required, will be cross-matched and reserved, and any medication will be made ready (in the same way that all the different materials are brought together in a factory). Any last-minute changes may require some degree of re-planning. For example, if the patient shows unexpected symptoms, observation may be necessary before the surgery can take place. Not only will this affect the patient's own treatment, but other patients' treatment may also have to be rescheduled (in the same way as machines will need rescheduling if a job is delayed in a factory). All these activities of scheduling, co-ordination and organization are concerned with the planning and control of the hospital.

> *** Operations principle**
> Planning and control involves scheduling, co-ordinating and organizing operations activities.

The difference between planning and control

Notice that we have chosen to treat 'planning and control' together. This is because the division between 'planning' and 'control' is not clear, either in theory or in practice. However, there are some general features that help to distinguish between the two. Planning is a formalization of what is intended to happen at some time in the future. But a plan does not guarantee that an event will actually happen. Rather it is a statement of intention. Although plans are based on expectations, during their implementation things do not always happen as expected. Customers change their minds about what they want and when they want it. Suppliers may not always deliver on time, process technology may fail, or staff may be absent through illness. Control is the process of coping with these types of change. It may mean that plans need to be redrawn in the short term. It may also mean that an 'intervention' will need to be made in the operation to bring it back 'on track' – for example, finding a new supplier who can deliver quickly, getting process technology up and running again, or moving staff from another part of the operation to cover for the absentees. Control activities make the adjustments which allow the operation to achieve the objectives that the plan has set, even when the assumptions on which the plan was based do not hold true.

> *** Operations principle**
> Planning and control are separate but closely related activities.

Long-, medium- and short-term planning and control

The nature of planning and control activities changes over time. In the very long term, operations managers make plans concerning what they intend to do, what resources they need, and what objectives they hope to achieve. The emphasis is on planning rather than control, because there is little to control as such. They will use forecasts of likely demand described in aggregated terms. For example, a hospital will make plans for '2,000 patients' without necessarily going into the details of the individual needs of those 2,000 patients. Similarly, the hospital might plan to have 100 nurses and 20 doctors but again without deciding on the specific attributes of the staff. Operations managers will focus mainly on volume and financial targets.

Medium-term planning and control is more detailed. It looks ahead to assess the overall demand which the operation must meet in a partially disaggregated manner. By this time, for example, the hospital must distinguish between different types of demand. The number of patients coming as accident and emergency cases will need to be distinguished from those requiring routine operations. Similarly, different categories of staff will have been identified and broad staffing levels in each category set. Just as important, contingencies will have been put in place which allow for slight deviations from the plans. These contingencies will act as 'reserve' resources and make planning and control easier in the short term.

In short-term planning and control, many of the resources will have been set and it will be difficult to make large changes. However, short-term interventions are possible if things are not going to plan. By this time, demand will be assessed on a totally disaggregated basis, with all types of surgical procedures treated as individual activities. More importantly, individual patients will have been identified by name, and specific time slots booked for their treatment. In making short-term interventions and changes to the plan, operations managers will be attempting to balance the quality, speed, dependability, flexibility and costs of their operation dynamically on an *ad hoc* basis. It is unlikely that they will have the time to carry out detailed calculations of the effects of their short-term planning and control decisions on all these objectives, but a general understanding of priorities will form the background to their decision making. Figure 10.2 shows how the control aspects of planning and control increase in significance closer to the date of the event.

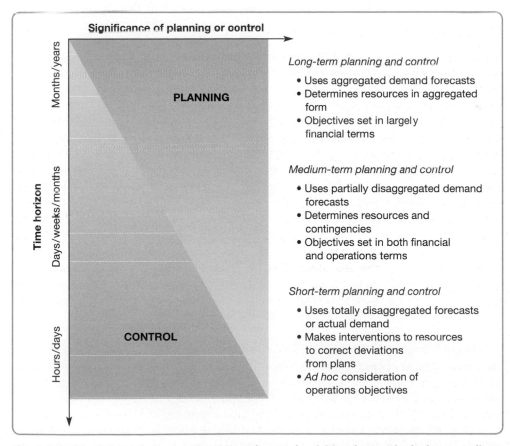

Figure 10.2 The balance between planning and control activities changes in the long, medium and short term

The volume–variety effect on planning and control

As we have found previously, the volume and variety characteristics of an operation will have an effect on its planning and control activities. Operations which produce a high variety of services or products in relatively low volume will have customers with different requirements and use different processes from operations which create standardized services or products in high volume (*see* Table 10.1).

Take two contrasting operations – an architects' practice and an electricity utility. The architects' high variety of customized services means they cannot produce designs in advance of customers requesting them. Because of this, the time it will take to finally deliver their services to customers will be relatively slow. Customers will understand this, but will expect to be consulted extensively as to their needs. The details and requirements of each job will emerge only as each individual building is designed to the client's requirements, so planning occurs on a relatively short-term basis. The individual decisions which are taken in the planning process will usually concern the timing of activities and events – for example, when a design is to be delivered, when building should start, when each individual architect will be needed to work on the design. Control decisions also will be at a relatively detailed level. A small delay in fixing one part of the design could have significant implications in many other parts of the job. For an architect, planning and control cannot be a totally routine matter; projects need managing on an individual basis. However, the robustness of the operation (that is, its vulnerability to serious disruption if one part of the operation fails) will be relatively high. There are probably plenty of other things to get on with if an architect is prevented from progressing one part of the job.

The electricity utility, on the other hand, is very different. Volume is high, production is continuous, and variety is non-existent. Customers expect instant 'delivery' whenever they plug in an appliance. The planning horizon in electricity generation can be very long. Major decisions regarding the capacity of power stations are made years in advance. Even the fluctuations in demand over a typical day can be forecast in advance. Popular television programmes can affect minute-by-minute demand and these are scheduled weeks or months ahead. The weather also affects demand, and is more uncertain, but can to some extent be predicted. Individual planning decisions made by the electricity utility are not concerned with the timing, but rather the volume of output. Control decisions will concern aggregated measures of output such as the total kilowatts of electricity generated, because the product is more or less homogeneous. However, the robustness of the operation is very low because, if a generator fails, the operation's capability of supplying electricity from that part of the operation also fails.

> **✱ Operations principle**
>
> The volume–variety characteristics of an operation will affect its planning and control activities.

Table 10.1 The volume–variety effects on planning and control

Volume	Variety	Customer responsiveness	Planning horizon	Major planning decision	Control decisions	Robustness
Low	High	Slow	Short	Timing	Detailed	High
↓	↓	↓	↓	↓	↓	↓
High	Low	Fast	Long	Volume	Aggregated	Low

'In many ways a major airline can be viewed as one large planning problem which is usually approached as many independent, smaller (but still difficult) planning problems. The list of things which need planning seems endless: crews, reservation agents, luggage, flights, through trips, maintenance, gates, inventory, equipment purchases. Each planning problem has its own considerations, its own complexities, its own set of time horizons, its own objectives, but all are interrelated.'

Air France has 80 flight planners working 24-hour shifts in their flight planning office at Roissy, Charles de Gaulle. Their job is to establish the optimum flight routes, anticipate any problems such as weather changes, and minimize fuel consumption. Overall the goals of the flight planning activity are first, and most important, safety, followed by economy and passenger comfort. Increasingly powerful computer programs process the mountain of data necessary to plan the flights, but in the end many decisions still rely on human judgement. Even the most sophisticated expert systems only serve as support for the flight planners. Planning Air France's schedule is a massive job. Just some of the considerations which need to be taken into account include the following:

Source: Shutterstock.com/Alhovik

● *Frequency* – for each airport how many separate services should the airline provide?
● *Fleet assignment* – which type of plane should be used on each leg of a flight?
● *Banks* – at any airline hub where passengers arrive and may transfer to other flights to continue their journey, airlines like to organize flights into 'banks' of several planes which arrive close together, pause to let passengers change planes, and all depart close together. So, how many banks should there be and when should they occur?
● *Block times* – a block time is the elapsed time between a plane leaving the departure gate at an airport and arriving at its gate in the arrival airport. The longer the allowed block time the more likely a plane will keep to schedule even if it suffers minor delays. However, longer block times also mean fewer flights can be scheduled.

● *Planned maintenance* – any schedule must allow time for planes to have time at a maintenance base.
● *Crew planning* – pilot and cabin crew must be scheduled to allocate pilots to fly planes on which they are licensed and to keep within maximum 'on duty' times for all staff.
● *Gate plotting* – if many planes are on the ground at the same time there may be problems in loading and unloading them simultaneously.
● *Recovery* – many things can cause deviations from any plan in the airline industry. Allowances must be built in to allow for recovery.

For flights within and between Air France's 12 geographic zones, the planners construct a flight plan that will form the basis of the actual flight only a few hours later. All planning documents need to be ready for the flight crew who arrive two hours before the scheduled departure time. Being responsible for passenger safety and comfort, the captain always has the final say and, when satisfied, co-signs the flight plan together with the planning officer.

THE EFFECT OF SUPPLY AND DEMAND ON PLANNING AND CONTROL

If planning and control is the process of reconciling demand with supply, then the nature of the decisions taken to plan and control an operation will depend on both the nature of demand and the nature of supply in that operation. In this next section, we examine some differences in demand and supply which can affect the way in which operations managers plan and control their activities.

Uncertainty in supply and demand

Uncertainty is important in planning and control because it makes it more difficult. Sometimes the supply of inputs to an operation may be uncertain. Local village carnivals, for example, rarely work to plan. Events take longer than expected, some of the acts scheduled in the programme may be delayed *en route*, and some traders may not even arrive. In other operations supply is relatively predictable, and the need for control is minimal. For example, cable TV services provide programmes to a schedule into subscribers' homes. It is rare to change the programme plan. Similarly demand may be unpredictable. A fast-food outlet inside a shopping centre does not know how many people will arrive, when they will arrive and what they will order. It may be possible to predict certain patterns, such as an increase in demand over the lunch and tea-time periods, but a sudden rainstorm that drives shoppers indoors into the centre could significantly and unpredictably increase demand in the very short term. Conversely, demand may be more predictable. In a school, for example, once classes are fixed and the term or semester has started, a teacher knows how many pupils are in the class. Both supply and demand uncertainty make planning and control more difficult, but a combination of supply *and* demand uncertainty is particularly difficult.

Dependent and independent demand

Some operations can predict demand with relative certainty because demand for their services or products is dependent upon some other factor which is known. This is known as dependent demand. For example, the demand for tyres in an automobile factory is not a totally random variable. The process of demand forecasting is relatively straightforward. It will consist of examining the manufacturing schedules in the car plant and deriving the demand for tyres from these. If 600 cars are to be manufactured on a particular day, then it is simple to calculate that 3,000 tyres will be demanded by the car plant (each car has 5 tyres) – demand is dependent on a known factor, i.e. the number of cars to be manufactured. Because of this, the tyres can be ordered from the tyre manufacturer to a delivery schedule which is closely related to the demand for tyres from the plant (as in Fig. 10.3). In fact, the demand for every part of the car plant will be derived from the assembly schedule for the finished cars. Other operations will act in a dependent demand manner because of the nature of the service or product which they provide. For example, a custom-made dressmaker will not buy fabric and make up dresses in many different sizes just in case someone comes along and wants to buy one. Nor will a high-class restaurant begin to cook food just in case a customer arrives and requests it. In both these cases, a combination of risk and the perishability of the product or service prevents the operation from starting to create the goods or services until it has a firm order. Planning and control in dependent demand situations is largely concerned with how the operation should respond when demand has occurred.

By contrast, some operations are subject to independent demand. They need to supply future demand without knowing exactly what that demand will be; or in the terminology of planning and control, they do not have firm 'forward visibility' of customer orders. For example, the Ace Tyre Company, which operates a drive-in tyre replacement service, will need to manage a stock of tyres. In that sense it is exactly the same task that faced the manager of tyre stocks in the car plant. However, demand is very different for Ace Tyres. It cannot predict either the volume or the specific needs of customers. It must make decisions on how many and what type of tyres to stock, based on demand forecasts and in light of the risks it is prepared to run of being out of stock. This is the nature of independent demand planning and control. It makes 'best guesses' concerning future demand, attempts to put the resources in place which can satisfy this demand, and attempts to respond quickly if actual demand does not match the forecast. Inventory planning and control (treated in Chapter 12) is typical of independent demand planning and control.

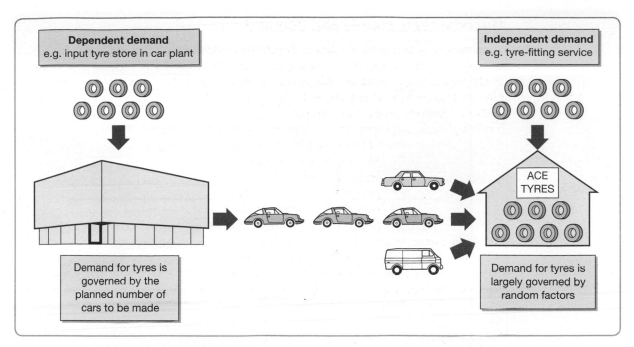

Figure 10.3 Dependent demand is derived from the demand for something else; independent demand is more random

Responding to demand

It is clear then that the nature of planning and control in any operation will depend how it responds to demand, which is in turn related to the type of services or products it produces. For example, an advertising agency will only start the process of planning and controlling the creation of an advertising campaign when the customer (or client, as the agency will refer to them) confirms the contract with the agency. The creative 'design' of the advertisements will be based on a 'brief' from the client. Only after the design is approved are the appropriate resources (director, scriptwriters, actors, production company. etc.) contracted. The actual shooting of the advertisement and post-production (editing, putting in the special effects, etc.) then goes ahead, after which the finished advertisements are 'delivered' through television slots. This is shown in Figure 10.4 as a 'Design, resource, create and deliver to order' operation.

Other operations might be sufficiently confident of the nature of demand, if not its exact details, to keep 'in stock' most of the resources it requires to satisfy its customers. Certainly it will keep its transforming resources, if not its transformed resources. However, it would still make the actual service or product only when it receives a firm customer order. For example, a website designer will have most of its resources (graphic designers, software developers, specialist development software, etc.) in place, but must still design, create and deliver the website after it understands its customer's requirements. (See the short case on Torchbox in Chapter 1.) This is shown in Figure 10.4 as a 'Design, create and deliver to order' operation.

Some operations offer relatively standard services or products, but do not create them until the customer has chosen which particular service or product to have. So a house builder who has standard designs might choose to build each house only when a customer places a firm order. Because the design of the house is relatively standard, suppliers of materials will have been identified, even if the building operation does not keep the items in stock itself. This is shown in Figure 10.4 as a 'Create and deliver to order' operation. In manufacturing it would be called a 'Make to order' operation.

Some operations have services or products that are so predictable that they can start to 'create' them before specific customer orders arrive. Possibly the best-known example of this is Dell Computers where customers can 'specify' their computer by selecting between product and receiving it, called the demand time, D, and the total throughput time from start to finish, P. Throughput time is how long the operation takes to design the service or product (if it is customized), obtain the resources, create and deliver it.

P and D times depend on the operation

P and D are illustrated for each type of operation in Figure 10.4. Generally the ratio of P to D gets larger as operations move from 'Design, resource, create and deliver to order' to 'Choose/collect from stock'. In other words, as one moves down this spectrum towards the 'Create to stock' and 'Choose/collect from stock' end, the operation has anticipated customer demand and already created the services and products, even though it has no guarantee that the anticipated demand will really happen. This is a particularly important point for the planning and control activity. The larger the $P{:}D$ ratio the more speculative the operation's planning and control activities will be. In its extreme form, the 'Choose/collect from stock' operation, such as a high-street retailer, has taken a gamble by designing, resourcing, creating and delivering (or more likely, paying someone else to do so) products to its shops before it has any certainty that any customers will want them. Contrast this with a 'Design, resource, create and deliver to order' operation, such as the advertising agency mentioned earlier. Here, D is the same as P and speculation regarding the volume of demand in the short term is eliminated because everything happens in response to a firm order. So by reducing their $P{:}D$ ratio, operations reduce their degree of speculative activity and also reduce their dependence on forecasting (although bad forecasting will lead to other problems).

But do not assume that when the $P{:}D$ ratio approaches 1, all uncertainty is eliminated. The volume of demand (in terms of the number of customer 'orders') may be known, but not the time taken to perform each 'order'. Take the advertising agency again: during each stage of the process, from design to delivery, it is common to have to seek the customer's approval and/or feedback many times during each stage. Moreover, there will almost certainly be some recycling back through stages as modifications are made. And, in a similar way to how simultaneous development works in new service and product design (see Chapter 5), a stage can be started before the previous one has been completed. So, for example, the video shoot director will have started prior to the artwork design being completed. This is illustrated in Figure 10.5. So here it is the timings that are uncertain.

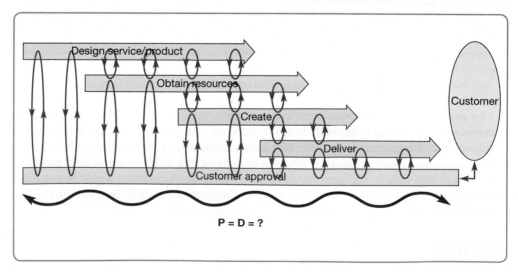

Figure 10.5 The relationship between stages in some 'Design, resource, create and deliver to order operations,' such as an advertising agency, can be complex with frequent consultation and unpredictable recycling

PLANNING AND CONTROL ACTIVITIES

Planning and control requires the reconciliation of supply and demand in terms of volumes, timing and quality. In this chapter we will focus on an overview of the activities that plan and control volume and timing (most of this part of the book is concerned with these issues). There are four overlapping activities: loading, sequencing, scheduling, and monitoring and control (*see* Fig. 10.6). Some caution is needed when using these terms. Different organizations may use them in different ways, and even textbooks in the area adopt different definitions. For example, some authorities term what

> **✳ Operations principle**
>
> Planning and control activities include loading, sequencing, scheduling, and monitoring and control.

we have called planning and control as 'operations scheduling'. However, the terminology of planning and control is less important than understanding the basic ideas described in the remainder of this chapter.

Loading

Loading is the amount of work that is allocated to a work centre. For example, a machine on the shop floor of a manufacturing business is available, in theory, 168 hours a week. However, this does not necessarily mean that 168 hours of work can be loaded onto that machine. Figure 10.7 shows what erodes this available time. For some periods the machine cannot be worked; for example, it may not be available on statutory holidays and weekends. Therefore, the load put onto the machine must take this into account. Of the time that the machine is available for work, other losses further reduce the available time. For example, time may be lost while changing over from making one component to another. If the machine breaks down, it will not be available. If there is machine reliability data available, this must also be taken into

> **✳ Operations principle**
>
> For any given level of demand a planning and control system should be able to indicate the implications for the loading on any part of the operation.

account. Sometimes the machine may be waiting for parts to arrive or be 'idling' for some other reason. Other losses could include an allowance for the machine being run below its optimum speed (for example, because it has not been maintained properly) and an allowance for the 'quality losses' or defects which the machine may produce. Of course, many of these losses (shown in Figure 10.6) should be small or non-existent in a well-managed operation. However, the valuable operating time available for productive working, even in the best operations, can be significantly below the maximum time available. This idea is taken further (in Chapter 11) when we discuss the measurement of capacity.

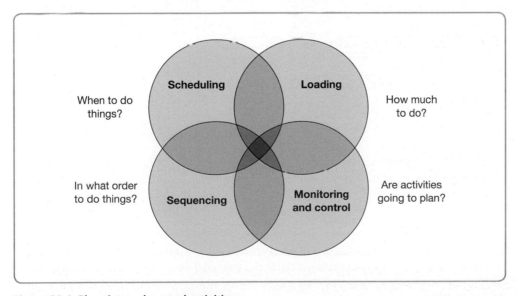

Figure 10.6 Planning and control activities

Figure 10.7 The reduction in the time available for valuable operating time

Finite and infinite loading

Finite loading is an approach which only allocates work to a work centre (a person, a machine, or perhaps a group of people or machines) up to a set limit. This limit is the estimate of capacity for the work centre (based on the times available for loading). Work over and above this capacity is not accepted. Figure 10.8 first shows how the load on the work centres is not allowed to exceed the capacity limit. Finite loading is particularly relevant for operations where:

- *it is possible to limit the load* – for example, it is possible to run an appointment system for a general medical practice or a hairdresser;
- *it is necessary to limit the load* – for example, for safety reasons only a finite number of people and weight of luggage are allowed on aircraft;
- *the cost of limiting the load is not prohibitive* – for example, the cost of maintaining a finite order book at a specialist sports car manufacturer does not adversely affect demand, and may even enhance it.

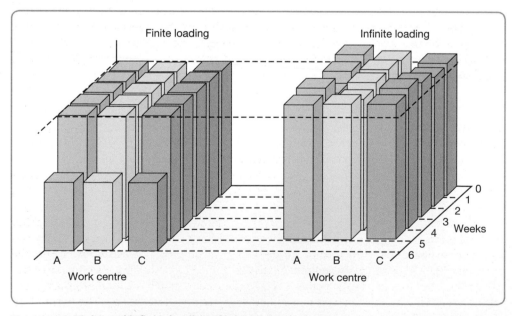

Figure 10.8 Finite and infinite loading of jobs on three work centres A, B and C. Finite loading limits the loading on each centre to their capacities, even if it means that jobs will be late. Infinite loading allows the loading on each centre to exceed their capacities to ensure that jobs will not be late

Infinite loading is an approach to loading work which does not limit accepting work, but instead tries to cope with it. The second diagram in Figure 10.8 illustrates this loading pattern where capacity constraints have not been used to limit loading so the work is completed earlier. Infinite loading is relevant for operations where:

- *it is not possible to limit the load* – for example, an accident and emergency department in a hospital should not turn away arrivals needing attention;
- *it is not necessary to limit the load* – for example, fast-food outlets are designed to flex capacity up and down to cope with varying arrival rates of customers. During busy periods, customers accept that they must queue for some time before being served. Unless this is extreme, the customers might not go elsewhere;
- *the cost of limiting the load is prohibitive* – for example, if a retail bank turned away customers at the door because a set number were inside, customers would feel less than happy with the service.

In complex planning and control activities where there are multiple stages, each with different capacities and with a varying mix arriving at the facilities, such as a machine shop in an engineering company, the constraints imposed by finite loading make loading calculations complex and not worth the considerable computational power which would be needed.

Sequencing

Whether the approach to loading is finite or infinite, when work arrives, decisions must be taken on the order in which the work will be tackled. This activity is termed 'sequencing'. The priorities given to work in an operation are often determined by some predefined set of rules, some of which are relatively complex. Some of these are summarized below.

Physical constraints

The physical nature of the inputs being processed may determine the priority of work. For example, in an operation using paints or dyes, lighter shades will be sequenced before darker shades. On completion of each batch, the colour is slightly darkened for the next batch. This is because darkness of colour can only be added to and not removed from the colour mix. Sometimes the mix of work arriving at a part of an operation may determine the priority given to jobs. For example, when fabric is cut to a required size and shape in garment manufacture, the surplus fabric would be wasted if not used for another product. Therefore, jobs that physically fit together may be scheduled together to reduce waste. The sequencing issue described in the short case 'Can airline passengers be sequenced?' is of this type.

Customer priority

Operations will sometimes use customer priority sequencing, which allows an important or aggrieved customer, or item, to be 'processed' prior to others, irrespective of the order of arrival of the customer or item. This approach is typically used by operations whose customer base is skewed, containing a mass of small customers and a few large, very important customers. Some banks, for example, give priority to important customers. Similarly, in hotels, complaining customers will be treated as a priority because their complaint may have an adverse effect on the perceptions of other customers. More seriously, the emergency services often have to use their judgement in prioritizing the urgency of requests for service. For example, Figure 10.10 shows the priority system used by a police force. Here the operators receiving emergency and other calls are trained to grade the calls into one of five categories. The response by the police is then organized to match the level of priority. The triage system in hospitals operates in a similar way (*see* the short case on 'The hospital triage system', p.304). However, customer priority sequencing, although giving a high level of service to some customers, may erode the service given to many others. This may lower the overall performance of the operation if work flows are disrupted to accommodate important customers.

Like many before him, Dr Jason Steffen, a professional astrophysicist from the world-famous Fermilab, was frustrated by the time it took to load him and his fellow passengers onto the aircraft. He decided to devise a way to make the experience a little less tedious. So, for a while, he neglected his usual work of examining extra-solar planets, dark matter and cosmology, and experimentally tested a faster method of boarding aircraft. He found that, by changing the sequence in which passengers are loaded onto the aircraft, airlines could potentially save both time and money. Using a computer simulation and the arithmetic techniques routinely used in his day-to-day job, he was able to find what seemed to be a superior sequencing method. In fact the most common way of boarding passenger planes proved to be the least efficient. This is called the 'block method' where blocks of seats are called for boarding, starting from the back. Previously other experts in the airline industry had suggested boarding those in window seats first followed by middle and aisle seats. This is called the Wilma method. But according to Dr Steffen's simulations, two things slow down the boarding process. The first is that passengers may be required to wait in the aisle while those ahead of them store their luggage before they can take their seat. The second is that passengers already seated in aisle or middle seats frequently have to rise

Source: Shutterstock.com/StudioSmart

and move into the aisle to let others take seats nearer the window. So Dr Steffen suggested a variant of the Wilma method that minimized the first type of disturbance and eliminated the second. He suggested boarding in alternate rows, progressing from the rear forward, window seats first. Using this approach (now called the Steffen method), first, the window seats for every other row on one side of the plane are boarded. Next, alternate rows of window seats on the opposite side are boarded. Then, the window seats in the skipped rows are filled in on each side. The procedure then repeats with the middle seats and the aisles. See Figure 10.9.

Block (conventional) method

Wilma method

Steffen method

Figure 10.9 The best way to sequence passengers onto an aircraft

Later, the effectiveness of the various approaches were tested using a mock-up of a Boeing 757 aircraft and 72 luggage-carrying volunteers. Five different scenarios were tested: 'block' boarding in groups of rows from back to front, one by one from back to front, the 'Wilma method', the Steffen method, and completely random boarding. In all cases, parent–child pairs were allowed to board first. It was assumed that families were likely to want to stay together. As Dr Steffen had predicted, the conventional block approach came out as the slowest, with the strict back-to-front approach not much better. Completely random boarding (unallocated seating), which is used by several low-cost airlines, fared much better, most probably because it randomly avoids space conflicts. The times for fully boarding the 70 passengers using each method were as follows: 'block' boarding – 6:54 minutes; back-to-front – 6:11 minutes; random boarding – 4:44 minutes; Wilma method – 4:13 minutes; Steffen method – 3:36 minutes.

The big question is, 'would passengers really be prepared to be sequenced in this way as they queue to board the aircraft?' Some airlines argue that directing passengers on to a plane is a little like herding cats. But if they could adopt Dr Steffen's system it would save time for customers and very significant amounts of money for airlines.

NORTHAMPTONSHIRE POLICE
INCIDENT GRADING

EMERGENCY

Grade One Incidents require immediate deployment and are subject to current KPI response targets.

Grade One Incidents are where: a) there is a threat to life b) crime is in progress or offender is still in the vicinity c) traffic accidents involving personal injury or where position of vehicles is likely to cause serious danger to other road users.

URGENT/PROMPT

Grade Two Incidents require immediate allocation. Responding resources will attend immediately or as soon as practicable.

Grade Two Incidents are incidents that do not fit the criteria for Grade One, but the individual circumstances of the incident, or the vulnerable nature of the victim/caller require prompt police attendance to resolve the situation, preserve evidence or reassure the caller/victim.

Grade Two Incidents would not usually warrant the use of blue lights and sirens.

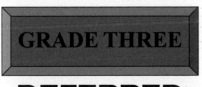

DEFERRED

Grade Three Incidents do not require an immediate attendance and include all incidents where deployment can be delayed for more than a few minutes and those that can be allocated by way of appointment.

It is vitally important that the caller is fully aware of the grade allocated to the incident, and where possible given an estimated time for police attendance at the incident.

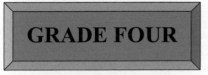

ADVICE

Grade Four Incidents require no deployment but are recorded for the information of an individual officer, sector, or for general information.

(Courtesy of Northamptonshire Police)

Figure 10.10 The call grading system for a police force

One of the hospital environments that is most difficult to schedule is the Accident and Emergency department, where patients arrive at random, without any prior warning, throughout the day. It is up to the hospital's reception and the medical staff to devise very rapidly a schedule which meets most of the necessary criteria. In particular, patients who arrive having had very serious accidents, or presenting symptoms of a serious illness, need to be attended to urgently. Therefore, the hospital will schedule these cases first. Less urgent cases – perhaps patients who are in some discomfort, but whose injuries or illnesses are not life-threatening – will have to wait until the urgent cases are treated. Routine non-urgent cases will have the lowest priority of all. In many circumstances, these patients will have to wait for the longest time, which may be many hours, especially if the hospital is busy. Sometimes these non-urgent cases may even be turned away if the hospital is too busy with more important cases. In situations where hospitals expect sudden influxes of patients, they have developed what is known as a triage system, whereby medical staff

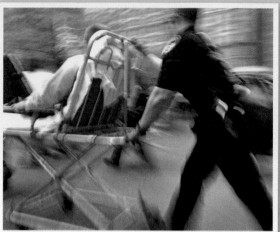

Source: Shutterstock.com/SV Luma

hurriedly sort through the patients who have arrived to determine which category of urgency each patient fits into. In this way a suitable schedule for the various treatments can be devised in a short period of time.

Due date (DD)

Prioritizing by due date means that work is sequenced according to when it is 'due' for delivery, irrespective of the size of each job or the importance of each customer. For example, a support service, such as a printing unit, will often ask when copies are required, and then sequence the work according to that due date. Due date sequencing usually improves the delivery dependability and average delivery speed. However, it may not provide optimal productivity, as a more efficient sequencing of work may reduce total costs. However, it can be flexible when new, urgent work arrives at the work centre.

Last in first out (LIFO)

Last in first out (LIFO) is a method of sequencing usually selected for practical reasons. For example, unloading an elevator is more convenient on a LIFO basis, as there is only one entrance and exit. However, it is not an equitable approach. Patients at hospital clinics may be infuriated if they see newly arrived patients examined first.

First in first out (FIFO)

Some operations serve customers in exactly the sequence they arrive in. This is called first in first out sequencing (FIFO), or sometimes 'first come, first served' (FCFS). For example, UK passport offices receive mail, and sort it according to the day when it arrived. They work through the mail, opening it in sequence, and process the passport applications in order of arrival. Queues in theme parks may be designed so that one long queue snakes around the lobby area until the row of counters is reached. When customers reach the front of the queue, they are served at the next free counter.

Longest operation time (LOT)

Operations may feel obliged to sequence their longest jobs first, called longest operation time sequencing. This has the advantage of occupying work centres for long periods. By contrast, relatively small jobs progressing through an operation will take up time at each work centre because of the need to change over from one job to the next. However, although longest operation time sequencing keeps utilization high, this rule does not take into account delivery speed, reliability or flexibility. Indeed, it may work directly against these performance objectives.

Shortest operation time first (SOT)

Most operations at some stage become cash constrained. In these situations, the sequencing rules may be adjusted to tackle short jobs first; this is called shortest operation time sequencing. These jobs can then be invoiced and payment received to ease cash-flow problems. Larger jobs that take more time will not enable the business to invoice as quickly. This has an effect of improving delivery performance, if the unit of measurement of delivery is jobs. However, it may adversely affect total productivity and can damage service to larger customers.

Judging sequencing rules

All five performance objectives, or some variant of them, could be used to judge the effectiveness of sequencing rules. However, the objectives of dependability, speed and cost are particularly important. So, for example, the following performance objectives are often used:

- meeting 'due date' promised to customer (dependability);
- minimizing the time the job spends in the process, also known as 'flow time' (speed);
- minimizing work-in-progress inventory (an element of cost);
- minimizing idle time of work centres (another element of cost).

Worked example

Steve Smith is a website designer in a business school. Returning from his annual vacation, five design jobs are given to him upon arrival at work (he finished all outstanding jobs before he left). He gives them the codes A to E. Steve has to decide in which sequence to undertake the jobs. He wants both to minimize the average time the jobs are tied up in his office and, if possible, to meet the deadlines (delivery times) allocated to each job.

His first thought is to do the jobs in the order they were given to him, i.e. first in first out (FIFO):

Sequencing Rule – First in First Out (FIFO)

Sequence of jobs	Process time (days)	Start time	Finish time	Due date	Lateness (days)
A	5	0	5	6	0
B	3	5	8	5	3
C	6	8	14	8	6
D	2	14	16	7	9
E	1	16	17	3	14
Total time in process		50	**Total lateness**		32
Average time in process (total/5)		12.5	**Average lateness (total/5)**		6.4

Alarmed by the average lateness, he tries the due date (DD) rule:

Sequencing Rule – Due Date (DD)

Sequence of jobs	Process time (days)	Start time	Finish time	Due date	Lateness (days)
E	1	0	1	3	0
B	3	1	4	5	0
A	5	4	9	6	3
D	2	9	11	7	4
C	6	11	17	8	9

	Total time in process	42	Total lateness	16
	Average time in process (total/5)	8.4	Average lateness (total/5)	3.2

Better! But Steve tries out the shortest operation time (SOT) rule:

Sequencing Rule – Shortest Operation Time (SOT)

Sequence of jobs	Process time (days)	Start time	Finish time	Due date	Lateness (days)
E	1	0	1	3	0
D	2	1	3	7	0
B	3	3	6	5	1
A	5	6	11	6	5
C	6	11	17	8	9

	Total time in process	38	Total lateness	15
	Average time in process (total/5)	7.6	Average lateness (total/5)	3

This gives the same degree of average lateness but with a lower average time in the process. Steve decides to use the SOT rule.

Comparing the results from the three sequencing rules described in the worked example, together with the two other sequencing rules described earlier and applied to the same problem, gives the results summarized in Table 10.2. The shortest operation time (SOT) rule resulted in both the best average time in process and the best (or least bad) in terms of average lateness. Although different rules will perform differently depending on the circumstances of the sequencing problem, in practice the SOT rule generally performs well.

Table 10.2 Comparison of five sequencing decision rules

Rule	Average time in process (days)	Average lateness (days)
FIFO	12.5	6.4
DD	8.4	3.2
SOT	7.6	3.0
LIFO	8.4	3.8
LOT	12.8	7.4

Scheduling

Having determined the sequence that work is to be tackled in, some operations require a detailed timetable showing at what time or date jobs should start and when they should end – this is scheduling. Schedules are familiar statements of volume and timing in many consumer environments. For example, a bus schedule shows that more buses are put on routes at more frequent intervals during rush-hour periods. The bus schedule shows the time each bus is due to arrive at each stage of the route. Schedules of work are used in operations where some planning is required to ensure that customer demand is met. Other operations, such as rapid-response service operations where customers arrive in an unplanned way, cannot schedule the operation in a short-term sense. They can only respond at the time demand is placed upon them.

The complexity of scheduling

The scheduling activity is one of the most complex tasks in operations management. First, schedulers must deal with several different types of resource simultaneously. Machines will have different capabilities and capacities; staff will have different skills. More importantly, the number of possible schedules increases rapidly as the number of activities and processes increases. For example, suppose one machine has five different jobs to process. Any of the five jobs could be processed first and, following that, any one of the remaining four jobs, and so on. This means that there are:

$$5 \times 4 \times 3 \times 2 = 120 \text{ different schedules possible}$$

In other words, for n jobs there are $n!$ (factorial n) different ways of scheduling the jobs through a single process. But when there are (say) two machines, there is no reason why the sequence on machine 1 would be the same as the sequence on machine 2. If we consider the two sequencing tasks to be independent of each other, for two machines there would be:

$$120 \times 120 = 14,400 \text{ possible schedules of the two machines and five jobs.}$$

So a general formula can be devised to calculate the number of possible schedules in any given situation, as follows:

$$\text{Number of possible schedules} = (n!)m$$

where n is the number of jobs and m is the number of machines.

In practical terms, this means that there are often many millions of feasible schedules, even for relatively small scheduling tasks. This is why scheduling rarely attempts to provide an 'optimal' solution but rather satisfies itself with an 'acceptable' feasible one.

Forward and backward scheduling

Forward scheduling involves starting work as soon as it arrives. Backward scheduling involves starting jobs at the last possible moment to prevent them from being late. For example, assume that it takes six hours for a contract laundry to wash, dry and press a batch of overalls. If the work is collected at 8.00 am and is due to be picked up at 4.00 pm, there are more than six hours available to do it. Table 10.3 shows the different start times of each job, depending on whether they are forward or backward scheduled.

The choice of backward or forward scheduling depends largely upon the circumstances. Table 10.4 lists some advantages and disadvantages of the two approaches. In theory, both materials requirements planning (MRP, see Chapter 14) and lean, or just-in-time, planning (JIT, see Chapter 15) use backward scheduling, only starting work when it is required. In practice, however, users of MRP have tended to allow too long for each task to be completed, and therefore each task is not started at the latest possible time. In comparison, JIT is started, as the name suggests, just in time.

> *** Operations principle**
> An operation's planning and control system should allow for the effects of alternative schedules to be assessed.

Table 10.3 The effects of forward and backward scheduling

Task	Duration	Start time (backwards)	Start time (forwards)
Press	1 hour	3.00 pm	1.00 pm
Dry	2 hours	1.00 pm	11.00 am
Wash	3 hours	10.00 am	8.00 am

Table 10.4 Advantages of forward and backward scheduling

Advantages of forward scheduling	Advantages of backward scheduling
● High labour utilization – workers always start work to keep busy	● Lower material costs – materials are not used until they have to be, therefore delaying added value until the last moment
● Flexible – the time slack in the system allows unexpected work to be loaded	● Less exposed to risk in case of schedule change by the customer ● Tends to focus the operation on customer due dates

Gantt charts

One crude but simple method of scheduling is by use of the Gantt chart. This is a simple device which represents time as a bar, or channel, on a chart. The start and finish times for activities can be indicated on the chart and sometimes the actual progress of the job is also indicated. The advantages of Gantt charts are that they provide a simple visual representation both of what should be happening and of what actually is happening in the operation. Furthermore, they can be used to 'test out' alternative schedules. It is a relatively simple task to represent alternative schedules (even if it is a far from simple task to find a schedule which fits all the resources satisfactorily). Figure 10.11 illustrates a Gantt chart for a specialist software developer. It indicates the progress of several jobs as they are expected to progress through five stages of the process. Gantt charts are not an optimizing tool, they merely facilitate the development of alternative schedules by communicating them effectively.

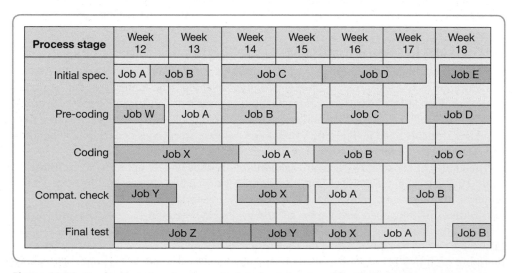

Figure 10.11 Gantt chart showing the schedule for jobs at each process stage

The life and times of a chicken salad sandwich – part one[6]

Pre-packed sandwiches are a growth product around the world as consumers put convenience and speed above relaxation and cost. But if you have recently consumed a pre-packed sandwich, think about the schedule of events which has gone into its making. For example, take a chicken salad sandwich. Less than five days ago, the chicken was on the farm unaware that it would never see another weekend. The Gantt chart schedule shown in Figure 10.12 tells the story of the sandwich, and (posthumously), of the chicken.

From the forecast, orders for non-perishable items are placed for goods to arrive up to a week in advance of their use. Orders for perishable items will be placed daily, a day or two before the items are required. Tomatoes, cucumbers and lettuces have a three-day shelf life so may be received up to three days before production. Stock is held on a strict first-in-first-out (FIFO) basis. If today is (say) Wednesday, vegetables are processed that have been received during the last three days. This morning the

Figure 10.12 Simplified schedule for the manufacture and delivery of a chicken salad sandwich

bread arrived from a local bakery and the chicken arrived fresh, cooked and in strips ready to be placed directly in the sandwich during assembly. Yesterday (Tuesday) it had been killed, cooked, prepared and sent on its journey to the factory. By midday orders for tonight's production will have been received on the internet. From 2.00 pm until 10.00 pm the production lines are closed down for maintenance and a very thorough cleaning. During this time the production planning team is busy planning the night's production run. Production for delivery to customers furthest away from the factory will have to be scheduled first. By 10 pm production is ready to start. Sandwiches are made on production lines. The bread is loaded into a conveyor belt by hand and butter is spread automatically by a machine. Next the various fillings are applied at each stage according to the specified sandwich 'design' (see Fig. 10.13). After the filling has been assembled the top slice of bread is placed on the sandwich and machine-chopped into two triangles, packed and sealed by machine. It is now early Thursday morning and by 2.00 am the first refrigerated lorries are already departing on their journeys to various customers. Production continues through until 2.00 pm on the Thursday, after which once again the maintenance and cleaning teams move in. The last sandwiches are dispatched by 4.00 pm on the Thursday. There is no finished goods stock.

Part two of the life and times of a chicken salad sandwich appears later (Chapter 14).

Figure 10.13 Design for a chicken salad sandwich

Scheduling work patterns

Where the dominant resource in an operation is its staff, then the schedule of work times effectively determines the capacity of the operation itself. The main task of scheduling, therefore, is to make sure that sufficient numbers of people are working at any point in time to provide a capacity appropriate for the level of demand at that point in time. This is often called staff rostering. Operations such as call centres, postal delivery, policing, holiday couriers, retail shops and hospitals will all need to schedule the working hours of their staff with demand in mind. This is a direct consequence of these operations having relatively high 'visibility' (we introduced this idea in Chapter 1). Such operations cannot store their outputs in inventories and so must respond directly to customer demand. For example, Figure 10.14 shows the scheduling of shifts for a small technical 'hot line' support service for a small software company. It gives advice to customers on their technical problems. Its service times are 4.00 hrs to 20.00 hrs on Monday, 4.00 hrs to 22.00 hrs Tuesday to Friday, 6.00 hrs to 22.00 hrs on Saturday, and 10.00 hrs to 20.00 hrs on Sunday. Demand is heaviest Tuesday to Thursday, starts to decrease on Friday, is low over the weekend and starts to increase again on Monday.

The scheduling task for this kind of problem can be considered over different timescales, two of which are shown in Figure 10.14. During the day, working hours need to be agreed with individual staff members. During the week, days off need to be agreed. During the year, vacations, training periods, and other blocks of time where staff are unavailable need to be agreed. All this has to be scheduled such that:

- capacity matches demand;
- the length of each shift is neither excessively long nor too short to be attractive to staff;

Figure 10.14 Shift scheduling in a home-banking enquiry service

- working at unsocial hours is minimized;
- days off match agreed staff conditions – in this example, staff prefer two consecutive days off every week;
- vacation and other 'time-off' blocks are accommodated;
- sufficient flexibility is built into the schedule to cover for unexpected changes in supply (staff illness) and demand (surge in customer calls).

Scheduling staff times is one of the most complex of scheduling problems. In the relatively simple example shown in Figure 10.14 we have assumed that all staff have the same level and type of skill. In very large operations with many types of skill to schedule and uncertain demand (for example, a large hospital) the scheduling problem becomes extremely complex. Some mathematical techniques are available but most scheduling of this type is, in practice, solved using heuristics (rules of thumb), some of which are incorporated into commercially available software packages.

Monitoring and controlling the operation

Having created a plan for the operation through loading, sequencing and scheduling, each part of the operation has to be monitored to ensure that planned activities are indeed happening. Any deviation from the plans can then be rectified through some kind of intervention in the operation, which itself will probably involve some re-planning. Figure 10.15 illustrates a simple view of control. The output from a work centre is monitored and compared with the plan which indicates what the work centre is supposed to be doing. Deviations from this plan are taken into account through a re-planning activity and the necessary interventions made to the work centre which will (hopefully) ensure that the new plan is carried out. Eventually, however, some further deviation from planned activity will be detected and the cycle is repeated.

> **✱ Operations principle**
>
> A planning and control system should be able to detect deviations from plans within a timescale that allows an appropriate response.

Push and pull control

One element of control, then, is periodic intervention into the activities of the operation. An important decision is how this intervention takes place. The key distinction is between intervention signals which push work through the processes within the operation and those which pull work only when it is required. In a push system of control, activities are scheduled by means of a central system and completed in line with central instructions, such as an MRP

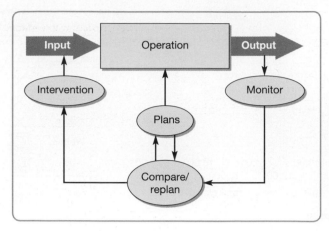

Figure 10.15 A simple model of control

system (*see* Chapter 14). Each work centre pushes out work without considering whether the succeeding work centre can make use of it. Work centres are co-ordinated by means of the central operations planning and control system. In practice, however, there are many reasons why actual conditions differ from those planned. As a consequence, idle time, inventory and queues often characterize push systems.

By contrast, in a pull system of control, the pace and specification of what is done are set by the 'customer' workstation, which 'pulls' work from the preceding (supplier) workstation. The customer acts as the only 'trigger' for movement. If a request is not passed back from the customer to the supplier, the supplier cannot produce anything or move any materials. A request from a customer not only triggers production at the supplying stage, but also prompts the supplying stage to request a further delivery from its own suppliers. In this way, demand is transmitted back through the stages from the original point of demand by the original customer.

The inventory consequences of push and pull Understanding the differing principles of push and pull is important because they have different effects in terms of their propensities to accumulate inventory in the operation. Pull systems are far less likely to result in inventory build-up and are therefore favoured by lean operations (*see* Chapter 15). To understand why this is so, consider an analogy: the 'gravity' analogy is illustrated in Figure 10.16. Here a push system is represented by an operation, each stage of which is on a lower level than the previous stage. When parts are processed by each stage, it pushes them down the slope to the next stage. Any delay or problem at that stage will result in the parts accumulating as inventory. In the pull system, parts cannot naturally flow uphill, so they can only progress if the next stage along deliberately pulls them forward. Under these circumstances, inventory cannot accumulate as easily.

> **❋ Operations principle**
>
> Pull control reduces the build-up on inventory between processes or stages.

Drum, buffer, rope

The drum, buffer, rope concept comes from the Theory of Constraints (TOC) and a concept called Optimized Production Technology (OPT) originally described by Eli Goldratt in his novel *The Goal*.[7] (We will deal more with his ideas in Chapter 14.) It is an idea that helps to decide exactly *where* in a process control should occur. Most do not have the same amount of work loaded onto each separate work centre (that is, they are not perfectly balanced). This means there is likely to be a part of the process which is acting as a bottleneck on the work flowing through the process. Goldratt argued that the bottleneck in the process should be the control point of the whole process. It is called the *drum* because it sets the 'beat' for the rest of the process to follow. Because it does not have sufficient capacity, a bottleneck is (or

A **push system** where material is moved on to the next stage as soon as it has been processed

A **pull system** where material is moved only when the next stage wants it

Figure 10.16 Push versus pull: the gravity analogy

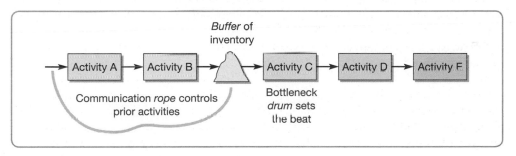

Buffer of inventory

Activity A → Activity B → Activity C → Activity D → Activity F

Communication *rope* controls prior activities

Bottleneck *drum* sets the beat

Figure 10.17 The drum, buffer, rope concept

should be) working all the time. Therefore, it is sensible to keep a *buffer* of inventory in front of it to make sure that it always has something to work on. Because it constrains the output of the whole process, any time lost at the bottleneck will affect the output from the whole process. So it is not worthwhile for the parts of the process before the bottleneck to work to their full capacity. All they would do is produce work which would accumulate further along in the process up to the point where the bottleneck is constraining the flow. Therefore, some form of communication between the bottleneck and the input to the process is needed to make sure that activities before the bottleneck do not overproduce. This is called the *rope* (*see* Fig. 10.17).

Critical commentary

Most of the perspectives on control taken in this chapter are simplifications of a far more messy reality. They are based on models used to understand mechanical systems such as car engines. But anyone who has worked in real organizations knows that organizations are not machines. They are social systems, full of complex and ambiguous interactions. Simple models such as these assume that operations objectives are always clear and agreed, yet organizations are political entities where different and often conflicting objectives compete. Local government operations, for example, are overtly political. Furthermore, the outputs from operations are not always easily measured. A university may be able to measure the number and qualifications of its students, for example, but it cannot measure the full impact of its education on their future happiness. Also, even if it is possible to work out an appropriate intervention to bring an operation back into 'control', most operations cannot perfectly predict what effect the intervention will have. Even the largest of burger bar chains does not know *exactly* how a new shift allocation system will affect performance. Also, some operations never do the same thing more than once anyway. Most of the work done by construction operations are one-offs. If every output is different, how can 'controllers' ever know what is supposed to happen? Their plans themselves are mere speculation.

CONTROLLING OPERATIONS IS NOT ALWAYS ROUTINE

The simple monitoring control model in Figure 10.15 helps us to understand the basic functions of the monitoring and control activity. But, as the critical commentary box above says, it is a simplification. Some simple routine processes may approximate to it, but many other operations do not. In fact, some of the specific criticisms cited in the critical commentary box provide a useful set of questions which can be used to assess the degree of difficulty associated with control of any operation. In particular:

● Is there consensus over what the operation's objectives should be?
● Are the effects of interventions into the operation predictable?
● Are the operation's activities largely repetitive?

Starting with the first question, are strategic objectives clear and unambiguous? It is not always possible (or necessarily desirable) to articulate every aspect of an operation's objectives in detail. Many operations are just too complex for that. Nor does every senior manager always agree on what the operation's objectives *should* be. Often the lack of a clear objective is because individual managers have different and conflicting interests. In social care organizations for example, some managers are charged with protecting vulnerable members of society, others with ensuring that public money is not wasted, and yet others may be required to protect the independence of professional staff. At other times, objectives are ambiguous because the strategy has to cope with unpredictable changes in the environment that make the original objectives redundant. A further assumption in the simplified control model is that there is some reasonable knowledge of how to bring about the desired outcome. That is, when a decision is made, one can predict its effects with a reasonable degree of confidence. In other words, operational control assumes that any interventions which are intended to bring a process back under control will indeed have the intended effect. Yet, this implies that the relationships between the intervention and the resulting consequence within the process are predictable, which in turn assumes that the degree of process knowledge is high. For example, if an organization decides to relocate in order to be more convenient for its customers, it may or may not prove to be correct. Customers may react in a manner that was not predicted. Even if customers seem initially to respond well to the new location there may be a lag before negative reactions become evident. In fact many operations decisions are taken about activities where the cause–effect relationship is only partly understood. The final assumption about control is that control interventions are made in a repetitive way and occur frequently (for example, checking on a process, hourly or daily). This means that the operation has the opportunity to learn how its interventions affect the process, which considerably facilitates control. However, some control situations are non-repetitive; for example, those involving unique services or products. So because the intervention, or the deviation from plan that caused it, may not be repeated, there is little opportunity for learning.

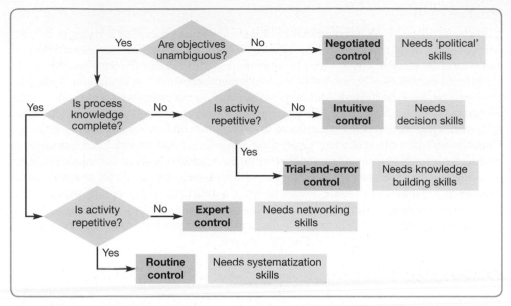

Figure 10.18 Control is not always routine; different circumstances require different types of control

Figure 10.18 illustrates how these questions can form a 'decision tree' type model that indicates how the nature of operations control mat be influenced.[8] Operational control is relatively straightforward: objectives are unambiguous, the effects of interventions are known, and activities are repetitive. This type of control can be done using predetermined conventions and rules. There are, however, still some challenges to successful routine control. It needs operational discipline to make sure that control procedures are systematically implemented. The main point though is that any divergence from the conditions necessary for routine control implies a different type of control.

> *** Operations principle**
>
> Planning and control is not always routine, especially when objectives are ambiguous; the effects of interventions into the operation are not predictable and activities not repetitive.

Expert control

If objectives are unambiguous, yet the effects of interventions relatively well understood, but the activity is not repetitive (for example, installing or upgrading software or IT systems), control can be delegated to an 'expert'; someone for whom such activities are repetitive because they have built their knowledge on previous experience elsewhere. Making a success of expert control requires that such experts exist and can be 'acquired' by the firm. It also requires that the expert takes advantage of the control knowledge already present in the firm and integrates his or her 'expert' knowledge with the support that potentially exists internally. Both of these place a stress on the need to 'network', both in terms of acquiring expertise and then integrating that expertise into the organization.

Trial-and-error control

If strategic objectives are relatively unambiguous, but effects of interventions not known, yet the activity is repetitive, the operation can gain knowledge of how to control successfully through its own failures. In other words, although simple prescriptions may not be available in the early stages of making control interventions, the organization can learn how to do it through experience. For example, if a fast-food chain is opening new stores into new markets, it may not be sure how best to arrange the openings at first. But if the launch is the first of several, the objective must be, not only to make a success of each launch, but equally (or more) important, it must learn from each experience. It is these knowledge-building skills that will ultimately determine the effectiveness of trial-and-error control.

Intuitive control

If objectives are relatively unambiguous (so it is clear what the operation is trying to do), but effects of control interventions are not known, and nor are they repetitive, learning by trial and error is not possible. Here control becomes more of an art than a science. And in these circumstances control must be based on the management team using its intuition to make control decisions. Many strategic operations processes fall into this category – for example, setting up a strategic supply partnership (see Chapter 13). Objectives are clear (jointly survive in the long term, make an acceptable return, and so on) but, not only are control interventions not repetitive and their effects not fully understood, sometimes the supplier's interests may be in conflict with yours. Yet, simply stating that 'intuition' is needed in these circumstances is not particularly helpful. Instinct and feelings are, of course, valuable attributes in any management team, but they are the result, at least partly, of understanding how best to organize their shared understanding, knowledge, and decision-making skills. It requires thorough decision analysis, not to 'mechanistically' make the decision, but to frame it so that connections can be made, consequences understood, and insights gained.

Negotiated control

The most difficult circumstance for strategic control is when objectives are ambiguous. This type of control involves reducing ambiguity in some way by making objectives less uncertain. Sometimes this is done simply by senior managers 'pronouncing' or arbitrarily deciding what objectives *should* be irrespective of opposing views. For example, controlling the activities of a child care service can involve very different views amongst the professional social workers making day-to-day decisions. Often a negotiated settlement may be sought which then can become an unambiguous objective. Alternatively outside experts could be used, either to help with the negotiations, or to remove control decisions from those with conflicting views. But, even within the framework of negotiation, there is almost always a political element when ambiguities in objectives exist. Negotiation processes will be, to some extent, dependent on power structures.

SUMMARY ANSWERS TO KEY QUESTIONS

MyOMLab *Check and improve your understanding of this chapter using self-assessment questions and a personalized study plan, a video case study, and an eText – all at* **www.myomlab.com**.

❯ What is planning and control?

- Planning and control is the reconciliation of the potential of the operation to supply products and services, and the demands of its customers on the operation. It is the set of day-to-day activities that run the operation on an ongoing basis.

❯ What is the difference between planning and control?

- A plan is a formalization of what is intended to happen at some time in the future. Control is the process of coping with changes to the plan and the operation to which it relates. Although planning and control are theoretically separable, they are usually treated together.
- The balance between planning and control changes over time. Planning dominates in the long term and is usually done on an aggregated basis. At the other extreme, in the short term, control usually operates within the resource constraints of the operation but makes interventions into the operation in order to cope with short-term changes in circumstances.

> How do supply and demand affect planning and control?

- The degree of uncertainty in demand affects the balance between planning and control. The greater the uncertainty, the more difficult it is to plan, and so greater emphasis must be placed on control.

- This idea of uncertainty is linked with the concepts of dependent and independent demand. Dependent demand is relatively predictable because it is dependent on some known factor. Independent demand is less predictable because it depends on the chances of the market or customer behaviour.

- The different ways of responding to demand can be characterized by differences in the $P:D$ ratio of the operation. The $P:D$ ratio is the ratio of total throughput time of services or products to demand time.

> What are the activities of planning and control?

- In planning and controlling the volume and timing of activity in operations, four distinct activities are necessary:
  - loading, which dictates the amount of work that is allocated to each part of the operation;
  - sequencing, which decides the order in which work is tackled within the operation;
  - scheduling, which determines the detailed timetable of activities and when activities are started and finished;
  - monitoring and control, which involve detecting what is happening in the operation, re-planning if necessary, and intervening in order to impose new plans. Two important types are 'pull' and 'push' control. Pull control is a system whereby demand is triggered by requests from a work centre's (internal) customer. Push control is a centralized system whereby control (and sometimes planning) decisions are issued to work centres which are then required to perform the task and supply the next workstation. In manufacturing, 'pull' schedules generally have far lower inventory levels than 'push' schedules.

- The ease with which control can be maintained varies between operations.

CASE STUDY *subText* Studios, Singapore (abridged)[9]

C.K. was clearly upset. Since he had founded *subText* in the fast growing South East Asian computer generated imaging (CGI) market, three years ago, this was the first time that he had needed to apologize to his clients. In fact, it had been more than an apology; he had agreed to reduce his fee, though he knew that didn't make up for the delay. He admitted that, up to that point, he hadn't fully realized just how much risk there was, both reputational and financial, in failing to meet schedule dates. It wasn't that either he or his team was unaware of the importance of reliability. On the contrary. 'Imagination', 'expertise' and 'reliability' all figured prominently in their promotional literature, mission statements, and so on. It was just that the 'imagination' and 'expertise' parts had seemed to be the things that had been responsible for their success so far. Of course, it had been bad luck that, after more than a year of perfect reliability (not one late job), the two that had been late in the first quarter of this year had been particularly critical. 'They were both for new clients', said C.K. 'And neither of them indicated just how important the agreed delivery date was to them. We should have known, or found out, I admit. But it's always more difficult with new clients, because without a track record with them, you don't really like even to admit the possibility of being late.'

The company

After studying computer science at the National University of Singapore, C.K. Ong had worked in CGI workshops in and around the Los Angeles area of California, after which he returned to Singapore to start *subText* Studios. At the heart of the company were the three 'core' departments that dealt sequentially with each job taken on. These three departments were 'Pre-production', 'Production' and 'Post-production'.

Pre-production was concerned with taking and refining the brief as specified by the client, checking with and liaising with the client to iron out any ambiguities in the brief, story-boarding the sequences, and obtaining outline approval of the brief from the client. In addition, pre-production also acted as account liaison with the client and were also responsible for estimating the resources and timing for each job. They also had nominal responsibility for monitoring the job through the remaining two stages, but generally they only did this if the client needed to be consulted during the production and post-production processes.

Production involved the creation of the imagery itself. This could be a complex and time-consuming process involving the use of state-of-the-art workstations and CGI software. Around 80 per cent of all production work was carried out in-house, but for some jobs other specialist workshops were contracted. This was only done for work that *subText* either could not do, or would find difficult to do.

Post-production had two functions: the first was to integrate the visual image sequences produced by Production with other effects such as sound effects, music, voice overs, etc; the second was to cut, edit, and generally produce the finished 'product' in the format required by the client.

Each of the three departments employed teams of two people. Pre-production had two teams, Production three teams, and Post-production two teams. For Pre-production and Post-production work, one team is always exclusively devoted to one job. *'We never allow either one team to be working on two jobs at the same time, or have both teams working on one job. It just doesn't work because of the confusion it creates. That doesn't apply to Production. Usually (but not always) the Production work can be parcelled up so that two or even all three of the teams could be working on different parts of it at the same time. Provided there is close co-ordination between the teams, and provided that they are all committed to pulling it together at the end, there should be a more or less inverse relationship between the number of bodies working on the job and the length of time it takes. In fact,*

Source: Shutterstock.com/Derek Audette

with the infamous "fifty-three slash F" job, that's exactly what we had to do. However, notwithstanding what I just said about shortening the time, we probably did lose some efficiency there by having all three teams working on it. Our teams generally work until the job is finished. That level of work is factored into the time estimates we make for each stage of the process. And, although we can be a little inaccurate sometimes, it's because this type of thing is difficult to estimate.' (C.K. Ong)

The fifty-three slash F job

The fifty-three slash F job, recently finished (late) and delivered to the client (dissatisfied), had been the source of much chaos, confusion and recrimination over the last two or three weeks. Although the job was only three days late, it had caused the client to postpone a presentation to its own client. Worse, *subText* had given only five days' notice of late delivery, trying until the last minute to pull back onto schedule.

The full name of the job that had given them so much trouble was 04/53/F. Table 10.5 shows the data for all the jobs started this year up to the current time (day 58 – every working day was numbered throughout the year). Figure 10.19 shows the schedule for this period. The job had been accepted on day 18 and had seemed relatively straightforward, although it was always clear that it would be a long production job. It was also clear that time was always going to be tight. There were 32 days in which to finish a job that was estimated to take 30 days.

'In hindsight we underestimated how much having three teams working on the production stage of this job at one point or other would increase its complexity. OK, it was not an easy piece of CGI to carry off, but we probably would have been OK if we had organized the CGI stage better. It was also real bad luck that, in our efforts to deliver the fifty-three slash F job on time, we also disrupted the fifty-four slash D job that turned out to be the only other new client we have had this year.' (C.K. Ong)

The job had proved difficult from the start. The pre-production stage took longer than estimated, mainly because the client's creative team changed just before the start of *subText* beginning the work. But it was the actual CGI itself that proved to be the major problem. Not only was the task intrinsically difficult, it was difficult to parcel it up into separate packages that could be co-ordinated for working on by the two teams allocated to the job. More seriously, it became apparent within two or three days of starting the production work that they would need the help of another

Table 10.5 *subText* Studios, Singapore – planning data for day 02 to day 58

Job (04)	Day in	Estimated total time	Actual total time	Due date	Actual delivery	Pre-prod		Prod		Post-prod	
						Est	Actual	Est	Actual	Est	Actual
06/A	−4	29	30	40	34	6	8	11	10	12	12
11/B	−4	22	24	42	31	4	5.5	7	7.5	11	11
04/C	2	31	30.5	43	40	9	9.5	12	13	10	9
54/D	5	28	34	55	58	10	12	12	17	6	5
31/E	15	34	25	68	57	10	11	12	14	12	–
53/F	18	32	49	50	53	6	10	18	28	8	11
24/G	25	26	20	70	–	9	11	9	9	8	–
22/H	29	32	26	70	–	10	12	14	14	8	–
22/I	33	30	11	75	–	10	11	12	–	8	–
09/J	41	36	14	81	–	12	14	14	–	10	–
20/K	49	40	–	89	–	12	-	14	–	14	–

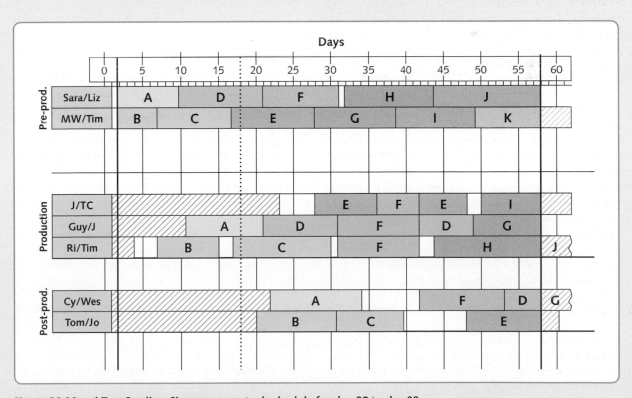

Figure 10.19 *subText* Studios, Singapore – actual schedule for day 02 to day 08

studio for some of the effects. Although the other studio was a regular supplier at short notice, this time they were too busy with their own work to help out. Help eventually came from a specialist studio in Hong Kong. *'The subcontracting delay was clearly a problem, but it was only halfway through the production phase that we first realized just how much difficulty the fifty-three slash F job was in. It was at that stage that we devoted all our production resources to finishing it. Unfortunately, even then, the job was late. The decision eventually to put all three teams on to the fifty-three slash F job was not easy because we knew that it would both disrupt other jobs and potentially cause more co-ordination problems.'*

'No way will we be doing that again'

'No way will we be doing that again', said C.K. to the core teams when they met to pick over what had gone wrong. *'We are desperately in need of a more professional approach to keeping track of our activities. There is no point in me telling everyone how good we are if we then let them down. The problem is that I don't want to encourage a "command and control" culture in the studio. We depend on all staff feeling that they have the freedom to explore seemingly crazy options that may just lead to something real special. We aren't a factory. But we do need to get a grip on our estimating so that we have a better idea of how long each job really will take. After that each of the core departments can be responsible for their own planning.'*

QUESTIONS

1 What went wrong with the fifty-three slash F job and how could the company avoid making the same mistakes again?

2 What would you suggest that *subText* do to tighten up their planning and control procedures?

PROBLEMS AND APPLICATIONS

MyOMLab

These problems and applications will help to improve your analysis of operations. You can find more practice problems as well as worked examples and guided solutions on MyOMLab at **www.myomlab.com**.

1 Re-read the 'operations management in practice' at the beginning of the chapter, 'Joanne manages the schedule', and also the short case on Air France (p. 293). What are the differences and what are the similarities between the planning and control task in these two operations?

2 A specialist sandwich retailer must order sandwiches at least 8 hours before they are delivered. When they arrive in the shop, they are immediately displayed in a temperature controlled cabinet. The average time that the sandwiches spend in the cabinet is 6 hours. What is the *P:D* ratio for this retail operation?

3 It is the start of the week and Marie, Willy and Silvie have three jobs to complete. The three of them can work on these jobs in any order. Job A requires 4 hours of Marie's time, 5 hours of Willy's time, and 3 hours of Silvie's time. Job B requires 2 hours of Marie's time, 8 hours of Willy's time, and 7 hours of Silvie's time. Job C requires 10 hours of Marie's time, 4 hours of Willy's time, and 5 hours of Silvie's time. Devise a schedule for Marie, Willy, and Sylvie that details when they will be working on each job. (Assume that they work 7 hours per day.)

4 For the example above, what is the loading on Marie, Willy and Silvie? If all the jobs have to be finished within 2 days, how much extra time must each of them work?

Step 1 – Make a list of all the jobs you have to do in the next week. Include in this list jobs relating to your work and/or study, jobs relating to your domestic life, in fact all the things you have to do.

Step 2 – Prioritize all these jobs on a 'most important' to 'least important' basis.

Step 3 – Draw up an outline schedule of exactly when you will do each of these jobs.

Step 4 – At the end of the week compare what your schedule said you *would* do with what you actually *have* done. If there is a discrepancy, why did it occur?

Step 5 – Draw up your own list of planning and control rules from your experience in this exercise in personal planning and control.

6 From your own experience of making appointments at your general practitioner's surgery, or by visiting whoever provides you with primary medical care, reflect on how patients are scheduled to see a doctor or nurse.
   a) What do you think planning and control objectives are for a general practitioner's surgery?
   b) How could your own medical practice be improved?

SELECTED FURTHER READING

Goldratt, E.Y. and Cox, J. (1984) *The Goal,* **North River Press Croton-on-Hudson, NY.** Don't read this if you like good novels but do read this if you want an enjoyable way of understanding some of the complexities of scheduling. It particularly applies to the drum, buffer, rope concept described in this chapter and it also sets the scene for the discussion of OPT in Chapter 14.

Kehoe, D.F. and Boughton, N.J. (2001) New paradigms in planning and control across manufacturing supply chains – the utilization of internet technologies, *International Journal of Operations & Production Management,* **vol. 21, issue 5/6, 582–593.**

Vollmann, T.E., Berry, W.L., Whybark, D.C. and Jacobs, F.R. (2004) *Manufacturing Planning and Control Systems for Supply Chain Management: The Definitive Guide for Professionals,* **McGraw-Hill Higher Education, New York.** The latest version of the 'bible' of manufacturing planning and control.

USEFUL WEBSITES

http://www.bpic.co.uk/ Some useful information on general planning and control topics.

http://www.apics.org The American professional and education body that has its roots in planning and control activities.

www.myomlab.com Test which sections you have mastered and which you need to review, with questions, a personalized study plan, video clips, revision tips, and cases.

www.opsman.org Useful materials.

http://operationsroom.wordpress.com/ Stanford University's take on topical operations stories.

www.iomnet.org The Institute of Operations Management site. One of the main professional bodies for the subject.

www.poms.org A US academic society for production and operations management. Academic, but some useful material, including a link to an encyclopedia of operations management terms.

http://sites.google.com/site/tomiportal/home One of the longest-established portals for the subject. Useful for academics and students alike.

 Now that you have finished reading this chapter, why not visit MyOMLab at www.myomlab.com where you'll find more learning resources to help you make the most of your studies and get a better grade.

11 Capacity management

Key questions

❯ What is capacity management?

❯ How is capacity measured?

❯ What are the ways of coping with demand fluctuation?

❯ How can operations plan their capacity level?

❯ How is capacity planning a queuing problem?

INTRODUCTION

Providing sufficient capability to satisfy current and future demand is a fundamental responsibility of operations management. Get the balance right between the capacity of an operation and the demand it is subjected to and it can satisfy its customers cost-effectively. Get it wrong and it could both fail to satisfy demand and have excessive costs. Capacity planning and control is also sometimes referred to as *aggregate* planning and control. This is because, at this level of planning and control, demand and capacity calculations are usually performed on an aggregated basis which does not discriminate between the different products and services that an operation might produce. The essence of the task is to reconcile, at a general and aggregated level, the supply of capacity with the level of demand which it must satisfy (*see* Fig. 11.1). There is also a supplement that deals with analytical queuing models, which is one way of considering capacity management, especially in some service operations.

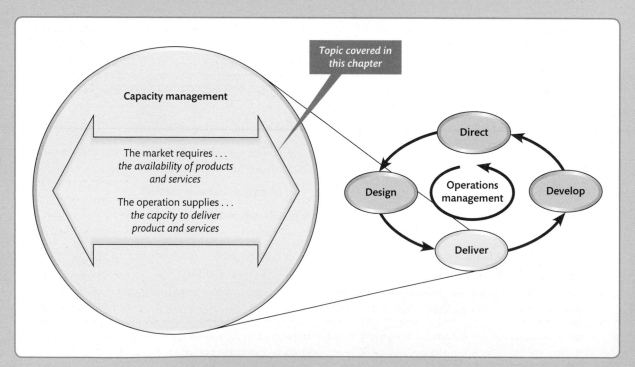

Figure 11.1 A definition of capacity planning and control

MyOMLab *Check and improve your understanding of this chapter using self-assessment questions and a personalized study plan, a video case study, and an eText – all at www.myomlab.com.*

Amazon's 'Cyber Monday'[1]

Founded as an online bookseller by Jeff Bezos, Amazon, now the world's biggest online retailer, started business in Europe in 1998. Since then the Seattle-based firm has experienced remarkable growth, employing around 40,000 people around the world and dominating a fiercely competitive consumer market, where its success is unquestionably based partly on its keen pricing. But low prices are not the only thing supporting Amazon's success. Without fast, accurate and efficient delivery it could not have secured its 'top e-retailer' position.

This is why Amazon devotes so much investment and effort into its fulfilment centres, customer service centres and software development centres across Europe, North America, Latin America and Asia. These organize the shipment of millions of individual items, from bird tables to baby clothes. (Amazon says that the exact number of different items it sells is difficult to define, especially if you take into account the articles that are offered via the 'marketplace', and changes every day.) Typical of Amazon's shipment operations is its 46,000-square-metre Milton Keynes warehouse in the UK, one of eight in Britain. In the warehouse products are stocked within its extensive shelving arrangement, with the position of every item referenced using a portable satellite navigation system. Amazon says that it saves time when their staff retrieve items. *The computer shows the shortest pick-path'*, said Arthur Valdez, the vice-president of Amazon's British operations. The item is then scanned and picked, after which it moves along a conveyor belt to be packed or gift-wrapped and then labelled. At this point an email is automatically sent to the customer informing them that their product is on its way.

Mr Valdez manages a network of fast-moving operations that must always maintain a tight control of its activities, but no time is more testing than the run-up to Christmas. The gift-buying habits of Western consumers mean that up to 40 per cent of annual sales value can come in the final three months of the year, with half of the multi-billion online Christmas sales taking place over the end of November and the first two weeks of December. The average number of articles being sold each day soars from 300,000 to, at its peak, 3.6 million being sold in one day. In the UK, this day – which it calls

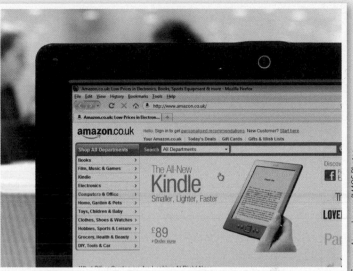

Source: Alamy Images/M4OS Photos

'Cyber Monday' – is at the beginning of December; or, to be more precise, 9 pm on that day, when shoppers, having normally been paid for the month and having spent the weekend browsing the high street, return from work to begin their Christmas shopping in earnest. It makes for a hectic time. *'A full truck is dispatched every 3 minutes and 24 seconds on our busiest trading day'*, says Mr Valdez. But careful forecasting can at least stop the Christmas peak being a surprise. And careful monitoring of customer behaviour has revealed a further trend – after 'Cyber Monday', now comes 'Boomerang Thursday', when customers start to return their unwanted items. *'As the online retail sector continues to grow, so too has consumer demand and confidence to return items, often before Christmas'*, says Mark Lewis, chief executive of CollectPlus, which allows customers to return items to a local convenience store. *'This suits retailers. They want to get* [items] *back as soon as possible, so they can sell them on.'* Mark Lewis says that half of his customers return items at off-peak times. *'It peaks at 7 pm. It reflects how we live our lives these days.'*

However, some retail analysts believe that the advance of technology in the form of mobile phone transactions and broadband has also meant the significance of 'Cyber Monday' and 'Boomerang Thursday' will diminish because such technology makes it easier to stagger transactions. But for Mr Valdez, it is continual vigilance that allows Amazon to keep up with demand trends. *'Every year it feels like* [Christmas starts on] *1 January. We are all year long focused on understanding the lessons learnt from the previous Christmas'*, he says.

WHAT IS CAPACITY MANAGEMENT?

The most common use of the word capacity is in the static, physical sense of the fixed *volume* of a container, or the space in a building. This meaning of the word is also sometimes used by operations managers. For example: a pharmaceutical manufacturer may invest in new 1,000-litre capacity reactor vessels; a property company purchases a 500-vehicle capacity city-centre car park; and a 'multiplex' cinema is built with 10 screens and a total capacity of 2,500 seats. Although these capacity measures describe the *scale* of these operations, they do not reflect the processing capacities of these investments. To do this we must incorporate a *time* dimension appropriate to the use of assets. So the pharmaceutical company will be concerned with the level of output that can be achieved using the 1,000-litre reactor vessel. If a batch of standard products can be produced every hour, the planned processing capacity could be as high as 24,000 litres per day. If the reaction takes four hours, and two hours are used for cleaning between batches, the vessel may only produce 4,000 litres per day. Similarly, the car park may be fully occupied by office workers during the working day, 'processing' only 500 cars per day. Alternatively, it may be used for shoppers staying on average only one hour, and theatre-goers occupying spaces for three hours, in the evening. The processing capacity would then be up to 5,000 cars per day. Thus the definition of the capacity of an operation is the *maximum level of value-added activity over a period of time* that the process can achieve under normal operating conditions.

Capacity constraints

Many organizations operate at below their maximum processing capacity, either because there is insufficient demand completely to 'fill' their capacity, or as a deliberate policy, so that the operation can respond quickly to every new order. Often, though, organizations find themselves with some parts of their operation operating below their capacity while other parts are at their capacity 'ceiling'. It is the parts of the operation that are operating at their capacity 'ceiling' which are the capacity constraint for the whole operation. For example, a retail superstore might offer a gift-wrapping service which at normal times can cope with all requests for its services without delaying customers unduly. At Christmas, however, the demand for gift-wrapping might increase proportionally far more than the overall increase in custom for the store as a whole. Unless extra resources are provided to increase the capacity of this micro-operation, it could constrain the capacity of the whole store.

> **✳ Operations principle**
>
> Any measure of capacity should reflect the ability of an operation or process to supply demand.

Planning and controlling capacity

Capacity planning and control is the task of setting the effective capacity of the operation so that it can respond to the demands placed upon it. This usually means deciding how the operation should react to fluctuations in demand. We have faced this issue before (in Chapter 6) where we examined long-term changes in demand and the alternative capacity strategies for dealing with the changes. These strategies were concerned with introducing (or deleting) major increments of physical capacity. We called this task long-term capacity strategy. Here we are treating the shorter timescale where capacity decisions are being made largely within the constraints of the physical capacity limits set by the operation's long-term capacity strategy.

Medium- and short-term capacity

Having established long-term capacity, operations managers must decide how to adjust the capacity of the operation in the medium term. This usually involves an assessment of the demand forecasts over a period of 2–18 months ahead, during which time planned output can be varied; for example, by changing the number of hours the equipment is used. In practice, however, few forecasts are accurate, and most operations also need to respond to changes in demand which occur over a shorter timescale. Hotels and restaurants have unexpected and apparently random changes in demand from night to night, but also know from experience that certain days are on average busier than others. So operations managers also have to make short-term capacity adjustments, which enable them to flex output for a short period, either on a predicted basis (for example, bank checkouts are always busy at lunchtimes) or at short notice (for example, a sunny warm day at a theme park).

Aggregate demand and capacity

The important characteristic of capacity management, as we are treating it here, is that it is concerned with setting capacity levels over the medium and short terms in aggregated terms. That is, it is making overall, broad capacity decisions, but is not concerned with all of the detail of the individual products and services offered. This is what 'aggregated' means – different products and services are bundled together in order to get a broad view of demand and capacity. This may mean some degree of approximation, especially if the mix of products or services being produced varies significantly (as we shall see later). Nevertheless, as a first step in management, aggregation is necessary. For example, a hotel might think of demand and capacity in terms of 'room nights per month'; this ignores the number of guests in each room and their individual requirements, but it is a good first approximation. A woollen knitwear factory might measure demand and capacity in the number of units (garments) it is capable of making per month, ignoring size, colour or style variations. Aluminium producers could use tonnes per month, ignoring types of alloy, gauge and batch size variation. The ultimate aggregation measure is money. For example, retail stores, who sell an exceptionally wide variety of products, use revenue per month, ignoring variation in spend, number of items bought, the gross margin of each item and the number of items per customer transaction. If all this seems very approximate, remember that most operations have sufficient experience of dealing with aggregated data to find it useful.

The objectives of capacity management

The decisions taken by operations managers in devising their capacity plans will affect several different aspects of performance:

- **Costs** will be affected by the balance between capacity and demand (or output level if that is different). Capacity levels in excess of demand could mean under-utilization of capacity and therefore high unit costs.
- **Revenues** will also be affected by the balance between capacity and demand, but in the opposite way. Capacity levels equal to or higher than demand at any point in time will ensure that all demand is satisfied and no revenue lost.
- **Working capital** will be affected if an operation decides to build up finished goods inventory prior to demand. This might allow demand to be satisfied, but the organization will have to fund the inventory until it can be sold.
- **Quality** of goods or services might be affected by a capacity plan which involved large fluctuations in capacity levels, by hiring temporary staff for example. The new staff and the disruption to the routine working of the operation could increase the probability of errors being made.
- **Speed** of response to customer demand could be enhanced, either by the build-up of inventories (allowing customers to be satisfied directly from the inventory rather than having to wait for items to be manufactured) or by the deliberate provision of surplus capacity to avoid queuing.
- **Dependability** of supply will also be affected by how close demand levels are to capacity. The closer demand gets to the operation's capacity ceiling, the less able it is to cope with any unexpected disruptions and the less dependable its deliveries of goods and services could be.
- **Flexibility**, especially volume flexibility, will be enhanced by surplus capacity. If demand and capacity are in balance, the operation will not be able to respond to any unexpected increase in demand.

Figure 11.2 The steps in capacity management

The steps of capacity management

The sequence of capacity management decisions which need to be taken by operations managers is illustrated in Figure 11.2. Typically, operations managers are faced with a forecast of demand which is unlikely to be either certain or constant. They will also have some idea of their own ability to meet this demand. Nevertheless, before any further decisions are taken, they must have quantitative data on both capacity and demand. So the first step will be to *measure the aggregate demand and capacity* levels for the planning period. The second step will be to *identify the alternative capacity plans* which could be adopted in response to the demand fluctuations. The third step will be to *choose the most appropriate capacity plan* for their circumstances.

HOW IS CAPACITY MEASURED?

Forecasting demand fluctuations

Although demand forecasting is usually the responsibility of the sales and/or marketing functions, it is a very important input into the capacity management decision, and so is of interest to operations managers. After all, without an estimate of future demand it is not possible to plan effectively for future events, only to react to them. It is therefore important to understand the basis and rationale for these demand forecasts. (See the supplement on forecasting after Chapter 6.) As far as capacity planning and control is concerned, there are three requirements from a demand forecast:

- *It is expressed in terms which are useful for capacity management.* If forecasts are expressed only in money terms and give no indication of the demands that will be placed on an operation's capacity, they will need to be translated into realistic expectations of demand, expressed in the same units as the capacity (for example, machine hours per year, operatives required, space, etc.).
- *It is as accurate as possible.* In capacity management, the accuracy of a forecast is important because, whereas demand can change instantaneously, there is a lag between deciding to change capacity and the change taking effect. Thus many operations managers are faced with a dilemma. In order to attempt to meet demand, they must often decide output in advance, based on a forecast which might change before the demand occurs, or worse, prove not to reflect actual demand at all.

- *It gives an indication of relative uncertainty.* Decisions to operate extra hours and recruit extra staff are usually based on forecast levels of demand, which could in practice differ considerably from actual demand, leading to unnecessary costs or unsatisfactory customer service. For example, a forecast of demand levels in a supermarket may show initially slow business that builds up to a lunchtime rush. After this, demand slows, only to build up again for the early evening rush, and it finally falls again at the end of trading. The supermarket manager can use this forecast to adjust (say) checkout capacity throughout the day. But although this may be an accurate average demand forecast, no single day will exactly conform to this pattern. Of equal importance is an estimate of how much actual demand could differ from the average. This can be found by examining demand statistics to build up a distribution of demand at each point in the day. The importance of this is that the manager now has an understanding of when it will be important to have reserve staff, perhaps filling shelves, but still on call to staff the checkouts should demand warrant it. Generally, the advantage of probabilistic forecasts such as this is that it allows operations managers to make a judgement between possible plans that would virtually guarantee the operation's ability to meet actual demand, and plans that minimize costs. Ideally, this judgement should be influenced by the nature of the way the business wins orders: price-sensitive markets may require a risk-avoiding cost-minimization plan that does not always satisfy peak demand, whereas markets that value responsiveness and service quality may justify a more generous provision of operational capacity.

Seasonality of demand

Most markets are influenced by some kind of seasonality – that means that they vary depending on the time of year. Sometimes the causes of seasonality are climatic (holidays), sometimes festive (gift purchases), sometimes financial (tax processing), or social, or political; in fact there are many factors that affect the volume of activity in everything from construction materials to clothing, from health care to hotels. It may be demand seasonality or supply seasonality, but in many organizations, capacity management is largely about coping with these seasonal fluctuations. These fluctuations in demand or supply may be reasonably forecastable, but some are usually also affected by unexpected variations in the weather and by changing economic conditions.

Consider the four different types of operation described previously: a woollen knitwear factory, a city hotel, a supermarket and an aluminium producer. Their demand patterns are shown in Figure 11.3. The woollen knitwear business and the city hotel both have seasonal sales demand patterns, but for different reasons: the woollen knitwear business because of climatic patterns (cold winters, warm summers) and the hotel because of demand from business people, who take vacations from work at Christmas and in the summer. The retail supermarket is a little less seasonal, but is affected by pre-vacation peaks and reduced sales during vacation periods. The aluminium producer shows virtually no seasonality, but is showing a steady growth in sales over the forecast period.

Weekly and daily demand fluctuations

Seasonality of demand occurs over a year, but similar predictable variations in demand can also occur for some products and services on a shorter cycle. The daily and weekly demand patterns of a supermarket will fluctuate, with some degree of predictability. Demand might be low in the morning, higher in the afternoon, with peaks at lunchtime and after work in the evening. Demand might be low on Monday and Tuesday, build up during the latter part of the week and reach a peak on Friday and Saturday. Banks, public offices, telephone sales organizations and electricity utilities all have weekly and daily, or even hourly, demand patterns which require capacity adjustment. The extent to which an operation will have to cope with very short-term demand fluctuations is partly determined by how long its customers are prepared to wait for their products or services. An operation whose customers are incapable of waiting, or unwilling to wait, will have to plan for very short-term demand fluctuations. Emergency services, for example, will need to understand the hourly variation in the demand for their services and plan capacity accordingly.

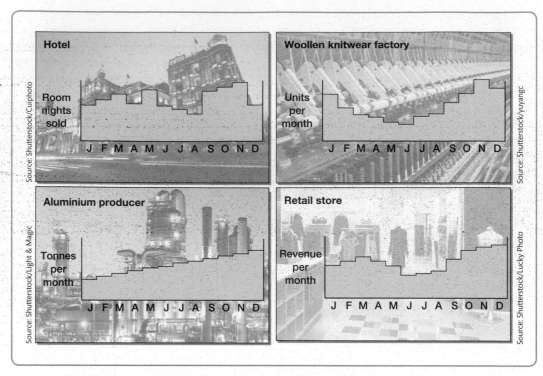

Figure 11.3 Aggregate demand fluctuations for four organizations

---

SHORT CASE   # Raining on their parade[2]

Some fluctuations in demand are predictable, others far less so. Amongst the most difficult to forecast, especially in the medium to long term that is of interest to business, is the weather. And many services and products are profoundly affected by the weather. Theme parks, garden centres, sunglasses, sunscreen, waterproof clothing and ice-cream are all obvious examples. Yet the range of operations interested in weather forecasting has expanded significantly. Energy utilities, soft drink producers and fresh food producers and retailers are all keen to purchase the latest weather forecasts. But so are operations such as banking call centres and mobile phone operators. It would appear that the demand for telephone banking falls dramatically when the sun shines, as does the use of mobile phones. A motorway catering group were surprised to find that their sales of hot meals fell predictably by €110,000 per day for each degree temperature rise above 20°C. Similarly, insurance companies have found it wise to sell their products when the weather is poor and likely customers are trapped indoors rather than relaxing outside in the sun, refusing to worry about the future. In the not-for-profit sector new understanding is being developed about the link between various illnesses and temperature. Here

temperature is often used as a predictor of demand. So, for example, coronary thrombosis cases peak two days after a drop in temperature, for strokes the delay is around five days, while deaths from respiratory infections peak twelve days after a temperature drop. Knowing this, hospital managers can plan for changes in their demand.

Because of this, meteorological services around the world now sell increasingly sophisticated forecasts to a wide range of companies. In the UK, the Meteorological Office offers an internet-based service for its customers. It is also used to help insurance companies price insurance policies to provide compensation against weather-related risk. Complex financial products called 'weather derivatives' are now available to compensate for weather-related uncertainty. The weather-derivatives industry hopes that farmers will insure against sun and rain that can affect the size of their harvest.

So, for example, an energy company could buy a financial option before winter where the seller pays the company a guaranteed sum of money if the temperature rises above a certain level. If the weather is mild and energy sales are low, the company gets compensation. If the weather is cold, the company loses the premium it has paid to the seller but makes up for it by selling more power at higher prices. However, as meteorologists point out, it is up to the individual businesses to use the information wisely. Only they have the experience to assess the full impact of weather on their operation.

Measuring capacity

The main problem with measuring capacity is the complexity of most operations. Only when the operation is highly standardized and repetitive is capacity easy to define unambiguously. So if a television factory produces only one basic model, the weekly capacity could be described as 2,000 Model A televisions. A government office may have the capacity to print and post 500,000 tax forms per week. A fast ride at a theme park might be designed to process batches of 60 people every three minutes – a capacity to convey 1,200 people per hour. In each case, an output capacity measure is the most appropriate measure because the output from the operation does not vary in its nature. For many operations, however, the definition of capacity is not so obvious. When a much wider range of outputs places varying demands on the process, for instance, output measures of capacity are less useful. Here input capacity measures are frequently used to define capacity. Almost every type of operation could use a mixture of both input and output measures, but in practice, most choose to use one or the other (*see* Table 11.1).

Table 11.1 Input and output capacity measures for different operations

Operation	Input measure of capacity	Output measure of capacity
Air-conditioner plant	Machine hours available	**Number of units per week**
Hospital	**Beds available**	Number of patients treated per week
Theatre	**Number of seats**	Number of customers entertained per week
University	**Number of students**	Students graduated per year
Retail store	**Sales floor area**	Number of items sold per day
Airline	**Number of seats available on the sector**	Number of passengers per week
Electricity company	Generator size	**Megawatts of electricity generated**
Brewery	Volume of fermentation tanks	**Litres per week**

Note: The most commonly used measure is shown in bold.

Capacity depends on activity mix

The hospital measures its capacity in terms of its resources, partly because there is not a clear relationship between the number of beds it has and the number of patients it treats. If all its patients required relatively minor treatment with only short stays in hospital, it could treat many people per week. Alternatively, if most of its patients required long periods of observation or recuperation, it could treat far fewer. Output depends on the mix of activities in which the hospital is engaged and, because most hospitals perform many different types of activities, output is difficult to predict. Certainly it is difficult to compare directly the capacity of hospitals which have very different activities.

> ✳ **Operations principle**
>
> Capacity is a function of service/product mix, duration, and product service specification.

Worked example

Suppose an air-conditioner factory produces three different models of air-conditioner unit: the deluxe, the standard and the economy. The deluxe model can be assembled in 1.5 hours, the standard in 1 hour and the economy in 0.75 hours. The assembly area in the factory has 800 staff hours of assembly time available each week.

If demand for deluxe, standard and economy units is in the ratio 2:3:2, the time needed to assemble $2 + 3 + 2 = 7$ units is:

$$(2 \times 1.5) + (3 \times 1) + (2 \times 0.75) = 7.5 \text{ hours}$$

The number of units produced per week is:

$$\frac{800}{7.5} \times 7 = 746.7 \text{ units}$$

If demand changes to a ratio of deluxe, economy, standard units of 1:2:4, the time needed to assemble $1 + 2 + 4 = 7$ units is:

$$(1 \times 1.5) + (2 \times 1) + (4 \times 0.75) = 6.5 \text{ hours}$$

Now the number of units produced per week is:

$$\frac{800}{6.5} \times 7 = 861.5 \text{ units}$$

Design capacity and effective capacity

The theoretical capacity of an operation – the capacity which its technical designers had in mind when they commissioned the operation – cannot always be achieved in practice. For example, a company coating photographic paper will have several coating lines which deposit thin layers of chemicals onto rolls of paper at high speed. Each line will be capable of running at a particular speed. Multiplying the maximum coating speed by the operating time of the plant gives the theoretical design capacity of the line. But in reality the line cannot be run continuously at its maximum rate. Different products will have different coating requirements, so the line will need to be stopped while it is changed over. Maintenance will need to be performed on the line, which will take out further productive time. Technical scheduling difficulties might mean further lost time. Not all of these losses are the operations manager's fault; they have occurred because of the market and technical demands on the operation. The actual capacity which remains, after such losses are accounted for, is called the effective capacity of operation. Not that these causes of reduction in capacity will be the only losses in the operation. Such factors as quality problems, machine breakdowns, absenteeism and other avoidable problems will all take their toll. This means that the

> ✳ **Operations principle**
>
> Useable capacity is rarely equal to theoretical or 'design' capacity.

actual output of the line will be even lower than the effective capacity. The ratio of the output actually achieved by an operation to its design capacity, and the ratio of output to effective capacity, are called, respectively, the utilization and the efficiency of the plant:

$$\text{Utilization} = \frac{\text{actual output}}{\text{design capacity}}$$

$$\text{Efficiency} = \frac{\text{actual output}}{\text{effective capacity}}$$

Worked example

Suppose the photographic paper manufacturer has a coating line with a design capacity of 200 square metres per minute, and the line is operated on a 24-hour day, 7 days per week (168 hours per week) basis.

Design capacity is $200 \times 60 \times 24 \times 7 = 2.016$ million square metres per week. The records for a week's production show the following lost production time:

1	Product changeovers (set-ups)	20 hrs
2	Regular preventative maintenance	16 hrs
3	No work scheduled	8 hrs
4	Quality sampling checks	8 hrs
5	Shift change times	7 hrs
6	Maintenance breakdown	18 hrs
7	Quality failure investigation	20 hrs
8	Coating material stockouts	8 hrs
9	Labour shortages	6 hrs
10	Waiting for paper rolls	6 hrs

During this week the actual output was only 582,000 square metres.

The first five categories of lost production occur as a consequence of reasonably unavoidable, planned occurrences and amount to a total of 59 hours. The last five categories are unplanned, and avoidable, losses and amount to 58 hours.

Measured in hours of production:

$$\text{Design capacity} = 168 \text{ hours per week}$$

$$\text{Effective capacity} = 168 - 59 = 109 \text{ hrs}$$

$$\text{Actual output} = 168 - 59 - 58 = 51 \text{ hrs}$$

$$\text{Utilization} = \frac{\text{actual output}}{\text{design capacity}} = \frac{51 \text{ hrs}}{168 \text{ hrs}} = 0.304 = 30\%$$

$$\text{Efficiency} = \frac{\text{actual output}}{\text{effective capacity}} = \frac{51 \text{ hrs}}{109 \text{ hrs}} = 0.468 = 47\%$$

Overall equipment effectiveness

The overall equipment effectiveness (OEE) measure is an increasingly popular method of judging the effectiveness of operations equipment. It is based on three aspects of performance:

- *the time* that equipment is available to operate;
- *the quality* of the product or service it produces;
- *the speed,* or throughput rate, of the equipment.

Overall equipment effectiveness is calculated by multiplying an availability rate by a performance (or speed) rate multiplied by a quality rate. Figure 11.4 uses the same categories of

Figure 11.4 Operating equipment effectiveness

'lost' time as were used in Figure 10.4 in the previous chapter. Some of the reduction in available capacity of a piece of equipment (or any process) is caused by time losses such as set-up and changeover losses (when the equipment or process is being prepared for its next activity), and breakdown failures when the machine is being repaired. Some capacity is lost through speed losses such as when equipment is idling (for example, when it is temporarily waiting for work from another process) and when equipment is being run below its optimum work rate. Finally, not everything processed by a piece of equipment will be error free. So some capacity is lost through quality losses.

Taking the notation in Figure 11.4:

$$OEE = a \times p \times q$$

For equipment to operate effectively, it needs to achieve high levels of performance against all three of these dimensions. Viewed in isolation, these individual metrics are important indicators of plant performance, but they do not give a complete picture of the machine's *overall* effectiveness. This can only be understood by looking at the combined effect of the three measures, calculated by multiplying the three individual metrics together. All these losses to the OEE performance can be expressed in terms of units of time – the design cycle time to produce one good part. So, a reject of one part has an equivalent time loss. In effect, this means that an OEE represents the valuable operating time as a percentage of the design capacity.

Worked example

In a typical 7-day period, the planning department programme a particular machine to work for 150 hours – its loading time. Changeovers and set-ups take an average of 10 hours and breakdown failures average 5 hours every 7 days. The time when the machine cannot work because it is waiting for material to be delivered from other parts of the process is 5 hours on average and during the period when the machine is running, it averages 90 per cent of its rated speed. Three per cent of the parts processed by the machine are subsequently found to be defective in some way.

$$\text{Maximum time available} = 7 \times 24 \text{ hours}$$
$$= 168 \text{ hours}$$
$$\text{Loading time} = 150 \text{ hours}$$
$$\text{Availability losses} = 10 \text{ hours(set-ups)} + 5 \text{ hrs(breakdowns)}$$
$$= 15 \text{ hours}$$
$$\text{So, total operating time} = \text{Loading time} - \text{Availability}$$
$$= 150 \text{ hours} - 15 \text{ hours}$$
$$= 135 \text{ hours}$$
$$\text{Speed losses} = 5 \text{ hours(idling)} + ((135 - 5) \times 0.1)(10\% \text{ of remaining time})$$
$$= 18 \text{ hours}$$
$$\text{So, net operating time} = \text{Total operating time} - \text{Speed losses}$$
$$= 135 - 18$$
$$= 117 \text{ hours}$$
$$\text{Quality losses} = 117(\text{Net operating time}) \times 0.03(\text{Error rate})$$
$$= 3.51 \text{ hours}$$
$$\text{So, valuable operating time} = \text{Net operating time} - \text{Quality losses}$$
$$= 117 - 3.51$$
$$= 113.49 \text{ hours}$$
$$\text{Therefore, availability rate} = a = \frac{\text{Total operating time}}{\text{Loading time}}$$
$$= \frac{135}{150} = 90\%$$
$$\text{and performance rate} = p = \frac{\text{Net operating time}}{\text{Total operating time}}$$
$$= \frac{117}{135} = 86.67\%$$
$$\text{and quality rate} = q = \frac{\text{Valuable operating time}}{\text{Net operating time}}$$
$$= \frac{113.49}{117} = 97\%$$
$$\text{OEE}(a \times p \times q) = 75.6\%$$

The London Eye is the world's largest observation wheel and one of the UK's most spectacular tourist attractions. The 32 passenger capsules, fixed on the perimeter of the 135-metre diameter rim, each hold 25 people. The wheel rotates continuously, so entry requires customers to step into the capsules which are moving at 0.26 metres per second, which is a quarter of normal walking speed. One complete 360-degree rotation takes 30 minutes, at the end of which the doors open and passengers disembark. Boarding and disembarkation are separated on the specially designed platform which is built out over the river. The attraction has a 'timed admissions booking system' (TABS) for both individual and group bookings. This allocates requests for 'flights' on the basis of half-hour time slots. At the time of writing, the London Eye is open every day except Christmas Day. Admission is from 10.00 am to 9.30 pm (for the 9.30 to 10.00 pm slot) in the summer, from the beginning of April to mid-September. For the rest of the year, the winter season, admission begins at 10.00 am, and last admissions are for the 5.30 to 6.00 pm slot. The London Eye forecasts anticipated that 2.2 million passengers would fly the London Eye in 2000, excluding January, which was reserved for final testing and admission of

Source: AL RF (Imagestate/Michael Duerinckx)

invited guests only. An early press release told journalists that the London Eye would rotate an average of 6,000 revolutions per year.

COPING WITH DEMAND FLUCTUATION

With an understanding of both demand and capacity, the next step is to consider the alternative methods of responding to demand fluctuations. There are three 'pure' options available for coping with such variation:

- Ignore the fluctuations and keep activity levels constant (level capacity plan).
- Adjust capacity to reflect the fluctuations in demand (chase demand plan).
- Attempt to change demand to fit capacity availability (demand management).

> ✳ **Operations principle**
>
> Capacity planning will use some mix of three 'pure' approaches, level capacity, chase demand, and demand management.

In practice, most organizations will use a mixture of all of these 'pure' plans, although often one plan might dominate. The short case 'Panettone: how Italy's bakers cope with seasonal demand' describes how one operation pursues some of these options.

Level capacity plan

In a level capacity plan, the processing capacity is set at a uniform level throughout the planning period, regardless of the fluctuations in forecast demand. This means that the same number of staff operate the same processes and should therefore be capable of producing the same aggregate output in each period. Where non-perishable materials are processed, but not immediately sold, they can be transferred to finished goods inventory in anticipation of sales at a later time. Thus this plan is feasible (but not necessarily desirable) for our examples of the woollen knitwear company and the aluminium producer (*see* Fig. 11.5).

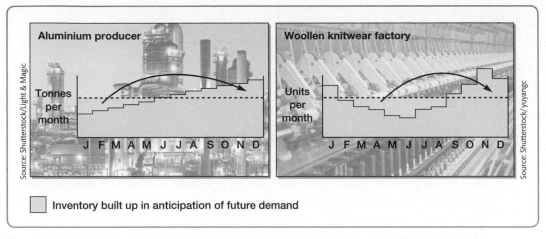

Inventory built up in anticipation of future demand

Figure 11.5 Level capacity plans which use anticipation inventory to supply future demand

Panettone: how Italy's bakers cope with seasonal demand[3]

Panettone has become a national symbol of the Italian Christmas. The light and fluffy dome-shaped confection is dotted with sultanas and candied citrus peel, and is *the* Italian Christmas cake. Traditionally made in Milan, Italy, about 40 million of them are consumed throughout Italy over the holiday period. Now, they are becoming popular around the world. Over a million are exported to the US, while an endorsement from Delia Smith, a celebrity chef, caused a surge in demand in Britain with a well-publicized recipe for trifle made with panettone. This boost to production is good news for the big Italian manufacturers, but although volumes are higher, the product is still seasonal, which poses a problem for even the experienced Milanese confectioners. Smaller 'artisan' producers simply squeeze a few batches of panettoni into their normal baking schedules as Christmas approaches. But for the large industrial producers who need to make millions for the Christmas season, it is not possible. And no pannetone manufacturer is larger than the Bauli group. It is one of the foremost manufacturers of confectionery in Europe. Founded over 70 years ago, and in spite of its mass production approach, it has a reputation for quality and technological improvement. The company's output of pannetone accounts for 38 per cent of Italian sales. The key to its success, according to the company, is in having 'combined the skill of home-made recipes with high technology [and] quality guaranteed by high standards that are unattainable in craftsman production, but that can only be reached by selecting top quality raw materials, by thousands of tests and checks on the entire production line and the production process'. In fact, the company says that its size is an advantage. 'High investment in research and technology allows us to manage natural fermentation and guarantee a uniform quality that artisanal bakeries find hard to achieve.'

In fact, although Bauli has diversified into year-round products like croissants and biscuits, it has acquired a leadership role in the production of products for festive occasions. Seasonal cakes account for over 50 per cent of its turnover of around €420 million. And so successful has it been in its chosen markets that in 2009 it bought Motta and Alemagna, the two big Milanese brands that pioneered the manufacture of panettone. So how does Bauli cope with such seasonality? Partly it is by hiring large numbers of temporary seasonal workers to staff its dedicated production lines. At peak times there can be 1,200 seasonal workers in the factory, in comparison to its permanent staff of around 800. It also starts to build up inventories of panettone before demand begins to increase for the Christmas peak. Production of panettone lasts about four months, starting in September. 'Attention to ingredients and the use of new technologies in production give a shelf-life of five months without preservatives', says Michele Bauli, deputy chairman, who comes from the firm's founding family. Temporary workers are also hired to bake other seasonal cakes such as the *colomba*, a dove-shaped Easter treat, which keeps them occupied for a month and a half in the spring.

Level capacity plans of this type can achieve the objectives of stable employment patterns, high process utilization, and usually also high productivity with low unit costs. Unfortunately, they can also create considerable inventory which has to be financed and stored. Perhaps the biggest problem, however, is that decisions have to be taken as to what to produce for inventory rather than for immediate sale. Will green woollen sweaters knitted in July still be fashionable in October? Could a particular aluminium alloy in a specific sectional shape still be sold months after it has been produced? Most firms operating this plan, therefore, give priority to only creating inventory where future sales are relatively certain and unlikely to be affected by changes in fashion or design. Clearly, such plans are not suitable for 'perishable' products, such as foods and some pharmaceuticals, for products where fashion changes rapidly and unpredictably (for example, fashion garments), or for customized products.

A level capacity plan could also be used by the hotel and supermarket, although this would not be the usual approach of such organizations, because it usually results in a waste of staff resources, reflected in low productivity. Because service cannot be stored as inventory, a level capacity plan would involve running the operation at a uniformly high level of capacity availability. The hotel would employ sufficient staff to service all the rooms, to run a full restaurant, and to staff the reception even in months when demand was expected to be well below capacity. Similarly, the supermarket would plan to staff all the checkouts, warehousing operations, and so on, even in quiet periods (*see* Fig. 11.6).

Low utilization can make level capacity plans prohibitively expensive in many service operations, but may be considered appropriate where the opportunity costs of individual lost sales

are very high; or example, in the high-margin retailing of jewellery and in (real) estate agents. It is also possible to set the capacity somewhat below the forecast peak demand level in order to reduce the degree of under-utilization. However, in the periods where demand is expected to exceed planned capacity, customer service may deteriorate. Customers may have to queue for long periods or may be 'processed' faster and less

Figure 11.6 Level capacity plans with under-utilization of capacity

sensitively. While this is obviously far from ideal, the benefits to the organization of stability and productivity may outweigh the disadvantages of upsetting some customers.

Chase demand plan

The opposite of a level capacity plan is one which attempts to match capacity closely to the varying levels of forecast demand. This is much more difficult to achieve than a level capacity plan, as different numbers of staff, different working hours, and even different amounts of equipment may be necessary in each period. For this reason, pure chase demand plans are unlikely to appeal to operations which manufacture standard, non-perishable products. Also, where manufacturing operations are particularly capital-intensive, the chase demand policy would require a level of physical capacity, all of which would only be used occasionally. It is for this reason that such a plan is less likely to be appropriate for the aluminium producer than for the woollen garment manufacturer (*see* Fig. 11.7). A pure chase demand plan is more usually adopted by operations which cannot store their output, such as customer-processing operations or manufacturers of perishable products. It avoids the wasteful provision of excess staff that occurs with a level capacity plan, and yet should satisfy customer demand throughout the planned period. Where output can be stored, the chase demand policy might be adopted in order to minimize or eliminate finished goods inventory.

Sometimes it is difficult to achieve very large variations in capacity from period to period. If the changes in forecast demand are as large as those in the hotel example (*see* Fig. 11.8), significantly different levels of staffing will be required throughout the year. This would mean

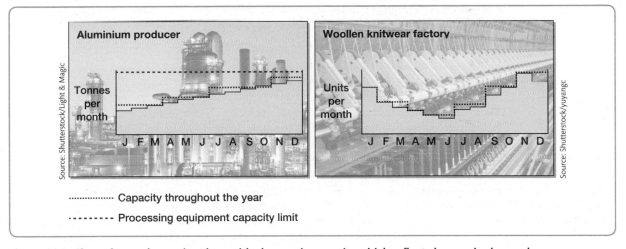

··············· Capacity throughout the year

- - - - - - - - Processing equipment capacity limit

Figure 11.7 Chase demand capacity plans with changes in capacity which reflect changes in demand

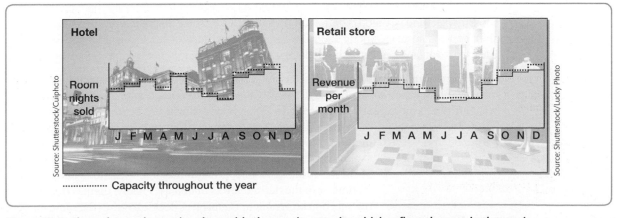

··············· Capacity throughout the year

Figure 11.8 Chase demand capacity plans with changes in capacity which reflect changes in demand employing part-time and temporary staff, requiring permanent employees to work longer hours, or even bringing in contract labour. The operations managers will then have the difficult task of ensuring that quality standards and safety procedures are still adhered to, and that the customer service levels are maintained.

Methods of adjusting capacity

The chase demand approach requires that capacity is adjusted by some means. There are a number of different methods for achieving this, although they may not all be feasible for all types of operation. Some of these methods are listed below.

Overtime and idle time Often the quickest and most convenient method of adjusting capacity is by varying the number of productive hours worked by the staff in the operation. When demand is higher than nominal capacity, overtime is worked, and when demand is lower than nominal capacity the amount of time spent by staff on productive work can be reduced. In the latter case, it may be possible for staff to engage in some other activity such as cleaning or maintenance. This method is only useful if the timing of the extra productive capacity matches that of the demand. For example, there is little to be gained in asking a retail operation's staff to work extra hours in the evening if all the extra demand is occurring during their normal working period. The costs associated with this method are either the extra payment which is normally necessary to secure the agreement of staff to work overtime, or in the case of idle time, the costs of paying staff who are not engaged in direct productive work. Further, there might be costs associated with the fixed costs of keeping the operation heated, lit and secure over the extra period staff are working. There is also a limit to the amount of extra working time which any workforce can deliver before productivity levels decrease. Annualized hours approaches, as described in the short case 'Annualized hours help Lowaters to retain its core team', are one way of flexing working hours without excessive extra costs.

Varying the size of the workforce If capacity is largely governed by workforce size, one way to adjust it is to adjust the size of the workforce. This is done by hiring extra staff during periods of high demand and laying them off as demand falls, or hire and fire. However, there are cost and ethical implications to be taken into account before adopting such a method. The costs of hiring extra staff include those associated with recruitment, as well as the costs of low productivity while new staff go through the learning curve. The costs of lay-off may include possible severance payments, but might also include the loss of morale in the operation and loss of goodwill in the local labour market. At a micro-operation level, one method of coping with peaks in demand in one area of an operation is to build sufficient flexibility into job design and job demarcation so that staff can transfer across from less busy parts of the operation. For example, the French hotel chain Novotel has trained some of its kitchen staff to escort customers from the reception area up to their rooms. The peak times for registering new customers coincide with the least busy times in the kitchen and restaurant areas.

Using part-time staff A variation on the previous strategy is to recruit part-time staff; that is, for less than the normal working day. This method is extensively used in service operations such as supermarkets and fast-food restaurants but is also used by some manufacturers to staff an evening shift after the normal working day. However, if the fixed costs of employment for each employee, irrespective of how long he or she works, are high, then using this method may not be worthwhile.

Subcontracting In periods of high demand, an operation might buy capacity from other organizations, called subcontracting. This might enable the operation to meet its own demand without the extra expense of investing in capacity which will not be needed after the peak in demand has passed. Again, there are costs associated with this method. The most obvious one is that subcontracting can be very expensive. The subcontractor will also want to make sufficient margin out of the business. A subcontractor may not be as motivated to deliver on time or to the desired levels of quality. Finally, there is the risk that the subcontractors might themselves decide to enter the same market.

> **✱ Operations principle**
> There are always costs, as well as benefits, associated with changing capacity levels.

To many, the idea of fluctuating the workforce to match demand, either by using part-time staff or by hiring and firing, is more than just controversial. It is regarded as unethical. It is any business's responsibility, they argue, to engage in a set of activities which are capable of sustaining employment at a steady level. Hiring and firing merely for seasonal fluctuations, which can be predicted in advance, is treating human beings in a totally unacceptable manner. Even hiring people on a short-term contract, in practice, leads to them being offered poorer conditions of service and leads to a state of permanent anxiety as to whether they will keep their jobs. On a more practical note, it is pointed out that, in an increasingly global business world where companies may have sites in different countries, those countries that allow hiring and firing are more likely to have their plants 'downsized' than those where legislation makes this difficult.

Manage demand plan

The most obvious mechanism of demand management is to change demand through price. Although this is probably the most widely applied approach in demand management, it is less common for products than for services. For example, some city hotels offer low-cost 'city break' vacation packages in the months when fewer business visitors are expected. Skiing and camping holidays are cheapest at the beginning and end of the season and are particularly expensive during school vacations. Ice-cream is 'on offer' in many supermarkets during the winter. The objective is invariably to stimulate off-peak demand and to constrain peak demand, in order to smooth demand as much as possible. Organizations can also attempt to increase demand in low periods by appropriate advertising. For example, turkey farmers in the UK and the USA make vigorous attempts to promote their products at times other than Christmas and Thanksgiving.

SHORT CASE   **Annualized hours help Lowaters to retain its core team[4]**

Lowaters Nursery is a garden plant and horticulture specialist in the south of England. Like any business that depends on seasonal weather conditions, it faces fluctuating demand for its services and products. It also prides itself on offering *'the best service in partnership with our customers, by communicating in a friendly professional manner and listening to our customers to provide the result required'* (Lowaters mission statement). But to maintain its quality of service throughout the seasonal ups and down in workload means keeping your core team happy and employed throughout the year. This is why Lowaters introduced its annualized hours scheme.

Source: Alistair Brandon-Jones

An annual hours work plan is a method of fluctuating capacity as demand varies throughout the year, without many of the costs associated with overtime or hiring temporary staff. It involves staff contracting to work a set number of hours per year rather than a set number of hours per week. The advantage of this is that the amount of staff time available to an organization can be varied throughout the year to reflect the real state of demand. Annual hours plans can also be useful when supply varies throughout the year.

Lowaters specialize in ornamental plants and employ around 25 people – most of them have been with the company for a long time and the company has a relatively low staff turnover of about 9 per cent per annum. Maria Fox, one of the management team at Lowaters, says that annualized hours give the company several advantages. *'It simplifies administration and gives us the flexibility we need to run the business while delivering some real advantages to the employees. They are all effectively on salary with fixed monthly payments. We can flex the hours worked over the year – when we are busy we work longer and when things are quiet, in the winter, they can take time off. Everyone other than directors is contracted to work 39 hours on average over 52 weeks of the year. This gives us a total of 2,028 hours that are available. In fact, supervisors are contracted to do a hundred more hours to cover planning and paperwork, making a total of 2,128.'*

The company created a simple spreadsheet that sets out the actual hours worked and compares them with a target distribution of the annualized hours expected to be worked over the year. This allows employees to see at a glance whether someone is over or under target. *'We email them a copy of their sheet at the beginning of the year so they can keep track of their own progress as they go'*, says Maria. *'It also allows us to keep track of how many hours they do. If at the end of the year they come in plus or minus 50 hours we simply adjust it up or down for the next year. If there is a bigger discrepancy than that we'll look at the job structure – or some retraining. We end up with more control over our wage budget and we can flex staff up and down according to weather and workload.'* It also gives flexibility to staff, claims Lowaters. Their salary doesn't vary from month to month and they can deal with time off for sickness because they have the whole year to make up their hours.

However, not all experiments with annualized hours have been as successful as that at Lowaters. In cases where demand is very unpredictable, staff can be asked to come in to work at very short notice. This can cause considerable disruption to social and family life. For example, at one news broadcasting company, the scheme caused problems. Journalists and camera crew who went to cover a foreign crisis found that they had worked so many hours, they were asked to take the whole of one month off to compensate. Since they had no holiday plans, many would have preferred to work.

Alternative products and services

Sometimes, a more radical approach is required to fill periods of low demand, such as developing alternative products or services which can be produced on existing processes, but have different demand patterns throughout the year (see the short case 'Getting the message' for an example of this approach). Most universities fill their accommodation and lecture theatres with conferences and company meetings during vacations. Ski resorts provide organized mountain activity holidays in the summer. Some garden tractor companies in the US now make snow movers in the autumn and winter. The apparent benefits of filling capacity in this way must be weighted against the risks of damaging the core product or service, and the operation must be fully capable of serving both markets. Some universities have been criticized for providing sub-standard, badly decorated accommodation which met the needs of impecunious undergraduates, but which failed to impress executives at a trade conference.

Mixed plans

Each of the three 'pure' plans is applied only where its advantages strongly outweigh its disadvantages. For many organizations, however, these 'pure' approaches do not match their required combination of competitive and operational objectives. Most operations managers are required simultaneously to reduce costs and inventory, to minimize capital investment, and yet to provide a responsive and customer-orientated approach at all times. For this reason, most organizations choose to follow a mixture of the three approaches. This can be best illustrated by the woollen knitwear company example (*see* Fig. 11.9). Here some of the peak

Figure 11.9 A mixed capacity plan for the woollen knitwear factory

demand has been brought forward by the company offering discounts to selected retail customers (manage demand plan). Capacity has also been adjusted at two points in the year to reflect the broad changes in demand (chase demand plan). Yet the adjustment in capacity is not sufficient to avoid totally the build-up of inventories (level capacity plan).

Yield management[5]

In operations which have relatively fixed capacities, such as airlines and hotels, it is important to use the capacity of the operation to maximize its potential to generate profit. One approach used by such operations is called yield management. It is really a variety of methods and analytical tools. The term is used in many service operations to mean techniques that can be used to allocate limited resources, among different categories of customers, such as business or leisure travellers. Because these techniques are used by operations with services that cannot be stored, yield management is sometimes called 'perishable asset revenue management' or simply 'revenue management'. But whatever name it goes by, the basic concept of yield management is based on the economic principle of supply and demand. When supplies are short, prices go up; when supply is high, prices go down. Yield management simply provides a systematic method for positioning customers within the supply–demand spectrum in such a way that they can obtain the highest yield for their services or products. So, a customer who has relatively little flexibility in his or her travel plans is the customer who is most likely to pay a higher price for airline tickets and hotel rooms. The customer with a great deal of flexibility is not as inclined to pay a higher price. Yield management is especially useful where:

● capacity is relatively fixed;
● the market can be fairly clearly segmented;
● the service cannot be stored in any way;
● the services are sold in advance;
● the marginal cost of making a sale is relatively low.

Companies which traditionally operate in seasonal markets can demonstrate some considerable ingenuity in their attempts to develop counter-seasonal products. One of the most successful industries in this respect has been the greetings card industry. Mother's Day, Father's Day, Halloween, Valentine's Day and other occasions have all been promoted as times to send (and buy) appropriately designed cards. Now, having run out of occasions to promote, greetings card manufacturers have moved on to 'non-occasion' cards, which can be sent at any time. These have the considerable advantage of being less seasonal, thus making the companies' seasonality less marked.

Hallmark Cards, one of the best-known card producers, has been the pioneer in developing non-occasion cards. Their cards include those intended to be sent from a parent to a child with messages such as 'Would a hug help?', 'Sorry I made you feel bad', and 'You're perfectly wonderful – it's your room that's a mess'. Other cards deal with more serious adult themes such as friendship ('You're more than a friend, you're just like family'), alcoholism ('This is hard to say, but I think you're a much neater person when you're not drinking'), or losing your job ('Don't think of it as losing your job. Think of it as a time out between stupid bosses'). Now Hallmark Cards have founded a 'loyalty marketing group' that 'helps companies communicate with their customers at an emotional level'. It promotes the use of greetings cards for corporate use, to show that customers and employees are valued.

The greetings card industry remains healthy, especially in some countries. Britons, for example, spend more than any other country on cards – sending 31 cards per person each year, according to the Greeting Card Association (GCA), an industry body. Now, prompted by new online 'greetings cards by email' or 'via online

Source: Shutterstock.com/Hannamariah

social networks' operations who offer a speedy service without buying a stamp, traditional card companies have also moved into the online business. And although card companies insist that e-cards do not pose a grave threat, because people use them as a supplement to physical cards or for less important dates, Hallmark and others are dealing with the threat by allowing customers to send free e-cards from their websites, but encouraging them to purchase annual subscriptions for access to 'special' or 'exclusive' card designs. Whatever else these products may be, they are not seasonal!

Airlines, for example, fit all these criteria. They adopt a collection of methods to try to maximize the yield (i.e. profit) from their capacity. These include the following:

- *Over-booking capacity*. Not every passenger who has booked a place on a flight will actually show up for the flight. If the airline did not fill this seat it would lose the revenue from it. Because of this, airlines regularly book more passengers onto flights than the capacity of the aircraft can cope with. If they over-book by the exact number of passengers who fail to show up, they have maximized their revenue under the circumstances. Of course, if more passengers show up than they expect, the airline will have a number of upset passengers to deal with (although they may be able to offer financial inducements for the passengers to take another flight). If they fail to over-book sufficiently, they will have empty seats. By studying past data on flight demand, airlines try to balance the risks of over-booking and under-booking.

- *Price discounting.* At quiet times, when demand is unlikely to fill capacity, airlines will also sell heavily discounted tickets to agents who then themselves take the risk of finding customers for them. In effect, this is using the price mechanism to affect demand.
- *Varying service types.* Discounting and other methods of affecting demand are also adjusted depending on the demand for particular types of service. For example, the relative demand for first-, business-, and economy-class seats varies throughout the year. There is no point discounting tickets in a class for which demand will be high. Yield management also tries to adjust the availability of the different classes of seat to reflect their demand. It will also vary the number of seats available in each class by upgrading or even changing the configuration of airline seats.

HOW CAN OPERATIONS PLAN THEIR CAPACITY LEVEL?

Before an operation can decide which of the capacity plans to adopt, it must be aware of the consequences of adopting each plan in its own set of circumstances. Two methods are particularly useful in helping to assess the consequences of adopting particular capacity plans:

- cumulative representations of demand and capacity;
- queuing theory.

Cumulative representations

Figure 11.10 shows the forecast aggregated demand for a chocolate factory which makes confectionery products. Demand for its products in the shops is greatest at Christmas. To meet this demand and allow time for the products to work their way through the distribution system, the factory must supply a demand which peaks in September, as shown. One method of assessing whether a particular level of capacity can satisfy the demand would be to calculate the degree of over-capacity below the graph which represents the capacity levels (areas A and C) and the degree of under-capacity above the graph (area B). If the total over-capacity is greater than the total under-capacity for a particular level of capacity, then that capacity could be regarded as adequate to satisfy demand fully, the assumption being that inventory has been accumulated in the periods of over-capacity. However, there are two problems with this approach. The first is that each month shown in Figure 11.10 may not

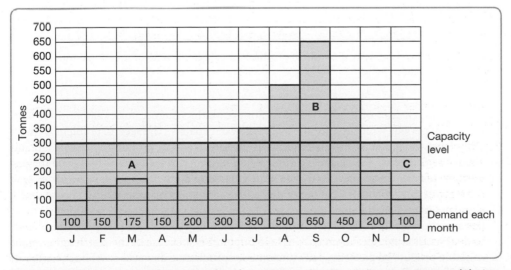

Figure 11.10 If the over-capacity areas (A+C) are greater than the under-capacity area (B), the capacity level seems adequate to meet demand. This may not necessarily be the case, however

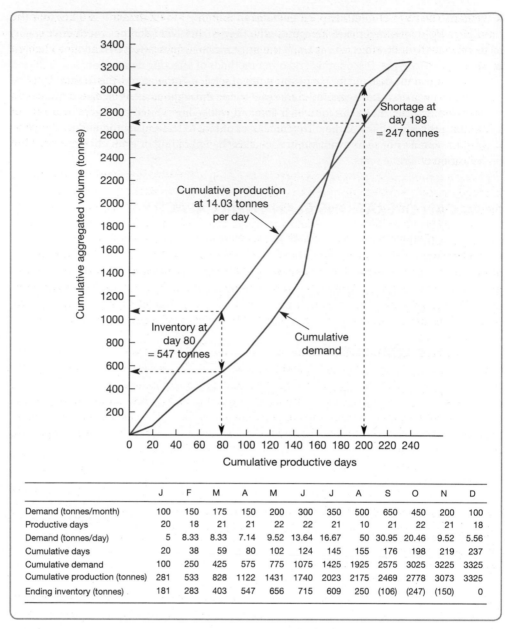

	J	F	M	A	M	J	J	A	S	O	N	D
Demand (tonnes/month)	100	150	175	150	200	300	350	500	650	450	200	100
Productive days	20	18	21	21	22	22	21	10	21	22	21	18
Demand (tonnes/day)	5	8.33	8.33	7.14	9.52	13.64	16.67	50	30.95	20.46	9.52	5.56
Cumulative days	20	38	59	80	102	124	145	155	176	198	219	237
Cumulative demand	100	250	425	575	775	1075	1425	1925	2575	3025	3225	3325
Cumulative production (tonnes)	281	533	828	1122	1431	1740	2023	2175	2469	2778	3073	3325
Ending inventory (tonnes)	181	283	403	547	656	715	609	250	(106)	(247)	(150)	0

Figure 11.11 A level capacity plan which produces shortages in spite of meeting demand at the end of the year

have the same amount of productive time. Some months (August, for example) may contain vacation periods which reduce the availability of capacity. The second problem is that a capacity level which seems adequate may only be able to supply products *after* the demand for them has occurred. For example, if the period of under-capacity occurred at the beginning of the year, no inventory could have accumulated to meet demand. A far superior way of assessing capacity plans is first to plot demand on a *cumulative* basis. This is shown as the blue line in Figure 11.11.

The cumulative representation of demand immediately reveals more information. First, it shows that although total demand peaks in September, because of the restricted number of available productive days, the peak demand per productive day occurs a month earlier in August. Second, it shows that the fluctuation in demand over the year is even greater than it seemed. The ratio of monthly peak demand to monthly lowest demand is 6.5:1, but the ratio of peak to lowest demand per productive day is 10:1. Demand per productive day is more relevant to operations managers, because productive days represent the time element of capacity.

The most useful consequence of plotting demand on a cumulative basis is that, by plotting capacity on the same graph, the feasibility and consequences of a capacity plan can be assessed. Figure 11.11 also shows a level capacity plan which produces at a rate of 14.03 tonnes per productive day. This meets cumulative demand by the end of the year. It would also pass our earlier test of total over-capacity being the same as or greater than under-capacity.

However, if one of the aims of the plan is to supply demand when it occurs, the plan is inadequate. Up to around day 168, the line representing cumulative production is above that representing cumulative demand. This means that at any time during this period, more product has been produced by the factory than has been demanded from it. In fact the vertical distance between the two lines is the level of inventory at that point in time. So by day 80,1,122 tonnes have been produced but only 575 tonnes have been demanded. The surplus of production above demand, or inventory, is therefore 547 tonnes. When the cumulative demand line lies above the cumulative production line, the reverse is true. The vertical distance between the two lines now indicates the shortage, or lack of supply. So by day 198, 3,025 tonnes have been demanded but only 2,778 tonnes produced. The shortage is therefore 247 tonnes.

For any capacity plan to meet demand as it occurs, its cumulative production line must always lie above the cumulative demand line. This makes it a straightforward task to judge the adequacy of a plan, simply by looking at its cumulative representation. An impression of the inventory implications can also be gained from a cumulative representation by judging the area between the cumulative production and demand curves. This represents the amount of inventory carried over the period. Figure 11.12 illustrates an adequate level capacity plan for the chocolate manufacturer, together with the costs of carrying inventory. It is assumed that inventory costs £2 per tonne per day to keep in storage. The average inventory each month is taken to be the average of the beginning- and end-of-month inventory levels, and the inventory-carrying cost each month is the product of the average inventory, the inventory cost per day per tonne and the number of days in the month.

> *** Operations principle**
>
> For any capacity plan to meet demand as it occurs, its cumulative production line must always lie above its cumulative demand line.

Comparing plans on a cumulative basis

Chase demand plans can also be illustrated on a cumulative representation. Rather than the cumulative production line having a constant gradient, it would have a varying gradient representing the production rate at any point in time. If a pure demand chase plan was adopted, the cumulative production line would match the cumulative demand line. The gap between the two lines would be zero and hence inventory would be zero. Although this would eliminate inventory-carrying costs, as we discussed earlier, there would be costs associated with changing capacity levels. Usually, the marginal cost of making a capacity change increases with the size of the change. For example, if the chocolate manufacturer wishes to increase capacity by 5 per cent, this can be achieved by requesting its staff to work overtime – a simple, fast and relatively inexpensive option. If the change is 15 per cent, overtime cannot provide sufficient extra capacity and temporary staff will need to be employed – a more expensive solution which also would take more time. Increases in capacity of above 15 per cent might only be achieved by subcontracting some work out. This would be even more expensive. The cost of the change will also be affected by the point from which the change is being made, as well as the direction of the change. Usually, it is less expensive to change capacity towards what is regarded as the 'normal' capacity level than away from it.

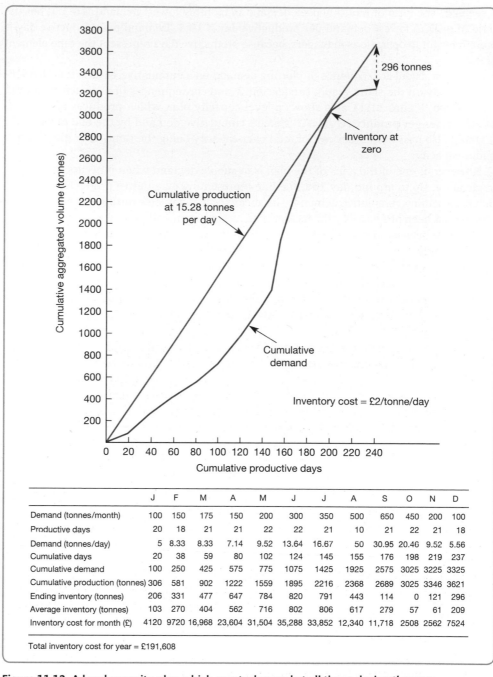

	J	F	M	A	M	J	J	A	S	O	N	D
Demand (tonnes/month)	100	150	175	150	200	300	350	500	650	450	200	100
Productive days	20	18	21	21	22	22	21	10	21	22	21	18
Demand (tonnes/day)	5	8.33	8.33	7.14	9.52	13.64	16.67	50	30.95	20.46	9.52	5.56
Cumulative days	20	38	59	80	102	124	145	155	176	198	219	237
Cumulative demand	100	250	425	575	775	1075	1425	1925	2575	3025	3225	3325
Cumulative production (tonnes)	306	581	902	1222	1559	1895	2216	2368	2689	3025	3346	3621
Ending inventory (tonnes)	206	331	477	647	784	820	791	443	114	0	121	296
Average inventory (tonnes)	103	270	404	562	716	802	806	617	279	57	61	209
Inventory cost for month (£)	4120	9720	16,968	23,604	31,504	35,288	33,852	12,340	11,718	2508	2562	7524

Total inventory cost for year = £191,608

Figure 11.12 A level capacity plan which meets demand at all times during the year

Worked example

Suppose the chocolate manufacturer, which has been operating the level capacity plan as shown in Figure 11.13, is unhappy with the inventory costs of this approach and decides to explore two alternative plans, both involving some degree of demand chasing.

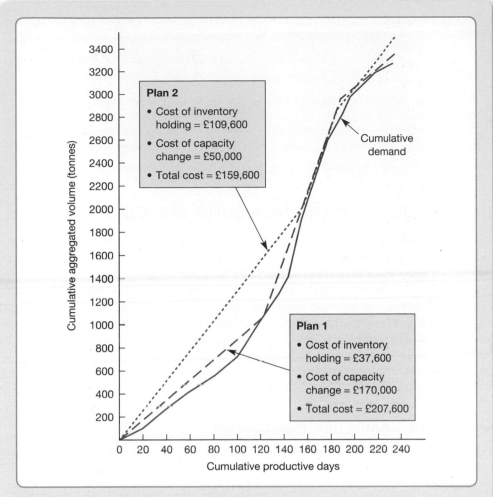

Figure 11.13 Comparing two alternative capacity plans

Plan 1

- Organize and staff the factory for a 'normal' capacity level of 8.7 tonnes per day.
- Produce at 8.7 tonnes per day for the first 124 days of the year, then increase capacity to 29 tonnes per day by heavy use of overtime, hiring temporary staff and some subcontracting.
- Produce at 29 tonnes per day until day 194, then reduce capacity back to 8.7 tonnes per day for the rest of the year.

The costs of changing capacity by such a large amount (the ratio of peak to normal capacity is 3.33:1) are calculated by the company as being:

Cost of changing from 8.7 tonnes/day to 29 tonnes/day = £110,000

Cost of changing from 29 tonnes/day to 8.7 tonnes/day = £60,000

Plan 2

- Organize and staff the factory for a 'normal' capacity level of 12.4 tonnes per day.
- Produce at 12.4 tonnes per day for the first 150 days of the year, then increase capacity to 29 tonnes per day by overtime and hiring some temporary staff.
- Produce at 29 tonnes/day until day 190, then reduce capacity back to 12.4 tonnes per day for the rest of the year.

The costs of changing capacity in this plan are smaller because the degree of change is smaller (a peak to normal capacity ratio of 2.34:1), and they are calculated by the company as being:

Cost of changing from 12.4 tonnes/day to 29 tonnes/day = £35,000

Cost of changing from 29 tonnes/day to 12.4 tonnes/day = £15,000

Figure 11.13 illustrates both plans on a cumulative basis. Plan 1, which envisaged two drastic changes in capacity, has high capacity change costs but, because its production levels are close to demand levels, it has low inventory carrying costs. Plan 2 sacrifices some of the inventory cost advantage of Plan 1 but saves more in terms of capacity change costs.

HOW IS CAPACITY PLANNING A QUEUING PROBLEM?

Cumulative representations of capacity plans are useful where the operation has the ability to store its finished goods as inventory. However, for operations where it is not possible to produce products and services *before* demand for them has occurred, a cumulative representation would tell us relatively little. The cumulative 'production' could never be above the cumulative demand line. At best, it could show when an operation failed to meets its demand. So the vertical gap between the cumulative demand and production lines would indicate the amount of demand unsatisfied. Some of this demand would look elsewhere to be satisfied, but some would wait. This is why, for operations which by their nature cannot store their output, such as most service operations, capacity planning and control is best considered using waiting or queuing theory.

Queuing or 'waiting line' management

When we were illustrating the use of cumulative representations for capacity planning and control, our assumption was that, generally, any production plan should aim to meet demand at any point in time (the cumulative production line must be above the cumulative demand line). Looking at the issue as a queuing problem (in many parts of the world queuing concepts are referred to as 'waiting line' concepts) accepts that, while sometimes demand may be satisfied instantly, at other times customers may have to wait. This is particularly true when the arrival of individual demands on an operation are difficult to predict, or the time to produce a product or service is uncertain, or both. These circumstances make providing adequate capacity at all points in time particularly difficult. Figure 11.14 shows the general form of this capacity issue. Customers arrive according to some probability distribution and wait to be processed (unless part of the operation is idle); when they have reached the front of the queue, they are processed by one of the n parallel 'servers' (their processing time also being described by a probability distribution), after which they leave the operation. There are many examples of this kind of system. Table 11.2 illustrates some of these. All of these examples can be described by a common set of elements that define their queuing behaviour.

The source of customers – sometimes called the calling population – is the source of supply of customers. In queue management 'customers' are not always human. 'Customers' could, for example, be trucks arriving at a weighbridge, orders arriving to be processed or machines waiting to be serviced, etc. The source of customers for a queuing system can be either *finite* or *infinite*. A finite source has a known number of possible customers. For example, if one maintenance person serves four assembly lines, the number of customers for the maintenance person is known, i.e. four. There will be a certain probability that one of the assembly lines will break down and need repairing. However, if one line really does break down the probability of another line needing repair is reduced because there are now only three lines to break down. So, with a finite source of customers, the probability of a customer arriving depends on the number of customers already being serviced. By contrast, infinite customer sources

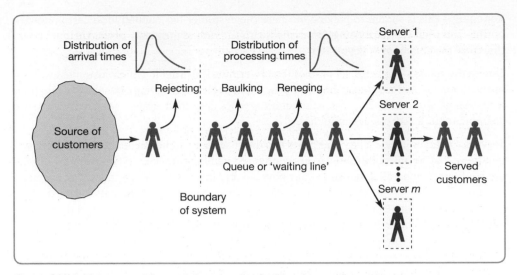

Figure 11.14 The general form of the capacity decision in queuing systems

Table 11.2 Examples of operations which have parallel processors

Operation	Arrivals	Processing capacity
Bank	Customers	Tellers
Supermarket	Shoppers	Checkouts
Hospital clinic	Patients	Doctors
Graphic artist	Commissions	Artists
Custom cake decorators	Orders	Cake decorators
Ambulance service	Emergencies	Ambulances with crews
Telephone switchboard	Calls	Telephonists
Maintenance department	Breakdowns	Maintenance staff

assume that there is a large number of potential customers so that it is always possible for another customer to arrive no matter how many are being serviced. Most queuing systems that deal with outside markets have infinite, or 'close-to-infinite', customer sources.

The arrival rate – is the rate at which customers needing to be served arrive at the server or servers. Rarely do customers arrive at a steady and predictable rate. Usually there is variability in their arrival rate. Because of this it is necessary to describe arrival rates in terms of probability distributions. The important issue here is that, in queuing systems, it is normal that at times no customers will arrive and at other times many will arrive relatively close together.

The queue – customers waiting to be served form the queue or waiting line itself. If there is relatively little limit on how many customers can queue at any time, we can assume that, for all practical purposes, an infinite queue is possible. Sometimes, however, there is a limit to how many customers can be in the queue at any one time.

Rejecting – if the number of customers in a queue is already at the maximum number allowed, then the customer could be rejected by the system. For example, during periods of heavy demand some websites will not allow customers to access part of the site until the demand on its services has declined.

Balking – when a customer is a human being with free will (and the ability to get annoyed) he or she may refuse to join the queue and wait for service if it is judged to be too long. In queuing terms this is called balking.

Reneging – this is similar to balking but here the customer has queued for a certain length of time and then (perhaps being dissatisfied with the rate of progress) leaves the queue and therefore the chance of being served.

Queue discipline – this is the set of rules that determine the order in which customers waiting in the queue are served. Most simple queues, such as those in a shop, use a *first-come-first-served* queue discipline. The various sequencing rules described earlier (see Chapter 10) are examples of different queue disciplines.

Servers – a server is the facility that processes the customers in the queue. In any queuing system there may be any number of servers configured in different ways. In Figure 11.14 servers are configured in parallel, but some may have servers in a series arrangement. For example, on entering a self-service restaurant you may queue to collect a tray and cutlery, move on to the serving area where you queue again to order and collect a meal, move on to a drinks area where you queue once more to order and collect a drink and then finally queue to pay for the meal. In this case you have passed through four servers (even though the first one was not staffed) in a series arrangement. Of course, many queue systems are complex arrangements of series and parallel connections. There is also likely to be variation in how long it takes to process each customer. Even if customers do not have differing needs, human servers will vary in the time they take to perform repetitive serving tasks. Therefore processing time, like arrival time, is usually described by a probability distribution.

Balancing capacity and demand

The dilemma in managing the capacity of a queuing system is how many servers to have available at any point in time in order to avoid unacceptably long queuing times or unacceptably low utilization of the servers. Because of the probabilistic arrival and processing times, only rarely will the arrival of customers match the ability of the operation to cope with them. Sometimes, if several customers arrive in quick succession and require longer-than-average processing times, queues will build up in front of the operation. At other times, when customers arrive less frequently than average and also require shorter-than-average processing times, some of the servers in the system will be idle. So even when the average capacity (processing capability) of the operation matches the average demand (arrival rate) on the system, both queues and idle time will occur.

If the operation has too few servers (that is, capacity is set at too low a level), queues will build up to a level where customers become dissatisfied with the time they are having to wait, although the utilization level of the servers will be high. If too many servers are in place (that is, capacity is set at too high a level), the time which customers can expect to wait will not be long but the utilization of the servers will be low. This is why the capacity planning and control problem for this type of operation is often presented as a trade-off between customer waiting time and system utilization. What is certainly important in making capacity decisions is being able to predict both of these factors for a given queuing system. The supplement to this chapter details some of the more simple mathematical approaches to understanding queue behaviour.

Variability in demand or supply

The variability, either in demand or capacity, as discussed above, will reduce the ability of an operation to process its inputs. That is, it will reduce its effective capacity. This effect was explained earlier (see Chapter 4) when the consequences of variability in individual processes were discussed. As a reminder, the greater the variability in arrival time or activity time at a process, the more the process will suffer both high throughput times and reduced utilization. This principle holds true for whole operations, and because long throughout times mean that queues will build up in the operation, high variability also affects

> ✳ **Operations principle**
>
> Variability, either in demand or capacity, will reduce effective capacity.

Figure 11.15 The effect of variability on the utilization of capacity

inventory levels. This is illustrated in Figure 11.15. The implication of this is that the greater the variability, the more extra capacity will need to be provided to compensate for the reduced utilization of available capacity. Therefore, operations with high levels of variability will tend to set their base level of capacity relatively high in order to provide this extra capacity.

Customer perceptions of queuing

Few of us like waiting. Yet queuing is something we all have to do. So if you have ever wondered if you are alone in particularly hating queuing, you are not – it's official. According to research involving 45,000 iPhone users who provided regular updates on their level of happiness via an app, it is one of the activities that most upsets us.[6] In fact of all the things that make us feel unhappy, queuing is beaten only by being in bed, sick. Yet, an important aspect of how they judge the service they receive from a queuing system is how they perceive the time spent queuing. It is well known that if you are told that you'll be waiting in a queue for twenty minutes and you are actually serviced

> **✳ Operations principle**
>
> Customer reactions to having to queue will be influenced by factors other than waiting time.

in ten minutes, your perception of the queuing experience will be more positive than if you were told that you would be waiting ten minutes but the queue actually took twenty minutes. Because of this, the management of queuing systems usually involves attempting to manage customers' perceptions and expectations in some way. One expert in queuing has come up with a number of principles that influence how customers perceive waiting times.

- Time spent idle is perceived as longer than time spent occupied.
- The wait before a service starts is perceived as more tedious than a wait within the service process.
- Anxiety and/or uncertainty heighten the perception that time spent waiting is long.
- A wait of unknown duration is perceived as more tedious than a wait whose duration is known.
- An unexplained wait is perceived as more tedious than a wait that is explained.
- The higher the value of the service for the customer, the longer the wait that will be tolerated.
- Waiting on one's own is more tedious than waiting in a group (unless you really don't like the others in the group!).

The dynamics of capacity management

Our emphasis so far has been on the planning aspects of capacity management. In practice, the management of capacity is a far more dynamic process which involves controlling and reacting to *actual* demand and *actual* capacity as it occurs. The capacity control process can be seen as a sequence of partially reactive capacity decisions. At the beginning of each period, operations management considers its forecasts of demand, its understanding of current capacity and, if appropriate, how much inventory has been carried forward from the previous period. Based on all this information, it makes plans for the following period's capacity. During the next period, demand might or might not be as forecast and the actual capacity of the operation might or might not turn out as planned. But whatever the actual conditions during that period, at the beginning of the next period the same types of decisions must be made, in the light of the new circumstances.

The success of capacity management is generally measured by some combination of costs, revenue, working capital and customer satisfaction (which goes on to influence revenue). This is influenced by the actual capacity available to the operation in any period and the demand for that period. However, capacity management is essentially a forward-looking activity. Overriding other considerations of what capacity strategy to adopt is usually the difference between the long- and short-term outlook for the volume of demand. If long-term outlook for demand is 'good' (in the sense that it is higher than current capacity can cope with) then it is unlikely that even 'poor' (demand less than capacity) short-term demand would cause an operation to make large, or difficult to reverse, cuts in capacity. Conversely if long-term outlook for demand is 'poor' (in the sense that it is lower than current capacity) then it is unlikely that even 'good' (demand more than capacity) short-term demand would cause an operation to take on large, or difficult to reverse, extra capacity. Figure 11.16 illustrates some appropriate capacity management strategies depending on the comparison of long- and short-term outlooks.

	Short-term outlook for volume		
	Decreasing below current capacity	Level with current capacity	Increasing above current capacity
Decreasing below current capacity	Reduce capacity (semi) permanently. For example; reduce staffing levels; reduce supply agreements.	Plan to reduce capacity (semi) permanently. For example, freeze recruitment; modify supply agreements.	Increase capacity temporarily. For example, increase working hours, and/or hire temporary staff; modify supply agreements.
Level with current capacity	Reduce capacity temporarily. For example, reduce staff working hours; modify supply agreements.	Maintain capacity at current level.	Increase capacity temporarily. For example, increase working hours, and/or hire temporary staff; modify supply agreements.
Increasing above current capacity	Reduce capacity temporarily. For example, reduce staff working hours, but plan to recruit; modify supply agreements.	Plan to increase capacity above current level; plan to increase supply agreements.	Increase capacity (semi) permanently. For example, hire staff; increase supply agreements.

Long-term outlook for volume

Figure 11.16 Capacity management strategies are partly dependent on the long- and short-term outlook for volumes

SUMMARY ANSWERS TO KEY QUESTIONS

Check and improve your understanding of this chapter using self-assessment questions and a personalized study plan, a video case study, and an eText – all at www.myomlab.com.

MyOMLab

⟩ What is capacity planning and control?

- It is the way operations organize the level of value-added activity which they can achieve under normal operating conditions over a period of time.

- It is usual to distinguish between a long-, medium- and short-term capacity decisions. Medium- and short-term capacity management where the capacity level of the organization is adjusted within the fixed physical limits which are set by long-term capacity decisions is sometimes called aggregate planning and control.

- Almost all operations have some kind of fluctuation in demand (or seasonality) caused by some combination of climatic, festive, behavioural, political, financial or social factors.

⟩ How is capacity measured?

- Either by the availability of its input resources or by the output which is produced. Which of these measures is used partly depends on how stable is the mix of outputs. If it is difficult to aggregate the different types of output from an operation, input measures are usually preferred.

- The usage of capacity is measured by the factors 'utilization' and 'efficiency'. A more recent measure is that of overall equipment effectiveness (OEE).

⟩ What are the ways of coping with demand fluctuation?

- Output can be kept level, in effect ignoring demand fluctuations. This will result in under-utilization of capacity where outputs cannot be stored, or the build-up of inventories where output can be stored.

- Output can chase demand by fluctuating the output level through some combination of overtime, varying the size of the workforce, using part-time staff and subcontracting.

- Demand can be changed, either by influencing the market through such measures as advertising and promotion, or by developing alternative products with a counter-seasonal demand pattern.

- Most operations use a mix of all these three 'pure' strategies.

⟩ How can operations plan their capacity level?

- Representing demand and output in the form of cumulative representations allows the feasibility of alternative capacity plans to be assessed.

⟩ How is capacity planning a queuing problem?

- In many operations, especially service operations, a queuing approach can be used to explore capacity strategies.

- Capacity control decisions are partly a function of the long- and short-term outlook for demand.

Blackberry Hill Farm

'Six years ago I had never heard of agri-tourism. As far as I was concerned, I had inherited the farm and I would be a farmer all my life.' (Jim Walker, Blackberry Hill Farm)

The 'agri-tourism' that Jim was referring to is 'a commercial enterprise at a working farm, or other agricultural centre, conducted for the enjoyment of visitors that generates supplemental income for the owner'. *'Farming has become a tough business'*, says Jim. *'Low world prices, a reduction in subsidies, and increasingly uncertain weather patterns have made it a far more risky business than when I first inherited the farm. Yet, because of our move into the tourist trade we are flourishing. Also ... I've never had so much fun in my life.'* But, Jim warns, agri-tourism isn't for everyone. *'You have to think carefully. Do you really want to do it? What kind of life style do you want? How open-minded are you to new ideas? How business-minded are you? Are you willing to put a lot of effort into marketing your business? Above all, do you like working with people? If you had rather be around cows than people, it isn't the business for you.'*

Source: AL RF (Imagestate/John Foxx Images)

History

Blackberry Hill Farm was a 200-hectare mixed farm in the south of England when Jim and Mandy Walker inherited it 15 years ago. It was primarily a cereal growing operation with a small dairy herd, some fruit and vegetable growing, and mixed woodland that was protected by local preservation laws. Six years ago it had become evident to Jim and Mandy that they might have to rethink how the farm was being managed. *'We first started a pick-your-own (PYO) operation because our farm is close to several large centres of population. Also the quantities of fruit and vegetables that we were producing were not large enough to interest the commercial buyers. Entering the PYO market was a reasonable success and, in spite of making some early mistakes, it turned our fruit and vegetable growing operation from making a small loss to making a small profit. Most importantly, it gave us some experience of how to deal with customers face-to-face and of how to cope with unpredictable demand. The biggest variable in PYO sales is weather. Most business occurs at the weekends between late spring and early autumn. If rain keeps customers away during part of those weekends, nearly all sales have to occur in just a few days.'*

Within a year of opening up the PYO operation Jim and Mandy had decided to reduce the area devoted to cereals and increase their fruit and vegetable growing capability. At the same time they organized a petting zoo that allowed children to mix with, feed and touch various animals.

'We already had our own cattle and poultry but we extended the area and brought in pigs and goats. Later we also introduced some rabbits, ponies and donkeys, and even a small bee-keeping operation.' At the same time the farm started building up its collection of 'farm heritage' exhibits. These were static displays of old farm implements and 'recreations' of farming processes together with information displays. This had always been a personal interest of Jim's and it allowed him to convert two existing farm outbuilding to create a 'Museum of Farming Heritage'.

The year after, they introduced tractor rides for visitors around the whole farm and extended the petting zoo and farming tradition exhibits further. But the most significant investment was in the 'preserving kitchen'. *'We had been looking for some way of using the surplus fruits and vegetables that we occasionally accumulated and also for some kind of products that we could sell in a farm shop. We started the preserving kitchen to make jams and fruit, vegetables and sauces preserved in jars. The venture was an immediate success. We started making just fifty kilogrammes of preserves a week; within three months that had grown to three hundred kilogrammes a week and we are now producing around a thousand kilogrammes a week, all under the "Blackberry Hill farm" label.'* The following year the preserving kitchen was extended and a viewing area added. *'It was a great attraction from the beginning'*, says Mandy. *'We employed ladies from the local village to make the preserves. They are all extrovert characters, so when we asked them to dress up in traditional "farmers' wives" type clothing they were happy to do it. The visitors love it, especially the good natured repartee with our ladies. The ladies also enjoy giving informal history lessons when we get school parties visiting us.'*

Table 11.3(a) Number of visitors last year

Month	Total visitors
January	1,006
February	971
March	2,874
April	6,622
May	8,905
June	12,304
July	14,484
August	15,023
September	12,938
October	6,687
November	2,505
December	3,777
Total	88,096
Average	7,341.33

Table 11.3(b) Farm opening times*

January–Mid-March	Wednesday–Sunday	10.00–16.00
Mid-March–May	Tuesday–Sunday	9.00–18.00
May–September	All week	8.30–19.00
October–November	Tuesday–Sunday	10.00–16.00
December	Tuesday–Sunday	9.00–18.00

*Special evening events, Easter, summer weekends and Christmas

With the last two years the farm had further extended its preserving kitchen, farm shop, exhibits and petting zoo. It had also introduced a small adventure playground for the children, a café serving drinks and its own produce, a picnic area and a small bakery. The bakery was also open to view by customers and staffed by bakers in traditional dress. 'It's a nice little visitor attraction', says Mandy, 'and it gives us another opportunity to squeeze more value out of our own products.' Table 11.3(a) shows last year's visitor numbers and Table 11.3(b) shows the farm's opening times.

Demand
The number of visitors to the farm was extremely seasonal. From a low point in January and February, when most people just visited the farm shop, the spring and summer months could be very busy, especially on public holidays.

The previous year Mandy had tracked the number of visitors arriving at the farm each day. 'It is easy to record the number of people visiting the farm attractions, because they pay the entrance charge. What we had not done before is include the people who just visited the farm shop and bakery that can be accessed both from within the farm and from the car park. We estimate that the number of people visiting the shop but not the farm ranges from 74 per cent in February down to around 15 per cent in August.' Figure 11.17 shows the number of visitors in the previous year's August. 'What our figures do not include are those people who visit the shop but don't buy anything. This is unlikely to be a large number.'

Mandy had also estimated the average stay at the farm and/or farm shop. She reckoned that in winter time the average stay was 45 minutes, but in August in climbed to 3.1 hours.

Current Issues
Both Jim and Mandy agreed that their lives had fundamentally changed over the last few years. Income from visitors and from the Blackberry Hill brand of preserves now accounted for 70 per cent of the farm's revenue. More importantly, the whole enterprise was significantly more profitable than it had ever been. Nevertheless, the farm faced a number of issues.

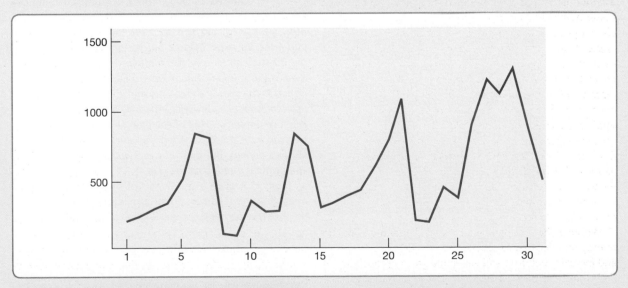

Figure 11.17 Daily number of visitors in August last year

Figure 11.18 Visitor arrivals on public holiday in August and a Wednesday in February

The first was the balance between its different activities. Jim was particularly concerned that the business remained a genuine farm. *'When you look at the revenue per hectare, visitor and production activities bring in far more revenue than conventional agricultural activities. However, if we push the agri-tourism too far we become no better than a theme park. We represent something more than this to our visitors. They come to us partly because of what we represent as well as what we actually do. I am not sure that we would want to grow much more. Anyway, more visitors would mean that we have to extend the car park. That would be expensive, and although it would be necessary, it does not directly bring in any more revenue. There are already parking problems during peak periods and we have had complaints from the police that our visitors park inappropriately on local roads.*

'There is also the problem of complexity. Every time we introduce a new attraction, the whole business gets that little bit more complex to manage. Although we enjoy it tremendously,

both Mandy and I are spreading ourselves thinly over an ever widening range of activities.' Mandy was also concerned about this. *'I'm starting to feel that my time is being taken up in managing the day-to-day problems of the business. This does not leave time either for thinking about the overall direction in which we should be going, or spending time talking with the staff. That is why we both see this coming year as a time for consolidation and for smoothing out the day-to-day problems of managing the business, particularly the queuing, which is getting excessive at busy times. That is why this year we are limiting ourselves to just one new venture for the business.'*

Staff management was also a concern for Mandy. The business had grown to over 80 (almost all part-time and seasonal) employees. *'We have become a significant employer in the area. Most of our employees are still local people working part-time for extra income but we are also now employing 20 students during the summer period and, last year, 8 agricultural students from Eastern Europe. But now, labour is short in this part of the country and it is becoming more difficult to attract local people, especially to produce Blackberry Hill farm preserves. Half of the preserving kitchen staff work all year, with the other employed during the summer and autumn periods. But most of them would prefer guaranteed employment throughout the year.'*

Table 11.4 gives more details of some of the issues of managing the facilities at the farm, and Table 11.5 shows the preserve demand and production for the previous year.

Where next?

By the 'consolidation' and improvement of 'day-to-day' activities, Jim and Mandy meant that they wanted to increase their revenue, while at the same time reducing the occasional

Table 11.4 The farm's main facilities and some of the issues concerned with managing them

Facility	Issues
Car park	85 car parking spaces, 4 x 40-seater tour bus spaces.
Fixed exhibits, etc. Recreation of old farmhouse kitchen, recreation of barnyard, old-fashioned milking parlour, various small exhibits on farming past and present, adventure playground, ice-cream and snack stands.	• Most exhibits in, or adjacent to the farm museum. • At peak times have helpers dressed in period costume to entertain visitors. • Feedback indicates customers find exhibits more interesting than they thought they would. • Visitors free to look when they wish absorbs demand from busy facilities.
Tractor rides One tractor towing decorated covered cart with maximum capacity of 30 people; tour takes around 20 minutes on average (including stops). Waits 10 minutes between tours except at peak times when tractor circulates continuously.	• Tractor acts both as transport and entertainment; approximately 60 per cent of visitors stay on for the whole tour, 40 per cent use it as 'hop-on hop-off' facility. • Overloaded at peak times, long queues building. • Feedback indicates it is popular, except for queuing. • Jim reluctant to invest in further cart and tractor
Pick-your-own area Largest single facility on the farm. Use local press, dedicated telephone line (answering machine) and website to communicate availability of fruit and vegetables. Checkout and weighing area next to farm shop, also displays picked produce and preserves, etc., for sale.	• Very seasonal and weather dependent, both for supply and demand. • Farm plans for a surplus over visitor demand, uses surplus in preserves. • Six weighing/paying stations at undercover checkout area. • Queues develop at peak times. Feedback indicates some dissatisfaction with this. • Can move staff from farm shop to help with checkout in busy periods, but farm shop also tends to be busy at the same time. • Considering using packers at pay stations to speed up the process.
Petting zoo Accommodation for smaller animals including sheep and pigs. Large animals (cattle, horses) brought to viewing area daily. Visitors can view all animals and handle/stroke most animals under supervision.	• Approximately 50 per cent of visitors view petting zoo. • Number of staff in attendance varies between 0 (off-peak) and 5 (peak periods). • The area can get congested during peak periods. • Staff need to be skilled at managing children.
Preserving kitchen Boiling vats, mixing vats, jar sterilizing equipment, etc. Visitor viewing area can hold 15 people comfortably. Average length of stay 7 minutes in off-season, 14 minutes in peak season.	• Capacity of kitchen is theoretically 4,500 kilogrammes per month on a 5-day week and 6,000 kilogrammes on a 7-day week. • In practice, capacity varies with season because of interaction with visitors. Can be as low as 5,000 kilogrammes on a 7-day week in summer, or up to 5,000 kilogrammes on a 5-day week in winter. • Shelf-life of products is on average 12 months. • Current storage area can hold 16,000 kilogrammes.
Bakery Contains mixing and shaping equipment, commercial oven, cooling racks, display stand, etc. Just installed doughnut-making machine. All pastries contain farm's preserved fruit.	• Starting to become a bottleneck since doughnut-making machine installed; visitors like watching it. • Products also on sale at farm shop adjacent to bakery. • Would be difficult to expand this area because of building constraints.
Farm shop and café Started by selling farm's own products exclusively. Now sells a range of products from farms in the region and wider. Started selling frozen menu dishes (lasagne, goulash, etc.) produced off-peak in the preserving kitchen.	• The most profitable part of the whole enterprise, Jim and Mandy would like to extend the retailing and café operation. • Shop includes area for cooking displays, cake decoration, fruit dipping (in chocolate), etc. • Some congestion in shop at peak times but little visitor dissatisfaction. • More significant queuing for café in peak periods. • Considering allowing customers to place orders before they tour the farm's facilities and collect their purchases later. • Retailing more profitable per square metre than café.

Table 11.5 Preserve demand and production (previous year)

Month	Demand (kg)	Cumulative demand (kg)	Production (kg)	Cumulative product (kg)	Inventory (kg)
January	682	682	4,900	4,900	4,218
February	794	1,476	4,620	9,520	8,044
March	1,106	2,582	4,870	14,390	11,808
April	3,444	6.026	5,590	19,980	13,954
May	4,560	10,586	5,840	25,820	15,234
June	6,014	16,600	5,730	31,550	14,950
July	9,870	26,470	5,710	37,260	10,790
August	13,616	40,086	5,910	43,170	3,084
September	5,040	45,126	5,730	48,900	3,774
October	1,993	47,119	1,570*	50,470	3,351
November	2,652	49,771	2,770*	53,240	3,467
December	6,148	55,919	4,560	57,800	1,881
Average demand	4,660			Average inventory	7,880

*Technical problems reduced production level

queues that they knew could irritate their visitors, preferably without any significant investment in extra capacity. They also were concerned to be able to offer more stable employment to the preserving kitchen 'ladies' throughout the year, who would produce at a near constant rate. However, they were not sure if this could be done without storing the products for so long that their shelf-life would be seriously affected. There was no problem with the supply of produce to keep production level, as less than 2 per cent of the fruit and vegetables that go into the preserves are actually grown on the farm. The remainder were bought at wholesale markets, although this was not generally understood by customers.

Of the many ideas being discussed as candidates for the 'one new venture' for next year, two were emerging as particularly attractive. Jim liked the idea of developing a Maize Maze, a type of attraction that had become increasingly popular in Europe and North America in the last five years. It involved planting a field of maize (corn) and, once grown, cutting through a complex serious of paths in the form of a maze. Evidence from other farms indicated that a maze would be extremely attractive to visitors and Jim reckoned that it could account for up to an extra 10,000 visitors during the summer period. Designed as a separate activity with its own admission charge, it would require an investment of around £20,000, but generate more than twice that in admission charges, as well as attracting more visitors to the farm itself.

Mandy favoured the alterative idea – that of building up their business in organized school visits. 'Last year we joined the National Association of Farms for Schools. Their advice is that we could easily become one of the top school attractions in this part of England. Educating visitors about farming tradition is already a major part of what we do. And many of our staff have developed the skills to communicate to children exactly what farm life used to be like. We would need to convert and extend one of our existing underused farm outbuildings to make a "school room" and that would cost between £30,000 and £35,000. And although we would need to discount our admission charge substantially, I think we could break even on the investment within around two years.'

QUESTIONS

1 How could the farm's day-to-day operations be improved?

2 What advice would you give Jim and Mandy regarding this year's 'new venture'?

PROBLEMS AND APPLICATIONS

MyOMLab

These problems and applications will help to improve your analysis of operations. You can find more practice problems as well as worked examples and guided solutions on MyOMLab at www.myomlab.com.

1. A local government office issues hunting licences. Demand for these licences is relatively slow in the first part of the year but then increases after the middle of the year before slowing down again towards the end of the year. The department works a 220-day year on a 5-days-a-week basis. Between working days 0 and 100, demand is 25 per cent of demand during the peak period which lasts between day 100 and day 150. After day 150, demand reduces to about 12 per cent of the demand during the peak period. In total, the department processes 10,000 applications per year. The department has 2 permanent members of staff who are capable of processing 15 licence applications per day. If an untrained temporary member of staff can only process 10 licences per day, how many temporary staff should the department recruit between days 100 and 150?

2. In the example above, if a new computer system is installed that allows experienced staff to increase their work rate to 20 applications per day, and untrained staff to 15 applications per day, (a) does the department still need 2 permanent staff, and (b) how many temporary members of staff will be needed between days 100 and 150?

3. A field service organization repairs and maintains printing equipment for a large number of customers. It offers one level of service to all its customers and employs 30 staff. The operations Marketing's Vice President has decided that in future the company will offer 3 standards of service: platinum, gold, and silver. It is estimated that platinum service customers will require 50 per cent more time from the company's field service engineers than the current service. The current service is to be called 'the gold service'. The silver service is likely to require about 80 per cent of the time of the gold service. If future demand is estimated to be 20 per cent platinum, 70 per cent gold, and 10 percent silver service, how many staff will be needed to fulfil demand?

4. Look again at the principles which govern customers' perceptions of the queuing experience. For the following operations, apply the principles to minimize the perceived negative effects of queuing:
   (a) a cinema;
   (b) a doctor's surgery;
   (c) waiting to board an aircraft.

5. Consider how airlines cope with balancing capacity and demand. In particular, consider the role of yield management. Do this by visiting the website of a low-cost airline, and for a number of flights price the fare that is being charged by the airline from tomorrow onwards. In other words, how much would it cost if you needed to fly tomorrow, how much if you needed to fly next week, how much if you needed to fly in two weeks, etc. Plot the results for different flights and debate the findings.

6. Calculate the overall equipment efficiency (OEE) of the following facilities by investigating their use:
   (a) a lecture theatre;
   (b) a cinema;
   (c) a coffee machine.
   Discuss whether it is worth trying to increase the OEE of these facilities and, if it is, how you would go about it.

SELECTED FURTHER READING

Brandimarte, P. and Villa, A. (1999) *Modelling Manufacturing Systems: From Aggregate Planning to Real Time Control*, Springer, New York. Very academic, although it does contain some interesting pieces if you need to get 'under the skin' of the subject.

Hopp, W.J. and Spearman, M.L. (2000) *Factory Physics*, 2nd edn, McGraw-Hill, New York. Very mathematical indeed, but includes some interesting maths on queuing theory.

Olhager, J., Rudberg, M. and Wikner, J. (2001) Long-term capacity management: linking the perspectives from manufacturing strategy and sales and operations planning, *International Journal of Production Economics*, vol. 69, issue 2, 215–225. Academic article, but interesting.

Vollmann, T., Berry, W., Whybark, D.C. and Jacobs, F.R. (2004) *Manufacturing Planning and Control Systems for Supply Chain Management: The Definitive Guide for Professionals*, McGraw-Hill Higher Education, New York. The latest version of the 'bible' of manufacturing planning and control. It's exhaustive in its coverage of all aspects of planning and control, including aggregate planning.

USEFUL WEBSITES

www.bis.gov.uk/policies/employment-matters/strategies Website of the Employment Relations Directorate who have developed a framework for employers and employees which promotes a skilled and flexible labour market founded on principles of partnership.

www.worksmart.org.uk/index.php This site is from the Trades Union Congress. Its aim is 'to help today's working people get the best out of the world of work'.

www.dol.gov/index.htm US Department of Labor's site with information regarding using part-time employees.

www.downtimecentral.com Lots of information on operational equipment efficiency (OEE).

www.myomlab.com Test which sections you have mastered and which you need to review, with questions, a personalized study plan, video clips, guided solutions, and cases.

www.opsman.org Useful materials.

http://operationsroom.wordpress.com Stanford University's take on topical operations stories.

www.iomnet.org The Institute of Operations Management site. One of the main professional bodies for the subject.

www.poms.org A US academic society for production and operations management. Academic, but some useful material, including a link to an encyclopedia of operations management terms.

Supplement to Chapter 11
Analytical queuing models

INTRODUCTION

Earlier (in the main part of Chapter 11) we described how the queuing approach (in the United States it would be called the 'waiting line approach') can be useful in thinking about capacity, especially in service operations. It is useful because it deals with the issue of variability, both of the arrival of customers (or items) at a process and of how long each customer (or item) takes to process. And where variability is present in a process (as it is in most processes, but particularly in service processes) the capacity required by an operation cannot easily be based on averages but must include the effects of the variation. Unfortunately, many of the formulae that can be used to understand queuing are extremely complicated, especially for complex systems, and are beyond the scope of this book. In fact, computer programs are almost always now used to predict the behaviour of queuing systems. However, studying queuing formulae can illustrate some useful characteristics of the way queuing systems behave.

NOTATION

Unfortunately there are several different conventions for the notation used for different aspects of queuing system behaviour. It is always advisable to check the notation used by different authors before using their formulae. We shall use the following notation:

t_a = average time between arrival

r_a = arrival rate (items per unit time) = $1/t_a$

c_a = coefficient of variation of arrival times

m = number of parallel servers at a station

t_e = mean processing time

r_e = processing rate (items per unit time) $- m/t_e$

c_e = coefficient of variation of process time

u = utilization of station = $r_a/r_e = (r_a t_e)/m$

WIP = average work in progress (number of items) in the queue

WIP_q = expected work in progress (number of times) in the queue

W_q = expected waiting time in the queue

W = expected waiting time in the system (queue time + processing time)

Some of these factors are explained later.

VARIABILITY

The concept of variability is central to understanding the behaviour of queues. If there were no variability there would be no need for queues to occur because the capacity of a process could be relatively easily adjusted to match demand. For example, suppose one member of staff (a server) serves customers at a bank counter who always arrive exactly every five minutes (i.e. 12 per hour). Also suppose that every customer takes exactly five minutes to be served, then because,

(a) the arrival rate is $\leq$ processing rate, and
(b) there is no variation

no customer need ever wait because the next customer will arrive when, or before, the previous customer leaves. That is, $\mathrm{WIP_q} = 0$.

Also, in this case, the server is working all the time, again because exactly as one customer leaves the next one is arriving. That is, $u = 1$.

Even with more than one server, the same may apply. For example, if the arrival time at the counter is 5 minutes (12 per hour) and the processing time for each customer is now always exactly 10 minutes, the counter would need two servers, and because,

(a) arrival rate is $\leq$ processing rate m, and
(b) there is no variation

again, $\mathrm{WIP_q} = 0$, and $u = 1$.

Of course, it is convenient (but unusual) if arrival rate/processing rate = a whole number. When this is not the case (for this simple example with no variation),

$$\text{Utilization} = \text{processing rate}/(\text{arrival rate multiplied by } m)$$

For example,

$$\text{if arrival rate, } r_a = 5 \text{ minutes}$$
$$\text{processing rate, } r_e = 8 \text{ minutes}$$
$$\text{number of servers, } m = 2$$
$$\text{then, utilization, } u = 8/(5 \times 2) = 0.8 \text{ or } 80\%$$

Incorporating variability

The previous examples were not realistic because the assumption of no variation in arrival or processing times very rarely occurs. We can calculate the average or mean arrival and process times but we also need to take into account the variation around these means. To do that we need to use a probability distribution. Figure S11.1 contrasts two processes with different arrival distributions. The units arriving are shown as people, but they could be jobs arriving at a machine, trucks needing servicing, or any other uncertain event. The top example shows low variation in arrival time where customers arrive in a relatively predictable manner. The bottom example has the same average number of customers arriving but this time they arrive unpredictably with sometimes long gaps between arrivals and at other times two or three customers arriving close together. Of course, we could do a similar analysis to describe processing times. Again, some would have low variation, some higher variation and others somewhere in between.

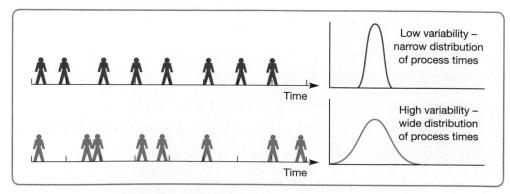

Figure S11.1 Low and high arrival variation

In Figure S11.1 high arrival variation has a distribution with a wider spread (called 'dispersion') than the distribution describing lower variability. Statistically the usual measure for indicating the spread of a distribution is its standard deviation, σ. But variation does not only depend on standard deviation. For example, a distribution of arrival times may have a standard deviation of 2 minutes. This could indicate very little variation when the average arrival time is 60 minutes. But it would mean a very high degree of variation when the average arrival time is 3 minutes. Therefore to normalize standard deviation, it is divided by the mean of its distribution. This measure is called the coefficient of variation of the distribution. So,

$$c_a = \text{coefficient of variation of arrival times} = \sigma_a/t_a$$
$$c_e = \text{coefficient of variation of processing times} = \sigma_e/t_e$$

INCORPORATING LITTLE'S LAW

Earlier (in Chapter 4) we discussed one of the fundamental laws of processes that describes the relationship between the cycle time of a process (how often something emerges from the process), the work-in-progress in the process and the throughput time of the process (the total time it takes for an item to move through the whole process including waiting time). It was called Little's law and it was denoted by the following simple relationship:

$$\text{Throughput time} = \text{work-in-progress} \times \text{cycle time}$$

Therefore,

$$\text{Work in-progress} = \text{throughput time/cycle time}$$

Or

$$\text{WIP} = T/C$$

We can make use of Little's law to help understand queuing behaviour. Consider the queue in front of a station.

Work-in-progress in the queue = the arrival rate at the queue (equivalent to $1/$cycle time) $\times$ waiting time in the queue (equivalent to throughput time)

$$\text{WIP}_q = r_a \times W_q$$

and

waiting time in the whole system = the waiting time in the queue + the average process time at the station

$$W = W_q + t_e$$

We will use this relationship later to investigate queuing behaviour.

TYPES OF QUEUING SYSTEM

Conventionally, queuing systems are characterized by four parameters:

A – the distribution of arrival times (or more properly interarrival times, the elapsed times between arrivals)

B – the distribution of process times

m – the number of servers at each station

b – the maximum number of items allowed in the system.

The most common distributions used to describe A or B are either,

    (a) the exponential (or Markovian) distribution denoted by M;

    (b) the general (for example normal) distribution denoted by G.

So, for example, an M/G/1/5 queuing system would indicate a system with exponentially distributed arrivals, process times described by a general distribution such as a normal distribution, with one server and a maximum number of items allowed in the system of 5. This type of notation is called Kendall's Notation.

Queuing theory can help us investigate any type of queuing system, but in order to simplify the mathematics, we shall here deal only with the two most common situations. Namely,

- M/M/m – the exponential arrival and processing times with m servers and no maximum limit to the queue.
- G/G/m – general arrival and processing distributions with m servers and no limit to the queue.

And first we will start by looking at the simple case when $m = 1$.

For M/M/1 queuing systems

The formulae for this type of system are as follows:

$$\text{WIP} = \frac{u}{1 - u}$$

Using Little's law,

$$\text{WIP} = \text{cycle time} \times \text{throughput time}$$

$$\text{Throughput time} = \text{WIP/cycle time}$$

Then

$$\text{Throughput time} = \frac{u}{1 - u} \times \frac{1}{r_a} = \frac{t_e}{1 - u}$$

and since throughput time in the queue = total throughput time − average processing time,

$$W_q = W - t_e$$

$$= \frac{t_e}{1 - u} - t_e$$

$$= \frac{t_e - t_e(1 - u)}{1 - u} = \frac{t_e - t_e - ut_e}{1 - u}$$

$$= \frac{u}{(1 - u)} t_e$$

again, using Little's law

$$\text{WIP}_q = r_a \times W_q = \frac{u}{(1 - u)} t_e r_a$$

and since

$$u = \frac{r_a}{r_e} = r_a t_e$$

$$r_a = \frac{u}{t_e}$$

then

$$\text{WIP}_q = \frac{u}{(1 - u)} \times t_e \times \frac{u}{t_e}$$

$$= \frac{(u^2)}{(1 - u)}$$

For M/M/m systems

When there are m servers at a station, the formula for waiting time in the queue (and therefore all other formulae) needs to be modified. Again, we will not derive these formulae but just state them.

$$W_q = \frac{u^{\sqrt{2(m+1)}-1}}{m(1-u)} t_e$$

From which the other formulae can be derived as before.

For G/G/1 systems

The assumption of exponential arrival and processing times is convenient as far as the mathematical derivation of various formulae is concerned. However, in practice, process times in particular are rarely truly exponential. This is why it is important to have some idea of how a G/G/1 and G/G/m queue behaves. However, exact mathematical relationships are not possible with such distributions. Therefore some kind of approximation is needed. The one here is in common use, and although it is not always accurate, it is for practical purposes. For G/G/1 systems the formula for waiting time in the queue is as follows:

$$W_q = \left(\frac{c_a^2 + c_e^2}{2}\right)\left(\frac{u}{1-u}\right)t_e$$

There are two points to make about this equation. The first is that it is exactly the same as the equivalent equation for an M/M/1 system but with a factor to take account of the variability of the arrival and process times. The second is that this formula is sometimes known as the VUT formula because it describes the waiting time in a queue as a function of:

    V – the variability in the queuing system,

    U – the utilization of the queuing system (that is demand versus capacity), and

    T – the processing times at the station.

In other words, we can reach the intuitive conclusion that queuing time will increase as variability, utilization or processing time increases.

For G/G/m systems

The same modification applies to queuing systems using general equations and m servers. The formula for waiting time in the queue is now as follows:

$$W_q = \left(\frac{c_a^2 + c_e^2}{2}\right)\left(\frac{u^{\sqrt{2(m+1)}-1}}{m(1-u)}\right)t_e$$

Worked example 1

'I can't understand it. We have worked out our capacity figures and I am sure that one member of staff should be able to cope with the demand. We know that customers arrive at a rate of around six per hour and we also know that any trained member of staff can process them at a rate of eight per hour. So why is the queue so large and the wait so long? Have at look at what is going on there please.'

    Sarah knew that it was probably the variation, both in customers arriving and in how long it took each of them to be processed, that was causing the problem. Over a two-day period when she was told that demand was more or less normal, she timed the exact arrival times and processing times of every customer. Her results were as follows:

The coefficient of variation, c_a of customer arrivals = 1

The coefficient of variation, c_a of processing time = 3.5

The average arrival rate of customers, r_a = 6 per hour

therefore the average inter-arrival time = 10 minutes

The average processing rate, r_a = 8 per hour

therefore the average processing time = 7.5 minutes

Therefore the utilization of the single server, u = 6/8 = 0.75

Using the waiting time formula for a G/G/1 queuing system

$$W_q = \left(\frac{1 + 12.25}{2}\right)\left(\frac{0.75}{1 - 0.75}\right)7.5$$

$$= 6.625 \times 3 \times 7.5 = 149.06 \text{ mins}$$

$$= 2.48 \text{ hours}$$

Also because,

$$WIP_q = \text{cycle time} \times \text{throughput time}$$

$$WIP_q = 6 \times 2.48 = 14.68$$

So, Sarah had found out that the average wait that customers could expect was 2.48 hours and that there would be an average of 14.68 people in the queue.

'OK, so I see that it's the very high variation in the processing time that is causing the queue to build up. How about investing in a new computer system that would standardized processing time to a greater degree? I have been talking with our technical people and they reckon that, if we invested in a new system, we could cut the coefficient of variation of processing time down to 1.5. What kind of a difference would this make?'

Under these conditions with $c_e = 1.5$:

$$W_q = \left(\frac{1 + 2.25}{2}\right)\left(\frac{0.75}{1 - 0.75}\right)7.5$$

$$= 1.625 \times 3 \times 7.5 = 36.56 \text{ mins}$$

$$= 0.61 \text{ hours}$$

Therefore,

$$WIP_q = 6 \times 0.61 = 3.66$$

In other words, reducing the variation of the process time has reduced average queuing time from 2.48 hours down to 0.61 hours and has reduced the expected number of people in the queue from 14.68 down to 3.66.

Worked Example 2

A bank wishes to decide how many staff to schedule during its lunch period. During this period customers arrive at a rate of 9 per hour and the enquiries that customers have (such as opening new accounts, arranging loans, etc.) take on average 15 minutes to deal with. The bank manager feels that 4 staff should be on duty during this period but wants to make sure that the customers do not wait more than 3 minutes on average before they are served.

The manager has been told by his small daughter that the distributions that describe both arrival and processing times are likely to be exponential. Therefore,

$$r_a = 9 \text{ per hour, therefore}$$
$$t_a = 6.67 \text{ minutes}$$
$$r_e = 4 \text{ per hour, therefore}$$
$$t_e = 15 \text{ minutes}$$

The proposed number of servers, $m = 4$

therefore the utilization of the system, $u = 9/(4 \times 4) = 0.5625$.

From the formula for waiting time for a M/M/m system,

$$W_q = \frac{u^{\sqrt{2(m+1)}-1}}{m(1-u)} t_e$$

$$W_q = \frac{0.5625^{\sqrt{10}-1}}{4(1-0.5625)} \times 0.25$$

$$= \frac{0.5625^{2.162}}{1.75} \times 0.25$$

$$= 0.042 \text{ hours}$$

$$= 2.52 \text{ minutes}$$

Therefore the average waiting time with 4 servers would be 2.52 minutes; that is well within the manager's acceptable waiting tolerance.

MyOMLab

Now that you have finished reading this chapter, why not visit MyOMLab at www.myomlab.com where you'll find more learning resources to help you make the most of your studies and get a better grade.

12

Inventory management

INTRODUCTION

Operations managers often have an ambivalent attitude towards inventories. On the one hand, they are costly, sometimes tying up considerable amounts of working capital. They are also risky because items held in stock could deteriorate, become obsolete or just get lost, and, furthermore, they take up valuable space in the operation. On the other hand, they provide some security in an uncertain environment that one can deliver items in stock, should customers demand them. This is the dilemma of inventory management: in spite of the cost and the other disadvantages associated with holding stocks, they do facilitate the smoothing of supply and demand. In fact they only exist because supply and demand are not exactly in harmony with each other (see Fig. 12.1).

Figure 12.1 This chapter covers inventory management

The blood bank's 'perfect storm'[1]

Inventory depends on both supply and demand, so when both are uncertain, inventory management poses particular challenges. And when, in addition, the consequences of running out of stock can affect people's health, then inventory management becomes a particularly vital task. Welcome to the world of the Blood Stocks Management Scheme of the National Health Service Blood and Transplant (NHSBT) that manages blood stocks across the blood supply chain in the UK. NHSBT is responsible for the collection, processing, testing and issuing of blood across England and North Wales. Each year approximately 2 million blood donations are collected from 1.4 million donors to supply hospitals with all the blood needed for accident and emergency situations and regular medical treatment.

Source: AL RF (PhotoDisc/Nick Rowe)

Many people owe their lives to transfusions that were made possible by the efficient management of blood, stocked in a supply network that stretches from donation centres through to hospital blood banks. The blood supply chain has three main stages:

- *Collection*, which involves recruiting and retaining blood donors, encouraging them to attend donor sessions and transporting the donated blood.
- *Processing*, which breaks blood down into its constituent parts.
- *Distribution*, which transports blood from blood centres to hospitals in response to both routine and emergency requests.

Inventory accumulates at all three stages, as well as in individual hospitals' blood banks. Within the supply chain some, less than 10 per cent, of donated red blood cells are lost. Much of this is due to losses in processing, but around 5 per cent is not used because it has 'become unavailable', mainly because it has been stored for too long. Part of the inventory management task is to keep this 'time expired' loss to a minimum. In fact most blood is lost when it is stored in hospital blood banks that are outside the service's direct control. Also, blood components will deteriorate over time. Platelets have a shelf life of only five days and demand can fluctuate significantly, which makes stock control particularly difficult. Even red blood cells, which have a shelf life of 35 days, may not be acceptable to hospitals if they are close to their 'use by date'. Stock accuracy is crucial. Giving a patient the wrong type of blood can be fatal.

At a local level demand can be affected significantly by accidents. One serious accident involving a cyclist used 750 units of blood, which completely exhausted the available supply (miraculously, he survived). Large-scale accidents usually generate a surge of offers from donors wishing to make immediate donations. There is also a more predictable seasonality to the donating of blood, however, with a low period during the summer vacation. During public holidays and sporting events blood donations drop. For example, on one day when the football World Cup quarter-final and Andy Murray's (a British tennis player) Wimbledon semi-final coincided, there was a 12 per cent drop in donations compared with the previous year. The summer of 2012 proved particularly difficult, with a cluster of events and public holidays between April and August, including the Queen's Jubilee, Euro 2012, the London Olympic Games and the Paralympic Games. Not only did these events reduce donations (supply), the increased number of visitors to London increased demand. Before the period, NHS Blood and Transplant said that the number of major events would create a *'perfect storm'* and dramatically impact the number of blood donations coming in. Assistant Director for Blood Donation, Jon Latham, said: *'Approximately 2 million units of blood will be needed by hospitals throughout 2012, and the equivalent of 500 extra donations will be needed each week in the first six months to help us build blood stocks and cover extra potential need from Olympic visitors.'*

WHAT IS INVENTORY?

Inventory is a term we use to describe the accumulations of materials, customers or information as they flow through processes or networks. Occasionally the term is also used to describe transforming resources, such as rooms in hotels or automobiles in a vehicle hire firm, but here we use the term for the accumulation of resources that flow through processes, operations or supply networks. Physical inventory (sometimes called 'stock') is the accumulation of physical materials such as components, parts, finished goods or physical (paper) information records. Queues are accumulations of customers, physical as in a queuing line or people in an airport departure lounge, or waiting for service at the end of phone lines. Databases are stores for accumulations of digital information, such as medical records or insurance details. Managing these accumulations is what we call 'inventory management'. And it's important. Material inventories in a factory can represent a substantial proportion of cash tied up in working capital. Reducing them can release large quantities of cash. However, reducing them too far can lead to customers' orders not being fulfilled. Customers held up in queues for too long can get irritated, angry, and possibly leave, so reducing revenue. Databases are critical for storing digital information and, while storage may be inexpensive, maintaining databases may not be.

All processes, operations and supply networks have inventories

Most things that flow do so in an uneven way. Rivers flow faster down steep sections or where they are squeezed into a ravine. Over relatively level ground they flow slowly, and form pools or even large lakes where there are natural or man-made barriers blocking its path. It's the same in operations. Passengers in an airport flow from public transport or their vehicles, then have to queue at several points, including check-in, security screening and immigration. They then have to wait (a queue even if they are sitting), again in the departure lounge as they are joined (batched) with other passengers to form a group of several hundred people who are ready to board the aircraft. They are then squeezed down the air bridge as they file in one at a time to board the plane. Likewise in a tractor assembly plant, stocks of components such as gearboxes, wheels, lighting circuits, etc., are brought into the factory in batches of 10 or 100 and are then stored next to the assembly line ready for use. Finished tractors will also be stored until the transporter comes to take them away in ones or 10s to the dealers or directly to the end customer. Similarly, a government tax department collects information about us and our finances from various sources, including our employers, our tax forms and information from banks or other investment companies, and stores this in databases until they are checked, sometimes by people, sometimes automatically, to create our tax codes and/or tax bills. In fact, because most operations involve flows of materials, customers and/or information, at some points they are likely to have material and information inventories and queues of customers waiting to be processed, see Table 12.1.

Inventories are often the result of uneven flows. If there is a difference between the timing or the rate of supply and demand at any point in a process or network then accumulations will occur. A common analogy is the water tank shown in Figure 12.2. If, over time, the rate of supply of water to the tank differs from the rate at which it is demanded, a tank of water (inventory) will be needed to maintain supply. When the rate of supply exceeds the rate of demand, inventory increases; when the rate of demand exceeds the rate of supply, inventory decreases. So if an operation or process can match supply and demand rates, it will also succeed in reducing its inventory levels. But most organizations must cope with unequal supply and demand, at least at some points in their supply chain.

There is a complication when using this 'water flow' analogy to represent flows and accumulations (inventories) of information. Inventories of information can either be stored because of uneven flow, in the same way as materials and people, or stored because the operation needs to use the information to process something in the future. For example, an internet retail operation will process each order it receives, and inventories of information may

Table 12.1 Examples of inventory held in processes, operations or supply networks

Process, operation or supply network	'Inventories'		
	Physical inventories	Queues of customers	Information in databases
Hotel	Food items, drinks, toilet items	At check-in and check-out	Customer details, loyalty card holders, catering suppliers
Hospital	Dressings, disposable instruments, blood	Patients on a waiting list, patients in bed waiting for surgery, patients in recovery wards	Patient medical records
Credit card application process	Blank cards, form letters	Customers waiting on the phone	Customers' credit and personal information
Computer manufacturer	Components for assembly, packaging materials, finished computers ready for sale	Customers waiting for delivery of their computer	Customers' details, supplier information

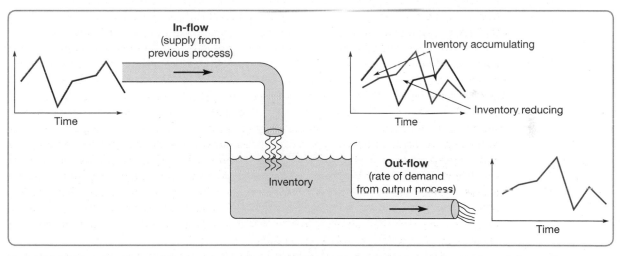

Figure 12.2 Inventory is created to compensate for the differences in timing between supply and demand

accumulate because of uneven flows, as we have described. But, in addition, during order processing customer details could be permanently stored in a database. This information will then be used, not only for future orders from the same customer, but also for other processes, such as targeting promotional activities. In this case the inventory of information had turned from a transformed resource into a transforming resource, because it is being used to transform other information rather than being transformed itself. So, whereas managing physical material concerns ordering and holding the right amounts of goods or materials to deal with the variations in flow, and managing queues is about the level of resources to deal with demand, a database is the accumulation of information but may not cause an interruption to the flow. Managing databases is about the organization of the data, its storage, security, and retrieval (access and search).

WHY SHOULD THERE BE ANY INVENTORY?

There are plenty of reasons to avoid accumulating inventory where possible. Table 12.2 identifies some of these, particularly those concerned with cost, space, quality, and operational/organizational issues.

So why have inventory?

On the face of it, it may seem sensible to have a smooth and even flow of materials, customers and information through operational processes and networks and thus not have any accumulations. In fact, inventories provide many advantages for both operations and their customers. If a customer has to go to a competitor because a part is out of stock or because they have had to wait too long or because the company insists on collecting all their personal details each time they call, the value of inventories seems undisputable. The task of operations management is to allow inventory to accumulate only when its benefits outweigh its disadvantages. The following are some of the benefits of inventory.

Physical inventory is an insurance against uncertainty Inventory can act as a buffer against unexpected fluctuations in supply and demand. For example, a retail operation can never forecast demand perfectly over the lead-time. It will order goods from its suppliers such that there is always a minimum level of inventory to cover against the possibility that demand will be greater than expected during the time taken to deliver the goods. This is buffer, or safety, inventory. It can also compensate for the uncertainties in the process of the supply of goods into the store. The same applies with the output inventories, which is why hospitals always have a supply of blood, sutures and bandages for immediate response to Accident and Emergency patients. Similarly, auto-servicing services, factories and airlines may hold selected critical spare parts inventories so that

> **✳ Operations principle**
>
> Inventory should only accumulate when the advantages of having it outweigh its disadvantages.

Table 12.2 Some reasons to avoid inventories

	'Inventories'		
	Physical inventories	*Queues of customers*	*Digital information in databases*
Cost	Ties up working capital and there could be high administrative and insurance costs	Primarily time-cost to the customer, i.e. wastes customers' time	Cost of set-up, access, updating and maintenance
Space	Requires storage space	Requires areas for waiting or phone lines for held calls	Requires memory capacity. May require secure and/or special environment
Quality	May deteriorate over time, become damaged or obsolete	May upset customers if they have to wait too long. May lose customers	Data may be corrupted or lost or become obsolete
Operational/ organizational	May hide problems (see lean synchronization – Chapter 15)	May put undue pressure on the staff and so quality is compromised for throughput	Databases need constant management; access control, updating and security

maintenance staff can repair the most common faults without delay. Again, inventory is being used as an 'insurance' against unpredictable events.

Physical inventory can counteract a lack of flexibility Where a wide range of customer options is offered, unless the operation is perfectly flexible, stock will be needed to ensure supply when it is engaged on other activities. This is sometimes called cycle inventory. For example, Figure 12.3 shows the inventory profile of a baker who makes three types of bread. Because of the nature of the mixing and baking process, only one kind of bread can be produced at any time. The baker will have to produce each type of bread in batches large enough to satisfy the demand for each kind of bread between the times when each batch is ready for sale. So, even when demand is steady and predictable, there will always be some inventory to compensate for the intermittent supply of each type of bread.

Physical inventory allows operations to take advantage of short-term opportunities Sometimes opportunities arise that necessitate accumulating inventory, even when there is no immediate demand for it. For example, a supplier may be offering a particularly good deal on selected items for a limited time period, perhaps because they want to reduce their own finished goods inventories. Under these circumstances a purchasing department may opportunistically take advantage of the short-term price advantage.

Physical inventory can be used to anticipate future demands Medium-term capacity management (covered in Chapter 11) may use inventory to cope with demand. Rather than trying to make a product (such as chocolate) only when it is needed, it is produced throughout the year ahead of demand and put into inventory until it is needed. This type of inventory is called anticipation inventory and is most commonly used when demand fluctuations are large but relatively predictable.

Physical inventory can reduce overall costs Holding relatively large inventories may bring savings that are greater than the cost of holding the inventory. This may be when bulk-buying gets the lowest possible cost of inputs, or when large order quantities reduce both the number of orders placed and the associated costs of administration and material handling. This is the basis of the 'economic order quantity' (EOQ) approach that will be treated later in this chapter.

Physical inventory can increase in value Sometimes the items held as inventory can increase in value and so become an investment. For example, dealers in fine wines are less reluctant to hold inventory than dealers in wine that does not get better with age. (However, it can be argued that keeping fine wines until they are at their peak is really part of the overall process rather than inventory as such.) A more obvious example is inventories of money. The many financial processes within most organizations will try to maximize the inventory of cash they hold because it is earning them interest.

Figure 12.3 Cycle inventory in a bakery

Physical inventory fills the processing 'pipeline' 'Pipeline' inventory exists because transformed resources cannot be moved instantaneously between the point of supply and the point of demand. When a retail store places an order, its supplier will 'allocate' the stock to the retail store in its own warehouse, pack it, load it onto its truck, transport it to its destination, and unload it into the retailer's inventory. From the time that stock is allocated (and therefore it is unavailable to any other customer) to the time it becomes available for the retail store, it is pipeline inventory. Especially in geographically dispersed supply networks, pipeline inventory can be substantial.

Queues of customers help balance capacity and demand This is especially useful if the main service resource is expensive, for example doctors, consultants, lawyers, or expensive equipment such as CAT scans. By waiting a short time after their arrival, and creating a queue of customers, the service always has customers to process. This is also helpful where arrival times are less predictable, for example where an appointment system is not used or not possible.

Queues of customers enable prioritization In cases where resources are fixed and customers are entering the system with different levels of priority, the formation of a queue allows the organization to serve urgent customers while keeping other less urgent ones waiting. In some circumstances it is not unusual to have to wait 3–4 hours for treatment in an Accident and Emergency ward, with more urgent cases 'jumping the queue' for treatment.

Queuing gives customers time to choose Time spent in a queue gives customers time to decide what products/services they require; for example, customers waiting in a fast-food restaurant have time to look at the menu so that when they get to the counter they are ready to make their order without holding up the server.

Queues enable efficient use of resources By allowing queues to form customers can be batched together to make efficient use of operational resources. For example, a queue for an elevator makes better use of its capacity; in an airport, by calling customers to the gate, staff can load the aircraft more efficiently and quickly.

Databases provide efficient multi-level access Databases are relatively cheap ways of storing information and providing many people with access, although there may be restrictions or different levels of access. The doctor's receptionist will be able to call up your records to check your name and address and make an appointment; the doctor will then be able to call up the appointment and your medical records; the pharmacist will be able to call up your name and prescriptions and cross-check for other prescriptions and known allergies, etc.

Databases of information allow single data capture There is no need to capture data at every transaction with a customer or supplier, though checks may be required.

Databases of information speed the process Amazon, for example, stores, if you agree, your delivery address and credit card information so that purchases can be made with a single click, making it fast and easy for the customer.

Reducing physical inventory

The objective of most operations managers who manage physical inventories is to reduce the overall level (and/or cost) of inventory whilst maintaining an acceptable level of customer service. Table 12.3 below identifies some of the ways in which inventory may be reduced.

The effect of inventory on return on assets

One can summarize the effects on the financial performance of an operation by looking at how some of the factors of inventory management impact on 'return on assets', a key financial performance measure. Figure 12.4 shows some of these factors.

Table 12.3 Some ways in which physical inventory may be reduced

Reason for holding inventory	Example	How inventory could be reduced
As an insurance against uncertainty	Safety stocks for when demand or supply is not perfectly predictable	• Improve demand forecasting • Tighten supply, e.g. through service level penalties
To counteract a lack of flexibility	Cycle stock to maintain supply when other products are being made	• Increase flexibility of processes, e.g. by reducing changeover times (see Chapter 11) • Using parallel processes producing output simultaneously (see Chapter 7)
To take advantage of relatively short-term opportunities	Suppliers offer 'time limited' special low-cost offers	• Persuade suppliers to adopt 'everyday low prices' (see Chapter 13)
To anticipate future demands	Build up stocks in low demand periods for use in high demand periods	• Increase volume flexibility by moving towards a 'chase demand' plan (see Chapter 11)
To reduce overall costs	Purchasing a batch of products in order to save delivery and administration costs	• Reduce administration costs through purchasing process efficiency gains • Investigate alternative delivery channels that reduce transport costs
To fill the processing 'pipeline'	Items being delivered to customer	• Reduce process time between customer request and dispatch of items • Reduce throughput time in the downstream supply chain (see Chapter 13)

- Inventory governs the operation's ability to supply its customers. The absence of inventory means that customers are not satisfied with the possibility of reduced revenue.
- Inventory may become obsolete as alternatives become available, or could be damaged, deteriorate, or simply get lost. This increases costs (because resources have been wasted) and reduces revenue (because the obsolete, damaged or lost items cannot be sold).
- Inventory incurs storage costs (leasing space, maintaining appropriate conditions, etc.). This could be high if items are hazardous to store (for example, flammable solvents, explosives, chemicals) or difficult to store requiring special facilities (for example, frozen food).
- Inventory involves administrative and insurance costs. Every time a delivery is ordered, time and costs are incurred.

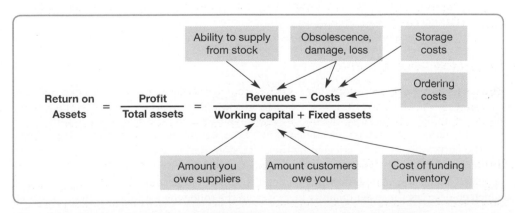

Figure 12.4 Inventory management has a significant effect on return on assets

- Inventory ties up money, in the form of working capital, which is therefore unavailable for other uses, such as reducing borrowings or making investment in productive fixed assets (we shall expand on the idea of working capital later).

- Inventory contracts with suppliers can dictate the timing of when suppliers need to be paid. If they require paying before the operation receives payment from *its* customers (as is normal), the difference between the amount the operation owes suppliers and the amount suppliers owe the operation adds to working capital requirements.

Day-to-day inventory decisions

Wherever inventory accumulates, operations managers need to manage the day-to-day tasks of managing inventory. Orders will be received from internal or external customers; these will be dispatched and demand will gradually deplete the inventory. Orders will need to be placed for replenishment of the stocks; deliveries will arrive and require storing. In managing the system, operations managers are involved in three major types of decision:

- *How much to order*. Every time a replenishment order is placed, how big should it be (sometimes called the *volume decision*)?
- *When to order*. At what point in time, or at what level of stock, should the replenishment order be placed (sometimes called the *timing decision*)?
- *How to control the system*. What procedures and routines should be installed to help make these decisions? Should different priorities be allocated to different stock items? How should stock information be stored?

HOW MUCH TO ORDER – THE VOLUME DECISION

To illustrate this decision, consider again the example of the food and drinks we keep at our home. In managing this inventory we implicitly make decisions on *order quantity*, which is how much to purchase at one time. In making this decision we are balancing two sets of costs: the costs associated with going out to purchase the food items and the costs associated with holding the stocks. The option of holding very little or no inventory of food and purchasing each item only when it is needed has the advantage that it requires little money since purchases are made only when needed. However, it would involve purchasing provisions several times a day, which is inconvenient. At the very opposite extreme, making one journey to the local superstore every few months and purchasing all the provisions we would need until our next visit reduces the time and costs incurred in making the purchase but requires a very large amount of money each time the trip is made – money which could otherwise be in the bank and earning interest. We might also have to invest in extra cupboard units and a very large freezer. Somewhere between these extremes there will lie an ordering strategy which will minimize the total costs and effort involved in the purchase of food.

Inventory costs

The same principles apply in commercial order-quantity decisions as in the domestic situation. In making a decision on how much to purchase, operations managers must try to identify the costs which will be affected by their decision. Earlier we examined how inventory decisions affect some of the important components of return on assets. Here we take a cost perspective and re-examine these components in order to determine which costs go up and which go down as the order quantity increases. In the following list, the first three costs will decrease as order size is increased, whereas the next four generally increase as order size is increased:

1 *Cost of placing the order*. Every time that an order is placed to replenish stock, a number of transactions are needed which incur costs to the company. These include preparing the order, communicating with suppliers, arranging for delivery, making payment, and maintaining internal records of the transaction. Even if we are placing an 'internal order' on part of our own operation, there are still likely to be the same types of transaction concerned with internal administration.

2 *Price discount costs*. Often suppliers offer discounts for large quantities and cost penalties for small orders.

3 *Stock-out costs*. If we misjudge the order-quantity decision and our inventory runs out of stock, there will be lost revenue (opportunity costs) of failing to supply customers. External customers may take their business elsewhere, internal customers will suffer process inefficiencies.

4 *Working capital costs*. After receiving a replenishment order, the supplier will demand payment. Of course, eventually, after we supply our own customers, we in turn will receive payment. However, there will probably be a lag between paying our suppliers and receiving payment from our customers. During this time we will have to fund the costs of inventory. This is called the *working capital* of inventory. The costs associated with it are the interest we pay the bank for borrowing it, or the opportunity costs of not investing it elsewhere.

5 *Storage costs*. These are the costs associated with physically storing the goods. Renting, heating and lighting the warehouse, as well as insuring the inventory, can be expensive, especially when special conditions are required, such as low temperatures or high security.

6 *Obsolescence costs*. When we order large quantities, this usually results in stocked items spending a long time stored in inventory. This increases the risk that the items might either become obsolete (in the case of a change in fashion, for example) or deteriorate with age (in the case of most foodstuffs, for example).

7 *Operating inefficiency costs*. According to just-in-time philosophies, high inventory levels prevent us seeing the full extent of problems within the operation. This argument is fully explored in Chapter 15.

It is worth noting that it may not be the same organization that incurs the costs. For example, sometimes suppliers agree to hold consignment stock. This means that they deliver large quantities of inventory to their customers to store but will only charge for the goods as and when they are used. In the meantime they remain the supplier's property so do not have to be financed by the customer, who does however provide storage facilities.

Inventory profiles

An inventory profile is a visual representation of the inventory level over time. Figure 12.5 shows a simplified inventory profile for one particular stock item in a retail operation. Every time an order is placed, Q items are ordered. The replenishment order arrives in one batch instantaneously. Demand for the item is then steady and perfectly predictable at a rate of D units per month. When demand has depleted the stock of the items entirely, another order of Q items instantaneously arrives, and so on. Under these circumstances:

The average inventory $= \dfrac{Q}{2}$ (because the two shaded areas in Fig 12.5 are equal)

The time interval between deliveries $= \dfrac{Q}{D}$

The frequency of deliveries $=$ the reciprocal of the time interval $= \dfrac{D}{Q}$

Figure 12.5 Inventory profiles chart the variation in inventory level

Mountains of grit[2]

Students of operations management from Singapore to Saudi Arabia will perhaps not have a full appreciation of how important this decision is in the colder parts of the world, but, believe me, road gritting is big news every winter where snow and ice can cause huge disruption to everyday life. But not every time it snows, and more interestingly, not every*where* it snows. The local government authorities around northern Europe and America differ significantly in how well they cope with freezing weather, usually by spreading grit (actually rock salt, a mixture of salt and grit) on the roads. So how do the authorities decide how much grit to stock up in preparation for winter, and when to spread it on the

roads? For example, in the UK, when snow is forecast, potential trouble spots are identified by networks of sensors embedded in the road surface to measure climatic conditions. Each sensor is connected by cable or mobile phone technology to an automatic weather station by the roadside. The siting of the sensors is important. They must be sited either on a representative stretch of road (no nearby trees, buildings or bridges, which offer some protection from the cold), or traditional cold spots. The weather stations then beam back data about air and road temperatures, wind speed and direction, and the wetness of roads. Salt levels are also measured to ensure that grit already spread has not been blown away by wind or washed away by rain. It has been known for cold weather to be forecast and the gritting trucks to be dispatched, only for the weather to change, with snow

turning to rain, which washed away the grit. Then when temperatures suddenly drop again the rain freezes on the road. But forecasting how much grit will be needed is even more difficult. Long-range weather forecasts are notoriously inaccurate, so no one knows just how bad a coming winter will be. To make matters worse, the need for road grit depends on more than just the total volume of snow. Local authorities can use the same amount of salt on one 30-cm snowfall as one 5-cm snowfall. Furthermore, the number of snowy days is important in determining how much grit will be needed. In the skiing areas of central Europe, most winter days will have snow predictably, while parts of the UK could have little or no snow one winter and many weeks of snow the next.

Supplies of road grit can also vary, as can its price. There are many reasons for this. Mainly of course, if a bad winter is forecast, all authorities in an area will want to buy the same grit, which will reduce supply and put prices up. Also salt mines can flood, especially in winter. Nor is it cheap to transport grit from one area to another; it is a low-value but heavy material. As a consequence some authorities organize purchasing groups to get better prices before the season starts. Getting more salt during the season may be possible but prices are higher and supply is not guaranteed. In addition, an authority has to decide how fast to use up its inventory of grit. At the start of the winter period, authorities may be cautious about gritting because, once used, the grit cannot be used again, and who knows what the weather will be like later in the season. But in the final analysis the decision of how large an inventory of grit to buy and how to use it is a balance between risks and consequences. Build up too big an inventory of grit and it may not all be used, with the cost of carrying it over to next year being borne by local taxpayers. Build up too small an inventory and incur the wrath of local voters when the roads are difficult to negotiate. Of course a perfect weather forecast would help!

The economic order quantity (EOQ) formula

The most common approach to deciding how much of any particular item to order when stock needs replenishing is called the economic order quantity (EOQ) approach. This approach attempts to find the best balance between the advantages and disadvantages of holding stock. For example, Figure 12.6 shows two alternative order-quantity policies for an item. Plan A, represented by the unbroken line, involves ordering in quantities of 400 at a time. Demand in this case is running at 1,000 units per year. Plan B, represented by the dotted line, uses smaller but more frequent replenishment orders. This time only 100 are ordered at a time, with orders being placed four times as often. However, the average inventory for plan B is one-quarter of that for plan A.

To find out whether either of these plans, or some other plan, minimizes the total cost of stocking the item, we need some further information, namely the total cost of holding one unit in stock for a period of time (C_h) and the total costs of placing an order (C_o). Generally, holding costs are taken into account by including:

- working capital costs
- storage costs
- obsolescence risk costs.

Order costs are calculated by taking into account:

- cost of placing the order (including transportation of items from suppliers if relevant);
- price discount costs.

Figure 12.6 Two alternative inventory plans with different order quantities (Q)

In this case the cost of holding stocks is calculated at £1 per item per year and the cost of placing an order is calculated at £20 per order.

We can now calculate total holding costs and ordering costs for any particular ordering plan as follows:

$$\text{Holding costs} = \text{holding cost/unit} \times \text{average inventory}$$

$$= C_h \times \frac{Q}{2}$$

$$\text{Ordering costs} = \text{ordering cost} \times \text{number of orders per period}$$

$$= C_o \times \frac{D}{Q}$$

$$\text{So, total cost, } C_t = \frac{C_h Q}{2} + \frac{C_o D}{Q}$$

We can now calculate the costs of adopting plans with different order quantities. These are illustrated in Table 12.4. As we would expect with low values of Q, holding costs are low but the costs of placing orders are high because orders have to be placed very frequently. As Q increases, the holding costs increase but the costs of placing orders decrease. Initially the decrease in ordering costs is greater than the increase in holding costs and the total cost falls. After a point, however, the decrease in ordering costs slows, whereas the increase in holding costs remains constant and the total cost starts to increase. In this case the order quantity, Q, which minimizes the sum of holding and order costs, is 200. This 'optimum' order quantity is called the *economic order quantity* (*EOQ*). This is illustrated graphically in Figure 12.7.

A more elegant method of finding the EOQ is to derive its general expression. This can be done using simple differential calculus as follows. From before:

$$\text{Total cost} = \text{holding cost} + \text{order cost}$$

$$C_t = \frac{C_h Q}{2} + \frac{C_o D}{Q}$$

The rate of change of total cost is given by the first differential of C_t with respect to Q:

$$\frac{dC_t}{dQ} = \frac{C_h}{2} - \frac{C_o D}{Q^2}$$

Table 12.4 **Costs of adoption of plans with different order quantities**

Demand (D) = 1,000 units per year Order costs (C₀) = £20 per order			Holding costs (Cₕ) = £1 per item per year		
Order quantity (Q)	Holding costs (0.5Q × C_h)	+	Order costs ((D/Q) × C_o)	=	Total costs
50	25		$20 \times 20 = 400$		425
100	50		$10 \times 20 = 200$		250
150	75		$6.7 \times 20 = 134$		209
200	100		$5 \times 20 = 100$		200*
250	125		$4 \times 20 = 80$		205
300	150		$3.3 \times 20 = 66$		216
350	175		$2.9 \times 20 = 58$		233
400	200		$2.5 \times 20 = 50$		250

* Minimum total cost.

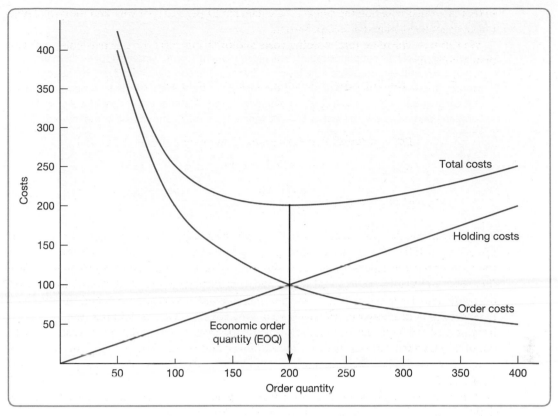

Figure 12.7 Graphical representation of the economic order quantity

The lowest cost will occur when $\dfrac{dC_t}{dQ} = 0$, that is:

$$0 = \frac{C_h}{2} - \frac{C_o D}{Q_o^2}$$

where Q_o = the EOQ. Rearranging this expression gives:

$$Q_o = \text{EOQ} = \sqrt{\frac{2C_o D}{C_h}}$$

When using the EOQ:

$$\text{Time between orders} = \frac{\text{EOQ}}{D}$$

$$\text{Order frequency} = \frac{D}{\text{EOQ}} \text{ per period}$$

Sensitivity of the EOQ

Examination of the graphical representation of the total cost curve in Figure 12.7 shows that, although there is a single value of Q which minimizes total costs, any relatively small deviation from the EOQ will not increase total costs significantly. In other words, costs will be near-optimum provided a value of Q which is reasonably close to the EOQ is chosen. Put another way, small errors in estimating either holding costs or order costs will not result in a significant deviation from the EOQ. This is a particularly convenient phenomenon because, in practice, both holding and order costs are not easy to estimate accurately.

> *** Operations principle**
>
> For any stock replenishment activity there is a theoretical 'optimum' order quantity that minimizes total inventory-related costs.

A building materials supplier obtains its bagged cement from a single supplier. Demand is reasonably constant throughout the year, and last year the company sold 2,000 tonnes of this product. It estimates the costs of placing an order at around £25 each time an order is placed, and calculates that the annual cost of holding inventory is 20 per cent of purchase cost. The company purchases the cement at £60 per tonne. How much should the company order at a time?

$$\text{EOQ for cement} = \sqrt{\frac{2C_oD}{C_h}}$$

$$= \sqrt{\frac{2 \times 25 \times 2{,}000}{0.2 \times 60}}$$

$$= \sqrt{\frac{100{,}000}{12}}$$

$$= 91.287 \text{ tonnes}$$

After calculating the EOQ the operations manager feels that placing an order for 91.287 tonnes *exactly* seems somewhat over-precise. Why not order a convenient 100 tonnes?

Total cost of ordering plan for Q = 91.287:

$$= \frac{C_hQ}{2} + \frac{C_oD}{Q}$$

$$= \frac{(0.2 \times 60) \times 91.287}{2} + \frac{25 \times 2{,}000}{91.287}$$

$$= £1{,}095.454$$

Total cost of ordering plan for Q = 100:

$$= \frac{(0.2 \times 60) \times 100}{2} + \frac{25 \times 2{,}000}{100}$$

$$= £1{,}100$$

The extra cost of ordering 100 tonnes at a time is £1,100 − £1095.45 = £4.55. The operations manager therefore should feel confident in using the more convenient order quantity.

Gradual replacement – the economic batch quantity (EBQ) model

Although the simple inventory profile shown in Figure 12.5 made some simplifying assumptions, it is broadly applicable in most situations where each complete replacement order arrives at one point in time. In many cases, however, replenishment occurs over a time period rather than in one lot. A typical example of this is where an internal order is placed for a batch of parts to be produced on a machine. The machine will start to produce the parts and ship them in a more or less continuous stream into inventory, but at the same time demand is continuing to remove parts from the inventory. Provided the rate at which parts are being made and put into the inventory (P) is higher than the rate at which demand is depleting the inventory (D) then the size of the inventory will increase. After the batch has been completed the machine will be reset (to produce some other part), and demand will continue to deplete the inventory level until production of the next batch begins. The resulting profile is shown in Figure 12.8. Such a profile is typical for cycle inventories supplied by batch processes, where

Figure 12.8 Inventory profile for gradual replacement of inventory

items are produced internally and intermittently. For this reason the minimum-cost batch quantity for this profile is called the economic batch quantity (EBQ). It is also sometimes known as the economic manufacturing quantity (EMQ), or the production order quantity (POQ). It is derived as follows:

$$\text{Maximum stock level} = M$$

$$\text{Slope of inventory build-up} = P - D$$

Also, as is clear from Figure 12.8:

$$\text{Slope of inventory build-up} = M \div \frac{Q}{P}$$

$$= \frac{MP}{Q}$$

So,

$$\frac{MP}{Q} = P - D$$

$$M = \frac{Q(P - Q)}{P}$$

$$\text{Average inventory level} = \frac{M}{2}$$

$$= \frac{Q(P - D)}{2P}$$

As before:

$$\text{Total cost} = \text{holding cost} + \text{order cost}$$

$$C_t = \frac{C_h Q(P - D)}{2P} + \frac{C_o D}{Q}$$

$$\frac{dC_t}{dQ} = \frac{C_h(P - D)}{2P} - \frac{C_o D}{Q^2}$$

Again, equating to zero and solving Q gives the minimum-cost order quantity EBQ:

$$\text{EBQ} = \sqrt{\frac{2C_o D}{C_h(1 - (D/P))}}$$

Worked example

The manager of a bottle-filling plant which bottles soft drinks needs to decide how long a 'run' of each type of drink to process. Demand for each type of drink is reasonably constant at 80,000 per month (a month has 160 production hours). The bottling lines fill at a rate of 3,000 bottles per hour, but take an hour to clean and reset between different drinks. The cost (of labour and lost production capacity) of each of these changeovers has been calculated at £100 per hour. Stock-holding costs are counted at £0.1 per bottle per month.

$$D = 80{,}000 \text{ per month}$$

$$= 500 \text{ per hour}$$

$$\text{EBQ} = \sqrt{\frac{2C_o D}{C_h(1 - (D/P))}}$$

$$= \sqrt{\frac{2 \times 100 \times 80{,}000}{0.1(1 - (500/3{,}000))}}$$

$$\text{EBQ} = 13{,}856$$

The staff who operate the lines have devised a method of reducing the changeover time from 1 hour to 30 minutes. How would that change the EBQ?

$$\text{New } C_o = £50$$

$$\text{New EBQ} = \sqrt{\frac{2 \times 50 \times 80{,}000}{0.1(1 - (500/3{,}000))}}$$

$$= 9{,}798$$

Critical commentary

The approach to determining order quantity which involves optimizing costs of holding stock against costs of ordering stock, typified by the EOQ and EBQ models, has always been subject to criticisms. Originally these concerned the validity of some of the assumptions of the model; more recently they have involved the underlying rationale of the approach itself. The criticisms fall into four broad categories, all of which we shall examine further:

● The assumptions included in the EOQ models are simplistic.
● The real costs of stock in operations are not as assumed in EOQ models.
● The models are really descriptive, and should not be used as prescriptive devices.
● Cost minimization is not an appropriate objective for inventory management.

Responding to the criticisms of EOQ

In order to keep EOQ-type models relatively straightforward, it was necessary to make assumptions. These concerned such things as the stability of demand, the existence of a fixed and identifiable ordering cost, that the cost of stock holding can be expressed by a linear function, shortage costs which were identifiable, and so on. While these assumptions are rarely strictly true, most of them can approximate to reality. Furthermore, the shape of the total cost curve has a relatively flat optimum point which means that small errors will not significantly affect the total cost of a near-optimum order quantity. However, at times the assumptions do pose severe limitations to the models. For example, the assumption of steady demand (or even demand which conforms to some known probability distribution) is untrue for a wide range of the operation's inventory problems. For example, a bookseller might be very happy to adopt an EOQ-type ordering policy for some of its most regular and stable products such as dictionaries and popular reference books. However, the demand patterns for many other books could be highly erratic, dependent on critics' reviews and word-of-mouth recommendations. In such circumstances it is simply inappropriate to use EOQ models.

Cost of stock

Other questions surround some of the assumptions made concerning the nature of stock-related costs. For example, placing an order with a supplier as part of a regular and multi-item order might be relatively inexpensive, whereas asking for a special one-off delivery of an item could prove far more costly. Similarly with stock-holding costs – although many companies make a standard percentage charge on the purchase price of stock items, this might not be appropriate over a wide range of stock-holding levels. The marginal costs of increasing stock-holding levels might be merely the cost of the working capital involved. On the other hand, it might necessitate the construction or lease of a whole new stock-holding facility such as a warehouse. Operations managers using an EOQ-type approach must check that the decisions implied by the use of the formulae do not exceed the boundaries within which the cost assumptions apply. Later (in Chapter 15) we explore the just-in-time approach that sees inventory as being largely negative. However, it is useful at this stage to examine the effect on an EOQ approach of regarding inventory as being more costly than previously believed. Increasing the slope of the holding cost line increases the level of total costs of *any* order quantity, but more significantly, shifts the minimum cost point substantially to the left, in favour of a lower economic order quantity. In other words, the less willing an operation is to hold stock on the grounds of cost, the more it should move towards smaller, more frequent ordering.

Using EOQ models as prescriptions

Perhaps the most fundamental criticism of the EOQ approach again comes from the Japanese-inspired 'lean' and JIT philosophies. The EOQ tries to optimize order decisions. Implicitly the costs involved are taken as fixed, in the sense that the task of operations managers is to find out what the true costs are rather than to change them in any way. EOQ is essentially a reactive approach. Some critics would argue that it fails to ask the right question. Rather than asking the EOQ question of 'What is the optimum order quantity?' operations managers should really be asking, 'How can I change the operation in some way so as to reduce the overall level of inventory I need to hold?' The EOQ approach may be a reasonable description of stock-holding costs but should not necessarily be taken as a strict prescription over what decisions to take. For example, many organizations have made considerable efforts to reduce the effective cost of placing an order. Often they have done this by working to reduce changeover times on machines. This means that less time is taken changing over from one product to the other, and therefore less operating capacity is lost, which in turn reduces the cost of the changeover. Under these circumstances, the order cost curve in the EOQ formula reduces and, in turn, reduces the effective economic order quantity. Figure 12.9 shows the EOQ formula represented graphically with increased holding costs (*see* the previous discussion) and reduced order costs. The net effect of this is to significantly reduce the value of the EOQ.

Should the cost of inventory be minimized?

Many organizations (such as supermarkets and wholesalers) make the most of their revenue and profits simply by holding and supplying inventory. Because their main investment is in the inventory it is critical that they make a good return on this capital, by ensuring that it has the highest possible 'stock turn' (defined later in this chapter) and/or gross profit margin. Alternatively, they may also be concerned to maximize the use of space by seeking to maximize the profit earned per square metre. The EOQ model does not address these objectives. Similarly, for products that deteriorate or go out of fashion, the EOQ model can result in excess inventory of slower-moving items. In fact the EOQ model is rarely used in such organizations,

Figure 12.9 If the true costs of stock holding are taken into account, and if the cost of ordering (or changeover) is reduced, the economic order quantity (EOQ) is much smaller

and there is more likely to be a system of periodic review (described later) for regular ordering of replenishment inventory. For example, a typical builders' supply merchant might carry around 50,000 different items of stock (SKUs). However, most of these cluster into larger families of items such as paints, sanitary ware, or metal fixings. Single orders are placed at regular intervals for all the required replenishments in the supplier's range, and these are then delivered together at one time. For example, if such deliveries were made weekly, then on average, the individual item order quantities will be for only one week's usage. Less popular items, or ones with erratic demand patterns, can be individually ordered at the same time, or (when urgent) can be delivered the next day by carrier.

SHORT CASE | Howard Smith Paper Group[3]

The Howard Smith Paper Group operates the most advanced warehousing operation within the European paper merchanting sector, delivering over 120,000 tonnes of paper annually. The function of a paper merchant is to provide the link between the paper mills and the printers or converters. This is illustrated in Figure 12.10. It is a sales- and service-driven business, so the role of the operation function is to deliver whatever the salesperson has promised to the customer. Usually, this means precisely the right product at the right time at the right place and in the right quantity. The company's operations are divided into two areas: 'logistics' that combines all warehousing and logistics tasks, and 'supply side' that includes inventory planning, purchasing and merchandising decisions.

Its main stocks are held at the national distribution centre, located in Northampton in the middle part of the UK. This location was chosen because it is at the centre of the company's main customer location and also because it has good access to motorways. The key to any efficient merchanting operation lies in its ability to do three things well. First, it must efficiently store the desired volume of required inventory. Second, it must have a 'goods inward' programme that sources the required volume of desired inventory. Third, it must be able to fulfil customer orders by 'picking' the desired goods fast and accurately from its warehouse. The warehouse is operational 24 hours per day, 5 days per week. A total of 52 staff are employed in the warehouse, including maintenance and cleaning staff. Skill sets are not an issue, since all pickers are trained for all tasks. This facilitates easier capacity management, since pickers can be deployed where most urgently needed. Contract labour is used on occasions, although this is less effective because the staff tend to be less motivated, and have to learn the job.

At the heart of the company's operations is a warehouse known as a 'dark warehouse'. All picking and movement within the dark warehouse is fully automatic and there is no need for any person to enter the high bay stores and picking area. The important difference with this warehouse operation is that pallets are brought to the pickers. Conventional paper merchants send pickers with handling equipment into the warehouse aisles for stock. A warehouse computer system (WCS) controls the whole operation without the need for human input. It manages pallet location and retrieval, robotic crane missions, automatic conveyors, bar-code label production and scanning, and all picking routines and priorities. It also calculates operator activity and productivity measures, as well as issuing documentation and planning transportation schedules.

The fact that all product is identified by a unique bar code means that accuracy is guaranteed. The unique user log-on ensures that any picking errors can be traced back to the name of the picker, to ensure further errors do not occur. The WCS is linked to the company's ERP system (we will deal with ERP in Chapter 14), such that once the order has been placed by a customer, computers manage the whole process from order placement to order dispatch.

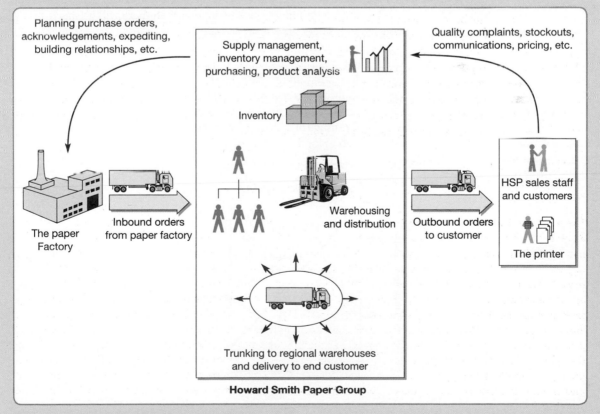

Figure 12.10 The role of the paper merchant

WHEN TO PLACE AN ORDER – THE TIMING DECISION

When we assumed that orders arrived instantaneously and demand was steady and predictable, the decision on when to place a replenishment order was self-evident. An order would be placed as soon as the stock level reached zero. This would arrive instantaneously and prevent any stock-out occurring. If replenishment orders do not arrive instantaneously, but have a lag between the order being placed and it arriving in the inventory, we can calculate the timing of a replacement order, as shown in Figure 12.11. The lead time for an order to arrive is in this case two weeks, so the re-order point (ROP) is the point at which stock will fall to zero minus the order lead time. Alternatively, we can define the point in terms of the level which the inventory will have reached when a replenishment order needs to be placed. In this case this occurs at a re-order level (ROL) of 200 items.

However, this assumes that both the demand and the order lead time are perfectly predictable. In most cases, of course, this is not so. Both demand and the order lead time are likely to vary to produce a profile which looks something like that in Figure 12.12. In these circumstances it is necessary to make the replenishment order somewhat earlier than would be the case in a purely deterministic situation. This will result in, on average, some stock still being in the inventory when the replenishment order arrives. This is buffer (safety) stock. The earlier the replenishment order is placed, the higher will be the expected level of safety stock (s) when the replenishment order arrives. But because of the variability of both lead time (t) and demand rate (d), there will sometimes be a higher-than-average level of safety stock and sometimes lower. The main consideration in setting safety stock is not so much the average level of stock when a replenishment order arrives but rather the probability that the stock will not have run out before the replenishment order arrives.

The key statistic in calculating how much safety stock to allow is the probability distribution which shows the lead-time usage. The lead-time usage distribution is a combination of the distributions which describe lead-time variation and the demand rate during the lead time. If safety stock is set below the lower limit of this distribution then there will be shortages every single replenishment cycle. If safety stock is set above the upper limit of the distribution, there

is no chance of stock-outs occurring. Usually, safety stock is set to give a predetermined likelihood that stock-outs will not occur. Figure 12.12 shows that, in this case, the first replenishment order arrived after t_1, resulting in a lead-time usage of d_1. The second replenishment order took longer, t_2, and demand rate was also higher, resulting in a lead-time usage of d_2. The third order cycle shows several possible inventory profiles for different conditions of lead-time usage and demand rate.

Figure 12.11 Re-order level (ROL) and re-order point (ROP) are derived from the order lead time and demand rate

Figure 12.12 Safety stock (*s*) helps to avoid stock-outs when demand and/or order lead time are uncertain

Worked example

A company which imports running shoes for sale in its sports shops can never be certain of how long, after placing an order, the delivery will take. Examination of previous orders reveals that out of 10 orders: one took one week, two took two weeks, four took three weeks, two took four weeks and one took five weeks. The rate of demand for the shoes also varies between 110 pairs per week and 140 pairs per week. There is a 0.2 probability of the demand rate being either 110 or 140 pairs per week, and a 0.3 chance of demand being either 120 or 130 pairs per week. The company needs to decide when it should place replenishment orders if the probability of a stock-out is to be less than 10 per cent.

Both lead time and the demand rate during the lead time will contribute to the lead-time usage. So the distributions which describe each will need to be combined. Figure 12.13 and

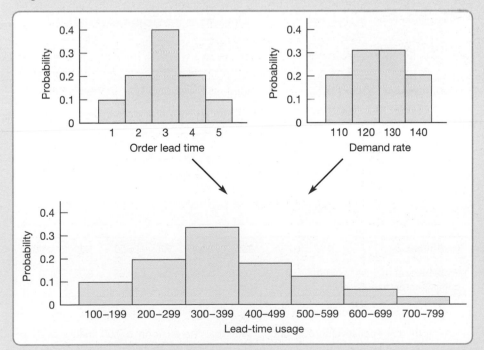

Figure 12.13 The probability distributions for order lead time and demand rate combine to give the lead-time usage distribution

Table 12.5 show how this can be done. Taking lead time to be either one, two, three, four or five weeks, and demand rate to be either 110, 120, 130 or 140 pairs per week, and also assuming the two variables to be independent, the distributions can be combined as shown in Table 12.5. Each element in the matrix shows a possible lead-time usage with the probability of its occurrence. So if the lead time is one week and the demand rate is 110 pairs per week, the actual lead-time usage will be $1 \times 110 = 110$ pairs. Since there is a 0.1 chance of the lead time being one week, and a 0.2 chance of demand rate being 110 pairs per week, the probability of both these events occurring is $0.1 \times 0.2 = 0.02$.

Table 12.5 Matrix of lead-time and demand-rate probabilities

			Lead-time probabilities				
			1	2	3	4	5
			0.1	0.2	0.4	0.2	0.1
Demand-rate probabilities	110	0.2	110 (0.02)	220 (0.04)	330 (0.08)	440 (0.04)	550 (0.02)
	120	0.3	120 (0.03)	240 (0.06)	360 (0.12)	480 (0.06)	600 (0.03)
	130	0.3	130 (0.03)	260 (0.06)	390 (0.12)	520 (0.06)	650 (0.03)
	140	0.2	140 (0.02)	280 (0.04)	420 (0.08)	560 (0.04)	700 (0.02)

We can now classify the possible lead-time usages into histogram form. For example, summing the probabilities of all the lead-time usages which fall within the range 100–199 (all the first column) gives a combined probability of 0.1. Repeating this for subsequent intervals results in Table 12.6.

Table 12.6 Combined probabilities

Lead-time usage	100–199	200–299	300–399	400–499	500–599	600–699	700–799
Probability	0.1	0.2	0.32	0.18	0.12	0.06	0.02

This shows the probability of each possible range of lead-time usage occurring, but it is the cumulative probabilities that are needed to predict the likelihood of stock-out (*see* Table 12.7).

Table 12.7 Combined probabilities

Lead-time usage X	100	200	300	400	500	600	700	800
Probability of usage being greater than X	1.0	0.9	0.7	0.38	0.2	0.08	0.02	0

Setting the re-order level at 600 would mean that there is only a 0.08 chance of usage being greater than available inventory during the lead time, i.e. there is a less than 10 per cent chance of a stock-out occurring.

Continuous and periodic review

The approach we have described to making the replenishment timing decision is often called the continuous review approach. This is because, to make the decision in this way, there must be a process to review the stock level of each item continuously and then place an order when the stock level reaches its re-order level. The virtue of this approach is that, although the timing of orders may be irregular (depending on the variation in demand rate), the order size (Q) is constant and can be set at the optimum economic order quantity. Such continual checking on inventory levels can be time-consuming, especially when there are many stock withdrawals compared with the average level of stock, but in an environment where all inventory records are computerized, this should not be a problem unless the records are inaccurate.

An alternative and far simpler approach, but one which sacrifices the use of a fixed (and therefore possibly optimum) order quantity, is called the periodic review approach. Here, rather than ordering at a predetermined re-order level, the periodic approach orders at a fixed and regular time interval. So the stock level of an item could be found, for example, at the end of every month and a replenishment order placed to bring the stock up to a predetermined level. This level is calculated to cover demand between the replenishment order being placed and the following replenishment order arriving. Figure 12.14 illustrates the parameters for the periodic review approach.

At time T_1 in Figure 12.14 the inventory manager would examine the stock level and order sufficient to bring it up to some maximum, Q_m. However, that order of Q_1 items will not arrive until a further time of t_1 has passed, during which demand continues to deplete the stocks. Again, both demand and lead time are uncertain. The Q_1 items will arrive and bring the stock up to some level lower than Q_m (unless there has been no demand during t_1). Demand then continues until T_2, when again an order Q_2 is placed which is the difference between the current stock at T_2 and Q_m. This order arrives after t_2, by which time demand has depleted the stocks further. Thus the replenishment order placed at T_1 must be able to cover for the demand which occurs until T_2 and t_2. Safety stocks will need to be calculated, in a similar manner to before, based on the distribution of usage over this period.

The time interval

The interval between placing orders, t_1, is usually calculated on a deterministic basis, and derived from the EOQ. So, for example, if the demand for an item is 2,000 per year, the cost of placing an order £25, and the cost of holding stock £0.5 per item per year:

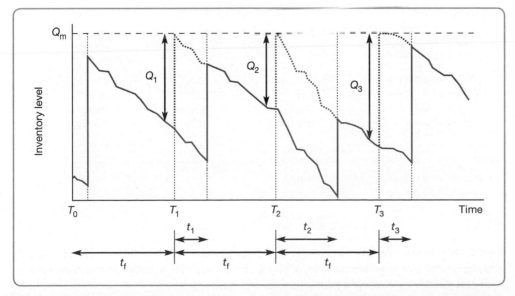

Figure 12.14 A periodic review approach to order timing with probabilistic demand and lead time

$$EOQ = \sqrt{\frac{2C_oD}{C_h}} = \sqrt{\frac{2 \times 2,000 \times 25}{0.5}} = 447$$

The optimum time interval between orders, t_f, is therefore:

$$t_f = \frac{EOQ}{D} = \frac{447}{2,000} \text{ years}$$

$$= 2.68 \text{ months}$$

It may seem paradoxical to calculate the time interval assuming constant demand when demand is, in fact, uncertain. However, uncertainties in both demand and lead time can be allowed for by setting Q_m to allow for the desired probability of stock-out based on usage during the period t_f + lead time.

Two-bin and three-bin systems

Keeping track of inventory levels is especially important in continuous review approaches to re-ordering. A simple and obvious method of indicating when the re-order point has been reached is necessary, especially if there are a large number of items to be monitored. The two- and three-bin systems illustrated in Figure 12.15 are such methods. The simple two-bin system involves storing the re-order point quantity plus the safety inventory quantity in the second bin and using parts from the first bin. When the first bin empties, that is the signal to order the next re-order quantity. Sometimes the safety inventory is stored in a third bin (the three-bin system), so it is clear when demand is exceeding that which was expected. Different 'bins' are not always necessary to operate this type of system. For example, a common practice in retail operations is to store the second 'bin' quantity upside-down behind or under the first 'bin' quantity. Orders are then placed when the upside-down items are reached.

 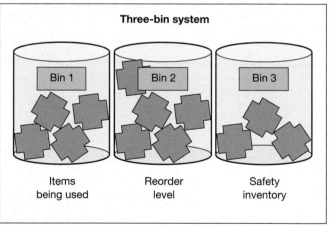

Figure 12.15 The two-bin and three-bin systems of re-ordering

HOW CAN INVENTORY BE CONTROLLED?

The models we have described, even the ones which take a probabilistic view of demand and lead time, are still simplified compared with the complexity of real stock management. Coping with many thousands of stocked items, supplied by many hundreds of different suppliers, with possibly tens of thousands of individual customers, makes for a complex and dynamic operations task. In order to control such complexity, operations managers have to do two things. First, they have to discriminate between different stocked items, so that they can apply a degree of control to each item which is appropriate to its importance. Second, they need to invest in an information-processing system which can cope with their particular set of inventory control circumstances.

Inventory priorities – the ABC system

In any inventory which contains more than one stocked item, some items will be more important to the organization than others. Some, for example, might have a very high usage rate, so if they ran out many customers would be disappointed. Other items might be of particularly high value, so excessively high inventory levels would be particularly expensive. One common way of discriminating between different stock items is to rank them by the usage value (their usage rate multiplied by their individual value). Items with a particularly high usage value are deemed to warrant the most careful control, whereas those with low usage values need not be controlled quite so rigorously. Generally, a relatively small proportion of the total range of items contained in an inventory will account for a large proportion of the total usage value. This phenomenon is known as the Pareto law (after the person who described it), sometimes referred to as the 80/20 rule. It is called this because, typically, 80 per cent of an operation's sales are accounted for by only 20 per cent of all stocked item types. The Pareto law is also used elsewhere in operations management (see, for example, Chapter 18). Here the relationship can be used to classify the different types of items kept in an inventory by their usage value. ABC inventory control allows inventory managers to concentrate their efforts on controlling the more significant items of stock:

- *Class A items* are those 20 per cent or so of high-usage-value items, which account for around 80 per cent of the total usage value.
- *Class B items* are those of medium usage value, usually the next 30 per cent of items, which often account for around 10 per cent of the total usage value.
- *Class C items* are those low-usage-value items which, although comprising around 50 per cent of the total types of items stocked, probably only account for around 10 per cent of the total usage value of the operation.

> **✳ Operations principle**
> Different inventory management decision rules are needed for different classes of inventory.

Worked example

Table 12.8 shows all the parts stored by an electrical wholesaler. The 20 different items stored vary in terms of both their usage per year and cost per item as shown. However, the wholesaler has ranked the stock items by their usage value per year. The total usage value per year is £5,569,000. From this it is possible to calculate the usage value per year of each item as a percentage of the total usage value, and from that a running cumulative total of the usage value as shown. The wholesaler can then plot the cumulative percentage of all stocked items against the cumulative percentage of their value. So, for example, the part with stock number A/703 is the highest value part and accounts for 25.14 per cent of the total inventory value. As a part, however, it is only one-twentieth or 5 per cent of the total number of items stocked. This item together with the next highest value item (D/012) account for only 10 per cent of the total number of items stocked, yet account for 47.37 per cent of the value of the stock, and so on.

Table 12.8 Warehouse items ranked by usage value

Stock no.	Usage (items/year)	Cost (£/item)	Usage value (£000/year)	% of total value	Cumulative % of total value
A/703	700	20.00	1 400	25.14	25.14
D/012	450	2.75	1 238	22.23	47.37
A/135	1 000	0.90	900	16.16	63.53
C/732	95	8.50	808	14.51	78.04
C/375	520	0.54	281	5.05	83.09
A/500	73	2.30	168	3.02	86.11
D/111	520	0.22	114	2.05	88.16
D/231	170	0.65	111	1.99	90.15
E/781	250	0.34	85	1.53	91.68
A/138	250	0.30	75	1.34	93.02
D/175	400	0.14	56	1.01	94.03
E/001	80	0.63	50	0.89	94.92
C/150	230	0.21	48	0.86	95.78
F/030	400	0.12	48	0.86	96.64
D/703	500	0.09	45	0.81	97.45
D/535	50	0.88	44	0.79	98.24
C/541	70	0.57	40	0.71	98.95
A/260	50	0.64	32	0.57	99.52
B/141	50	0.32	16	0.28	99.80
D/021	20	0.50	10	0.20	100.00
Total			5,569	100.00	

This is shown graphically in Figure 12.16. Here the wholesaler has classified the first four part numbers (20 per cent of the range) as Class A items and will monitor the usage and ordering of these items very closely and frequently. A few improvements in order quantities or safety stocks for these items could bring significant savings. The six next part numbers C/375 through to A/138 (30 per cent of the range) are to be treated as Class B items with slightly less effort devoted to their control. All other items are classed as Class C items whose stocking policy is reviewed only occasionally.

Figure 12.16 Pareto curve for items in a warehouse

Although annual usage and value are the two criteria most commonly used to determine a stock classification system, other criteria might also contribute towards the (higher) classification of an item:

- *Consequence of stock-out*. High priority might be given to those items which would seriously delay or disrupt other operations, or the customers, if they were not in stock.
- *Uncertainty of supply*. Some items, although of low value, might warrant more attention if their supply is erratic or uncertain.
- *High obsolescence or deterioration risk*. Items which could lose their value through obsolescence or deterioration might need extra attention and monitoring.

Some more complex stock classification systems might include these criteria by classifying on an A, B, C basis for each. For example, a part might be classed as A/B/A meaning it is an A category item by value, a class B item by consequence of stock-out and a class A item by obsolescence risk.

Critical commentary

This approach to inventory classification can sometimes be misleading. Many professional inventory managers point out that the Pareto law is often misquoted. It does not say that 80 per cent of the SKUs (stock keeping units) account for only 20 per cent of inventory value. It accounts for 80 per cent of inventory 'usage' or throughput value; in other words sales value. In fact it is the slow-moving items (the C category items) that often pose the greatest challenge in inventory management. Often these slow-moving items, although only accounting for 20 per cent of sales, require a large part (typically between one-half and two-thirds) of the total investment in stock. This is why slow-moving items are a real problem. Moreover, if errors in forecasting or ordering result in excess stock in 'A class' fast-moving items, it is relatively unimportant in the sense that excess stock can be sold quickly. However, excess stock in a slow-moving C item will be there a long time. According to some inventory managers, it is the A items that can be left to look after themselves; it is the B and even more the C items that need controlling.

Measuring inventory

In our example of ABC classifications we used the monetary value of the annual usage of each item as a measure of inventory usage. Monetary value can also be used to measure the absolute level of inventory at any point in time. This would involve taking the number of each item in stock, multiplying it by its value (usually the cost of purchasing the item) and summing the value of all the individual items stored. This is a useful measure of the investment that an operation has in its inventories but gives no indication of how large that investment is relative to the total throughput of the operation. To do this we must compare the total number of items in stock against their rate of usage. There are two ways of doing this. The first is to calculate the amount of time the inventory would last, subject to normal demand, if it were not replenished. This is sometimes called the number of weeks' (or days', months', years', etc.) *cover* of the stock. The second method is to calculate how often the stock is used up in a period, usually one year. This is called the stock turn or turnover of stock and is the reciprocal of the stock-cover figure mentioned earlier.

A small specialist wine importer holds stocks of three types of wine, Chateau A, Chateau B and Chateau C. Current stock levels are 500 cases of Chateau A, 300 cases of Chateau B, and 200 cases of Chateau C. Table 12.9 shows the number of each held in stock, their cost per item and the demand per year for each.

Table 12.9 Stock, cost and demand for three stocked items

Item	Average number in stock	Cost per item (£)	Annual demand
Chateau A	500	3.00	2,000
Chateau B	300	4.00	1,500
Chateau C	200	5.00	1,000

$$\text{The total value of stock} = \Sigma(\text{average stock level} \times \text{cost per item})$$
$$= (500 \times 3) + (300 \times 4) + (200 \times 5)$$
$$= 3{,}700$$

The amount of *stock cover* provided by each item stocked is as follows (assuming 50 sales weeks per year):

$$\text{Chateau A, stock cover} = \frac{\text{stock}}{\text{demand}} = \frac{500}{2{,}000} \times 50 = 12.5 \text{ weeks}$$

$$\text{Chateau B, stock cover} = \frac{\text{stock}}{\text{demand}} = \frac{300}{1{,}500} \times 50 = 10 \text{ weeks}$$

$$\text{Chateau C, stock cover} = \frac{\text{stock}}{\text{demand}} = \frac{200}{1{,}000} \times 50 = 10 \text{ weeks}$$

The *stock turn* for each item is calculated as follows:

$$\text{Chateau A, stock turn} = \frac{\text{demand}}{\text{stock}} = \frac{2{,}000}{500} = 4 \text{ times/year}$$

$$\text{Chateau B, stock turn} = \frac{\text{demand}}{\text{stock}} = \frac{1{,}500}{300} = 5 \text{ times/year}$$

$$\text{Chateau C, stock turn} = \frac{\text{demand}}{\text{stock}} = \frac{1{,}000}{200} = 5 \text{ times/year}$$

To find the average stock cover or stock turn for the total items in the inventory, the individual item measures can be weighted by their demand levels as a proportion of total demand (4,500). Thus:

$$\text{Average stock cover} = \left(125 \times \frac{2{,}000}{4{,}500}\right) + \left(10 \times \frac{1{,}500}{4{,}500}\right) + \left(10 \times \frac{1{,}000}{4{,}500}\right)$$

$$= 11.11$$

$$\text{Average stock turn} = \left(4 \times \frac{2{,}000}{4{,}500}\right) + \left(5 \times \frac{1{,}500}{4{,}500}\right) + \left(5 \times \frac{1{,}000}{4{,}500}\right)$$

$$= 4.56$$

Inventory information systems

Most inventories of any significant size are managed by computerized systems. The many relatively routine calculations involved in stock control lend themselves to computerized support. This is especially so since data capture has been made more convenient through the use of bar-code readers and the point-of-sale recording of sales transactions. Many commercial systems of stock control are available, although they tend to share certain common functions.

Updating stock records

Every time a transaction takes place (such as the sale of an item, the movement of an item from a warehouse into a truck, or the delivery of an item into a warehouse), the position, status and possibly value of the stock will have changed. This information must be recorded so that operations managers can determine their current inventory status at any time.

Generating orders

The two major decisions we have described previously, namely how much to order and when to order, can both be made by a computerized stock control system. The first decision, setting the value of how much to order (Q), is likely to be taken only at relatively infrequent intervals. Originally almost all computer systems automatically calculated order quantities by using the EOQ formulae covered earlier. Now more sophisticated algorithms are used, often using probabilistic data and based on examining the marginal return on investing in stock. The system will hold all the information which goes into the ordering algorithm but might periodically check to see if demand or order lead times, or any of the other parameters, have changed significantly and recalculate Q accordingly. The decision on when to order, on the other hand, is a far more routine affair which computer systems make according to whatever decision rules operations managers have chosen to adopt: either continuous review or periodic review. Furthermore, the systems can automatically generate whatever documentation is required, or even transmit the re-ordering information electronically through an electronic data interchange (EDI) system.

Generating inventory reports

Inventory control systems can generate regular reports of stock value for the different items stored, which can help management monitor its inventory control performance. Similarly, customer service performance, such as the number of stock-outs or the number of incomplete orders, can be regularly monitored. Some reports may be generated on an exception basis. That is, the report is only generated if some performance measure deviates from acceptable limits.

Forecasting

Inventory replenishment decisions should ideally be made with a clear understanding of forecast future demand. The inventory control system can compare actual demand against forecast and adjust the forecast in the light of actual levels of demand. Control systems of this type are treated in more detail later (see Chapter 14).

Common problems with inventory systems

Our description of inventory systems has been based on the assumption that operations (a) have a reasonably accurate idea of costs such as holding cost, or order cost, and (b) have accurate information that really does indicate the actual level of stock and sales. But data inaccuracy often poses one of the most significant problems for inventory managers. This is because most computer-based inventory management systems are based on what is called the perpetual inventory principle. This is the simple idea that stock records are (or should be) automatically updated every time that items are recorded as having been received into an inventory or taken out of the inventory. So,

opening stock level + receipts in − dispatches out = new stock level.

Any errors in recording these transactions and/or in handling the physical inventory can lead to discrepancies between the recorded and actual inventory, and these errors are perpetuated until physical stock checks are made (usually quite infrequently). In practice there are many opportunities for errors to occur, if only because inventory transactions are numerous. This means that it is surprisingly common for the majority of inventory records to be inaccurate. The underlying causes of errors include:

- keying errors; entering the wrong product code
- quantity errors; a mis-count of items put into or taken from stock
- damaged or deteriorated inventory not recorded as such, or not correctly deleted from the records when it is destroyed
- the wrong items being taken out of stock, but the records not being corrected when they are returned to stock
- delays between the transactions being made and the records being updated
- items stolen from inventory (common in retail environments, but also not unusual in industrial and commercial inventories).

SUMMARY ANSWERS TO KEY QUESTIONS

MyOMLab

Check and improve your understanding of this chapter using self-assessment questions and a personalized study plan, a video case study, and an eText – all at **www.myomlab.com**.

❯ What is inventory?

- Inventory, or stock, is the stored accumulation of the transformed resources in an operation. Sometimes the words 'stock' and 'inventory' are also used to describe transforming resources, but the terms *stock control* and *inventory control* are nearly always used in connection with transformed resources.

- Almost all operations keep some kind of inventory, most usually of materials but also of information and customers (customer inventories are normally called queues).

❯ Why should there be any inventory?

- Inventory occurs in operations because the timing of supply and the timing of demand do not always match. Inventories are needed, therefore, to smooth the differences between supply and demand.

- There are five main reasons for keeping inventory:
  - to cope with random or unexpected interruptions in supply or demand (buffer inventory);
  - to cope with an operation's inability to make all products simultaneously (cycle inventory);
  - to allow different stages of processing to operate at different speeds and with different schedules (de-coupling inventory);
  - to cope with planned fluctuations in supply or demand (anticipation inventory);
  - to cope with transportation delays in the supply network (pipeline inventory).

- Inventory is often a major part of working capital, tying up money which could be used more productively elsewhere.
- If inventory is not used quickly, there is an increasing risk of damage, loss, deterioration, or obsolescence.
- Inventory invariably takes up space (for example, in a warehouse), and has to be managed, stored in appropriate conditions, insured, and physically handled when transactions occur. It therefore contributes to overhead costs.

〉 How much should be ordered?

- This depends on balancing the costs associated with holding stocks against the costs associated with placing an order. The main stock-holding costs are usually related to working capital, whereas the main order costs are usually associated with the transactions necessary to generate the information to place an order.
- The best-known approach to determining the amount of inventory to order is the economic order quantity (EOQ) formula. The EOQ formula can be adapted to different types of inventory profile using different stock behaviour assumptions.
- The EOQ approach, however, has been subject to a number of criticisms regarding the true cost of holding stock, the real cost of placing an order, and the use of EOQ models as prescriptive devices.

〉 When should an order be placed?

- Partly this depends on the uncertainty of demand. Orders are usually timed to leave a certain level of average safety stock when the order arrives. The level of safety stock is influenced by the variability of both demand and the lead time of supply. These two variables are usually combined into a lead-time usage distribution.
- Using re-order level as a trigger for placing replenishment orders necessitates the continual review of inventory levels. This can be time-consuming and expensive. An alternative approach is to make replenishment orders of varying size but at fixed time periods.

〉 How can inventory be controlled?

- The key issue here is how managers discriminate between the levels of control they apply to different stock items. The most common way of doing this is by what is known as the ABC classification of stock. This uses the Pareto principle to distinguish between the different values of, or significance placed on, types of stock.
- Inventory is usually managed through sophisticated computer-based information systems which have a number of functions: the updating of stock records, the generation of orders, the generation of inventory status reports and demand forecasts. These systems critically depend on maintaining accurate inventory records.

supplies4medics.com

Founded almost 20 years ago, supplies4medics.com has become one of Europe's most successful direct mail suppliers of medical hardware and consumables to hospitals, doctors' and dentists' surgeries, clinics, nursing homes and other medical-related organizations. Its physical and online catalogues list just over 4,000 items, categorized by broad applications such as 'hygiene consumables' and 'surgeons' instruments'. Quoting their website:

*'We are **the** pan-European distributors of wholesale medical and safety supplies . . . We aim to carry everything you might ever need; from nurses' scrubs to medical kits, consumables for operations, first aid kits, safety products, chemicals, fire-fighting equipment, nurse and physicians' supplies, etc. Everything is at affordable prices – and backed by our very superior customer service and support – **supplies4medics** is your ideal source for all medical supplies. Orders are normally despatched same-day, via our European distribution partner, the Brussels Hub of DHL. You should therefore receive your complete order within one week, but you can request next day delivery if required, for a small extra charge. You can order our printed catalogue on the link at the bottom of this page, or shop on our easy-to-use online store.'*

Last year turnover grew by over 25 per cent to about 120 million euro, a cause for considerable satisfaction in the company. However, profit growth was less spectacular; and market research suggested that customer satisfaction, although generally good, was slowly declining. Most worrying, inventory levels had grown faster than sales revenue, in percentage terms. This was putting a strain on cash flow, requiring the company to borrow more cash to fund the rapid growth planned for the next year. Inventory holding is estimated to be costing around 15 per cent per annum, taking account of the cost of borrowing, insurance, and all warehousing overheads.

Pierre Lamouche, the Head of Operations, summarized the situation faced by his department: *'As a matter of urgency, we are reviewing our purchasing and inventory management systems! Most of our existing re-order levels (ROL) and re-order quantities (ROQ) were set several years ago, and have never been recalculated. Our focus has been on rapid growth through the introduction of new product lines. For more recently introduced items, the ROQs were based only on forecast sales, which actually can be quite misleading. We estimate that it costs us, on average, 50 euros to place and administer every purchase order, since most suppliers are still not able to take orders over the internet or by EDI. In the meantime, sales of some products have grown fast, whilst*

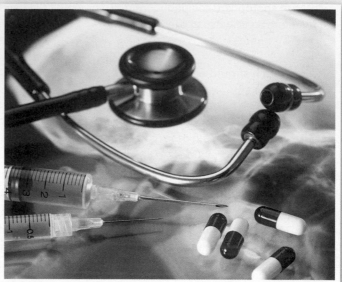

Source: AL RF (Imagemore Co., Ltd)

others have declined. Our average inventory (stock) cover is about 10 weeks, but . . . amazingly . . . we still run out of critical items! In fact, on average, we are currently out of stock of about 500 SKUs (Stock Keeping Units) at any time. As you can imagine, our service level is not always satisfactory with this situation. We really need help to conduct a review of our system, so have employed a mature intern from the local business school to review our system. He has first asked my team to provide information on a random, representative sample of 20 items from the full catalogue range, which is copied below.'

QUESTIONS

1 **Prepare a spreadsheet-based ABC analysis of usage value. Classify as follows:**

   A-items: top 20% of usage value
   B-items: next 30% of usage value
   C-items: remaining 50% of usage value

2 **Calculate the inventory weeks for each item, for each classification, and for all the items in total. Does this suggest that Pierre Lomouche's estimate of inventory weeks is correct?**

3 **If so, what is your estimate of the overall inventory at the end of the base year, and how much might that have increased during the year?**

4 **Based on the sample, analyse the underlying causes of the availability problem described in the text.**

5 **Calculate the EOQs for the A-items.**

6 **What recommendations would you give to the company?**

Table 12.10 Representative sample of 20 catalogue Items

Sample number	Catalogue reference number*	Sales unit description**	Sales unit cost (Euro)	Last 12 months' sales (units)	Inventory as at last year end (units)	Re-order quantity (units)
1	11036	Disposable Aprons (10pk)	2.40	100	0	10
2	11456	Ear-loop Masks(Box)	3.60	6,000	120	1,000
3	11563	Drill Type 164	1.10	220	420	250
4	12054	Incontinence Pads Large	3.50	35,400	8,500	10,000
5	12372	150ml Syringe	11.30	430	120	100
6	12774	Rectal Speculum 3 Prong	17.40	65	20	20
7	12979	Pocket Organiser Blue	7.00	120	160	500
8	13063	Oxygen Trauma Kit	187.00	40	2	10
9	13236	Zinc Oxide Tape	1.50	1,260	0	50
10	13454	Dual Head Stethoscope	6.25	10	16	25
11	13597	Disp. Latex Catheter	0.60	3,560	12	20
12	13999	Roll-up Wheelchair Ramp	152.50	12	44	50
13	14068	WashClene Tube	1.40	22,500	10,500	8,000
14	14242	Cervical Collar	12.00	140	24	20
15	14310	Head Wedge	89.00	44	2	10
16	14405	Three-Wheel Scooter	755.00	14	5	5
17	14456	Neonatal Trach. Tube	80.40	268	6	100
18	14675	Mouldable Strip Paste	10.20	1250	172	100
19	14854	Sequential Comp. Pump	430.00	430	40	50
20	24943	Toilet Safety Frame	25.60	560	18	20

* Reference numbers are allocated sequentially as new items are added to catalogue.
** All quantities are in sales units (e.g. item, box, case, pack).

PROBLEMS AND APPLICATIONS

These problems and applications will help to improve your analysis of operations. You can find more practice problems as well as worked examples and guided solutions on MyOMLab at www.myomlab.com.

MyOMLab

1 An electronics circuit supplier buys microchips from a large manufacturer. Last year the company supplied 2,000 specialist D/35 chips to customers. The cost of placing an order is $50 and the annual holding cost is estimated to be $2.4 per chip per year. How much should the company order at a time, and what is the total cost of carrying inventory of this product?

2 Jollyfrighteningmasks.com is an internet supplier of uncannily realistic masks. One of its most profitable lines is the 'Zombie'. Demand for this product is 15,000 per year, the cost of holding the product is estimated to be €25 per year and the cost of placing an order €75. How many 'Zombie' masks should the company order at a time?

3   Jollyfrighteningmasks.com works a 44-week year. If the lead time between placing an order for 'Zombie' masks and receiving them is two weeks, what is the re-order point for the 'Zombie' mask?

4   The Super Pea Canning Company produces canned peas. It uses 10,000 litres of green dye per month. Because of the hazardous nature of this product it needs special transport; therefore the cost of placing an order is €2,000. If the storage costs of holding the dye are €5 per litre per month, how much dye should be ordered at a time?

5   Estimate the annual usage value and average inventory level (or value) and space occupied by 20 representative items of food used within your household, or that of your family. Using Pareto analysis, categorize this into usage-value groups (e.g. A,B,C), and calculate the average stock turn for each group. Does this analysis indicate a sensible use of capital and space, and if not, what changes might you make to the household's shopping strategy?

6   Obtain the last few years' Annual Report and Accounts (you can usually download these from the company's website) for two materials-processing operations (as opposed to customer or information processing operations) within one industrial sector. Calculate each operation's stock–turnover ratio and the proportion of inventory to current assets over the last few years. Try to explain what you think are the reasons for any differences and trends you can identify and discuss the likely advantages and disadvantages for the organizations concerned.

SELECTED FURTHER READING

Emmett, S. and Granville, D. (2007) *Excellence in Inventory Management: How to Minimise Costs and Maximise Service*, **Cambridge Academic, Cambridge.** Practical guide.

Flores, B.E. and Whybark, D.C. (1987) Implementing multiple criteria ABC analysis, *Journal of Operations Management*, **vol. 7, no. 1.** An academic paper but one that gives some useful hints on the practicalities of ABC analysis.

Muller, M. (2011) *Essentials of Inventory Management*, **2nd edn, Amacom, New York.** Straightforward treatment.

Waters, D. (2003) *Inventory Control and Management*, **John Wiley & Sons Ltd, Chichester.** Conventional but useful coverage of the topic.

Wild, T. (2002) *Best Practice in Inventory Management*, **Butterworth-Heinemann, Oxford.** A straightforward and readable practice-based approach to the subject.

USEFUL WEBSITES

www.inventoryops.com/dictionary.htm   A great source for information on Inventory Management and Warehouse Operations.

www.mapfornonprofits.org   General 'private' site on operations management, but with some good content.

www.apics.org   Site of APICS: a US 'educational society for resource managers'.

http://www.inventorymanagement.com Site of the Centre for Inventory management. Cases and links.

www.myomlab.com Test which sections you have mastered and which you need to review, with questions, a personalized study plan, video clips, revision tips, and cases.

www.poms.org A US academic society for production and operations management. Academic, but some useful material, including a link to an encyclopedia of operations management terms.

MyOMLab *Now that you have finished reading this chapter, why not visit MyOMLab at www.myomlab.com where you'll find more learning resources to help you make the most of your studies and get a better grade.*

13 Supply chain management

Key questions

> What is supply chain management?

> What are the activities of supply chain management?

> How can the relationship between operations in a supply chain affect the way it works?

> How do supply chains behave in practice?

> How can supply chains be improved?

INTRODUCTION

How is it that businesses such as Apple, Toyota, Dell and Zara achieve notable results in competitive markets? Partly, it is down to their services and products, but partly it is because of how they organize the way they supply them. This is what supply chain management is concerned with – the way operations managers have to look beyond a purely internal view and look at the performance of suppliers, and suppliers' suppliers, as well as customers, and customers' customers. In addition, increasingly operations are outsourcing many of their activities, buying more of their services and materials from outside specialists. So the way they manage the supply of products and services to their own operations becomes increasingly important, as does the integration of their distribution activities. Earlier (Chapter 6) we raised the strategic and structural issues of supply network management; this chapter considers the more 'infrastructural' issues of planning and controlling the individual chains in the supply network.

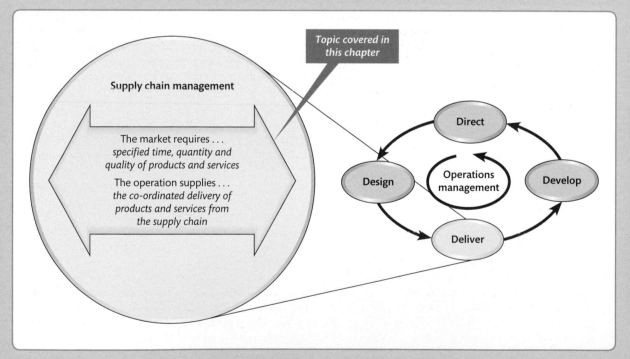

Figure 13.1 This chapter covers supply chain management

Ocado[1]

It was greeted as an announcement that reinforced the importance of Ocado's high-tech operations processes. Mark Richardson, the head of Ocado's technology operation, had been promoted to the newly-created role of Operations Director. It was also seen as reflecting the urgent need for Ocado to get its state-of-the-art distribution centre operating at full efficiency. The company's on-time delivery performance, although still better than its rivals, had been slipping in the months prior to the announcement. This had been an unusual experience for Ocado, which was the only dedicated online supermarket in the UK and the largest dedicated online supermarket in the world. It had succeeded in reshaping the final 'business-to-consumer' configuration of the traditional food supply chain in its UK home market, and in the process had become one of the most successful online grocers in the world. Tim Steiner, the Chief Executive Officer of Ocado, said: 'For a business that didn't deliver to its first customer until 2002 I'm immensely proud of where Ocado has got to in a few years. To now have our achievements recognized globally is a great accolade for all of our 4,500-strong team.'

But it was not the first. Back in 1999 an internet grocer called Webvan erupted on to the scene in California. It gained considerable publicity and more than a billion US dollars from backers wanting to join in what promised to be the exciting new world of online retailing. However, it proved far more difficult than Webvan's management and investors thought to make a totally new form of supply chain work. Although its market value had been as high as 15 billion US dollars, by February 2001 Webvan filed for bankruptcy protection with $830 million in accumulated losses. Yet Ocado has thrived. One of its first decisions was to enter into a branding and sourcing arrangement with Waitrose, a leading high-quality UK supermarket, from where the vast majority of Ocado's products are still sourced. But, just as important, it has developed a supply process that provides both relative efficiency and high levels of service. (A typical Ocado delivery has a lower overall carbon footprint than walking to your local supermarket.) Most online grocers fulfil web orders by gathering goods from the shelf of a local supermarket and then loading them in a truck for delivery. By contrast, from its distribution centre in Hatfield, 20 miles north of London, it offers 'doorstep' delivery

Source: Alamy Images/Justin Kase

of grocery products through its supply process, to over one-and-a-half million registered customers' homes. The orders are centrally picked from a single, state-of-the-art, highly automated warehouse (the customer fulfilment centre or 'CFC'). This is a space the size of 10 football pitches; a 15-km system of conveyor belts handles upwards of 8,000 grocery containers an hour, which are then shipped to homes, mainly in the southern part of the UK. The largely automated picking process, which was developed by its own software engineers, allows the company to pick and prepare groceries for delivery up to seven times faster than its rivals. Making its deliveries of more than 21,000 different products from a central location means it can carry more items than smaller local stores, which are more likely to run out of stock. Also fresh or perishable items that are prepared centrally will have a longer 'shelf-life'. Ocado's food waste, at 0.3 per cent of sales, is the lowest in the industry. The structural advantage of this supply arrangement means that 99 per cent of all orders are fulfilled accurately. Just as important as the physical distribution to the customers' door is the ease of use of the company's website (Ocado.com) and the convenience of booking a delivery slot. Ocado offers reliable one-hour, next-day timeslots in an industry where two-hour timeslots prevail. This is made possible thanks, again, to the centralized model and world-class processes, systems and controls. The company says that its website is designed to be simple to use and intuitive. Smart lists personalized to each customer offer prompts and ideas so that the absence of any in-store inspiration becomes irrelevant.

For a pre-registered customer, a weekly shop can be completed in less than five minutes. The site also has an extensive range of recipes, including some on video, and ideas such as craft activities and lunchbox fillers. Ocado makes a conscious effort to recruit people with customer service skills and then train them as drivers rather than vice versa. Drivers, known as Customer Service Team Members, are paid well above the industry norm and are empowered to process refunds and deal with customer concerns on the doorstep. Yet although as many as one million separate items are picked for individual customer orders every day, there are fewer than 80 mistakes.

It was the decision to increase the capacity of this distribution centre that had proved problematic. When its construction started to run behind schedule a vital part of Ocado's supply network was affected. The automated systems had suffered from teething problems, capacity had been restricted, delivery performance adversely influenced, and hiring the extra staff to handle orders had affected profitability. Because Ocado operates what it calls its 'hub and spoke' supply system, its central CFC (hub) serving regional (spoke) distribution points means that it is particularly vulnerable to disruption at its 'hubs'. In contrast with traditional 'bricks-and-mortar' supermarkets (Ocado has no 'physical' shops) it delivers direct to customers from its distribution centre rather than from stores. This has led some commentators to label Ocado 'the new Amazon'. 'Not so', say others. 'In some ways it's actually more complex than Amazon's operation. Amazon built a dominant brand in the US, the world's biggest market, by selling books and CDs, which essentially you just stick in an envelope and put a stamp on. That is not the same as having a highly automated warehouse with expensive machines and a huge fleet of delivery vans taking the goods to every house.'

WHAT IS SUPPLY CHAIN MANAGEMENT?

Supply chain management is the management of the interconnection of organizations that relate to each other through upstream and downstream linkages between the processes that produce value to the ultimate consumer in the form of products and services. It is a holistic approach to managing across company boundaries. Earlier (in Chapter 6) we used the term 'supply network' to refer to all the operations that were linked together so as to provide goods and services through to the end customers. In this chapter we deal with the 'ongoing' flow of goods and services through this network along individual channels or strands of that network. In large organizations there can be many hundreds of strands of linked operations passing through the operation. These strands are more commonly referred to as supply chains. An analogy often used to describe supply chains is that of the 'pipeline'. Just as liquids flow through a pipeline, so physical goods (and services, but the metaphor is more difficult to imagine) flow down a supply chain. Long pipelines will, of course, contain more liquid than short ones. So, the time taken for liquid to flow all the way through a long pipeline will be longer than if the pipeline was shorter. Stocks of inventory held in the supply chain can be thought of as analogous to storage tanks. On its journey through the supply chain pipeline, products are processed by different operations in the chain and also stored at different points.

Internal and external supply chains

Although we described supply chains as an interconnection of 'organizations', this does not necessarily mean that these 'organizations' are distinctly separate entities belonging to and managed by different owners. Earlier (in Chapter 1) we pointed out how the idea of networks can be applied, not just at the supply network level of 'organization-to-organization' relationships, but also at the 'process-to-process' within-operation level and even at the 'resource-to-resource' process level. Also we introduced the idea of internal customers and suppliers. Put these two related ideas together and one can understand how some of the issues that we will be discussing in the context of 'organization-to-organization' supply chains can also provide insight into internal 'process-to-process' supply chains.

> ✳ Operations principle
>
> The supply chain concept applies to the internal relationships between processes as well as the external relationships between operations.

Tangible and intangible supply chains

Almost all the books, blogs and articles on supply chain management deal with relationships between what we called 'material transformation' operations; that is operations concerned with the creation, movement, storage or sale of physical products. But (as we demonstrated in Chapter 6) the idea of supply networks (and therefore, supply chains) applies equally to operations with largely or exclusively intangible inputs and outputs; such as retail shopping malls, banks, insurance providers, health-care operations, consultants, universities, and so on. All these operations have suppliers and customers, they all purchase services, they all have to choose how they get their services to consumers; in other words they all have to manage their supply chains. Of course, all supply chains, even ones that transform physical items, have service elements – again (referring back to Chapter 1) most operations supply a mixture of products *and* services. So, although we, like most authors, focus primarily on supply chains that transform physical items, remember that many of the ideas discussed also have relevance for 'pure' services that supply intangibles.

> *** Operations principle**
>
> The supply chain concept applies to non-physical flows between operations and processes as well as physical flows.

Supply chain management objectives

All supply chain management shares one common, and central, objective – to satisfy the end customer. All stages in a chain must eventually include consideration of the final customer, no matter how far an individual operation is from the end customer. When a customer decides to make a purchase, he or she triggers action back along the whole chain. All the businesses in the supply chain pass on portions of that end-customer's money to each other, each retaining a margin for the value it has added. Each operation in the chain should be satisfying its own customer, but also making sure that eventually the end customer is also satisfied.

For a demonstration of how end-customer perceptions of supply satisfaction can be very different from that of a single operation, or part of an operation, examine the customer 'decision tree' in Figure 13.2. It charts the hypothetical progress of a hundred customers requiring service (or products) as they progress through the business's internal supply chain. The business's product design department is responsible for designing products that appeal to potential customers (80 per cent success); the production planning department is responsible for ensuring that sufficient products are scheduled to meet demand (70/80 = 85.5 per cent success). Sales are responsible for negotiating a price and delivery estimate that satisfies customers (20/70 = 28.6 per cent success); Manufacturing is responsible for meeting customer orders (18/20 = 90 per cent success); finally Distribution should deliver to customers on time (16/18 = 88.9 per cent success). So, performance, as seen by manufacturing operations, represented by the shaded part of the diagram looks relatively acceptable. It has received 20 orders, 18 of which were produced as promised (on time, and in full). However, originally 100 customers had requested service, 20 of whom found the business did not make appropriate products, 10 of whom could not be served because the products were not scheduled to be available, 50 of whom were not satisfied with the price and/ or delivery (of whom 10 placed an order notwithstanding). Of the 20 orders received, 18 were produced as promised but 2 were not received as promised (delayed or damaged in transport). So what seems a 90 per cent manufacturing operation performance is in fact an 8 per cent performance from the customer's perspective. And this is just the internal supply chain. Include the cumulative effect of similar reductions in performance for all the external operations in a chain, and the probability that the end customer is adequately served could become remote. The point here is that the performance both of the supply chain as a whole, and its constituent operations, should be judged in terms of how all end-customer needs are satisfied.

> *** Operations principle**
>
> The performance of an operation in a supply chain does not necessarily reflect the performance of the whole supply chain.

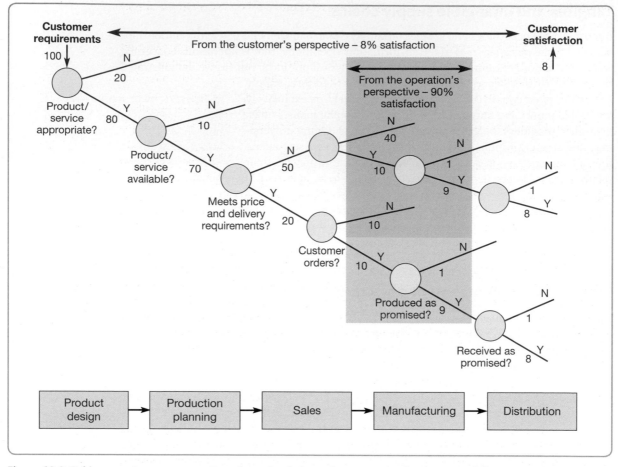

Figure 13.2 Taking a customer perspective of supply chain performance can lead to very different conclusions

Supply chains and the five operations performance objectives

Meeting the requirements of end customers requires the supply chain to achieve appropriate levels of the five operations performance objectives; quality, speed, dependability, flexibility, and cost.

Quality The quality of a product or service when it reaches the customer is a function of the quality performance of every operation in the chain that supplied it. Errors in each stage of the chain can multiply in their effect on end-customer service, so if each of 7 stages in a supply chain has a 1 per cent error rate, only 93.2 per cent of products or services will be of good quality on reaching the end customer (i.e. 0.99^7). This is why, only by every stage taking some responsibility for its own *and its suppliers'* performance, can a supply chain achieve high end customer quality.

Speed This has two meanings in a supply chain context. The first is how fast customers can be served, an important element in any business's ability to compete. However, fast customer response can be achieved simply by over-resourcing or over-stocking within the supply chain. For example, very large stocks in a retail operation can reduce the chances of stock-out to almost zero, so reducing customer waiting time virtually to zero. Similarly, an accounting firm may be able to respond quickly to customer demand by having a very large number of accountants on standby waiting for demand that may (or may not) occur. An alternative perspective on speed is the time taken for goods and services to move through the chain. So, for example, products that move quickly down a supply chain will spend little time as inventory because to achieve fast throughput time, material cannot dwell for significant periods as inventory. This in turn reduces inventory-related costs in the supply chain.

Dependability Like speed, one can almost guarantee 'on-time' delivery by keeping excessive resources, such as inventory, within the chain. However, dependability of throughput time is a much more desirable aim because it reduces uncertainty within the chain. If the individual operations in a chain do not deliver as promised on time, there will be a tendency for customers to over-order, or order early, in order to provide some kind of insurance against late delivery. This is why delivery dependability is often measured as 'on time, in full' in supply chains.

Flexibility In a supply chain context is usually taken to mean the chain's ability to cope with changes and disturbances. Very often this is referred to as supply chain agility. The concept of agility includes previously discussed issues such as focusing on the end customer and ensuring fast throughput and responsiveness to customer needs. But, in addition, agile supply chains are sufficiently flexible to cope with changes, either in the nature of customer demand or in the supply capabilities of operations within the chain.

Cost In addition to the costs incurred within each operation, the supply chain as a whole incurs additional costs that derive from each operation in a chain doing business with each other. These may include such things as the costs of finding appropriate suppliers, setting up contractual agreements, monitoring supply performance, transporting products between operations, holding inventories, and so on. Many developments in supply chain management, such as partnership agreements or reducing the number of suppliers, are attempts to minimize transaction costs.

THE ACTIVITIES OF SUPPLY CHAIN MANAGEMENT

The history of supply chain management is one of several separate activities coming together under a single overarching concept; consequently, some of the terms used in supply chain management overlap in the sense that they refer to common parts of the total supply network. So it is useful to distinguish between the different terms used in the topic. These are illustrated in Figure 13.3. *Supply chain management* co-ordinates all the operations on the supply side and the demand side. *Purchasing and supply management* deals with the operation's interface with its supply markets. *Physical distribution management* may mean supplying immediate customers, while *logistics* is an extension that often refers to materials and information flow down through a distribution channel, to the retail store or consumers (increasingly common because of the growth of internet-based retailing). The term *third-party logistics*(TPL) indicates outsourcing to a specialist logistics company. *Materials management* is a more limited term and refers to the flow of materials and information only through the immediate supply chain.

Purchasing (procurement) and supply management

At the supply end of the business, purchasing (sometimes called 'procurement') buys in materials and services from suppliers. Typically the volume and value of these purchases are increasing as organizations concentrate on their 'core tasks'. Purchasing managers provide a vital link between the operation itself and its suppliers. They must understand the requirements of all the processes within the operation and also the capabilities of the suppliers (sometimes thousands in numbers) who could potentially provide products and services for the operation. Purchasing can have a very significant impact on any operation's costs, and therefore profits. To illustrate the impact that price-conscious purchasing can have on profits, consider a simple operation with the following financial details:

Total sales	£10,000,000
Purchased services and materials	£7,000,000

Figure 13.3 Some of the terms used to describe the management of different parts of the supply chain

Salaries	£2,000,000
Overheads	£500,000

Therefore, profit = £500,000. Profits could be doubled to £1 million by any of the following:

increase sales revenue by up to 100 per cent

decrease salaries by 25 per cent

decrease overheads by 100 per cent

decrease purchase costs by 7.1 per cent.

A doubling of sales revenue does sometimes occur in very fast-growing markets, but this would be regarded by most sales and marketing managers as an exceedingly ambitious target. Decreasing the salaries bill by a quarter is likely to require substantial alternative investment – for example, in automation – or reflect a dramatic reduction in medium- to long-term sales. Similarly, a reduction in overheads by 100 per cent is unlikely to be possible over the short to medium term without compromising the business. However, reducing purchase costs by 7.1 per cent, although a challenging objective, is usually far more of a realistic option than the other actions. The reason purchase price savings can have such a dramatic impact on total profitability is that the costs of purchasing services and materials are such a large proportion of total costs. The higher are the proportion of purchase costs, the more profitability can be improved in this way. Figure 13.4 illustrates this.

> **✲ Operations principle**
>
> The higher the proportion of an operations costs that are represented by bought-in services and products, the more important is the purchasing activity.

Supplier selection

Choosing appropriate suppliers should involve trading off alternative attributes. Rarely are potential suppliers so clearly superior to their competitors that the decision is self-evident. Most businesses find it best to adopt some kind of supplier 'scoring' or assessment procedure.

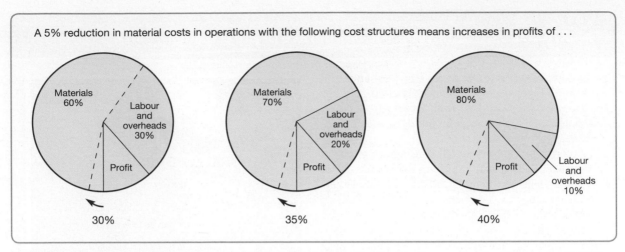

A 5% reduction in material costs in operations with the following cost structures means increases in profits of . . .

Figure 13.4 The larger the level of material costs as a proportion of total costs, the greater the effect on profitability of a reduction in material costs

This should be capable of rating alternative suppliers in terms of factors such as those in Table 13.1.

Choosing suppliers should involve evaluating the relative importance of all these factors. So, for example, a business might choose a supplier who, although more expensive than alternative suppliers, has an excellent reputation for on-time delivery, because that is more appropriate to the way the business competes itself, or because the high level of supply dependability allows the business to hold lower stock levels, which may even save costs overall. Other trade-offs may be more difficult to calculate. For example, a potential supplier may have high levels of technical capability, but may be financially weak, with a small but finite risk of going out of business. Other suppliers may have little track record of supplying the products or services required, but show the managerial talent and energy for potential customers to view developing a supply relationship as an investment in future capability.

Table 13.1 Factors for rating alternative suppliers

Short-term ability to supply	*Longer-term ability to supply*
Range of products or services provided	Potential for innovation
Quality of products or services	Ease of doing business
Responsiveness	Willingness to share risk
Dependability of supply	Long-term commitment to supply
Delivery and volume flexibility	Ability to transfer knowledge as well as products and services
Total cost of being supplied	Technical capability
Ability to supply in the required quantity	Operations capability
	Financial capability
	Managerial capability

Climbing The North Face of purchasing[2]

Few outdoor clothing brands have had the impact of The North Face since it was founded over 40 years ago in San Francisco. Now, The North Face is part of the VF Corporation, a $9 billion giant that dominates the leisurewear garment market.

According to the influential WebTogs blog, *'one of the brilliant things about The North Face jackets is that no matter whether you're off to battle with some subzero temperatures or just to chill out and take a load off there is always a North Face jacket to accompany you and keep you warm and snug'*. Named for the coldest, most unforgiving side of northern hemisphere mountains, its range of high-performance outdoor apparel, equipment and footwear has developed a reputation for durability, fashionable styling, and increasingly, sustainable sourcing of its materials. VF Corporation's claim is that they 'responsibly manage the industry's most efficient and complex supply chain, which spans multiple geographies, product categories and distribution channels'.

In particular, The North Face are keen to promote sustainable purchasing in their supply chain management. Their commitment to sustainability, they say, comes from a desire to protect the natural places associated with how and where their products are used and from their concern about the effects of climate change. As a sign of their determination to pursue sustainable purchasing, The North Face have partnered with the independent bluesign® standard, a Swiss-based organization that promotes, *'maximum resource productivity with a view to environmental protection, health and safety* [and represents] *an assurance for manufacturers and retailers that today's quality criteria are fulfilled in the best possible way and that applicable regulations and limits are complied with.'* The idea of bluesign® is to tackle the sustainability at its roots and exclude substances and practices which are potentially hazardous to human health or the environment from all processes in the garment supply

Source: Shutterstock.com/cappi thompson

chain. So to be considered as a supplier to The North Face any factory must meet the rigorous, independent bluesign® standard which ensures that suppliers address harmful chemicals at the fabric level and meet demanding requirements for consumer and worker safety, efficient resource use and environmental protection. But it is not only the monitoring of suppliers that is important in meeting sustainability targets, say The North Face – product and process innovation is also vital. *'For example'*, they say, *'our Venture jacket is a great illustration of innovation going hand-in-hand with environmental sustainability. We reduced the synthetic compounds in the membrane of our Venture product line by 50 per cent by incorporating castor oil, a renewable resource. The castor bean plant, widely grown throughout the tropics, produces oil from its seeds that provides an effective substitute for half of the petroleum-derived materials in the waterproof membrane of our best-selling Venture product line.'*

Worked example

A hotel chain has decided to change its supplier of cleaning supplies because its current supplier has become unreliable in its delivery performance. The two alternative suppliers that it is considering have been evaluated, on a 1–10 scale, against the criteria shown in Table 13.2. That also shows the relative importance of each criterion, also on a 1–10 scale. Based on this evaluation, Supplier B has the superior overall score.

Table 13.2 Weighted supplier selection criteria for the hotel chain

Factor	Weight	Supplier A score	Supplier B score
Cost performance	10	8 (8 × 10 = 80)	5 (5 × 10 = 50)
Quality record	10	7 (7 × 10 = 70)	9 (9 × 10 = 90)
Delivery speed promised	7	5 (5 × 7 = 35)	5 (5 × 7 = 35)
Delivery speed achieved	7	4 (4 × 7 = 28)	8 (8 × 7 = 56)
Dependability record	8	6 (6 × 8 = 48)	8 (8 × 8 = 64)
Range provided	5	8 (8 × 5 = 40)	5 (5 × 5 = 25)
Innovation capability	4	6 (6 × 4 = 24)	9 (9 × 4 = 36)
Total weighted score		325	356

SINGLE- AND MULTI-SOURCING

An important decision facing most purchasing managers is whether to source each individual product or service from one or more than one supplier, known, respectively, as single-sourcing and multi-sourcing. Some of the advantages and disadvantages of single- and multi-sourcing are shown in Table 13.3.

It may seem as though companies who multi-source do so exclusively for their own short-term benefit. However, this is not always the case: multi-sourcing can bring benefits to both supplier and purchaser in the long term. For example, Robert Bosch GmbH, the German automotive components business, required that subcontractors do no more than 20 per cent of their total business with them.

> ✳ **Operations principle**
>
> Supplier selection should reflect overall supply chain objectives.

Table 13.3 Advantages and disadvantages of single- and multi-sourcing

	Single-sourcing	Multi-sourcing
Advantages	• Potentially better quality because more SQA possibilities • Strong relationships which are more durable • Greater dependency encourages more commitment and effort • Better communication • Easier to co-operate on new product/service development • More scale economies • Higher confidentiality	• Purchaser can drive price down by competitive tendering • Can switch sources in case of supply failure • Wide sources of knowledge and expertise to tap
Disadvantages	• More vulnerable to disruption if a failure to supply occurs • Individual supplier more affected by volume fluctuations • Supplier might exert upward pressure on prices if no alternative supplier is available	• Difficult to encourage commitment by supplier • Less easy to develop effective SQA • More effort needed to communicate • Suppliers less likely to invest in new processes • More difficult to obtain scale economies

This was to prevent suppliers becoming too dependent and allow volumes to be fluctuated without pushing the supplier into bankruptcy. However, there has been a trend for purchasing functions to reduce the number of companies supplying any one part or service.

Purchasing, the internet and e-procurement

For some years, electronic means have been used by businesses to confirm purchased orders and ensure payment to suppliers. The rapid development of the internet, however, opened up the potential for far more fundamental changes in purchasing behaviour. Partly this was as the result of supplier information made available through the internet. By making it easier to search for alternative suppliers, the internet changed the economics of the search process and offers the potential for wider searches. It also changed the economics of scale in purchasing. For example, purchasers requiring relatively low volumes find it easier to group together in order to create orders of sufficient size to warrant lower prices. E-procurement is the generic term used to describe the use of electronic methods in every stage of the purchasing process from identification of requirement through to payment, and potentially to contract management. Suppliers are seeing e-procurement as a means to make buying from them easier for their customers and more profitable for themselves. For example IBM, the technology provider, sees e-procurement as an opportunity for more effective business-to-business integration. In particular, it says, e-procurement offers the following advantages.[3]

- Convenient and efficient electronic ordering – in other words, it's easier to buy from them.
- Shorter requisition and fulfilment cycles – in other words, it's faster to buy from them.
- Centralized spending controls – in other words, it's easier to keep track of what you are buying from them.
- Standardized global IT catalogue – in other words, it's less confusing to buy from them, because you can cut out things that you are not interested in buying.

In addition, e-procurement can be integrated with other IT systems (see Chapter 14 on enterprise resource planning). And, of course, it gives lower purchasing costs and improved efficiency, because purchasing staff spend less time on the procurement activity. Note, however, that lowering prices (purchase costs to the buyer) is only one of the benefits of e-procurement. The cost savings from purchased goods may be the most visible advantages of e-procurement, but some managers say that it is just the tip of the iceberg. It can also be far more efficient because purchasing staff are no longer chasing purchase orders and performing routine administrative tasks. Much of the advantage and time savings comes from the decreased need to re-enter information, from streamlining the interaction with suppliers and from having a central repository for data with everything contained in one system. Purchasing staff can negotiate with vendors faster and more effectively. Online auctions can compress negotiations from months to one or two hours, or even minutes.

Electronic marketplaces

E-procurement has grown largely because of the development over the last 10 years of electronic marketplaces (also sometimes called infomediaries or cybermediaries). These operations that have emerged in business-to-business commerce offer services to both buyers and sellers. They have been defined as 'an information system that allows buyers and sellers to exchange information about prices and product (and service) offerings, and the firm operating the electronic market place acts as in intermediary'.[4] They can be categorized as consortium, private, or third party.

- A private e-marketplace is where buyers or sellers conduct business in the market only with its partners and suppliers by previous arrangement.
- The consortium e-marketplace is where several large businesses combine to create an e-market place controlled by the consortium.
- A third party e-marketplace is where an independent party creates an unbiased, market-driven e-marketplace for buyers and sellers in an industry.

The scope of e-procurement

The influence of the internet on purchasing behaviour is not confined to when the trade actually takes place over the internet. It is also an important source of purchasing information, even if the purchase is actually made by using more traditional methods. Also, even though many businesses have gained advantages by using e-procurement, it does not mean that everything should be bought electronically. When businesses purchase very large amounts of strategically important products or services, they will negotiate multi-million-euro deals, which involve months of discussion, arranging for deliveries up to a year ahead. In such environments, e-procurement adds little value. Deciding whether to invest in e-procurement applications (which can be expensive) depends on what is being bought, say some authorities. For example, simple office supplies such as pens, paper clips and copier paper may be appropriate for e-procurement, but complex, made-to-order engineered components are not. Four questions seem to influence whether e-procurement will be appropriate.[5]

- *Is the value of the spend high or low?* High spending on purchased products and services give more potential for savings from e-procurement.
- *Is the product or commodity highly substitutable or not?* When products and services are 'substitutable' (there are alternatives), e-procurement can identify and find lower cost alternatives.
- *Is there a lot of competition or a little?* When several suppliers are competing, e-procurement can manage the process of choosing a preferred supplier more effectively and with more transparency.
- *How efficient are your internal processes?* When purchasing processes are relatively inefficient, e-procurement's potential to reduce processing costs can be realized.

Global sourcing

One of the major supply chain developments of recent years has been the expansion in the proportion of products and services which businesses are willing to source from outside their home country; this is called global sourcing. It is the process of identifying, evaluating, negotiating and configuring supply across multiple geographies. Traditionally, even companies who exported their goods and services all over the world (that is, they were international on their demand side) still sourced the majority of their supplies locally (that is, they were not international on their supply side). This has changed – companies are now increasingly willing to look further afield for their supplies, and for very good reasons. Most companies report a 10 per cent to 35 per cent cost saving by sourcing from low-cost-country suppliers.[6] There are a number of other factors promoting global sourcing:

- The formation of trading blocks in different parts of the world has had the effect of lowering tariff barriers, at least within those blocks. For example, the single market developments within the European Union (EU), the North American Free Trade Agreement (NAFTA) and the South American Trade Group (MERCOSUR) have all made it easier to trade internationally within the regions.
- Transportation infrastructures are considerably more sophisticated and cheaper than they once were. Super-efficient port operations in Rotterdam and Singapore, for example integrated road–rail systems, jointly developed auto-route systems and cheaper air freight, have all reduced some of the cost barriers to international trade.
- Perhaps most significantly, far tougher world competition has forced companies to look at reducing their total costs. Given that in many industries bought-in items are the largest single part of operations costs, an obvious strategy is to source from wherever is cheapest.

There are of course problems with global sourcing. The risks of increased complexity and increased distance need managing carefully. Suppliers who are a significant distance away need to transport their products across long distances. The risks of delays and hold-ups can be far greater than when sourcing locally. Also negotiating with suppliers whose native language is different from one's own makes communication more difficult and can lead to misunderstandings over contract terms. Therefore global sourcing decisions require businesses to balance cost, performance, service and risk factors, not all of which are obvious. These factors are important in global sourcing because of non-price or 'hidden' cost factors such as cross-border freight and handling fees, complex inventory stocking and handling requirements, and even more complex administrative, documentation and regulatory requirements. The factors that must be understood and included in evaluating global sourcing opportunities are as follows:

- **Purchase price** – the total price, including transaction and other costs related to the actual product or service delivered.
- **Transportation costs** – transportation and freight costs, including fuel surcharges and other costs of moving products or services from where they are produced to where they are required.
- **Inventory carrying costs** – storage, handling, insurance, depreciation, obsolescence, and other costs associated with maintaining inventories, including the opportunity costs of working capital (see Chapter 12).
- **Cross-border taxes, tariffs, and duty costs** – sometimes called 'landed costs', which are the sum of duties, shipping, insurance and other fees and taxes for door-to-door delivery.
- **Supply performance** – the cost of late or out-of-specification deliveries, which, if not managed properly, can offset any price gains attained by shifting to an offshore source.
- **Supply and operational risks** – including geopolitical factors, such as changes in country leadership; trade policy changes; the instability caused by war and/or terrorism or natural disasters and disease, all of which may disrupt supply.

Global sourcing and social responsibility

Although the responsibility of operations to ensure that they only deal with ethical suppliers has always been important, the expansion of global sourcing has brought the issue into sharper focus. Local suppliers can (to some extent) be monitored relatively easily. However, when suppliers are located around the world, often in countries with different traditions and ethical standards, monitoring becomes more difficult. Not only that, but there may be genuinely different views of what is regarded as ethical practice. Social, cultural and religious differences can easily make for mutual incomprehension regarding each other's ethical perspective. This is why many companies are putting significant effort into articulating and clarifying their supplier selection policies. The short case on Levi Strauss's policy is typical of an enlightened organization's approach to global sourcing.

Logistics, physical distribution management and distribution

Ever since businesses started making physical products they have had to arrange for the movement of raw materials to their operations and finished products to their destination, as well as organize their protection, storage and inventory control. This is variously called logistics, physical distribution management, or simply distribution. But whatever term is used it generally includes six inter-related activities as follows:

- **Transportation** – physically moving products or materials between operations by some means such as road, rail or air transportation. Usually this involves deciding on the appropriate balance between the cost of transportation and the level of delivery service (quality, speed, dependability, flexibility) offered.
- **Storage** – keeping an appropriate amount of inventory of products or materials so that they can be delivered to the next stage in the supply chain. We dealt with this in some detail earlier (see Chapter 12).
- **Warehousing** – providing suitable accommodation (for example, distribution centres) in which to store inventory. This involves deciding on the location, capacity and capabilities of warehouse operations.

Our Global Sourcing and Operating Guidelines help us to select business partners who follow workplace standards and business practices that are consistent with our company's values. These requirements are applied to every contractor who manufactures or finishes products for Levi Strauss & Co. Trained inspectors closely audit and monitor compliance among approximately 600 cutting, sewing, and finishing contractors in more than 60 countries . . . The numerous countries where Levi Strauss & Co. has existing or future business interests present a variety of cultural, political, social and economic circumstances . . . The Country Assessment Guidelines help us assess any issue that might present concern in light of the ethical principles we have set for ourselves. Specifically, we assess how . . . the . . . Health and Safety Conditions, Human Rights Environment, the Legal System and the Political, Economic and Social Environment would protect the company's commercial interests and brand/corporate image. The company's employment standards state that they will only do business with partners who adhere to the following guidelines:

Source: Alamy Images/Helen Sessions

- *Child Labor.* Use of child labor is not permissible. Workers can be no less than 15 years of age and not younger than the compulsory age to be in school. We will not utilize partners who use child labor in any of their facilities.
- *Prison Labor/Forced Labor.* We will not utilize prison or forced labor in contracting relationships in the manufacture and finishing of our products. We will not utilize or purchase materials from a business partner utilizing prison or forced labor.
- *Disciplinary Practices.* We will not utilize business partners who use corporal punishment or other forms of mental or physical coercion.
- *Working Hours.* While permitting flexibility in scheduling, we will identify local legal limits on work hours and seek business partners who do not exceed them

except for appropriately compensated overtime. Employees should be allowed at least one day off in seven.
- *Wages and Benefits.* We will only do business with partners who provide wages and benefits that comply with any applicable law and match the prevailing local manufacturing or finishing industry practices.
- *Freedom of Association.* We respect workers' rights to form and join organizations of their choice and to bargain collectively. We expect our suppliers to respect the right to free association and the right to organize and bargain collectively without unlawful interference.
- *Discrimination.* While we recognize and respect cultural differences, we believe that workers should be employed on the basis of their ability to do the job, rather than on the basis of personal characteristics or beliefs. We will favor business partners who share this value.
- *Health & Safety.* We will only utilize business partners who provide workers with a safe and healthy work environment. Business partners who provide residential facilities for their workers must provide safe and healthy facilities.

- **Materials handling** – ensuring that, within the warehouse or distribution centre, the movement and storage of products or materials is handled efficiently. This involves deciding on a suitable layout of items within the warehouse, choosing appropriate materials-handling technology and organizing warehouse staff's jobs to promote efficiency and safety; for example, minimizing the distance walked to fulfil orders.
- **Security** – protecting items from damage or theft. When items are being physically moved they can accidentally be damaged, so it is necessary to provide suitable protective packaging as well as design-handling equipment that minimizes the chances of damage. Similarly, both movement and storage provide opportunities for criminal theft, so security arrangement need to be made.

- **Order processing and communication** – as we stressed earlier, information is an important part of any supply chain; no more so than when items are being moved or stored. It is vital that the location and condition of items are communicated to all parties in the supply chain who need the information for their own planning purposes,

Physical distribution management and the internet

The potential offered by internet communications in physical distribution management has had two major effects. The first is to make information available more readily along the distribution chain. This means that the transport companies, warehouses, suppliers and customers who make up the chain can share knowledge of where goods are in the chain. This allows the operations within the chain to co-ordinate their activities more readily, with potentially significant cost savings. For example, an important issue for transportation companies is 'back-loading'. When the company is contracted to transport goods from A to B, its vehicles may have to return from B to A empty. Back-loading means finding a potential customer who wants their goods transported from B to A in the right time-frame. Companies which can fill their vehicles on both the outward and return journeys will have significantly lower costs per distance travelled than those whose vehicles are empty for half the total journey. The second impact of the internet has been in the 'business-to-consumer' (B2C, *see* the discussion on supply chain relationships later) part of the supply chain. While the last few years have seen an increase in the number of goods bought by consumers online, most goods still have to be physically transported to the customer. Often early e-retailers ran into major problems in the order fulfilment task of actually supplying their customers. Partly this was because many traditional warehouse and distribution operations were not designed for e-commerce fulfilment. Supplying a conventional retail operation requires relatively large vehicles to move relatively

---

SHORT CASE   ## TDG serving the whole supply chain[8]

TDG are specialists in providing *third-party* logistics services to the growing number of manufacturers and retailers who choose not to do their own distribution. Instead they outsource to companies like TDG, who have operations spread across 250 sites that cover the UK, Ireland, France, Spain, Poland and Holland, employ 8,000 employees and use 1,600 vehicles. They provide European logistics services through their own operations in the Netherlands and Ireland and, with the support of alliance partners, in several other European companies.

Source: Alamy Images/Justin Kase

'There are a number of different types of company providing distribution services', says David Garman, Chief Executive Officer of TDG , 'each with different propositions for the market. At the simplest level, there are the "haulage" and "storage" businesses. These companies either move goods around or they store them in warehouses. Clients plan what has to be done and it is done to order. One level up from the haulage or storage operations are the physical distribution companies, who bring haulage and storage together. These companies collect clients' products, put them into storage facilities and deliver them to the end customer as and when required. After that there are the companies who offer contract logistics. As a contract logistics service provider you are likely to be dealing with the more sophisticated clients who are looking for better quality facilities and management and the capability to deal with more complex operations. One level further large quantities of goods from warehouses to shops. Distributing to individual customers requires a large number of smaller deliveries.

RELATIONSHIPS BETWEEN OPERATIONS IN A SUPPLY CHAIN

One of the key issues within a supply chain is how relationships with immediate suppliers and customers should be managed. The behaviour of the supply chain as a whole is, after all, made up of the relationships which are formed between individual pairs of operations in the chain. It is important, therefore, to have some framework which helps us to understand the different ways in which supply chain relationships can be developed.

Business or consumer relationships?

The growth in e-commerce has established broad categorization of supply chain relationships. This happened because internet companies have categorized market sectors defined by who is supplying whom. This categorization distinguishes between relationships that are the final link in the supply chain, involving the ultimate consumer, and those involving two commercial businesses. It results in four types of relationships:

- **Business-to-business (B2B) relationships** are by far the most common in a supply chain context. These relationships involve businesses trading products (or components) and services with each other, possibly using some of the e-procurement exchange networks discussed earlier.
- **Business-to-consumer (B2C) relationships** are the end of the supply chain where businesses sell products and services to final consumers. This could include both 'bricks-and-mortar' retailers and online retailers.
- **Consumer-to-business (C2B) relationships** involve consumers informing businesses of their opinions, ideas, or needs, or in some other way creating value to the business. It includes consumers posting their needs on the internet (sometimes stating the price they are willing to pay) and companies then decide whether to offer. For example, when consumers write reviews of services or products, this provides useful information, not only to other consumers, but also to the provider. C2B relationships also include crowdsourcing, where a business, in effect, outsources activities to an undefined (and generally large) network of people (see Chapter 5).
- **Customer-to-customer (C2C) or peer-to-peer (P2P) relationships** are where consumers post items or services for sale to other consumers, and/or bid to purchase them. Examples include online exchanges, auction services and file-sharing services. The most common example of C2C is the online auction. Usually a third party, such as eBay, facilitates the transaction.

In this chapter we deal almost exclusively with B2B relationships.

Types of business to business relationship

A convenient way of categorizing supply chain relationships is to examine the extent and nature of what a company chooses to buy in from suppliers. Two dimensions are particularly important – *what* the company chooses to outsource, and *who* it chooses to supply it. In terms of *what* is outsourced, key questions are: 'How many activities are outsourced?' (from doing everything in-house at one extreme, to outsourcing everything at the other extreme); and 'How important are the activities outsourced?' (from outsourcing only trivial activities at one extreme, to outsourcing even core activities at the other extreme). In terms of *who* is chosen to supply products and services, again two questions are important: 'How many suppliers will be used by the operation?' (from using many suppliers to perform the same set of activities at one extreme, through to only one supplier for each activity at the other extreme); and 'How close are the relationships?' (from 'arm's length' relationships at one extreme, through to close and intimate relationships at the other extreme). Figure 13.5 illustrates this way of characterizing relationships.

Contracting and relationships

There are two basic ingredients of supply arrangements that are connected to the horizontal axis of Figure 13.5; they are 'contracts' and 'relationships'. Whatever arrangement with its suppliers a firm chooses to take, it can be described by the balance between contracts and relationships (*see* Fig. 13.6). They complement each other, but can cause major problems with suppliers if they are not balanced. The more a supply agreement is market-based with purchases based on relatively short-term arrangements, the more the agreement is likely to be defined in a detailed contract. By contracts we mean explicit – usually written and formal – documents that specify the legally binding obligations and roles of both parties in a relationship. The more a supply agreement is based on long-term, usually exclusive, agreements, the more broad, trust-based partnership agreements are appropriate. In any one operation a range of different approaches will be required.

> **✳ Operations principle**
>
> All supply chain relationships can be described by the balance between their 'contractual' and 'partnership' elements.

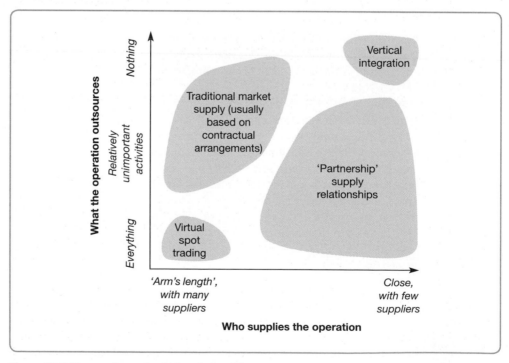

Figure 13.5 Types of supply chain relationship

'Market-based' or 'transactional'
supply arrangements

'Partnership' supply
arrangements

Emphasis predominantly on
relationships

Emphasis predominantly on
contracting

Figure 13.6 Supply arrangements are a balance between contracting and relationship

Market-based supply relationships

The very opposite of performing an operation in-house is to purchase goods and services from outside in a 'pure' market fashion, often seeking the 'best' supplier every time it is necessary to purchase. Each transaction effectively becomes a separate decision, and the agreement between buyer and seller can be very short term. Once the goods or services are delivered and payment is made, there may be no further trading between the parties. The advantages of traditional market supplier relationships are usually seen as follows:

- They maintain competition between alternative suppliers. This promotes a constant drive between suppliers to provide best value.
- A supplier specializing in a small number of products or services (or perhaps just one), but supplying them to many customers, can gain natural economies of scale.
- This enables the supplier to offer the products and services at a lower price than would be obtained if customers performed the activities themselves on a smaller scale.
- There is inherent flexibility in outsourced supplies. If demand changes, customers can simply change the number and type of suppliers. This is a far faster and simpler alternative to having to redirect their internal activities.
- Innovations can be exploited no matter where they originate. Specialist suppliers are more likely to come up with innovative products and services which can be bought in faster and cheaper than would be the case if the company were itself trying to innovate.
- They help operations to concentrate on their core activities. One business cannot be good at everything. It is sensible therefore to concentrate on the important activities and outsource the rest.

There are, however, disadvantages in buying in a totally 'free market' manner:

- There may be supply uncertainties. Once an order has been placed, it is difficult to maintain control over how that order is fulfilled.
- Choosing who to buy from takes time and effort. Gathering sufficient information and making decisions continually are, in themselves, activities which need to be resourced.
- There are strategic risks in subcontracting activities to other businesses. An over-reliance on outsourcing can 'hollow out' the company, leaving it with no internal capabilities which it can exploit in its markets.
- Short-term relationships may be used on a trial basis when new companies are being considered as more regular suppliers. Also, many purchases which are made by operations are one-off or very irregular. For example, the replacement of all the windows in a company's office block would typically involve this type of competitive-tendering market relationship. In some public sector operations, purchasing is still based on short-term contracts. This is mainly because of the need to prove that public money is being spent as judiciously as

possible. However, this short-term, price-orientated type of relationship can have a downside in terms of ongoing support and reliability. This may mean that a short-term 'least cost' purchase decision will lead to long-term high cost.

Virtual operations

An extreme form of outsourcing operational activities is that of the virtual operation. Virtual operations do relatively little themselves, but rely on a network of suppliers who can provide products and services on demand. A network may be formed for only one project and then disbanded once that project ends. For example, some software and internet companies are virtual in the sense that they buy in all the services needed for a particular development. This may include not only the specific software development skills but also such things as project management, testing, applications prototyping, marketing, physical production, and so on. Much of the Hollywood film industry also operates in this way. A production company may buy and develop an idea for a movie, but it is created, edited and distributed by a loose network of agents, actors, technicians, studios and distribution companies. The advantage of virtual operations is their flexibility and the fact that the risks of investing in production facilities are far lower than in a conventional operation. However, without any solid base of resources, a company may find it difficult to hold onto and develop a unique core of technical expertise. The resources used by virtual companies will almost certainly be available to competitors. In effect, the core competence of a virtual operation can only lie in the way it is able to manage its supply network.

'Partnership' supply relationships

Partnership relationships in supply chains are sometimes seen as an attempt to achieve some of the closeness and co-ordination efficiencies of vertical integration, while at the same time attempting to achieve a relationship that has a constant incentive to improve. Partnership relationships are defined as: *'relatively enduring inter-firm cooperative agreements, involving flows and linkages that use resources and/or governance structures from autonomous organizations, for the joint accomplishment of individual goals linked to the corporate mission of each sponsoring firm'*. What this means is that suppliers and customers are expected to co-operate, even to the extent of sharing skills and resources, to achieve joint benefits beyond those they could have achieved by acting alone. At the heart of the concept of partnership lies the issue of the *closeness* of the relationship. Partnerships are close relationships, the degree of which is influenced by a number of factors, as follows:

- *Sharing success.* An attitude of shared success means that both partners work together in order to increase the total amount of joint benefit they receive, rather than manoeuvring to maximize their own individual contribution.
- *Long-term expectations.* Partnership relationships imply relatively long-term commitments, but not necessarily permanent ones.
- *Multiple points of contact.* Communication between partners is not only through formal channels, but may take place between many individuals in both organizations.
- *Joint learning.* Partners in a relationship are committed to learn from each other's experience and perceptions of the other operations in the chain.
- *Few relationships.* Although partnership relationships do not necessarily imply single sourcing by customers, they do imply a commitment on the part of both parties to limit the number of customers or suppliers with whom they do business. It is difficult to maintain close relationships with many different trading partners.
- *Joint co-ordination of activities.* Because there are fewer relationships, it becomes possible jointly to co-ordinate activities such as the flow of materials or service, payment, and so on.
- *Information transparency.* An open and efficient information exchange is seen as a key element in partnerships because it helps to build confidence between the partners.
- *Joint problem solving.* Although partnerships do not always run smoothly, jointly approaching problems can increase closeness over time.

- *Trust*. This is probably the key element in partnership relationships. In this context, trust means the willingness of one party to relate to the other on the understanding that the relationship will be beneficial to both, even though that cannot be guaranteed. Trust is widely held to be both the key issue in successful partnerships, but also, by far, the most difficult element to develop and maintain.

Customer relationship management (CRM)

There is a story (which may or may not be true) that is often quoted to demonstrate the importance of using information technology to analyse customer information. It goes like this: Wal-Mart, the huge US-based supermarket chain, did an analysis of customers' buying habits and found a statistically significant correlation between purchases of beer and purchases of diapers (nappies), especially on Friday evenings. The reason? Fathers were going to the supermarket to buy nappies for their babies, and because fatherhood restricted their ability to go out for a drink as often, they would also buy beer. Supposedly this led the supermarket to start locating nappies next to the beer in their stores, resulting in increased sales of both.

Whether it is true or not, it does illustrate the potential of analysing data to understand customers. This is the basis of customer relationship management (CRM). It is a method of learning more about customers' needs and behaviours in order to develop stronger relationships with them. Although CRM usually depends on information technology, it is misleading to see it as a 'technology'. Rather it is a process that helps to understand customers' needs and develop ways of meeting those needs while maximizing profitability. CRM brings together all the disparate information about customers so as to gain insight into their behaviour and their value to the business. It helps to sell products and services more effectively and increase revenues by:

- providing services and products that are exactly what your customers want;
- retaining existing customers and discovering new ones;
- offering better customer service;
- cross-selling products more effectively.

CRM tries to help organizations understand who their customers are and what their value is over a lifetime. It does this by building a number of steps into its customer interface processes. First, the business must determine the needs of its customers and how best to meet those needs. For example, banks may keep track of its customers' age and lifestyle so that it can offer appropriate products like mortgages or pensions to them when they fit their needs. Second, the business must examine all the different ways and parts of the organization where customer-related information is collected, stored and used. Businesses may interact with customers in different ways and through different people. For example, sales people, call centres, technical staff, operations and distribution managers may all, at different times, have contact with customers. CRM systems should integrate this data. Third, all customer-related data must be analysed to obtain a holistic view of each customer and identify where service can be improved.

Critical commentary

Despite its name, some critics of CRM argue that the greatest shortcoming is that it is insufficiently concerned with directly helping customers. CRM systems are sold to executives as a way to increase efficiency, force standardized processes and gain better insight into the state of the business. But they rarely address the need to help organizations resolve customer problems, answer customer questions faster, or help them solve their own problems. This may explain the trend towards a shift in focus from automating internal front-office functions to streamlining processes such as online customer support.

HOW DO SUPPLY CHAINS BEHAVE IN PRACTICE?

A fundamental question in supply chain management is: 'How should supply chains be managed when operations compete in different ways in different markets?' One answer, proposed by Professor Marshall Fisher of Wharton Business School, is to organize the supply chains serving those individual markets in different ways.[9] He points out that many companies have seemingly similar products which, in fact, compete in different ways. Shoe manufacturers may produce classics which change little over the years, as well as fashions which last only one or two seasons. Chocolate manufacturers have stable lines which have been sold for 50 years, but also product 'specials' associated with an event or film release, maybe selling only for a few months. Demand for the former products will be relatively stable and predictable, but demand for the latter will be far more uncertain. Also, the profit margin commanded by the innovative product will probably be higher than that of the more functional product. However, the price (and therefore the margin) of the innovative product may drop rapidly once it has become unfashionable in the market. The supply chain policies which are seen to be appropriate for functional products and innovative products are termed by Fisher 'efficient supply chain policies' and 'responsive supply chain policies', respectively. Efficient supply chain policies include keeping inventories low, especially in the downstream parts of the network, so as to maintain fast throughput and reduce the amount of working capital tied up in the inventory. What inventory there is in the network is concentrated mainly in the manufacturing operation, where it can keep utilization high and therefore manufacturing costs low. Information must flow quickly up and down the chain from retail outlets back up to the manufacturer so that schedules can be given the maximum amount of time to adjust efficiently. The chain is then managed to make sure that products flow as quickly as possible down the chain to replenish what few stocks are kept downstream. By contrast, responsive supply chain policy stresses high service levels and responsive supply to the end customer. The inventory in the network will be deployed as closely as possible to the customer. In this way, the chain can still supply even when dramatic changes occur in customer demand. Fast throughput from the upstream parts of the chain will still be needed to replenish downstream stocks. But those downstream stocks are needed to ensure high levels of availability to end customers. Figure 13.7 illustrates how the different supply chain policies match the different market requirements implied by functional and innovative products.

> ❉ **Operations principle**
>
> 'Functional' products require lean supply chain management: 'innovative' products require agile supply chain management.

The bullwhip effect – supply chain dynamics

The 'bullwhip effect' is used to describe how a small disturbance at the downstream end of a supply chain causes increasingly large disturbances, errors, inaccuracies and volatility as it works its way upstream. Its main cause is an understandable desire by the different links in the supply chain to manage their production rates and inventory levels sensibly. To demonstrate this, examine the production rate and stock levels for the supply chain shown in Table 13.4. This is a four-stage supply chain where an original equipment manufacturer (OEM) is served by three tiers of suppliers. The demand from the OEM's market has been running at a rate of 100 items per period, but in period 2 demand reduces to 95 items. All stages in the supply chain work on the principle that they will keep in stock one period's demand (a simplification but not a gross one). The 'stock' column shows the starting stock at the beginning, and the finish stock at the end, of the period. At the beginning of period 2, the OEM has 100 units in stock. Demand in period 2 is 95 and the OEM must produce enough to finish up at the end of the period with 95 in stock (this being the new demand rate). To do this, it need only manufacture 90 items; these, together with 5 items taken out of the starting stock, will supply demand and leave a finished stock of 95 items and the OEM can operate at a steady rate of 95 items per period. Note, however, that a change in demand of only 5 items has produced a fluctuation of 10 items in the OEM's production rate.

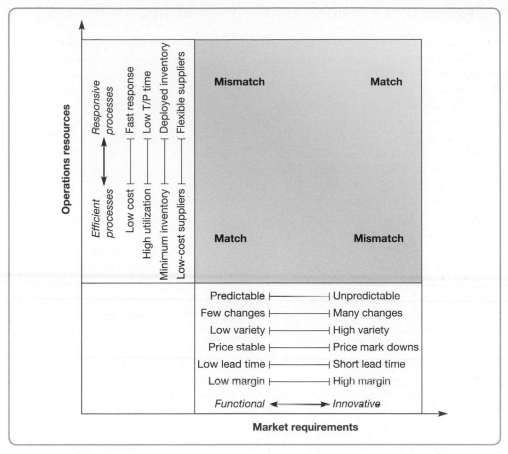

Figure 13.7 Matching the operations resources in the supply chain with market requirements
Source: Adapted from Fisher, M.C. (1997) What is the Right Supply Chain for Your Product? *Harvard Business Review*, March–April, 105–116.

Now carry this same logic through to the first-tier supplier. At the beginning of period 2, the second-tier supplier has 100 items in stock. The demand which it has to supply in period 2 is derived from the production rate of the OEM. This has dropped down to 90 in period 2. The first-tier supplier therefore has to produce sufficient to supply the demand of 90 and leave one month's demand (now 90 items) as its finish stock. A production rate of 80 items per month will achieve this. It will therefore start period 3 with an opening stock of 90 items, but the demand from the OEM has now risen to 95 items. It therefore has to produce sufficient to fulfil this demand of 95 items and leave 95 items in stock. To do this, it must produce 100 items in period 3. This logic can be extended right back to the third-tier supplier. The further back up the supply chain an operation is placed, the more drastic are the fluctuations caused by the relatively small change in demand from the final customer. The decision of how much to produce each month was governed by the following relationship:

Total available for sale in any period = Total required in the same period
Starting stock + Production rate = Demand + Closing stock
Starting stock + Production rate = 2 × Demand (because closing stock must be
equal to demand)
Production rate = 2 × Demand − Starting stock

This relatively simple exercise does not include any time lag between a demand occurring in one part of the supply chain and it being transmitted to its supplier. In practice there will be such a lag, and this will make the fluctuations even more marked.

✱ Operations principle
Demand fluctuations become progressively amplified as their effects work back up the supply chain.

Table 13.4 Fluctuations of production levels along supply chain in response to small change in end-customer demand

Period	Third-tier supplier		Second-tier supplier		First-tier supplier		Original equipment mfr		Demand
	Prodn.	Stock	Prodn.	Stock	Prodn.	Stock	Prodn.	Stock	
1	100	100	100	100	100	100	100	100	100
		100		100		100		100	
2	20	100	60	100	80	100	90	100	95
		60		80		90		95	
3	180	60	120	80	100	90	95	95	95
		120		100		95		95	
4	60	120	90	100	95	95	95	95	95
		90		95		95		95	
5	100	90	95	95	95	95	95	95	95
		95		95		95		95	
6	95	95	95	95	95	95	95	95	95
		95		95		95		95	

Note all operations keep one period's inventory.

Miscommunication in the supply chain

Whenever two operations in a supply chain arrange for one to provide products or services to the other, there is the potential for misunderstanding and miscommunication. This may be caused simply by not being sufficiently clear about what a customer expects or what a supplier is capable of delivering. There may also be more subtle reasons stemming from differences in perception of seemingly clear agreements. The effect is analogous to the children's game of 'Chinese whispers'. The first child whispers a message to the next child who, whether he or she has heard it clearly or not, whispers an interpretation to the next child, and so on. The more children the message passes between, the more distorted it tends to become. The last child says out loud what the message is, and the children are amused by the distortion of the original message. Figure 13.8 shows the bullwhip effect in a typical supply chain, with relatively small fluctuations in the market causing increasing volatility further back in the chain.

HOW CAN SUPPLY CHAINS BE IMPROVED?

Traditionally, the objective of supply chain management is to be able to do the right thing at the right time and in the right place. At one time operations achieved this by planning for excess resources (for example, large inventories in warehouses) that could be used as and when required. Now operations are more concerned with making the supply chain more

Figure 13.8 Typical supply chain dynamics

effective, delivering services and products only when and where they were needed. Yet, at the same time, with the advent of global sourcing, the task of organizing supply chains has become more complex as activities crossed international borders. This is why supply chain improvement has become such an important topic for most businesses. Some of the improvement effort has been focused on improved information systems that permit supply chain managers to know more precisely and faster exactly items which are in the chain. Some efforts have involved improving relationships with suppliers. But, at a more fundamental level, supply chain performance improvement often requires an attempt to understand the complexity of supply chain processes and to co-ordinate activities throughout the chain.

The SCOR model

The Supply Chain Operations Reference Model (SCOR) is a broad, but highly structured and systematic, framework to supply chain improvement that has been developed by the Supply Chain Council (SCC), a global non-profit consortium. The framework uses a methodology, diagnostic and benchmarking tools that are widely accepted for evaluating supply chain activities. The SCOR model allows its users to improve, and communicate supply chain management practices within and between all operations by using standard terminology and definitions. Companies that have used the model include BP, AstraZeneca, Shell, SAP AG, Siemens AG, and Bayer. The model uses three well-known individual techniques turned into an integrated approach. These are:

- business process modelling;
- benchmarking performance;
- best practice analysis.

Business process modelling

SCOR represents each 'link' in the supply chain as made up of five types of process, each process being a 'supplier–customer' relationship (*see* Fig. 13.9).

- 'Source' is the procurement, delivery, receipt and transfer of raw material items, subassemblies, product and/or services.
- 'Make' is the transformation process of adding value to products and services through mixing production operations processes.
- 'Deliver' processes perform all customer-facing order management and fulfilment activities, including outbound logistics.
- 'Plan' processes manage each of these customer–supplier links and balance the activity of the supply chain. They are the supply and demand reconciliation process, which includes prioritization when needed.

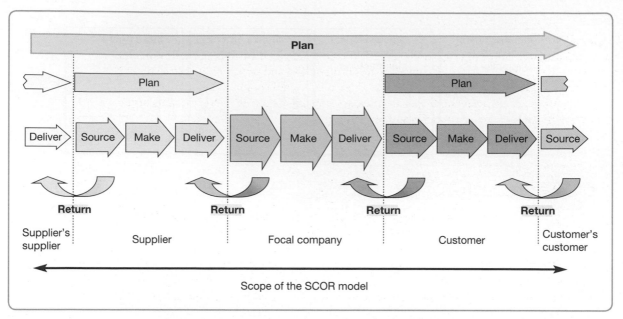

Figure 13.9 Matching the operations resources in the supply chain with market requirements

- 'Return' processes look after the reverse logistics flow of moving material back from end customers upstream in the supply chain because of product defects or post-delivery customer support.

All these processes are modelled at increasingly detailed levels from level 1 through to more detailed process modelling at level 3.

Benchmarking performance

Performance metrics in the SCOR model are also structured by level, as is process analysis. Level 1 metrics are the yardsticks by which an organization can measure how successful it is in achieving its desired positioning within the competitive environment, as measured by the performance of a particular supply chain. These level 1 metrics are the key performance indicators (KPIs) of the chain and are created from lower-level diagnostic metrics (called level 2 and level 3 metrics) which are calculated on the performance of lower-level processes. Some metrics do not 'roll up' to level 1; these are intended to diagnose variations in performance against plan.

Best practice analysis

Best practice analysis follows the benchmarking activity that should have measured the performance of the supply chain processes and identified the main performance gaps. Best practice analysis identifies the activities that need to be performed to close the gaps. SCC members have identified more than 400 'best practices' derived from their experience. The definition of a 'best practice' in the SCOR model is one that:

- is current – neither untested (emerging) nor outdated;
- is structured – it has clearly defined goals, scope and processes;
- is proven – there has been some clearly demonstrated success;
- is repeatable – it has been demonstrated to be effective in variuos contexts;
- has an unambiguous method – the practice can be connected to business processes, operations strategy, technology, supply relationships, and information or knowledge management systems;
- has a positive impact on results – operations improvement can be linked to KPIs.

Benefits of the SCOR model

Claimed benefits from using the SCOR model include: improved process understanding and performance; improved supply chain performance; increased customer satisfaction and retention; a decrease in required capital; better profitability and return on investment; and increased productivity. And, although most of these results could arguably be expected when any company starts focusing on business processes improvements, SCOR proponents argue that using the model gives an above-average and supply-focused improvement.

The effects of e-business on supply chain management practice[10]

New information technology applications combined with internet-based e-business have transformed the supply chain management practice. Largely, this is because they provide better and faster information to all stages in the supply chain. Information is the lifeblood of supply chain management. Without appropriate information, supply chain managers cannot make the decisions that co-ordinate activities and flows through the chain. Without appropriate information, each stage in the supply chain has relatively few cues to tell them what is happening elsewhere in the chain. To some extent, they are 'driving blind' and having to rely on the most obvious of mismatches between the activities of different stages in the chain (such as excess inventory) to inform their decisions. Conversely, with accurate and 'near real-time' information, the disparate elements in supply chains can integrate their efforts to the benefit of the whole chain and, eventually, the end customer. Just as importantly, the collection, analysis, and distribution of information using e-business technologies is far less expensive to arrange than previous, less automated methods. Table 13.5 summarizes some of the effects of e-business on three important aspects of supply chain management – business and market information flow, product and service flow, and the cash flow that comes as a result of product and service flow.

Information-sharing

One of the reasons for the fluctuations in output described in the example earlier was that each operation in the chain reacted to the orders placed by its immediate customer. None of the operations had an overview of what was happening throughout the chain. If information had been available and shared throughout the chain, it is unlikely that such wild fluctuations would have occurred. It is sensible therefore to try to transmit information throughout the chain so that all the operations can monitor true demand, free of these distortions. An obvious improvement is to make information on end-customer demand available to upstream

Table 13.5 Some effects of e-business on supply chain management practice

	Market/sales information flow	Product/service flow	Cash flow
Supply-chain-related activities	• Understanding customers' needs • Designing appropriate products/services • Demand forecasting	• Purchasing • Inventory management • Throughput/waiting times • Distribution	• Supplier payments • Customer invoicing • Customer receipts
Beneficial effects of e-business practices	• Better customer relationship management • Monitoring real-time demand • Online customization • Ability to co-ordinate output with demand	• Lower purchasing administration costs • Better purchasing deals • Reduced bullwhip effect • Reduced inventory • More efficient distribution	• Faster movement of cash • Automated cash movement • Integration of financial information with sales and operations activities

operations. Electronic point-of-sale (EPOS) systems used by many retailers attempt to do this. Sales data from checkouts or cash registers is consolidated and transmitted to the warehouses, transportation companies and supplier manufacturing operations that form its supply chain. Similarly, electronic data interchange (EDI) helps to share information (*see* the short case on Seven-Eleven Japan). EDI can also affect the economic order quantities shipped between operations in the supply chain.

SHORT CASE   Seven-Eleven Japan's agile supply chain[11]

Seven-Eleven Japan (SEJ) is that country's largest and most successful retailer. The average amount of stock in an SEJ store is between 7 and 8.4 days of demand, a remarkably fast stock turnover for any retailer. Industry analysts see SEJ's agile supply chain management as being the driving force behind its success. It is an agility that is supported by a fully integrated information system that provides visibility of the whole supply chain and ensures fast replenishment of goods in its stores customized exactly to the needs of individual stores. As a customer comes to the checkout counter the assistant first keys in the customer's gender and approximate age and then scans the bar codes of the purchased goods. This sales data is transmitted to the Seven-Eleven headquarters through its own high-speed lines. Simultaneously, the store's own computer system

Source: Shutterstock.com/Tupungato

records and analyses the information so that store managers and headquarters have immediate point-of-sale information. This allows both store managers and headquarters to, hour by hour, analyse sales trends, any stock-outs, the types of customer buying certain products, and so on. The headquarters computer aggregates all this data by region, product and time so that all parts of the supply chain, from suppliers through to the stores, has the information by the next morning. Every Monday, the company chairman and top executives review all performance information for the previous week and develop plans for the up-coming week. These plans are presented on Tuesday morning to SEJ's 'operations field counsellors; each of which is responsible for facilitating performance improvement in around eight stores. On Tuesday afternoon the field counsellors for each region meet to decide how they will implement the overall plans for their region. On Tuesday night the counsellors fly back to their regions and by next morning are visiting their stores to deliver the messages developed at headquarters to help the stores implement their plans.

SEJ's physical distribution is also organized on an agile basis. The distribution company maintains radio communications with all drivers and SEJ's headquarters keeps track of all delivery activities. Delivery times and routes are planned in great detail and published in the form of a delivery timetable. On average each delivery takes only 1.5 minutes at each store, and drivers are expected to make their deliveries within 10 minutes of scheduled time. If a delivery is late by more than 3 minutes the distribution company has to pay the store a fine equivalent to the gross profit on the goods being delivered. The agility of the whole supply system also allows SEJ headquarters and the distribution company to respond to disruptions. For example, on the day of the Kobe earthquake, SEJ used 7 helicopters and 125 motorcycles to rush through a delivery of 64,000 rice balls to earthquake victims.

Channel alignment

Channel alignment means the adjustment of scheduling, material movements, stock levels, pricing and other sales strategies so as to bring all the operations in the chain into line with each other. This goes beyond the provision of information. It means that the systems and methods of planning and control decision making are harmonized through the chain. For example, even when using the same information, differences in forecasting methods or purchasing practices can lead to fluctuations in orders between operations in the chain. One way of avoiding this is to allow an upstream supplier to manage the inventories of its downstream customer. This is known as vendor-managed inventory (VMI). So, for example, a packaging supplier could take responsibility for the stocks of packaging materials held by a food manufacturing customer. In turn, the food manufacturer takes responsibility for the stocks of its products which are held in its customer's, the supermarket's, warehouses.

Operational efficiency

'Operational efficiency' means the efforts that each operation in the chain can make to reduce its own complexity, reduce the cost of doing business with other operations in the chain, and increase throughput time. The cumulative effect of these individual activities is to simplify throughput in the whole chain. For example, imagine a chain of operations whose performance level is relatively poor: quality defects are frequent, the lead time to order products and services is long, delivery is unreliable, and so on. The behaviour of the chain would be a continual sequence of errors and effort wasted in replanning to compensate for the errors. Poor quality would mean extra and unplanned orders being placed, and unreliable delivery and slow delivery lead times would mean high safety stocks. Just as important, most operations managers' time would be spent coping with the inefficiency. By contrast, a chain whose operations had high levels of operations performance would be more predictable and have faster throughput, both of which would help to minimize supply chain fluctuations. One of the most important approaches to improving the operational efficiency of supply chains is known as time compression. This means speeding up the flow of materials down the chain and the flow of information back up the chain. The supply chain dynamics effect we observed in Table 13.4 was due partly to the slowness of information moving back up the chain.

Supply chain vulnerability

One of the consequences of the agile supply chain concept has been to take more seriously the possibility of supply chain risk and disruption. The concept of agility includes consideration of how supply chains have to cope with common disruptions such as late deliveries, quality problems, incorrect information, and so on. Yet far more dramatic events can disrupt supply chains. Global sourcing means that parts are shipped around the world on their journey through the supply chain. Microchips manufactured in Taiwan could be assembled to printed circuit boards in Shanghai, which are then finally assembled into a computer in Ireland. Perhaps most significantly, there tends to be far less inventory in supply chains that could buffer interruptions to supply. According to Professor Martin Christopher, an authority on supply chain management, *'Potentially the risk of disruption has increased dramatically as the result of a too-narrow focus on supply chain efficiency at the expense of effectiveness. Unless management recognizes the challenge and acts upon it, the implications for us all could be chilling.'*[12] These 'chilling' effects can arise as a result of disruptions such as natural disasters, terrorist incidents, industrial or direct action such as strikes and protests, accidents such as fire in a vital component supplier's plant, and so on. Of course, many of these disruptions have always been present in business. It is the increased vulnerability of supply chains that has made many companies place more emphasis on understanding supply chain risks.

SHORT CASE   **Tsunami disrupts Japan's global supply chains**[13]

The volcanic ash from Iceland that disrupted air transport across Europe provided a preview of how natural disasters could throw global supply chains into disarray; especially those that had adopted the lean, low-inventory, just-in-time philosophy. That was in 2010. Yet the following year an even more severe disaster caused chaos in all supply chains with a Japanese connection; and that is a lot of supply chains. It was a quadruple disaster: an earthquake off Japan's eastern coast, one of the largest ever recorded, caused a tsunami that killed thousands of people and caused a meltdown at a nearby nuclear power plant, which necessitated huge evacuations and nationwide power shortages. The effect on global supply networks was immediate and drastic. The Sony Corporation shut down some of its operations in Japan because of the ongoing power shortages and announced that it was giving its staff time off during the summer (when air-conditioning needs are high) to save energy. Japanese automobile companies were among the worst affected. Toyota suspended production at most of its Japanese plants, reduced and then suspended output from its North American and European operations. Nissan said it would be suspending its UK production for three days at the end of the month due to a shortfall of parts from Japan. Honda announced that it was halving production at its factory in Swindon in the south of England. However, the disruption was not as severe as it might have been. Honda said that the vast majority of the parts used in Swindon are made in Europe, and added that its flexible working policy would

Source: Shutterstock.com/justasc

allow it to make up for the lost production later in the year. 'Thanks to a working-time agreement, there will be no loss of earnings for the workforce while the company cuts production', said Jim D'Avila, regional officer for the Unite union.

In the longer term, the disruption caused a debate amongst practitioners about how supply chains could be made more robust. Hans-Paul Bürkner, chief of the Boston Consulting Group, said, *'It is very important now to think the extreme. You have to have some buffers.'* Some commentators even drew parallels with financial meltdowns, claiming that, just as some financial institutions proved 'too big to fail', some Japanese suppliers may be too crucial to do without. For example, at the time of the disruption, two companies, Mitsubishi Gas Chemical and Hitachi Chemical, controlled about 90 per cent of the market for a speciality resin used to make the microchips that go in to smartphones and other devices. Both firms' plants were damaged and the effect was felt around the world. So maybe suppliers who have near-monopolies on vital components should spread their production facilities geographically. Similarly, businesses that rely on single suppliers should perhaps be more willing to split their orders between two or more suppliers.

SUMMARY ANSWERS TO KEY QUESTIONS

Check and improve your understanding of this chapter using self-assessment questions and a personalized study plan, a video case study, and an eText – all at www.myomlab.com.

❯ What is supply chain management?

- Supply chain management is a broad concept which includes the management of the entire supply chain from the supplier of raw material to the end customer.

❯ What are the activities of supply chain management?

- Its component activities include purchasing, physical distribution management, logistics, materials management and customer relationship management (CRM).

❯ How can the relationship between operations in a supply chain affect the way it works?

- Supply networks are made up of individual pairs of buyer–supplier relationships. The use of internet technology in these relationships has led to a categorization based on a distinction between business and consumer partners. Business-to-business (B2B) relationships are of the most interest in operations management terms. They can be characterized on two dimensions – what is outsourced to a supplier, and the number and closeness of the relationships.

- Traditional market supplier relationships are where a purchaser chooses suppliers on an individual periodic basis. No long-term relationship is usually implied by such 'transactional' relationships, but it makes it difficult to build internal capabilities.

- Virtual operations are an extreme form of outsourcing where an operation does relatively little itself and subcontracts almost all its activities.

- Partnership supplier relationships involve customers forming long-term relationships with suppliers. In return for the stability of demand, suppliers are expected to commit to high levels of service. True partnerships are difficult to sustain and rely heavily on the degree of trust which is allowed to build up between partners.

- Supply arrangements between supply chain actors is a mix of contracting and relationships.

- Customer relationship management (CRM) is a method of learning more about customers' needs and behaviours in order to develop stronger relationships with them. It brings together all information about customers to gain insight into their behaviour and their value to the business.

❭ How do supply chains behave in practice?

- Marshall Fisher distinguishes between functional markets and innovative markets. He argues that functional markets, which are relatively predictable, require efficient supply chains, whereas innovative markets, which are less predictable, require 'responsive' supply chains.

- Supply chains exhibit a dynamic behaviour known as the 'bullwhip' effect. This shows how small changes at the demand end of a supply chain are progressively amplified for operations further back in the chain.

❭ How can supply chains be improved?

- The Supply Chain Operations Reference Model (SCOR) is a highly structured framework for supply chain improvement that has been developed by the Supply Chain Council (SCC).

- The model uses three well-known individual techniques turned into an integrated approach. These are:
  - business process modelling;
  - benchmarking performance;
  - best practice analysis.

- To reduce the 'bullwhip' effect, operations can adopt some mixture of three co-ordination strategies:
  - *information-sharing*: the efficient distribution of information throughout the chain can reduce demand fluctuations along the chain by linking all operations to the source of demand;
  - *channel alignment*: this means adopting the same or similar decision-making processes throughout the chain to co-ordinate how and when decisions are made;
  - *operational efficiency*: this means eliminating sources of inefficiency or ineffectiveness in the chain; of particular importance is 'time compression', which attempts to increase the throughput speed of the operations in the chain.
  - Increasingly, supply risks are being managed as a countermeasure to their vulnerability.

CASE STUDY   Supplying fast fashion[14]

Garment retailing has changed. No longer is there a standard look that all retailers adhere to for a whole season. Fashion is fast, complex and furious. Different trends overlap and fashion ideas that are not even on a store's radar screen can become 'must haves' within six months. Many retail businesses with their own brands, such as H&M and Zara, sell up-to-the-minute fashionability and low prices, in stores that are clearly focused on one particular market. In the world of fast fashion, catwalk designs speed their way into high-street stores at prices anyone can afford. The quality of the garment means that it may only last one season, but fast-fashion customers don't want yesterday's trends. As *Newsweek* puts it, *'being a "quicker picker-upper" is what made fashion retailers H&M and Zara successful. [They] thrive by practicing the new science of "fast fashion"; compressing product development cycles as much as six times.'* But the retail operations that customers see are only the end part of the supply chains that feeds them. And these have also changed.

At its simplest level, the fast-fashion supply chain has four stages. First, the garments are designed, after which they are manufactured; they are then distributed to the retail outlets where they are displayed and sold in retail operations designed to reflect the businesses' brand values. In this short case we examine two fast-fashion operations, Hennes and Mauritz (known as H&M) and Zara, together with United Colours of Benetton (UCB) – a similar chain, but with a different market positioning.

Benetton. Almost fifty years ago, Luciano Benetton took the world of fashion by storm by selling the bright, casual sweaters designed by his sister across Europe (and later the rest of the world), promoted by controversial advertising. By 2005 the Benetton Group was present in 120 countries throughout the world. Selling casual garments, mainly under its United Colours of Benetton (UCB) and its more fashion-orientated Sisley brands, it produces 110 million garments a year, over 90 per cent of them in Europe. Its retail network of over 5,000 stores produces revenue of around €2 billion. Benetton products are seen as less 'high fashion' but higher quality and durability, with higher prices, than H&M and Zara.

H&M. Established in Sweden in 1947, they now sell clothes and cosmetics in over 1,000 stores in 20 countries around the world. The business concept is 'fashion and quality at the best price'. With more than 40,000 employees, and revenues of around SEK 60,000 million, its biggest market is Germany, followed by Sweden and the UK. H&M are seen by many as the originator of the fast-fashion concept. Certainly they have years of experience at driving down the price of up-to-the-minute fashions. 'We ensure the best price', they say, 'by having few middlemen, buying large volumes, having extensive experience of the clothing industry, having a great knowledge of which goods should be bought from which markets, having efficient distribution systems, and being cost-conscious at every stage.'

Zara. The first store opened almost by accident in 1975 when Amancio Ortega Gaona, a women's pyjama manufacturer, was left with a large cancelled order. The shop he opened was intended only as an outlet for cancelled orders. Now, Inditex, the holding group that includes the Zara brand, has over 1,300 stores in 39 countries with sales of over €3 billion. The Zara brand accounts for over 75 per cent of the group's total retail sales, and is still based in northwest Spain. By 2003 it had become the world's fastest-growing volume garment retailer. The Inditex group also has several other branded chains, including Pull and Bear and Massimo Dutti. In total it employs almost 40,000 people in a business that is known for a high degree of vertical integration compared with most fast-fashion companies. The company believes that it is their integration along the supply chain that allows them to respond to customer demand fast and flexibly while keeping stock to a minimum.

Source: Shutterstock.com/InnervisionArt

Design

All three businesses emphasize the importance of design in this market. Although not *haute couture*, capturing design trends is vital to success. Even the boundary between high and fast fashion is starting to blur. In 2004 H&M recruited high fashion designer Karl Lagerfeld, previously noted for his work with more exclusive brands. For H&M his designs were priced for value rather than exclusivity. '*Why do I work for H&M? Because I believe in inexpensive clothes, not "cheap" clothes,*' said Lagerfeld. Yet most of H&M's products come from over 100 designers in Stockholm who work with a team of 50 pattern designers, around 100 buyers and a number of budget controllers. The department's task is to find the optimum balance between the three components comprising H&M's business concept – fashion, price and quality. Buying volumes and delivery dates are then decided.

Zara's design functions are organized in a different way to most similar companies. Conventionally, the design input comes from three *separate* functions: the designers themselves, market specialists and buyers who place orders on to suppliers. At Zara the design stage is split into three product areas: women's, men's and children's garments. In each area, designers, market specialists and buyers are co-located in design halls that also contain small workshops for trying out prototype designs. The market specialists in all three design halls are in regular contact with Zara retail stores, discussing customer reaction to new designs. In this way, the retail stores are not the end of the whole supply chain but the beginning of the design stage of the chain. Zara's around 300 designers, whose average age is 26, produce approximately 40,000 items per year of which about 10,000 go into production.

Benetton also has around 300 designers, who not only design for all their brands, but also are engaged in researching new materials and clothing concepts. Since 2000 the company has moved to standardize their range globally. At one time more than 20 per cent of its ranges were customized to the specific needs of each country; now only between 5 and 10 per cent of garments are customized. This reduced the number of individual designs offered globally by over 30 per cent, strengthening the global brand image and reducing production costs.

Both H&M and Zara have moved away from the traditional industry practice of offering two 'collections' a year, for spring/summer and autumn/winter. Their 'seasonless cycle' involves the continual introduction of new products on a rolling basis throughout the year. This allows designers to learn from customers' reactions to their new products and incorporate them quickly into more new products. The most extreme version of this idea is practised by Zara. A garment will be designed and a batch manufactured and 'pulsed' through the supply chain. Often the design is never repeated; it may be modified and another batch produced, but there are no 'continuing' designs as such. Even Benetton have increased the proportion of what they call 'flash' collections, small collections that are put into its stores during the season.

Manufacturing

At one time Benetton focused its production on its Italian plants. Then it significantly increased its production outside Italy to take advantage of lower labour costs. Non-Italian operations include factories in North Africa, Eastern Europe and Asia. Yet each location operates in a very similar manner. A central, Benetton-owned, operation performs some manufacturing operations (especially those requiring expensive technology) and co-ordinates the more labour-intensive production activities that are performed by a network of smaller contractors (often owned and managed by ex-Benetton employees). These contractors may in turn subcontract some of their activities. The company's central facility in Italy allocates production to each of the non-Italian networks, deciding what and how much each is to produce. There is some specialization; for example, jackets are made in Eastern Europe while T-shirts are made in Spain. Benetton also has a controlling share in its main supplier of raw materials, to ensure fast supply to its factories. Benetton are also known for the practice of dyeing garments after assembly rather than using dyed thread or fabric. This postpones decisions about colours until late in the supply process so that there is a greater chance of producing what is needed by the market.

H&M does not have any factories of its own, but instead works with around 750 suppliers. Around half of production takes place in Europe and the rest mainly in Asia. It has 21 production offices around the world that between them are responsible for co-ordinating the suppliers who produce over half a billion items a year for H&M. The relationship between production offices and suppliers is vital, because it allows fabrics to be bought in early. The actual dyeing and cutting of the garments can then be decided at a later stage in the production The later an order can be placed on suppliers, the less the risk of buying the wrong thing. Average supply lead times vary from three weeks up to six months, depending on the nature of the goods. However, 'the most important thing', they say, 'is to find the optimal time to order each item. Short lead times are not always best. [For] some high-volume fashion basics, it is to our advantage to place orders far in advance. Trendier garments require considerably shorter lead times.'

Zara's lead times are said to be the fastest in the industry, with a 'catwalk to rack' time as little as 15 days. According to one analyst this is because they 'own most of the manufacturing capability used to make their products, which they use as a means of exciting and stimulating customer demand'. About half of Zara's products are produced in its network of 20 Spanish factories, which, like at Benetton, tended to concentrate on the more capital intensive operations such as cutting and dyeing. Subcontractors are used for most labour-intensive operations like sewing. Zara buy around 40 per cent of their fabric from its own wholly-owned subsidiary, most of which is in undyed form for dyeing after assembly. Most Zara factories and their subcontractors work on a single-shift system to retain some volume flexibility.

Distribution

Both Benetton and Zara have invested in highly automated warehouses, close to their main production centres, that store, pack and assemble individual orders for their retail networks. These automated warehouses represent a major investment for both companies. In 2001, Zara caused some press comment by announcing that it would open a second automated warehouse even though, by its own calculations, it was only using about half its existing warehouse capacity. More recently, Benetton caused some controversy by announcing that it was exploring the use of RFID tags to track its garments.

At H&M, while the stock management is primarily handled internally, physical distribution is subcontracted. A large part of the flow of goods is routed from production site to the retail country via H&M's transit terminal in Hamburg. Upon arrival the goods are inspected and allocated to the stores or to the centralized store stockroom. The centralized store stockroom, within H&M referred to as 'Call-Off warehouse', replenishes stores on item level according to what is selling.

Retail

All H&M stores (average size 1,300 square metres) are owned and solely run by H&M. The aim is to 'create a comfortable and inspiring atmosphere in the store that makes it simple for customers to find what they want and to feel at home'. This is similar to Zara stores, although they tend to be smaller (average size, 800 square metres). Perhaps the most remarkable characteristic of Zara stores is that garments rarely stay in the store for longer than two weeks. Because product designs are often not repeated and produced in relatively small batches, the range of garments displayed in the store can change radically every two or three weeks. This encourages customers both to avoid delaying a purchase and to revisit the store frequently.

Since 2000 Benetton has been reshaping its retail operations. At one time the vast majority of Benetton retail outlets were small shops run by third parties. Now these small stores have been joined by several Benetton-owned and -operated, larger stores (1,500 to 3,000 square metres). These mega-stores can display the whole range of Benetton products and reinforce the Benetton shopping experience.

QUESTION

1 **Compare and contrast the approaches taken by H&M, Benetton and Zara to managing their supply chain.**

PROBLEMS AND APPLICATIONS

These problems and applications will help to improve your analysis of operations. You can find more practice problems as well as worked examples and guided solutions on MyOMLab at www.myomlab.com.

1   'Look, why should we waste our time dealing with suppliers who can merely deliver good product, on time, and in full? There are any number of suppliers who can do that. What we are interested in is developing a set of suppliers who will be able to supply us with suitable components for the generation of products that comes after the next products we launch. It's the underlying capability of suppliers that we are really interested in.'

(a)   Devise a set of criteria that this manager could use to evaluate alternative suppliers.

(b)   Suggest ways in which she could determine how to weight each criterion.

2   Three managers are attending a seminar on 'Getting More Value from Your Purchasing Function'. One manager is from a large retail bank, one is from a general hospital and the third is from a printing company. At the seminar they were discussing their problems during coffee:

'This is really useful; I think that even a relatively small reduction in our bought-in supplies bill could have a major impact on the profitability of our printing company.'

'Yes, I agree the hospital will also benefit from an exercise that would reduce the bought-in supplies bill. At the moment it accounts for almost 30 per cent of all our expenditure.'

'Yes, at the bank we spend almost 20 per cent of our expenditure on bought-in supplies. Given that our profit is 20 per cent of our total revenue, any saving in bought-in supplies would be valuable.'

'I have to say that profits are not so high in the printing industry. Our profits are only 10 per cent of sales revenue. However, with bought-in supplies accounting for 70 per cent of our total costs, I am sure that any reduction in bought-in supplies costs will be useful.'

Which of these three managers would benefit most from a 5 per cent reduction in their bought-in supplies bill?

3   The example of the bullwhip effect shown in Table 13.4 shows how a simple 5 per cent reduction in demand at the end of the supply chain causes fluctuations that increase in severity the further back an operations is placed in the chain.

(a)   Using the same logic and the same rules (i.e. all operations keep one period's inventory), what would the effect on the chain be if demand fluctuated period by period between 100 and 95? That is, period 1 has a demand of 100, period 2 has a demand of 95, period 3 a demand of 100, period 4 a demand of 95, and so on?

(b)   What happens if all operations in the supply chain decided to keep only half of the period's demand as inventory?

4   If you were the owner of a small local retail shop, what criteria would you use to select suppliers for the goods which you wish to stock in your shop? Visit three shops which are local

to you and ask the owners how they select their suppliers. In what way were their answers different from what you thought they might be?

 Visit a C2C auction site (for example, eBay) and analyse the function of the site in terms of the way it facilitates transactions. What does such a site have to get right to be successful?

SELECTED FURTHER READING

Andersen, M. and Skjoett-Larsen, T. (2009) Corporate social responsibility in global supply chains, *Supply Chain Management: An International Journal*, vol. 14, issue 2, 75–86. A good review of the topic.

Chopra, S. and Meindl, P. (2009) *Supply Chain Management*, 4th edn, Pearson Prentice Hall, Upper Saddle River, NJ. One of the best of the specialist texts.

Christopher, M. (2011) *Logistics and Supply Chain Management: Creating Value-Adding Networks*, FT Prentice Hall, Harlow. Updated version of a classic that gives a comprehensive treatment on supply chain management from a distribution perspective by one of the gurus of supply chain management.

Fisher, M.L. (1997) What is the right supply chain for your product?, *Harvard Business Review*, vol. 75, no. 2. A particularly influential article that explores the issue of how supply chains are not all the same.

Green, K.W. Jr, Whitten, D. and Inman, R.A. (2008) The impact of logistics performance on organizational performance in a supply chain context, *Supply Chain Management: An International Journal*, vol. 13, issue 4, 317–327. What it says in the title.

USEFUL WEBSITES

www.cio.com/topic/3207/Supply_Chain_Management Site of CIO's Supply Chain Management Research Center. Topics include procurement and fulfilment, with case studies.

www.gsb.stanford.edu/scforum Stanford University's supply chain forum. Interesting debate.

www.rfidc.com Site of the RFID Centre that contains RFID demonstrations and articles to download.

www.spychips.com Vehemently anti-RFID site. If you want to understand the nature of some activists' concern over RFID, this site provides the arguments.

www.cips.org The Chartered Institute of Purchasing and Supply (CIPS) is an international organization, serving the purchasing and supply profession and dedicated to promoting best practice. Some good links.

www.myomlab.com Test which sections you have mastered and which you need to review, with questions, a personalized study plan, video clips, revision tips, and cases.

www.opsman.org Useful materials.

http://operationsroom.wordpress.com/ Stanford University's take on topical operations stories.

 Now that you have finished reading this chapter, why not visit MyOMLab at www.myomlab.com where you'll find more learning resources to help you make the most of your studies and get a better grade.

Enterprise resource planning (ERP)

Key questions

> **What is ERP?**

> **How did ERP develop?**

> **How should ERP systems be implemented?**

INTRODUCTION

One of the most important issues in planning and controlling operations is managing the sometimes vast amounts of information generated by the activity. It is not just the operations function that is the author and recipient of this information – almost every other function of a business will be involved. So, it is important that all relevant information that is spread throughout the organization is brought together. Then it can inform planning and control decisions such as when activities should take place, where they should happen, who should be doing them, how much capacity will be needed, and so on. This is what enterprise resource planning (ERP) does. It grew out of a set of calculations known as material requirements planning (MRP), which is described in the supplement to this chapter.

Figure 14.1 This chapter covers enterprise resource planning (ERP)

MyOMLab

Check and improve your understanding of this chapter using self-assessment questions and a personalized study plan, a video case study, and an eText – all at www.myomlab.com.

It may not be a glamorous business, but pet food is certainly big business. It is also competitive, with smaller suppliers battling against the giants like Nestlé. One of the most successful of the smaller European producers of dog food is Butcher's Pet Care, located in the Midlands of the UK, which takes a positive moral and ethical approach towards the dog food they produce. It also needs to be super-efficient at co-ordinating its production and distribution if it is to compete with larger rivals. Listen to how Butcher's IT manager, Malcolm Burrows, explains his vision of how its ERP system helps it do this.

Source: Alistair Brandon-Jones

Why implement a new ERP system?

'There were specific goals that needed to be achieved, as the legacy systems created long processes, and it was an issue to find out what was in the warehouse, etc.' A lot of manual planning tasks took place outside of the system, whereas now the planning, the enterprise resource planning (ERP), and the scheduling of material coming in is a lot better.

What were the benefits of the new ERP system?

'We're definitely getting a better view of what stock we're holding, and a much quicker response in being able to change product fore-ordering. As you can probably guess, within an environment whereby we are supplying to super-markets and supply chains, there are regularly promotions that affect the manufacturing demand we produce to, and it's a fairly quick turnaround. So from that point of view, the system does have a core value in that we can respond and meet requirements much quicker and easier.'

What were the challenges in implementing the ERP system?

'It was a very big cultural change for the staff . . . As with any ERP system, business and process mapping is crucial.

The interesting challenges were working out how we needed to change to get the best out of the system, and that we had agreed a timeline for its implementation.'

How did you train staff to use the system?

'We had a core project team, and they were the "champions" who had to go out and then work within their areas. [The] IT [department] really cannot dictate that; [users] need to be able to have that autonomy to say "this is how we want to operate it". We will get involved if there are technical queries, but otherwise the "champions" [are in charge].'

WHAT IS ERP?

An easy way of thinking about enterprise resource planning (ERP) is to imagine that you have decided to hold a party in two weeks' time and expect about 40 people to attend. As well as drinks, you decide to provide sandwiches and snacks. You will probably do some simple calculations, estimating guests' preferences and how much people are likely to drink and eat. You may already have some food and drink in the house which you will use, so you will take that into account when making your shopping list. If any of the food is to be cooked from a recipe, you may have to multiply up the ingredients to cater for 40 people. Also, you may also wish to take into account the fact that you will prepare some of the food the week before and freeze it, while you will leave the rest to either the day before or the day of the party. So, you will need to decide when each item is required so that you can shop in time. In fact planning a party requires a series of interrelated decisions about the volume (quantity) and timing of the materials needed. This is the basis of the foundation concept for ERP, called materials requirement planning (MRP). It is a process that helps companies make volume and timing calculations (similar to those in the party, but on a much larger scale, and with a greater degree of complexity). But your planning may extend beyond 'materials'. You may want to hire in a sound system from a local supplier – you will have to plan for this. The party also has financial implications. You may have to agree a temporary increase to your credit card limit. Again, this requires some forward planning and calculations of how much it is going to cost, and how much extra credit you require. Both the equipment and financial implications may vary if you increase the number of guests. But, if you postpone the party for a month, these arrangements will change. Also there are also other implications of organizing the party. You will need to give friends, who are helping with the organization, an idea of when they should come and for how long. This will depend on the timing of the various tasks to be done (making sandwiches, etc.).

So, even for this relatively simple activity, the key to successful planning is how we generate, integrate and organize all the information on which planning and control depends. Of course in business operations it is more complex than this. Companies usually sell many different products to many hundreds of customers who are likely to vary their demand for the products. This is a bit like organizing 200 parties one week, 250 the next and 225 the following week, all for different groups of guests with different requirements who keep changing their minds about what they want to eat and drink. This is what ERP does: it helps companies 'forward-plan' these types of decisions and understand all the implications of any changes to the plan.

HOW DID ERP DEVELOP?

Enterprise resource planning is the latest, and the most significant, development of the original materials requirements planning (MRP) philosophy. The (now) large companies which have grown almost exclusively on the basis of providing ERP systems include SAP and Oracle. Yet to understand ERP, it is important to understand the various stages in its development, summarized in Figure 14.2. The original MRP became popular during the 1970s, although the planning and control logic that underlies it had, by then, been known for some time. What popularized MRP was the availability of computer power to drive the basic planning and control mathematics. We will deal with MRP in detail in the supplement to this chapter; it uses product information in the form of a bill of materials (BOM) which is similar to the 'component structure' (discussed in Chapter 5), together with demand information in the form of a master production schedule (MPS).

Manufacturing resource planning (MRP II) expanded out of MRP during the 1980s. Again, it was a technology innovation that allowed the development. Local-area networks (LANs, *see* Chapter 8), together with increasingly powerful desktop computers, allowed a much

Figure 14.2 The development of ERP

higher degree of processing power and communication between different parts of a business. Also MRP II's extra sophistication allowed the forward modelling of 'what-if' scenarios. The strength of MRP and MRP II lay always in the fact that it could explore the *consequences* of any changes to what an operation was required to do. So, if demand changed, the MRP system would calculate all the 'knock-on' effects and issue instructions accordingly. This same principle also applies to ERP, but on a much wider basis. Enterprise resource planning (ERP) has been defined as:

> '*a complete enterprise-wide business solution. The ERP system consists of software support modules such as: marketing and sales, field service, product design and development, production and inventory control, procurement, distribution, industrial facilities management, process design and development, manufacturing, quality, human resources, finance and accounting, and information services. Integration between the modules is stressed without the duplication of information.*'[2]

Some authorities caution against taking a naive view of ERP. Look at this view:

> '*Enterprise resource planning software, or ERP, doesn't live up to its acronym. Forget about planning – it doesn't do much of that – and forget about resource, [it is] a throwaway term. But remember the enterprise part. This is ERP's true ambition. It attempts to integrate all departments and functions across a company onto a single computer system that can serve all those different departments' particular needs.*'[3]

So ERP systems allow decisions and databases from all parts of the organization to be integrated so that the consequences of decisions in one part of the organization are reflected in the planning and control systems of the rest of the organization (*see* Fig. 14.3). ERP is the equivalent of the organization's central nervous system, sensing information about the condition of different parts of the business and relaying the information to other parts of the business that need it. The information is updated in real time by those who use it and yet is always available to everyone connected to the ERP system.

Also, the potential of web-based communication has provided a further boost to ERP development. Many companies have suppliers, customers and other businesses with whom they collaborate who themselves have ERP-type systems. An obvious development is to allow these

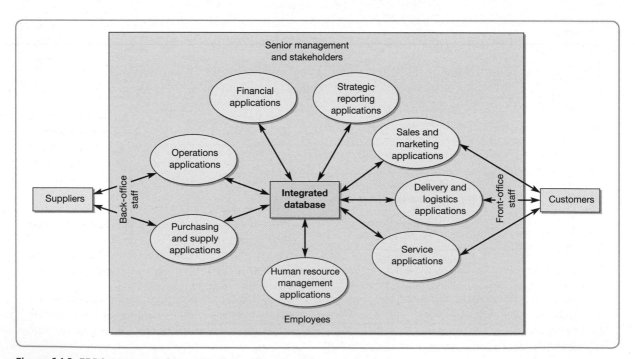

Figure 14.3 ERP integrates information from all parts of the organization

systems to communicate. However, the technical, as well as organizational and strategic, consequences of this can be formidable. Nevertheless, many authorities believe that the true value of ERP systems is only fully exploited when such web-integrated ERP (known by some people as 'collaborative commerce', or c-commerce) becomes widely implemented.

The benefits of ERP

ERP is generally seen as having the potential to very significantly improve the performance of many companies in many different sectors. This is partly because of the very much enhanced visibility that information integration gives, but it is also a function of the discipline that ERP demands. Yet this discipline is itself a 'double-edged' sword. On one hand, it 'sharpens up' the management of every process within an organization, allowing best practice (or at least common practice) to be implemented uniformly through the business. No longer will individual idiosyncratic behaviour by one part of a company's operations cause disruption to all other processes. On the other hand, it is the rigidity of this discipline that is both difficult to achieve and (arguably) inappropriate for all parts of the business. Nevertheless, the generally accepted benefits of ERP are usually held to be the following:

- Because software communicates across all functions, there is absolute visibility of what is happening in all parts of the business.

SHORT CASE **SAP and its partners**[4]

The largest European software company, based in Walldorf, Germany, SAP's growth over the years has matched the popularity of the ERP systems which are still the foundation of its success. Founded by five former IBM engineers in 1972, SAP launched its groundbreaking SAP R/1 system one year later. This was followed by SAP R/2 in 1979 and R/3 in 1992. In 1999 SAP anticipated the influence of the internet on network integration with its 'mySAP.com' product. Now customers in more than 120 countries run SAP 'business software' applications. These range, as the company phrases it, from distinct solutions addressing the needs of small businesses and mid-size companies, to suite offerings for global organizations. SAP defines 'business software' as comprising enterprise resource planning and related applications such as supply chain management, customer relationship management, product life-cycle management, and supplier relationship management.

SAP is well known for developing a network of 'business partners' to develop new products, sell its 'solutions', implement them into customers' operations, provide service, educate end users, and several other activities. There are various categories of partnerships:

- *Global alliances.* SAP global alliance partners are themselves global leaders and are therefore strategic partners with significant global presence. Membership is by invitation only.
- *Original equipment manufacturers (OEM).* This is for independent software vendors who integrate SAP

Source: Shutterstock.com/Monkey Business

technologies with their own products. OEM partners may add on, bundle, host, or embed SAP software.
- *Solution providers.* These partners offer customized solutions (a combination of business, technical or application expertise) that include SAP software.
- *Complementary technology partners.* These partners provide complete, technically verified turnkey (out-of-the-box) software solutions that extend and add value to SAP solutions.
- *Volume resellers.* These partners resell all or part of the SAP software portfolio and derive their primary revenue from licence sales.
- *Authorized education.* Partners are authorized by SAP to provide official training and education services to ensure that customers' employees gain optimal training.

- The discipline of forcing business-process-based changes (Chapters 1 and 18 look at business process) is an effective mechanism for making all parts of the business more efficient.
- There is better 'sense of control' of operations that will form the basis for continuous improvement (albeit within the confines of the common process structures).
- It enables far more sophisticated communication with customers, suppliers, and other business partners, often giving more accurate and timely information.
- It is capable of integrating whole supply chains, including suppliers' suppliers and customers' customers.

In fact, although the integration of several databases lies at the heart of ERP's power, it is nonetheless difficult to achieve in practice. This is why ERP installation can be particularly expensive. Attempting to get new systems and databases to talk to old (sometimes called *legacy*) systems can be very problematic. Not surprisingly, many companies choose to replace most, if not all, their existing systems simultaneously. New common systems and relational databases help to ensure the smooth transfer of data between different parts of the organization. In addition to the integration of systems, ERP usually includes other features which make it a powerful planning and control tool:

- It is based on a client–server architecture; that is, access to the information systems is open to anyone whose computer is linked to central computers.
- It can include decision support facilities (see Chapter 8) which enable operations decision makers to include the latest company information.
- It is often linked to external extranet systems, such as the electronic data interchange (EDI) systems, which are linked to the company's supply chain partners.
- It can be interfaced with standard applications programs which are in common use by most managers, such as spreadsheets, etc.
- Often, ERP systems are able to operate on most common platforms such as Windows or UNIX, or Linux.

SHORT CASE — The life and times of a chicken salad sandwich – part two[5]

Earlier (in Chapter 10) we looked at the schedule for the manufacture of a chicken salad sandwich. This concentrated on the lead times for the ordering of the ingredients and the manufacturing schedule for producing the sandwiches during the afternoon and night-time of each day for delivery during the evening and the night-time, and the morning of the following day. But that is only one half of the story, the half that is concerned with planning and controlling the timing of events. The other half concerns how the sandwich company manages the *quantity* of ingredients to order, the quantity of sandwiches to be made, and the whole chain of implications for the whole company. In fact, this sandwich company uses an ERP system that has at its core an MRP II package. This MRP II system has the two normal basic drivers of, first, a continually updated sales forecast, and, second, a product structure database. In this case the product structure and/or bill of materials is the 'recipe' for the sandwich, within the company this database is called the 'Recipe Management System'. The 'recipe' for the chicken sandwich (its bill of materials), is shown in Table 14.1.

Figure 14.4 shows the ERP system used by this sandwich company. Orders are received from customers

Source: Alamy Images/Numb

electronically through the EDI system. These orders are then checked through what the company calls a Validation System that checks the order against current product codes and expected quantities to make sure that the customer has not made any mistakes, such as forgetting to order some products (this happens surprisingly often). After validation the orders are transferred through the central database to the MRP II system that performs

Table 14.1 Bill of materials for a chicken salad sandwich

FUNCTION: MBIL		MULTI-LEVEL BILL INQUIRY					
PARENT: BTE80058		UM:EA	DESC:		HE CHICKEN SALAD TRY		LA
RV:			RUNLT:		0 FIXED LT: 0		
PLNR: LOU			PLN POL: N		DRWG: WA1882		

LEVEL 1…5 …10	PT USE	SEQN	COMPONENT	CT	PARTIAL DESCRIPTION	QTY	UM
1	PACK	010	FTE80045	P	H.E. CHICKENS	9	EA
2	ASSY	010	MBR–0032	P	BREAD HARVESTE	2	SL
3	HRPR	010	RBR–0023	N	BREAD HARVESTE	.4545455	EA
2	ASSY	020	RDY–0001	N	SPREAD BUTTER	.006	KG
2	ASSY	030	RMA–0028	N	MAYONNAISE MYB	.01	KG
2	ASSY	040	MFP–0016	P	CHICKEN FRESH	.045	KG
3	HRPR	010	RFP–0008	N	CHICKEN FRESH	1	KG
	ASSY	050	MVF–0063	P	TOMATO SLICE 4	3	SL
3	ALTI	010	RVF–0026	P	TOMATOES PRE–S	.007	KG
4	HRPR	010	RVF–0018	N	TOMATOES	1	KG
2	ASSY	060	MVF–0059	P	CUCUMBER SLICE	2	SL
3	ALTI	010	RVF–0027	P	CUCUMBER SLICE	.004	KG
4	TRAN	010	RVF–0017	N	CUCUMBER	1	KG
2	ASSY	070	MVF–0073	P	LETTUCE COS SL	.02	KG
3	HRPR	010	RVF–0015	N	LETTUCE COS	1	KG
2	ASSY	080	RPA–0070	N	WEBB BASE GREY	.00744	KG
2	ASSY	090	RPA–0071	N	WEBB TOP WHITE	.0116	KG
2	ASSY	100	RLA–0194	N	LABEL SW H	1	EA
2	ASSY	110	RLA–0110	N	STICKER NE	1	EA
1	PACK	010	RPA–0259	N	SOT LABELL	1	EA
1	PACK	030	RPA–0170	N	TRAY GREEN	1	EA

the main requirements breakdown. Based on these requirements and forecasted requirements for the next few days, orders are placed to the company's suppliers for raw materials and packaging. Simultaneously, confirmation is sent to customers, accounts are updated, staffing schedules are finalized for the next two weeks (on a rolling basis), customers are invoiced, and all this information is made available both to the customers' own ERP systems and the transportation company's planning system.

Interestingly, the company, like many others, found it difficult to implement its ERP system. 'It was a far bigger job than we thought', according to the company's operations director. 'We had to change the way we organized our processes so that they would fit in with the ERP system that we bought. But that was relatively easy compared to making sure that the system integrated with our customers', suppliers' and distributors' systems. Because some of these companies were also implementing new systems at the time, it was like trying to hit a moving target.' However, three years after the start of implementation, the whole process was working relatively smoothly.

Figure 14.4 The ERP structure for the sandwich company

ERP changes the way companies do business

Arguably the most significant issue in many companies' decision to buy an off-the-shelf ERP system is that of its compatibility with the company's current business processes and practices. The advice that is emerging from the companies that have adopted ERP (either successfully or unsuccessfully) is that it is extremely important to make sure that their current way of doing business will fit (or can be changed to fit) with a standard ERP package. In fact, one of the most common reasons for companies to decide not to install ERP is that they cannot reconcile the assumptions in the software of the ERP system with their core business processes. If, as most businesses find, their current processes do not fit, they can do one of two things. They could change their processes to fit the ERP package. Alternatively, they could modify the software within the ERP package to fit their processes. Both of these options involve costs and risks. Changing business practices that are working well will involve reorganization costs as well introducing the potential for errors to creep into the processes. Adapting the software will both slow down the project and introduce potentially dangerous software 'bugs' into the system. It would also make it difficult to upgrade the software later on.

> **✳ Operations principle**
>
> ERP systems are only fully effective if the way a business organizes its processes is aligned with the underlying assumption of its ERP system.

Why did companies invest in ERP?

If one accepts only some of the criticisms of ERP outlined in the critical commentary box below, it does pose the question as to why companies have invested such large amounts of money in it. Partly it was the attraction of turning the company's information systems into a 'smooth running and integrated machine'. The prospect of such organizational efficiency is attractive to most managers, even if it does presuppose a very simplistic model of how organizations work in practice. After a while, although organizations could now see the formidable problems in ERP implementation, the investments were justified on the basis that, 'even if we gain no significant advantage by investing in ERP, we will be placed at a disadvantage by *not* investing in it because all our competitors are doing so'. There is probably some truth in this; sometimes businesses have to invest just to stand still.

Web-integrated ERP

Perhaps the most important justification for embarking on ERP is the potential it gives the organization to link up with the outside world. For example, it is much easier for an operation to move into internet-based trading if it can integrate its external internet systems into

Far from being the magic ingredient which allows operations to fully integrate all their information, ERP is regarded by some as one of the most expensive ways of getting zero or even negative return on investment. For example, the American chemicals giant, Dow Chemical, spent almost half a billion dollars and seven years implementing an ERP system which became outdated almost as soon as it was implemented. One company, FoxMeyer Drug, claimed that the expense and problems which it encountered in implementing ERP eventually drove it into bankruptcy. One problem is that ERP implementation is expensive. This is partly because of the need to customize the system, understand its implications on the organization, and train staff to use it. Spending on what some call the *ERP ecosystem* (consulting, hardware, networking and complementary applications) has been estimated as being twice the spending on the software itself. But it is not only the expense which has disillusioned many companies, it is also the returns they have had for their investment. Some studies show that the vast majority of companies implementing ERP are disappointed with the effect it has had on their businesses. Certainly many companies find that they have to (sometimes fundamentally) change the way they organize their operations in order to fit in with ERP systems. This organizational impact of ERP (which has been described as the corporate equivalent of root-canal work) can have a significantly disruptive effect on the organization's operations.

its internal ERP systems. However, as has been pointed out by some critics of the ERP software companies, ERP vendors were not prepared for the impact of e-commerce and had not made sufficient allowance in their products for the need to interface with internet-based communication channels. The result of this has been that whereas the internal complexity of ERP systems was designed only to be intelligible to systems experts, the internet has meant that customers and suppliers (who are non-experts) are demanding access to the same information. So, important pieces of information such as the status of orders, whether products are in stock, the progress of invoicing, etc., need to be available, via the ERP system, on a company's website.

One problem is that different types of external company often need different types of information. Customers need to check the progress of their orders and invoicing, whereas suppliers and other partners want access to the details of operations planning and control. Not only that, but they want access all the time. The internet is always there, but web-integrated ERP systems are often complex and need periodic maintenance. This can mean that every time the ERP system is taken offline for routine maintenance or other changes, the website also goes offline. To combat this some companies configure their ERP and e-commerce links in such a way that they can be decoupled, so that ERP can be periodically shut down without affecting the company's web presence.

SHORT CASE | SAP at Rolls-Royce[6]

Rolls-Royce is one of the world's largest manufacturers of the gas turbines that are used to propel civil aircraft, military aircraft, ships, and in power generation as well as many other uses. They are exceptionally complex products, typically with around 25,000 parts, and hundreds of assemblies and sub-assemblies, and their production is equally complex with over 600 external suppliers and thousands of work centres in many different locations. This makes planning a complex task, which is why Rolls-Royce was one of the earliest users of computers to help with the task. Traditionally the company had developed its own software; however, this had become increasingly expensive compared with buying off-the-shelf systems. It was also risky because customized and complex software could be difficult to update and often could not exchange or share data. So, the company decided to implement a standard enterprise resource planning (ERP) system from the market-leading German SAP company. Because it was a 'commercial' off-the-shelf system it would force the company to adopt a standardized approach. Also it would fully integrate all the company's systems, and updates would be made available by SAP. Finally, the whole organization would be able to use a single database, reducing duplication and errors. The database modules included product information, resource information (plant assets, capacities of machines, all human resource data, etc.), inventory, external suppliers, order processing information, and external sales.

Yet the company knew that many ERP implementations had been expensive disasters. 'We were determined to ensure that this did not happen in Rolls-Royce', said Julian Goulder, who led the implementation. 'The project was too important to us; it was the largest single element within our strategic investment plan. So, we had a core technical team that led the design of the systems, and a large implementation team that was spread

Source: Shutterstock.com/ID1974

around the businesses. We always made sure that we communicated the changes throughout the company and used extensive education and training. We also phased the implementation to avoid any risky "big-bang" approach. There was an extensive data "clean-up" to ensure accuracy and integrity of existing information, and all existing processes were reviewed and standardized. In fact, this implementation forced us to re-examine all of our processes, to make sure that they fitted the SAP system. Within operations we have already seen a significant reduction in inventory, improved customer service, and substantially improved business information and controls.'

Supply chain ERP

The step beyond integrating internal ERP systems with immediate customers and suppliers is to integrate all the ERP and similar systems along a supply chain. Of course, this can never be straightforward and is often exceptionally complicated. Not only do different ERP systems have to communicate together, they have to integrate with other types of system. For example, sales and marketing functions often use systems such as customer relationship management (CRM, see Chapter 13) that manage the complexities of customer requirements, promises and transactions. Getting ERP and CRM systems to work together is itself often difficult. Sometimes the information from ERP systems has to be translated into a form that CRM and other e-commerce applications are able to understand. Nevertheless, such web-integrated ERP, or c-commerce (collaborative commerce), applications are emerging and starting to make an impact on the way companies do business. Although a formidable task, the benefits are potentially great. The costs of communicating between supply chain partners could be dramatically reduced and the potential for avoiding errors as information and products move between partners in the supply chain is significant. Yet as a final warning note, it is well to remember that, although integration can bring all the benefits of increased transparency in a supply chain, it may also transmit systems failure. If the ERP system of one operation within a supply chain fails for some reason, it may block the effective operation of the whole integrated information system throughout the chain.

> ✱ **Operations principle**
>
> The effectiveness of ERP systems depends partly on suppliers' and customers' ERP systems.

IMPLEMENTATION OF ERP SYSTEMS

By their nature, ERP systems are designed to address problems of information fragmentation. Therefore any ERP system will be complex and difficult to get right. Implementing this type of system will necessarily involve crossing organizational boundaries and integrating internal processes that cover many, if not all, functional areas of a business. Building a single system that simultaneously satisfies the requirements of operations managers, marketing and sales managers, finance managers and everyone else in the organization is never going to be easy. It is likely that each function will have its own set of processes and well-understood system that has been designed for its specific needs. Moving everyone onto a single, integrated system that runs off a single database is going to be potentially very unpopular. Furthermore, few people like change, and ERP asks almost everyone to change how they do their jobs. If ERP implementation was not difficult there would not be so many reports of the failure of ERP implementations, or even the complete abandonment of systems.

One of the key issues in ERP implementation is what critical success factors (CSFs) should be managed to increase the chances of a successful implementation. In this case, CSFs are those things that the organization must 'get right' in order for the ERP system to work effectively. Much of the research in this area has been summarized by Finney and Corbett[7] who distinguish between the broad, organization-wide, or strategic, factors, and the more project-specific, or tactical, factors. These are shown in Table 14.2.

Of course, some of these CSFs could be appropriate for any kind of complex implementation, whether of an ERP system, or some other major change to an operation. But that is the point.

SHORT CASE	What a waste[8]

Not only can ERP implementation go wrong, even when undertaken by experienced professionals, sometimes it can end up in the law courts. Waste Management, Inc. is the leading provider of waste and environmental services in North America. In 2008 it announced that it was suing SAP (see earlier short case) over the failure of an ERP implementation. Waste Management said that it was seeking the recovery of more than $100 million in project expenses as well as 'the savings and benefits that the SAP software was promised to deliver to Waste Management'. It said that SAP promised that the software could be fully implemented throughout all of Waste Management within 18 months, and that

Source: AL RF (PhotoDisc/Tracy Montana)

its software was an 'out-of-the-box' solution that would meet Waste Management's needs without any customization or enhancements.

Waste Management signed a sales pact with SAP in October, 2005, but according to Waste Management, 'Almost immediately following execution of the agreements, the SAP implementation team discovered significant "gaps" between the software's functionality and Waste Management's business requirements. Waste Management has discovered that these gaps were already known to the product development team in Germany even before the SLA (service level agreement) was signed.' But members of SAP's implementation team had reportedly blamed Waste Management for the functional gaps and had submitted change orders requiring that Waste Management pay for fixing them.

Table 14.2 Strategic and tactical critical success factors (CSF) related to successful ERP implementation

Strategic critical success factors	*Tactical critical success factors*
• Top-management commitment and support – strong and committed leadership at the top-management level is essential to the success of an ERP implementation.	• Balanced team – the need for an implementation team that spans the organization, as well as one that possesses a balance of business and IT skills.
• Visioning and planning – articulating a business vision to the organization, identifying clear goals and objectives, and providing a clear link between business goals and systems strategy.	• Project team – there is a critical need to put in place a solid, core implementation team that is comprised of the organization's 'best and brightest' individuals. These individuals should have a proven reputation and there should be a commitment to 'release' these individuals to the project on a full-time basis.
• Project champion – the individual should possess strong leadership skills as well as business, technical and personal managerial competencies.	• Communication plan – planned communication among various functions and organizational levels (specifically between business and IT personnel) is important to ensure that open communication occurs within the entire organization, as well as with suppliers and customers.
• Implementation strategy and timeframe – implement the ERP under a time-phased approach.	
• Project management – the ongoing management of the implementation plan.	• Project cost planning and management – it is important to know up front exactly what the implementation costs will be and dedicate the necessary budget.
• Change management – this concept refers to the need for the implementation team to formally prepare a change management programme and be conscious of the need to consider the implications of such a project. One key task is to build user acceptance of the project and a positive employee attitude. This might be accomplished through education about the benefits and need for an ERP system. Part of this building of user acceptance should also involve securing the support of opinion leaders throughout the organization. There is also a need for the team leader to effectively negotiate between various political turfs. Some authorities also stress that in planning the ERP project, it must be looked upon as a change management initiative, not an IT initiative.	• IT infrastructure – it is critical to assess the IT readiness of the organization, including the architecture and skills. If necessary, infrastructure might need to be upgraded or revamped.
	• Selection of ERP – the selection of an appropriate ERP package that matches the business's processes.
	• Consultant selection and relationship – some authorities advocate the need to include an ERP consultant as part of the implementation team.
	• Training and job redesign – training is a critical aspect of an implementation. It is also necessary to consider the impact of the change on the nature of work and the specific job descriptions.
	• Troubleshooting/crises management – it is important to be flexible in ERP implementations and to learn from unforeseen circumstances, as well as be prepared to handle unexpected crisis situations. The need for troubleshooting skills will be an ongoing requirement of the implementation process .

Based on Sherry Finney and Martin Corbett (2007) ERP implementation: a compilation and analysis of critical success factors, *Business Process Management Journal*, vol. 13, no. 3, 2007, 329–347.

ERP implementation certainly has some specific technical requirements, but good ERP implementation practice is very similar to other complicated and sensitive implementation. Again, what is different about ERP is that it is enterprise-wide, so implementation should always be considered on an enterprise-wide level. Therefore there will at all times be many different stakeholders to consider, each with their own concerns. That is why implementing an ERP system is always going to be an exercise in change management. Only if the anxieties of all relevant groups are addressed effectively will the prospect of achieving superior system performance be high.

At a purely practical level, many consultants who have had to live through the difficulties of implementing ERP have summarized their experiences. The following list of likely problems with an ERP implementation is typical (and really does reflect reality):[9]

- The total cost is likely to be underestimated.
- The time and effort to implement it is likely to be underestimated.
- The resourcing from both the business and the IT function is likely to be higher than anticipated.
- The level of outside expertise required will be more than anticipated.
- The changes required to business processes will be greater than expected.
- Controlling the scope of the project will be more difficult than expected.
- There will never be enough training.
- The need for change management is not likely to be recognized until it is too late, and the changes required to corporate culture are likely to be grossly underestimated. (This is the single biggest failure point for ERP implementations.)

SUMMARY ANSWERS TO KEY QUESTIONS

Check and improve your understanding of this chapter using self-assessment questions and a personalized study plan, a video case study, and an eText - all at www.myomlab.com.

MyOMLab

❯ What is ERP?

- ERP is an enterprise-wide information system that integrates all the information from many functions needed for planning and controlling operations activities. This integration around a common database allows for transparency.
- It often requires very considerable investment in the software itself, as well as its implementation. More significantly, it often requires a company's processes to be changed to bring them in line with the assumptions built into the ERP software.

❯ How did ERP develop?

- ERP can be seen as the latest development from the original planning and control approach, known as materials requirements planning (MRP).
- Although ERP is becoming increasingly competent at the integration of internal systems and databases, there is the even more significant potential for integration with other organizations' ERP (and equivalent) systems.
- In particular, the use of internet-based communication between customers, suppliers and other partners in the supply chain has opened up the possibility of web-based integration.

● Because ERP systems are designed to address problems of information fragmentation, implementation will be complex, crossing organizational boundaries.

● There are a number of critical success factors (CSFs) that the organization must 'get right' in order for the ERP system to work effectively. Some of these are broad, organization-wide, or strategic, factors. Others are more project-specific, or tactical, factors.

CASE STUDY   Psycho Sports Ltd

Peter Townsend knew that he would have to make some decisions pretty soon. His sports goods manufacturing business, Psycho Sports, had grown so rapidly over the last two years that he would soon have to install some systematic procedures and routines to manage the business. His biggest problem was in manufacturing control. He had started off making specialist high-quality table tennis bats but now made a wide range of sports products, including tennis balls, darts and protective equipment for various games. Furthermore, his customers, once limited to specialist sports shops, now included some of the major sports retail chains. *'We really do have to get control of our manufacturing. I keep getting told that we need what seems to be called an MRP system. I wasn't sure what this meant and so I have bought a specialist production control book from our local bookshop and read all about MRP principles. I must admit, these academics seem to delight in making simple things complicated. And there is so much jargon associated with the technique, I feel more confused now than I did before.*

Source: Shutterstock.com/Chen WS

'Perhaps the best way forward is for me to take a very simple example from my own production unit and see whether I can work things out manually. If I can follow the process through on paper then I will be far better equipped to decide what kind of computer-based system we should get, if any!'

Peter decided to take as his example one of his new products: a table tennis bat marketed under the name of the 'high-resolution' bat, but known within the manufacturing unit more prosaically as Part Number 5654. Figure 14.5 shows the product structure for this table tennis bat, showing the table tennis bat made up of two main assemblies: a handle assembly and a face assembly. In order to bring the two main assemblies together to form the finished bat, various fixings are required, such as nails, connectors, etc.

The gross requirements for this particular bat are shown below. The bat is not due to be launched until Week 13 (it is now Week 1), and sales forecasts have been made for the first 23 weeks of sales:

Weeks 13–21 inclusive, 100 per week
Weeks 22–29 inclusive, 150 per week
Weeks 30–35 inclusive, 200 per week.

Peter also managed to obtain information on the current inventory levels of each of the parts which made up the finished bat, together with cost data and lead times. He was surprised, however, how long it took him to obtain this information. *'It has taken me nearly two days to get hold of all the information I need. Different people held it, nowhere was it conveniently put together, and sometimes it was not even written down. To get the inventory data, I actually had to go down to the stores and count how many parts were in the boxes.'*

Figure 14.5 Product structure for bat 5654

The data Peter collected was as shown in Table 14.3.

Peter set himself six exercises which he knew he would have to master if he was to understand fully the basics of MRP.

Exercise 1

Draw up:

(a) the single-level bill of materials for each level of assembly;

(b) a complete indented bill of materials for all levels of assembly.

Exercise 2

(a) Create the materials requirements planning records for each part and sub-assembly in the bat.

(b) List any problems that the completed MRP records identify.

(c) What alternatives are there that the company could take to solve any problems? What are their relative merits?

Table 14.3 Inventory, cost and lead-time information for parts

Part no.	Description	Inventory	EQ	LT	Std cost
5645	Bat	0	500	2	12.00
0499	Handle assy	0	400	3	4.00
7754	Shaft	15	1,000	5	1.00
0955	Connector	350	5,000	4	0.02
9110	Nail	120	5,000	4	0.01
8744	Rivet	3,540	5,000	4	0.01
0772	Face assy	0	250	4	5.00
1821	Handle	0	500	4	2.00
6511	Rubber face	0	2,000	10	0.50
2547	Wooden inner	10	300	7	1.50
8561	Foam panel	0	1,000	8	0.50

LT = lead time for ordering (in weeks); EQ = economic quantity for ordering; Std cost = standard cost in £.

Exercise 3

Based on the first two exercises, create another set of MRP records, this time allowing one week's safety lead time for each item: that is, ensuring the items are in stock the week prior to when they are required.

Exercise 4

Over the time period of the exercise, what effect would the imposition of a safety lead time have on average inventory value?

Exercise 5

If we decided that our first task was to reduce inventory costs by 15 per cent, what action would we recommend? What are the implications of our action?

Exercise 6

How might production in our business be smoothed?

QUESTIONS

1 Why did Peter have such problems getting to the relevant information?

2 Perform all the exercises which Peter set for himself. Do you think he should now fully understand MRP?

PROBLEMS AND APPLICATIONS

MyOMLab

These problems and applications will help to improve your analysis of operations. You can find more practice problems as well as worked examples and guided solutions on MyOMLab at **www.myomlab.com**.

1 Your company has developed a simple, but amazingly effective mango peeler. It is constructed from a blade and a supergrip handle that has a top piece and a bottom piece. The assembled mango peeler is packed in a simple recycled card pack. All the parts simply clip together and are bought in from suppliers, who can deliver the parts within one week of orders being placed. Given enough parts, your company can produce products within a day of firm orders being placed. Initial forecasts indicate that demand will be around 500 items per week.
   (a) Draw a component structure and bill of materials for the mango peeler.
   (b) Develop a master production schedule for the product.
   (c) Develop a schedule indicating when and how many of each component should be ordered (your scheduler tells you that the economic order quantity, EOQ, for all parts is 2,500).

2 The mango peeler described above was a huge success. Demand is now level at 800 items per week. You now have also developed two further products, a melon baller and a passion fruit pulper. Both new products use the same handle, but have their own specially designed handle and pack. Demand for the new products is expected to be 400 items per week. Also your suppliers have indicated that, because of the extra demand, they will need two weeks to deliver orders. Similarly, your own assembly department is now taking a week to assemble the products.
   (a) Draw new component structures and bills of material for the new products.
   (b) Develop a master production schedule for all the products.
   (c) Develop a schedule indicating when and how many of each component should be ordered.

3 Using a cookery book, choose three similar, fairly complex, recipe items such as layered and decorated gateaux (cakes) or desserts. For each, construct the indented bill of materials and identify all the different materials, sub-assemblies and final products with one set of part numbers (i.e. no duplication). Using the times given in the recipes (or your own estimates), construct a table of lead times (e.g. in minutes or hours) for each stage of production and for

procurement of the ingredients. Using these examples (and a bit of your own imagination!), show how this information could be used with an MRP system to plan and control the batch production processes within a small cake or dessert factory making thousands of each product every week. Show part of the MRP records and calculations that would be involved.

4   **(Advanced)** Working in a small study group, construct a model of the information systems that you think would be needed to plan and control the most important day-to-day operations and finances of a large university or college. In particular, identify and include at least three processes that cross departmental and functional boundaries, and show how ERP might be used to improve the quality, speed, dependability, flexibility, and/or costs of such processes. Then discuss:

(a) If ERP is not already in use at your chosen organization, should it be introduced, and if so why? What would the difficulties be in doing this, and how could they be overcome?

(b) If ERP is already in use, what advantages and disadvantages are already apparent to the staff (e.g. ask a lecturer, an administrator, and a support services manager, such as someone who runs cleaning or catering services).

SELECTED FURTHER READING

Bradford, M. (2010) *Modern ERP: Select, Implement & Use Today's Advanced Business Systems*, lulu.com. A good solid class text.

Davenport, T.H. (1998) **Putting the enterprise into the enterprise system**, *Harvard Business Review*, July–August. Covers some of the more managerial and strategic aspects of ERP.

Koch, C. and Wallgum, T. (2007) **ERP definition and solutions**, www.cio.com. *CIO.com* has some really useful articles; this is one of the most thought-provoking.

Srivastava, D. and Batra A. (2010) *ERP Systems*, I K International Publishing House Pvt. Ltd, New Delhi. An in-depth study of ERP systems and its benefits, including implementation.

Turbit, N. (2005) **ERP implementation – the traps, the project perfect white paper collection**, www.projectperfect.com.au. Practical (and true).

Vollmann, T.E., Berry, W.L., Whybark, D.C. and Jacobs, F.R. (2004) *Manufacturing Planning and Control Systems for Supply Chain Management: The Definitive Guide for Professionals*, McGraw-Hill, New York. The latest version of the 'bible' of manufacturing planning and control. Explains the 'workings' of MRP and ERP in detail.

USEFUL WEBSITES

www.bpic.co.uk Some useful information on general planning and control topics.

www.cio.com/article/40323/ERP-Definition_and_Solutions Several descriptions and useful information on ERP-related topics.

www.erpfans.com Yes, even ERP has its own fan club! Debates and links for the enthusiast.

www.sap.com/index.epx 'Helping to build better businesses for more than three decades', SAP has been the leading worldwide supplier of ERP systems for ages. They should know how to do it by now!

www.sapfans.com Another fan club, this one is for SAP enthusiasts.

www.apics.org The American professional and education body that has its roots in planning and control activities.

www.myomlab.com Test which sections you have mastered and which you need to review, with questions, a personalized study plan, video clips, revision tips, and cases.

INTRODUCTION

Materials requirements planning (MRP) is an approach to calculating how many parts or materials of particular types are required and what times they are required. This requires data files which, when the MRP program is run, can be checked and updated. Figure S14.1 shows how these files relate to each other. The first inputs to materials requirements planning are customer orders and forecast demand. MRP performs its calculations based on the combination of these two parts of future demand. All other requirements are derived from, and dependent on, this demand information.

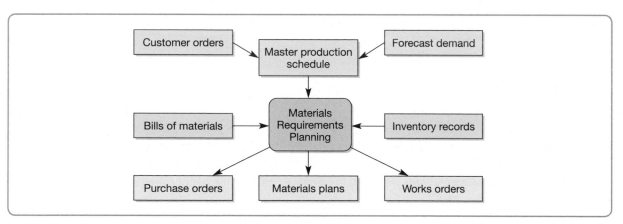

Figure S14.1 Materials requirements planning (MRP) schematic

MASTER PRODUCTION SCHEDULE

The master production schedule (MPS) forms the main input to materials requirements planning and contains a statement of the volume and timing of the end products to be made. It drives all the production and supply activities that eventually will come together to form the end products. It is the basis for the planning and utilization of labour and equipment, and it determines the provisioning of materials and cash. The MPS should include all sources of demand, such as spare parts, internal production promises, etc. For example, if a manufacturer of earth excavators plans an exhibition of its products and allows a project team to raid the stores so that it can build two pristine examples to be exhibited, this is likely to leave the factory short of parts. MPS can also be used in service organizations. For example, in a hospital theatre there is a master schedule that contains a statement of which operations are planned and when. This can be used to provision materials for the operations, such as sterile instruments, blood and dressings. It may also govern the scheduling of staff for operations.

The master production schedule record

Master production schedules are time-phased records of each end product, which contain a statement of demand and currently available stock of each finished item. Using this information, the available inventory is projected ahead in time. When there is insufficient inventory to satisfy forward demand, order quantities are entered on the master schedule line. Table S14.1 is a simplified example of part of a master production schedule for one item. In the first row the known sales orders and any forecast are combined to form 'Demand'. The second row, 'Available', shows how much inventory of this item is expected to be in stock at the end of each weekly period. The opening inventory balance, 'On hand', is shown separately at the bottom of the record. The third row is the master production schedule, or MPS; this shows how many finished items need to be completed and available in each week to satisfy demand.

Table S14.1 Example of a master production schedule

	Week number								
	1	2	3	4	5	6	7	8	9
Demand	10	10	10	10	15	15	15	20	20
Available	20	10	0	0	0	0	0	0	0
MPS	0	0	10	10	15	15	15	20	20
On hand	30								

Chase or level master production schedules

In the example in Table S14.1, the MPS increases as demand increases and aims to keep available inventory at 0. The master production schedule is 'chasing' demand (see Chapter 11) and so adjusting the provision of resources. An alternative 'levelled' MPS for this situation is shown in Table S14.2. Level scheduling involves averaging the amount required to be completed to smooth out peaks and troughs; it generates more inventory than the previous MPS.

Table S14.2 Example of a 'level' master production schedule

	Week number								
	1	2	3	4	5	6	7	8	9
Demand	10	10	10	10	15	15	15	20	20
Available	31	32	33	34	30	26	22	13	4
MPS	11	11	11	11	11	11	11	11	11
On hand	30								

Available to promise (ATP)

The master production schedule provides the information to the sales function on what can be promised to customers and when delivery can be promised. The sales function can load known sales orders against the master production schedule and keep track of what is available to promise (ATP) (see Table S14.3). The ATP line in the master production schedule shows the maximum that is still available in any one week, against which sales orders can be loaded.

Table S14.3 Example of a level master production schedule including available to promise

					Week number				
	1	**2**	**3**	**4**	**5**	**6**	**7**	**8**	**9**
Demand	10	10	10	10	15	15	15	20	20
Sales orders	10	10	10	8	4				
Available	31	32	33	34	30	26	22	13	4
ATP	31	1	1	3	7	11	11	11	11
MPS	11	11	11	11	11	11	11	11	11
On hand	30								

THE BILL OF MATERIALS (BOM)

From the master schedule, MRP calculates the required volume and timing of assemblies, sub-assemblies and materials. To do this it needs information on what parts are required for each product. This is called the 'bill of materials'. Initially it is simplest to think about these as a product structure. The product structure in Figure S14.2 is a simplified structure showing the parts required to make a simple board game. Different 'levels of assembly' are shown with the finished product (the boxed game) at level 0, the parts and sub-assemblies that go into the boxed game at level 1, the parts that go into the sub-assemblies at level 2, and so on.

A more convenient form of the product structure is the 'indented bill of materials'. Table S14.4 shows the whole indented bill of materials for the board game. The term

Figure S14.2 Product structure for the Treasure Hunt game

Table S14.4 Indented bill of materials for board game

Part number: 00289

Description: Board game

Level: 0

Level	Part number	Description	Quantity
0	00289	Board game	1
. 1	10077	Box lid	1
. 1	10089	Box base assy	1
. . 2	20467	Box base	1
. . 2	10062	TV label	1
. . 2	23988	Inner tray	1
. 1	10023	Quest cards set	1
. 1	10045	Character set	1
. 1	10067	Die	2
. 1	10062	TV label	1
. 1	10033	Game board	1
. 1	10056	Rules booklet	1

'indented' refers to the indentation of the level of assembly, shown in the left-hand column. Multiples of some parts are required; this means that MRP has to know the required number of each part to be able to multiply up the requirements. Also, the same part (for example, the TV label, part number 10062) may be used in different parts of the product structure. This means that MRP has to cope with this commonality of parts and, at some stage, aggregate the requirements to check how many labels in total are required.

INVENTORY RECORDS

MRP calculations need to recognize that some required items may already be in stock. So, it is necessary, starting at level 0 of each bill, to check how much inventory is available of each finished product, sub-assembly and component, and then to calculate what is termed the 'net' requirements; that is, the extra requirements needed to supplement the inventory so that demand can be met. This requires that three main inventory records are kept: the item master file, which contains the unique standard identification code for each part or component; the transaction file, which keeps a record of receipts into stock, issues from stock and a running balance; and the location file, which identifies where inventory is located.

THE MRP NETTING PROCESS

The information needs of MRP are important, but it is not the 'heart' of the MRP procedure. At its core, MRP is a systematic process of taking this planning information and calculating the volume and timing requirements which will satisfy demand. The most important element

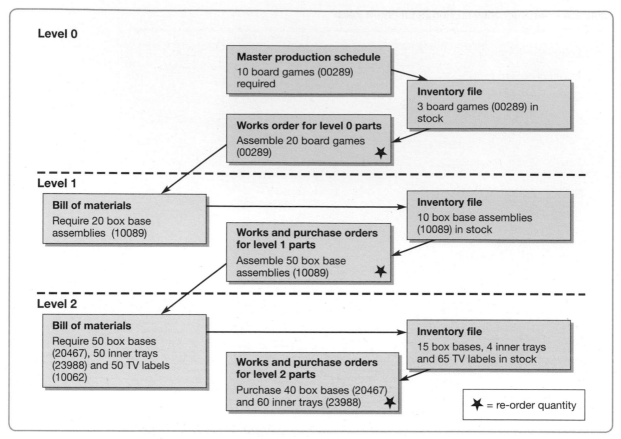

Level 0

Master production schedule
10 board games (00289)
required

Inventory file
3 board games (00289) in
stock

Works order for level 0 parts
Assemble 20 board games
(00289) ✴

Level 1

Bill of materials
Require 20 box base
assemblies (10089)

Inventory file
10 box base assemblies
(10089) in stock

Works and purchase orders
for level 1 parts
Assemble 50 box base
assemblies (10089) ✴

Level 2

Bill of materials
Require 50 box bases
(20467), 50 inner trays
(23988) and 50 TV labels
(10062)

Inventory file
15 box bases, 4 inner trays
and 65 TV labels in stock

Works and purchase orders
for level 2 parts
Purchase 40 box bases (20467)
and 60 inner trays (23988) ✴

✴ = re-order quantity

Figure S14.3 Example of the MRP netting process for the board game

of this is the MRP netting process. Figure S14.3 illustrates the process that MRP performs to calculate the volumes of materials required. The master production schedule is 'exploded', examining the implications of the schedule through the bill of materials, checking how many sub-assemblies and parts are required. Before moving down the bill of materials to the next level, MRP checks how many of the required parts are already available in stock. It then generates 'works orders', or requests, for the net requirements of items. These form the schedule which is again exploded through the bill of materials at the next level down. This process continues until the bottom level of the bill of materials is reached.

Back-scheduling

In addition to calculating the volume of materials required, MRP also considers when each of these parts is required; that is, the timing and scheduling of materials. It does this by a process called back-scheduling which takes into account the lead time (the time allowed for completion of each stage of the process) at every level of assembly. Again using the example of the board game, assume that 10 board games are required to be finished by a notional planning day which we will term day 20. To determine when we need to start work on all the parts that make up the game, we need to know all the lead times that are stored in MRP files for each part (*see* Table S14.5).

Using the lead-time information, the programme is worked backwards to determine the tasks that have to be performed and the purchase orders that have to be placed. Given the lead times and inventory levels shown in Table S14.5, the MRP records shown in Figure S14.4 can be derived.

Table S14.5 Back-scheduling of requirements in MRP

Part no.	Description	Inventory on hand day 0	Lead time (days)	Re-order quantity
00289	Board game	3	2	20
10077	Box lid	4	8	25
10089	Box base assy	10	4	50
20467	Box base	15	12	40
23988	Inner tray	4	14	60
10062	TV label	65	8	100
10023	Quest cards set	4	3	50
10045	Character set	46	3	50
10067	Die	22	5	80
10033	Game board	8	15	50
10056	Rules booklet	0	3	80

MRP CAPACITY CHECKS

The MRP process needs a feedback loop to check whether a plan was achievable and whether it has actually been achieved. Closing this planning loop in MRP systems involves checking production plans against available capacity and, if the proposed plans are not achievable at any level, revising them. All but the simplest MRP systems are now closed-loop systems. They use three planning routines to check production plans against the operation's resources at three levels:

- Resource requirements plans (RRPs) involve looking forward in the long term to predict the requirements for large structural parts of the operation, such as the numbers, locations and sizes of new plants.
- Rough-cut capacity plans (RCCPs) are used in the medium to short term, to check the master production schedules against known capacity bottlenecks, in case capacity constraints are broken. The feedback loop at this level checks the MPS and key resources only.
- Capacity requirements plans (CRPs) look at the day-to-day effect of the works orders issued from the MRP on the loading individual process stages.

00289: Treasure Hunt game   Assembly lead time = 2   Re-order quantity = 20

Day Number:	0	1	2	3	4	5	6	7	8	9	10	11	12	13	14	15	16	17	18	19	20
Requirements Gross																					10
Scheduled Receipts																					
On hand Inventory	3	3	3	3	3	3	3	3	3	3	3	3	3	3	3	3	3	3	3	3	13
Planned Order Release																			20		

10077: Box lid   Purchase lead time = 8   Re-order quantity = 25

Day Number:	0	1	2	3	4	5	6	7	8	9	10	11	12	13	14	15	16	17	18	19	20
Requirements Gross																			20		
Scheduled Receipts																					
On hand Inventory	4	4	4	4	4	4	4	4	4	4	4	4	4	4	4	4	4	4	9	9	9
Planned Order Release											25										

10089: Box base assembly   Assembly lead time = 4   Re-order quantity = 50

Day Number:	0	1	2	3	4	5	6	7	8	9	10	11	12	13	14	15	16	17	18	19	20
Requirements Gross																			20		
Scheduled Receipts																					
On hand Inventory	10	10	10	10	10	10	10	10	10	10	10	10	10	10	10	10	10	10	40	40	40
Planned Order Release															50						

20467: Box base   Purchase lead time = 12   Re-order quantity = 40

Day Number:	0	1	2	3	4	5	6	7	8	9	10	11	12	13	14	15	16	17	18	19	20
Requirements Gross															50						
Scheduled Receipts																					
On hand Inventory	15	15	15	15	15	15	15	15	15	15	15	15	15	15	5	5	5	5	5	5	5
Planned Order Release			40																		

23988: Inner tray   Purchase lead time = 14   Re-order quantity = 60

Day Number:	0	1	2	3	4	5	6	7	8	9	10	11	12	13	14	15	16	17	18	19	20
Requirements Gross															50						
Scheduled Receipts																					
On hand Inventory	4	4	4	4	4	4	4	4	4	4	4	4	4	4	14	14	14	14	14	14	14
Planned Order Release	60																				

10062: TV label   Purchase lead time = 8   Re-order quantity = 100

Day Number:	0	1	2	3	4	5	6	7	8	9	10	11	12	13	14	15	16	17	18	19	20
Requirements Gross															50				20		
Scheduled Receipts																					
On hand Inventory	65	65	65	65	65	65	65	65	65	65	65	65	65	65	15	15	15	15	95	95	95
Planned Order Release											100										

10023: Quest card set   Purchase lead time = 3   Re-order quantity = 50

Day Number:	0	1	2	3	4	5	6	7	8	9	10	11	12	13	14	15	16	17	18	19	20
Requirements Gross																			20		
Scheduled Receipts																					
On hand Inventory	4	4	4	4	4	4	4	4	4	4	4	4	4	4	4	4	4	4	34	34	34
Planned Order Release															50						

10045: Character set   Purchase lead time = 3   Re-order quantity = 50

Day Number:	0	1	2	3	4	5	6	7	8	9	10	11	12	13	14	15	16	17	18	19	20
Requirements Gross																			20		
Scheduled Receipts																					
On hand Inventory	46	46	46	46	46	46	46	46	46	46	46	46	46	46	46	46	46	46	26	26	26
Planned Order Release																					

10067: Die   Purchase lead time = 5   Re-order quantity = 80

Day Number:	0	1	2	3	4	5	6	7	8	9	10	11	12	13	14	15	16	17	18	19	20
Requirements Gross																			40		
Scheduled Receipts																					
On hand Inventory	3	3	3	3	3	3	3	3	3	3	3	3	3	3	3	3	3	3	3	3	13
Planned Order Release														80							

10033: Game board   Purchase lead time = 15   Re-order quantity = 50

Day Number:	0	1	2	3	4	5	6	7	8	9	10	11	12	13	14	15	16	17	18	19	20
Requirements Gross																			20		
Scheduled Receipts																					
On hand Inventory	8	8	8	8	8	8	8	8	8	8	8	8	8	8	8	8	8	8	38	38	38
Planned Order Release			50																		

10056: Rules booklet   Purchase lead time = 3   Re-order quantity = 80

Day Number:	0	1	2	3	4	5	6	7	8	9	10	11	12	13	14	15	16	17	18	19	20
Requirements Gross																			20		
Scheduled Receipts																					
On hand Inventory	0	0	0	0	0	0	0	0	0	0	0	0	0	0	0	0	0	0	60	60	60
Planned Order Release															80						

Figure S14.4 Extract of the MRP records for the board game

SUMMARY

- MRP stands for materials requirements planning which is a dependent demand system that calculates materials requirements and production plans to satisfy known and forecast sales orders. It helps to make volume and timing calculations based on an idea of what will be necessary to supply demand in the future.
- MRP works from a master production schedule which summarizes the volume and timing of end products or services. Using the logic of the bill of materials (BOM) and inventory records, the production schedule is 'exploded' (called the MRP netting process) to determine how many sub-assemblies and parts are required, and when they are required.
- Closed-loop MRP systems contain feedback loops which ensure that checks are made against capacity to see if plans are feasible.
- MRP II systems are a development of MRP. They integrate many processes that are related to MRP, but which are located outside the operation's function.

MyOMLab

Now that you have finished reading this chapter, why not visit MyOMLab at www.myomlab.com where you'll find more learning resources to help you make the most of your studies and get a better grade.

15

Lean synchronization

Key questions

❯ What is lean synchronization?

❯ How does lean synchronization eliminate waste?

❯ How does lean synchronization apply throughout the supply network?

❯ How does lean synchronization compare with other approaches?

INTRODUCTION

This chapter examines an approach that we call 'lean synchronization' or just 'lean'. It was originally called 'just-in-time' (JIT) when it started to be adopted outside its birthplace, Japan. It is, at the same time, a philosophy, a method of operations planning and control and an approach to improvement. Lean synchronization aims to meet demand instantaneously, with perfect quality and no waste. This involves supplying products and services in perfect synchronization with the demand for them. These principles were once a radical departure from traditional operations practice, but have now become orthodox in promoting the synchronization of flow through processes, operations and supply networks. Figure 15.1 places lean synchronization in the overall model of operations management.

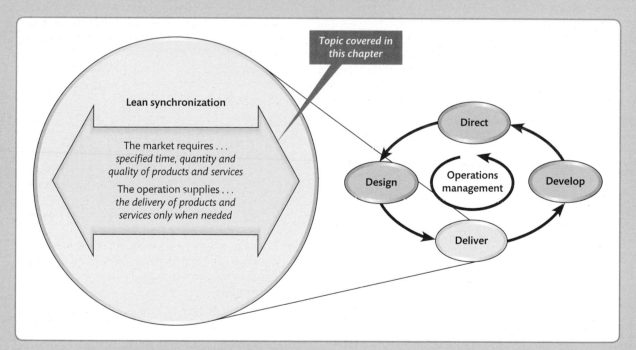

Figure 15.1 This chapter covers lean synchronization

Seen as the leading practitioner and the main originator of the lean approach, the Toyota Motor Company has progressively synchronized all its processes simultaneously to give high-quality, fast throughput and exceptional productivity. It has done this by developing a set of practices that has largely shaped what we now call 'lean' or 'just-in-time' but which Toyota calls the Toyota Production System (TPS). The TPS has two themes, 'just-in-time' and 'jidoka'. Just-in-time is defined as the rapid and co-ordinated movement of parts throughout the production system and supply network to meet customer demand. It is operationalized by means of *heijunka* (levelling and smoothing the flow of items), *kanban* (signalling to the preceding process that more parts are needed) and *nagare* (laying out processes to achieve smoother flow of parts throughout the production process). *Jidoka* is described as 'humanizing the interface between operator and machine'. Toyota's philosophy is that the machine is there to serve the operator's purpose. The operator should be left free to exercise his/her judgement. Jidoka is operationalized by means of fail-safeing (or machine jidoka), line-stop authority (or human jidoka), and visual control (at-a-glance status of production processes and visibility of process standards).

Toyota believe that both just-in-time and jidoka should be applied ruthlessly to the elimination of waste, where waste is defined as 'anything other than the minimum amount of equipment, items, parts and workers that are absolutely essential to production'. Fujio Cho of Toyota identified seven types of waste that must be

Source: Alamy Images/Hannu Li vaar

eliminated from all operations processes. They are, waste from over-production, waste from waiting time, transportation waste, inventory waste, processing waste, waste of motion, and waste from product defects. Beyond this, authorities on Toyota claim that its strength lies in understanding the differences between the tools and practices used with Toyota operations and the overall philosophy of their approach to lean synchronization. This is what some have called the apparent paradox of the Toyota production system, 'namely, that activities, connections and production flows in a Toyota factory are rigidly scripted, yet at the same time Toyota's operations are enormously flexible and adaptable. Activities and processes are constantly being challenged and pushed to a higher level of performance, enabling the company to continually innovate and improve.'

One influential study of Toyota identified four rules that guide the design, delivery, and development activities within the company:[1]

- *Rule one* – all work shall be highly specified as to content, sequence, timing, and outcome.
- *Rule two* – every customer-supplier connection must be direct and there must be an unambiguous yes or no method of sending requests and receiving responses.
- *Rule three* – the route for every product and service must be simple and direct.
- *Rule four* – any improvement must be made in accordance with the scientific method, under the guidance of a teacher, and at the lowest possible level in the organization.

WHAT IS LEAN SYNCHRONIZATION?

Synchronization means that the flow of items (materials, information or customers) that constitute services and products always delivers exactly what customers want (perfect quality), in exact quantities (neither too much nor too little), exactly when needed (not too early or too late), and exactly where required (not to the wrong location). *Lean* synchronization is to do all this at the lowest possible cost. It results in items flowing rapidly and smoothly through processes, operations and supply networks.

Synchronization, 'lean' and 'just-in-time'

Different terms are used to describe what here we call lean synchronization. Our definition – *'lean synchronization aims to meet demand instantaneously, with perfect quality and no waste'* – could also be used to describe the general concept of 'lean', or 'just-in-time' (JIT). The concept of 'lean' stresses the elimination of waste, while 'just-in-time' emphasizes the idea of producing items only when they are needed. But all three concepts overlap to a very large degree, and no definition fully conveys the full implications for operations practice. Here we use the term lean synchronization because it best describes the impact of these ideas on flow and delivery.

The benefits of synchronized flow

When first introduced, the lean synchronization (often called just 'lean' or 'just-in-time') approach was relatively radical, even for large and sophisticated companies. Now the lean approach is being adopted outside its traditional high-volume and manufacturing roots. But wherever it is applied, the principles remain the same. The best way to understand how lean synchronization differs from more traditional approaches to managing flow is to contrast the two simple processes in Figure 15.2. The traditional approach assumes that each stage in the process will place its output in an inventory that 'buffers' that stage from the next one downstream in the process. The next stage down will then (eventually) take outputs from the inventory, process them, and pass them through to the next buffer inventory. These buffers are there to insulate each stage from its neighbours, making each stage relatively independent so that if, for example, stage A stops operating for some reason, stage B can continue, at least for a time. The larger the buffer inventory, the greater the degree of insulation between the stages. This insulation has to be paid for in terms of inventory and slow throughput times because items will spend time waiting in the buffer inventories.

But, the main argument against this traditional approach lies in the very conditions it seeks to promote, namely the insulation of the stages from one another. When a problem occurs at one stage, the problem will not immediately be apparent elsewhere in the system. The responsibility for solving the problem will be centred largely on the people within that stage, and the consequences of the problem will be prevented from spreading to the whole system.

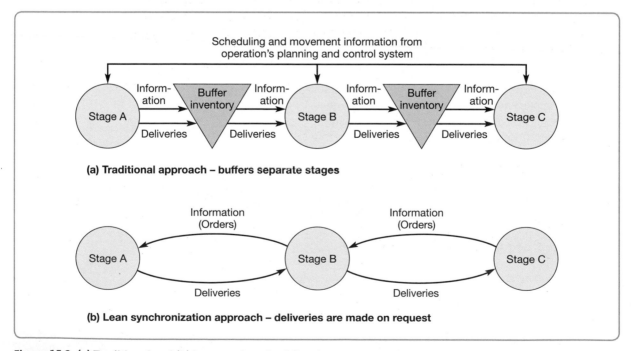

Figure 15.2 (a) Traditional and (b) lean synchronized flow between stages

However, contrast this with the pure lean synchronized process illustrated in Figure 15.2. Here items are processed and then passed directly to the next stage in a synchronized manner 'just-in-time' for them to be processed further. Problems at any stage have a very different effect in such a system. Now if stage A stops processing, stage B will notice immediately and stage C very soon after. Stage A's problem is now quickly exposed to the whole process, which is immediately affected by the problem. This means that the responsibility for solving the problem is no longer confined to the staff at stage A. It is now shared by everyone, considerably improving the chances of the problem being solved, if only because it is now too important to be ignored. In other words, by preventing items accumulating between stages, the operation has increased the chances of the intrinsic efficiency of the plant being improved. Non-synchronized approaches seek to encourage efficiency by protecting each part of the process from disruption. The lean synchronized approach takes the opposite view. Exposure of the system (although not suddenly, as in our simplified example) to problems can both make them more evident and change the 'motivation structure' of the whole system towards solving the problems. Lean synchronization sees accumulations of inventory as a 'blanket of obscurity' that lies over the production system and prevents problems being noticed. This same argument can be applied when, instead of queues of material, or information (inventory), an operation has to deal with queues of customers.

> *** Operations principle**
> Buffer inventory used to insulate stages or processes localizes the motivation to improve.

Now think of the logic behind the explanation above. There are four interrelated ideas that 'mesh' with each other to form a logical chain. First, between each stage, it is the downstream 'customer' stage that signals the need for action. It is the customer who, in effect, 'pulls' items through the process. The starting point of the lean philosophy is a customer focus. Second, this customer 'pull' encourages items to flow through the process in a synchronized manner (rather than dwelling as inventory). Third, the smooth synchronized flow and resulting reduction in inventory affects the motivation to improve because stages are no longer decoupled. Fourth, the increased motivation to improve exposes waste and encourages its elimination. These four related ideas are illustrated in Figure 15.3, and we will discuss them further in the rest of this chapter.

The river and rocks analogy

The idea of obscuring effects of inventory is often illustrated diagrammatically, as in Figure 15.4. The many problems of the operation are shown as rocks in a river bed that cannot be seen because of the depth of the water. The water in this analogy represents the inventory

Figure 15.3 The four elements of lean

Figure 15.4 Reducing the level of inventory (water) allows operations management (the ship) to see the problems in the operation (the rocks) and work to reduce them

in the operation. Yet, even though the rocks cannot be seen, they slow the progress of the river's flow and cause turbulence. Gradually reducing the depth of the water (inventory) exposes the worst of the problems which can be resolved, after which the water is lowered further, exposing more problems, and so on. The same argument will also apply for the flow between whole processes, or whole operations. For example, stages A, B and C in Figure 15.2 could be a supplier operation, a manufacturer and a customer's operation, respectively.

Lean synchronization and capacity utilization

Lean synchronization has many benefits but these come at the cost of capacity utilization. Return to the process shown in Figure 15.2. When stoppages occur in the traditional system,

the buffers allow each stage to continue working and thus achieve high-capacity utilization. The high utilization does not necessarily make the process as a whole produce more. Often extra 'production' goes into buffer inventories. In a lean process, any stoppage will affect the whole process. This will necessarily lead to lower-capacity utilization, at least in the short term. However, there is no point in producing output just for its own sake. Unless the output is useful and causes the operation as a whole to produce saleable products, there is no point in producing it anyway. In fact, producing just to keep utilization high is not only pointless, it is counter-productive, because the extra inventory produced merely serves to make improvements less likely. Figure 15.5 illustrates the two approaches to capacity utilization.

The involvement of everyone

Lean proponents frequently stress the importance of involving all staff in the lean approach. In this way it is similar to other improvement-based concepts such as 'total quality', which is discussed in detail later (see Chapter 17). However, the lean approach to people management is very much influenced by its Japanese origins, which is evident both from the terminology and the concepts themselves. So, for example, the original lean advocates called their approach the 'respect-for-humans' system. It encourages (and often requires) team-based problem-solving, job enrichment (by including maintenance and set-up tasks in operators' jobs), job rotation and multi-skilling. The intention is to encourage a high degree of personal responsibility, engagement and 'ownership' of the job. Similarly, what are called 'basic

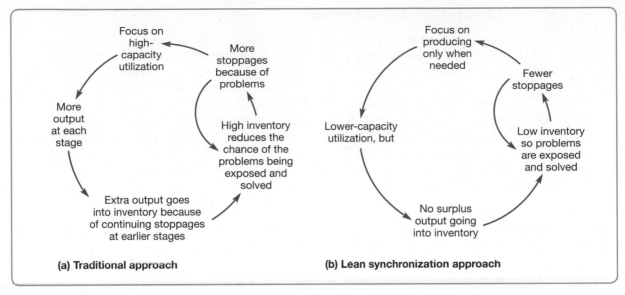

Figure 15.5 The different views of capacity utilization in (a) traditional and (b) JIT approaches to operations

working practices' are sometimes used to implement the 'involvement of everyone' principle. These include the following:

- **Discipline** – in following work standards, critical for the safety of staff and the environment, and for quality.
- **Flexibility** – to expand responsibilities to the extent of people's capabilities.
- **Equality** – in how all staff are treated (which is why some lean companies wear uniforms).
- **Autonomy** – allowing delegation to people involved in direct activities.
- **Development** – of staff to create a more capable workforce.
- **Quality of working life (QWL)** – to include involvement in decision making, security of employment and enjoyment of working area facilities.
- **Creativity** – as one of the indispensable elements of motivation.
- **Total people involvement** – where staff take on more responsibility by participating in activities such as the selection of new recruits, dealing directly with suppliers and customers over schedules, quality issues and delivery information, spending improvement budgets and planning and reviewing work done each day through communication meetings.

Critical commentary

Not all commentators see lean-influenced people-management practices as entirely positive. The lean approach to people management can be viewed as patronizing. It may be, to some extent, less autocratic than some Japanese management practices dating from earlier times. However, it is certainly not in line with some of the job design philosophies which place a high emphasis on contribution and commitment (as described in Chapter 9). Even in Japan the lean approach is not without its critics. Kamata wrote an autobiographical description of life as an employee at a Toyota plant called *Japan in the Passing Lane*.[2] His account speaks of *'the inhumanity and the unquestioning adherence'* of working under such a system. Similar criticisms have been voiced by some trade union representatives.

Continuous improvement

Lean objectives are often expressed as ideals, such as our definition: 'to meet demand instantaneously with perfect quality and no waste'. While any operation's current performance may be far removed from such ideals, a fundamental lean belief is that it is possible to get closer to them over time. Without such beliefs to drive progress, lean proponents claim improvement is more likely to be transitory than continuous. This is why the concept of continuous improvement is such an important part of the lean philosophy. If its aims are set in terms of ideals which individual organizations may never fully achieve, then the emphasis must be on the way in which an organization moves closer to the ideal state. The Japanese word for continuous improvement is kaizen, and it is a key part of the lean philosophy. It is explained fully later (see Chapter 18).

Perspectives on lean

So what exactly is lean? Actually this is not a straightforward question because it can be viewed as three things: a philosophy; a method of planning and control with useful prescriptions of how to manage day-to-day operations; and a set of improvement tools.

Lean is a philosophy of how to run operations It is a coherent set of principles that are founded on smoothing flow through processes by doing all the simple things well, on gradually doing them better, on meeting customer needs exactly and (above all) on squeezing out waste every step of the way. Three key issues define the lean philosophy: the involvement of staff in the operation; the drive for continuous improvement; and the elimination of waste. Other chapters look at the first two issues. We devote the majority of the remainder of this chapter to the central idea of the elimination of waste.

Lean is a method of planning and controlling operations Many lean ideas are concerned with how items (materials, information, customers) flow through operations; and more specifically, how operations managers can manage this flow. For this reason lean can be viewed as a method of planning and control. Yet it is planning and control activity that is done in pursuit of lean's philosophical aims (see above). Unco-ordinated flow causes unpredictability, and unpredictability causes waste because people hold inventory, capacity or time, to protect themselves against it. So lean planning and control uses several methods to achieve synchronized flow and reduce waste. Above all it uses 'pull' control which was described earlier (see Chapter 10), in contrast to MRP (described in Chapter 14) which relies on 'push' control. This is usually achieved using some sort of kanban system (described later). In addition, the other lean planning and control methods which promote smooth flow include levelled scheduling and delivery, and mixed modelling (again described later).

Lean is a set of tools that improve operations performance The 'engine room' of the lean philosophy is a collection of improvement tools and techniques which are the means for cutting out waste. There are many techniques which could be termed 'lean techniques' and, again, many of them follow on naturally and logically from the overall lean philosophy. What is just as important to understand is how the introduction of lean as a philosophy helped to shift the focus of operations management generally towards viewing improvement as its main purpose. In addition, the rise of lean ideas gave birth to techniques that have now become mainstream in operations management. Some of these tools and techniques are well known outside the lean sphere and are covered in other chapters of this book.

Lean in service

Lean (or just-in-time as it was called then) originated in the Japanese manufacturing sector, most prominently, although not exclusively, at Toyota. Japan's attitude towards waste ('make every grain of rice count'), together with its position as a crowded and virtually naturally resourceless country, produced ideal conditions in which to devise an approach to manufacturing that emphasizes low waste and high added value. Yet, as we have pointed out before, service operations form the vast majority of any developed economy's activity. So how can lean principles be applied to service operations, often dealing in intangibles? The idea of lean factory operations is relatively easy to understand. Waste is evident in over-stocked inventories, excess scrap, badly sited machines and so on. In services it is less obvious; inefficiencies are more difficult to see. Yet most of the principles and techniques of lean synchronization, although often described in the context of manufacturing operations, are also applicable to service settings. Many of the examples of lean philosophy and lean techniques in service industries are directly analogous to those found in manufacturing industries because physical items are being moved or processed in some way. Also many principles of lean can be illustrated by referring to common practice in service operations. For example, supermarkets usually replenish their shelves only when customers have taken sufficient products off the shelf. The movement of goods from the 'back office' store to the shelf is triggered only by the 'empty-shelf' demand signal. This is an excellent example of one of a key lean principle – pull control (explained in Chapter 10, but also central to lean, see later). In fact, some of the philosophical underpinning to lean synchronization can also be seen as having its equivalent in the service sector. Take, for example, the role of inventory. The comparison between manufacturing systems that hold large stocks of inventory between stages and those that did not centred on the effect which inventory had on improvement and problem-solving. Exactly the same argument can be applied when, instead of queues of material (inventory), an operation has to deal with queues of information, or even customers. With its customer focus, standardization, continuous quality improvement, smooth flow and efficiency, lean thinking has direct application in all operations, manufacturing or service. Bradley Staats and David Upton of Harvard Business School have studied how lean ideas can be applied in service operations.[3] They make three main points:

> ✳ **Operations principle**
>
> Lean is widely used in service operations, but may need adapting.

- In terms of operations and improvements, the service industries in general are a long way behind manufacturing.
- Not all lean manufacturing ideas translate from factory floor to office cubicle. For example, tools such as empowering manufacturing workers to 'stop the line' when they encounter a problem is not directly replicable when there is no line to stop.
- Adopting lean operations principles alters the way a company learns through changes in problem-solving, co-ordination through connections, and pathways and standardization.

HOW DOES LEAN SYNCHRONIZATION ELIMINATE WASTE?

Arguably the most significant part of the lean philosophy is its focus on the elimination of all forms of waste. Waste can be defined as any activity that does not add value. For example, studies often show that as little as 5 per cent of total throughput time is actually spent directly adding value. This means that for 95 per cent of its time, an operation is adding cost to the service or product, not adding value. Such calculations can alert even relatively efficient operations to the enormous waste which is dormant within all operations. This same phenomenon applies as much to service processes as it does to manufacturing ones. Relatively simple requests, such as applying for a driving licence, may only take a few minutes to actually process, yet take days (or weeks) to be returned.

> ✳ **Operations principle**
>
> Simple, transparent flow exposes sources of waste.

Muda, mura, muri

As so often in lean philosophy, Japanese terms are often used to describe core ideas. And waste elimination is certainly a core lean idea. The terms *muda*, *mura*, and *muri* are Japanese words conveying three causes of waste that should be reduced or eliminated.

- *Muda*. These are activities in a process that are wasteful because they do not add value to the operation or the customer. The main causes of these wasteful activities are likely to be poorly communicated objectives (including not understanding the customer's requirements), or the inefficient use of resources. The implication of this is that, for an activity is to be effective, it must be properly recorded and communicated to whoever is performing it.
- *Mura*. This means 'lack of consistency' or unevenness that results in periodic overloading of staff or equipment. So, for example, if activities are not properly documented so that different people at different times perform a task differently then, not surprisingly, the result of the activity may be different. The negative effects of this are similar to a lack of dependability (see Chapter 2).
- *Muri*. This means absurd or unreasonable. It is based on the idea that unnecessary or unreasonable requirements put on a process will result in poor outcomes. The implication of this is that appropriate skills, effective planning, accurate estimation of times and schedules will avoid this 'muri' overloading waste. In other words, waste can be caused by failing to carry out basic operations planning tasks such as prioritizing activities (sequencing), understanding the necessary time (scheduling) and resources (loading) to perform activities. All these issues are discussed in Chapter 10.

These three causes of waste are obviously related. When a process is inconsistent (mura), it can lead to the overburdening of equipment and people (muri) which, in turn, will cause all kinds of non-value-adding activities (muda).

The seven types of waste

Muda, mura and muri are three *causes* of waste; Toyota have identified seven *types* of waste, which have been found to apply in many different types of operations – both service and production – and which form the core of lean philosophy:

1. *Over-production*. Producing more than is immediately needed by the next process in the operation is the greatest source of waste according to Toyota.
2. *Waiting time*. Equipment efficiency and labour efficiency are two popular measures which are widely used to measure equipment and labour waiting time, respectively. Less obvious is the amount of waiting time of items, disguised by operators who are kept busy producing WIP which is not needed at the time.
3. *Transport*. Moving items around the operation, together with the double and triple handling of WIP, does not add value. Layout changes which bring processes closer together and improvements in transport methods and workplace organization can all reduce waste.
4. *Process*. The process itself may be a source of waste. Some operations may only exist because of poor component design, or poor maintenance, and so could be eliminated.
5. *Inventory*. All inventory should become a target for elimination. However, it is only by tackling the causes of inventory that it can be reduced.
6. *Motion*. An operator may look busy but sometimes no value is being added by the work. Simplification of work is a rich source of reduction in the waste of motion.
7. *Defectives*. Quality waste is often very significant in operations. Total costs of quality are much greater than has traditionally been considered, and it is therefore more important to attack the causes of such costs. This is discussed further later (Chapter 17).

Between them, these seven types of waste contribute to four barriers to any operation achieving lean synchronization. They are: waste from irregular (non-streamlined) flow, waste from inexact supply, waste from inflexible response, and waste from variability. We will examine each of these barriers to achieving lean synchronization.

Looking for waste (and kaizen opportunities) – gemba

Gemba (also sometimes called 'ganba'), when roughly translated from the Japanese, means 'the actual place' where something happens. It is a term often used in lean philosophy or in improvement generally, to convey the idea that, if you really want to understand something, you go to where it actually takes place. Only then can a true appreciation of the realities of improvement opportunities be gained. Lean improvement advocates often use the idea of 'the gemba walk' to make problems visible. By this they mean that managers should regularly visit the place where the job is done to seek out waste. (The western idea of 'management by walking around' is similar.) The concept of gemba is also used in new service or product development to mean that designers should go to where the service happens, or where the product is used, to develop their ideas.

✳ Operations principle

There is no substitute for seeing the way processes actually operate in practice.

Eliminate waste through streamlined flow

The smooth flow of materials, information and people in the operation is a central idea of lean synchronization. Long process routes provide opportunities for delay and inventory build-up, add no value, and slow down throughput time. So, the first contribution any operation can make to streamlining flow is to reconsider the basic layout of its processes. Primarily, reconfiguring the layout of a process to aid lean synchronization involves moving it down the 'natural diagonal' of process design that was discussed earlier (see Chapter 4). Broadly speaking, this means moving from functional layouts towards cell-based layouts, or from cell-based layouts towards line layouts. Either way, it is necessary to move towards a layout that brings more systematization and control to the process flow. At a more detailed level, typical layout techniques include placing workstations close together so that inventory physically just cannot build up because there is no space for it to do so, and arranging workstations in such a way that all those who contribute to a common activity are in sight of each other and can provide mutual help (for example, by facilitating movement between workstations to balance capacity).

Examine all elements of throughput time

Throughput time is often taken as a surrogate measure for waste in a process. The longer that items being processed are held in inventory, moved, checked, or subject to anything else that does not add value, the longer they take to progress through the process. So, looking at exactly what happens to items within a process is an excellent method of identifying sources of waste.

Value stream mapping (also known as 'end-to-end' system mapping) is a simple but effective approach to understanding the flow of material and information as a product or service has value added as it progresses through a process, operation, or supply chain. It visually maps a product or services 'production' path from start to finish. In doing so it records, not only the direct activities of creating products and services, but also the 'indirect' information systems that support the direct process. It is called 'value stream' mapping because it focuses on value-adding activities and distinguishes between value-adding and non-value-adding activities. It is similar to process mapping (see Chapter 4) but different in four ways:

- It uses a broader range of information than most process maps.
- It is usually at a higher level (5–10 activities) than most process maps.
- It often has a wider scope, frequently spanning the whole supply chain.
- It can be used to identify where to focus future improvement activities.

A value stream perspective involves working on (and improving) the 'big picture', rather than just optimizing individual processes. Value stream mapping is seen by many practitioners as a starting point to help recognize waste and identify its causes. It is a four-step technique that identifies waste and suggests ways in which activities can be streamlined. First, it involves identifying the value stream (the process, operation or supply chain) to map. Second, it involves physically mapping a process, then above it mapping the information flow that enables the process to occur. This is the 'current state' map. Third, problems are diagnosed and changes suggested, making a 'future state' map that represents the improved process, operation or supply chain. Finally, the changes are implemented. Figure 15.6 shows a value stream

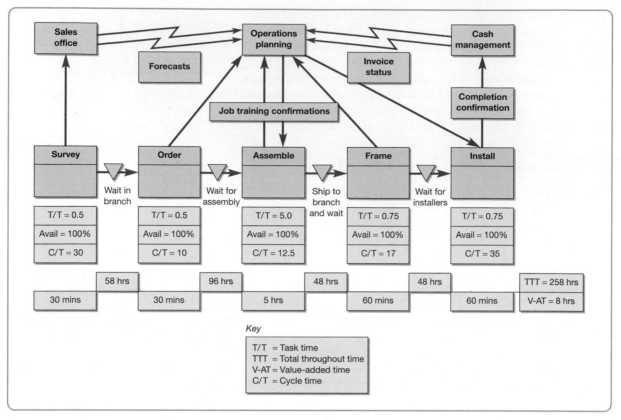

Figure 15.6 Value stream map for an industrial air-conditioning installation service

map for an industrial air-conditioning installation service. The service process itself is broken down into five relatively large stages and various items of data for each stage are marked on the chart. The type of data collected here does vary, but all types of value stream map compare the total throughput time with the amount of value-added time within the larger process. In this case, only 8 of the 258 hours of the process is value-adding.

Example: airline maintenance[4] Aircraft maintenance is important. Planes have a distressing tendency to fall out of the sky unless they are checked, repaired and generally maintained regularly. So the overriding objective of the operations that maintain aircraft must be the quality of maintenance activities. But it is not the *only* objective. Improving maintenance turnaround time can reduce the number of aircraft an airline needs to own, because they are not out of action for as long. Also, the more efficient the maintenance process, the more profitable is the activity and the more likely it is that a major airline with established maintenance operations can create additional revenue streams by doing maintenance for other airlines. Figure 15.7 shows how one airline maintenance operation applied lean principles to achieve all these objectives. The objectives of the lean analysis were to preserve, or even improve, quality levels, while at the same time improving the cost of maintaining airframes and increasing the availability of airframes by reducing turnaround time.

The lean analysis focused on identifying waste in the maintenance process. Two findings emerged from this. First, the sequence of activities on the airframe itself was being set by the tasks identified in the technical manuals supplied by the engine, body and control system manufacturers, and other suppliers. No one had considered all the individual activities together to work out a sequence that would save maintenance staff time and effort. The overall sequence of activities was defined and allocated with structured work preparation of tools, materials, and equipment. Figure 15.7 shows the path taken by maintenance staff before and

Before:
- Maintenance staff follow the steps as detailed in the technical documentation.
- The overall sequence of tasks is not optimized.
- Preparation work and set-ups included as part of the task.

After:
- The overall sequence of tasks is defined and allocated to minimize non-value-added.
- Preparation work and set-ups may be done ahead of time to minimize aircraft contact time.
- Increased productivity and reduced aircraft waiting time.

Figure 15.7 Aircraft maintenance procedures subject to waste reduction analysis

after the lean analysis. Second, maintenance staff would often be waiting until the airframe became available. Yet some of the preparatory work and set-ups did not need to be done while the airframe was present. Therefore, why not get maintenance staff to do these tasks when they would otherwise be waiting before the airframe became available? The result of these changes was a substantial improvement in cost and availability. In addition, work preparation was conducted in a more rigorous and routine manner, and maintenance staff were more motivated because many minor frustrations and barriers to their efficient working were removed.

Visual management

Visual management is one of the lean techniques designed to make the current and planned state of the operation or process transparent to everyone, so that anyone (whether working in the process or not) can very quickly see what is going on. It usually employs some kind of visual sign, such as a noticeboard, computer screen, or simply lights or other signals which convey what is happening. Although a seemingly trivial and usually simple device, visual management has several benefits, such as helping to:

- act as a common focus for team meetings;
- demonstrate methods for safe and effective working practice;
- communicate to everyone how performance is being judged;
- assess at a glance the current status of the operation;
- understand tasks and work priorities;
- judge your and others' performance;
- identify the flow of work – what has been and is being done;
- identify when something is not going to plan;
- show what agreed standards should be;
- provide real-time feedback on performance to everyone involved;
- reduce the reliance on formal meetings.

Example: web-based retailing As an example of how visual management works, a finance office in a web-based retailer was having problems. Service levels were low, and complaints high, as the office attempted to deal with payments from customers, invoices from suppliers, requests for information from its distribution centre; all while demand was increasing. It was agreed that the office's processes were chaotic and poorly managed, with little understanding of priorities or how each member of staff was contributing. To remedy this state of affairs, first the manager responsible for the office tried to bring clarity to the process, defined individual and team roles and started establishing visual management. Collectively the staff mapped processes and set performance objectives. These objectives were shown on a large board placed so everyone in the office could see it. At the end of each day, process supervisors updated the board with each process's performance for the day. Also indicated on the board were visual representations of various improvement projects being carried out by the teams. Every morning, staff gathered in what was called 'the morning huddle' to discuss the previous day's performance, identify how it could be improved, review the progress of ongoing improvement projects, and plan for the upcoming day's work.

The above example illustrates the three main functions of visual management:

- To act as a communication mechanism.
- To encourage commitment to agreed goals.
- To facilitate co-operation between team members.

An important technique that is used to ensure flow visibility is the use of simple but highly visual signals, indicating that a problem has occurred, together with the operational authority to stop the process. For example, on an assembly line, if an employee detects some kind of quality problem, he or she could activate a signal that illuminates a light (called an 'andon' light) above the workstation and stops the line. Although this may seem to reduce the efficiency of the line, the idea is that this loss of efficiency in the short term is less than the accumulated losses of allowing defects to continue on in the process. Unless problems are tackled immediately, they may never be corrected.

Use small-scale simple process technology

There may also be possibilities to encourage smooth streamlined flow through the use of small-scale technologies. That is, using several small units of process technology (for example, machines), rather than one large unit. Small machines have several advantages over large ones. First, they can process different products and services simultaneously. For example, in Figure 15.8 one large machine produces a batch of A, followed by a batch of B, and followed by a batch of C. However, if three smaller machines are used they can each produce A, B, or C

Figure 15.8 Using several small machines rather than one large one allows simultaneous processing, is more robust, and is more flexible

simultaneously. The system is also more robust. If one large machine breaks down, the whole system ceases to operate. If one of the three smaller machines breaks down, it is still operating at two-thirds effectiveness. Small machines are also easily moved, so that layout flexibility is enhanced, and the risks of making errors in investment decisions are reduced. However, investment in capacity may increase in total because parallel facilities are needed, so utilization may be lower (see the earlier arguments).

SHORT CASE Lean hospitals[5]

In one of the increasing number of health-care services to adopt lean principles, the Bolton Hospitals National Health Service trust in the north of the UK has reduced one of its hospital's mortality rate in one injury by more than a third. David Fillingham, chief executive of Bolton Hospitals NHS trust, said, '*We had far more people dying from fractured hips than should have been dying.*' The trust then greatly reduced its mortality rate for fractured neck of femur by re-designing the patient's stay in hospital to reduce or remove the waits between 'useful activities'. The mortality rate fell from 22.9 per cent to 14.6 per cent, which is the equivalent of 14 more patients surviving every six months. At the same time, the average length of stay fell by a third from 34.6 days to 23.5 days. The trust held five 'rapid improvement events', involving employees from across the organization who spent several days examining processes and identifying alternative ways how to improve them. Some management consultants were also used but strictly in an advisory role. In addition, third-party experts were brought in. These included staff from the Royal Air Force, who had been applying lean principles to running aircraft carriers. The value of these outsiders was not only their expertise – 'They asked all sorts of innocent, naïve questions', said Mr Fillingham, 'to which, *often, no member of staff had an answer.*' Other lean-based improvement initiatives included examining the patient's whole experience from start to finish so that delays (some of which could prove fatal) could be removed on their journey to the operating theatre, radiology processes were speeded up and unnecessary paperwork was eliminated. Cutting the length of stay and reducing process complications should also start to reduce costs, although Mr Fillingham says that it could take several years for the savings to become substantial. Not only that, but staff are said to be helped by the changes because they can spend more time helping patients rather than doing non-value-added activities.

Meanwhile at Salisbury district hospital in the south of the UK, lean principles have reduced delays in waiting for the results of tests from the ultrasound department. Waiting lists have been reduced from 12 weeks to between 2 weeks and zero after an investigation showed that 67 per cent of demand was coming from

Source: Alamy Images/Art Kowalsky

just 5 per cent of possible ultrasound tests: abdominal, gynaecological and urological. So all work was streamed into routine 'green' streams and complex 'red' ones. This is like having different traffic lanes on a motorway dedicated to different types of traffic with fast cars in one lane and slow trucks in another. Mixing both types of work is like mixing fast cars and slow-moving trucks in all lanes. The department then concentrated on doing the routine 'green' work more efficiently. For example, the initial date scan used to check the age of a foetus took only two minutes, so a series of five-minute slots were allocated just for these. 'The secret is to get the steady stream of high-volume, low-variety chugging down the ultrasound motorway', says Kate Hobson, who runs the department. Streaming routine work in this way has left more time to deal with the more complex jobs, yet staff are not overloaded. They are more likely to leave work on time and also believe that the department is doing a better job, all of which has improved morale, says Kate Hobson. 'I think people feel their day is more structured now. It's not that madness, opening the doors and people coming at you.' Nor has this more disciplined approach impaired the department's ability to treat really urgent jobs. In fact it has stopped leaving space in its schedule for emergencies – the now standard, short waiting time is usually sufficient for urgent jobs.

Eliminate waste through matching supply and demand exactly

The value of the supply of services or products is always time-dependent. Something that is delivered early or late often has less value than something that is delivered exactly when it is needed. For example, parcel delivery companies charge more for guaranteed faster delivery. This is because our real need for the delivery is often for it to be as fast as possible. The closer to instantaneous delivery we can get, the more value the delivery has for us and the more we are willing to pay for it. In fact delivery of information earlier than it is required can be even more harmful than late delivery because it results in information inventories that serve to confuse flow through the process. For example, an Australian tax office used to receive applications by mail, open the mail and send it through to the relevant department who, after processing it, sent it to the next department. This led to piles of unprocessed applications building up within its processes, causing problems in tracing applications and losing them, sorting through and prioritizing applications, and worst of all, long throughput times. Now they only open mail when the stages in front can process it. Each department requests more work only when they have processed previous work.

> *** Operations principle**
>
> Delivering only and exactly what is needed and when it is needed smoothes flow and exposes waste.

Pull control

The exact matching of supply and demand is often best served by using 'pull control' wherever possible (discussed in Chapter 10). At its simplest, consider how some fast-food restaurants cook and assemble food and place it in the warm area only when the customer-facing server has sold an item. Production is being triggered only by real customer demand. Some construction companies make it a rule to call for material deliveries to its sites only the day before those items are actually needed. This not only reduces clutter and the chances of theft, it speeds up throughput time and reduces confusion and inventories. The essence of pull control is to let the downstream stage in a process, operation or supply network pull items through the system rather than have them 'pushed' to them by the supplying stage. As Richard Hall, an authority on lean operations, put it, *'Don't send nothing nowhere, make 'em come and get it.'*[6]

Kanbans

The use of kanbans is one method of operationalizing pull control. Kanban is the Japanese for card or signal. It is sometimes called the 'invisible conveyor' that controls the transfer of items between the stages of an operation. In its simplest form, it is a card used by a customer stage to instruct its supplier stage to send more items. Kanbans can also take other forms. In some Japanese companies, they are solid plastic markers or even coloured ping-pong balls. Whichever kind of kanban is being used, the principle is always the same: the receipt of a kanban triggers the movement, production or supply of one unit or a standard container of units. If two kanbans are received, this triggers the movement, production or supply of two units or standard containers of units, and so on. Kanbans are the only means by which movement, production or supply can be authorized. Some companies use 'kanban squares'. These are marked spaces on the shop floor or bench that are drawn to fit one or more work pieces or containers. Only the existence of an empty square triggers production at the stage that supplies the square. As one would expect, at Toyota the key control tool is its kanban system. The kanban is seen as serving three purposes:

- It is an instruction for the preceding process to send more.
- It is a visual control tool to show up areas of over-production and lack of synchronization.
- It is a tool for kaizen (continuous improvement). Toyota's rules state that 'the number of kanbans should be reduced over time'.

There are a number of methods of using kanbans, of which the 'single-card system' is most often used because it is by far the simplest system to operate. Figure 15.9 shows the operation of a single-card kanban system. At each stage (only two stages are shown, A and B) there is a work centre and an area for holding inventory. All production and inventory are contained

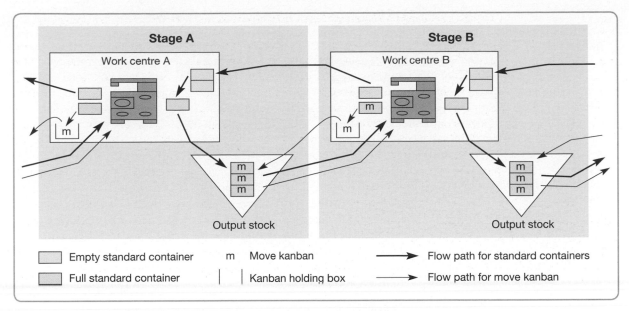

Figure 15.9 The operation of the single-card kanban system of pull control

in standard containers, all of which contain exactly the same number of parts. When stage B requires some more parts to work on, it withdraws a standard container from the output stock point of stage A. After work centre B has used the parts in the container, it places the move kanban in a holding area and sends the empty container to the work centre at stage A. The arrival of the empty containers at stage A's work centre is the signal for production to take place at work centre A. The move kanban is taken from the holding box back to the output stock point of stage A. This acts as authorization for the collection of a further full container to be moved from the output stock of stage A through to the work centre at stage B. Two closed loops effectively control the flow of materials between the stages. The move kanban loop (illustrated by the thin arrows) keeps materials circulating between the stages, and the container loop (illustrated by the thicker arrows) connects the work centres with the stock point between them and circulates the containers, full from A to B and empty back from B to A. This sequence of actions and the flow of kanbans may at first seem complicated. However, in practice their use provides a straightforward and transparent method of calling for material only when it is needed and limiting the inventory which accumulates between stages. The number of kanbans put into the loops between the stages or between the stock points and the work centres is equal to the number of containers in the system and therefore the inventory which can accumulate. Taking a kanban out of the loop has the effect of reducing the inventory.

SHORT CASE **Kanban control at Torchbox web designers[7]**

Torchbox is an independently-owned web-design and development company based in Oxfordshire (see the short case in Chapter 1 'Torchbox: award-winning web designers' for more details). It provides high-quality, cost-effective and ethical solutions for its clients. And although it is a company that relies on its staff's creative capabilities, this does not mean that lean techniques have no place in its operations. On the contrary, it makes full use of the 'kanban' approach to controlling its work as it progresses through the web-design process. *'We know that kanban control originated from car manufacturers like Toyota, but our development teams can also benefit from its basic principles'*, says Edward Kay, the Head of Production at Torchbox. *'It is a way of scheduling work based on what needs to be produced and what resources are available to produce it with. At Torchbox we use a large magnetic* whiteboard (called the "kanban board") to track completed features through each stage of the design process; from discovery through development, design, demo, deployment and on to the finish of the design (called the "done" stage). Each feature has its own paper slip which physically moves across the board, held in place with a magnet. You can't have more features in progress than the number of magnets you have to hold them in place, so the principle is enforced with a physical limitation. When one feature enters the "done" column, another one can be pulled through into "discovery". There's a pulling process, where completing work allows you to start on something new.'

At the start of every day, the team has a stand-up meeting at the kanban board where each member quickly runs through what they did the day before, and what they'll do in the coming day. Each developer has a few tokens which they place on the features they're working on. This helps link up the 'big picture' of how a design's features are developing, with the 'little picture' of what each developer is working on each day, and helps teams to make sure that all work being done is being tracked across the board.

'One of the big benefits of using kanban,' says Edward Kay, 'is that because we're visualizing the steps a feature goes through to be completed, we're able to see where the bottlenecks are that work gets held up on. Because we can see where work is being held up, we're then able to continually improve our processes to make sure we're working

Source: Shutterstock.com/alphaspirit

as efficiently as possible. If we're finding that a project's features keep getting held up in the design stage, we can bring more designers onto the project to widen the bottleneck. Using kanban with feature-driven development helps us constantly deliver value to our clients. This more measured and controlled approach to handling and controlling incoming work helps ensure that every hour we work produces an hour's worth of value. Ultimately, it's all about delivering great products on time and to budget, and kanban is a great tool to help achieve this.'

Eliminate waste through flexible processes

Responding exactly and instantaneously to customer demand implies that operations resources need to be sufficiently flexible to change both what they do and how much they do of it without incurring high cost or long delays. In fact, flexible processes (often with flexible technologies) can significantly enhance smooth and synchronized flow. For example, new publishing technologies allow professors to assemble printed and e-learning course material customized to the needs of individual courses or even individual students. In this case flexibility is allowing small customized batches to be delivered 'to order'. In another example, a firm of lawyers used to take ten days to prepare its bills for customers. This meant that customers were not asked to pay until ten days after the work had been done. Now they use a system that, every day, updates each customer's account. So, when a bill is sent it includes all work up to the day before the billing date. The principle here is that process inflexibility also delays cash flow.

<table>
<tr><td>

✳ Operations principle

Changeover flexibility reduces waste and smoothes flow.

</td></tr>
</table>

Reduce changeover times[8]

For many processes, increasing flexibility means reducing the time taken to change over the process from one activity to the next. And changeover time can usually be reduced, sometimes radically. For example, compare the time it takes you to change the tyre on your car with the time taken by a Formula 1 team. Changeover time reduction can be achieved by a variety of methods such as the following:

● **Measure and analyse changeover activities.** Sometimes simply measuring the current changeover times, recording them and analysing exactly what activities are performed can help to improve changeover times.

- **Separate external and internal activities.** 'External' activities are simply the activities that can be carried out while the process is continuing. For example, processes could be getting ready for the next customer or job while waiting for the next one (see the example of aircraft maintenance described earlier). 'Internal' activities are those which cannot be carried out while the process is going on (such as interviewing the customer while completing a service request for the previous customer). By identifying and separating internal and external activities, the intention is to do as much as possible while the step/process is continuing.
- **Convert internal to external activities**. The other common approach to changeover time reduction is to convert work which was previously performed during the changeover to work that is performed outside the changeover period. There are three major methods of achieving the transfer of internal setup work to external work:
  - Pre-prepare activities or equipment instead of having to do it during changeover periods.
  - Make the changeover process intrinsically flexible and capable of performing all required activities without any delay.
  - Speed up any required changes of equipment, information or staff, for example, by using simple devices.
- **Practise changeover routines**. Not surprisingly, the constant practice of changeover routines and the associated learning curve effect tends to reduce changeover times.

Fast changeovers are particularly important for airlines because they can't make money from aircraft that are sitting idle on the ground. It is called 'running the aircraft hot' in the industry. For many smaller airlines, the biggest barrier to running hot is that their markets are not large enough to justify passenger flights during the day and night. So, in order to avoid aircraft being idle over night, they must be used in some other way. That was the motive behind Boeing's 737 'Quick Change' (QC) aircraft. With it, airlines have the flexibility to use it for passenger flights during the day and, with less than a one-hour changeover (set-up) time, use it as a cargo airplane throughout the night. Boeing engineers designed frames that hold entire rows of seats that could smoothly glide on and off the aircraft, allowing 12 seats to be rolled into place at once. When used for cargo, the seats are simply rolled out and replaced by special cargo containers designed to fit the curve of the fuselage and prevent damage to the interior. Before reinstalling the seats the side walls are thoroughly cleaned so that, once the seats are in place, passengers cannot tell the difference between a QC aircraft and a normal 737. Some airlines particularly value the aircraft's flexibility. It allows them to provide frequent reliable services in both passenger and cargo markets. So the aircraft that has been carrying passengers during the day can be used to ship freight during the night.

Eliminate waste through minimizing variability

One of the biggest causes of the variability that will disrupt flow and prevent lean synchronization is variation in the quality of items. This is why a discussion of lean synchronization should always include an evaluation of how quality conformance is ensured within processes, what was referred to as 'mura' earlier. In particular, the principles of statistical process control (SPC) can be used to understand quality variability. (Chapter 17 and its supplement on SPC examine this subject, so in this section we shall focus on other causes of variability.) The first of these is variability in the mix of items moving through processes, operations, or supply networks.

Level schedules as much as possible

Levelled scheduling (or heijunka) means keeping the mix and volume of flow between stages at an even rate over time. For example, instead of producing 500 items in one batch to cover the needs for the next three months, levelled scheduling would require the process to produce items on a regular basis that satisfied demand. Thus, the principle of levelled scheduling is very straightforward; however, the requirements to put it into practice are quite severe, although the benefits resulting from it can be substantial. The move from conventional to levelled scheduling is illustrated in Figure 15.10. Conventionally, if a mix of items were required

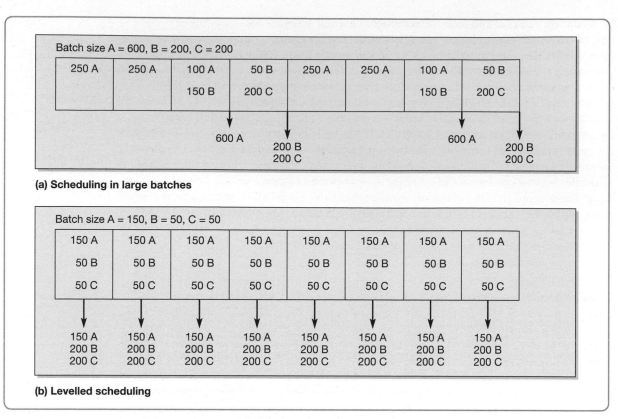

Batch size A = 600, B = 200, C = 200

250 A	250 A	100 A	50 B	250 A	250 A	100 A	50 B
		150 B	200 C			150 B	200 C

600 A

200 B
200 C

600 A

200 B
200 C

(a) Scheduling in large batches

Batch size A = 150, B = 50, C = 50

150 A	150 A	150 A	150 A	150 A	150 A	150 A	150 A
50 B	50 B	50 B	50 B	50 B	50 B	50 B	50 B
50 C	50 C	50 C	50 C	50 C	50 C	50 C	50 C

150 A	150 A	150 A	150 A	150 A	150 A	150 A	150 A
200 B	200 B	200 B	200 B	200 B	200 B	200 B	200 B
200 C	200 C	200 C	200 C	200 C	200 C	200 C	200 C

(b) Levelled scheduling

Figure 15.10 Levelled scheduling equalizes the mix of items made each day

in a time period (usually a month), a batch size would be calculated for each item and the batches produced in some sequence. Figure 15.10(a) shows three items that are produced in a 20-day time period in an operation.

$$\text{Quantity of item A required} = 3,000$$
$$\text{Quantity of item B required} = 1,000$$
$$\text{Quantity of item C required} = 1,000$$

$$\text{Batch size of item A} = 600$$
$$\text{Batch size of item B} = 200$$
$$\text{Batch size of item C} = 200$$

Starting at day 1, the unit commences producing item A. During day 3, the batch of 600 As is finished and dispatched to the next stage. The batch of Bs is started but is not finished until day 4. The remainder of day 4 is spent making the batch of Cs and both batches are dispatched at the end of that day. The cycle then repeats itself. The consequence of using large batches is, first, that relatively large amounts of inventory accumulate within and between the units, and second, that most days are different from one another in terms of what they are expected to produce (in more complex circumstances, no two days would be the same).

Now suppose that the flexibility of the unit could be increased to the point where the batch sizes for the items were reduced to a quarter of their previous levels without loss of capacity (*see* Fig. 15.10(b)):

$$\text{Batch size of item A} = 150$$
$$\text{Batch size of item B} = 50$$
$$\text{Batch size of item C} = 50$$

A batch of each item can now be completed in a single day, at the end of which the three batches are dispatched to their next stage. Smaller batches of inventory are moving between each stage, which will reduce the overall level of work-in-progress in the operation. Just as significant, however, is the effect on the regularity and rhythm of production at the unit. Now every day in the month is the same in terms of what needs to be processed. This makes planning and control of each stage in the operation much easier. For example, if on day 1 of the month the daily batch of As was finished by 11.00 am, and all the batches were successfully completed in the day, then the following day the unit will know that, if it again completes all the As by 11.00 am, it is on schedule. When every day is different, the simple question 'Are we on schedule to complete our processing today?' requires some investigation before it can be answered. However, when every day is the same, everyone in the unit can tell whether production is on target by looking at the clock. Control becomes visible and transparent to all, and the advantages of regular, daily schedules can be passed to upstream suppliers.

Level delivery schedules

A similar concept to levelled scheduling can be applied to many transportation processes. For example, a chain of convenience stores may need to make deliveries of all the different types of products it sells every week. Traditionally it may have dispatched a truck loaded with one particular product around all its stores so that each store received the appropriate amount of the product that would last them for one week. This is equivalent to the large batches discussed in the previous example. An alternative would be to dispatch smaller quantities of all products in a single truck more frequently. Then, each store would receive smaller deliveries more frequently, inventory levels would be lower and the system could respond to trends in demand more readily because more deliveries means more opportunity to change the quantity delivered to a store. This is illustrated in Figure 15.11.

Adopt mixed modelling where possible

The principle of levelled scheduling can be taken further to give a repeated mix of outputs – what is known as mixed modelling. Suppose that processes can be made so flexible that they achieve the ideal of a 'batch' size of one. The sequence of individual items emerging from the process could be reduced progressively as illustrated in Figure 15.12. This would produce a steady stream of each item flowing continuously from the process. However, the sequence of items does not always fall as conveniently as in Figure 15.12. The unit processing times for each item are not usually identical and the ratios of required volumes are less convenient. For example, if a process is required to process items A, B and C in the ratio 8:5:4, it could produce 800 of A, followed by 500 of B, followed by 400 of A, or 80A, 50B, and 40C. But ideally, to sequence the items as smoothly as possible, it would produce in the order . . . BACABACABACABACAB . . . repeated. . . repeated . . . etc. Doing this achieves relatively smooth flow (but does rely on significant process flexibility).

Figure 15.11 Delivering smaller quantities more often can reduce inventory levels

Figure 15.12 Levelled scheduling and mixed modelling: mixed modelling becomes possible as the batch size approaches one

Keep things simple – the 5 Ss

The **5-S terminology** comes originally from Japan, and although the translation into English is approximate, they are generally taken to represent the following:

1. **Sort** (*seiri*). Eliminate what is not needed and keep what is needed.
2. **Straighten** (*seiton*). Position things in such a way that they can be easily reached whenever they are needed.
3. **Shine** (*seiso*). Keep things clean and tidy; no refuse or dirt in the work area.
4. **Standardize** (*seiketsu*). Maintain cleanliness and order – perpetual neatness
5. **Sustain** (*shitsuke*). Develop a commitment and pride in keeping to standards.

The 5 Ss can be thought of as a simple housekeeping methodology to organize work areas that focuses on visual order, organization, cleanliness and standardization. It helps to eliminate all types of waste relating to uncertainty, waiting, searching for relevant information, creating variation and so on. By eliminating what is unnecessary, and making everything clear and predictable, clutter is reduced, needed items are always in the same place, and work is made easier and faster.

Adopt total productive maintenance (TPM)

Total productive maintenance aims to eliminate the variability in operations processes caused by the effect of breakdowns. TPM is treated later (see Chapter 19).

LEAN SYNCHRONIZATION APPLIED THROUGHOUT THE SUPPLY NETWORK

Although most of the concepts and techniques discussed in this chapter are devoted to the management of stages *within* processes and processes *within* an operation, the same principles can apply to the whole supply chain. In this context, the stages in a process are the whole businesses, operations or processes between which products flow. And as any business starts to approach lean synchronization it will eventually come up against the constraints imposed by the lack of lean synchronization of the other operations in its supply chain. So, achieving further gains must involve trying to spread lean synchronization practice outward to its partners in the chain. Ensuring lean synchronization throughout an entire supply network is clearly a far more demanding task than doing the same within a single process. It is a complex task. And it becomes more complex as more of the supply chain embraces the lean philosophy. The nature of the interaction between whole operations is far more complex than between individual stages within a process. A far more complex mix of products and services is likely to be being provided and the whole network is likely to be subject to a less predictable set of potentially disrupt events. To make a supply chain lean means more than making each operation in the chain lean. A collection of localized lean operations rarely leads to an overall lean chain. Rather, one needs to apply the lean synchronization philosophy to the supply chain as a whole. Yet the advantages from truly lean chains can be significant.

And essentially the principles of lean synchronization are the same for a supply chain as they are for a process. Fast throughput throughout the whole supply network is still valuable and will save cost throughout the supply network. Lower levels of inventory will still make it easier to achieve lean synchronization. Waste is just as evident (and even larger) at the level of the supply network and reducing waste is still a worthwhile task. Streamline flow, exact matching of supply and demand, enhanced flexibility, and minimizing variability are all still tasks that will benefit the whole network. The principles of pull control can work between whole operations in the same way as they can between stages within a single process. In fact, the principles and the techniques of lean synchronization are essentially the same no matter what level of analysis is being used. And because lean synchronization is being implemented on a larger scale, the benefits will also be proportionally greater.

One of the weaknesses of lean synchronization is that it is difficult to achieve when conditions are subject to unexpected disturbance. This is especially a problem with applying lean synchronization principles in the context of the whole supply network. Whereas unexpected fluctuations and disturbances do occur within operations, local management has a reasonable degree of control that it can exert in order to reduce them. Outside the operation, within the supply network, it is far more difficult. Nevertheless, it is generally held that, although the task is more difficult and although it may take longer to achieve, the aim of lean synchronization is just as valuable for the supply network as a whole as it is for an individual operation.

Lean supply chains are like air traffic control systems[9]

The concept of the lean supply chain has been likened to an air traffic control system, in that it attempts to provide continuous 'real-time visibility and control' to all elements in the chain. This is the secret of how the world's busiest airports handle thousands of departures and arrivals daily. All aircraft are given an identification number that shows up on a radar map. Aircraft approaching an airport are detected by the radar and contacted using radio. The control tower precisely positions the aircraft in an approach pattern which it co-ordinates. The radar detects any small adjustments that are necessary, which are communicated to the aircraft. This real-time visibility and control can optimize airport throughput while maintaining extremely high safety and reliability.

Contrast this to how most supply chains are co-ordinated. Information is captured only periodically, probably once a day, and any adjustments to logistics and output levels at the various operations in the supply chain are adjusted, and plans rearranged accordingly. But imagine what would happen if this was how the airport operated, with only a 'radar snapshot' once a day. Co-ordinating aircraft with sufficient tolerance to arrange take-offs and landings every two minutes would be out of the question. Aircraft would be jeopardized, or alternatively, if aircraft were spaced further apart to maintain safety, throughput would be drastically reduced. Yet this is how most supply chains have traditionally operated. They use a daily 'snapshot' from their ERP systems (see Chapter 14 for an explanation of ERP). This limited visibility means operations must either space their work out to avoid 'collisions' (i.e. missed customer orders), thereby reducing output, or they must 'fly blind', thereby jeopardizing reliability.

Remember the section on supply chain vulnerability earlier (see Chapter 13) where it was argued that lean principles can be taken to an extreme. When just-in-time ideas first started to have an impact on operations practice in the West, some authorities advocated the reduction of between-process inventories to zero. While in the long term this provides the ultimate in motivation for operations managers to ensure the efficiency and reliability of each process stage, it does not admit the possibility of some processes always being intrinsically less than totally reliable. An alternative view is to allow inventories (albeit small ones) around process stages with higher than average uncertainty. This at least allows some protection for the rest of the system. The same ideas apply to just-in-time delivery between factories. Severe disruption to supply chains, as from the effects of the Japanese tsunami, caused many overseas Japanese factories to close down for a time because of a shortage of key parts.

LEAN SYNCHRONIZATION COMPARED WITH OTHER APPROACHES

Either as a broad philosophy or a practical method of operations planning and control, lean synchronization is not the only approach that is used in practice. There are other approaches that can be used to underpin operations improvement and operations planning and control. We will describe how lean compares with other improvement approaches later (see Chapter 18). Here we look briefly at two alternatives to lean synchronization as a planning and control method: the theory of constraints (TOC), and material requirements planning (MRP) (which we examined in the supplement to Chapter 14).

Lean synchronization and the theory of constraints

A central idea of lean synchronization is the smooth flow of items through processes, operations and supply networks. Any bottleneck will disrupt this smooth progress. Therefore, it is important to recognize the significance of capacity constraints to the planning and control process. This is the idea behind the theory of constraints (TOC) which has been developed to focus attention on the capacity constraints or bottleneck parts of the operation. By identifying the location of constraints, working to remove them, then looking for the next constraint, an operation is always focusing on the part that critically determines the pace of output. The approach which uses this idea is called optimized production technology (OPT). Its development and the marketing of it as a proprietary software product were originated by Eliyahu Goldratt.[10] OPT is a computer-based technique and tool which helps to schedule production systems to the pace dictated by the most heavily loaded resources – that is, bottlenecks. If the rate of activity in any part of the system exceeds that of the bottleneck, then items are being produced that cannot be used. If the rate of working falls below the pace at the bottleneck, then the entire system is under-utilized. There are principles underlying OPT which demonstrate this focus on bottlenecks:

1. Balance flow, not capacity. It is more important to reduce throughput time rather than achieving a notional capacity balance between stages or processes.
2. The level of utilization of a non-bottleneck is determined by some other constraint in the system, not by its own capacity. This applies to stages in a process, processes in an operation, and operations in a supply network.
3. Utilization and activation of a resource are not the same. According to the TOC a resource is being utilized only if it contributes to the entire process or operation creating more

output. A process or stage can be activated in the sense that it is working, but it may only be creating stock or performing other non-value-added activity.

4. An hour lost (not used) at a bottleneck is an hour lost forever out of the entire system. The bottleneck limits the output from the entire process or operation, therefore the under-utilization of a bottleneck affects the entire process or operation.

5. An hour saved at a non-bottleneck is a mirage. Non-bottlenecks have spare capacity anyway. Why bother making them even less utilized?

6. Bottlenecks govern both throughput and inventory in the system. If bottlenecks govern flow, then they govern throughput time, which in turn governs inventory.

7. You do not have to transfer batches in the same quantities as you produce them. Flow will probably be improved by dividing large production batches into smaller ones for moving through a process.

8. The size of the process batch should be variable, not fixed. Again, from the EBQ model, the circumstances that control batch size may vary between different products.

9. Fluctuations in connected and sequence-dependent processes add to each other rather than averaging out. So, if two parallel processes or stages are capable of a particular average output rate, in parallel, they will never be able to achieve the same average output rate.

10. Schedules should be established by looking at all constraints simultaneously. Because of bottlenecks and constraints within complex systems, it is difficult to work out schedules according to a simple system of rules. Rather, all constraints need to be considered together.

OPT uses the terminology of 'drum, buffer, rope' to explain its planning and control approach. We explained this idea earlier (see Chapter 10). The bottleneck work centre becomes a 'drum', beating the pace for the rest of the factory. This 'drum beat' determines the schedules in non-bottleneck areas, pulling through work (the rope) in line with the bottleneck capacity, not the capacity of the work centre. A bottleneck should never be allowed to be working at less than full capacity; therefore, inventory buffers should be placed before it to ensure that it never runs out of work.

The five steps of the theory of constraints

As a practical method of synchronizing flow, TOC emphasizes the following five steps:[11]

1. *Identify the system constraint* – the part of a system that constitutes its weakest link; it could be a physical constraint or even a decision-making or policy constraint.

2. *Decide how to exploit the constraint* – obtain as much capability as possible from the constraint, preferably without expensive changes. For example, reduce or eliminate any non-productive time at the bottleneck.

3. *Subordinate everything to the constraint* – the non-constraint elements of the process are adjusted to a level so that the constraint can operate at maximum effectiveness. After this, the overall process is evaluated to determine if the constraint has shifted elsewhere in the process. If the constraint has been eliminated, go to step 5.

4. *Elevate the constraint* – 'elevating' the constraint means eliminating it. This step is only considered if steps 2 and 3 have not been successful. Major changes to the existing system are considered at this step.

5. *Start again from step 1.*

Table 15.1 shows some of the differences between the theory of constraints and lean synchronization. Arguably, the main contribution of TOC to smooth, synchronized flow is its inclusion of the idea that the effects of bottleneck constraints (a) must be prioritized, and (b) can 'excuse' inventory, if it means maximizing the utilization of the bottleneck. Nor (unlike ERP/MRP, for example) does it necessarily require large investment in new information technology. Further, because it attempts to improve the flow of items through a process, it can release inventory that in turn releases invested capital. Claims of the financial payback from OPT are often based on this release of capital and fast throughput.

Table 15.1 Theory of constraints compared with lean synchronization[12]

	Theory of constraints	Lean synchronization
Overall objectives	To increase profit by increasing the throughput of a process or operation	To increase profit by adding value from the customers' perspective
Measures of effectiveness	• Throughput • Inventory • Operating expense	• Cost • Throughput time • Value-added efficiency
Achieve improvement by...	Focusing on the constraints (the 'weakest links') in the process	Eliminating waste and adding value by considering the entire process, operation or supply network
How to implement	A five-step, continuous process (see above) emphasizing acting locally	Continuous improvement emphasizing the whole supply network

Lean synchronization and MRP

The operating philosophies of lean synchronization and MRP do seem to be fundamentally opposed. Lean synchronization encourages a 'pull' system of planning and control, whereas MRP is a 'push' system. Lean synchronization has aims which are wider than the operations planning and control activity, whereas MRP is essentially a planning and control 'calculation mechanism'. Yet the two approaches can reinforce each other in the same operation, provided their respective advantages are preserved. The irony is that lean synchronization and MRP have similar objectives. JIT scheduling aims to connect the new network of internal and external supply processes by means of invisible conveyors so that parts only move in response to co-ordinated and synchronized signals derived from end-customer demand. MRP seeks to meet projected customer demand by directing that items are only produced as needed to meet that demand. However, there are differences. MRP is driven by the master production schedule, which identifies future end-item demand. It models a fixed lead-time environment, using the power of the computer to calculate how many of, and when, each part should be made. Its output is in the form of time-phased requirements plans that are centrally calculated and co-ordinated. Parts are made in response to central instructions. Day-to-day disturbances, such as inaccurate stock records, undermine MRP authority and can make the plans unworkable. While MRP is excellent at planning, it is weak at control. On the other hand, lean synchronization scheduling aims to meet demand instantaneously through simple control systems based on kanban. If the total throughput time (P) is less than the demand lead time (D), then lean synchronization systems should be capable of meeting that demand. But if the $P{:}D$ ratio is greater than 1, some speculative production will be needed. And if demand is suddenly far greater than expected for certain products, the JIT system may be unable to cope. Pull scheduling is a reactive concept that works best when independent demand has been levelled and dependent demand synchronized. While lean synchronization may be good at control, it is weak on planning.

MRP is also better at dealing with complexity, as measured by numbers of items being processed. It can handle detailed requirements even for 'strangers'. Lean synchronization pull scheduling is less capable of responding instantaneously to changes in demand as the part count, options and colours increase. Therefore, lean synchronization production systems favour designs based on simpler product structures with high parts commonality. Such disciplines challenge needless complexity, so that more parts may be brought under pull-scheduling control.

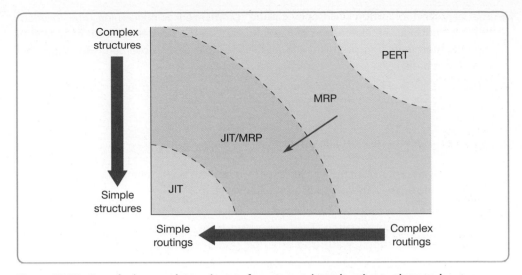

Figure 15.13 Complexity as a determinant of an appropriate planning and control system

Source: from Voss, C.A. and Harrison, A. (1987) Strategies for implementing JIT, in Voss, C.A. (ed.) *Just-In-Time Manufacture*, IFS/Springer-Verlag

When to use lean synchronization, MRP and combined systems

Figure 15.13 distinguishes between the complexity of product structures and the complexity of the flow path routings through which they must pass.[13] Simple product structures which have routings with high repeatability are prime candidates for pull control. Lean synchronization can easily cope with their relatively straightforward requirements. As structures and routings become more complex, so the power of the computer is needed in order to break down product structures and so assign orders to suppliers. In many environments, it is possible to use pull scheduling for the control of most internal materials. Again, prime candidates for pull control are materials which are used regularly each week or each month. Their number can be increased by design standardization, as indicated by the direction of the arrow in Figure 15.13. As structures and routings become even more complex, and parts usages become more irregular, so the opportunities for using pull scheduling decrease. Very complex structures require networking methods like PERT (program evaluation and review technique – see Chapter 16) for planning and control.

SUMMARY ANSWERS TO KEY QUESTIONS

Check and improve your understanding of this chapter using self-assessment questions and a personalized study plan, a video case study, and an eText – all at www.myomlab.com.

MyOMLab

❯ What is lean synchronization?

● Lean synchronization is an approach to operations which tries to meet demand instantaneously with perfect quality and no waste. It is an approach which differs from traditional operations practices insomuch as it stresses waste elimination and fast throughput, both of which contribute to low inventories.

● The ability to deliver just in time not only saves working capital (through reducing inventory levels) but also has a significant impact on the ability of an operation to improve its intrinsic efficiency.

- The lean synchronization philosophy can be summarized as concerning three overlapping elements: (a) the elimination of waste in all its forms, (b) the inclusion of all staff of the operation in its improvement, and (c) the idea that all improvement should be on a continuous basis.
- Most of the ideas of lean synchronization are directly applicable to service operations.

〉 How does lean synchronization eliminate waste?

- The most significant part of the lean philosophy is its focus on the elimination of all forms of waste, defined as any activity that does not add value.
- Lean synchronization identifies seven types of waste that, together, form four barriers to achieving lean synchronization. They are: waste from irregular (non-streamlined) flow, waste from inexact supply, waste from inflexible response, and waste from variability.

〉 How does lean synchronization apply throughout the supply network?

- Most of the concepts and techniques of lean synchronization, although usually described as applying to individual processes and operations, also apply to the whole supply network.
- The concept of the lean supply chain has been likened to an air traffic control system, in that it attempts to provide continuous 'real-time visibility and control' to all elements in the chain.

〉 How does lean synchronization compare with other approaches?

- There are other approaches that attempt to perform the same function as lean synchronization. Two alternatives to lean synchronization as a planning and control method are the theory of constraints (TOC) and material requirements planning (MRP).
- Although both TOC and MRP may seem to be different approaches, they can be combined.
- The way in which they can be combined depends on the complexity of product structures, the complexity of product routing, the volume–variety characteristics of the operation and the level of control required.

CASE STUDY The National Tax Service (NTS)[14]

The National Tax Service (NTS) was the government agency that assessed and collected taxes from citizens and businesses. The organization was committed to providing an excellent service by applying the tax laws fairly and making it simple and convenient for their 'customers' to fulfil their tax obligations. Its staff aimed to be polite, prompt, competent, clear and consistent. The NTS had a set of service standards including answering 85 per cent of calls within 1 minute, replying to 80 per cent of emails within 5 working days and processing refunds within 30 days. In return it expected its customers to complete their tax returns promptly, give accurate and complete information, keep proper records and pay their tax on time.

Despite the organization's success in meeting its service standards, Max Serwotka, director of the NTS, explained his reasons for initiating the Lean Programme: *'We are under pressure from the government not only to make substantial cost savings but also improve the service we provide to citizens and businesses. I attended a lean workshop some time ago and I reckon the principles of lean and its benefits could be applied directly to us. So I appointed a lean consultancy to help us implement a Lean Programme. They informed me that a Lean Programme should be able to deliver, within 12 months, a 30 per cent improvement in productivity, reduce backlogs and improve consistency in our processing capabilities, and improve the customer experience. They recommended a three-step approach: first, redesign our service delivery processes to eliminate waste and variability; second, change management processes to create a structure that will help implement and sustain improvements; and third, change the mindsets of leaders and front-line staff to support the new systems and deliver continuous improvement.'*

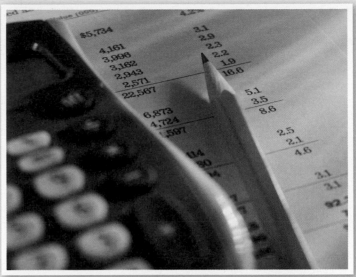

Source: AL RF (Photolibrary.com/Tetra)

The consultants began by running a number of events including start-up events (SUE) with senior managers to explain the principles of lean, the approach to be taken and to establish an operational performance focus, as well as a series of two-day performance improvement events (PIE) for front-line staff to engage them in the process and identify the first set of issues to work on. These were followed by task team events (TTE) where task teams were set up, facilitated by the consultants, to focus on a few of the issues that were raised. These events were rolled out rapidly across the organization and supported with a number of workshops aimed at giving the members of the task teams skills in a number of techniques, including process-mapping, problem-solving, waste identification and project management. The objective was to make the Lean Programme self-sustaining within one year.

The initial response to the programme was extremely positive, as one senior manager related: *'For a long time the NTS has been focused on staff and things like hours of working and flexibility of hours; we have always looked at it from a staff perspective. Under the Lean Programme we are looking at things from a customer perspective. The aim is to deal immediately with customers' tax returns and queries and meet the government's "demand" for tax revenues from us, with no problems or errors, at minimum cost. Although we set the deadlines for tax returns and payments, our customers should set the pace and initiate the flow of activities.'*

Within six months of the start of the Programme members of staff seemed to be less than enthusiastic. Comments from front-line staff included: *'We went to a workshop where we did an exercise with bits of paper and coloured dots, making "products" from them to meet requests from "customers". It was all good fun and we all enjoyed it. But it didn't work when we came back to our desks. We do our jobs differently because every tax return is different. We can't see the principles working here.'* And *'Lean can't work in a tax office. The*

consultants have worked in manufacturing and in hospitals, but not a tax office.'

Max had good contacts with the local university and asked Professor Kaz Khalid and her team to assess how well the Lean Programme was going. Within a few months the team had visited 10 tax offices, 3 regional processing centres and the central processing centre. They interviewed 137 staff, including senior managers and front line staff, to gain an understanding of what they thought of the Lean Programme, what its aims were and how well it had succeeded in meeting those aims. Their conclusion was that even though the Lean Programme had made an impact there were significant issues that still needed to be addressed. This presented a new set of challenges for Max. Their report stated: *'The Lean Programme has engaged and challenged people but it is not the foundation for lean that it was designed to be. The Programme is not applying all the principles of lean, and the NTS has a considerable way to go before it can describe itself as a lean organization. However, this does not mean that "Lean" is not working; there has been a movement in the right direction, but it has a considerable way to go.'* The team's key findings included:

- Senior managers don't appear to be engaged with the Programme, though they appear to understand the nature of lean and the Lean Programme much better than the front-line staff.
- While some processes and practices have been modified and made clearer, there have been only marginal benefits in terms of productivity and the customer experience.
- The focus of the task teams appears to have been mainly concerned with waste reduction rather than a focus on the customer; indeed there has been no consultation or involvement with customers and key stakeholders.
- A few areas have seen improvements in productivity but these have not been shared with other parts of the organization.

- Many of the key processes were seen to be 'centrally owned' so staff felt they were unable to influence them.
- Staff seem to welcome the workshops and the problem-solving skills they were developing but they voiced frustration that when they made suggestions they were not followed through.

Some of the quotes contained in the report were as follows:

'The improvements were supposedly going to be massive and many of the senior managers thought changes would be very difficult to implement, knowing how the organization worked. Then negativity crept in with managers and staff, and so the improvements didn't actually come about.'

'There isn't much support from the consultants. We analyse problems and make suggestions but there doesn't seem to be any way of making the changes.'

'A lot of front-line staff seemed worried about joining the task teams. There was a view that jobs might be at risk.'

'We have heard about this lean initiative but we have not been consulted or involved.'

'We heard that one of the sites had made some changes and removed some waste, but it had upset so many taxpayers that they had changed things back. We started to be worried about making any changes.'

'We have daily meetings now but they don't seem to serve any purpose. We discuss targets and quality, but most of the time we talk about things we got wrong.'

'How can we move to a "pull" system when we have such a big backlog of work?'

'The targets are simply not achievable. We can never succeed whatever we do.'

However, there had been some successes. The introduction of quality managers had helped identify problems and errors early and help staff better understand what to do. Managers also indicated that the Programme was helping them identify those in the team who worked well and those who were struggling. At three of the sites, managers mentioned that teamworking had improved, with teams becoming more integrated, with a better team spirit because they better understood the processes they were involved in. The removal of waste had also had some success at a few sites with non-value-adding elements of some processes being removed. In terms of customer focus the senior managers referred to 'the customer' and understood the need to deliver better service. However, many members of the front-line staff were struggling with the notion of 'the customer'. Some quotes were as follows:

'We find it difficult to understand "the customer". We don't actually use the word but we hear it more often now.'

'We deal with bits of paper not customers.'

'We never see the customer and most people don't even talk to a customer, so it's just a bit of paper or a screen. Sometimes we forget that there is a customer at the other end.'

'The taxpayers are told they have to pay. We are supposed to call them customers, but they're not.'

'We have more of a realization about customer focus than we ever had. I am not saying that we are there yet, but we are getting there.'

Max summarized his views. *'Since the start of the programme productivity has hardly increased; we still have the same backlog of work. However, quality has improved a little. There are now many more quality checks during the process with dedicated quality managers doing the checking. Now feedback on errors and problems is much faster so staff are now learning from their mistakes. From the point of view of our customers, things must have got better. However, we are a long, long way from achieving what this Programme set out to achieve. I was taught that there are three key stages to lean; engage, establish and embed. Far from engaging our staff we appear to have alienated some of them. Questions are now being asked by members of the government about the costs and benefits of the Lean Programme and my head is on the line.'*

PROBLEMS AND APPLICATIONS

MyOMLab *These problems and applications will help to improve your analysis of operations. You can find more practice problems as well as worked examples and guided solutions on MyOMLab at www.myomlab.com.*

1 Think about the last time that you travelled by air. Analyse the journey in terms of value-added time (actually going somewhere) and non-value-added time (the time spent queuing, etc.) from the time you left home to the exact time you arrived at your ultimate destination. Calculate the value-added time for the journey.

2 A simple process has four stages – A, B, C, and D. The average amount of work needed to process items passing through these stages is as follows: stage A = 68 minutes, stage B = 55 minutes, stage C = 72 minutes, and stage D = 60 minutes. A spotcheck on the work-in-progress between each stage reveals the following: between stages A and B there are 82 items, between stages B and C there are 190 items, and between stages C and D there are 89 items.

   a. Using Little's law (see Chapter 4), calculate the throughput time of the process.

   b. What is the throughput efficiency of the process?

3 In the example above, the operations manager in charge of the process re-allocates the work at each stage to improve the 'balance' of the process. Now each stage has an average of 64 minutes of work. Also, the work-in-progress in front of stages B, C, and D is 75, 80, and 82 units respectively. How has this changed the throughput efficiency of the process?

4 A production process is required to produce 1,400 of product X, 840 of product Y, and 420 of product Z in a 4-week period. If the process works 7 hours per day and 5 days per week, devise a mixed model schedule, in terms of the number of each products required to be produced every hour, that would satisfy demand.

5 Revisit the 'Operations in action' at the beginning of this chapter, and (a) list all the different techniques and practices which Toyota adopts, and (b) describe how operations objectives (quality, speed, dependability, flexibility, cost) are influenced by the practices which Toyota adopts.

6 Consider how set-up reduction principles can be used on the following:

   a. changing a tyre at the side of the road (following a puncture);

   b. cleaning out an aircraft and preparing it for the next flight between an aircraft on its inbound flight landing and disembarking its passengers, and the same aircraft being ready to take-off on its outbound flight;

   c. the time between the finish of one surgical procedure in a hospital's operating theatre, and the start of the next one;

   d. the 'pitstop' activities during a Formula 1 race (how does this compare to (a) above?).

SELECTED FURTHER READING

Ahlsrom, P. (2004) Lean service operations: translating lean production principles to service operations, *International Journal of Services, Technology and Management*, vol. 5, nos 5/6. Explains how lean can be used in services.

Bicheno, J. and Holweg, M. (2009) *The Lean Toolbox: The Essential Guide to Lean Transformation*, **4th edn, Picsie Press, Buckingham, England.** A manual of lean techniques; very much a 'how to do it' book, and none the worse for it.

Holweg, M. (2007) The genealogy of lean production, *Journal of Operations Management*, **vol. 25, 420–437.** An excellent overview of how lean ideas developed.

Liker, J. (2003) *The Toyota Way: 14 Management Principles from the World's Greatest Manufacturer*, **McGraw-Hill Education, New York.**

Schonberger, R.J. (1996) *World Class Manufacturing: The Next Decade*, **The Free Press, New York.** As above (and above that) but more speculative.

Spear, S. and Bowen, H.K. (1999) Decoding the DNA of the Toyota Production System, *Harvard Business Review*, **September–October.** Revisits the leading company as regards JIT practice and re-evaluates the underlying philosophy behind the way it manages its operations. Recommended.

Womack, J.P., Jones, D.T. and Roos, D. (1990) *The Machine that Changed the World*, Rawson Associates, New York. Arguably the most influential book on operations management practice of the last 50 years. Firmly rooted in the automotive sector but did much to establish Lean.

Womack, J.P. and Jones, D.T. (1996) *Lean Thinking: Banish Waste and Create Wealth in Your Corporation*, Simon and Schuster, New York. Some of the lessons from *The Machine that Changed the World* but applied in a broader context.

USEFUL WEBSITES

www.lean.org Site of the Lean Enterprise Institute, set up by one of the founders of the Lean thinking movement.

www.iee.org The site of the Institution of Electrical Engineers (which includes manufacturing engineers, surprisingly) has material on this and related topics, as well as other issues covered in this book.

www.mfgeng.com The Manufacturing Engineering site.

www.myomlab.com Test which sections you have mastered and which you need to review, with questions, a personalized study plan, video clips, revision tips, and cases.

www.opsman.org Useful materials.

http://operationsroom.wordpress.com/ Stanford University's take on topical operations stories.

www.iomnet.org The Institute of Operations Management site. One of the main professional bodies for the subject.

www.poms.org A US academic society for production and operations management. Academic, but some useful material, including a link to an encyclopedia of operations management terms.

MyOMLab *Now that you have finished reading this chapter, why not visit MyOMLab at www.myomlab.com where you'll find more learning resources to help you make the most of your studies and get a better grade.*

16 Project management

Key questions

> What is project management?

> How are projects planned and controlled?

> What is network planning?

INTRODUCTION

Here we deal with the planning and control of operations that occupy the low-volume–high-variety end of the continuum which we introduced earlier (Chapter 4). These 'project' operations are engaged in complex, sometimes large-scale, activities with a defined beginning and end. The pioneers of managing project operations were the engineers and planners who worked on complex defence and construction projects. Now their methods are used on projects as diverse as new product launches, education projects and movie making. Project management is important because all managers will, at some point, get involved with managing projects (see Fig. 16.1).

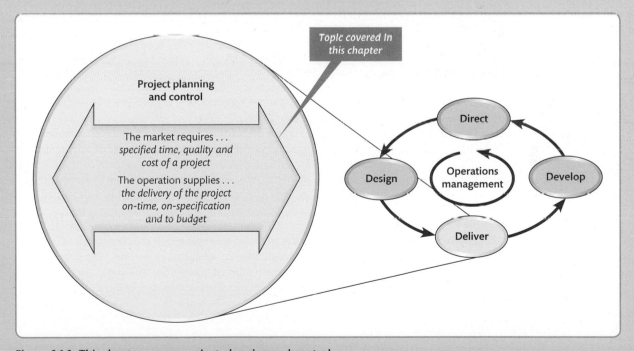

Figure 16.1 This chapter covers project planning and control

The Millau bridge[1]

For decades French motorists called the little bridge at Millau 'the Millau cork'. It held up all the traffic on what should have been one of the busiest north–south routes through France. No longer. In place of the little bridge is one of the most impressive and beautiful civil engineering successes of the last century. Lord Foster, the bridge's architect, described it as having the *'delicacy of a butterfly'*, with the environment dominating the scene rather than the bridge. And although the bridge appears to float on the clouds, it is also a remarkable technical achievement. At 300 metres it is the highest road bridge in the world, weighing 36,000 tonnes. The central pillar is higher than the Eiffel Tower, and took only three years to complete, notwithstanding the new engineering techniques that were needed.

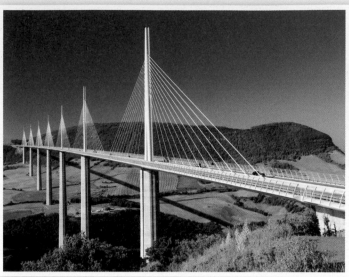

Source: Shutterstock.com/Richard Semik

The bridge was completed on time and on budget. It also had proved the effectiveness of its new construction technique. The traditional method of building this type of bridge (called a 'cable stay' bridge) involves building sections of the roadway on the ground and using cranes to put them in position. Because of its height, 300 metres above the valley floor, a new technique had to be developed. First, the towers were built in the usual way, with steel reinforced concrete. The roadway was built on the high ground at either side of the valley and then pushed forward into space as further sections were added, until it met with precision (to the nearest centimetre) in the centre. This technique had never been tried before and it carried engineering risks, which added to the complexity of the project management task.

It all began with a massive recruitment drive. *'People came from all over France for employment. We knew it would be a long job. We housed them in apartments and houses in and around Millau. Guarantees were given to all the tenants and a unit was set up to help everyone with the paperwork involved in this. It was not unusual for a worker to be recruited in the morning and have his apartment available the same evening with electricity and a telephone available.'* (Jean-Pierre Martin, Chief Engineer of Groupe Eiffage and Director of Building) Over 3,000 workers contributed to the project, with 500 of them on the project site, working in all weather to complete the project on time. *'Every day I would ask myself what was the intense force that united these men'*, said Jean-Pierre Martin. *'They had a very strong sense of pride and they belonged to a community that was to build the most beautiful construction in the world. It was never necessary to shout at them to get them to work. Life on a construction site has many ups and downs. Some days we were frozen. Other days we were subjected to a heatwave. But even on days of bad weather, one had to force them to stay indoors. Yet often they would leave their lodgings to return to work.'*

Many different businesses were involved in building the bridge. All of them needed co-ordinating in such a way that they would co-operate towards the common goal, but yet avoid any loss of overall responsibility. Jean-Pierre Martin came up with the idea of nine autonomous work groups. One group was placed at the foot of each of the seven piles that would support the bridge and two others at either end. The motto adopted by the teams was *'rigueur et convivialité'* – rigorous quality and friendly co-operation. *'The difficulty with this type of project is keeping everyone enthusiastic throughout its duration. To make this easier we created these small groups. Each of the 9 teams' shifts were organized in relays between 7 and 14 hours, and 14 and 21 hours.'* So, to maintain the good atmosphere, no expense was spared to celebrate important events in the construction of the viaduct, for example, or a pile, or another piece of road completed. Sometimes, to boost the morale of the teams, and to celebrate these important events, Jean-Pierre would organize a *'méchouis'* – a spit roast of lamb, especially popular with the many workers who were of North African origin.

WHAT IS PROJECT MANAGEMENT?

First, what is a project? A project is a set of activities with a defined start point and a defined end state, which pursues a defined goal and uses a defined set of resources. Technically many small-scale operations management endeavours, taking minutes or hours, conform to this definition of a project. However, in this chapter we will be examining the management of larger-scale projects taking days, months or years. Large-scale (and therefore complex) undertakings consume a relatively large amount of resources, take a long time to complete and typically involve interactions between different parts of an organization. Projects come in many and various forms, including the following:

- organizing emergency aid to earthquake victims;
- producing a television programme;
- designing an aircraft;
- running a one-week course in project management;
- relocating a factory;
- refurbishing an hotel;
- installing a new information system.

What do projects have in common?

To a greater or lesser extent, all the projects listed above have some elements in common. They all have *an objective,* a definable end result or output that is typically defined in terms of cost, quality and timing. They are all *unique.* A project is usually a 'one-off', not a repetitive undertaking. Even 'repeat' projects, such as the construction of another chemical plant to the same specification, will have distinctive differences in terms of resources used and the actual environment in which the project takes place. They are all of a *temporary nature.* Projects have a defined beginning and end, so a temporary concentration of resources is needed to carry out the undertaking. Once their contribution to the project objectives has been completed, the resources are usually redeployed. They will all have some degree of *complexity.* Many different tasks are required to be undertaken to achieve a project's objectives. The relationship between all these tasks can be complex, especially when the number of separate tasks in the project is large. Finally, all projects have to cope with some *uncertainty.* All projects are planned before they are executed and therefore carry an element of risk. A 'blue sky' research project carries the risk that expensive, high-technology resources will be committed with no worthwhile outcome.

At this point it is worth pointing out the distinction between 'projects' and 'programmes'. A programme, such as a continuous improvement programme, has no defined end point. Rather it is an ongoing process of change. Individual projects may be individual sub-sections of an overall programme, but 'programme management' will overlay and integrate the individual projects. Generally, it is a more difficult task in the sense that it requires resource co-ordination, particularly when multiple projects share common resources, as emphasized in the following quotation:

'Managing projects is, it is said, like juggling three balls – cost, quality, and time. Programme management . . . is like organizing a troupe of jugglers all juggling three balls and swapping balls from time to time.'[2]

A typology of projects

Figure 16.2 illustrates a typology for projects according to their *complexity* – in terms of size, value and the number of people involved in the project – and their uncertainty of achieving the project objectives of cost, time and quality.

The typology helps to give a rational presentation of the vast range of undertakings where project management principles can be applied. It also gives a clue to the nature of the projects

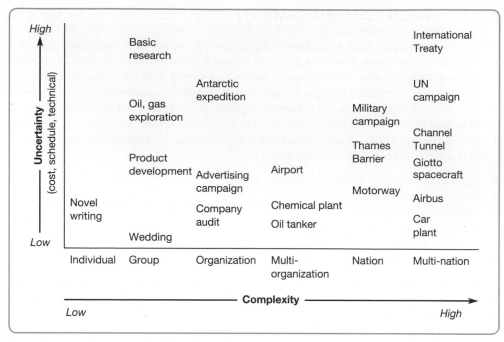

Figure 16.2 A typology of projects

Source: Adapted from Nicholas, J.M. and Steyn, H. (2012) *Project Management for Engineering, Business and Technology,* 4th ed., Routledge, p. 6, Figure 1.3.

and the difficulties of managing them. Uncertainty particularly affects project planning, and complexity particularly affects project control.

Projects with *high uncertainty* are likely to be especially difficult to define and set realistic objectives for. If the exact details of a project are subject to change during the course of its execution, the planning process is particularly difficult. Resources may be committed, times may be agreed, but if the objectives of the project change or the environmental conditions change, or if some activity is delayed, then all the plans which were made prior to the changes will need to be redrawn. When uncertainty is high, the whole project planning process needs to be sufficiently flexible to cope with the consequences of change. For example, the implementation of a political treaty in the European Union is subject to the ratification of all the member governments. Politics being an uncertain business, any of the member countries might either fail to ratify the treaty or attempt to renegotiate it. The central planners at EU headquarters must therefore have contingency plans in place which indicate how they might have to change the 'project' to cope with any political changes.

Projects with *high levels of complexity* need not necessarily be difficult to plan, although they might involve considerable effort; controlling them can be problematic, however.

As projects become more detailed, with many separate activities, resources and groups of people involved, the scope for things to go wrong increases. Furthermore, as the number of separate activities in a project increases, the ways in which they can impact on each other increases exponentially. This increases the effort involved in monitoring each activity. It also increases the chances of overlooking some part of the project which is deviating from the plan. Most significantly, it increases the 'knock-on' effect of any problem.

The (only partly joking) 'laws of project management' which were issued by the American Production and Inventory Control Society give a flavour of uncertain and complex projects:

1 No major project is ever installed on time, within budget, or with the same staff that started it. Yours will not be the first.

2 Projects progress quickly until they become 90 per cent complete, then they remain at 90 per cent complete forever.

3 One advantage of fuzzy project objectives is that they let you avoid the embarrassment of estimating the corresponding costs.

4 When things are going well, something will go wrong. When things just cannot get any worse, they will. When things appear to be going better, you have overlooked something.

5 If the project content is allowed to change freely, the rate of change will exceed the rate of progress.

6 No system is ever completely debugged. Attempts to debug a system inevitably introduce new bugs that are even harder to find.

7 A carelessly planned project will take three times longer to complete than expected; a carefully planned project will take only twice as long.

8 Project teams detest progress reporting because it vividly manifests their lack of progress.

Successful project management

There are some points of commonality in project success and failure, which allow us to identify some general points which seem to minimize the chances of a project failing to meet its objectives. The following factors are particularly important:[3]

- *Clearly defined goals*: including the general project philosophy or general mission of the project, and a commitment to those goals on the part of the project team members.
- *Competent project manager*: a skilled project leader who has the necessary interpersonal, technical and administrative skills.
- *Top-management support*: top-management commitment for the project that has been communicated to all concerned parties.
- *Competent project team members*: the selection and training of project team members, who between them have the skills necessary to support the project.
- *Sufficient resource allocation*: resources, in the form of money, personnel, logistics, etc., which are available for the project in the required quantity.
- *Adequate communications channels*: sufficient information is available on project objectives, status, changes, organizational conditions and clients' needs.
- *Control mechanisms*: the mechanisms which are in place to monitor actual events and recognize deviations from plan.
- *Feedback capabilities*: all parties concerned with the project are able to review the project's status and make suggestions and corrections.
- *Responsiveness to clients*: all potential users of the project are concerned with and are kept up to date on the project's status.
- *Troubleshooting mechanisms*: a system or set of procedures which can tackle problems when they arise, trace them back to their root cause and resolve them.
- *Project staff continuity*: the continued involvement of key project personnel through its life. Frequent turnover of staff can dissipate the team's acquired learning.

Project managers

In order to co-ordinate the efforts of many people in different parts of the organization (and often outside it as well), all projects need a project manager. Many of a project manager's activities are concerned with managing human resources. The people working in the project team need a clear understanding of their roles in the (usually temporary) organization. Controlling an uncertain project environment requires the rapid exchange of relevant information with the project stakeholders, both within and outside the organization. People, equipment and other resources must be

> ✳ **Operations principle**
> The activity of project management requires interpersonal as well as technical skills.

identified and allocated to the various tasks. Undertaking these tasks successfully makes the management of a project a particularly challenging operations activity. Five characteristics in particular are seen as important in an effective project manager:[4]

- background and experience which are consistent with the needs of the project;
- leadership and strategic expertise, in order to maintain an understanding of the overall project and its environment, while at the same time working on the details of the project;
- technical expertise in the area of the project in order to make sound technical decisions;
- interpersonal competence and the people skills to take on such roles as project champion, motivator, communicator, facilitator and politician;
- proven managerial ability in terms of a track record of getting things done.

HOW ARE PROJECTS PLANNED AND CONTROLLED?

Figure 16.3 shows the stages in project management, four of which are relevant to project planning and control:

Stage 1   Understanding the project environment – internal and external factors which may influence the project.

Stage 2   Defining the project – setting the objectives, scope and strategy for the project.

Stage 3   Project planning – deciding how the project will be executed.

Stage 4   Technical execution – performing the technical aspects of the project.

Stage 5   Project control – ensuring that the project is carried out according to plan.

We shall examine project planning and control under the headings of stages 1, 2, 3 and 5 (stage 4, the technical execution of the project, is determined by the specific technicalities of individual projects.) However, it is important to understand that the stages are not a simple sequential chain of steps. Project management is essentially an *iterative* process. Problems or changes which become evident in the control stage may require replanning and may even cause modifications to the original project definition.

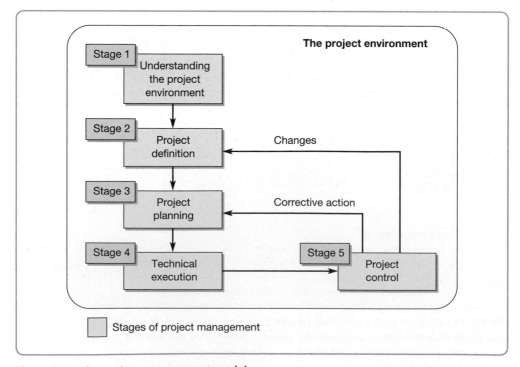

Figure 16.3 The project management model

Stage 1 – Understanding the project environment

The project environment comprises all the factors which may affect the project during its life. It is the context and circumstances in which the project takes place. Understanding the project environment is important because the environment affects the way in which a project will need to be managed and (just as important) the possible dangers that may cause the project to fail. Environmental factors can be considered under the following four headings:

- *Geo-social environment* – geographical, climatic and cultural factors that may affect the project.
- *Econo-political environment* – the economic, governmental and regulatory factors around which the project takes place.
- *Business environment* – industrial, competitive, supply network and customer expectation factors that shape the likely objectives of the project.
- *Internal environment* – the individual company's strategy and culture, the resources available and the interaction with other projects that will influence the project.

Stakeholders

One way of operationalizing the importance of understanding a project's environment is to consider the various 'stakeholders' who have some kind of interest in the project. The stakeholders in any project are the individuals and groups who have an interest in the project process or outcome. All projects will have stakeholders and complex projects will have many. They are likely to have different views on a project's objectives that may conflict with other stakeholders'. At the very least, different stakeholders are likely to stress different aspects of a project. So, as well an ethical imperative to include as many people as possible in a project from an early stage, it is often useful in preventing objections and problems later in the project. Moreover, there can be significant direct benefits from using a stakeholder-based approach. Project managers can use the opinions of powerful stakeholders to shape the project at an early stage. This makes it more likely that they will support the project, and can also improve its quality. Communicating with stakeholders early and frequently can ensure that they fully understand the project and understand potential benefits. Stakeholder support may even help to win more resources, making it more likely that projects will be successful. Perhaps most important, one can anticipate stakeholder reaction to various aspects of the project, and plan the actions that could prevent opposition, or build support.

> **✱ Operations principle**
> All projects have stakeholders with different interests and priorities.

Some (even relatively experienced) project managers are reluctant to include stakeholders in the project management process, preferring to 'manage them at a distance' rather than allow them to interfere with the project. Others argue that the benefits of stakeholder management are too great to ignore and many of the risks can be moderated by emphasizing the responsibilities as well as the rights of project stakeholders. For example, one information technology company formally identifies the rights and responsibilities of project stakeholders as shown in Table 16.1.

> **✱ Operations principle**
> Project stakeholders have responsibilities as well as rights.

Managing stakeholders

Managing stakeholders can be a subtle and delicate task, requiring significant social and, sometimes, political skills. But it is based on three basic activities: identifying, prioritizing and understanding the stakeholder group.

Identify stakeholders Think of all the people who are affected by your work, who have influence or power over it, or have an interest in its successful or unsuccessful conclusion. Although stakeholders may be both organizations and people, ultimately you must communicate with people. Make sure that you identify the correct individual stakeholders within a stakeholder organization.

Table 16.1 The rights and responsibilities of stakeholders in one IT company

The rights of stakeholders	*The responsibilities of project stakeholders*
1 To expect developers to learn and speak their language	1 Provide resources (time, money, etc.) to the project team
2 To expect developers to identify and understand their requirements	2 Educate developers about their business
3 To receive explanations of artefacts that developers use as part of working with project stakeholders, such as models they create with them (e.g. user stories or essential UI prototypes), or artefacts that they present to them (e.g. UML deployment diagrams)	3 Spend the time to provide and clarify requirements
	4 Be specific and precise about requirements
	5 Make timely decisions
	6 Respect a developer's assessment of cost and feasibility
	7 Set requirement priorities
4 To expect developers to treat them with respect	8 Review and provide timely feedback regarding relevant work artefacts of developers
5 To hear ideas and alternatives for requirements	9 Promptly communicate changes to requirements
6 To describe characteristics that make the product easy to use	10 Own their organization's software processes: to both follow them and actively help to fix them when needed
7 To be presented with opportunities to adjust requirements to permit reuse, reduce development time, or to reduce development costs	
8 To be given good-faith estimates	
9 To receive a system that meets their functional and quality needs	

Prioritize stakeholders Many people and organizations will be affected by a project. Some of these may have the power either to block or advance the project. Some may be interested in what you are doing, others may not care. Map out stakeholders using the power–interest grid (see later), and classify them by their power and by their interest in the project.

Understand key stakeholders It is important to know about key stakeholders. One needs to know how they are likely to feel about and react to the project. One also needs to know how best to engage them in the project and how best to communicate with them.

The power–interest grid

One approach to discriminating between different stakeholders, and more important, how they should be managed, is to distinguish between their power to influence the project and their interest in doing so. Stakeholders who have the power to exercise a major influence over the project should not ever be ignored. At the very least, the nature of their interest, and their motivation, should be well understood. But not all stakeholders who have the power to exercise influence over a project will be interested in doing so, and not everyone who is interested in the project has the power to influence it. The power–interest grid, shown in Figure 16.4, classifies stakeholders simply in terms of these two dimensions. Although there will be graduations between them, the two dimensions are useful in providing an indication of how stakeholders can be managed in terms of four categories.

Stakeholders' positions on the grid gives an indication of how they might be managed. High-power, interested groups must be fully engaged, with the greatest efforts made to satisfy them.

> **✳ Operations principle**
> Different stakeholder groups will need managing differently.

High-power, less-interested groups require enough effort to keep them satisfied, but not so much that they become bored or irritated with the message. Low-power, interested groups need to be kept adequately informed, with checks to ensure that no major issues are arising. These groups may be very helpful with the detail of the project. Low-power, less-interested groups need monitoring, but without excessive communication. Some key questions that can help to understand high-priority stakeholders include the following:

- What financial or emotional interest do they have in the outcome of the project? Is it positive or negative?

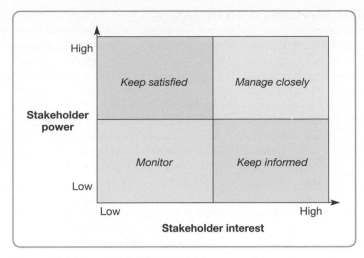

Figure 16.4 The stakeholder power–interest grid

- What motivates them most of all?
- What information do they need?
- What is the best way of communicating with them?
- What is their current opinion of the project?
- Who influences their opinions? Do some of these influencers therefore become important stakeholders in their own right?
- If they are not likely to be positive, what will win them around to support the project?
- If you don't think you will be able to win them around, how will you manage their opposition?

The Workhouse at The National Trust[5]

'Our projects can be funded by a variety of sources, involve the sensitive restoration of literally irreplaceable buildings, need a clear vision of how to reconcile historical integrity with commercial viability, and rely on the support of volunteers, our members and the community. It isn't surprising that we need to involve all stakeholders all the way through the project.' (Leigh Rix, Project Manager, The Workhouse)

The National Trust of England, Wales and Northern Ireland was formed in 1895 with the objective to preserve places of historic interest or natural beauty permanently for the nation to enjoy. 'The Workhouse' was one of its more intriguing projects. Originally built in 1824, for over 150 years it housed the local poor. But by 1997 this nationally important protected building was under threat of being turned into residential apartments. In order to aid the understanding of poverty for this and future generations the National Trust purchased The Workhouse with the intention of bringing this important part of

social history to a modern generation. 'Our vision for The Workhouse was to take a building that originally nobody wanted to enter and create a heritage facility that anyone would want to visit and where everyone is welcome.'

Leigh Rix and his project team understood from their previous experience that careful and sensitive stakeholder management was often key to the success of this type of project. The team drew up a list of stakeholders and set out to win them over with their enthusiasm for the project. They invited local people to attend meetings, explained the vision and took them to look round the site. Out of these meetings they met people with knowledge of the history of the site and sometimes with a personal connection with the building. A woman in her 90s had worked as an assistant matron, aged 14, in the 1920s. More surprisingly a woman in her 30s had lived there as recently as the 1970s when her family were homeless. Finding these links allowed the project team to re-examine their interpretation of the building and incorporate real people's stories into the presentation of the building's history.

With the need for so much, often technically difficult, building work another key group of stakeholders were the builders. Before work started the curator took all the building staff on the same tour of the site as they had taken

the various groups of VIPs who provided the funding. *'Involving the builders in the project sparked a real interest in the project and the archaeological history of the site. Often they would come across something interesting, tell the foreman who would involve an archaeologist, and so preserve an artefact that might otherwise have been destroyed. They took a real interest in their work; they felt involved.'*

The project was completed on time and within the original budget, but Leigh Rix was particularly pleased with the 'quality' of the finished project. *'It may seem like a time-consuming and expensive activity to involve all stakeholders right at the start of a project, particularly when they seem to have conflicting needs and interests. Yet, as with many of our projects, it is worth the effort. Looking back, identifying and involving the stakeholders not only allowed the project to be completed on time and within budget, it improved the eventual quality in ways we could not have anticipated.'*

Stage 2 – Project definition

Before starting the complex task of planning and executing a project, it is necessary to be clear about exactly what the project is – its definition. This is not always straightforward, especially in projects with many stakeholders. Three different elements define a project:

- its objectives – the end state that project management is trying to achieve;
- its scope – the exact range of the responsibilities taken on by project management;
- its strategy – how project management is going to meet its objectives.

Project objectives

Objectives help to provide a definition of the end point which can be used to monitor progress and identify when success has been achieved. They can be judged in terms of the five performance objectives – quality, speed, dependability, flexibility and cost. However, flexibility is regarded as a 'given' in most projects which, by definition, are to some extent one-offs, and speed and dependability are compressed to one composite objective – 'time'. This results in what are known as the 'three objectives of project management' – cost, time and quality. Figure 16.5 shows the 'project objectives triangle' with these three types of project marked.

The relative importance of each objective will differ for different projects. Some aerospace projects, such as the development of a new aircraft, which impact on passenger safety, will place a very high emphasis on quality objectives. With other projects, for example a research project that is being funded by a fixed government grant, cost might predominate. Other projects emphasize

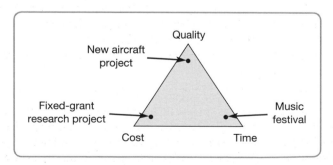

Figure 16.5 The project objectives triangle

time: for example, the organization of an open-air music festival has to happen on a particular date if the project is to meet its objectives. In each of these projects, although one objective might be particularly important, the other objectives can never be totally forgotten.

Good objectives are those which are clear, measurable and, preferably, quantifiable. Clarifying objectives involves breaking down project objectives into three categories – the purpose, the end results, and the success criteria. For example, a project that is expressed in general terms as 'improve the budgeting process' could be broken down into:

- *Purpose* – to allow budgets to be agreed and confirmed prior the annual financial meeting.
- *End result* – a report that identifies the causes of budget delay, and which recommends new budgeting processes and systems.
- *Success criteria* – the report should be completed by 30 June, meet all departments' needs and enable integrated and dependable delivery of agreed budget statements. Cost of the recommendations should not exceed $200,000.

Project scope

The scope of a project identifies its work content and its products or outcomes. It is a boundary-setting exercise which attempts to define the dividing line between what each part of the project will do and what it won't do. Defining scope is particularly important when part of a project is being outsourced. A supplier's scope of supply will identify the legal boundaries within which the work must be done. Sometimes the scope of the project is articulated in a formal 'project specification'. This is the written, pictorial and graphical information used to define the output, and the accompanying terms and conditions.

Project strategy

The third part of a project's definition is the project strategy, which defines, in a general rather than a specific way, how the project is going to meet its objectives. It does this in two ways: by defining the phases of the project, and by setting milestones, and/or 'stagegates'. Milestones are important events during the project's life. Stagegates are the decision points that allow the project to move onto its next phase. A stagegate often launches further activities and therefore commits the project to additional costs, etc. Milestone is a more passive term, which may herald the review of a part-complete project or mark the completion of a stage, but does not necessarily have more significance than a measure of achievement or completeness. At this stage the actual dates for each milestone are not necessarily determined. It is useful, however, to at least identify the significant milestones and stagegates, either to define the boundary between phases or to help in discussions with the project's customer.

Stage 3 – Project planning

The planning process fulfils four distinct purposes:

1 It determines the cost and duration of the project. This enables major decisions to be made – such as the decision whether to go ahead with the project at the start.
2 It determines the level of resources which will be needed.
3 It helps to allocate work and to monitor progress. Planning must include the identification of who is responsible for what.
4 It helps to assess the impact of any changes to the project.

Planning is not a one-off process. It may be repeated several times during the project's life as circumstances change; nor is replanning a sign of project failure or mismanagement. In uncertain projects, in particular, it is a normal occurrence. In fact, later stage plans typically mean that more information is available, and that the project is becoming less uncertain. The process of project planning involves five steps (*see* Fig. 16.6).

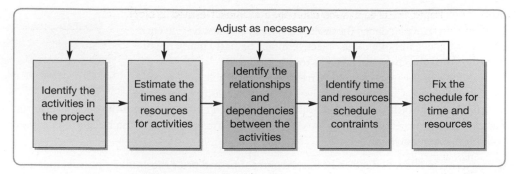

Figure 16.6 Stages in the planning process

Identify activities – the work breakdown structure

Most projects are too complex to be planned and controlled effectively unless they are first broken down into manageable portions. This is achieved by structuring the project into a 'family tree', along similar lines to the component structure (Chapter 5), but which specifies major tasks or sub-projects. These in turn are divided up into smaller tasks until a defined, manageable series of tasks, called a *work package*, is arrived at. Each work package can be allocated its own objectives in terms of time, cost and quality. The output from this is called the work breakdown structure (WBS). The WBS brings clarity and definition to the project planning process. It shows 'how the jigsaw fits together'. It also provides a framework for building up information for reporting purposes.

Example project
As a simple example to illustrate the application of each stage of the planning process, let us examine the following domestic project. The project definition is:

● *purpose:* to make breakfast in bed;
● *end result:* breakfast in bed of boiled egg, toast and orange juice;
● *success criteria:* plan uses minimum staff resources and time, and product is high-quality (egg freshly boiled, warm toast, etc.);
● *scope:* project starts in kitchen at 6.00 am, and finishes in bedroom; needs one operator and normal kitchen equipment.

The work breakdown structure is based on the above definition and can be constructed as shown in Figure 16.7.

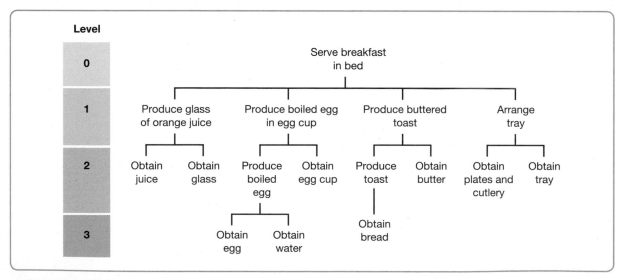

Figure 16.7 A work breakdown structure for a simple domestic project

Table 16.2 Time and resources estimates for a 'breakfast-in-bed' project

Activity	Effort (person-min)	Duration (min)
Butter toast	1	1
Pour orange juice	1	1
Boil egg	0	4
Slice bread	1	1
Fill pan with water	1	1
Bring water to boil	0	3
Toast bread	0	2
Take loaded tray to bedroom	1	1
Fetch tray, plates, cutlery	1	1

Estimate times and resources

The next stage in planning is to identify the time and resource requirements of the work packages. Without some idea of how long each part of a project will take and how many resources it will need, it is impossible to define what should be happening at any time during the execution of the project. Estimates are just that, however – a systematic best guess, not a perfect forecast of reality. Estimates may never be perfect but they can be made with some idea of how accurate they might be.

Example project
Returning to our very simple example 'breakfast-in-bed' project, the activities were identified and times estimated as in Table 16.2. While some of the estimates may appear generous, they take into account the time of day and the state of the operator.

Probabilistic estimates
The amount of uncertainty in a project has a major bearing on the level of confidence which can be placed on an estimate. The impact of uncertainty on estimating times leads some project managers to use a probability curve to describe the estimate. In practice, this is usually a positively skewed distribution, as in Figure 16.8. The greater the risk, the greater the range of the distribution. The natural tendency of some people is to produce *optimistic* estimates, but these will have a relatively low probability of being correct because they

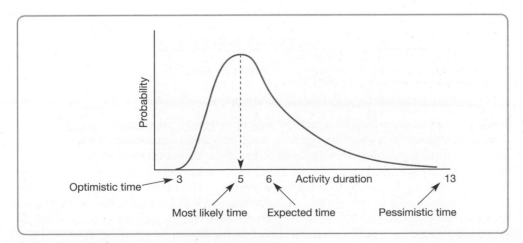

Figure 16.8 Probability distribution of time estimates

represent the time which would be taken if *everything* went well. *Most likely* estimates have the highest probability of proving correct. Finally, *pessimistic* estimates assume that almost everything which could go wrong does go wrong. Because of the skewed nature of the distribution, the expected time for the activity will not be the same as the most likely time.

Critical commentary

When project managers talk of 'time estimates', they are really talking about guessing. By definition, planning a project happens in advance of the project itself. Therefore, no one really knows how long each activity will take. Of course, some kind of guess is needed for planning purposes. However, some project managers believe that too much faith is put in time estimates. The really important question, they claim, is not how long *will* something take, but how long *could* something take without delaying the whole project. (We deal with this issue partially when we discuss the concept of float later in the chapter.) Also, if a single most likely time estimate is difficult to estimate, then using three, as one does for probabilistic estimates, is merely over-analysing what is highly dubious data in the first place.

Identify relationships and dependencies

All the activities which are identified as comprising a project will have some relationship with one another that will depend on the logic of the project. Some activities will, by necessity, need to be executed in a particular order. For example, in the construction of a house, the foundations must be prepared before the walls are built, which in turn must be completed before the roof is put in place. These activities have a *dependent* or *series* relationship. Other activities do not have any such dependence on each other. The rear garden of the house could probably be prepared totally independently of the garage being built. These two activities have an *independent* or *parallel* relationship.

Example project

Table 16.2 identified the activities for the breakfast preparation project. The list shows that some of the activities must necessarily follow others. For example, 'boil egg' cannot be carried out until 'fill pan with water' and 'bring water to boil' have been completed. Further logical analysis of the activities in the list shows that there are two major 'chains', where activities must be carried out in a definite sequence:

Slice bread – Toast bread – Butter toast

Fill pan with water – Bring water to boil – Boil egg

Both of these sequences must be completed before the activity 'take loaded tray to bedroom'. The remaining activities ('Pour orange juice' and 'Fetch tray, plates, cutlery') can be done at any time provided that they are completed before 'Take loaded tray to bedroom'. An initial project plan might be as shown in Figure 16.9. Here, the activities have been represented as blocks of time in proportion to their estimated durations. From this, we can see that the 'project' can be completed in nine minutes. Some of the activities have spare time (called float) indicated by the dotted line. The sequence 'Fill pan – Boil water – Boil egg – Bedroom' has no float, and is called the *critical path* of the project. By implication, any activity which runs late in this sequence would cause the whole project to be delayed accordingly.

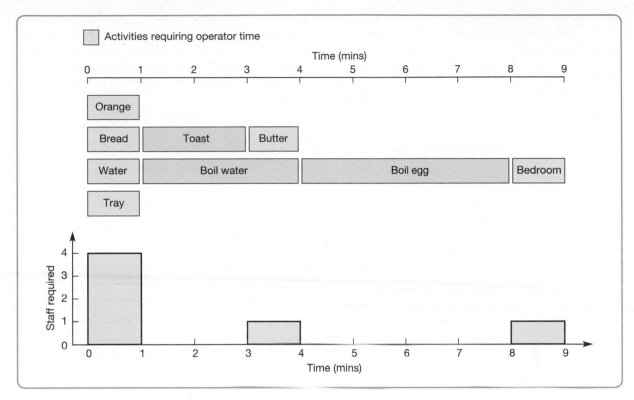

Figure 16.9 Initial project plan for a simple project, with resources

Identify schedule constraints

Once estimates have been made of the time and effort involved in each activity, and their dependencies identified, it is possible to compare project requirements with the available resources. The finite nature of critical resources – such as special skills – means that they should be taken into account in the planning process. This often has the effect of highlighting the need for more detailed replanning. There are essentially two fundamental approaches:

- *Resource-constrained.* Only the available resource levels are used in resource scheduling, and are never exceeded. As a result, the project completion may slip. Resource-limited scheduling is used, for example, when a project company has its own highly specialized assembly and test facilities.
- *Time-constrained.* The overriding priority is to complete the project within a given time. Once normally available resources have been used up, alternative ('threshold') resources are scheduled.

Example project

Returning to the breakfast-in-bed project, we can now consider the resource implications of the plan in Figure 16.9. Each of the four activities scheduled at the start (pour orange, cut bread, fill pan, fetch tray) consumes staff resources. There is clearly a resource-loading problem, because the project definition states that only one person is available. This is not an insuperable difficulty, however, because there is sufficient float to move some of the activities. A plan with levelled resources can be produced, as shown in Figure 16.10. All that has been necessary is to delay the toast preparation by one minute, and to use the elapsed time during the toasting and water-boiling processes to pour orange and fetch the tray.

Fix the schedule

Project planners should ideally have a number of alternatives to choose from. The one which best fits project objectives can then be chosen or developed. For example, it may be appropriate to examine both resource-limited and time-limited options. However, it is not always

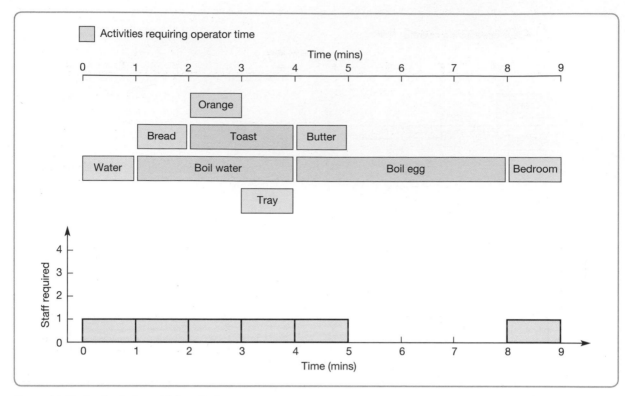

Figure 16.10 Revised plan with levelled resources

possible to examine several alternative schedules, especially in very large or very uncertain projects, as the computation could be prohibitive. However, modern computer-based project management software is making the search for the best schedule more feasible.

Example project

A further improvement to the plan can be made. Looking again at the project definition, the success criteria state that the product should be 'high-quality'. In the plan shown in Figure 16.10, although the egg is freshly boiled, the toast might be cold. An 'optimized' plan which would provide hot toast would be to prepare the toast during the 'boil egg' activity. This plan is shown in Figure 16.11.

Stage 5 – Project control

The stages in project planning and control have so far all taken place before the actual project takes place. This stage deals with the management activities which take place during the execution of the project. Project control is the essential link between planning and doing. It involves three sets of decisions:

● how to *monitor* the project in order to check on its progress;
● how to *assess the performance* of the project by comparing monitored observations of the project with the project plan;
● how to *intervene* in the project in order to make the changes that will bring it back to plan.

Project monitoring

Project managers have first to decide what they should be looking for as the project progresses. Usually a variety of measures are monitored. To some extent, the measures used will depend on the nature of the project. However, common measures include current expenditure to date,

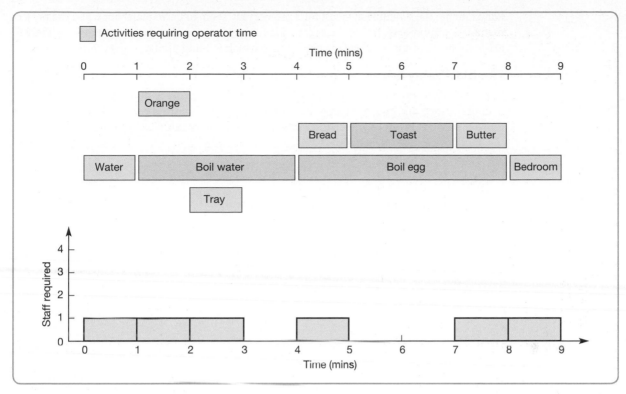

Figure 16.11 Revised plan with levelled resources and warm toast

supplier price changes, amount of overtime authorized, technical changes to project, inspection failures, number and length of delays, activities not started on time, missed milestone, etc. Some of these monitored measures affect mainly cost, some mainly time. However, when something affects the quality of the project, there are also time and cost implications. This is because quality problems in project planning and control usually have to be solved in a limited amount of time.

Assessing project performance

The monitored measures of project performance at any point in time need to be assessed so that project management can make a judgement concerning overall performance. A typical planned cost profile of a project through its life is shown in Figure 16.12. At the beginning of a project some activities can be started, but most activities will be dependent on finishing. Eventually, only a few activities will remain to be completed. This pattern of a slow start followed by a faster pace with an eventual tail-off of activity holds true for almost all projects, which is why the rate of total expenditure follows an S-shaped pattern as shown in Figure 16.13, even when the cost curves for the individual activities are linear. It is against this curve that actual costs can be compared in order to check whether the project's costs are being incurred to plan. Figure 16.12 shows the planned and actual cost figures compared in this way. It shows that the project is incurring costs, on a cumulative basis, ahead of what was planned.

Intervening to change the project

If the project is obviously out of control in the sense that its costs, quality levels or times are significantly different from those planned, then some kind of intervention is almost certainly likely to be required. The exact nature of the intervention will depend on the technical characteristics of the project, but it is likely to need the advice of all the people who would be affected. Given the interconnected nature of projects – a change to one part of the project will have knock-on effects elsewhere – this means that interventions often require wide consultation. Sometimes intervention is needed even if the project looks to be proceeding according to plan.

For example, the schedule and cost for a project may seem to be 'to plan', but when the project managers project activities and cost into the future, they see that problems are very likely to arise. In this case it is the *trend* of performance which is being used to trigger intervention.

The MacLeamy Curve[6]

It has been accepted for many years by professional project managers that a project becomes more difficult to change as it progresses. The more developed it becomes, the more a project develops internal connections and complexities; therefore changing one

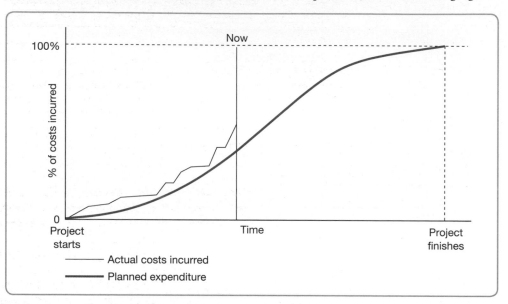

Figure 16.12 Comparing planned and actual expenditure

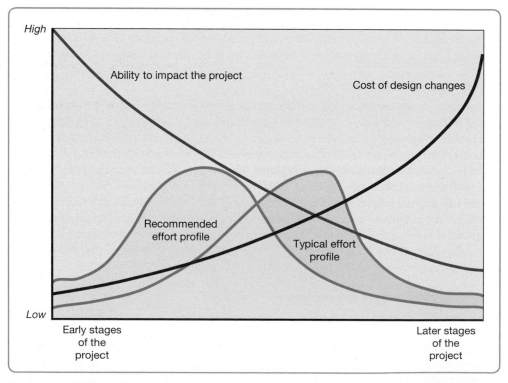

Figure 16.13 The MacLeamy Curve

Source: adapted from *Collaboration, Integrated Information, and the Project Life Cycle in Building Design and Construction and Operation*, Construction Users Roundtables (CURT)

part of the project is more likely to have implications in other parts of the project. Patrick MacLeamy, the boss of the architecture firm HOK, drew a set of curves based on this observation (although previous authors had also proposed similar curves). The idea is that, as the project moves forward, the cost of making changes to the original project plan increases, but the ability of project managers to influence the project goes down. The key point made by MacLeamy is that project managers focus their effort too late, during the time when design changes are relatively costly. Instead, they should move their efforts forward in the project, frontloading it, in order to reduce the cost of any changes to the project specification (*see* Fig. 16.13).

SHORT CASE   Imagineering projects at Disney[7]

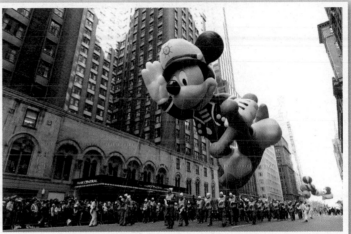

Source: Shutterstock.com/Scott Cornell

Ever since the creation of famous characters such as Mickey Mouse and Snow White, the Disney Corporation has been synonymous with innovative quality entertainment. At the Walt Disney Studios and Parks, persuasive stories come alive and technology and artistry work together to delight visitors and audiences alike. Nowhere is this more true than Walt Disney's 'Imagineering' operation ('Imagineering' is a word that combines 'imagination' and 'engineering'), which, in effect, is the research and development arm of Walt Disney Parks and Resorts. It is responsible for creating many of the more significant attractions, shows, fireworks displays and parades at the Disney theme parks. Their complex and often innovative attractions will be closely scrutinized by thousands or millions of Disney's 'guests', so it is vital to pay attention to details. A famous Walt Disney saying is that a guest may not notice a specific (sometimes tiny) detail, but he or she will notice when the detail isn't there. This means that they need to be created with skill, creativity, and equally importantly, professional project management. Walt Disney World's Imagineering Department's project managers work with the interactive technologies, the park staff, special-effects wizards, digital designers and others to create an interactive experience for the guests. Although many of the projects are technical in nature, project managers work with a wide range of different disciplines from construction to marketing.

David Van Wyk is the vice president of project management for Walt Disney Imagineering and he fully understands the importance of effective project management. '*Without it*', he says '*how can we be as relevant tomorrow as we are today? How can we meet and exceed guest expectations in a changing world? We have somewhere between 140 and 150 different skill sets in Imagineering, including engineers, creative staff, artists,* architects, accountants, writers, theme and new media specialists, and more. A culture of interdisciplinary co-ordination with diverse stakeholders aims to interact and socialize to understand issues and problems. We have developed and keep working on a culture of collaboration. We do not have an NIH (not invented here) culture.'* The Imagineering group is very much aware of the implications of the MacLeamy Curve (see earlier) which highlights the idea that cost increases while the ability to change decreases over the life of the project. So it is important to solve issues earlier in the design process, when it's more economical to make changes, especially those involving equipment. Which is why, says David Van Wyk, '*we seek to incorporate more peer review earlier in the engineering-design process. We also look for on-time delivery, getting it right before it gets to the field, with a strong start, strong finish, and careful resource allocation*'. All of which makes it important to develop excellent relationships with partners and make sure that they, and all stakeholders, fully subscribe to the objectives of predictability, collaboration, impeccable co-ordination, prompt decision making, collective quality, and just-in-time delivery.

WHAT IS NETWORK PLANNING?

The process of project planning and control is greatly aided by the use of techniques which help project managers to handle its complexity and time-based nature. The simplest of these techniques is the Gantt chart (or bar chart) which we introduced earlier (see Chapter 10). Gantt charts are the simplest way to exhibit an overall project plan, because they have excellent visual impact and are easy to understand. They are also useful for communicating project plans and status to senior managers as well as for day-to-day project control. Later techniques, most of which go under the collective name of network analysis, are now used, almost universally, to help plan and control all significant projects, but can also prove helpful in smaller ventures. The two network analysis methods we will examine are the critical path method (CPM) or analysis (CPA) and programme evaluation and review technique (PERT).

Critical path method (CPM)

As project complexity increases, so it becomes necessary to identify the relationships between activities. It becomes increasingly important to show the logical sequence in which activities must take place. The critical path method (CPM) models the project by clarifying the relationships between activities diagrammatically. The first way we can illustrate this is by using arrows to represent each activity in a project. For example, examine the simple project in Figure 16.14 which involves the decoration of an apartment. Six activities are identified together with their relationships. The first, activity *a*, 'Remove furniture', does not require any of the other activities to be completed before it can be started. However, activity *b*, 'Prepare bedroom', cannot be started until activity *a* has been completed. The same applies to activity *d*, 'Prepare the kitchen'. Similarly activity *c*, 'Paint bedroom', cannot be started until activity *b* has been completed. Nor can activity *e*, 'Paint the kitchen', be started until the kitchen has been prepared. Only when both the bedroom and the kitchen have been painted can the apartment be furnished again. The logic of these relationships is shown as an arrow diagram,

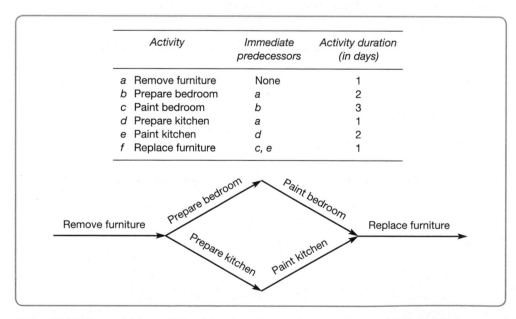

Activity	Immediate predecessors	Activity duration (in days)
a Remove furniture	None	1
b Prepare bedroom	*a*	2
c Paint bedroom	*b*	3
d Prepare kitchen	*a*	1
e Paint kitchen	*d*	2
f Replace furniture	*c, e*	1

Figure 16.14 The activities, relationships, durations and arrow diagram for the project 'decorate apartment'

where each activity is represented by an arrow (the length of the arrows is not proportional to the duration of the activities).

This arrow diagram can be developed into a network diagram as shown in Figure 16.15. At the tail (start) and head (finish) of each *activity* (represented by an arrow) is a circle which represents an event. Events are moments in time which occur at the start or finish of an activity. They have no duration and are of a definite recognizable nature. Networks of this type are composed only of activities and events.

The rules for drawing this type of network diagram are fairly straightforward:

Rule 1 An event cannot be reached until all activities leading to it are complete. Event 5 in Figure 16.15 is not reached until activities *c* and *e* are complete.

Rule 2 No activity can start until its tail event is reached. In Figure 16.15 activity *f* cannot start until event 5 is reached.

Rule 3 No two activities can have the same head and tail events. In Figure 16.16 activities *x* and *y* cannot be drawn as first shown; they must be drawn using a dummy activity.

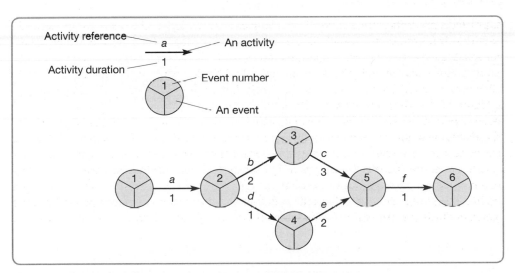

Figure 16.15 A network diagram for the project 'decorate apartment'

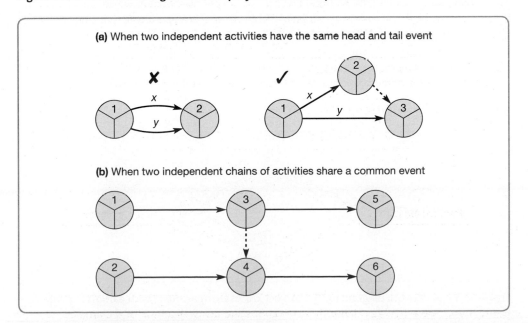

Figure 16.16 When dummy activities are necessary

These have no duration and are usually shown as a dotted line arrow. They are used either for clarity of drawing or to keep the logic of the diagram consistent with that of the project.

The critical path

In all network diagrams where the activities have some parallel relationships, there will be more than one sequence of activities which will lead from the start to the end of the project. These sequences of activities are called *paths* through the network. Each path will have a total duration which is the sum of all its activities. The path which has the longest sequence of activities is called the critical path of the network (note that it is possible to have more than one critical path if they share the same joint longest time). It is called the critical path because any delay in any of the activities on this path will delay the whole project. In Figure 16.15, therefore, the critical path through the network is *a, b, c, f*, which is seven days long. This is the minimum duration of the whole project. By drawing the network diagram we can:

- identify which are the particularly important activities;
- calculate the duration of the whole project.

Calculating float

Earlier in the chapter we described the flexibility to change the timings of activities, which is inherent in various parts of a project, as float. We can use the network diagram to calculate this for each activity. The procedure is relatively simple:

1. Calculate the earliest and latest event times for each event. The earliest event time (EET) is the very earliest the event could possibly occur if all preceding activities are completed as early as possible. The latest event time (LET) is the latest time that the event could possibly take place without delaying the whole project.
2. Calculate the 'time window' within which an activity must take place. This is the time between the EET of its tail event and the LET of its head event.
3. Compare the actual duration of the activity with the time window within which it must take place. The difference between them is the float of the activity.

Consider again the simple network example. The critical path is the sequence of activities *a, b, c, f*. We can calculate the EET and LET for each event as shown in Figure 16.17. If activity *a* starts at time 0, the earliest it can finish is 1 because it is a one-day activity. If activity *b* is started immediately, it will finish at day 3 (EET of tail event + duration, 1 + 2). Activity *c* can then start at day 3 and because it is of three days' duration it will finish at day 6. Activity *e* also has event number 5 as its head event so we must also calculate the EET of activity *e*'s tail event. This is determined by activity *d*. If activity *d* starts at day 1 (the earliest it can) it will

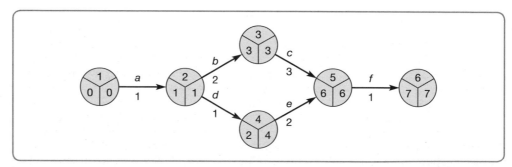

Figure 16.17 A network diagram for the project 'decorate apartment' with earliest and latest event times

finish at day 2. So the EET of event number 4 is day 2. If activity *e* is started immediately, it will then finish at day 4. Event number 5 cannot occur, however, until both *e* and *c* have finished, which will not be until day 6 (*see* rule 1 above). Activity *f* can then start and will finish at day 7.

The LETs can be calculated by using the reverse logic. If event number 6 *must* occur no later than day 7, the LET for event number 5 is day 6. Any later than this and the whole project will be delayed. Working back, if activity *c* must finish by day 6 it cannot start later than day 3, and if activity *b* must finish by day 3 it must start by day 1. Similarly, if activity *e* is to finish by day 6 it must start no later than day 4, and if activity *d* is to finish by day 4 it must start no later than day 3. Now we have two activities with event number 2 as their tail event, one of which needs to start by day 1 at the latest, the other by day 3 at the latest. The LET for event number 2, therefore, must be the smaller of the two. If it was delayed past this point, activity *b*, and therefore the whole project, would be delayed.

Worked example

The chief surveyor of a firm that moves earth in preparation for the construction of roads has identified the activities and their durations for each stage of an operation to prepare a difficult stretch of motorway (*see* Table 16.3). The surveyor needs to know how long the project will take and which are the critical activities.

Table 16.3 Road construction activities

Activity	Duration (days)	Preceding activities
A	5	–
B	10	–
C	1	–
D	8	B
E	10	B
F	9	B
G	3	A, D
H	7	A, D
I	4	F
J	3	F
K	5	C, J
L	8	H, E, I, K
M	4	C, J

Figure 16.18 shows the network diagram for the project. Drawing these diagrams from the type of information in Table 16.3 is a matter of sketching the logic of the relationships between the activities on a piece of paper until it conforms to the relationships as stated, and then drawing the diagram again in a neater fashion. So, for example, A, B and C have no predecessors and therefore are the activities that can be commenced at the beginning of the project. Activities D, E and F all can start after the completion of activity B, and so on. The diagram also shows the latest and earliest event times for the activities. It shows that the critical path for the project is the sequence of activities B, F, J, K, L. The total length of the project is 35 days, this being the length of the critical path sequence of activities.

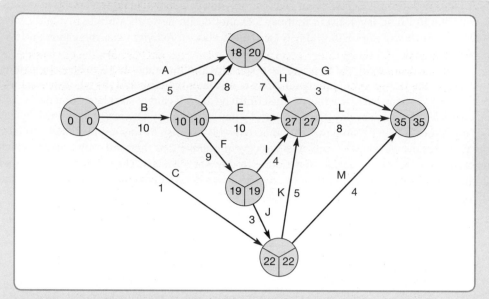

Figure 16.18 Network diagram for the motorway project

Critical commentary

The idea that all project activities can be identified as entities with a clear beginning and a clear end point and that these entities can be described in terms of their relationship with each other is an obvious simplification. Some activities are more or less continuous and evolve over time. For example, take a simple project such as digging a trench and laying a communications cable in it. The activity 'dig trench' does not have to be completed before the activity 'lay cable' is started. Only two or three metres of the trench needs to be dug before cable laying can commence. A simple relationship, but one that is difficult to illustrate on a network diagram. Also, if the trench is being dug in difficult terrain, the time taken to complete the activity, or even the activity itself, may change, to include rock-drilling activities for example. However, if the trench cannot be dug because of rock formations, it may be possible to dig more of the trench elsewhere, a contingency not allowed for in the original plan. So, even for this simple project, the original network diagram may reflect neither what *will* happen nor *could* happen.

Activity on node networks

The network we have described so far uses arrows to represent activities and circles at the junctions or nodes of the arrows to represent events. This method is called the activity on arrow (AoA) method. An alternative method of drawing networks is the activity on node (AoN) method. In the AoN representation, activities are drawn as boxes, and arrows are used to define the relationships between them. There are three advantages to the AoN method:

- It is often easier to move from the basic logic of a project's relationships to a network diagram using AoN rather than using the AoA method.
- AoN diagrams do not need dummy activities to maintain the logic of relationships.
- Most of the computer packages which are used in project planning and control use an AoN format.

An AoN network of the 'apartment decorating' project is shown in Figure 16.19.

Example

The implementation of a new logistics operation involves the purchase of a fleet of trucks, the design of new routes and the building of a new distribution centre and associated handling equipment. Figure 16.20 provides an AoN network for the project. The *earliest start times* for

Figure 16.19 Activity on node network diagram for project 'decorate apartment'

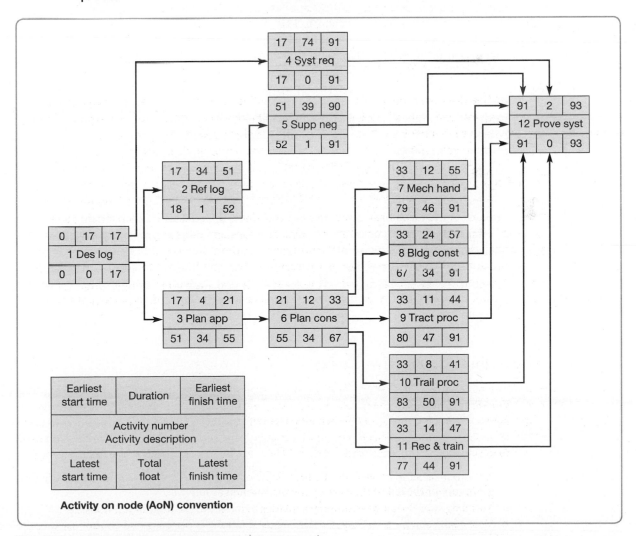

Figure 16.20 New logistics operation: precedence network

each activity are found by working from left to right across the network. Each start event can begin at $t = 0$. At a 'merge' event (where two or more activities come together, as at event 12), use the latest completion date of the various activities which lead into it. Earliest finish times of a 'burst' activity (such as activity 6, where five succeeding activities literally 'burst' out) are carried forward to form the earliest start dates of the succeeding activities (7 through 11). The *latest start times* for each activity are found by working back from right to left across the network. The earliest start time for the final event on the network is often used as the latest start time for that event as well. At a 'merge' event (such as event 6), use the earliest completion date of the various activities.

First, we carry out a *forward pass* of the network (i.e. proceed from left to right). Activity 1 is given a start date of week 0. The earliest finish is then week 17, because the duration is 17 weeks. The earliest start date for activity 2 must then also be week 17. Activity 5 starts at $17 + 34$, the duration for activity 2. Activity 4 is in parallel with activity 2, and can start at the same time. The rest of the forward pass is straightforward until we reach activity 12. Here, seven activities merge, so we must use the highest earliest finish of the activities which lead into it as the earliest start time for activity 12. This is 91 (the earliest finish time for activity 4). Since the duration of activity 12 is two weeks, the earliest finish time for the whole network is 93 weeks.

Now we can carry out a *backward pass* by assuming that the latest finish time is also 93 weeks (the bottom right-hand box on activity 12). This means that there is no 'float', i.e. the difference between the earliest and latest start dates for this activity is zero. Hence, the latest start time is also week 91. This gets down-dated into activities 7 through 11, which have week 91 as the latest finish time. The difference between week 91 and the various earliest finish times for these activities means that there is float on each one. That is, they can start much later than indicated by the earliest start dates. On the backward pass, activity 6 forms a merge event for activities 7 through 11. Take the lowest latest start time from these activities, i.e. week 67, as the latest finish time for activity 6. If all goes well, and the analysis is correct, there should also be zero float for activity 1. The *critical path* for the network is then the line which joins the activities with minimum float, i.e. activities 1, 4 and 12.

Programme evaluation and review technique (PERT)

The programme evaluation and review technique, or PERT as it is universally known, is a technique that recognizes that activity durations and costs in project management cannot be forecast perfectly, so probability theory should be used. In this type of network the duration of each activity is estimated on an optimistic, a most likely and a pessimistic basis, as shown in Figure 16.21. If it is assumed that these time estimates are consistent with a beta probability distribution, the mean and variance of the distribution can be estimated as follows:

$$t_e = \frac{t_o + 4t_l + t_p}{6}$$

where

t_e = the expected time for the activity

t_o = the optimistic time for the activity

t_l = the most likely time for the activity

t_p = the pessimistic time for the activity

The variance of the distribution (V) can be calculated as follows:

$$V = \frac{(t_p - t_o)^2}{6^2} = \frac{(t_p - t_o)^2}{36}$$

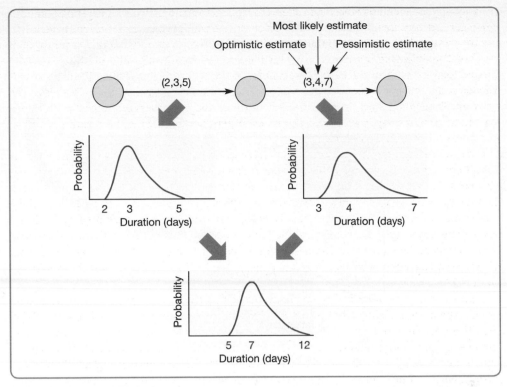

Figure 16.21 Probabilistic time estimates can be summed to give a probabilistic estimate for the whole project

The time distribution of any path through a network will have a mean which is the sum of the means of the activities that make up the path, and a variance which is a sum of their variances. In Figure 16.21:

$$\text{The mean of the first activity} = \frac{2 + (4 \times 3) + 5}{6} = 3.17$$

$$\text{The variance of the first activity} = \frac{(5 - 2)^2}{36} = 0.25$$

$$\text{The mean of the second activity} = \frac{3 + (4 \times 4) + 7}{6} = 4.33$$

$$\text{The variance of the second activity} = \frac{(7 - 3)^2}{36} = 0.44$$

$$\text{The mean of the network distribution} = 3.17 + 4.33 = 7.5$$

$$\text{The variance of the network distribution} = 0.25 + 0.44 = 0.69$$

It is generally assumed that the whole path will be normally distributed.

The advantage of this extra information is that we can examine the 'riskiness' of each path through a network as well as its duration. For example, Figure 16.22 shows a simple two-path network. The top path is the critical one; the distribution of its duration is 10.5 with a variance of 0.06 (therefore a standard deviation of 0.245). The distribution of the non-critical path has a mean of 9.67 and a variance of 0.66 (therefore a standard deviation of 0.812). The implication of this is that there is a chance that the non-critical path could in reality be critical. Although we will not discuss the probability calculations here, it is possible to determine the probability of any sub-critical path turning out to be critical when the project actually takes place. However, on a practical level, even if the probability calculations are judged not

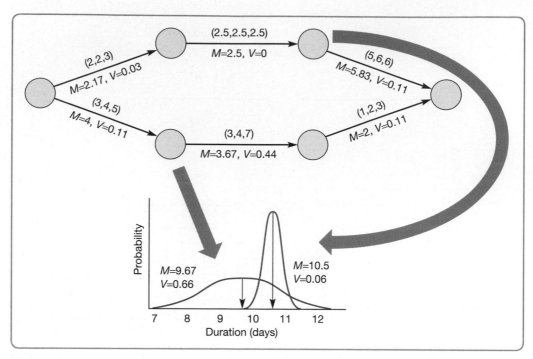

Figure 16.22 One path in the network can have the longest expected duration while another path has the greater variance

to be worth the effort involved, it is useful to be able to make an approximate assessment of the riskiness of each part of a network.

Introducing resource constraints

The logic which governs network relationships is primarily derived from the technical details of the project as we have described. However, the availability of resources may impose its own constraints, which can materially affect the relationships between activities. Figure 16.23 shows a simple two-path network with details of both the duration of each activity and the number of staff required to perform each activity. The total resource schedule is also shown. The three activities on the critical path, *a*, *c*, and *e*, have been programmed into the resource schedule first. The remaining activities all have some float and therefore have flexibility as to when they are performed.

The resource schedule in Figure 16.23 has the non-critical activities starting as soon as is possible. This results in a resource profile which varies from seven staff down to three. Even if seven staff are available, the project manager might want to even out the loading for organizational convenience. If the total number of staff available is less than seven, however, the project will need rescheduling. Suppose only five staff are available. It is still possible to complete the project in the same time, as shown in Figure 16.24. Activity *b* has been delayed until after activity *a* has finished. This results in a resource profile which varies only between four and five staff and is within the resourcing limit of five staff.

However, in order to achieve this it is necessary to *require* activity *b* to start only when activity *a* is completed. This is a logic constraint which, if it were included in the network, would change it as shown in Figure 16.24. In this network all activities are critical, as indeed one can see from the resource schedule.

Crashing networks

Crashing (accelerating) activities in networks is the process of reducing time spans on critical path activities so that the project is completed in less time. Usually, crashing activities incurs extra cost. This can be as a result of such actions as overtime working, acquiring

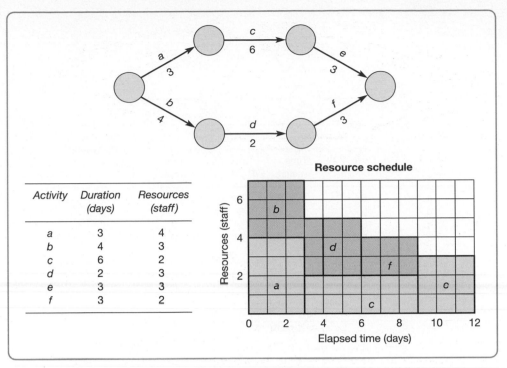

Figure 16.23 Resource profile of a network assuming that all activities are started as soon as possible

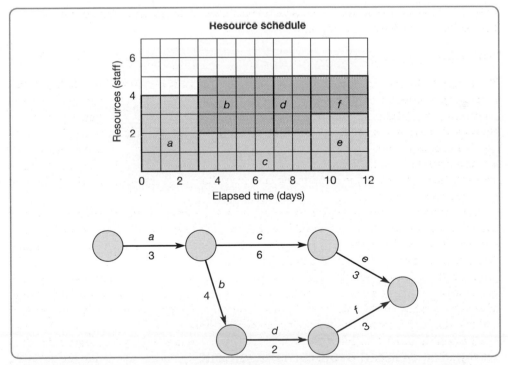

Figure 16.24 Resource profile of a network with non-critical activities delayed to fit resource constraints; in this case this effectively changes the network logic to make all activities critical

additional resources, such as manpower, or using subcontractors. Figure 16.25 shows an example of crashing a simple network. For each activity the duration and normal cost are specified, together with the (reduced) duration and (increased) cost of crashing them. Not all activities are capable of being crashed; here activity *e* cannot be crashed. The critical path

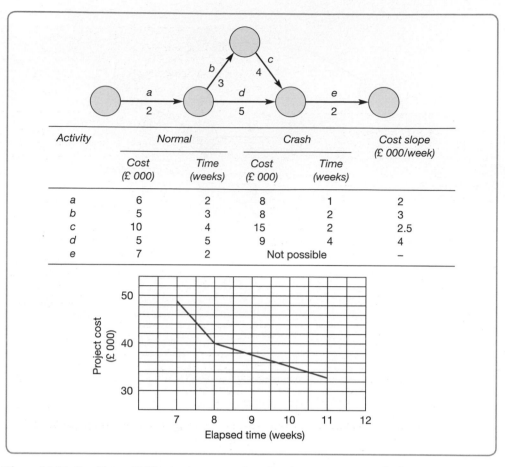

Figure 16.25 Crashing activities to shorten project time becomes progressively more expensive

is the sequence of activities *a*, *b*, *c*, *e*. If the total project time is to be reduced, one of the activities on the critical path must be crashed. In order to decide which activity to crash, the 'cost slope' of each is calculated. This is the cost per time period of reducing durations. The most cost-effective way of shortening the whole project then is to crash the activity on the critical path which has the lowest cost slope. This is activity *a*, the crashing of which will cost an extra £2,000 and will shorten the project by one week. After this, activity *c* can be crashed, saving a further two weeks and costing an extra £5,000. At this point all the activities have become critical and further time savings can only be achieved by crashing two activities in parallel. The shape of the time–cost curve in Figure 16.25 is entirely typical. Initial savings come relatively inexpensively if the activities with the lowest cost slope are chosen. Later in the crashing sequence the more expensive activities need to be crashed and eventually two or more paths become jointly critical. Inevitably by that point, savings in time can only come from crashing two or more activities on parallel paths.

Computer-assisted project management

For many years, since the emergence of computer-based modelling, increasingly sophisticated software for project planning and control has become available. The rather tedious computation necessary in network planning can relatively easily be performed by project planning models. All they need are the basic relationships between activities, together with timing and resource requirements for each activity. Earliest and latest event times, float and other characteristics of a network can be presented, often in the form of a Gantt chart. More significantly, the speed of computation allows for frequent updates to project plans. Similarly,

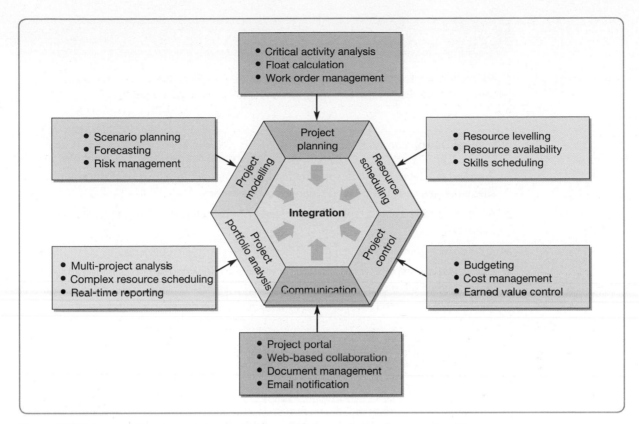

Figure 16.26 Some of the elements integrated in enterprise project management systems

if updated information is both accurate and frequent, such computer-based systems can also provide effective project control data. More recently, the potential for using computer-based project management systems for communication within large and complex projects has been developed in so-called enterprise project management (EPM) systems.

Figure 16.26 illustrates just some of the elements that are integrated within EPM systems. Most of these activities have been treated in this chapter. Project planning involves critical path analysis and scheduling, an understanding of float, and the sending of instructions on when to start activities. Resource scheduling looks at the resource implications of planning decisions and the way projects may have to be changed to accommodate resource constraints. Project control includes simple budgeting and cost management together with more sophisticated earned value control. However, EPM also includes other elements. Project modelling involves the use of project planning methods to explore alternative approaches to a project, identifying where failure might occur and exploring the changes to the project which may have to be made under alternative future scenarios. Project portfolio analysis acknowledges that, for many organizations, several projects have to be managed simultaneously. Usually these share common resources. Therefore, not only will delays in one activity within a project affect other activities in that project, they may also have an impact on a completely different project which is relying on the same resource. Finally, integrated EPM systems can help to communicate problems, both within a project, and to outside organizations which may be contributing to the project. Much of this communication facility is web-based. Project portals can allow all stakeholders to transact activities and gain a clear view of the current status of a project. Automatic notification of significant milestones can be made by email. At a very basic level, the various documents that specify parts of the project can be stored in an online library. Some people argue that it is this last element of communication capabilities that is the most useful part of EPM systems.

MyOMLab   *Check and improve your understanding of this chapter using self-assessment questions and a personalized study plan, a video case study, and an eText – all at* **www.myomlab.com.**

❯ What is project management?

- A project is a set of activities with a defined start point and a defined end state, which pursues a defined goal and uses a defined set of resources.

- All projects can be characterized by their degree of complexity and the inherent uncertainty in the project.

- Project management is the activity of planning and controlling projects.

- Project management has five stages, four of which are relevant to project planning and control: understanding the project environment; defining the project; planning the project; technical execution of the project (not part of project planning and control); and project control.

❯ How are projects planned and controlled?

- It is important to understand the environment in which a project takes place for two reasons. First, the environment influences the way a project is carried out, often through stakeholder activity. Second, the nature of the environment in which a project takes place is the main determinant of the uncertainty surrounding it.

- Projects can be defined in terms of their objectives (the end state which project management is trying to achieve), scope (the exact range of the responsibilities taken on by project management), and strategy (how project management is going to meet the project objectives).

- Project planning involves five stages:
  - identifying the activities within a project;
  - estimating times and resources for the activities;
  - identifying the relationship and dependencies between the activities;
  - identifying the schedule constraints;
  - fixing the schedule.

❯ What is network planning?

- Network planning and Gantt charts are the most common project management techniques. The former (using either the activity on arrow or activity on node format) is particularly useful for assessing the total duration of a project and the degree of flexibility or float of the individual activities within the project. The most common method of network planning is called the critical path method (CPM).

- The logic inherent in a network diagram can be changed by resource constraints.

- Network planning models can also be used to assess the total cost of shortening a project where individual activities are shortened.

- The process of project control involves three sets of decisions: how to monitor the project in order to check its progress; how to assess the performance of the project by comparing monitored observations to the project plan; and how to intervene in the project in order to make the changes which will bring it back to plan.

● Enterprise project management systems can be used to integrate all the information needed to plan and control projects.

CASE STUDY | United Photonics Malaysia Sdn Bhd

Introduction

Anuar Kamaruddin, COO of United Photonics Malaysia (EPM), was conscious that the project in front of him was one of the most important he had handled for many years. The number and variety of the development projects under way within the company had risen sharply in the last few years, and although they had all seemed important at the time, this one – the 'Laz-skan' project – clearly justified the description given it by the President of United Photonics Corporation, the US parent of UPM: *'the make or break opportunity to ensure the division's long-term position in the global instrumentation industry'*.

The United Photonics Group

United Photonics Corporation had been founded in the 1920s (as the Detroit Gauge Company), a general instrument and gauge manufacturer for the engineering industry. By expanding its range into optical instruments in the early 1930s, it eventually moved also into the manufacture of high-precision and speciality lenses, mainly for the photographic industry. Its reputation as a specialist lens manufacturer led to such a growth in sales that by 1969 the optical side of the company accounted for about 60 per cent of total business and it ranked as one of the top two or three optics companies of its type in the world. Although its reputation for skilled lens-making had not diminished since then, the instrument side of the company had come to dominate sales once again in the 80s and 90s.

UPM product range

UPM's product range on the optical side included lenses for inspection systems which were used mainly in the manufacture of microchips. These lenses were sold both to the inspection system manufacturers and to the chip manufacturers themselves. They were very high-precision lenses; however, most of the company's optical products were specialist photographic and cinema lenses. In addition about 15 per cent of the company's optical work was concerned with the development and manufacture of 'one or two off' extremely high precision lenses for defence

contracts, specialist scientific instrumentation, and other optical companies. The Group's instrument product range consisted largely of electromechanical assembles with an increasing emphasis on software-based recording, display and diagnostic abilities. This move towards more software-based products had led the instrument side of the business towards accepting some customized orders. The growth of this part of the instrumentation had resulted in a special development unit being set up: the Customer Services Unit (CSU) who modified, customized, or adapted products for those customers who required an unusual application. Often CSU's work involved incorporating the company's products into larger systems for a customer.

In 1995 United Photonics Corporation had set up its first non-North American facility just outside Kuala Lumpur in Malaysia. United Photonics Malaysia Sdn Bhd (UPM) had started by manufacturing sub-assemblies for Photonics instrumentation products, but soon had developed into a laboratory for the modification of United Photonics products for customers throughout the Asian region. This part of the Malaysian business was headed by T.S. Lim, a Malaysian engineer who had taken his postgraduate qualifications at Stanford and three years ago moved back to his native KL to head up the Malaysian outpost of the CSU, reporting directly to Bob Brierly, the Vice-President of Development, who ran the main CSU in Detroit. Over the last three years, T.S. Lim and his small team of engineers had gained quite a reputation for innovative development. Bob Brierly was delighted with their enthusiasm. *'Those guys really do know how to make things happen. They are giving us all a run for our money.'*

The Laz-skan project

The idea for Laz-skan had come out of a project which T.S. Lim's CSU had been involved with in 2004. At that time the CSU had successfully installed a high-precision Photonics lens into a character recognition system for a large clearing bank. The enhanced capability which the lens and software modifications had given had enabled the bank to scan documents even when they were not correctly aligned. This had led to CSU proposing the development of a 'vision metrology' device that could optically scan a product at some point in the manufacturing process, and check the accuracy of up to 20 individual dimensions. The geometry of the product to be scanned, the dimensions to be gauged and the tolerances to be allowed could all be programmed into the control-logic of the device. T.S. Lim's team were convinced that the idea could have considerable potential. The proposal, which the CSU team had called the Laz-skan project, was put forward to Bob Brierly in August 2004. Brierly both saw the potential value of the idea and was again impressed by the CSU team's enthusiasm. *'To be frank, it was their evident enthusiasm that influenced me as much as anything. Remember that the Malaysian CSU had only been existence for two years at this time – they were a group of keen but relatively young engineers. Yet their proposal was well thought out and, on reflection, seemed to have considerable potential.'*

In November 2004 Lim and his team were allocated funds (outside the normal budget cycle) to investigate the feasibility of the Laz-skan idea. Lim was given one further engineer and a technician, and a three-month deadline to report to the board. In this time he was expected to overcome any fundamental technical problems, assess the feasibility of successfully developing the concept into a working prototype, and plan the development task that would lead to the prototype stage.

The Lim investigation

T.S. Lim, even at the start of his investigation, had some firm views as to the appropriate 'architecture' for the Laz-skan project. By 'architecture' he meant the major elements of the system, their functions, and how they related to each other. The Laz-skan system architecture would consider five major sub-systems: the lens and lens mounting, the vision support system, the display system, the control logic software, and the documentation.

T.S. Lim's first task, once the system's overall architecture was set, was to decide whether the various components in the major sub-systems would be developed in-house, developed by outside specialist companies from UPM's specifications, or bought in as standard units and if necessary modified in-house. Lim and his colleagues made these decisions themselves, while recognizing that a more consultative process might have been preferable. *'I am fully aware that ideally we should have made more use of the expertise within the company to decide how units were to be developed. But within the time available we just did not have the chance to explain the product concept, explain the choices, and wait for already busy people to come up with a recommendation. Also there was the security aspect to think of. I'm sure our employees are to be trusted but the more people who know about the project, the more chance there is for leaks. Anyway, we did not see our decisions as final. For example, if we decided that a component was to be bought in and modified for the prototype building stage it does not mean that we can't change our minds and develop a better component in-house at a later stage.'* By February 2005, TS's small team had satisfied themselves that the system could be built to achieve their original technical performance targets. Their final task before reporting to Brierly would be to devise a feasible development plan.

Planning the Laz-skan development

As a planning aid the team drew up a network diagram for all the major activities within the project from its start through to completion, when the project would be handed over to Manufacturing Operations. This is shown in Figure 16.27 and the complete list of all events in the diagram is shown in Table 16.4. The duration of all the activities in the project were estimated either by T.S. Lim or (more often) by him consulting a more experienced engineer back in Detroit. While he was reasonably confident in the estimates, he was keen to stress that they were just that – estimates.

Two drafting conventions on these networks need explanation. The three figures in brackets by each activity arrow represent the 'optimistic', 'most likely', and 'pessimistic' times (in weeks) respectively. The left-side figure in the event circles indicates the earliest time the event could take place and the figure in the right side of the circles indicates the latest time the event could take place without delaying the whole project. Dotted lines represent 'dummy' activities. These are nominal activities which have no time associated with them and are there either to maintain the logic of the network or for drafting convenience.

1 The lens (events 5-13-14-15)

The lens was particularly critical since the shape was complex and precision was vital if the system was to perform up to its intended design specification. T.S. Lim was relying heavily upon the skill of the Group's expert optics group in Pittsburg to produce the lens to the required high tolerance. Since

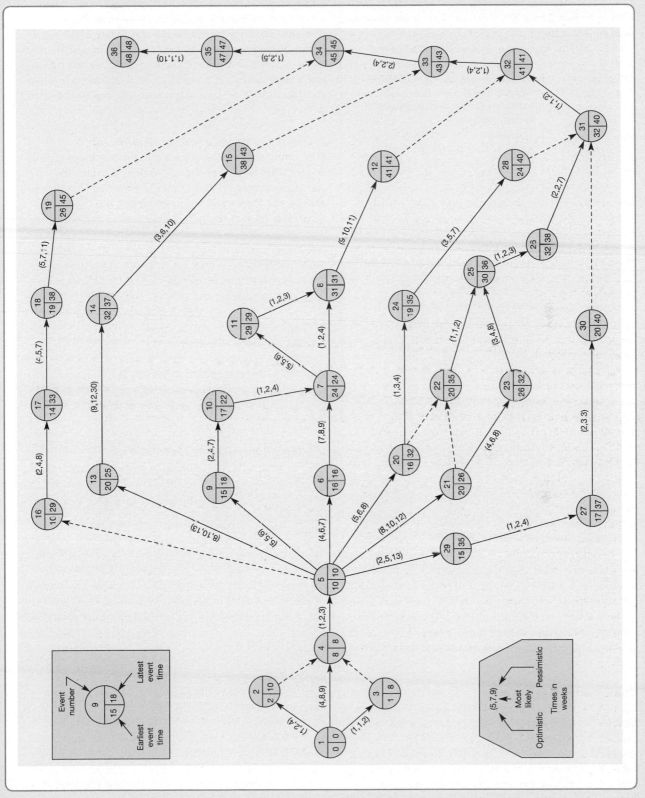

Figure 16.27 Some of the elements integrated in enterprise project management systems

Table 16.4 Event listing for the Laz-skan project

Event number	Event description
1	Start systems engineering
2	Complete interface transient tests
3	Complete compatibility testing
4	Complete overall architecture block and simulation
5	Complete costing and purchasing tender planning
6	End alignment system design
7	Receive S/T/G, start synch mods
8	Receive Triscan/G, start synch mods
9	Complete B/A mods
10	Complete S/T/G mods
11	Complete Triscan/G mods
12	Start laser sub-system compatibility tests
13	Complete optic design and specification, start lens manufacture
14	Complete lens manufacture, start lens housing S/A
15	Lens S/A complete, start tests
16	Start technical specifications
17	Start help routine design
18	Update engineering mods
19	Complete doc sequence
20	Start vision routines
21	Start interface (trinsic) tests
22	Start system integration compatibility routines
23	Coordinate trinsic tests
24	End interface development
25	Complete alignment integration routine
26	Final alignment integration data consolidation
27	Start interface (tmnsic) programming
28	Complete alignment system routines
29	Start tmnsic comparator routines
30	Complete (interface) trinsic coding
31	Begin all logic system tests
32	Start cycle tests
33	Lens S/A complete
34	Start assembly of total system
35	Complete total system assembly
36	Complete final tests and dispatch

what in effect was a trial-and-error approach was involved in their manufacture, the exact time to manufacture would be uncertain. T.S. Lim realized this. *'The lens is going to be a real problem. We just don't know how easy it will be to make the particular geometry and precision we need. The optics people won't commit themselves even though they are regarded as some of the best optics technicians in the world. It is a relief that lens development is not amongst the "critical path" activities.'*

2 Vision support system (events 6-7-8-12, 9-5, 11)

The vision support system included many components which were commercially available, but considerable engineering effort would be required to modify them. Although the development design and resting of the vision support system was complicated, there was no great uncertainty in the individual activities, or therefore the schedule of completion. If more funds were allocated to their development, some tasks might even be completed ahead of time.

3 The control software (events 20 to 26, 28)

The control software represented the most complex task, and the most difficult to plan and estimate. In fact, the software development unit had little experience of this type of work but (partly in anticipation of this type of development) had recently recruited a young software engineer with some experience of the type of work which would be needed for Laz-skan. He was confident that any technical problems could be solved even though the system needs were novel, but completion times would be difficult to predict with confidence.

4 Documentation (events 5-16-17-18-19)

A relatively simple sub-system, 'documentation' included specifying and writing the technical manuals, maintenance routines, online diagnostics, and 'help desk' information. It was a relatively predictable activity, part of which was subcontracted to technical writers and translation companies in Kuala Lumpur.

5 Display system (events 29-27-30)

The simplest of the sub-systems to plan, the display system, would need to be manufactured entirely out of the company and tested and calibrated on receipt.

Market prospects

In parallel with T.S. Lim's technical investigation, Sales and Marketing had been asked to estimate the market potential of Laz-skan. In a very short time, the Laz-skan project had aroused considerable enthusiasm within the function, to the extent that Halim Ramli, the Asian Marketing Vice President, had taken personal charge of the market study. The major conclusions from this investigation were:

(a) The global market for Laz-skan type systems was unlikely to be less than 50 systems per year in 2008, climbing to more than 200 per year by 2012.

(b) The volume of the market in financial terms was more difficult to predict, but each system sold was likely to represent around US$300,000 of turnover.

(c) Some customization of the system would be needed for most customers. This would mean greater emphasis on commissioning and post-installation service than was necessary for UPM's existing products.

(d) Timing the launch of Laz-skan would be important. Two 'windows of opportunity' were critical. The first and most important was the major world trade show in Geneva in April 2006. This show, held every two years, was the most prominent show-case for new products such as Laz-skan. The second related to the development cycles of the original equipment manufacturers who would be the major customers for Laz-skan. Critical decisions would be taken in the fall of 2006. If Laz-skan was to be incorporated into these companies' products it would have to be available from October 2006.

The Laz-skan go ahead

At the end of February 2005 UPM considered both the Lim and the Ramli reports. In addition estimates of Laz-skan's manufacturing costs had been sought from George Hudson, the head of Instrument Development. His estimates indicated that Laz-skan's operating contribution would be far higher than the company's existing products. The board approved the immediate commencement of the Laz-skan development through to prototype stage, with an initial development budget of US$4.5m. The objective of the project was to 'build three prototype Laz-skan systems to be "up and running" for April 2006'.

The decision to go ahead was unanimous. Exactly how the project was to be managed provoked far more discussion. The Laz-skan project posed several problems. First, engineers had little experience of working on such a major project. Second, the crucial deadline for the first batch of prototypes meant that some activities might have to be been accelerated, an expensive process that would need careful judgement. A very brief investigation into which activities could be accelerated had identified those where acceleration definitely would be possible and the likely cost of acceleration (*see* Table 16.5). Finally, no one could agree either whether there should be a single project leader, which function he or she should come from, or how senior the project leader should be. Anuar Kamaruddin knew that these decisions could affect the success of the project, and possibly the company, for years to come.

Table 16.5 Acceleration opportunities for Laz-skan

Activity	Acceleration cost (US$/week)	Likely maximum activity time, with acceleration (weeks)	Normal most likely time (weeks)
5–6	23,400	3	6
5–9	10,500	2	5
5–13	25,000	8	10
20–24	5,000	2	3
24–28	11,700	3	5
33–34	19,500	1	2

QUESTIONS

1 Who do you think should manage the Laz-skan Development Project?

2 What are the major dangers and difficulties that will be faced by the development team as they manage the projects towards its completion?

3 What can they do about these dangers and difficulties?

PROBLEMS AND APPLICATIONS

These problems and applications will help to improve your analysis of operations. You can find more practice problems as well as worked examples and guided solutions on MyOMLab at www.myomlab.com.

MyOMLab

1 The activities, their durations and precedences for designing, writing and installing a bespoke computer database are shown in Table 16.6. Draw a Gantt chart and a network diagram for the project and calculate the fastest time in which the operation might be completed.

2 A business is launching a new product. The launch will require a number of related activities as follows – hire a sales manager (5 weeks), require the sales manager to recruit sales people (4 weeks), train the sales people (7 weeks), select an advertising agency (2 weeks), plan an advertising campaign with the agency (4 weeks), conduct the advertising campaign (10 weeks), design the packaging of the product (4 weeks), set up packing operation (12 weeks), pack enough products for the launch stock (8 weeks), order the launch quantity of products from the manufacturer (13 weeks), select distributors for the product (9 weeks), take initial orders from the distributors (3 weeks), despatch the initial orders to the distributors (2 weeks).
(a) What is the earliest time that the new product can be introduced to the market?

Table 16.6 Bespoke computer database activities

Activity	Duration (weeks)	Activities that must be completed before it can start
1 Contract negotiation	1	–
2 Discussions with main users	2	1
3 Review of current documentation	5	1
4 Review of current systems	6	2
5 Systems analysis (a)	4	3, 4
6 Systems analysis (b)	7	5
7 Programming	12	5
8 Testing (prelim)	2	7
9 Existing system review report	1	3, 4
10 System proposal report	2	5, 9
11 Documentation preparation	19	5, 8
12 Implementation	7	7, 11
13 System test	3	12
14 Debugging	4	12
15 Manual preparation	5	11

(b) If the company hire trained salesmen who do not need further training, could the product be introduced 7 weeks earlier?

(c) How long could one delay selecting the advertising agency?

3 In the example above, if the sales manager cannot be hired for 3 weeks, how will that affect the total project?

4 In the previous example, if the whole project launch operation is to be completed as rapidly as possible, what activities must have been completed by the end of week 16?

5 Identify a project of which you have been part (for example, moving apartments, a holiday, dramatic production, revision for an examination, etc.).

(a) Who were the stakeholders in this project?

(b) What was the overall project objective (especially in terms of the relative importance of cost, quality and time)?

(c) Were there any resource constraints?

(d) Looking back, how could you have managed the project better?

6 Identify your favourite sporting team (Manchester United, the Toulon rugby team, or if you are not a sporting person, choose any team you have heard of). What kind of projects do you think they need to manage? For example, merchandising, sponsorship, etc. What do you think are the key issues in making a success of managing each of these different types of project?

SELECTED FURTHER READING

There are hundreds of books on project management. They range from the introductory to the very detailed and from the managerial to the highly mathematical. Here are two general (as opposed to mathematical) books which are worth looking at.

Maylor, H. (2003) *Project Management*, 3rd edn, Financial Times Prentice Hall, Harlow.

Newton, R. (2005) *Project Manager: Mastering the Art of Delivery in Project Management*, FT Prentice Hall, Harlow.

USEFUL WEBSITES

http://apm.org.uk The UK Association for Project Management. Contains a description of what professionals consider to be the body of knowledge of project management.

http://pmi.org The Project Management Institute's home page. An American association for professionals. Insights into professional practice.

http://ipma.ch The International Project Management Association, based in Zurich. Some definitions and links.

www.comp.glam.ac.uk/staff/dwfarth/projman.htm A great site with lots of interesting stuff on software, project management and related issues, but also very good for general project management.

www.myomlab Test which sections you have mastered and which you need to review, with questions, a personalized study plan, video clips, revision tips, and cases.

www.opsman.org Useful materials.

http://operationsroom.wordpress.com/ Stanford University's take on topical operations stories.

www.iomnet.org The Institute of Operations Management site. One of the main professional bodies for the subject.

www.poms.org A US academic society for production and operations management. Academic, but some useful material, including a link to an encyclopedia of operations management terms.

Now that you have finished reading this chapter, why not visit MyOMLab at www.myomlab.com where you'll find more learning resources to help you make the most of your studies and get a better grade.

17

Quality management

Key questions

> What is quality and why is it so important?

> How can quality problems be diagnosed?

> What steps lead towards conformance to specification?

> What is total quality management (TQM)?

INTRODUCTION

Quality is the only one of the five 'operations performance criteria' to have its own dedicated chapter in this book. There are two reasons for this. First, in some organizations a separate function is devoted exclusively to the management of quality. Second, quality is a key concern of almost all organizations. High-quality services or products can give an organization a considerable competitive edge. Good quality reduces the costs of rectification, waste, complaints and returns and, most importantly, generates satisfied customers. Some operations managers believe that, in the long run, quality is the most important single factor affecting an organization's performance relative to its competitors.

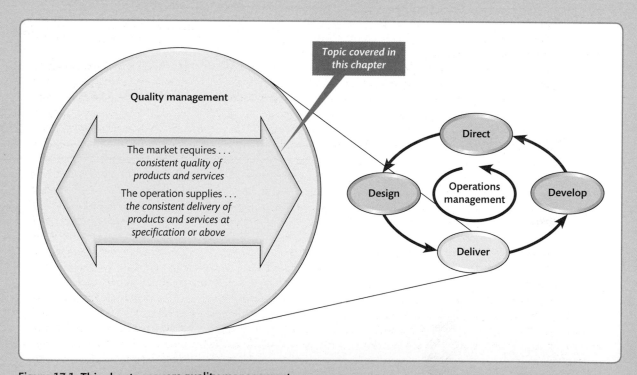

Figure 17.1 This chapter covers quality management

MyOMLab *Check and improve your understanding of this chapter using self-assessment questions and a personalized study plan, a video case study, and an eText – all at www.myomlab.com.*

Quality at the Four Seasons Canary Wharf[1]

The first Four Seasons Hotel opened over 45 years ago. Since then the company has grown to 81 properties in 34 countries. Famed for its quality of service, the hotel group has won countless awards including the prestigious Zagat survey, numerous AAA Five Diamond Awards and it is also one of only 14 organizations that have been on the *Fortune* magazine's list of '100 Best Companies to Work For' every year since it launched in 1998, thus ranking as 'top hotel chain' internationally. From its inception the group has had the same guiding principle, 'to make the quality of our service our competitive advantage'. The company has what it calls its Golden Rule: 'Do to others (guests and staff) as you would wish others to do to you'. It is a simple rule, but it guides the whole organization's approach to quality.

'*Quality service is our distinguishing edge and the company continues to evolve in that direction. We are always looking for better, more creative and innovative ways of serving our guests*', says Michael Purtill, the General Manager of the Four Seasons Hotel Canary Wharf in London. '*We have recently refined all of our operating standards across the company, enabling us to further enhance the personalized, intuitive service that all our guests receive. All employees are empowered to use their creativity and judgement in delivering exceptional service and making their own decisions to enhance our guests' stay. For example, one morning an employee noticed that a guest had a flat tyre on their car and decided on his own accord to change it for them, which was very much appreciated by the guest.*

'*The golden rule means that we treat our employees with dignity, respect and appreciation. This approach encourages them to be equally sensitive to our guests' needs and offer sincere and genuine service that exceeds expectations. Just recently one of our employees accompanied a guest to the hospital and stayed there with him for the entire afternoon. He wanted to ensure that the guest wasn't alone and was given the medical attention he needed. The following day that same employee took the initiative to return to the hospital (even though it was his day off) to visit and made sure that the guest's family in America was kept informed about his progress. We ensure that we have an ongoing focus on recognizing these successes and publicly praise and celebrate all individuals who deliver these warm, spontaneous, thoughtful touches.*

'*At Four Seasons we believe that our greatest asset and strength are our people. We pay a great deal of attention to selecting the right people with an attitude that takes great pride in delivering exceptional service. We know that motivated and happy employees are essential to our service*

Source: AL RF (Imagestate/John Foxx)

culture and are committed to developing our employees to their highest potential. Our extensive training programmes and career development plans are designed with care and attention to support the individual needs of our employees as well as operational and business demands. In conjunction with traditional classroom-based learning, we offer tailor-made internet-based learning featuring exceptional quality courses for all levels of employee. Such importance is given to learning and development that the hotel has created two specialized rooms, designated to learning and development. One is intended for group learning and the other is equipped with private computer stations for internet-based individual learning. There is also a library equipped with a broad variety of hospitality-related books, CDs and DVDs that can be taken home at any time. This encourages our employees to learn and develop at an individual pace. This is very motivating for our employees and in the same instance their development is invaluable to the growth of our company. Career-wise, the sky is the limit and our goal is to build lifelong, international careers with Four Seasons.

'*Our objective is to exceed guest expectations and feedback from our guests and our employees is an invaluable barometer of our performance. We have created an in-house database that is used to record all guest feedback (whether positive or negative). We also use an online guest survey and guest comment cards which are all personally*

WHAT IS QUALITY AND WHY IS IT SO IMPORTANT?

It is worth revisiting some of the arguments which were presented earlier (Chapter 2) regarding the benefits of high quality. This will explain why quality is seen as being so important by most operations. Figure 17.2 illustrates the various ways in which quality improvements can affect other aspects of operations performance. Revenues can be increased by better sales and enhanced prices in the market. At the same time, costs can be brought down by improved efficiencies, productivity and the use of capital. So, a key task of the operations function must be to ensure that it provides quality goods and services, both to its internal and external customers.

The operation's view of quality

There are many definitions of quality: here we define it as *'consistent conformance to customers' expectations'*. The use of the word 'conformance' implies that there is a need to meet a clear specification. Ensuring a service or product conforms to specification is a key operations task. 'Consistent' implies that conformance to specification is not an *ad hoc* event but that the service or product meets the specification because quality requirements are used to design and run the processes that produce services or products. The use of 'customers' expectations' recognizes that the service or product must take the views of customers into account, which

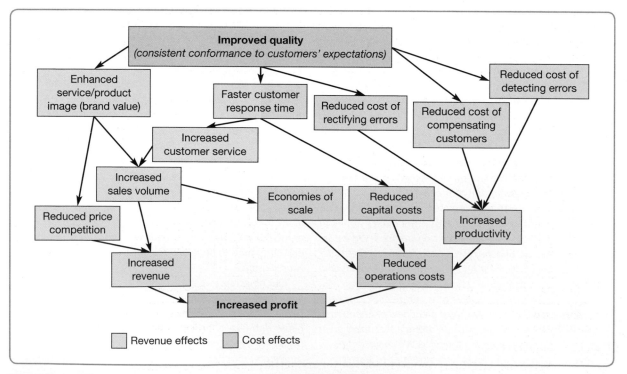

Figure 17.2 Higher quality has a beneficial effect on both revenues and costs

may be influenced by price. Also note the use of the word 'expectations' in this definition, rather than needs or wants.

Customers' view of quality

Past experiences, individual knowledge and history will all shape customers' expectations. Furthermore, customers may each *perceive* a service or product in different ways. One person may perceive a long-haul flight as an exciting part of a holiday; the person on the next seat may see it as a necessary chore to get to a business meeting. So quality needs to be understood from a customer's point of view because, to the customer, the quality of a particular service or product is whatever he or she perceives it to be. If the passengers on a skiing charter flight perceive it to be of good quality, despite long queues at check-in or cramped seating and poor meals, then the flight really is of good perceived quality.[2] Also customers may be unable to judge the 'technical' specification of the service or product and so use surrogate measures as a basis for their perception of quality. For example, a customer may find it difficult to judge the technical quality of dental treatment, except insofar as it does not give any more trouble. The customer may therefore perceive quality in terms the demeanour of the dentist and technician and how they were treated.

> **✴ Operations principle**
>
> Quality is multi-faceted; its individual elements differ for different operations.

Reconciling the operation's and the customer's views of quality

The operation's view of quality is concerned with trying to meet customer expectations. The customer's view of quality is what he or she *perceives* the service or product to be. To create a unified view, quality can be defined as the degree of fit between customers' expectations and customer perception of the service or product.[3] Using this idea allows us to see the customers' view of quality of (and, therefore, satisfaction with) the service or product as the result of the customers comparing their expectations of the service or product with their perception of how it performs. This is not always straightforward; see the short case 'Tea and Sympathy'. Also, if the service or product experience was better than expected then the customer is satisfied and quality is perceived to be high. If the service or product was less than his or her expectations then quality is low and the customer may be dissatisfied. If the service or product matches expectations then the perceived quality of the service or product is seen to be acceptable. These relationships are summarized in Figure 17.3.

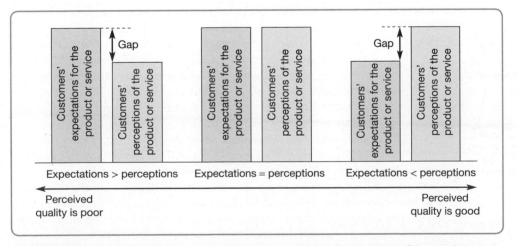

Figure 17.3 Perceived quality is governed by the magnitude and direction of the gap between customers' expectations and their perceptions of the service or product

Defining quality in terms of perception and expectation can sometimes reveal some surprising results. For example, Tea and Sympathy is a British restaurant and café in the heart of New York's West Village. Over the last 10 years it has become a fashionable landmark in a city with one of the broadest range of restaurants in the world. Yet it is tiny, with around a dozen tables packed into an area little bigger than the average British sitting room. Not only expatriate Brits but also native New Yorkers and celebrities queue to get in. As the only British restaurant in New York, it has a novelty factor, but also it has become famous for the unusual nature of its service. *'Everyone is treated in the same way'*, says Nicky Perry, one of the two ex-Londoners who run it. *'We have a firm policy that we don't take any shit.'* This robust attitude to the treatment of customers is reinforced by 'Nicky's Rules' which are printed on the menu.

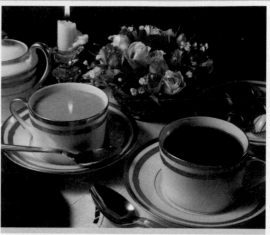

Source: AL RF (PhotoDisc/Mitch Hrdlicka)

1 Be pleasant to the waitresses – remember Tea and Sympathy girls are always right.

2 You will have to wait outside the restaurant until your entire party is present: no exceptions.

3 Occasionally, you may be asked to change tables so that we can accommodate all of you.

4 If we don't need the table you may stay all day, but if people are waiting it's time to naff off.

5 These rules are strictly enforced. Any argument will incur Nicky's wrath. You have been warned.

Most of the waitresses are also British and enforce Nicky's Rules strictly. If customers object they are thrown out. Nicky says that she has had to train 'her girls' to toughen up. *'I've taught them that when people cross the line they can tear their throats out as far as I'm concerned. What we've discovered over the years is that if you are really sweet, people see it as a weakness. People get thrown out of the restaurant about twice a week and yet customers still queue for the genuine shepherd's pie, a real cup of tea, and of course the service.'*

Both customers' expectations and perceptions are influenced by a number of factors, some of which cannot be controlled by the operation and some of which, to a certain extent, can be managed. Figure 17.4 shows some of the factors that will influence the gap between expectations and perceptions. This model of customer-perceived quality can help us understand how operations can manage quality and identifies some of the problems in so doing. The bottom part of the diagram represents the operation's 'domain' of quality and the top part the customer's 'domain'. These two domains meet in the actual service or product, which is provided by the organization and experienced by the customer. Within the operation's domain, management is responsible for designing the service or product and providing a specification of the quality to which the service or product has to be created. Within the customer's domain, his or her expectations are shaped by such factors as previous experiences with the particular service or product, the marketing image provided by the organization and word-of-mouth information from other users. These expectations are internalized as a set of quality characteristics.

> ✳ **Operations principle**
>
> Perceived quality is governed by the magnitude and direction of the gap between customers' expectations and their perceptions of a product or service.

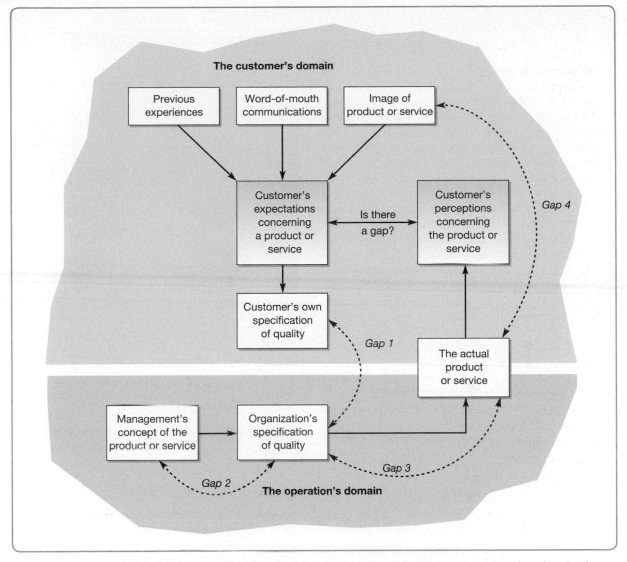

The customer's domain

Figure 17.4 The customer's domain and the operations domain in determining the perceived quality, showing how the gap between customers' expectations and their perception of a service or product could be explained by one or more gaps elsewhere in the model

Source: Adapted from Parasuraman, A. *et al.* (1985) A Conceptual Model of Service Quality and Implications for Future Research, *Journal of Marketing*, vol. 49, Fall.

Magic Moments is a small but successful wedding photography business. Its owner, Richard Webber, has seen plenty of changes over the last 20 years. *'In the past, my job involved taking a few photos during the wedding ceremony and then formal group shots outside. I was rarely at a wedding for more than two hours. Clients would select around 30 photos to go in a standard wedding album. It was important to get the photos right, because that was really the only thing I was judged on. Now it's different.*

I usually spend all day at a wedding, and sometimes late into the evening as well. This creates a very different dynamic with the wedding party, as you're almost like another guest. Whilst the bride and groom are still my primary concern, other guests at the wedding are also important. The challenge is to find the right balance between getting the best photos possible whilst being as discreet as possible. I could spend hours getting the perfect picture, but annoy everyone in the process. It's difficult, because clients judge you on both the technical quality of your work and the way you interact with everyone on the day. The product has changed too. Clients receive a CD or memory stick with around 500 photos taken during the day. Also I can give them a choice of 10 albums in different sizes, ranging from 30–100 photos. This year, I have started offering photo books which allow a much greater level of customization and have proved popular for younger couples. For the future, I'm considering offering albums with wedding items such as invitations, confetti, and menus, and individual paintings created from photographs. Obviously I would have to outsource the paintings. I'm also going to upgrade our website, so wedding guests can order photos and related products online. This will generate revenue and act as a good marketing tool. My anxiety is that advertising this additional service at the wedding will be seen as being too commercial, even if it's actually of benefit to guests.

'One of the biggest problems for the business is the high level of demand in the summer months. Weekends in June, July and August are often booked up two years in advance. One option is to take on additional photographers during busy periods. However, the best ones are busy themselves. The concern is that the quality of the service I offer would deteriorate. A large part of the business is about how one relates to clients and that's hard to replicate. Having been to so many weddings, I often offer clients advice on various

Source: Alistair Brandon-Jones

aspects of their wedding, such as locations, bands, caterers, and florists. However, with development, wedding planning is clearly an area that could be profitable to the business. Of course, another option is to move beyond weddings into other areas, such as school photos, birthdays, celebrations, or studio work.'

HOW CAN QUALITY PROBLEMS BE DIAGNOSED?[5]

Figure 17.4 also shows how quality problems can be diagnosed. If the perceived quality gap is such that customers' perceptions of the service or product fail to match their expectations of it, then the reason (or reasons) must lie in other gaps elsewhere in the model as follows.

Gap 1: The customer's specification–operation's specification gap. Perceived quality could be poor because there may be a mismatch between the organization's own internal quality specification and the specification which is expected by the customer. For example, a car may be designed to need servicing every 10,000 kilometres but the customer may expect 15,000 kilometre service intervals.

Gap 2: The concept–specification gap. Perceived quality could be poor because there is a mismatch between the service or product concept (see Chapter 5) and the way the organization has specified quality internally. For example, the concept of a car might have been for an inexpensive, energy-efficient means of transportation, but the inclusion of a climate control system may have both added to its cost and made it less energy-efficient.

Gap 3: The quality specification–actual quality gap. Perceived quality could be poor because there is a mismatch between actual quality and the internal quality specification (often called 'conformance to specification'). For example, the internal quality specification for a car may be that the gap between its doors and body, when closed, must not exceed 7 mm. However, because of inadequate equipment, the gap in reality is 9 mm.

Gap 4: The actual quality–communicated image gap. Perceived quality could be poor because there is a gap between the organization's external communications or market image and the actual quality delivered to the customer. This may be because the marketing function has set unachievable expectations or operations is not capable of the level of quality expected by the customer. For example, an advertising campaign for an airline might show a cabin attendant offering to replace a customer's shirt on which food or drink has been spilt, whereas such a service may not in fact be available should this happen.

CONFORMANCE TO SPECIFICATION

Conformance to specification means providing a service or producing a product to its design specification. It is usually seen as the most important contribution that operations management can make to the customer's perception of quality. We shall examine how it can be achieved in the remainder of this chapter by describing quality management as six sequential steps. (This chapter, and Chapters 18, 19 and 20 will deal with these steps.)

ACHIEVING CONFORMANCE TO SPECIFICATION

Achieving conformance to specification requires the following steps:

Step 1 Define the quality characteristics of the service or product.

Step 2 Decide how to measure each quality characteristic.

Step 3 Set quality standards for each quality characteristic.

Step 4 Control quality against those standards.

Step 5 Find and correct causes of poor quality.

Step 6 Continue to make improvements.

Step 1 – Define the quality characteristics

Much of the 'quality' of a service or product will have been specified in its design and can be summarized by a set of quality characteristics. Table 17.1 shows a list of the quality characteristics which are generally useful. Also many services have several elements, each with their own quality characteristics, and to understand the quality characteristics of the whole service it is necessary to understand the individual characteristics within and between each element of the whole service. For example, Figure 17.5 shows some of the quality characteristics for a web-based online grocery shopping service.

Step 2 – Decide how to measure each characteristic

These characteristics must be defined in such a way as to enable them to be measured and then controlled. This involves taking a very general quality characteristic such as 'appearance' and breaking it down, as far as one can, into its constituent elements. 'Appearance' is difficult to measure as such, but 'colour match', 'surface finish' and 'number of visible scratches' are all capable of being described in a more objective manner. They may even be quantifiable. Other quality characteristics pose more difficulty. The 'courtesy' of airline staff, for example, has no objective quantified measure. Yet operations with high customer contact, such as airlines, place a great deal of importance on the need to ensure courtesy in their staff. In cases like this, the operation will have to attempt to measure customer *perceptions* of courtesy.

Variables and attributes

The measures used by operations to describe quality characteristics are of two types: variables and attributes. Variable measures are those that can be measured on a continuously variable scale (for example, length, diameter, weight or time). Attributes are those which are assessed by judgement and are dichotomous, i.e. have two states (for example, right or wrong, works or does not work, looks OK or not OK). Table 17.2 (p. 544) categorizes some of the measures which might be used for the quality characteristics of the automobile and the airline journey.

Table 17.1 Quality characteristics for an automobile, bank loan, and an air journey

Quality characteristic	Car (material transformation process)	Bank loan (information transformation process)	Air journey (customer transformation process)
Functionality – how well the service or product does its job	Speed, acceleration, fuel consumption, ride quality, road-holding, etc.	Interest rate, terms and conditions	Safety and duration of journey, onboard meals and drinks, car and hotel booking services
Appearance – the sensory characteristics of the service or product: its aesthetic appeal, look, feel, etc.	Aesthetics, shape, finish, door gaps, etc	Aesthetics of information, website, etc.	Decor and cleanliness of aircraft, lounges and crew
Reliability – the consistency of the product's or service's performance over time	Mean time to failure	Keeping promises (implicit and explicit)	Keeping to the published flight times
Durability – the total useful life of the service or product	Useful life (with repair)	Stability of terms and conditions	Keeping up with trends in the industry
Recovery – the ease with which problems with the service or product can be resolved	Ease of repair	Resolution of service failures	Resolution of service failures
Contact – the nature of the person-to-person contact which might take place	Knowledge and courtesy of sales staff	Knowledge and courtesy of branch and call centre staff	Knowledge, courtesy and sensitivity of airline staff

Step 3 – Set quality standards

When operations managers have identified how any quality characteristic can be measured, they need a quality standard against which it can be checked; otherwise they will not know whether it indicates good or bad performance. The quality standard is that level of quality which defines the boundary between acceptable and unacceptable. Such standards may well be constrained by operational factors such as the state of technology in the factory, and the cost limits of making the product. At the same time, however, they need to be appropriate to the expectations of customers. But quality judgements can be difficult. If one airline passenger out of every 10,000 complains about the food, is that good because 9,999 passengers out of 10,000 are satisfied? Or is it bad because, if one passenger complains, there must be others who, although dissatisfied, did not bother to complain? And if that level of complaint is similar to other airlines, should it regard its quality as satisfactory?

Step 4 – Control quality against those standards

After setting up appropriate standards the operation will then need to check that the products or services conform to those standards; doing things right, first time, every time. This involves three decisions:

1 Where in the operation should they check that it is conforming to standards?
2 Should they check every service or product or take a sample?
3 How should the checks be performed?

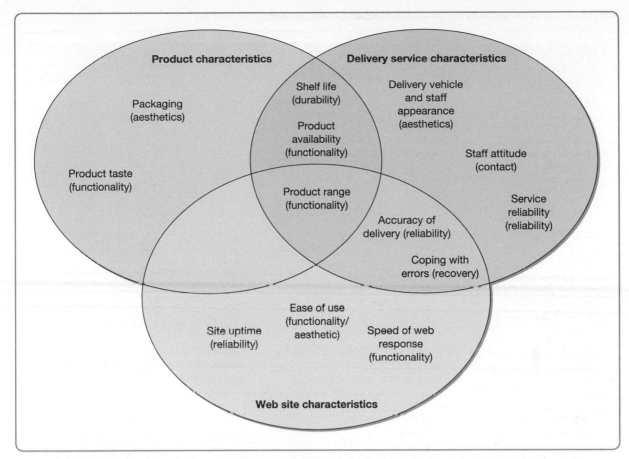

Figure 17.5 Quality characteristics for an online grocery shopping service, including its website through which orders are placed, the products that are sold through the site, and the delivery service that transports purchases to the customer

Where should the checks take place?

At the start of the process incoming resources may be inspected to make sure that they are to the correct specification. For example, a car manufacturer will check that components are of the right specification. A university will screen applicants to try to ensure that they have a high chance of getting through the programme. During the process checks may take place before a particularly costly process, prior to a 'difficult to check' process, immediately after a process with a high defective rate, before potential damage or distress might be caused, and so on. Checks may also take place after the process itself to ensure that customers do not experience non-conformance.

Check every product and service or take a sample?

While it might seem ideal to check every single service or product, a sample may be more practical for a number of reasons:

- It might be dangerous to inspect everything. A doctor, for example, checks just a small sample of blood – rather than taking all of a patient's blood! The characteristics of this sample are taken to represent those of the rest of the patient's blood.
- Checking everything might destroy the product or interfere with the service. Not every light bulb is checked for how long it lasts, as it would destroy every bulb. Waiters do not check that customers are enjoying the meal every 30 seconds.
- Checking everything can be time-consuming and costly. It may not be feasible to check all output from a high-volume machine or to check the feelings of every bus commuter every day.

Table 17.2 Variable and attribute measures for quality characteristics

Quality Characteristic	Car		Airline journey	
	Variable	*Attribute*	*Variable*	*Attribute*
Functionality	Acceleration and braking characteristics from test bed	Is the ride quality satisfactory?	Number of journeys which actually arrived at the destination (i.e. didn't crash!)	Was the food acceptable?
Appearance	Number of blemishes visible on car	Is the colour to specification?	Number of seats not cleaned satisfactorily	Is the crew dressed smartly?
Reliability	Average time between faults	Is the reliability satisfactory?	Proportion of journeys which arrived on time	Were there any complaints?
Durability	Life of the car	Is the useful life as predicted?	Number of times service innovations lagged competitors	Generally, is the airline updating its services in a satisfactory manner?
Recovery	Time from fault discovered to fault repaired	Is the serviceability of the car acceptable?	Proportion of service failures resolved satisfactorily	Do customers feel that staff deal satisfactorily with complaints?
Contact	Level of help provided by sales staff (1 to 5 scale)	Did customers feel well served (yes or no)?	The extent to which customers feel well treated by staff (1 to 5 scale)	Did customers feel that the staff were helpful (yes or no)?

SHORT CASE

The Swiss Army Knife: 'Our best means of protection is quality'[6]

It is known all over the world for its usefulness, and its quality. The famous Swiss Army Knife, which traces its history back to 1891, is made by the Victorinox Company in its factory in the small Swiss town of Ibach, Kanton Schwyz. The company has numerous letters from its customers testifying to their product's quality and durability. The following story from one engineer is typical. *'I was installing a new piece of equipment in a sewage treatment plant. One morning, as I was crossing the bridge over the aeration tank of the treatment plant, I saw that the setting on one of the instruments was incorrect. I took out my Swiss Army Knife to make the necessary adjustment. The knife slipped out of my hand and fell into the aeration tank whose function is to oxidize organic waste – the oxidizing environment is extremely corrosive to metals. Four years later, I received a small parcel with a note from the supervisor of the plant. They had emptied the aeration tank and* *found my knife at the bottom. The parcel contained the knife which was in astonishingly good condition. The plastic casing and cover had only suffered very minor damage. I can assure you that very few products could have survived treatment like this; the components would have dissolved or simply disappeared.'*

Today, the Victorinox factory assembles 27,000 knives a day (plus nearly 100,000 other items). More than 450 steps are required in its manufacture. But times have not been easy for the Victorinox Company. Airport security restrictions after 9/11 hit sales of the knife. *'Our sales plummeted almost overnight'*, says Carl Elsener, the Company's CEO and the great-grandson of its founder. *'All airport shops were suddenly banned from selling knives and we lost 30 per cent of our income that came from spontaneous airport purchases.'* But rather than shut down some of its production lines and get rid of

Source: Shutterstock.com/Hana

Flash foldable USB drives. Another major threat to sales that has been growing is the appearance on the market of fake 'Swiss Army' knives, made mostly in China. Many of them look similar to the original; they even have the familiar Swiss cross on the handle.

So what is their defence against these fakes? 'Quality', says Carl Elsener. 'We have exhausted all legal means for the brand protection of our popular products. Our best means of protection is quality which remains unsurpassed and speaks louder than words.'

And the three components of the 'Victorinox quality control system' is at the heart of this quality defence. First, incoming materials are checked to conform to quality specifications. Non-conforming products are identified, evaluated and reviewed according to set procedures. Only steel and plastic which comply with Victorinox rigorous quality standards are used in the manufacturing of the products. Second, process control is employed at all stages of the production process. Third, the Final Inspection Department employs 50–60 people who are responsible for ensuring that all products conform to requirements. Any non-conforming products are isolated and identified. Non-conforming parts are repaired or replaced at the repair department.

a considerable chunk of its workforce to cut costs (the factory hasn't fired a single person for economic reasons in all of the 125 years of its existence), Victorinox developed new products, including laser-fronted ballpoint pens, bladeless 'in-flight' knives, Swiss Memory and Swiss

Also, 100 per cent checking may not guarantee that all defects will be identified. Sometimes it is intrinsically difficult. For example, although a physician may undertake the correct testing procedure, he or she may not necessarily diagnose a (real) disease. Nor is it easy to notice everything. For example, try counting the number of 'e's on this page. Count them again and see if you get the same score.

Type I and type II errors

Although it reduces checking time, using a sample to make a decision about quality does have its own inherent problems. Like any decision activity, we may get the decision wrong. Take the example of a pedestrian waiting to cross a street. He or she has two main decisions: whether to continue waiting or to cross. If there is a satisfactory break in the traffic and the pedestrian crosses then a correct decision has been made. Similarly, if that person continues to wait because the traffic is too dense then he or she has again made a correct decision. There are two types of incorrect decisions or errors, however. One incorrect decision would be if he or she decides to cross when there is not an adequate break in the traffic, resulting in an accident – this is referred to as a type I error. Another incorrect decision would occur if he or she decides not to cross even though there was an adequate gap in the traffic – this is called a type II error. In crossing the road, therefore, there are four outcomes, which are summarized in Table 17.3.

Table 17.3 Type I and type II errors for a pedestrian crossing the road

| Decision | Road conditions | |
	Unsafe	Safe
Cross	Type I error	Correct decision
Wait	Correct decision	Type II error

Type I errors are those which occur when a decision was made to do something and the situation did not warrant it. Type II errors are those which occur when nothing was done, yet a decision to do something should have been taken as the situation did indeed warrant it. For example, if a school's inspector checks the work of a sample of 20 out of 1,000 pupils and all 20 of the pupils in the sample have failed, the inspector might draw the conclusion that all the pupils have failed. In fact, the sample just happened to contain 20 out of the 50 students who had failed the course. The inspector, by assuming a high fail rate, would be making a type I error. Alternatively, if the inspector checked 20 pieces of work all of which were of a high standard, he or she might conclude that all the pupils' work was good despite having been given, or having chosen, the only pieces of good work in the whole school. This would be a type II error. Although these situations are not likely, they are possible. Therefore any sampling procedure has to be aware of these risks (see the short case on 'Surgical statistics').

How should the checks be performed?

In practice most operations will use some form of sampling to check the quality of their services or products. The most common approach for checking the quality of a sample service or product so as to make inferences about all the output from an operation is called statistical process control (SPC). SPC is concerned with sampling the process during the production of the goods or the delivery of service. Based on this sample, decisions are made as to whether the process is 'in control', that is, operating as it should be. A key aspect of SPC is that it looks at the variability in the performance of processes to check whether the process is operating as it should do (known as the process being 'in control'). In fact variability (or more specifically, reducing variability) is one of the most important objectives of quality improvement. For an illustration of this see the short case 'What a giveaway'. SPC is explained in detail in the supplement to this chapter.

SHORT CASE | **Surgical statistics[7]**

Understanding the nature of type I and type II errors is an essential part of any surgeon's quality planning. Take the well-known appendectomy operation, for example. This is the removal of the appendix when it becomes infected or inflamed. Removal is necessary because of the risk of the appendix bursting and causing peritonitis, a potentially fatal poisoning of the blood. The surgical procedure itself is a relatively simple operation with expected good results but there is always a small risk associated with any invasive surgery needing a general anaesthetic. In addition, like any surgical procedure, it is expensive. The cost of the USA's approximately quarter-of-a-million appendectomies averages out to around $4,500 per operation. Unfortunately, appendicitis is difficult to diagnose accurately. Using standard X-ray procedures a definite diagnosis can only be obtained about 10 per cent of the time. But now a new technique, developed in the Massachusetts General Hospital in Boston, claims to be able to identify 100 per cent of true appendicitis cases before surgery is carried out. The new technique (Focused Appendix Computed Tomography) uses spiral X-ray images together with a special dye. It scans only the relevant part of the body, so exposure to radiation is not as major an issue as with conventional X-ray techniques.

Source: AL RF (Imagemore Co., Ltd)

The technique can also help in providing an alternative diagnosis when an appendectomy is not needed. Most significantly, the potential cost savings are very great. The test itself costs less than $250 which means that one single avoided surgery pays for around 20 tests.

Go round any supermarket and look at all the products that are packaged, bottled, or otherwise 'filled' into their containers. Bottled drinks, detergent, bags of vegetables, cans of paint: they are all put in their containers in the manufacturing operations that produce them. And this filling or packing process is, in most countries, governed by strict government regulations. When a package claims to have a certain amount of product, customers have a right to expect that it really does include that amount; otherwise they are paying for something that they are not getting. On any product sold that has an 'e' after its claimed weight printed on the container, the law states that the average weight must be greater than the declared weight on the container, with the average weight being determined by sampling. The problem is that the technology used to fill packages is not always totally consistent. There is always some degree of variation in the amount 'dispensed'. So, if packers or fillers want to conform to legal weights and measures stipulations on minimum fill levels, they must build in a margin of safety into filling levels in order to overcome the variation of the filling technology. This margin of safety

is known as 'giveaway' or 'over-fill'. Experts in this technology estimate that this kind of routine over-filling can mean that 3 per cent of an operation's output can literally be given away in this manner. This idea is illustrated in Figure 17.6.

Figure 17.6 Average fill to meet minimum fill requirements has to be larger when process variability is large, resulting in 'giveaway'

Typical of the type of operation that has benefited from reducing the amount of variation in its processes, and therefore the amount of giveaway, is the food producer Quick Food Products. Founded in 1988 by immigrants from the Caribbean, it specializes in producing Jamaican patties with a range of meat, vegetable and fish fillings. Now it has expanded its range to include producing patties for the British-based Nigerian community, as well as patties certified to carry the halal label, indicating compliance with Muslim religious requirements. However, the firm had a problem – it needed extra capacity to manufacture and fill the new patties, but it was reluctant to spend the large sums that would be necessary to install new filling lines. To help it solve the problem, Quick Food Products called in operations improvement consultants. The consultants soon realized that there was too much variation in the weight of filling in the patties, and that reducing the variation in filling quantities could make significant savings – both in terms of reducing cost and in freeing-up capacity. Maxine Chapman, one of the consultants, says, '*It wasn't a big technical problem, but more a question of agreeing best operating-practices, and then using them.*' And the improvement at Quick Foods is not a one-off. '*Time and again*', she says, '*significant improvements in the performance of filling and packing lines can be achieved by applying simple tools consistently, and through a better understanding of the parameters of the equipment that you're dealing with.*'

Step 5 and 6 – Find and correct causes of poor quality and continue to make improvements

The final two steps in our list of quality management activities are, in some ways, the most important yet also the most difficult. They also blend into the general area of operations improvement. The material covered later (in Chapters 18, 19 and 20) all have contributions to make to these two steps. Nevertheless, there is an aspect of quality management that has been particularly important in shaping how quality is improved and the improvement activity made self-sustaining. This is total quality management (TQM). The remainder of the main body of this chapter is devoted to TQM.

TOTAL QUALITY MANAGEMENT (TQM)

Total quality management (TQM) was one of the earliest of the current wave of management 'fashions'. Its peak of popularity was in the late 80s and early 90s. As such it has suffered from something of a backlash in recent years and there is little doubt that many companies adopted TQM in the simplistic belief that it would transform their operations performance overnight. Yet the general precepts and principles that constitute TQM are still the dominant mode of organizing operations improvement. The approach we take here is to stress the importance of the 'total' in total quality management and how it can guide the agenda for improvement.

TQM as an extension of previous practice

TQM can be viewed as a logical extension of the way in which quality-related practice has progressed (*see* Fig. 17.7). Originally quality was achieved by inspection – screening out defects before they were noticed by customers. The quality control (QC) concept developed a more systematic approach to not only detecting, but also treating, quality problems. Quality assurance (QA) widened the responsibility for quality to include functions other than direct operations. It also made increasing use of more sophisticated statistical quality techniques. TQM included much of what went before but developed its own distinctive themes. We will use some of these themes to describe how TQM represents a clear shift from traditional approaches to quality.

What is TQM?

TQM is 'an effective system for integrating the quality development, quality maintenance and quality improvement efforts of the various groups in an organization so as to enable production and service at the most economical levels which allow for full customer satisfaction'.[9] However, it was the Japanese who first made the concept work on a wide scale and subsequently popularized the approach and the term 'TQM'. It was then developed further by several so-called 'quality gurus'. Each 'guru' stressed a different set of issues, from which emerged the TQM approach. It is best thought of as a philosophy of how to approach quality improvement. This philosophy, above everything, stresses the 'total' of TQM. It is an approach that puts quality at the heart of everything that is done by an operation including all activities within an operation. This totality can be summarized by the way TQM lays particular stress on the following:

- meeting the needs and expectations of customers;
- covering all parts of the organization;

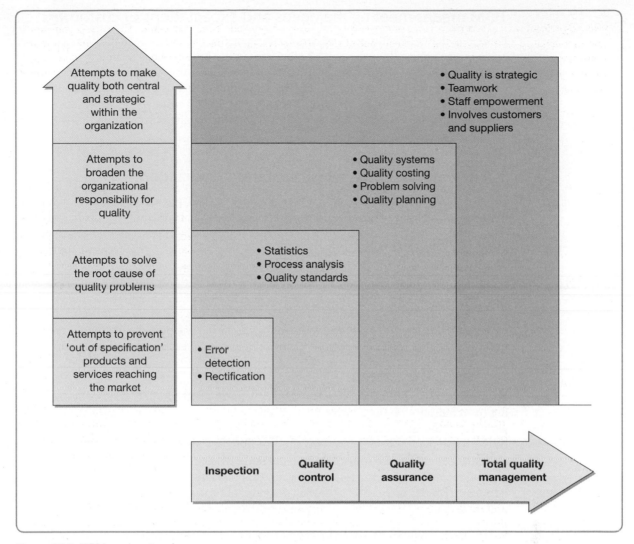

Figure 17.7 TQM as an extension

- including every person in the organization;
- examining all costs which are related to quality, especially failure costs and getting things 'right first time';
- developing the systems and procedures which support quality and improvement;
- developing a continuous process of improvement (this will be treated in the broader context of improvement, in Chapter 18).

Not surprisingly, several researchers have tried to establish how much of a relationship there is between adopting total quality management and the performance of the organization. One of the best-known studies[10] found that there was a positive relationship between the extent to which companies implement TQM and its overall performance. It found that TQM practices did indeed have a direct effect on operating performance but managers should implement TQM as a whole set of ideas rather than simply picking a few techniques to implement. The same study also suggests that where TQM does not prove successful in improving performance the problems could be the result of poor implementation rather than in the TQM practices themselves, and that a serious commitment on the part of top management to TQM is a prerequisite for success.

TQM means meeting the needs and expectations of customers

Earlier we defined quality as 'consistent conformance to customers' expectations'. Therefore any approach to quality management must necessarily include the customer perspective. In TQM this customer perspective is particularly important. It may be referred to as 'customer centricity' (discussed briefly in Chapter 18) or the 'voice of the customer'. However it is called, TQM stresses the importance of starting with an insight into customer needs, wants, perceptions, and preferences. This can then be translated into quality objectives and used to drive quality improvement.

TQM means covering all parts of the organization

For an organization to be truly effective, every single part of it, each department, each activity, each person and each level, must work properly together, because every person and every activity affects and in turn is affected by others. One of the most powerful concepts that has emerged from various improvement approaches is the concept of the internal customer/supplier. This is recognition that everyone is a customer within the organization and consumes goods or services provided by other internal suppliers, and everyone is also an internal supplier of goods and services for other internal customers. The implication of this is that errors in the service provided within an organization will eventually affect the service or product which reaches the external customer.

> **∗ Operations principle**
>
> An appreciation of, involvement in, and commitment to quality should permeate the entire organization.

Service level agreements

Some organizations bring a degree of formality to the internal customer concept by encouraging (or requiring) different parts of the operation to agree service level agreements (SLAs) with each other. SLAs are formal definitions of the dimensions of service and the relationship between two parts of an organization. The type of issues which would be covered by such an agreement could include response times, the range of services, dependability of service supply, and so on. Boundaries of responsibility and appropriate performance measures could also be agreed. For example, an SLA between an information systems support unit and a research unit in the laboratories of a large company could define such performance measures as:

- the types of information network services which may be provided as 'standard';
- the range of special information services which may be available at different periods of the day;
- the minimum 'up-time', i.e. the proportion of time the system will be available at different periods of the day;
- the maximum response time and average response time to get the system fully operational should it fail;
- the maximum response time to provide 'special' services, and so on.

Critical commentary

While some see the strength of SLAs as the degree of formality they bring to customer–supplier relationships, there also some clear drawbacks. The first is that the 'pseudo-contractual' nature of the formal relationship can work against building partnerships (*see* Chapter 13). This is especially true if the SLA includes penalties for deviation from service standards. Indeed, the effect can sometimes be to inhibit rather than encourage joint improvement. The second, and related, problem is that SLAs, again because of their formal documented nature, tend to emphasize the 'hard' and measurable aspects of performance rather than the 'softer' but often more important aspects. So a telephone may be answered within four rings, but how the caller is treated, in terms of 'friendliness', may be far more important.

TQM means including every person in the organization

Every person in the organization has the potential to contribute to quality and TQM was amongst the first approach to stress the centrality of harnessing everyone's potential contribution to quality. There is scope for creativity and innovation even in relatively routine activities, claim TQM proponents. The shift in attitude which is needed to view employees as the most valuable intellectual and creative resource which the organization possesses can still prove difficult for some organizations. Yet most advanced organizations do recognize that quality problems are almost always the results of human error. Even Google can fall victim to human error: see the short case 'Even Google suffers "human error"'.

TQM means all costs of quality are considered

The costs of controlling quality may not be small, whether the responsibility lies with each individual, or a dedicated quality control department. It is therefore necessary to examine all the costs and benefits associated with quality (in fact 'cost of quality' is usually taken to refer to both costs and benefits of quality). These costs of quality are usually categorized as *prevention costs, appraisal costs, internal failure costs* and *external failure costs*.

Prevention costs are those costs incurred in trying to prevent problems, failures and errors from occurring in the first place. They include such things as:

- identifying potential problems and putting the process right before poor quality occurs;
- designing and improving the design of products and services and processes to reduce quality problems;
- training and development of personnel in the best way to perform their jobs;
- process control through SPC.

Appraisal costs are those costs associated with controlling quality to check to see if problems or errors have occurred during and after the creation of the service or product. They might include such things as:

- the setting up of statistical acceptance sampling plans;
- the time and effort required to inspect inputs, processes and outputs;

Even Google suffers 'human error'[11]

For a 40-minute period one busy Saturday in January, all search results on Google, the most popular search engine in the world, were flagged as potentially harmful, with users warned that the site 'may harm your computer'. Users were being warned that all search results were dangerous and advised to pick another one. Google's search service had been hit by technical problems, with users unable to access search results.

So what had happened? *'It was human error'*, wrote Marissa Mayer, Vice President of Search Products and User Experience, on the official Google blog. Google work with an organization called stopbadware.org who find out, using customer complaints, which sites install malicious software on people's computers and which therefore should carry a warning. The list of dangerous sites is regularly updated and handed to Google. But when Google updated the list on this Saturday, it

Source: Shutterstock.com/Annette Shaff

mistakenly flagged all sites as potentially dangerous. *'We will carefully investigate this incident and put more robust file-checks in place to prevent it from happening again'*, said Marissa Mayer.

- obtaining processing inspection and test data;
- investigating quality problems and providing quality reports;
- conducting customer surveys and quality audits.

Internal failure costs are failure costs associated with errors which are dealt with inside the operation. These costs might include such things as:

- the cost of scrapped parts and material;
- reworked parts and materials;
- the lost production time as a result of coping with errors;
- lack of concentration due to time spent troubleshooting rather than improvement.

External failure costs are those which are associated with an error going out of the operation to a customer. These costs include such things as:

- loss of customer goodwill affecting future business;
- aggrieved customers who may take up time;
- litigation (or payments to avoid litigation);
- guarantee and warranty costs;
- the cost to the company of providing excessive capability (too much coffee in the pack or too much information to a client).

The relationship between quality costs

In traditional quality management it was assumed that failure costs reduce as the money spent on appraisal and prevention increases. Furthermore, it was assumed that there is an *optimum* amount of quality effort to be applied in any situation, which minimizes the total costs of quality. The argument is that there must be a point beyond which diminishing returns set in – that is, the cost of improving quality gets larger than the benefits which it brings. Figure 17.8(a) sums up this idea. As quality effort is increased, the costs of providing the effort – through extra quality controllers, inspection procedures, and so on – increases proportionally. At the same time, however, the cost of errors, faulty products, and so on, decreases because there are fewer of them. However, TQM proponents believe that this logic is flawed. First, it implies that failure and poor quality are acceptable. Why, TQM proponents argue, should any operation accept the *inevitability* of errors? Some occupations seem to be able to accept a zero-defect standard. No one accepts that pilots are allowed to crash a certain proportion of their aircraft, or that nurses will drop a certain proportion of the babies they deliver. Second, it assumes that costs are known and measurable. In fact, putting realistic figures to the cost of quality is not a straightforward matter. Third, it is argued that failure costs in the traditional model are greatly underestimated. In particular, all the management time wasted by failures and the loss of concentration it causes are rarely accounted for. Fourth, it implies that prevention costs are inevitably high because it involves expensive inspection. But why should quality not be an integral part of everyone's work rather than employing extra people to inspect it? Finally, the 'optimum-quality level' approach, by accepting compromise, does little to challenge operations managers and staff to find ways of improving quality. Put these corrections into the optimum-quality effort calculation and the picture looks very different (*see* Fig. 17.8). If there is an 'optimum', it is a lot further to the right, in the direction of putting more effort (but not necessarily cost) into quality.

> **∗ Operations principle**
>
> Effective investment in preventing quality errors can significantly reduce appraisal and failure costs.

The TQM quality cost model

TQM rejects the optimum-quality level concept and strives to reduce all known and unknown failure costs by preventing errors and failure taking place. Rather than looking for 'optimum' levels of quality effort, TQM stresses the relative balance between different types of quality cost. Of the four cost categories, two (costs of prevention and costs of appraisal) are open

Figure 17.8 (a) The traditional cost of quality model, and (b) the traditional cost of quality model, with adjustments to reflect TQM criticisms

to managerial influence, while the other two (internal costs of failure and external costs of failure) show the consequences of changes in the first two. So, rather than placing most emphasis on appraisal (so that 'bad products and service don't get through to the customer') TQM emphasizes prevention (to stop errors happening in the first place). That is because the more effort that is put into error prevention, the more internal and external failure costs are reduced. Then, once confidence has been firmly established, appraisal costs can be reduced. Eventually even prevention costs can be stepped down in absolute terms, though prevention remains a significant cost in relative terms. Figure 17.9 illustrates this idea. Initially

SHORT CASE   Deliberate defectives

A story which illustrates the difference in attitude between a TQM and a non-TQM company has become almost a legend among TQM proponents. It concerns a plant in Ontario, Canada, of IBM, the computer company. It ordered a batch of components from a Japanese manufacturer and specified that the batch should have an acceptable quality level (AQL) of three defective parts per thousand. When the parts arrived in Ontario they were accompanied by a letter which expressed the supplier's bewilderment at being asked to supply defective parts as well as good ones. The letter also explained that they had found it difficult to make parts which were defective, but had indeed managed it. These three defective parts per thousand had been included and were wrapped separately for the convenience of the customer.

Source: AL RF (Imagestate/John Foxx)

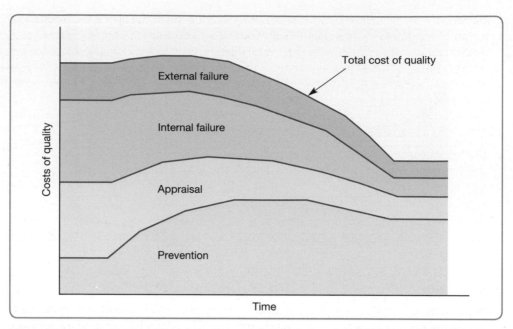

Figure 17.9 Increasing the effort spent on preventing errors occurring in the first place brings a more than equivalent reduction in other cost categories

total quality costs may rise as investment in some aspects of prevention – mainly training – is increased. However, a reduction in total costs can quickly follow.

Getting things 'right first time'

Accepting the relationships between categories of quality cost as illustrated in Figure 17.9 have a particularly important implication for how quality is managed. It shifts the emphasis from *reactive* (waiting for something to happen) to *proactive* (doing something before anything happens). This change in the view of quality costs has come about with a movement from an inspect-in (appraisal-driven) approach to a design-in (getting it right first time) approach.

Developing the systems and procedures which support quality and improvement

The emphasis on highly formalized systems and procedures to support TQM has declined in recent years, yet one aspect is still active for many companies. This is the adoption of the ISO 9000 standard. And although ISO 9000 can be regarded as a stand-alone issue, it is very closely associated with TQM.

The ISO 9000 approach

The ISO 9000 series is a family of standards compiled by the International Organization for Standardization (ISO) which is the world's largest developer and publisher of International Standards, based in Geneva, Switzerland. According to the ISO 'the standards represent an international consensus on good quality management practices. It consists of standards and guidelines relating to quality management systems and related supporting standards'. To be precise, it is the 'ISO 9001:2008' standard that provides the set of standardized requirements for a quality management system which should apply to any organization, regardless of size, or whether it is in the private or public sector. It is the only standard in the family against which organizations can be certified – although certification is not a compulsory requirement of the standard.

Its purpose when it was first framed was to provide an assurance to the purchasers of products or services that they have been produced in such a way that they meet their requirements. The best way to do this, it was argued, was to define the procedures, standards and characteristics of the management control system which governs the operation. Such a system would help to ensure that quality was 'built into' the operation's transformation processes. Rather than using different standards for different functions within a business, it takes a 'process' approach that focuses on outputs from any operation's process rather than detailed procedures. This process orientation requires operations to define and record core processes and sub-processes (in a manner very similar to the 'hierarchy of processes' principle that was outlined in Chapter 1). In addition, processes are documented using the process mapping approach (as described in Chapter 4). It also stresses four other principles:

- Quality management should be *customer-focused*. Customer satisfaction should be measured through surveys and focus groups and improvement against customer standards should be documented.

- Quality performance should be *measured*. In particular, measures should relate both to processes that create products and services and customer satisfaction with those products and services. Furthermore, measured data should be analysed in order to understand processes.

- Quality management should be *improvement-driven*. Improvement must be demonstrated in both process performance and customer satisfaction.

- Top management must demonstrate their commitment to maintaining and continually improving management systems. This commitment should include communicating the importance of meeting customer and other requirements, establishing a quality policy and quality objectives, conducting management reviews to ensure the adherence to quality policies, and ensuring the availability of the necessary resources to maintain quality systems.

The ISO illustrates the benefits of the standard as follows: '*Without satisfied customers, an organization is in peril! To keep customers satisfied, the organization needs to meet their requirements. The ISO 9001:2008 standard provides a tried and tested framework for taking a systematic approach to managing the organization's processes so that they consistently turn out product that satisfies customers' expectations.*'[12] In addition, it is also seen as providing benefits both to the organizations adopting it (because it gives them detailed guidance on how to design their control procedures) and especially to customers (who have the assurance of knowing that the products and services they purchase are produced by an operation working to a defined standard). Further, it may also provide a useful discipline to stick to 'sensible' process-orientated procedures which lead to error reduction, reduced customer complaints and reduced costs of quality, and may even identify existing procedures which are not necessary and can be eliminated. Moreover, gaining the certificate demonstrates that the company takes quality seriously; it therefore has a marketing benefit.

Critical commentary

Notwithstanding its widespread adoption (and its revision to take into account some of its perceived failing), ISO 9000 is not seen as beneficial by all authorities, and is still subject to some specific criticisms. These include the following:

The continued use of standards and procedures encourages 'management by manual' and over-systematized decision making.

The whole process of documenting processes, writing procedures, training staff and conducting internal audits is expensive and time-consuming.

Similarly, the time and cost of achieving and maintaining ISO 9000 registration are excessive.

It is too formulaic. It encourages operations to substitute a 'recipe' for a more customized and creative approach to managing operations improvement.

MyOMLab *Check and improve your understanding of this chapter using self-assessment questions and a personalized study plan, a video case study, and an eText – all at www.myomlab.com.*

❯ What is quality and why is it so important?

- The definition of quality used in this book defines quality as 'consistent conformance to customers' expectations'. It is important because it has a significant impact on profitability.

❯ How can quality problems be diagnosed?

- At a broad level, quality is best modelled as the gap between customers' expectations concerning the service or product and their perceptions concerning the service or product.
- Modelling quality this way will allow the development of a diagnostic tool which is based around the perception–expectation gap. Such a gap may be explained by four other gaps:
  - the gap between a customer's specification and the operation's specification;
  - the gap between the service or product concept and the way the organization has specified it;
  - the gap between the way quality has been specified and the actual delivered quality;
  - the gap between the actual delivered quality and the way the service or product has been described to the customer.

❯ What steps lead towards conformance to specification?

- There are six steps:
  - define quality characteristics;
  - decide how to measure each of the quality characteristics;
  - set quality standards for each characteristic;
  - control quality against these standards;
  - find and correct the causes of poor quality;
  - continue to make improvements.
- Most quality planning and control involves sampling the operations performance in some way. Sampling can give rise to erroneous judgements which are classed as either type I or type II errors. Type I errors involve making corrections where none are needed. Type II errors involve not making corrections where they are in fact needed.

❯ What is total quality management (TQM)?

- TQM is 'an effective system for integrating the quality development, quality maintenance and quality improvement efforts of the various groups in an organization so as to enable production and service at the most economical levels which allow for full customer satisfaction'.
- It is best thought of as a philosophy that stresses the 'total' of TQM and puts quality at the heart of everything that is done by an operation.

- 'Total' in TQM means the following:
  - meeting the needs and expectations of customers;
  - covering all parts of the organization;
  - including every person in the organization;
  - examining all costs which are related to quality, and getting things 'right first time';
  - developing the systems and procedures which support quality and improvement;
  - developing a continuous process of improvement.

CASE STUDY

Turnround at the Preston plant[13]

Introduction
'Before the crisis, production monitoring was done to please the client, not for problem-solving. Data readouts were brought to production meetings and we would all look at then, but none of us were looking behind the data.' (Chief Operating Officer (COO), Preston plant)

The Preston plant was located in Preston, Vancouver. Precision-coated papers for specialist printing uses accounted for the majority of the plant's output. The plant used state-of-the-art coating machines that allowed very precise coatings to be applied to bought-in rolls of paper. After coating, the coated rolls were cut into standard sizes.

The curl problem
In the spring of 2008, Hewlett-Packard (the plant's main customer) informed the plant of problems it had encountered with paper curling under conditions of low humidity. There had been no customer complaints. HP's own personnel had noticed the problem, but they took the problem seriously. Over the next eight months the plant's Production staff worked to isolate the cause of the problem and improve systems that monitored processing metrics. By January 2009 the process was producing acceptable product, yet it had not been a good year for the plant. Although volumes were buoyant, the plant was making a loss of around $10 million a year. In October 2008, Tom Branton was appointed as COO.

Slipping out of control
Although the curl problem was solved, productivity, scrap and re-work levels were poor. In response to this, operations managers increased the speed of the line in order to raise productivity. 'Looking back, changes were made without any proper discipline, there was no real concept of control and the process was allowed to drift. Our culture said, "If it's within specification then it's OK", and we were very diligent in making sure that the product which was shipped was

Source: AL RF (PhotoDisc/Kim Steele)

in specification. However, Hewlett-Packard gets "process data" which enables them to see exactly what is happening right inside your operation. We were also getting all the data but none of it was being internalized. By contrast, HP has a "capability mentality". They say, "You might be capable of making this product but we are thinking two or three product generations forward and asking ourselves, do we want to invest in this relationship for the future?"' (Tom Branton). The spring of 2009 was eventful. First, Hewlett-Packard asked the plant to carry out preliminary work for a new paper to supply its next generation of printers, known as the Viper project. Second, the plant was acquired by the Rendall Group, who was not impressed by what they found. The plant had been making a loss for two years and had incurred HP's disapproval over the curl issue. They made it clear that, if the plant did not get the Viper contract, its future looked bleak. Meanwhile, in the plant, the chief concern was plant productivity, but also

HP was starting to make complaints about quality levels. Yet HP's attitude caused bewilderment in the production team. 'When HP asked questions about our process the operations guys would say, "Look we're making roll after roll of paper, it's within specification and we've got 97 per cent up-time. What's the problem?"' (COO, Preston Plant). But it was not until summer that the full extent of HP's disquiet was made clear. 'I will never forget that day in June of 2009. I was with HP in Chicago and during the meeting one of their engineers handed me some of the process data that we had to supply with every batch of product, and said, "Here's your latest data. We think you're out of control and you don't know that you're out of control and we think that HP is looking at this data more than you are." He was absolutely right.' (Tom Branton)

The crisis

Tom immediately set about the task of bringing the plant back under control. They first of all decided to go back to the conditions which the monitoring system indicated had prevailed in January, when the curl problem had been solved and before productivity pressures had caused the process to be adjusted. At the same time, production worked on ways of implementing unambiguous 'shut-down rules' which would indicate to operators when a line should be halted if they were in doubt about operating quality.

'At one point in May of 2009 we had to throw away 64 jumbo rolls of out-of-specification product. That's over $400,000 of product scrapped in one run. That was because operators had been afraid to shut the line down. Either that or they had tried to tweak the line while it was running to get rid of the defect. The shut-down system says, "We are not going to operate when we are not in a state of control." Prior to that, our operators just couldn't win. If they failed to keep the process running we would say, "You've got to keep productivity up." If they kept the machines running but had quality problems as a result, we criticized them for making garbage. Now you get into far more trouble for violating process procedures than for not meeting productivity targets. We did two further things. First, each production team started holding daily reviews of processing data and some "first pass" analysis of the data. Second, one day a month we brought all three shifts together, looked at the processing data and debated the implications of production data. Some people got nervous because we were not producing anything. But for the first time you got operators from the three shifts, together with the production team, talking about operating issues. We also invited HP up to attend these meetings. Remember these weren't staged meetings; it was the first time these guys had met together and there was plenty of heated discussion, all of which the Hewlett-Packard representatives witnessed.' (Engineer, Preston plant)

In spite of the changes, morale on the shop floor was good. At last something positive was happening. By September 2009 the process was coming under control, the efficiency of the plant was improving, as was its outgoing quality level, its on-time delivery and its responsiveness to customer orders and its inventory levels. Yet the Preston team did not have

time to enjoy their emerging success. In September of 2009 Hewlett-Packard announced that the plant would not get the Viper project because of their discomfort about quality levels, and Rendall formally made their decision on the future of the plant. 'We lost 10 million dollars in 2009. We had also lost the Viper project. It was no surprise when they made the decision to shut the plant down. I told the senior management team that we would announce it, in April of 2010. The irony was that we knew that we had already turned the corner. It would take perhaps three or four months, but we were convinced that we would become profitable.' (Tom Branton)

Convincing the rest of the world

Notwithstanding the closure decision, the management team in Preston set about the task of convincing both HP and Rendall that the plant could be viable. They figured it would take three things. First, it was vital that they continue to improve quality. Second, costs had to be brought down further. Third, the plant had to create a portfolio of new product ideas.

Improving quality further involved establishing full statistical process analysis into the process monitoring system. It also meant establishing quality consciousness and problem-solving tools throughout the plant. 'We had people out there, technologists and managers, who saw themselves as concerned with investment projects rather than the processes that were affected. But taking time out and discussing process performance and improvement, we got used to discussing the basic capabilities that we needed to improve.' (Tom Branton)

Working on cost reduction was inevitably going to be painful. The first task was to get an understanding of what should be an appropriate level of operating costs.

'We went through a zero-based assessment to decide what ideal processes would look like. By the way, in hindsight, cutting numbers had a greater impact on cost than the payroll saving figures seem to suggest. If you really understand your process, when you cut people it cuts complexity and makes things clearer to understand. Although most staff had not been told of the closure decision, they were left in no doubt that the plant had its back to the wall. We were careful to be very transparent. We made sure that everyone knew whether they would be affected or not. I did lots of walking around explaining the company's position. There were tensions and some negative reactions from the people who had to leave. Yet most accepted the business logic of what we were doing.' (Tom Branton)

By December of 2009 there were 40 per cent fewer people in the plant than 2 months earlier. All departments were affected. Surprisingly the quality department shrank more than most, moving from 22 people down to 9. 'When the plant was considering downsizing they asked me, "How can we run a lab with 6 technicians?" Remember that at this time we had 22 technicians. I said, "Easy. We get production to make good product in the first place, and then we don't have to control all the garbage."' (Quality Manager, Preston plant)

Several new product ideas were investigated, including some that were only possible because of the plant's enhanced capability. The most important of these became known as 'Ecowrap', a recyclable protective wrap aimed at the Japanese market. It was technically difficult, but the plant's new capabilities allowed it to develop appropriate coatings at a cost that made the product attractive.

Out of the crisis

In spite of their trauma in the fall, the plant's management team faced Christmas of 2009 with increasing satisfaction, if not optimism, for the plant's future. In December they made an operational profit for the first time for over two years. By spring of 2010 even HP, at a corporate level, were starting to look more favourably on the Preston plant. More significantly, HP had asked the plant to start work on trials for a new product – 'heavyweight' paper. April 2010 was a good month for the plant. It had chalked up three months of profitability and HP formally gave the heavyweight ink-jet paper contract to Preston, and were generally more upbeat about the future. At the end of April, Rendall reversed their decision to close the plant.

The future

The year 2010 was a profitable one for the plant, by the end of which they had captured 75 per cent of Hewlett-Packard's US-printing-paper business and were being asked to work on several other large projects. 'Hewlett-Packard now seems very keen to work with us. It has helped us with our own suppliers also. We have already given considerable assistance to our main paper supplier to improve their own internal process control procedures. Recently we were in a meeting with people from all different parts of HP. There was all kinds of confidential information going around. But you could never tell that there was an outsider (us) in the room. They were having arguments amongst themselves about certain issues and no one could have been there without feeling that basically we were a part of that company. In the past they've always been very close with some information. Basically the change is all down to their new-found trust in our capabilities.' (Tom Branton)

QUESTIONS

1 What are the most significant events in the story of how the plant survived because of its adoption of quality-based principles?

2 The plant's processes eventually were brought under control. What were the main benefits of this?

3 SPC is an operational level technique for ensuring quality conformance. How many of the benefits of bringing the plant under control would you class as strategic?

PROBLEMS AND APPLICATIONS

These problems and applications will help to improve your analysis of operations. You can find more practice problems as well as worked examples and guided solutions on MyOMLab at www.myomlab.com.

MyOMLab

(Read the supplement on statistical process control before attempting these problems.)

1 A call centre for a bank answers customers' queries about their loan arrangements. All calls are automatically timed by the call centre's information system and the mean and standard deviation of call lengths is monitored periodically. The bank have decided that only on very rare occasions should calls be less than 0.5 minutes because customers would think this was impolite, even if the query was so simple that it could be answered in this time. Also, the bank reckoned that it was unlikely that any query should ever take more than 7 minutes to answer satisfactorily. The figures for last week's calls show that the mean of all call lengths was 3.02 minutes and the standard deviation was 1.58 minutes. Calculate the C_p and the C_{pk} for the call centre process.

2 In the above call centre, if the mean call length changes to 3.2 minutes and the standard deviation to 0.9 minutes, how does this affect the C_p and C_{pk}? Do you think this is an appropriate way for the bank to monitor its call centre performance?

3 A vaccine production company has invested in an automatic tester to monitor the impurity levels in its vaccines. Previously all testing was done by hand on a sample of batches of serum. According to the company's specifications, all vaccine must have impurity levels of less than 0.03 milligrams per 1,000 litres. In order to test the effectiveness of its new automatic sampling

equipment, the company runs a number of batches through the process with known levels of impurity. The table below shows the level of impurity of each batch and whether the new process accepted or rejected the batch. From this data, estimate the type I and type II error levels for the process.

0.035 (rejected)	0.028 (accepted)	0.031 (accepted)	0.029 (accepted)	0.028 (accepted)	0.034 (accepted)	0.031 (accepted)
0.040 (rejected)	0.011 (accepted)	0.028 (rejected)	0.025 (accepted)	0.019 (accepted)	0.018 (accepted)	0.033 (rejected)
0.022 (accepted)	0.029 (rejected)	0.012 (accepted)	0.034 (accepted)	0.027 (accepted)	0.017 (accepted)	0.021 (accepted)
0.031 (rejected)	0.015 (accepted)	0.037 (rejected)	0.030 (accepted)	0.025 (accepted)	0.034 (rejected)	0.020 (accepted)

4   A utility has a department who do nothing but change the addresses of customers on the company's information systems when customers move house. The process is deemed to be in control at the moment and a random sample of 2,000 transactions shows that 2.5 per cent of these transactions had some type of error. If the company are to use statistical process control to monitor error levels, calculate the mean, upper control level (UCL) and lower control level (LCL) for their SPC chart.

5   Find two products, one a manufactured food item (for example, a pack of breakfast cereals, packet of biscuits, etc.) and the other a domestic electrical item (for example, electric toaster, coffee maker, etc.):
   (a)   Identify the important quality characteristics for these two products.
   (b)   How could each of these quality characteristics be specified?
   (c)   How could each of these quality characteristics be measured?

6   Many organizations check up on their own level of quality by using 'mystery shoppers'. This involves an employee of the company acting the role of a customer and recording how they are treated by the operation. Choose two or three high-visibility operations (for example, a cinema, a department store, the branch of a retail bank, etc.) and discuss how you would put together a mystery shopper approach to testing their quality. This may involve you determining the types of characteristics you would wish to observe, the way in which you would measure these characteristics, an appropriate sampling rate, and so on. Try out your mystery shopper plan by visiting these operations.

SELECTED FURTHER READING

ASQ Quality Press (2010) *Seven Basic Quality Tools*, ASQ Quality Press, Milwaukee, WI. Very much a 'how to do it' handbook.

Dale, B.G., van der Wiele, T. and van Waarden, J. (2007) *Managing Quality*, 5th edn, Wiley-Blackwell, Oxford. This is the latest version of a long-established, comprehensive and authoritative text.

Garvin, D.A. (1988) *Managing Quality*, The Free Press, New York. Somewhat dated now but relates to our discussion at the beginning of this chapter.

USEFUL WEBSITES

http://www.quality-foundation.co.uk The British Quality Foundation is a not-for-profit organization promoting business excellence.

http://www.juran.com The Juran Institute's mission statement is to provide clients with the concepts, methods and guidance for attaining leadership in quality.

http://www.asq.org/ The American Society for Quality site. Good professional insights.

http://www.quality.nist.gov/ American Quality Assurance Institute. Well-established institution for all types of business quality assurance.

http://www.gslis.utexas.edu/~rpollock/tqm.html Non-commercial site on total quality management with some good links.

http://www.iso.org/iso/en/ISOOnline.frontpage Site of the International Standards Organization that runs the ISO 9000 and ISO 14,000 families of standards. ISO 9000 has become an international reference for quality management requirements.

www.myomlab.com Test which sections you have mastered and which you need to review, with questions, a personalized study plan, video clips, revision tips, and cases.

INTRODUCTION

Statistical process control (SPC) is concerned with checking a service or product during its creation. If there is reason to believe that there is a problem with the process, then it can be stopped and the problem can be identified and rectified. For example, an international airport may regularly ask a sample of customers if the cleanliness of its restaurants is satisfactory. If an unacceptable number of customers in one sample are found to be unhappy, airport managers may have to consider improving its procedures. Similarly, an automobile manufacturer will periodically check whether a sample of door panels conforms to its standards so it knows whether the machinery which produces them is performing correctly.

CONTROL CHARTS

The value of SPC is not just to make checks of a single sample but to monitor the quality over a period of time. It does this by using control charts, to see if the process seems to be performing as it should, or alternatively if it is 'out of control'. If the process does seem to be going out of control, then steps can be taken *before* there is a problem. Actually, most operations chart their quality performance in some way. Figure S17.1, or something like it, could be found in almost any operation. The chart could, for example, represent the percentage of customers in a sample of 1,000 who, each month, were dissatisfied with the restaurant's cleanliness. While the amount of dissatisfaction may be acceptably small, management should be concerned

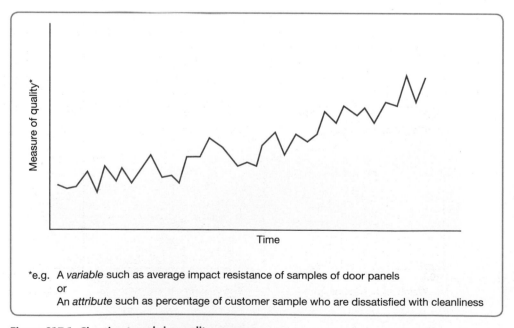

*e.g. A *variable* such as average impact resistance of samples of door panels
   or
   An *attribute* such as percentage of customer sample who are dissatisfied with cleanliness

Figure S17.1 Charting trends in quality measures

that it has been steadily increasing over time and may wish to investigate why this is so. In this case, the control chart is plotting an attribute measure of quality (satisfied or not). Looking for trends is an important use of control charts. If the trend suggests the process is getting steadily worse, then it will be worth investigating the process. If the trend is steadily improving, it may still be worthy of investigation to try to identify what is happening that is making the process better. This information might then be shared with other parts of the organization, or, on the other hand, the process might be stopped as the cause could be adding unnecessary expense to the operation.

VARIATION IN PROCESS QUALITY

Common causes

The processes charted in Figure S17.1 showed an upwards trend. But the trend was neither steady nor smooth: it varied – sometimes up, sometimes down. All processes vary to some extent. No machine will give precisely the same result each time it is used. People perform tasks slightly differently each time. Given this, it is not surprising that the measure of quality will also vary. Variations which derive from these *common causes* can never be entirely eliminated (although they can be reduced). For example, if a machine is filling boxes with rice, it will not place *exactly* the same weight of rice in every box it fills. When the filling machine is in a stable condition (that is, no exceptional factors are influencing its behaviour) each box could be weighed and a histogram of the weights could be built up. Figure S17.2 shows how the histogram might develop. The first boxes weighed could lie anywhere within the natural variation of the process but are more likely to be close to the average weight (*see* Fig. S17.2a). As more boxes are weighed they clearly show the tendency to be close to the process average (*see* Fig. S17.2b and S17.2c). After many boxes have been weighed they form a smoother distribution (Fig. S17.2d), which can be drawn as a histogram (Fig. S17.2e), which will approximate to the underlying process variation distribution (Fig. S17.2f).

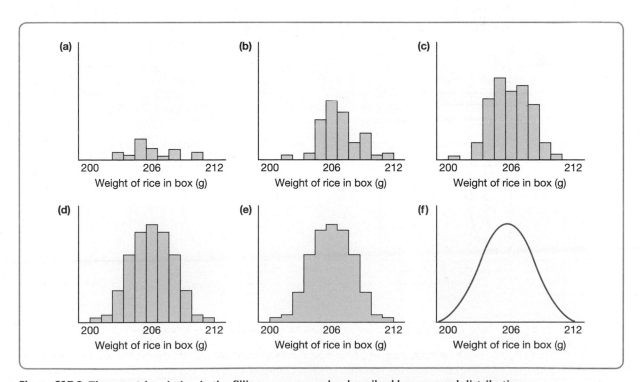

Figure S17.2 The natural variation in the filling process can be described by a normal distribution

Usually this type of variation can be described by a normal distribution with 99.7 per cent of the variation lying within ± 3 standard deviations. In this case, the weight of rice in the boxes is described by a distribution with a mean of 206 grams and a standard deviation of 2 grams. The obvious question for any operations manager would be: 'Is this variation in the process performance acceptable?' The answer will depend on the acceptable range of weights which can be tolerated by the operation. This range is called the specification range. If the weight of rice in the box is too small then the organization might infringe labelling regulations; if it is too large, the organization is 'giving away' too much of its product for free.

Process capability

Process capability is a measure of the acceptability of the variation of the process. The simplest measure of capability (C_p) is given by the ratio of the specification range to the 'natural' variation of the process (i.e. ±3 standard deviations):

$$C_p = \frac{UTL - LTL}{6s}$$

where

$$UTL = \text{the upper tolerance limit}$$
$$LTL = \text{the lower tolerance limit}$$
$$s = \text{the standard deviation of the process variability.}$$

Generally, if the C_p of a process is greater than 1, it is taken to indicate that the process is 'capable', and a C_p of less than 1 indicates that the process is not 'capable', assuming that the distribution is normal (*see* Fig. S17.3a, S17.3b and S17.3c).

The simple C_p measure assumes that the average of the process variation is at the mid-point of the specification range. Often the process average is offset from the specification range,

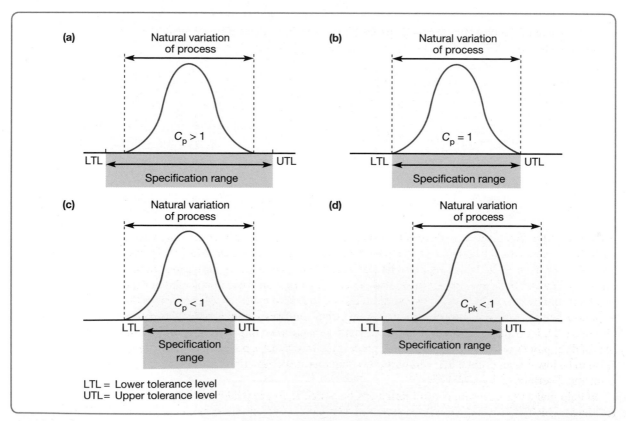

Figure S17.3 Process capability compares the natural variation of the process with the specification range which is required

however (*see* Fig. S17.3d). In such cases, *one-sided* capability indices are required to understand the capability of the process:

$$\text{Upper one-sided index } C_{pu} = \frac{UTL - X}{3s}$$

$$\text{Lower one-sided index } C_{pl} = \frac{X - LTL}{3s}$$

where X = the process average.

Sometimes only the lower of the two one-sided indices for a process is used to indicate its capability (C_{pk}):

$$C_{pk} = \min(C_{pu}, C_{pl})$$

Worked example

In the case of the process filling boxes of rice, described previously, process capability can be calculated as follows:

$$\text{Specification range} = 214 - 198 = 16\,g$$
$$\text{Natural variation of process} = 6 \times \text{standard deviation}$$
$$= 6 \times 2 = 12\,g$$
$$C_p = \text{process capability}$$
$$= \frac{UTL - LTL}{6s}$$
$$= \frac{214 - 198}{6 \times 2} = \frac{16}{12}$$
$$= 1.333$$

If the natural variation of the filling process changed to have a process average of 210 grams but the standard deviation of the process remained at 2 grams:

$$C_{pu} = \frac{214 - 210}{3 \times 2} = \frac{4}{6} = 0.666$$
$$C_{pl} = \frac{210 - 198}{3 \times 2} = \frac{12}{6} = 2.0$$
$$C_{pk} = \min(0.666, 2.0)$$
$$= 0.666$$

Assignable causes of variation

Not all variation in processes is the result of common causes. There may be something wrong with the process which is assignable to a particular and preventable cause. Machinery may have worn or been set up badly. An untrained person may not be following prescribed procedures. The causes of such variation are called *assignable causes*. The question is whether the results from any particular sample, when plotted on the control chart, simply represent the variation due to common causes or due to some specific and correctable, *assignable* cause. Figure S17.4, for example, shows the control chart for the average impact resistance of samples of door panels taken over time. Like any process the results vary, but the last three points seem to be lower than usual. So, is this natural (common cause) variation, or the symptom of some more serious (assignable) cause?

To help make this decision, control limits can be added to the control chart (the red dotted lines) which indicates the expected extent of 'common-cause' variation. If any points lie outside these control limits (the shaded zone) then the process can be deemed out of control in the sense that variation is likely to be due to assignable causes. These control limits could

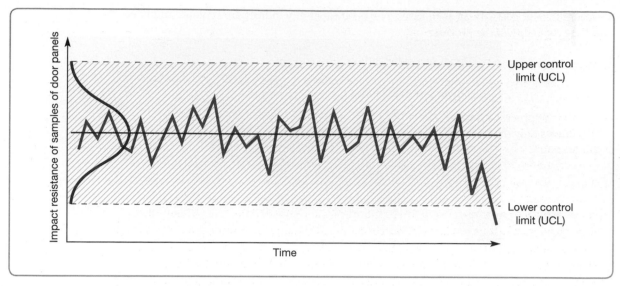

Figure S17.4 Control chart for the impact resistance of door panels, together with control limits

be set intuitively by examining past variation during a period when the process was thought to be free of any variation which could be due to assignable causes. But control limits can also be set in a more statistically revealing manner. For example, if the process which tests door panels had been measured to determine the normal distribution which represents its common-cause variation, then control limits can be based on this distribution. Figure S17.4 also shows how control limits can be added; here put at ±3 standard deviations (of the population of sample means) away from the mean of sample averages. It shows that the probability of the final point on the chart being influenced by an assignable cause is very high indeed. When the process is exhibiting behaviour which is outside its normal 'common-cause' range, it is said to be 'out of control'. Yet there is a small but finite chance that the (seemingly out of limits) point is just one of the rare but natural results at the tail of the distribution which describes perfectly normal behaviour. Stopping the process under these circumstances would represent a type I error because the process is actually in control. Alternatively, ignoring a result which in reality is due to an assignable cause is a type II error (*see* Table S17.1).

Control limits are usually set at three standard deviations either side of the population mean. This would mean that there is only a 0.3 per cent chance of any sample mean falling outside these limits by chance causes (that is, a chance of a type I error of 0.3 per cent). The control limits may be set at any distance from the population mean, but the closer the limits are to the population mean, the higher the likelihood of investigating and trying to rectify a process which is actually problem-free. If the control limits are set at two standard deviations, the chance of a type I error increases to about 5 per cent. If the limits are set at one standard deviation then the chance of a type I error increases to 32 per cent. When the control limits are placed at ±3 standard deviations away from the mean of the distribution which describes 'normal' variation in the process, they are called the upper control limit (UCL) and lower control limit (LCL).

Table S17.1 Type I and type II errors in SPC

Decision	Actual process state	
	In control	*Out of control*
Stop process	Type I error	Correct decision
Leave alone	Correct decision	Type II error

When its originators first described SPC more than half a century ago, the key issue was only to decide whether a process was 'in control' or not. Now, we expect SPC to reflect common sense as well as statistical elegance and promote continuous operations improvement. This is why two (related) criticisms have been levelled at the traditional approach to SPC. The first is that SPC seems to assume that any values of process performance which lie within the control limits are equally acceptable, while any values outside the limits are not. However, surely a value close to the process average or 'target' value will be more acceptable than one only just within the control limits. For example, a service engineer arriving only 1 minute late is a far better 'performance' than one arriving 59 minutes late, even if the control limits are 'quoted time $\pm$ one hour'. Also, arriving 59 minutes late would be almost as bad as 61 minutes late! Second, a process always within its control limits may not be deteriorating, but is it improving? So rather than seeing control limits as fixed, it would be better to view them as a reflection of how the process is being improved. We should expect any improving process to have progressively narrowing control limits.

Why variability is a bad thing

Assignable variation is a signal that something has changed in the process which therefore must be investigated. But normal variation is itself a problem because it masks any changes in process behaviour. Figure S17.5 shows the performance of two processes, both of which are subjected to a change in their process behaviour at the same time. The process on the left has such a wide natural variation that it is not immediately apparent that any change has taken place. Eventually it will become apparent because the likelihood of process performance violating the lower (in this case) control limit has increased, but this may take some time. By contrast, the process on the right has a far narrower band of natural variation. Because of this, the same change in average performance is more easily noticed (both visually and statistically). So, the narrower the natural variation of a process, the more obvious are changes in the behaviour of that process. And the more obvious are process changes, the easier it is to understand how and why the process is behaving in a particular way. Accepting any variation in any process is, to some degree, admitting to ignorance of how that process works.

> *** Operations principle**
>
> High levels of variation reduce the ability to detect changes in process performance.

Figure S17.5 Low process variation allows changes in process performance to be readily detected

CONTROL CHARTS FOR ATTRIBUTES

Attributes have only two states – 'right' or 'wrong', for example – so the statistic calculated is the proportion of wrongs (p) in a sample. (This statistic follows a binomial distribution.) Control charts using p are called 'p-charts'. In calculating the limits, the population mean ($\bar{p}$) – the actual, normal or expected proportion of 'defectives' or wrongs to rights – may not be known. Who knows, for example, the actual number of city commuters who are dissatisfied with their journey time? In such cases the population mean can be estimated from the average of the proportion of 'defectives' ($\bar{p}$), from m samples each of n items, where m should be at least 30 and n should be at least 100:

$$\bar{p} = \frac{p^1 + p^2 + p^3 + \ldots + p^n}{m}$$

One standard deviation can then be estimated from:

$$\sqrt{\frac{\bar{p}(1 - \bar{p})}{n}}$$

The upper and lower control limits can then be set as:

$$\text{UCL} = \bar{p} + 3 \text{ standard deviations}$$
$$\text{LCL} = \bar{p} - 3 \text{ standard deviations}$$

Of course, the LCL cannot be negative, so when it is calculated to be so it should be rounded up to zero.

Worked example

A credit card company deals with many hundreds of thousands of transactions every week. One of its measures of the quality of service it gives its customers is the dependability with which it mails customers' monthly accounts. The quality standard it sets itself is that accounts should be mailed within two days of the 'nominal post date' which is specified to the customer. Every week the company samples 1,000 customer accounts and records the percentage which was not mailed within the standard time. When the process is working normally, only 2 per cent of accounts are mailed outside the specified period, that is, 2 per cent are 'defective'.

Control limits for the process can be calculated as follows:

$$\text{Mean proportion defective, } \bar{p} = 0.02$$
$$\text{Sample size } n = 1,000$$
$$\text{Standard deviation } s = \sqrt{\frac{\bar{p}(1 - \bar{p})}{n}}$$
$$= \sqrt{\frac{0.02(0.98)}{1,000}}$$
$$= 0.004$$

With the control limits at $\bar{p} \pm 3s$:

$$\text{Upper control limit (UCL)} = 0.02 + 3(0.0044) = 0.0332$$
$$= 3.32\%$$

and

$$\text{lower control limit (LCL)} = 0.02 - 3(0.0044) = 0.0068$$
$$= 0.68\%$$

Figure S17.6 shows the company's control chart for this measure of quality over the last few weeks, together with the calculated control limits. It also shows that the process is in control. Sometimes it is more convenient to plot the actual number of defects (c) rather than the proportion (or percentage) of defectives, on what is known as a c-chart. This is very similar to the p-chart but the sample size must be constant and the process mean and control limits are calculated using the following formulae:

$$\text{Process mean } \bar{c} = \frac{c_1 + c_2 + c_3 + \ldots + c_m}{m}$$

$$\text{Control limits} = \bar{c} \pm 3\sqrt{\bar{c}}$$

where

$$c = \text{number of defects}$$
$$m = \text{number of samples}$$

Figure S17.6 Control chart for the percentage of customer accounts which are mailed outside their two-day period

CONTROL CHART FOR VARIABLES

The most commonly used type of control chart employed to control variables is the $\bar{X} - R$ chart. In fact this is really two charts in one. One chart is used to control the sample average or mean ($\bar{X}$). The other is used to control the variation within the sample by measuring the range (R). The range is used because it is simpler to calculate than the standard deviation of the sample.

The means ($\bar{X}$) chart can pick up changes in the average output from the process being charted. Changes in the means chart would suggest that the process is drifting generally away from its supposed process average, although the variability inherent in the process may not have changed (*see* Fig. S17.7).

The range (R) chart plots the range of each sample, that is, the difference between the largest and the smallest measurement in the samples. Monitoring sample range gives an indication of whether the variability of the process is changing, even when the process average remains constant (*see* Fig. S17.7).

Control limits for variables control chart

As with attributes control charts, a statistical description of how the process operates under normal conditions (when there are no assignable causes) can be used to calculate control limits. The first task in calculating the control limits is to estimate the grand average or population mean ($\bar{\bar{X}}$) and average range ($\bar{R}$) using m samples each of sample size n.

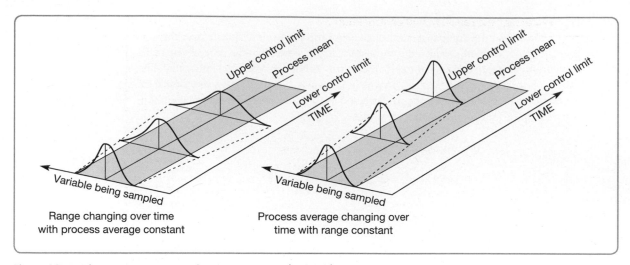

Figure S17.7 The process mean or the process range (or both) can change over time

The population mean is estimated from the average of a large number (m) of sample means:

$$\bar{\bar{X}} = \frac{X_1 + X_2 + \ldots + X_m}{m}$$

The average range is estimated from the ranges of the large number of samples:

$$\bar{R} = \frac{R_1 + R_2 + \ldots + R_m}{m}$$

The control limits for the sample means chart are:

$$\text{Upper control limit (UCL)} = \bar{\bar{X}} + A_2\bar{R}$$
$$\text{Lower control limit (LCL)} = \bar{\bar{X}} - A_2\bar{R}$$

The control limits for the range charts are:

$$\text{Upper control limit } (UCL) = D_4\bar{R}$$
$$\text{Lower control limit } (LCL) = D_3\bar{R}$$

The factors A_2, D_3 and D_4 vary with sample size and are shown in Table S17.2.

The LCL for the means chart may be negative (for example, temperature or profit may be less than zero) but it may not be negative for a range chart (or the smallest measurement in the sample would be larger than the largest). If the calculation indicates a negative LCL for a range chart then the LCL should be set to zero.

Table S17.2 Factors for the calculation of control limits

Sample size n	A_2	D_3	D_4
2	1.880	0	3.267
3	1.023	0	2.575
4	0.729	0	2.282
5	0.577	0	2.115
6	0.483	0	2.004
7	0.419	0.076	1.924
8	0.373	0.136	1.864
9	0.337	0.184	1.816
10	0.308	0.223	1.777
12	0.266	0.284	1.716
14	0.235	0.329	1.671
16	0.212	0.364	1.636
18	0.194	0.392	1.608
20	0.180	0.414	1.586
22	0.167	0.434	1.566
24	0.157	0.452	1.548

Worked example

GAM (Groupe As Maquillage) is a contract cosmetics company, based in France but with plants around Europe, which manufactures and packs cosmetics and perfumes for other companies. One of its plants, in Ireland, operates a filling line which automatically fills plastic bottles with skin cream and seals the bottles with a screw-top cap. The tightness with which the screw-top cap is fixed is an important part of the quality of the filling-line process. If the cap is screwed on too tightly, there is a danger that it will crack; if screwed on too loosely it might come loose when packed. Either outcome could cause leakage of the product during its journey between the factory and the customer. The Irish plant had received some complaints of product leakage which it suspected was caused by inconsistent fixing of the screw-top caps on its filling line. The 'tightness' of the screw tops could be measured by a simple test device which recorded the amount of turning force (torque) that was required to unfasten the tops. The company decided to take samples of the bottles coming out of the filling-line process, test them for their unfastening torque and plot the results on a control chart. Several samples of four bottles were taken during a period when the process was regarded as being in control. The following data were calculated from this exercise:

$$\text{The grand average of all samples } \overline{\overline{X}} = 812 \text{ g/cm}^3$$
$$\text{The average range of the sample } \overline{R} = 6 \text{ g/cm}^3$$

Control limits for the means (X) chart were calculated as follows:

$$\text{UCL} = \overline{\overline{X}} + A_2\overline{R}$$
$$= 812 + (A_2 \times 6)$$

From Table S17.2, we know, for a sample size of four, $A_2 = 0.729$. Thus:

$$\text{UCL} = 812 + (0.729 \times 6)$$
$$= 816.37$$

$$\text{LCL} = \overline{\overline{X}} - (A_2\overline{R})$$
$$= 812 - (0.729 \times 6)$$
$$= 807.63$$

Control limits for the range chart (R) were calculated as follows:
$$UCL = D_4 \times \overline{R}$$
$$= 2.282 \times 6$$
$$= 13.69$$

$$LCL = D_3\overline{R}$$
$$= 0 \times 6$$
$$= 0$$

After calculating these averages and limits for the control chart, the company regularly took samples of four bottles during production, recorded the measurements and plotted them as shown in Figure S17.8. The control chart revealed that only with difficulty could the process average be kept in control. Occasional operator interventions were required. Also the process range was moving towards (and once breaking) the upper control limit. The process seemed to be becoming more variable. After investigation it was discovered that, because of faulty maintenance of the line, skin cream was occasionally contaminating the torque head (the part of the line which fitted the cap). This resulted in erratic tightening of the caps.

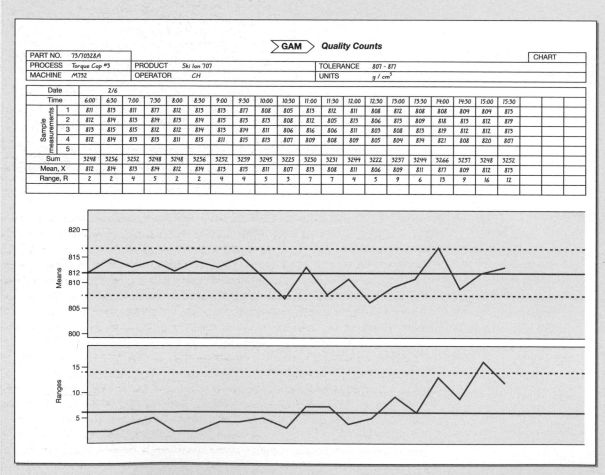

Figure S17.8 The completed control form for GAM's torque machine showing the mean ($\overline{X}$) and range ($\overline{R}$) charts

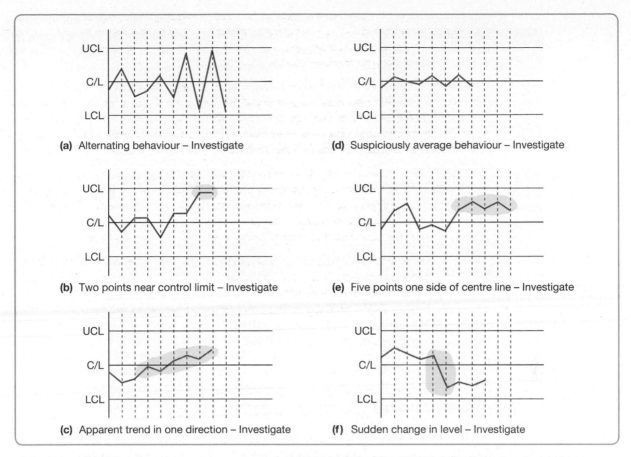

(a) Alternating behaviour – Investigate

(d) Suspiciously average behaviour – Investigate

(b) Two points near control limit – Investigate

(e) Five points one side of centre line – Investigate

(c) Apparent trend in one direction – Investigate

(f) Sudden change in level – Investigate

Figure S17.9 In addition to points falling outside the control limits, other unlikely sequences of points should be investigated

Interpreting control charts

Plots on a control chart which fall outside control limits are an obvious reason for believing that the process might be out of control, and therefore for investigating the process. This is not the only clue which could be revealed by a control chart, however. Figure S17.9 shows some other patterns which could be interpreted as behaviour sufficiently unusual to warrant investigation.

PROCESS CONTROL, LEARNING AND KNOWLEDGE

In recent years the role of process control, and SPC in particular, has changed. Increasingly, it is seen not just as a convenient method of keeping processes in control, but also as an activity which is fundamental to the acquisition of competitive advantage. This is a remarkable shift in the status of SPC. Traditionally it was seen as one of the most *operational*, immediate and 'hands-on' operations management techniques. Yet it is now being connected with an operation's *strategic* capabilities. This is how the logic of the argument goes:

> *** Operations principle**
> Statistical-based control gives the potential to enhance process knowledge.

1 SPC is based on the idea that process variability indicates whether a process is in control or not.
2 Processes are brought into *control* and improved by progressively reducing process variability. This involves eliminating the assignable causes of variation.

3 One cannot eliminate assignable causes of variation without gaining a better understanding of how the process operates. This involves *learning* about the process, where its nature is revealed at an increasingly detailed level.

4 This learning means that process knowledge is enhanced, which in turn means that operations managers are able to predict how the process will perform under different circumstances. It also means that the process has a greater capability to carry out its tasks at a higher level of performance.

5 This increased *process capability* is particularly difficult for competitors to copy. It cannot be bought 'off-the-shelf'. It only comes from time and effort being invested in controlling operations processes. Therefore, process capability leads to strategic advantage.

In this way, process control leads to learning which enhances process knowledge and builds difficult-to-imitate process capability.

SUMMARY

- Statistical process control (SPC) involves using control charts to track the performance of one or more quality characteristics in the operation. The power of control charting lies in its ability to set control limits derived from the statistics of the natural variation of processes. These control limits are often set at ± 3 standard deviations of the natural variation of the process samples.

- Control charts can be used for either attributes or variables. An attribute is a quality characteristic which has two states (for example, right or wrong). A variable is one which can be measured on a continuously variable scale.

- Process control charts allow operations managers to distinguish between the 'normal' variation inherent in any process and the variations which could be caused by the process going out of control.

SELECTED FURTHER READING

Woodall, W.H. (2000) Controversies and contradictions in statistical process control. Paper presented at the Journal of Quality Technology Session at the 44th Annual Fall Technical Conference of the Chemical and Process Industries Section and Statistics Section of the American Society for Quality and the Section on Physical & Engineering Sciences of the American Statistical Association in Minneapolis, Minnesota, 12–13 October, 2000. Academic but interesting.

USEFUL WEBSITES

www.asq.org The American Society for Quality site. Good professional insights.

Now that you have finished reading this chapter, why not visit MyOMLab at www.myomlab.com where you'll find more learning resources to help you make the most of your studies and get a better grade.

Source: Getty Images/Jasper James

Part Four
IMPROVEMENT

Even the best operation will need to improve because the operation's competitors will also be improving. This part of the book looks at how managers can make their operation perform better, how they can stop it failing, and how they can bring their improvement activities together.

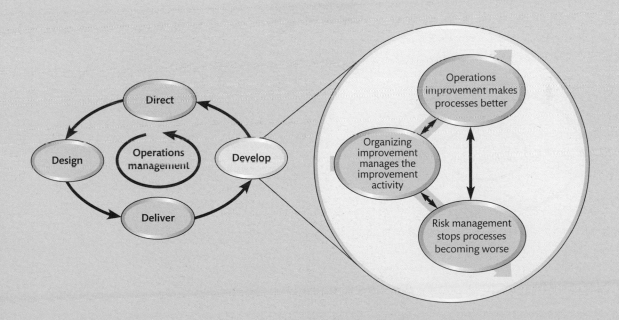

INTRODUCTION

Even when an operation's strategy is set, its design finalized and its deliveries planned and controlled, the operations manager's task is not finished. All operations, no matter how well managed, are capable of being improved. In fact, in recent years the emphasis amongst operations professionals has shifted markedly towards making improvement one of their main responsibilities. In this part of the book we treat improvement activities in three stages. First, this chapter looks at the elements commonly found in various improvement approaches, examines four of the more widely used approaches, shows how these approaches fit together, then illustrates some of the techniques which can be adopted to improve the operation. Second, Chapter 19 looks at improvement from another perspective, that is, how operations can improve by managing the risks of getting worse. Finally, Chapter 20 looks at how improvement activities can be organized, supported and implemented. These three stages are interrelated as shown in Figure 18.1.

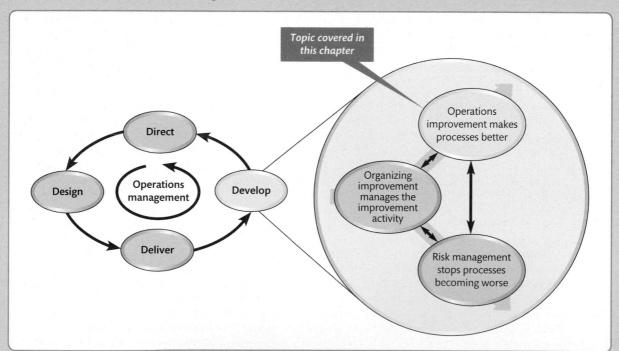

Figure 18.1 Operations improvement

Delivering global optimization at TNT[1]

When you are in the business of express parcel delivery, operations improvement is not an option; it's a necessity if you are going to survive. Customers tend to be less than understanding if their package is late, or, worse, doesn't arrive at all. Costs, especially fuel, are on a rising curve. Competitors are getting better all the time. Setting up a global network of hubs and routes takes immense amounts of capital, and because global networks are expensive to maintain, demand has to be kept high just to break even. In addition, increasingly society expects such companies to reduce their carbon emissions. So it's a 'no brainer': delivery operations must continually be reducing costs, improving levels of service to delight customers, and deploying its resources in a manner as close to optimum as possible. This is why TNT Express started the Global Optimization Programme (known as the GO Programme) to optimize its complete logistic chain. Within this programme TNT Express aims to improve how it makes vehicle routing, hub operations, scheduling and customer service decisions all over the world by sharing best practices of the different businesses and by developing its improvement methods.

TNT Express is a package delivery service with 80,000 employees, headquartered in the Netherlands, which operates air and road networks in Europe, China, South America, the Asia-Pacific region and the Middle East. Although the company had been achieving broadly acceptable cost and service levels of performance for a number of years, by 2005 the company realized that it was not making full use of the type of analytical quantitative modelling tools that its competitors, such as Federal Express and UPS, had been using for years. It became clear that TNT Express was very late in adopting such techniques by the standards of competitor companies. Yet some parts of the company *had* been engaged in using analytical improvement tools. In Italy, TNT Express had launched its drive to optimize how it used the domestic road network to improve operational performance. Using the success in Italy as a foundation, TNT Express decided to formalize the company's improvement efforts by establishing its Global Optimization (GO) project. Just as important was the company's decision that improvement through the use of analytics must not be relegated to the sidelines as the preserve of a few specialists, but that it should be at the core of the business. However, specialist help would clearly be needed, so the company partnered with ORTEC, providers of advanced planning and optimization software solutions. With experience in providing solutions that set out to optimize the kind of

Source: Alamy Images/Apex News and Pictures Agency

activities at the heart of TNT Express's operations, such as fleet routing and dispatch, vehicle and pallet loading, workforce scheduling, delivery forecasting, and network planning, ORTEC helped provide the 'analytical muscle' needed for such complex operations.

But operations improvement is not just a matter of solving analytical puzzles; it must also engage with people in the organization. To accomplish this, the company established two people-focused initiatives called 'the GO Communities of Practice' and 'the GO-Academy'. The GO Communities of Practice was a network of individuals who had similar responsibilities, but in different parts of the world. The Community of Practice groups meet around three times a year to learn from each other's experience in applying improvement analytics in various parts of the world, with sometimes different conditions. The GO-Academy was developed to overcome some degree of resistance to the improvement initiative (not unusual with such initiatives). The objective of the academy was *'to train employees in optimization principles and, at a high level, to acquaint them with the available optimization tools, without trying to turn them into mathematicians'*. Over a two-year period participants from throughout the company have been encouraged to promote and explain the improvement initiative throughout the organization. The academy's courses are run jointly with Tilburg University in the southern part of the Netherlands.

And has all this improvement effort been worthwhile? Very much so, says TNT Express. It carried out 200 network optimization projects in one year. In the seven years after the introduction of the GO initiative, operations' decision-making quality has significantly improved and resulted in €207 million in cost savings and saved 60 million kilometres of mileage and 54 million kg of CO_2 emissions.

WHY IS IMPROVEMENT SO IMPORTANT IN OPERATIONS MANAGEMENT?

Why is operations improvement so important? Well, who doesn't want to get better? And businesses are (or should be) just the same as people – they generally want to get better. Not just for the sake of their own excellence, although that may be one factor, but mainly because improving operations performance has such an impact on what any organization is there to do. Emergency services want to reach distressed people faster and treat them better because by doing so they are fulfilling their role more effectively. Package delivery businesses like TNT Express want to deliver more reliably, at lower cost and reducing emissions because it means happier customers, higher profits and less pollution. Development charities want to target their aid and campaign for improvement in human conditions as wisely and efficiently as possible because more money will find its way to beneficiaries rather than be wasted or consumed in administration. Not surprising then that the whole emphasis of operations management has shifted towards emphasizing improvement. Operations managers are judged not only on how they meet their ongoing responsibilities of producing products and services to acceptable levels of quality, speed, dependability, flexibility, and cost, but also on how they improve the performance of the operations function overall.

> **✳ Operations principle**
>
> Performance improvement is the ultimate objective of operations and process management.

Why the focus on improvement?

Various reasons have been suggested to explain the shift towards a focus on improvement in professional operations managers' activities:

- There is a perceived increase in the intensity of competitive pressures (or 'value for money' in not-for-profit or public sector operations). In fact, economists argue about whether markets are really getting more competitive. As far as improvement is concerned it doesn't matter; there is a *perception* of increased competitive pressure, and certainly the owners of operations (shareholders or governments) are less likely to tolerate poor returns or value for money.
- The nature of world trade is changing. Economies such as China, India and Brazil are emerging as both producers and consumers of products and services. This has had a number of effects that have impacted more developed economies. It has introduced cost pressures in countries with relatively expensive labour and infrastructure costs; it has introduced new challenges for global companies, such as managing complex supply chains; and it has accelerated demand for resources (materials, food, energy) pushing up (or destabilizing) prices for these commodities.
- New technology has both introduced opportunities to improve operations practice and disrupt existing markets. Look at how operations in the music business have had to adapt their working practices to downloading and music streaming.
- The interest in operations improvement has resulted in the development of many new ideas and approaches to improving operations which have, in turn, focused attention on improvement. The more ways there are to improve operations, the more operations will be improved.
- The scope of operations management has widened from a subject associated largely with manufacturing to one that embraces all types of enterprise and processes in all functions of the enterprise. Because of this extended scope, operations managers have seen how they can learn from each other, even if their operations and processes seem, at first glance, different.

The Red Queen effect

In 1973 the scientist Leigh Van Valen was looking to describe a discovery that he had made while studying marine fossils. He had established that, no matter how long a family of animals had already existed, the probability that the family will become extinct is unaffected. In other words, the struggle for survival never gets easier. However well a species fits with its environment, it can never relax. The analogy that Van Valen drew came from *Alice's Adventures through the Looking Glass* by Lewis Carroll. In the book, Alice encounters living chess pieces and, in particular, the 'Red Queen'.

> *'Well, in our country,'* said Alice, still panting a little, *'you'd generally get to somewhere else – if you ran very fast for a long time, as we've been doing'. 'A slow sort of country!'* said the Queen. *'Now, here, you see, it takes all the running you can do, to keep in the same place. If you want to get somewhere else, you must run at least twice as fast as that!'*[2]

In many respects this is like business. Improvements and innovations may be imitated or countered by competitors. For example, in the automotive sector, the quality of most firms' products is very significantly better than it was two decades ago. This reflects the improvement in those firm's operations processes. Yet their relative competitive position has in many cases not changed. Those firms that have improved their competitive position have improved their operations performance *more than* competitors. Where improvement has simply matched that of competitors, survival has been the main benefit. The implications for operations improvement are clear. It is even more important, especially when competitors are actively improving their operations.

An important distinction in the approach taken by individual operations is that between radical or 'breakthrough' improvement, on one hand, and continuous or 'incremental' improvement on the other.

Radical or breakthrough change

Radical breakthrough improvement (or 'innovation'-based improvement, as it is sometimes called) is a philosophy that assumes that the main vehicle of improvement is major and dramatic change in the way the operation works. The introduction of a new, more efficient machine in a factory, the total redesign of a computer-based hotel reservation system, and the introduction of an improved degree programme at a university are all examples of breakthrough improvement. The impact of these improvements is relatively sudden, abrupt and represents a step change in practice (and hopefully performance). Such improvements are rarely inexpensive, usually calling for high investment of capital, often disrupting the ongoing workings of the operation, and frequently involving changes in the product/service or process technology. The bold line in Figure 18.2(a) illustrates the pattern of performance with several breakthrough improvements. The improvement pattern illustrated by the dotted line in Figure 18.2(a) is regarded by some as being more representative of what really occurs when operations rely on pure breakthrough improvement. Breakthrough improvement places a high value on creative solutions. It encourages free thinking and individualism. It is a radical philosophy insomuch as it fosters an approach to improvement which does not accept many constraints on what is possible. 'Starting with a clean sheet of paper', 'going back to first principles' and 'completely rethinking the system' are all typical breakthrough improvement principles.

> *** Operations principle**
> Performance improvement sometimes requires radical change.

Continuous or incremental improvement

Continuous improvement, as the name implies, adopts an approach to improving performance which assumes many small incremental improvement steps. For example, modifying the way a product is fixed to a machine to reduce changeover time, simplifying the question sequence when taking a hotel reservation, and rescheduling the assignment completion dates on a university course so as to smooth the students' workload are all examples of incremental improvements. While there is no guarantee that such small steps towards better performance will be followed by other steps, the whole philosophy of continuous improvement attempts to ensure that they will be. Continuous improvement is not concerned with promoting small improvements *per se*. It does view small improvements, however, as having one significant advantage over large ones – they can be followed relatively painlessly by other small improvements (*see* Fig. 18.2(b)). Continuous improvement is also known as kaizen. Kaizen is a Japanese

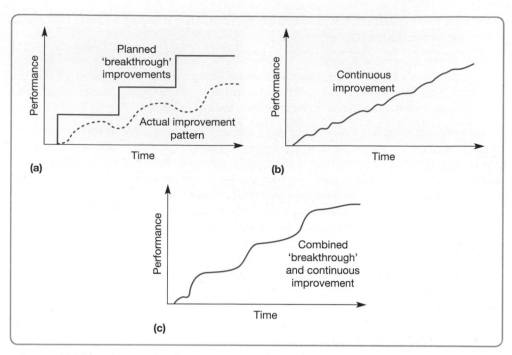

Figure 18.2 (a) 'Breakthrough' improvement, (b) 'continuous' improvement and (c) combined improvement patterns

word, the definition of which is given by Masaaki Imai[3] (who has been one of the main proponents of continuous improvement) as follows: '*Kaizen means improvement. Moreover, it means improvement in personal life, home life, social life and work life. When applied to the workplace, kaizen means continuing improvement involving everyone – managers and workers alike.*'

In continuous improvement it is not the *rate* of improvement which is important; it is the *momentum* of improvement. It does not matter if successive improvements are small; what does matter is that every month (or week, or quarter, or whatever period is appropriate) some kind of improvement has actually taken place.

The structure of improvement ideas

There have been hundreds of ideas relating to operations improvement that have been proposed over the last few decades. To understand how these ideas relate to each other it is important to distinguish between:

- The broad approaches to improvement – some improvement approaches have been used for over a century (for example, some work study approaches, see Chapter 9), while others are relatively recent (for example, Six Sigma, explained later).
- The elements contained within improvement approaches – do not think that approaches to improvement are different in all respects. There are many elements that are common to several approaches.
- The improvement techniques – there are many 'step-by-step' techniques and tools that can be used to find improved ways of doing things; some of these use quantitative modelling and others are more qualitative.

Improvement methodologies are often associated with repetitive operations. Performing the same task repeatedly means that there are plenty of opportunities to 'get it right'. The whole idea behind continuous improvement derives from this simple idea. By contrast operations that have to perform more difficult activities, especially those that call for expert judgement and diagnostic ability, must call for equally complex improvement approaches, right? Well, no, according to Atul Gawande, a physician at the prestigious Johns Hopkins Hospital. Mr Gawande thinks that the very opposite is true. Although medicine is advancing at an astounding rate and medical journals produce learned papers adding the results of advanced research to an ever-expanding pool of knowledge, the medical profession overall does not always have a reliable method for learning from its mistakes. Atul Gawande's idea is that his, and similar 'knowledge-based' professions, are in danger of sinking under the weight of facts. Scientists are accumulating more and more information and professions are fragmenting into ever narrower specialisms.

Mr Gawande tells the story of Peter Pronovost, a specialist in critical care at Johns Hopkins Hospital, who in 2001 tried to reduce the number of patients who were becoming infected on account of the use of intravenous central lines. There are five steps that medical teams can take to reduce the chances of contracting such infections. Initially Pronovost simply asked nurses to observe whether doctors took the five steps. What they found was that, at least a third of the time, they missed one or more of the steps. So nurses were authorized to stop doctors who had missed out any of the steps, and, as a matter of course, ask whether existing intravenous central lines should be reviewed. As a result of applying these simple checklist-style rules, the ten-day line-infection rates went down from 11 per cent to zero. In one hospital, it was calculated that, over a year, this simple method had prevented 43 infections, 8 deaths and saved about $2 million. Using the same checklist approach the hospital identified and applied the method to other activities. For example, a check in which nurses asked patients about their pain levels led to untreated pain reducing from 41 per cent to 3 per cent. Similarly, the simple checklists method helped the average length of patient stay in intensive care to fall by half. When Pronovost's approach was adopted by other hospitals, within 18 months, 1,500 lives and $175 million had been saved.

Mr Gawande describes checklists used in this way as a 'cognitive net' – a mechanism that can help prevent experienced people from making errors due to flawed memory and attention, and ensure that teams work together. Simple checklists are common in other professions. Civil engineers use them to make certain that complicated structures are assembled on schedule. Chefs use them to make sure that food is prepared exactly to the customers' taste. Airlines use them to make sure that pilots take off safely and also to learn from, now relatively rare, crashes. Indeed, Mr Gawande is happy to acknowledge that checklists are not a new idea. He tells the story of the prototype of the Boeing B17 Flying Fortress that crashed after take-off on its trial flight in 1935. Most experts said that the bomber was 'too complex to fly'. Facing bankruptcy, Boeing investigated and discovered that, confronted with four engines rather than two, the pilot forgot to release a vital locking mechanism. But Boeing created a pilot's checklist, in which the fundamental actions for the stages of flying were made a mandated part of the pilot's job. In the following years, B17s flew almost 2 million miles without a single accident. Even for pilots, many of whom are rugged individualists, says Mr Gawande, it is usually the application of routine procedures that saves planes when things go wrong, rather than 'hero-pilotry' so fêted by the media. It is discipline rather than brilliance that preserves life. In fact, it is discipline that leaves room for brilliance to flourish.

The best way to understand improvement is to deal with the elements contained within improvement approaches first, see how they come together to form broad approaches to improvement, and then examine some typical improvement techniques.

The section following that (see pages 588–598) will then show how these elements are combined to form different improvement approaches.

THE KEY ELEMENTS OF OPERATIONS IMPROVEMENT

The elements of improvement are the individual basic fundamental ideas of improvement. Think of these elements of improvement as the building blocks of the various improvement approaches that we shall look at later. Here we explain some, but not all (there are lots), of the more common elements in use today.

Improvement cycles

An important element within some improvement approaches is the use of a literally never-ending process of repeatedly questioning and re-questioning the detailed working of a process or activity. This repeated and cyclical questioning is usually summarized by the idea of the improvement cycle, of which there are many, but two are widely used models – the PDCA cycle (sometimes called the Deming Cycle, named after the famous quality 'guru', W.E. Deming) and the DMAIC (pronounced De-Make) cycle, made popular by the Six Sigma approach (see later). The PDCA cycle model is shown in Figure 18.3(a). It starts with the P (for plan) stage, which involves an examination of the current method or the problem area being studied. This involves collecting and analysing data so as to formulate a plan of action which is intended to improve performance. Once a plan for improvement has been agreed, the next step is the D (for do) stage. This is the implementation stage during which the plan is tried out in the operation. This stage may itself involve a mini-PDCA cycle as the problems of implementation are resolved. Next comes the C (for check) stage where the new implemented solution is evaluated to see whether it has resulted in the expected performance improvement. Finally, at least for this cycle, comes the A (for act) stage. During this stage the change is consolidated or standardized if it has been successful. Alternatively, if the change has not been successful, the lessons learned from the 'trial' are formalized before the cycle starts again.

The DMAIC cycle is in some ways more intuitively obvious than the PDCA cycle insomuch as it follows a more 'experimental' approach. The DMAIC cycle starts with (D), defining the problem or problems, partly to understand the scope of what needs to be done and partly to define exactly the requirements of the process improvement. Often at this stage a formal goal or target for the improvement is set. After definition comes (M), the measurement stage. This stage involves validating the problem to make sure that it really is a problem worth solving, using data to refine the problem and measuring exactly what is happening. Once these measurements have been established, they can be (A), analysed. The analysis stage is sometimes seen as an opportunity to develop hypotheses as to what the root causes of the problem really are. Such hypotheses are

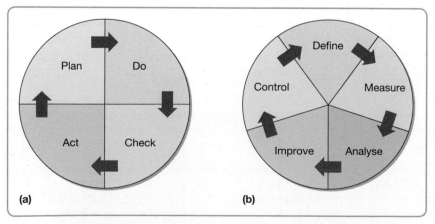

Figure 18.3 (a) The plan–do–check–act, or 'Deming' improvement cycle, and (b) the define–measure–analyse–improve–control, or DMAIC Six-Sigma improvement cycle

validated (or not) by the analysis and the main root causes of the problem identified. Once the causes of the problem are identified, work can begin on (I), improving the process. Ideas are developed to remove the root causes of problems, solutions are tested and those solutions that seem to work are implemented, formalized and results measured. The improved process needs then to be continually monitored and (C), controlled, to check that the improved level of performance is sustained. After this point the cycle starts again and defines the problems which are preventing further improvement. Remember though, it is the last point about both cycles that is the most important – the cycle starts again. It is only by accepting that in a continuous improvement philosophy these cycles quite literally never stop that improvement becomes part of every person's job.

A process perspective

Even if some improvement approaches do not explicitly or formally include the idea that taking a process perspective should be central to operations improvement, almost all do so implicitly. This has two major advantages. First, it means that improvement can be focused on what actually happens rather than which part of the organization has responsibility for what happens. In other words, if improvement is not reflected in the process of creating products and services, then it is not really improvement as such. Second, as we have mentioned before, all parts of the business manage processes. This is what we call operations as activity rather than operations as a function. So, if improvement is described in terms of how processes can be made more effective, those messages will have relevance for all the other functions of the business in addition to the operations function.

End-to-end processes

Some improvement approaches take the process perspective further and prescribe exactly how processes should be organized. One of the more radical prescriptions of Business Process Re-engineering (BPR, see later), for example, is the idea that operations should be organized around the total process which adds value for customers, rather than the functions or activities which perform the various stages of the value-adding activity. We have already pointed out the difference between conventional processes within a specialist function, and an end-to-end business process (in Chapter 1). Identified customer needs are entirely fulfilled by an 'end-to-end' business process. In fact the processes are designed specifically to do this, which is why they will often cut across conventional organizational boundaries. Figure 18.4 illustrates this idea.

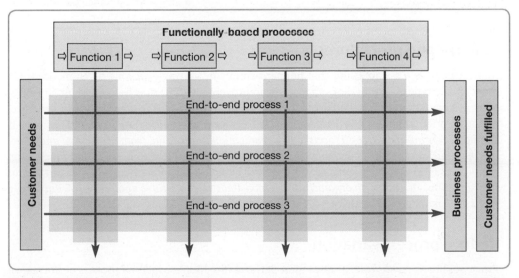

Figure 18.4 BPR advocates reorganizing (re-engineering) micro operations to reflect the natural customer-focused business processes

Evidence-based problem-solving

In recent years there has been a resurgence of the use of quantitative techniques in improvement approaches. Six Sigma (see later) in particular promotes systematic use of (preferably quantitative) evidence. Yet Six Sigma is not the first of the improvement approaches to use quantitative methods (some of the TQM gurus promoted statistical process control, for example), although it has done a lot to emphasize the use of quantitative evidence. In fact much of the considerable training required by Six Sigma consultants is devoted to mastering quantitative analytical techniques. However, the statistical methods used in improvement activities do not always reflect conventional academic statistical knowledge as such. They emphasize observational methods of collecting data and the use of experimentation to examine hypotheses. Techniques include graphical methods, analysis of variance, and two-level factorial experiment design. Underlying the use of these techniques is an emphasis on the scientific method, responding only to hard evidence, and using statistical software to facilitate analysis.

Customer centricity

There is little point in improvement unless it meets the requirements of the customers. However, in most improvement approaches, meeting the expectations of customers means more than this. It involves the whole organization in understanding the central importance of customers to its success and even to its survival. Customers are seen, not as being external to the organization, but as the most important part of it. However, the idea of being customer-centric does not mean that customers must be provided with everything that they want. Although 'What's good for customers' may frequently be the same as 'What's good for the business', it is not always. Operations managers are always having to strike a balance between what customers would like and what the operation can afford (or wants) to do.

Voice of the customer (VOC)

The 'voice of the customer' (VOC) is an idea that is closely related to the idea of customer centricity. The term means capturing a customer's requirements, expectations, perceptions and preferences in some depth. Sometimes a VOC exercise is done as part of new service and product development as part of Quality Function Deployment (QFD) (explained in Chapter 5). Sometimes it is part of a more general improvement activity. There are several ways to do this, but it usually involves using market research to derive a comprehensive set of customer requirements, which is ordered into a hierarchical structure, often prioritized to indicate the relative importance of different aspects of operations performance.

Systems and procedures

Improvement is not something that happens simply by getting everyone to 'think improvement'. Some type of system that supports the improvement effort may be needed. An improvement system (sometimes called a 'quality system') is defined as: *'the organizational structure, responsibilities, procedures, processes and resources for implementing quality management.*[5] It should . . . *define and cover all facets of an organization's operation, from identifying and meeting the needs and requirements of customers, design, planning, purchasing, manufacturing, packaging, storage, delivery and service, together with all relevant activities carried out within these functions. It deals with organization, responsibilities, procedures and processes. Put simply* [it] *is good management practice.*[6]

Reduce process variation

Processes change over time, as does their performance. Some aspect of process performance (usually an important one) is measured periodically (either as a single measurement or as a small sample of measurements). These are then plotted on a simple timescale. This has a number of advantages. The first is to check that the performance of the process is, in itself, acceptable (capable). They can also be used to check if process performance is changing over time, and to check on the extent of the variation in process performance. Earlier (in Chapter 17) we illustrated how random variation in the performance of any process could obscure what was really happening within the process. So a potentially useful method of identifying improvement opportunities is to try and identify the sources of random variation in process performance. Statistical process control is one way of doing this.

Synchronized flow

This is another idea that we have seen before (in Chapter 15, as part of the lean philosophy). Synchronized flow means that items in a process, operation or supply network flow smoothly and with even velocity from start to finish. This is a function of how inventory accumulates within the operation. Whether inventory is accumulated in order to smooth differences between demand and supply, or as a contingency against unexpected delays, or simply to batch for purposes of processing or movement, it all means that flow becomes asynchronous. It waits as inventory rather than progressing smoothly on. Once a state of perfect synchronization of flow has been achieved, it becomes easier to expose any irregularities of flow which may be the symptoms of more deep-rooted underlying problems.

Emphasize education/training

Several improvement approaches stress the idea that structured training and organization of improvement should be central to improvement. Not only should the techniques of improvement be fully understood by everyone engaged in the improvement process, the business and organizational context of improvement should also be understood. After all, how can one improve without knowing what kind of improvement would best benefit the organization and its customers? Furthermore, education and training has an important part to play in motivating all staff towards seeing improvement as a worthwhile activity. Some improvement approaches in particular place great emphasis on formal education. Six Sigma, for example (see later), and its proponents often mandate a minimum level of training (measured in hours) that they deem necessary before improvement projects should be undertaken.

Perfection is the goal

Almost all organization-wide improvement programmes will have some kind of goal or target that the improvement effort should achieve. And while targets can be set in many different ways, some improvement authorities hold that measuring process performance against some kind of absolute target does most for encouraging improvement. An 'absolute target' literally means the theoretical level of perfection – for example, zero errors, instant delivery, delivery absolutely when promised, infinite flexibility, zero waste, etc. Of course, in reality such perfection may never be achievable. That is not the point. What is important is that current performance can be calibrated against this target of perfection in order to indicate how much more improvement is possible. Improving (for example) delivery accuracy by 5 per cent may seem good until it is realized that only an improvement of 30 per cent would eliminate all late deliveries.

Waste identification

All improvement approaches aspire to eliminate waste. In fact, any improvement implies that some waste has been eliminated, where waste is any activity that does not add value. But the identification and elimination of waste is sometimes a central feature. For example (as we discussed in Chapter 15) it is arguably the most significant part of the lean philosophy.

Include everybody

Harnessing the skills and enthusiasm of every person and all parts of the organization seems an obvious principle of improvement. The phrase 'quality at source' is sometimes used, stressing the impact that each individual has on improvement. The contribution of all individuals in the organization may go beyond understanding their contribution to 'not make mistakes'. Individuals are expected to bring something positive to improving the way they perform their jobs. The principles of 'empowerment' are frequently cited as supporting this aspect of improvement. When Japanese improvement practices first began to migrate in the late 1970s, this idea seemed even more radical. Yet now it is generally accepted that individual creativity and effort from all staff represents a valuable source of development. However, not all improvement approaches have adopted this idea. Some authorities believe that a small number of internal improvement consultants or specialists offer a better method of organizing improvement. However, these two ideas are not incompatible. Even with improvement specialists used to lead improvement efforts, the staff who actually operate the process can still be used as a valuable source of information and improvement ideas.

Develop internal customer–supplier relationships

One of the best ways to ensure that external customers are satisfied is to establish the idea that every part of the organization contributes to external customer satisfaction by satisfying its own internal customers. This idea was introduced in earlier, as was the related concept of service level agreements (SLAs) (Chapter 17). It means stressing that each process in an operation has a responsibility to manage these internal customer–supplier relationships. They do this primarily by defining as clearly as possible what their own and their customers' *requirements* are. In effect this means defining what constitutes 'error-free' service – the quality, speed, dependability and flexibility required by internal customers.

THE BROAD APPROACHES TO MANAGING IMPROVEMENT

Many of the elements described above are present in one or more of the commonly used approaches to improvement. Some of these approaches have already been described. For

> **✳ Operations principle**
>
> There is no one universal approach to improvement.

example, both lean (Chapter 15) and TQM (Chapter 17) have been discussed in some detail. In this section we will briefly re-examine TQM and lean, specifically from an improvement perspective, and also add two further approaches – Business Process Re-engineering (BPR) and Six Sigma.

Total quality management as an improvement approach

Total quality management was one of the earliest management 'fashions'. Its peak of popularity was in the late 80s and early 90s. As such it has suffered from something of a backlash in recent years. Yet the general precepts and principles that constitute TQM are still hugely influential. Few, if any, managers have not heard of TQM and its impact on improvement. Indeed, TQM has come to be seen as an approach to the way operations and processes should be managed and improved, generally. Even if TQM is not the label given to an improvement initiative, many of its elements will almost certainly have become routine. It is best thought of as a philosophy of how to approach improvement. This philosophy, above everything, stresses the 'total' of TQM. It is an approach that puts quality (and indeed improvement generally) at the heart of everything that is done by an operation. As a reminder, this totality can be summarized by the way TQM lays particular stress on the following elements (see Chapter 17):

- meeting the needs and expectations of customers;
- improvement covers all parts of the organization (and should be group-based);

Heineken International produces and sells beer around the world with growing sales, especially in its Heineken and Amstel brands. However, sales growth can put pressure on any company's operations. For example, Heineken's Zoeterwoude facility, a packaging plant that fills bottles and cans in the Netherlands, has had to increase its volume by between 8 and 10 per cent per year on a regular basis. In a competitive market, the company faced two challenges. First, it needed to improve its operations processes to reduce its costs. Second, because it would have taken a year to build a new packaging line, it needed to improve the efficiency of its existing lines in order to increase its capacity. So, improving line efficiency was vital if the plant was to cut its costs and create the extra capacity it needed to delay investment in a new packaging line.

Source: Shutterstock.com/Valentyn Volkov

The objective of the improvement project was to improve the plant's operational equipment efficiency (OEE) (see Chapter 11 for a discussion of OEE) by 20 per cent. Setting a target of 20 per cent was seen as important because it was challenging yet achievable, as well as meeting the cost and capacity objectives of the project. It was also decided to focus the improvement project around two themes: (a) obtaining accurate operational data that could be converted into useful business information on which improvement decisions could be based; and (b) changing the culture of the operation to promote fast and effective decision making. This would help people at all levels in the plant to have access to accurate and up-to-date information as well as encouraging staff to focus on the improvement of how they do their job rather than just 'doing the job'. Before the improvement, project staff at the Zoeterwoude plant had approached problem-solving as an ad hoc activity, only to be done when circumstances made it unavoidable. By contrast, the improvement initiative taught the staff on each packaging line to use various problem-solving techniques such as cause-effect and Pareto diagrams (discussed later in this chapter). Other techniques included the analysis of improved equipment maintenance and failure mode and effective analysis (FMEA). (Both are discussed in Chapter 19.)

'Until we started using these techniques', says Wilbert Raaijmakers, Heineken Netherlands Brewery Director, 'there was little consent regarding what was causing any problems. There was poor communication between the various departments and job grades. For example, maintenance staff believed that production stops were caused by operating errors, while operators were of the opinion that poor maintenance was the cause.' The use of better information, analysis and improvement techniques helped the staff to identify and treat the root causes of problems. With many potential improvements to make, staff teams were encouraged to set priorities that would reflect the overall improvement target. There was also widespread use of benchmarking performance against targets periodically so that progress could be reviewed.

At the end of 12 months the improvement project had achieved its objectives of a 20 per cent improvement in OEE, not just for one packaging line but for all nine. This allowed the plant to increase the volume of its exports and cut its costs significantly. Not only that, but other aspects of the plant's performance improved. Up to that point, the plant had gained a reputation for poor delivery dependability. After the project it was seen by the other operations in its supply chain as a much more reliable partner. Yet Wilbert Raaijmakers still sees room for improvement. 'The optimization of an organization is a never-ending process. If you sit back and do the same thing tomorrow as you did today, you'll never make it. We must remain alert to the latest developments and stress the resulting information to its full potential.'

- improvement includes every person in the organization (and success is recognized);
- including all costs of quality;
- getting things 'right first time', i.e. designing-in quality rather than inspecting it in;
- developing the systems and procedures which support improvement.

Lean as an improvement approach

The idea of 'lean' spread beyond its Japanese roots and became fashionable in the West at about the same time as TQM. And although its popularity has not declined to the same extent as TQM, over 25 years of experience have diminished the excitement once associated with the approach. But, unlike TQM, it was seen initially as an approach to be used exclusively in manufacturing. Now, lean has become fashionable as an approach that can be applied in service operations. As a reminder (see Chapter 15), the lean approach aims to meet demand instantaneously, with perfect quality and no waste. The key elements of the lean when used as an improvement approach are as follows:

- customer-centricity;
- internal customer–supplier relationships;
- perfection is the goal;
- synchronized flow;
- reduce variation;
- include all people;
- waste elimination.

Some organizations, especially now that lean is being applied more widely in service operations, view waste elimination as the most important of all the elements of the lean approach. In fact, they sometimes see the lean approach as consisting almost exclusively of waste elimination. What they fail to realize is that effective waste elimination is best achieved through changes in behaviour. It is the behavioural change brought about through synchronized flow and customer triggering that provides the window onto exposing and eliminating waste.

Business process re-engineering (BPR)

The idea of business process re-engineering originated in the early 1990s when Michael Hammer proposed that, rather than using technology to automate work, it would be better applied to doing away with the need for the work in the first place ('don't automate, obliterate'). In doing this he was warning against establishing non-value-added work within an information technology system where it would be even more difficult to identify and eliminate. All work, he said, should be examined for whether it adds value for the customer and if not processes should be redesigned to eliminate it. In doing this BPR was echoing similar objectives in both scientific management and, more recently, lean approaches. But BPR, unlike those two earlier approaches, advocated radical changes rather than incremental changes to processes. Shortly after Hammer's article, other authors developed the ideas, again the majority of them stressing the importance of a radical approach to elimination of non-value-added work.

BPR has been defined as:[8] '*the fundamental rethinking and radical redesign of business processes to achieve dramatic improvements in critical, contemporary measures of performance, such as cost, quality, service and speed*'. But there is far more to it than that. In fact, BPR was a blend of a number of ideas which had been current in operations management for some time. Lean concepts, process flow charting, critical examination in method study, operations network management and customer-focused operations all contribute to the BPR concept. It was the potential of information technologies to enable the fundamental redesign of processes, however, which acted as the catalyst in bringing these ideas together. It was the information technology that allowed radical process redesign, even if many of the methods used to achieve the redesign had been explored before. The main principles of BPR can be summarized in the following points:

- Rethink business processes in a cross-functional manner which organizes work around the natural flow of information (or materials or customers).
- Strive for dramatic improvements in performance by radically rethinking and redesigning the process.
- Have those who use the output from a process perform the process. Check to see if all internal customers can be their own supplier rather than depending on another function

in the business to supply them (which takes longer and separates out the stages in the process).

● Put decision points where the work is performed. Do not separate those who do the work from those who control and manage the work.

Example[9]

We can illustrate this idea of reorganizing (or re-engineering) around business processes through the following simple example. Figure 18.5(a) shows the traditional organization of a trading company which purchases consumer goods from several suppliers, stores them, and

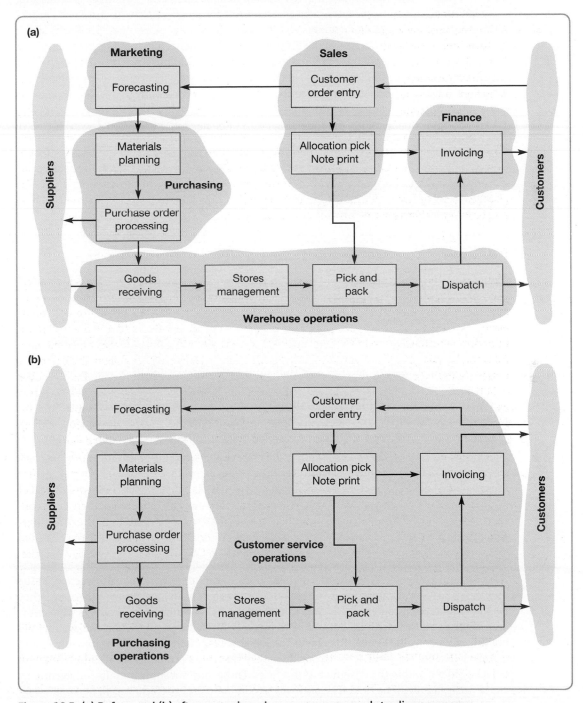

Figure 18.5 (a) Before and (b) after re-engineering a consumer goods trading company

sells them on to retail outlets. At the heart of the operation is the warehouse which receives the goods, stores them, and packs and dispatches them when they are required by customers. Orders for more stock are placed by Purchasing which also takes charge of materials planning and stock control. Purchasing buys the goods based on a forecast which is prepared by Marketing, which takes advice from the Sales department which is processing customers' orders. When a customer does place an order, it is the Sales department's job to instruct the warehouse to pack and dispatch the order and tell the Finance department to invoice the customer for the goods. So, traditionally, five departments (each a micro-operation) have between them organized the flow of materials and information within the total operation. But at each interface between the departments there is the possibility of errors and miscommunication arising. Furthermore, *who is responsible for looking after the customer's needs?* Currently, three separate departments all have dealings with the customer. Similarly, *who is responsible for liaising with suppliers?* This time two departments have contact with suppliers.

Eventually the company reorganized around two essential business processes. The first process (called purchasing operations) dealt with everything concerning relationships with suppliers. It was this process's focused and unambiguous responsibility to develop good working relationships with suppliers. The other business process (called customer service operations) had total responsibility for satisfying customers' needs. This included speaking 'with one voice' to the customer.

Critical commentary

BPR has aroused considerable controversy, mainly because BPR sometimes looks only at work activities rather than at the people who perform the work. Because of this, people become 'cogs in a machine'. Many of these critics equate BPR with the much earlier principles of scientific management, pejoratively known as 'Taylorism'. Generally these critics mean that BPR is overly harsh in the way it views human resources. Certainly there is evidence that BPR is often accompanied by a significant reduction in staff. Studies at the time when BPR was at its peak often revealed that the majority of BPR projects could reduce staff levels by over 20 per cent. Often BPR was viewed as merely an excuse for getting rid of staff. Companies that wished to 'downsize' were using BPR as the pretext, putting the short-term interests of the shareholders of the company above either their longer-term interests or the interests of the company's employees. Moreover, a combination of radical redesign together with downsizing could mean that the essential core of experience was lost from the operation. This left it vulnerable to any marked turbulence since it no longer possessed the knowledge and experience of how to cope with unexpected changes.

Six Sigma

The Six Sigma approach was first popularized by Motorola, the electronics and communications systems company. When it set its quality objective as 'total customer satisfaction' in the 1980s, it started to explore what the slogan would mean to its operations processes. They decided that true customer satisfaction would only be achieved when its products were delivered when promised, with no defects, with no early-life failures, and when the product did not fail excessively in service. To achieve this, Motorola initially focused on removing manufacturing defects. However, it soon came to realize that many problems were caused by latent defects, hidden within the design of its products. These may not show initially but eventually could cause failure in the field. The only way to eliminate these defects was to make sure that design specifications were tight (i.e. narrow tolerances) and its processes very capable.

Motorola's Six Sigma quality concept was so named because it required the natural variation of processes (± 3 standard deviations) to be half their specification range. In other words, the specification range of any part of a product or service should be ± 6 the standard deviation of the process (see Chapter 17). The Greek letter sigma (σ) is often used to indicate the standard deviation of a process, hence the Six Sigma label. Figure 18.6 illustrates the effect of progressively narrowing process variation on the number of defects produced by the process, in terms of defects per million. The defects per million measure is used within the Six Sigma approach to emphasize the drive towards a virtually zero defect objective.[10] Now the definition of Six Sigma has widened to well beyond this rather narrow statistical perspective. General Electric (GE), who were probably the best known of the early adopters of Six Sigma, defined it as '*A disciplined methodology of defining, measuring, analysing, improving, and controlling the quality in every one of the company's products, processes, and transactions – with the ultimate goal of virtually eliminating all defects.*' So, now Six Sigma should be seen as a broad improvement concept rather than a simple examination of process variation, even though this is still an important part of process control, learning and improvement.

Measuring performance

The Six Sigma approach uses a number of related measures to assess the performance of operations processes.

- **A defect** is a failure to meet customer required performance (defining performance measures from a customer's perspective is an important part of the Six Sigma approach).
- **A defect unit or item** is any unit of output that contains a defect (i.e. only units of output with no defects are not defective; defective units will have one or more than one defects).
- **A defect opportunity** is the number of different ways a unit of output can fail to meet customer requirements (simple products or services will have few defect opportunities, but very complex products or services may have hundreds of different ways of being defective).
- **Proportion defective** is the percentage or fraction of units that have one or more defect.
- **Process yield** is the percentage or fraction of total units produced by a process that are defect free (i.e. $1 -$ proportion defective).
- **Defect per unit (DPU)** is the average number of defects on a unit of output (the number of defects divided by the number of items produced).
- **Defects per opportunity** is the proportion or percentage of defects divided by the total number of defect opportunities (the number of defects divided by (the number items produced $\times$ the number of opportunities per item)).
- **Defects per million opportunities (DPMO)** is exactly what it says, the number of defects which the process will produce if there were one million opportunities to do so.
- **The Sigma measurement**[11] is derived from the DPMO and is the number of standard deviations of the process variability that will fit within the customer specification limits.

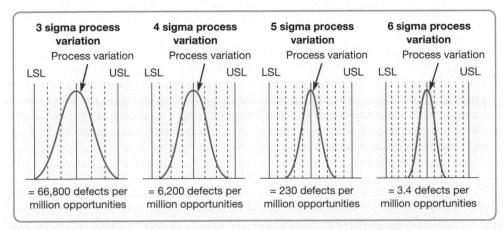

Figure 18.6 Process variation and its impact on process defects per million

An insurance process checks details of insurance claims and arranges for customers to be paid. It samples 300 claims at random at the end of the process. They find that 51 claims had one or more defects and there were 74 defects in total. Four types of error were observed, coding errors, policy conditions errors, liability errors and notification errors.

$$\text{Proportion defective} = \frac{\text{Number of defects}}{\text{Number of units processed}}$$

$$= \frac{51}{300} = 0.17 \ (17\% \text{ defective})$$

$$\text{Yield} = 1 - \text{proportion of defectives}$$

$$= 1 - 0.17 = 0.83 \text{ or } (83\% \text{ yield})$$

$$\text{Defects per unit} = \frac{\text{Number of defects}}{\text{Numer of units processed}}$$

$$= \frac{74}{300} = 0.247 \ (\text{or } 24.7) \text{ DPU}$$

$$\text{Defects per opportunity} = \frac{\text{Number of defects}}{\text{Number of units produced} \times \text{Number of opportunities}}$$

$$= \frac{74}{300 \times 4} = 0.062 \text{ DPO}$$

$$\text{Defects per million opportunities} = \text{DPO} \times 10^6$$

$$= 62{,}000 \text{ DPMO}$$

Although the scope of Six Sigma is disputed, elements frequently associated with Six Sigma include the following:

- **Customer-driven objectives.** Six Sigma is sometimes defined as 'the process of comparing process outputs against customer requirements'. It uses a number of measures to assess the performance of operations processes. In particular it expresses performance in terms of defects per million opportunities (DPMO).
- **Use of evidence.** Although Six Sigma is not the first of the new approaches to operations to use statistical methods it has done a lot to emphasize the use of quantitative evidence.
- **Structured improvement cycle.** The structured improvement cycle used in Six Sigma is the DMAIC cycle.
- **Process capability and control.** Not surprisingly, given its origins, process capability and control is important within the Six Sigma approach.
- **Process design.** Latterly Six Sigma proponents also include process design into the collection of elements that define the Six Sigma approach.
- **Structured training and organization of improvement.** The Six Sigma approach holds that improvement initiatives can only be successful if significant resources and training are devoted to their management.

The 'martial arts' analogy

The terms that have become associated with Six Sigma experts (and denote their level of expertise) are, Master Black Belt, Black Belt and Green Belt. Master Black Belts are experts in the use of Six Sigma tools and techniques as well as how such techniques can be used and implemented. Primarily Master Black Belts are seen as teachers who can not only guide improvement projects, but also coach and mentor Black Belts and Green Belts who are closer to the day-to-day improvement activity. They are expected to have the quantitative analytical skills to help with Six Sigma techniques and also the organizational and interpersonal skills to teach and mentor. Given their responsibilities, it is expected that Master Black Belts are employed full-time on their improvement activities. Black Belts can take a direct hand in organizing improvement teams. Like Master Black Belts, Black Belts are expected to develop their quantitative analytical skills and also act as coaches for Green Belts. Black Belts are dedicated full-time to improvement, and although opinions vary on how many Black Belts should be employed in an operation, some organizations recommend one Black Belt for every hundred employees. Green Belts work within improvement teams, possibly as team leaders. They have significant amounts of training, although less than Black Belts. Green Belts are not full-time positions; they have normal day-to-day process responsibilities but are expected to spend at least 20 per cent of their time on improvement projects.

SHORT CASE   Six Sigma at Xchanging[12]

'I think Six Sigma is powerful because of its definition; it is the process of comparing process outputs against customer requirements. Processes operating at less than 3.4 defects per million opportunities means that you must strive to get closer to perfection and it is the customer that defines the goal. Measuring defects per opportunity means that you can actually compare the process of, say, a human resources process with a billing and collection process.' Paul Ruggier, Head of Process at Xchanging, is a powerful advocate of Six Sigma, and credits the success of the company, at least partly, to the approach.

Xchanging is one of a new breed of companies operating as an outsourcing business for 'back-office' functions for a range of companies, such as Lloyds of London, the insurance centre. Xchanging's business proposition is for the client company to transfer the running of the whole, or part, of their back office to Xchanging, either for a fixed price or one determined by cost savings achieved. The challenge Xchanging face is to run that back office in a more effective and efficient manner than the client company had managed in the past. So, the more effective Xchanging is at running the processes, the greater its profit. To achieve these efficiencies Xchanging offers, on a larger scale, a higher level of process expertise, focus and investment in technology. But above all, they offer a Six Sigma approach. 'Everything we do can be broken down into a process', says Paul Ruggier. 'It may be more straightforward in a manufacturing business; frankly they've been using a lot of Six Sigma tools and techniques for decades. But the concept of process improvement is relatively new in many service companies. Yet the concept is powerful. Through the implementation of this approach we have achieved 30 per cent productivity improvements in 6 months.'

The company also adopts the Six Sigma terminology for its improvement practitioners – Master Black Belts,

Source: Shutterstock.com/Kzenon

Black Belts and Green Belts. Attaining the status of Black Belt is very much sought after as well as being fulfilling, says Rebecca Whittaker, who is a Master Black Belt at Xchanging. 'At the end of a project it is about having a process which is redesigned to such an extent, that is simplified and consolidated and people come back and say, "It's so much better than it used to be." It makes their lives better and it makes the business results better and those are the things that make being a Black Belt worthwhile.'

Rebecca was recruited by Xchanging along with a number of other Master Black Belts as part of a strategic decision to kick-start Six Sigma in the company. It is seen as a particularly responsible position by the company and Master Black Belts are expected to be well versed in the Six Sigma techniques and be able to provide the training and know-how to develop other staff within the company. In Rebecca's case, she has been working as a Six Sigma facilitator for five years, initially as a Green Belt then as a Black Belt.

Typically a person identified as having the right analytical and interpersonal skills will be taken off their job for at least a year, trained and immersed in the concepts of improvement and then sent to work with line staff as project manager/facilitator. Their role as Black Belt will be to guide the line staff to make improvements in the way they do the job. One of the new Black Belts at Xchanging, Sarah Frost, is keen to stress the responsibility she owes to the people who will have to work in the improvement process. '*Being a Black Belt is about being a project manager. It is about working with the staff and combining our skills in facilitation and our knowledge of the Six Sigma process with their knowledge of the business. You always have to remember that you will go on to another project but they* [process staff] *will have to live with the new process. It is about building solutions that they can believe in.*'

Critical commentary

One common criticism of Six Sigma is that it does not offer anything that was not available before. Its emphasis on improvement cycles comes from TQM, its emphasis on reducing variability comes from statistical process control, its use of experimentation and data analysis is simply good quantitative analysis. The only contribution that Six Sigma has made, argue its critics, is using the rather gimmicky martial arts analogy of Black Belt, etc., to indicate a level of expertise in Six Sigma methods. All Six Sigma has done is package pre-existing elements together in order for consultants to be able to sell it to gullible chief executives. In fact it's difficult to deny some of these points. Maybe the real issue is whether it is really a criticism. If bringing these elements together really does form an effective problem-solving approach, why is this a problem?

Six Sigma is also accused of being too hierarchical in the way it structures its various levels of involvement in the improvement activity (as well as the dubious use of martial-arts-derived names such as Black Belt). It is also expensive. Devoting such large amounts of training and time to improvement is a significant investment, especially for small companies. Nevertheless, Six Sigma proponents argue that the improvement activity is generally neglected in most operations and, if it is to be taken seriously, it deserves the significant investment implied by the Six Sigma approach. Furthermore, they argue, if operated well, Six Sigma improvement projects run by experienced practitioners can save far more than their cost. There are also technical criticisms of Six Sigma, most notably that in purely statistical terms the normal distribution which is used extensively in Six Sigma analysis does not actually represent most process behaviour. Other technical criticisms (that are not really the subject of this book) imply that aiming for the very low levels of defects per million opportunities, as recommended by Six Sigma proponents, is far too onerous.

Differences and similarities

In this text we have chosen to very briefly explain four improvement approaches. It could have been more. Enterprise resource planning (ERP, see Chapter 14), total preventive maintenance (TPM, see Chapter 19), lean Sigma (a combination of lean and Six Sigma), and others could have been added. But these four constitute a representative sample of the most commonly used approaches. Nor do we have the space to describe them fully. But there are clearly some common elements between some of these approaches that we have described. Yet there are also differences between them in that each approach includes a different set of elements and therefore a different emphasis and these differences need to be understood. For example, one important

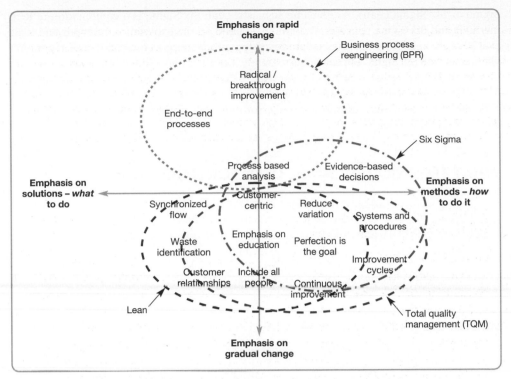

Figure 18.7 The four approaches on the two dimensions of improvement

difference relates to whether the approaches emphasize a gradual, continuous approach to change, or whether they recommend a more radical 'breakthrough' change. Another difference concerns the aim of the approach. What is the balance between whether the approach emphasizes *what* changes should be made or *how* changes should be made? Some approaches have a firm view of what is the best way to organize the operation's processes and resources. Other approaches hold no particular view on what an operation should do but rather concentrate on how the management of an operation should decide what to do. Indeed we can position each of the elements and the approaches that include them. This is illustrated in Figure 18.7. The approaches differ in the extent that they prescribe appropriate operations practice. BPR, for example, is very clear in what it is recommending. Namely, that all processes should be organized on an end-to-end basis. Its focus is *what* should happen rather than *how* it should happen. To a slightly lesser extent lean is the same. It has a definite list of things that processes should or should not be – waste should be eliminated, inventory should be reduced, technology should be flexible, and so on. Contrast this with both Six Sigma and TQM which focus to a far greater extent on *how* operations should be improved. Six Sigma in particular has relatively little to say about what is good or bad in the way operations resources are organized (with the possible exception of emphasizing the negative effects of process variation). Its concern is largely the way improvements should be made: using evidence, using quantitative analysis, using the DMAIC cycle, and so on. They also differ in terms of whether they emphasize gradual or rapid change. BPR is explicit in its radical nature. By contrast TQM and lean both incorporate ideas of continuous improvement. Six Sigma is relatively neutral on this issue and can be used for small or very large changes.

> **✻ Operations principle**
>
> There is significant overlap between the various approaches to improvement in terms of the improvement elements they contain.

Lean Sigma[13]

As if to emphasize the shared elements of the various approaches to operations improvement, some organizations are blending two or more approaches to form hybrids that try and combine their best characteristics. The best known of these is Lean Sigma (also called Lean Six

Sigma or Six Sigma Lean). As its name suggests, Lean Six Sigma is a combination of lean methods and Six Sigma concepts. It attempts to build on the experience, methods and tools that have emerged from the several decades of operational improvement and implementation using lean and Six Sigma approaches separately. Lean Sigma includes the waste reduction, fast throughput time and impact of Lean with the data-driven rigour and variation control of Six Sigma. Some organizations also include other elements from other approaches. For example, the continuous improvement and error-free quality orientation of TQM is frequently included into the concept.

WHAT TECHNIQUES CAN BE USED FOR IMPROVEMENT?

> ✳ **Operations principle**
>
> Improvement is facilitated by relatively simple analytical techniques.

All the techniques described in this book and its supplements can be regarded as 'improvement' techniques. However, some techniques are particularly useful for improving operations and processes generally. Here we select some techniques which either have not been described elsewhere or need to be reintroduced in their role of helping operations improvement particularly.

Scatter diagrams

Scatter diagrams provide a quick and simple method of identifying whether there is evidence of a connection between two sets of data: for example, the time at which you set off for work every morning and how long the journey to work takes. Plotting each journey on a graph which has departure time on one axis and journey time on the other could give an indication of whether departure time and journey time are related, and if so, how. Scatter diagrams can be treated in a far more sophisticated manner by quantifying how strong the relationship between the sets of data is. But, however sophisticated the approach, this type of graph only identifies the existence of a relationship, not necessarily the existence of a cause–effect relationship. If the scatter diagram shows a very strong connection between the sets of data, it is important evidence of a cause–effect relationship, but not proof positive. It could be coincidence!

Example: Kaston Pyral Services Ltd (A)

Kaston Pyral Services Ltd (KPS) installs and maintains environmental control, heating and air-conditioning systems. It has set up an improvement team to suggest ways in which it might improve its levels of customer service. The improvement team had completed its first customer satisfaction survey. The survey asked customers to score the service they received from KPS in several ways. For example, it asked customers to score services on a scale of 1 to 10 on promptness, friendliness, level of advice, etc. Scores were then summed to give a 'total satisfaction score' for each customer – the higher the score, the greater the satisfaction. The spread of satisfaction scores puzzled the team and they considered what factors might be causing such differences in the way their customers viewed them. Two factors were put forward to explain the differences:

(a) the number of times in the past year the customer had received a preventive maintenance visit;
(b) the number of times the customer had called for emergency service.

All this data was collected and plotted on scatter diagrams as shown in Figure 18.8. It shows that there seems to be a clear relationship between a customer's satisfaction score and the number of times the customer was visited for regular servicing. The scatter diagram in Figure 18.8(b) is less clear. Although all customers who had very high satisfaction scores had made very few emergency calls, so had some customers with low satisfaction scores. As a result of this analysis, the team decided to survey customers' views on its emergency service.

Figure 18.8 Scatter diagrams for customer satisfaction versus (a) number of preventive maintenance calls and (b) number of emergency service calls

Process maps (flow charts)

Process maps (sometimes called flow charts in this context) can be used to give a detailed understanding prior to improvement. They were described earlier (in Chapter 4) and are widely used in improvement activities. The act of recording each stage in the process quickly shows up poorly organized flows. Process maps can also clarify improvement opportunities and shed further light on the internal mechanics or workings of an operation. Finally, and probably most importantly, they highlight problem areas where no procedure exists to cope with a particular set of circumstances.

Example: Kaston Pyral Services Ltd (B)

As part of its improvement programme the team at KPS is concerned that customers are not being served well when they phone in with minor queries over the operation of their heating systems. These queries are not usually concerned with serious problems, but often concern minor irritations which can be equally damaging to the customers' perception of KPS's service. Figure 18.9 shows the process map for this type of customer query. The team found the map illuminating. The procedure had never been formally laid out in this way before, and it showed up three areas where information was not being recorded. These are the three points marked with question marks on the process map in Figure 18.9. As a result of this investigation, it was decided to log all customer queries so that analysis could reveal further information on the nature of customer problems.

Cause–effect diagrams

Cause–effect diagrams are a particularly effective method of helping to search for the root causes of problems. They do this by asking what, when, where, how and why questions, but also add some possible 'answers' in an explicit way. They can also be used to identify areas where further data is needed. Cause–effect diagrams (which are also known as 'Ishikawa diagrams') have become extensively used in improvement programmes. This is because they provide a way of structuring group brainstorming sessions. Often the structure involves identifying possible causes under the (rather old-fashioned) headings of: machinery, manpower, materials, methods and money. Yet in practice, any categorization that comprehensively covers all relevant possible causes could be used.

Example: Kaston Pyral Services Ltd (C)

The improvement team at KPS was working on a particular area which was proving a problem. Whenever service engineers were called out to perform emergency servicing for a customer, they took with them the spares and equipment which they thought would be necessary to repair the system. Although engineers could never be sure exactly what materials and equipment

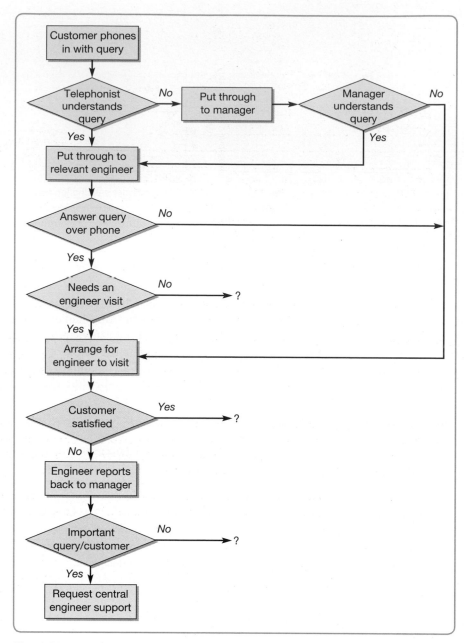

Figure 18.9 Process map for customer query

they would need for a job, they could guess what was likely to be needed and take a range of spares and equipment which would cover most eventualities. Too often, however, the engineers would find that they needed a spare that they had not brought with them. The cause–effect diagram for this particular problem, as drawn by the team, is shown in Figure 18.10.

Pareto diagrams

In any improvement process, it is worthwhile distinguishing what is important and what is less so. The purpose of the Pareto diagram (first introduced in Chapter 12) is to distinguish between the 'vital few' issues and the 'trivial many'. It is a relatively straightforward technique which involves arranging items of information on the types of problem or causes of problem into their order of importance (usually measured by frequency of occurrence). This can be used to highlight areas where further decision making will be useful. Pareto analysis is based

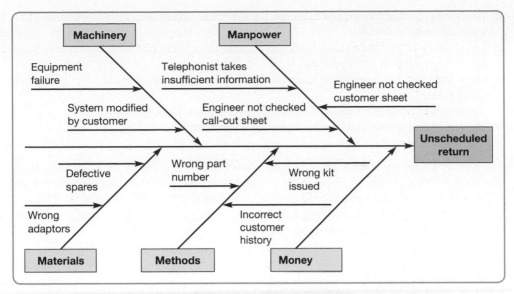

Figure 18.10 Cause–effect diagram of unscheduled returns at KPS

on the phenomenon of relatively few causes explaining the majority of effects. For example, most revenue for any company is likely to come from relatively few of the company's customers. Similarly, relatively few of a doctor's patients will probably occupy most of his or her time.

Example: Kaston Pyral Services Ltd (D)

The KPS improvement team which was investigating unscheduled returns from emergency servicing (the issue described in the cause–effect diagram in Figure 18.11) examined all occasions over the previous 12 months on which an unscheduled return had been made. They categorized the reasons for unscheduled returns as follows:

1 The wrong part had been taken to a job because, although the information which the engineer received was sound, he or she had incorrectly predicted the nature of the fault.

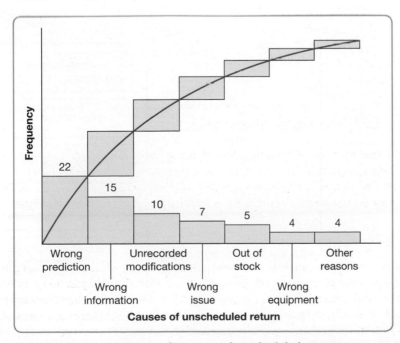

Figure 18.11 Pareto diagram for causes of unscheduled returns

2 The wrong part had been taken to the job because there was insufficient information given when the call was taken.

3 The wrong part had been taken to the job because the system had been modified in some way not recorded on KPS's records.

4 The wrong part had been taken to the job because the part had been incorrectly issued to the engineer by stores.

5 No part had been taken because the relevant part was out of stock.

6 The wrong equipment had been taken for whatever reason.

7 Any other reason.

The relative frequency of occurrence of these causes is shown in Figure 18.11. About a third of all unscheduled returns were due to the first category, and more than half the returns were accounted for by the first and second categories together. It was decided that the problem could best be tackled by concentrating on how to get more information to the engineers which would enable them to predict the causes of failure accurately.

Why–why analysis

Why–why analysis starts by stating the problem and asking *why* that problem has occurred. Once the reasons for the problem occurring have been identified, each of the reasons is taken in turn and again the question is asked *why* those reasons have occurred, and so on. This procedure is continued until either a cause seems sufficiently self-contained to be addressed by itself or no more answers to the question 'Why?' can be generated.

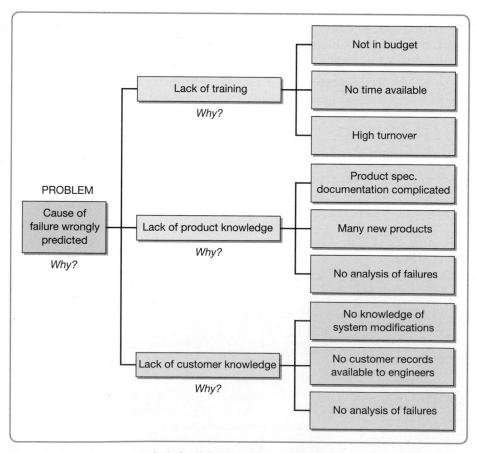

Figure 18.12 Why–why analysis for 'failure wrongly predicted'

Example: Kaston Pyral Services Ltd (E)

The major cause of unscheduled returns at KPS was the incorrect prediction of reasons for the customer's system failure. This is stated as the 'problem' in the why–why analysis in Figure 18.12. The question is then asked, why was the failure wrongly predicted? Three answers are proposed: first, that the engineers were not trained correctly; second, that they had insufficient knowledge of the particular product installed in the customer's location; and third, that they had insufficient knowledge of the customer's particular system with its modifications. Each of these three reasons is taken in turn, and the questions are asked, why is there a lack of training, why is there a lack of product knowledge, and why is there a lack of customer knowledge? And so on.

SUMMARY ANSWERS TO KEY QUESTIONS

Check and improve your understanding of this chapter using self-assessment questions and a personalized study plan, a video case study, and an eText – all at www.myomlab.com.

MyOMLab

❯ Why is improvement so important in operations management?

- Improvement is now seen as the prime responsibility of operations management. Of the four areas of operations management activity (direct, design, deliver and develop) the focus of most operations managers has shifted towards 'develop', that is, improvement. Furthermore all operations management activities are really concerned with improvement in the long term. And all four activities are really interrelated and interdependent. Also, companies in many industries are having to improve simply to retain their position relative to their competitors. This is sometimes called the 'Red Queen' effect.

- A common distinction is between radical or breakthrough improvement on one hand, and continuous or incremental improvement on the other.

❯ What are the key elements of operations improvement?

- There are many 'elements' that are the building blocks of improvement approaches. The ones described in this chapter are:
  - Improvement cycles;
  - a process perspective;
  - end-to-end processes;
  - radical change;
  - evidence-based problem-solving;
  - customer centricity;
  - systems and procedures;
  - reduce process variation;
  - synchronized flow;
  - emphasize education/training;
  - perfection is the goal;
  - waste identification;
  - include everybody;
  - develop internal customer–supplier relationships.

〉 What are the broad approaches to managing improvement?

- What we have called 'the broad approaches to improvement' are relatively coherent collections of some of the 'elements' of improvement. The four most common are total quality management (TQM), lean, business process re-engineering (BPR) and Six Sigma.

- BPR is a typical example of the radical approach to improvement. It attempts to redesign operations along customer-focused processes rather than on the traditional functional basis. The main criticisms are that it pays little attention to the rights of staff who are the victims of the 'downsizing' which often accompanies BPR, and that the radical nature of the changes can strip out valuable experience from the operation.

- Total quality management was one of the earliest management 'fashions' and has suffered from a backlash, but the general precepts and principles of TQM are still influential. It is an approach that puts quality (and indeed improvement generally) at the heart of everything that is done by an operation.

- Lean was seen initially as an approach to be used exclusively in manufacturing, but has become seen as an approach that can be applied in service operations. Also lean, when first introduced, was radical, and counter-intuitive. The idea that inventories had a negative effect, and that throughput time was more important than capacity utilization, was difficult to accept by the more traditionally minded. So, as lean ideas have been gradually accepted, we have likewise come to be far more tolerant of ideas that are radical and/or counter-intuitive.

- Six Sigma is 'A disciplined methodology of defining, measuring, analysing, improving, and controlling the quality in every one of the company's products, processes, and transactions – with the ultimate goal of virtually eliminating all defects'. First popularized by Motorola, it was so named because it required that the natural variation of processes (± 3 standard deviations) should be half their specification range. In other words, the specification range of any part of a product or service should be ± 6 the standard deviation of the process. Now the definition of Six Sigma has widened beyond its statistical origins. It should be seen as a broad improvement concept rather than a simple examination of process variation, even though this is still an important part of process control, learning and improvement.

- There are differences between these improvement approaches. Each includes a different set of elements and therefore a different emphasis. They can be positioned on two dimensions. The first is whether the approaches emphasize a gradual, continuous approach to change or a more radical 'breakthrough' change. The second is whether the approach emphasizes *what* changes should be made or *how* changes should be made.

〉 What techniques can be used for improvement?

- Many of the techniques described throughout this book could be considered improvement techniques, for example statistical process control (SPC).

- Techniques often seen as 'improvement techniques' include: scatter diagrams, flow charts, cause–effect diagrams, Pareto diagrams, and why–why analysis.

GCR Insurance

'This is not going to be like last time. Then, we were adopting an improvement programme because we were told to. This time it's our idea and, if it's successful, it will be us that are telling the rest of the group how to do it.' (Tyko Mattson, Six Sigma Champion, GCR)

Tyko Mattson was speaking as the newly appointed 'Champion' at GCR Insurance, who had been charged with *'steering the Six Sigma programme until it is firmly established as part of our ongoing practice'.* The previous improvement initiative that he was referring to dated back many years to when GCR's parent company, Wichita Mutual Insurance, had insisted on the adoption of total quality management (TQM) in all its businesses. The TQM initiative had never been pronounced a failure and had managed to make some improvements, especially in customers' perception of the company's levels of service. However, the initiative had 'faded out' during the 1990s and, even though all departments still had to formally report on their improvement projects, their number and impact were now relatively minor.

Source: AL RF (Alamy Images/Ingram)

History

GCR Insurance was founded in 1922 to provide insurance for building contractors and construction companies, initially in German-speaking Europe and then in North America. In the early 1950s it started to grow partly because it moved into larger (sometimes very large) construction insurance in the industrial, oil, petrochemical and power-plant construction areas. In 1983 it absorbed the group's existing construction insurance businesses. By 2000 it had been bought by the Wichita Mutual Group and had established itself as one of the leading providers of insurance for construction projects, especially complex, high-risk projects where contractual and other legal issues, physical exposures and design uncertainty needed 'customized' insurance responses. Providing such insurance needed particular knowledge and skills from specialists including construction underwriters, loss adjusters, engineers, international lawyers, and specialist risk consultants. Typically, the company would insure losses resulting from contractor failure, related public liability issues, delays in project completion, associated litigation, other litigation (such as ongoing asbestos risks) and negligence issues.

The company's headquarters were in Geneva and housed all major departments, including sales and marketing, underwriting, risk analysis, claims and settlement, financial control, general admin, specialist and general legal advice, and business research. There were also 37 local offices around the world, organized into 4 regional areas: North America; South America; Europe Middle East and Africa; and Asia. These regional offices provided localized help and advice directly to clients and also to the 890 agents that GCR used worldwide.

The previous improvement initiative

When Wichita Mutual had insisted that CGR adopt a TQM initiative, it had gone as far as to specify exactly how it should do it and which consultants should be used to help establish the programme. Tyko Mattson shakes his head as he describes it. *'I was not with the company at that time but, looking back, it's amazing that it ever managed to do any good. You can't impose the structure of an improvement initiative from the top. It has to, at least partially, be shaped by the people who are going to be involved in it. But everything had to be done according to the handbook. The cost of quality was measured for different departments according to the handbook. Everyone had to learn the improvement techniques that were described in the handbook. Everyone had to be part of a quality circle that was organized according to the handbook. We even had to have annual award ceremonies where we gave out special "certificates of merit" to those quality circles that had achieved the type of improvement that the handbook said they should.'* The TQM initiative had been run by the 'quality committee', a group of eight people with representatives from all the major departments at head office. Initially, it had spent much of its time setting up the improvement groups and organizing training in quality techniques. However, soon it had become swamped by the work needed to evaluate which improvement suggestions should be implemented. Soon the workload associated with assessing improvement ideas had become so great that the company decided to allocate small improvement budgets to each department on a quarterly basis that they could spend without reference to the quality committee. Projects requiring larger investment, or that had a significant impact on other parts of the business, still needed to be approved by the committee before they were implemented.

Department improvement budgets were still used within the business and improvement plans were still required from each department on an annual basis. However, the quality committee had stopped meeting a few years ago and the annual award ceremony had become a general communications meeting for all staff at the headquarters. 'Looking back', said Tyko, 'the TQM initiate faded away for three reasons. First, people just got tired of it. It was always seen as something extra rather than part of normal business life, so it was always seen as taking time away from doing your normal job. Second, many of the supervisory and middle management levels never really bought into it, I guess because they felt threatened. Third, only a very few of the local offices around the world ever adopted the TQM philosophy. Sometimes this was because they did not want the extra effort. Sometimes, however, they would argue that improvement initiatives of this type may be OK for head office processes, but not for the more dynamic world of supporting clients in the field.'

The Six Sigma initiative

Early in 2005 Tyko Mattson, who for the last two years had been overseeing the outsourcing of some of GCR's claims processing to India, had attended a conference on 'Operations Excellence in Financial Services', and had heard several speakers detail the success they had achieved through using a Six Sigma approach to operations improvement. He had persuaded his immediate boss, Marie-Dominique Tomas, the Head of Claims for the company, to allow him to investigate its applicability to GCR. He had interviewed a number of other financial services who had implemented Six Sigma as well as a number of consultants and in September 2005 had submitted a report entitled 'What is Six Sigma and how might it be applied in GRC?' Extracts from this are included in Appendix 1. Marie-Dominique Tomas was particularly concerned that they should avoid the mistakes of the TQM initiative. 'Looking back, it is almost embarrassing to see how naive we were. We really did think that it would change the whole way that we did business. And although it did produce some benefits, it absorbed a large amount of time at all levels in the organization. This time we want something that will deliver results without costing too much or distracting us from focusing on business performance. That is why I like Six Sigma. It starts with clarifying business objectives and works from there.'

By late 2005 Tyko's report had been approved both by GCR and by Wichita Mutual's main board. Tyko had been given the challenge of carrying out the recommendations in his report, reporting directly to GCR's executive board. Marie-Dominique Tomas was cautiously optimistic. 'It is quite a challenge for Tyko. Most of us on the executive board remember the TQM initiative and some are still sceptical concerning the value of such initiatives. However, Tyko's gradualist approach and his emphasis on the "three-pronged" attack on revenue, costs, and risk impressed the board. We now have to see whether he can make it work.'

APPENDIX
Extract from 'What is Six Sigma and how might it be applied in GCR?'

Six Sigma – pitfalls and benefits

Some pitfalls of Six Sigma
It is not simple to implement, and is resource-hungry. The focus on measurement implies that the process data is available and reasonably robust. If this is not the case it is possible to waste a lot of effort in obtaining process performance data. It may also over-complicate things if advanced techniques are used on simple problems.

It is easier to apply Six Sigma to repetitive processes – characterized by high volume, low variety and low visibility to customers. It is more difficult to apply Six Sigma to low volume, higher variety and high visibility processes where standardization is harder to achieve and the focus is on managing the variety.

Six Sigma is not a 'quick fix'. Companies that have implemented Six Sigma effectively have not treated it as just another new initiative but as an approach that requires the long-term systematic reduction of waste. Equally, it is not a panacea and should not be implemented as one.

Some benefits of Six Sigma
Companies have achieved significant benefits in reducing cost and improving customer service through implementing Six Sigma.

Six Sigma can reduce process variation, which will have a significant impact on operational risk. It is a tried and tested methodology, which combines the strongest parts of existing improvement methodologies. It lends itself to being customized to fit [each] individual company's circumstances.

For example, Mestech Assurance has extended their Six Sigma initiative to examine operational risk processes.

Six Sigma could leverage a number of current initiatives. The risk-self-assessment methodology, Sarbanes Oxley, the process library, and our performance metrics work are all laying the foundations for better knowledge and measurement of process data.

Six Sigma – key conclusions for GCR

Six Sigma is a powerful improvement methodology. It is not all new but what it does do successfully is to combine some of the best parts of existing improvement methodologies, tools and techniques. Six Sigma has helped many companies achieve significant benefits.

Six Sigma could help GCR significantly improve risk management because it focuses on driving errors and exceptions out of processes.

Six Sigma has significant advantages over other process improvement methodologies:

- It engages senior management actively by establishing process ownership and linkage to strategic objectives. This is seen as integral to successful implementation in the literature and by all companies interviewed who had implemented it.
- It forces a rigorous approach to driving out variance in processes by analysing the root cause of defects and errors and measuring improvement.
- It is an 'umbrella' approach, combining all the best parts of other improvement approaches.

Implementing Six Sigma across GCR is not the right approach

Companies who are widely quoted as having achieved the most significant headline benefits from Six Sigma were already relatively mature in terms of process management. Those companies, who understood their process capability, typically had achieved a degree of process standardization and had an established process improvement culture.

Six Sigma requires significant investment in performance metrics and process knowledge. GCR is probably not yet sufficiently advanced. However, we are working towards a position where key process data are measured and known and this will provide a foundation for Six Sigma.

A targeted implementation is recommended because:

Full implementation is resource-hungry. Dedicated resource and budget for implementation of improvements is required. Even if the approach is modified, resource and budget will still be needed, just to a lesser extent. However, the evidence is that the investment is well worth it and pays back relatively quickly.

There was strong evidence from companies interviewed that the best implementation approach was to pilot Six Sigma, and select failing processes for the pilot. In addition,

previous internal piloting of implementations has been successful in GCR – we know this approach works within our culture.

Six Sigma would provide a platform for GSR to build on and evolve over time. It is a way of leveraging the ongoing work on processes, and the risk methodology (being developed by the Operational Risk Group). This diagnostic tool could be blended into Six Sigma, giving GCR a powerful model to drive reduction in process variation and improved operational risk management.

Recommendations

It is recommended that GCR management implement a Six Sigma pilot. The characteristics of the pilot would be as follows:

- A tailored approach to Six Sigma that would fit GCR's objectives and operating environment. Implementing Six Sigma in its entirety would not be appropriate.
- The use of an external partner: GCR does not have sufficient internal Six Sigma, so, external experience will be critical to tailoring the approach, and providing training.
- Establishing where GCR's Sigma performance is now. Different tools and approaches will be required to advance from 2 to 3 Sigma than those required to move from 3 to 4 Sigma.
- Quantifying the potential benefits. Is the investment worth making? What would a 1 Sigma increase in performance vs. risk be worth to us?
- Keeping the methods simple, if simple will achieve our objectives. As a minimum for us that means Team Based Problem Solving and basic statistical techniques.

Next steps

1 Decide priority and confirm budget and resourcing for initial analysis to develop a Six Sigma risk improvement programme in 2006.
2 Select external partner experienced in improvement and Six Sigma methodologies.
3 Assess GCR current state to confirm where to start in implementing Six Sigma.
4 Establish how much GCR is prepared to invest in Six Sigma and quantify the potential benefits.
5 Tailor Six Sigma to focus on risk management.
6 Identify potential pilot area(s) and criteria for assessing its suitability.
7 Develop a Six Sigma pilot plan.
8 Conduct and review the pilot programme.

QUESTIONS

1 **How does the Six Sigma approach seem to differ from the TQM approach adopted by the company almost 20 years ago?**

2 **Is Six Sigma a better approach for this type of company?**

3 **Do you think Tyko can avoid the Six Sigma initiative suffering the same fate as the TQM initiative?**

PROBLEMS AND APPLICATIONS

MyOMLab *These problems and applications will help to improve your analysis of operations. You can find more practice problems as well as worked examples and guided solutions on MyOMLab at **www.myomlab.com**.*

1 Sophie was sick of her daily commute. 'Why', she thought 'should I have to spend so much time in a morning stuck in traffic listening to some babbling halfwit on the radio? We can work flexi-time after all. Perhaps I should leave the apartment at some other time?' So resolved, Sophie deliberately varied her time of departure from her usual 8.30. Also, being an organized soul, she recorded her time of departure each day and her journey time. Her records are shown in Table 18.1.

(a) Draw a scatter diagram that will help Sophie decide on the best time to leave her apartment.

(b) How much time per (5 day) week should she expect to be saved from having to listen to a babbling halfwit?

Table 18.1 Sophie's journey times (in minutes)

Day	Leaving time	Journey time	Day	Leaving time	Journey time	Day	Leaving time	Journey time
1	7.15	19	6	8.45	40	11	8.35	46
2	8.15	40	7	8.55	32	12	8.40	45
3	7.30	25	8	7.55	31	13	8.20	47
4	7.20	19	9	7.40	22	14	8.00	34
5	8.40	46	10	8.30	49	15	7.45	27

2 The Printospeed Laser printer company was proud of its reputation for high-quality products and services. Because of this it was especially concerned with the problems that it was having with its customers returning defective toner cartridges. About 2,000 of these were being returned every month. Its European service team suspected that not all the returns were actually the result of a faulty product, which is why the team decided to investigate the problem. Three major problems were identified. First, some users were not as familiar as they should have been with the correct method of loading the cartridge into the printer, or in being able to solve their own minor printing problems. Second, some of the dealers were also unaware of how to sort out minor problems. Third, there was clearly some abuse of Printospeed's 'no-questions-asked' returns policy. Empty toner cartridges were being sent to unauthorized refilling companies who would sell the refilled cartridges at reduced prices. Some cartridges were being refilled up to five times and were understandably wearing out. Furthermore, the toner in the refilled cartridges was often not up to Printospeed's high quality standards.

(a) Draw a cause–effect diagram that includes both the possible causes mentioned, and any other possible causes that you think worth investigating.

(b) What is your opinion of the alleged abuse of the 'no-questions-asked' returns policy adopted by Printospeed?

3 Think back to the last product or service failure that caused you some degree of inconvenience. Draw a cause–effect diagram that identifies all the main causes of why the failure could have occurred. Try to identify the frequency with which such causes happen. This could be done by talking with the staff of the operation that provided the service. Draw a Pareto diagram that indicates the relative frequency of each cause of failure. Suggest ways in which the operation could reduce the chances of failure.

SELECTED FURTHER READING

George, M.L., Rowlands, D. and Kastle, B. (2003) *What Is Lean Six Sigma?* McGraw-Hill Professional, New York. Very much a quick introduction on what Lean Six Sigma is and how to use it.

Goldratt, E.M. and Cox, J. (2004) *The Goal: A Process of Ongoing Improvement*, Gower, Aldershot. Updated version of a classic.

Hendry, L. and Nonthaleerak, P. (2004) Six Sigma: literature review and key future research areas, Lancaster University Management School, Working Paper, 2005/044 http://www.lums.lancs.ac.uk/publications/. Good overview of the literature on Six Sigma.

Hindo, B. (2007) At 3M, a struggle between efficiency and creativity: how CEO George Buckley is managing the yin and yang of discipline and imagination, *Business Week*, June 2011. Readable article from the popular business press.

Pande, P.S., Neuman, R.P. and Cavanagh, R. (2002) *Six Sigma Way Team Field Book: An Implementation Guide for Project Improvement Teams*, McGraw-Hill Professional, New York. Obviously based on the Six Sigma principle (and related to the book by the same author team recommended in Chapter 17), this is a unashamedly practical guide to the Six Sigma approach.

Paper, D.J., Rodger, J.A. and Pendharkar, P.C. (2001) A BPR case study at Honeywell, *Business Process Management Journal*, vol. 7, no. 2, 85–99. Interesting, if somewhat academic, case study.

Xingxing Zu , Fredendall, L.D. and Douglas, T.J. (2008) The evolving theory of quality management: the role of Six Sigma, *Journal of Operations Management*, 26, 630–650. As it says . . .

USEFUL WEBSITES

www.processimprovement.com Commercial site but some content that could be useful.

www.kaizen-institute.com Professional institute for kaizen. Gives some insight into practitioner views.

www.mxawards.org The Manufacturing Excellence Awards site. Dedicated to rewarding excellence and best practice in UK manufacturing. Obviously manufacturing biased, but some good examples.

www.ebenchmarking.com Benchmarking information.

www.quality.nist.gov American National Institute of Standards and Technology. Well-established institution for all types of business quality assurance.

www.balancedscorecard.org Site of an American organization with plenty of useful links.

www.myomlab.com Test which sections you have mastered and which you need to review, with questions, a personalized study plan, video clips, revision tips, and cases.

www.opsman.org Useful materials.

http://operationsroom.wordpress.com/ Stanford University's take on topical operations stories.

www.poms.org A US academic society for production and operations management. Academic, but some useful material, including a link to an encyclopedia of operations management terms.

Now that you have finished reading this chapter, why not visit MyOMLab at www.myomlab.com where you'll find more learning resources to help you make the most of your studies and get a better grade.

Risk management

INTRODUCTION

No matter how much effort is put into improving operations, there is always a risk that something unexpected or unusual will happen that could reverse much, if not all, of the improvement effort. So, one obvious way of improving operations performance is by reducing the risk of failure (or of failure causing disruption) within the operation. Understanding and managing risk in operations can be seen as an improvement activity, even if it is in an 'avoiding the negative effects of failure' sense. But there is also a more conspicuous reason why risk management is increasingly a concern of operations managers. The sources of risk and the consequences of risk are becoming more difficult to handle. From sudden changes in demand to the bankruptcy of a key supplier, from terrorist attacks to cybercrime, the threats to normal smooth running of operations are not getting fewer. Nor are the consequences of such events becoming less serious. Sharper cost cutting, lower inventories, higher levels of capacity utilization, increasingly effective regulation, and attentive media can all serve to make the costs of operational failure greater. So for most operations managing risks is not just desirable, it is essential. But the risks to the smooth running of operations are not confined to major events. Even in less critical situations, having dependable processes can give a competitive advantage. And in this chapter we examine both the dramatic and more routine risks that can prevent operations working as they should. Figure 19.1 shows how this chapter fits into the operation's improvement activities.

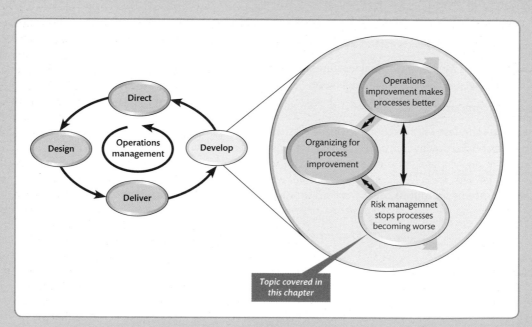

Figure 19.1 This chapter covers risk management

Cadbury's salmonella outbreak[1]

In June 2007, Cadbury, founded by a Quaker family in 1824, and now part of Kraft, one of the world's biggest food companies, was fined £1 million plus costs of £152,000 for breaching food safety laws in a national salmonella outbreak that infected 42 people, including children aged under 10, who became ill with a rare strain of Salmonella montevideo. '*I regard this as a serious case of negligence*', the judge said. '*It therefore needs to be marked as such to emphasize the responsibility and care which the law requires of a company in Cadbury's position.*' One prominent lawyer announced that '*Despite Cadbury's attempts to play down this significant fine, make no mistake it was intended to hurt and is one of the largest of its kind to date. This reflects no doubt the company's high profile and the length of time over which the admitted breach took place, but will also send out a blunt warning to smaller businesses of the government's intentions regarding enforcement of food safety laws.*'

Source: Shutterstock.com/Max Photographer

Before the hearing, the company had, in fact, apologized, offering its 'sincere regrets' to those affected, and pleaded guilty to nine food safety offences. But at the beginning of the incident it had not been so open: one of the charges faced by Cadbury, who said it had co-operated fully with the investigation, admitted that it failed to notify the authorities of positive tests for salmonella as soon as they were known within the company. While admitting its mistakes, a spokesman for the confectioner emphasized that the company had acted in good faith, a point supported by the judge when he dismissed a prosecution suggestion that Cadbury had introduced the procedural changes that led to the outbreak simply as a cost-cutting measure. Cadbury, through its lawyers, said: '*Negligence we admit, but we certainly do not admit that this was done deliberately to save money and nor is there any evidence to support that conclusion.*' The judge said Cadbury had accepted that a new testing system, originally introduced to improve safety, was a '*distinct departure from previous practice*', and was '*badly flawed and wrong*'. In a statement Cadbury said: '*Mistakenly, we did not believe that there was a threat to health and thus any requirement to report the incident to the authorities – we accept that this approach was incorrect. The processes that led to this failure ceased from June last year and will never be reinstated.*'

The company was not only hit by the fine and court costs, it had to bear the costs of recalling from sale one million chocolate bars that may have been contaminated, and face private litigation claims brought by its consumers who were affected. Cadbury said it lost around £30 million because of the recall and subsequent safety modifications, not including any private litigation claims. The London *Times* reported on the case of Shaun Garratty, one of the people affected. A senior staff nurse, from Rotherham, he spent seven weeks in hospital critically ill and now he fears that his nursing career might be in jeopardy. *The Times* reported him as being '*pleased that Cadbury's had admitted guilt but now wants to know what the firm is going to do for him*'. Before the incident, it said, he was a fitness fanatic and went hiking, cycling, mountain biking or swimming twice a week. He always took two bars of chocolate on the trips, usually a Cadbury's Dairy Milk and a Cadbury's Caramel bar. He also ate one as a snack each day at work. '*My gastroenterologist told me if I had not been so fit I would have died*', said Mr Garratty. '*Six weeks after being in hospital they thought my bowel had perforated and I had to have a laparoscopy. I was told my intestines were inflamed and swollen.*' Even after he returned to work he has not fully recovered. According to one medical consultant, the illness had left him with a form of irritable bowel syndrome that could take 18 months to recover.

WHAT IS RISK MANAGEMENT?

Risk management is about identifying things that could go wrong, stopping them going wrong, reducing the consequences when things do go wrong, and recovering after things have gone wrong. It is important because there is always a chance that things might go wrong, which is why operations managers spend so much time trying to prevent things going wrong. They attempt to minimize both the likelihood of failure and the effect it will have, although the method of coping with failure will depend on how serious its consequences are, and how likely it is to occur. At a minor level, every small error in the delivered product or service from the operation could be considered a failure. The whole area of quality management is concerned with reducing this type of 'failure'. Other failures will have more impact on the opera-

> ✳ **Operations principle**
>
> Failure will always occur in operations; recognizing this does not imply accepting or ignoring it.

tion, even if they do not occur very frequently. A server failure can seriously affect service and therefore customers, which is why system reliability is such an important measure of performance for IT service providers. And, if we class a failure as something that has negative consequences, some are so serious we class them as disasters, such as freak weather conditions, air crashes, and acts of terrorism. These 'failures' are treated increasingly seriously by businesses, not necessarily because their likelihood of occurrence is high (although it may be at certain times and in certain places), but because their impact is so negative.

Here we are concerned with all types of failure other than those with relatively minor consequences. This is illustrated in Figure 19.2. Some of these failures are irritating, but relatively unimportant, especially those close to the bottom left-hand corner of the matrix in Figure 19.2. Other failures, especially those close to the top right-hand corner of matrix, are normally avoided by all businesses because embracing such risks would be clearly foolish. In between these two extremes is where most operations-related risks occur. We shall be treating various aspects of these types of failure, and in particular how they can be moved in the direction of arrows in Figure 19.2.

From an operations perspective, risk is caused by some type of failure, and there are many different sources of failure in any operation. But dealing with failures, and therefore

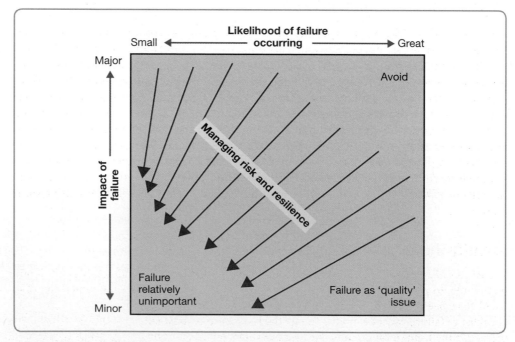

Figure 19.2 How failure is managed depends on its likelihood of occurrence and the negative consequences of failure

Figure 19.3 Risk management involves failure prevention, mitigating the negative consequences of failure, and failure recovery

managing risk, generally involves four sets of activities. The first is concerned with understanding what failures could potentially occur in the operation and assessing their seriousness. The second task is to examine ways of preventing failures occurring. The third is to minimize the negative consequences of failure (called failure or risk 'mitigation'). The final task is to devise plans and procedures that will help the operation to recover from failures when they do occur. The remainder of this chapter deals with these four tasks, see Figure 19.3.

ASSESSING THE POTENTIAL CAUSES OF AND RISKS FROM FAILURE

The first aspect of risk management is to understand the potential sources of risk. This means assessing where failure might occur and what the consequences of failure might be. Often it is a 'failure to understand failure' that results in unacceptable risk. Each potential cause of failure needs to be assessed in terms of how likely it is to occur and the impact it may have. Only then can measures be taken to prevent or minimize the effect of the more important potential failures. The classic approach to assessing potential failures is to inspect and audit operations activities. Unfortunately, inspection and audit cannot, on their own, provide complete assurance that undesirable events will be avoided. The content of any audit has to be appropriate, the checking process has to be sufficiently frequent and comprehensive and the inspectors have to have sufficient knowledge and experience. But whatever approach to risk is taken, it can only be effective if the organizational culture that it is set in fully supports a 'risk-aware' attitude.

Identify the potential causes of failure

The causes of some failure are purely random, like lightning strikes, and are difficult, if not impossible, to predict. However, the vast majority of failures are caused by something that could have been avoided. So, as a minimum starting point, a simple checklist of failure causes is useful. In fact the root cause of most failure is usually human failure of some type; nevertheless, identifying failure sources usually requires a more evident checklist, which is why failure sources are often classified as: failures of supply; internal failures such as those deriving from human, organizational and technological sources; failures deriving from the design of products and services; failures deriving from customer failures; and general environmental failures.

Supply failure

Supply failure means any failure in the timing or quality of goods and services delivered into an operation. For example, suppliers delivering the wrong or faulty components, outsourced call centres suffering a telecoms failure, disruption to power supplies, and so on. It can be an important source of failure because of increasing dependence on outsourced activities in most industries. Also, global sourcing usually means that parts are shipped around the world on their journey through the supply chain. Microchips manufactured in Taiwan could be assembled to printed circuit boards in Shanghai which are then finally assembled into a computer in Ireland. At the same time, many industries are suffering increased volatility in demand. Perhaps most significantly there tends to be far less inventory in supply chains that could buffer interruptions to supply. According to one authority on supply chain management, *'Potentially the risk of disruption has increased dramatically as the result of a too-narrow focus on supply chain efficiency at the expense of effectiveness.'*[2]

Human failures

There are two broad types of human failure. The first is where key personnel leave, become ill, die, or in some way cannot fulfil their role. The second is where people are doing their job but are making mistakes. Understanding risk in the first type of failure involves identifying the key people without whom operations would struggle to operate effectively. These are not always the most senior individuals, but rather those fulfilling crucial roles that require special skills or tacit knowledge. Human failure through 'mistakes' also comes in two types: errors and violations. 'Errors' are mistakes in judgement, where a person should have done something different. For example, if the manager of a sports stadium fails to anticipate dangerous crowding during a championship event. 'Violations' are acts which are clearly contrary to defined operating procedure. For example, if a maintenance engineer fails to clean a filter in the prescribed manner, it is eventually likely to cause failure. Catastrophic failures are often caused by a combination of errors and violations. For example, one kind of accident, where an aircraft appears to be under control and yet still flies into the ground, is very rare (once in two million flights). For this type of failure to occur, first, the pilot has to be flying at the wrong

---

SHORT CASE   **Risk and human error**[3]

If you are an anxious flyer, or of a nervous disposition, stop reading now . . .

When American pilot George La Perle turned up for work at Heathrow, he was so drunk that he didn't know where he was supposed to fly his transatlantic passenger plane. At his trial, the judge, Phillip Matthews, jailed him for six months saying, *'You knew that you were about to co-pilot a Boeing 767 across the Atlantic with all that entails, yet you had consumed alcohol which, at the time that you arrived at Heathrow Airport, was showing that you were four times over the prescribed aviation limit. The consequences for the passengers on that plane, if you had piloted for any stage of that journey, which was a distinct possibility bearing in mind that is what you were employed to do, were potentially catastrophic.'*

Source: Asset Library (AL)/Sozaijiten

altitude (error). Second, the co-pilot would have to fail to cross-check the altitude (violation). Third, air traffic controllers would have to miss the fact that the plane was at the wrong altitude (error). Finally, the pilot would have to ignore the ground proximity warning alarm in the aircraft, which can be prone to give false alarms (violation).

Organizational failure

Organizational failure is usually taken to mean failures of procedures and processes and failures that derive from a business's organizational structure and culture. This is a huge potential source of failure and includes almost all operations and process management. In particular, failure in the design of processes (such as bottlenecks causing system overloading) and failures in the resourcing of processes (such as insufficient capacity being provided at peak times) need to be investigated. But there are also many other procedures and processes within an organization that can make failure more likely. For example, remuneration policy may motivate staff to work in a way that, although increasing the financial performance of the organization, also increases the risk of failure. Examples of this can range from sales people being so incentivized that they make promises to customers that cannot be fulfilled, through to investment bankers being more concerned with profit than the risks of financial overexposure. This type of risk can derive from an organizational culture that minimizes consideration of risk, or it may come from a lack of clarity in reporting relationships.

Technology and facilities failures

By 'technology and facilities' we mean all the IT systems, machines, equipment, and buildings of an operation. All are liable to failure, or breakdown. The failure may be only partial, for example a machine that has an intermittent fault. Alternatively, it can be what we normally regard as a 'breakdown – a total and sudden cessation of operation. Either way, its effects could bring a large part of the operation to a halt. For example, a computer failure in a supermarket chain could paralyse several large stores until it is fixed.

Product and service design failures

In its design stage, a product or service might look fine on paper; only when it has to cope with real circumstances might inadequacies become evident. Of course, during the design process, potential risk of failure should have been identified and 'designed out'. But one only has to look at the number of 'product recalls' or service failures to understand that design failures are far from uncommon. Sometimes this is the result of a trade-off between fast time-to-market performance and the risk of the product or service failing in operation. And, while no reputable business would deliberately market flawed products or services, equally most businesses cannot delay a product or service launch indefinitely to eliminate every single small risk of failure.

Customer failures

Not all failures are (directly) caused by the operation or its suppliers. Customers may 'fail' in that they misuse products and services. For example, an IT system might have been well designed, yet the user could treat it in a way that causes it to fail. Customers are not 'always right'; they can be inattentive and incompetent. However, merely complaining about customers is unlikely to reduce the chances of this type of failure occurring. Most organizations will accept that they have a responsibility to educate and train customers, and to design their products and services so as to minimize the chances of failure.

Environmental disruption

Environmental disruption includes all the causes of failure that lie outside of an operation's direct influence. This source of potential failure has risen to near the top of many firms' agenda since 11 September 2001 and the global 'credit crunch' of 2008. As operations become increasingly integrated (and increasingly dependent on integrated technologies such as information technologies), businesses are more aware of the critical events and malfunctions that have the potential to interrupt normal business activity and even stop the entire company. Risks in this category include everything from cybercrime to hurricanes, from terrorism to political change.

E-security[4]

Any advance in processes or technology creates risks. No real advance comes without risk, threats, and even danger. This applies particularly to e-business. In almost all businesses information has become critical. So, information security management has become a particularly high priority. But herein lies the problem. The internet, which is the primary medium for conducting e-business, is by design an open non-secure medium. Since the original purpose of the internet was not for commercial purposes, it is not designed to handle secure transactions. So there is a trade-off between providing wider access through the internet and the security concerns it generates. Three developments have amplified e-security concerns. First, increased connectivity (who does not rely on internet-based systems?) means that everyone has at least the potential to 'see' everyone else. Organizations want to make enterprise systems and information more available to internal employees, business partners and customers (see Chapter 14 on ERP). Second, there has been a loss of 'perimeter' security as more people work from home or through mobile communications. For example, some banks have been targeted by criminals seeking to exploit home working, as a hitherto overlooked flaw in corporate security firewalls. Hackers had hoped to exploit lower levels of security in home computers to burrow into corporate networks. Third, for some new, sometimes unregulated, technologies, such as some mobile networks, it takes time to discover all possible sources of risk. The internet, after all, is an open system and the rapid rate of development of new software and systems often means that users do not have an adequate knowledge about software and systems architecture. This makes users oblivious to potential vulnerabilities that can lead to serious security breaches.

Yet there is an increasing customer awareness of data security and data confidentiality which means that companies are viewing e-business security as a potential marketing advantage. One specialist in this area, Forrester Research, reported that 74 per cent of online consumers said that online security is an important consideration in choosing a financial service provider.

Post-failure analysis

One of the critical activities of operations and process resilience is to understand why a failure has occurred. This activity is called post-failure analysis. It is used to uncover the root cause of failures. This includes such activities as the following:

- Accident investigation, where large-scale national disasters like oil tanker spillages and airplane accidents are investigated using specifically trained staff.
- Failure traceability, where procedures ensure that failures can be traced back to where they originated.
- Complaint analysis, where complaints (and compliments) are used as a valuable source for detecting the root causes of failures of customer service.
- Fault tree analysis, where a logical procedure starts with a failure or a potential failure and works backwards to identify all the possible causes and therefore the origins of that failure. Fault tree analysis is made up of branches connected by two types of nodes: AND nodes and OR nodes. The branches below an AND node all need to occur for the event above the node to occur. Only one of the branches below an OR node needs to occur for the event above the node to occur. Figure 19.4 shows a simple tree identifying the possible reasons for a filter in a heating system not being replaced when it should have been.

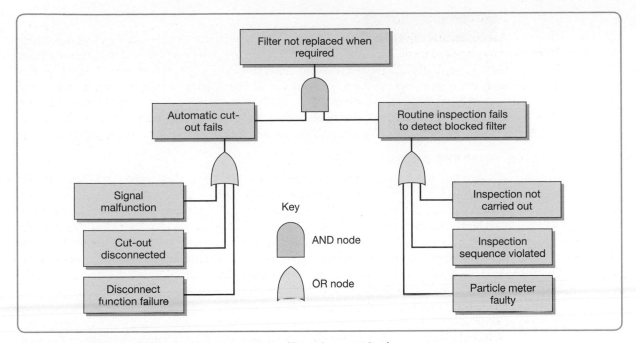

Figure 19.4 Fault tree analysis for failure to replace filter when required

Likelihood of failure

The difficulty of estimating the chance of a failure occurring varies greatly. Some failures are well understood through a combination of rational causal analysis and historical performance. For example, a mechanical component may fail within 10 to 17 months of its installation in 99 per cent of cases. Other types of failure are far more difficult to predict. The chances of a fire in a supplier's plant are (hopefully) low, but how low? There will be some data concerning fire hazards in this type of plant, but the estimated probability of failure will be subjective.

'Objective' estimates

Estimates of failure based on historical performance can be measured in three main ways: failure rates – how often a failure occurs; reliability – the chances of a failure occurring; and availability – the amount of available useful operating time. 'Failure rate' and 'reliability' are different ways of measuring the same thing – the propensity of an operation, or part of an operation, to fail. Availability is one measure of the consequences of failure in the operation.

Failure rate

Failure rate (FR) is calculated as the number of failures over a period of time. For example, the security of an airport can be measured by the number of security breaches per year, and the failure rate of an engine can be measured in terms of the number of failures divided by its operating time. It can be measured either as a percentage of the total number of products tested or as the number of failures over time:

$$FR = \frac{\text{number of failures}}{\text{total number of products tested}} \times 100$$

or

$$FR = \frac{\text{number of failures}}{\text{operating time}}$$

A batch of 50 electronic components is tested for 2,000 hours. Four of the components fail during the test as follows:

Failure 1 occurred at 1,200 hours

Failure 2 occurred at 1,450 hours

Failure 3 occurred at 1,720 hours

Failure 4 occurred at 1,905 hours

$$\text{Failure rate (as a percentage)} = \frac{\text{number of failures}}{\text{number tested}} \times 100 = \frac{4}{50} \times 10 = 8\%$$

The total time of the test $= 50 \times 2,000 = 100,000$ component hours

But:

one component was not operating $2,000 - 1,200 = 800$ hours

one component was not operating $2,000 - 1,450 = 550$ hours

one component was not operating $2,000 - 1,720 = 280$ hours

one component was not operating $2,000 - 1,905 = 95$ hours

Thus:

$$\text{Total non-operating time} = 1,725 \text{ hours}$$

$$\text{Operating time} = \text{total time} - \text{non-operating time}$$

$$= 100,000 - 1,725 = 98,275 \text{ hours}$$

$$\text{Failure rate (in time)} = \frac{\text{number of failures}}{\text{operating time}} = \frac{4}{98,275}$$

$$= 0.000041$$

Bath-tub curves

Sometimes failure is a function of time. For example, the probability of an electric lamp failing is relatively high when it is first used, but if it survives this initial stage, it could still fail at any point, and the longer it survives, the more likely its failure becomes. The curve which describes failure probability of this type is called the bath-tub curve. It comprises three distinct stages: the 'infant-mortality' or 'early-life' stage where early failures occur caused by defective parts or improper use; the 'normal-life' stage when the failure rate is usually low and reasonably constant, and caused by normal random factors; the 'wear-out' stage when the failure rate increases as the part approaches the end of its working life and failure is caused by the ageing and deterioration of parts. Figure 19.5 illustrates three bath-tub curves with slightly different characteristics. Curve A shows a part of the operation which has a high initial infant-mortality failure but then a long, low-failure, normal life followed by the gradually increasing likelihood of failure as it approaches wear-out. Curve B is far less predictable. The distinction between the three stages is less clear, with infant-mortality failure subsiding only slowly and a gradually increasing chance of wear-out failure. Failure of the type shown in curve B is far more difficult to manage in a planned manner. The failure of operations which rely more on human resources than on technology, such as some services, can be closer to curve C. They may be less susceptible to component wear-out but more so to staff complacency as the service becomes tedious and repetitive.

Reliability

Reliability measures the ability to perform as expected over time. Usually the importance of any particular failure is determined partly by how interdependent the other parts of the

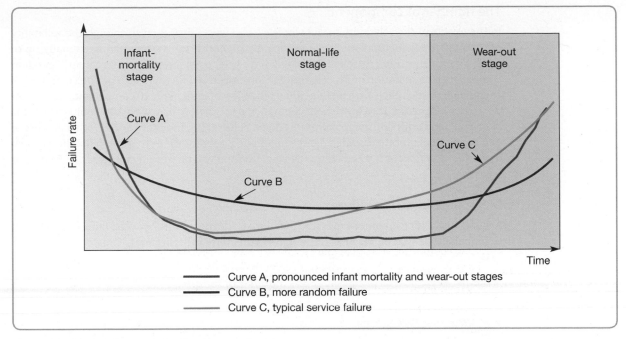

Figure 19.5 Bath-tub curves for three types of process

system are. With interdependence, a failure in one component will cause the whole system to fail. So, if an interdependent system has n components each with their own reliability, $R_1, R_2, \ldots, R_n$, the reliability of the whole system, R_s, is given by:

$$R_s = R_1 \times R_2 \times R_2 \times \ldots \times R_n$$

where

R_1 = reliability of component 1

R_2 = reliability of component 2

etc.

Worked example

An automated pizza-making machine in a food manufacturer's factory has five major components, with individual reliabilities (the probability of the component not failing) as follows:

Dough mixer	Reliability = 0.95
Dough roller and cutter	Reliability = 0.99
Tomato paste applicator	Reliability = 0.97
Cheese applicator	Reliability = 0.90
Oven	Reliability = 0.98

If one of these parts of the production system fails, the whole system will stop working. Thus the reliability of the whole system is:

$$R_s = 0.95 \times 0.99 \times 0.97 \times 0.90 \times 0.98$$
$$= 0.805$$

The number of components

In the example, the reliability of the whole system was only 0.8, even though the reliability of the individual components was significantly higher. If the system had been made up of more components, then its reliability would have been even lower. The more interdependent components an operation or process has, the lower its reliability will be. For one composed of components which each have an individual reliability of 0.99, with 10 components the system reliability will shrink to 0.9, with 50 components it is below 0.8, with 100 components it is below 0.4, and with 400 components it is down below 0.05. In other words, with a process of 400 components (not unusual in a large automated operation), even if the reliability of each individual component is 99 per cent, the whole system will be working for less than 5 per cent of its time.

Mean time between failures

An alternative (and common) measure of failure is the mean time between failures (MTBF) of a component or system. MTBF is the reciprocal of failure rate (in time). Thus:

$$\text{MTBF} = \frac{\text{operating hours}}{\text{number of failures}}$$

> ### Worked example
>
> In the earlier worked example which was concerned with electronic components, the failure rate (in time) of the electronic components was 0.000041. For that component:
>
> $$\text{MTBF} = \frac{1}{0.000041} = 24{,}390.24 \text{ hours}$$
>
> That is, a failure can be expected once every 24,390.24 hours on average.

Availability

Availability is the degree to which the operation is ready to work. An operation is not available if it has either failed or is being repaired following failure. There are several different ways of measuring it depending on how many of the reasons for not operating are included. Lack of availability because of planned maintenance or changeovers could be included, for example. However, when 'availability' is being used to indicate the operating time excluding the consequence of failure, it is calculated as follows:

$$\text{Availability } (A) = \frac{\text{MTBF}}{\text{MTBF} + \text{MTTR}}$$

where:

   MTBF = the mean time between failures of the operation

   MTTR = the mean time to repair, which is the average time taken to repair the operation, from the time it fails to the time it is operational again.

> ### Worked example
>
> A company which designs and produces display posters for exhibitions and sales promotion events competes largely on the basis of its speedy delivery. One particular piece of equipment which the company uses is causing some problems. This is its large platform colour laser

printer. Currently, the mean time between failures of the printer is 70 hours and its mean time to repair is 6 hours. Thus:

$$\text{Availability} = \frac{70}{70 + 6} = 0.92$$

The company has discussed its problem with the supplier of the printer who has offered two alternative service deals. One option would be to buy some preventive maintenance (*see* later for a full description of preventive maintenance) which would be carried out each weekend. This would raise the MTBF of the printer to 90 hours. The other option would be to subscribe to a faster repair service which would reduce the MTTR to 4 hours. Both options would cost the same amount. Which would give the company the higher availability?

With MTBF increased to 90 hours:

$$\text{Availability} = \frac{90}{90 + 6} = 0.938$$

With MTTR reduced to 4 hours:

$$\text{Availability} = \frac{70}{70 + 4} = 0.946$$

Availability would be greater if the company took the deal which offered the faster repair time.

'Subjective' estimates

Failure assessment, even for subjective risks, is increasingly a formal exercise that is carried out using standard frameworks, often prompted by health and safety, environmental, or other regulatory reasons. These frameworks are similar to the formal quality inspection methods associated with quality standards like ISO 9000 that often implicitly assume unbiased objectivity. However, individual attitudes to risk are complex and subject to a wide variety of influences. In fact, many studies have demonstrated that people are generally very poor at making risk-related judgements. Consider the success of state and national lotteries. The chances of winning, in nearly every case, are so low as to make the financial value of the investment entirely negative. If a player has to drive their car in order to purchase a ticket, they may be more likely to be killed or seriously injured than they are to win the top prize. But, although people do not always make rational decisions concerning the chances of failure, this does not mean abandoning the attempt. But it does mean that one must understand the limits to overly rational approaches to failure estimation; for example, how people tend to pay too much attention to dramatic low-probability events and overlook routine events. Even when 'objective' evaluations of risks are used, they may still cause negative consequences. For example, when the oil giant Royal-Dutch Shell took the decision to employ deep-water disposal in the North Sea for their Brent Spar Oil Platform, they felt that they were making a rational operational decision based upon the best available scientific evidence concerning environmental risk. Unfortunately Greenpeace disagreed and put forward an alternative 'objective analysis' showing significant risk from deep-water disposal. Eventually Greenpeace admitted their evidence was flawed but by that time Shell had lost the public relations battle and had altered their plans.

> *** Operations principle**
> Subjective estimates of failure probability are better than no estimates at all.

Critical commentary

The idea that failure can be detected through in-process inspection is increasingly seen as only partially true. Although inspecting for failures is an obvious first step in detecting them, it is not even close to being 100 per cent reliable. Accumulated evidence from research and practical examples consistently indicates that people, even when assisted by

▶

technology, are not good at detecting failure and errors. This applies even when special attention is being given to inspection. For example, airport security was significantly strengthened after 11 September 2001, yet one in ten lethal weapons that were entered into airports' security systems (in order to test them) were not detected. *'There is no such thing as 100 per cent security, we are all human beings,'* says Ian Hutcheson, the Director of Security at Airport Operator BAA. No one is advocating abandoning inspection as a failure detection mechanism. Rather it is seen as one of a range of methods of preventing failure.

Failure mode and effect analysis

One of the best-known approaches to assessing the relative significance of failure is failure mode and effect analysis (FMEA). Its objective is to identify the factors that are critical to various types of failure as a means of identifying failures before they happen. It does this by providing a 'checklist' procedure built around three key questions for each possible cause of failure:

- What is the likelihood that failure will occur?
- What would the consequence of the failure be?
- How likely is such a failure to be detected before it affects the customer?

Based on a quantitative evaluation of these three questions, a risk priority number (RPN) is calculated for each potential cause of failure. Corrective actions, aimed at preventing failure, are then applied to those causes whose RPN indicates that they warrant priority, (*see* Fig. 19.6).

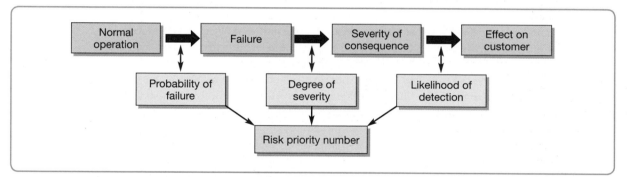

Figure 19.6 Procedure for failure mode and effects analysis (FMEA)

Worked example

Part of an FMEA exercise at a transportation company has identified three failure modes associated with the failure of 'goods arriving damaged' at the point of delivery:

- Goods not secured (failure mode 1).
- Goods incorrectly secured (failure mode 2).
- Goods incorrectly loaded (failure mode 3).

The improvement group which is investigating the failures allocates scores for the probability of the failure mode occurring, the severity of each failure mode, and the likelihood that they will be detected using the rating scales shown in Table 19.1, as follows:

Probability of occurrence

Failure mode 1	5
Failure mode 2	8
Failure mode 3	7

Table 19.1 Rating scales for FMEA

A. Occurrence of failure		
Description	Rating	Possible failure occurrence
Remote probability of occurrence	1	0
It would be unreasonable to expect failure to occur		
Low probability of occurrence	2	1:20,000
Generally associated with activities similar to previous ones with a relatively low number of failures	3	1:10,000
Moderate probability of occurrence	4	1:2,000
Generally associated with activities similar to previous	5	1:1,000
ones which have resulted in occasional failures	6	1:200
High probability of occurrence	7	1:100
Generally associated with activities similar to ones		
which have traditionally caused problems	8	1:20
Very high probability of occurrence	9	1:10
Near certainty that major failures will occur	10	1:2

B. Severity of failure	
Description	Rating
Minor severity	1
A very minor failure which would have no noticeable effect on system performance	
Low severity	2
A minor failure causing only slight customer annoyance	3
Moderate severity	4
A failure which would cause some customer	5
dissatisfaction, discomfort or annoyance, or would	6
cause noticeable deterioration in performance	
High severity	7
A failure which would engender a high degree of	8
customer dissatisfaction	
Very high severity	9
A failure which would affect safety	
Catastrophic	10
A failure which may cause damage to property, serious injury or death	

C. Detection of failure		
Description	Rating	Probability of detection
Remote probability that the defect will reach the customer	1	0 to 15%
(It is unlikely that such a defect would pass through inspection, test or assembly)		
Low probability that the defect will reach the	2	6 to 15%
customer	3	16 to 25%
Moderate probability that the defect will reach the	4	26 to 35%
customer	5	36 to 45%
	6	46 to 55%
High probability that the defect will reach the	7	56 to 65%
customer	8	66 to 75%
Very high probability that the defect will reach the	9	76 to 85%
customer	10	86 to 100%

Severity of failure

Failure mode 1	6
Failure mode 2	4
Failure mode 3	4

Probability of detection

Failure mode 1	2
Failure mode 2	6
Failure mode 3	7

The RPN of each failure mode is calculated:

Failure mode 1 (goods not secured)	$5 \times 6 \times 2 = 60$
Failure mode 2 (goods incorrectly secured)	$8 \times 4 \times 5 = 160$
Failure mode 3 (goods incorrectly loaded)	$7 \times 4 \times 7 = 196$

Priority is therefore given to failure mode 3 (goods incorrectly loaded) when attempting to eliminate the failure.

PREVENTING FAILURE

Once a thorough understanding of the causes and effects of failure has been established, the next responsibility of operations managers is to try to prevent the failures occurring in the first place. The obvious way to do this is to systematically examine any processes involved and 'design out' any failure points. (Many of the approaches used in Chapters 4 and 5 on process and product/service design and Chapter 17 on quality management can be used to do this.) In this section we will look at three further approaches to reducing risk by trying to prevent failure: building redundancy into a process; 'fail-safeing' some of the activities in the process; and maintaining the physical facilities in the process.

Redundancy

Building in redundancy to an operation means having back-up systems or components in case of failure. It can be expensive and is generally used when the breakdown could have a critical impact. It means doubling or even tripling some parts of a process or system in case one component fails. Nuclear power stations, spacecraft and hospitals all have auxiliary systems in case of an emergency. Some organizations also have 'back-up' staff held in reserve in case someone does not turn up for work. Rear brake lighting sets in buses and trucks contain two bulbs to reduce the likelihood of not showing a red light. Human bodies contain two of some organs – kidneys and eyes, for example – both of which are used in 'normal operation' but the body can cope with a failure in one of them. The reliability of a component together with its back-up is given by the sum of the reliability of the original component and the likelihood that the back-up component will both be needed *and* be working.

$$R_{a+b} = R_a + (R_b \times P(\text{failure}))$$

where

$$R_{a+b} = \text{reliability of component } a \text{ with its back-up component } b$$
$$R_a = \text{reliability of } a \text{ alone}$$
$$R_b = \text{reliability of back-up component } b$$
$$P(\text{failure}) = \text{the probability that component } a \text{ will fail and therefore component } b \text{ will be needed}$$

The food manufacturer in the earlier worked example has decided that the cheese depositor in the pizza-making machine is so unreliable that it needs a second cheese depositor to be fitted to the machine which will come into action if the first cheese depositor fails.

The two cheese depositors (each with reliability = 0.9) working together will have a reliability of:

$$0.9 + [0.9 \times (1 - 0.9)] = 0.99$$

The reliability of the whole machine is now:

$$0.95 \times 0.99 \times 0.97 \times 0.99 \times 0.98 = 0.885$$

Redundancy is often used for servers, where system availability is particularly important. In this context, the industry uses three main types of redundancy:

- **Hot standby** – where both primary and secondary (backup) systems run simultaneously. The data is copied to the secondary server in real time so that both systems contain identical information.
- **Warm standby** – where the secondary system runs in the background to the primary system. Data is copied to the secondary server at regular intervals, so there are times when both servers do not contain exactly the same data.
- **Cold standby** – where the secondary system is only called upon when the primary system fails. The secondary system receives scheduled data backups, but less frequently than a warm standby, so cold standby is mainly used for non-critical applications.

Fail-safeing

The concept of fail-safeing has emerged since the introduction of Japanese methods of operations improvement. Called poka-yoke in Japan (from *yokeru,* to prevent, and *poka,* inadvertent errors), the idea is based on the principle that human mistakes are to some extent inevitable. What is important is to prevent them becoming defects. Poka-yokes are simple (preferably inexpensive) devices or systems which are incorporated into a process to prevent inadvertent operator mistakes resulting in a defect. Typical poka-yokes are such devices as:

> * **Operations principle**
> Simple methods of fail-safeing can often be the most cost effective.

- limit switches on machines which allow the machine to operate only if the part is positioned correctly;
- gauges placed on machines through which a part has to pass in order to be loaded onto, or taken off, the machine – an incorrect size or orientation stops the process;
- digital counters on machines to ensure that the correct number of cuts, passes or holes have been machined;
- checklists which have to be filled in, either in preparation for, or on completion of, an activity;
- light beams which activate an alarm if a part is positioned incorrectly.

More recently, the principle of fail-safeing has been applied to service operations. Service poka-yokes can be classified as those which 'fail-safe the server' (the creator of the service) and those which 'fail-safe the customer' (the receiver of the service). Examples of fail-safeing the server include:

- colour-coding cash register keys to prevent incorrect entry in retail operations;
- the McDonald's french-fry scoop which picks up the right quantity of fries in the right orientation to be placed in the pack;

- trays used in hospitals with indentations shaped to each item needed for a surgical procedure – any item not back in place at the end of the procedure might have been left in the patient;
- the paper strips placed round clean towels in hotels, the removal of which helps house-keepers to tell whether a towel has been used and therefore needs replacing.

Examples of fail-safeing the customer include:

- the locks on aircraft lavatory doors, which must be turned to switch the light on;
- beepers on ATMs to ensure that customers remove their cards;
- height bars on amusement rides to ensure that customers do not exceed size limitations;
- outlines drawn on the walls of a child-care centre to indicate where toys should be replaced at the end of the play period;
- tray stands strategically placed in fast-food restaurants to remind customers to clear their tables.

Critical commentary

Much of the previous discussion surrounding the prevention of failure has assumed a 'rational' approach. In other words, it is assumed that operations managers and customers alike will put more effort into preventing failures that are either more likely to occur or more serious in their consequences. Yet this assumption is based on a rational response to risk. In fact, being human, managers often respond to the perception of risk rather than its reality. For example, Table 19.2 shows the cost of each

Table 19.2 The cost per life saved of various safety (failure prevention) investments

Safety investment	Cost per life (€M)
Advanced train protection system	30
Train protection warning systems	7.5
Implementing recommended guidelines on rail safety	4.7
Implementing recommended guidelines on road safety	1.6
Local authority spending on road safety	0.15

life saved by investment in various road and rail transportation safety (in other words, failure prevention) investments. The table shows that investing in improving road safety is very much more effective than investing in rail safety. And while no one is arguing for abandoning efforts on rail safety, it is noted by some transportation authorities that actual investment reflects more the public perception of rail deaths (low) compared with road deaths (very high).

Maintenance

Maintenance is how organizations try to avoid failure by taking care of their physical facilities. It is an important part of most operations' activities, particularly in operations dominated by their physical facilities such as power stations, hotels, airlines and petrochemical refineries. The benefits of effective maintenance include enhanced safety, increased reliability, higher quality (badly maintained equipment is more likely to cause errors), lower operating costs (because regularly serviced process technology is more efficient), a longer lifespan for process technology, and higher 'end value' (because well-maintained facilities are generally easier to dispose of into the second-hand market).

The three basic approaches to maintenance

In practice an organization's maintenance activities will consist of some combination of the three basic approaches to the care of its physical facilities. These are run to breakdown (RTB), preventive maintenance (PM) and condition-based maintenance (CBM).

Run to breakdown maintenance. As its name implies, this involves allowing the facilities to continue operating until they fail. Maintenance work is performed only after failure has taken place. For example, the televisions, bathroom equipment and telephones in a hotel's guest rooms will probably only be repaired when they fail. The hotel will keep some spare parts and the staff available to make any repairs when needed. Failure in these circumstances is neither catastrophic (although perhaps irritating to the guest) nor so frequent as to make regular checking of the facilities appropriate.

Preventive maintenance. This attempts to eliminate or reduce the chances of failure by servicing (cleaning, lubricating, replacing and checking) the facilities at pre-planned intervals. For example, the engines of passenger aircraft are checked, cleaned and calibrated according to a regular schedule after a set number of flying hours. Taking aircraft away from their regular duties for preventive maintenance is clearly an expensive option for any airline. The consequences of failure while in service are considerably more serious, however. The principle is also applied to facilities with less catastrophic consequences of failure. The regular cleaning and lubricating of machines, even the periodic painting of a building, could be considered preventive maintenance.

Condition-based maintenance. This attempts to perform maintenance only when the facilities require it. For example, continuous process equipment, such as that used in coating photographic paper, is run for long periods in order to achieve the high utilization necessary for cost-effective production. Stopping the machine to change, say, a bearing when it is not strictly necessary to do so would take it out of action for long periods and reduce its utilization. Here condition-based maintenance might involve continuously monitoring the vibrations, for example, or some other characteristic of the line. The results of this monitoring would then be used to decide whether the line should be stopped and the bearings replaced.

Mixed maintenance strategies

Each approach to maintaining facilities is appropriate for different circumstances. RTB is often used where repair is relatively straightforward (so the consequence of failure is small), where regular maintenance is very costly, or where failure is not at all predictable (failure is just as likely to occur after repair as before). PM is used where the cost of unplanned failure is high and where failure is not totally random. CBM is used where the maintenance activity is expensive, either because of the cost of providing the maintenance itself, or because of the disruption which the maintenance activity causes to the operation. Most operations adopt a mixture of these approaches. Even an automobile uses all three approaches (*see* Fig. 19.7). Light bulbs and fuses are normally replaced only when they fail. Engine oil is subject to preventive maintenance at a regular service. Finally, most drivers also monitor the condition of the car, for example by measuring the amount of tread on the tyre.

Breakdown *versus* preventive maintenance

The balance between preventive and breakdown maintenance is usually set to minimize the total cost of breakdown. Infrequent preventive maintenance will cost little to provide but will result in a high likelihood (and therefore cost) of breakdown maintenance. Conversely,

Figure 19.7 A mixture of maintenance approaches is often used – in a car, for example

very frequent preventive maintenance will be expensive to provide but will reduce the cost of having to provide breakdown maintenance (*see* Fig. 19.8(a)). The total cost of maintenance appears to minimize at an 'optimum' level of preventive maintenance. However, the cost of providing preventive maintenance may not increase quite so steeply as indicated in Figure 19.8(a). The curve assumes that it is carried out by a separate set of people (skilled maintenance staff) from the 'operators' of the facilities. Furthermore, every time preventive maintenance takes place, the facilities cannot be used productively. This is why the slope of the curve increases, because the maintenance episodes start to interfere with the normal working of the operation. But in many operations some preventive maintenance can be performed by the operators themselves (which reduces the cost of providing it) and at times which are convenient for the operation (which minimizes the disruption to the operation). The cost of breakdowns could also be higher than is indicated in Figure 19.8(a). Unplanned breakdowns may do more than necessitate a repair and stop the operation; they can take away stability from the operation which prevents it being able to improve itself. Put these two ideas together and the minimizing total curve and maintenance cost curve look more like

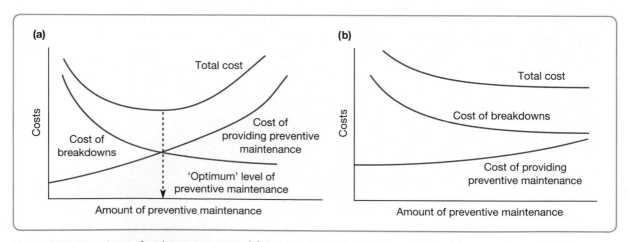

Figure 19.8 Two views of maintenance costs. (a) One model of the costs associated with preventive maintenance shows an optimum level of maintenance effort. (b) If routine preventive maintenance tasks are carried out by operators and if the real cost of breakdowns is considered, the 'optimum' level of preventive maintenance shifts towards higher levels

Figure 19.8(b). The emphasis is shifted more towards the use of preventive maintenance than run-to-breakdown maintenance.

Total productive maintenance

Total productive maintenance (TPM) is 'the productive maintenance carried out by all employees through small group activities', where productive maintenance is 'maintenance management which recognizes the importance of reliability, maintenance and economic efficiency in plant design'.[5] In Japan, where TPM originated, it is seen as a natural extension in the evolution from run-to-breakdown to preventive maintenance. TPM adopts some of the teamworking and empowerment principles discussed earlier (in Chapter 9), as well as a continuous improvement approach to failure prevention (as discussed in Chapter 18). It also sees maintenance as an organization-wide issue, to which staff can contribute in some way. It is analogous to the total quality management approach (discussed in Chapter 17).

The five goals of TPM

TPM aims to establish good maintenance practice in operations through the pursuit of 'the five goals of TPM':

1 *Improve equipment effectiveness* by examining all the losses which occur.
2 *Achieve autonomous maintenance* by allowing staff to take responsibility for some of the maintenance tasks and for the improvement of maintenance performance.
3 *Plan maintenance* with a fully worked out approach to all maintenance activities.
4 *Train all staff in relevant maintenance skills* so that both maintenance and operating staff have all the skills to carry out their roles.
5 *Achieve early equipment management* by 'maintenance prevention' (MP), which involves considering failure causes and the maintainability of equipment during its design, manufacture, installation and commissioning.

Reliability-centred maintenance

Reliability-centred maintenance (RCM) uses the pattern of failure for each type of failure mode of a part of a system to dictate the approach to its maintenance. For example, take the process illustrated in Figure 19.9. This is a simple shredding process which prepares vegetables prior to freezing. The most significant part of the process which requires the most maintenance attention is the cutter sub-assembly. However, there are several modes of failure which could lead to the cutters requiring attention. Sometimes they require changing simply because they have worn out through usage, sometimes they have been damaged by small stones entering the process, sometimes they have shaken loose because they were not fitted correctly. The failure patterns for these three failure modes are very different, as illustrated in Figure 19.9. Certainly, 'wear out' can be managed by timing preventive maintenance intervals just prior to the increased likelihood of failure. But this approach would not help prevent stone damage which could happen at any time with equal likelihood. The approach here would be to prevent stones getting to the cutters in the first place, perhaps through fixing a screen. The failure pattern for the cutters shaking loose is different again. If the cutters have been incorrectly fitted, it would become evident soon after the fitting. Again, preventive maintenance is unlikely to help here; rather effort should be put into ensuring that the cutters are always correctly fitted, perhaps by organizing more appropriate training of staff. The approach of RCM is sometimes summarized as, 'if we cannot stop it from happening, we had better stop it from mattering'. In other words, if maintenance cannot either predict or even prevent failure, and the failure has important consequences, then efforts need to be directed at reducing the impact of the failure.

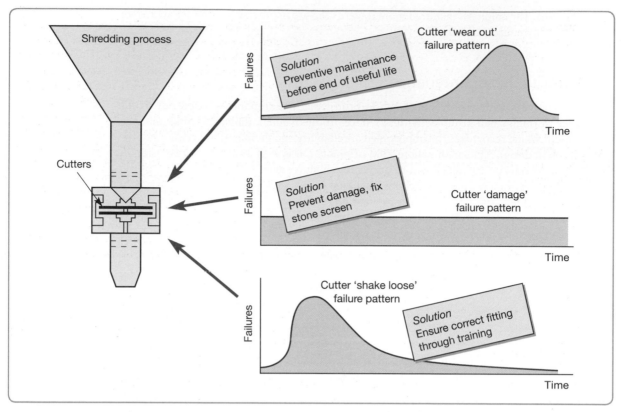

Figure 19.9 One part in one process can have several different failure modes, each of which requires a different approach

Lifting maintenance performance[6]

Back in 1853 Elisha Graves Otis introduced the world's first safety elevator in Yonkers, New York. It was to have a remarkable impact on the world's skylines. Without elevators, the skyscraping buildings that dominate most modern cities would probably never have been developed. Given the number of elevators in regular use throughout the world and the Otis Company's position as a leading supplier, Otis is the world's leading people mover. And Otis is very much aware that every time we enter an elevator we are trusting our lives to the people who designed and made it, and, more immediately, the people who maintain it. Without effective maintenance the elevators which are often on duty every minute of every day would literally be death traps. Central to the Otis philosophy of maintenance is its 'Otis Maintenance Management System' (OMMS), a programme that takes into account its clients' elevators' maintenance needs. Using this system Otis can customize inspection and

Source: Shutterstock.com/March Cattle

maintenance schedules for up to 12 years of operation or 5 million trips in advance. Maintenance procedures are determined by each elevator's individual pattern of use. Frequency of trips, the loads carried by the elevator and conditions of use, are all incorporated to determine the frequency and nature of maintenance activities. Because no component part of any equipment is perfect, Otis also monitors the life-cycle characteristics of all its elevators' components. This information on wear and failure is made available to its customers via its 24-hour communications centre and website. This ongoing understanding of component life also is used to update maintenance schedules.

With Otis's call service, when an elevator has a problem, a technician can be on their way to a customer's facility within minutes. Its 24-hours-a-day, 7-days-a-week service handles over 1.2 million calls a year and can get the elevators back in service on average within two and half hours. Also the Otis on-site monitoring equipment system is a sophisticated and interconnected system of sensors, monitors, hardware and software that collects, records, analyses and communicates hundreds of different system functions. If the system detects a problem it automatically makes a service call, calling out a technician who has been provided with the information collected by the system which will be used to help identify the component causing the problem. 'Around-the-clock response is important', says Otis, 'because problems don't keep office hours . . . [the remote sensing] . . . system detects deteriorating components, identifies intermittent anomalies, notes the small nuisances that . . . would have gone undetected . . . It identifies most potential problems before they occur.'

HOW CAN OPERATIONS MITIGATE THE EFFECTS OF FAILURE?

Risk, or failure, mitigation means isolating a failure from its negative consequences. It is an admission that not all failures can be avoided. However, in some areas of operations management, relying on mitigation, rather than prevention, is unfashionable. For example, 'inspection' practices in quality management were based on the assumption that failures were inevitable and needed to be detected before they could cause harm. Modern total quality management places much more emphasis on prevention. Yet, in operations and process resilience, mitigation can be vital when used in conjunction with prevention in reducing overall risk.

Risk mitigation actions

The nature of the action taken to mitigate failure will obviously depend on the nature of the risk. In most industries technical experts have established a classification of risk mitigation actions that are appropriate for the types of risk likely to be suffered. So, for example, in agriculture, government agencies and industry bodies have published mitigation strategies for such risks as the outbreak of crop disease, contagious animal infections, and so on. Such documents will outline the various mitigation actions that can be taken under different circumstances and detail exactly who are responsible for each action. Although these classifications tend to be industry-specific, the following generic categorization gives a flavour of the types of mitigation actions that may be generally applicable.

Mitigation planning is the activity of ensuring that all possible failure circumstances have been identified and the appropriate mitigation actions identified. It is the overarching activity that encompasses all subsequent mitigation actions, and may be described in the form of a decision tree or guide rules.

Economic mitigation includes actions such as insurance against losses from failure, spreading the financial consequences of failure, and 'hedging' against failure. Insurance is the best known of these actions and is widely adopted, although ensuring appropriate insurance and effective claims management is a specialized skill in itself. Hedging often takes the form of financial instruments; for example, a business may purchase a financial 'hedge' against the price risk of a vital raw material deviating significantly from a set price.

Containment (spatial) means stopping the failure physically spreading to affect other parts of an internal or external supply network. Preventing contaminated food from spreading through the supply chain, for example, will depend on real-time information systems that provide traceability data.

Containment (temporal) means containing the spread of a failure over time. It particularly applies when information about a failure or potential failure needs to be transmitted without undue delay. For example, systems that give advanced warning of hazardous weather such as snow storms must transmit such information to local agencies such as the police and road clearing organizations in time for them to stop the problem causing excessive disruption.

Loss reduction covers any action that reduces the catastrophic consequences of failure by removing the resources that are likely to suffer those consequences. For example, the road signs that indicate evacuation routes in the event of severe weather, or the fire drills that train employees in how to escape in the event of an emergency, may not reduce all the consequences of failure, but can help in reducing loss of life or injury.

Substitution means compensating for failure by providing other resources that can substitute for those rendered less effective by the failure. It is a little like the concept of redundancy that was described earlier, but does not always imply excess resources if a failure has not occurred. For example, in a construction project, the risk of encountering unexpected geological problems may be mitigated by the existence of a separate work plan that is invoked only if such problems are found.

HOW CAN OPERATIONS RECOVER FROM THE EFFECTS OF FAILURE?

In parallel with considering how to prevent failures occurring, operations managers need to decide what they will do when failures do occur. This activity is called failure recovery. All types of operation can benefit from well-planned recovery. For example, a construction company whose mechanical digger breaks down can have plans in place to arrange a replacement from a hire company. The breakdown might be disruptive, but not as much as it might have been if the operations manager had not worked out what to do. Recovery procedures will also shape customers' perceptions of failure. Even where the customer sees a failure, it may not necessarily lead to dissatisfaction. Indeed, in many situations, customers may well accept that things do go wrong. If there is a metre of snow on the train lines, or if the restaurant is particularly popular, we may accept that the product or service does not work. It is not necessarily the failure itself that leads to dissatisfaction but often the organization's response to the

> **✳ Operations principle**
>
> Successful failure recover can yield more benefits than if the failure had not occurred.

breakdown. While mistakes may be inevitable, dissatisfied customers are not. A failure may even be turned into a positive experience. A good recovery can turn angry, frustrated customers into loyal ones. One research project used four service scenarios and examined the willingness of customers to use an organization's services again.[7] The four scenarios were:

1 The service is delivered to meet the customers' expectations and there is full satisfaction.
2 There are faults in the service delivery but the customer does not complain about them.
3 There are faults in the service delivery and the customer complains but he/she has been fobbed off or mollified. There is no real satisfaction with the service provider.
4 There are faults in the service delivery and the customer complains and feels fully satisfied with the resulting action taken by the service providers.

Customers who are fully satisfied and do not experience any problems (1) are the most loyal, followed by complaining customers whose complaints are resolved successfully (4). Customers who experience problems but don't complain (2) are in third place and last of all come customers who do complain but are left with their problems unresolved and feelings of dissatisfaction (3).

Recovery in high-visibility services

The idea of failure recovery has been developed particularly in service operations. As one specialist put it, '*If something goes wrong, as it often does, will anybody make special efforts to get it right? Will somebody go out of his or her way to make amends to the customer? Does anyone make an effort to offset the negative impact of a screw-up?*'[8] It has also been suggested that service recovery does not just mean 'return to a normal state' but to a state of enhanced perception. All breakdowns require the deliverer to jump through a few hoops to get the customer back to neutral. More hoops are required for victims to recover. Operations managers need to recognize that all customers have recovery expectations that they want organizations to meet. Recovery needs to be a planned process. Organizations therefore need to design appropriate responses to failure, linked to the cost and the inconvenience caused by the failure to the customer, which will meet the needs and expectations of the customer. Such recovery processes need to be carried out either by empowered front-line staff or by trained personnel who are available to deal with recovery in a way which does not interfere with day-to-day service activities.

Failure planning

Identifying how organizations can recover from failure is of particular interest to service operations because they can turn failures around to minimize the effect on customers or even to turn failure into a positive experience. It is also of interest to other industries, however, especially those where the consequences of failure are particularly severe. Bulk chemical manufacturers and nuclear processors, for example, spend considerable resources in deciding how they will cope with failures. The activity of devising the procedures which allow the operation to recover from failure is called failure planning. It is often represented by stage models, one of which is represented in Figure 19.10. We shall follow it through from the point where failure is recognized.

Discover   The first thing any manager needs to do when faced with a failure is to discover its exact nature. Three important pieces of information are needed: first of all, what exactly has happened; second, who will be affected by the failure; and, third, why did the failure occur? This last point is not intended to be a detailed inquest into the causes of failure (that comes later) but it is often necessary to know something of the causes of failure in case it is necessary to determine what action to take.

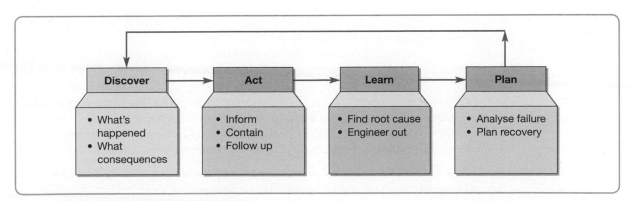

Figure 19.10   The stages in failure planning

Act The discover stage could only take minutes or even seconds, depending on the severity of the failure. If the failure is a severe one with important consequences, we need to move on to doing something about it quickly. This means carrying out three actions, the first two of which could be carried out in reverse order, depending on the urgency of the situation. First, tell the significant people involved what you are proposing to do about the failure. In service operations this is especially important where the customers need to be kept informed, both for their peace of mind and to demonstrate that something is being done. In all operations, however, it is important to communicate what action is going to happen so that everyone can set their own recovery plans in motion. Second, the effects of the failure need to be contained in order to stop the consequences spreading and causing further failures. The precise containment actions will depend on the nature of the failure. Third, there needs to be some kind of follow-up to make sure that the containment actions really have contained the failure.

Learn As discussed earlier in this chapter, the benefits of failure in providing learning opportunities should not be underestimated. In failure planning, learning involves revisiting the failure to find out its root cause and then engineering out the causes of the failure so that it will not happen again. This is the key stage for much failure planning.

Plan Learning the lessons from a failure is not the end of the procedure. Operations managers need formally to incorporate the lessons into their future reactions to failures. This is often done by working through 'in theory' how they would react to failures in the future. Specifically, this involves first identifying all the possible failures which might occur (in a similar way to the FMEA approach). Second, it means formally defining the procedures which the organization should follow in the case of each type of identified failure.

Business continuity

Many of the ideas behind failure, failure prevention and recovery are incorporated in the growing field of business continuity. This aims to help operations avoid and recover from disasters while keeping the business going, an issue that has risen to near the top of many firms' agenda since 11 September 2001. As operations become increasingly integrated (and increasingly dependent on integrated technologies such as information technologies), critical failures can result from a series of related and unrelated events and combine to disrupt totally a company's business. These events are the critical malfunctions which have the potential to interrupt normal business activity and even stop the entire company, such as: natural disasters; fire, power or telecommunications failure; corporate crime; theft; fraud; sabotage; computer system failure; bomb blast, scare or other security alert; key personnel leaving or becoming ill or dying; key supplier ceasing trading; contamination of product or processes and so on. The procedures adopted by business continuity experts are very similar to those described in this chapter:

- *Identify and assess risks* to determine how vulnerable the business is to various risks and take steps to minimize or eliminate them.
- *Identify core business processes* to prioritize those that are particularly important to the business and which, if interrupted, would have to be brought back to full operation quickly.
- *Quantify recovery times* to make sure staff understand priorities (for example, get the customer ordering system back into operation before the internal email).
- *Determine resources needed* to make sure that resources will be available when required.
- *Communicate* to make sure that everyone in the operation knows what to do if disaster strikes.

One response to the threat of such large-scale failures has been a rise in the number of companies offering 'replacement office' operations. These are fully equipped offices, often with access to a company's current management information and with normal internet and telephone communications links. They are fully working offices but with no people. Should a customer's main operation be affected by a disaster, business can continue in the replacement facility within days or even hours. The provision of this type of replacement office is, in effect, a variation of the 'redundancy' approach to reducing the impact of failure that was discussed earlier in this chapter.

Disaster recovery

Sometimes the term 'disaster recovery' is used as being synonymous with business continuity, but in fact is a subset that is focused on dealing with technology infrastructure. Disaster recovery is concerned with the action plans and procedures that are put in place to prepare for the recovery (or continuance) of critical information technology and systems after a natural or human-induced disaster that has interrupted normal operation. Redundant or replacement systems and IT capacity may be 'reserved' and data stored in more than one location. Cloud-computing-based business resilience is increasingly being sold as providing rapid recovery time and relatively low costs.

SUMMARY ANSWERS TO KEY QUESTIONS

Check and improve your understanding of this chapter using self-assessment questions and a personalized study plan, a video case study, and an eText – all at **www.myomlab.com**.

MyOMLab

❯ What is risk management?

- Risk management is about things going wrong and what operations can do to stop things going wrong. Or, more formally, *'the process which aims to help organizations understand, evaluate and take action on all their risks with a view to increasing the probability of their success and reducing the likelihood of failure'*.

- It consists of four broad activities:
  - understanding what failures could occur;
  - preventing failures occurring;
  - minimizing the negative consequences of failure (called risk 'mitigation');
  - recovering from failures when they do occur.

❯ How can operations assess the potential causes of, and risks from, failure?

- There are several causes of operations failure, including design failures, facilities failure, staff failure, supplier failure, customer failure and environmental disruption.

- There are three ways of measuring failure. 'Failure rates' indicate how often a failure is likely to occur. 'Reliability' measures the chances of a failure occurring. 'Availability' is the amount of available and useful operating time left after taking account of failures.

- Failure over time is often represented as a failure curve. The most common form of this is the so-called 'bath-tub curve' which shows the chances of failure being greater at the beginning and end of the life of a system or part of a system.

- Failure analysis mechanisms include accident investigation, product liability, complaint analysis, critical incident analysis, and failure mode and effect analysis (FMEA).

❯ How can failures be prevented?

- There are four major methods of improving reliability: designing out the fail points in the operation; building redundancy into the operation; 'fail-safeing' some of the activities of the operation; and maintenance of the physical facilities in the operation.

- Maintenance is the most common way operations attempt to improve their reliability, with three broad approaches. The first is running all facilities until they break down and then repairing them, the second is regularly maintaining the facilities even if they have not broken down, and the third is monitoring facilities closely to try to predict when breakdown might occur.

- Two specific approaches to maintenance have been particularly influential: total productive maintenance (TPM) and reliability-centred maintenance (RCM).

❯ How can operations mitigate the effects of failure?

- Risk, or failure, mitigation means isolating a failure from its negative consequences.

- Risk mitigation actions include:
  - mitigation planning;
  - economic mitigation;
  - containment (spatial and temporal);
  - loss reduction;
  - substitution.

❯ How can operations recover from the effects of failure?

- Recovery can be enhanced by a systematic approach to discovering what has happened to cause failure, acting to inform, contain and follow up the consequences of failure, learning to find the root cause of the failure and preventing it taking place again, and planning to avoid the failure occurring in the future.

- The idea of 'business continuity' planning is a common form of recovery planning.

CASE STUDY | **Slagelse Industrial Services (SIS)**

Slagelse Industrial Services (SIS) had become one of Europe's most respected die-casters of zinc, aluminium and magnesium parts and a supplier for hundreds of companies in many industries, especially automotive and defence. The company cast and engineer precision components by combining the most modern production technologies with precise tooling and craftsmanship. Slagelse Industrial Services (SIS) began life as a classic family firm set up by Erik Paulsen, who opened a small manufacturing and die-casting business in his hometown of Slagelse, a town in east Denmark, about 100 km southwest of Copenhagen. He had successfully leveraged his skills and passion for craftsmanship over many years whilst serving a variety of different industrial and agricultural customers. His son, Anders, had spent nearly 10 years working as a production engineer for a large automotive parts supplier in the UK, but eventually returned to Slagelse to take over the family firm. Exploiting his experience in mass manufacturing, Anders spent years building the firm into a larger-scale industrial component manufacturer but retained his father's commitment to quality and customer service. After 20 years he sold the firm to a UK-owned industrial conglomerate and within 10 years it had doubled in size again and now employed in the region of 600 people and had a turnover approaching £200 million. Throughout this period the firm had continued to target their products into niche industrial markets where their emphasis upon product quality and dependability meant they were less vulnerable to price and cost pressures. However in 2009, in the midst of difficult economic times and widespread industrial restructuring, they had been encouraged to bid for higher-volume, lower-margin work. This process was not very successful but eventually culminated in a tender for the design and production of a core metallic element of a child's toy (a 'transforming' robot).

Source: Shutterstock.com/anyunov

Interestingly the client firm, Alden Toys, was also a major customer for other businesses owned by SIS's corporate parent. They were adopting a preferred supplier policy and intended to have only one or two purchase points for specific elements in their global toy business. They had a high degree of trust in the parent organization and, on visiting the SIS site, were impressed by the firm's depth of experience and commitment to quality. In 2010, they selected SIS to complete the design and begin trial production.

'Some of us were really excited by the prospect . . . but you have to be a little worried when volumes are much greater than anything you've done before. I guess the risk seemed OK because in the basic process steps, in the type of product if you like, we were making something that felt very similar to what we'd been doing for many years.' (SIS Operations Manager)

'Well, obviously we didn't know anything about the toy market but then again we didn't really know all that much about the auto industry or the defence sector or any of our traditional customers before we started serving them. Our key competitive advantage, our capabilities, call it what you will, they are all about keeping the customer happy, about meeting and sometimes exceeding specification.' (SIS Marketing Director)

The designers had received an outline product specification from Alden Toys during the bid process and some further technical detail afterwards. Upon receipt of this final brief, a team of engineers and managers confirmed that the product could and would be manufactured using an up-scaled version of current production processes. The key operational challenge appeared to be accessing sufficient (but not too much) capacity. Fortunately, for a variety of reasons, SIS's parent company was very supportive of the project and promised to underwrite any sensible capital expenditure plans. Although this opinion of the nature of the production challenge was widely accepted throughout the firm (and shared by Alden Toys and SIS's parent group), it was left to one specific senior engineer to actually sign both the final bid and technical completion documentation. By early 2011, the firm had begun a trial period of full-volume production. Unfortunately, as would become clear later, during this design validation process SIS had effectively sanctioned a production method that would prove to be entirely inappropriate for the toy market; but it was not until 12 months later that any indication of problems began to emerge.

Throughout both North America and Europe, individual customers began to claim that their children had been 'poisoned' whilst playing with the end product. The threat of litigation was quickly levelled at Alden Toys and the whole issue rapidly became a 'full-blown' child health scare. A range of pressure groups and legal damage specialists supported and acted to aggregate the individual claims. Although similar accusations had been made before, the litigants and their supporters focused in on the recent changes made to the production process at SIS and in particular the role of Alden Toys in managing their suppliers.

'It's all very well claiming that you trust your suppliers but you simply cannot have the same level of control over another firm in another country. I am afraid that this all comes down to simple economics, that Alden Toys put its profits before children's health. Talk about trust . . . parents trusted this firm to look out for them and their families and have every right to be angry that boardroom greed was more important!' (Legal spokesperson for US litigants when being interviewed on UK TV consumer rights show)

Under intense media pressure, Alden Toys rapidly convened a high-profile investigation into the source of the contamination. It quickly revealed that an 'unauthorized' chemical had been employed in an apparently trivial metal cleaning and preparation element of the SIS production process. Although, when interviewed by the US media, the parent firm's legal director emphasized there was 'no causal link established or any admission of liability by either party', Alden Toys immediately withdrew their order and began to signal an intent to bring legal action against SIS and its parent. This action brought an immediate end to production in this part of the operation and the inspection (and subsequent official and legal visits) had a crippling impact upon the productivity of the whole site. The competitive impact of the failure was extremely significant. After over a year of production, the new product accounted for more than a third (39 per cent) of the factory's output. In addition to major cash-flow implications, the various investigations took up lots of managerial time and the reputation of the firm was seriously affected. As the site operations manager explained, even their traditional customers expressed concerns.

'It's amazing but people we had been supplying for 30 or 40 years were calling me up and asking "what's going on?"

and that they were worried about what all this might mean for them . . . these are completely different markets!'

QUESTIONS

1 What operational risks did SIS face when deciding to become a strategic supplier for Alden Toys?

2 What control problems did they encounter in implementing this strategy (pre- and post-investigation)?

PROBLEMS AND APPLICATIONS

MyOMLab

These problems and applications will help to improve your analysis of operations. You can find more practice problems as well as worked examples and guided solutions on MyOMLab at www.myomlab.com.

1 'We have a test bank where we test batches of 100 of our products continuously for 7 days and nights. This week only 3 failed, the first after 10 hours, the second after 72 hours, and the third after 1,020 hours.' What is the failure rate in percentage terms and in time terms for this product?

2 An automatic testing process takes samples of ore from mining companies and subjects them to four sequential tests. The reliability of the four different test machines that perform the tasks is different. The first test machine has a reliability of 0.99, the second has a reliability of 0.92, the third has a reliability of 0.98, and the fourth a reliability of 0.95. If one of the machines stops working, the total process will stop. What is the reliability of the total process?

3 For the product testing example in Problem 1, what is the mean time between failures (MTBF) for the products?

4 Conduct a survey amongst colleagues, friends and acquaintances of how they cope with the possibility that their computers might 'fail', either in terms of ceasing to operate effectively, or in losing data. Discuss how the concept of redundancy applies in such failure.

5 In terms of its effectiveness at managing the learning process, how does a university detect failures? What could it do to improve its failure detection processes?

SELECTED FURTHER READING

Dhillon, B.S. (2002) *Engineering Maintenance: A Modern Approach*, Technomic Publishing Company, Lancaster, PA. A comprehensive book for the enthusiast that stresses the 'cradle-to-grave' aspects of maintenance.

Evans, D. (2012) *Risk Intelligence: How to Live with Uncertainty*, Atlantic Books, London. Looks at what the author claims to be a special kind of intelligence for dealing with risk and uncertainty.

Li, J., Yu, K., Wang, L. and Song, H. (2007) Research on operational risk management for equipment, *Journal of Academy of Armored Force Engineering*, vol. 21, no. 2, 8–11. Not as dull as it sounds. Deals with risks in military operations including complex equipment systems.

Regester, M. and Larkin, J. (2005), *Risk Issues and Crisis Management: A Casebook of Best Practice*, Kogan Page, London. Aimed at practising managers, with lots of advice. Good for getting the flavour of how it is in practice.

Smith, D.J. (2000) *Reliability, Maintainability and Risk*, **Butterworth-Heinemann, Oxford.** A comprehensive and excellent guide to all aspects of maintenance and reliability.

USEFUL WEBSITES

www.smrp.org Site of the Society for Maintenance and Reliability Professionals. Gives an insight into practical issues.

www.sre.org American Society of Reliability Engineers. The newsletters give insights into reliability practice.

http://facultyweb.berry.edu/jgrout/pokayoke.html The poka-yoke page of John Grout. Some great examples, tutorials, etc.

www.rspa.com/spi/SQA.html Lots of resources, involving reliability and poka-yoke.

http://sra.org Site of the Society for Risk Analysis. Very wide scope, but interesting.

www.hse.gov.uk/risk Health and Safety Executive of the UK government.

www.theirm.org The home page of the Institute of Risk Management.

www.myomlab.com Test which sections you have mastered and which you need to review, with questions, a personalized study plan, video clips, revision tips, and cases.

Now that you have finished reading this chapter, why not visit MyOMLab at www.myomlab.com where you'll find more learning resources to help you make the most of your studies and get a better grade.

20 Organizing for improvement

Key questions

> Why does improvement need organizing?

> How should the improvement effort be linked to strategy?

> What information is needed for improvement?

> What should be improvement priorities?

> How can organizational culture affect improvement?

> What are the key implementation issues?

INTRODUCTION

This is the third, and final, chapter devoted to operations improvement. It examines some of the managerial issues associated with how improvement can be organized. There are no techniques as such in this chapter. Nor are all the issues dealt with easily defined. Rather it covers the 'soft' side of improvement. But do not dismiss this as in any way less important. In practice it is often the 'soft' stuff that determines the success or failure of improvement efforts. Moreover, the 'soft' stuff can be more difficult to get right than the 'hard', more technique-based, aspects of improvement. The 'hard' stuff is hard, but the 'soft' stuff is harder!

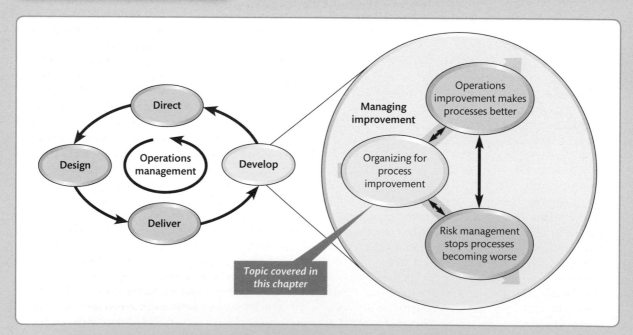

Figure 20.1 This chapter covers the management of improvement

Improving Sonae Corporation's retail operations

(Adapted, with permission, from an original case by Professors Rui Soucasaux Sousa and Sofia Salgado Pinto, Católica Porto Business School, Portugal.)

The retail industry may not seem to be the most likely setting for the use of improvement approaches more usually associated with manufacturing, but Sonae Corporation's Continente supermarkets' 22,500 employees have demonstrated that any type of business can benefit from operations improvement initiatives. Operating 170 stores and 2 state-of-the-art distribution centres, Continente stores have become a benchmark in Portugal for superior customer service and competitive prices.

Source: Shutterstock.com/Adisa

Sonae's operations improvement programme was originally a response to changes in Portuguese labour laws which required companies to provide a minimum of 35 hours of training per year, per worker. Jaime Maia, Sonae's Human Resource Director, was keen that the training should be 'on-the-job' rather than being based in the classroom. He asked a consulting firm, the Kaizen Institute (KI) to help, first by observing daily operations at several retail stores. The results were surprising. KI uncovered a significant amount of waste (or 'muda' as KI called it, adopting lean terminology, see Chapter 15). It was clear that there was potential for a programme combining training with process improvement. However, when Jaime Maia and KI presented their ideas to the Chief Operations Officer (COO), their photographs showing several examples of waste caused some discomfort; after all, they were the most successful retailer in Portugal. Despite some scepticism, the COO decided to invite KI to explain the programme to a senior management team. Several managers argued that lean principles would not work in retail because, unlike a manufacturing plant, the retail environment was too turbulent and dynamic. Yet, eventually the COO decided to give the improvement initiative a chance.

Within a store several processes keep the operation running smoothly. 'Back-office' processes include unloading trucks, routing goods to sales areas or the warehouses, cleaning activities, shelf replenishment and store decoration (for specific seasons or promotions). 'Front-office' processes include the sales areas for various types of goods, and the supporting checkout and customer service areas. Key operational goals include the efficient use of store space, increasing sales per square metre of store space, and customer satisfaction. The first stage of the programme involved workshops for store managers that focused on three store processes – goods reception, shelf replenishment activities carried out with the store closed, and shelf replenishment activities carried out during the day with the store open. Simple lean tools such as 5 S and visual management (see Chapter 15) were used, as was the idea of 'gemba', or working out improvements in the workplace. After a seminar, each store manager had to go back and work with his/her team to develop and provide training sessions to the workforce, based on a 'lean manual', define an action plan and schedule, identify the most obvious problem areas in the store, and select the lean tools to be applied. As Jaime Maia explained, *'Improvements were suggested by store managers, top down. But those ideas were immediately enriched and put into action by the teams in the stores, bringing about further improvements in a continuous fashion.'*

After just one year there had been an 'explosion of creativity' in the stores, leading to significant benefits. Productivity had increased, inventory was reduced, as were stock-outs, and customer satisfaction increased. As Jaime Maia put it, continuous improvement *'stimulates a good attitude and a constant sense of critique'*. A typical improvement project concerned the company's shelf replenishing policy. Initially, Sonae believed that the best way to minimize stock-outs was to continuously replenish shelves as sales took place. This meant that sales shelves were replenished frequently in small quantities during the day. However, this has a number of disadvantages. In particular, product movements are constrained by customer flows and by the need to keep the store clean and tidy at all times. So a new replenishment policy was tested. *'The store is fully loaded before the morning opening. From then on, we just need to perform minimal stock maintenance during the day. There is a time of the day at which a shelf may appear to be quite empty. However, typically, there is no need to replenish the shelf, but simply bring the products from the back to the front of the shelf, or from the upper shelves to the eye-level shelves'*, explained Nuno Almeida, Regional Operations Manager. Fast-moving goods continue to be replenished during the day with the store open, but they represent only a small proportion of the total number of goods displayed at a store

With the success of the programme, Sonae decided to expand it by including all areas in the stores, introducing additional improvement practices such as total preventive maintenance (see Chapter 19), and most significantly, involving all employees in the programme. A formal steering group for the improvement initiative was created, and halfway through each year it developed an action plan for the following year, with monthly general meetings and a video-conference meeting being held every two weeks to assess progress. Substantial improvements in performance continued, but the main breakthrough came from the widespread involvement of employees, which led to a greater feeling of success. Yet progress was not uniform. When KI conducted an audit of some stores to assess the level of lean implementation they found a large variation between stores, ranging from a score of 87 per cent implementation for the best store, down to 37 per cent implementation for the store with most improvement potential. So the steering group decided that their priority should now be to improve the consistency of improvement implementation across stores, with more emphasis on benchmarking and learning.

And the future? *'One challenge'*, said Jaime Maia, *'is to sustain the motivation for the programme across the organization, after years of continuous successes.'* He also felt the programme was reaching a new turning point and needed to be reinvented. Until now, lean principles had been applied mainly to materials flows and workplace organization. Could lean principles be extended to customer flows?

WHY THE IMPROVEMENT EFFORT NEEDS ORGANIZING

Improvement does not just happen. It needs organizing and it needs implementing. It also needs a purpose that is well thought through and clearly articulated. Although much operations improvement will take place at an operational level, it may be small scale and incremental. Nevertheless, it must be placed in some kind of context. That is, it should be clear *why* improvement is happening as well as what it consists of. This means linking the improvement to the overall strategic objectives of the organization. This is why we start this chapter by thinking about improvement in a strategic context. Improvement must also be based on sound information. If the performance of operations and the processes within them are to be improved, one must first be able to define and measure exactly what we mean by 'performance'. Furthermore, benchmarking one's own activities and performance against other organizations' activities and performance can both lead to valuable insights and help to quantify progress. It also helps to answer some basic improvement questions such as: who should be in charge of it, when it should take place, and how one should go about ensuring that improvement really does impact the performance of the organization. This is why in this section we will deal with such issues as measuring performance, benchmarking, prioritization, learning and culture, and the role of systems of procedures in the implementation process.

Remember also that the issue of how improvement should be organized is not a new concern. It has been a concern of management writers for decades. For example, W.E. Deming (considered in Japan to be the father of quality control) asserted that quality starts with top management and is a strategic activity.[1] It is claimed that much of the success in terms of quality in Japanese industry was the result of his lectures to Japanese companies in the 1950s.[2] Deming's basic philosophy is that quality and productivity increase as 'process variability' (the unpredictability of the process) decreases. In his *14 points for quality improvement*, he emphasizes the need for statistical control methods, participation, education, openness and purposeful improvement:

1 Create constancy of purpose.
2 Adopt new philosophy.
3 Cease dependence on inspection.

4 End awarding business on price.
5 Improve constantly the system of production and service.
6 Institute training on the job.
7 Institute leadership.
8 Drive out fear.
9 Break down barriers between departments.
10 Eliminate slogans and exhortations.
11 Eliminate quotas or work standards.
12 Give people pride in their job.
13 Institute education and a self-improvement programme.
14 Put everyone to work to accomplish it.

LINKING IMPROVEMENTS TO STRATEGY

At one level, the objective of any improvement is obvious – it tries to make things better! But, does this mean better in every way or better in some specific manner? And how much better does better mean? This is why we need some more general framework to put any organization's improvement efforts into a broader context; preferably one that brings together an overall operation's performance with its market objectives. After all, at a strategic level, the whole purpose of operations improvement is to make operations performance better serve its markets. Figure 20.2(a) illustrates this idea by showing diagrammatically the approximate alignment or 'fit' between an operation's performance and the requirements of its markets.

> *** Operations principle**
> Without strategic clarity, key performance indicators cannot be appropriately targeted.

The vertical dimension represents the level of market requirements that reflect the intrinsic needs of customers or their expectations. This includes such factors as the strength of brand/reputation, the degree of market differentiation and the extent of plausible market promises. Moving along this dimension indicates a broadly enhanced level of market performance. The horizontal scale represents the level of the organization's operations performance. This includes such things as its ability to achieve its competitive objectives and the efficiency with which it uses its resources. Again, moving along the dimension indicates a broadly enhanced level of operations performance and therefore operations capabilities. Be careful, however, in using this diagrammatic representation. It is a conceptual model rather than a practical tool. It is intended merely to illustrate some ideas around the concept of strategic improvement. In terms of the framework illustrated in Figure 20.2(a), improvement means three things:

1 **Achieving 'alignment'.** This means achieving an approximate balance between 'required market performance' and 'actual operations performance'. The diagonal line in Figure 20.2(a) therefore represents a 'line of fit' with market and operations in balance.
2 **Achieving 'sustainable' alignment.** It is not enough to achieve some degree of alignment to a single point in time. Equally important is whether operations processes could adapt to the new market conditions.
3 **Improving overall performance.** If the requirements placed on the organization by its markets are relatively undemanding, then the corresponding level of operations performance will not need to be particularly high, while the more demanding the level of market requirements, the greater will have to be the level of operations performance. But most firms would see their overall strategic objectives as achieving alignment at a level that implies some degree of long-term competitive success. In Figure 20.2(b) point A represents alignment at a low level, while point B represents alignment at a higher level. The assumption in most firms' operations strategies is that point B is a more desirable position than point A because it is more likely to represent a financially successful position. High levels of market performance achieved as a result of high levels of operations performance is generally more difficult for competitors to match.

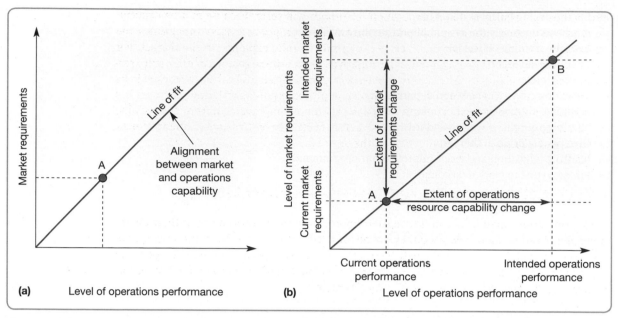

Figure 20.2 In operations improvement should achieve 'fit' between market requirements and operations performance

Deviating from the line of fit

During the improvement path from A to B in Figure 20.2 it may not be possible to maintain the balance between market requirements and operations performance. Sometimes the market may expect something that the operation cannot (temporarily) deliver. Sometimes operations may have capabilities that cannot be exploited in the market. At a strategic level, there are risks deriving from any deviation from the 'line of fit'. For example, delays in the improvement to a new website could mean that customers do not receive the level of service they were promised. This is shown as position X in Figure 20.3. Under these circumstances, the

Figure 20.3 Deviation from the 'line of fit' between market requirements and operations performance can expose the operation to risk

risk to the organization is that its reputation (or brand) will suffer because market expectations exceed the operation's capability to perform at the appropriate level. At other times, the operation may make improvements before they could be fully exploited in the market. For example, the same online retailer may have improved its website so that it can offer extra services, such as the ability to customize products, before those products have been stocked in its distribution centre. This means that, although an improvement to its ordering processes has been made, problems elsewhere in the company prevent the improvement from giving value to the company. This is represented by point Y in Figure 20.3. In both instances, improvement activity needs to move the operation back to the line of fit.

WHAT INFORMATION IS NEEDED FOR IMPROVEMENT?

Before operations managers can devise their approach to the improvement of their operations, they need to know how good they are already. The urgency, direction and priorities of improvement will be determined partly by whether the current performance of an operation is judged to be good, bad or indifferent. Therefore all operations need some kind of performance measurement as a prerequisite for improvement.

Performance measurement

Performance measurement is the process of *quantifying action*, where measurement means the process of quantification and the performance of the operation is assumed to derive from actions taken by its management.[3] Performance here is defined as the degree to which an operation fulfils the five performance objectives at any point in time, in order to satisfy its customers. Some kind of *performance measurement* is a prerequisite for judging whether an operation is good, bad or indifferent. Without performance measurement, it would be impossible to exert any control over an operation on an ongoing basis. A performance measurement system that gives no help to ongoing improvement is only partially effective. The polar diagrams (which we introduced in Chapter 2) in Figure 20.4 illustrate this concept. The five performance objectives which we have used throughout this book can be regarded as the dimensions of overall performance that satisfy customers. The market's needs and expectations of each performance objective will vary. The extent to which an operation meets market requirements will also vary. In addition, market requirements and the operation's performance could change over time. In Figure 20.4 the operation is originally almost meeting the requirements of the market as far as quality and flexibility are concerned, but

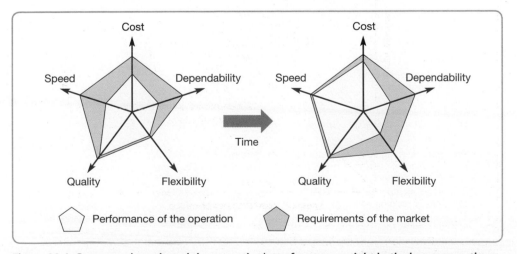

Figure 20.4 Customers' needs and the operation's performance might both change over time

is under-performing on its speed, dependability and cost. Sometime later the operation has improved its speed and cost to match market requirements but its flexibility no longer matches market requirements, not because it has deteriorated in an absolute sense but because the requirements of the market have changed.

Performance measurement, as we are treating it here, concerns three generic issues:

- What factors to include as performance measures?
- Which are the most important performance measures?
- What detailed measures to use?

What factors to include as performance measures?

The five generic performance objectives – quality, speed, dependability, flexibility and cost – can be broken down into more detailed measures, or they can be aggregated into 'composite' measures, such as 'customer satisfaction', 'overall service level' or 'operations agility'. These composite measures may be further aggregated by using measures such as 'achieve market objectives', 'achieve financial objectives', 'achieve operations objectives' or even 'achieve overall strategic objectives'. The more aggregated performance measures have greater strategic relevance insomuch as they help to draw a picture of the overall performance of the business, although by doing so they necessarily include many influences outside those that operations performance improvement would normally address. The more detailed performance measures are usually monitored more closely and more often, and although they provide a limited view of an operation's performance, they do provide a more descriptive and complete picture of what should be and what is happening within the operation. In practice, most organizations will choose to use performance targets from throughout the range. This idea is illustrated in Figure 20.5.

Choosing the important performance measures

One of the problems of devising a useful performance measurement system is trying to achieve some balance between having a few key measures on one hand (straightforward and simple, but may not reflect the full range of organizational objectives), and, on the other hand, having many detailed measures (complex and difficult to manage, but capable of conveying many nuances of performance). Broadly, a compromise is reached by making sure that there

Figure 20.5 Performance measures can involve different levels of aggregation

is a clear link between the operation's overall strategy, the most important (or 'key') performance indicators (KPIs) that reflect strategic objectives, and the bundle of detailed measures that are used to 'flesh out' each key performance indicator. Obviously, unless strategy is well defined it is difficult to 'target' a narrow range of key performance indicators.

What detailed measures to use?

The five performance objectives – quality, speed, dependability, flexibility and cost – are really composites of many smaller measures. For example, an operation's cost is derived from many factors, which could include the purchasing efficiency of the operation, the efficiency with which it converts materials, the productivity of its staff, the ratio of direct to indirect staff, and so on. All of these measures individually give a partial view of the operation's cost performance, and many of them overlap in terms of the information they include. However, each of them does give a perspective on the cost performance of an operation that could be useful either to identify areas for improvement or to monitor the extent of improvement. If an organization regards its 'cost' performance as unsatisfactory, disaggregating it into 'purchasing efficiency', 'operations efficiency', 'staff productivity', etc. might explain the root cause of the poor performance. Table 20.1 shows some of the partial measures which can be used to judge an operation's performance.

Table 20.1 Some typical partial measure of performance

Performance objective	Some typical measures
Quality	Number of defects per unit Level of customer complaints Scrap level Warranty claims Mean time between failures Customer satisfaction score
Speed	Customer query time Order lead time Frequency of delivery Actual *versus* theoretical throughput time Cycle time
Dependability	Percentage of orders delivered late Average lateness of orders Proportion of products in stock Mean deviation from promised arrival Schedule adherence
Flexibility	Time needed to develop new products/services Range of products/services Machine changeover time Average batch size Time to increase activity rate Average capacity/maximum capacity Time to change schedules
Cost	Minimum delivery time/average delivery time Variance against budget Utilization of resources Labor productivity Added value Efficiency Cost per operation hour

The balanced scorecard approach

Generally operations performance measures have been broadening in their scope. It is now generally accepted that the scope of measurement should, at some level, include external as well as internal, long-term as well as short-term, and 'soft' as well as 'hard' measures. The best-known manifestation of this trend is the 'balanced scorecard' approach taken by Kaplan and Norton.

> 'The balanced scorecard retains traditional financial measures. But financial measures tell the story of past events, an adequate story for industrial age companies for which investments in long-term capabilities and customer relationships were not critical for success. These financial measures are inadequate, however, for guiding and evaluating the journey that information age companies must make to create future value through investment in customers, suppliers, employees, processes, technology, and innovation.'[4]

As well as including financial measures of performance, in the same way as traditional performance measurement systems, the balanced scorecard approach also attempts to provide the important information that is required to allow the overall strategy of an organization to be reflected adequately in specific performance measures. In addition to financial measures of performance, it also includes more operational measures of customer satisfaction, internal processes, innovation and other improvement activities. In doing so it measures the factors behind financial performance which are seen as the key drivers of future financial success. In particular, it is argued that a balanced range of measures enables managers to address the following questions (*see* Fig. 20.6):

- How do we look to our shareholders (financial perspective)?
- What must we excel at (internal process perspective)?
- How do our customers see us (the customer perspective)?
- How can we continue to improve and build capabilities (the learning and growth perspective)?

The balanced scorecard attempts to bring together the elements that reflect a business's strategic position, including product or service quality measures, product and service development times, customer complaints, labour productivity, and so on. At the same time it attempts to avoid performance reporting becoming unwieldy by restricting the number of measures

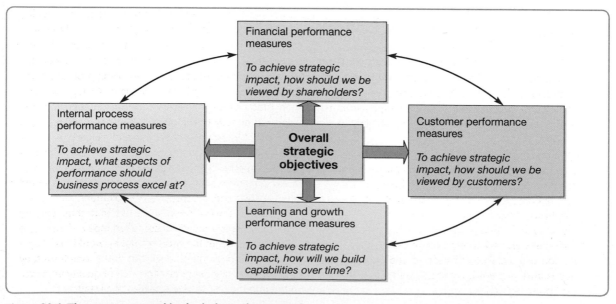

Figure 20.6 The measures used in the balanced scorecard

and focusing especially on those seen to be essential. The advantages of the approach are that it presents an overall picture of the organization's performance in a single report and, by being comprehensive in the measures of performance it uses, encourages companies to take decisions in the interests of the whole organization rather than sub optimizing around narrow measures.

SHORT CASE   Taxing quality[5]

Operations effectiveness is just as important an issue in public sector operations as it is for commercial companies. People have the right to expect that their taxes are not wasted on inefficient or inappropriate public processes. This is especially true of the tax collecting system itself. It is never a popular organization in any country, and tax payers can be especially critical when the tax collection process is not well managed. This was very much on the minds of the Aarhus Region Customs and Tax unit (Aarhus CT) when they developed their award-winning quality initiative. The Aarhus Region is the largest of Denmark's 29 local customs and tax offices. It acts as an agent for central government in collecting taxes in a professional and efficient manner while being able to respond to tax payers' queries. Aarhus CT must *'keep the user (customer) in focus'*, they say. *'Users must pay what is due – no more, no less and on time. But users are entitled to fair control and collection, fast and efficient case work, service and guidance, flexible employees, polite behaviour and a professional telephone service.'* The Aarhus CT approach to managing its quality initiative was built around a number of key points:

Source: Shutterstock.com/Ioana Davies

- A recognition that poor quality processes cause waste both internally and externally.
- A determination to adopt a practice of regularly surveying the satisfaction of its users. Employees were also surveyed, both to understand their views on quality and to check that their working environment would help to instill the principles of high-quality service.
- Although a not-for-profit organization, quality measures included measuring the organization's adherence to financial targets as well as error reporting.
- Internal processes were redefined and redesigned to emphasize customer needs and internal staff requirements. For example, Aarhus CT was the only tax region in Denmark to develop an independent information process that was used to analyse customers' needs and 'prevent misunderstanding in users' perception of legislation'.

- Internal processes were designed to allow staff the time and opportunity to develop their own skills, exchange ideas with colleagues and take on greater responsibility for management of their own work processes.

The organization set up what it called its 'Quality Organization' (QO) structure that spanned all divisions and processes. The idea of the QO was to foster staff commitment to continuous improvement and to encourage the development of ideas for improving process performance. Within the QO was the Quality Group (QG). This consisted of four managers and four process staff, and reported directly to senior management. It also set up a number of improvement groups and suggestion groups consisting of managers as well as process staff. The role of the suggestion groups was to collect and process ideas for improvement which the improvement groups would then analyse and, if appropriate, implement.

Aarhus CT were keen to stress that their Quality Groups would eventually become redundant if they were to be successful. In the short term they would maintain a stream of improvement ideas, but in the long term they should have fully integrated the idea of quality improvement into the day-to-day activities of all staff.

Setting target performance

A performance measure means relatively little until it is compared against some kind of target. Knowing that only 1 document in 500 is sent out to customers containing an error tells

us relatively little unless we know whether this is better or worse than we were achieving previously, and whether it is better or worse than other similar operations (especially competitors) are achieving. Setting performance targets transforms performance measures into performance 'judgements'. Several approaches to setting targets can be used, including the following:

- **Historically based targets** – targets that compare current against previous performance.
- **Strategic targets** – targets set to reflect the level of performance that is regarded as appropriate to achieve strategic objectives.
- **External performance-based targets** – targets set to reflect the performance that is achieved by similar, or competitor, external operations.
- **Absolute performance targets** – targets based on the theoretical upper limit of performance.

One of the problems in setting targets is that different targets can give very different messages regarding the improvement being achieved. So, for example, in Figure 20.7, one of an operation's performance measures is 'delivery' (in this case defined as the proportion of orders delivered on time). The performance for one month has been measured at 83 per cent, but any judgement regarding performance will be dependent on the performance targets. Using a *historical* target, when compared to last year's performance of 60 per cent, this month's performance of 83 per cent is good. But, if the operation's *strategy* calls for a 95 per cent delivery performance, the actual performance of 83 per cent looks decidedly poor. The company may also be concerned with how they perform against *competitors'* performance. If competitors are currently averaging delivery performances of around 80 per cent, the company's performance looks rather good. Finally, the more ambitious managers within the company may wish to at least try to seek perfection. Why not, they argue, use an *absolute* performance standard of 100 per cent delivery on time? Against this standard the company's actual 83 per cent again looks disappointing.

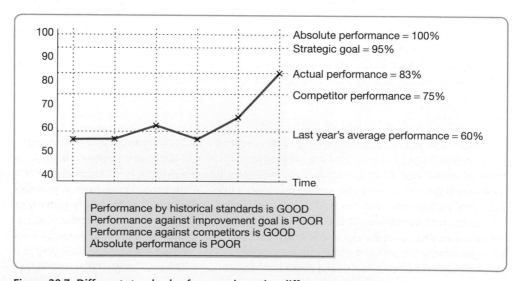

Figure 20.7 Different standards of comparison give different messages

Performance measurement and performance management

It is worth noting the difference between performance *measurement*, which we describe here, and performance *management*. They are closely related (and sometimes are confused with each other). Performance management is broader than performance measurement. It is the *'process of assessing progress toward achieving predetermined goals. It involves building on that process, adding the relevant communication and action on the progress achieved against these predetermined goals. It helps organizations achieve their strategic goals'.*[6] The objectives of performance management are to ensure co-ordination and coherence between individual, process or team objectives and overall strategic and organizational objectives. But more than that, performance management attempts to influence decisions, behaviours and skills development so that individuals and processes are better equipped to meet strategic objectives.

Benchmarking

Benchmarking is 'the process of learning from others' and involves comparing one's own performance or methods against other comparable operations. It is a broader issue than setting performance targets, and includes investigating other organizations' operations practice in order to derive ideas that could contribute to performance improvement. Its rationale is based on the idea that (a) problems in managing processes are almost certainly shared by processes elsewhere, and (b) that there is probably another operation somewhere that has developed a better way of doing things. For example, a bank might learn some things from a supermarket about how it could cope with demand fluctuations during the day. Benchmarking is essentially about stimulating creativity in improvement practice.

> **✱ Operations principle**
>
> Improvement is aided by contextualizing processes and operations performance through some kind of benchmarking.

Types of benchmarking

There are many different types of benchmarking (which are not necessarily mutually exclusive), some of which are listed below:

- *Internal benchmarking* is a comparison between operations or parts of operations which are within the same total organization.
- *External benchmarking* is a comparison between an operation and other operations which are part of a different organization.
- *Non-competitive benchmarking* is benchmarking against external organizations which do not compete directly in the same markets.
- *Competitive benchmarking* is a comparison directly between competitors in the same, or similar, markets.
- *Performance benchmarking* is a comparison between the levels of achieved performance in different operations.
- *Practice benchmarking* is a comparison between an organization's operations practices, or way of doing things, and those adopted by another operation.

Benchmarking as an improvement tool

Although benchmarking has become popular, some businesses have failed to derive maximum benefit from it. Partly this may be because there are some misunderstandings as to what benchmarking actually entails. First, it is not a 'one-off' project. It is best practised as a continuous process of comparison. Second, it does not provide 'solutions'. Rather, it provides ideas and information that can lead to solutions. Third, it does not involve simply copying or imitating other operations. It is a process of learning and adapting in a pragmatic manner. Fourth, it means devoting resources to the activity. Benchmarking cannot be done without some investment, but this does not necessarily mean allocating exclusive responsibility to a set of highly paid managers. In fact, there can be advantages in organizing staff at all levels to investigate and collate information from benchmarking targets.

It can be argued that there is a fundamental flaw in the whole concept of benchmarking. Operations that rely on others to stimulate their creativity, especially those that are in search of 'best practice', are always limiting themselves to currently accepted methods of operating or currently accepted limits to performance. In other words, benchmarking leads companies only as far as others have gone. 'Best practice' is not 'best' in the sense that it cannot be bettered, it is only 'best' in the sense that it is the best that one can currently find. Indeed accepting what is currently defined as 'best' may prevent operations from ever making the radical breakthrough or improvement that takes the concept of 'best' to a new and fundamentally improved level. This argument is closely related to the concept of breakthrough improvement discussed later in this chapter. Furthermore, methods or performance levels that are appropriate in one operation may not be in another. Because one operation has a set of successful practices in the way it manages its process does not mean that adopting those same practices in another context will prove equally successful. It is possible that subtle differences in the resources within a process (such as staff skills or technical capabilities) or the strategic context of an operation (for example, the relative priorities of performance objectives) will be sufficiently different to make the adoption of seemingly successful practices inappropriate.

WHAT SHOULD BE IMPROVEMENT PRIORITIES?

Earlier (in Chapter 3), when discussing the 'market requirements' perspective, we identified two major influences on the way in which operations decide on their improvement priorities:

- the needs and preferences of customers;
- the performance and activities of competitors.

The consideration of customers' needs has particular significance in shaping the objectives of all operations. The fundamental purpose of operations is to create goods and services in such a way as to meet the needs of their customers. What customers find important, therefore, the operation should also regard as important. If customers for a particular product or service prefer low prices to wide range, then the operation should devote more energy to reducing its costs than to increasing the flexibility which enables it to provide a range of products or services. The needs and preferences of customers shape the *importance* of operations objectives within the operation.

The role of competitors is different from that of customers. Competitors are the points of comparison against which the operation can judge its performance. From a competitive viewpoint, as operations improve their performance, the improvement which matters most is that which takes the operation past the performance levels achieved by its competitors. The role of competitors then is in determining achieved *performance*.

Both importance and performance have to be brought together before any judgement can be made as to the relative priorities for improvement. Just because something is particularly important to its customers does not mean that an operation should necessarily give it immediate priority for improvement. It may be that the operation is already considerably better than its competitors at serving customers in this respect. Similarly, just because an operation is not very good at something when compared with its competitors' performance, it does not necessarily mean that it should be immediately improved. Customers may not particularly value this aspect of performance. Both importance and performance need to be viewed together to judge the prioritization of objectives.

✳ **Operations principle**

Improvement priorities are determined by importance for customers and performance against competitors or similar operations.

Judging importance to customers

Earlier (Chapter 3) we introduced the idea of order-winning, qualifying and less important competitive factors. *Order-winning competitive factors* are those which directly win business for the operation. *Qualifying competitive factors* are those which may not win extra business if the operation improves its performance, but can certainly lose business if performance falls below a particular point, known as the qualifying level. *Less important competitive factors*, as their name implies, are those which are relatively unimportant compared with the others. In fact, to judge the relative importance of its competitive factors, an operation will usually need to use a slightly more discriminating scale. One way to do this is to take our three broad categories of competitive factors – order-winning, qualifying and less important – and to divide each category into three further points representing strong, medium and weak positions. Figure 20.8(a) illustrates such a scale.

Judging performance against competitors

At its simplest, a competitive performance standard would consist merely of judging whether the achieved performance of an operation is better than, the same, or worse than that of its competitors. However, in much the same way as the nine point importance scale was derived, we can derive a more discriminating nine-point performance scale, as shown in Figure 20.8(b).

The importance–performance matrix

The priority for improvement which each competitive factor should be given can be assessed from a comparison of their importance and performance. This can be shown on an importance–performance matrix which, as its name implies, positions each competitive factor according to its scores or ratings on these criteria. Figure 20.9 shows an importance–performance matrix divided into zones of improvement priority. The first zone boundary is the

(a) Importance scale for competitive factors		(b) Performance scale for competitive factors	
Rating	**Description**	**Rating**	**Description**
1	Provides a crucial advantage to customers	1	Considerably better than similar organizations
2	Provides an important advantage to customers	2	Clearly better than similar organizations
3	Provides a useful advantage to customers	3	Marginally better than similar organizations
4	Needs to be up to good industry standards	4	Sometimes marginally better than similar organizations
5	Needs to be up to median industry standards	5	About the same as most similar organizations
6	Needs to be within close range of rest of industry	6	Slightly worse than the average of similar organizations
7	Not usually important but could become so	7	Usually marginally worse than similar organizations
8	Very rarely considered by customers	8	Generally worse than most similar organizations
9	Never considered by customers	9	Consistently worse than similar organizations

Figure 20.8 Nine-point scales for judging importance and performance

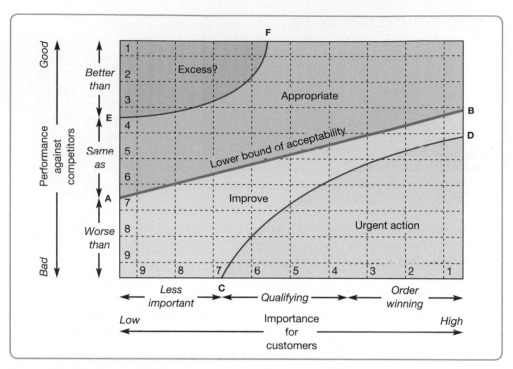

Figure 20.9 Priority zones in the importance–performance matrix

'lower bound of acceptability' shown as line AB in Figure 20.9. This is the boundary between acceptable and unacceptable performance. When a competitive factor is rated as relatively unimportant (8 or 9 on the importance scale), this boundary will in practice be low. Most operations are prepared to tolerate performance levels which are 'in the same ballpark' as their competitors (even at the bottom end of the rating) for unimportant competitive factors. They only become concerned when performance levels are clearly below those of their competitors. Conversely, when judging competitive factors which are rated highly (1 or 2 on the importance scale), they will be markedly less sanguine at poor or mediocre levels of performance. Minimum levels of acceptability for these competitive factors will usually be at the lower end of the 'better than competitors' class. Below this minimum bound of acceptability (AB) there is clearly a need for improvement; above this line there is no immediate urgency for any improvement. However, not all competitive factors falling below the minimum line will be seen as having the same degree of improvement priority. A boundary approximately represented by line CD represents a distinction between an urgent priority zone and a less urgent improvement zone. Similarly, above the line AB, not all competitive factors are regarded as having the same priority. The line EF can be seen as the approximate boundary between performance levels which are regarded as 'good' or 'appropriate' on one hand and those regarded as 'too good' or 'excess' on the other. Segregating the matrix in this way results in four zones which imply very different priorities:

- **The 'appropriate' zone.** Competitive factors in this area lie above the lower bound of acceptability and so should be considered satisfactory.
- **The 'improve' zone.** Lying below the lower bound of acceptability, any factors in this zone must be candidates for improvement.
- **The 'urgent-action' zone.** These factors are important to customers but performance is below that of competitors. They must be considered as candidates for immediate improvement.
- **The 'excess?' zone.** Factors in this area are 'high performing', but not important to customers. The question must be asked, therefore, whether the resources devoted to achieving such a performance could be used better elsewhere.

EXL Laboratories is a subsidiary of an electronics company. It carries out research and development as well as technical problem-solving work for a wide range of companies, including companies in its own group. It is particularly keen to improve the level of service which it gives to its customers. However, it needs to decide which aspect of its performance to improve first. It has devised a list of the most important aspects of its service:

- **The quality of its technical solutions** – the perceived appropriateness by customers.
- **The quality of its communications with customers** – the frequency and usefulness of information.
- **The quality of post-project documentation** – the usefulness of the documentation which goes with the final report.
- **Delivery speed** – the time between customer request and the delivery of the final report.
- **Delivery dependability** – the ability to deliver on the promised date.
- **Delivery flexibility** – the ability to deliver the report on a revised date.
- **Specification flexibility** – the ability to change the nature of the investigation.
- **Price** – the total charge to the customer.

EXL assigned a score to each of these factors using the 1–9 scale described in Figure 20.8 and then turned their attention to judging the laboratory's performance against competitor organizations. Although they have benchmarked information for some aspects of performance, they have to make estimates for the others. Both these scores are shown in Figure 20.10.

EXL Laboratories plotted the importance and performance ratings it had given to each of its competitive factors on an importance–performance matrix. This is shown in Figure 20.11. It shows that the most important aspect of competitiveness – the ability to deliver sound technical solutions to its customers – falls comfortably within the appropriate zone. Specification flexibility and delivery flexibility are also in the appropriate zone, although only just. Both delivery speed and delivery dependability seem to be in need of improvement as each is below the minimum level of acceptability for their respective importance positions. However, two competitive factors, communications and cost/price, are clearly in need of immediate improvement. These two factors should therefore be assigned the most urgent priority for improvement. The matrix also indicates that the company's documentation could almost be regarded as 'too good'.

Figure 20.10 Rating 'importance to customers' and 'performance against competitors' on the nine-point scales for EXL Laboratories

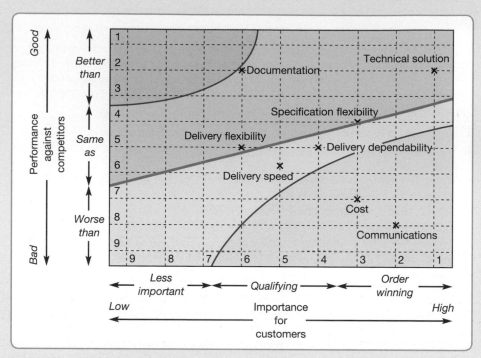

Figure 20.11 The importance–performance matrix for EXL Laboratories

The matrix may not reveal any total surprises. The competitive factors in the 'urgent-action' zone may be known to be in need of improvement already. However, the exercise is useful for two reasons:
1 It helps to discriminate between many factors which may be in need of improvement.
2 It gives purpose and structure to the debate on improvement priorities.

The sandcone theory

As well as approaches that base improvement priority on an operation's specific circumstances, some authorities believe that there is also a generic 'best' sequence of improvement. The best-known theory is called *the sandcone theory*,[7] so called because the sand is analogous to management effort and resources. Building a stable sandcone needs a stable foundation of quality, upon which one can build layers of dependability, speed, flexibility and cost (*see* Fig. 20.12). Building up improvement is thus a cumulative process, not a sequential one. Moving on to the second priority for improvement does not mean dropping the first, and so on. According to the sandcone theory, the first priority should be *quality*, since this is a precondition to all lasting improvement. Only when the operation has reached a minimally acceptable level in quality should it then tackle the next issue, that of internal *dependability*. Importantly though, moving on to include dependability in the improvement process will actually require further improvement in quality. Once a critical level of dependability is reached, enough to provide some stability to the operation, the next stage is to improve the *speed* of internal throughput, but again only while continuing to improve quality and dependability further. Soon it will become evident that the most effective way to improve speed is through improvements in response *flexibility*, that is, changing things within the operation faster. Again, including flexibility in the improvement process should not divert attention from continuing to work further on quality, dependability and speed. Only now, according to the sandcone theory, should *cost* be tackled head on.

Figure 20.12 The sandcone model of improvement; cost reduction relies on a cumulative foundation of improvement in the other performance objectives

HOW CAN ORGANIZATIONAL CULTURE AFFECT IMPROVEMENT?

It is generally held by most organizational theorists that an organization's ability to improve its operations performance depends to a large extent on its 'culture'. By 'organizational culture' we here mean *'the pattern of shared basic assumptions . . . that have worked well enough to be considered valid'*,[8] or, as some put it, *'the way we do things around here'*. Professor Gerry Johnson[9] is more specific, describing the elements of organizational culture as follows:

- the organization's mission and values;
- its control systems;
- its organizational structures, hierarchies, and processes;
- its power structures;
- its symbols, logos and designs including its symbols of power;
- its rituals, meetings and routines;
- its stories and myths that develop about people and events.

So, organizational culture and improvement are clearly related. A receptive organizational culture that encourages a constant search for improved ways to do things nurtures improvement. At the same time the organization's view of improvement is an important indication of its culture. But what is meant by 'an improvement culture'? Here we look at two aspects: first, the various elements that make up an improvement culture; second, the recurring theme of 'learning' as a key element of improvement culture.

Building an improvement capability

The ability to improve, especially on a continuous basis, is not something which always comes naturally to operations managers and staff. There are specific abilities, behaviours and actions which need to be consciously developed if improvement is to sustain over the long term. Bessant and Caffyn[10] distinguish between what they call 'organizational abilities' (the capacity or aptitude to adopt a particular approach to continuous improvement), 'constituent behaviours' (the routines of behaviour which staff adopt and which reinforce the approach to continuous improvement) and 'enablers' (the procedural devices or techniques used to progress the continuous improvement effort). They identify six generic organizational abilities, each with its own set of constituent behaviours. These are identified in Table 20.2. Examples of enablers are the improvement techniques that were described earlier (in Chapter 18).

Table 20.2 Continuous improvement (CI) abilities and some associated behaviours

Organizational ability	Constituent behaviours
Getting the CI habit Developing the ability to generate sustained involvement in CI	People use formal problem-finding and -solving cycle People use simple tools and techniques People use simple measurement to shape the improvement process Individuals and/or groups initiate and carry through CI activities – they participate in the process Ideas are responded to in a timely fashion – either implemented or otherwise dealt with Managers support the CI process through allocation of resources Managers recognize in formal ways the contribution of employees to CI Managers lead by example, becoming actively involved in design and implementation of CI Managers support experiment by not punishing mistakes, but instead encouraging learning from them
Focusing on CI Generating and sustaining the ability to link CI activities to the strategic goals of the company	Individuals and groups use the organization's strategic objectives to prioritize improvements Everyone is able to explain what the operation's strategy and objectives are Individuals and groups assess their proposed changes against the operation's objectives Individuals and groups monitor/measure the results of their improvement activity CI activities are an integral part of the individual's or group's work, not a parallel activity
Spreading the word Generating the ability to move CI activity across organizational boundaries	People co-operate in cross-functional groups People understand and share an holistic view (process understanding and ownership) People are orientated towards internal and external customers in their CI activity Specific CI projects with outside agencies (customers, suppliers, etc.) take place Relevant CI activities involve representatives from different organizational levels
CI on the CI system Generating the ability to manage strategically the development of CI	The CI system is continually monitored and developed There is a cyclical planning process whereby the CI system is regularly reviewed and amended There is periodic review of the CI system in relation to the organization as a whole Senior management make available sufficient resources (time, money, personnel) to support the continuing development of the CI system The CI system itself is designed to fit within the current structure and infrastructure When a major organizational change is planned, its potential impact on the CI system is assessed
Walking the talk Generating the ability to articulate and demonstrate CI's values	The 'management style' reflects commitment to CI values When something goes wrong, people at all levels look for reasons why, rather than blame individuals People at all levels demonstrate a shared belief in the value of small steps and that everyone can contribute, by themselves being actively involved in making and recognizing incremental improvements
Building the learning organization Generating the ability to learn through CI activity	Everyone learns from their experiences, both good and bad Individuals seek out opportunities for learning/personal development Individuals and groups at all levels share their learning The organization captures and shares the learning of individuals and groups Managers accept and act on all the learning that takes place Organizational mechanisms are used to deploy what has been learned across the organization

Improvement as learning

Note that many of the abilities and behaviours described in Table 20.2 are directly or indirectly related to learning in some way. This is not surprising given that operations improvement implies some kind of intervention or change to the operation, and change will be evaluated in terms of whatever improvement occurs. This evaluation adds to our knowledge of how the operation really works, which in turn increases the chances that future interventions will also result in improvement. (This idea of an improvement cycle was discussed in Chapter 18). What is important is to realize that it is a learning process, and it is crucial that improvement is organized so that it encourages, facilitates and exploits the learning that occurs during improvement. This requires us to recognize that there is a distinction between single- and double-loop learning.[11]

> **✳ Operations principle**
>
> There can be no intentional improvement without learning.

Single- and double-loop learning

Single-loop learning occurs when there is a repetitive and predictable link between cause and effect. Statistical process control (see Chapter 17), for example, measures output characteristics from a process, such as product weight, telephone response time, etc. These can then be used to alter input conditions, such as supplier quality, manufacturing consistency, staff training, with the intention of 'improving' the output. Every time an operational error or problem is detected, it is corrected or solved, and more is learned about the process. However, this happens without questioning or altering the underlying values and objectives of the process, which may, over time, create an unquestioning inertia that prevents it adapting to a changing environment. Double-loop learning, by contrast, questions the fundamental objectives, service or even the underlying culture of the operation. This kind of learning implies an ability to challenge existing operating assumptions in a fundamental way. It seeks to re-frame competitive assumptions and remain open to any changes in the competitive environment. But being receptive to new opportunities sometimes requires abandoning existing operating routines which may be difficult to achieve in practice, especially as many operations reward experience and past achievement (rather than potential) at both an individual and group level. Figure 20.13 illustrates single- and double-loop learning.

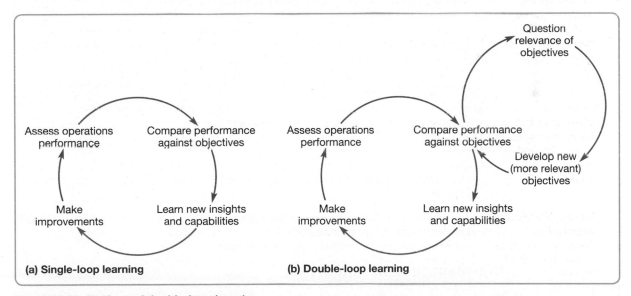

Figure 20.13 Single- and double-loop learning

KEY IMPLEMENTATION ISSUES

Not all of the improvement initiatives which are launched by organizations, often with high expectations, will go on to fulfil their potential of having a major impact on performance. Estimates of the failure of improvement efforts range from half to 80 per cent. Yet, although there are many examples of improvement efforts that have failed, there are also examples of

Learning from Formula 1[12]

As driving jobs go, there could be no bigger difference than between Formula 1 racing drivers weaving their way through some of the fastest competitors in the world and a supermarket truck driver quietly delivering beans, beer and bacon to distribution centres and stores. But they have more in common than one would suspect. Both Formula 1 and truck drivers want to save fuel, either to reduce pit-stops (Formula 1) or keep delivery costs down (Heavy Goods Vehicles). And although grocery deliveries in the suburbs do not seem as thrilling as racing round the track at Monza, the computer-assisted simulation programs developed by the Williams Formula 1 team are being deployed to help Sainsbury's (a British supermarket group) drivers develop the driving skills that could potentially cut its fuel bill by up to 30 per cent. The simulator technology, which allows realistic advanced training to be conducted in a controlled environment, was developed originally for the advanced training of Formula 1 drivers and was developed and extended at the Williams Technology Centre in Qatar. It can now train drivers to a high level of professional driving skills and road safety applications.

Source: Shutterstock.com/Natursports

Williams F1's Chief Executive, Alex Burns, commented, '*Formula 1 is well recognized as an excellent technology incubator. It makes perfect sense to embrace some of the new and emerging technologies that the Williams Technology Centre in Qatar is developing from this incubator to help Sainsbury's mission to* reduce its energy consumption and enhance the skills and safety of those supporting its crucial logistics operation.' Sainsbury's energy-related improvement programmes tackle energy supply (for example, wind, solar and geothermal energy) as well as energy consumption (for example, switching to LED lighting, CO_2 refrigeration, etc.). Learning from Formula 1 will help Sainsbury's to improve further in the field of energy efficiency. Roger Burnley, Sainsbury's retail and logistics director, said, '*We are committed to reducing our environmental impact and as a result, we are often at the very forefront of technological innovation. By partnering with Williams F1, we can take advantage of some of the world's most advanced automotive technology, making our operations even more efficient and taking us a step closer to meeting our CO_2 reduction targets.*'

successful implementations. So why do some improvement efforts disappoint? Some reasons we have already identified – an organizational culture that discourages any change, for example. But there are some more tangible causes of implementation failure. The remainder of this chapter will be devoted to some of these.

Top-management support

The importance of top-management support goes far beyond the allocation of resources to the programme; it sets the priorities for the whole organization. If the organization's senior managers do not understand and show commitment to the programme, it is only understandable that others will ask why they should do so. Usually this is taken to mean that top management must:

- understand and believe in the benefits of the improvement approach;
- communicate the principles and techniques of improvement;
- participate in the improvement process;
- formulate and maintain a clear 'improvement strategy'.

This last point is particularly important. Without thinking through the overall purpose and long-term goals of improvement it is difficult for any organization to know where it is going. An improvement strategy is necessary to provide the goals and guidelines which help to keep improvement efforts in line with strategic aims. Specifically, the improvement strategy should have something to say about the competitive priorities of the organization, the roles and improvement responsibilities of all parts of the organization, the resources available for improvement, and its overall improvement philosophy.

Senior managers may not fully understand the improvement approach

Earlier (Chapter 18) we described how there were several (related) improvement approaches. Each of these approaches is the subject of several books that describe them in great detail. There is no shortage of advice from consultants and academics as to how they should be used. Yet it is not difficult to find examples of where senior management have used one or more of these approaches without fully understanding them. The details of Six Sigma or lean, for example, are not simply technical matters. They are fundamental to how appropriate the approach could be in different contexts. Not every approach fits every set of circumstances. So understanding in detail what each approach means must be the first step in deciding whether it is appropriate.

Avoid excessive 'hype'

Operations improvement has, to some extent, become a fashion industry with new ideas and concepts continually being introduced as offering a novel way to improve business performance. There is nothing intrinsically wrong with this. Fashion stimulates and refreshes, through introducing novel ideas. Without it, things would stagnate. The problem lies not with new improvement ideas, but rather with some managers becoming a victim of the process, where some new idea will entirely displace whatever went before. Most new ideas have something to say, but jumping from one fad to another will not only generate a backlash against any new idea, but also destroy the ability to accumulate the experience that comes from experimenting with each one. Avoiding becoming an improvement fashion victim is not easy.

Improvement or quality awards

Various bodies have sought to stimulate improvement through establishing improvement (sometimes called 'quality') awards. The three best-known awards are the Deming Prize, the Malcolm Baldrige National Quality Award and the European Quality Award.

The Deming Prize

The Deming Prize was instituted by the Union of Japanese Scientists and Engineers in 1951 and is awarded to those companies, initially in Japan, but more recently opened to overseas companies, which have successfully applied 'company-wide quality control' based upon statistical quality control. There are 10 major assessment categories: policy and objectives; organization and its operation; education and its extension; assembling and disseminating of information; analysis; standardization; control; quality assurance; effects; and future plans. The applicants are required to submit a detailed description of quality practices. This is a significant activity in itself and some companies claim a great deal of benefit from having done so.

The Malcolm Baldrige National Quality Award

In the early 1980s the American Productivity and Quality Center recommended that an annual prize, similar to the Deming Prize, should be awarded in America. The purpose of the awards was to stimulate American companies to improve quality and productivity, to

The idea of including all staff in the process of improvement has formed the core of many improvement approaches. One of the best-known ways of this is the 'Work-Out' approach that originated in the US conglomerate GE. Jack Welch, the then boss of GE, reputedly developed the approach to recognize that employees were an important source of brainpower for new and creative ideas, and as a mechanism for *'creating an environment that pushes towards a relentless, endless company-wide search for a better way to do everything we do'*. The Work-Out programme was seen as a way to reduce the bureaucracy often associated with improvement and *'giving every employee, from managers to factory workers, an opportunity to influence and improve GE's day-to-day operations'*. According to Welch, Work-Out was meant to help people stop *'wrestling with the boundaries, the absurdities that grow in large organizations. We're all familiar with those absurdities: too many approvals, duplication, pomposity, waste. Work-Out in essence turned the company upside down, so that the workers told the bosses what to do. That forever changed the way people behaved at the company. Work-Out is also designed to reduce, and ultimately eliminate, all of the waste hours and energy that organizations like GE typically expend in performing day-to-day operations.'* GE also used what it called 'town meetings' of employees. And although proponents of Work-Out emphasize the need to modify the specifics of the approach to fit the context in which it is applied, there is a broad sequence of activities implied within the approach:

Source: Shutterstock.com/Prill

- Staff, other key stakeholders and their manager hold a meeting away from the operation (a so-called 'off-siter').
- At this meeting the manager gives the group the responsibility to solve a problem or set of problems shared by the group but which are ultimately the manager's responsibility.
- The manager then leaves and the group spend time (maybe two or three days) working on developing solutions to the problems, sometimes using outside facilitators.
- At the end of the meeting, the responsible manager (and sometimes the manager's boss) rejoins the group to be presented with its recommendations.
- The manager can respond in three ways to each recommendation: 'yes', 'no', or 'I have to consider it more'. If it is the last response the manager must clarify what further issues must be considered and how and when the decision will be made.

Work-Out programmes are expensive: outside facilitators, off-site facilities and the payroll costs of a sizeable group of people meeting away from work can be substantial, even without considering the potential disruption to everyday activities. But arguably the most important implications of adopting Work-Out are cultural. In its purest form Work-Out reinforces an underlying culture of fast (and, some would claim, superficial) problem-solving. It also relies on full and near universal employee involvement and empowerment, together with direct dialogue between managers and their subordinates. What distinguishes the Work-Out approach from the many other types of group-based problem-solving is fast decision making and the idea that managers must respond immediately and decisively to team suggestions. But some claim that it is intolerant of staff and managers who are not committed to its values. In fact, it is acknowledged in GE that resistance to the process or outcome is not tolerated and that obstructing the efforts of the Work-Out process is *'a career-limiting move'*.

recognize achievements, to establish criteria for a wider quality effort and to provide guidance on quality improvement. The main examination categories are: leadership; information and analysis; strategic quality planning; human resource utilization; quality assurance of products and services; quality results; and customer satisfaction. The process, like that of the Deming Prize, includes a detailed application and site visits.

The EFQM Excellence Model

In 1988, 14 leading Western European companies formed the European Foundation for Quality Management (EFQM). An important objective of the EFQM is to recognize quality achievement. Because of this, it launched the European Quality Award (EQA), awarded to the most successful exponent of total quality management in Europe each year. To receive a prize, companies must demonstrate that their approach to total quality management has contributed significantly to satisfying the expectations of customers, employees and others with an interest in the company for the past few years. In 1999, the model on which the European Quality Award was based was modified and renamed the EFQM Excellence Model, or Business Excellence Model. The changes made were not fundamental but did attempt to reflect some new areas of management and quality thinking (for example, partnerships and innovation) and placed more emphasis on customer and market focus. It is based on the idea that the outcomes of quality management in terms of what it calls 'people results', 'customer results', 'society results' and 'key performance results' are achieved through a number of 'enablers'. These enablers are leadership and constancy of purpose, policy and strategy, how the organization develops its people, partnerships and resources, and the way it organizes its processes. These ideas are incorporated in the EFQM Excellence Model as shown in Figure 20.14. The five enablers are concerned with how results are being achieved, while the four 'results' are concerned with what the company has achieved and is achieving.

Self-assessment

The European Foundation for Quality Management (EFQM) defines self-assessment as '*a comprehensive, systematic, and regular review of an organization's activities and results referenced against a model of business excellence*'; in its case the model shown in Figure 20.14. The main advantage of using such models for self-assessment seems to be that companies find it easier to understand some of the more philosophical concepts of TQM when they are translated into specific areas, questions and percentages. Self-assessment also allows organizations to measure their progress in changing their organization and in achieving the benefits of TQM. An important aspect of self-assessment is an organization's ability to judge the relative importance of the assessment categories to its own circumstances. The EFQM Excellence Model originally placed emphasis on a generic set of weighting for each of its nine categories. With the increasing importance of self-assessment, the EFQM moved to encourage organizations using its model to allocate their own weightings in a rational and systematic manner.

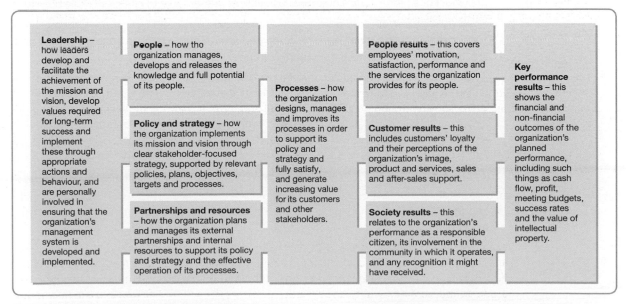

Figure 20.14 The EFQM Excellence Model

MyOMLab *Check and improve your understanding of this chapter using self-assessment questions and a personalized study plan, a video case study, and an eText – all at www.myomlab.com.*

❭ Why does improvement need organizing?

● Improvement does not just happen by itself. It needs organizing, information must be gathered so that improvement is treating the most appropriate issues, responsibility for looking after the improvement effort must be allocated, and resources must be allocated. It must also be linked to the organization's overall strategy. Without these decisions, it is unlikely that real improvement will take place.

❭ How should the improvement effort be linked to strategy?

● At a strategic level, the whole purpose of operations improvement is to make operations performance better serve its markets. Therefore there should be approximate alignment or 'fit' between an operation's performance and the requirements of its markets. In fact, improvement should do three things to achieve this:

1 It should achieve an approximate balance between 'required market performance' and 'actual operations performance'.
2 It should make this alignment 'sustainable' over time.
3 It should 'move up' the line of fit, the assumption being that high levels of market performance, achieved as a result of high levels of operations performance, are difficult for competitors to match.

❭ What information is needed for improvement?

● It is unlikely that for any operation a single measure of performance will adequately reflect the whole of a performance objective. Usually operations have to collect a whole bundle of partial measures of performance.

● Each partial measure then has to be compared against some performance standard. There are four types of performance standard commonly used:

1 historical standards, which compare performance now against performance sometime in the past;
2 target performance standards, which compare current performance against some desired level of performance;
3 competitor performance standards, which compare current performance against competitors' performance;
4 absolute performance standards, which compare current performance against its theoretically perfect state.

● The process of benchmarking is often used as a means of obtaining competitor performance standards.

❯ What should be improvement priorities?

● Improvement priorities can be determined by bringing together the relative importance of each performance objective or competitive factor as judged by customers, with the performance which the operation achieves as compared with its competition. This idea can be consolidated on an 'importance–performance matrix'.

● The 'sandcone model' provides an alternative approach to prioritization. It recommends that improvement should cumulatively emphasize quality, dependability, speed, flexibility, and then cost.

❯ How can organizational culture affect improvement?

● An organization's ability to improve its operations performance depends to a large extent on its 'culture', that is *the pattern of shared basic assumptions . . . that have worked well enough to be considered valid*. A receptive organizational culture that encourages a constant search for improved ways to do things can encourage improvement.

● According to Bessant and Caffyn there are specific abilities, behaviours and actions which need to be consciously developed if improvement is to sustain over the long term.

● Many of the abilities and behaviours related to an improvement culture relate to learning in some way. The learning process is important because it encourages, facilitates and exploits the learning that occurs during improvement. This involves two types of learning – single- and double loop learning:
  ● Single-loop learning occurs when there is a repetitive and predictable link between cause and effect.
  ● Double-loop learning questions the fundamental objectives, service or even the underlying culture of the operation.

❯ What are the key implementation issues?

● Improvement efforts often fail (estimates range from half to 80 per cent of programmes failing). Included in the reasons for this are the following:
  ● Top-management support may be lacking.
  ● Senior managers may not fully understanding the improvement approach.
  ● The improvement may be 'hyped up' excessively, leading to unrealistic (and therefore unrealized) expectations.
  ● Implementation problems may not be anticipated.

● So-called 'quality awards' and models may contribute towards implementation of improvement by providing a focused structure for organizations to assess their improvement efforts. The best known of these is probably the EFQM (Business) Excellence Model. This is based on a nine-point model which distinguishes between the 'enablers' of quality and the 'results' of quality. It is often now used as a self-certification model.

Re-inventing Singapore's Libraries[14]

By Professors Robert Johnston, Warwick Business School, Chai Kah Hin and Jochen Wirtz, National University of Singapore, and Christopher Lovelock, Yale University.

The National Library Board (NLB) in Singapore oversees the management of the national, reference, regional, community, and children's libraries, as well as over 30 libraries belonging to government agencies, schools and private institutions. Over the last 15 years the NLB has completely changed the nature of libraries in Singapore and its work has been used as a blueprint for many other libraries across the world. Yet it was not always like this. In 1995 libraries in Singapore were traditional, quiet places full of old books where you went to study or borrow books if you could not afford to buy them. There were long queues to have books stamped or returned and the staff seemed unhelpful and unfriendly. But today, things are very different. There are cafés in libraries to encourage people to come in, browse and sit down with a book, and libraries in community centres (putting libraries where the people are). The NLB has developed specialist libraries aimed at children and libraries in shopping malls aimed at attracting busy 18–35 year olds into the library while they are shopping. There are libraries dedicated to teenagers, one of the most difficult groups to entice into the library. These have even been designed by the teenagers themselves so they include drinks machines, cushions and music systems. The library also hosts a wide range of events, from mother and baby reading sessions to rock concerts, to encourage a wide range of people into the library.

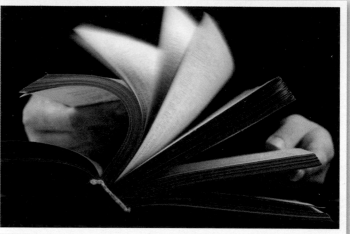

Source: Shutterstock.com/Silver-John

'We started this journey back in 1995 when Dr Christopher Chia was appointed as Chief Executive. Looking back, we were a very traditional public service. Our customers used words like "cold" and "unfriendly", though, in fairness, our staff were working under great pressure to deal with the long queues for books and to answer enquiries on library materials posed by our customers. Christopher Chia and his team made a study of the problems, undertook surveys and ran focus groups. They then began to address the challenges with vision and imagination through the application of the project management methodology and the innovative use of technology. Staff involvement and contribution was key to the success of the transformation. We knew where we wanted to go, and were committed to the cause.' (Ms Ngian Lek Choh, the Deputy Chief Executive and Director of the National Library)

Underpinning many of the changes was the NLB's innovative use of technology. It was the first public library in the world to prototype radio-frequency identification (RFID) to create its Electronic Library Management System (ELiMS).

RFID is an electronic system for automatically identifying items. It uses RFID tags, or transponders, which are contained in smart labels consisting of a silicon chip and coiled antenna. They receive and respond to radio-frequency queries from an RFID transceiver, which enables the remote and automatic retrieval, storing and sharing of information (see Chapter 8). RFID tags are installed in its 10 million books, making it one of the largest users of the technology in the world. Customers spend very little time queuing, with book issuing and returns automated. Indeed books can be returned to any of the NLB's 24-hour book drops (which look a bit like ATM machines) where RFID enables not only fast and easy returns but also fast and easy sorting. The NLB has also launched a mobile service via SMS (text messaging). This allows users to manage their library accounts anytime and anywhere through their mobile phones. They can check their loan records, renew their books, pay library payments, and get reminder alerts to return library items before the due-date.

Improving its services meant fully understanding the library's customers. Customers were studied using surveys and focus groups to understand how the library added value for customers, how customers could be segmented, the main learning and reading motivators, and people's general reading habits. And feedback from customers, both formal and informal, is an important source of design innovation – as are ideas from staff. Everyone in NLB, from the Chief Executive to the Library Assistant, is expected to contribute to work improvement and innovations. So much so that innovation has become an integral part of NLB's culture, leading to a steady stream of both large and small innovations. In order to facilitate this, the Chief Executive holds 'express-o' discussions with staff. He also has a strategy called 'ask stupid questions' (ASQ) which encourages staff to challenge what is normally accepted. Dr Varaprasad, the Chief Executive, commented, '*In my view there are no stupid questions, there are only stupid answers! What we try to do is engage the staff by letting them feel they can ask stupid questions and that they are entitled to an answer.*'

The NLB also makes use of small improvement teams to brainstorm ideas and test them out with colleagues from other libraries across the island. Good ideas attract financial rewards from S$5 to $1,000. One such idea was using a simple system of coloured bands on the spines of books (representing the identification number of each book) which make it much easier to shelve the books in the right places and also spot books that have been misplaced by customers. Staff are also encouraged to travel overseas to visit other libraries to learn about how they use their space, their programmes and collections, attend and speak at conventions and also visit very different organizations to get new ideas. The automatic book return, for example, was an idea borrowed and modified from the Mass Rapid Transport stations in Hong Kong where, with the flash of a card, the user is identified and given access across the system. NLB applied a similar line of thought for seamless check-in and check-out of books and a return-anywhere concept. NLB harvests ideas from many different industries including logistics, manufacturing, IT and supermarkets. However, some elements of NLB's improvement process have changed. In the early days their approach to implementing ideas was informal and intuitive. It is now much more structured. Now, each good idea that comes forward is managed as a project, starting with a 'proof of concept' stage, which involves selling the idea to management and checking with a range of people that the idea seems feasible. Then the services or processes are re-engineered, often involving customers or users. The new concepts are then prototyped and piloted, allowing managers to gather customer feedback to enable them to assess, refine and, if appropriate, develop them for other sites.

QUESTIONS

1 How would the culture of NLB have changed in order for it to make such improvements?

2 Where did the ideas for improvement originate? And how did NLB encourage improvement ideas?

3 Why, do you think, has the improvement process become more systematic over the years?

4 What could be the biggest challenges to NLB's improvement activities in the future?

PROBLEMS AND APPLICATIONS

These problems and applications will help to improve your analysis of operations. You can find more practice problems as well as worked examples and guided solutions on MyOMLab at www.myomlab.com.

MyOMLab

1 Reread the short case in this chapter on 'Taxing quality' (p. 649) which describes the improvement initiative carried out by the Aarhus region customs and tax unit.

    (a) How does the idea of a customer-focused approach to improvement need to be adapted for a customs and tax unit?

    (b) Generally, how might the ideas of improvement organization outlined in this chapter need to be adapted for public sector operations such as this one?

2 What are the differences and similarities between the approach taken by the Aarhus customs and tax unit and the example described in the 'Operations in practice' on 'Improving Sonae Corporation's retail operations' at the start of the chapter?

3 Compare and contrast the approaches taken by GE in their Work-Out approach described in the short case (p. 662) and that taken in the 'Learning from Formula 1' short case (p. 660).

4 Ruggo carpets encourage continuous improvement based around the 'drive for customer focus'. The company's total quality process has graduated from 'total customer satisfaction' through 'total customer delight' to its present form – 'bridging the gap', which is effectively a 'where we are' and 'where we should be' yardstick for the company. Developments in the warehouse are typical. The supervisor has been replaced by a group leader who acts as a 'facilitator',

working within the team. They are also trained to carry out their own job plus five others. Fixed hours are a thing of the past, as is overtime. At peak times the team works the required hours to dispatch orders, and at off-peak times the team can leave when work is completed. Dispatch labels and address labels are computer-generated and the carpets are bar-coded to reduce human error. Each process within the warehouse has been analysed and re-engineered.

(a) What is implied by the progression of the company's three initiatives from 'total customer satisfaction' to 'total customer delight' to 'bridging the gap'?

(b) Evaluate this example against the criteria included in the Business Excellence Model.

5   Look through the financial or business pages of a (serious) newspaper and find examples of businesses that have 'deviated from the line of fit', as described in the early part of this chapter.

6   Devise a performance measurement scheme for the performance of the course you are following.

SELECTED FURTHER READING

Barrows, E. and Neely, A. (2012) *Managing Performance in Turbulent Times: Analytics and Insight*, John Wiley & Sons, Hoboken, NJ. Linking performance management with business strategy.

Deming, W.E. (1986) *Out of the Crisis*, MIT Press, Cambridge, MA. One of the gurus. It had a huge impact in its day. Read it if you want to know what all the fuss was about.

Kaplan, R.S. and Norton, D.P. (2001) *The Strategy Focused Organization*, Harvard Business School Press, Boston, MA.

Neely, A.D. and Adams, C. (2001) The performance prism perspective, *Journal of Cost Management*, vol. 25, no. 1, 7–15.

Neely, A. (2011) *Business Performance Measurement: Unifying Theory and Integrating Practice*, 2nd edn, Cambridge University Press, Cambridge. A collection of (academic) papers reviewing developments in the theory and practice of performance measurement and management.

Schein, E.H. (2004) *Organizational Culture and Leadership*, 3rd edn, Jossey-Bass, San Francisco. A classic.

USEFUL WEBSITES

www.quality-foundation.co.uk The British Quality Foundation is a not-for-profit organization promoting business excellence.

www.juran.com The Juran Institute's mission statement is to provide clients with the concepts, methods and guidance for attaining leadership in quality.

www.asq.org The American Society for Quality site. Good professional insights.

www.quality.nist.gov American Quality Assurance Institute. Well-established institution for all types of business quality assurance.

www.myomlab.com Test which sections you have mastered and which you need to review, with questions, a personalized study plan, video clips, revision tips, and cases.

www.opsman.org Useful materials.

http://operationsroom.wordpress.com/ Stanford University's take on topical operations stories.

www.iomnet.org The Institute of Operations Management site. One of the main professional bodies for the subject.

www.poms.org A US academic society for production and operations management. Academic, but some useful material, including a link to an encyclopedia of operations management terms.

www.gslis.utexas.edu/~rpollock/tqm.html Non-commercial site on total quality management with some good links.

www.iso.org Site of the International Standards Organization that runs the ISO 9000 and ISO 14000 families of standards. ISO 9000 has become an international reference for quality management requirements.

MyOMLab

Now that you have finished reading this chapter, why not visit MyOMLab at www.myomlab.com where you'll find more learning resources to help you make the most of your studies and get a better grade.

21 Operations and corporate social responsibility (CSR)

Part Five
CORPORATE SOCIAL RESPONSIBILITY

The ultimate test for any operations manager is whether he or she can develop an operation which meets the challenges and decisions that lie ahead for the organization. In the preceding text, we have outlined many of these challenges and decisions, and placed them in the context of the nature and purpose of operations management. In this final part of the book we examine an issue that is far wider than operations management, but with which operations management is intimately connected – corporate social responsibility (CSR). It is important to operations management because, of all the functions of any organization, it is operations management that can have the most practical impact on its CSR performance.

21 Operations and corporate social responsibility (CSR)

Key questions

❯ What is corporate social responsibility (CSR)?

❯ How does the wider view of corporate social responsibility influence operations management?

❯ How can operations managers analyse CSR issues?

INTRODUCTION

Operations managers face many new challenges as the economic, social, political, and technological environment changes. Many of these decisions and challenges seem largely economic in nature. What will be the impact on our costs of adding a new product or service feature? Can we generate an acceptable return if we invest in new technology? Other decisions have more of a 'social' aspect. How do we make sure that all our suppliers treat their staff fairly? And some have an environmental impact. Are we doing enough to reduce our carbon footprint? Yet the 'economic' decisions also have a 'social' aspect to them. Will a new product feature make end-of-life recycling more difficult? Will the new technology increase pollution? Similarly the 'social' decisions must be made in the context of their economic consequences. Sure, we want suppliers to treat staff well and, OK, we want to reduce our environmental impact, but we also need to make a profit. And this is the great dilemma of CSR. How do operations managers try to be, simultaneously, economically viable whilst being environmentally and socially responsible?

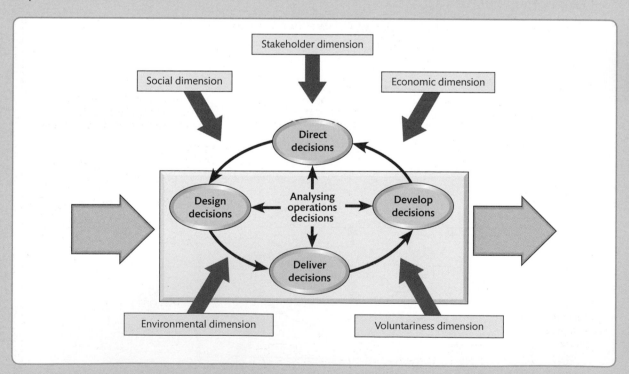

Figure 21.1 This chapter covers corporate social responsibility

For those readers who live in regions of the world where Marmite is not a big seller, Marmite is 'a nutritious savoury spread that contains B vitamins, enjoyable in a sandwich, on toast, bread or even as a cooking ingredient'. It is not to everyone's taste, which is why it is advertised with the line *'you'll either love it or hate it'*. But behind the clever advertising, Marmite, which is part of Unilever, the large food company, is a pioneer in recycling the leftovers from its production process to generate energy at the factory where it is made. The factory is in Burton upon Trent in the UK and every year around 18,000 tonnes of solidified Marmite deposit is left adhering to the surfaces of the machines and handling equipment that are used to produce the product. For years this residue was cleaned off and then either flushed into the sewerage system or sent to landfill sites. Then Unilever installed an anaerobic digester. This is a composter that allows the

waste by-product to be digested by microbes that feed on the waste. As they do, they release methane which is burned in a boiler which is connected to a generator that produces power. The system also captures the waste heat that comes through the exhaust and helps heat the

Waste Marmite recycled to an anaerobic digester

The bugs in the anaerobic digester 'eat' the waste Marmite and produce methane

Energy produced helps to heat factory

Methane burned to produce power

Figure 21.2 Waste product recycling at Marmite

factory's water system. But the Marmite example is just one part of Unilever's 'Sustainable Living Plan', first published in 2010. Since then it has published an update every year on the progress it is making globally and nationally towards meeting its Sustainable Living Plan targets.

Unilever publishes its performance against its Sustainable Living Plan targets as falling into three categories. The first is *'areas where we are making genuinely good progress'*. In 2012 these included sustainable sourcing, nutrition and eco-efficiency (including the Marmite project). The second category is *'areas where we have had to consider carefully how to reach our targets but are now ready to scale up'*. In 2012 this included a programme to increase the recycling rates of aerosols, encouraging more local councils to collect aerosols kerbside. *'However'*, the report admitted, *'we have more to do, working in partnership with industry, government and NGOs to help to increase recycling and recovery rates'.* The third category is *'areas where we are finding it difficult to make progress and will need to work with others to find solutions'.* This included targets that require consumer behaviour change, such as encouraging people to eat foods with lower salt levels or reducing the use of heated water in showering and washing clothes.

Amanda Sourry, Unilever UK and Ireland Chairman, said: *'The old view of growth at any cost is unacceptable; today the only responsible way to do business is through sustainable growth. It's for this reason that the Unilever Sustainable Living Plan is not just a bolt-on strategy, it's our blueprint for the future. Today's progress update shows that we've made some fantastic steps forward, particularly in the areas of sustainable sourcing, health and nutrition and reducing greenhouse gases. Just one year into the decade-long plan, we are proud of our achievements so far but there's still much more to do.'*

WHAT IS CORPORATE SOCIAL RESPONSIBILITY?

Although operations management is seen by some as being concerned largely with the routine aspects of business, it is in fact at the very forefront of almost all the new challenges to business practice. This is because – whether it is new technologies, new approaches to organizing resources, changing market and environmental circumstances, changing regulatory frameworks, or shifts in how society views business practices – operations will have to understand the consequences of these changes and respond to them. That is why it is useful to reflect on current and future trends and how they will impact on operations management in practice. Of course we could pick any number of issues that may become more important in the future and examine how operations management will have to respond. By definition, the future is unknown, so who knows what will be important in the future? However, one issue in particular has risen to the top of the list of things that concern many, if not most, businesses, regulatory authorities, governments and citizens generally. That issue is 'how should the relationship between business and wider society be viewed, assessed and (if possible) managed?' This issue is generally referred to as corporate social responsibility (or simply CSR).

Defining CSR

Surprisingly, for such an important topic, there is no universally accepted definition of CSR. Here are just some that give a flavour of how CSR is seen:

> *'CSR is the business contribution to our sustainable development goals. Essentially it is about how business takes account of its economic, social and environmental impacts in the way it operates – maximizing the benefits and minimizing the downsides. Specifically, we see CSR as the voluntary actions that business can take, over and above compliance with minimum legal requirements, to address both its own competitive interests and the interests of wider society.' (UK Government)*

> *'Corporate social responsibility is the continuing commitment by business to behave ethically and contribute to economic development while improving the quality of life of the workforce and their families as well as of the local community and society at large.'[2]*

> *'Corporate social responsibility . . . is listening and responding to the needs of a company's stakeholders. This includes the requirements of sustainable development. We believe that building good relationships with employees, suppliers and wider society is the best guarantee of long-term success. This is the backbone of our approach to CSR.'[3]*

Table 21.1 The five dimensions and example phrases

The 'dimensions' of CSR	What the definition refers to	Typical phrases used in the definition
The environmental dimension	The natural environment and 'sustainability' of business practice	'a cleaner environment' 'environmental stewardship' 'environmental concerns in business operations'
The social dimension	The relationship between business and society in general	'contribute to a better society' 'integrate social concerns in their business operations' 'consider the full scope of their impact on communities'
The economic dimension	Socio-economic or financial aspects, including describing CSR in terms of its impact on the business operation	'preserving the profitability' 'contribute to economic development'
The stakeholder dimension	Considering all stakeholders or stakeholder groups	'interaction with their stakeholders' 'how organizations interact with their employees, suppliers, customers and communities' 'treating the stakeholders of the firm'
The voluntariness dimension	Actions not prescribed by law. Doing more than you have to	'based on ethical values' 'beyond legal obligations' 'voluntary'

'CSR is a company's commitment to operating in an economically, socially and environmentally sustainable manner whilst balancing the interests of diverse stakeholders.'[4]

'[Our vision is to] . . . enable the profitable and responsible growth of our airports. One of our six strategies to achieve that purpose is to earn the trust of our stakeholders. Corporate responsibility is about how we manage our social and environmental impacts as part of our day-to-day business, in order to earn that trust.'[5]

'CSR is about how companies manage the business processes to produce an overall positive impact on society.'[6]

'Corporate social responsibility is the commitment of businesses to contribute to sustainable economic development by working with employees, their families, the local community and society at large to improve their lives in ways that are good for business and for development.'[7]

'CSR is a concept whereby companies integrate social and environmental concerns in their business operations and in their interaction with their stakeholders on a voluntary basis.'[8]

Although there are so many definitions, according to Alexander Dahlsrud of the Norwegian University of Science and Technology[9] almost all of them involve five 'dimensions' of CSR, as shown in Table 21.1. We will use these dimensions, first to explore CSR in general and, second, to explore the role of operations management specifically in CSR.

We have already mentioned some of these dimensions (in Chapter 2) when we discussed the 'triple bottom line' concept that includes the environmental dimension, the social dimension and the economic dimension. Here we are simply extending the idea to include the stakeholder dimension and the voluntariness dimension. However, most CSR professionals would view the triple bottom line categories as being the most important. For example, see the short case on Holcim.

> *** Operations principle**
>
> Corporate social responsibility should be a factor in every organization's operations activities.

Holcim works with the 'triple bottom line'[10]

Holcim is a global company, based in Switzerland, employing around 80,000 people, with production sites in around 70 countries. It is one of the world's leading manufacturers and distributors of cement and aggregates (for example, crushed stone, gravel and sand). It also supplies ready-mix concrete and asphalt as well as offering consulting, research, trading, engineering and other services. But, along with other companies in this sector, Holcim faces some considerable challenges in pursuing its CSR objectives. After all, cement manufacture is an activity that has a significant impact on almost every aspect of sustainability and social responsibility. Concrete is the second most used resource in the world after water. As the chief ingredient in concrete, cement is therefore a key requirement of modern society, but its manufacture is a resource- and energy-intensive process. This possibly explains why Holcim put so much effort into its sustainable development strategies. It aspires, it says, *'to be the world's most respected and attractive company in our industry, creating value for all our stakeholders. Placing sustainable development at the core of our business strategy aims to enhance this value, safeguards our reputation and contributes to continued success'*. Holcim's strategy and their approach to value creation attempts to integrate economic, environmental and social impacts. These are the three elements of what has become known as the 'triple bottom line'.

Triple bottom line accounting for company performance first came to prominence in John Elkington's 1998 book, *Cannibals with Forks: The Triple Bottom Line of 21st*

Source: Shutterstock.com/aodaodaodaod

Century Business.[11] It advocated expanding the conventional financial reporting conventions to include ecological and social performance in addition to financial performance. To achieve their triple bottom line business goals, Holcim have established a set of group-wide performance targets. But, before targets are met, the company aim to understand their current performance. They do this by establishing consistent measurement and reporting techniques, as well as implementing management systems to monitor progress toward their goals. Yet CSR-related performance measurement systems should not, say Holcim, be separate from the more conventional business systems. To work effectively, CSR performance systems are integrated into overall business processes and supported by appropriate training.

The environmental dimension of CSR

Environmental sustainability (according to the World Bank) means *'ensuring that the overall productivity of accumulated human and physical capital resulting from development actions more than compensates for the direct or indirect loss or degradation of the environment'*, or (according to the Brundtland Report From the United Nations) it is *'meeting the needs of the present without compromising the ability of future generations to meet their own needs'*. Put more directly, it is generally taken to mean the extent to which business activity negatively impacts on the natural environment. It is clearly an important issue, not only because of the obvious impact on the immediate environment of hazardous waste, and air, and even noise, pollution, but also because of the less obvious, but potentially far more damaging, issues around global warming.

From the perspective of individual organizations, the challenging issues of dealing with sustainability are connected with the scale of the problem and the general perception of 'green' issues. First, the scale issue is that cause and effect in the environmental sustainability area are judged at different levels. The effects of, and arguments for, environmentally sustainable activities are felt at a global level, while those activities themselves are essentially local. It has been argued that it is difficult to use the concept at a corporate or even at the regional level. Second, there is a paradox with sustainability-based decisions, which is that the more the public become sensitized to the benefits of firms acting in an environmentally sensitive way, the more those firms are tempted to exaggerate their environmental credentials: the so-called 'greenwashing' effect.

One way of demonstrating that operations, in a fundamental way, is at the heart of environmental management is to consider the total environmental burden (EB) created by the totality of operations activities:[12]

$$EB = P \times A \times T$$

where

P = the size of the population

A = the affluence of the population (a proxy measure for consumption)

T = technology (in its broadest sense, the way products and services are made and delivered, in other words operations management)

Achieving sustainability means reducing, or at least stabilizing, the environmental burden. Considering the above formula, this can only be done by decreasing the human population, lowering the level of affluence and therefore consumption, or changing the technology used to create products and services. Decreasing population is not feasible. Decreasing the level of affluence would not only be somewhat unpopular, but would also make the problem worse because low levels of affluence are correlated with high levels of birth rate. The only option left is to change the way goods and services are created.

The social dimension of CSR

The fundamental idea behind the social dimension of CSR is not simply that there is a connection between businesses and the society in which they operate (defined broadly) – that is self-evident. Rather it is that businesses should accept that they bear some responsibility for the impact they have on society and balance the external 'societal' consequences of their actions with the more direct internal consequences, such as profit.

Society is made up of organizations, groups and individuals. Each is more than a simple unit of economic exchange. Organizations have responsibility for the general well-being of society beyond short-term economic self-interest. At the level of the individual, this means devising jobs and work patterns which allow individuals to contribute their talents without undue stress. At a group level, it means recognizing and dealing honestly with employee representatives. This principle also extends beyond the boundaries of the organization. Any business has a responsibility to ensure that it does not knowingly disadvantage individuals in its suppliers or trading partners. Businesses are also a part of the larger community, often integrated into the economic and social fabric of an area. Increasingly, organizations are recognizing their responsibility to local communities by helping to promote their economic and social well-being. And of the many issues that affect society at large, arguably the one that has had the most profound effect on the way business has developed over the last few decades has been the globalization of business activity.

Globalization

The International Monetary Fund defines globalization as 'the growing economic interdependence of countries worldwide through increasing volume and variety of cross-border transactions in goods and services, free international capital flows, and more rapid and widespread diffusion of technology'. It reflects the idea that the world is a smaller place to do business in. Even many medium-sized companies are sourcing and selling their products and services on a global basis. Considerable opportunities have emerged for operations managers to develop both supplier and customer relationships in new parts of the world. All of which is exciting but it also poses many problems. Globalization of trade is considered by some to be the root cause of exploitation and corruption in many developing countries. Others see it as the only way of spreading the levels of prosperity enjoyed by developed countries throughout the world.

The ethical globalization movement seeks to reconcile the globalization trend with how it can impact on societies. Typical aims include the following:

- Acknowledging shared responsibilities for addressing global challenges and affirming that our common humanity doesn't stop at national borders.
- Recognizing that all individuals are equal in dignity and have the right to certain entitlements, rather than viewing them as objects of benevolence or charity.
- Embracing the importance of gender and the need to pay attention to the often different impacts of economic and social policies on women and men.
- Affirming that a world connected by technology and trade must also be connected by shared values, norms of behaviour and systems of accountability.

The economic dimension of CSR

If business could easily adopt a more CSR-friendly position without any economic consequences, there would be no debate. But there *are* economic consequences to taking socially responsible decisions. Some of these will be positive, even in the short term. Others will be negative in the sense that managers believe that there is a real cost in the short term (to their companies specifically). Investment in CSR is a short-term issue, whereas payback from the investment may (possibly) be well into the future, although this is no different from other business investment, except for the uncertain payback and timescale. But also, the investment is made largely by the individual business, whereas the benefits are enjoyed by everyone (including competitors). Yet the direct business benefits of adopting a CSR philosophy are becoming more obvious as public opinion is more sensitized to business's CSR behaviour. Similarly stock market investors are starting to pay more attention. According to Geoffrey Heal of Columbia Business School, some stock market analysts, who research the investment potential of companies' shares, have started to include environmental, social and governance issues into their stock valuations. Further, $1 out of every $9 under professional management in America now involves an element of 'socially responsible investment'.[13]

The stakeholder dimension of CSR

Earlier (in Chapter 2) we looked at the various stakeholder groups from whose perspective operations performance could be judged. The groups included shareholders, directors/top management, staff, staff representative bodies (e.g. trade unions), suppliers (of materials, services, equipment, etc.), regulators (e.g. financial regulators), government (local, national, regional), lobby groups (e.g. environmental lobby groups), and society in general. Later (in Chapter 16) we took this idea further in the context of project management (although the ideas work throughout operations management) and examined how different stakeholders could be managed in different ways. However, two further points should be made here. The first is that a basic tenet of CSR is that a broad range of stakeholders should be considered when making business decisions. In effect, this means that purely economic criteria are insufficient for a socially acceptable outcome. The second is that such judgements are not straightforward. While the various stakeholder groups will obviously take different perspectives on decisions, their perspective is a function not only of their stakeholder classification, but also of their cultural background. What might be unremarkable in one country's or company's ethical framework could be regarded as highly dubious in another's. Nevertheless, there is an emerging agenda of ethical issues to which, at the very least, all managers should be sensitive.

> ❋ **Operations principle**
>
> Effective corporate social responsibility requires an understanding of all the organization's operations stakeholders.

The voluntary dimension of CSR

In most of the world's economies, regulation requires organizations to conform to CSR standards. So, should simply conforming to regulatory requirement be regarded as CSR? Or should social responsibility go beyond merely complying with legally established regulations? In fact most authorities on CSR emphasize its voluntary nature. But this idea is not uncontested. Certainly some do not view CSR as *only* a voluntary activity. They stress the need for a mixture of voluntary and regulatory approaches. Globally, companies, they say, have, in practice, significant power and influence yet '*their socially responsible behaviour does not reflect the accountability they have as a result of their size. Fifty-one of the largest 100 global economies are corporations . . . so . . . corporate power is significantly greater than those of most national governments and plays a dominant role in sectors that are of significance for national economies, especially of developing countries, which may be dependent on a few key sectors.*'[14]

THE WIDER VIEW OF CORPORATE SOCIAL RESPONSIBILITY

The concept of corporate social responsibility permeates operations management. Almost every decision taken by operations managers and every issue discussed in this book influences, and is influenced by, the various dimensions of CSR. In this section we identify and illustrate just some of the operations topics that have a significant relationship with CSR. We shall again use the five 'dimensions' of CSR.

> **✳ Operations principle**
>
> Operations managers have a significant impact on the organization's corporate social responsibility efforts.

Operations and the environmental dimension of CSR

Operations managers cannot avoid responsibility for environmental protection generally, or their organization's environmental performance more specifically. It is often operational failures which are at the root of pollution disasters and operations decisions (such as product design) which impact on longer-term environmental issues. The pollution-causing disasters which make the headlines seem to be the result of a whole variety of causes – oil tankers run aground, nuclear waste is misclassified, chemicals leak into a river, or gas clouds drift over industrial towns. But in fact they all have something in common. They were all the result of an operational failure. Somehow operations procedures were inadequate. Less dramatic in the short term, but perhaps more important in the long term, is the environmental impact of

---

SHORT CASE   **Hewlett-Pockard's recycling programme**[15]

HP began recycling hardware as far back as 1987, when it was the only major computer manufacturer to operate its own recycling facility. Since then they have recovered over 2.3 billion pounds (1.04 billion kg) of products for reuse or recycling. Its recycling program seeks to reduce the environmental impact of its products and minimize waste going to landfills by helping customers discard products conveniently in an environmentally sound manner. Recovered materials, after recycling, have been used to make products, including auto body parts, clothes hangers, plastic toys, fence posts, and roof tiles. In 2010, they manufactured over 310 million HP LaserJet and ink cartridges that contained content from their 'closed-loop' recycling process. HP sees its recycling service as providing an easy way to recycle. Their specially developed state-of-the-art processes are designed to make sure that computer hardware, empty HP printing supplies and other items are recycled responsibly.

Source: Shutterstock.com/RA2 Studio

The HP recycling programme includes such customer friendly features as recycling HP Inkjet and LaserJet cartridges for free; recycling *any* brand of computer hardware, being able to use their online ordering tool to request recycling services, and recycling HP Large Format and Banner Media for free.

products which cannot be recycled and processes which consume large amounts of energy – again, both issues which are part of the operations management's broader responsibilities.

Again, it is important to understand that broad issues such as environmental responsibility are intimately connected with the day-to-day decisions of operations managers. Many of these are concerned with waste. Operations management decisions in product and service design significantly affect the utilization of materials both in the short term as well as in long-term recyclability. Process design influences the proportion of energy and labour that is wasted as well as materials wastage. Planning and control may affect material wastage (packaging being wasted by mistakes in purchasing, for example), but also affects energy and labour wastage. Improvement, of course, is dedicated largely to reducing wastage. Here environmental responsibility and the conventional concerns of operations management coincide. Reducing waste, in all its forms, may be environmentally sound but it also saves cost for the organization.

At other times, decisions can be more difficult. Process technologies may be efficient from the operations point of view but may cause pollution, the economic and social consequences of which are borne by society at large. Such conflicts are usually resolved through regulation

Table 21.2 Some environmental considerations of operations management decisions

Decision area	Some environmental issues
Product/service design	• Recyclability of materials • Energy consumption • Waste material generation
Network design	• Environmental impact of location • Development of suppliers in environmental practice • Reducing transport-related energy
Layout of facilities	• Energy efficiency
Process technology	• Waste and product disposal • Noise pollution • Fume and emission pollution • Energy efficiency
Job design	• Transportation of staff to/from work • Development in environmental education
Planning and control (including MRP, JIT and project planning and control)	• Material utilization and wastage • Environmental impact of project management • Transport pollution of frequent JIT supply
Capacity planning and control	• Over-production waste of poor planning • Local impact of extended operating hours
Inventory planning and control	• Energy management of replenishment transportation • Obsolescence and wastage
Supply chain planning and control	• Minimizing energy consumption in distribution • Recyclability of transportation consumables
Quality planning and control and TQM	• Scrap and wastage of materials • Waste in energy consumption
Failure prevention and recovery	• Environmental impact of process failures • Recovery to minimize impact of failures

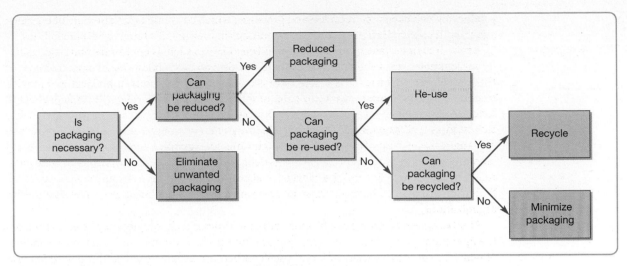

Figure 21.3 Identifying waste minimization in packaging

and legislation. Not that such mechanisms are always effective – there is evidence that just-in-time principles applied in Japan may have produced significant economic gains for the companies which adopted them, but at the price of an overcrowded and polluted road system. Table 21.2 identifies some of the issues concerned with environmental responsibility in each of the operations management decision areas. Figure 21.3 illustrates how one set of operations managers studied the reduction in the wastage of materials and energy, as well as the external environmental impact of their packaging policies.

Green reporting[16]

Until recently, relatively few companies around the world provided information on their environmental practices and performance. Now environmental reporting is increasingly common. One estimate is that around 35 per cent of the world's largest corporations publish reports on their environmental policies and performance. Partly, this may be motivated by an altruistic desire to cause less damage to the planet. However, what is also becoming accepted is that green reporting makes good business sense.

ISO 14000

Another emerging issue in recent years has been the introduction of the ISO 14000 standard. It has a three-section environmental management system which covers initial planning, implementation and objective assessment. Although it has had some impact worldwide, it is largely limited to Europe.

ISO 14000 makes a number of specific requirements, including the following:

- a commitment by top-level management to environmental management;
- the development and communication of an environmental policy;
- the establishment of relevant legal and regulatory requirements;
- the setting of environmental objectives and targets;
- the establishment and updating of a specific environmental programme, or programmes, geared to achieving the objectives and targets;
- the implementation of supporting systems such as training, operational control and emergency planning;
- regular monitoring and measurement of all operational activities;
- a full audit procedure to review the working and suitability of the system.

The similarity of ISO 14000 to the quality procedures of ISO 9000 is a bit of a giveaway. ISO 14000 can contain all the problems of ISO 9000 (management by manual, obsession with procedures rather than results, a major expense to implement it, and, at its worst, the formalization of what was bad practice in the first place). But ISO 14000 also has some further problems. The main one is that it can become a 'badge for the smug'. It can be seen as 'all there is to do to be a good environmentally sensitive company'. At least with quality standards like ISO 9000 there are real customers continually reminding the business that quality does matter. Pressures to improve environmental standards are far more diffuse. Customers are not likely to be as energetic in forcing good environmental standards on suppliers as they are in forcing the good-quality standards from which they benefit directly. Instead of this type of procedure-based system, surely the only way to influence a practice which has an effect on a societal level is through society's normal mechanism – legal regulation. If quality suffers, individuals suffer and have the sanction of not purchasing goods and services again from the offending company. With bad environmental management, we all suffer. Because of this, the only workable way to ensure environmentally sensitive business policies is by insisting that our governments protect us. Legislation, therefore, is the only safe way forward.

Operations and the social dimension of CSR

The way in which an operation is managed has a significant impact on its customers, the individuals who work for it, the individuals who work for its suppliers and the local community in which the operation is located. The dilemma is how can operations be managed to be profitable, responsible employers and be good neighbours? As in the previous section, we will look particularly at globalization, primarily because the world is a smaller place; very few operations do not either source from or sell to foreign markets. So, how do operations managers cope with this expanded set of opportunities?

Globalization and operations decisions

Most of the decision areas we have covered in this book have an international dimension to them. Often this is simply because different parts of the world with different cultures have different views on the nature of work. So, for example, highly repetitive work on an assembly line may be unpopular in parts of Europe, but it is welcome as a source of employment in other parts of the world. Does this mean that operations should be designed to accommodate the cultural reactions of people in different parts of the world? Probably. Does this mean that we are imposing lower standards on less wealthy parts of the world? Well, it depends on your point of view. The issue, however, is that cultural and economic differences do impact on the day-to-day activities of operations management decision making.

Ethical globalization

If all this seems at too high a level for a humble subject like operations management, look at Table 21.3 and consider how many of these issues have an impact on day-to-day decision making. If a company decides to import some of its components from a Third World country, where wages are substantially cheaper, is this a good or a bad thing? Local trade unions might oppose the 'export of jobs'. Shareholders would, presumably, like the higher profits. Environmentalists would want to ensure that natural resources were not harmed. Everyone with a social conscience would want to ensure that workers from a Third World country were not exploited (although one person's exploitation is another's very welcome employment opportunity). Such decisions

Table 21.3 Some social considerations of operations management decisions

Decision area	Some social issues
Product/service design	• Customer safety • Social impact of product
Network design	• Employment implications of location • Employment implications of plant closure • Employment implications of vertical integration
Layout of facilities	• Staff safety • Disabled access
Process technology	• Staff safety • Noise damage • Repetitive/alienating work
Job design	• Staff safety • Workplace stress • Repetitive/alienating work • Unsocial working hours • Customer safety (in high contact operations)
Planning and control (including MRP, lean and project planning and control)	• What priority to give customers waiting to be served • Unsocial staff working hours • Workplace stress • Restrictive organizational cultures
Capacity planning and control	• 'Hire and fire' employment policies • Working hours fluctuations • Unsocial working hours • Service cover in emergencies • Relationships with subcontractors • 'Dumping' of products below cost
Inventory planning and control	• Price manipulation in restricted markets • Warehouse safety
Supply chain planning and control	• Honesty in supplier relationships • Transparency of cost data • Non-exploitation of developing country suppliers • Prompt payment to suppliers
Quality planning and control and TQM	• Customer safety • Staff safety • Workplace stress
Failure prevention and recovery	• Customer safety • Staff safety

are made every day by operations managers throughout the world. Table 21.3 identifies just some of the social responsibility issues for each of the major decision areas covered in this book.

Operations and the economic dimension of CSR

Operations managers are at the forefront of trying to balance any costs of CSR with any benefits. In a practical sense this means attempting to understand where extra expenditure will be necessary in order to adopt socially responsible practices against the savings and/or benefits that will accrue from these same practices. Here it is useful to divide operations-related costs into input, transformation (or processing), and output costs.

The Gap between perception, reality and intention[17]

It is expensive to manufacture garments in developed countries where wages, transport and infrastructure costs are high. It is also a competitive market. As customers, most of us look to secure a good deal when we shop. This is why most garments sold in developed countries are actually made in less developed countries. Large retail chains such as Gap select suppiers who can deliver acceptable quality at a cost that allows both them and the chain to make a profit. But what if the supplier achieves this by adopting practices that, while not unusual in the supplier's country, are unacceptable to consumers? Then, in addition to any harm to the victims of the practice, the danger to the retail chain is one of 'reputational risk'. This is what happened to the garment retailer Gap when a British newspaper ran a story under the headline, *'Gap Child Labour Shame'*. The story went on, *'An Observer investigation into children making clothes has shocked the retail giant and may cause it to withdraw apparel ordered for Christmas. Amitosh concentrates as he pulls the loops of thread through tiny plastic beads and sequins on the toddler's blouse he is making. Dripping with sweat, his hair is thinly coated in dust. In Hindi his name means "happiness". The hand-embroidered garment on which his tiny needle is working bears the distinctive logo of international fashion chain Gap. Amitosh is 10.*

Within two days Gap responded as follows: *'Earlier this week . . . an allegation* [was made] *of child labor at a facility in India. An investigation was immediately launched . . . a very small portion of one order . . . was apparently subcontracted to an unauthorized subcontractor*

Source: Shutterstock.com/Viorel Sima

without the company's knowledge . . . in direct violation of [our] *agreement under* [our] *Code of Vendor Conduct. We strictly prohibit the use of child labor. This is a non-negotiable for us – and we are deeply concerned and upset by this allegation. As we've demonstrated in the past, Gap has a history of addressing challenges like this head-on. In 2006, Gap Inc. ceased business with 23 factories due to code violations. We have 90 people located around the world whose job is to ensure compliance with our Code of Vendor Conduct.'*

Input costs. CSR-related costs are often associated with the nature of the relationship between an operation and its suppliers. As in the example of Gap above, socially responsible behaviour involves careful monitoring of all suppliers so as to ensure that their practices conform with what is generally accepted as good practice (although this does vary in different parts of the world) and does not involve dealing with ethically questionable sources. All this requires extra costs of monitoring, setting up audit procedures, and so on. The benefits of doing this are related to the avoidance of reputational risk. Good audit procedures allow firms to take advantage of lower input costs while avoiding the promotion of exploitative practices. In addition, from an ethical viewpoint, one could also argue that it provides employment and promotes good practice in developing parts of the world.

Transformation (processing) costs. Many operations' processes are significant consumers of energy and produce (potentially) significant amounts of waste. It is these two aspects of processing that may require investment, for example, in new energy-saving processes, but will generate a return, in the form of lower costs, in the longer term. Also in this category could be included staff-related costs, such as those that promote staff well-being, work–life balance, diversity, etc. Again, although promoting these staff-related issues may have a cost, it will also generate economic benefits associated with committed staff and the multi-perspective benefits associated with diversity. In addition, of course, there are ethical benefits of reducing energy consumption, promoting social equality and so on.

Output costs. Two issues are interesting here. First is that of 'end-of-life' responsibility. Either through legislation or consumer pressure, businesses are having to invest in processes that recycle or reuse their products after disposal. Second, there is a broader issue of businesses being expected to try and substitute services in place of products. A service that hires or leases equipment for example, is deemed to be a more efficient user of resources than one that produces and sells the same equipment, leaving it to customers to use the equipment efficiently. (This issue is close to that of servitization mentioned in Chapter 1.) While both of these trends involve costs to the operation, they also can generate revenue. Taking responsibility for end-of-life collection and disposal allows companies to better understand how their products have been used. Substituting services for products can be more problematic, but offers the possibility of generating revenue through the services themselves. In addition, ethically, both these trends could result in a more effective and efficient use of global resources.

Operations and the stakeholder dimension of CSR

As we discussed earlier (in Chapter 2), almost all stakeholder groups will, in some way or other, be affected by operations decisions. Here we summarize just some of these effects.

Customers' welfare is directly affected by many operations decisions. The most obvious is that their safety might be compromised. If a product is badly assembled or if the equipment used in a service (such as a rail transport system) is not maintained, customers can come to harm. But customer safety is influenced by more than good manufacturing or maintenance practice; it could also be affected by the degree to which an operation discloses the details of its activities. When should an airline admit that it has received bomb threats? At a less serious level, the ethical framework of operations decisions can affect the fairness with which customers are treated. For example, should a bank discriminate between different customers in order to give priority to those from whom they can make more profit?

Staff are constantly exposed to the ethical framework of the organization throughout their working lives. Organizations have a duty to their staff to prevent their exposure to hazards at work. This means more than preventing catastrophic physical injuries; it means that organizations must take into account the longer-term threat to staff health from, say, repetitive strain injury (RSI) due to short-cycle, repetitive work motions. A more subtle ethical duty to staff is the operation's responsibility to avoid undue workplace stress. Stress could be caused through not providing employees with the information which allows them to understand the rationale and consequences of operations decisions, or expecting staff to take decisions for which they are not equipped. Again, many staff-related ethical decisions are not straightforward. Should an operation be totally honest with its staff regarding future employment changes when doing so might provoke a labour dispute, or signal the company's intentions to its competitors?

Suppliers are always a source of ethical dilemma for the operation. Is it legitimate to put suppliers under pressure not to trade with other organizations, either to ensure that you get focused service from them or to deny competitors this source of supply? Also, do you have any right to impose your own ethical standards on your suppliers, for example, because you would not wish to exploit workers in developing countries? How much effort should you put into making sure that your suppliers are operating as you would? More significantly, would you be prepared to pay a higher price for their product or service if it meant them abandoning what you regard as unethical practice?

The community also has a right to expect its organizations to adopt a responsible attitude. Yet there are often difficult trade-offs between commercial and societal objectives. However, businesses could claim that prospering commercially is also a very valuable contribution to society, as is stated by Rolls-Royce in this extract from their CSR policy: *'The most significant contribution Rolls-Royce makes in the field of Corporate Social Responsibility comes from the wealth created by maintaining the 35,000 highly-skilled jobs which arise from our business activities, mainly in the UK, North America, Germany and the Nordic Countries. In 2004 our global wage bill was £1.5 billion. In addition, the company's activities support thousands of jobs throughout our global supply chain.'*

Operations and the voluntary dimension of CSR

Some critics of corporate behaviour claim that CSR is meaningless if it involves nothing more than what is required by legislation, or even simple good management. Unless it hurts, they seem to be saying, it does not count as true CSR. So, how should operations managers view CSR? In one survey[18] the most popular response was that CSR was 'a necessary cost of doing business'. In other words, operations managers see it as something that has to be done because it is required either by legislation or through company policy. There is very little element of voluntariness in this response. Certainly there is no evidence that respondents who think this way see any advantage in going beyond what is strictly required. However, the second most popular response (running the first one very close) is that CSR gives the company something of a distinctive position in the market. In other words, there are market-based advantages in adopting CSR. While this is positive it is somewhat self-serving. CSR is seen simply as something that enhances a brand position rather than something that tackles serious problems from a largely ethical perspective. After that, with less than half the scores of the first two categories of response, is that of CSR being meaningless if it includes what we would do anyway. This is true voluntarism. Perhaps CSR proponents will take comfort from the fact that a very small percentage of respondents thought that CSR was 'a waste of money'.

What does not come out in the survey, but is well worth considering, is that CSR activities can provide some genuine operations-based advantages. But moving beyond the minimum of engagement in CSR can provide real operations-based benefits. The obvious one, as we have mentioned before, is that in some ways the interests of CSR and those of the firm very obviously coincide. Energy saving, minimizing transport costs, avoiding reputational-risk-laden issues, and so on, are the 'low hanging fruit' of CSR. But beyond this there may be advantages for businesses that regularly monitor the environment (including business environment) generally and keep in touch with and aware of what is happening in the world. CSR can only encourage this. Finally, it may be that operations who 'push the envelope' of their own processes in order to improve their ethical behaviour are also the ones with the greater process knowledge. In other words, moving beyond the strict minimum of CSR behaviour may be one of the best signs of competent operations management. Reportedly, some stock market analysts believe that examining the excellence of a company's CSR policy may be helpful in assessing the quality of its management more generally.

HOW CAN OPERATIONS MANAGERS ANALYSE CSR ISSUES?

It should already be apparent that CSR is both important and yet difficult to analyse. It is an issue on which not everyone holds similar views. It involves a partially understood relationship between cause and effect. It often involves conflicting short-term and long-term costs and benefits. More than anything else, it is complex, involving operational, strategic, socio-economic, and geopolitical aspects. How then can operations managers attempt to understand CSR issues? It will certainly involve operations managers in mastering new skills and analytical techniques. Yet there are existing concepts (some of which are covered in this text) that can be used to enhance our understanding of CSR. Here we have space only to look at two of them – trade-off theory and risk management.

Trade-offs and CSR

Earlier (in Chapter 3) we introduced the idea of trade-offs and how the concept of the 'efficient frontier' could help with an understanding of operations strategy. It can also help with an understanding of CSR. Figure 21.4 illustrates the idea of trade-offs between the financial and the ethical performance of any operations. The first point to make is that there are relatively extreme positions on both financial and ethical performance. On the side of those who believe that CSR is essentially a distraction for business, the most famous

Figure 21.4 To what extent do ethical and financial performance trade off?

quote comes from Milton Friedman, the famous economist, who said: 'The business of busi-ness is business. A society that puts equality before freedom will get neither. A society that puts freedom before equality will get a high degree of both.' In the opposite corner, representing those who believe that business should only exist in the context of a broader set of social responsibilities, is the founder of Body Shop, Anita Roddick. She said: 'In terms of power and influence . . . there is no more powerful institution in society than business . . . The busi-ness of business should not be about money, it should be about responsibility. It should be about public good, not private greed.'

In between these two positions, most businesses try and reach some degree of compromise. In this sense they are 'repositioning' themselves on an efficient frontier as in Figure 21.4(a). As pointed out earlier (in Chapter 3), repositioning an operation on the efficient frontier is sometimes necessary as the demands of the market (or environment) change. Also (as we pointed out in Chapter 3), it is possible either to adopt an extreme position at either end of the efficient frontier (that is, designing a focused operation) or to try to break through the efficient frontier through operations improvement activities. In this case, it is increasingly difficult to focus exclusively on either financial or ethical performance. Societal pressure and issues of reputational risk are defining minimum ethical standards while tough market conditions and stockholder expectations are defining minimum financial standards. Thus exercising improvement creativity to try to become better at financial and ethical perfor-mance simultaneously could be argued to be the only realistic option for most businesses (see Fig. 21.4(b)).

Risk management

Although treating CSR as risk management is frowned on by some experts, it is likely that, in practice, many companies, while doing their best to adopt ethical standards, are certainly influenced by the reputational risks of unethical behaviour. Look at this quotation from one

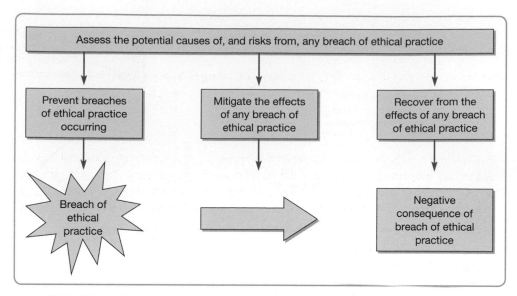

Figure 21.5 CSR as risk management

report on the subject: '*Most of the rhetoric on CSR may be about doing the right thing and trumping competitors, but much of the reality is plain risk management. It involves limiting the damage to the brand and the bottom line that can be inflicted by a bad press and consumer boycotts, as well as dealing with the threat of legal action.*'[19] Given this, it is worth reminding ourselves of how we described risk management earlier (in Chapter 19). Figure 21.5 summarizes an operations view of risk management as it could be applied to CSR. Essentially it involves thinking through and planning for four steps:

1 *Assess the potential causes of and risks from any breach of ethical practice.* The first stage in any risk management is to look at what could go wrong. In this case, exactly what could the operation do that would fall short of sound ethical practice? One of the main problems here is that different stakeholders will judge what sound ethical practice is differently.

2 *Prevent breaches of ethical practice occurring.* This is where an operation's basic process and cultural ability to follow procedures is tested. An operation that has designed its processes to deliver appropriate levels of performance, has resourced those processes adequately and kept the processes under continual review is less likely to suffer breaches of ethical standards. By contrast, operations with poorly defined or out-of-date process records will find it difficult to identify where breaches of procedure are likely to occur.

3 *Mitigate the effects of any breach of ethical practice.* Mitigation means reducing the negative consequences of failure. If a breach of ethical standards does occur, how can its effects be minimized? Again, one refers back to the details of mitigation (outlined in Chapter 19), but it is worthwhile pointing out that a history of genuine efforts to maintain ethical standards can help to diffuse failures when they do occur. Look back at the example of Gap earlier. The fact that Gap had a history of penalizing suppliers who breached its ethical codes must have helped to diffuse the failure in one supplier's ethical standards when it did occur.

4 *Recover from the effects of any breach of ethical practice.* As with any other recovery activity, it is important to be prompt, honest, and genuinely penitent. The worst thing that any company could do is try and 'cover up' any ethical failure. Rather, it is important to understand what has happened, honestly examine why the failure has occurred and learn the lessons that can prevent it happening in the future.

Check and improve your understanding of this chapter using self-assessment questions and a personalized study plan, a video case study, and an eText all at www.myomlab.com.

MyOMLab

❯ What is corporate social responsibility (CSR)?

● CSR is about how business takes account of its economic, social and environmental impacts in the way it operates – maximizing the benefits and minimizing the downsides. It is the voluntary actions that business can take, over and above compliance with minimum legal requirements, to address both its own competitive interests and the interests of wider society.

● Although there are many definitions of CSR, they usually include five 'dimensions':
  - the environmental dimension;
  - the social dimension;
  - the economic dimension;
  - the stakeholder dimension;
  - the voluntariness dimension.

❯ How does the wider view of corporate social responsibility influence operations management?

● The concept of corporate social responsibility permeates almost every decision taken by operations managers.

● Most dramatic environmental contamination disasters are caused by operational failure. In a broader sense, all operations management decisions have some kind of environmental impact.

● Increasingly, companies are making formal reports and statements relating to their environmental practice. Operations managers are often responsible for providing the basic information for these reports. The environmental management system ISO 14000 is being adopted by a wide range of organizations. Operations managers will often have to implement these standards.

● Corporate social responsibility includes understanding the effects of operations management decisions on all stakeholder groups.

● Although globalization is an emotive issue, operations managers are affected in all the decision areas by aspects of globalization.

● Operations managers are at the forefront of trying to balance any costs of CSR with any benefits. This means attempting to understand where extra expenditure will be necessary in order to adopt socially responsible practices against the savings and/or benefits that will accrue from these same practices.

● Groups who are affected by ethical management practice include the organization, the customers, staff, suppliers, the wider community and the organization's shareholders.

● Some authorities claim that CSR is meaningless if it involves nothing more than what is required by legislation, or even simple good management.

❯ How can operations managers analyse CSR issues?

● Analysing CSR issues is difficult in the context of operations management decisions, partly because of the complexity of those issues. Two models that were introduced in earlier chapters, and can be used to understand how to approach CSR, are trade-off analysis (including the idea of the efficient frontier) and risk management.

CSR as it is presented

The following are extracts from the corporate social responsibility corporate websites of four reputable companies.

HSBC (bank)

For HSBC CSR means *'addressing the expectations of our customers, shareholders, employees and other stakeholders in managing our business responsibly and sensitively for long-term success . . . [this involves] . . . listening to our stakeholders [which] helps us to develop our business in ways that will continue to appeal to customers, investors, employees and other stakeholders . . . We believe the world is a rich and diverse place. The better our workforce reflects this diversity, the better we can anticipate and meet our customers' needs . . . Involving our employees in the community brings many benefits. Our employees gain in understanding, confidence and self-esteem. And being recognized in the community as good corporate citizens and employers helps HSBC to attract great people who in turn can provide great service to our customers.'*

Orange (mobile telecoms operator)

'As part of our commitment to corporate social responsibility and to the communities we operate in, Orange have developed a framework in the UK called community futures, which is about enabling people to participate more fully in society. It provides a co-ordinated approach to our corporate community involvement, bringing together all activities undertaken by our employees and the company. Community futures covers three core areas – charity, community futures awards and education. Many people with sensory disabilities find it difficult to participate fully in society. Communication is clearly key to improving lives and we believe our expertise in this area can make a real difference. Therefore, we have chosen sensory disability, with a focus on the visually and hearing impaired, as the single issue for national campaigning in the UK. Orange support local projects around the country that are working to make a difference to people with sensory disabilities. Through the provision of awards, Orange seek to recognize and reward innovative community projects that use communication to enable people with sensory disabilities to participate more fully in society. Education plays a key role in any community, bringing it together. It helps people participate more fully in society by improving the ability to communicate.'

John Lewis Partnership (retailer)

'The Partnership was ahead of its time in recognizing that commercial success depended on showing the highest level of good citizenship in its behaviour within the community. Today we are best known for the fact that our business is owned for the benefit of our employees, but we know that to cut our way through tough competitive conditions, we have to continue to prize sound relationships with our customers and suppliers, and sustain a keen sense of civic responsibility.'

Source: Corbis/Ultraf

Pearson (education company)

'We see two big environmental challenges facing the planet. The first is climate change and the second is resource use. . . Climate change impacts such as extreme weather patterns and water scarcity affect people everywhere, with developing countries the most vulnerable. . . We operate in more than 70 countries and we are seeing a growing global recognition of the effects of climate change whether from our investors or by policymakers and how this is starting to change the business landscape. New regulations are emerging – as are the expectations of the people who work at Pearson and who buy our products and services. . . The second challenge is lack of resources. It is sobering to note this estimate by the World Wildlife Fund: if every country in the world consumed materials at the same rate as the UK, it would take three planets to sustain our way of life. All countries have legitimate aspirations to grow and provide opportunity, but that they do so in a sustainable fashion, should be of deep concern to us all.'

QUESTIONS

1 What are the similarities and differences between these statements?

2 Why do large companies like these go to so much trouble to invest in CSR?

3 Some companies have been the target of anti-globalization violence. What is likely to make a company such a target?

These problems and applications will help to improve your analysis of operations. You can find more practice problems as well as worked examples and guided solutions on MyOMLab at www.myomlab.com.

MyOMLab

Try debating the following points:

- Business ethics is a contradiction in terms.
- For-profit companies have a primary responsibility to their shareholders; social responsibility therefore only makes sense when it is in the commercial interests of companies.
- Life would be considerably simpler if we went back to serving our own national markets rather than global ones.
- Anti-capitalist globalization protesters are basically conservatives who are frightened by the modern world. Throughout history there have been people like this.
- Soon all organizations will be global organizations. The internet will see to that.
- The modern corporation cannot separate itself from the society in which it operates. We are entering the mature age of capitalism, where business objectives must reflect the interests of all their stakeholders.
- The only way to get firms to be environmentally responsible is by taxing them for the environmental damage they do.
- The best way to encourage firms to be environmentally responsible is by educating customers only to buy products and services from environmentally responsible companies.
- How can operations managers ever be creative in their response to CSR? To do their job well, they have to be dull, technologically obsessed and sad. They ought to get a life.

SELECTED FURTHER READING

Crane, A., McWilliams, A., Matten, D. and Siegel, D.S. (editors) (2009) *The Oxford Handbook of Corporate Social Responsibility* (Oxford Handbooks in Business and Management), OUP, Oxford. An authoritative review of the academic research on CSR.

Harvard Business Review (2003) *Harvard Business Review on Corporate Responsibility*, Harvard Business School Press, Boston, MA.

Kotler, P. and Lee, N. (2005) *Corporate Social Responsibility: Doing the Most Good for Your Company and Your Cause*, John Wiley & Sons, Inc., Hoboken, NJ.

McWilliams, A. and Siegel, D. (2001) Corporate social responsibility: a theory of the firm perspective, *Academy of Management Review*, vol. 26, no. 1, 117–127. Discusses the 'ideal' level of CSR, which managers can determine using cost–benefit analysis.

USEFUL WEBSITES

www.imf.org The International Monetary Fund website. Not a neutral in the globalization debate, but some well-argued commentary.

www.ifg.org Site of the International Forum on Globalization (IFG), an 'alliance of 60 leading activists, scholars, economists, researchers and writers formed to stimulate new thinking, joint activity, and public education in response to economic globalization'. They don't like it, but their discussions are interesting.

http://sd.defra.gov.uk The UK government's site.

www.technologyreview.com MIT's online technology review. Full of interesting stuff (if you like technology, that is).

www.kmworld.com A knowledge management journal with articles and links.

www.myomlab.com Test which sections you have mastered and which you need to review, with questions, a personalized study plan, video clips, revision tips, and cases.

www.opsman.org Useful materials.

http://operationsroom.wordpress.com/ Stanford University's take on topical operations stories.

www.ft.com Good for researching topics and companies.

www.economist.com *The Economist*'s site, well written and full of interesting stuff about business generally.

MyOMLab

Now that you have finished reading this chapter, why not visit MyOMLab at www.myomlab.com where you'll find more learning resources to help you make the most of your studies and get a better grade.

Notes on chapters

Chapter 1

1 Sources include: company website (2012); Baraldi, E. (2008) Strategy in Industrial Networks: Experiences from IKEA, *California Management Review*, vol. 50, no. 4; IKEA plans to end 'stressful shopping', *London Evening Standard*, 24 April 2006; Walley, P. and Hart, K. (1993) *IKEA (UK) Ltd*, Loughborough University Business School.

2 Sources include: discussions with Tom Dyson and Olly Willans of Torchbox, to whom we are grateful for their advice and assistance.

3 Sources include: MSF website (2011), www.msf.org.uk; Beaumont, P. (2011) Médecins sans Frontières book reveals aid agencies' ugly compromises, *Guardian*, 20 November.

4 Sources include: First Direct social media newsroom website, www.newsroom.firstdirect.com; Hill-Wilson, M. (2011) First Direct and instilling a customer service DNA, Institute of Customer Service, 5 January; First Direct collaborates with customers online (2011) http://itsopen.co.uk/about.

5 Sources include: Goodman, M. (2011) Pret Smile, it will pay for everyone, *Sunday Times*, 6 March; Pret A Manger website, www.pret.com.

6 Sources include: Johnston, R. and Staughton. R. (2009) Establishing and developing strategic relationships – the role of operations managers, *International Journal of Operations and Production Management*, vol. 29, no. 6; Wyganowska, J. (2008) The Top 10 Skills of Effective Operations Managers, Recreation Management, www.recmanagement.com/200802gc04.php; Operationsmanagers.com (2011) The 5 Key Personality Traits of Operations Managers, http://careers-in-business.com/omskill.htm.

7 An earlier version of this case appeared in Johnston, R., Chambers, S., Harland, C., Harrison, A. and Slack N. (2003) *Cases in Operations Management,* 3rd edn, Financial Times Prentice Hall, Harlow.

Chapter 2

1 Sources include: BBC website (2008) BA managers leave after T5 fiasco, 15 April; Browning, A. (2008) How do you clear a bags backlog? BBC website, 19 April; Yeoman, F. and Hines, N. (2008) Heathrow T5 disruption to continue over weekend, Times Online, 28 March; Done, K. (2008) BA to cancel hundreds more flights from T5, *Financial Times*, 30 March 30; Done, K. (2008) Long haul to restore BA's reputation, *Financial Times*, 28 March; Robertson, D. (2008) Why Heathrow's T5 disaster provide a lesson for Dubai's T3, *The Times*, 29 November.

2 The phrase 'the triple bottom line' was first used in 1994 by John Elkington, the founder of a British consultancy called SustainAbility. Read Elkington, J., *Cannibals with Forks: The Triple Bottom Line of 21st Century Business*, Capstone, Oxford, 1997. Also good is, Savitz, A.W. and Weber, K. (2006) *The Triple Bottom Line: How Today's Best-Run Companies Are Achieving Economic, Social and Environmental Success—and How You Can Too*, Jossey-Bass, San Francisco, CA.

3 Sources include: *Economist* (2012) Firms with benefits: A new sort of caring, sharing company gathers momentum, 7 January; Patagonia website, www.patagonia.com.

4 Jensen, M.C. (2001) Value Maximization, Stakeholder Theory, and the Corporate Objective Function, *Journal of Applied Corporate Finance*, vol. 14, no. 3, 7–21.

5 We are grateful to Nick Fuge for his time giving us this information.

6 Sources include: Marlinson, C. (2006) The Golden Hour, *Sunday Times*, 21 September.

7 Sources include: Levitz, J. (2011) Inside UPS's Weather Machine, *Wall Street Journal*, 23 December.

8 Sources include: mymuesli website, http://uk.mymuesli.com/muesli.

9 Sources include: John Hendry-Pickup of Aldi.

10 Sources include: Moore, M. (2012) 'Mass suicide' protest at Apple manufacturer Foxconn factory, *Daily Telegraph*, 12 January; Suicides at Foxconn, *Economist*, 27 May 2010.

11 Source: Miles, A. and Baldwin, T. (2002) Spidergram to check on police forces, *The Times*, 10 July.

12 Source: Skinner, W. (1985) *Manufacturing: The Formidable Competitive Weapon*, John Wiley, London.

13 We are grateful to the management of the Penang Mutiara. The case is for illustrative purposes, and some hotel practices may have changed since the writing of the case.

Chapter 3

1 Sources include: the 'I hate Ryanair' website, www.ihateryanair.org/ryanair-recent-passenger-reviews; press releases, Ryanair; Keenan, S. (2002) 'How Ryanair put its passengers in their place, *The Times*, 19 June; Flextronics website.

2 Hayes, R.H. and Wheelwright, S.C. (1984) *Restoring our Competitive Edge*, John Wiley, London.

3 For a more thorough explanation, *see* Slack, N. and Lewis, M. (2011) *Operations Strategy*, 3rd edn, Financial Times Prentice Hall, Harlow.

4 Mintzberg, H. and Waters, J.A. (1995) Of Strategies: Deliberate and Emergent, *Strategic Management Journal*, July/Sept.

5 Sources include: Poeter, D. (2011) Apple stores' secret sauce spilled, PC Mag.com, 15 June; Lipschutz, K. (2011) Apple's retail philosophy: employees reveal calculated culture, *Adweek*, 15 June; Johnson, R. (2011) What I learned building the Apple store, HBR Blog network, 21 November.

6 Also called critical success factors by some authors.

7 Source: Hill, T. (1993) *Manufacturing Strategy*, 2nd edn, Macmillan.

8 There is a vast literature which describes the resource-based view of the firm. For example, *see* Barney, J. (1991) The resource-based model of the firm: origins, implications and prospect, *Journal of Management*, vol. 17, no. 1; or Teece, D.J. and Pisano, G. (1994) The dynamic capabilities of firms: an introduction, *Industrial and Corporate Change*, vol. 3, no. 3.

9 Source: Lifting the bonnet, *Economist*, 7 October 2006.

10 Source: Barney, J. (1991) The resource-based model of the firm: origins, implications and prospect, *Journal of Management*, vol. 17, no. 1.

11 Sources include: Satariano, A. and Burrows, P. (2011) Apple's supply-chain secret? Hoard lasers, *Bloomberg Businessweek*, 3 November; Elmer-DeWitt, P. (2011) How Apple became a monopsonist, CNN News, 5 July; Lariviere, M. (2011) Operations: Apple's secret sauce?, *The Operations Room*, 4 November.

12 Slack, N. and Lewis, M.A. (2011) *Operations Strategy*, 3rd edn, Financial Times Prentice Hall, Harlow.

13 Weick, K.E. (1990) Cartographic myths in organization, in Huff, A. (ed) *Mapping Strategic Thought*, Wiley, London.

14 This case was written by Shirley Johnston, 2009. It is based on a real organization and all names and places have been changed.

Chapter 4

1 Source: Horovitz, A. (2002) Fast Food World Says Drive-Through is the Way to Go, *USA Today*, 3 April.

2 The term 'takt time' comes from Toyota, the automobile company. It is their adaptation of the German word 'tak-tzeit', originally meaning 'clock cycle'.

3 Associated Press (2012) Standardised bed chart 'could prevent hundreds of hospital deaths', *Guardian*, 27 July.

4 Sources include: Ecover website, www.the-splash.co.uk; Osborne, H. (2006) Spick'n'span ethics, *Guardian*, 17 November.

5 Hayes, R.H. and Wheelwright, S.C. (1984) *Restoring our Competitive Edge*, John Wiley.

6 One note of caution regarding this idea: although logically coherent, it is a conceptual model rather than something that can be 'scaled'. Although it is intuitively obvious that deviating from the diagonal increases costs, the precise amount by which costs will increase is very difficult to determine.

7 Sources include: Davey, J. (2010) Today we built a house every hour, *Sunday Times*, 31 January; Persimmon company website; Brown, G. (2010) Space4 growth gives boost to former car sector workers, *Birmingham Post*, 27 August.

8 The Workflow Management Coalition (2009) website: www.wfmc.org.

9 *Economist*, A new departure for London's airports, 21 August 2008.

Chapter 5

1 Sources include: Marsh, P. (2011) Dyson heater seen as the key to tech refocus, *Financial Times*, 15 September; Dyson website, www.dyson.co.uk.

2 Henderson, R.M. and Clark, K.B. (1990) Architectural innovation: The reconfiguration of existing product technologies and the failure of established firms. *Administrative Science Quarterly*, vol. 35(1), 9–22.

3 Sources include: *Economist* (2012) The last Kodak moment?, 14 January; Wright, M. (2010) Kodak develops: A film giant's self-reinvention, *Wired* magazine, 15 February.

4 Sources: many thanks to Mark Taber for his advice; *Economist* (2006) Open, but not as usual, 16 March; Kisiel, R. (2008) BMW wants joint effort to develop open-source in-vehicle platform, *Automotive News Europe*, 23 October.

5 Sources include: *Economist* (2008) A people business, print edition, 25 September; de Castella, T. (2010) Should we trust the wisdom of crowds, BBC News magazine, 5 July.

6 Sources include: BBC (2001) Square fruit stuns Japanese shoppers, BBC website, 15 June; Poulter, S. (2006) Square melons on the way, *Daily Mail*, 3 August.

7 With thanks to George Northwood, Manager of Daniel Hersheson's Mayfair salon.

8 Source: *Economist* (2002) Think local, 13 April.

9 Bennis, W. and Biederman, P.W., *Organising Genius: The Secrets of Creative Collaboration*, Addison-Wesley, 1997; new edn, Nicholas Brealey, 1998.

10 Sources include: *The Times* (2006) Timeline – Airbus A380 'superjumbo', 26 October; BBC news website (2006) Q&A: A380 delays, 30 October; BBC news website (2007) Q&A: Airbus job cuts, 28 February; Hollinger, P. and Wiesmann, G. (2008) Airbus is hampered by cultural differences, *Financial Times*; *Economist* (2008) Airbus Marathon Man, 17 July; *Economist* (2008) Boeing and Airbus – swings and roundabouts, 27 November.

Chapter 6

1 Sources include: Taylor, P. (2012) Customer must be king in the web world, *Financial Times*, 24 January.

2 Sources include: *Economist* (2009) HTC, Upwardly mobile, 9 July.

3 Bacon, G., Machan, I. and Dnyse, J. (2008) Offshore challenges, Manufacturing, The Institute of Electrical Engineers, January.

4 Sources include: Devendra Damle; *Economist* (2008) Nano wars, 28 August; *Economist* (2008) The one-lakh car, 10 January; *Economist* (2008) A new home for the Nano, 9 October.

5 Sources include: *Economist* (2011) Clusters flustered – global competition seems to be weakening the benefits of being in a cluster, 14 April; Deutsche Bank Research (2010) Global financial centres after the crisis, 2 August; *Economist* (2009) Britain and Formula 1 – cluster champs, 22 October; Wendling, M. (2011) Can 'Silicon Roundabout' challenge Silicon Valley? BBC News website, 8 September.

6 Sources include: Blakely, R. (2010) Britain can learn from India's assembly-line heart operations, says doctor, *The Times*, 14 May; *Economist* (2011) Economies of scale made steel – the economics of very big ships, 12 November.

7 This case was prepared using published sources of information. It does not reflect the views of the Walt Disney company, who should not be held responsible for the accuracy or interpretation of any of the information or views

contained in the case. It is not intended to illustrate either good or bad management practice.

Supplement to Chapter 6

1 Linstone, H.A. and Turoof, M. (1975) *The Delphi Method: Techniques and Applications*, Addison-Wesley, Reading, MA.
2 Hogarth, R.M. and Makridakis, S. (1981) Forecasting and Planning: An Evaluation, *Management Science*, vol. 27, 115–38.
3 Hogarth, R.M. and Makridakis, S., *op. cit.*
4 Armstrong, J.S. and Grohman, M.C. (1972) A Comparative Study of Methods for Long-Range Market Forecasting, *Management Science*, vol. 19, no. 2, 211–21.

Chapter 7

1 Sources: Paul Walley, our colleague in the Operations Management Group at Warwick Business School; Irisys website (2009) www.irisys.co.uk; Martin, P. (2000) How supermarkets make a meal of you, *Sunday Times*, 4 November.
2 Jonathon Carr-Brown, French factory surgeon cuts NHS queues, *Sunday Times*, 23 October 2005.
3 Koontz, C., Retail interior layout for libraries, *Info Today*, 27 January 2012, www.infotoday.com/mls/jan05/koontz.shtml
4 Dawson, C., For Toyota, patriotism and profits may not mix, *Wall Street Journal*, 29 November 2011.
5 Gurman, M., Apple Store coming to London's world-famous Harrods department store, *inShare*, 19 January 2012.
6 Sources: Interviews with company staff and Johnston, R., Chambers, S., Harland, C., Harrison, A. and Slack, N. (2003) *Cases in Operations Management* (3rd edn), Financial Times Prentice Hall.
7 Bitner, M.J. (1992) Servicescapes: the impact of physical surroundings on customers and employees, *Journal of Marketing*, 56, 57–7.
8 Sources include: Hirasuna, D. VW's Transparent Factory; *@issue: The Online Journal of Business and Design*, 19 March 2012; Markus, F. VW's transparent factory, *Car and Driver*, September 2003.
9 A longer version of this case first appeared in Slack *et al* (2005) *Operations and Process Management*, Pearson, Harlow.

Chapter 8

1 Sources include: *Economist*, I, robot-manager, Schumpeter column, print edition, 31 March 2011; *Economist*, Marathon machine – unskilled workers are struggling to keep up with technological change, print edition, 19 November 2011; Brynjolfsson, E. and McAfee, A. (2011) Race Against The Machine: How the Digital Revolution is Accelerating Innovation, Driving Productivity, and Irreversibly Transforming Employment and the Economy, Digital Frontier Press; Kageyama, Y., Canon moves toward robots-only production for digital cameras, *Toronto Star*, 14 May 2012.
2 Associated Press, Robotic milking machines, CBS News site, 11 February 2009.
3 Loh Den, My new favorite barber: QB House, denniland.com, 25 June 2008.

4 Sources include: Moskvitch, K., Internet of Things blurs the line between bits and atoms, BBC news website, 3 June 2011; Chui, M., Löffler, M. and Roberts, R., The Internet of Things, *McKinsey Quarterly*, March 2010; Evans-Pughe, C., M2M and the Internet of Things, *Engineering and Technology*, vol. 6, issue 9, 12 September 2011.
5 'SAP IOT Definition', SAP Research, http://services.future-internet.eu/images/1/16/A4_Things_Haller.pdf.
6 Sources include: www.news-medical.net/; www.telemedicine.com; Studstill, K., Future of health: remote diagnostics, *PSFK Consulting*, 2 August 2010.
7 Staff columnist, Barriers to telemedicine limit patient access to quality care, *Patient Safety and Quality Healthcare (PSQH)*, 22 January 2012, www.psqh.com/barriers-to-telemedicine-limit-patient-access-to-quality-care.html.
8 Dosi, G., Teece, D. and Winter, S.G., Towards a theory of corporate coherence, in Dosi, G., Giametti, R. and Toninelli, P.A. (eds) (1992) *Technology and Enterprise in a Historical Perspective*, Oxford University Press.
9 Walley, P. and Amin, V. (1994) Automation in a Customer Contact Environment, *International Journal of Operations and Production Management*, vol. 14, no. 5, 86–100.
10 *Economist*, Help! There's nobody in the cockpit, 21 December 2002.
11 Chew, W.B., Leonard-Barton, D. and Bohn, R.E., Beating Murphy's Law, *Sloan Management Review*, vol. 5, Spring 1991.

Chapter 9

1 Sources include: company website; The Sunday Times Best Companies to work for, W.L. Gore & Associates (UK), *The Sunday Times*, 8 March 2009; Simon Caulkin, Gore Tex gets made without managers, *The Observer*, Sunday 2 November 2008; Nick Smith, Profile: W.L. Gore, The Institution of Engineering and Technology Knowledge network, 21 October 2008.
2 Accenture website, www.accenture.com.
3 Ulrich, D. (1997) *Human Resource Champions: The Next Agenda for Adding Value and Delivering Results*, Harvard Business School Press, Boston.
4 Source: Fuzzy maths, *The Economist*, 13 May 2006.
5 The Health and Safety Executive (HSE) of the UK government, www.hse.gov.uk/stress.
6 Based on work from the Advisory, Conciliation and Arbitration Service, ACAS.
7 Morgan describes these and other metaphors in Gareth Morgan (1986) *Images of Organization*, Sage.
8 Hoxie, R.F. (1915) *Scientific Management and Labour*, D. Appleton, Washington, DC.
9 Adapted from Hackman, J.R., Oldham, G., Janson, R. and Purdy, K. (1975) A new strategy for job enrichment, *California Management Review*, vol. 17, no. 3.
10 Bowen, D.E. and Lawler, E.E. (1992) The empowerment of service workers: what, why, how and when, *Sloan Management Review*, vol. 33, no. 3, 31–9.
11 Sources include: company website; The Times Best 100 Companies, www.thetimes100.co.uk.
12 Kobrick, J.L. and Fine, B.J. (1983) Climate and human performance, in Oborne, D.J. and Gruneberg, M.M. (eds) *The Physical Environment and Work*, John Wiley.

Chapter 10

1 Source: Interview with Joanne Cheung, Steve Deeley and other staff at Godfrey Hall, BMW Dealership, Coventry.

2 Sources: Jean Farman (1999) 'Les Coulisses du Vol', Air France. Talk presented by Richard E Stone, NorthWest Airlines at the IMA Industrial Problems Seminar, 1998.

3 Sources include: *Economist* (2012) Taxis and technology – dispatching the middleman, Economist Babbage Science blog, 17 March 2012; myTaxi website.

4 The concept of P:D ratios comes originally from Shingo, S. (1981) *Study of Toyota Production Systems*, Japan Management Association; and was extended by Mather, K. (1988) *Competitive Manufacturing*, Prentice Hall.

5 Sources include: *Economist* (2011) Please be seated: A faster way of boarding planes could save time and money, print edition, 3 September 2011; Palmer, J., Tests show fastest way to board passenger planes, BBC website, BBC News, 31 August 2011.

6 Source: Thanks to Lawrence Wilkins for this example.

7 Goldratt, E.Y. and Cox, J. (1984) *The Goal*, North River Press, Great Barrington, Mass.

8 Based on an original model described in Hofstede, G. (1981) Management control of public and not-for-profit activities, *Accounting, Organizations and Society*, vol. 6, no. 3, 193–211.

9 The original version of this case appears in Slack, N., Brandon-Jones, A., Johnston, R. and Betts, A. (2012) *Operations and Process Management*, 3rd edn, Pearson.

Chapter 11

1 Sources include: *Economist* (2011) Amazon: the Wal-Mart of the web, 1 October; Amazon website (2011); Ralph, A. (2011) Too many unhappy returns, *The Times*, 26 November.

2 Sources include: *Economist* (2012) Weather derivatives: come rain or shine, the outlook for the business of hedging against the elements, print edition, 4 February; Davies, P.J., Poorer states hedge against costs of extreme weather, *Financial Times*, 21 November 2011; Jackson, H., Weather derivatives are hot, *Wall Street Journal*, 13 February 2002.

3 Sources include: *Economist* (2009) A piece of cake: Panettone season arrives, print edition, 10 December; Bauli website, www.bauligroup.it/en/.

4 Sources include: *Horticulture Week* (2010) Grower guide tackles problem of building sustainable workforces, 14 May; Growing Jobs website http://growingjobs.org/.

5 Sources include: The effect of yield management on hotel chains, Event To Go website, retrieved 7 July 2012, www.eventogo.com/tips/business/yield-management.php.

6 Flyn, C., Queuing: pinpointing our 'appiest moments, *The Sunday Times*, 6 November 2011.

Chapter 12

1 Sources include: BBC News website, Blood bank 'perfect storm' threat for 2012, 28 December 2011; Stanger, S.H.W, Wilding, R., Yates, N. and Cotton, S. (2012) What drives perishable inventory management performance? Lessons learnt from the UK blood supply chain, *Supply Chain Management: An International Journal*, vol. 17, 2, 107–123.

2 Sources include: BBC Magazine website, How do they know when to grit roads?, December 2010; Grimm, E. (2009) Prepare for winter, *Daily Chronicle*, 30 November 2009.

3 With special thanks to John Mathews, Howard Smith Paper Group.

Chapter 13

1 Sources include: Pratley, N., Ocado: buy two problems get one free, *Guardian*, 23 January 2012.

2 Sources include: The North Face website, http://uk.thenorthface.com/blog/uk/en/sustainability.

3 Source: IBM website, www.ibm.com.

4 Garcia-Dastugue, S.J. and Lambert, D.M. (2003) Internet-enabled coordination in the supply chain, *Industrial Marketing Management*, vol. 3, 32.

5 Wheatley, C., How to know if e-procurement is right for you, *CIO* Magazine, 15 June 2003.

6 Minahan, T., Global sourcing: what you need to know to make it work, www.CIO.com, 11 August 2003.

7 Source: www.levistrauss.com/responsibility/conduct/guidelines.

8 Source: Interview with David Garman, September 2006.

9 Fisher, M.L. (1997) What is the right supply chain for your product, *Harvard Business Review*, March–April.

10 Basu, A and Siems. F. (2004), The impact of e-business technologies on supply chain operations, Working Paper 0404, The Reserve Bank of Dallas, November.

11 Source: Lee, H.L. and Whang, S. (2001) Demand chain excellent: a tale of two retailers, *Supply Chain Management Review*, 3 January.

12 Christopher, M. (2002) Business is failing to manage supply chain vulnerability, *Odyssey*, Issue 16, June.

13 Sources include: *Economist* (2011) Broken links – the disruption to manufacturers worldwide from Japan's disasters will force a rethink of how they manage production, print edition, 31 March; BBC News website (2011) Sony considers two-week shutdown due to power shortages: production at some of Japan's biggest companies has been affected by power shortages, 11 April; BBC News website (2011) Toyota motors has suspended production at most of its plants in Japan and also reduced output at its North American and European factories, 11 April.

14 All information taken from each company's website.

Chapter 14

1 Sources include: My way – IT at Butcher's Pet Care, *Engineering and Technology Magazine*, Vol. 4 (13) (Allan, K. 2009), 21 July; company website.

2 Wight, O. (1984) *Manufacturing Resource Planning: MRP II*, Oliver Wight Ltd.

3 Koch, C. and Wailgum, T. (2007) ERP definition and solutions, www.cio.com.

4 SAP website, www.sap.com.

5 Based on information kindly provided by Lawrence Wilkins.

6 With thanks to Julian Goulder, Director, Logistics Processes and IT, Rolls-Royce.

7 Based on a review of the research in this area by Finney, S. and Corbett, M. (2007) ERP implementation: a compilation and analysis of critical success factors, *Business Process Management Journal*, vol. 13, no. 3, 329–347.

8 Kanaracus, C. (2008) Waste Management sues SAP over ERP implementation, *InfoWorld*, 27 March.

9 Turbit, N. (2005) ERP implementation – the traps, The Project Perfect White Paper Collection, www.projectperfect.com.au.

Chapter 15

1 Spear, S. and Bowen, H.K. (1999) Decoding the DNA of the Toyota production system, *Harvard Business Review*, Sept–Oct.

2 Kamata, S. (1983) *Japan in the Passing Lane: An Insider's Account of Life in a Japanese Auto Factory*, Allen and Unwin.

3 Staats, B. and Upton, D. (2007) Lean principles and software production: Evidence from Indian software services, Harvard Working Paper, Harvard Business School.

4 Corbett, S. (2004) Applying lean in offices, hospitals, planes, and trains, presentation at the Lean Service Summit, Amsterdam, 24 June.

5 Source: Mathieson, S.A. (2006) NHS should embrace lean times, *Guardian*, 8 June.

6 Quoted in: Schonberger, R. (1982) *Japanese Manufacturing Techniques*, The Free Press.

7 Sources include: Interview with Edward Kay, Tom Dyson and Olly Willans of Torchbox, January 2012; Torchbox website, www.torchbox.com/blog/kanban-project-management. We are grateful to everyone at Torchbox for their help and allowing us access to their operation.

8 Set-up time reduction is also called single minute exchange of dies (SMED), because this was the objective in some manufacturing operations.

9 This great metaphor seems to have originated from the consultancy '2think', www.2think.biz/index.htm.

10 Goldratt, E.M. and Cox, J. (1986) *The Goal*, North River Press.

11 Goldratt, E.M. (1990) *What Is This Thing Called Theory of Constraints and How Should It Be Implemented?* Great Barrington, Mass.: The North River Press.

12 Adapted from: Rattner, S. (2009) What is the theory of constraints, and how does it compare to lean thinking?, The Lean Enterprise Institute, at www.leanvs.com/tocvsleanthinking.pdf.

13 Voss, C.A. and Harrison, A. (1987) Strategies For Implementing JIT, in Voss, C.A. (editor) *Just-In-Time Manufacture*, IFS/Springer-Verlag.

14 This case is based on a real organization and was written by Professors Robert Johnston, Warwick Business School, and Zoe Radnor, Loughborough University, with the help of Giovanni Bucci, AtoZ Business Consultancy, 2012. All names and places have been changed.

Chapter 16

1 Source: Slack, A., Popping the Millau Cork, translated and adapted from Le Figaro Entreprises, 15 December 2004.

2 From Nicholas, J.M. (1990) *Managing Business and Engineering Projects: Concepts and Implementation*, Prentice Hall.

3 Based on Pinto, J.K. and Slevin, D.P. (1987) Critical success factors in successful project implementation, *IEEE Transactions on Engineering Management*, vol. 34, no. 1.

4 Weiss, J.W. and Wysocki, R.K. (1992) *Five-Phase Project Management: A Practical Planning and Implementation Guide*, Addison-Wesley.

5 Source: Interview with Leigh Rix, Project Manager, The Workhouse.

6 Sources include: Davis, D. (2011) The MacLeamy curve: digital morphogenesis, evolving architecture through computation, The blog of nz Architecture, posted 15.10.2011.

7 Sources include: Boyes, W., David Van Wyk shares the Disney Imagineering project management process, www.controlglobal.com, 29 June 2011; Hoske, M.T. What do Walt Disney Imagineering and NASA space travel have in common? Engineering inspiration, *Control Engineering*, 22 September 2011, at www.controleng.com.

Chapter 17

1 Source: Interview with Michael Purtill, the General Manager of the Four Seasons Hotel Canary Wharf in London. We are grateful for Michael's cooperation (and for the great quality of service at his hotel!).

2 Parasuraman, A., Zeithaml, V.A. and Berry, L.L. (1985) A conceptual model of service quality and implications for future research, *Journal of Marketing*, vol. 49, Fall, 41–50; and Gummesson, E. (1987) Lip service: a neglected area in services marketing, *Journal of Services Marketing*, vol. 1, no. 1, 19–23.

3 Berry, L.L. and Parasuraman, A. (1991) *Marketing Services: Competing Through Quality*, The Free Press.

4 Mechling, L. (2002) Get ready for a storm in a tea shop, *Independent*, 8 March 2002; company website.

5 Based on Parasuraman, A., *op. cit.*

6 Sources include: Vitaliev, V., The much-loved knife, *Engineering and Technology Magazine*, 21 July 2009; Victorinox website (2012) 'The Victorinox Quality System'.

7 Source: Dobson, R., Scan avoids needless appendectomy, *The Sunday Times*, 23 February 1997.

8 Sources include: Wheatley, M., Filling time on the production line, *Engineering and Technology Magazine*, 8 November 2010.

9 Feigenbaum, A.V. (1986) *Total Quality Control*, McGraw-Hill, New York.

10 Kaynak, H. (2003) The relationship between total quality management practices and their effects on firm performance, *Journal of Operations Management*, vol. 21, 405–435.

11 BBC News website, 'Human error' hits Google search, http://news.bbc.co.uk, 31 January 2009.

12 Source: ISO website, www.iso.org/iso/iso_9000_essentials.

13 This case is based on a real situation, but data have been changed for reasons of commercial confidentiality.

Chapter 18

1 Sources include: Boyd, E.A., Award-winning analytics, *Analytics Magazine*, May/June 2012; Poppelaars, J., Supply chain wide optimization at TNT Express, proceedings of the Euroma Conference, Amsterdam, 2–4 July 2012; TNT Corporate website (2012), TNT Express win the 2012 Edelman Award.

2 Carroll, L. (1871) *Alice Through the Looking Glass*.

3 Imai, M. (1986) *Kaizen – The Key to Japan's Competitive Success*, McGraw-Hill.

4 Sources: Gawande, A. (2010) *The Checklist Manifesto: How to Get Things Right,* Profile Books; Aaronovitch, D., The Checklist Manifesto: review, *The Times*, 23 January 2010.

5 International Standards Organization, *ISO 8402*, 1986.

6 Dale, B.G. (1994) Quality management systems, in Dale B.G. (editor) *Managing Quality*, Prentice Hall.

7 Sources include: Company website, www.heinekeninternational.com.

8 Davenport, T., Re-engineering – the fad that forgot people, *Fast Company*, November 1995.

9 Based on an example in Kruse, G., Fundamental innovation, *Manufacturing Engineer*, February 1995.

10 These defects per million (DPM) figures assume that the mean and/or SD may vary over the long term so the 3 sigma DPM is actually based on 1.5 sigma and 6 sigma on 4.5 sigma. These distributions are assumed to be 'one-tailed' as the shift is usually one direction.

11 See Note 10 above.

12 Source: Interviews with Paul Ruggier, Rebecca Whittaker and Sarah Frost, Xchanging.

13 There are many books and publications that explain the benefits of combining lean and Six Sigma. For example, see Byrne, G., Lubowe, D. and Blitz, A. (2007) Driving operational innovation using lean Six Sigma, IBM Institute for Business Value; Brue, G. (2005) *Six Sigma for Managers: 24 Lessons to Understand and Apply Six Sigma Principles in Any Organization*, McGraw-Hill Professional Education Series.

Chapter 19

1 Sources include: Herman, M. and Jordan, D., Cadbury fined £1 million over salmonella outbreak, Times Online, 16 July 2007; and Elliot, V., Cadbury admits hygiene failures over salmonella in chocolate bars, *The Times*, 16 June 2007.

2 Christopher, M. (2002) Business is failing to manage supply chain vulnerability, *Odyssey*, Issue 16, June.

3 Source: Mail Online, Drunk pilot didn't know where he was meant to be flying his plane, 24 January 2011.

4 Information for this section is based partly on a private communication from Ben Betts of ht2.com.

5 Nahajima, S. (1988) *Total Productive Maintenance*, Productivity Press.

6 Source: Otis website, www.otis.com.

7 Armistead, C.G. and Clark, G. (1992) *Customer Service and Support*, Prentice Hall.

8 Judge, E., Instant replacements to make it business as usual – from new offices to key staff, *The Times*, 15 February 2003.

Chapter 20

1 Deming, W.E. (1982) *Quality, Productivity and Competitive Position*, MIT Center for Advanced Engineering Study.

2 Deming, W.E. (1986) *Out of Crisis*, MIT Center for Advanced Engineering Study.

3 Based on Neely, A. (1993) *Performance Measurement System Design – Theory and Practice*, Manufacturing Engineering Group, Cambridge University, April.

4 Kaplan, R.S. and Norton, D.P. (1993) *The Balanced Scorecard*, Harvard Business School Press, Boston, MA.

5 Source: The EFQM website, www.efqm.org.

6 Bourne, M., Franco, M. and Wilkes, J. (2003) Corporate performance management, *Measuring Business Excellence*, vol. 7, no.3, 15.

7 Ferdow, K. and de Meyer, A. (1990) Lasting improvement in manufacturing, *Journal of Operations Management*, vol. 9, no. 2.

8 Schein, E.H. (2004) *Organizational Culture and Leadership*, 3rd edn, Jossey-Bass.

9 Johnson, G. (1988) Rethinking incrementalism, *Strategic Management Journal*, vol. 9, 75–91.

10 Bessant, J. and Caffyn, S. (1997) High involvement innovation, *International Journal of Technology Management*, vol. 14, no. 1.

11 Argyris, C. and Schön, D. (1978) *Organizational Learning*, Addison-Wesley, Reading, MA.

12 Sources include: West, K., Formula One trains van drivers, *The Times*, 1 May 2011; f1network.net, www.f1network.net/main/s107/st164086.htm.

13 For further details of this approach see, Schaninger, W.S., Harris, S.G. and Niebuhr, R.L. (2000) Adapting General Electric's Workout for use in other organizations: a template, www.isixsigma.com; Quinn, J. (1994) What a workout! *Sales and Marketing Management*, Performance Supplement, November, 58–63; Stewart, T. (1991) GE keeps those ideas coming, *Fortune*, 124 (4), 40–45.

14 The authors gratefully acknowledge the valuable assistance of Teo Yi Wen, Department of Industrial and Systems Engineering, NUS. The authors would like to thank the interviewees for their participation in this project and Johnson Paul and Sharon Foo for facilitating the research. All Rights Reserved, National Library Board Singapore and the Authors, 2009.

Chapter 21

1 Sources include: West, K., Turn up the heat with Marmite, *Sunday Times*, 2 October 2011; Unilever's sustainable living report (2012) www.unilever.co.uk/sustainable-living.

2 World Business Council for Sustainable Development, at www.wbcsd.org.

3 Marks and Spencer's, at www.marksandspencer.com.

4 CSR Asia, at www.csr-asia.com.

5 BAA, airport operator, at www.baa.com.

6 Mallen Baker, a writer, speaker and strategic advisor on CSR, www.mallenbaker.net.

7 International Finance Corporation.

8 European Commission.

9 Dahlsrud, A. (2006) How corporate social responsibility is defined: an analysis of 37 definitions, *Corporate Social Responsibility and Environmental Management*, vol. 12, no. 2.

10 Source: Holcim press releases.

11 Elkington, J. (1998) *Cannibals with Forks: The Triple Bottom Line of 21st Century Business*, New Society Publishers.

12 Ehrlich, P. and Commoner, B., as quoted in Hart, S.L. (1997) Strategies for a sustainable world, *Harvard Business Review*, Jan–Feb.

13 *Economist* (2008) Just good business, 17 January 2008.

14 Traidcraft Exchange (2001) EU Corporate Social Responsibility: a Green Paper, at www.traidcraft.co.uk.

15 Sources include: HP website, www8.hp.com/us/en/hp-information/environment/product-recycling.html.

16 Based on Kolk, A. (2000) *The Economics of Environmental Management*, Financial Times, Prentice Hall. Also see www.globalreporting.org.

17 Sources include: Company website; McDougall, D. (2007) Gap child labour shame, *Observer*, 28 October 2007.

18 Economist Intelligence Unit, Corporate Social Responsibility, January 2008.

19 Economist Intelligence Unit (2008) Why CSR?

Glossary

5 S's: a simple housekeeping methodology to organize work areas. Originally translated from the Japanese, they are generally taken to mean sort, strengthen, shine, standardized, and sustain. The aim is to reduce clutter in the workplace.

ABC inventory control: an approach to inventory control that classes inventory by its usage value and varies the approach to managing it accordingly.

Acceptance sampling: a technique of quality sampling that is used to decide whether to accept a whole batch of products (and occasionally services) on the basis of a sample; it is based on the operation's willingness to risk rejecting a 'good' batch and accepting a 'bad' batch.

Activity: as used in project management, it is an identifiable and defined task, used together with event activities to form network planning diagrams.

Aggregated planning and control: a term used to indicate medium-term capacity planning that aggregates different products and services together in order to get a broad view of demand and capacity.

Agility: the ability of an operation to respond quickly and at low cost as market requirements change.

Allowances: term used in work study to indicate the extra time allowed for rest, relaxation and personal needs.

Andon: a light above a workstation that indicates its state, whether working, waiting for work, broken down, etc.; andon lights may be used to stop the whole line when one station stops.

Annual hours: a type of flexitime working that controls the amount of time worked by individuals on an annual rather than a shorter basis.

Anthropometric data: data that relate to people's size, shape and other physical abilities, used in the design of jobs and physical facilities.

Anticipation inventory: inventory that is accumulated to cope with expected future demand or interruptions in supply.

Appraisal costs: those costs associated with checking, monitoring and controlling quality to see if problems or errors have occurred, an element within quality-related costs.

Attributes of quality: measures of quality that can take one of two states, for example, right or wrong, works or does not work, etc.

B Corps: an abbreviation for Benefit Corporations; those that have a clear and unequivocal social benefit.

Back-office: the low-visibility part of an operation.

Backward scheduling: starting jobs at a time when they should be finished exactly when they are due, as opposed to forward scheduling.

Balanced scorecard (BSC): in addition to financial performance, the balanced scorecard also includes assessment of customer satisfaction, internal processes and innovation and learning.

Balancing loss: the quantification of the lack of balance in a production line, defined as the percentage of time not used for productive purposes with the total time invested in making a product.

Bar code: a unique product code that enables a part or product type to be identified when read by a bar-code scanner.

Basic time: the time taken to do a job without any extra allowances for recovery.

Batch processes: processes that treat batches of products together, and where each batch has its own process route.

Bath-tub curve: a curve that describes the failure probability of a product, service or process and indicates relatively high probabilities of failure at the beginning and at the end of the life cycle.

Behavioural job design: an approach to job design that takes into account individuals' desire to fulfil their needs for self-esteem and personal development.

Benchmarking: the activity of comparing methods and/or performance with other processes in order to learn from them and/or assess performance.

Bill of materials (BOM): a list of the component parts required to make up the total package for a product or service together with information regarding their level in the product or component structure and the quantities of each component required.

Blueprinting: a term often used in service design to mean process mapping.

Bottleneck: the capacity-constraining stage in a process; it governs the output of the whole process.

Bottom-up: the influence of operational experience on operations decisions.

Brainstorming: an improvement technique where small groups of people put forward ideas in a creative free-form manner.

Break-even analysis: the technique of comparing revenues and costs at increasing levels of output in order to establish the point at which revenue exceeds cost, that is, the point at which it 'breaks even'.

Breakthrough improvement: an approach to improving operations performance that implies major and dramatic change in the way an operation works; for example, business process re-engineering (BPR) is often associated with this type of improvement, also known as innovation-based improvement, contrasted with continuous improvement.

Broad definition of operations: all the activities necessary for the fulfilment of customer requests.

Buffer inventory: an inventory that compensates for unexpected fluctuations in supply and demand; can also be called safety inventory.

Bullwhip effect: the tendency of supply chains to amplify relatively small changes at the demand side of a supply chain such that the disruption at the supply end of the chain is much greater.

Business continuity: the procedures adopted by businesses to mitigate and recover from the effects of major failures.

Business process outsourcing (BPO): the term that is applied to the outsourcing of whole business processes; this need not mean a change in location of the process, sometimes it involves an outside company taking over the management of processes that remain in the same location.

Business process re-engineering (BPR): the philosophy that recommends the redesign of processes to fulfil defined external customer needs.

Business processes: processes, often that cut across functional boundaries, which contribute some part to fulfilling customer needs.

Business strategy: the strategic positioning of a business in relation to its customers, markets and competitors, a subset of corporate strategy.

Capacity: the maximum level of value-added activity that an operation, or process, or facility is capable of over a period of time.

Capacity lagging: the strategy of planning capacity levels such that they are always less than or equal to forecast demand.

Capacity leading: the strategy of planning capacity levels such that they are always greater than or equal to forecast demand.

Cause–effect diagrams: a technique for searching out the root cause of problems, it is a systematic questioning technique, also known as Ishikawa diagrams.

Cell layout: locating transforming resources with a common purpose such as processing the same types of product, serving similar types of customer, etc., together in close proximity (a cell).

Centre-of-gravity method of location: a technique that uses the physical analogy of balance to determine the

geographical location that balances the weighted importance of the other operations with which the one being located has a direct relationship.

Chase demand: an approach to medium-term capacity management that attempts to adjust output and/or capacity to reflect fluctuations in demand.

Cluster analysis: a technique used in the design of cell layouts to find which process groups fit naturally together.

Clusters: where similar companies with similar needs locate relatively close to each other in the same geographical area.

Co-creation: where the customer or customers play an important part in the character of the product or service offering.

Combinatorial complexity: the idea that many different ways of processing products and services at many different locations or points in time combine to result in an exceptionally large number of feasible options; the term is often used in facilities layout and scheduling to justify non-optimal solutions (because there are too many options to explore).

Commonality: the degree to which a range of products or services incorporate identical components (also called 'parts commonality').

Community factors: those factors that are influential in the location decision that relate to the social, political and economic environment of the geographical position.

Competitive factors: the factors such as delivery time, product or service specification, price, etc. that define customers' requirements.

Component structure: *see* 'Product structure'.

Computer-aided design (CAD): a system that provides the computer ability to create and modify product, service or process drawings.

Computer-integrated manufacturing (CIM): a term used to describe the integration of computer-based monitoring and control of all aspects of a manufacturing process, often using a common database and communicating via some form of computer network.

Concept generation: a stage in the product and service design process that formalizes the underlying idea behind a product or service.

Contracting relationships: relationship between operations in a supply network that rely on formal and/or legal contracts that specify obligations and roles.

Concurrent engineering: *see* 'Simultaneous development'.

Condition-based maintenance: an approach to maintenance management that monitors the condition of process equipment and performs work on equipment only when it is required.

Content of strategy: the set of specific decisions and actions that shape the strategy.

Continuous improvement: an approach to operations improvement that assumes many, relatively small, incremental improvements in performance, stressing the momentum of improvement rather than the rate of improvement; also known as 'kaizen', often contrasted with breakthrough improvement.

Continuous processes: processes that are high-volume and low-variety; usually products made on a continuous process are produced in an endless flow, such as petrochemicals or electricity.

Continuous review: an approach to managing inventory that makes inventory-related decisions when inventory reaches a particular level, as opposed to period review.

Control: the process of monitoring operations activity and coping with any deviations from the plan; usually involves elements of replanning.

Control charts: the charts used within statistical process control to record process performance.

Control limits: the lines on a control chart used in statistical process control that indicate the extent of natural or common-cause variations; any points lying outside these control limits are deemed to indicate that the process is likely to be out of control.

Co-opetition: an approach to supply networks that defines businesses as being surrounded by suppliers, customers, competitors, and complementors.

Core functions: the functions that manage the three core processes of any business: marketing, product/service development and operations.

Corporate social responsibility: how business takes account of its economic, social and environmental impacts.

Corporate strategy: the strategic positioning of a corporation and the businesses within it.

CRAFT: Computerized Relative Allocation of Facilities Technique, a heuristic technique for developing good, but non-optimal, solutions.

Crashing: a term used in project management to mean reducing the time spent on critical path activities so as to shorten the whole project.

Create-to-order: *see* 'Make-to-order'.

Critical path: the longest sequence of activities through a project network, it is called the critical path because any delay in any of its activities will delay the whole project.

Critical path method (CPM): a technique of network analysis.

Crowdsourcing: the act of taking an activity traditionally performed by a designated agent and outsourcing it to a large group of people in the form of an open call.

Customer contact skills: the skills and knowledge that operations staff need to meet customer expectations.

Customer relationship management (CRM): a method of learning more about customers' needs and behaviours by analysing sales information.

Customization: the variation in product or service design to suit the specific need of individual customers or customer groups.

Cycle inventory: inventory that occurs when one stage in a process cannot supply all the items it produces simultaneously and so has to build up inventory of one item while it processes the others.

Cycle time: the average time between units of output emerging from a process.

Decision support system (DSS): a management information system that aids or supports managerial decision-making; it may include both databases and sophisticated analytical models.

De-coupling inventory: the inventory that is used to allow work centres or processes to operate relatively independently.

Delivery: the ativities that plan and control the transfer of products and services to customers.

Delivery flexibility: the operation's ability to change the timing of the delivery of its services or products.

Demand management: an approach to medium-term capacity management that attempts to change or influence demand to fit available capacity.

Demand side: the chains of customers, customers' customers, etc. that receive the products and services produced by an operation.

Dependability: delivering, or making available, products or services when they were promised to the customer.

Dependent demand: demand that is relatively predictable because it is derived from some other known factor.

Design acceptability: the attractiveness to the operation of a process, product or service.

Design capacity: the capacity of a process or facility as it is designed to be, often greater than effective capacity.

Design concept: the set of expected benefits to the customer encapsulated in a product or service design.

Design feasibility: the ability of an operation to produce a process, product or service.

Design funnel: a model that depicts the design process as the progressive reduction of design options from many alternatives down to the final design.

Design package: the component products, services and parts within a product or service design that provide the benefits to the customer.

Design screening: the evaluation of alternative designs with the purpose of reducing the number of design options being considered.

Development: a collection of operations activities that improve products, services and processes.

Directing: operations activities that create a general understanding of an operation's strategic purpose and performance.

Disaster recovery: term is used in a similar way to business continuity, but is concerned largely with action plans and procedures for the recovery of critical information technology and systems after a natural or human-induced disaster.

Diseconomies of scale: a term used to describe the extra costs that are incurred in running an operation as it gets larger.

Disintermediation: the emergence of an operation in a supply network that separates two operations that were previously in direct contact.

Disruptive technologies: technologies which in the short term cannot match the performance required by customers but may improve faster than existing technology to make that existing technology redundant.

Distributed processing: a term used in information technology to indicate the use of smaller computers distributed around an operation and linked together so that they can communicate with each other, the opposite of centralized information processing.

Division of labour: an approach to job design that involves dividing a task down into relatively small parts, each of which is accomplished by a single person.

DMAIC cycle: increasingly used improvement cycle model, popularized by the Six Sigma approach to operations improvement.

Do or buy: the term applied to the decision on whether to own a process that contributes to a product or service, or, alternatively, outsource the activity performed by the process to another operation.

Downstream: the other operations in a supply chain between the operation being considered and the end customer.

Drum, buffer, rope: an approach to operations control that comes from the theory of constraints (TOC) and uses the bottleneck stage in a process to control materials movement.

Earned-value control: a method of assessing performance in project management by combining the costs and times achieved in the project with the original plan.

E-business: the use of internet-based technologies either to support existing business processes or to create entirely new business opportunities.

E-commerce: the use of the internet to facilitate buying and selling activities.

Economic batch quantity (EBQ): the amount of items to be produced by a machine or process that supposedly minimizes the costs associated with production and inventory holding.

Economic bottom line: the part of the triple bottom line that assesses an organization's economic performance, usually in financial terms.

Economic order quantity (EOQ): the quantity of items to order that supposedly minimizes the total cost of inventory management, derived from various EOQ formulae.

Economy of scale: the manner in which the costs of running an operation decrease as it gets larger.

Effective capacity: the useful capacity of a process or operation after maintenance, changeover and other stoppages and loading have been accounted for.

Efficient frontier: the convex line which describes current performance trade-offs between (usually two) measures of operations performance.

EFQM excellence model: a model that identifies the categories of activity that supposedly ensure high levels of quality; now used by many companies to examine their own quality-related procedures.

Electronic marketplaces: also sometimes called infomediaries or cybermediaries, websites that offer services to both buyers and sellers, usually in B2B markets.

Emergent strategy: a strategy that is gradually shaped over time and based on experience rather than theoretical positioning.

Empowerment: a term used in job design to indicate increasing the authority given to people to make decisions within the job or changes to the job itself.

End-to-end business processes: processes that totally fulfil a defined external customer need.

Enterprise project management (EPM): software that integrates all the common activities in project management.

Enterprise resource planning (ERP): the integration of all significant resource planning systems in an organization that, in an operations context, integrates planning and control with the other functions of the business.

Environmental bottom line: the element of the triple bottom line that assesses an organization's performance in terms of how it affects the natural environment.

E-procurement: the use of the internet to organize purchasing; this may include identifying potential suppliers and auctions as well as the administrative tasks of issuing orders etc.

Ergonomics: a branch of job design that is primarily concerned with the physiological aspects of job design, with how the human body fits with process facilities and the environment; can also be referred to as human factors, or human factors engineering.

Ethernet: a technology that facilitates local-area networks that allows any device attached to a single cable to communicate with any other devices attached to the same cable; also now used for wireless communication that allows mobile devices to connect to a local-area network.

European Quality Award (EQA): a quality award organized by the European Foundation for Quality Management (EFQM), it is based on the EFQM excellence model.

Events: points in time within a project plan; together with activities, they form network planning diagrams.

Evidence-based problem solving: using statistical methods and hard data as a basis for improvement.

Expert systems (ES): computer-based problem-solving systems that, to some degree, mimic human problem-solving logic.

External failure costs: those costs that are associated with an error or failure reaching a customer, an element within quality-related costs.

Extranets: computer networks that link organizations together and connect with each organization's internal network.

Facilitating products: products that are produced by an operation to support its services.

Facilitating services: services that are produced by an operation to support its products.

Fail-safeing: building in, often simple, devices that make it difficult to make the mistakes that could lead to failure; also known by the Japanese term 'poka-yoke'.

Failure analysis: the use of techniques to uncover the root cause of failures; techniques may include accident investigation, complaint analysis, etc.

Failure mode and effect analysis (FMEA): a technique used to identify the product, service or process features that are crucial in determining the effects of failure.

Failure rate: a measure of failure that is defined as the number of failures over a period of time.

Fault tree analysis: a logical procedure starts with a failure or potential failure and works backwards to identify its origins.

Finite loading: an approach to planning and control that only allocates work to a work centre up to a set limit (usually its useful capacity).

First-tier: the description applied to suppliers and customers that are in immediate relationships with an operation with no intermediary operations.

Fixed cost break: the volumes of output at which it is necessary to invest in operations facilities that bear a fixed cost.

Fixed-position layout: locating the position of a product or service such that it remains largely stationary, while transforming resources are moved to and from it.

Flexibility: the degree to which an operation's process can change what it does, how it is doing it, or when it is doing it.

Flexible manufacturing systems (FMS): manufacturing systems that bring together several technologies into a coherent system, such as metal cutting and material handling technologies; usually their activities are controlled by a single governing computer.

Flexi-time working: increasing the possibility of individuals varying the time during which they work.

Focus group: a group of potential product or service users, chosen to be typical of its target market who are formed to test their reaction to alternative designs.

Forward scheduling: loading work onto work centres as soon as it is practical to do so, as opposed to backward scheduling.

Four-stage model of operations contribution: model devised by Hayes and Wheelwright that categorizes the degree to which operations management has a positive influence on overall strategy.

Front-office: the high-visibility part of an operation.

Functional layout: layout where similar resources or processes are located together (sometimes called process layout).

Functional operations: the idea that every function in an organization uses resources to produce products and services for (internal) customers, therefore, all functions are, to some extent, operations.

Functional strategy: the overall direction and role of a function within the business; a subset of business strategy.

Gantt chart: a scheduling device that represents time as a bar or channel on which activities can be marked.

Gemba: also sometimes called Gamba, term used to convey the idea of going to where things actually take place as a basis for improvement.

Globalization: the extension of operations' supply chain to cover the whole world.

Heijunka: *see* 'Levelled scheduling'.

Henderson–Clark Model: innovation theory that distinguishes between knowledge of the components of an idea and knowledge of how the components fit together.

Heuristics: 'rules of thumb' or simple reasoning short cuts that are developed to provide good but non-optimal solutions, usually to operations decisions that involve combinatorial complexity.

Hierarchy of operations: the idea that all operations processes are made up of smaller operations processes.

High-level process mapping: an aggregated process map that shows broad activities rather than detailed activities (sometimes called an 'outline process map').

Hire and fire: a (usually pejorative) term used in medium-term capacity management to indicate varying the size of the workforce through employment policy.

House of quality: *see* 'Quality function deployment'.

Human factors engineering: an alternative term for ergonomics.

Human resource strategy: the overall long-term approach to ensuring that an organization's human resources provide a strategic advantage.

Immediate supply network: the suppliers and customers that have direct contact with an operation.

Importance–performance matrix: a technique that brings together scores that indicate the relative importance and relative performance of different competitive factors in order to prioritize them as candidates for improvement.

Improvement cycles: the practice of conceptualizing problem solving as used in performance improvement in terms of a never-ending cyclical model, for example the PDCA cycle or the DMAIC cycle.

Independent demand: demand that is not obviously or directly dependent on the demand for another product or service.

Indirect process technology: technology that assists in the management of processes rather than directly contributes to the creation of products and services, for example information technology that schedules activities.

Indirect responsibilities of operations management: the activities of collaborating with other functions of the organization.

Infinite loading: an approach to planning and control that allocates work to work centres irrespective of any capacity or other limits.

Information technology (IT): any device, or collection of devices, that collects, manipulates, stores or distributes information, nearly always used to mean computer-based devices.

Infrastructural decisions: the decisions that concern the operation's systems, methods and procedures and shape its overall culture.

Innovation: the act of introducing new ideas to products, services, or processes.

Innovation S-Curve: the curve that describes the impact of an innovation over time.

Input resources: the transforming and transformed resources that form the input to operations.

Intangible resources: the resources within an operation that are not immediately evident or tangible, such as relationships with suppliers and customers, process knowledge, new product and service development.

Interactive design: the idea that the design of products and services on one hand, and the processes that create them on the other, should be integrated.

Internal customers: processes or individuals within an operation that are the customers for other internal processes or individuals' outputs.

Internal failure costs: the costs associated with errors and failures that are dealt with inside an operation but yet cause disruption; an element within quality-related costs.

Internal suppliers: processes or individuals within an operation that supply products or services to other processes or individuals within the operation.

Internet of Things: the integration of physical objects into an information network where the physical objects become active participants in business processes.

Inventory: also known as stock, the stored accumulation of transformed resources in a process; usually applies to material resources but may also be used for inventories of information; inventories of customers or customers of customers are usually queues.

ISO 9000: a set of worldwide standards that established the requirements for companies' quality management systems; last revised in 2000, there are several sets of standards.

ISO 14000: an international standard that guides environmental management systems and covers initial planning, implementation and objective assessment.

Job design: the way in which we structure the content and environment of individual staff members' jobs within the workplace and the interface with the technology or facilities that they use.

Job enlargement: a term used in job design to indicate increasing the amount of work given to individuals in order to make the job less monotonous.

Job enrichment: a term used in job design to indicate increasing the variety and number of tasks within an individual's job; this may include increased decision-making and autonomy.

Job rotation: the practice of encouraging the movement of individuals between different aspects of a job in order to increase motivation.

Jobbing processes: processes that deal with high variety and low volumes, although there may be some repetition of flow and activities.

Just-in-time (JIT): a method of planning and control and an operations philosophy that aims to meet demand instantaneously with perfect quality and no waste.

Kaizen: Japanese term for continuous improvement.

Kanban: Japanese term for card or signal; it is a simple controlling device that is used to authorize the release of materials in pull control systems such as those used in JIT.

Keiretsu: a Japanese term used to describe a coalition of companies which form a supply network around a large manufacturer and can include service companies such as banks as well as conventional suppliers.

Lead-time usage: the amount of inventory that will be used between ordering replenishment and the inventory arriving, usually described by a probability distribution to account for uncertainty in demand and lead time.

Lean: (also known as Lean Synchronization) an approach to operations management that emphasizes the continual elimination of waste of all types, often used interchangeably with just-in-time (JIT); it is more an overall philosophy whereas JIT is usually used to indicate an approach to planning and control that adopts lean principles.

Lean Sigma: a blend of improvement elements from lean and Six Sigma.

Less important factors: competitive factors that are neither order-winning nor qualifying; performance in them does not significantly affect the competitive position of an operation.

Level capacity plan: an approach to medium-term capacity management that attempts to keep output from an operation or its capacity constant, irrespective of demand.

Levelled scheduling: the idea that the mix and volume of activity should even out over time so as to make output routine and regular, sometimes known by the Japanese term 'heijunka'.

Life-cycle analysis: a technique that analyses all the production inputs, life-cycle use of a product and its final disposal in terms of total energy used and wastes emitted.

Line balancing: the activity of attempting to equalize the load on each station or part of a line layout or mass process.

Line layout: a more descriptive term for what is technically a product layout.

Line of fit: an alternative name for the 'natural' diagonal of the product process matrix.

Little's law: the mathematical relationship between throughput time, work-in-process and cycle time (throughput time equals work-in-process × cycle time).

Loading: the amount of work that is allocated to a work centre.

Local-area network (LAN): a communications network that operates, usually over a limited distance, to connect devices such as PCs, servers, etc.

Location: the geographical position of an operation or process.

Logistics: a term in supply chain management broadly analogous to physical distribution management.

Long-term capacity management: the set of decisions that determine the level of physical capacity of an operation in whatever the operation considers to be long-term; this will vary between industries, but is usually in excess of one year.

Long thin process: a process designed to have many sequential stages, each performing a relatively small part of the total task; the opposite of short fat process.

MacLeamy curve: a model that conveys the idea that, as projects move forward, the cost of making changes to the original project plan increases but the ability of project managers to influence the project goes down.

Maintenance: the activity of caring for physical facilities so as to avoid or minimize the chance of those facilities failing.

Make-to-order: operations that produce products only when they are demanded by specific customers.

Make-to-stock: operations that produce products prior to their being demanded by specific customers.

Management information systems (MIS): information systems that manipulate information so that it can be used in managing an organization.

Manufacturing resource planning (MRP II): an expansion of materials requirement planning to include greater integration with information in other parts of the organization and often greater sophistication in scheduling calculations.

Market requirements: the performance objectives that reflect the market position of an operation's products or services, also a perspective on operations strategy.

Matrix organizational forms: hybrids of M form and U form organizations.

Mass customization: the ability to produce products or services in high volume, yet vary their specification to the needs of individual customers or types of customer.

Mass processes: processes that produce goods in high volume and relatively low variety.

Mass services: service processes that have a high number of transactions, often involving limited customization, for example mass transportation services, call centres, etc.

Master production schedule (MPS): the important schedule that forms the main input to material requirements planning, it contains a statement of the volume and timing of the end products to be made.

Materials requirement planning (MRP): a set of calculations embedded in a system that helps operations make volume and timing calculations for planning and control purposes.

Mean time between failures (MTBF): operating time divided by the number of failures; the reciprocal of failure rate.

Method study: the analytical study of methods of doing jobs with the aim of finding the 'best' or an improved job method.

M-form organization: an organizational structure that groups together either its resources needed to produce a product or service group, or those needed to serve a particular geographical area in separate divisions.

Milestones: term used in project management to denote important events at which specific reviews of time, cost and quality can be made.

Mitigation: a term used in risk management to mean isolating a failure from its negative consequences.

Mix flexibility: the operation's ability to produce a wide range of products and services.

Modular design: the use of standardized sub-components of a product or service that can be put together in different ways to create a high degree of variety.

MRP netting process: the process of calculating net requirements using the master production schedule and the bills of materials.

Muda: all activities in a process that are wasteful because they do not add value to the operation or to the customer.

Mura: a term meaning lack of consistency or unevenness that results in periodic overloading of staff or equipment.

Muri: waste because of unreasonable requirements placed on a process that will result in poor outcomes.

Multi-skilling: increasing the range of skills of individuals in order to increase motivation and/or improve flexibility.

Multi-sourcing: the practice of obtaining the same type of product, component, or service from more than one supplier in order to maintain market bargaining power or continuity of supply.

Network analysis: overall term for the use of network-based techniques for the analysis and management of projects; for example, includes critical path method (CPM) and programme evaluation and review technique (PERT).

N-form organization: networked organizational structures where clusters of resources have delegated responsibility for the strategic management of those resources.

Off-shoring: sourcing products and services from operations that are based outside one's own country or region.

Open sourcing: products or services developed by an open community, including users.

Operations function: the arrangement of resources that are devoted to the production and delivery of products and services.

Operations management: the activities, decisions and responsibilities of managing the production and delivery of products and services.

Operations managers: the staff of the organization who have particular responsibility for managing some or all of the resources which compose the operation's function.

Operations resource capabilities: the inherent ability of operations processes and resources; also a perspective on operations strategy.

Operations strategy: the overall direction and contribution of the operation's function with the business; the way in which market requirements and operations resource capabilities are reconciled within the operation.

Optimized production technology (OPT): software and concept originated by Eliyahu Goldratt to exploit his theory of constraints (TOC).

Order fulfilment: all the activities involved in supplying a customer's order, often used in e-retailing but now also used in other types of operation.

Order-winners: the competitive factors that directly and significantly contribute to winning business.

Outline process map: *see* 'High-level process mapping'.

Outsourcing: the practice of contracting out to a supplier work previously done within the operation.

Overall equipment effectiveness (OEE): a method of judging the effectiveness of how operations equipment is used.

Pareto law: a general law found to operate in many situations that indicates that 20 per cent of something causes 80 per cent of something else, often used in inventory management (20 per cent of products produce 80 per cent of sales value) and improvement activities (20 per cent of types of problems produce 80 per cent of disruption).

Partnership: a type of relationship in supply chains that encourages relatively enduring co-operative agreements for the joint accomplishment of business goals.

Parts commonality: *see* 'Commonality'.

Parts family coding: the use of multi-digit codes to indicate the relative similarity between different parts, often used to determine the process route that a part takes through a manufacturing operation.

PDCA cycle: stands for Plan, Do, Check, Act cycle, perhaps the best known of all improvement cycle models.

P:D ratio: a ratio that contrasts the total length of time customers have to wait between asking for a product or service and receiving it (D) and the total throughput time to produce the product or service (P).

Performance management: similar but broader to performance measurement but also attempts to influence decisions behaviour and skills development so that individuals and processes are better equipped to meet objectives.

Performance measurement: the activity of measuring and assessing the various aspects of a process or whole operation's performance.

Performance objectives: the generic set of performance indicators that can be used to set the objectives or judge the performance of any type of operation; although there are alternative lists proposed by different authorities, the five performance objectives as used in this book are quality, speed, dependability, flexibility and cost.

Performance standards: a defined level of performance against which an operation's actual performance is compared; performance standards can be based on historical performance, some arbitrary target performance, the performance of competitors, etc.

Periodic review: an approach to making inventory decisions that defines points in time for examining inventory levels and then makes decisions accordingly, as opposed to continuous review.

Perpetual inventory principle: a principle used in inventory control that inventory records should be automatically updated every time items are received or taken out of stock.

Physical distribution management: organizing the integrated movement and storage of materials.

Pipeline inventory: the inventory that exists because material cannot be transported instantaneously.

Planning: the formalization of what is intended to happen at some time in the future.

Plant-within-a-plant: a similar term to a cell layout but sometimes used to indicate a larger clustering of resources, *see also* 'Shop-within-a-shop'.

Poka-yoke: Japanese term for fail-safeing.

Polar diagram: a diagram that uses axes, all of which originate from the same central point, to represent different aspects of operations performance.

Predetermined motion–time systems (PMTS): a work measurement technique where standard elemental times obtained from published tables are used to construct a time estimate for a whole job.

Preliminary design: the initial design of a product or service that sets out its main components and functions, but does not include many specific details.

Prevention costs: those costs that are incurred in trying to prevent quality problems and errors occurring, an element within quality-related costs.

Preventive maintenance: an approach to maintenance management that performs work on machines or facilities at regular intervals in an attempt to prevent them breaking down.

Principles of motion economy: a checklist used to develop new methods in work study that is intended to eliminate elements of the job, combine elements together, simplify the activity or change the sequence of events so as to improve efficiency.

Processes: an arrangement of resources that produces some mixture of products and services.

Process capability: an arithmetic measure of the acceptability of the variation of a process.

Process design: the overall configuration of a process that determines the sequence of activities and the flow of transformed resources between them.

Process distance: the degree of novelty required by a process in the implementation of a new technology.

Process hierarchy: the idea that a network of resources form processes, networks of processes form operations, and networks of operations form supply networks.

Process layout: alternative (misleading) name for functional layout.

Process mapping: describing processes in terms of how the activities within the process relate to each other (may also be called 'process blueprinting' or 'process analysis').

Process mapping symbols: the symbols that are used to classify different types of activity; they usually derive either from scientific management or information-systems flow-charting.

Process of operations strategy: how operations strategies are put together, often divided into formulation, implementation, monitoring, and control.

Process outputs: the mixture of goods and services produced by processes.

Process technology: the machines and devices that create and/or deliver goods and services.

Process types: terms that are used to describe a particular general approach to managing processes; in manufacturing these are generally held to be project, jobbing, batch, mass and continuous processes; in services they are held to be professional services, service shops and mass services.

Production flow analysis (PFA): a technique that examines product requirements and process grouping simultaneously to allocate tasks and machines to cells in cell layout.

Process variability: the degree to which activities vary in their time or nature in a process.

Productivity: the ratio of what is produced by an operation or process to what is required to produce it, that is, the output from the operation divided by the input to the operation.

Product layout: locating transforming resources in a sequence defined by the processing needs of a product or service.

Product–process matrix: a model derived by Hayes and Wheelwright that demonstrates the natural fit between volume and variety of products and services produced by an operation on one hand, and the process type used to produce products and services on the other.

Product/service flexibility: the operation's ability to introduce new or modified products and services.

Product/service life cycle: a generalized model of the behaviour of both customers and competitors during the life of a product or service; it is generally held to have four stages: introduction, growth, maturity and decline.

Product structure: diagram that shows the constituent component parts of a product or service package and the order in which the component parts are brought together (often called components structure).

Product technology: the embedded technology within a product or service, as distinct from process technology.

Professional services: service processes that are devoted to producing knowledge-based or advice-based services, usually involving high customer contact and high customization; examples include management consultants, lawyers, architects, etc.

Programme: as used in project management, it is generally taken to mean an ongoing process of change comprising individual projects.

Programme evaluation and review technique (PERT): a method of network planning that uses probabilistic time estimates.

Project: a set of activities with a defined start point and a defined end state which pursue a defined goal using a defined set of resources.

Project manager: competent project managers are vital for project success.

Project processes: processes that deal with discrete, usually highly customized, products.

Prototyping: an initial design of a product or service devised with the aim of further evaluating a design option.

Pull control: a term used in planning and control to indicate that a workstation requests work from the previous station only when it is required, one of the fundamental principles of just-in-time planning and control.

Purchasing: the organizational function, often part of the operations function, that forms contracts with suppliers to buy in materials and services.

Push control: a term used in planning and control to indicate that work is being sent forward to workstations as soon as it is finished on the previous workstation.

Qualified worker: term used in work study to denote a person who is accepted as having the necessary physical attributes, intelligence, skill, education and knowledge to perform the task.

Qualifiers: the competitive factors that have a minimum level of performance (the qualifying level) below which customers are unlikely to consider an operation's performance satisfactory.

Quality: there are many different approaches to defining this. We define it as consistent conformance to customers' expectations.

Quality characteristics: the various elements within the concept of quality, such as functionality, appearance, reliability, durability, recovery, etc.

Quality function deployment (QFD): a technique used to ensure that the eventual design of a product or service actually meets the needs of its customers (sometimes called 'house of quality').

Quality loss function (QLF): a mathematical function devised by Genichi Taguchi that includes all the costs of deviating from a target performance.

Quality-related costs: an attempt to capture the broad cost categories that are affected by, or affect, quality, usually categorized as prevention costs, appraisal costs, internal failure costs and external failure costs.

Quality sampling: the practice of inspecting only a sample of products or services produced rather than every single one.

Quality variables: measures of quality that can be measured on a continuously variable scale, for example length, weight, etc.

Queuing theory: a mathematical approach that models random arrival and processing activities in order to predict the behaviour of queuing systems (also called 'waiting line theory').

Rating: a work study technique that attempts to assess a worker's rate of working relative to the observer's concept of standard performance – controversial and now accepted as being an ambiguous process.

Received variety: the variety that occurs because the process is not designed to prevent it.

Recovery: the activity (usually a predetermined process) of minimizing the effects of an operation's failure.

Red Queen effect: the idea that improvement is relative; a certain level of improvement is necessary simply to maintain one's current position against competitors.

Redundancy: the extent to which a process, product or service has systems or components that are used only when other systems or components fail.

Relationship chart: a diagram used in layout to summarize the relative desirability of facilities to be close to each other.

Reliability: when applied to operations performance, it can be used interchangeably with 'dependability'; when used as a measure of failure it means the ability of a system, product or service to perform as expected over time; this is usually measured in terms of the probability of it performing as expected over time.

Reliability-centred maintenance: an approach to maintenance management that uses different types of maintenance for different parts of a process depending on their pattern of failure.

Remainder cell: the cell that has to cope with all the products that do not conveniently fit into other cells.

Re-order level: the level of inventory at which more items are ordered, usually calculated to ensure that inventory does not run out before the next batch of inventory arrives.

Re-order point: the point in time at which more items are ordered, usually calculated to ensure that inventory does not run out before the next batch of inventory arrives.

Repeatability: the extent to which an activity does not vary.

Repetitive strain injury (RSI): damage to the body because of repetition of activities.

Research and development (R&D): the function in the organization that develops new knowledge and ideas and operationalizes the ideas to form the underlying knowledge on which product, service and process designs are based.

Resource distance: the degree of novelty required of an operation's resources during the implementation of a new technology or process.

Resource-based view (RBV): the perspective on strategy that stresses the importance of capabilities (sometimes known as core competences) in determining sustainable competitive advantage.

Resource-to-order: operations that buy-in resources and produce only when they are demanded by specific customers.

Reverse engineering: the taking apart or deconstruction of a product or service in order to understand how it has been produced (often by a competing organization).

Robots: automatic manipulators of transformed resources whose movement can be programmed and reprogrammed.

Rostering: a term used in planning and control, usually to indicate staff scheduling, the allocation of working times to individuals so as to adjust the capacity of an operation.

Run-to-breakdown maintenance: an approach to maintenance management that only repairs a machine or facility when it breaks down.

SAP: a German company which is the market leader in supplying ERP software, systems and training.

Scheduling: a term used in planning and control to indicate the detailed timetable of what work should be done, when it should be done and where it should be done.

Scientific management: a school of management theory dating from the early twentieth century; more analytical and systematic than 'scientific' as such, sometimes referred to (pejoratively) as Taylorism, after Frederick Taylor who was influential in founding its principles.

SCOR model: a broad but highly structured and systematic framework of supply chain improvement developed by the Supply Chain Council.

Second-tier: the description applied to suppliers and customers who are separated from the operation only by first-tier suppliers and customers.

Sequencing: the activity within planning and control that decides on the order in which work is to be performed.

Service level agreements (SLAs): formal definitions of the dimensions and levels of service that should be provided by one process or operation to another.

Servicescape: a term used to describe the look and feel of the environment within an operation.

Service shops: service processes that are positioned between professional services and mass services, usually with medium levels of volume and customization.

Set-up reduction: the process of reducing the time taken to change over a process from one activity to the next; also called 'single-minute exchange of dies' (SMED) after its origins in the metal pressing industry.

Seven types of waste: types of waste identified by Toyota, they are overproduction, waiting time, transport, process waste, inventory, motion, and defectives.

Shop-within-a-shop: an operations layout that groups facilities that have a common purpose together; the term was originally used in retail operations but is now some- times used in other industries, very similar to the idea of a cell layout.

Short fat processes: processes designed with relatively few sequential stages, each of which performs a relatively large part of the total task; the opposite of long thin processes.

Simulation: the use of a model of a process, product or service to explore its characteristics before the process, product or service is created.

Simultaneous development: overlapping these stages in the design process so that one stage in the design activity can start before the preceding stage is finished, the intention being to shorten time to market and save design cost (also called 'simultaneous engineering' or 'concurrent engineering').

Single-minute exchange of dies (SMED): alternative term for set-up reduction.

Single-sourcing: the practice of obtaining all of one type of input product, component, or service from a single supplier, as opposed to multi-sourcing.

Six Sigma: an approach to improvement and quality management that originated in the Motorola Company but which was widely popularized by its adoption in the GE Company in America. Although based on traditional statistical process control, it is now a far broader 'philosophy of improvement' that recommends a particular approach to measuring, improving and managing quality and operations performance generally.

Skunkworks: a small, focused development team who are taken out of their normal working environment.

Social bottom line: the element of the triple bottom line that assesses the performance of a business in relation to the people and the society with which it has contact; and/or environmental mission and a legal responsibility to respect the interests of workers, the community and the environment as well as shareholders.

Social responsibility: the incorporation of the operation's impact on its stakeholders into operations management decisions.

Spatially variable costs: the costs that are significant in the location decision that vary with geographical position.

Speed: the elapsed time between customers requesting products or services and their receiving them.

Stakeholders: the people and groups of people who have an interest in the operation and who may be influenced by, or influence, the operation's activities.

Standardization: the degree to which processes, products or services are prevented from varying over time.

Standard performance: term used in work measurement to indicate the rate of output that qualified workers will achieve without over-exertion as an average over the working day provided they are motivated to apply themselves, now generally accepted as a very vague concept.

Standard time: a term used in work measurement indicating the time taken to do a job and including allowances for recovery and relaxation.

Statistical process control (SPC): a technique that monitors processes as they produce products or services and attempts to distinguish between normal or natural variation in process performance and unusual or 'assignable' causes of variation.

Stock: alternative term for inventory.

Strategic decisions: those which are widespread in their effect, define the position of the organization relative to its environment and move the organization closer to its long-term goals.

Structural decisions: the strategic decisions which determine the operation's physical shape and configuration, such as those concerned with buildings, capacity, technology, etc.

Subcontracting: when used in medium-term capacity management, it indicates the temporary use of other operations to perform some tasks, or even produce whole products or services, during times of high demand.

Supplier quality assurance (SQA): the activity of monitoring and improving levels of quality of the products and services delivered by suppliers; also used to assess supply capability when choosing between alternative suppliers.

Supply chain: a linkage or strand of operations that provides goods and services through to end-customers; within a supply network several supply chains will cross through an individual operation.

Supply chain dynamics: the study of the behaviour of supply chains, especially the level of activity and inventory levels at different points in the chain; its best known finding is the bullwhip effect.

Supply chain risk: a study of the vulnerability of supply chains to disruption.

Supply network: the network of supplier and customer operations that have relationships with an operation.

Supply side: the chains of suppliers, suppliers' suppliers, etc. that provide parts, information or services to an operation.

Support functions: the functions that facilitate the working of the core functions, for example accounting and finance, human resources, etc.

Sustainability: the ability of a business to create acceptable profit for its owners as well as minimizing the damage to the environment and enhancing the existence of the people with whom it has contact.

Synthesis from elemental data: work measurement technique for building up a time from previously timed elements.

Systemization: the extent to which standard procedures are made explicit.

Taguchi method: a design technique that uses design combinations to test the robustness of a design.

takt time: (similar to cycle time) the time between items emerging from a process, usually applied to 'paced' processes.

Tangibility: the main characteristic that distinguishes products (usually tangible) from services (usually intangible).

Telemedicine: the ability to provide interactive health care utilizing modern telecommunications technology.

Teleworking: the ability to work from home using telecommunications and/or computer technology.

Theory of constraints (TOC): philosophy of operations management that focuses attention on capacity constraints or bottleneck parts of an operation; uses software known as 'optimized production technology' (OPT).

Three-D printing: also known as additive manufacturing, a technology that produces three-dimensional objects by laying down layer upon layer of material.

Throughput efficiency: the work content needed to produce an item in a process expressed as a percentage of total throughput time.

Throughput time: the time for a unit to move through a process.

Time study: a term used in work measurement to indicate the process of timing (usually with a stopwatch) and rating jobs; it involves observing times, adjusting or normalizing each observed time (rating) and averaging the adjusted times.

Time to market (TTM): the elapsed time taken for the whole design activity, from concept through to market introduction.

Top-down: the influence of the corporate or business strategy on operations decisions.

Total productive maintenance (TPM): an approach to maintenance management that adopts a similar holistic approach to total quality management (TQM).

Total quality management (TQM): a holistic approach to the management of quality that emphasizes the role of all parts of an organization and all people within an organization to influence and improve quality; heavily influenced by various quality 'gurus', it reached its peak of popularity in the 1980s and 1990s.

Total supply network: all the suppliers and customers who are involved in supply chains that 'pass through' an operation.

Trade-off theory: the idea that the improvement in one aspect of operations performance comes at the expense of deterioration in another aspect of performance, now substantially modified to include the possibility that in the long term different aspects of operations performance can be improved simultaneously.

Transformation process model: model that describes operations in terms of their input resources, transforming processes and outputs of goods and services.

Transformed resources: the resources that are treated, transformed or converted in a process, usually a mixture of materials, information and customers.

Transforming resources: the resources that act upon the transformed resources, usually classified as facilities (the buildings, equipment and plant of an operation) and staff (the people who operate, maintain and manage the operation).

Triple bottom line: (also known as people, plants, and profit) the idea that organizations should measure themselves on social and environmental criteria as well as financial ones.

Two-handed process chart: a type of micro-detailed process map that shows the motion of each hand used in an activity on a common timescale.

U-form organization: an organizational structure that clusters its resources primarily by their functional purpose.

Upstream: the other operations in a supply chain that are towards the supply side of the operation.

Usage value: a term used in inventory control to indicate the quantity of items used or sold multiplied by their value or price.

Utilization: the ratio of the actual output from a process or facility to its design capacity.

Valuable operating time: the amount of time at a piece of equipment or work centre that is available for productive working after stoppages and inefficiencies have been accounted for.

Value-added throughput efficiency: the amount of time an items spends in a process having value added to it expressed as a percentage of total throughput time.

Value engineering: an approach to cost reduction in product design that examines the purpose of a product or service, its basic functions and its secondary functions.

Value stream map: a mapping process that aims to understand the flow of material and information through a process or series of processes, it distinguishes between value-added and non-value-added times in the process.

Variation: the degree to which the rate or level of output varies from a process over time, a key characteristic in determining process behaviour.

Variety: the range of different products and services produced by a process, a key characteristic that determines process behaviour.

Vertical integration: the extent to which an operation chooses to own the network of processes that produce a product or service; the term is often associated with the 'do or buy' decision.

Virtual operation: an operation that performs few, if any, value-adding activities itself, rather it organizes a network of supplier operations, seen as the ultimate in outsourcing.

Virtual prototype: a computer-based model of a product, process or service that can be tested for its characteristics before the actual process, product or service is produced.

Visibility: the amount of value-added activity that takes place in the presence (in reality or virtually) of the customer, also called 'customer contact'.

Visual management: an approach to making the current and planned state of an operation or process transparent to everyone.

Voice of the customer (VOC): capturing a customer's requirements, expectations and perceptions and using them as improvement targets within an operation.

Volume: the level or rate of output from a process, a key characteristic that determines process behaviour.

Volume flexibility: the operation's ability to change its level of output or activity to produce different quantities or volumes of products and services over time.

Waiting line theory: an alternative term for queuing theory.

Web-integrated ERP: enterprise resource planning that is extended to include the ERP-type systems of other organizations such as customers and suppliers.

Weighted-score method of location: a technique for comparing the attractiveness of alternative locations that allocates a score to the factors that are significant in the decision and weights each score by the significance of the factor.

Wide-area networks (WANs): similar to local-area networks (LANs) but with a greater reach, usually involving elements outside a single operation.

Work breakdown structure: the definition of, and the relationship between, the individual work packages in project management; each work package can be allocated its own objectives that fit in with the overall work breakdown structure.

Work content: the total amount of work required to produce a unit of output, usually measured in standard times.

Workflow: process of design of information-based processes.

Work-in-progess (WIP): the number of units within a process waiting to be processed further (also called 'work-in-process').

Work measurement: a branch of work study that is concerned with measuring the time that should be taken for performing jobs.

Work study: the term generally used to encompass method study and work measurement, derived from the scientific management school.

World Wide Web (WWW): the protocols and standards that are used on the internet for formatting, retrieving, storing and displaying information.

Yield management: a collection of methods that can be used to ensure that an operation (usually with a fixed capacity) maximizes its potential to generate profit.

Zero defect: the idea that quality management should strive for perfection as its ultimate objective even though in practice this will never be reached.

Index

Page numbers in **bold** refer to entries in the Glossary.